Contents

Introduction

Experiences have always been at the heart of the Rough Guide concept. When we started writing Rough Guides we wanted to share the kind of travel that we had been doing ourselves. Our aim was to put a destination's culture at centre stage: to highlight the clubs and bars where you could hear local music, the places you could eat and drink with people you hadn't come on holiday with and the festivals that could show you unique traditions as well as a good time. We wanted to push travel a bit further, inspiring our readers to get away from the established routes, even if that meant getting lost occasionally, and seek something that little bit more special and authentic – in short, to settle for nothing less than an ultimate travel experience.

What makes the best kind of travel experience? Well, it should be something you would recommend to others, something you would want to tell your friends or family about: an experience that you'll always remember. It could be about the sense of awe you felt the first time you set eyes on an iconic building or looked out across a stunning landscape; it might be the camaraderie of joining the locals at a football match, or the epic train ride you took to get there; it might be rainforest zipwiring, or soaring over the desert in a hot-air balloon; or even just enjoying a simple meal with new people in a perfect setting.

It's possible to have some of the best travel experiences without going very far at all. Travel isn't only about distance and long-haul flights. But the most meaningful moments often take place when we move away from the familiar, where even the most run-of-the-mill situations and events take on an exotic quality. It's no coincidence that so many of the experiences we feature in this book have some degree of cultural engagement. They're driven by taste, but also opportunity: some are very easy to do; others less so; they can be seasonal events that happen once each year; they can be almost wilfully remote. What they have in common is that they are all Rough Guide writers' personal recommendations, accumulated over the thirty years of our existence. For this second edition, we've added over two hundred new experiences from around the world. They are intended to evoke the same excitement in you that they did in us.

James Smart
Editor

GETTING AWAY FROM IT ALL ON SKELLIG MICHAEL • GIGGING IN GLASGOW • MOONWALKING IN JERSEY • FEELING INSIGNIFICANT AT THE BRITISH MUSEUM • CLUBBING IN LONDON • BE HUMBLED IN DURHAM • SUPPING GUINNESS IN DUBLIN • WANDERING BORROWDALE IN THE LAKE DISTRICT • FISH AND CHIPS: THE TRUE ENGLISH FAVOURITE • HIKING THE PENNINE WAY • SANDWOOD BAY: BRITAIN'S MOST MYSTERIOUS BEACH • CYCLING IN THE NEW FOREST • DRESSING UP FOR ROYAL ASCOT • TOASTING BAD WEATHER IN THE SCOTTISH HIGHLANDS • RAMBLING ON DARTMOOR • HORSING ABOUT AT THE COMMON RIDINGS • PUNTING ON THE CAM • GUNPOWDER, TREASON AND PLOT: LEWES BONFIRE NIGHT • PLAYING THE OLD COURSE AT ST. ANDREWS • LOSING YOURSELF IN CONNEMARA • CLIMB THE HIGHEST LIGHTHOUSE IN BRITAIN • TRUNDLING ALONG THE WEST HIGHLAND RAILWAY • DAYDREAMING IN OXFORD • FLYING WITH BA TO BARRA AND BEYOND • INTO THE VALLEY: HEARING A WELSH CHOIR • WALKING IN THE MOUNTAINS OF MOURNE • HOARDING BOOKS IN HAY-ON-WYE • FREEDIVING IN THE ROYAL NAVY'S SETT • CHASING CHEESE IN GLOUCESTER • HITTING THE STREETS FOR THE NOTTING HILL CARNIVAL • GO WEST: HIKING THE PEMBROKESHIRE COAST PATH • CALLING IN THE HEAVIES AT THE HIGHLAND GAMES • HOLKHAM MAGIC • WALK LONDON'S HIDDEN HIGHWAYS • BURNING RUBBER AT THE ISLE OF MAN TT • WINNING THE PREHISTORIC LOTTERY • SURFING THE SEVERN BORE • BARGING DOWN THE BARROW • WATCHING THE HURLING AT CROKE PARK • WALKING THE WALLS OF CONWY CASTLE • BREATHING IN THE SEA AIR IN TOBERMORY • FOLLOW IN THE FOOTSTEPS OF KINGS AND QUEENS AT BATH SPA • FOLKING OUT UNDER THE SUGAR LOAF • FINDING HEAVEN ON EARTH IN CORNWALL • FOLLOWING THE OYSTER TRAIL IN GALWAY • SOAKING UP THE EDINBURGH FESTIVAL • ENJOYING THE SEASONS OF THE SCILLIES • HIGHLAND FLING: GETTING PERSONAL WITH BEN NEVIS • SEE THE BELFAST MURALS • MOUNTAIN BIKING WELSH TRAILS • GETTING AWAY FROM IT ALL ON SKELLIG MICHAEL • GIGGING IN GLASGOW • MOONWALKING IN JERSEY • FEELING INSIGNIFICANT AT THE BRITISH MUSEUM • CLUBBING IN LONDON • BE HUMBLED IN DURHAM • SUPPING GUINNESS IN DUBLIN • WANDERING BORROWDALE IN THE LAKE DISTRICT • FISH AND CHIPS: THE TRUE ENGLISH FAVOURITE • HIKING THE PENNINE WAY • SANDWOOD BAY: BRITAIN'S MOST MYSTERIOUS BEACH • CYCLING IN THE NEW FOREST • DRESSING UP FOR ROYAL ASCOT • TOASTING BAD WEATHER IN THE SCOTTISH HIGHLANDS • RAMBLING ON DARTMOOR • HORSING ABOUT AT THE COMMON RIDINGS • PUNTING ON THE CAM • GUNPOWDER, TREASON AND PLOT: LEWES BONFIRE NIGHT • PLAYING THE OLD COURSE AT ST. ANDREWS • LOSING YOURSELF IN CONNEMARA

SCOTLAND

011 Sandwood Bay: Britain's most mysterious beach

002 Gigging in Glasgow

NORTHERN IRELAND

006 Be humbled in Durham

035 Burning rubber at the Isle of Man TT

020 Losing yourself in Connemara

039 Watching the hurling at Croke Park

IRELAND

WALES

ENGLAND

043 Folking out under the Sugar Loaf

025 Into the valley: hearing a Welsh choir

034 Walk London's hidden highways

044 Finding heaven on Earth in Cornwall

JERSEY

001 GETTING AWAY FROM IT ALL ON
Skellig Michael

IRELAND The jagged twin pyramids of the Skellig Islands rise abruptly out of the Atlantic Ocean, 6 miles off the southwest tip of Ireland. Little Skellig is a teeming, noisy bird sanctuary, home to around 50,000 gannets and now officially full (the excess have had to move to another island off County Wexford). In tranquil contrast, neighbouring Skellig Michael shelters one of the most remarkable hermitages in the world.

In the late seventh or early eighth century, a monastery was somehow built on this inhospitable outcrop, in imitation of the desert communities of the early Church fathers – and indeed, continuing the practices of Ireland's druids, who would spend long periods alone in the wilderness. Its design is a miracle of ingenuity and devotion. On small artificial terraces, the dry-stone beehive huts were ringed by sturdy outer walls, which deflected the howling winds and protected the vegetable patch made of bird droppings; channels crisscrossed the settlement to funnel rainwater into cisterns. Monks – up to fifteen of them at a time – lived here for nearly five hundred years, withstanding anything the Atlantic could throw at them – including numerous Viking raids. In the twelfth century, however, a climatic change made the seas even rougher, while pressure was brought to bear on old, independent monasteries such as Skellig Michael to conform, and eventually the fathers adopted the Augustinian rule and moved to the mainland.

The beauty of a visit to the island is that it doesn't require a huge leap to imagine how the monks might have lived. You still cross over from the mainland on small, slow boats, huddling against the spray. From the quay, 650 steps climb almost vertically to the monastery, whose cells, chapels and refectory remain largely intact after 1300 years. The island even has residents, at least in the summer: friendly guides, employed by the Office of Public Works to give talks to visitors, sometimes stay out here for weeks at a time, making the most of the spiritual solitude.

002 Gigging in Glasgow

SCOTLAND Pop stars, travelling from coach to bar and from plane to arena, are notoriously oblivious about the city they happen to be performing in. There are countless stories of frontmen bellowing "Hello, Detroit!" when they're actually in Toronto. But some places have a genuine buzz about them. London is fine, but all too often its crowds sit back and wait to be impressed. If you want real passion, vibrant venues and bands who really play out of their skin, Glasgow is where it's at.

Scotland's biggest city has an alternative rock pedigree that few can match. Primal Scream, Franz Ferdinand, the Jesus & Mary Chain, Simple Minds, Snow Patrol and Belle & Sebastian have all sprung from a city that *Time* magazine has described as Europe's "secret capital" of rock music. Its gig scene, which stretches from gritty pubs to arty student haunts, marvellous church halls to cavernous arenas, is enthusiastic, vociferous and utterly magnetic. Nice 'N' Sleazy and King Tut's Wah Wah Hut (where Alan McGee first spotted Oasis) are legendary in their own right, but if one venue really defines the city, it's the Barrowland.

Opened in the 1930s as a ballroom (which explains the fine acoustics), it was the hunting ground of the killer known as "Bible John" in the late sixties. It's still a fairly rough-and-ready place – the Barras market is just outside, and its location in the Celtic heartland of Glasgow's East End makes it a favoured venue for rambunctious traditional bands. Shane McGowan's been there, drinking lurid cocktails, his slurred vocals drowned out by a roaring crowd. So have Keane, flushed at the success of their piano-pop debut, and looking bemused at the small fights that broke out near the front at their performance.

Of course, most gigs finish without the drama getting violent. With a 2000-person capacity that's atmospheric but intimate, and without any seats or barriers to get in the way of the music or the pogoing, the Barrowland is a wonderful place to see a live performance, full of energy and expectation. I've seen PJ Harvey transfix the crowd, the Streets provoke wall-to-wall grins, the Mars Volta prompt walkouts, Leftfield play spine-shaking bass and Echo and the Bunnymen cement their return with dark majesty. Go get some memories of your own.

003 Moonwalking in Jersey

THE CHANNEL ISLANDS It was one small step for man. A little jump down from the harbour wall at La Rocque in Jersey's southeast corner and we were out onto the expanse of sand bars and gullies that surround the largest of the Channel Islands, standing on a rocky seabed with distinctly no sea. In the fading light some one-and-a-half miles from shore loomed Seymour Tower, our destination for the night, and beyond that, forming a crease on the horizon, the waiting Atlantic.

Jersey has one of the highest tidal ranges in the world, and twice a day, when the ocean beats a hasty retreat back into the Gulf of St Malo, the island almost doubles in size. In its wake, the water leaves a lunar landscape of twisted rock and muddy tidal flats, seemingly barren but in fact home to an astonishing variety of marine life: scuttling, swimming, hiding or just hanging on for dear

life. The southeast coast's sheltered waters act as a sanctuary for sea bass, sole and turbot, and as we picked our path across the rock we spotted spider crabs and snakelocks anemones, their green tentacles wafting in the shallow pools.

The sense of discovery is intensified by the knowledge that this is all so temporary, all too fleeting – within a few hours, the ocean will be back and the channels we're weaving through will be under 30ft of water. We sought refuge in Seymour Tower, built in the eighteenth century to defend the island from the French (the Normandy coast lies just 15 miles away), scrambling up the rocks to the safety inside. Out there in the darkness, growing louder by the minute, was the sea, creeping over sandbanks at first but then surging through gullies, swirling around us faster and faster until it pounded on the walls below.

004 Feeling insignificant at the British Museum

ENGLAND The first thing that strikes you about the British Museum is its enormity. From the moment you step through the gates into the sprawling front courtyard and gaze up at the imposing Greek Revival portico with its towering Ionic columns, you are humbled. With 2.5 miles of exhibits that span civilizations across the globe from ancient times to the modern day, this museum is not to be sniffed at.

Head to the Great Court, where gleaming white stone and sleek marble floors reflect the light streaming down through the state-of-the-art glass-and-steel roof; the bright white glare reflected off every shiny surface is almost blinding. Straight ahead, the central Round Reading Room, a remnant of the British Library that originally resided here, offers old-fashioned solace in the midst of this stark modernity. Its small door beckons you in to a space of wood-panelled, book-lined walls enclosed by an immense dome, which towers overhead in

soothing hues of pale sky blue and eggshell white.

Move on to the exhibit galleries, where you'll encounter an entirely different type of largesse; here, in the endless labyrinth of display rooms, the achievements of past civilizations cannot fail to instil a sense of awe. As you crane your neck to take in the full height of the Greeks' gargantuan statues and admire the skilfully carved friezes Lord Elgin pilfered from the Parthenon, it's easy to feel belittled by the sheer grandeur of it all; cowering in front of the perfectly preserved Egyptian mummies and soaking up the significance of the code-breaking Rosetta Stone, you can almost feel the vast weight of history pressing down upon you. Hours later you re-enter the modern world through the colonnaded portico feeling exhausted and a great deal less important, yet exhilarated by the marvels mankind has wrought.

ENGLAND From superclubs to sweaty backrooms, hip-hop to hardcore, there's a London club-night guaranteed to get you throwing shapes on the dance floor. Genres like dubstep and electro are riding high, but with pop, indie, metal, drum'n'bass, soul, salsa and classic house all prominent, it's not hard to find your niche. Some of the superclubs that dominated the nineties have crumbled, but institutions such as Thames-set *Matter*, the revitalised *Ministry of Sound* and *Fabric* show no signs of slowing down. They aren't cheap – and it can be worth buying tickets in advance to avoid the queues – but if you want world-famous DJs on knee-trembling sound systems they're a must. *Fabric*'s labyrinthine rooms in particular are packed with phemonenal DJs come the weekend, most of them relishing the freedom the clued-up management and up-for-it crowd give them to play adventurous sets.

London's fierce local loyalties are backed by fine scenes that top almost anything in the overpriced, cheese-dripping West End. Up north, Camden is the indie scene's eclectic epicentre. South of the river, Elephant and Castle and London Bridge are the home of scruffy converted arches and warehouses with a friendly, dressed-down vibe. The east veers on the theatrical, with trendy Hoxtonites striding out in vintage frocks and dramatic make-up, as pop, electro and dubstep collide in weird and wonderful ways. Meanwhile, small venues and boho chic are the order of the day west in Notting Hill, with an eclectic soundtrack of soulful funk, broken beat and world music.

But don't get too hung up on geography. There are fine clubs in most postcodes – you'll just need to dig around a bit. There's no need to stop at dawn, either, with after-parties promoted outside the larger clubs at closing time. There's really no excuse for staying in.

CLUBBING IN
London

005

ENGLAND Durham Cathedral is now something of a celebrity to millions who've never even set foot in the Northeast, having appeared as Hogwarts' detention hall, courtyard and Quidditch practice arena in the Harry Potter films. This recent brush with fame, however, is a mere blink in the cathedral's centuries-old history, as Durham stands as one of the greatest and most enduring achievements of Norman architectural engineering.

Looming over this university city like a gentle giant, the cathedral offers a haven of calm from the narrow, bustling streets. Boasting the enormous lion-shaped sanctuary door knocker that, when rapped, would guarantee desperate fugitives 37 days of refuge, the North Porch Door opens onto the broad Norman nave, flanked by immense pillars, deeply carved with geometric grooves. Lighting up the east wall of the cathedral is the magnificent rose window, below which you'll find the final resting place of the north's popular saint, St Cuthbert; the monk from Lindisfarne, famed for his healing hands, was deposited here in 1104 after a protracted and somewhat unceremonious tour of the country in his coffin (he had died in 687).

A hike up the Central Tower is worth the wear on the thigh muscles; 325 steps spiral up for 223 feet, where you're greeted with a superb panoramic view of the surrounding county, Wearside – claustrophobics be warned: the steps are extremely steep and narrow. The entrance to the tower is in the South Transept, next to Prior Castell's colourful sixteenth-century clock, decorated with a Scottish thistle: the last remaining testament to Durham's sticky involvement in the Civil War, when Cromwell used the cathedral to imprison 3000 Scottish soldiers.

At night, the Cathedral takes on an entirely new persona: bathed in artificial light, it dominates the skyline in haunting magnitude. To experience the cathedral in all its auricular glory, aim to visit around 5pm for the Evensong service, when you can enjoy the enchanting refrains of the university choristers. And if you're after more magic – this time in the culinary sense – the *Almshouses* café is located just across the grassy Palace Green (a perennial stage for streaking students). Sublime. The cake selection that is, not the streakers.

007 Supping Guinness in Dublin

IRELAND Rain lashing a grey Dublin Friday. *The Palace*, etched in glass, promises refuge. In quick. No trouble catching the barman's eye, "A pint, please". As he slowly begins to pour, time to take in the handsome room: mirrored screens sectioning the bar discreetly, Victorian mahogany twirling everywhere. I eavesdrop while the half-poured Guinness stands to one side to settle: the Dublin–Mayo match on Sunday, brutal tailbacks on the M50, bin charges. More patience needed when the glass is full, waiting for the black-and-white turmoil to calm itself; drawings of writers Flann O'Brien and Patrick Kavanagh, old *Palace* regulars, stare down.

I settle myself in the back room, under a glass roof that floods light in and noisily reminds me of the drenching I'm missing. Clutching my pint, I think of the philosopher, struggling with the problem of consciousness, who compared beer in a glass to the brain, the mind or soul to the froth on top – same physical stuff, but in essence quite different. Surely he can't have been Irish – this dark, malty liquid seems barely on speaking terms with the creamy, white top. A twist in the tale, perhaps only possible in "God's own country": as I sup my way through the black stuff, the froth persists, sinking slowly down the glass.

Same again? A fine pint, but was it the best Guinness in Dublin – and so, I suppose, the world? Some say it's better round the corner at *Mulligan's*, where it's been sanctified by generations of *Irish Times* journalists. Or is the travel-shy liquid happier at *Ryan's*, just across the river from the brewery? And what about the brewery's own panoramic bar? There you get a manicured pint, as its maker intended, with views over the city and the Wicklow Mountains thrown in.

Now, what was I meant to be doing this afternoon?

008 Wandering Borrowdale in the Lake District

ENGLAND Eighteenth-century Romantic poet Thomas Gray described the narrowest part of Borrowdale – the so-called Jaws of Borrowdale – as "a menacing ravine whose rocks might, at any time, fall and crush a traveller". Gray obviously didn't get out much, for more than anything Borrowdale is characterized by its sylvan beauty, the once glaciated hills smoothed off by the ancient ice. Some have dubbed it the most beautiful valley in England, and it's easy to see why on the gentle walks that weave across the flat valley floor. Some of the best are around Derwentwater, its mountain backdrop, wooded slopes and quaint ferry service making it one of the prettiest lakes in the area.

Ever since Victorian times, visitors have flocked to the Bowder Stone, a 2000-ton glacial erratic probably carried south from Scotland in the last Ice Age. This cube of andesitic lava is perched so precariously on one edge that it looks ready to topple at any moment. Wooden steps give access to its thirty-foot summit where the rock has been worn smooth by hundreds of thousands of feet.

Immediately north, a circular walk takes in an area boasting the densest concentration of superb views in the Lake District. The most spectacular is from Walla Crag – vistas stretch over Derwentwater up to the Jaws of Borrowdale.

North of the Bowder Stone, a small tumbling stream is spanned by Ashness Bridge, an ancient stone-built structure designed for packhorses. With its magnificent backdrop of Derwentwater and the rugged beauty of the northern fells, it's one of the most photographed scenes in the entire Lake District.

009 Fish and chips: the true English favourite

ENGLAND Whatever you may think of fish and chips – that it's been surpassed as the quintessential English dish by chicken vindaloo, or that it's a stodgy recipe for a surefire heart attack – there's something undeniably appealing about it. This hot, greasy, starchy mess, smothered with salt and drenched in vinegar, can satisfy like nothing else.

Quite frankly, you'll probably be served a lot of awful fish and chips along the way. This despite the fact that this seaside fare is on a bit of a roll, even, heaven forbid, nearly fashionable. All kinds of chefs, buoyed by the renaissance in British cuisine, have been trying their hand at dressing up the humble dish. Indeed, noted gourmet Rick Stein – who has his own fish and chips restaurant on the southwest coast in Padstow – has compared serving up good fish and chips to presenting a plate of Helford oysters with a bottle of Premier Cru Chablis.

Fish and chips has pretty much always meant cod, followed by traditional substitutes such as skate, plaice, haddock and bottom-feeding rock salmon (the appealing way of saying "catfish" or "dogfish"). Overfishing of cod and other species has meant some places increasingly giving gurnard, pollock and whiting their turn in the fryer, so don't limit yourself to the classic staples.

As for the batter that coats the fish, flour and water is standard, though you might find yeast and beer batter or matzo meal in the most outré of places. What's the basic chip? Thick-cut potatoes, preferably cooked in beef dripping – and, of course, coated in a light layer of grease and liberal lashings of salt and vinegar.

010 Hiking the Pennine Way

ENGLAND After two weeks' walking through rain and shine (and with moods to match), the final day of the Pennine Way, Britain's oldest and longest long-distance footpath, is upon you: a 27-mile marathon over the desolate Cheviot Hills. It's a challenging finale but the narcotic effects of mounting euphoria ought to numb your multiple aches. Anyway, if you're one of the few who've made it this far, you'll not give up now.

The Pennine Way begins at the village of Edale in Derbyshire's Peak District and meanders 270 miles north to Kirk Yetholm beneath the Cheviot Hills and a mile across the Scottish border. Along its course, it leads through some of England's most beautiful and least crowded countryside. In the early stages, it passes the birthplace of the English Industrial Revolution, and today stone slabs from the derelict mills and factories have been recycled into winding causeways over the once notorious moorland peat bogs. This is Brontë country, too, grim on a dank, misty day but bleakly inspiring

when the cloud lifts.

The mires subside to become the rolling green pastures and dry-stone walls of the Yorkshire Dales that rise up to striking peaks like the 2278ft-high Pen-y-ghent – the "Mountain of the Winds".

The limestone Dales in turn become the wilder northern Pennines, where no one forgets stumbling onto the astounding glaciated abyss of High Cup Nick. The Way's final phase begins with an invigorating stage along the 2000-year-old Hadrian's Wall before ending with the calf-wrenching climax over the Cheviots.

Walking the wilds is exhilarating but staying in pretty villages along the way is also a highlight. Again and again you'll find yourself transported back to a bygone rural idyll of village shops, church bells and, of course, pubs. Memories of mud and glory will pass before your eyes as you stagger the last few yards onto Kirk Yetholm's village green, stuff your reviled backpack in the bin and turn towards the inviting bar at the *Border Hotel*.

011 Sandwood Bay: Britain's most mysterious beach

SCOTLAND Cape Wrath: a name that epitomizes nature at its harshest, land and sea at their most unforgiving. In fact, the name Wrath denotes a "turning-point" in Old Norse, and the Vikings regarded this stockade of vertical rock in the most northwesterly corner of Scotland as a milestone in their ocean-going voyages. As such, they were surely among the first travellers to come under the spell of Sandwood Bay, the Cape's most elemental stretch of coastline.

Here, across a mile-long breach in the headland, blow Britain's most remote sands, flanked by epic dunes and a slither of shimmering loch; a beach of such austere and unexpected elegance, scoured so relentlessly by the Atlantic and located in such relative isolation, that it scarcely seems part of the Scottish mainland at all. The freestanding impudence of the hulking stack of stone that is Am Buachaille ("the Herdsman"), rearing some 240ft out of the sea off the bay's southern tip, is fantastical in itself.

Even on the clearest of summer days, when shoals of cumuli race shadows across the foreshore, you are unlikely to encounter other visitors save for the odd sandpiper. You might not be entirely alone though; whole galleons are said to be buried in the sand, and a cast of mermaids, ghostly pirates and grumbling sailors have filled accounts of the place for as long as people have frequented it. Though the last mermaid sighting was in 1900 (attributed to a local shepherd, Alexander Gunn, who famously stuck by his story till death), the sheer scale and magnetism of the Sandwood panorama – accessible only on foot via a desolate, four-mile path – may just throw you a supernatural encounter of your own.

Whether you camp wild in the haunted ruins of an old crofter's cottage, or merely stroll the sand in the teeth of an untrammelled westerly, the presence of the bay is undeniable. Or maybe it's just the feeling that you're standing at the edge of the known world, a turning point between the familiar and the inexplicable.

012 Cycling in the New Forest

ENGLAND Covering a wedge of land between Bournemouth, Southampton and the English Channel, the New Forest offers some of Britain's most exhilarating cycling country, with a chance to lose yourself amid a network of roads, gravelled paths and bridleways, and 150 miles of car-free cycle tracks. Here, you can indulge your wild side, surrounded by a leafy world remote from modern-day stresses. Spring brings budding growth to the area and the ground is swathed in delicate colour, while autumn paints the forest in gorgeous hues of red and brown. Your travels will take you past tidy thatched cottages on quiet wooded lanes onto exposed heathland with magnificent views and dotted with deer. The 40mph speed limit on forest roads makes for a safe and unhassled ride, picnic spots are ubiquitous, and the occasional pub provides

more substantial refreshment.

England's newest national park has been a protected wilderness for nigh on a thousand years: William the Conqueror appropriated the area as a hunting reserve (his son, William Rufus, was killed here by an arrow in an apparent accident). The area has changed little since Norman times and is a superb place to spot wildlife: amid terrain ranging from thick woodland to bogs, heath and grassland strewn with bracken and gorse, the forest is home to around 2000 fallow, roe, red and sika deer, not to mention some 3000 wild ponies, and numerous sheep, cattle, pigs and donkeys.

Park up the car and pedal off; go fast or take your time; map out routes or ride at random – you're the boss on this invigorating escape into freedom.

Dressing up for *Royal Ascot*

ENGLAND Picture the scene: the pop and fizz of hundreds of champagne bottles, the sweet smell of trampled grass, show-stopping millinery, royalty and celebrities mingling cheerfully with the crowds, and, of course, the steaming coats of snorting, cavorting thorough-breds. You couldn't be anywhere other than Royal Ascot.

Featuring the very best horses and jockeys from all over the globe, Royal Ascot is the cream of British horseracing – speed, agility and nail-biting finishes, this is entertainment in pure equine form. None of the five days' races is commercially sponsored, and many reflect their regal origins: the Queen Anne Stakes (the first race of the meeting, in honour of the course's founder), the Coronation Stakes and the Queen's Vase (named for the accession of Queen Victoria). Each day at 2pm sharp, the present-day queen, a racehorse owner herself, helps put the "Royal" in "Royal Ascot" as she arrives in an open-top horse-drawn carriage, leading a procession from Windsor Castle down the middle of the course.

Ascot may be the world's finest horseracing meet, but the majority of people are here for the social scene, the fine dining and the fashion show. Come equipped with a killer outfit – and an equally killer hat (the bigger, and more outrageous, the better) – and you'll fit right in. All that remains is to pack a sumptuous picnic, to be munched with friends by the side of the car (preferably a Porsche). But if you'd rather avoid the stress of providing your own fancy fodder, dine on lobster, smoked salmon or beef in one of the restaurants, accompanied by a bottle of champagne – just one of the 170,000 that'll be quaffed that day. Good going, isn't it?

Scottish Highlands

014

SCOTLAND First, be glad that it rains so much in Scotland. Without the rain the rivers here wouldn't run – the Livet, the Fiddich, the Spey. Without the rain the glens wouldn't be green and the barley wouldn't grow tall and plump.

Be glad it's damp here in Scotland. Peat needs a few centuries sitting in a bog to come out right. Then a breeze, and a wee bit of sun, to dry it. You burn it, with that delicious reek – the aroma – to dry the malted barley. Earth, wind and fire.

And be glad it's cold here too. Whisky was being made in these hills for centuries before refrigeration. Cool water to condense the spirit. After all, if you're going to leave liquid sitting around in wooden barrels for ten or more years, you don't want it too warm. The evaporation – "the angels' share" – is bad enough. Still, it makes the idea of "taking the air" in Speyside rather more appealing.

And if it weren't cold and wet and damp, you wouldn't appreciate being beside that roaring fire and feeling the taste for something to warm the cockles. Here's a heavy glass for that dram, that measure. How much? More than a splash, not quite a full pour. Look at the colour of it: old gold.

Taste it with your nose first; a whisky expert is called a "noser" rather than a "taster". Single malts have all sorts of smells and subtleties and flavours: grass, biscuits, vanilla, some sweet dried fruit, a bit of peat smoke. Drinking it is just the final act.

Aye, with a wee splash of water. The spirit overpowers your tastebuds otherwise. A drop, to soften it, unlock the flavours. Not sacrilege – the secret. Water.

Is it still raining?

Let me pour you another.

015 Rambling on Dartmoor

ENGLAND In the middle of that most genteel of counties, Devon, it comes as something of a shock to encounter the 365 square miles of raw granite, barren bogland and rippling seas of heather that make up Dartmoor. The feeling of space is intimidating. If you want to declutter your mind and energize your body, the recipe is simple: invest in a pair of hiking boots, switch off your mobile and set out on an adventure into the primitive heart of Britain. The briefest of journeys onto the moor is enough to take in the dusky umbers of the landscape, flecked by yellow gorse and purple heather and threaded by flashes of moorland stream, all washed in a moist and misty light. Even the gathering haze that precedes rain appears otherworldly, while the moor under a mantle of snow and illuminated by a crisp wintry light is spellbinding.

Your walk will take you from picturesque, hideaway hamlets such as Holne and Buckland-in-the-Moor to bare wilderness and blasted crag within a few strides. There are some surprising examples of architecture, too, including the authentically Norman Okehampton Castle and the wholly fake Castle Drogo, built by Lutyens in the early twentieth century in the style of a medieval fortress. But by far the most stirring man-made relics to be found are the Bronze and Iron Age remains, a surprising testimony to the fact that this desolate expanse once hummed with activity: easily accessible are the grand hut circles of Grimspound, where Conan Doyle set a scene from his Sherlock Holmes yarn, *The Hound of the Baskervilles*.

The best way to explore is on an organized walk led by a knowledgeable guide, often focusing on a theme, from birdwatching to orienteering, to painting. It's a first-rate way to get to grips with the terrain and discover facets of this vast landscape that you'd never encounter on your own. Alternatively, equip yourself with a decent map and seek out your own piece of Dartmoor. You may not see another soul for miles, but you'll soon absorb its slow, soothing rhythm.

016 Horsing about at the Common Ridings

SCOTLAND The Common Ridings of the Scottish Border towns of Hawick, Selkirk, Jedburgh and Lauder are one of Britain's best-kept secrets – an equestrian extravaganza that combines the danger of Pamplona's Fiesta de San Fermin and the drinking of Munich's Oktoberfest. Commemorating the days when the Scots needed early warnings of attacks from their expansionist neighbours, the focus of each event is a dawn horseback patrol of the commons and fields that mark each town's boundaries. Selkirk may boast the largest number of riders, and Lauder might be the oldest event, but Hawick is always the first – and the best attended – of them all.

At dawn on each day of the ridings, a colourful and incredibly noisy drum and fife band marches around the streets to shake people from their sleep and, more importantly, to allow plenty of time for the riders, and virtually the entire town population, to get down to the pub – they open at 6am – and stock up on the traditional breakfast of "Curds and Cream" (rum and milk). Suitably fortified, over two hundred riders – all exquisitely attired in cream jodhpurs, black riding boots, tweed jackets and white silk neckerchiefs – mount their horses and gallop at breakneck speed around the ancient lanes and narrow streets of town, before heading out into the fields to continue the racing in a slightly more organized manner.

By early evening, and with the racing done for the day, the spectators and riders stagger back into Hawick to reacquaint themselves with the town's pubs, an activity that most people approach with gusto. Stumbling out onto the street at well past midnight, you should have just enough time for an hour or two of shuteye before the fife band strikes up once more and it's time to do it all over again.

017 Punting on the Cam

ENGLAND The experienced professional punter – propelling boatloads of tourists along Cambridge's River Cam – speaks of the simple sensory pleasure to be found in the interaction of the firm riverbed, the massive punting pole (wielded with a masterful delicacy) and the punt itself, pushing against the springy upthrust of the gentle waters. In fact, it is like driving a people carrier with a joystick from a seat where the luggage would usually go.

Your punt will naturally be attracted to other punts, blocking the river under the sarcastic gaze of the city's youth, who stop to watch your ineptitude from one of the many pretty bridges. Your response should be to affect an ironic detachment; something achieved more easily when you console yourself with the idea that perhaps punting was never meant to be done well. The point is to drift with languorous unconcern, admiring the beautiful college gardens and architecture, while disguising incompetence as abstraction and reverie.

This slow river is lined with some of the grandest architecture in the country. You recline almost at the water's level as the great buildings rear around you in a succession of noble set-pieces. Perhaps the two most notable sights are the chapel at King's College, a structure of forbidding single-minded authority, and Christopher Wren's library for Trinity College, which has the same rigorous perfection that some may find refreshing (others overwhelming).

When you're done punting, the colleges are wonderful places to explore, if they'll let you in; the rules of access vary from college to college and season to season, although you can always behave as if you have a perfect right to walk wherever you like and see what happens.

018 Gunpowder, treason and plot: Lewes Bonfire night

ENGLAND The first week of November sees one of the eccentric English's most irresponsible, unruly and downright dangerous festivals – Bonfire Night. Up and down the country, human effigies are burned in back gardens and fireworks are set off – all in the name of Guy Fawkes' foiled attempt to blow up the Houses of Parliament in 1605 – but in the otherwise peaceful market town of Lewes, things are taken to extremes. Imagine a head-on collision between Halloween and Mardi Gras and you're well on your way to picturing Bonfire Night, Lewes-style.

Throughout the evening, smoke fills the Lewes air, giving the steep and narrow streets an eerie, almost medieval feel. As the evening draws on, rowdy torch-lit processions make their way through the streets, pausing to hurl barrels of burning tar into the River Ouse before dispersing to their own part of town to stoke up their bonfires.

Establishment propaganda in the aftermath of the so-called Gunpowder Plot ensured that Fawkes' name was forever associated with treason and treachery, and that "bone fires" – featuring burnings in effigy of villains of the day – became inextricably linked with his name. As the societies head for their own bonfires, they are each trailed by huge papier-mâché figures. Crammed full of fireworks themselves, these "guys" are defended by a number of "prelates", who fearlessly bat the rockets thrown at them by members of rival societies back into the crowd.

Forget the limp burgers of mainstream displays and lame sparklers suitable for use at home – for a real pyrotechnic party, Lewes is king.

019 Playing the old course at St Andrews

SCOTLAND There are several courses where you have to play a round at least once to call yourself a true golf devotee (Pine Valley, Pebble Beach and Augusta National to name but a few), but the Old Course at St Andrews is still "the one". Just walking out onto the first tee sends shivers down the spine, as you think how many feet, legendary or otherwise, have squared up to send a ball hurtling into the blustery winds before you.

St Andrews is the home of golf – the game's equivalent to Wembley or Wimbledon, a venue that is part of the mythology of the sport. The contemporary view may be that golf courses should be manufactured, created and sculpted, but St Andrews had a very different designer of sorts, in the form of nature itself. Here, the landscape is the course. It may not have the charm or the aesthetics of its American counterparts but it has real character. There's barely a tree to be seen, so the atmosphere is quite different from many modern courses. Similarly, there's little water around aside from Swilcan Burn, which has to be traversed on the 18th fairway, and the adjacent bruise-black waters of the North Sea.

This perceived lack of obstacles doesn't mean there's little to test the most experienced of players though; the course is filled with hidden humps, bumps and dips, and there are man-made challenges, too – the infamous Road Hole Bunker on the 17th being the most notorious. Any obstacle that requires a ladder to escape from must be pretty hardcore.

They've been teeing off here for around three hundred years and you'd guess it hasn't changed much at all, which is one of the things that makes this such a unique sporting experience. Be sure to take a local caddie, though – that way, he can worry about whether you should be using a 9-iron or a pitching wedge, and you can concentrate on absorbing the significance of it all.

020 Losing yourself in Connemara

IRELAND On the far western edge of Europe, the starkly beautiful region of Connemara is a great place to get lost. Cut off from the rest of Ireland by the 25-mile barrier of Lough Corrib, the lie of the land at first looks simple, with two statuesque mountain ranges, the Maam Turks and the Twelve Bens, bordered by the deep fjord of Killary Harbour to the north.

The coast, however, is full of jinks and tricks, a hopeless maze of inlets, peninsulas and small islands. Dozens of sparkling lakes and vast blanket bogs covered in purple moor grass further blur the distinction between land and water. Throw in a fickle climate, which can turn from blazing sunshine to grey, soaking mist in the time it takes to buy a loaf of bread, and the carefree sense of disorientation is complete.

This austere, infertile land was brutally depopulated by starvation, eviction and emigration during the Great Famine of the 1840s. Even when dramatist J.M. Synge visited in the early twentieth century, he considered any farming here to be like "the freak of an eccentric". Today, these wild and lonely margins are the ultimate fulfilment of visitors' romantic dreams of Ireland, with enough variety to warrant weeks of exploration.

Cycling on the quiet backroads – many of which were built to provide employment during the Famine – is probably the best way to get to know the area. At an even gentler pace, the outlandishly contorted geology provides great diversity for walkers, ranging from tough, high-level treks in the mountains to scenic hikes up isolated hummocks such as Errisbeg and Tully Hill.

ENGLAND Its tower stands almost 100ft tall, but what really lifts Old Light above the rest of Britain's lighthouses is the 400ft hulk of granite on which it's perched. Set on the wild island of Lundy, eleven miles off the Devon coast, Old Light's great height ended up crippling it: the lantern spent much of its time obscured by soupy fogs and was replaced in 1897 by lower lights at the north and south of the island.

Old Light may be in retirement, but it's still the highest lighthouse in Britain, and visitors can reap the rewards of its failure with a visit to its lofty lamp chamber. Climb the 147 narrow, stone steps and ease into a deckchair to take in the dizzying panorama of the island plummeting into a gaping ocean. Or venture up at sunset to witness orange skies silhouetting the surrounding coastlines of Wales, Cornwall, Devon and Somerset.

Being atop Old Light isn't just about gawping at the views, though. The experience begins as you slip away from the mainland aboard HMS *Oldenburg*. If you're lucky dolphins will ride the bow wave, or you might spot a basking shark. You disembark in a place with only a score of permanent residents and little regard for modern trappings. Walking is the only means of transport – a fact emphasized by the gruelling incline to the verdant plateau that caps the island.

Lundy is Norse for "Puffin Island" and these bright-beaked birds can be spotted during April and May. Wildlife is far from sparse at other times of year, though, with seals hauling themselves onto rocks above which kittiwakes, fulmars and shags soar. Lundy ponies, Soay sheep and feral deer roam the wild terrain, and in the kelp forests of the surrounding sea lies one of only three Marine Nature Reserves in the UK.

Come on a daytrip if you must, but once the ferry leaves the island really turns on its magic. Rest your head in a converted pigsty, a castle or the keeper's quarters of the lighthouse. Or better yet, in a place where there's no electricity after midnight, be a true Robinson Crusoe and camp out under the stars.

021

022

SCOTLAND Even in a country as scenic as Scotland, you might not expect to combine travelling by train with classic views of the Scottish Highlands; the tracks are down in the glens, after all, tracing the lower contours of the steep-sided scenery. On the other hand, you might have to crane your neck occasionally, but at least you don't have to keep your eyes on the road. And you can always get out for a wander; in fact, some of the stations on the West Highland line are so remote that no public road connects them. At each stop, a handful of deerstalkers, hikers, mountain bikers, photographers or day-trippers might get on or off. It'll be a few hours until the next train comes along, but that's not a problem. There's a lot to take in.

The scenery along the West Highland Railway is both epic in its breadth and compelling in its imagery. You travel at a very sedate pace in a fairly workaday train carriage from the centre of Glasgow and its bold Victorian buildings, along the banks of the gleaming Clyde estuary, up the thickly wooded loch shores of Argyll, across the desolate heathery bogs of Rannoch Moor and deep into the grand natural architecture of the Central Highlands, their dappled birch forests fringing green slopes and mist-enveloped peaks.

After a couple of hours, the train judders gently into the first of its destinations, Fort William, set at the foot of Britain's highest peak, Ben Nevis. The second leg of the journey is a gradual pull towards the Hebrides. At Glenfinnan, the train glides over an impressive 21-arch viaduct, most famous these days for conveying Harry Potter on the *Hogwarts Express*. Not long afterwards, the line reaches the coast, where there are snatched glimpses of bumpy islands and silver sands, before you pull into the fishing port of Mallaig, with seagulls screeching overhead in the stiff, salty breeze, and the silhouette of Skye emerging from across the sea.

TRUNDLING ALONG

the **West Highland Railway**

023 Daydreaming in Oxford

ENGLAND Christchurch meadow at dusk and the timing is impeccable. The light is perfect – the harsh midday sun has softened, and now, rather than glinting off the spires and turrets of Merton and Corpus Christi colleges, it seems almost to embrace them, revealing their sharp angles and intricate carvings. They jut proudly above the quiet parklands and sports grounds, and the majestic Tom Tower of Christchurch presides graciously over the centre of Oxford. The noise of the city centre (just minutes to the north) has melted away completely. This is Oxford University at its best; the time when its touristy title "the city of dreaming spires" doesn't seem so overblown after all.

Such fleeting glimpses of this centuries-old seat of learning, right in the midst of a thoroughly modern city, are both disarming and exhilarating. For a brief time, the colleges shed any contemporary associations and you can imagine what it would have been like to study here, long before cars clogged the narrow streets and camera-toting tourists swarmed amongst the cloisters. The spires acquire a greater significance, appearing to reach up, high into the sky, almost signifying the pursuit of knowledge.

Back at ground level there's plenty more to stimulate the imagination and fire up the intellect. Wander down Oxford's narrow alleys and into its quiet corners, where you'll feel the presence of generations of scholars who've gone before. Duck into the *Eagle and Child* pub, where J.R.R. Tolkien and C.S. Lewis hobnobbed; stroll the echoing walkways of Magdalen College, through which politician William Hague and Nobel Laureate Seamus Heaney rushed to tutorials; and visit the cavernous dining hall at Christchurch, where the likes of John Locke and Albert Einstein once ate, but which is now more famous as Hogwarts' hall in the Harry Potter films. In Oxford, however, facts are far better than fiction.

024 Flying with BA to Barra and beyond

SCOTLAND BA8855 is perhaps the oddest scheduled domestic flight in Britain. It is a twenty-seater propeller plane that takes off daily from Glasgow and lands an hour later directly on the beach at Barra, the southernmost island of the Western Isles, also known as the Outer Hebrides. There is no airstrip, nor are there even any lights on the sand, and the flight times shift to fit in with the tide tables, because at high tide the runway is submerged.

Even if Barra were a dreary destination, the flight would be worth taking simply for the views it gives of Scotland's beautiful west coast and the islands of Mull, Skye, Rum and Eigg. It's probably also the only British Airways flight on which the person who demonstrates the safety procedures then turns around, gets into the cockpit and flies the plane.

The Western Isles is the only part of Britain – and one of only a few in the world – where you can experience a truly stunning landscape in solitude; a hundred-mile-long archipelago consisting of a million exquisitely beautiful acres with a population that would leave Old Trafford stadium two-thirds empty.

Give yourself a week to drive slowly up through the island chain, from Barra to Eriskay, site of the famous "Whisky Galore" shipwreck (both the real and the fictional one), then South Uist to Benbecula, to North Uist, and finally to Harris and Lewis. Some islands are linked by causeways (all of which have "Beware: Otters Crossing" traffic signs), others by car ferries. Stop if you can at *Scarista House*, a gourmet paradise set alongside a vast, perpetually empty white sandy beach in the midst of a walker's Eden.

025 Into the valley: hearing a Welsh choir

WALES The road into Senghenydd from the imposing Welsh castle town of Caerphilly snakes along the side of a steep slope that drops into a rocky valley below. Lined with red-toned terraced houses constructed from local stone, the village almost clings to the hillside, and though coal mining died out here long ago, the landscape still bears its scars. You may need to pause on the high street to allow stray sheep to cross the road – this is one of Britain's most rural corners.

Senghenydd is home to the Aber Valley Male Voice Choir, and though the choir gives concerts all over the world, it is here in the village's ex-servicemen's club that the sound is created and honed to perfection. The 59 men, many of them second- or third-generation choristers, perform everything from sombre hymns to 'Bohemian Rhapsody'. Singing in both English and Welsh, their voices swell in four-part harmonies, as rich and complex as an orchestra.

Male voice choirs are a Welsh institution, part of the lives of thousands of working men from Snowdonia to the Rhondda. The choirs grew from the companionship and community spirit forged by the men who worked down the mines of the south and the quarries of the north.

Times have changed, but they are still going strong. The choir in Senghenydd practises twice a week (the men come as much for the camaraderie as for the music), and visitors are welcome to drop in on a rehearsal – an intimate and moving experience. The high proportion of silver hair in the choir ranks might raise concern about whether the younger generation will carry on the tradition. But with nearly 150 male voice choirs in a land just short of three million people, this unique part of Welsh life is in no danger of disappearing.

Walking in the mountains of

MOURNE

NORTHERN IRELAND The mountains rise above the seaside town of Newcastle like green giants, with Slieve Donard the highest, almost three thousand feet above the sandy strand of Dundrum Bay. Donard is just one of more than twenty peaks in County Down's Kingdom of Mourne (as the tourist office likes to call it), with a dozen of them towering over two thousand feet. Conveniently grouped together in a range that is just seven miles broad and about fourteen miles long, they are surprisingly overlooked – especially by many locals. On foot, in a landscape with no interior roads, you feel as if you have reached a magical oasis of high ground, a pure space that is part *Finian's Rainbow* and part Middle Earth.

Cutting across the heart of the Mournes is a dry-stone wall, part of a 22-mile barrier built in the 1920s to keep livestock out of the water catchment for the Silent Valley Reservoir. When a mist rolls off the sea, or a rain squall hits hard, the wall is a shelter, and a guide.

This is a wet place where the Glen River flows from the flanks of Slieve Commedagh and through Donard Wood. Some slopes are bog, and ragged black-faced sheep shelter behind clumps of golden gorse. Up here, peregrines ride on the wind and sharp-beaked ravens hope to scavenge the corpse of a lamb or two. Tied to the earth, you can follow the Brandy Pad, a scenic smugglers' track leading over the mountains from the Bloody River through Hare's Gap and down again to Clonachullion. This is ancient land, and prehistoric cairns and stone graves – said to mark the resting place of Irish chiefs – dot the hills, peering through the mist to meet you.

027

HOARDING BOOKS IN
Hay-on-Wye

028 Freediving in the Royal Navy's SETT

ENGLAND It's 100 feet deep and filled with warm, clear water. The Royal Navy Submarine Escape Training Tank (SETT) in Gosport does what it says on the label, but it's also a perfect place to practise freediving, with safety ropes for swimmers to hold onto as they fin down in preparation for trying the sport in the sea. Fans of Luc Besson's cult movie *Le Grand Bleu*, spearfishermen and scuba divers all get drawn to freediving because it is a purer, simpler way to experience the tranquillity of the underwater world – you just hold your breath and go. The training tank is like a giant space rocket filled with shimmering water, luring you to dive into the depths.

029 Chasing cheese in Gloucester

ENGLAND Cooper's Hill Cheese-Rolling, an organized bout of cheese chasing down a grassy mound in Gloucestershire, is one of Britain's best-known festivals, and possibly its most bizarre – a totem, somehow, of a country of eccentric and long-established events. It's certainly in the best spirit of British amateurism: anyone can enter, and all they have to do is fling themselves down a precipitous hill after an eighteen-pound wheel of Double Gloucester. The first one to reach it wins – and no prizes for guessing what.

030 Hitting the streets for the Notting Hill Carnival

ENGLAND It starts sometime in August, when the first of the after-party posters materialize along Ladbroke Grove and the plink-plonk rhythms of steelband rehearsals filter through the clamour of Portobello market. By the time the crowd barriers appear on street corners and the shop-owners begin covering their windows with party-scarred plywood, the feeling of anticipation is almost tangible: Carnival is coming. These familiar old streets are about to be transformed into a wash of colour, sound, movement and pure, unadulterated joy that makes this huge street festival the highlight of London's party calendar.

Carnival Sunday morning and in streets eerily emptied of cars, sound-system guys, still bleary-eyed from the excesses of last night's warm-up parties, wire up their towering stacks of speakers, while fragrant smoke wafts from the stalls of early-bird jerk chicken chefs. And then a bass line trembles through the morning air, and the trains begin to disgorge crowds of revellers, dressed to impress and brandishing their whistles and horns. Some head straight for the sound systems, spending the entire day moving from one to the other and stopping wherever the music takes them. Streets lined by mansion blocks become canyons of sound, and all you can see is a moving sea of people, jumping and blowing whistles as wave after wave of music ripples through the air.

But the backbone of Carnival is mas, the parade of costumed bands that winds its way through the centre of the event. Crowds line up along the route, and Ladbroke Grove becomes a seething throng of floats and flags, sequins and feathers, as the mas (masquerade) bands cruise along, their revellers dancing up a storm to the tunes bouncing from the music trucks. And for the next two days, the only thing that matters is the delicious, anarchic freedom of dancing on the London streets.

WALES Though a drive through the electrically green countryside that surrounds Hay-on-Wye makes for a perfectly lovely afternoon, a more potent draw is the sleepy Welsh town's mouthwatering amount of printed matter: with over a million books crammed into its aging stores, quaint, cobblestoned Hay-on-Wye (Y Gelli, in Welsh) is a bibliophilic Mecca to be reckoned with. Dusty volumes are packed in like sardines, some of them in shops tucked away down alleyways verdant with moss and mildew. Mouldering British cookbooks fight for shelf space with plant-taxonomy guides, romance novels and pricey but lavishly produced first editions.

To unearth these treasures the intrepid bookhunter need only meander into one of the many bookshops that liberally dot the town. And with a human-to-bookshop ratio of around 40:1, there's a lot of choice. Mystery aficionados should check out Murder & Mayhem, while a visit to The Poetry Bookshop is *de rigueur* for fans of verse. One of the largest and most diverse collections can be found at the Hay Cinema Bookshop – rickety mini staircases, two sprawling floors and a labyrinthine series of rooms loosely divided by subject matter, creates a unique book-browsing space that seems to exist outside of the space-time continuum for the way in which it can so wholly consume an afternoon. Stay long enough and your faith that there's an underlying logic to the bookshelves' progression from "Fifteenth-century Russian History" to "British Water Fowl" to "Erotica" will grow wonderfully, psychotically strong.

Topic-driven pilgrimages aside, a visit to the two outdoor secondhand bookshops in front of crumbling Hay Castle is unmissable. Ringed by stone ramparts, the castle – nearly 1000 years old – provides a striking backdrop as you rifle through scads of books eclectic in appearance as much as theme.

031 Go west: hiking the Pembrokeshire Coast Path

WALES The Pembrokeshire Coast Path fringes Britain's only coastal national park, which has resisted the onslaught of the twenty-first century in all but a few hotspots such as Tenby and St David's (and even these remain remarkably lovely). Get out and stride along part of the 143-mile trail and you'll soon appreciate this evocative and spectacular edge of Wales.

Long golden surf beaches easily rival those of California; the clear green seas are the habitat of seals, whales, dolphins, sharks and, in summer, exotic species such as sunfish and even seahorses. Further offshore, you'll spot islands that are home to internationally important seabird colonies. You can wander atop the highest sea cliffs in Wales, bent into dramatic folds by ancient earth movements; and in the hamlets, harbours and villages you pass through along the way, there are plenty of charming pubs and restaurants at which to refuel.

This variety is one of the best things about the coast path, which offers something for everyone – and not just in summer. The off-season can provide the thrilling spectacle of mighty Atlantic storms dashing thirty-foot waves against the sea cliffs as you fight your way along an exhilaratingly wind-lashed beach, whilst the next day the sun could be glittering in a clear blue sky with seabirds wheeling and screeching overhead. Take time out from your hike to relax and enjoy views across the Atlantic, which, other than the occasional lighthouse dotting the horizon, have remained unchanged since St Patrick sailed from Whitesands Beach to Ireland.

To walk the full length of the path takes up to two weeks and, surprisingly, involves more ascent than climbing Mount Everest, but even just a half-day outing along the trail is worth the effort and acts as a reminder that Britain boasts some of the finest coastline in the world.

032 Calling in the heavies at the Highland Games

SCOTLAND Throughout Scotland, not just in the Highlands, summer signals the onset of the Highland Games, from the smallest village get-togethers to the Giant Cowal Highland Gathering in Dunoon, which draws a crowd of 10,000. Urbanites might blanch at the idea of al fresco Scottish country dancing, but with dog trials, tractors, fudge stalls and more cute animals than you could toss a caber at, the Highland Games are a guaranteed paradise for kids.

It's thought that the games originated in the eleventh century as a means of selecting soldiers through trials of strength and endurance. These events were formalized in the nineteenth century, partly as a result of Queen Victoria's romantic attachment to Highland culture:

a culture that had in reality been brutally extinguished following the defeat of the Jacobites at Culloden.

The military origins of the games are recalled in displays of muscle-power by bulky bekilted local men, from tossing the caber (ie tree trunk) to hurling hammers and stones, and pitching bales of straw over a raised pole. Music and dance are also integral to the games, with pipe bands and small girls – kitted out in waistcoats, kilts and long woolly socks – performing reels and sword dances. You might also see showjumping, as well as sheepdogs being put through their paces, while the agricultural shows feature prize animals, from sleek ponies with intricate bows tied in their manes and tails to curly- horned rams.

033 Holkham Magic

ENGLAND Is Holkham Bay in north Norfolk the best beach in Britain? It must certainly be the broadest. At high tide, you follow the private road from Holkham Hall, walk through a stretch of woods and expect to find the sea at your feet. But it is – literally – miles away: two miles at the very least, shimmering beyond a huge expanse of dunes, pools, flat sands and salt marsh. If it's your first visit, it may seem oddly familiar – for this was the location for Gwyneth Paltrow's walk along the sands, as Viola, at the end of *Shakespeare in Love*.

The amazing thing about Holkham is that, even with the filming of a Hollywood movie in full swing, you could have wandered onto the beach and not noticed. It is that big. You saunter off from the crowds near the road's end and within a few minutes you're on your own, splashing through tidal pools, picking up the odd shell, or, if it's

warm enough, diving into the sea. You can walk along the beach all the way to Wells (to the east) or Overy Staithe (west), or drop back from the sea and follow trails through woods of Corsican pines. Just beware going out onto the sandbanks when there's a rising tide; it comes in alarmingly fast.

Birdlife is exceptional around Holkham – which is a protected reserve – and you'll see colonies of pink-footed and Brent geese in winter, as well as oystercatchers, little terns, and many other birds. And if you head down the coast to Cley-next-the-Sea or to Blakeney, you'll find even more riches, accompanied by rows of twitchers, camped behind binoculars. Take time to walk out to the hides at Cley Marshes, or for a boat ride to Blakeney Point, where you can watch several hundred common and grey seals basking on the mud.

ENGLAND Go to Venice or Amsterdam, and you can hardly cross a street without tumbling into a canal. In London, you have to dig deeper. The Regent's Canal stretches from chichi Maida Vale to Thames-side Limehouse, cutting past London Zoo's aviaries, Camden's pop kids, Islington restaurants and Hackney high-rises on its way. Built in the early nineteenth century to connect London's docks with the Grand Union Canal to Birmingham, its traffic was almost entirely lost to truck and rail by the 1950s.

Now (mostly) cleaned up, the canal and its tributaries feel like a wonderfully novel way to delve into a compelling, overexposed city. That's in part down to its submerged nature: much of its length is below street level, hidden by overgrown banks. Spend time by the water's edge and you feel utterly removed from the road and rail bridges above. When the route rises up or spews you back onto the street momentarily, you catch a brief glimpse of people seemingly oblivious to the green serpent that stretches across their city.

It's not all idyllic: for every lovely patch of reeds or drifting duck, there's a bobbing beer can or the unmistakable judder of traffic though. Stroll the busier stretches on a summer Sunday, when the walkers, cyclists and barges are out, and the canal can feel more like an artery than an escape route. But this is a dynamic, breathing space: its energy is what makes it so vital, and makes the moments of quiet feel so special.

There are countless highlights: the spire of St Pancras station, soaring over a surprisingly secluded corner near King's Cross; Mile End's picturesque nature reserve; and the bridges and wharfs that connect Limehouse to the Isle of Dogs. The poet Paul Verlaine thought the isle's vast docks and warehouses classical in their majesty, calling them "astonishing...Tyre and Carthage all rolled in to one". Turned into smart flats or left to crumble, they are no longer the heartbeat of an industrial nation, but with their forgotten corners and fascinating history, they still feel magical.

WALK LONDON'S
hidden highways

034

BURNING RUBBER AT THE **TT**
Isle of Man

ENGLAND For fifty weeks of the year, the Isle of Man is a sleepy little place. Locals leave their doors unlocked, they stop to chat in the street, and they know the name of their next-door neighbour's cat. But for two weeks in summer, everything changes, as forty thousand visitors – with twelve thousand motorcycles – cross the Irish Sea and turn this quiet island into a rubber-burning, beer-swilling, eardrum-bursting maelstrom of a motorcycle festival.

The TT (Tourist Trophy) has been screeching round the Isle of Man for a hundred years, but only came about thanks to the island's political peculiarity. The Isle of Man is a Crown Dependency, but not a part of the UK or the EU – it has its own parliament and its own laws. And so when, in the early days of the automobile, the UK forbade motor racing on its public roads and imposed a speed limit of 20mph, race organizers made their way over the water.

And they've never left, although the race they devised in 1907 would be impossible to initiate today. It's the kind of event that drives health and safety officers to drink: the 37-mile Mountain Course, which competitors lap several times, is no carefully cambered track – it's an ordinary road that winds its way through historic towns, screams along country roads, climbs up hills and takes in two hundred bends, many of which are not lined by grass or pavement but by bone-mashing, brain-spilling brick walls. And the fastest riders complete the course at an average speed of 120mph.

Sad to say, they don't all reach the finish line. Around two hundred riders have taken their final tumble on the roads of the TT, and islanders will delight in describing the details to you over a pint of local Bushey's beer. They'll also tell you that, while many of their fellow Manx folk love the adrenalin, the triumph and the tragedy of those two weeks in summer, others are less enthusiastic. The combination of road closures and roistering bikers drives these malcontents to blow the dust from their door keys, to lock up their homes and seek refuge elsewhere – taking their daughters with them.

036 Winning the prehistoric lottery

IRELAND Every year in Ireland, thousands of people do the Newgrange lottery. Entry is by application form, with the draw made in October by local schoolchildren. And the prize? The lucky winners are invited to a bleak, wintry field in the middle of County Meath on the longest night of the year, to huddle into a dank and claustrophobic tunnel and wait for the sun to come up.

It's not just any old field, though, but part of Brú na Boinne, one of Europe's most important archeological sites. A slow bend in the River Boyne cradles this extraordinary ritual landscape of some forty Neolithic mounds, which served not only as graves but also as spiritual and ceremonial meeting places for the locals, five thousand years ago.

The tunnel belongs to the most famous passage mound, Newgrange, which stretches over 273ft in diameter, weighs 200,000 tons in total and is likely to have taken forty years to build. The lottery winners get to experience the annual astronomical event for which the tomb's passage was precisely and ingeniously designed: through a roofbox over the entrance, the first rays of the rising sun on the winter solstice shine unerringly into the burial chamber in the heart of the mound, 65ft away at the end of the passage.

Not everyone gets to win the lottery, of course, so throughout the year as part of an entertaining guided tour of the mound, visitors are shown an electrically powered simulation of the solstice dawn in the central chamber. Once you've taken the tour and seen the impressive visitor centre, the perfect complement is to drive 19 miles west to the Loughcrew Cairns, a group of thirty similar mounds that are largely unexcavated. Here, you borrow a torch and the key to the main passage tomb, Cairn T, and you'll almost certainly have the place to yourself. With views of up to sixteen counties on a clear day, you can let your imagination run wild in an unspoilt and enigmatic landscape.

037 Surfing the Severn Bore

ENGLAND Autumn mist swirls across the placid waters of the River Severn, and a kingfisher flits along the river bank in a spark of colour. Gradually, from downriver, a noise like the murmuring of a distant crowd develops into a roar, then suddenly a mighty wall of brown water appears across the entire width of the river, topped here and there by a creamy curl where the wave is racing to get ahead of itself.

This is the Severn Bore, one of the longest and biggest tidal bores in the world. It's a startling spectacle when you're watching from the river bank. If you're actually in the river, it can be terrifying.

The river, though, is where you'll be if you choose to surf the Bore. Since the sixties, surfers from all over the world have made their way to the Severn to catch this remarkable wave. It occurs on the biggest tides of the year when Atlantic waters from the Bristol Channel surge up the Severn Estuary at as much as 12mph and become funnelled between the ever-narrowing river banks to create one of Britain's most bizarre natural phenomena.

If the equinoxes coincide with big Atlantic swells, the wave may be as much as six-feet high, tearing off overhanging tree branches, sweeping away sections of river bank and providing a ride that can last for several miles. It's a challenge even for a competent surfer. Non-surfers will want to stay bankside, from where the Bore is simply a strange and magnificent sight.

038 Barging down the Barrow

IRELAND There's a point on the River Barrow in County Kildare, about halfway between the country towns of Athy and Carlow, when you realize that you're in the middle of absolutely nowhere. A quick flick of the engine into neutral and you're surrounded by silence, nothing but the soothing slosh of water as the barge's bow glides slowly through the reeds. Flanked on both sides by trees and rolling fields of verdant emerald green, there's only one thing to do: sit back and soak up the solitude.

For nearly two hundred years, steel-boarded barges have plied the Grand Canal network, first transporting peat to Dublin and beyond, and latterly ferrying holidaymakers through the languid countryside. A week spent cruising along the Grand Canal and down the River Barrow, one of the most beautiful navigable stretches in Europe, is time spent recharging the soul: after a few early-morning maintenance checks, just undo the moorings, start up the engine and off you go, slowly chugging your way to the next ruined castle or cosy local.

Idle days make for idle ways, and the beauty of barging is that you have to do very little to keep your thirty-foot vessel on the straight and narrow. Manoeuvring through a set of double locks without taking the whole thing with you provides a brief lull in the languor – racks have to be cranked, sluices opened and pawls closed, all while the driver holds the barge steady to avoid getting beached on the back sill – but the rest of the day is spent cruising the backwaters of middle Ireland at a leisurely 5mph.

But if you're going to get nowhere fast, there can surely be fewer places better than the Barrow. Yellow iris, cuckoo flower and heavily scented meadowsweet line the river banks, herons let your barge get tantalizingly close before launching off across the water, and there's a traditional pub at every turn, each serving finer Guinness than the last.

039 Watching the hurling at Croke Park

IRELAND The player leaps like a basketball star through a crowd of desperate opponents and flailing sticks. Barely visible to the naked eye, the arcing ball somehow lodges in his upstretched palm. Dropping to the ground, he shimmies his way out of trouble, the ball now delicately balanced on the flat end of his hurley, then bang! With a graceful, scything pull, he slots the ball through the narrow uprights, seventy yards away.

Such is the stuff of Irish boyhood dreams, an idealized sequence of hurling on continual rewind. With similarities to lacrosse and hockey – though it's not really like either – hurling is a thrilling mix of athleticism, timing, outrageous bravery and sublime skill. Said to be the fastest team game in the world, it can be readily enjoyed by anyone with an eye for sport.

The best place to watch a match is Dublin's vast Croke Park, the iconic headquarters of the GAA (Gaelic Athletic Association).

In this magnificent, 80,000-seater stadium, you'll experience all the colour, banter and passion of inter-county rivalry. And before the game, you can visit the excellent GAA Museum to get up to speed on hurling and its younger brother, Gaelic football, ancient sports whose renaissance was entwined with the struggle for Irish independence. Here, you'll learn about the first Bloody Sunday in 1920, when British troops opened fire on a match at this very ground, killing twelve spectators and one of the players. You'll be introduced to the modern-day descendants of Cúchulain, the greatest warrior-hero of Irish mythology, who is said to have invented hurling: star players of the last century including flat-capped Christy Ring of Cork and more recent icons such as Kilkenny's D.J. Carey. And finally, you can attempt to hit a hurling ball yourself – after a few fresh-air shots, you'll soon appreciate the intricate skills the game requires.

040 Walking the walls of Conwy Castle

WALES Up on Conwy Castle's battlements the wind whips around the eight solid towers that have stood on this rocky knoll for over seven hundred years. It's a superb spot with long views out across the surrounding landscape, but look down from the castle's magnificent curtain walls and you'll also see all the elements that combined to make Conwy one of the most impressive fortresses of its day.

The castle occupies an important site, beside the tidal mud flats of the Conwy Estuary where pearl mussels have been harvested for centuries. To the south lie the northern peaks of Snowdonia, the mountains where the Welsh have traditionally sought refuge from invaders such as the Norman English, who built this castle around 1283. Conwy formed a crucial link in Edward I's "Iron Ring" of eight castles around North Wales, designed to finally crush the last vestiges of Welsh resistance to his rule. Gazing upon this imposing fortress, which took just five years to build and is still largely intact,

it isn't hard to understand why he was successful.

A key part of the castle's design was its integration with the town, so that the two could support each other, and from the battlements a three-quarter-mile ring of intact town walls, punctuated with 21 towers, loops out from the base of the castle, encircling Conwy's old town. For centuries, the Welsh were forced to live outside the town walls while the English prospered within; the latter left behind a fine legacy in the form of the fourteenth-century half-timbered Aberconwy House and Plas Mawr, Britain's best-preserved Elizabethan town house.

Finish off the day by heading into town and walking a circuit of the thirty-foot-high town walls. Start at the very highest point (tower 13), where you get a superb view across the slate roofs of the town to the castle, and wander down towards the river where a pint on the quay outside the *Liverpool Arms* is *de rigueur* on a fine evening.

041 Breathing in the sea air in Tobermory

SCOTLAND On the old stone fishing pier in Tobermory, on the island of Mull, a very affordable indulgence is available: queue at the fish and chip van and order a scallop supper. It'll be served in brown paper, just like the classic (but more mundane) takeaway fish and chips, and you'll probably have to perch on the harbour wall to eat them, but you get a meal of steaming chips and sweet, tender scallops, gathered from the surrounding waters a few hours previously, as well as free views across the prettiest port on the west coast of Scotland.

Close by, fishing boats are tied up at the pier, pyramids of lobster creels piled up in their sterns. Out in the bay, yachts sit on their moorings, while large inflatable boats with deep-throated outboard engines circle near the jetty, ready to take passengers on an evening spin out into the surrounding waters to look for seals, porpoises,

dolphins, basking sharks and, quite possibly, minke or killer whales.

Along the waterfront, tall handsome houses are painted in vibrant blue, pink, yellow, red or gleaming white. No matter what the weather, they're an uplifting, if slightly garish, sight. The rest of the village – the grand castellated hotel, cosy guesthouses, the arts centre with its background vibe of uplifting Gaelic songs – is perched on a hillside that rises sharply from the water. Toil up the short but steep switchback roads of the upper village and you'll be treated to increasingly impressive views of the bay, the wave-creased Sound of Mull and empty hills beyond. Venture even further, across the heathery golf course on the fringes of the village, and dramatic glimpses of the strewn islands and ragged coast to the north and west begin to appear. It's not a bad way to walk off supper.

Follow in the footsteps of **kings and queens** at Bath Spa

042

ENGLAND For almost twenty years at the end of the last century, Britain's most famous spa town had no thermal baths. The opening of the new Thermae Bath Spa in 2006, at the centre of this World Heritage City, was therefore a watershed in Bath's history. Once the haunt of the Roman elite who founded the city 2000 years ago, and later frequented by British Royalty like Elizabeth I and Charles II, Britain's only natural thermal spa boasts a uniquely soothing atmosphere with gentle lighting and curative vapours, the surrounding grandeur testament to the importance given to these therapeutic waters.

The spa's centrepiece is its rooftop pool, where on cold winter evenings the Twilight bathing package allows you to enjoy majestic views of Bath's Abbey and its genteel Georgian architecture through wisps of rising steam from the pool's 33.5˚C water. The Celts thought that the goddess Sul was the force behind the spring, but we now know that the waters probably fell as rain in the nearby Mendip Hills some 10,000 years ago, before being pushed 2km upwards through bedrock and limestone to arrive at the pools enriched with minerals and hot enough to treat respiratory, muscular and skin problems.

The new spa's remarkable design contrasts existing listed Georgian buildings and colonnades with contemporary glass curves and fountains, employing local Bath stone to impressive effect. The covered Minerva Bath provides thermal water jets for shoulder massage, while you can indulge in an astonishing variety of massages and treatments like reiki, shiatsu, body wraps and flotation in the classical Hot Bath, built in 1778 and restored with twelve treatment rooms and a striking glass ceiling. Elsewhere, four steam rooms offer eucalyptus, mint and lavender scents, and there is a giant thermal shower to reinvigorate the soul. When you've had your fill of relaxation, the old Roman Baths nearby are well worth a visit, too – they offer one of the world's best-preserved insights into Roman culture, complete with authentic Latin graffiti.

WALES Convertibles sell better in Britain than in much of the Mediterranean. That might make it sound like the inhabitants of this damp island are stupid. A kinder explanation is that they just enjoy the sunshine when it comes – an impression that will have struck anyone who's attended a pop festival in the UK with the force of a stage diver. The tales of the rains that swallowed tents at Glastonbury in 2005 and turned 2008's Bestival into a treacherous mudbath rapidly acquired legendary proportions. When the sun shines and the right band are onstage, people tell fewer stories, but the smiles are as broad as they come. And Green Man, which has had its share of blissful warmth and endless drizzle, is the pick of the festive crop.

Sat between Abergavenny and the Brecon Beacons, its estate location feels classically picturesque, but hills including the iconic Sugar Loaf rear around the site, giving that touch of the wilderness. Its capacity (10,000 at last count) is big enough to bestow a sense of occasion but small enough to mean you might manage to find your tent and friends, which will prove a relief to anyone who's spent hours trekking Glastonbury's acres. There's no big branding here, and the staff spend more time helping you out than telling you what you can't do – even the toilets are decidedly bearable. Green Man also manages the neat trick of being family- and hedonist-friendly – the DJ tent booms through the witching hours, but kids will enjoy the stalls, gardens and children's parades.

Indeed, while many festivals that try to be all things to all people end up tying themselves in knots, Green Man pulls out some crackers. There aren't many stadium headliners here, but the intriguing assortment of folk veterans, psychedelic hipsters and bluesy rockers have been picked by organisers who care deeply about their music. They've seen Animal Collective get the crowd frugging to swelling math-rock, Richard Thompson play nimble songs of love and loss, Bon Iver bring his Vermont laments to a sunny Saturday and Spiritualized rock out in the downpour. Worth the risk of rain? You bet.

043

FOLKING OUT UNDER THE SUGAR LOAF

044 Finding heaven on Earth in Cornwall

ENGLAND A disued clay pit may seem like an odd location for Britain's very own ecological paradise, but then everything about Cornwall's Eden Project is refreshingly far from conventional. From the conception of creating a unique ecosystem that could showcase the diversity of the world's plant life, through to the execution – a set of bulbous, alien-like, geodesic biomes wedged into the hillside of a crater – the designers have never been less than innovative.

The gigantic humid tropics biome, the largest conservatory in the world, is kept at a constant temperature of 30°c. Besides housing lofty trees and creepers that scale its full 160ft height, it takes visitors on a journey through tropical agriculture from coffee growing to the banana trade, to rice production and finding a cure for leukaemia. There's even a life-size replica of a bamboo Malaysian jungle home, and a raffia African rondavel (a makeshift straw hut field workers use when tending their crops and animals).

The smaller biome reconstitutes the Mediterranean, California and parts of South Africa under one roof (unusually composed of Telon-coated "ETFE cushions"), showing how arid regions have been cultivated for centuries in order to fill the world's supermarket shelves. There's also a well-informed introduction to the evils of the tobacco trade, and the centrepiece is a joyful homage to the god of wine, Bacchus, with wild, twisting sculptural installations of a Bacchanalian orgy surrounded by vines. The outdoor biome continues the focus on sustainable ethics, with an introduction to biofuels, such as rapeseed, and willow coppicing, a sustainable way of obtaining wood.

Perhaps all this research and construction represents how future generations will exist? You'd better Adam'n'Eve-it. Maybe we've already taken our chunk of the apple or maybe, with a visit to the Eden Project, we've enough information to create change in our everyday lives and look after our very own biome: planet Earth.

045 Following the Oyster Trail in Galway

IRELAND A canny bit of marketing may lie behind the origins of the Galway International Oyster Festival, but Ireland's longest-running and greatest gourmet extravaganza continues to celebrate the arrival of the new oyster season in the finest way possible: with a three-day furore of drinking, dancing and crustacean guzzling.

Just after midday in Eyre Square, Galway's mayor cracks open the first oyster of the season, knocks it back in one gulp, and declares the festival officially open – just as he has done since the 1950s, when the festival's devisers were searching for something that could extend the tourist season into September. A parade of marching bands, vintage cars, oyster openers, dignitaries and the like then makes its way down the town's main street and along the bank of the River Corrib, its destination the festival marquee, and the World Oyster Opening Championship.

All this pomp, however, is purely a sideshow, albeit a colourful one, to the weekend's main attraction, the Guinness Oyster Trail – the real backbone of the party and one of the greatest Irish pub crawls ever devised. The Trail consists of some thirty boozers dotted around the town, each providing a host of live music, comedy and dance acts over the entire period and, more importantly, offering free oysters with a pint of Guinness – every pub on the Oyster Trail employs a full-time oyster-opener throughout the weekend, who frantically and ceaselessly liberates the delicious creatures from their shells.

The traditional objective is to down a pint and a couple of oysters in every pub along the Trail over the three days – that's around thirty pints and up to one hundred oysters. If you can do this and still make it down for breakfast on the Sunday morning, you need never prove yourself again.

046 Soaking up the Edinburgh Festival

SCOTLAND People talk about culture vultures flocking to the Edinburgh Festival in August, but the truth is that for an event this big you need the stamina of an ox, the appetite of a hippo and the nocturnal characteristics of an owl. The sheer scale and diversity of what's going on in the Scottish capital each August can be hard to digest properly – over half a dozen separate festivals take place simultaneously featuring thousands of different shows in more than two hundred venues. Not to mention the street acts, the buskers, the bizarrely dressed leafleters – and the simple fascination to be had just watching it all swirl around you.

How do you do the Festival without fear of disappointment or exhaustion? Book early for something significant in the International Festival, perhaps one of the world's great philharmonic orchestras at the Usher Hall. Wander into the tented Book Festival in gracious Charlotte Square and enjoy a reading and erudite discussion with a favourite author. Take a chance on an intriguing-sounding piece

of theatre by a company you've never heard of in a venue you struggle to find. After all, you've scoured the reviews in the papers over a couple of cappuccinos in a pleasant café and found a four-star show you can fit in before the new film by that director you've admired for a while.

Pick up a last-minute offer on cheap tickets for a comedian you've seen do a nearly hilarious slot on telly, then join the crowds shuffling up the Royal Mile to the nightly Military Tattoo, thrilling its multinational audience with pomp, ceremony and massed pipe bands, rounded off with fireworks crashing around the castle's battlements.

Time for more? There's probably a risqué cabaret going on at one of the Fringe venues, or a crazy Hungarian folk band stomping its way into the wee small hours in a folk club. But if you're going to do it all again tomorrow, then find a quiet corner of a cosy, wood-panelled pub and order a dram of whisky. Good stuff, this culture.

047 Enjoying the seasons of the Scillies

ENGLAND It's no exaggeration to say that, from London, you can get to the Caribbean quicker than the Scillies. But then, that's part of the appeal. You take the night train down to Penzance and then hop on the Scillonian ferry (not for the queasy) or the helicopter out over the Atlantic.

What awaits depends very much on the weather. The Scillies out of season are bracing, as wind and rain batter these low island outcrops. Wrapped in waterproofs, you can still have fun, squelching over wet bracken and spongy turf to odd outcrops of ruined castles, or picking through the profusion of shells on the beaches. And if you can afford a room at the *Hell Bay Hotel* on Bryher, then you can top off the day with a first-rate meal while gazing at original sculptures and paintings by Barbara Hepworth and Ivor Hitchens.

In summer, when the sun's out, it's a very different scene, and you can swim, go boating, even learn to scuba dive – the water is crystal clear and there are numerous wrecks. It can be a cheap holiday, too, since for only a few pounds you can pitch a tent at the Bryher campsite and enjoy one of the loveliest views in Europe. From there, wander down to the *Fraggle Rock* pub for a pint of Timothy Taylors and a crab sandwich, and then, if the tide's right, wade across to the neighbouring island of Tresco, and explore the subtropical Abbey Gardens.

I keep stressing Bryher, as that's my island. Scilly-fans are fiercely loyal. But you can have almost as good a time on St Martin's, which has arguably the best beaches, or on the diminutive St Agnes, with its wind-sculpted granite and a brilliantly sited pub, *The Turk's Head*. St Mary's doubtless has devotees, too, but with the islands' main town, regular roads and cars, it lacks essential isolated romance. For that, you'll find me on Bryher.

048 Highland fling: getting personal with Ben Nevis

SCOTLAND Scots delight in telling you that Ben Nevis means "venomous hill" in Gaelic, and the name seemed spot on that bleak February morning, with clouds blanketing the peak and an icy wind whistling across from the Atlantic. At 4406ft, Britain's highest mountain is a bairn by Alpine standards, but hiking the Highland giant is not to be scoffed at; the trail ascends relentlessly from sea level past murky lochans, boulder-strewn plateaux and jaw-dropping gullies. Guidebooks say it's best to walk "The Ben" in summer, but if you're prepared for Arctic conditions, there's nothing like winter for a wee adventure.

The dewy greenery of Glen Nevis slowly faded and Highland cattle shrunk to specks on the landscape as I scaled the rocky track skirting Meall an t-Suidhe hill. Each step took me closer to a brooding sky; clouds occasionally peeled back to reveal snow-clad Glencoe and the steely waters of Loch Linnhe. After a steady climb into the gloom, a wave of relief washed over me as I glimpsed the halfway lochan – prematurely perhaps, as soon after I hit the snow. I'd expected a light dusting at the summit, but certainly not two hours of stomping through knee deep, hard-packed powder on the plateau. The trail had all but vanished in the white, my toes were numb, and only frozen footprints were left to guide me.

Exhausted yet exhilarated, I plopped myself down next to the cairn at the top just in time to see the sun pierce a hole in the clouds. As if on cue, shafts of light illuminated the rolling Munroes and the deep blue lochs studding the valley, casting shadows on the distant crags of the Cairngorms. It only lasted for a few minutes but made all the hard slog worth it. In the late afternoon, climbers were still scrambling up the treacherous North Face. But I'd done my intrepid bit. Now it was time to kick back and enjoy the view from my balcony over Britain.

049 See the Belfast Murals

NORTHERN IRELAND Mention the Falls Road and Shankill districts of Belfast, and up flash images of bitter sectarian street battles between the pro-British, Protestant Loyalists and the pro-Irish, largely Catholic Republicans. These close neighbours have long used wall paintings to stake territorial claims, and now that Belfast is back on the tourist agenda, the murals have become a star attraction.

Walking west from central Belfast to the Republican Falls Road, you can't miss the huge painted images adorning almost all end-terrace walls. Some are tributes to the fallen, while others commemorate specific incidents such as the 1981 prison hunger strike when Bobby Sands became a Republican martyr, along with nine comrades. Elsewhere, "Free Ireland" slogans depict wrists shackled by manacles labelled "Made in Britain". The message could hardly be clearer.

A few steps up the side streets north of the Falls Road you hit the Peace Line, a fortified boundary of razor wire and CCTV cameras that separates the road from Loyalist Shankill. The heavy steel gates are now left open, hopefully permanently.

There's an altogether more militaristic feel to Shankill, with guns on almost every mural. Union Jacks are ubiquitous, even on the kerbstones, and one whole housing estate is ringed by red, white and blue kerbing. Most murals also bear the red hand of Ulster, which forms the centrepiece of the Ulster Flag and features on the emblems of both the UVF and UDA paramilitary organizations.

In these districts, passions run high and you'd think it would feel unsettling being a rubbernecking tourist in a place that has witnessed so much bloodshed. But most people are just pleased that you're interested. If you feel at all intimidated or want a deeper insight, opt for one of the excellent taxi tours that visit both districts.

Mountain biking

WALES It's not often that the modest mountains of Wales can compete with giants like the Alps or the Rockies, but when it comes to mountain biking, the trails that run through the craggy peaks of Snowdonia, the high moorlands of the Cambrian Mountains, and the deep, green valleys of South Wales are more than a match for their loftier counterparts. Indeed, the International Mountain Biking Association has long rated Wales as one of the planet's top destinations.

Over the last decade or so, a series of purpose-built mountain biking centres has been created throughout the country, providing world-class riding for everyone from rank beginner through to potential-world-cup downhiller. From easy, gently undulating trails along former rail lines that once served the heavy industry of the South Wales valleys, to the steep, rooty, rocky single tracks that run through the cloud-shadowed hills of North Wales, this is mountain biking at its finest.

Take a centre such as Coed-y-Brenin in Snowdonia National Park. You can ride all day here through deep pine forests, beside tumbling cascades, and alongside open pastures whose vistas stretch from the blue-green water of the Irish Sea to the misty mountaintops of the Snowdon range – and that just covers a couple of trails at only one of seven mountain bike centres located around the country.

The tracks have been designed to be ridden year round – despite the country's (somewhat) undeserved reputation for inclement weather, Welsh trails, like Welsh riders, can deal with anything that's thrown at them, and they remain open in all conditions. That's not to say you should wait for the next downpour – hit the trails when the sun is shining, when the views stretch far into the distance, and you'll begin to understand why this really is some of the finest mountain biking on Earth.

NEED to know

001 Boats run out to the Skelligs, usually between May and September, from several points on the Kerry coast, including Ballinskelligs and Portmagee.

002 The Barrowland is at 244 Gallowgate, Glasgow (ⓦ www.glasgow-barrowland .com).

003 Jersey Walk Adventures (ⓦ www.jerseywalkadventures.co.uk) run "moonwalks" to Seymour Tower on the evening low tide two or three times a month; accommodation in the tower is in basic bunks. Return daywalks on the morning low tide are also available.

004 For entrance hours and exhibition details, contact the British Museum on ☎ +44 (0) 207 323 8000 or go to ⓦ www.britishmuseum.org.

005 Check out *Fabric* (ⓦ www.fabriclondon.com); *Ministry of Sound* (ⓦ www.ministryofsound.com); *Matter* (ⓦ www.matterlondon.com). After-clubs run at *Aquarium* (ⓦ www.clubaquarium.co.uk) and *Egg* (ⓦ www.egglondon.net), among other venues. For online listings, try ⓦ www.timeout.com/london and ⓦ www.londonnet.co.uk.

006 For more info, see ⓦ www.durhamcathedral.co.uk.

007 *The Palace*, 21 Fleet St; *Mulligan's*, 8 Poolbeg St; *Ryan's*, 28 Parkgate St; *Guinness Storehouse*, off Belleview; see ⓦ www.guinness-storehouse.com.

008 Borrowdale is in the heart of the Lake District, running south of Keswick for eight miles. Parking is limited so catch the local bus from Keswick.

009 Two to try: Stein's Fish & Chips, South Quay, Padstow, Cornwall (ⓦ www.rickstein.com); Anstruther Fish Bar, 42-44 Shore Street, Anstruther, Fife (ⓦ www.anstrutherfishbar.co.uk).

010 Most people walk the Pennine Way in 2 to 3 weeks, covering daily distances of 12 to 20 miles.

011 Access is via the car park at Blairmore, a few miles from Kinlochbervie, Sutherland. There are no local facilities but you can hike eight miles north to the Ozone Café, located in the Cape Wrath lighthouse. Cape Wrath itself is used as an MOD air bombing range and access is restricted at times; call the range's freephone information line, ☎ +44 (0) 800 833 300, to check ahead.

012 You can rent bikes at several points around the New Forest, with helmets, child seats and other equipment included in the price. See ⓦ www.thenewforest .co.uk for more details.

013 Royal Ascot begins on the third Tuesday in June. For tickets, contact ☎ +44 (0) 870 727 1234 or check out ⓦ www.ascot.co.uk.

014 Speyside's Malt Whisky Trail (ⓦ www.maltwhisky trail.com) points you in the direction of seven working distilleries offering guided tours.

015 Contact the High Moorland Visitor Centre (☎ +44 (0) 1822 890414, ⓦ www.dartmoor-npa.gov.uk) for details of guided walks or to order a copy of the free annual *Dartmoor Guide*.

016 The Common Ridings are usually held in June. For more details, see ⓦ www.hawickcommonriding.com.

017 Punts can be hired from stations at Mill Lane and Magdalene Bridge, and at other points in the city centre.

018 Bonfire Night is held on November 5, unless this falls on a Sunday, when it moves to November 6. For more info, see ⓦ www.lewesbonfirecouncil.org.uk.

019 Players need to enter a ballot to get a tee-off time – visit ⓦ www.standrews.org.uk or call ☎ +44 (0) 1334 466666.

020 For further information about Connemara, go to ⓦ www.connemara.net.

021 See ⓦ www.lundyisland.co.uk for more info and ⓦ www.landmarktrust.org.uk for accommodation details. Depart from Ilfracombe or Bideford on board the MS *Oldenburg* between March and Oct. From Nov to mid-March a helicopter service runs from Hartland Point.

022 Trains run from Glasgow on the West Highland Line to Fort William and then onto Mallaig (5hr journey time).

023 Oxford is northwest of London and easily accessible by bus from Victoria Station (1hr 30min) or train from Paddington Station (1hr).

024 See ⓦ www.isleofbarra.com for more about Barra and ⓦ www.scaristahouse.com for info on *Scarista House*.

025 For a closer look at the Aber Valley Male Voice Choir, see ⓦ www.aber-valleymvc.co.uk.

026 For more information on Mourne, see ⓦ www .mournelive.com.

027 Hay-on-Wye straddles the English–Welsh border, twenty miles from Hereford. Murder & Mayhem, 5 Lion Street; The Poetry Bookshop, Ice House, Brook Street; Hay Cinema Bookshop, Castle Street.

028 The SETT tank is located in Gosport, near Portsmouth. See ⓦ www.royal-navy.mod.uk/server/show /nav.3097 for details.

029 Cooper's Hill Cheese-Rolling starts at noon on the end-of-May bank holiday Monday. See ⓦ www.cheese -rolling.co.uk for more.

030 See ⓦ www.nottinghillcarnival.biz for a wealth of information on the carnival.

031 For more info, go to ⓦ www.pcnpa.org.uk.

032 Highland Games are held from May to September – the big gatherings include Braemar (ⓦ www .braemargathering.org) and Cowal (ⓦ www.cowalgath ering.com).

033 For a picnic lunch on the beach, stock up at the wonderful Picnic Fayre deli in Cley-next-the-Sea.

034 The London Canal Museum, 12-13 New Wharf Road (ⓦ www.canalmuseum.org.uk) offers information

and exhibits. Useful tube stops from which to explore the canal, from west to east, include Warwick Avenue, Camden Town, Angel, Mile End and Limehouse.

035 TT race week is the first week of June; for more information, see ⓦ www.iomtt.com.

036 The Brú na Bóinne visitor centre (ⓦ www.herit ageireland.ie) is 10km southwest of Drogheda in Co. Meath. The Loughcrew Cairns, near Oldcastle, are accessible only with your own transport – pick up the key for Cairn T from the coffee shop at Loughcrew Gardens (ⓦ www.loughcrew.com).

037 The largest bores occur at the September and March equinoxes. Go to ⓦ www.severn-bore.co.uk for more details.

038 For more information on the Barrow itself, and for details of barge rental companies, see ⓦ www.iwai.ie.

039 For information about matches and museum entry, go to ⓦ www.crokepark.ie or ⓦ www.gaa.ie.

040 For entry hours and admission fees to Conwy Castle, see ⓦ www.cadw.wales.gov.uk.

041 A ferry runs to Mull from the west-coast port of Oban (6 or 7 daily; 46min). For more info, see ⓦ www .calmac.co.uk.

042 Prices start at £24 for a two-hour spa session in the New Royal Bath (including access to the rooftop pool, Minerva Bath, steam rooms and restaurant). The smaller, historic Cross Bath lies opposite the main complex with its own facilities; a one-and-a-half hour session here costs £14. See ⓦ www.thermaebathspa. com for more details.

043 Green Man takes place every year, generally in late August. See ⓦ www.thegreenmanfestival.co.uk for more details.

044 For more information, check out ⓦ www.eden project.com, or the unofficial, but useful, ⓦ www.eden-project.co.uk.

045 See ⓦ www.galwayoysterfest.com for event information and booking forms.

046 For more on Edinburgh's festivals and the Military Tattoo, go to ⓦ www.edinburghfestivals.co.uk or ⓦ www.edintattoo.co.uk.

047 From June to September, you need to book well ahead for accommodation – especially for the *Hell Bay Hotel* on Bryher (☎ +44 (0) 1720 424122, ⓦ www.hell bay.co.uk).

048 The website ⓦ www.visit-fortwilliam.co.uk has a webcam permanently trained on Ben Nevis as well as plenty of information on climbing the mountain.

049 Big E's Belfast Taxi Tours (☎ +44 (0) 79 68 477924, ⓦ www.big-e-taxitours.com).

050 For info on the best riding in Wales, go to ⓦ www .mbwales.com or ⓦ www.visitwales.co.uk/active.

GOOD to know

FIVE GREAT FILMS

How Green Was My Valley (1941). You can almost imagine you're in South Wales in Western director John Ford's family saga, even though he filmed it in California.

Brief Encounter (1945). Elegant romance set in stiff-upper-lip 1940s England; a chance meeting at a train station sparks a deep but impossible love affair between two married people.

Withnail and I (1987). Bruce Robinson's mordant cult comedy is a classic 1960s period piece that moves from London via a wonderfully deserted M1 to the Lake District.

Trainspotting (1996). Witty, brilliant adaptation of Irvine Welsh's druggy novel set in an Edinburgh far from the tourist picture book.

The Wind That Shakes the Barley (2006). Palme d'Or-winning drama about the Irish Civil War of the 1920s.

WHAT'S IN A NAME?

The **British Isles** is a term that encompasses the whole of England, Scotland, Wales and Ireland. **Britain** (or Great Britain) refers only to Scotland, England and Wales. The United Kingdom (UK), on the other hand, is a political term and includes all of Britain and Northern Ireland. **Éire** is the official (Gaelic) term for the **Republic of Ireland** (all of Ireland, except Northern Ireland).

"The English never draw a line without blurring it"

Winston Churchill

CLASSIC COUNTRY RETREATS

Dalhousie Castle, Midlothian, Scotland Historic thirteenth-century castle where guests can dine in the Dungeon Restaurant and handle hawks and owls in the Falconry. Ⓦwww.dalhousie castle.co.uk.

The Lamb Inn, Burford, England This ancient Cotswold inn has its very own English country garden and a sophisticated restaurant. Ⓦwww .cotswold-inns-hotels.co.uk.

Ballymaloe House, near Cork, Ireland Charming family-run country house hotel set on a 200-acre farm that is just as famous for its award-winning restaurant. Ⓦwww.ballymaloe.ie.

The Gurnard's Head, near Zennor, England Cosy Cornish retreat with an outstanding restaurant and a stunning costal location, perfect for bracing walks. Ⓦwww.gurnardshead.co.uk.

"To travel hopefully is a better thing than to arrive, and the true success is to labour"

Robert Louis Stevenson

LAW OF THE LAND

Britain possesses a long and rich history that stretches back thousands of years, and many of today's laws date back just as far, though sadly, they are rarely upheld:

• It is illegal to enter the Houses of Parliament dressed in a suit of armour.

• By law, all London taxi drivers must ask their passengers if they have smallpox or the plague.

• If a dead whale is found anywhere on the British coast the tail belongs to the Queen, in case she needs the bones for a new corset.

SUMMER MUSIC FESTIVALS

Barely a week goes by over the summer months when there isn't some sort of outdoor shindig going on. The big names – **Reading** and **Leeds**, **T in the Park** and the two **V** events – tend to draw the largest crowds and most currently favoured acts, while other mid-sized events such as the revived **Isle of Wight Festival** and its late-season Isle of Wight brother, **Bestival**, fill in the gaps. August's **The Big Chill** is, as you might expect, a more laid-

back, family-orientated affair. Then there's the niche dos, including the splendid **Green Man** (experience Ⓞ43), alongside Reading's world-music extravaganza **WOMAD**, and the notoriously hard-to-get-tickets-to **Cambridge Folk Festival**, both in July. Others include **Creamfields** for dance fans, **All Tomorrow's Parties** for underground rock weirdness and the **Brecon Jazz Festival** for jazz sounds.

CELEBRITY CHEF-OWNED RESTAURANTS

Fifteen, London, Jamie Oliver. Jamie's flagship enterprise takes on unemployed kids to train as chefs, who wouldn't normally get a chance to do so – and it works. Trattoria-style food. Ⓦwww.fifteenrestaurant.com.

The Seafood Restaurant, Padstow, Rick Stein Rick may monopolize the eating establishments in this Cornish seaside town, but The Seafood Restaurant is considered one of Britain's best places to eat fish. Ⓦwww.rickstein.com.

Le Manoir aux Quat' Saisons, Raymond Blanc Exquisite modern French cuisine is the order of the day at this two-Michelin-starred hotel and restaurant near Oxford. Ⓦwww.manoir.com.

The Fat Duck, Bray, Heston Blumenthal Famous for his adventurous tasting menu, and unusual combinations such as egg and bacon ice cream, Blumenthal's culinary explorations have earnt his restaurant three Michelin stars. Ⓦwww.fatduck.co.uk.

WILD BEASTS

The most fearsome wild mammal in Britain and Ireland today is the **badger**, while the largest is the **red deer**. So not much to worry about then. The islands once boasted a much wider variety of mammals: **wolves** survived in Scotland and Ireland up until the eighteenth century, and **brown bears** and **lynxes** used to roam the countryside in pre-Roman times. Although lynxes were last seen in the British Isles around two thousand years ago, many people believe there are still big cats roaming wild. The most notorious is the **Beast of Bodmin Moor**, a black, panther-like creature which reputedly lives in Cornwall.

KAFFEE UND KUCHEN IN A VIENNESE KAFFEEHAUS • LORDING IT IN THE LOIRE VALLEY • EXPLORING THE PREHISTORIC CAVE ART OF PECH-MERLE • GOING UNDERGROUND IN THE CASEMATES DU BOCK • TASTING WINES THAT ARE FIT FOR A PRINCE • LOUNGING ABOARD THE GLACIER EXPRESS • LISTENING TO MOZART IN SALZBURG • PETIT TRAIN JAUNE: FOLLOWING THE NARROW GAUGE ROAD • BATHING IN THE BALTIC • HAVING A BEER IN BRUSSELS • REMINISCING IN THE WORLD'S MOST FAMOUS CEMETERY • DEFYING GRAVITY ON THE SEMMERING RAILWAY • GETTING NAKED IN CAP D'AGDE • ART AFTER DARK: AN EVENING IN THE LOUVRE • SWIMMING UNDER THE PONT DU GARD • THE FRIEDRICHSBAD: THE BEST BATHS IN BADEN-BADEN • SKIING THE STREIF • MUD, GLORIOUS MUD • HORSING ABOUT AT THE POLO WORLD CUP ON SNOW • ARS ELECTRONICA CENTRE: LOSING GRIP ON REALITY • THE CRESTA RUN: SLEDGING WITH A DIFFERENCE • PEDALLING AND PICNICKING ALONG THE LOIRE • BEACH BAR HOPPING IN HAMBURG • SNOW WONDER: PODDING IT UP IN THE SWISS ALPS • ONE RING TO RULE THEM ALL • CLIMBING MONT ST-MICHEL • COW-FIGHTING AT THE COMBAT DES REINES • CHAMPAGNE TASTING IN ÉPERNAY • GATHERING FRIENDS FOR A SWISS FONDUE • BRAVING THE HEIGHTS OF BONIFACIO • GETTING GROOVY AT THE MONTREUX JAZZ FESTIVAL • SCHLOSS NEUSCHWANSTEIN, THE ULTIMATE FAIRY-TALE CASTLE • TREATING YOUR SENSES AT A CHRISTKINDLMARKT • BUNGEEING OFF THE VERZASCA DAM • CANOEING DOWN THE DORDOGNE • IMPRESSIONIST PAINTINGS AT THE MUSÉE D'ORSAY • CYCLING IN THE DUTCH COUNTRYSIDE • DOWNING A STEIN OR TEN AT THE OKTOBERFEST • WASHING IT DOWN WITH CIDER IN NORMANDY • GORGING ON CHOCOLATES IN BRUSSSELS • PLAYBOYS AND PETROLHEADS: THE MONACO GRAND PRIX • MUSH! MUSH! HUSKY SLEDDING IN THE SWISS ALPS • ASSEMBLING A PICNIC FROM SARLAT MARKET • MACAROONS FOR HER MAJESTY • FREEWHEELING IN THE UPPER DANUBE VALLEY • HIKING CORSICA'S GR20 • COMMUNING WITH CARNAC'S PREHISTORIC PAST • GETTING SERIOUS IN THE ARDENNES • BIG FOOT: SNOWSHOEING THROUGH THE BLACK FOREST • THE CATHAR CASTLES OF LANGUEDOC-ROUSSILLON • THE JEWEL OF BERRY: CATHÉDRALE ST-ETIENNE • PAYING YOUR RESPECTS IN NORMANDY • CRANKING UP THE VOLUME ON QUEEN'S DAY • MAROONED ON SEIN: THE ISLAND AT THE EDGE OF THE WORLD • GOING TO THE MEDIEVAL MOVIES • KAYAKING ACROSS THE BORDERS ON LAKE CONSTANCE • WINE-TASTING IN BORDEAUX • ON THE ART TRAIL IN THE CÔTE D'AZUR • JOINING THE GILLES AT BINCHE CARNIVAL • KAFFEE UND KUCHEN IN A VIENNESE KAFFEEHAUS • LORDING IT IN THE LOIRE VALLEY • EXPLORING THE PREHISTORIC

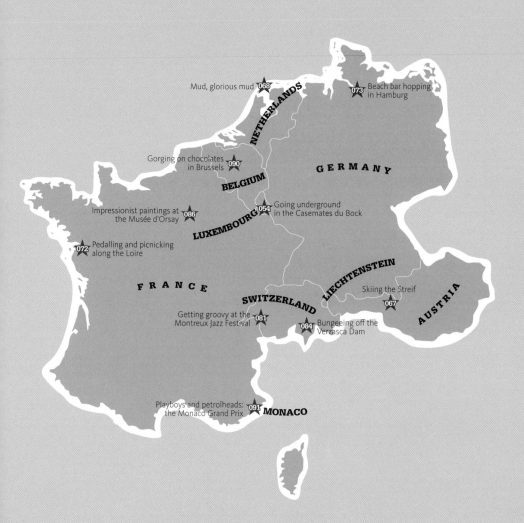

Mud, glorious mud 068

073 Beach bar hopping
in Hamburg

NETHERLANDS

GERMANY

Gorging on chocolates 090
in Brussels

BELGIUM

Impressionist paintings at 086
the Musée d'Orsay

054 Going underground
in the Casemates du Bock

LUXEMBOURG

072 Pedalling and picnicking
along the Loire

LIECHTENSTEIN

FRANCE

Skiing the Streif

SWITZERLAND

067

AUSTRIA

Getting groovy at the 081
Montreux Jazz Festival

084 Bungeeing off the
Verzasca Dam

Playboys and petrolheads: 091
the Monaco Grand Prix **MONACO**

KAFFEE UND KUCHEN
IN A VIENNESE KAFFEEHAUS

AUSTRIA As refined as afternoon tea and as sacred as the Japanese tea ceremony, *Kaffee und Kuchen* – coffee and cake – is the most civilized of Viennese rituals. It is not an experience to be rushed, and should you try, the archetypal grumpy Viennese waiter will surely sabotage your efforts. *Kaffee und Kuchen* is as much a cultural as a culinary ex perience.

The cafés are destinations in their own right: the grand, nineteenth-century *Café Central*, the suave *Café Landtmann* and the gloomy, bohemian *Café Hawelka* are as distinct from each other as *Topfenstrudel* is from *Gugelhupf*. In these memorable surroundings, there are newspapers to be read and very likely, fevered artistic or political discussions to be had. Trotsky, it is said, planned world revolution over *Kaffee und Kuchen* in Vienna, though the contrast between the revolutionary intent and the bourgeois trappings must have been richly comic.

The coffee-and-cake culture is unique to Austria. For coffee, you may order a cappuccino, but you'll endear yourself to your waiter if instead you go for a *Mélange*, which is the closest Austrian equivalent. The choice is bewildering: there are *Einspänner, kleiner* or *grosser Brauner*, and even the *Kaisermélange* with egg yolk and brandy. Whatever you order, you'll most likely also get a small glass of water with your coffee.

The cakes are made with care from high-quality ingredients. It doesn't make them any healthier, but at least it ensures that the assault on your arteries is likely to be an enjoyable one. *Apfelstrudel* and the unexpectedly bitter, chocolate *Sachertorte* are reliable and ubiquitous, ideally eaten with a heap of *schlagobers* (whipped cream) on the side. More exotic creations include the multilayered almond-sponge *Esterhazytorte* and the caramel-topped *Dobostorte*.

For all their sugary delights, an air of gloom pervades many Viennese cafés: part nostalgia for vanished imperial glories but also surely an acknowledgement of the transitory nature of sensual pleasure. Because finishing a hot, pungently sour cherry strudel is a small death, the last delicious forkful as full of sorrow and yearning as anything by Mahler.

052 Lording it in the Loire Valley

FRANCE You can't translate the word château. "Castle" is too warlike, "palace" too regal – and besides, they're all so different: some are grim and broken keeps, others lofty Gothic castles or exquisite Renaissance manor houses. Many are elegant country residences whose tall, shuttered windows overlook swathes of rolling parkland. And a few – the finest – are magnificent royal jewels set in acre upon acre of prime hunting forest.

Today, the aristocracy no longer lord it over every last village in France, but a surprising number still cling to their ancestral homes. Some eke out a living offering tours, and the most fascinating châteaux are not always the grandest palaces but the half-decrepit country homes of faded aristocrats who will show off every stick of furniture, or tell you stories of their ancestors in the very chapel where they themselves will one day be buried.

Some owners, enticingly, even offer bed and breakfast. You get a vividly personal sense of France's patrician past when you wake up and see the moonlight shining through the curtains of your original, seventeenth-century four-poster – as at the Château de Brissac in Anjou. Or when you gaze from your leaded window down an ancient forest ride in the Manoir de la Rémonière in Touraine, or draw a chair up to the giant stone bedroom fireplace at the perfectly tumbledown Château de Chémery, near Blois.

As for the great royal residences, most are now cold and empty. National monuments like Chambord, a "hunting lodge" with a chimney for every day of the year, or Fontainebleau, where the *Mona Lisa* once hung in the royal bathroom, are the stunning but faded fruits of a noble culture that cherished excellence and had the money to pay for it in spades. But thanks to the tourist trade, many châteaux are recovering their former glory. The French state now scours auction houses all over the world for the fine furnishings flogged off by the wagon-load after the Revolution. Once empty and echoing, the royal palaces will soon be gilded once more – if not, perhaps, occupied.

053 Exploring the prehistoric cave art of Pech-Merle

FRANCE Imagine a cave in total darkness. Then a tiny flame from a tar torch appears, piercing the blackness, and a small party of men carrying ochre pigment and charcoal crawl through the labyrinth. They select a spot on the cold, damp walls and start to paint, using nothing but their hands and a vivid imagination. Finished, they gather their torches and leave their work to the dark.

Until now. A mind-blowing 25,000 years later, you can stand in the Grotte de Pech-Merle and admire this same astonishing painting: two horses, the right-hand figure with a bold, naturalistic outline that contrasts with the decidedly abstract black dots – two hundred of them – that fill up its body and surround the head. The whole thing is circled, enigmatically, by six handprints, while a red fish positioned above its back adds to the sense of the surreal.

Short of inventing a time machine, this is the closest you'll get to the mind of Stone Age man. And it's this intimacy, enhanced by the cool dimness of the cave, that makes a visit here so overwhelming. Unlike Lascaux in the Dordogne, Pech-Merle allows visitors to view the original art, and the so-called dotted horses are just the best-known of the cave's mesmerizing ensemble of seven hundred paintings, finger drawings and engravings of bison, mammoths and horses.

It was once common to think of prehistoric peoples as brutish, shaggy-haired cavemen waving clubs, but some 30,000 years ago here in France, they were busy creating the world's first naturalistic and abstract art. No one's sure just why they made these paintings, but it's possible that the tranquil, womb-like caves were sacred places linked to fertility cults, the drawings divided into male and female symbols suffused with Paleolithic mythology. But new theories suggest something far more prosaic: that the paintings were made primarily by teenage boys who had the subjects of hunting and women foremost on their minds. Perhaps Pech-Merle's most poignant treasure backs this up – the footprint of an adolescent boy, captured in clay he left the cave one evening, some 25,000 years ago.

054 Going underground in the Casemates du Bock

LUXEMBOURG The network of dark, damp tunnels below Luxembourg City's tenth-century castle – the Rocher du Bock – remain a clear legacy of the country's strategic position in Europe. Narrow stone staircases twist down underground, leading into a maze of cave-like chambers and passageways. The Spanish began the casemates in 1644, carving them out of the rock to house soldiers and cannons – fortifications that successive European powers continued to build upon. Eventually spanning 23km, the tunnels were partially destroyed after military withdrawal, though they later provided vital shelter for the people of Luxembourg during both world wars. Now a World Heritage Site, what remains of the underground ramparts is eerie, claustrophobic and utterly fascinating.

055 Tasting wines that are fit for a prince

LIECHTENSTEIN Sandwiched between Switzerland and Austria, the principality of Liechtenstein may be pint-sized, but it has plenty of treats up its Alpine sleeves. There's the scenic mountain backdrop, for one, and the appealingly stodgy cuisine – the highlight being *käsknöpfle* (cheese-laden dumplings), which are as good a way as any to line your stomach for a visit to the prince's wine cellars. Prince Hans-Adam II, resident of the mountaintop medieval castle that looks down imperiously on the state's capital, Vaduz, boasts one of the finest vineyards in the Rhine Valley, with optimum conditions for growing Pinot Noir and Chardonnay. If you fail to score a personal invitation to the castle, a visit to the prince's Hofkellerei winery for a tasting of its fine vintages, is a highly satisfying second best.

056 Lounging aboard the Glacier Express

SWITZERLAND The Swiss are often chided for not being much good at, say, football, jokes or wars – but two things they do better than just about anyone are mountains and trains. Combine the two, and you're onto a winner.

We were booked on the Glacier Express; there were pristine blue skies that morning at St Moritz and our state-of-the-art panoramic carriage awaited. Vast windows extended from knee level right up around the top of the coach; from any seat the views were all-encompassing. As we got going, we didn't feel like passengers, stuck behind glass, but rather travellers, engaged in the scenery.

The journey started under sparkling sunshine beside the River Inn, whose waters tumble east to join the Danube; here, amidst the wild Alpine forests, it's the slenderest of mountain brooks. Every sightline was dominated by sky-blue, snow-white and pine-green. By mid-morning, we were rolling on alongside the young Rhine, crossable here by a single stepping stone.

As forests, wild gorges, snowy peaks and huddled villages trundled past, the train climbed effortlessly into the bleak high country, above the treeline. After lunch onboard, we downed a warming schnapps as we crested the Oberalp Pass – 2033m above sea level, though still dwarfed by a thousand more metres of craggy cliffs. Rolling down the other side, the snow lay thick on the village roofs below.

By mid-afternoon, our carriage was quiet: fingers were laced over bellies and there were a few yawns. But still the scenery was compulsive: we gazed down into a bottomless ravine and then craned our necks to take in the soaring summits, framed against a still-perfect Alpine blue sky.

As the train pulled into the little village of Zermatt, we caught our first glimpse of the iconic, pyramidal Matterhorn, and celebrated our arrival – with a Toblerone, naturally.

057 Listening to Mozart in Salzburg

AUSTRIA Wolfgang Amadeus Mozart was the original musical prodigy, an eighteenth-century pop idol whose fame took him to Vienna, Prague and the capitals of Europe, and in the years since his death he has become an industry. No Mozart connection, however slight, is ignored. There are Mozart views to savour, Mozart chocolates to devour and any amount of Mozart kitsch to consume. Brushing all that aside, however, the music remains. And there is no better place to hear it than in Mozart's beautiful, Baroque home town.

Mozart was the Salzburg-born son of a court musician who swiftly recognized his son's musical ability – junior gave his first performance before the court of Prince-Archbishop Sigismund Graf von Schrattenbach, amid the splendour of the Salzburg Residenz, at the tender age of six. These days, the best opportunity for serious fans to hear Mozart in Salzburg is during the annual Mozartwoche

(Mozart Week), which takes place at the Mozarteum and the Festspielhaus around the time of the composer's birthday (January 27), and which each year focuses on a particular aspect of the composer's work.

You can hear his music in glorious historic surroundings at any time of the year. Much the most luxurious are the candlelit Mozart dinner concerts in the hall of the *Stiftskeller St Peter* restaurant in St Peter monastery, where you eat food prepared according to recipes from the 1900s while opera singers in eighteenth-century costume perform arias and duets from *Don Giovanni*, *The Marriage of Figaro* and *The Magic Flute*. Occasional dinner concerts are also held in the mighty medieval fortress that towers above the city. But if you're in more reflective mood, the *Mozart Requiem* is regularly performed at the Kollegienkirche, the university church whose Baroque magnificence matches in stone the splendour of Mozart's genius.

058 Petit Train Jaune: following the narrow gauge road

FRANCE As small and perfectly formed as its wind-in-the-hair views are vast, the fondly named Petit Train Jaune ("Little Yellow Train") has been pitting narrow gauge track against the vertiginous rock of deepest French Catalonia for a century and counting. Best enjoyed in summer, when at least one of the train's spartan, buttercup-yellow carriages travels open-topped, the squeamish can still savour spectacular vistas from the enclosed comfort of a gleaming modern equivalent. Not so much a train journey as a slow-motion roller-coaster ride, its 63km route is a vital resource for remote communities and a magnet for tourists, climbing from medieval Villefranche-de-Conflent on the Têt Valley floor, to the heights of La Tour-de-Carol on the Pyrenean frontier with Spain. Dwarfed by sun-baked limestone colossi and cleaving to ever more impossibly narrow ledges, it offers a hugely exhilarating perspective of the country's lesser-known, ravishingly wild scenery, shadowed by the magisterial bulk of Mount Canigou. Better still the train proceeds on its three-hour journey at the kind of speed (55km/h maximum) conducive to actually appreciating it all, or

even getting off at one of the tiny stations to explore.

Idyllically sited hot springs, many unregulated and known only to locals, steam all over this area; near the request-stop of Thuès-les-Bains especially, you might spot dripping villagers crossing the rail tracks, clearly judging their natural hot-tub eyrie to be worth the risk. If, after a soak, you have the energy to hike up the opposite side of the valley, enchanting and little-visited hamlets like Canaveilles and Llar offer tantalizing views of the journey still to come. The train crosses this chasm twice on its way up to Mont Louis, France's highest fortified town: via a sliver of track atop a slender stone aqueduct and across a vertigo-inducing suspension bridge. Once you've crested France's loftiest station, Bolquère, at some 1.5km above the Mediterranean, your ride pans out over the plateau of Cerdagne, which basks in an incredible 3000 hours of annual sunshine. Here, near journey's end, you're almost in Spain, or at least Spanish Catalonia, even as the train's red-trimmed livery – not to mention the continuity of the Pyrenean landscape – makes the distinction superfluous.

Bathing in the Baltic

GERMANY Carved balconies like lace, swaggering villas in spacious gardens and an absurdly long pier. Who would've thought "Herring Village" would be so glitzy? Indeed, who would've imagined such *Bäderarchitektur* (spa architecture) in a backwater like Usedom, a little-known island in the Baltic Sea? Yet during the latter half of the nineteenth century, as German aristocracy went crazy for seawater spa cures, Heringsdorf and adjacent Ahlbeck morphed from fishing villages into the St-Tropez of the Baltic. When Kaiser Friedrich Wilhelm III began holidaying here, earning the villages their collective name *Kaiserbäder* (Emperor's spas), the Prussian elite followed.

Aristocrats and industrialists set aside six weeks every summer to wet an imperial ankle in *Badewanne Berlins* ("Berlin's bathtub"). You can almost smell the moustache wax along Delbrückstrasse in Heringsdorf. A des res of its day, synonymous with status, the promenade is a glimpse of the Second Empire at the height of its pomp. Mosaics glitter in the pediment of Neoclassical Villa Oechler at No. 5; it doesn't stretch the imagination far to visualize the glittering garden balls hosted before the palatial colonnades of

Villa Oppenheim; and the Kaiser himself took tea at Villa Staudt located at No. 6. Only breeze-block architecture bequeathed by the German Democratic Republic in the centre spoils things here – top apparatchiks built hotel blocks for workers and took the grand villas for themselves.

Reunification has returned health cures and gloss to the resorts; Ahlbeck in particular has emerged as a stylish spa retreat for Berlin's city slickers. If you sit in a traditional *Strandkörbe* wicker seat, scrunching sugar white sand between your toes – imperial villas on one side, Germans promenading continental Europe's longest pier on the other – you'd be forgiven for thinking the *Kaiserbäder* are back to normal. Not quite.

Usedom has acquired a new reputation of late. In 2008 the world's first nudist flights landed at its airport and a minor diplomatic spat occurred when Poles strolled across the newly dismantled border to see sizzling sausages of a very unexpected kind. Sure, *Freikörperkultur* (literally "Free Body Culture") is restricted to specified areas, but you can almost hear the Kaiser splutter into his Schnapps.

Having a

beer

in Brussels

BELGIUM Don't just ask for a beer in Belgium – your request will be met with a blank stare. Because no one produces such a wide range of beers as they do here: there are lagers, wheat beers, dark amber ales, strong beers brewed by Trappist monks, fruit beers and even beers mixed with grapes. Some beers are fermented in the cask, others in the bottle and corked champagne-like. And each beer has its own glass, specifically developed to enhance the enjoyment of that particular brew.

Brussels is the best place to try all of them, including its own beery speciality, Lambic, a flattish concoction that is brewed in open barrels and fermented with the naturally occurring yeasts in the air of the Payottenland (the area around Brussels). It's not much changed from the stuff they drank in Bruegel's time, and a few glasses is enough to have you behaving like one of the peasants in his paintings – something you can do to your heart's content at *La Bécasse*, down an alley not far from the Grande-Place, or at the *Cantillon Brewery* in the Anderlecht district, where they still brew beer using these old methods, and which you can visit on regular tours.

You can taste another potent brew, Gueuze, a sparkling, cidery affair, at *La Mort Subite*, a dodgy-sounding name for a comfortable fin-de-siècle café; your ale will be served with brisk efficiency by one of the ancient staff, and while you sip it you can munch on cubes of cheese with celery salt or cold meats like jellied pigs' cheeks. After this aperitif, make your way to *In't Spinnekopke*, a restaurant that cooks everything in beer, and has lots to drink as well, or just head for *Delirium*, which serves over two thousand different types of beer, a quarter of which are Belgian.

061 Reminiscing in the world's most famous cemetery

FRANCE In 1900, a few days before he passed away, Oscar Wilde declared he was "fighting a duel to the death" with the wallpaper in his St-Germain hotel room. "One or other of us", he remarked, "has to go." The poet's final resting place – Division 89 in Père-Lachaise, one of the world's largest and most famous cemeteries – seems far more likely to have met with his approval. Home to a string of notables including composer Frédéric Chopin, singer Edith Piaf, playwright Molière, and authors Marcel Proust and Honoré de Balzac, Père-Lachaise sits proudly on a hill in eastern Paris, exerting a distinct melancholic charm. Covering more than 47,000 square metres and boasting its own street signs and cobbled paths, the "city of the dead" attracts around two million visitors a year.

Wilde's tomb – marked by a Pharaonic winged messenger, designed by Jacob Epstein – attracts a steady stream of admirers, many of whom show their affection for the acerbic poet by leaving a lipstick kiss or scrawled tribute on it. A sober verse from *The Ballad of Reading Gaol*, which Wilde wrote after serving two years hard labour for gross indecency, is inscribed on the tomb, while the messenger's missing appendage is reputedly used as a paperweight in the cemetery director's office. The grave of ex-Doors singer Jim Morrison is protected from similarly adoring fans – who leave behind smouldering cigarettes, candles and flowers – by a security guard.

The most poignant monuments in Père-Lachaise, however, are found in Division 97, the "*coin des martyrs*". Here, amid neatly tended flower gardens and towering trees, are moving memorials to Resistance fighters and victims of Nazi concentration camps. Nearby, in Division 76, a modest plaque on a stone wall, the *Mur de Fédérés*, marks where, after a dramatic chase through the cemetery, the final 147 troops of the 72-day Paris Commune uprising were lined up and executed in 1871; the spot remains a potent symbol for the Left. Visit first thing in the morning, and you can wander undisturbed amongst the graves and enjoy the sweeping views of Paris in peace.

062 Defying gravity on the Semmering Railway

AUSTRIA You don't need a train spotter to tell you that the Semmering Railway is a little bit special. Running 42km between the towns of Gloggnitz and Murzzuschlag, the line – a World Heritage Site – winds through the last surge of the eastern Austrian Alps before they taper off into the Hungarian plains. Of course, the mountain landscape is spectacular, but the railway itself rightly grabs your attention.

Built between 1848 and 1854, it is a daring feat of civil engineering that uses sixteen viaducts (several supported by two-storey arches), fifteen tunnels and over one hundred curved stone bridges to surmount the 460m difference in height. The engineer was Carlo di Ghega, a man who pushed the technical boundaries during the pioneering heyday of railway construction.

The track had to rise up over a kilometre-high mountain pass – which then became the highest altitude that could be reached by railway in the world – and overcome extreme radii and upward gradients. Twenty thousand workmen laboured to carve the vision from the limestone rock; such was the feat that afterwards it was triumphantly claimed that there was now nowhere that a railway could not be built.

The Semmering Railway is a harmonious blend of technology and nature. It created the first modern tourism phenomenon, as the rural idyll became readily accessible to the Viennese elite. The steam engines that once worked the rails were replaced by electricity in 1959, but the architecture of the grand old line remains. The quality of the old tunnels and viaducts means they have been used continuously, and as you make the ninety-minute journey, it takes little to imagine that you're inside a stately old engine as it curves around the exhilarating Kalte Rinne or Krauselklause viaducts.

063 Getting naked in Cap d'Agde

FRANCE Awkward to pronounce, difficult to place on a map and virtually impossible to describe to friends when you return home, Cap d'Agde's legendary nudist resort is one of the world's most unique places to stay. Of a size and scale befitting a small town, the Cap offers an ostentatious expression of alternative living. But this is no sect. The 60,000-odd naked people who come here during the height of summer often have nothing more in common than a sunburnt bottoms and a desire to express themselves in unconventional ways.

The resort's sprawling campsite is generally the domain of what the French like to call *bios*: the hardy souls who arrive at the Cap when the nights are still chilly and leave when the last leaves have fallen from the trees. They love their body hair as much as they hate their clothes, are invariably the naked ones in the queue at the post office, and don't mind the odd strand of spaghetti getting tangled up in their short and curlies at lunch. These textile-loathing *bios* share the Cap with a very different breed, who are occasionally found at the campsite, but usually prefer the privacy of apartments or hotel rooms. During the day, these libertines gather at the northern end of the Cap's 2km-long beach. For them, being naked is a fashion statement as much as a philosophy: smooth bodies, strategically placed tattoos and intimate piercings are the order of the day – and sex on the beach is not necessarily a cocktail.

In the evenings, the *bios* prefer to play a game of pétanque, cook dinner and go to bed early. Meanwhile, as the last camp stoves are cooling down, a few couples might be spotted slipping out of the campsite dressed in leather, PVC, lacy lingerie and thigh-high stiletto boots to join the throngs of more adventurous debauchees who congregate nightly in the Cap's bars, restaurants and notoriously wild swingers' clubs for a night of uninhibited fun and frolicking.

Art after dark:
an evening in the Louvre

064

FRANCE If getting up close to the *Mona Lisa* was never easy, in the wake of *Da Vinci Code* fever it's now almost as challenging as the puzzle at the heart of Dan Brown's blockbuster. But come on a Wednesday or Friday evening for one of the Louvre's late openings, and you'll find things considerably quieter.

Make your way along the shadowy, labyrinthine corridors to the outstanding Italian collection, where the famous Grande Galerie, its blonde parquet stretching into the dark distance, displays all the great names in Italian Renaissance art: Mantegna, Botticelli, Titian, Bellini, Raphael, Veronese. And then, of course, there's Leonardo's *Mona Lisa* herself – without the daytime swarms, you may get the opportunity to truly appreciate this strange and beguiling painting.

065 Swimming under the Pont du Gard

FRANCE A monumentally graceful section of the Roman aqueduct that once supplied Nîmes with fresh water, the Pont du Gard is an iconic structure, a tribute both to the engineering prowess of its creators and, with its lofty, elegant triple-tiered arches, to their aesthetic sensibilities. Though mostly long-gone today, the aqueduct originally cut boldly through the countryside for a staggering 50km, across hills, through a tunnel and over rivers. The bridge has endured, though, providing inspiration for the masons and architects who, over the centuries, travelled from all over France to see it, meticulously carving their names and home towns into the weathered, pale gold stone.

A fancy visitor centre gives you the lowdown on the construction of the bridge, but a better way to get up close and personal to this architectural marvel is to follow the hundreds of French visitors who descend on a sunny day: make for the rocky banks of the River Gard,

don your swimming gear and take to the water. The tiers of arches rise high above you and to either side, with just one of the six lower arches making a superbly confident step across the river. Propelled by the gentle current of the reassuringly shallow Gard, you can float right under the arch, which casts a dense shadow onto the turquoise water. Beyond the bridge the river widens, and fearless kids leap from the rocks adjoining the aqueduct into the deepening waters, while families tuck into lavish picnics on the banks.

The splendour of the Pont du Gard made eighteenth-century philosopher and aqueduct enthusiast Rousseau wish he'd been born a Roman – perhaps he chose to ignore the fact that the bridge was built by slave labour. Better to be a twenty-first-century visitor – the only labour you'll have to expend is a bit of backstroke as you look up at what is still, after 2000 years, one of France's most imposing monuments.

066 The Friedrichsbad: the best baths in Baden-Baden

GERMANY Time does strange things in southwest Germany. Even before Einstein hit on his Theory of Relativity in Ülm, Mark Twain had realized something was up after taking to the waters in the smart spa town of Baden-Baden. "Here at the Friedrichsbad," he wrote, "you lose track of time within ten minutes and track of the world within twenty."

Nearly 2000 years after the Romans tapped curative waters in this corner of the Black Forest, Twain swore that he left his rheumatism in Baden-Baden (literally, the "Baths of Baden"). England physios also considered Friedrichsbad sessions good enough to fast-track the return of injured striker Wayne Rooney for the World Cup in 2006. But regardless of whether a visit to the Roman-Irish mineral baths is for relaxation or rheumatism, as Twain noted, minutes melt into hours once inside. Midway through the full sixteen-stage programme, schedules are mere memories as you float in the circular pool of the Kuppelbad, whose marble walls and columns, creamy caryatids and sculpted cupola make it seem more minor Renaissance cathedral than spa centrepiece. By the final stage, time is meaningless and locations are a blur, as you drift prune-like and

dozy between a sequence of mineral water baths, showers, scrubs and saunas of ever-decreasing temperatures.

If time warps inside the Friedrichsbad, the spa itself is a throwback to when Baden-Baden was a high rollers' playground – Kaisers and Tzars flocked here for the summer season, Queen Victoria promenaded parks planted in ball-gown colours, Strauss and Brahms staged gala concerts, and Dostoevsky tried his luck in a Versailles-styled casino. With such esteemed visitors, the town's steam room suddenly looked rather frumpy. So in 1877, Grand Duke Friedrich I cut the opening ribbons to his spa, the most modern bathing house in Europe but with all the palatial trimmings: hand-painted tiles or arches and colonnades that alluded to the decadence of antiquity.

Be warned: for all its stately appearance, you need to leave your inhibitions at the Friedrichsbad door: bathing is nude and frequently mixed. Which can be just as much of a shock as the penultimate plunge into 18˚C waters. Or the realization as you emerge tingling and light-headed that, actually, the five hours you thought you spent inside were only three.

067 Skiing the Streif

AUSTRIA It never looked this icy on TV. And it certainly never looked this steep. But then cameras have a way of warping reality: they make people look ever so slightly bigger; and they make downhill-skiing runs look a lot, lot tamer.

And Kitzbühel's "Streif" is far from tame. A legendary downhill course that makes up one third of the Hahnenkammrennen, the most popular series of races on the skiing World Cup circuit, Streif is a challenging run in the same way that Everest is a difficult climb.

Buoyed by the bravado of a late-night *gluwein*, you have somehow talked yourself into giving it a crack. But now your legs are gone, and you can't seem to shake the image of an alpine rescue team scraping you off the slopes. 3, 2, 1. And you plunge down the slope, scooping up powder in the widest snowplough the course has ever seen. The

Mausefalle (Mousetrap) is swiftly negotiated – too swiftly for your liking – and you're on your way, the rushing wind making your eyes stream as you whizz through Steilhang and down Alte Schneise. Perfect edging and exact timing is the key to success here. Most amateurs have neither, and sure enough you skitter across an icy patch, your trailing ski almost catching an edge. There isn't time to think of the mess you'd have made if it had done.

Building up sufficient speed to carry you through Brückenschuß and Gschößwiese, a section of the course most commentators maliciously describe as "flat", you descend on the Hausbergkante – a jump, followed by a difficult left-hand turn over a large rise in the terrain – and then its down the Rasmusleitn, to the finish line. You punch the air and wave to the imaginary crowd. Piece of cake.

MUD, *glorious* MUD

THE NETHERLANDS You can wallow in it, make pies with it, even smear it all over your face. But in The Netherlands they have a different use for mud. They walk across it for fun, striking out from the coast of Friesland at low tide to the Wadden Islands, a string of four islands between 10km and 20km offshore: an energetic pastime that goes right to the heart of the Dutch fascination with water and, well, primeval ooze.

It's a tough but rewarding pastime, and one you're not allowed to do on your own. Only experienced guides are allowed across the mudflats: the depth of the stuff is variable and the tides inconsistent – sometimes there's not much margin for error between tides – and in any case despite all the mud there are always deep channels left behind, even at low tide, and it pays to know where they are. You also have to get up early: most group treks start around 6am, and can take anything from three to six hours to reach your final destination. You need to be properly equipped: knee-high socks and high-top trainers are a good idea, as is a warm sweater and cagoule; and a complete change of clothes stashed in a watertight pack. It's freezing when you start and can be pretty hot by the time you finish, so dress in layers. But above all wear shorts; whatever happens you're going to get covered in mud, so you may as well not weigh yourself down with mud-caked trousers.

Real hard-cases go to Terschelling, one of the prettiest and liveliest islands, but at 18km and six hours also by far the most gruelling choice, especially as for a lot of the time you're wading through water rather than mud; in fact they don't let you try it unless you've already completed the easier trip to Ameland, which takes about half the time and manages mostly to avoid the water. On the other side, a tractor will take you to a café in the main village where you can devour one of the best and most well-earned late breakfasts of your life.

069 Horsing about at the Polo World Cup on Snow

SWITZERLAND Polo may not be the "Sport of Kings", but you need to have money to play it – and possibly even more to follow it. But all good glitterati make the pilgrimage to St Moritz on the last weekend of January for the sport's top tournament: the annual Polo World Cup on Snow.

Held on the town's frozen lake, the event pulls in aristocratic punters from all over Europe to sip champagne and cheer on one of the four teams battling it out for the coveted championship title and the Cartier trophy. Competition is ferocious, and the players hurl themselves and their steeds into some spectacular duels, but the biggest bonus is that they're doing it all on an icy, snow-covered surface. Start saving now and you may just have enough money to treat your grandchildren to a trip.

070 Ars Electronica Centre: losing grip on reality

AUSTRIA Pegging yourself as the Museum of the Future is, in our ever-changing world, bold. Brash, even. And that's exactly what the Ars Electronica Centre in Linz is. Dedicated to new technology, and its influence within the realms of art, few museums on Earth have their fingers quite as firmly on the pulse.

The Ars features over fifty interactive installations, from warring robots to displays that enable you to create your own cyberspace project, but everyone comes here for the CAVE (Cave Automatic Visual Environment), the only exhibition of its kind that's open to the public. This room, measuring – cutely enough – 3m cubed, is at the cutting-edge of virtual reality; the simulation uses technology so advanced – 3-D projections dance across the walls and along the floor, as you navigate through virtual solar systems and across artificial landscapes – that you feel like you're part of the installation.

071 The Cresta Run: sledging with a difference

SWITZERLAND Are you man enough for this challenge? Requiring great upper body strength and stamina, the Cresta Run in St Moritz is strictly only for those with the XY chromosome – women have been banned since 1929. Oh, and you also have to be fearless, a bit of a thrill-seeker and slightly crazy.

Positioned on a skeleton toboggan, hurtling headfirst down a sheet-hard ice track at speeds of up to a terrifying 145km/h, you will probably wonder, hysterically, if you'll ever see your loved ones again. Shoulders braced – for the very natural fear of being propelled skywards at every perilous twist and turn – you'd be hard pushed to find a more adrenalin-filled ride.

Unbelievably, the majority of racers make it down the death-defying, 1.2km run in one piece. But even so, the sane amongst us will be content just to watch.

FRANCE The French call the Loire the "last wild river in France" for its winter habit of destructive flooding. In summer, however, it's hard to imagine anything gentler or more cultivated. The river meanders placidly between golden sandbanks where little white terns wheel and dive and herons fish in the shallows. At the water's edge stand grey-leaved willows and tall, fluttery poplars. The climate is idyllically temperate, vines comb the hillsides on all sides, and every mile or so brings another village built in creamy tufa stone, huddled around its church, or another well-to-do little town overlooked by a resplendent château.

Two hundred years ago the Loire thrummed with river traffic, but these days the freight has all taken to the roads and railways, leaving the old stone quays blissfully empty. New traffic, however, is returning to the banks. A delightful cycle network, *La Loire à Vélo* ("The Loire by bike"), now runs for some 800km – on minor roads or dedicated paths, and always at an easy gradient – from the hills above Sancerre, where you can try exquisite Sauvignon Blanc wines and *crottin de chavignol* goats' cheese, westwards to the Breton coast below Nantes, where refreshing Muscadet and mussels await.

As you pedal from provincial hotel to *chambre d'hôte* (bed and breakfast), perhaps staying at or visiting the odd Renaissance masterpiece château here and there, you can pause to sample regional specialities: the little battered whitebait-like fish of *friture de Loire*, mushrooms grown in local caves, and endless goats' cheeses ranging from creamy fresh to the well-aged and truly goaty. Then there are the wines: the fresh reds of Chinon and Bourgueil, redolent of raspberries and violets; Anjou's summery rosé; the joyful sparklers of Vouvray and Saumur; and the deep, honeyed sweet whites made with the Chenin Blanc grape. Pedalling and picnicking: there's no finer way to taste the slow pace of rural France.

PEDALLING *and* PICNICKING *along the* LOIRE

072

Beach bar hopping IN HAMBURG

GERMANY Move over Paris Plage. Although media reports heap praise upon its strip of sun, Seine and sand, the North European city that has a better claim to be the spiritual home of the urban beach is Hamburg. Every April tens of thousands of tonnes of sand are imported as miniature seaside paradises appear in the heart of Germany's second city. The doors open at the end of May and so begins another summer of beach bar hopping Hamburg-style.

Having spent their weekends on sandy strips beside the River Elbe since the late-1800s, Hamburg residents have long known about urban beach culture. But the reason why no other German city does the *Stadtstrand* (city beach) with such panache comes down to character. That Hamburg is simultaneously a sophisticated media metropolis and a rollicking port city produces a beach bar scene that ranges from glamour to grunge without sacrificing the key element – good times. Think sand, sausages and *Strandkörbe* (traditional wicker seats) to a soundtrack of funk and house beats. Ibiza it is not, but then nor is it trying to be.

Your flip-flops on, head to the river in port-turned-nightlife district St Pauli to begin at *Strand Pauli* (Hafenstr. 89). A year-round institution near the ferry port, it combines retro lampshades, castaway style and views of the ninth largest container port in the world – Hamburg in a nutshell. Next stop west on the beach bar crawl is slicker *Hamburg City Beach Club* (Grosse Elbstr. 279), all potted palms, day beds and aviator sunglasses, from where it's a short walk to the former docks in Altona. Behind the beach volleyball pitch are relaxed *Hamburg del Mar* (Van-der-Smissen-Str. 4) and *Lago Bay* (same address), which aspires towards Ibiza but scores most for a small swimming pool. A tip wherever you go: sunset is popular, so arrive early, buy a drink and settle in.

Not that it's all imported sand and urban chic. At the end of the road in Övelgönne further west still is *Altona's Strandperle* (Schulberg 2). Sure it's a glorified shack, but no one minds when it's on a genuine river beach to make Paris Plage look like a glorified sandpit. Now, what was the German for "*c'est magnifique*"?

074 Snow wonder: podding it up in the Swiss Alps

SWITZERLAND You can barely see *Whitepod*, a zero-impact, luxury "camp", until you're almost upon it, so well is it camouflaged against the deep snows of this tranquil forest setting, high in the Alps and far from any roads.

Each pod – eight of them make up the camp – is a mini geodesic dome sheathed in white canvas, a sturdy, igloo-shaped construction set on a raised wooden platform. But this is no wilderness campsite: the emphasis is squarely on modern, five-star comforts. Inside each pod – heated by its own wood-burning stove – you get a proper king-size bed with multiple fluffy down covers and comfortable armchairs, along with an iPod and designer toiletries.

So far, so typical of the ski industry – hardly the world's most environmentally sound, with all those snow cannon and piste-grooming machines, not to mention traffic jams on Alpine roads. But *Whitepod*, the idea of a Swiss entrepreneur, is different: no concrete is used in the pods, so there is no impact on the ground beneath, and everything is sourced locally, from the logs to the solar power to the organic food.

For showers, meals and relaxing with other guests, you cross to the wooden chalet in the centre of the site, which has been updated inside – all soft lighting, comfortable lounging and chic designer touches. The atmosphere is great – out in the wild woods, boasting spectacular views of the mountains, yet with every comfort taken care of in an understated, very Swiss way.

075 One Ring to rule them all

GERMANY Guests who have probably waited ten years for tickets to the Bayreuth Festival approach expectantly up a hillside. At the top a flag rises and falls in the breeze, a large letter W emblazoned on it. Groups gather outside to take in the last fresh air they will breathe for several hours, sparkling in their very best – you will never have seen so many diamonds. The atmosphere is eager and anticipatory, but certainly not light-hearted. Richard Wagner saw attending his operas as more than entertainment. It's also a ritual, part of an almost sacred experience.

Held annually, the festival was conceived by Richard Wagner not just to showcase his work but to restore a spiritual dimension to materialistic European culture. The Festspielhaus building itself is an enclosed amphitheatre, built on a relative shoestring in brick and wood as Wagner's patrons couldn't afford more substantial materials. In spite of this, it has superb acoustics – Wagner, who designed it, would not have settled for anything less. Inside, there are no boxes or balconies in the white-columned auditorium, just a single rake of seating for 1800 spectators. Seats are wooden and hard (many people bring cushions) and the acts are long. Wagner dispensed with the idea of a bell to call the audience to their seats. Instead, fifteen minutes before each act begins, a small brass ensemble plays a fanfare based on a key phrase from the upcoming act. They repeat it again twice, at ten and five minutes before the curtain rises.

The lights dim – Wagner revolutionized opera production by insisting on no distracting illumination in the auditorium – and the orchestra, hidden below a curved wooden canopy, begins. *Das Rheingold*, which opens Wagner's mighty *Ring Cycle*, is always played without interval and usually lasts two and a half hours. There will be four evenings like this, fifteen hours of uncompromising, highly emotional music each night. Whatever your feelings about Wagner the man, you will emerge from each performance of his music a changed person.

076 Climbing Mont St-Michel

FRANCE Wondrously unique yet as recognizable as the Eiffel Tower, Mont St-Michel and its harmonious blend of natural and man-made beauty has been drawing tourists and pilgrims alike to the Normandy coast for centuries. Rising some eighty metres from the waters of the bay that bears its name, this glowering granite outcrop has an entire commune clinging improbably to its steep boulders, its tiers of buildings topped by a magnificent Benedictine abbey.

From a few kilometres away, the sheer scale of the Mont provides an almost surreal backdrop to the rural tranquillity of Normandy – a startling welcome for the first-time visitor. And as you approach along the causeway that connects the Mont to the rest of France, the grandeur of this World Heritage Site becomes all the more apparent. Up close, the narrow, steepening streets offer an architectural history lesson, with Romanesque and Gothic buildings seemingly built one on top of the other.

Perched at the summit is the abbey itself, gushingly described by Guy de Maupassant as "the most wonderful Gothic building ever made for God on this earth". Although the first church was founded here in 709, today's abbey was constructed between the eleventh and thirteenth centuries, under Norman and subsequently French patronage. And as much as it's an aesthetic delight, the abbey is also a place of serenity: less than a third of the 3.5 million tourists that flock here each year actually climb all the way up to see it, and it remains a perfect place to be still and contemplate the Mont's glorious isolation.

Looking out from Mont St-Michel, as you watch the tides rolling in around its base – "like a galloping horse", said Victor Hugo – you can understand why medieval pilgrims would risk drowning to reach it, and why no invading force has ever succeeded in capturing the rock. It's a panorama to be savoured – as fine a sight as that of the Mont itself, and one that'll stay with you for a long time.

Cow-fighting

at the

COMBAT DES REINES

077

SWITZERLAND A peculiarly Swiss sport, cow-fighting is said to have originated when the villages of the Valais region used to get together to see whose cow was the most suited to lead the herd up to summer pasture. Nowadays, it's a far more serious business, with farmers breeding animals specifically to fight for the cash – and kudos – that taking the prestigious "Queen of the Herd" title entails. Despite the image of two heavyweight heifers going at it, it's a rather civilized event: no one gets hurt, least of all the cows, and spectating is accompanied by a good (and rather un-Swiss-like) amount of roaring and drinking.

But the real showpiece of the season, the top battle of the bovines, is the *Combat des Reines*. Held in Martigny's large ancient Roman amphitheatre, it's the culmination of hundreds of cattle fights that have been going on all summer, the winner of which brings a whole new (literal) meaning to the term "cash cow".

078 Champagne tasting in Épernay

FRANCE Champagne is an exclusive drink, in all senses of the word, what with its upmarket associations and the fact that it can be made only from the grapes grown in the Champagne region of northern France. The centre of champagne production is Épernay, a town that's made much of its association with the fizzy stuff, and where all the maisons of the well-known brands are lined up along the appropriately named Avenue de Champagne.

All of these champagne houses offer tours and tastings, and one of the best places to indulge is at the *maison* of Moët et Chandon, arguably the best-known brand in the world. The splendid, cathedral-like cellars afford suitable dignity to this most regal of drinks, while the multilingual guides divulge the complexities of blending different grapes and vintages to maintain a consistency of flavour from one year to the next. During the tasting, an enthusiastic sommelier explains the subtleties of flavour in the different *cuvées*, and although the whole experience can feel rather impersonal, it's nonetheless an essential part of any visit to the region.

For an altogether more exclusive experience, head 15km or so north of Épernay to the village of Bligny. Here, the eighteenth-century Château de Bligny is the only one in France still producing its own champagne and, if you call ahead, you can arrange a private tour. Driving through the wrought-iron gates and up the scrunchy gravel driveway, a sense of understated class strikes you immediately, and things only get classier as you're taken through the tastefully furnished rooms and vaulted cellars, and shown the family's cherished champagne flute collection. A tasting of several prize-winning vintages, taken in the opulent drawing room, is of course included, and as you savour your second glass, you'll doubtless conclude that there's no better place to get a flavour of the heady world of champagne than the home ground of this "drink of kings".

079 Gathering friends for a Swiss fondue

SWITZERLAND No one takes cheese as seriously as the Swiss. Elsewhere, cheese is one element within a more complex meal. In Switzerland, cheese is the meal – and fondue is the classic cheese feast. Pick a cold night and gather some friends: fondue is a sociable event, designed to ward off the Alpine chill with hot comfort food, warming alcohol and good company. No Swiss would dream of tackling one alone. In French, *fondre* means "to melt": fondue essentially comprises a pot of molten cheese that is brought to the table and kept bubbling over a tiny burner. To eat it, you spear a little cube of bread or chunk of potato with a long fork, swirl it through the cheese, twirl off the trailing ends and pop it into your mouth.

Those are the basics. But you'll find there's a whole ritual surrounding fondue consumption that most Swiss take alarmingly seriously. To start with, no one can agree on ingredients: the classic style is a *moitié-moitié*, or "half-and-half" – a mixture of Gruyère and Emmental – but many folk insist on nutty Vacherin Fribourgeois playing a part, and hardy types chuck in a block of stinking Appenzeller. Then there's the issue of what kind of alcohol to glug into the pot: kirsch (cherry spirit) is common, but French-speaking Swiss prefer white wine, while German speakers from the Lake Constance orchards stick firmly to cider.

Once that's decided and the pot is bubbling, everyone drinks a toast, the Swiss way: with direct eye contact as you say the other person's name – no mumbling or general clinking allowed! Then give your bread a good vigorous spin through the cheese (it helps stop the mixture separating), but lose it off your fork and the drinks are on you.

If the whole thing sounds like a recipe for a stomachache, you'd be spot-on: imagine roughly 250g (half a pound) of molten cheese solidifying inside you. There's a reason for the traditional *coup de milieu* – everyone downing a shot of alcohol halfway through the meal: if it doesn't help things settle, at least it masks the discomfort.

080 Braving the heights of Bonifacio

FRANCE A mere eleven kilometres separate the northernmost extremity of Sardinia from the iconic white cliffs of Bonifacio, on Corsica's wild southern tip. In fine weather, the straits can seem languid, like a lake of sapphire-coloured oil. But when the weather is up, as it was the first time I made the ferry crossing from Santa Teresa di Gallura, the ferocity of the currents ripping through this treacherous sea lane remind you that, to generations of mariners, Bonifacio was a symbol of salvation.

Rearing vertically from the waves, the striated chalk escarpments form a wall of dazzling brilliance, even on dull, stormy days. A row of ancient Genoese houses squeezes close to their edge, looking aloof and not a little smug – despite the fact the chalk beneath has crumbled away in colossal chunks, leaving the structures hanging precariously over expanses of cobalt sea and razor-sharp rock.

Rounding the harbour mouth, the waves grow suddenly still and the ferry seems to glide the last couple of hundred metres into port. Under the vast, sand-coloured ramparts of Bonifacio's citadel, tourists stroll along a quayside lined with rows of luxury yachts and pretty stone tenements sporting pastel-painted shutters. Wafts of coffee, grilled fish and freshly baked bread drift out of the waterfront cafés as you climb from the port up the steps of the Montée Rastello to Bonifacio's *haute ville*.

Most people are in a hurry to peak inside the gateway at the top, at the narrow alleyways, tiny cobbled squares and delicate campanile of the Église Sainte-Marie-Majeur. But the town never looks quite as wonderful as it does from the cliffs around it. Follow the path that strikes left of the Montée into the maquis, an ocean of scrub rolling away to the mountains inland, and – as your ferry pitches and rolls its way out of the harbour – you'll be rewarded with one of the most magnificent seascapes in the entire Mediterranean.

081 Getting groovy at the Montreux Jazz Festival

SWITZERLAND Backed by craggy hills and jutting out into the eastern tip of Lake Geneva, Montreux's setting is almost as stylish as its famous festival. But then few things are quite as cool as the Montreux Jazz Festival, one of Europe's most prestigious music events and a showcase for emerging talent as much as well established stars.

This is jazz, but not as you may know it – everything from hip-hop to acid jazz, gospel, techno, reggae and African jazz get an airing, and you can groove the days away on samba and salsa boats that head out onto the town's lake every afternoon. Jazz runs deep in Montreux – one of the venues is called the Miles Davis Hall – and the festival continues to expand and diversify, featuring a bewildering range of workshops and an A-List line-up. Herbie Hancock and John McLaughlin are just two of the more regular artists from a cast of around two thousand.

082 Schloss Neuschwanstein, the ultimate fairy-tale castle

GERMANY If you could only visit one castle in the world, then Schloss Neuschwanstein must be it. Boldly perched on a rocky outcrop high above the Bavarian village of Hohenschwangau, the *schloss* lords it over some of the most spectacular countryside in the country. It looks every bit the storybook castle, a forest of capped grey granite turrets rising from a monumental edifice. And the all-important intriguing background? Built in 1869 as a refuge from reality by King Ludwig II, a crazed monarch who compared himself to the mythical medieval "Grail King" Parzival, Neuschwanstein ticks that box, too.

083 Treating your senses at a Christkindlmarkt

AUSTRIA The sweet, heady tang of gluwein penetrates the frosty air, fairy lights twinkle in the dwindling light and children scurry past munching on delicious *vanillekipel* (vanilla cookies coated in sugar): I'm standing in the middle of an Austrian Christkindlmarkt, absorbing the festive, merry atmosphere. Even though it's freezing cold, I'm reluctant to cover my nose with my thick woollen scarf – the smells swirling around this little wonderland are just too good to miss.

In the weeks leading up to Christmas, marketplaces across the country fill with stalls selling arts and crafts and delicious Austrian delicacies. I wander through the hustle and bustle, from stall to stall, occasionally munching on a bit of strudel and sipping my warming gluwein. I should probably take some home as Christmas gifts, but I have a funny feeling that these just might not make it as far as the wrapping paper.

084
BUNGEEING
off the Verzasca Dam

SWITZERLAND Sweaty palms. I had sweaty palms then, looking out over the edge, and I still get sweaty palms just thinking about it.

It was a fresh, sunny afternoon, and I'd driven up from Locarno, on the Swiss shores of Lake Maggiore. As the road climbed through sun-dappled pine forest, the giant wall of the Verzasca Dam came into view. I parked and walked out onto the dam.

To my right lay a calm blue lake, framed by wooded slopes, with the high, snowy Alps looming in the distance. But on my left the ground fell away into a dry, yawning chasm; between me and a valley mouth was empty air – not forgetting the razor-sharp rocks littering the ravine far below. And, halfway along the dam, people were flinging themselves off into this space.

Switzerland has a reputation as a placid place, docile even. It's all cheese, chocolate and cowbells. Swiss people – so the stereotype would have it – don't take risks; they exploit calculated investment opportunities.

The Verzasca Dam blows that stereotype into thin air. Never mind Australia or New Zealand – this is the world's highest bungee jump, fully 220m (722ft) high. If you've seen *Goldeneye*, you might remember it from the opening sequence. But 007 used a stunt double. You don't.

It's a mind-bending prospect. While I was watching, one jumper took a look over the edge and retreated; another was sitting quietly, trying to gather her courage. People who did leap seemed to take an age to fall, swan-diving out into nothingness, their howls echoing up off the dam.

I wish I could report that I met the Verzasca challenge. But I didn't. Sweaty palms, you see. Just standing on the edge looking down was challenging enough for me.

CANOEING down the Dordogne

FRANCE Have you ever fancied paddling in speckled sunlight past ancient châteaux and honey-hued villages, stopping off for a spot of gentle sightseeing and ending the day with a well-earned gastronomic extravaganza? If so, then canoeing down the Dordogne river in southwest France is just the ticket.

For a 170km stretch from Argentat down to Mauzac the river provides classic canoeing. The scenery is glorious and varied, there are umpteen first-class sights within a stone's throw of the water and the choice of accommodation ranges from convivial campsites and rustic village inns to luxury hotels in converted châteaux. The free-flowing river also offers a variety of canoeing conditions to suit beginners upwards, and though it's hardly white-water rafting, some of the Dordogne's rapids are sufficiently challenging, particularly in spring and early summer, to give at least a *frisson* of excitement.

Keen canoeists should start at Argentat, from where it takes roughly ten days to paddle downstream. The river here is fast, fun and more or less crowd-free. Beyond Beaulieu the current eases back as the river widens, and the first limestone outcrops and sandy beaches – perfect for a picnic lunch – start to appear. Souillac marks the beginning of the most famous – and busiest – stretch of river. If you can only spare one day, then paddle from Souillac, or Domme, to Beynac where the river loops beneath beetling cliffs from which medieval fortresses keep watch from their dizzying eyries. At water level you glide past walnut orchards, duck farms and houses drenched in geraniums.

The crowds fall behind as you slip past Beynac. There are fewer sights and the scenery is more mellow, though the Dordogne has one final treat in store at Limeuil where it splits into two great channels that meander across the floodplain. Leave your canoe behind and head for the limestone cliffs for a bird's-eye view of this classic Dordogne scene.

086 Impressionist paintings at the Musée d'Orsay

FRANCE Forget the Louvre, it's not a patch on the Musée d'Orsay – or so you'll be told. Maybe this is down to continued bitterness towards futuristic glass pyramids, but it's probably more about the understated elegance of the Musée d'Orsay itself. Located in a renovated turn-of-the-century railway station, the museum's splendid collection of vibrant Impressionist canvases are displayed in much more intimate surroundings, right up under the roof in a wing whose attic-like feel is far less formal and imposing than the Louvre.

A wander through the compact Impressionist and Post-Impressionist galleries provides an astonishingly comprehensive tour of the best paintings of the period, the majority of them easily recognizable classics like Van Gogh's *Starry Night* or Renoir's *Dance at Le Moulin de la Galette*. Even better, these are paintings you can really engage with, their straightforward style and vibrant, life-like scenes drawing you into the stories they tell. It's easy to forget where you are and, transfixed, reach out a finger to trace the chunky swirls of paint that make up Van Gogh's manic skies; you might even catch yourself imitating the movements of Degas' delicate ballerinas as they dance across the walls, sweeping their arms in arcs above their heads and pointing their tiny toes.

When the intricate grandeur of Monet's Rouen Cathedral looms above you and reinstates a sense of decorum, it's almost as if you were standing under the imposing bulk of the old building itself. Exhilaration returns as you're transported to the tropics by Gauguin's disarming Tahitian maids, who eye you coyly from the depths of the jungle. But don't get so caught up in the stories that you forget the incredible artistic prowess on display; stick your nose right up to Seurat's dotted *Cirque*, then inch slowly backwards and, as the yellow-clad acrobats appear with their white horse, you'll feel the immense genius of the pioneer of pointillism.

087 Cycling in the Dutch countryside

THE NETHERLANDS If you like the idea of cycling, but would rather cut off both arms and legs than bike up a mountain, then perhaps The Netherlands is the perfect place for you – especially if you're also scared of traffic. The most cycle-friendly country in the world, Holland has a fantastically well-integrated network of cycle paths that make it simple for even the rawest cycling greenhorns to get around by bike, and to enjoy its under-rated and sometimes swooningly beautiful vast skies, flat pastures and huge expanses of water. If you don't want to go far, get hold of a Dutch-style bike, gearless and with back pedal brakes or bring your own and follow the country's network of 26 well-signposted, long-distance or LF (*landelijke fietroutes*) paths, which connect up the whole country so you never have to go near a main road. The Netherlands is a small country and it's easy to cover 50km or so a day, maybe more if you're fit enough and have a decent bike – the sit-up-and-beg Dutch variety are only really suitable for short distances. The one thing holding you back may be the wind, which can whip across the Dutch dykes and polders. But there's nothing quite like the feeling of your first Heineken of the evening after a long day's cycle. *Tot ziens!*

088 Downing a stein or ten at the Oktoberfest

GERMANY The world's largest public festival, the Munich Oktoberfest, kicks off on the penultimate Saturday in September and keeps pumping day after day for a full two weeks. Known locally as the "Wies'n" after the sprawling Theresienwiese park in which it takes place, it was first held to celebrate the wedding of local royalty but is now an unadulterated celebration of beer and Bavarian life, attracting almost six million visitors and seeing as many million litres of beer disappear in sixteen days.

At the heart of the festival are fourteen enormous beer tents where boisterous crowds sit at long benches, elbow to elbow, draining one huge litre-capacity glass or "stein" after another. If you're up for annihilation, head to the Hofbrau tent at a weekend, go for the ten-stein challenge and join in with the thousands of young bloods braying for beer. If you actually want to remember your time in Munich, or to encounter some real Germans, pitch up midweek and take in two or three of the other beer tents. Whenever and wherever you go, you can count on one thing for sure – within two *steins* you'll be laughing with your neighbours like long-lost buddies and banging the table in time with the Oompah bands.

The busiest time to visit Oktoberfest is the first weekend, when the "Grand Entry of the Oktoberfest Landlords and Breweries" starts the whole thing off as participants attired in Bavarian finery (lederhosen, basically), decorated carriages, curvaceous waitresses on horse-drawn floats and booming brass bands from each of the beer tents parade through town, joined by several thousand thirsty locals and international party-goers.

The local mayor gets things going by tapping the first barrel of Oktoberfest beer at the park's entrance and declaring "Ozapftis", which means "it's been tapped", but translates more accurately as, "Why doesn't everybody get as wasted as possible in my town for the next two weeks and don't worry about the mess because we'll clear up?" Huge cheers rise up from the crowd as the mad dash to the cavernous beer tents begins.

089 Washing it down with cider in Normandy

FRANCE Normandy is to cider what Bordeaux is to wine. Sparkling, crisp and refreshing, it's the perfect foil to the artery-clogging food that Normans also do rather well – and as some of France's best food and drink comes from the rolling hills and green meadows of Normandy's Pays d'Auge, dining at a country restaurant in these parts is an experience not to miss.

The bottle of cider plonked down by your waiter may look as distinguished as a fine champagne, but don't stand on ceremony: open it quickly and take a good swig while it's still cold.

Norman cider is typically sweeter and less alcoholic than its English cousin, but it's the invigorating fizz that tickles the back of the throat and bubbles up through the nose that you'll remember.

You could try a *kir normand*: cider mixed with cassis – a more sophisticated and delicious French take on that old student favourite, "snakebite and black".

Make sure that you have a full glass ready for the arrival of your *andouilles* starter: although it won't necessarily enhance the taste of assorted blood and guts in a sausage, a generous gulp of cider will help get it down. Pork and cider, on the other hand, is one of the classic combinations of Norman cooking. Opt for some pork chops to follow and they come drowned in a thick, deliciously satisfying sauce with as much cream in it as cider. At this point, you may be offered the *trou normand*: a shot of Calvados apple brandy that helps digestion, apparently by lighting a fire in the pit of your stomach that burns through even the toughest *andouilles'* intestines. The *trou* clears just enough room for a slice of Camembert or Pont-l'Evêque, two of the famous cheeses produced in the Pays d'Auge, before you can finally leave the table, full and just a bit wobbly.

090 Gorging on chocolates in Brussels

BELGIUM The Mayans may have invented chocolate long ago, but Belgium is today its world headquarters, and nowhere more so than Brussels, whose temples to the art of the brown stuff are second to none. It's not just a tourist thing, although within the vicinity of the Grande-Place you could be forgiven for thinking so. Chocolate is massively popular in Belgium, and even the smallest town has at least a couple of chocolate shops; in fact, the country has two thousand all told, and produces 172,000 tonnes of chocolate every year. You may think that this would make for a nation of obese lardcakes, especially as Belgium's other favourite thing is beer (not even mentioning the country's obsession with *pommes frites*). However, whatever your doctor may tell you, chocolate in moderation is quite healthy. It reduces cholesterol and is easily digested; some claim it's an aphrodisiac as well.

So what are you waiting for? Everyone has their favourite chocolatier – some swear by Neuhaus, while others rely on good old Leonidas, which has a shop on every corner in Brussels – but

Godiva is perhaps the best-known Belgian name, formed in the early 1900s by Joseph Draps, one of whose descendants now runs a chocolate museum on the Grande-Place. Once you've checked that out (and gobbled down a few free samples), make for the elegant Place du Grand Sablon, with not only a Godiva outlet, but also the stylish shop of Pierre Marcolini, who produces some of the best chocs in the city, if not the world. *Wittamer*, also on Place du Grand Sablon, doesn't just do chocolates, and in fact you can sip coffee and munch on a chocolate-covered choux pastry at its rather nice café; you're probably best off saving that big box of *Wittamer*'s delicious pralines for later... though trying just a few now surely can't hurt. If you're not feeling queasy by this point, stop at *Planète Chocolate*, on rue du Lombard, where you can find the city's most exotic and adventurous flavours – pepper, rose, various kinds of tea – as well as watch the chocolate-making process in action, followed by (what else?) the obligatory tasting. Moderation be damned.

091 Playboys and petrolheads: the Monaco Grand Prix

MONACO From the hotel-sized yachts in the harbour to the celebrity-filled Casino, the Grand Prix in Monaco is more than a motor race – it's a three-day playboy paradise. The Monaco crown is still the most sought after in motor-racing circles, although today's event is as much a showcase for the richest men and women on the planet as it is for the drivers.

Set amongst the winding streets of the world's second smallest and most densely populated principality, this is the most glamorous and high-profile date on the Formula One calendar. Attracting a global television audience of millions, the cars roar their way around the city centre at four-times the speed the streets were designed for. The circuit is blessed with some of the most historic and memorable corners in motor racing: St Devote, Mirabeau, La Rascasse, Casino and, of course, the Tunnel. Part of Monaco's appeal is its renowned difficulty. Three-times Formula One World

Champion Nelson Piquet once described tackling the circuit as like, "riding a bicycle around your living room".

Watching this gladiatorial spectacle around the Portier corner is particularly thrilling – one of the few possible, if unlikely, overtaking points on the course – seeing the cars' flaming exhausts before they disappear into the Tunnel, the deafening roar of the engines echoing behind. But one of the best and cheapest places to watch the race is the standing-only Secteur Rocher, a grassy area on a hill above the last corner – Rascasse – at the circuit's western end, which offers fine views and attracts the most passionate F1 supporters. The cars look pretty small from up here, but watching them sweep past is incredible. And afterwards you can climb down for a stroll or drive around the circuit, which is reopened to traffic every evening: just don't imagine you're Michael Schumacher – the normal speed limit still applies.

Mush! Mush! *Husky sledding in the Swiss Alps*

SWITZERLAND I don't think he actually said "Mush! Mush!" – all I caught was a little click of the teeth and a high-pitched cry – but the dogs still howled and yapped and took off through the snow like hounds out of hell. We were up at 3000m, whisking across the snowfields on a sled drawn by eight huskies yoked in pairs. Earlier, the musher, René, had pointed out the different breeds to us – most were regular huskies, with their pale coats and blue eyes, but he also had several stocky, dark-pelted Greenlands. It was about ten degrees below freezing, under a crystal-clear blue sky – really too warm for them: these dogs prefer temperatures nearer minus thirty.

The sled was a simple affair, a couple of metres long, with a platform at the back for the musher to stand on with reins in hand and us sitting below, facing the bobbing tails of the rearmost pair of dogs. We whooshed along: what a great way to travel! Human and dog working together, in a spectacular natural setting of high peaks and grand panoramas.

Even on that short ride, we could see the pack at work: René had yoked an adolescent trainee alongside one of the old matriarchs at the front, and she was doling out some training of her own, with the odd nip to keep the young'un in line.

As we arrived back at base, the rest of the pack set up a frantic howling to greet the returnees, who stood, tongues out, panting clouds of steamy breath. They looked fantastic – I wanted to set off again into the wilderness and never come back.

092

FRANCE Ready for lunch? Given the range and quality of foodstuffs available from small producers in France, there's nothing better than to buy your own picnic at a local market – and no better place to do it than Sarlat. This medieval town tucked in a fold of hills on the edge of the Dordogne Valley hosts one of the biggest and best markets in southwest France.

For centuries people have been flocking to Sarlat market, where the banter is just as likely to be in local dialect as in French. The stalls under their jaunty parasols groan with local produce, from a rainbow array of seasonal fruit and vegetables to home-baked cakes and the famous pâté de foie gras, the fattened liver of goose or duck.

Let your nose guide you first to the charcuterie van selling aromatic pork or venison sausage and locally cured ham. There are terrines of *rillettes*, a coarse duck or goose pâté, and melt-in-the-mouth foie gras, sometimes laced with truffles, the "black diamonds of Périgord". Next up is the farmer tempting customers with tasty slivers of cheese. The regional speciality is *cabécou*, a small, flat medallion of goats' cheese, but you'll also find creamy ewes'-milk cheese from the Pyrenees and Salers and Bleu d'Auvergne from the Massif Central.

A few tomatoes – still sun-warm and packed with flavour – and a cucumber make a quick salad. Then you need bread. Traditionalists will opt for a crusty *pain de campagne*, but wholemeal baguettes and rye or seed-speckled granary breads are just as prevalent. While you're at it, ask for some wedges of walnut cake or *pastis*, a lip-smacking apple tart topped with crinkled pastry and more than a hint of Armagnac.

Last stop is the fruit stall, groaning with the season's bounty, from the first cherries of spring through summer strawberries to autumn's apples, pears and fat Chasselas grapes. Now tear yourself away to find a sunny spot on the banks of the Dordogne – not forgetting the wine and corkscrew of course. Bon appétit!

094 Macaroons for her majesty

FRANCE It's 5.30pm on a Friday, and a queue stretches out through the door of Ladurée, on rue Royale near the place de la Madeleine. If you're wondering what the fuss is about, just take one look at the display of fabulous cakes and pastries – so renowned are Ladurée's confections that foodies will cross Paris for them and patiently wait their turn to have their purchases packed into elegant boxes.

If you feel you've earned yourself a sightseeing break, you could bypass the queue and head for the adjoining *salon de thé* or tea room, though the English translation hardly does justice to this luxurious parlour dating from 1862, decorated with gilt-edged mirrors, marble-topped tables and ceiling frescoes.

Once you're installed at your table, surrounded by elegantly coiffed grandes dames sporting Hermès scarves and fashionistas flanked by designer bags, a waitress in a long polka-dotted apron will take your order and flash you a complicitous look as you name your desired confection. You could let yourself be tempted by any number of heavenly gateaux, but if you've never tasted them, it's Ladurée's famous *macarons* (macaroons) that you should try. Nothing like the stodgy coconut-heavy cookies that you may know from back home, these are delicate almondy biscuits with a delicious ganache filling – at once crunchy and gooey. They come in a variety of flavours and pastel colours – the chocolate and blackcurrant are the best – and, like designer fashion collections, new flavours are launched each season.

More extravagant creations are also available, such as the *saint-honoré rose-framboise*; made of choux pastry, Chantilly, raspberry compote and raspberries, and topped off with a rose petal, it has all the flouncy froufrou of a dress from the court of Versailles. Perhaps unsurprising, then, that Ladurée was appointed the official pâtissier for Sofia Coppola's film *Marie Antoinette*. "Let them eat cake!", the French queen was supposed to have said. And when the cakes are this good, it's hard to imagine why you'd want to eat anything else.

095 Freewheeling in the Upper Danube Valley

GERMANY When Germans wax lyrical about the Rhine and Bavarian Alps, they're just trying to keep you out of the Upper Danube Valley. Few know that Strauss's beloved Blue Danube waltzes into the picture in the Black Forest; and fewer still that one of its most awe-inspiring stretches is tucked away in rural Swabia. Here, limestone pinnacles and cave-riddled crags force you to look up.

Looking up, I discovered, is tempting but can also be treacherous if you're pedalling along the banks, lose your balance and barely manage to escape a head-on collision with a cliff. Breathtaking – in every sense of the word. I freewheeled from Fridingen, following the loops and bends of the Danube river through evergreen valleys speckled with purple thistles. There's something special about a place that, for all its beauty, remains untouched by tourism. Aside from the odd farmer bidding me "*Guten Tag*", I was alone in discovering this Daliesque landscape; where surreal rock formations and deep crevasses punctuate shady pine and birch forests. A soft breeze blew across the cliffs and I could hear the distant hammering of woodpeckers.

Pulling up at a bend in the river, I paused to dangle my toes into the tingling water streaked pink and gold. Towering 200m above was the gravity-defying Burg Bronnen, a medieval castle clinging precipitously to a rocky outcrop and seemingly hanging on for dear life. There was no way I was going to be able to lug my bike up there. No matter, I might still make it to the Benedictine abbey in Beuron if I notched it up a gear. Then again, maybe not. Out here in the sticks, time no longer mattered. I slipped back into my saddle and slowly continued to trace the Danube's curves; the late afternoon sun silhouetted turrets, pinnacles and treetops.

096 Hiking Corsica's GR20

FRANCE We'd set out in pre-dawn darkness to ascend the spectacular head of the Vallée d'Asco, ringed by peaks nudging 3000m. High above, an enfolding wall of snow-streaked granite glowed crimson in the first rays of daylight. Small flocks of mouflon sheep were already grazing overhead, sending small pebbles spiralling down the cliffs as we began the first pass of the day.

The view from the col was astounding. Looking northwards along the serrated ridge-tops of the watershed, tiers of shadowy summits receded to a sea the colour of lapis. The light was exceptionally vivid all the way to the horizon, where a front of white cloud was floating above the French Riviera.

Except it wasn't cloud. As a glance through the binoculars confirmed, the white apparition in the distance was in fact the southern reaches of the Alps – a staggering 250km away. What we'd assumed was a small yacht on its way to St-Tropez or Toulon was in fact a massive car ferry the size of a block of flats. The realization was overwhelming, completely overturning our sense of space and scale.

Seeing the Alps from such a distance may have been a one-off, but every day on the GR20 – France's famous *haute route* across the Mediterranean island of Corsica – brings astonishing moments. The ingenious red-and-white waymarks lead you across terrain of incredible variety. On a typical *étape* you could climb passes nearly 2.5km high, picnic by frozen glacial lakes, skinny dip in mountain streams, skid down eternal snow patches and come face to face at the bottom with a wild boar.

Best of all, at the end of it, having hauled yourself through all fifteen *étapes*, you can rest your aching bones in some of the most translucent turquoise waters in the entire Mediterranean.

097 Communing with Carnac's prehistoric past

FRANCE Created around 3300 BC, Carnac's three alignments of over two thousand menhirs comprise the greatest concentration of standing stones in the world. Come here in the summer and you'll encounter crowds and boundary ropes. But visit during the winter and you can wander among them freely – and if you arrive just after sunrise, when the mist still clings to the coast, you'll be accompanied by nothing but the birds and the sounds of the local farms waking up.

Just to the north of town, where the stones of Le Ménec alignment are at their tallest, you can walk between broken megalithic walls that stand twice your height. Stretching for more than one hundred metres from one side to the other and extending for over a kilometre, the rows of stones might first seem part of a vast art installation. Each is weathered and worn by five thousand years of Atlantic storms, and their stark individuality provides a compelling contrast to the symmetry of the overall arrangement. But it's hard to believe there wasn't something religious about them.

It's possible that the stones had some sort of ritual significance, linked to the numerous tombs and dolmens in the area; or they may have been the centre of a mind-blowing system to measure the precise movements of the moon – we simply don't know.

At the northwest end of the third and final alignment, Kerlescan, don't turn back as most visitors do. Keep walking to where the stones peter out in the thick, damp woodland of Petit Ménec, and the moss- and lichen-smothered menhirs seem even more enchanting, half hidden in the leaves. There's something incredibly stirring about these rows of megalithic monuments, and something mystical – it's that feeling you get when you walk into a quiet church, the sense of being in a spiritual place. And the knowledge that they were placed here for reasons we don't understand sends shivers down your spine.

098 Getting serious in the Ardennes

BELGIUM Home of the EU, and for most people Europe's most boring country, Belgium is hardly the most obvious choice for an activity holiday. Yet the thickly wooded hills of its southernmost region, the Ardennes, are one of the country's biggest surprises: sharply scenic, with peaks of exposed limestone, criss-crossed with waymarked footpaths, busy with wildlife, and cut through by fast-flowing rivers, it's a hiker's and kayaker's – even a climber's – heaven.

First off, just walk. There is fantastic hiking all over the Ardennes, and at La Roche-en-Ardennes you can undertake any number of relatively easy hikes that loop out from the town; Rochefort, too, whose most popular walk is named after the Belgian King Albert I who was famously killed in a climbing accident in the Ardennes in the 1930s, is a great centre for both easy and more difficult treks. But at Rochehaut, northwest of Bouillon, the hikes get more serious, indeed the paths that follow the valley of the Semois river are definitely not for the fainthearts, with some very steep climbs, some of which you have to negotiate by means of handrails and fixed ladders, ropes and footbridges. But it's well worth the effort, and the scenery is so spectacular, looking down on the sweeping meanders of the river, that you have to pinch yourself that, yes, you're still in Belgium.

Scramble down to Bouillon from here for a spot of kayaking – a good place to start if you're new to the sport. There are several outfits renting craft, and they'll let you loose downriver and then pick you up at the end of the day, though be warned that in high summer it can be crowded and the water levels very low. If you're still feeling energetic, spurn the outfitter's minibus, and walk back to Bouillon, picking up one of any number of trails that lead back to the town, and maybe even stopping for a beer on the way. You may need to wade through some fast-flowing rapids to get served, but, hey, that's Belgium.

099 Big foot: snowshoeing through the Black Forest

GERMANY There's nothing more satisfying than being the first person to step on deep virgin snow. Except, perhaps, being able to step on it without sinking to your thighs. The solution? Snowshoes: clumsy tennis-racket contraptions that have morphed into lighter, high-tech models with snazzy spikes and the power to glide. Forget the adrenalin rush of bombing down the Alps; snowshoeing offers silent winter thrills in frozen forests and the chance to see a country's wild side. I'd picked the Black Forest in Germany, a winter wonderland of fir-clad hills custom-made for this low-impact sport.

Just for the "wow factor", I decided to hike the forest's highest peak, 1493m Feldberg, geared up for snowshoers like me, with mile upon mile of well-marked trails. Leaving civilization behind, I took my first giant steps through layers of crunchy powder, little by little adapting to the shuffle and swoosh of my snowshoes in quiet exhilaration. More confident now, I attempted a few Bambi-style leaps and bounces down a smooth white slope. Heart racing and cheeks glowing, it dawned on me that I'd have to climb back up that hill. Damn.

I've seen some big trees in my time, but Black Forest firs beat them all – Goliaths standing to attention, their branches thick with gloopy snow as though someone got a bit carried away with the icing sugar. I flopped beneath one of them, slurping hot tea and enjoying the isolation of being out of my depth in snow and surrounded by utter silence. Taking long, rhythmic strides past fox prints, deer poo and stacks of fresh-cut timber, I finally emerged at Feldberg's summit. Ahead, the panorama opened up to reveal glacier-carved valleys framed by the pointy Alps and Vosges. Behind me, a solitary set of footprints twinkled in the midday sun.

THE CATHAR CASTLES OF
Languedoc-Roussillon

100

FRANCE It's hard to forget the first time you catch a glimpse of the Château de Peyrepertuse. In fact, it takes a while before you realize that this really is a castle, not just some fantastic rock formation sprouting from the mountaintop. But it's no mirage – 800 years ago, men really did haul slabs of stone up here to build one of the most hauntingly beautiful fortresses in Europe.

In medieval France, war was frequent, life often violent – the point of castles, obviously enough, was to provide a degree of protection from all of that. Location was all-important – and the Cathar lords of Languedoc-Roussillon took this to ludicrous extremes, building them in seemingly impossible places. How they even laid foundations boggles the mind. Approach on foot, from the village of Duilhac, and you'll soon see why. Improbably perched on the edge of a long, rocky ridge, it's surrounded by a sheer drop of several hundred metres, and its outer walls cleverly follow the contours of the mountain, snaking around the summit like a stone

viper. Inside, at the lower end, is the main keep, a solid grey cube of rock that looks like it could withstand a battering from smart bombs, never mind medieval cannon. But to really appreciate the fortress, you have to get closer.

It's a sweaty hour-long hike to the top, but when you clamber through the main entrance and onto the upper keep, the views from the battlements are stupendous: here, where the mountain ends in a vast, jagged stub of granite, there are no walls – you'd need wings to attack from this side.

Ironically, even castles like this couldn't protect the Cathars. In the early thirteenth century, this Christian cult was virtually exterminated after forty years of war and a series of massacres that were brutal even by medieval standards. Peyrepertuse was surrendered in 1240, but the fact that it still survives, as impressive now as it must have been centuries ago, is testament to the Cathars' ingenious building skills and their passionate struggle for freedom.

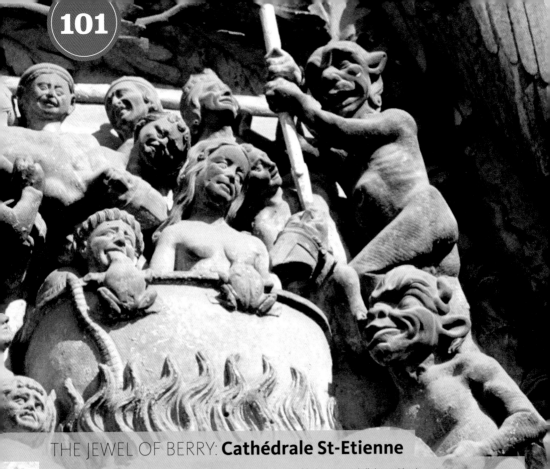

THE JEWEL OF BERRY: **Cathédrale St-Etienne**

FRANCE A flat plain at the very heart of France, stranded between the verdant Loire Valley and the abundant hillsides of Burgundy, the Berry region has become a byword for provincial obscurity. This really is *La France profonde*, the cherished "deep France", whose peasant traditions continue to resist the modernization that threatens – so they say – to engulf the nation. You can drive for miles here without seeing anything except open fields and modest farmhouses.

As you approach the miniature regional capital of Bourges, however, a mighty landmark begins to reveal itself. Looming over the fields, allotments and low houses is a vast Gothic cathedral, its perfect skeleton of flying buttresses and keel-like roof giving it the look of a huge ship in dry dock. A stupendous relic of the inexorable, withdrawing tide of power and belief, its preposterous size and wealth of detailing prove that the Berry was not always a backwater. In the early thirteenth century, when the cathedral was built, this was a powerful and wealthy region – and Bourges'

archbishops wanted all the world to know it.

At the foot of the impossibly massive west front, five great portals yawn open, their deep arches fringed by sculptures. You could spend hours gazing at the central portal, which depicts the Last Judgement in appalling detail, complete with snake-tailed and wing-arsed devils, and damned souls – some wearing bishops' mitres – screaming from the bottom of boiling cauldrons.

Inside, the prevailing mood is one of quieter awe. The magnificent nave soars to an astonishing 38 metres, and is ringed by two tall aisles. No matter where you look, smooth-as-bone columns power their way from marble floor to tent-like vault, their pale stone magically dappled with colours cast by some of Europe's finest, oldest and deepest-hued stained glass. Behind the high altar, at the very heart of the cathedral and at the very centre of France, the apse holds these jewels of the Berry: precious panels of coloured glass, their images of the Crucifixion, the Last Judgement, the Apocalypse and of Joseph and his coat glowing like gemstones.

102 Paying your respects in Normandy

FRANCE Apart from the German stronghold of Pointe du Hoc, where gleeful kids take time out from building sandcastles to clamber over the rubble of battered bunkers, the D-Day landing beaches – Sword, Juno, Gold, Omaha and Utah – contain few physical traces of their bloody past. It's almost as though the cheery banality of summertime in the seaside towns along this stretch of the Norman coast has grown like poppies over the painful memories of June 6, 1944. The beaches are dotted with gaily painted wooden bathing huts; the odd windsurfer braves the choppy waters; walkers ramble along the dunes; families up from Paris eat *moules frites* at beachside terraces – all a far cry from those horrible events as re-enacted in the shocking opening scene of *Saving Private Ryan*.

But while the sands are consumed by summer's frivolity, the cemeteries built to bury the D-Day dead serve as sanctuaries for those who don't want to forget. People shuffle in silence across the well-manicured lawns of the American burial ground on a cliff overlooking Omaha, where rows of perfectly aligned white crosses sweep down to the cliff's edge and appear to continue for miles into the sea. In the church-like peace and tranquillity, broken only by the sharp cries of seagulls, uniformed veterans remember fallen comrades and lost husbands and fathers. Even the children, too young to even understand the sacrifices made, are humbled by the solemnity of their surroundings, affording only glancing and indifferent looks at the kites swirling in the breeze before returning to the poignantly simple white crosses that have made the grown-ups so quiet.

103 Cranking up the volume on Queen's Day

THE NETHERLANDS Every April 30, Amsterdam, a city famed for its easy-going, fun-loving population, manages to crank the party volume a few notches higher in a street party that blasts away for a full 24 hours. Held to celebrate the official birthday of the Dutch monarch, Queen's Day is traditionally the one time each year when the police are forbidden from interfering with any activity, no matter how outrageous; and, of course, it's always a challenge to see where they really draw the line.

Stages piled high with huge sound systems take over every available open space, blasting out the beats all day and night – the main stages are on Rembrandtplein and particularly Thorbeckplein, Leidseplein, Nieuwmarkt and Museumplein – and whatever your inclination, you'll find enough beer-chugging, pill-popping and red-hot partying to satisfy the most voracious of appetites. There are only two rules: you must dress as ridiculously as possible, preferably in orange, the Dutch national colour, which adorns virtually every building, boat and body on the day; and you must drink enough beer not to care.

The extensive and picturesque canals are one of the best things about Amsterdam, and Queen's Day makes the most of them, as boating restrictions are lifted (or perhaps just ignored) and everyone goes bananas on the water – rowingboats, barges and old fishing vessels crammed with people, crates of beer and booming sound systems, pound their way along the canals like entrants in some particularly disorganized aquatic carnival. Your mission is to get on board, as they're a great way to get around – pick one with good tunes and people you like the look of. Or just hang out with everyone else and watch the boats come and go: crowds gather on the larger bridges and canal junctions to cheer as each bizarre vessel passes – Prinsengracht is a good canal, with Reguliersgracht and Prinsengracht a particularly chaotic and enjoyable intersection.

104 Marooned on Sein: the island at the edge of the world

FRANCE Of the many isolated islands dotted off the coast of Brittany, the tiny, flat-as-a-pancake Île de Sein has to be the most romantic and mysterious. A slender sliver, silhouetted against the sunset, Sein lies 8km west of the rocky Pointe du Raz, Brittany's westernmost promontory. Nowhere rising more than 6m above the surrounding sea, for much of its 2.5km length the island is little broader than the concrete breakwater that serves as its central spine. Each fresh tide seems likely to wash right over the land and its very grip on existence seems so tenuous it's hard to believe anyone could survive here. However, over three hundred islanders make their living from the sea, fishing for scallops, lobster and crayfish. Indeed, the island has long been inhabited; Roman sources tell of a shrine served by nine virgin priestesses, and it's said to have been the last refuge of the Druids in Brittany.

Setting off to Sein on a misty morning feels like sailing off the edge of the world. Having picked their way along a chain of lonely lighthouses, ferries draw in at the one, tight-knit village, hunched with its back to the open ocean. There are no cars – the rugged stone houses snuggle so close that no vehicle could squeeze between them – and even bicycles are not permitted.

Although low tide uncovers a small sandy beach in one of the harbours, there's little to the village itself, and most visitors stride off to enjoy the ravishing coastal scenery, where land, sea and sky meld together in a whirl of white surf. The tiny agricultural terraces of the eastern tip, connected by a pencil-thin natural causeway, have long been overgrown with sparse yellow broom – you'll probably have the place to yourself as you explore the myriad rock pools. A longer walk west leads to the Phare de Goulenez lighthouse; though it's not open to visitors, the lighthouse is an oddly comforting presence here at the very edge of the island, as the ocean claws and drags at the black, seaweed-strewn boulders, and the screaming seagulls return from their forays over the infinite Atlantic.

105 Going to the medieval movies

FRANCE A world apart from piles of old stones, paintings of curly-wigged fat men or pungent-smelling châteaux, seeing the *Bayeux Tapestry* is more like going to the movies than trotting round a traditional tourist sight. Wrapped around a half-lit wall like a medieval IMAX theatre, it's protected by a glass case and dim lighting, while a deep, movie-trailer voice gives a blow-by-blow headphone commentary of the kings, shipwrecks and gory battles depicted in the comic-strip-like scenes.

The nuns who are thought to have embroidered this 70m strip of linen chronicling William of Normandy's conquest of England could hardly have guessed that, nearly a millennium later, people would be lining up to marvel at their meticulous artwork and impeccable storytelling.

But like Shakespeare's plays, the *Bayeux Tapestry* is one of history's timeless treasures. Okay, so the characters are two-dimensional, the ancient colours hardly HD and the scenes difficult to decipher without the commentary, but it's captivating nonetheless. William looks every bit the superhero on the back of his huge horse, while King Harold, with his dastardly moustache, appears the archetypal villain, his arrow in the eye a just dessert.

The wonderful detail adds intriguing layers to the main theme: the appearance of Halley's Comet as a bad omen when Harold is crowned king builds up the suspense, while the apparent barbecuing of kebabs on the beach has led some historians to argue that the tapestry is considerably newer than first thought. Whether this is true is of no great importance – the images are as engrossing now as they ever were, and on exiting the theatre, even the staunchest of Brits might feel enthused enough to be secretly pleased that a brave Frenchman crossed the Channel to give Harold his comeuppance. And in this way, the *Bayeux Tapestry* has lost none of its power as one of the finest pieces of propaganda the world has ever seen.

106 Kayaking across the borders on Lake Constance

GERMANY, SWITZERLAND & AUSTRIA Germany drifted behind me and I spied Switzerland ahead – their red-and-white flag fluttering in the breeze. Like whales in a fish pond, approaching ferries created tidal waves that thrashed both sides of my kayak and rocked it so hard that I thought the dreaded Eskimo Roll was imminent. Still, I was loving every minute of it. But then it's hard not to love Lake Constance, Europe's third largest lake, where you can wake up on the beach in Germany, cool off with a swim in Switzerland and still make it to Austria in time for a schnitzel dinner with alpine views.

Ahhh, this was the life – summer on the turquoise lake, rotating my paddle, stabbing the rippling water with a double-edged blade and pulling back with the strength of bionic woman. A floating speck on this mother of a lake, I felt as inconspicuous as a fly on the wall (albeit one in a dazzling red life jacket); passing sailing boats full of – surely not! – nude Germans sunbathing on deck, swanky yachts where über-cool Zurich day-trippers in designer shades popped corks, and families frolicking in the water and grilling *bratwurst* in horseshoe-shaped bays.

Allensbach's onion-domed church faded and I was heading for the fruit-growing island of Reichenau, a World Heritage Site famed for its twin-towered Benedictine abbey. Too attached to my kayak to get out and explore, I skirted around the marshes and propelled the craft towards Mannenbach in Switzerland, to dive into the deliciously cold water and picnic on the shore. I reached the fringes of Wollmatinger Ried nature reserve, as the late afternoon sun glinted on my kayak's name – *Wolke Sieben* (Cloud Number Nine). Well it's not far off, I thought. Nearer than Austria, anyway.

107 Wine-tasting in Bordeaux

FRANCE Margaux, Pauillac, Sauternes, St-Émilion – some of the world's most famous wines come from the vineyards encircling Bordeaux. So famous, in fact, that until recently, most châteaux didn't bother about marketing their wares. But times are changing: faced with greater competition and falling demand, more and more are opening their doors to the public. It has never been easier to visit these châteaux and sample the wines aptly described as "bottled sunlight".

Ranging from top-rank names such as Mouton-Rothschild and Palmer to small, family-run concerns, there are plenty to choose from. Some make their wine according to time-honoured techniques; others are ultra high-tech, with gleaming, computer-controlled vats and automated bottling lines – and there are a growing number of organic producers, too. All are equally rewarding. During the visit you'll learn about soil types and grape varieties, about fermentation, clarification and the long, complicated process which transforms grapes into wine.

Though you rarely get to see inside the châteaux themselves, several offer other attractions to draw in the punters, from wine or wine-related museums to introductory wine-tasting classes (this being France, you can sometimes sign up children for the latter, too). And because not everyone is just here for the wine, there are also art galleries, sculpture parks, hot-air balloon trips and, around St-Émilion, underground quarries to explore.

All visits, nevertheless, end in the tasting room. In top-rank châteaux, an almost reverential hush descends as the bottles are lovingly poured out. The aficionados swirl glasses and sniff the aromas, take a sip, savour it and then spit it out. If you feel like it, an appreciative nod always goes down well. And often, you will feel like it – because despite all the detailed scientific explanations of how they're produced, the taste of these wines suggests that magic still plays a part.

108 On the art trail in the Côte d'Azur

FRANCE Like most of Renoir's work, it's instantly appealing, with a dazzling range of colour and a warmth that radiates out from the canvas. A hazy farmhouse at the end of a driveway, framed by leafy trees and bathed in sunny pastel tones, *La Ferme des Collettes* is one of the artist's most famous paintings, perfectly evoking a hot, balmy day in the south of France.

But what makes this watercolour extra special is its location: it's one of eleven on show in the actual *ferme* depicted in the painting, a mansion in Cagnes-sur-Mer where the celebrated Impressionist lived and worked from 1907 until his death, and which is now the Musée Renoir. Step outside and you step right into the picture, bathed in the same bright light and warm Mediterranean air.

And then there's Picasso. Probably the greatest painter of the twentieth century, he spent a prolific year at the Château Grimaldi in Antibes, a short drive south of Nice. Now the Musée Picasso, it's packed with work from that period – the creative energy of *Ulysses*

and his Sirens, a 4m-high representation of the Greek hero tied to the mast of his ship, is simply overwhelming. But it's hard to stare at something this intense for long, and you'll soon find yourself drifting to the windows – and the same spectacular view of the ocean that inspired Picasso sixty years ago.

Ever since pointillist Paul Signac beached his yacht at St-Tropez in the 1880s, the Côte d'Azur has inspired more writers, sculptors and painters than almost anywhere on the planet. If you want to follow in their footsteps, Nice is the place to start, home to Henri Matisse for much of his life. Resist the temptations of the palm-fringed promenade and head inland to the Musée Matisse, a striking maroon-toned building set in the heart of an olive grove. Among the exotic works on display, *Nature morte aux grenades* offers a powerful insight into the intense emotional connection Matisse established with this part of France, his vibrant use of raw, bold colour contrasting beautifully with the rough, almost clumsy style.

109
JOINING THE **Gilles** at **Binche Carnival**

BELGIUM Taking place in February or March, the four-hundred-year-old Binche Carnival is a magic combination of the country's national preoccupation with beer – outdoor beer tents are stacked high with a huge variety of Belgian brews – and a bizarre tradition that dates back to the Middle Ages.

The spectacular March of the Gilles is a parade of six hundred peculiarly and identically dressed men – the Gilles – strange, giant-like figures who dominate this event, all wearing the same wax masks, along with green glasses and moustaches, apparently in the style of Napoleon III. On Mardi Gras, groups of Gilles gather in the Grand-Place to dance around in a huge circle, or *rondeau*, holding

hands and tapping their wooden-clogged feet in time to the beat of the drum. The drummers, or *tamboureurs*, are situated in the middle of the circle, as are a smaller *rondeau* of petits Gilles. Get inside the circles if you can; here, you're perfectly placed to get dragged in with Gilles as they head into the town hall to ritually remove their masks. In the afternoon, they emerge to lead the Grand Parade, sporting tall hats, elaborately adorned with ostrich feathers, and clutching wooden baskets filled with oranges, which they throw with gusto into the crowd, covering everyone in blood-red juice and pulp. Be warned, though, that this ferocious "battle" is a decidedly one-sided affair – it's not done to throw them back.

NEED to know

051 *Café Central*, 1, Herrengasse 14; *Café Landtmann*, 1, Dr-Karl-Lueger-Ring 4; *Café Hawelka*, 1, Dorothergasse 6.

052 Château de Brissac, Brissac-Quincé (❂www .chateau-brissac.fr); Château de Chémery, Loir-et-Cher (❂www.chateaudechemery.com); Manoir de la Rémonière, near Azay-le-Rideau (❂www.manoirdela remoniere.com).

053 Grotte de Pech-Merle (❂www.quercy.net /pechmerle) is two hours' drive north of Toulouse.

054 The Casemates du Bock are open daily between March and October from 10am to 5pm.

055 Tours of the winery are available for ten people or more; see ❂www.hofkellerei.li for details.

056 The Glacier Express runs daily between St Moritz and Zermatt; full details at ❂www.glacierexpress.ch.

057 Mozartwoche (❂www.mozarteum.at); Fortress concerts (❂www.mozartfestival.at); dinner concerts at Stiftskeller St Peter & Mozart Requiem at the Kollegienkirche (❂www.salzburg-concerts.com)

058 See ❂www.trains-touristiques.sncf.com/train _jaune.htm for current timetable and fares. Note that the original open-topped carriages only run in summer and that many of the smaller stations are request stops only.

059 Usedom is 2.5 hours by car or train from Berlin; change at Züssow to reach Heringsdorf and Ahlbeck by rail. The resorts' website is ❂www.drei -kaiserbaeder.de.

060 *La Bécasse*, rue de Tabora 11; *Cantillon Brewery*, rue Gheude 56; *La Mort Subite*, rue Montagne-aux-Herbes Potagères 7; *In't Spinnekopke*, Place Jardin aux Fleurs 1; *Delirium*, Impasse de la Fidelité 4a.

061 The cemetery is open Mon–Fri 8am–5.30pm, Sat 8.30am–5.30pm and Sun 9am–5.30pm. Nearest metro stations are Père-Lachaise and Phillipe-Auguste. For more info, visit ❂www.parisinfo.com and ❂www .paris.fr, or for a virtual tour of the cemetery, see ❂www.pere-lachaise.com.

062 A single, one-way, first-class Gloggnitz to Murzzuschlag ticket costs €17. Book at ❂www.oebb.at.

063 Cap d'Agde is on France's Mediterranean coast, 60km southwest of Montpellier. For more visit ❂www .naturist.de.

064 The Louvre's "nocturnes" are on Wednesdays and Fridays. See ❂www.louvre.fr for more information.

065 For more information, visit ❂www.pontdugard.fr.

066 For opening times and massage costs, see ❂www.roemisch-irisches-bad.de.

067 The Streif run is in the resort of Kitzbühel (❂www.kitzbuhel.com); the most convenient airport is Munich.

068 For more information, and to organize tours, see ❂www.wadlopen.net or ❂www.wadlopen.com.

069 Go to ❂www.polostmoritz.com for full details.

070 You can find opening times, prices and other information at ❂www.aec.at.

071 The Cresta Run is open from December to March.

See ❂www.cresta-run.com for more.

072 Détours de Loire (❂www.locationdevelos.com) will drop you off, with bikes, at the location of your choice. See ❂www.loire-a-velo.fr for more.

073 Scheduled flights link Hamburg to airports in London, Bristol, Manchester, Edinburgh and Dublin. Beach bars open from noon to midnight between May and September.

074 Whitepod is located near Villars, in southwestern Switzerland. See ❂www.whitepod.com for details.

075 Tickets from €28.50 to €208. Apply for a booking form via ☎+49 921 202 21, 11am–noon, Mon–Fri. Bayreuth does not accept credit cards so you will have to transfer money. See ❂www.bayreuther-festspiele. de for the application deadline – usually mid-October the year before. First-time applicants are advised to get their forms in by the end of September at the latest.

076 See ❂www.ot-montsaintmichel.com for more.

077 For more on cow-fighting go to ❂www .switzerland.isyours.com/e/guide/valais/cowfighting .html.

078 The tourist office in Épernay (❂www.ot-epernay. fr) has information on touring the town's champagne houses.

079 Fribourg is the best place to try a classic style moitié-moitié; the pick of the bunch is the excellent *Gothard* at 18 Rue du Pont-Muré.

080 Ferries from Santa Teresa di Gallura in Sardinia run daily, year round. Corsica's airport is at Figari, 17km north of Bonifacio. For more, go to ❂www.bonifacio.fr.

081 ❂www.montreuxjazz.com has information on schedules, tickets and everything else.

082 The castle is a 20min walk from Hohenschwangau, in south Bavaria. See ❂www.neuschwanstein.de.

083 ❂www.austrianchristmasmarkets.co.uk has the full lowdown (and links) on Austria's Christmas markets.

084 The Verzasca Dam lies just east of Locarno, in southern Switzerland. Visit ❂www.trekking.ch /eng/007.asp for more information.

085 Numerous canoe rental companies set up along the Dordogne in summer offering rental by the day or half-day.

086 Check ❂www.musee-orsay.fr for entry prices and opening times.

087 The Dutch motoring organization, the ANWB, publishes a series of cycle maps that covers the whole country. Bike rental costs around €32 a week.

088 For more info, check out ❂www.oktoberfest.de.

089 The Route du Cidre is a 40km loop in the Pays d'Auge. For more information, visit ❂www.calvados -tourisme.com.

090 *Godiva*, Place du Grand Sablon 47– 48; *Pierre Marcolini*, rue des Minimes 1; *Wittamer*, Place du Grand Sablon 12; *Planète Chocolate*, rue du Lombard 24.

091 The Monaco Grand Prix is held annually in May. For tickets, visit ❂www.formula1.com.

092 Loschadej's Huskypower (June–Oct; ❂www .huskypower.ch) operates on the Diablerets Glacier, in southwestern Switzerland.

093 Sarlat main food market takes place on Saturday 8am–1pm.

094 Ladurée (❂www.laduree.fr) is at 16 rue Royale.

095 The trails in the Upper Danube Valley are mostly flat and well signposted. Valley Bike (❂www .valleybike.de) in Hausen am Tal near Beuron rents mountain bikes.

096 The GR20 stretches for some 170km and is open from June until mid-October. Most people need between ten and twelve days to complete it.

097 The Route des Alignements follows the course of the three main alignments. There's a visitor centre at the Alignements de Kermario.

098 See ❂www.belgiumtheplaceto.be, ❂www .wallonie-tourism.be/accueil/en and ❂www.grsentiers .org for more.

099 You can rent snowshoes and poles from the Haus der Natur in Feldberg. Check out ❂www.naturpark -suedschwarzwald.de for more details on the trails and maps.

100 Château de Peyrepertuse sits above the village of Duilhac. See ❂www.chateau-peyrepertuse.com.

101 The cathedral is open April–Sept 8.30am-7.15pm; Oct–March 8.15am–5.45pm. Entrance is free.

102 The Normandy landing beaches stretch west from the mouth of the River Orne near Caen to the Cotentin Peninsula south of Cherbourg. Informative tours are offered by the Caen Memorial (❂www .memorial-caen.fr).

103 Amsterdam's main clubs lay on special Queen's Day nights – pick up a copy of the free listings magazine *NL20* when you arrive.

104 Daily ferries make the hour-long crossing to Sein from Audierne on the mainland (summer €30, winter €20; ❂www.pennarbed.fr). The island has two lovely inexpensive hotels, the d'Armen (❂www.hotel -armen.net), which has a good restaurant, and Les Trois Dauphins (❂www.hoteliledesein.com).

105 See ❂www.chateau-guillaume-leconquerant.fr for opening hours and entry prices.

106 Rudolf Albiez in Radolfzell Harbour rents kayaks (❂www.bootsvermietung-radolfzell.de).

107 Local tourist offices and Maisons du Vin provide lists of producers offering vineyard visits. Most visits are free, though more famous châteaux may charge a small fee.

108 For more, visit ❂www.chez.com/renoir/cagnes. htm, ❂www.musee-matisse-nice.org, or ❂www.antibes -juanlespins.com/eng/culture/musees/picasso.

109 See ❂www.carnavaldebinche.be for more info.

GOOD to know

FROMAGE FORMIDABLE

Cheese is a French obsession. More *fromage* is consumed here than in any other European nation, at 23kg per person per year, while France produces over 500 types of highly prized regional varieties, from Normandy's soft, creamy Camembert and Brie to Vieux Boulogne, an unpasteurized, beer-washed concoction that's widely held to be one of the smelliest in the world.

FAMOUS BELGIANS

Plastic Bertrand (1954–) Who can forget Plastic's one-hit wonder "Ca Plane Pour Moi", which was Belgium's biggest punk hit in 1977. After nearly twenty years in the Walloon wilderness he made a comeback in the late 1990s and beccame a presenter on French TV.

Eddy Merckx (1945–) Regularly voted the greatest ever Belgian by both Flemish- and French-speakers, Merckx is perhaps the greatest competitive cyclist of all time. He won both the Tour de France and Giro d'Italia five times and is still involved in the sport as a race commentator.

Adolphe Sax (1814–1894) Soul and jazz music would have been much the poorer without the contribution of Adolphe Sax, who invented the saxophone in Dinant in 1846. You can pay homage at his house – now a museum – in the sleepy Ardennes town.

Georges Simenon (1903–1989) Famous philanderer (he apparently slept with 10,000 women) and creator of the classically deadpan European detective Maigret, Simenon hailed from Liege but spent most of his adult life in Paris, where he set most of his books.

> "How can anyone govern a nation that has 246 different kinds of cheese?"
>
> **Charles de Gaulle**
>
> There are now between 350 and 1000 French cheeses, depending on your definition

MAKING A PIG OF YOURSELF

Held every August at Trie-sur-Baise in the Mini-Pyrenees and drawing a loyal cult following, the **French Pig Squealing Championships** are one of France's most bizarre "fêtes folles", and sees participants act like pigs, competing on the basis of oinks, grunts and even, disturbingly, simulated suckling and mating.

DUTCH WONDER

According to the American Society of Civil Engineers, the **North Sea Protection Works** in the Netherlands is one of the Seven Modern Wonders of the World. This unique and complex system of dams, floodgates and storm surge barriers protects the Netherlands from the North Sea. The main features are a 30km-long dam to block the Zuider Zee, and the Eastern Schelde Barrier, 3km of gates between huge concrete piers.

GREAT FRENCH PHILOSOPHERS

René Descartes (1596–1650) Best known for claiming "I think therefore I am", Descartes was a leading proponent of rationalism – using the rational mind rather than the unreliable senses to deduct scientific truth, as the empiricists advocated.

Blaise Pascal (1623–1662) Starting his career as a scientist, Pascal began the Pensées ("Thoughts"), after a religious epiphany in 1654, attacking Descartes' rationalism with Pascal's Wager – the concept that it is always better to believe in God, as the expected benefit from that belief is always greater than atheism.

Voltaire (1694–1778) Leading light of the French Enlightenment, and author of satires such as *Candide*, Voltaire is best known for his defence of religious freedom.

Jean-Paul Sartre (1905–1980) One of the founders of existentialism, but also lauded for his works of fiction and political activism, he refused the Nobel Prize for Literature in 1964, saying he had never accepted honours before and did not want to be associated with establishment institutions.

Jacques Derrida (1930–2004) The controversial founder of deconstruction proposed the "Death of the Author" and explored the gap between language and meaning.

> "It is impossible to overlook the extent to which civilization is built upon a renunciation of instinct"
>
> **Sigmund Freud**

BEER AND WINE

Essen, **Germany**, has the highest beer consumption of any city in the world with an astonishing 230 litres drunk per person per year. **Belgium** has the greatest number of beer varieties, including the decidedly punchy Trappist ale Westvleteren, which weighs in at around 12% alcohol, although Samichlaus, a brew produced each year in Austria for Christmas is more alcoholic, at 14%.

France is the largest wine-producing country in the world by value, and is also its biggest consumer. But its crown may be slipping: in terms of export volume, Italy and Spain now lead the pack.

SPORTS TO TRY

Boules, France The best-known type of boules is pétanque; played on a gravel surface, players toss metal balls to land as close as possible to a wooden-ball target.

Hornussen, Switzerland An outlandish mix of golf and baseball: one player launches a puck along a curved track with a long cane; others try to hit it with large wooden balls before it touches the ground. The game's name ("hornet") comes from the sound of the whizzing puck.

Korfball, Belgium and the Netherlands Like an egalitarian netball: two teams of four men and four women each try to score baskets against each other.

HEART OF STONE: LOSING YOURSELF IN DEEPEST IBERIA • WASHING AWAY THE CIDER HOUSE BLUES • BIG-GAME FISHING IN THE ATLANTIC • DANCING TILL DAWN AT BENICÀSSIM • SEEING STARS IN SAN SEBASTIÁN • PLAYING WITH FIRE AT LAS FALLAS • MODERNISME AND MAÑANA: GAUDÍ'S SAGRADA FAMILIA • TOBOGGANING WITHOUT SNOW • FLAMENCO: BACKSTREETS AND GYPSY BEATS • COUNTING DOLPHINS IN THE MEDITERRANEAN • IN SEARCH OF THE PERFECT TART • THE LOST STREET OF RIO HONOR DE CASTILLA • GAWPING AT THE GUGGENHEIM • TRAM 28: TAKING A RIDE THROUGH LISBON'S HISTORIC QUARTERS • HEADING FOR THE HEIGHTS IN THE PICOS DE EUROPA • DISCOVERING THE CONQUISTADORS' SPOILS • STOP! IT'S HAMMER TIME AT THE FESTA DE SÃO JOÃO • PORTRAITS AND PURGATORY AT THE PRADO • GOING FOR YOUR GUNS IN ALMERÍA • TAPAS CRAWLING IN MADRID • MARVELLING INSIDE THE MEZQUITA • PRAY MACARENA! EASTER IN SEVILLE • MOORISH GRANADA: EXPLORING THE ALHAMBRA • SURFING THE COAST OF LIGHT: FROM TARIFA TO TANGIER • EXPLORING MYSTICAL SINTRA • GOING UNDER THE RADAR IN ANCIENT CÁDIZ • RUNNING WITH THE BULLS • GETTING LOST IN THE PILGRIM'S PALACE • SURREAL LIFE AT THE DALÍ MUSEUM • SEEING SUMMER OFF IN STYLE: IBIZA'S CLOSING PARTIES • HIKING IN THE PYRENEES • TAKING TO THE STREETS OF TENERIFE • PAINTING THE TOWN RED AT LA TOMATINA • MEDITERRANEAN HIGHS: PUIG DE MARIA • THE ART OF LAVA: CÉSAR MANRIQUE'S LANZAROTE • BROWSING LA BOQUERIA • A DROP OF THE BARD'S STUFF: DRINKING SHERRY SPANISH STYLE • ABOVE THE CLOUDS ON PICO RUIVO • CLEARING YOUR CALENDAR FOR BACALHAU • WAGING WINE WAR IN LA RIOJA • HIKING THE ANCIENT FORESTS OF LA GOMERA • CYCLING FOR THE SOUL: EL CAMINO DE SANTIAGO • CRUISING THROUGH THE COTO DE DOÑANA • HEART OF STONE: LOSING YOURSELF IN DEEPEST IBERIA • WASHING AWAY THE CIDER HOUSE BLUES • BIG-GAME FISHING IN THE ATLANTIC • DANCING TILL DAWN AT BENICÀSSIM • SEEING STARS IN SAN SEBASTIÁN • PLAYING WITH FIRE AT LAS FALLAS • MODERNISME AND MAÑANA: GAUDÍ'S SAGRADA FAMILIA • TOBOGGANING WITHOUT SNOW • FLAMENCO: BACKSTREETS AND GYPSY BEATS • COUNTING DOLPHINS IN THE MEDITERRANEAN • IN SEARCH OF THE PERFECT TART • THE LOST STREET OF RIO HONOR DE CASTILLA • GAWPING AT THE GUGGENHEIM • TRAM 28: TAKING A RIDE THROUGH LISBON'S HISTORIC QUARTERS • HEADING FOR THE HEIGHTS IN THE PICOS DE EUROPA • DISCOVERING THE CONQUISTADORS' SPOILS • STOP! IT'S HAMMER TIME AT THE FESTA DE SÃO JOÃO • PORTRAITS AND PURGATORY AT THE PRADO • GOING FOR YOUR GUNS IN ALMERÍA

The Iberian Peninsula
110–152

MADEIRA

117 Tobogganing without snow

CANARY ISLANDS

PORTUGAL

123 Tram 28: taking a ride through Lisbon's historic quarters

124 Heading for the heights in the Picos de Europa

122 Gawping at the Guggenheim

ANDORRA

S P A I N

110 Heart of stone: losing yourself in deepest Iberia

129 Tapas crawling in Madrid

145 Browsing La Boqueria

142 Painting the town red at La Tomatina

BALEARIC ISLANDS

131 Pray Macarena! Easter in Seville

135 Going under the radar in ancient Cádiz

Heart of stone:

LOSING YOURSELF IN DEEPEST IBERIA

PORTUGAL The Beira Baixa is a land of burning plains and granite visions, isolated in one of the most remote corners of Western Europe, where the Spanish border blurs under a broiling sun. Here, if you search hard enough, you'll find at least two of the most startling medieval villages in Europe: Monsanto – Mon Sanctus in Latin – is truly a sacred hill; you can feel it in the air, in the very fabric of its ancient houses and the long life of its inhabitants. Even as you drive past the cork trees below its flanks, their valuable bark sliced away to reveal an ochre core, this mini-citadel grips the imagination and quickens the blood. It is a village built into the earth, not on it: the famous Casa de Uma Só Telha – the house with only one tile – boasts a roof consisting of a single slab of granite. No surprise that its flower-buttoned facades once won it the title "most Portuguese village", or that mystery and superstition permeate the draughts of warm air rising from the rocks In the relative cool of evening. A few octogenarian villagers still sell *marafonas*, rag dolls traditionally hung over doorways to "scare thunder storms, sorcery and the fox". While you're unlikely to come across many foxes, far less sorcery, you might just hear the high, ululating strangeness of one of these old women accompanying herself on the *adufe*, a square, tambourine-like percussion instrument of Moorish origin, once common in Alentejo and Trás-os-Montes yet now largely confined to the Beira Baixa; or be regaled by toothless men old enough to remember their fathers holding off Vatua hordes in Mozambique. Had the "most Portuguese village" competition not been scrapped after envious howls of protest, it would surely, sooner or later, have been scooped by Sortelha, some 35km to the north. A walled horseshoe of ancient history on a 45-degree angle, it's the kind of place that sends your brain spinning: silent, sleeping streets and Vesuvian hulks of stone piling down upon garden, upon pantiled roof, upon carved stairwell; a film set waiting to happen. At its apex sits *Bar Campanario*, a tiny stone hostelry hiding one of the world's most atmospheric terraces, its infinite views wheeling endlessly across the primordial plain-scape beyond, and only ghosts for company.

111 Washing away the cider house blues

SPAIN The Basques are a proud people. And boy do they take pride in their regional produce. Which is why they have the finest fish on the Spanish coast, the tastiest tapas across Iberia – and some of the most scrumptious cider in all of Europe. Prohibited under the Franco regime, cider is back with a bang – or, at least, with a sharp, mouth-watering fizz. The beauty of Basque cider is that it's succulently simple. There are no must or extracts here, no gas or sweeteners added. Just a blend of three types of apple: bitter, sour and sweet, all lovingly combined in the perfect proportions.

The best cider is drunk on site: head out to the orchards of Astigarraga and spend the day at one of the area's many *sagardotegiak*, or cider houses, drinking the golden liquor straight from *kupelas* (large barrels). Empty the glass each time with one quick gulp – it preserves the cider's *txinparta*: its colour, bouquet and that tangy, tantalizing taste.

112 Big-game fishing in the Atlantic

THE AZORES Way out in the Atlantic, a thousand miles off the coast of Portugal, the string of volcanic islands that make up the Azores is probably the only part of the European Union in which you can go big-game fishing – and for blue marlin, too, the mother of all large fish, weighing in at 150 kilos or more.

The islands regularly host the European and World Big Game Championships if you want to see how it's done. Alternatively, you can hire a boat and a skipper and try your own luck; the abundance of marlin in summer, as well as shark and swordfish year round – make the Azores a game-fishers' paradise. And while you're waiting for them to bite, keep an eye out for the dolphins and whales that frolic just offshore.

113 Dancing till dawn at Benicàssim

SPAIN One thing it isn't is peaceful. The music goes on till 8am, and by 10am most tents are too hot to sleep in, sweat dripping from skin to sleeping mat and back. By day, you eat tapas in bars and snooze in precious patches of shade at the nearby beach. But the awesomely entertaining four-day Festival International de Benicàssim is really about the night-time, about strolling, Spanish-style, between Anglo-American rock bands (the Pixies, Radiohead and the Arctic Monkeys have starred in recent years) and local musicians, flexing your limbs in the numerous dance tents and drinking with strangers under the bright lights of stalls. You'll regret it in the morning, of course – but morning has probably already arrived.

114 Seeing stars in San Sebastián

SPAIN Many who make their way to the genteel resort of San Sebastián, in Spain's Basque region, have one thing on their mind: food. Within the country, País Vasco – as the Basque area is known – has always been recognized as serving Spain's finest cuisine. The city in fact boasts the most impressive per capita concentration of Michelin stars in the world, a recognition that its deep-rooted gastronomic tradition has finally come of age.

Juan Mari Arzak is widely regarded as the one who kicked it all off back in the 1970s. Long the holder of three of those cherished stars, his *Arzak* restaurant remains the parlour-informal, family-friendly temple of audacious yet almost always recognizably Basque food; a meal here is a thrilling affair. Deftly incorporating line-caught fruits of the Cantabrian sea, the flora and fauna of the Basque countryside and flavours from further afield, Arzak and his daughter Elena are as likely to cook with smoked chocolate, cardamom, dry ice-assisted sauces and ash-charred vinaigrette

as the signature truffles and foie gras. Bold, subversive takes on Spanish classics – strawberry gazpacho anyone? – confound and exhilarate while longstanding favourites like truffle-distilled poached egg are so flawlessly presented you'll hesitate to slice into them. And despite the gourmet prices, the ratio of gregarious locals to foodie pilgrims means there's little scope for snobbery.

Still, if cost is an issue, you can experience San Sebastián's epicurean passions by way of a *txikiteo*, the Basque version of a tapas crawl. You can taste your way through a succession of tempting *pintxos* – their name for the baroque miniatures on offer – at hearteningly unpretentious bars such as *Txepetxa*, *Ganbara* and *La Cuchara de San Telmo*, in the *parte vieja* (old town). Marinated anchovies with sea urchin roe, papaya or spider crab salad, tumblers of viscous garlic broth and earthy wild mushroom confit come with a tiny price tag – just a few euros – but with lasting reward.

115 Playing with fire at Las Fallas

SPAIN While Wicker Man fever has only crept back into Britain over the last decade or so, Catholic Spain has traditionally held faster to old habits, synchronizing Saints' days with ancient seasonal rites.

The most famous – and noisiest – festival of all is Las Fallas: in mid-March Valencia's streets combust in a riot of flame and firecrackers, ostensibly in celebration of St Joseph. As a recent local article put it: "Gunpowder is like blood for any Valencian Festival", and that goes double for Las Fallas; it's (barely) controlled pyromania on a scale unrivalled anywhere in Europe, a festival where the neighbourhood firemen are on overtime and beauty sleep is in short supply.

If you're not still partying from the night before, a typical Fallas day will see you rudely awakened at 7am by the galumphing cacophony of a brass band (perhaps it's no coincidence that the shawm – an ancestor of the oboe – was originally employed by Arab armies

as an early form of psychological warfare). By 2pm sharp, you'll be part of the baying mob in the Plaza Ayuntamiento, standing gape-mouthed in anticipation of the Mascletà, a daily round of colour and seismic blasts. The *fallas* themselves are huge satirical tableaux peopled by *ninots*, or allegorical figures – everyone from voluptuous harlots to George W. Bush – painstakingly crafted out of wood, wax, papier-mâché and cardboard. They're exhibited by their respective Casals Faller – the grass-roots community houses which run the festival – during nightly street parties, before all five hundred of them literally go up in smoke; the Cremà (the burning) represents the festival's climax, kicking off at midnight on March 19.

If the heady aroma of cordite, wood-fired paella, *buñuelos* (pumpkin fritters) and industrial-strength drinking chocolate is all too much for you, you can always view the *fallas* that got away (one gets a reprieve each year) in the quieter – and saner – environs of the city's Museu Faller.

116 Modernisme and mañana: Gaudí's Sagrada Familia

SPAIN If you've ever been at the mercy of a Spanish tradesman, or merely tried to buy a litre of milk after midday, you'll know that the Iberian concept of time is not just slightly elastic but positively twangy. The master of twang, however, has to be Antoni Gaudí i Cornet, the Catalan architect whose *pièce de résistance* is famously still under construction more than a century after he took the project on: "My client is not in a hurry" was his jocular riposte to the epic timescale.

Conceived as a riposte to secular radicalism, the Temple Expiatori de la Sagrada Família consumed the final decade and a half of a life that had become increasingly reclusive. Gaudí couldn't have imagined that a new millennium would find his creation feted as a wonder of the post-modern world, symbolic of a Barcelona reborn and the single most popular tourist attraction in Spain. Craning your neck up to the totemic, honeycomb-gothic meltdown of the Sagrada Família's towers today, it's perhaps not

so difficult to believe that Gaudí was a nature-loving vegetarian as well as an ardent Catholic and nationalist. By subsuming the organic intricacy of cellular life, his off-kilter modernisme wields a hypnotic, outlandish power, a complexity of design that entwines itself around your grey matter in a single glance. Which is half its charm; if you don't fancy dodging sweaty tourists and piles of mosaics in progress, simply take a constitutional around the exterior. Personally masterminded by Gaudí before his death, the Nativity facade garlands its virgin birth with microcosmic stone flora, a stark contrast to the Cubist austerity of the recently completed Passion facade.

The main reward for venturing inside is an elevator ride up one of the towers, a less tiring, crowded and claustrophobic experience than taking the stairs (hundreds of them!), leaving you with sufficient energy to goggle at the city through a prism of threaded stone and ceramics.

Tobogganing without snow

117

MADEIRA However you make the 560m climb to Monte, a hillside town hanging quietly over Madeira's verdant capital, Funchal, there's only one way to get back down. Well, you could test your driving skills on the impossibly steep streets, or risk vertigo as you dangle high above eucalyptus trees in a flimsy-looking cable car, but neither option is as downright whacky as taking a toboggan. There's no snow, of course – this is a subtropical paradise – but thanks to some typically resourceful thinking you're not going to need it, as the road becomes your black run and instead of using the latest winter sports gear, you'll be hurtling towards sea level in a giant wicker basket.

This might seem an unlikely pursuit on Madeira – an island that's better known for sleepy resorts than extreme sports. But ever since the first wooden sledge made the 6km journey between Monte and Funchal in 1850, tobogganing has picked up speed. In fact, it's now one of the island's biggest draws. So when you find

yourself at the bottom of the stairs that lead to Nossa Senhora do Monte, an imposing white church in the heart of town, look out for the swarm of tourists and take your place in the queue.

This is where the fun begins, and where you'll meet the two guys who'll be pushing your toboggan. They're locals, with bright white clothes and sun-dried skin. Usually, they're smoking. But when it's their turn to guide a sledge through the streets they spring into life, throwing their weight behind the job. At first, progress is slow. Then gravity takes over, powering you to speeds of up to 48 km/h, and their only mission is to stop you pounding into cars, frightened dogs and any other obstacles that weave in front of your basket. When you think you're going too fast to stop (there aren't any real brakes here), your wheezing guides will dig their rubber boots into the tarmac – giving you the first chance to jump out, look down and admire the sparkling blue Atlantic that stretches out before you.

Flamenco:
BACKSTREETS AND GYPSY BEATS

SPAIN With Diego El Cigala cleaning up at the Grammys, Catalan gypsy-punks Ojos de Brujo scooping a BBC Radio 3 World Music Award and Enrique Morente jamming with Sonic Youth in Valencia, the socio-musico-cultural phenomenon that is Spanish flamenco has never been hotter. Like any improvisational art form (particularly jazz, with which it often shares a platform), it's most effective in the raw, on stage, as hands and heels thwack in virile syncopation, a guitar bleeds unfathomable flurries of notes and the dancer flaunts her disdain with a flourish of ruffled silk.

Those who are in serious search of the elusive *duende* may find themselves faced with a surfeit of touristy options, but genuine flamenco is almost always out there if you look hard enough. Madrid is home to producer extraodinaire Javier Limón and his Casa Limón label, and the capital city boasts such famous *tablaos* as *Casa Patas*, *Corral de la Morería* and *El Corral de la Pacheca*,

where Hollywood actors are as ubiquitous as the tiles and white linen. Less pricey and more accommodating to the spirit of the *juerga* (spontaneous session) is the wonderful *La Soleá*, where both local and out-of-town enthusiasts test their mettle. Festivals to look out for include the annual Flamenco Pa'Tos charity bash and the Suma Flamenca event that farms out shows to Madrid's wider communidad.

One of Spain's biggest festivals is Seville's La Bienal de Flamenco, an award-winning event held from mid-September to mid-October. In the city itself, *Los Gallos* is one of the oldest tablaos, but it's worth scouring the cobbled backstreets for *La Carbonería*, a former coal merchants where free flamenco pulls in a volubly appreciative scrum of locals and tourists, or heading to the old gyspy quarter of Triana where *barrio* hangouts like *Casa Anselma* exult in Seville's home-grown form, the "Sevillana".

119 Counting dolphins in the Mediterranean

SPAIN "Sighting!" shouts Captain Ricardo Sagarminaga, as the dorsal fins flicker into view. Moments later, a hundred striped dolphins are speeding alongside the boat, leaping out of the waves and riding the wake of the bow. On board *Toftevaag*, our antique wooden ketch, a very international crew of volunteers and scientists springs into action. The Dane grabs the sonar reader, the American opens the behaviour log, the Spaniard sets up her SLR, and the Brit slaps on the factor 40. It's going to be a long, hot afternoon of serious dolphin counting.

The volunteers, mostly office workers in need of some sea air, have set sail off the southern coast of Spain with the international environmental charity Earthwatch to play at being marine biologists for a dozen days. On board, we help scientists to monitor dolphin populations, pollution levels and the impact of overfishing. Photo-identifications, behavioural notes, skin swabs, environmental data and oceanographic readings are all gathered during the frequent sightings, and are transformed into impressive graphs and reports by the captain's wife, marine biologist Dr. Ana Cañadas. In 2000, Ana and Ricardo's research into a decline in dolphin populations persuaded the Spanish government to create a Marine Protected Area in this region. Today, the couple continue to monitor and manage the area, working alongside visiting scientists, volunteers and local fishing communities.

For us volunteers, working on the boat is no easy ride – assisting the scientists during sightings, cooking and cleaning for the whole crew – in a sweltering galley – sleeping onboard in cramped bunks and setting sail at 7am. But awe-inspiring encounters are practically guaranteed. Common, bottlenose and striped dolphins, pilot whales, sperm whales and loggerhead turtles are all regularly sighted from the boat, and we leave the *Toftevaag* with a greater understanding of marine conservation issues, and with memories of wild dolphins leaping from the open sea.

120 In search of the perfect tart

PORTUGAL I like to ensure I have a tart in every port of call when I visit Portugal. It is a surprise, however, to see these very same tarts making an appearance near my UK home. For *pastéis de nata* – custard cream tarts to you and me – are becoming Portugal's hottest export since Ronaldo. To have them at their best, though, means seeking out their ancestral home in Portugal.

The Portuguese lay claim to introducing the British to tea and cakes after Catherine of Bragança showed the English court how to do it in the seventeenth century. But Portuguese pastries are more akin to those in North Africa, largely based around almonds and very sweet egg-based toppings. Despite their often risqué names – such as *Papas de Anjo* (Angel's Breasts) – many recipes were honed in convent kitchens, including *pastéis de nata*, which are made with sweet, egg-based custard, best served slightly warm, lightly caramelized, in a crispy pastry casing.

In Porto's Belle Époque *Café Majestic*, *pastéis de nata* arrive on silver trays borne by bow-tied waiters, fresh from glass counters stashed with row upon row of comforting *bolos* (cakes). Another good spot for *pastéis* is *Café Aliança* near Faro's harbour, now slightly down at heel but little changed from when Simone de Beauvoir and Fernando Pessoa used to hang out here in the 1930s.

But to find the best *pastéis* of all means following in the footsteps of the great Portuguese navigators, to their famous departure point at Belém in Lisbon's western suburbs. Here, the *Antiga Confeitaria de Belém* has been serving *pastéis* – here called *pastéis de Belém* – since 1837, using their own secret recipe acquired from a nearby monastery. Come on a Sunday and it feels as if the whole of Lisbon has descended for their small and sublimely crisp tarts, served on marble table tops, each with their own shakers – one for cinnamon and one for icing sugar. Somehow, the cavernous warren of tiled rooms seems to absorb the throngs with ease, despite the queues for takeaway tarts, lovingly dispensed in cardboard tubes.

121 The lost streets of Rio Honor de Castilla

SPAIN Long before Spanish–Portuguese borders were abandoned to EU integration and the elements, the good folk of Rio Honor de Castilla and Rio de Onor lived as though they'd never existed. Isolated at the tip of Spain's Old Castille and Portugal's Trás-os-Montes regions, these two villages-in-one effectively ignored political frontiers while the rest of Europe tore itself apart. Nowadays any lawbreaking that goes on is subject to respective national laws rather than the traditional fines in wine, but the unique egalitarian systems and language (Rionorês, a hybrid of Portuguese and the Castillian dialect of Leonese) stand as a testament to the absurdity of arbitrary division.

Though the young people have long departed, the old ways survive and there's a tangible sense that things have always been done differently: in contrast to neighbouring villages, the leathery, black-clad elders are garrulous and inquisitive. They still tend a central plot of land and lead their animals through dung-clotted streets, stabling them below their sagging schist houses. The few narrow streets on either side of the settlement are among the most haunting in the whole of the Iberian peninsula; untold years of cross-cultural birth, life, work and death linger in the mountain air, even as the population peters out.

If you're linguistically equipped, you can savour the novelty of speaking Portuguese in the tiny, ancient bar and Castillian in the grocery store where, true to type, the owner – not so used to the company of *guiris* – can talk for Spain (or Portugal). A stone bridge is all that separates the two villages; how long they can work together to stave off the ravages of depopulation is another question. For now at least, though, visiting Rio Honor de Castilla and Rio de Onor is a fascinating, hugely atmospheric step back in time.

122 Gawping at the Guggenheim

SPAIN In the same way Glasgow outlived a grimy past to become the darling of America's travel media, Bilbao gambled on the cultural dollar and won. By becoming the first European city to fully embrace New York's Guggenheim franchise, it transformed itself from a briny, rusting behemoth into a modern art mecca. Frank O. Gehry's brief was to draw the gaze of the world; his response was an audacious, ingenious conflation of Bilbao's past and future, a riverine citadel moulded from titanium and limestone, steel and glass. Up close it appears as an urban planner's daydream gone delightfully wrong; viewed from the opposite bank of the river it assumes the guise of a gilded, glittering ark. But it all depends on your mood and the notoriously unpredictable Basque weather: on other days it broods like a computer-generated *Marie Celeste*, or glints rudely like a capricious cross between Monty Python and El Dorado. Gehry extends the aquatic theme by subsuming Bilbao's historic waterway into his design, so you can also take its measure by means of the nifty raised walkway and the connecting bridge, Puente de la Salve.

By the main entrance sits Jeff Koons' *Puppy*, an oversized, overstuffed floral statue, lost in an eternal siesta. Even the entrance is surreal, descending into the museum's huge atrium and voluminous galleries where, inevitably, the contents are rarely afforded quite as much attention as the surroundings. In amidst the rotated collections of Abstract Expressionism and Pop Art, interactive installations and excitable knots of foreign students, the powers that be continue to envisage the wordless horror of Picasso's *Guernica* as a centrepiece, even if it still languishes in Madrid. *Guernica* or no, every city and its satellite is now clamouring for a piece of the Guggenheim action – stand up Guadalajara, sit down Rio – but Spain remains the titanium template, proof that Bilbao's ship has finally come in.

123 Tram 28: taking a ride through Lisbon's historic quarters

PORTUGAL Just as you should arrive in Venice on a boat, it is best to arrive in Lisbon on a tram, from the point where many people leave it for good: at Prazeres, by the city's picturesque main cemetery. Get a taxi to the suburban terminus of tram 28 for one of the most atmospheric public-transport rides in the world: a slow-motion roller coaster into the city's historic heart.

Electric trams first served Lisbon in 1901, though the route 28 fleet are remodelled 1930s versions. The polished wood interiors are gems of craftsmanship, from the grooved wooden floors to the shiny seats and sliding window panels. And the operators don't so much drive the trams as handle them like ancient caravels, adjusting pulleys and levers as the streetcar pitches and rolls across Lisbon's wavy terrain. As tram 28 rumbles past the towering dome of the Estrela Basilica, remember the famous bottoms that have probably sat exactly where you are: the writers Pessoa and Saramago, the singer Mariza, footballers Figo and Eusebio.

You reach central Lisbon at the smart Chiado district, glimpses of the steely Tagus flashing into view between the terracotta roof tiles and church spires. Suddenly you pitch steeply downhill, the tram hissing and straining against the gradients of Rua Vítor Cordon, before veering into the historic downtown Baixa district. Shoppers pile in and it's standing room only for newcomers, but those already seated can admire the row of traditional shops selling sequins and beads along Rua da Conceição through the open windows.

Now you climb past Lisbon's ancient cathedral and skirt the hilltop castle, the vistas across the Tagus estuary below truly dazzling. The best bit of the ride is yet to come though, a weaving, grinding climb through the Alfama district, Lisbon's village-within-a-city where most roads are too narrow for cars. Entering Rua das Escolas Gerais, the street is just over tram width, its shopfronts so close that you can almost lean out and take a tin of sardines off the shelves.

124 Heading for the heights in the Picos de Europa

SPAIN Defining the topography of Asturias and Cantabria, and even nudging into neighbouring León, the Parque Nacional Picos de Europa throws a lot of limestone weight around for a comparatively compact range.

It's also stubbornly diverse and disarmingly magnificent, long the destination of choice for not only discerning European trekkers and climbers but also cavers, who are drawn to the 1km-plus depths of its tentacle-like drainage system. Much like the parks of northern Portugal, the Picos shelter countless stone-clad villages and hamlets which the land has sustained for centuries and where the trekking industry is comparatively recent. But the layered vista of beech-forested valleys, flinty summer pasture and incongruous lunar peaks makes the range particularly alluring and deceptively benign.

The history likewise generates its own mystique, literally enshrined in stone at the pilgrimage site of Covadonga on the park's far western fringe. This was where, in the early eighth century, the beleaguered Christians allegedly took their first Moorish scalp and kick-started the Reconquista.

You don't have to be a believer to wonder at the beauty of the Picos, although a sense of divine presence might help, especially in negotiating the forbidding, 1.5km-deep chasm that is the Cares Gorge. It remains the definitive Picos experience, usually accessed from the village of Caín, from where the most impressive bridges and tunnels are in easy reach. As griffon vultures tailspin high overhead, well-fed day-trippers and the occasional heavily laden hiker pick their way along a path audaciously gouged out of the cliff face. The gorge forms a natural boundary between the less visited western mountains and the central massif, where the official daddy of the Picos, Torre Cerredo, is outclassed by its rakish, orange-bronzed rival, the Naranjo de Bulnes. The Naranjo is a perennial favourite with climbers, although even they have been known to succumb to the less arduous thrill of the *teleférico*, which shudders up more than 750 metres of sheer cliff.

125 Discovering the conquistadors' spoils

SPAIN In any account of Extremadura's history, a neat parallel is usually drawn between the austerity of the landscape and the savagery of the conquistadors who were born and raised there. The alternately broiling and bitterly cold plains hold an allure that's hard to shake off, and the contrast with the towns is striking. Both Trujillo and Cáceres remain synonymous with conquistador plunder, rich in lavish *solares* (mansions) built by New World returnees. Cáceres is UNESCO-protected, but Trujillo is even prettier, and its sons more infamous. This was the birthplace of Francisco Pizarro, illiterate conqueror of Peru and scourge of the Incas.

While a bronze likeness coolly surveys the Plaza Mayor, the legacy of his less bloodthirsty half-brother, Hernando, is more imposing: the Palacio de la Conquista lords it over the square, its richly ornamented facade adorned with a doomed Atahualpa (the last Inca ruler) and spuriously sage-like busts of both Pizarro siblings – the ultimate expression of local *hombres* made good.

Nearby is the Palacio de Orellana-Pizarro, transformed from a fortress into a conquistador's des res by Francisco's cousin Juan, and crowned by an exquisite Renaissance balcony.

Keeping it in the family was important in Cáceres: the town's most impressive mansion, the Casa de Toledo-Moctezuma, is a work of mannerist indulgence and august grandeur, a place with royal Aztec connections where the son of conquistador Juan Cano (an acolyte of Hernán Cortés) and Doña Isabel (daughter of the Mexican emperor) settled down with his Spanish bride. Across the old town, the gorgeous honeyed-gothic facade of the Casa de los Golfínes de Abajo dates back to the years immediately prior to the New World voyages.

These days, the wealth of the Indies arrives in the form of sweet music: the world music jamboree that is WOMAD flings open its doors in Cáceres for four days each May. With consummate irony, it's possible to bask in balmy Latin American sounds, surrounded by mansions financed by Latin American gold.

126 Stop! It's hammer time at the Festa de São João

PORTUGAL The old cliché that Porto works while Lisbon plays is redundant on June 24, when Portugal's second city teaches the capital a thing or two about having fun. The Festa de São João is a magnificent display of midsummer madness – one giant street party, where bands of hammer-wielding lunatics roam the town, and every available outdoor space in Porto is given over to a full night of eating, drinking and dancing to welcome in the city's saint's day.

By the evening of June 23, the *tripeiros*, as the residents of Porto are known, are already in the party mood. A tide of whistle-blowing, hammer-wielding people begins to seep down the steep streets towards the river. No one seems to know the origin of the tradition of hitting people on the head on this day, but what was traditionally a rather harmless pat with a leek has evolved into a somewhat firmer clout with a plastic hammer. You should know that everyone has a plastic hammer, and everyone wants to hit someone else with it.

People begin dancing to the live music by the Rio Douro while it's still light, banging their hammers on metal café tables to the rhythm of Latin and African sounds. Elsewhere, live music performances vary from pop and rock to traditional folk music and choral singing, and as darkness falls, exploding fireworks thunder through the night sky above the glowing neon of the port wine lodges over the Douro.

Midnight sees the inevitable climax of fireworks, but the night is far from over. As dawn approaches, the emphasis shifts further west to the beach of Praia dos Ingleses in the suburb of Foz do Douro. Here, there's space to participate in the tradition of lighting bonfires for São João, with youths challenging each other to jump over the largest flames. As the beach party rumbles on, pace yourself and before you know it the crowds will start to thin slightly and the first signs of daylight will appear on the horizon. Congratulations. You've made it through to the day of São João itself.

127 Portraits and purgatory at the Prado

SPAIN Opened in 1819 at the behest of Ferdinand VII, Madrid's El Prado has long been one of the world's premier art galleries, with a collection so vast only a fraction of its paintings can be exhibited at any one time. Among those treasures – gleaned largely from the salons of the Spanish nobility – are half of the complete works of Diego Velázquez, virtuoso court painter to Felipe IV. Such was the clamour surrounding a 1990 exhibition that half a million people filed through the turnstiles; those locked out clashed with civil guards. What Velázquez himself would've made of it all is hard to say; in his celebrated masterpiece *Las Meninas*, he peers out inscrutably from behind his own canvas, dissolving the boundaries between viewer and viewed, superimposing scene upon reflected scene. Strung out over two floors, the works of Francisco de Goya

are equally revolutionary, ranging from sensous portraiture to piercing documents of personal and political trauma. It's difficult to imagine public disorder over his infamous *Pinturas Negras*, nor do they attract the spectatorial logjams of *Las Meninas*, yet they're not works you'll forget in a hurry. The terrible magnetism of paintings like *The Colossus* and *Saturn Devouring One of His Sons* is easier to comprehend in the context of their creation, as the last will and testament of a deaf and disillusioned old man, fearful of his own flight into madness. Originally daubed on the walls of his farmhouse, the black paintings take to extremes motifs that Goya had pioneered: *Tres de Mayo* is unflinching in depicting the tawdry horror of war, its faceless Napoleonic executioners firing a fusillade that echoes into the twenty-first century.

128 Going for your guns in Almería

SPAIN The only genuine desert in Europe, Almería's merciless canyons and moonscape gulches did, once upon a time in the Spanish Wild West, play host to Hollywood. Back in the Sixties, Spaghetti Western don Sergio Leone shot his landmark trilogy here, climaxing with *The Good, the Bad and the Ugly*. Since this golden era, the place has had the occasional flash of former glories: Alex Cox revisited the terrain in the Eighties with his all-star spaghetti parody *Straight to Hell*, and Sean Connery pitched up for *Indiana Jones and the Last Crusade*.

Spanish director Alex de la Iglesia's critically acclaimed *800 Bullets* actually subsumed Almerían cinema's rise and fall into its plot, centring on the Fort Bravo studios/Texas Hollywood, where the most authentic film-set experience is still to be had. It's a gloriously eerie, down-at-heel place, which, likely as not, you'll have to yourself. Unfortunately, there's no explanation as to which sets were used in which films, but the splintered wood, fading paintwork and general dilapidation certainly feels genuine. A wholesale Mexican compound complete with a blinding white mission chapel is the atmospheric centrepiece; close your eyes and you can just about smell the gunpowder.

A couple of kilometres down the road is Mini-Hollywood, the sanitized big daddy of the region's three film-set theme parks, with a must-see museum of original poster art. And Leone diehards will want to complete the tour with a visit to nearby Western Leone, which houses the extant debris of the man's masterpiece, *Once Upon a Time in the West*. Hopeless cowboys (and girls) can even take a four-day horseriding tour into the desert, scouting various locations amid breathtakingly desolate scenery.

129 Tapas crawling in Madrid

SPAIN Tapas crawling is to the Spaniard what pub crawling is to the northern European, with the added bonus that you're not literally crawling by the end of the night, or at least you shouldn't be if you've faithfully scoffed a titbit with each drink.

In Granada and assorted hinterlands they're still a complimentary courtesy; in the rest of the country a free lunch has gone the way of the siesta and the peseta. But if you're going to pay for your nibbles, Madrid offers one of the meanest tapas crawls in the land, starting from the central Puerta del Sol. In and around the narrow streets between Sol and Plaza Santa Ana you can tuck into fluffy fried prawns and erm...more prawns (*al ajillo*, in garlic), washed down by heady house wine at the Lilliputian *Casa del Abuelo* (c/Victoria 12). Unpretentious, atmospheric bars also serving authentic bites are *Las Bravas* (c/Alvarez Gato 3), a former barbers turned fried-potato-in-spicy-sauce specialist with a closely guarded recipe, and *La Oreja de Oro* (c/Victoria 9), which translates as "The Golden Ear", but in fact serves ears of the conspicuously edible variety. The fried pigs' parts are a concession to local tastes, but the rest of the menu – including Ribeiro wine served in bowls and pimientos de Padrón (unpredictably hot fried peppers) – wears its Galician colours proudly. If cartilage doesn't tickle your tastebuds, it's probably worth taking a little detour back to the western edge of the Plaza Mayor for *Mesón del Champiñones* (Cava de San Miguel 17), an earthy *taberna* that's been doling out mouthwatering pan-fried mushrooms and sangría for longer than most Madrileños can remember. Even older is *Taberna de Antonio Sanchez* (c/Mesón de Paredes 13) in nearby Lavapiés, a bullfighters' den dating from 1830, where the dark wood walls are heavy with scarred taurine trophies from long-forgotten duels. For something less queasy to finish up, cut back east to *Taberna de Dolores* (Plaza de Jesús 4), where the slender Roquefort and anchovy canapés will ensure you wake up with fearsome breath, if not a hangover.

130 Marvelling inside the Mezquita

SPAIN La Mezquita: a name that evokes the mystery and grace of Córdoba's famous monument so much more seductively than the English translation. It's been a while since the Great Mosque was used as such (1236 to be exact), but at one time it was not only the largest in the city – dwarfing a thousand others – but in all al-Andalus and nigh on the entire world.

Almost a millennium later, its hallucinatory interior still hushes the garrulous into silence and the jaded into awe, a dreamscape of candy-striped arches piled upon arches, sifting light from shadow. Since the Christians took over it's been mostly shadow, yet at one time the Mezquita's dense grove of recycled Roman columns was open to the sunlight, creating a generous, arboreal harmony with its courtyard and wider social environment. Today's visitors still enter through that same orange blossom compound, the Patio de los Naranjos, proceeding through the Puerta de las Palmas where they doff their cap rather than removing their shoes. As your eyes adjust to the gloom, you're confronted with a jasper and marble forest, so constant, fluid and deceptively symmetrical in design that its ingenious system of secondary supporting arches barely registers. Gradually, the resourcefulness of the Muslim architects sinks in, the way they improvised on the inadequacy of their salvaged pillars, inversely propping up the great weight of the roof arches and ceiling.

That first flush of wonder ebbs slightly once you stumble upon an edifice clearly out of step with the Moorish scheme of things, if gracious enough in its own right. In 1523, despite fierce local opposition, the more zealous Christians finally got their revenge by tearing out the Mosque's heart and erecting a Renaissance cathedral. Carlos V's verdict was damning: "you have destroyed something that was unique in the world". Thankfully they left intact the famous Mihrab, a prayer niche of sublime perfection braided by Byzantine mosaics and roofed with a single block of marble. Like the Mezquita itself, its beauty transcends religious difference.

Pray Macarena!

131

EASTER IN SEVILLE

SPAIN The Spanish flock may be wavering but, being Catholic and proud, they take their religious festivals as seriously as they did in the days when a pointy hat meant the Inquisition. "Semana Santa" (or Holy Week) is the most spectacular of all the Catholic celebrations, and Seville carries it off with an unrivalled pomp and ceremony. Conceived as an extravagant antidote to Protestant asceticism, the festivities were designed to steep the common man in Christ's Passion, and it's the same today – the dazzling climax to months of preparation. You don't need to be a Christian to appreciate the outlandish spectacle or the exquisitely choreographed attention to detail. Granted, if you're not expecting it, the sight of massed hooded penitents can be disorientating and not a little disturbing – rows of eyes opaque with concentration, feet stepping slavishly in time with brass and percussion. But Holy Week is also about the *pasos*, or floats, elaborate slow-motion platforms graced with piercing, tottering images of Jesus and the Virgin Mary, swathed in Sevillano finery. All across Seville, crowds hold their collective breath as they anticipate the moment when their local church doors are thrown back and the *paso* commences its unsteady journey, the *costaleros* (or bearers) sweating underneath, hidden from view. With almost sixty *cofradías*, or brotherhoods, all mounting their own processions between Palm Sunday and Good Friday, the city assumes the guise of a sacred snakes-and-ladders board, criss-crossed by caped, candlelit columns at all hours of the day and night, heavy with the ambrosial scent of incense and orange blossom, and pierced by the plaintive lament of the *saetas*, unaccompanied flights of religious song sung by locals on their balconies. Regardless of where the processions start they all converge on Calle Sierpes, the commercial thoroughfare jammed with families who've paid for a front-seat view. From here they proceed to the cathedral, where on Good Friday morning the whole thing reaches an ecstatic climax with the appearance of "La Macarena", the protector of Seville's bullfighters long before she graced the pop charts.

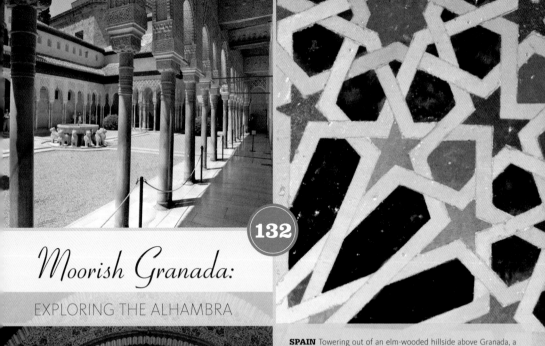

Moorish Granada:

EXPLORING THE ALHAMBRA

SPAIN Towering out of an elm-wooded hillside above Granada, a snowy Sierra Nevada behind, there are few more iconic images of Spain than the ochre-tinted enclave of the Alhambra. By the time the last Moorish prince, Boabdil, was scolded (by his mother) with the immortal line "Do not weep like a woman for what you could not defend like a man", a succession of Nasrid rulers had expanded upon the bare bones of the Alcazaba (or citadel). In doing so they created an exalted wonder of the world, elevating its inhabitants with voluptuous waterways and liberating inscriptions.

Yet its current status as the country's most revered monument is due at least in part to Washington Irving, a sometime American diplomat in Madrid better known for writing *The Legend of Sleepy Hollow*. In the mid-nineteenth century, at a time when no one gave the place a second glance, Irving recognized its faded glamour, completing his *Tales of the Alhambra* in the abandoned palace.

Now over five thousand visitors wander through the restored complex every day, its chambers and gardens once again alive with cosmopolitan chatter if not free-flowing verse. No amount of words, however, can approximate the sensual charge of seeing the Palacios Nazaries, the best preserved palace of the Nasrid dynasty, for the first time. As a building, the palace's function was to concentrate the mind on the oneness of God, and nowhere is this more apparent than the Patio de los Leones courtyard. Here Arabic calligraphy sweeps across the stucco with unparalleled grace, stalactite vaulting dazzles in its intricate irregularity and white marble lions guard a symbolic representation of paradise. The sweet irony is that none of it was built to last, its simple adobe and wood in harmony with the elements and in stark contrast to the Alcazaba fortress opposite, the impregnable looking towers of which have defined the Granada skyline for centuries.

133 Surfing the coast of light: from Tarifa to Tangier

SPAIN No Spanish town is more synonymous with wind than Tarifa. Facing down Morocco across the Gibraltar Straits, it's both a windsurfing magnet and a suicide blackspot where the relentless gusting can literally drive people mad. But don't let that put you off; you're more likely to be driven to distraction in the concrete inferno of Costas Brava, Blanca or Sol, an orgy of development from which the Costa de la Luz has thus far abstained. In contrast, Tarifa is a whitewashed rendezvous, a chimerical canvas where the Med meets the Atlantic, the Poniente wind meets the Levante and Africa meets Europe. Even as muscled windsurfers ride the tide and live large, the Rif Mountains of *kif* farms and Paul Bowles-imagined Gothic loom across the waves like emissaries of another, darker star.

Climatic conditions for wind- and kitesurfing are optimal in the afternoon and early evening once the Levante hits its stride, although beginners are usually schooled in the morning. There are several rental places in Tarifa itself, and other facilities further up the crescent of bleached-sand beach. When the sun goes down, Tangier's lights start beckoning, and it is possible (just) to get your afternoon's surfing fix before heading to Morocco for the evening, avoiding the daytime scrum of quayside touts, and arriving just as sunset breathes new energy into the city's pavement cafés.

Stumbling into a harshly daylit street from a hotel you entered in darkness, the culture shock hits hard. Despite its seedy reputation, Tangier is a fascinating place, where you can meditate over William Burroughs and mint tea, take an incorrigibly polite tour of an Anglican church, zone out on *gnawa* music and make the medina *muezzin* your dawn alarm. And once you've experienced Morocco, the sight of Tarifa's harbour walls and bulging sails on your return seems even more illusory, more a continuation of North Africa than an outpost of Europe.

134 Exploring mystical Sintra

PORTUGAL Inspiration for a host of writers – including Lord Byron and William Beckford – Sintra, the former summer retreat of Portuguese monarchs, is dotted with palaces and surrounded by a series of wooded ravines. Now one of Europe's finest UNESCO World Heritage sites, Sintra has been a centre for cult worship for centuries: the early Celts named it Mountain of the Moon after one of their gods, and the hills are scattered with ley lines and mysterious tombs. Locals say batteries drain noticeably faster here and light bulbs pop with monotonous regularity. Some claim it is because of the angle of iron in the rocks, others that it is all part of the mystical powers that lurk in Sintra's hills and valleys. There are certainly plenty of geographical and meteorological quirks: house-sized boulders litter the landscape as if thrown by giants, while a white cloud – affectionately known as "the queen's fart" – regularly hovers over Sintra's palaces even on the clearest summer day.

The fairy-tale Palácio da Pena on the heights above town, with its dizzy views over the surrounding woodlands, looks like something from *Shrek*, complete with elaborate walkways, domes and drawbridges. Inside, its kitsch decor is kept just as it was when Portugal's last monarch, Manuel, fled at the birth of the republic. Quinta da Regaleira, a private estate from the turn of the twentieth century, is no less extraordinary. The gardens of this landowner's mansion hide the Initiation Well, entered via a revolving stone door. Inside, a moss-covered spiral staircase leads to a subterranean tunnel that resurfaces by a lake – a bizarre and mysterious place, which, like all of Sintra, shelters tales as fantastical as the buildings.

135 Going under the radar in ancient Cádiz

SPAIN On a roll-call of Spain's most glamorous cities, Cádiz would struggle to make the top twenty, never mind the top ten. But don't be put off, for the charms of Europe's oldest conurbation – with three millennia behind it and counting – are understated. The first thing that strikes you is location. A fist-shaped promontory jutting out into the Bay of Cádiz was the obvious site for a seaport, and the city's connections with the briny have driven its history.

The thing to do on arrival is to take a stroll along the narrow cobbled streets pickled in centuries of *andaluz* sunshine. With few grandiose buildings to catch the eye, Cádiz's fascination lies in the vernacular, the everyday. Mirador-fronted facades painted in pastel shades, atmospheric alleys, and an old quarter largely unchanged since the great days of the seventeenth-century Spanish empire. Here you'll find elegant turreted houses from which lookouts once scanned the horizon for ships and their valuable cargoes.

The city's inhabitants, breezy working-class folk, are impossible not to love and admire. They spring out of bed each morning seemingly unable to contain their glee at the prospect of spending another day among fellow *gaditanos* (from the city's ancient name "Gadir"). Meeting on the street they kiss, hug and even sing to each other, riotously so during the city's spectacular February Carnival. And this infectious vitality is nowhere more evident than in the bustling nineteenth-century Mercado Central where stalls display a mind-boggling cornucopia of fish and crustaceans, fruit and vegetables.

For a pit stop, nearby bars are just the place for a fino and a tasty tapa – Bar Manteca, run by a retired *torero*, is a wonderful example. Here, beneath walls covered with bullfighting memorabilia, tapas, such as a mouthwatering *chorizo ibérico*, arrive on greaseproof paper. Cádiz is also a flamenco city and a visit to a *peña*, or club, is a must. Peña la Perla is one of several offering a warm *gaditano* welcome. You'll be able to down fino into the early hours while being entertained with classic *cante jondo* flamenco singing and some electrifying dancing.

136 Running with the bulls

SPAIN For one week each year the Spanish town of Pamplona parties so hard that the foothills of the nearby Pyrenees start shaking. The scariest, loudest and most raucous party you'll ever come across, the Fiesta de San Fermín, held in honour of Pamplona's patron saint, has been celebrated since the early sixteenth century. But it's the daily ritual of the notoriously dangerous *encierro* (bull run) – the most prominent feature of the event for at least two hundred years and something of a rite of passage for young men of the region – that gets all the attention.

Nothing can prepare you for your first Pamplona experience: the constant flow of beer and sangría, the outrageous drunken partying, the hordes of excited people in the streets, and, most

of all, the early morning terror of the bull run. It only lasts about three-and-a-half minutes but is pure adrenaline all the way, with half-a-dozen bulls running 800m or so to the town's main bullring behind several thousand would-be heroes. The first bull run is held on the morning of July 7, after which the ritual of all-night partying followed by a morning bull run followed by a few hours sleep is repeated until July 14, when there's a solemn closing ceremony. There are also bullfights every evening, a naked procession to protest at the cruelty of the whole event and regular drunken diving from one of the statues in the main square. You've got to hand it to the Spanish – they certainly know how to host a phenomenal party.

137 Getting lost in the Pilgrim's Palace

SPAIN Though you may well get lost in the sprawling *Parador de Santiago de Compostela*, you certainly won't mind if you do. This is medieval Spain in all its gold-flecked grandeur – a post-sherry saunter from the echoing banquet hall has you padding down crimson-carpeted hallways lined with heavy tapestries and presided over by stern-faced busts of a veritable who's who of Spanish history. And that's just one wing.

The golden-granite parador was built in 1499 for Queen Isabella and King Ferdinand as the Hostal dos Reis Católicos, a royal hospital that provided refuge and relief to all the foot-blistered pilgrims who streamed into this damp northwestern corner of Spain. Five centuries on, travellers still seek shelter here – though now high-thread-count sheets and heated towel racks are part of the package.

This hospice-turned-haute-hotel is the grande dame of Spain's *paradores*, a chain of government-run hotels – now numbering nearly 100 – established in the 1920s. The aim was both to provide accommodation in Spain's more remote, pastoral areas, and to revive and maintain ancient edifices, from castles and convents

to monasteries and manor houses, that might otherwise fall into ruin. Today, staying in a parador not only offers the chance to bed down in a historical monument, but also helps ensure its survival.

Suites here are fit for a king – literally: kick back on canopied, four-poster beds like those once warmed by Spanish monarchs, tug on a tassel to turn on the light, catch your reflection in an antique mirror. Having catered to devout pilgrims, the parador is awash in spiritual nooks: leafy, hushed cloisters offer moments of absolute stillness in the late afternoon, as shadows fall across the stone pillars, one by one.

The parador shares the Praza do Obradoiro with the city's splendid cathedral. All roads to Santiago lead to this Baroque behemoth, where the mortal remains of St James are supposedly buried. Roam the Romanesque interior – all the more memorable when the massive *botafumeiro* (incense burner) is being used: hung on ropes as thick as well-fed pythons, it's swung in a wide arc across the transept, a rite originally performed to perfume the dishevelled, pungent pilgrims as they filed into the cathedral. These days, a scented bath at the parador should suffice.

138 Surreal life at the Dalí museum

SPAIN Nothing can ready you for the sheer volume of outwardly respectable, smart-casual tourists crowding desperately around the unwholesome creations of Catalonia's most eccentric, outrageous and egotistical son. Within a salmon pink, egg-topped palace ("like Elton John's holiday home", quipped one visitor) in the heart of Figueres, class and generation gaps dissolve as young and old strain to aim their cameras at a siren-like Queen of Persia riding barefoot atop an Al Capone car. In the back seat, wet and hollow-chested passengers look like they have tussled with *Day of the Triffids* just one time too many. As the irreverence of the exhibits triggers an irreverence of the spirit, standard gallery politesse goes out the window. A funhouse-like *frisson* takes its place as frumpy pensioners queue to climb a staircase and gape at a distorted approximation of Mae West's face; gangling students make what they will of an incongruous Duke Ellington album sleeve, an Alice Cooper hologram

and a gilded monkey skeleton; and designer-tagged señoritas jostle for a good position to crane their necks, point and click at a kitschy, fleshy footed self-portrait reaching for the heavens. Even if you're only dimly aware of Dalí's liquefied Surrealism, an hour in the man's domain will convince you that queasy paintings like the candle-faced *Cosmic Athletes* were dredged from one of the most singular subconscious minds of the twentieth century, one unhitched from the Surrealist vanguard in favour of his own, brilliantly christened "paranoiac-critical" method.

Like Gaudí before him, Salvador Dalí's monument was also his last, reclusive refuge. The man is actually buried in the crypt, right below your feet, and it's easy to imagine his moustachioed ghost prowling the half-moon corridors, bug-eyed and impish, revelling in the knowledge that his lurid mausoleum is Spain's most sought-after art spectacular after the Prado.

BALEARIC ISLANDS Ibiza's summer clubbing season is an orgy of hedonism, full of beats, late nights and frazzled young things. It reaches a messy climax in September, when the main club promoters and venues host a series of seratonin-sapping parties to round things off and extract a few final euros from their battered punters. These end-of-season events tend to attract an older clubbing crowd, who prefer to hop over to Ibiza for a cheeky long weekend, avoiding the gangs of teenage pill-monsters that descend on the island in late July and August. The British rave dinosaurs join a resident hardcore of Ibizan clubbers and an international cast of party freaks and techno geeks, all brought together by a common appetite for dance music.

Where you go depends on your tastes. In San Antonio, the young crowd gathers at *Eden* and *Es Paradis*, whose entire dancefloor is flooded just before sunrise, while in the village of San Rafael, *Amnesia*'s essential closing party usually throws open its doors for free after 4am – the last worn-out dancers are often still there come mid-afternoon. Just across the road, *Privilege*, the world's biggest club, parted ways with the famously debauched Manumission in 2008, but still throws closing parties for crowds of up to 10,000. In a laudable attempt to inject fresh energy into the scene, Ibiza Rocks has added live music, including Florence and the Machine and Pendulum, to the mix in recent years. Across the island in Ibiza Town, the elegant *Pacha* has the cream of the world's best DJs, including Erick Morillo and David Guetta, cranking things up to delirious levels. Four kilometres south of Ibiza Town, the after-party at *Space* usually gets going around 8am, with punters donning shades and getting down on the legendary terrace before moving inside, where the walls quiver to progressive techno.

The *Space* closing party was once *the* event in the Ibiza club calendar but lately it has lost out to the hardcore action down at *DC10*. The no-frills club has had regular battles with the authorities over licensing, but it's gained a loyal crowd of the hippest partiers (and most outrageous mullets) in Ibiza).

SEEING SUMMER OFF IN STYLE:

Ibiza's 139
closing parties

SPAIN When is a national park not a national park? Catalunya's Parc Nacional d'Aigüestortes i Estany de Sant Maurici doesn't make the grade internationally, yet under any other definition it fits the bill spectacularly. Soaring and plunging amidst a rarefied conclave of snow-veined peaks near the French border, it's one of the most bracingly handsome stretches of the Pyrenean range. Apart from the hydroelectric works that preclude wider official status, the park remains unspoilt habitat for such singular fauna as the Alpine marmot and the Pyrenean desman, an aquatic mole which forages in glacial streams. The entire 140-square-kilometre reach is studded with high-altitude lakes, fir and pine trees blanketing the lower slopes, beneath barbarous granite pinnacles reaching 2400 metres.

If, as likely, you approach from the east at Espot, you'll save yourself blistered feet by negotiating the lengthy paved road into the park by 4WD-taxi. Once the road ends, a warren of trails fans out from the cobalt waters of the Estany de Sant Maurici, with conveniently sited refuges at several of the intersections. Bisected by a main road and tunnel, the range then lunges westwards towards the equally impressive Parque Nacional de Ordesa y Monte Perdido. Inaugurated in 1918, it gets the nod from UNESCO and the attention of climbers looking to tackle its vertigo-stricken, Wild West-gone-alpine canyons, which thunder with glacial meltwater in late spring. Those with a less adventurous head for heights can admire the limestone strangeness from the depths of the Ordesa Gorge, where an unusual east–west orientation funnels in damp Atlantic air and supports unexpectedly lush vegetation; access is most common from the west, via the village of Torla. Some 10km further south, Añisclo, an equally breathtaking and far less tourist-trodden canyon, can be accessed via a minor road turning off at Sarvisé. Sequestered in its hulking gorge wall is the hermitage of San Urbez, bearing witness to the days when the park was an untrammelled wilderness, home to mystics rather than wardens.

141 Taking to the streets of Tenerife

CANARY ISLANDS A small island two hundred miles off the African coast, Tenerife seems an unlikely spot for one of the world's largest carnival parties. Yet festivals are in Tenerife's blood – it hosts over three hundred of them – and in the run-up to Lent, over a quarter of a million revellers converge on the capital, Santa Cruz, dressed in costumes so elaborate and cumbersome that they often need trolleys to hold them up.

Absorbed by their quest for winter sun, most tourists are oblivious to the goings-on in Santa Cruz. Those who do make the trip to the capital for carnival usually leave after the formal events finish – certainly before the night really gets going, when stages along the Plaza de España pump out vibrant salsa rhythms, and street kiosks play dance music until dawn. The gregarious locals will be more than happy to party with you, though, as long as you're in fancy dress: you'll be well provided for by the stores along Santa Cruz's main pedestrian drag, Calle del Castillo.

Carnival doesn't really kick off until the Friday before Shrove Tuesday, with an opening parade of bands and floats. After everyone's recovered from the weekend parties, the flagship event of the official carnival is the *Coso* or "Grand Procession", a lively five-hour cavalcade of floats, bands, dancing troupes and entertainers that dances its way along the dockside road on the afternoon of Shrove Tuesday itself. The following night's Burial of the Sardine is a tongue-in-cheek event centred on a huge wood-and-paper fish and its cortege of wailing priests and "widows" – mostly moustachioed men in drag. Failing to bow to the onset of Lent, the carnival doesn't reach its climactic end until the following weekend, when some of the festival's most intense partying follows a kids' parade on the Saturday and a seniors' parade on the Sunday.

142 Painting the town red at La Tomatina

SPAIN On the last Wednesday of every August, 130,000 kilos of over-ripe tomatoes are hurled around the alleyways of Buñol until the tiny town's streets are ankle deep in squelching fruit. What started in the 1940s as an impromptu food fight between friends has turned into one of the most bizarre and downright infantile fiestas on earth, a world-famous summer spectacular in which thirty thousand or so finger-twitching participants try to dispose of the entire EU tomato mountain by way of a massive hour-long food fight.

Locals, young and old, spend the morning attaching protective plastic sheeting to their house fronts, draping them over the balconies and bolting closed the shutters. By midday, the town's plaza and surrounding streets are brimming to the edges with a mass of overheated humans, and the chant of "To-ma-te, To-ma-te" begins to ring out across the town.

As the church clock chimes noon, dozens of trucks rumble into the plaza, disgorging their messy ammunition onto the dusty streets. And then all hell breaks. There are no allies, no protection, nowhere to hide; everyone – man or woman, young or old – is out for themselves. The first five minutes is tough going: the tomatoes are surprisingly hard and they actually hurt until they have been thrown a few times. Some are fired head-on at point-blank range, others sneakily aimed from behind, and the skilled lobber might get one to splat straight onto the top of your head. After what seems like an eternity, the battle dies down as the tomatoes disintegrate into an unthrowable mush. The combatants slump exhausted into a dazed ecstasy, grinning inanely at one another and basking in the glory of the battle. But the armistice is short-lived as another truck rumbles into the square to deposit its load. Battle commences once more, until the next load of ammunition is exhausted. Six trucks come and go before the final ceasefire. All in all, it only lasts about an hour, but it's probably the most stupidly childish hour you'll ever enjoy as an adult.

143 Mediterranean highs: Puig de Maria

BALEARIC ISLANDS I flung open the green shutters and took a deep breath: honeysuckle and pine. And another: incense, zesty lemons and the smell of the sea. The early Mallorcan sun bathed the bricks of Puig de Maria monastery in gold light, and the sense of calm was overwhelming; only the clang of goat bells broke the morning silence. Sipping my *cafecito* on the terrace, I could pick out the half-moon Bay of Pollença, Alcúdia, and the Formentor peninsula, flicking out into Mediterranean like a knobbly dragon's tail.

Rising 300m above Pollença, this hilltop retreat in Mallorca's northeast corner has done well to keep a low profile: it's blissfully quiet, barely touched by tourism and has arguably the best 360-degree panoramas on the island. As I slipped into a hermit's shoes for a few days, my life took on a different rhythm. Once I'd explored the secluded courtyards, the beamed fifteenth-century refectory and the silent gothic chapel, there was little left to see. And the feeling was liberating. Those lazy days spilled into lazy nights on the cobbled patio – eating paella, drinking Rioja and watching the stars twinkle above and the bays twinkle below.

At Puig de Maria, solitude is real and your senses become more alert – from the rustle of the trees and the crackling of an open fire to the feeling of stones slipping underfoot on the steep trail that weaves down to the valley. The buzz of the coast seems a million miles away and you're more likely to encounter buzzards than Brits abroad. The only way to reach the peak is to brave the hairpin bends zigzagging up to the monastery's car park, then walk the rest on foot, or take the pilgrim's way – an hour's hot hike through pine forest. But it's worth every bit to experience the Mallorca that once was and, far from Magaluf's madding crowd, thankfully still is.

THE ART OF LAVA:
César Manrique's Lanzarote

CANARY ISLANDS Nature has treated Lanzarote harshly over the centuries. Violent volcanic eruptions have ripped the island apart, leaving much of its surface area twisted, charred and strewn with lava. Gaze up at the mighty Timanfaya cone and you feel connected to the centre of the Earth. To César Manrique (1919–1992), Lanzarote's influential painter, sculptor, designer and conservationist, the island's other-worldly lava landscapes were an inspiration. His abstract paintings – some of which hang in MIAC (Museo Internacional de Arte Contemporáneo) in Arrecife's Castillo de San José and FCM (Fundación César Manrique) in the Taro de Tahíche – are powerfully suggestive of furiously boiling rock. Manrique's greatest legacy is a circuit of large-scale artistic and architectural creations, designed on Lanzarote in the 1960s. Taking the island's stark natural aesthetic as a starting point, he moulded and enhanced sections of the terrain into public works of avant-garde art: sculptures, galleries, gardens and meeting places.

The Taro de Tahíche – Manrique's former home – nestles into a lava flow from the 1730s and is a fascinating building to visit. Its facade resembles a traditional Canarian house, but step inside and you find yourself in a light-drenched, glass-walled space hung with greats such as Picasso and Miró. Panoramic windows offer lava views so dramatic they threaten to upstage the paintings. Downstairs there's a perfect ornamental pool and a playboy lair sculpted out of natural caves.

A tour of Manrique's Lanzarote will take you to the Juguetes del Viento, jaunty mechanical sculptures which rotate in the brisk Atlantic breeze; the Jardín de Cactus, Manrique's flamboyant cactus garden; the Mirador del Río, a clifftop lookout; and *El Diablo*, a volcano-powered restaurant. Best of all is the *Jameos del Agua*, deep in the island's northern volcanic badlands. Here, Manrique transformed a series of roofless lava caves and a mysterious subterranean lagoon into a strikingly imaginative rock-walled restaurant, bar and meeting place.

BROWSING LA BOQUERIA

SPAIN It happens to most newcomers: noses flare, eyes widen and pulses quicken upon entering La Boqueria, Barcelona's cathedral to *comida fresca* (fresh food). Pass through the handsome Modernista cast-iron gateway and you're rapidly sucked in by the raw, noisy energy of the cavernous hall, the air dense with the salty tang of the sea and freshly spilled blood. As they say in these parts, if you can't find it in La Boqueria, you can't find it anywhere: pyramids of downy peaches face whole cow heads – their eyes rolled back – and hairy curls of *rabo de toro* (bulls' tails). Pale-pink piglets are strung up by their hind legs, snouts pointing south, while *dorada* (sea bream) twitch on beds of ice next to a tangle of black eels.

The Mercat de Sant Josep, as it's officially called, was built in 1836 on the site of a former convent, though records show that there had been a market here since the thirteenth century. Its devotees are as diverse as the offerings: bargain-hunting grandmas rooting through dusty bins; *gran cocineros* (master chefs) from around Europe palming eggplants and holding persimmons up to the light; and droves of wide-eyed visitors weaving through the hubbub. At its core, though, La Boqueria is a family affair. Ask for directions and you might be told to turn right at Pili's place, then left at the Oliveros brothers. More than half of the stalls – and attendant professions – have been passed down through generations for over a century.

When it comes time to eat, do it here. The small bar-restaurants tucked away in La Boqueria may be low on frills, but they serve some of the finest market-fresh Catalan fare in the city. Flames lick over the dozens of orders crammed onto the tiny grill at *Pinotxo*, a bustling bar that has been around since 1940. Pull up a stool, and choose from the day's specials that are rattled off by various members of the extended family, like the affable, seventy-something Juanito. Tuck into bubbling *samfaina*, a Catalan ratatouille, or try *cap i pota*, stewed head and hoof of pig. As the afternoon meal winds down, Juanito walks the bar, topping up glasses from a jug of red wine. There's a toast – "Salud!" – and then everyone takes long, warming swallows, as all around the shuttered market sighs to a close.

146 A drop of the bard's stuff: drinking sherry Spanish style

SPAIN Sixteenth-century England mightn't have been so green and pleasant for Spain's Armada but at least Shakespeare was busy lauding its wine. Falstaff's avowal of the properties of "sherris-sack" should probably be taken with a pincho of salt, but there's nothing quite like a chilled glass of fino in the Andalucían shade. The vineyards from which it derives are among the oldest on Earth, surviving the disapproval of Moorish rulers, the ravages of civil war and a phylloxera epidemic, only to face a twenty-first-century market saturated with trendy New World competition. Downsized but unbowed, they still occupy the famous sherry triangle bounded by the southwestern towns of Jerez de la Frontera, San Lúcar de Barrameda and El Puerto de Santa María, intent on attracting a younger, hipper market. And why not; the sickly cream sherries mouldering in British cupboards are a world away from the lithe tang of a fino or bleached-dry manzanilla, which dance on the palette and flirt coquettishly with tapas. In terms of sprucing up sherry's rather fusty image (at least outside Spain), González Byass have been leading the way with their rebranding of the famed Tio Pepe. Their cobbled lanes and dim, vaulted cellars are among the oldest in Jerez, one of the most atmospheric – if touristy – places to sample a fino or an almond-nutty amontillada straight from the *bota* (sherry cask); you can even anoint your soles with some of their hallowed grapes during the September harvest. And if you're still hankering after the kind of tipple granny used to pour, nose out the chocolatey bitter-richness of a dry oloroso instead. Falstaff would approve.

147 Above the clouds on Pico Ruivo

MADEIRA A local challenge is to build a snowman on your bonnet, then drive to the beach for a swim before it melts. There are not many places where you can be in the mountains at ten in the morning and bathing in the sea by eleven, but such is the height of Madeira's peaks that in winter this is often possible.

More often associated with its dazzling flora and year-round sunshine, Madeira also boasts some of Europe's most dramatic mountain ranges. Long extinct volcanic peaks jut to nearly 2000m above the warm Atlantic waters, and one of the island's greatest walks is a dizzy footpath linking its highest points.

The walk to the island's highest peak, Pico Ruivo, is well signed and immediately dramatic, following a high ridge across a volcanic landscape. Skeletal bones of basalt columns and sills jut out of the soft, reddish ferrous soil, but as you climb, the scenery is far from barren. In summer, the path is lined with miniature pink geraniums, weird interlocking leaves of house leeks and the contorted trunks of ancient heather trees.

The 11km path is endlessly varied, sometimes following steps up steep inclines, or skirting cliffs along terrifyingly narrow (but thankfully fenced) ledges. Despite the cool mountain air, you soon feel the heat of the high sun and it can be thirsty work, though you can shelter in caves, once used by shepherds. At times, the track passes through rock tunnels hewn through dramatic outcrops.

After some five hours, you reach a government rest house just below the final ascent to Pico Ruivo. At 1862m, this is the highest point on Madeira, and on clear days it's possible to see both the north and south coasts of the Portuguese island from here, though more often the view is over a fluffy landscape of billowing clouds.

148 Clearing your calendar for bacalhau

PORTUGAL On Lisbon's Rua do Arsenal, whole window displays are lined with what looks like crinkly grey cardboard. The smell is far from alluring, but from these humble slabs of cod the Portuguese are able to conjure up an alleged 365 different recipes for *bacalhau*, one for each day of the year. Reassuringly, none of this mummified fish dates back to when it first became popular in the 1500s, when the Corte Real brothers sailed as far as Newfoundland for its rich cod banks. To preserve the fish for the journey back, the brothers salted and dried it – the result was an instant hit both with Portuguese landlubbers and navigators, who could safely store it for their long explorations of the new world.

Nowadays, *bacalhau* is the national dish, served in just about every restaurant in the country and every family home on Christmas Day. Even in Setúbal – where harbour restaurants are stacked with the fresh variety – salted cod appears on most menus, bathed in water for up to two days, and then its skin and bones pulled away from the swelled and softened flesh, before being boiled and strained into a fishy goo.

Some *bacalhau* dishes can be an acquired taste. My first experience was in a restaurant on the mosaic-paved old town of Cascais, where my stolid *bacalhau com grau* (boiled with chick peas) nearly put me off for life. But start with *rissóis de bacalhau* (cod rissoles), commonly served as a bar snack, and you'll soon be hooked. Then move on to *bacalhau com natas* (baked with cream) or *bacalhau a brás* (with fried potatos, olives and egg) and there's no looking back.

With fourteen *bacalhau* options on its menu, *Sabores a Bacalhau*, in Lisbon's Parque das Nações, is a good place to start. In a restaurant swathed in decorative *azulejos* tiles appropriately showing sea creatures, a waiter tells me, "Bacalhau is like the Kama Sutra. There may be hundreds of different variations, but you get to know the two or three types that are enjoyable!". Only the Portuguese could compare *bacalhau* with sex, but you can't argue that it is good.

SPAIN For grape gourmets, it might seem a terrible waste of wine, but each year several villages in La Rioja spend an entire day soaking each other in the stuff. One of the truly great events of the Spanish summer, the Wine War (La Batalla del Vino) is the modern-day remnant of ancient feuds between the wine town of Haro and its Riojan neighbours. A wine-fight of epic – and historic – proportions.

The festival begins with what must be one of the most bizarre religious processions anywhere: the congregation – as many as five thousand people, mostly dressed in white – comes armed not with Bibles, crucifixes and rosary beads but with an ingenious array of wine-weapons, ranging from buckets, water pistols and bota bags (wine-skin bottles) to agricultural spraying equipment.

The battle is thick and fast, with warring factions drenching each other with medium-bodied Rioja. In theory, the townsfolk of Haro are battling it out with those of neighbouring Miranda de Ebro, but in the good-humoured but frantic battle that rages, there are no obvious sides, and no winners or losers. Instead, the object is perfectly straightforward: to squirt, hose, blast or throw some 25,000 litres of what is presumably not vintage *vino tinto* over as many people as possible.

You won't be spared as a spectator, so you may as well join in. At the very least, come armed with a water pistol, though be warned that the locals have perfected the art of the portable water cannon, and can practically blast you off your feet from five metres. But what a way to go.

150 Hiking the ancient forests of La Gomera

CANARY ISLANDS Though an easy ferry ride from Tenerife, La Gomera, the smallest of Spain's Canary Islands, is one of Europe's most remote corners. Indeed, this is where a number of 1960s American draft dodgers sought refuge, and it remains a perfect place to get away from it all. In its centre the ancient forests of the Parque Nacional De Garajonay unfold, a tangled mass of moss-cloaked laurel trees thriving among swirling mists to produce an eerie landscape straight out of a Tolkien novel.

The park is best explored along the rough paths that twist between the many labyrinthine root systems. Embark on its finest hike, a 9km trek that's manageable in about four hours if you use a bus or taxi to access the start (a road intersection called Pajarito) and finish points. The lush route takes in the island's central peak, Garajonay; from its summit, you can enjoy immense views looking out over dense tree canopy to neighbouring islands, including Tenerife's towering volcano Mount Teide – at 3718m, Spain's highest point. From Garajonay's peak, follow a crystal-clear stream through thick, dark forest to the cultivated terraces around the hamlet of El Cedro.

Here you can camp, get a basic room or even rent a no-frills cottage – but be sure to at least pause at its rustic bar. Settled on a wooden bench, try some thick watercress soup sprinkled with the traditional bread-substitute *gofio*, a flour made from roasted grains.

Beyond El Cedro the valley opens up to the craggy and precipitous landscape that surrounds the town of Hermigua. The terrain around here is so difficult that for centuries a whistling language thrived as a means of communication, but today catching a bus back to your base – via dizzyingly steep hillside roads – is an easy matter.

151 Cycling for the soul: El Camino de Santiago

SPAIN Traditionally, pilgrimage meant hoofing it, wayfaring the hard way. Yet most Catholic authorities will tell you there's nothing particularly sinful about making it easier on yourself. You could roughly trace Spain's Camino de Santiago, or Way of St James, by car ... but then taking full advantage of the fringe benefits – discount accommodation and gorgeous red wine – would prove difficult. The answer? Get on your bike.

With reasonable fitness and not a little tenacity, the mantra of two wheels good four wheels bad can take you far, on a religious pilgrimage route that pretty much patented European tourism back in the Middle Ages. The most popular section begins at the Pyrenean Monastery of Roncesvalles, rolling right across northwestern Spain to the stunning (and stunningly wet) Galician city of Santiago de Compostela, where the presence of St James's mortal remains defines the whole exercise. Pack your mac, but spare a thought for the pre-Gortex, pre-Penny Farthing millions who tramped through history, walking 500 miles to lay down at Santiago's door.

Bikers can expect a slight spiritual snag: 200km to qualify for a purgatorial reprieve (twice the minimum for walkers – allow two to three weeks), but by the time you're hurtling down to Pamplona with a woody, moist Basque wind in your hair, purgatory will be the last thing on your mind. Granted, the vast, windswept plains between Burgos and León have greater potential for torment, but by then you'll have crossed the Ebro and perhaps taken a little detour to linger amongst the vineyards of La Rioja, fortifying your weary pins with Spain's most acclaimed wine.

The Camino was in fact responsible for spreading Rioja's reputation, as pilgrims used to slake their thirst at the monastery of Santo Domingo de la Calzada. The medieval grapevine likewise popularized the Romanesque architecture for which the route is celebrated; today many of the monasteries, convents and churches house walkers and cyclists. Once you're past the Cebreiro pass and into Celtic-green Galicia, rolling past hand-ploughed plots and slate-roofed villages, even a bike will seem new-fangled amidst rhythms that have scarcely changed since the remains of St James first turned up in 813.

152 Cruising through the Coto de Doñana

SPAIN The supposed site of the lost city of Atlantis, the preserve of the Duchess of Alba, Goya's muse, and a favourite hunting haunt of seventeenth-century monarchs Felipe IV and Felipe V, Andalucía's Coto de Doñana was also, up until recently, the infamous domain of malaria-carrying mosquitos.

While many of Spain's wetland areas were drained in the fight against the disease, which put paid to many a royal and was only eradicated in 1964, the swampy triangle that is the Río Guadalquivir delta escaped with its water and wildlife intact. Five years after the area was declared disease-free, almost 350 square kilometres came under the aegis of the Parque Nacional de Doñana, Spain's largest national park. Today, the area is both a UNESCO World Heritage Site and Biosphere Reserve, and encompasses more than 770 square kilometres. Illuminated by the hallucinatory glare of the Costa de la Luz sun, it's a place of tart air and buckled horizons, with that almost mystical lure encountered in unbroken landscapes.

Bordered by the urban centres of Seville, Huelva and Cádiz, it suffers the kind of man-made encroachments from which remoter parks are immune, so it's likely your visit will be confined to a guided tour in an incongruously militaristic 4WD bus. Yet as your driver barrels past sand dunes, sun-blind lagoons and pine stands with typically brusque abandon, you can rest easy in the knowledge that the flamingos, wild boars, tortoises, red deer, mongooses and vultures that reside here are otherwise left in peace. Eking out a living alongside them are small, endangered populations of imperial eagles and Iberian lynx, as well as a rude array of migratory birds that alight in flooded marshes on their way back from West Africa in winter and spring. How many of them you actually see will depend on luck, season and a good pair of binoculars; just remember to pack that repellent.

NEED to know

110 The Beira Baixa region lies more or less equidistant between Coimbra and the Spanish town of Cáceres. Monsanto is accessible via (infrequent) bus from the regional hub of Castelo Branco, Sortelha via a €12–15 taxi ride from nearby Sabugal.

111 The nearest main town to Astigarraga is San Sebastián. The cider season lasts mid-Jan–May. Devotees should check out www.sagardotegiak.com.

112 The tourist board website www.azores.com has lots of details on the islands, including material on fishing.

113 The official festival website www.fiberfib.com has all the details you need on lineups, tickets, etc.

114 *Arzak*, Avda Alcalde Elosegui 273 (☎+34 943 278 465, www.arzak.es).

115 Las Fallas is held annually March 12–19: see www.fallasfromvalencia.com for more details.

116 For opening hours and entry fees, see www .sagradafamilia.org.

117 The cable car from Funchal Bay to Monte is open daily (except Christmas Day) 10am–6pm. For more information, visit www.madeiracablecar.com or call ☎+351 291 780 280.

118 In Madrid: *Corral de la Morería* c/Moreriacutea 17; *El Corral de la Pacheca* c/Juan Ramón Jiménez 26; *La Soleá* c/Cava Baja 34. In Seville: *Los Gallos* Plaza de Santa Cruz; *La Carbonería* c/Levíes 18; *Casa Anselma* c/Pagés del Corro 49.

119 Earthwatch (www.earthwatch.org) recruits and supplies volunteers to established conservation projects around the world.

120 *Café Majestic*, Rua de Santa Catarina, Porto; *Café Aliança*, Rua Dr. F. Gomes 6–11, Faro; *Antiga Confeitaria de Belém*, Rua de Belém 90, Belém, Lisbon.

121 Rio Honor de Castilla/Rio de Onor is a twenty-minute taxi ride from the Leonese fortress town of Puebla de Sanabria.

122 The Guggenheim is located in Bilbao's Abandoi-barra district; see www.guggenheim-bilbao.es.

123 Tram 28 runs from roughly 6am to 11pm. Check www.carris.pt for fares.

124 www.asturiaspicosdeeuropa.com is a useful English-language site.

125 Most mansions are restricted to exterior viewing. WOMAD (www.womad.org) is held during the first fortnight in May.

126 Go to www.portoturismo.pt for more on the São João festival and on Porto itself.

127 The Museo del Prado (www.museodelprado.es) is on Paseo del Prado; the nearest metros are Atocha and Banco de España.

128 Texas Hollywood opening hours and entry costs can be found at www.fort-bravo.com.

129 Peak tapas times are noon–2pm and 8–10pm.

130 Check www.infocordoba.com for up-to-date entry costs and other details.

131 The official programme is available from newsstands in Seville; local newspapers also print timetables and maps.

132 The Alhambra is open throughout the year; advance booking recommended (www.alhambra -patronato.es).

133 FRS (www.frs.es) run ferries between Tarifa and Tangier (up to 7 daily; 35min).

134 Sintra is just 45 minutes by train from Lisbon's Rossio or Sete Rios stations.

135 For more info on Cádiz and the Carnaval, see www.cadizturismo.com or www.andalucia.es/ carnaval-de-cadiz. *Bar Manteca*, Corralon de Carros, 66; *Peña la Perla*, c/Carlos Ollero s/n.

136 The mobile tourist office in Plaza del Castillo has a timetable of events and map. See www.sanfermin. com for more information.

137 You'll find *paradores* throughout Spain; for further information check www.parador.es.

138 www.salvador-dali.org has details of opening hours and entry fees.

139 The Ibiza closing parties take place in the last three weeks of September; DJ, Pacha and MixMag magazines have listings.

140 Both parks are free but vehicular access to Aigüestortes is prohibited.

141 The official carnival website – www.carnaval tenerife.es – has history and and photos as well as up-to-date info on the next carnival.

142 See www.latomatina.com for info on Tomatina tours and plenty of photos and videos of the event.

143 The Puig de Maria monastery is open Tues–Sun 10am–1pm & 4–7pm and admission costs €4.

144 MIAC, *Jameos del Agua*, Jardín de Cactus, Mirador del Río and *El Diablo* (Montañas del Fuego) are open daily; visitor details can be found at www.centros-turisticos.com. FCM (www.fcmanrique.org) is open Nov–Jun: Mon–Sat 10am–6pm, Sun 10am–3pm; Jul–Oct daily 10am–7pm (€8).

145 La Boqueria has a website – www.boqueria.info – and is open Monday-Saturday 8am–8.30pm.

146 Jerez de la Frontera lies 85km south of Seville, with which it has regular bus connections.

147 Details of walking companies are available on the tourist-board website www.madeiratourism.org.

148 *Sabores a Bacalhau*, Rua da Pimenta 47, Parque das Nações (☎+351 218 957 290; closed Tues.)

149 Haro's Wine War takes place on June 29; see www.haro.org for more details.

150 La Gomera lies 28km from Tenerife and is served by regular daily ferries. See www.fredolsen.es for more info.

151 Credentials (or Pilgrim's Passport) are available from Roncesvalles Monastery for a few euros, entitling you to free or very cheap hostal accommodation.

152 Daily four-hour bus tours depart from the reception centre at El Acebuche, 4km north of the coastal resort of Matalascañas (☎+34 959 430 432).

GOOD to know

THE SIESTA

Contrary to popular belief, the Spanish *siesta*, or early afternoon nap, originated in the Alentejo region of Portugal. Although the practice is being eroded due to economic demands, in much of Spain you'll still find **nothing doing** between 2 and 5pm. The shutdown is generally spent over a long lunch rather than in the sack, but a recent national commission blamed the lengthy lunch hour for sleep deprivation (due to working later at night and going to bed later), attendant low productivity and even increased physical and mental illness. It looks unlikely, however, that leisurely afternoons will be abandoned with any great enthusiasm, and the Portuguese have even formed a pressure group to defend them.

"Waking up earlier won't make the sun rise faster"

Spanish proverb

FIVE BEAUTIFUL BEACHES

Bolonia Costa de la Luz, Tarifa, Spain Relentless wind keeps the crowds away at this remote, very low-key quasi-resort, flanked by the Roman ruins of Baelo Claudia.

Playa de Oyambre Comillas, Cantabria, Spain A great white escape from Santander, popular with surfers.

Praia de São Rafael, Albufeira, Portugal Stunning cove beach a couple of kilometres west of town, dotted with wave-etched sandstone pillars.

Ponta da Calheta–Penado do Sono, Porto Santo, Madeira A 6km stretch of golden sand fringes the southeast coast of this little island, 75km off Madeira.

Xilloi O Vecedo, Lugo, Spain Crystal clear, blue-flag bay buffered by emerald cliffs.

SPORT

Spain and Portugal are nations of **fútbol** obsessives, and while the latter has top teams in Benfica and Porto, Spain is home to a league that has long been the envy of Europe. Barcelona and Real Madrid remain two of the biggest names in world football and the Spanish national team's perenially underwhelming tournament form turned in 2008, when they won the European Championships in confident style.

THE SPANISH CIVIL WAR

A bloody prelude to World War II, the Spanish Civil War broke out in July 1936 and lasted until beleaguered Republican forces surrendered on April 1, 1939. An uneasy coalition of liberals, socialists, Communists and anarchists had fought alongside the army, loyal to the leftist Popular Front government, against a Nationalist uprising by **General Francisco Franco**. He was supported by the landed gentry, Carlist monarchists, fascists and the majority of Catholic priests. The fact that the Nationalists were aided by Italy, Germany and Portugal (albeit strategically), and the Republicans by the USSR, also made it a prelude to the Cold War, while the International Brigades (foreign volunteers fighting on the Republican side) demonstrated the passions aroused by the conflict worldwide. Franco's victory inaugurated almost four decades of dictatorship and isolation, shaping modern Spanish life and politics.

FIVE FOODS TO TRY

Churros, Spain Strips of fried dough dunked in viscous chocolate.

Pastéis de nata, Portugal Custard tarts with a caramelized topping.

Jamón serrano, Spain Cured ham, perfected in Extremadura.

Caldeirada de Lulas, Madeira Local take on the Portuguese stew, with squid instead of fish, and added ginger.

Bacalhau, Portugal Salted cod, cooked in hundreds of mouthwatering ways.

MADEIRA WINE

The **fortified wine** Madeira was discovered after table wine bound for the East Indies was "cooked" in the extreme heat onboard ship. Surprisingly, the wine improved with the heat, and until the end of the nineteenth century, Madeira was made by transporting wine to Indonesia and back to achieve the right temperature.

"Better a red face than a black heart"

Portuguese proverb

FIVE OF THE BEST BOOKS ON SPAIN

Homage to Catalonia *George Orwell* Gripping first-person account of the Spanish Civil War, unflinching in its portrayal of internecine conflict.

The New Spaniards *John Hooper* Exhaustive and perceptive analysis of pretty much every facet of life in post-Franco Spain.

Our Lady of the Sewers *Paul Richardson* With a brief "to sieve out the ancient, perverse and eccentric from the new, nice and normal" how could he fail? Engrossing, casually hilarious and outrageously well informed.

Sacred Roads *Nicholas Shrady* A book on global pilgrimages rather than Spain, but Shrady's winter journey along the *camino francés* remains one of the most lucid contemporary accounts in print.

Voices of the Old Sea *Norman Lewis* With tender humour and pristine prose, Lewis recreates the lost world of post-war peasant and fishing communities soon to be eclipsed by tourism.

IBERIAN INGENUITY

Perhaps the most famous of Spanish inventions is the **six-string guitar**, although they've also brought us the submarine, graded lenses for glasses and the humble lollipop. Portugal's finest invention is the **caravel**, a small, nimble vessel that was the preferred ship of the early explorers.

DANISH DELIGHTS: TIVOLI'S FAIRGROUND ATTRACTION • FEELING THE HEAT IN A FINNISH SAUNA • SNORKELLING "THE RIFT" • TREKKING TO DOOR MOUNTAIN • HEARING WOLVES HOWL • RIDING THE WINTER ICE ABOARD AN ARCTIC ICEBREAKER • ROPE RAFTS ON THE KLARÄLVEN • PUFFIN AND PANTIN' • SLEEPING WITH THE FISHES AT UTTER INN • FJORD FOCUS: TOURING THE WESTERN WATERWAYS • NAVIGATING A SWEDISH SMÖRGÅSBORD • JOINING THE FESTIVITIES ON NORWEGIAN NATIONAL DAY • WATCHING HAMLET IN KRONBORG SLOT • TESTING YOUR TASTEBUDS IN REYKJAVÍK • PLUNGING FROM MOUNTAIN TO FJORD ON THE FLÅMSBANA • SUMMER SAILING IN THE STOCKHOLM ARCHIPELAGO • A TO B BY CROSS-COUNTRY SKI • CREATIVE CUISINE AT NOMA • CRUISING THE COOLEST COAST IN EUROPE • CHRISTMAS IN THE HAPPIEST PLACE IN THE WORLD • DEBUNKING MYTHS IN KVERKFJÖLL • A TOAST TO VIKINGS IN BORNHOLM • SOAKING IN LAKE MÝVATN'S HOT SPRINGS • SEEING THE LIGHT AT JUTLAND'S EDGE • WHALE WATCHING IN HÚSAVÍK • BREAKFASTING WITH THE STARS AT THE GRAND HOTEL • PARTYING AT THE WORLD'S LARGEST SÁMI FESTIVAL • HIKING THE BESSEGGEN RIDGE • DANISH DELIGHTS: TIVOLI'S FAIRGROUND ATTRACTION • FEELING THE HEAT IN A FINNISH SAUNA • SNORKELLING "THE RIFT" • TREKKING TO DOOR MOUNTAIN • HEARING WOLVES HOWL • RIDING THE WINTER ICE ABOARD AN ARCTIC ICEBREAKER • ROPE RAFTS ON THE KLARÄLVEN • PUFFIN AND PANTIN' • SLEEPING WITH THE FISHES AT UTTER INN • FJORD FOCUS: TOURING THE WESTERN WATERWAYS • NAVIGATING A SWEDISH SMÖRGÅSBORD • JOINING THE FESTIVITIES ON NORWEGIAN NATIONAL DAY • WATCHING HAMLET IN KRONBORG SLOT • TESTING YOUR TASTEBUDS IN REYKJAVÍK • PLUNGING FROM MOUNTAIN TO FJORD ON THE FLÅMSBANA • SUMMER SAILING IN THE STOCKHOLM ARCHIPELAGO • A TO B BY CROSS-COUNTRY SKI • CREATIVE CUISINE AT NOMA • CRUISING THE COOLEST COAST IN EUROPE • CHRISTMAS IN THE HAPPIEST PLACE IN THE WORLD • DEBUNKING MYTHS IN KVERKFJÖLL • A TOAST TO VIKINGS IN BORNHOLM • SOAKING IN LAKE MÝVATN'S HOT SPRINGS • SEEING THE LIGHT AT JUTLAND'S EDGE • WHALE WATCHING IN HÚSAVÍK • BREAKFASTING WITH THE STARS AT THE GRAND HOTEL • PARTYING AT THE WORLD'S LARGEST SÁMI FESTIVAL • HIKING THE BESSEGGEN RIDGE • DANISH DELIGHTS: TIVOLI'S FAIRGROUND ATTRACTION • FEELING THE HEAT IN A FINNISH SAUNA • SNORKELLING "THE RIFT" • TREKKING TO DOOR MOUNTAIN • HEARING WOLVES HOWL • RIDING THE WINTER ICE ABOARD AN ARCTIC ICEBREAKER • ROPE RAFTS ON THE KLARÄLVEN • PUFFIN AND PANTIN' • SLEEPING WITH THE FISHES

177 Whale watching in Húsavík

155 Snorkelling "The Rift"

ICELAND

Puffin and pantin' 160

FAROE ISLANDS

Partying at the world's largest Sámi festival

179

Fjord focus: touring the western waterways 162

158 Riding the winter ice aboard an Arctic icebreaker

NORWAY

SWEDEN

FINLAND

164

Joining the festivities on Norwegian national day

157 Hearing wolves howl

159 Rope rafts on the Klarälven

DENMARK

174 A toast to Vikings in Bornholm

153 Danish delights: Tivoli's fairground attractions

DENMARK Not many cities have a roller coaster, a pirate ship and an 80m-high carousel slap bang in their centre, but Copenhagen is home to Tivoli – probably the best fairground in the world. The famous pleasure gardens have dished out fun and thrills to a bewitched public since 1843 – to the deeply patriotic Danes they're a national treasure, while most foreign visitors are lured through the gates by the charming mix of old and new: pretty landscaped gardens, fairground stalls, pantomime theatres and old-fashioned rickety rides rub shoulders with brash, high-octane newcomers such as the Golden Tower, which will have you plunging vertically from a height of sixty metres, and the Demon – a stomach-churning three-loop roller coaster.

But the rides are just the icing on the cake – whether you're grabbing a hot dog or candy floss from the fast-food stands or splashing out in one of the thirty or so restaurants, eating is also part of the Tivoli experience. Music plays a big role, too, be it jazz and blues in the bandstands, Friday night rock on the open-air stage or the more stellar offerings of Tivoli Koncertshal, with its big-name international acts – anyone from Anne-Sophie Mutter to Beck. In October, the whole place is festooned with pumpkins, ghouls and witches for a Halloween-themed extravaganza, and in the weeks around Christmas, the festive spirit is cranked up with spectacular lighting displays, a Christmas Market, a skating rink by the Chinese pagoda and all sorts of tasty Christmas nibbles and warming *glögg*, while the braziers and torches help keep the worst of the Danish winter at bay.

Even if fairs usually leave you cold, you can't fail to be won over by the innocent pleasures of Tivoli. On a fine summer's night, with the twinkling illuminations, music drifting across the flowerbeds and fireworks exploding overhead, it's nothing short of magical.

154 Feeling the heat in a Finnish sauna

FINLAND There are over half a million saunas in Finland – that's one for every ten Finns – and they have played an integral part in Finnish life for centuries. Finns believe the sauna to be an exorcism of all ills, and there's certainly nothing quite like it for inducing a feeling of serenity.

Always a single-sex affair in public, the sauna is a wonderfully levelling experience since everybody is naked (it's insisted upon for hygiene reasons). After first showering, take a paper towel or a small wooden tray and place this on one of the benches inside, arranged in the form of a gallery, before you sit down. This stops the benches from burning your skin. Traditionally a sauna is heated by a wood-burning stove which fills the room with a rich smell of wood smoke. However, more often than not, modern saunas are electrically heated, typically to around 80–90ºC, a claustrophobic, lung-filling heat. Every so often, when the air gets too dry, water is thrown onto the hot stones that sit on top of the stove, which then hiss furiously and cause a blast of steam.

By this point you'll be sweating profusely, streams pouring off you and pooling on the ground, prompting the next stage in your sauna experience – lashing yourself with birch twigs. The best saunas provide bathers with small birch branches, with leaves still on, with which you gently strike yourself to increase blood circulation. The fresh smell of the birch in the hot air, coupled with the tingling feeling on the skin, is wondrously sensual. Traditionally, Finns end their sauna by mercilessly plunging straight into the nearest lake or, in winter, by rolling in the icy snow outside – the intense searing cold that follows the sweltering heat creating a compelling, addictive rush at the boundary of pleasure and pain.

155 Snorkelling "The Rift"

ICELAND Few places on Earth can match Silfra for snorkelling. The setting is unique, a fissure crack running between the American and Eurasian continents, its precise location changing with the shifting of the plates each year. But it's the water – or more accurately, the stunning clarity of the water – that makes this site remarkable.

Silfra has arguably the finest visibility anywhere in the world. Crystal is cloudy in comparison. The temperature helps, hovering at around 3°C, as does the water's glacial purity – it takes two thousand years to get here, drip-feeding its way through fields of lava. In fact, the combination creates a clarity so intense that people have been known to experience vertigo on entering the water, suspended like astronauts over a gully that seemingly drops away into the very centre of the Earth.

156 Trekking to Door Mountain

ICELAND At the wild and sparsely inhabited eastern edge of Iceland, the granite crag of Dyrfjoll towers above the natural amphitheatre known as Stórurð (the Elves' Bowl). One edge is sharp and steep, the other a flattened tabletop, and in between, the giant square gap that earns the whole its name: Door Mountain. Hewn by a glacier millions of years ago, the gap is two hundred metres lower than the surrounding cliffs. Heather crowned with blueberries lines the route to Door Mountain, and there are sweeping views across the Héradsflói valley, a vast moorland plain where strands of meltwater from Europe's largest glacier shine like silver threads on a brown blanket. Few roads cross this landscape, and it remains the last great wilderness in Europe.

Hearing 157 wolves howl

SWEDEN Deep in the Swedish birch forest your mind can begin to play tricks. As the shadows lengthen and a chill creeps into the pine-scented air you're reminded of the folk tales that originated here, from gnomes and trolls to the siren call of the *Tallemaja* or "Lady of the Woods". But there is one much-mythologized creature very much alive in the forest – the *varg* or wolf.

Once thought to be in league with the Devil and all but wiped out across Scandinavia by the 1960s, wolves have staged a remarkable comeback. There are now around two hundred spread across the wilds of central and southern Sweden, all descendants of a single pack from Finland. Your best chance of encountering them is in the forests of Bergslagen, just a couple of hours from Stockholm, and home to the country's predator research centre. Here you can track wolves with local experts, spending the night in a cosy tipi or *lavvu*, lulled to sleep (or not) by the howling of the pack.

The camp's location depends on where wolves have been spotted in recent days – they can cover up to 60km in a day so it's crucial to find the best spot. After a short lecture by scientists at the research centre, it's time to head out on the prowl. Close encounters are rare, as wolves are notoriously shy and can smell humans from 3km away, but you are almost guaranteed to find fresh paw prints and experience the eerie sense of being watched. As dusk descends it's time to hike back to the warmth of the tipi in time to hear the wolves howl. Clambering into your sleeping bag, it's hard not to feel a shiver as this bizarre aria begins – a mournful yet comforting sound, once heard across Europe and now, perhaps, set to return.

Riding the winter ice aboard an Arctic icebreaker

FINLAND Outside, in the cold winter air, a community of red-suited humans looking for all the world like miniature Teletubbies are flapping about the icebergs. Up on deck, warmly dressed passengers shudder and scan the horizon, their breath nearly crystallizing the moment it hits the air. In the distance, a slender elk springs from the shore onto the ice, darting across the frozen sea.

Breaking the silence of the Finnish Arctic is the *Sampo*, a colossal 76m-long, 3500-tonne icebreaker that rides on top of the frozen sea, bearing down on the ice and breaking it into chunks like bits of frosty white chocolate. The jagged, fragmented shards – up to a metre thick in some parts – crash and scrape along the steel hull as the vessel cruises on past them towards the sea's deepest waters.

Built in 1960 in Helsinki, the *Sampo* plied through iced-over routes to the Arctic Sea for three decades before becoming a tourist attraction. Today, it is the only Arctic icebreaker in the world to accept passengers, leading the intrepid on four-hour guided tours through the frigid waters of the Gulf of Bothnia, the only European sea to freeze every winter – which can happen as early as October.

The ship's northerly location means things get cold – as low as -40°C at water-level. But this doesn't deter curious visitors from descending the ship out onto the ice, slipping into the frozen waters and floating there in the ship-issue red puffy drysuits. It's just like being four again; the only thing missing is a rubber duckie.

159 Rope rafts on the Klarälven

SWEDEN Boating is so much more satisfying when you've built the barge you're travelling in. On the Klarälven, Sweden's longest river, you can construct a raft big enough to carry six people, using just a dozen ropes and logs, and the guidance of an expert instructor.

You can put the boat together in a morning and be on the water for the afternoon, but a five- or eight-day trip gives you the opportunity to both enjoy tranquil Värmland (Sweden's most southerly wilderness) and head onto dry land to explore the villages along the Klarälven. You can sleep overnight under canvas on your moored craft or in a tent by the river.

Rapids and whirlpools provide moments of real excitement, but much of the trip is a slow meander. This was one of the last Swedish rivers where timber was floated downstream to sawmills, and you'll be travelling at the same gentle pace, keeping an eye out for beavers and elk as the forests and marshes slip by.

160 Puffin and pantin'

FAROE ISLANDS It is mating season on the unspoilt Faroe Islands, about 300km north of Scotland in the windswept, weather-tossed North Atlantic. Heavy waves batter tall, chalky cliffs. Clouds of seagulls sweep through the skies, touching down on fields of purple orchids, flanked by traditional, brightly coloured houses with roofs of turf. Pairs of puffins, their feathers ruffled from the raging sea, wash up on the island, standing proud and rubbing their beaks together in displays of matrimony. The show has just begun. For the next four months, these curious seabirds will mate, nest and raise their offspring on the towering Vestmanna cliffs. They will spend their days diving in and out of the sea, digging burrows, bringing home fish suppers and preparing for migration in late August. All of which makes for great viewing. Boats chug out here from Tórshavn, so you can gaze up at the thousands of nesting birds, hanging on to the crags of the 450m-high cliffs far above.

161 Sleeping with the fishes at Utter Inn

SWEDEN In many ways, the *Utter Inn* is your archetypal Swedish house: its walls are wood-panelled and painted red, there's a white gabled roof, and the location – propped on a little island in the middle of Lake Malaren – is classic Scandinavia.

But things get slightly surreal once you look out of the window of the hotel's solitary room. A large Baltic salmon glides past, followed by a huge shoal of smelt. The orange soles of ducks' feet wheel through the water above. These are not your average lakeside views, but then you're not actually lakeside. The island is a pontoon, the red house just the tip of the architectural iceberg: *Utter Inn* lies three metres below the surface of the lake. A night spent here is literally like living life in a goldfish bowl.

162 Fjord focus: touring the western waterways

NORWAY Everything about the Geirangerfjord is dramatic, even the approach: zigzagging up through the mountains from Åndalsnes before throwing yourself round a series of hair-raising bends as you descend the aptly named Ørnevegen, or Eagle's Highway, the fjord glittering like a precious gem below.

The Geirangerfjord, a great slice of deep blue carved into the crystalline rock walls and snaking out in an "S" shape as it weaves west, is one of the region's smallest fjords and one of its most beautiful. From the pretty little village that marks its eastern end, ferries set out on the 16km trip along the fjord west to Hellesylt. On a summer's day, as the ferry eases away from the wooden pier and chugs off slowly through the passage, waterfalls cascading down the sheer walls on either side and dolphins playing in the bow waves –

as they have done since the first cruise ship found its way up here in 1869 – it's easy to see why UNESCO considered this to be the archetypal fjord, awarding it World Heritage status in 2005, jointly with Nærøyfjord .

As beautiful as it is, Geirangerfjord is just one sliver of water in a network of stunning strands, and you need to see a few fjords to appreciate their magnificence as a whole. Head south for Nærøyfjord, the narrowest fjord in the world, where you can savour the emerald-green waters close up, in a kayak. Or hop in the car and glide across on a tiny ferry, over nearby Norddalsfjord, or – to the south – glass-like Lustrafjord, the wind whipping off the water as you stand at the very mouth of the boat, the imposing silhouette of Urnes' Viking stave church looming ever closer.

163 Navigating a Swedish smörgåsbord

SWEDEN Offhand, how many different ways can you think of to prepare herring or salmon? The two fish are staples of the *smörgåsbord* and, at last count, there were well over 120 varieties being used in restaurants and kitchens across Sweden.

The Swedish *smörgåsbord* (literally "buttered table") is a massive all-you-can-eat buffet where you can sample almost anything under the midnight sun, from heaving plates of fish and seafood – pickled, curried, fried or cured – to a dizzying assortment of eggs, breads, cheeses, salads, pâtés, terrines and cold cuts, and even delicacies such as smoked reindeer and caviar.

You're best off arriving early and on an empty stomach. Just don't pile everything high onto your plate at once – remember that the tradition is as much celebratory social ritual as it is one of consumption. That means cleansing your palate first with a shot of ice-cold aquavit (caraway-flavoured schnapps), then drinking beer

throughout – which as it happens goes especially well with herring, no matter the preparation.

Plan to attack your food in three separate stages – cold fish, cold meats and warm dishes – as it's generally not kosher to mix fish and meat dishes on the same plate. Layer some slices of herring onto a bit of rye bread, and side it with a boiled potato, before moving on to smoked or roasted salmon, jellied eel or roe. Follow this with any number of cold meats such as liver pâté, cured ham and oven-baked chicken. Then try a hot item or two – Swedish meatballs, wild mushroom soup, perhaps Janssons *frestelse* ("Jansson's temptation"), a rich casserole of crispy matchstick potatoes, anchovies and onion baked in a sweet cream. Wind down with a plate of cheese, crackers and crisp Wasa bread and, if you can still move, fruit salad, pastries or berry-filled pies for dessert, capped by a cup of piping hot coffee. Then feel free to pass out.

164 Joining the festivities on Norwegian National Day

NORWAY The seventeenth of May is just another day to most people, but in Oslo (and all across Norway for that matter) it's an eagerly anticipated annual event: Norwegian National Day. A celebration of the signing of the Norwegian Constitution, National Day is a joyous and rather rambunctious affair. It has the usual parades, bands, street parties and food stalls you'd expect, plus a healthy dose of patriotic singing and flag waving. Children are allowed as much ice cream as they can ingest, and Oslo's half a million inhabitants come out in their droves. But the twist in Norway is all in the togs.

Walk out of your door on the big day and you'll feel as if you've accidentally stumbled onto the set of a historical costume drama, with everyone dressed head to toe in traditional dress. Women bustle about in floor-length woollen dresses in vibrant reds, greens, blues and purples, their laced-up bodices adorned with intricate embroidery. Little boys run around in plus fours and woollen waistcoats to

match their fathers while teenagers, depending on their year in school, wear traditional fishermen's overalls in fire-engine red and peacock blue. The effect is disconcerting at first and then, frankly, wonderful as everyone takes part and the city is completely transformed.

Don't worry if you've not got the gear, and certainly don't try to buy an outfit for the occasion as they cost hundreds (if not thousands) of euros and are passed down in Norwegian families from generation to generation. Just steer clear of jeans and wear something nice and you'll blend right in. The best advice is to go with the flow: clap along with the packs of teenagers chanting traditional Norwegian songs; smile at the children strutting by, their faces scrubbed clean and hair done perfectly for the occasion; bow and nod to the waved greetings of the royal family from the balcony of the palace; and above all let yourself be dragged into the spontaneous and joyous revelry all around.

Watching **Hamlet** in **Kronborg Slot**

DENMARK "To be or not to be: that is the question." Walking through the hallowed halls of the sixteenth-century Kronborg Slot in northeastern Denmark you're likely to hear that famous phrase time and again. For it was here that Shakespeare's *Hamlet* was purportedly set; scores of visitors now come to marvel at this UNESCO World Heritage Site, and few can resist citing the tragic prince's most famous line. Even better, though, is if you time your visit to catch one of the annual performances of the play in the dramatically sited castle grounds, overlooking the sea – the spine-tingling authenticity of the Bard's characters coming to life in their original setting is theatre at its finest.

166 Testing your tastebuds in Reykjavík

ICELAND "Icelandic cuisine" promised the menu outside *Laekjar-brekka*, a Reykjavík institution for over thirty years, and while I didn't exactly know what that meant, the opportunity for an adventurous eater was too good to pass up.

I ordered the house appetizer, which the cheerful waitress promptly delivered – a dubious-looking platter of reindeer carpaccio, marinated trout and smoked puffin. On the plate were three piles: greyish flaked fish (obviously the trout), some thin red disks with a dark outline, and a few short black strips that looked as if they came from the dark, bruised sections of a beet. The trout was very tasty, but truth be told, a bit common. I guessed the circular option was the reindeer. It was actually quite good, with a rich, outdoorsy flavour that lingered.

I stabbed a piece of must-be-the-puffin with my fork. A bit more sturdy than I'd expected. It didn't have a smell, so I wasn't prepared for what my mouth told me it tasted like. It had the consistency of well-done steak, and a strong, oily-fishy flavour, a combination that could politely be described as "conflicting". I kept eating it, certain that the taste would change, so that I could at least deem it "not bad" in a quirky culinary sort of way. It didn't.

Delighting in my expression, the waitress happily informed me that puffin paled in comparison to some of the country's other "delicacies". Real daredevil diners, it seems, skip the orange-beaked bird and tuck straight into *hakarl* (rotten shark meat that's buried for six months) or pickled ram's testicles. Those, I promised my stomach, would have to wait for the next trip.

167 Plunging from mountain to fjord on the Flåmsbana

NORWAY The brakes grind then release and you're off, squeaking and squealing down a roller-coaster-like track for what might just be the train ride of your life. This is the Flåmsbana, a shiny, pine-green pleasure train that plunges nearly a kilometre in a mere fifty minutes. The unforgettable ride takes you from the heady frozen heights of the Norwegian mountains in Myrdal right down to the edge of the icy-blue waters of the Aurlandsfjord in the picturesque village of Flåm.

On the train, the old-fashioned carriage interior is wood-panelled and fitted with wide, high-backed benches which transport you back to the 1920s when the train was first built; it took over four years to lay the 20km track which spirals and zigzags down around hairpin bends and through twenty hand-dug tunnels during the course of its short journey. As you might imagine the views are spectacular; to accommodate this, enormous, over-sized windows were fitted to

ensure you don't miss a thing, regardless of where you happen to be seated.

As it runs all year, the train is a lifeline in the winter months for fjord inhabitants who were previously cut off by the long frozen winters. But for the best views, stick to late spring and summer when the ice and snow-melt create majestic, crashing waterfalls (don't miss the close-range view of Kjosfossen) that seem to leap and spring from every crevice in the sheer, verdant cliffs.

The Flåmsbana offers an experience that's at the same time glamorous, hair-raising and magical. The dizzy inclines and thunderous soundtrack of crashing waterfalls will give even the most seasoned rider a shiver of excitement, and if you can't help but conjure up images of runaway trains, just remember there are five independent sets of brakes – a necessary precaution and a very reassuring feature.

168 Summer sailing in the Stockholm archipelago

SWEDEN The truly amazing thing about the Vikings was that they ever decided to leave home. With warm sunshine, cool breezes and the smell of fresh pine drifting across verdant landscapes of hillocks and heather, Scandinavia boasts some of Europe's most alluring summers. Few experiences can top a week spent exploring the nooks and crannies of the Baltic, ending each day on the stern of a ship against a jaw-dropping sunset.

Splayed out across 25,000 islands, islets and skerries – only 150 of which are inhabited – the Stockholm archipelago is made up of thickly wooded inner islands and more rugged, bare and windblown atolls further out. During the day, you'll ply the waters in ferries, sailboats or kayaks, while at night you can either take to your berth or hop ashore to spend the night in a rustic inn, cottage or campsite.

Depart from Stockholm's marina and follow the day-trippers to

Vaxholm, just an hour away, where an imposing sixteenth-century fortress citadel towers over a charming wharf loaded with art galleries, shops and several excellent restaurants. Another 10km on is Grinda, less crowded and great for swimming, and just next door, Viggsö, a tiny green islet where the members of ABBA penned many of their hit songs. Sail east to Sandhamn, a paradise for the yachting fraternity and home to sandy beaches that rival those of the Med. Wend your way south of here to Fjärdlång, a 3.5km-long pine-filled nature reserve ideal for bird-watchers, kayakers and hikers, before heading just inland to Kymmendö, a tiny outcrop of fifteen residents that Strindberg called "paradise on Earth"; you can hire a cycle and pedal to his tiny cottage. Or push on further out into the sparkling waters for Björnö, where small sandy cove beaches, dense reed beds, lush hillocks and undiscovered oak forests await.

169 A to B by cross-country ski

NORWAY With 30,000km of marked trails, Norway is the true home of cross-country skiing, the original and most effective means of getting yourself across snowbound winter landscapes. And it's easier and less daunting to learn than the more popular downhill variety (well, more popular outside Scandinavia – here, everyone is a cross-country skier from the age of 2).

As your skills develop, you'll soon want to take on more challenging hills (both up and down) and to test yourself a little more – there are different techniques for using cross-country skis on the flat, downhill and uphill.

And once you've mastered the basics, a truly beautiful winter world will open up. Popular ski resorts such as Voss, to the east of Bergen, offer a plethora of cross-country tracks, which snake their way under snow-shrouded forests and round lowland hills, while

the Peer Gynt Ski Region, north of Lillehammer, has over 600km of marked trails winding through pine-scented forests, alongside frozen lakes and over huge whaleback mountains.

It may sound blindingly obvious, but try to go in the depths of winter, for in this season the low angle of the midwinter sun creates beautiful pastel shades of lilac, mauve and purple on the deep, expansive folds of hard-packed powder, especially at the start and end of the day.

Ski trails are graded for difficulty and length so you won't bite off more than you can chew, and you'll usually find various ski *hütte* (huts) along the way, where you can stop for a warming loganberry juice. As your skills develop, you may even want to take on a multiday tour, staying overnight at cosy mountain lodges and discovering the high country of Scandinavia in marvellously traditional fashion.

170 Creative cuisine at NOMA

DENMARK Danish cuisine hasn't always scored top marks for imagination, but *Noma* in Copenhagen is now a magnet for gourmands the world over. In 2007 it earned its second Michelin star, and in 2010 it was named as the best restaurant in the world by *Restaurant* magazine. Being tucked away in a fashionably derelict corner of a capital city has its advantages, and during a quiet lunch you could walk in, take your pick of tables, and enjoy a meal more sophisticated, delicate, inspired and, ultimately, delicious, than anything you could find in Milan, Marseille or Madrid.

"Noma" is an abbreviation for *Nordisk mad*, or Nordic food, and those two words are restaurant dogma: every single ingredient, from the familiar (salt and butter) to the foraged (sea buckthorn and Gotland truffle) comes from the region. So, musk ox appears with caramelized apples and woodruff, crispy pig's tail is married with pickled flowers, and instead of olive oil, chef René Redzepi infuses rapeseed oil with herbs and drizzles it over salads.

Noma's style of cooking could be called molecular gastronomy, that culinary sleight-of-hand where sauces are solids and everything is foamed, but the toys in its kitchen are used judiciously, to expand the possibilities of food. Take the beef neck seared to a perfectly bloody rare: it shouldn't be possible – neck is one of the toughest cuts of meat, and should never see a sauté pan – but Redzepi simmers it sous vide at 58 degrees for 36 hours with Gammel Dansk, the bitter digestif, then finishes it over a high flame, and it has the deep flavour of an all-day stew but the texture of a fillet.

As the meal unfolds, Scandinavia seems as bountiful as Tuscany. There are bright sorrel leaves the size of clovers, raw shrimps in cucumber water, impossibly sweet Faroe Island langoustines, and wild mushrooms shaved paper-thin. Then cloudberries appear with wild thyme, and an elderberry cake might be accompanied by tarragon ice cream in a heavy copper bowl; when nobody was looking, Danish cuisine caught up with Danish design.

171 Cruising the coolest coast in Europe

NORWAY For over a hundred years, the *Hurtigrute* boat service has made the dramatic voyage from Bergen in the western fjords of Norway to Kirkenes, deep within the Arctic Circle and hard up against the Russian border. It's a beautiful trawl up the coast, past towering peaks and deep-blue fjords, the views growing more spectacular with every passing knot.

This is far from your average cruise. Quoits are distinctly absent from the upper deck and there are no afternoon salsa classes with the crew; entertainment comes instead in the form of the pounding ocean and some truly staggering scenery. The *Hurtigrute* calls in at 35 ports on the way – some thriving cities steeped in maritime history, others little more than a jetty and a cluster of uniform wooden houses painted in the ubiquitous red. Joining the boat at Bodø in the far north of Norway you're ensured a spectacular start.

Easing gently out of Bodø and into the Norwegian Sea, the boat turns starboard for the Lofoten Islands, the soaring crags of the Lofotenveggen – a jagged wall of mountains that stretches 160km along the shore – looming ever closer. Hopping in and out of a couple of rustic fishing villages along the coast, it then squeezes through the Vesterålen Islands, almost rubbing its bows along the sheer cliff-faces that line the Trollfjord, before pushing on to Tromsø, a teeming metropolis compared with the sparse settlements left behind. From here, the *Hurtigrute* sets off on its final leg, stopping for a couple of hours at Nordkaap, a desolate spot that marks the northernmost point in mainland Europe, before traversing the Barents Sea. Finally, six days after leaving Bergen and 67 hours from Bodø, it triumphantly chugs into the uniformly lacklustre town of Kirkenes, concrete proof – after such a journey – that it is often better to travel than to arrive.

172 Christmas in the happiest place in the world

DENMARK What is happiness? It depends on whom you ask, of course, but the Danes seem to have it figured out. According to yearly surveys, petite Denmark consistently emerges as the happiest place in the world. It makes sense really. This is the country that invented Lego, after all. Danes enjoy free healthcare and education, and punctual, spotless public transport. They make good beer and better smoked herring. No wonder all those apple-cheeked blondes cycling the cobbled streets are beaming.

And then there's the Danish Christmas, or *Jul*, which ties it all together with a fat red bow. If happiness starts with the slow warmth of anticipation, then December's the month to be here. Meander through any town, large or small, and the holiday fervour is palpable: wreaths heavy with berries hang on front doors; delicate paper cutouts of snowflakes dangle from ceilings; and fragrant Christmas trees are bedecked in wooden angels and white candles.

In these northern reaches of the globe, frigid temperatures are a given. But in Denmark, a dusting of snow on the thatched roofs and bright-red mailboxes only adds to the allure.

Mischief is also in the air: as any Danish kid knows, when a sock goes missing, or when the milk suddenly spills as if an invisible hand has pushed it, then the nimble *nisser* (elves) are up to their tricks again – and will be unless you leave a bowl of porridge out before going to bed.

Christmas is celebrated on the evening of December 24, with a feast of roast duck stuffed with oranges or prunes, followed by creamy rice pudding. Then, everyone rises from the table and, in the Danish tradition, forms a ring around the Christmas tree. The singing begins, softly at first, as young and old start to dance, circling the tree and swaying together, small hands in big ones – a moment of sharing that is happiness, no matter whom you ask.

Debunking myths in Kverkfjöll

ICELAND As you approach the entrance to the Kverkfjöll Glacier Caves, in Iceland's stark interior, you may begin to understand why local myths of trolls and mystical beings are given a surprising amount of credence. Beneath a drooping archway of ice, a shadowy cavern is partly obscured by wisps of sulphurous steam – an eerie, almost magical scene, but one entirely of nature's doing. Lurking deep beneath is a frighteningly active volcano whose intense heat melts ice from the base of the glacier, creating rivers of warm water that burrow through the ice as easily as a hot knife through butter. The tunnels and caverns etched by the rivers are enthralling frozen palaces that stretch for over 2km into the glacier.

The caves, situated along the northern edge of the Vatnajökull Glacier at the end of a rough track that passes barren lava fields and volcanic badlands, are not to be taken lightly. Falling ice, swollen rivers and toxic gases can make the caves dangerous, and it is best to explore them with an experienced guide.

Inside the air feels muggy and slightly intoxicating; given the heat, it's surprising to touch the cave walls and find them numbingly cold. Every surface is dimpled like a choppy sea, sculpted by heat and steam, but as smooth as glass. Slowly your eyes adjust to the light, and you are struck by dazzling shades of blue, from ultramarine to the deepest blue-black. As you make your way in, following tunnels that twist and turn, filtered light gives the ice an unnatural glow. Above the noise of crampons and the echo of running water you can hear the groans of the ice as it is slowly moulded by pressure and geothermal heat – the elements, not trolls, hard at work.

173

174 A toast to Vikings in Bornholm

DENMARK Thick smoke wafts over the rows of slender herring, as their silvery scales warm into a golden red. The flushed Dane, in coveralls and clogs, prods the alderwood embers with a long pole swathed in rags at one end. Inside the smokehouse, it's damp and dark, not much larger than a garden shed – and just as basic. Then again, so is the herring preparation – here on the wave-lashed Danish island of Bornholm, this tradition of fish meeting fire owes a debt to the island's first Viking inhabitants, who pulled up in their longboats a millennium ago.

The little kingdom has come a long way. These days, bright ferries filled with sun-seekers pull up to an island that embodies Denmark's penchant for all things *hygellig*, or "cosy and warm": brick-tiled roofs top custard-yellow half-timbered houses, lace curtains frame doll's-house windows and, in the quiet harbour, fishing boats bob to the squawks of gulls circling lazily above. Off in the distance, slender smokehouse chimneys punctuate the low-rise landscape, snorting smoke into the bright northern sky.

Emerge from the tangled Almindingen forest and you'll come across places like Gudhjem, or "God's Home" – just what you might expect if the Man Upstairs were to design his perfect village, especially when the last gasp of sunlight strikes the cobblestone streets. The island's twelfth-century round churches (*rundkirke*) – whitewashed fortresses capped with ink-black conical roofs – lend a stylized, medieval splendour to the otherwise tidy pastureland that surrounds them.

While the Vikings' table manners likely raised a few eyebrows – they didn't use plates or utensils except for the knives they pulled from their sheaths – today, or so the saying goes, the only time you'll see a Dane with a knife in hand is when he has a fork in the other. Still, as you feast on "Sun over Gudhjem" (smoked herring on dark bread, topped with a quivering egg and raw onions), washed down with glass after glass of chilled Tuborg, you may feel some distant connection to those helmet-wearing voyagers. They did know a thing or two about having a good time.

175 Soaking in Lake Mývatn's hot springs

ICELAND Most people visit Iceland in summer, when once or twice a week it actually stops raining and the sun shines in a way that makes you think, briefly, about taking off your sweater. The hills show off their green, yellow and red gravel faces to best effect, and you can even get around easily without a snowplough. But if you really want to see what makes this odd country tick, consider a winter visit. True, you'll find many places cut off from the outside world until Easter, people drinking themselves into oblivion to make those endless nocturnal stretches race by (though they do the same thing in summer, filled with joy at the endless daylight) and tourist information booths boarded up until the thaw. On the other hand, you can do some things in winter that you will never forget.

Up in the northeast, Lake Mývatn is surrounded by craters, boiling mud pools and other evidence of Iceland's unstable tectonics. Near its northeast shore lie crevasses, flooded by thermal springs welling up out of the earth. They are too hot for summer bathing, but in winter the water temperature drops to just within human tolerance, and the springs are best visited in a blizzard, when you'll need to be well rugged up against the bitter, driving wind and swirling snow. Clamber up the steep slope and look down over the edge: rising steam from the narrow, flooded fissure five metres below has built up a thick ice coating, so it's out with the ice axes to cut footholds for the climb down to a narrow ledge, where you undress in the cold and, shivering, ease yourself into the pale-blue water. And then... heaven! You tread water and look up into the falling snow and weird half-light, your damp hair nearly frozen but your body flooded with heat. Five minutes later, you clamber out, feeling so hot you're surprised that the overhanging ice sheets haven't started to melt.

176 Seeing the light at Jutland's edge

DENMARK The fishing town of Skagen could have been torn from the pages of a Hans Christian Andersen fairy tale: half-timbered houses line the cobblestone streets and lemon-yellow daffodils bob behind white picket fences. Wander beyond the tidy hamlet, though, and the wilder side of northern Jutland reveals itself: here, the icy Baltic Sea pounds the shore, whipped up by powerful gales. At Grenen Point, you can saunter along a pale finger of sand and plant your feet in the frothy coupling of two seas, the Skagerrak and Kattegat. And just south of Skagen lies the largest migrating sand dune in northern Europe. Thanks to the strong winds, the Råbjerg Mile moves eastward at the rate of about fifteen metres a year, collecting loose debris in its path, like a giant mop.

But it's the region's luminous skies that have long seduced artists, starting with the Skagen painters – or Danish Impressionists – who arrived in the late 1800s. Viggo Johansen, Anna and Michael Ancher, and P.S. Krøyer all immortalized the remote seaside village, capturing its everyday coastal existence – burly fishermen unloading the daily catch, women in high-necked gowns with parasols strolling the beach – amid milky-white sand dunes glowing under an incandescent light.

You can view their paintings at the Skagens Museum, founded in 1908, which features the world's largest collection of works by these great Danes. The beautifully designed space abounds with windows and skylights to maximize the natural sunlight, so you can admire their portrayals of Skagen's ethereal glow in a room that's bathed in it, and then gaze out of the window to see the real thing.

Next to the museum sits the whitewashed, country-style *Brøndum's Hotel*, a favourite hangout of the bohemian artists – who enjoyed long, loose luncheons here – and still the social heart of town. Settle at one of the outdoor tables, and after a couple of Tuborgs you may also be inspired to pull out the paintbrushes and capture the bright northern skies yawning above you.

177 Whale watching in Húsavík

ICELAND The fact that in Icelandic the word for beached whale is the same as that for jackpot or windfall may give you some clue as to how these seaborne beasts are seen by the locals. Yes, you may well find whale on the menu in Iceland's restaurants – but thanks to a temporary moratorium on whaling back in the enlightened nineties, whalers were forced to seek alternative sources of income and at that point the whale-watching industry was born.

Sadly the moratorium was lifted in 2006, but stocks remain high – and consequently so do sightings. Head out to sea and across Skjálfandi Bay from Húsavík on the island's north coast and thanks to experienced local guides who know every inch of this blustery bay, your opportunities of seeing at least one gentle giant are good.

Unlike many other countries, Iceland plays host to numerous different species of whale, which makes scanning the waterline that much more interesting. The species you're most likely to see is the (relatively) small minke whale, which favours shallow waters near the coast and is very inquisitive, often bringing its head out of the water to watch the boat. The massive blue whale (the largest animal on Earth), vast fin whale (the second largest), square-headed sperm whale and the killer whale are also often sighted, but the biggest creature you'll probably spot is the humpback. Humpback whales are famous for their entertaining behaviour and lively acrobatics, and this is the species most likely to breach, leaping out of the water to expose its whole body, often up to seventeen metres in length.

As if that wasn't quite enough marine life for one trip, there are also dolphins, puffins and other seabirds in this lively bay – more than enough to keep those binoculars busy, and to put a big salty smile on your face as you return to shore for dinner. Just remember to order carefully if you've fallen in love with these graceful creatures.

178 Breakfasting with the stars at the Grand Hotel

SWEDEN Ever since the Nobel Prizes were first awarded in 1901, the winners have stayed at Stockholm's *Grand Hotel*. And for good reason. Set on the waterfront at Blasieholmshamnen, the hotel has one of the most spectacular city views in the world. Straight ahead is the Swedish Royal Palace, the parliament building and the small island of Gamla Stan, Stockholm's old town with its narrow lanes and cobbled alleys. From the large picture windows of its fine dining room, the Veranda, you can watch the bustle of the promenade and the small boats ferrying people out to the islands of the archipelago.

No one of consequence visits Stockholm without staying at the *Grand*, and the signatures in the guest book read like an almanac of twentieth-century life. There is music: Leonard Bernstein, Herbert von Karajan, Bruce Springsteen, Elton John, Michael Jackson, Tina Turner and Bono. There is literature: Hemingway, Steinbeck, Beckett and Camus. And there is global politics: Mandela, Churchill, Thatcher, Chirac and the Dalai Lama. For many it is the Hollywood connection that makes the location special: Charlie Chaplin, Grace Kelly, Alfred Hitchcock, Ingrid Bergman and Greta Garbo are some of the stars that have stayed here.

As if the guest book wasn't enough to tempt you with delusions of celebrity, the *Grand* has another secret: it serves what is probably the best breakfast in all of Europe. Naturally you can order the usual things: eggs coddled, fried, poached, boiled and served with bacon, ham, toast, muffins, crumpets, waffles and mushrooms. As well as this there are crunchy Swedish crispbreads, fresh croissants, rigorously wholesome mueslis and porridge. Home-made pâtés, marmalades and jams moisten the palate. And then there is herring – pickled or curried in a mouth-watering number of ways – as well as cold cuts and terrines. The choice seems endless, with more than 120 hot and cold dishes to sample. Sitting at a table by the window in the glass-walled Veranda, you begin your day with an infusion of fine tea, crisp white linen and that subtle Scandinavian light.

179 Partying at the world's largest Sámi festival

FINLAND Once Lapland has begun to awaken from its long winter hibernation, as the days begin to get longer and the sun breaks away from below the horizon, everyone who's anyone collects on the shores of Lake Ounasjärvi in the far reaches of the Arctic to celebrate all there is to celebrate about the North. Held in one form or another in Lapland since the end of the fourteenth century, the week-long festival of Marianpäivät (St Mary's Days) that takes place in late March in the northern Finnish town of Hetta (also known as Enontekiö or Heahttá) comprises the largest Sámi party of the year. While Sámi are a minority population in Hetta, the festival fills the town to the brim with traditional nomadic people from all over the region – Russian Lapland included – who come donned in shawls, reindeer-fur moccasins and kolts, their multi-coloured, knee-length skirts sewn from broadcloth, frieze and velvet.

The fete is inaugurated out on the frozen lake with everyone's favourite wintertime activity: a reindeer lassoing contest. As the original inhabitants of Lapland, the Sámi are the world's most famous reindeer herders, and the festival is a meeting point for them to mingle, swap stories and talk shop before their annual spring migration journeys. To keep everyone entertained there are reindeer races, visits to the local saunas and pubs, exhibitions of ice carving, displays of traditional art and also performances of Sámi *joiking* (or *juoiggus* in Sámi), the nomads' distinctive mode of singing, whose sound lies somewhere between a yelp and a yodel. If at the end of all this you're still up for more Sámi culture, venture northwest to Kaaresuvanto in April to take part in the annual ice-fishing competition, where families camp out in the middle of the ice for hours at a time, their fishing lines dropped into large holes cut smack into the frozen lake.

NORWAY As trekking goes, the beginning of the Besseggen Ridge is a breeze: sitting on the bow of a little tug as it chugs along picturesque Lake Gjende in central Norway's Jotunheimen Nasjonalpark, you'd be forgiven for wondering what all the fuss is about – this is, after all, Norway's best-known day hike, in the country's most illustrious national park. But then the boat drops you off at a tiny jetty and you start the hike up the hill, knowing that each step takes you closer to the crest – a threadline precipice that'll turn even the toughest mountaineer's legs to jelly.

You'll need a good head for heights, but it's not a technically difficult walk: the path is generally wide and well marked by intermittent cairns, splashed with fading red "T"s. After the initial climb away from the jetty, the route levels out before ascending again across boulder-strewn terrain until – some 2.5 hours into the

trek – you arrive at the base of the ridge itself.

The actual clamber up the ridge takes about half an hour, though the Norwegian youngsters who stride past, frighteningly upright, seem to do it much more quickly. It's incredibly steep and requires a lot of heaving yourself up and over chest-high ledges; in places, the rock just drops away into thin air. But the views are some of the finest in Norway: a wide sweep of jagged peaks and rolling glaciers, and, far, far below, Lake Gjende, glinting green on sunny days but more often – thanks to the upredictably moody weather up here – resembling a menacing pool of cold, hard steel.

From there on, the going is comparatively easy, and you'll probably scamper the remaining few kilometres back to Gjendesheim, your energy bolstered by the biggest adrenaline boost you have had in a very long time.

NEED to know

153 For opening hours and entrance fees, see ⓦwww.tivoli.dk.

154 Most public swimming pools in Finland have a sauna: check out Kotiharjun (Tues–Fri 2–8pm, Sat 1–7pm) on Harjutorinkatu street in Helsinki.

155 Diving Iceland (ⓦwww.dive.is) organizes snorkelling trips into Silfra.

156 For more information on the area, see ⓦwww.east.is.

157 The "Howling with wolves" two-day tour is offered by ⓦwww.naturetravels.co.uk, with regular dates in summer and others available on request.

158 March is the best month to board, when the ice is at its thickest. Don't forget your sunglasses – the glare of the sun off snow-covered ice can be harsh – and some chapstick. ⓦwww.sampotours.com.

159 Minimum ten people for two rafts. The tour begins at Gunnerud, 95km north of Karlstad, from where you'll be taken to the raft building site. For details visit ⓦwww.vildmark.se.

160 Puffins are best viewed on an organized boat tour from Tórshavn; see ⓦwww.visittorshavn.fo/uk for a list of operators.

161 The *Utter Inn* is situated at Lake Malaren, in Vasteras, an hour or so from Stockholm and costs from 1150kr a night. Call ⓣ+46 (0) 21 830 023 for more details.

162 Geirangerfjord is in southwestern Norway, 9hr by bus from Bergen. Naerøyfjord and Lustrafjord are 3hr and 5hr respectively from Bergen.

163 Try *Ulriksdals Wårdshus*, Slottspark (ⓦwww.ulriksdalswardshus.se), 10min north of Stockholm in Solna.

164 Oslo's main tourist office is in the centre, behind the Rådhus at Fridtjof Nansens plass 5 (ⓦwww.visitoslo.com).

165 The website ⓦ www.ses.dk/en/SlotteOgHaver/Slotte/Kronborg is a good port of call for information on Kronborg Slot.

166 *Laekjarbrekka* is at Bankstraeti 2 (ⓦwww.laekjarbrekka.is).

167 To get to the Flåmsbana take the train from Bergen to Myrdal (via Voss). You can buy your ticket all the way through to Flåm at the Bergen train station, which means you'll be able to jump right on the train when you arrive in Myrdal. ⓦwww.flaamsbana.no.

168 A Båtluffarkortet pass gets you five days of unlimited ferry travel; alternatively, you can hire a sailboat from any number of outfits in Stockholm. Visit ⓦwww.skargardsstiftelsen.se for accommodation on the islands.

169 Most cross-country ski areas offer lessons and have skis and boots available for hire. For more information on Voss, see ⓦwww.visitvoss.no.

170 *Noma* is at Strandgade 93, 1401 Copenhagen K (ⓦwww.noma.dk).

171 See ⓦwww.hurtigruten.com for fares and sailing schedules.

172 A number of Copenhagen restaurants offer Christmas dinner specials; for details, check with the tourist office, at Vesterbrogade 4a (ⓦwww.visitcopenhagen.com).

173 The tourist information centre in Reykjavík (ⓦwww.visiticeland.com) can provide information on guides and tour companies.

174 Ferries travel daily to Bornholm from Ystad, in southern Sweden (1hr 15min), and from Køge, south of Copenhagen (overnight).

175 Mývatn is about 6hr by road from Reykjavík, and 2hr from the nearest town, Akureyri. Buses run in summer; you'll have to hire a car during the rest of the year.

176 Skagens Museum (ⓦwww.skagensmuseum.dk); *Brøndum's Hotel* ⓦwww.broendums-hotel.dk; Danish language only).

177 Húsavík's two main whale-watching operators are Gentle Giants (ⓦwww.gentlegiants.is) and North Sailing Húsavík (ⓦwww.northsailing.is). Both operate daily from May to September and trips last around three hours. Temperatures rarely creep above 10°C even in summer, so wrap up warm.

178 Menus and reservations for breakfast at the *Grand Hotel* via ⓦwww.grandhotel.se.

179 You can fly from Helsinki to Hetta via Rovaniemi, or take the train from Helsinki to Kolari, and then a bus to Hetta. For information on the festival, contact Enontekiö Tourist Information (ⓦwww.tosilappi.fi).

180 Jotunheimen Nasjonalpark is accessed via Gjendesheim, 90km southwest of Otta. The Lake Gjende boat runs from late June to mid-Sept (ⓣ+44 (0) 6123 8509).

GOOD to know

SCANDINAVIAN OR NORDIC?

In linguistic terms, **Skandinavien** is an Old Norse term describing the ancient territories of the Norsemen – the Danes, Swedes and Norwegians. Technically, however, Iceland and the Faroe Islands are also included in this, and Greenland, Shetland and Orkney also share some cultural affinities. "Scanvinavica" is the Latin word for the peninsula shared by Norway, Sweden and northern Finland. "The Nordic Countries" came into being as a term with the creation of the Nordic Council in the 1950s. It includes Finland and Iceland and is the most politically correct and accepted term to include the five main countries of the region. But "Scandinavia" still trumps other descriptions when it comes to conjuring up romantic notions of cold, mountainous landscapes of forests, fjords and glaciers.

FINE DESIGN

Arne Jacobsen, whose cradle-like Egg Chair put Scandinavian design on the map in the 1950s, leads the Danish pack, while the architectural works of **Jørn Utzon** (Sydney Opera House) and **Henning Larsen** (Copenhagen Opera House) make striking statements on modern life amid their urban landscapes. The oh-so-practical aesthetic of long-standing Swedish brand **IKEA** is now firmly planted in the homes of millions of people around the world, although the exuberant designs of Finnish textile and clothier **Marimekko** are fast becoming sought-after objects for the high-class home owner.

WHO'S YOUR DADDY?

Patronymics (last names derived from the father's name) were widely employed in the Scandinavian countries for hundreds of years. Fathers would pass on their first names to their sons, to which -sen in Denmark and Norway and -son in Sweden were added, while women used the suffix -datter, -dottir or -dotter to indicate who their father was. Family names became a legal necessity in the nineteenth century, and only in Iceland and the Faroe Islands has the age-old custom been kept alive.

WHAT DAY IS IT?

English derives four of its days of the week from the names of Norse gods: Tiu (Tuesday), Odin (Wednesday), Thor (Thursday) and Freya (Friday).

"Football is a fertility festival. Eleven sperm trying to get into the egg. I feel sorry for the goalkeeper" **Björk**

FIVE CLASSIC READS

The Unknown Soldier, Vainö Linna
The Fairy Tale of My Life, Hans Christian Andersen
Hunger, Knut Hamsun
Pippi Longstocking, Astrid Lindgren
The Kalevala, Elias Lonnröt

FIVE MODERN READS

Borderliners, Peter Høeg
Sophie's World, Jostein Gaarder
Under the Snow, Kerstin Ekman
The Year of Hare, Arto Paasilinna
The Sun, My Father, Nils-Aslak Valkeapää

TOP VIKING SITES

Denmark, Norway and Sweden were the centres of Viking rule and strategic strongholds for the regulation of shipping and piracy, and there are traces of Viking societies and communities all over the place.
Jelling Stones, Denmark Large runic stones erected more than 1000 years ago by King Gorm the Old, and featuring the first written mention of the nation called "Danmark".
Ladby Skibet, Denmark Underground tenth-century tomb – the only Viking ship burial mound ever to be discovered in Denmark – containing the remains of a Viking chieftain and his longboat.
Trelleborg, Denmark Ring fortress, noted for the mathematical precision of its construction, dating back to 980 AD and the reign of Harald Bluetooth.
Birka, Sweden The oldest town in Sweden and an important early Viking trade centre. Nearby Hovgarden contains the remains of thousands of Viking burial mounds.
Vikingeskibsmuseet, Norway Spectacular museum in Oslo housing near-complete reconstructions from several buried Viking ships recovered from Tune, Gokstad, Oseberg and Borre.

SOCIAL WELFARE

The Scandinavian **welfare model** refers to the way in which the Nordic countries organize and finance their social security systems, public health services and education. The principle is based on the Lutheran ideal that benefits should be given universally to all citizens, supported by a taxation system that has both a broad basis of taxation and a high taxation burden – around 46 percent for most workers – ultimately bringing about greater wealth distribution.

FIVE HOT SUMMER MUSIC FESTIVALS

Roskilde Festival, Demark Early July. A four-day party for nearly 100,000 people with some of the biggest rock bands in the world, plus plenty of newcomers. Ⓦwww.roskilde-festival.com.
Copenhagen Jazz Festival, Denmark Mid-July. The capital's largest festival, showcasing everything from live bebop to spoken-word poetry. Ⓦwww.festival.jazz.dk.
Savonlinna Opera Festival, Finland July. One of Europe's liveliest and most prestigious opera festivals, with many of the classics of European opera performed within the walls of a fifteenth-century castle. Ⓦwww.operafestival.fi.
Malmö Festival, Sweden Mid-Aug. Over 250 concerts and around 1.5 million visitors over eight days. Best of all, it's free. Ⓦwww.malmofestivalen.se.
Telemark Folk Music Festival, Norway Mid-July. Folk enthusiasts converge to catch several dozen concerts of world folk music, with a focus on the rich tradition of Nordic dancing. Ⓦwww.telemarkfestivalen.no.

BEAN FEASTS AND ORANGE FIGHTS • LOSE YOURSELF AT MYSTRA • ALL YOU CAN EAT – WITH MUSIC! • THIS IS THE LIGHT: EASTER CELEBRATIONS IN LOUTRÓ • PLAY CRUSOE IN THE ADRIATIC'S REMOTEST REACHES • BEARS AND BOARS: TREKKING IN THE ABRUZZO NATIONAL PARK • UNCOVERING THE ROMANI SECRETS OF ŠUTKA • VISITING FEDERICO'S PALACE IN URBINO • GOING WITH THE FLOW OF SAN GENNARO • BALKAN BRASS MADNESS IN GUČA • GET THE MEASURE OF THE MEDICI IN THE UFFIZI • GETTING LOST IN DIOCLETIAN'S PALACE • INSIDE A METAPHOR: TROY • EXTREME MEASURES AND REVOLUTIONARY ART IN PADUA • PARADISE REGAINED: ITALY'S OLDEST NATIONAL PARK • STALAGMITES, STALACTITES AND A HUMAN FISH • THE COLOSSEUM IN WINTER • A NIGHT OUT ON INDEPENDENCE STREET • GET DOWN AND DIRTY IN DALYAN • GRAND MASTER FLASH • THE DIVINE DANCERS OF CALABRIA • TREAD THE PLITVICE BROADWALKS • WORKING UP A LAVA ON STROMBOLI • BOMB SHELTERS FOR COMPANY: HIKING THE OHRID BORDER • SHARING THE LOVES OF THE GODS AT THE PALAZZO FARNESE • SOLVING THE MYSTERIES OF POMPEII • SNUFFLING FOR TRUFFLES IN PIEMONTE • BUNKERING DOWN IN DURRES • PLAYING FOR HIGH STAKES AT SIENA'S IL PALIO • SOMETHING FISHY IN MARSAXLOKK • INTO THE LAGOON: VENICE'S OTHER ISLANDS • VISITING THE HOME OF PIZZA • MUSIC, DANCE AND DRAMA IN ANCIENT ASPENDOS • HEADING INTO DEEPEST MAFIA COUNTRY • CONQUERING MOUNT OLYMPUS • BRAVING THE MIDDAY SUN IN ROCK-HEWN LECCE • THE PEACE OF PAESTUM • HAGGLE WITH HORROR IN ISTANBUL • LIVING IT UP ON THE AMALFI COAST • TACKLING OLD MR THREE HEADS • NUTS, SOCKS AND MISTLETOE BRANDY: JOINING THE TRUFFLE TRAIN IN BUZET • CALLED BY RUMI: DERVISHES IN ISTANBUL • LIVE LIKE A DOGE: ONE NIGHT AT THE DANIELI • TECHNO AND TURBO-FOLK: HAVING A BLAST IN BELGRADE • MONASTERIES IN THE AIR • HOT COALS FOR CONSTANTINE • SAUNTERING THROUGH THE RUINS OF ANI • CHEWING THE FAT: A GLUTTON'S TOUR OF BOLOGNA • ISLAND-HOPPING ON THE AEGEAN • LOCKED UP IN LJUBLJANA • MONASTIC MOUNT ÁTHOS • CAPPADOCIA: LAND OF THE FAIRY CHIMNEYS • IN THE FOOTSTEPS OF ODYSSEUS ON ITHACA • THE MURALS OF TIRANA'S TOWER BLOCKS • CLASSICAL DRAMA AT EPIDAVROS • STRIKING OIL IN EDIRNE • STUDENICA'S MAGIC MONASTERIES • ROAM OSTIA ANTICA • FACE TO FACE WITH THE GODS IN SICILY • ENJOYING DA VINCI'S LAST SUPPER • RAFTING THE TARA CANYON • TAKE THE IRON WAY OVER THE ALPS • TOURING THE TUSCAN HILL TOWNS • GOING UNDERGROUND IN SARAJEVO • KAYAKING IN THE BAY OF KOTOR • DOING PENANCE IN THE SISTINE CHAPEL • GORGING ON FROGS AND EELS IN THE NERETVA DELTA • VENICE: EUROPE'S FIRST MODERN CITY? • WORSHIP THE CATHEDRALS OF THE MEGALITHIC • CELEBRATING THE BIENNALE • SOLDIERS, MONKS, AND FRESCOED SQUID IN KOSOVO'S MONASTERIES • SHOPPING WITH STYLE IN MILAN • BEAN FEASTS AND ORANGE

Southeast Europe
181–252

Tackling old Mr Three Heads **220**

SLOVENIA

CROATIA

SERBIA

BOSNIA-HERZEGOVINA

Balkan brass madness in Guča **190**

244 Going underground in Sarajevo

ITALY

KOSOVO

The Colosseum in winter **197**

MONTENEGRO

The murals of Tirana's tower blocks **234**

F.Y.R.O.M

A night out on Independence Street **198**

226 Hot coals for Constantine

ALBANIA

TURKEY

GREECE

Heading into deepest mafia country **214**

Island-hopping on the Aegean **229**

MALTA

Bean feasts and orange fights

181

ITALY One of Italy's biggest and most peculiar carnival celebrations takes place in Ivrea, not far from Turin. On the Sunday before Shrove Tuesday the town fills with revellers who tuck into bowls of beans ladled out from giant cauldrons in the main square before taking part in a humongous orange fight, which starts at the same time each afternoon for the next three days. Anyone and anything is fair game here, and by the end of each day everyone is covered in pulp and drenched in freshly squeezed juice; there's nowhere to walk that's not swimming in vitamin C, and the air is full of the bitter smell of oranges. On Shrove Tuesday it finishes with a huge procession and a celebratory bonfire in the square.

182 Lose yourself at Mystra

GREECE The Peloponnese is littered with ancient sites, but arguably none is quite as evocative as Mystra, a ruined Byzantine city that dates back to the mid-thirteenth century. It's an intriguing place to explore, strung down a steep hillside and extraordinarily intact, with crumbling mansions and tiny churches that sport monumental frescoes, as well as an ancient convent at its heart that is still inhabited by half a dozen nuns. It's not overcrowded, and you can lose yourself in its alleys and arches – which is just what you should do, maybe combining a visit with some hiking in the nearby beautiful and remote Langhada Pass between Kalamata and Sparta, said to be a route taken by Telemachus in *The Odyssey*.

183 All you can eat – with music!

ITALY There's no better way to unwind after Florence's legendary Uffizi Gallery than by eating the food of one of Italy's top chefs, Fabio Picchi, whose restaurant has been feeding hungry locals for years. There's a posh restaurant and a much cheaper trattoria at the same location, both serving delicious takes on traditional Tuscan cuisine (no pasta), but the place you might prefer to try is his latest venture, the *Teatro del Sale*, where you scoff as much as you like for around €25 and be entertained at the same time. You can order wine, but otherwise the food is just brought to you course by course – pasta or risotto to start, followed by a meat dish and then dessert, after which you're treated to a programme of music, poetry or Italian drama.

184 This is the light: Easter celebrations in Loutró

GREECE A faint glimmer of flame behind the altar of the darkened church and the black-clad *papás* appears, holding aloft a lighted taper and chanting "Avto to Fos" – "This is the Light of the World". Thus Easter Sunday begins at the stroke of midnight in a tiny chapel in the small seaside village of Loutró, southern Crete. Minutes earlier, the congregation and entire village had been plunged into darkness.

Now, as the priest ignites the first candle and the flame is passed from neighbour to neighbour, light spreads through the church again. As the congregation pours out into the street the candlelight is distributed to every home along with the cry of "Christos Anesti" ("Christ is Risen"). It's an extraordinary experience – a symbolic reawakening of brightness and hope with clear echoes of more ancient rites of spring – and within minutes wilder celebrations begin; firecrackers are thrown and traditional dishes devoured to break the week-long fast that the more devout have observed.

The rituals of the Greek Orthodox Church permeate every aspect of Greek society, but never so clearly as at Easter. As a visitor you are inevitably drawn in, especially in a place as small as Loutró – accessible only by boat or on foot – where the locals go out of their way to include you.

After a few hours' sleep you wake to the smell of lambs and goats roasting on spits. As they cook, the wine and beer flow freely until the whole village, locals and visitors alike, join the great feasts to mark the end of Lent.

185
Play Crusoe
in the Adriatic's remotest reaches

CROATIA Around day three you get it. For the first 48 hours or so your mind skitters, unaccustomed to the sudden stillness. Back at home, a week's isolation seems the antidote to the hurly-burly of everyday life, but the reality of empty seascapes and silence is still a mild shock. Then, after a couple of days, time seems to loosen and days assume a delicious ease. *Fijaka*, the Croats call it; a mood of pure languid contentment.

Remote, getaway holidays are the secrets of Croatian tourism. Usually week-long breaks on uninhabited islands, they are the ultimate escape in a country of insanely popular rivieras. The question is how far away you get.

If isolation feels like exile choose the Kornati islands in central Dalmatia, where the neighbours are just beyond your bay. Hire a former fishermen's cottage in this national park and you are ferried from Murter then left to pootle about your cove in peace. Bar a gas lamp or two, light and water are of the natural variety, while food comes from whatever provisions you have brought or whatever

takes your hook. George Bernard Shaw wrote that the islands were the crowning glory of God's Creation, built "out of tears, stars and breath". On a still, velvety night only the latter half seems dubious.

For true Robinson Crusoe types, however, there's little in Europe that compares to Palagruža. They say that Diomedes, Odysseus's friend and the bravest of the Greeks who sacked Troy, sheathed his sword for good on this mid-Adriatic islet, and archaeology confirms an antique settlement. Nowadays the only resident is a lighthouse keeper who lets two simple apartments to adventurers eager to experience Croatia's most distant island, a nature reserve that is closer to Italy than the Croatian mainland 120km away.

With a week to explore an island you could circuit in an hour – rummaging through the Mediterranean scrub that fuzzes its rocky fin, peering over 90m cliffs – you can't help but discover a golden beach. And what beaches, washed by the cleanest seas in the Mediterranean but without a sunbather in sight: the shock comes when you return to the real world.

186 Bears and boars: trekking in the Abruzzo National Park

ITALY The Apennines stretch for some thirteen hundred kilometres down the very spine of Italy. They are the country at its roughest and least showy. But these mountains are far from dull. In their loftiest and most rugged stretch, in the central region of Abruzzo, two hours from Rome, you'll find peaks rising up from gentle pastures, and swathes of beech woodland that roll up from deep valleys before petering out just short of the steepest ridges.

Romans come to the Parco Nazionale d'Abruzzo to walk, climb and enjoy rustic foods like wild boar prosciutto and local sheep's cheese, washed down by the hearty Montepulciano d'Abruzzo wine. Foreign visitors are rare, and you can walk for hours without seeing another person. This tranquillity isn't lost on the park's wildlife. Chamois, roe deer, martens and even wolves have found a haven here, and the park is one of the last refuges in Western Europe of the Marsican brown bear. They haven't survived by

being easy to spot. After the furtive lynx – an animal which stalks its prey by night before launching an attack that can only be described as explosive – bears are among the park's most elusive creatures. You may be lucky enough to see one briefly, tantalizingly exposed while crossing an open mountain ridge. You're more likely, however, to find just paw prints or rocks overturned in the hunt for moths.

The best base is Pescasseroli, a ridge-top village with a cluster of homely hotels and a park visitor centre. From here, you can hike straight into the forest and up along the long ridge that crests and falls from Monte Petroso (2247m) to the aptly named Monte Tranquillo (1830m) and on to Monte Cornacchia (2003m). Or you can take a bicycle on hundreds of kilometres of rough roads that thread through the area – by which time you'll have earned your plate of wild boar.

187 Uncovering the Romani secrets of Šutka

FYROM As you take your first steps into the Macedonian district of Šutka, you may find yourself rubbing your eyes in disbelief. In many ways, this is more like India than Europe: tradespeople cry their wares through a cacophony of parping motorbikes, livestock roam streets strewn with litter and crisscrossed with drying laundry, and the area's houses – or at least those that have not yet collapsed – have been given coat after coat of gaudy paint. This is one of the Continent's most impoverished and dilapidated corners, but its curious charms are enticing an increasing number of foreign adventurers.

Lying just west of the Macedonian capital of Skopje, the district of Šuto Orizari, more commonly referred to as Šutka, is home to almost twenty thousand people, the majority of whom are of Roma extraction. This makes it the world's largest Gypsy community, as well as the only one governed by a Romani mayor. The bustling daily market disguises a rampant unemployment rate – most

youngsters dream of living abroad, and overseas remittances form a substantial chunk of the local economy. Late spring and early summer are the most popular periods for those born in Šutka to return home, and is also the best time for travellers to catch a glimpse of two of the area's prize attractions: weddings and music.

For a small, poor area, it's amazing how many weddings take place in Šutka – in warmer months there seems to be at least one every afternoon. The most lavish take place at the district hotel, though you may also find one going on in an abandoned shipping container. Big or small, all weddings feature hour after hour of Romani dancing, accompanied by braying brass and fleet-fingered guitar chords. Šutka is one of Macedonia's foremost centres of song and dance, and musicians from the area tend to mop up most of the national awards. Events run to no fixed schedule, but head along on a sunny afternoon and you may be in luck – just follow your ears, and enjoy the inevitably warm Roma hospitality.

188 Visiting Federico's Palace in Urbino

ITALY Having evolved from a patchwork of city-states, Italy is littered with amazing palaces raised by local rulers, but none is more stunning than the Palazzo Ducale in Urbino. Baldassarre Castiglione, whose sixteenth-century handbook of courtly etiquette, *Il Cortegiana* (The Courtier), is set in the palace, reckoned it to be the most beautiful in all Italy, and few would disagree with that verdict.

Dominating this attractive little university town in the heart of the rural province of Marche, the Palazzo Ducale was commissioned in 1468 by Federico da Montefeltro, one of the most remarkable men of his era. A brilliant soldier, Federico kept the coffers of Urbino full by selling his military services, but he was also a man of genuine learning and a great patron of the arts. A friend of the great architect and theorist Leon Battista Alberti, he regarded architecture as the highest form of aesthetic activity, and studied the subject so thoroughly that it was written of him that "no lord or gentleman of his own day knew as much about it as he did." His residence – designed primarily by the otherwise obscure Luciano Laurana – is

an unforgettable testimony to his discernment.

From the street it's not an especially handsome building, but once you step into the Cortile d'Onore you'll see what this place is all about: elegant, exquisitely crafted yet unostentatious, it's the perfect blend of practicality and discreet grandeur. Inside, many of the rooms are occupied by the Galleria Nazionale delle Marche, where one of the prize exhibits is a portrait of Federico by Pedro Berruguete – he's painted, as always, in profile, having lost his right eye in battle. In Federico's private suite of rooms you'll see paintings by the finest of all the artists he sponsored, Piero della Francesca, including the enigmatic *Flagellation*. Two adjoining chapels – one dedicated to Apollo and the Muses, the other to the Christian God – are indicative of the complexity of the duke's world-view, as is the astounding Studiolo, where wall panels of inlaid wood create some startling illusory perspectives – you'll see some delicately hued landscapes of Urbino here, and portraits of great men ranging from Homer and Petrarch to Solomon and St Ambrose.

189 Going with the flow of San Gennaro

ITALY The capital of the South, Naples is quite unlike anywhere else in Italy. It's a city of extremes, fiercely Catholic, its streets punctuated by bright neon Madonnas cut into niches and its miraculous cults regulating the lives of people here almost much as they did in Rome's pagan days. None more so than the cult of San Gennaro, Naples' patron saint, whose dried blood, kept in a vial in the cathedral, appears to spontaneously liquefy three times a year, thereby ensuring the city's safety for the months to come. It is supposed to take place on the first Saturday in May, on September 19 – San Gennaro's feast day – and also on December 16, and the liquefaction (or otherwise) of San Gennaro's blood is the biggest event in the city's calendar by far, attended by the great and the good of the city, not to mention a huge press corps.

The blood liquefies during a Mass, which you can attend if you get to the Duomo early enough (ie the middle of the night). The doors open at 9am, when a huge crowd will have gathered, and you're ushered into the church by armed *carabinieri*, who then stand guard at the high altar while the service goes on, the priest placing the vial containing the saint's blood on a stand and occasionally taking it down to see if anything has happened, while the faithful, led by a group of devout women called the "parenti di San Gennaro", chant prayers for deliverance. The longer it takes, the worse the portents for the city are.

If it doesn't liquefy at all... well, you will know all about it. It didn't happen in 1944, the last time Vesuvius erupted, and in 1980, when a huge earthquake struck the city, so people are understandably jumpy. Luckily, the blood has been behaving itself for the past couple of decades, a period which has coincided to some extent with the city's resurgence. As the mayor of Naples commented: "it's a sign that San Gennaro is still protecting our city, a strong sign of hope and an encouragement for everyone to work for the common good." You may not believe in any of it, of course, but being here amid the hype, the hope and the ceremony is an experience like no other.

190 Balkan brass madness in Guča

SERBIA Bars, restaurants and tents blast out hard Romani funk, punters slap dinar notes onto the heads of sweat-soaked musicians, and men and women of all ages and dispositions form a *kolo* – a joyous, fast-paced circular formation dance. For one week each summer, the otherwise tranquil village of Guča (pronounced "goo-chah"), located some 250km south of the Serbian capital Belgrade, is transformed into the undisputed party capital of the Balkans. Guča is home to the Dragačevo Trumpet Festival, the largest, loudest – and quite possibly, craziest – event of its kind anywhere in the world. Essentially a celebration of folk and brass music from across the Balkans, principally Serbia, it stars dozens of bands competing for the coveted Golden Trumpet.

The king of Guča, and the finest trumpet player of his generation, is Boban Marković who, with his fabulous twelve-piece orchestra – which includes his teenage son Marko – has scooped the Golden Trumpet several times. Such has been their dominance that they no longer bother competing for the big prize, though they do still make the occasional feted appearance. Marković is typical of the large number of Roma, musicians that attend Guča, and who make this event the rocking spectacle that it is. With their ecstatic, turbo-charged Gypsy sounds, these outrageously talented and charismatic performers provide a potent sonic odyssey – indeed, Miles Davis was once famously moved to remark "I never knew a trumpet could be played like that." Welcome to Guča, welcome to brass madness.

191 Get the measure of the Medici in the Uffizi

ITALY It's a simple equation: Florence was the centre of the Italian Renaissance; the Medici were the greatest art patrons of Renaissance Florence; their collection was bequeathed to the city by the last Medici, Anna Maria Lodovica; therefore the Uffizi Gallery – which occupies offices (*uffizi*) built for the Medici in 1560 – is the greatest display of Renaissance painting in the world. Which is why the Uffizi attracts more visitors than any other building in Italy – more than one and a half million of them every year.

The key to enjoying the Uffizi is to book your ticket in advance and to ration yourself; if you try to see everything you'll barely be able to skate over the surface. For your first visit, limit yourself to the first eighteen rooms or so – this will take you as far as the Bronzino portraits in the octagonal Tribuna. Arranged more or less chronologically, the Uffizi encapsulates the genesis of the Renaissance in a room of three altarpieces of the Maestà (Madonna Enthroned) by Duccio, Cimabue and Giotto. After a diversion through the exquisite late Gothic art of Simone Martini and Gentile da Fabriano, the narrative of the Renaissance resumes with Paolo Uccello's *The Battle of San Romano* and continues with Piero della Francesca, Filippo Lippi (and his son Filippino), and of course Botticelli: it doesn't matter how many times you've seen photos of them, the *Primavera* and the *Birth of Venus* will stop you in your tracks. And there's still Leonardo da Vinci to come before you reach the halfway point.

Should you decide to make a dash to the end, you'll see a remarkable collection of Venetian painting (Giorgione, Giovanni Bellini, Paolo Veronese, Tintoretto and no fewer than nine Titians), a clutch of fabulous Mantegnas and Raphaels, and the extraordinary Doni Tondo, the only easel painting Michelangelo ever came close to completing. Ahead of you are fabulous pieces by Dürer, Holbein and Cranach, del Sarto and Parmigianino, Caravaggio and Rembrandt, Goya and Chardin. Wherever you stop in the Uffizi, there's a masterpiece staring you in the face.

192 Getting lost in Diocletian's Palace

CROATIA Try imagining Pompeii as a functioning twenty-first-century city, and you'll get a good idea of what the Croatian port of Split looks like. At its heart lies a confusing warren of narrow streets, crooked alleys and Corinthian-style colonnades that looks like a computer-generated reconstruction of an archeological dig. High-street shops, banks, restaurants and bars seem stuffed into this structure like incongruous afterthoughts.

Split began life as the purpose-built palace of Roman Emperor Diocletian, who retired here after his abdication in 305 AD. When marauding Avars sacked the nearby city of Salona in 615, fleeing inhabitants sought refuge within the palace walls, improvising a home in what must have been the most grandiose squat of all time. Diocletian's mausoleum was turned into a cathedral, the Temple of Jupiter became a baptistery, and medieval tenement blocks were built into the palace walls.

Nowadays the palace's crumbling courtyards provide the perfect setting for some of the best bars in the Mediterranean. The only problem is that Split's maze-like street plan makes it head-scratchingly difficult to navigate your way back to the welcoming drinking hole you discovered the previous night. Split folk themselves possess a highly developed nocturnal radar, flitting from one place to the next without ever staying anywhere long enough to make it look as if they haven't got a better party to go to.

The best way not to get disoriented is to locate Dosud, a split-level zigzag of an alley in the southwestern corner of the palace. Here you'll find ultra-trendy *Puls*, which, with its post-industrial interior and cushion-splashed stone-stepped terrace, is an essential stop on any bar crawl; and its polar opposite, *Tri Volta*, a resolutely old-fashioned local that has long catered to neighbourhood bohemians. In between the two is *Ghetto*, a temple to graffiti art with a beautiful flower-filled courtyard which occasionally hosts alfresco gigs. History doesn't record whether Diocletian was much of a drinker, but this proudly pagan emperor would surely have approved of Split's enduring appetite for Bacchic indulgence.

193 Inside a metaphor: Troy

TURKEY Zeki, the Çanakkale taxi driver, sighed when I said our destination was Truva, but he was still willing to take our fare. Later, careening along in his battered Fiat, he asked why Westerners seemed compelled to visit the desolate plateau overlooking the Dardanelles. "Rage", said my wife, separating our fighting boys. "It's all about rage", she emphasized as our two warriors lapsed into sullen silence. The answer was ingenious. Rage is mentioned in the first sentence of *The Iliad* and is the dominant emotion throughout. It's this abstract power that makes the story of the ancient city so compelling and still so relevant. Look from Troy out towards the distant sea and you realize the importance of this strategic position between Europe and Asia. Whether the city burned for a sea tax or "possession of a charming whore", there can be little doubt it would have been passionately fought over.

Yet my wife missed Zeki's point. Turkey contains remains of scores of civilizations and empires stretching from prehistory to the twentieth century. When compared to Ayia Sophia or the ruins at Ephesus, the broken walls protruding from sunburnt Hissarlik Hill seem unspectacular. Still, a century of excavation has breathed life back into the ruins. Walking around the site with Dr Manfred Korfmann's *A Tour of Troia* is insightful, but it is the fierce glory of Troy that captures the imagination. Considered the first and possibly greatest literary work about war, Homer's tale is the prototype of human conflict. The epic has supplied the themes of literature, art and cinema from Euripides to Shakespeare, and from Eugene O'Neill to Wolfgang Petersen. Stand upon the sloped ramparts, look down upon the broad Troad plain, and it is easy to imagine a besieging army gathering below. And for kids, there is the wooden horse to clamber inside, inspiring curiosity in the story in another generation.

194 Extreme measures and revolutionary art in Padua

ITALY It could be argued that the frescoes in Padua's Cappella degli Scrovegni are the single most significant sequence of paintings in all of Italy. The masterpiece of Giotto, these pictures mark the point at which the spirit of humanism began to subvert the stylized, icon-like conventions of medieval art – Giotto's figures are living, breathing people who inhabit a three-dimensional world, and for many subsequent artists, such as Masaccio and Michelangelo, the study of Giotto was fundamental to their work. But in addition to being of supreme importance, the frescoes are immensely fragile, having been infiltrated by damp rising from the swampy ground on which the chapel is built, and by moisture exhaled by millions of admiring tourists. Extraordinary measures have been taken to save the chapel from further damage: only 25 visitors at a time are allowed in, for just a quarter of an hour, and entrance is via an elaborate airlock.

The chapel was commissioned in 1303 by Enrico Scrovegni in atonement for the usury of his father, who died screaming "give me the keys to my strong box" and was denied a Christian burial. As soon as the walls were built, Giotto was commissioned to cover every inch of the interior with illustrations of the lives of Jesus, Mary and Joachim (Mary's father), and the story of the Passion, arranged in three tightly knit tiers and painted against a backdrop of saturated blue. There's little precedent in Western art for the psychological tension of these scenes – the exchange of glances between the two shepherds in *The Arrival of Joachim* is particularly powerful, as are the tender gestures of *Joachim and Anna at the Golden Gate* and *The Visit of Mary to Elizabeth*. And look out for what's said to be Giotto's self-portrait in the fresco of the *Last Judgement* – he's among the redeemed, fourth from the left at the bottom.

195 Paradise regained: Italy's oldest national park

ITALY Treading where once only royals and aristocrats could set foot is an everyday occurrence in Italy: once-forbidding palaces, castles and gardens are now open to all. One of the most exhilarating former royal enclaves is a celebration of the sheer wonder of nature, the Parco del Gran Paradiso – a pristine alpine wilderness that lies within yodelling distance of the Swiss Alps and Mont Blanc.

King Vittorio Emanuele II donated what had been the private hunting grounds of the House of Savoy to the Italian state in 1922. The rapacious royals had managed to see off the entire population of bears and wolves, but the scimitar-horned ibex – now the majestic symbol of the park – and the park's other native mountain goat species, the chamois, survived, and now thrive in the protected environment. Even the golden eagle has been reintroduced, and currently numbers about ten pairs, while you may also encounter cuddly-looking marmots, which, along with perky martens, are the preferred quarry of the major birds of prey.

In winter, the park is a paradise for skiers, particularly those of the cross-country variety, who embark from the enticing village of Cogne. But most visitors come to the park in the warmer months, when the rocky heights are spectacularly pure and hundreds of species of vibrant wildflowers dazzle the eye – and when you're also more likely to spot wildlife. The verdant valley slopes and vertiginous ridges are all traversable by kilometres of walking and hiking trails of all degrees of difficulty, which in turn link to numerous refuges where you can spend the night. There's mountaineering, too, throughout all of the ten valleys. You could try an assault on the 4000m-high summit of Gran Paradiso itself – not a particularly difficult ascent if you have the right equipment, and guides – or the more gentle trek up to the sanctuary of San Besso, a two-hour hike to over 2000m, where the church and refuge nestle under a primeval overhanging massif.

196 Stalagmites, stalactites and a human fish

SLOVENIA Of Slovenia's many show caves, none has quite the pulling power of Postojna, located in the heart of the country's beguiling Karst region. And, at more than 20km long, it is Europe's most expansive cave system. Writing about Postojna in the seventeenth century, the great Slovene polymath Janez Vajkard Valvasor remarked: "in some places you see terrifying heights, elsewhere everything is in columns so strangely shaped as to seem like some creepy-crawly, snake or other animal in front of one", an apt description for this immense grotto – a jungle of impossibly shaped stalactites and stalagmites, Gothic columns and translucent stone draperies, all of which are the result of millions of years of erosion of the permeable limestone surface by rainwater. Postojna has been Slovenia's most emblematic tourist draw ever since Emperor Franz Josef I set foot here in 1819, though the smudged signatures etched into the craggy walls would indicate an earlier human presence in the caves, possibly as far back as the thirteenth century.

Visiting the cave first entails a 2km-long ride through narrow tunnels on the open-topped cave train – a somewhat more sophisticated version of the hand-pushed wagons used in the nineteenth century – before you emerge into vast chambers of formations and colours. Among them is the Beautiful Cave, which takes its name from the many lustrous features on display; the Spaghetti Hall, so-called because of its thousands of dripping, needle-like formations; and the Winter Chamber, which is home to a beast of a stalagmite called "Brilliant", on account of its dazzling snow-white colour.

Despite all this, Postojna's most prized asset, and most famous resident, is *Proteus anguinus*, aka the Human Fish. This enigmatic 25cm-long, pigmentless amphibian has a peculiar snake-like appearance, with two tiny pairs of legs – hence the name – and a flat, pointed fin to propel itself through water. Almost totally blind, and with a lifespan approaching one hundred years, it can also go years without food, though it's been known to dabble in a spot of cannibalism. Indeed, the abiding memory for many visitors to Postojna is of this most bizarre and reclusive of creatures slinking about its dimly lit tank.

197 The Colosseum in winter

ITALY Is there a more recognizable architectural profile in existence? Featured on everything from Olympic medals to Italy's five-euro coin, the Colosseum has been the model for just about every stadium built since. Even our word "arena" derives from the Latin word for sand, which was used to soak up the blood of the unfortunate gladiators and various beasts who died here.

The Colosseum wasn't good enough for the film director Ridley Scott, who decided it was too small for the film *Gladiator* and had a larger replica mocked up in Malta instead. But for the rest of the world it does nicely as a reminder of the spectacular brutality of the Roman world, home as it was to its gladiatorial games and the ritual slaughter of exotic animals by the ton. The emperor Trajan was perhaps the most bloodthirsty ruler to raise his thumb here: his games of 108–109 AD consumed around 11,000 animals and involved 10,000 gladiators. The bloodbaths may have gone out of fashion, but the Colosseum's magnificent architecture has lost none of its power. The Romans were not known for their diminutive constructions, but this is by far the largest building they produced – and probably the cleverest too, ingeniously designed so that its 60,000 spectators could exit in around twenty minutes.

Nowadays it's a bit of a Disneyland of kiss-me-quick gladiators and long queues, so visit out of season, preferably on a weekday as soon as it opens, when there's no one around. Coming here on a gloomy January morning may not have quite the same appeal as a sunny day in spring or summer, but wandering alone through the Colosseum's grand corridors and gazing down into its perfectly proportioned arena gives you the chance to appreciate this seminal building at its best.

TURKEY You've had a satisfying day or two's heavy sightseeing in Istanbul's historic Sultanahmet district. You're culturally replete – but have a nagging feeling that you've missed something. The locals. Just what the hell do they do in this metropolis of fifteen million souls?

To find out, head across the Golden Horn to Independence Street (İstiklal Caddesi), the nation's liveliest thoroughfare. Lined with nineteenth-century apartment blocks and churches, and with a cute red turn-of-the-twentieth-century tramway, it was the fashionable centre of Istanbul's European quarter before independence, and it is now where young Istanbulites (it has the youngest population of any European city) come to shop, eat, drink, take in a film, club, gig and gawk, 24/7.

By day, bare-shouldered girls in Benetton vests, miniskirts and Converse All Stars mingle with Armani-clad businessmen riding the city's financial boom, and music stores and fashion boutiques blare out the latest club sounds onto the shopper-thronged street. At night the alleyways off the main drag come to life. Cheerful tavernas serve noisy diners (the Turks are great talkers) wonderful meze, fish and lethal raki. Later, blues, jazz and rock venues, pubs and clubs burst into life – with the streets even busier than in daylight hours. You won't see many head-scarved women here, and the call to prayer will be drowned by thumping Western sounds. But though Islam may have lost its grip on Istanbul's westernized youth, traditional Turkish hospitality survives even on Independence Street, and you may find yourself being offered a free beer or two. This is Istanbul's happening European heart; no wonder it has been heralded as "Europe's Hippest City".

A night out on

198 Independence Street

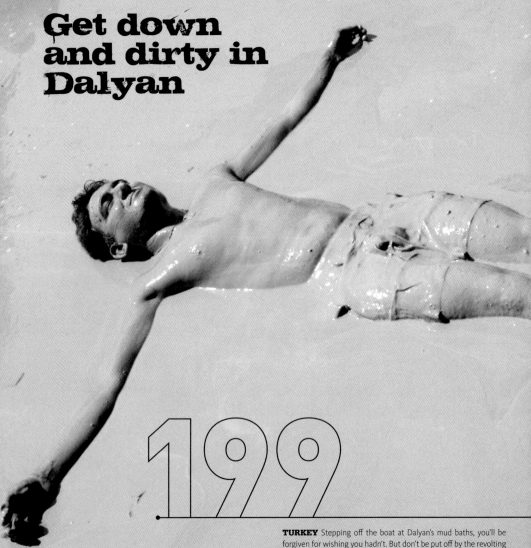

Get down and dirty in Dalyan

199

TURKEY Stepping off the boat at Dalyan's mud baths, you'll be forgiven for wishing you hadn't. But don't be put off by the revolting rotten-egg stench of the sulphur pools – after a revitalizing day here, you'll be gagging for more. The instructions are simple – roll in the mud, bake yourself in the sun till your mud cast cracks, shower off and then dunk yourself in the warm, therapeutic waters of the sulphur pool. Not only will your skin be baby-soft and deliciously tingly, you will also revert to behaving like a big kid: a huge mud bath can mean only one thing – a giant mud fight.

200 Grand Master Flash

MALTA The Knights of Malta didn't set out to create Christianity's most ornate building, but Valetta's St John's Co-Cathedral has become their defining legacy. Its interior contains such florid detail that the walls seem ablaze, while the floor is a screaming patchwork of tombstones, all uniquely rendered in dense inlaid marble. Once an austere shrine, the transformation to grand monument took place in the seventeenth century when Malta's defences were complete, and the Knights – the cream of Europe's aristocrats – embraced the exuberant Baroque style that was sweeping Catholic Europe. They courted some of the best artists to work on their church, enticing Caravaggio, whose *Beheading of St John the Baptist* is arguably one of the finest paintings of the seventeenth century.

Each side-chapel was assigned to a different regional group of nights, known as a *langue*, and each competed to outperform the others. Busts of Grand Masters are mounted among lions, angels, lances and trumpets in an orgy of self-aggrandizement. It's overwhelming: stepping outdoors into the bright Maltese light leaves you giddy and disoriented.

201 The divine dancers of Calabria

ITALY Ecstasies of the cult of Dionysus, the god of divine madness, flourish still in the fishing hamlet of Gioiosa Ionica, which hugs the Ionian Sea on the instep of Italy's boot. A legacy of the ancient Greeks, the wholly incongruous excuse for this pre-Christian bacchanal is the festival of the fourteenth-century Saint Roch, who with his dog ministered to plague victims. Every August, in the crushing summer light and heat, skimpily clad devotees throng the tiny hilltown's cobbled lanes, packing around the church at the top. When his life-size effigy breaches the portal, snare drums pound a tattoo and participants roar "Roccu, Roccu, Roccu, viva Santu Roccu! Non mi toccare che non ti toccu!" ("Roc, Roc, Roc, long live Saint Roc! Don't touch me and I won't touch you!"). Suddenly everyone leaps into a frenzied *tarantella*, an ancient fertility dance officially banned by the Church, which imitates the mating ritual of the partridge, once considered the most lascivious of creatures.

202 Tread the Plitvice boardwalks

CROATIA Plitvice Lakes National Park, some 80km from the Adriatic, is Croatia's most enticing natural attraction. Like a colossal water garden, this 8km string of sixteen crystal-clear, turquoise lakes descends through some of Europe's most primeval forests (complete with brown bears, if you know where to look), connected by rushing waterfalls and linked by footpaths, wooden bridges and walkways. Kids love the park, and Plitvice's limestone geology makes it unique, and has brought it UNESCO World Heritage Site status. As such, visiting is a well-organized affair, with big crowds in the summer. But the lakes have a minor-key majesty that makes the crowds bearable, and out of season they can be relatively quiet. By using the shuttle buses and boats, you can see much of the park in a day, taking the bus to the upper lakes and walking down. Better still, spend a few days here: there's a cluster of hotels near the middle, and private rooms in nearby villages, meaning you can get up early to enjoy the lakes in all their pristine, untouched glory.

203 Working up a lava on Stromboli

ITALY Stromboli is the most active volcano in Europe, and on clear nights its worms of red lava are visible from many kilometres away. If there was anywhere mankind was not meant to go, surely it was the crater of an active volcano. And yet the lure was irresistible.

The steady, three-hour climb to the top proved not to be difficult. We walked through aromatic maquis, passing wild roses, fig trees, prickly pears and clumps of capers. The sky was clear, the sea blue and the breathtaking view spanned Mount Etna and Calabria. I was wondering what I'd been scared of, when a resounding crash, like an iron door slamming, reminded me. I jumped. Mario the guide turned round: "Don't worry, it's normal". I tried to look as though walking up an erupting volcano were the most natural thing in the world.

Abruptly, the vegetation ended. We stopped to don heavy clothes and helmets, and follow the final ridge. At the top, all I could see were clouds of steam. Then, suddenly, four spouts of fire threw up a fountain of glowing boulders that drew tracks of light across the sky. Mario chose that moment to start talking on the radio. A panicked thought: we were in danger. But no, this was Stromboli, and things were normal – he was discussing dinner.

204 Bomb shelters for company: hiking the Ohrid border

ALBANIA & FYROM Albania and Macedonia are two of Europe's undiscovered gems. Sparsely-populated lands of chunky mountains and pastoral scenery, the two countries share not just a border but a gargantuan body of water: jaw-dropping Lake Ohrid, a majestic, sea-like expanse ringed by muscular peaks. The lake itself is no secret, and the main base – gorgeous little Ohrid town, on the Macedonian side – has witnessed something of a tourist boom, but there's still plenty of room for adventure.

You can wake literally feet from the lake in Ohrid town, the bedroom ceiling ashimmer with reflected sunlight. After an early lakeside breakfast of fish and strong coffee, a bus-taxi combo will get you to the Albanian border. High up in the mountains, this crossing sees very little traffic, which makes the hour-long walk to the main Tirana road something of a pleasure: brisk winds, occasional views of the lake – and the sudden realization that horses seem larger and much scarier in the wild. Also in evidence are clusters of dome-like bomb shelters, built in their hundreds of thousands during the despotic, isolationist rule of Enver Hoxha.

On the main road, there's little option but to flag down a shared minibus known as a *furgon* for the lakeside ride to Pogradec, a pleasant town on Ohrid's southern shore. It's tempting to overnight here and catch a sunset that throws the lake into a glistening expanse of reds and yellows, but on we press – after a delicious Albanian lunch of lamb *qöfte*, yoghurt-like *kos* and Turkish coffee, it's time to start hiking once more, this time back to Macedonia.

Despite the length of the walk – around twelve kilometres – the time flies by, with Ohrid's gentle waves lapping the shore to the left, and bomb shelter after bomb shelter to the right. Somehow, it's hard not to miss these reinforced concrete buddies once back in Macedonian territory, but on hand to mitigate any sadness is the stunning monastery of Sveti Naum, which has sat by the lake for over a thousand years, and from a distance appears to be made of gingerbread and cookies. From the monastery, occasional buses run back to Ohrid town, where there's plenty of Macedonian wine to toast the fantastic 88km route around one of the prettiest lakes in Europe.

205 Sharing the loves of the Gods at the Palazzo Farnese

ITALY One of the greatest art experiences in Italy is also one of its best-kept secrets. And for that you have to thank not the Italians, but the French, whose embassy has occupied Rome's Palazzo Farnese for the past century or so.

Inside, Annibale Carracci's remarkable ceiling fresco, *The Loves of the Gods*, was until relatively recently almost entirely off-limits, open only to scholars, VIPs and those with a proven interest in Renaissance art. Now, with a little planning, it's possible to see it for yourself on a tour. Though this is only in French and Italian, it gives access to perhaps the most extraordinary piece of work you'll see in Rome apart from the Sistine Chapel – and you get to view it with a small group of art lovers rather than a huge scrum of other tourists.

The work was commissioned from the then unknown Bolognese painter Annibale Carracci, by Odoardo Farnese at the turn of the sixteenth century to decorate one of the rooms of the palace. It's a work of magnificent vitality, and it seems almost impossible that it could be the work of just one man. In fact, it wasn't. Annibale devised the scheme and did the main ceiling, but the rest was finished by his brother and cousin, Agostino and Lodovico, and assistants like Guido Reni and Guercino, who went on to become some of the most sought-after artists of the seventeenth century.

The central painting, with its complex and dramatically arranged figures, great swathes of naked flesh and vivid colours, is often seen as the first great work of the Baroque era, a fantastic, fleshy spectacle of virtuoso technique and perfect anatomy. The main painting, centring on the marriage of Bacchus and Ariadne, which is supposed to represent the binding of the Aldobrandini and Farnese families, leaps out of its frame in an erotic hotchpotch of cavorting, surrounded by similarly fervent works illustrating various classical themes. Between and below them, nude figures peer out – amazing exercises in perspective that almost seem to stand alongside you in the room. Carracci was paid a pittance for the work, and died a penniless drunk shortly after finishing it, but the triumph of its design, and the amazing technical accomplishment of its painting, shines brighter than ever.

SOLVING THE MYSTERIES OF POMPEII

ITALY Pity the poor folk picking through the rubble of the Forum in Rome. To make the most of the ruins there you have to use your imagination. In the ancient Roman resort town of Pompeii, however, it's a little easier. Pompeii was famously buried by Vesuvius in 79 AD, and the result is perhaps the best-preserved Roman town anywhere, with a street plan that is easy to discern – not to mention wander – and a number of palatial villas that are still largely intact. It's crowded, not surprisingly, but is a large site, and it's quite possible to escape the hordes and experience the strangely still quality of Pompeii, sitting around ancient swimming pools, peering at frescoes and mosaics still standing behind the counters of ancient shops.

Finish up your visit at the incredible Villa of Mysteries, a suburban dwelling just outside the ancient city. Its layout is much the same as the other villas of the city, but its walls are decorated with a cycle of frescoes that give a unique insight into the ancient world – and most importantly they are viewable *in situ*, unlike most of the rest of Pompeii's mosaics and frescoes, which have found their way to Naples' archeological museum. No one can be sure what these pictures represent, but it's thought that they show the initiation rites

of a young woman preparing for marriage. Set against deep ruby-red backgrounds, and full of marvellously preserved detail, they are dramatic and universal works, showing the initiate's progress from naïve young girl to eligible young woman. But above all they tell a story – one that speaks to us loud and clear from 79 AD.

206

>> Southeast Europe

207 Snuffling for truffles in Piemonte

ITALY One of Italy's great seasonal events is the autumn truffle season, when Italian gastronomes descend upon the historic town of Alba in search of the white Piemontese *tartufo* or truffle. The *tuber magnatum pico* develops in cool damp chalky soil 10–15cm underground, and is only found in this part of Piemonte. Local farmers use specially trained dogs or *tabui* (literally "bastards") to sniff them out in the oak and hazelnut forests near Alba, usually at night – not only because the whole thing is tremendously secretive but also because fully mature truffles are said to emit a stronger perfume after dark.

On the final weekend in October, the market for truffles in Alba's old centre is at its peak. Once inside the covered venue, the experience is a sensory overload. Never again will you whiff so many truffles – or truffle products – in such a confined space. But buying one of these little gastronomic gems can be stressful. Prices are steep – €3000–4000 a kilo – and the market traders as sharp as they come. They'll happily let you pick up and smell as many truffles as you wish, but learning how to discern a decent truffle's characteristics isn't easy – your best bet is to watch how the locals do it. Truffles must be consumed within ten days of their discovery and should be brownish-white in colour and clean of dirt – greyish truffles are old truffles. They should be firm to the touch and knobbly in texture; a spongy truffle must be eaten that day or not at all. Look out also for any holes which might have been filled with dirt to increase the weight. Above all, be sure to smell the truffle thoroughly: a mature specimen will possess a strong and nutty bouquet. If you feel the need for a second opinion, the "Quality Commission" in the centre of the market will take a look for you. You might think they would shave off a small piece. But that's not needed. All they do is remove the truffle from the paper towel, place it on the scales, test the firmness between the thumb and index finger, and, finally, put it as close to the nose as physically possible and *SNIFF*. Once authenticated, the truffle is placed in a numbered paper bag.

Is it really worth all the hype? Well, the taste is sensual, earthy and curiously moreish, whether it's shaved thinly over pasta, or as the basis of various oils, cream sauces and butters. And where else could you get to eat something quite so gloriously expensive?

208 Bunkering down in Durres

ALBANIA A small, rickety Ferris wheel now turns on the spot in Skanderbeg Square where Enver Hoxha's colossal gilded statue once stood. After his death in 1985, the dictator's busts were gradually removed from public view and the National Historical Museum in Tirana was "ideologically renovated". However, despite the cosmetic surgery, Albania just can't seem to shrug off one legacy of Hoxha's brutal brand of Stalinism.

The ultra-paranoid dictator covered Albania's pretty rural landscape with over 700,000 bunkers – one for every four citizens – to protect his people from invading hordes of imperialists, fascists and counter-revolutionaries. The enemy tanks never arrived, but the bunkers were built so strongly that to this day few have been removed. These small concrete domes occupy every possible vantage point in the rolling countryside that flanks the road between the capital and the port city of Durres on the Adriatic coast: gloomy relics of the old regime that have been reinvented to represent the spirit of the new Albania.

The rusty ledge of one bunker's entrance is lined with pretty potted flowers, while rows of tomatoes grow defiantly around it. Inside, candles struggle to stay alight in the stale air, scarcely lighting the table around which a family of five, who have chosen to call this suffocating box home, are eating dinner. Other bunkers are painted with jaunty murals or emblazoned with the colours of football teams or lovers' names: unambiguous expressions of the new priorities in Albanians' lives. A young couple emerge from a solitary bunker on the brow of a hill, walk down to a beaten-up Mercedes parked by the roadside and stop for a lingering kiss before driving back to Tirana.

And at Durres, the odd imperialist tourist freshly arrived on the ferry from Italy sips beer and listens to one ABBA hit after another in the dark, slightly dank surroundings of a beachside bunker bar, as Hoxha turns lividly in his grave.

209 Playing for high stakes at Siena's Il Palio

ITALY Siena's famous bareback horserace – Il Palio – is a highly charged, death-defying dash around the boundary of the city's majestic Piazza del Campo. It's also likely to be the most rabidly partisan event you'll ever witness. Twice every summer riders elected by each of the city's ancient districts – the *contrade* – compete in a bid to win the much prized "Palio" or banner. Sounds like fun? It is. But the Palio is not just a bit of tourist fluff. On the two days that the race takes place – as well as throughout the exacting year-long preparations – the Sienese are playing for very high stakes indeed, and the air positively crackles with the seriousness of it all.

There's a parade around the piazza at 5pm, with banner hurlers – *bandierati* – from each *contrada*, accompanied by the chimes of the bell tower, after which the square is a riot of colour until the "War Chariot", drawn by two pairs of white oxen, displays the prize for the coming contest. The race itself takes only ninety seconds to complete, and the only rule is that there are no rules: practically any sort of violence toward rival riders or animals is permitted, and anything short of directly interfering with another jockey's reins or flinging a rider to the ground is seen as fair game. Each jockey carries a special whip or *nerbo* – by tradition fashioned from the skin of a bull's penis and thus thought to give a particularly deep sting, not to mention conferring super-potency on its wielder. The course is so treacherous, with its sharp turns and sloping, slippery surfaces that often fewer than half of the participants finish. But in any case it's only the horse that matters – the beast that crosses the line first (even without its rider) is the winner, after which the residents of the victorious district sing, dance and celebrate their victory into the small hours.

MALTA Bobbing in the sea, staring at passers-by, the eyes of a *luzzu* appear to follow you as you walk along the promenade in Marsaxlokk – Malta's premier fishing port. Traditionally painted in red, blue and yellow, with the odd patch of green, boats line the waterfront of this otherwise small village on Malta's southeast coast. The *luzzu* is one of Malta's national symbols and featured on the country's lira coins before the adoption of the euro. Originally equipped with sails, today the boats are motorized and some double as transport for tourists. Said to be the eye of Osiris, the Phoenician god of protection from evil, the *luzzu*'s eye is thought to save the boat's owners from the dangers of the sea.

A natural harbour, Marsaxlokk is home to over 250 registered fishing vessels, from the traditional *luzzu* to larger *skunas* and smaller *fregatinas* (rowing boats), in which you'll see men sitting, close to shore, handreels dangling over the side, hoping to take a catch in the pristine water. On a bright day, the sun dances off the water, drawing out the colours of the boats and reflecting off the fishing nets splayed out to dry.

If you wish to escape the glare of the *luzzus*' eyes, head towards the local market for a spot of shopping. Once purely a fish market where local fishermen sell their daily catch, Sunday is now the best day to purchase all types of aquatic produce, with other days of the week a better bet for stocking up on souvenirs including handmade bags constructed from recycled fishing nets and dyed a rainbow of colours. Once you're done strolling along the promenade, duck into one of the many restaurants along the waterfront – this is, unsurprisingly, the perfect town in which to eat fish.

SOMETHING FISHY IN
Marsaxlokk

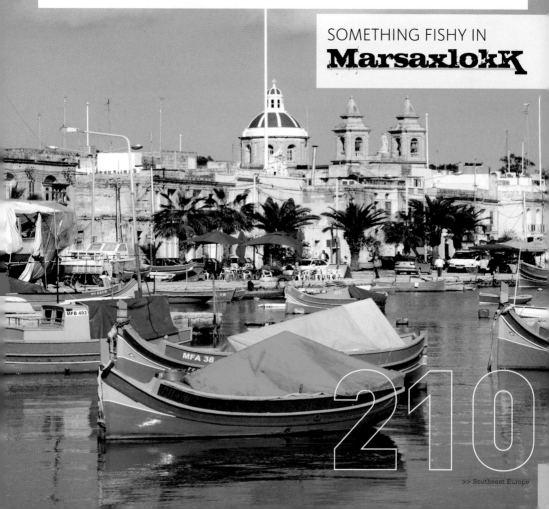

210

Into the lagoon:
Venice's other islands

ITALY You'd be mad to go to Venice and never set foot in a boat. Yet many visitors do a lot of footwork up and down little bridges, and spend little time on the water. The spectacular solution is to take the splendid jaunt down the Canal Grande on the *vaporetto* water bus (forget the overpriced, touristy gondolas), but to get a real taste of Venice you've got to plunge off in search of the city's outlying islands. When you stand at the rail of a *vaporetto* and see the city's built-up banks receding into a mirage of summer haze or winter fog, you'll start to feel the true strangeness of the place. And when your boat bumps back against the quay, and you hear the squeak of the rope tightening round the mooring posts and the distinctive rattle of the passenger gate, you may start to feel that little bit at home.

A few minutes' ride to the south of the city curls the Giudecca, a spine of joined-up islets whose broad, canalside *fondamente* gaze across at Venice's sun-drenched southern skirts. Set into the Giudecca are two serene churches by the great Renaissance architect Andrea Palladio, while a stone's throw away, on the island of San Giorgio Maggiore, stands his monastery church of St George, its tower offering a fine view across the water to the Palazzo Ducale.

North of Venice, the *vaporetti* forge deeper into the lagoon, stopping first at the strange, silent cemetery island of San Michele, where the tombs are shaded by tall cypresses and guarded by high brick walls. The island-complex of Murano is like a scaled-down Venice, complete with its own modest Canal Grande; it's known for its coloured glassware, which you can see being blown. Continuing north feels like steaming into Venice's past. Tiny, brightly painted Burano still has working fishing boats, while lonely Torcello preserves Venice's original cathedral, founded in the seventh century; gazing from its campanile across the primeval mud-flats and shallows, it's possible to feel afresh the miracle of Venice's emergence from the waters.

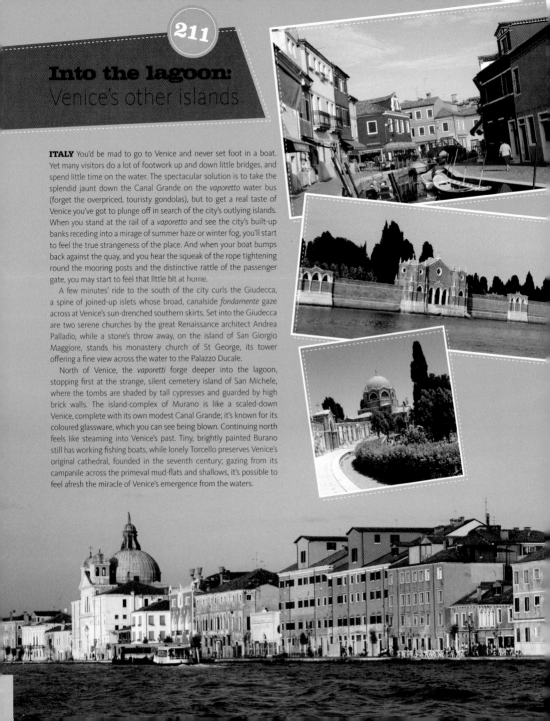

212 Visiting the home of pizza

ITALY A simple dish of bread dough spread with tomatoes and mozzarella cheese cooked in the hottest oven you can muster, pizza is probably the most widespread – and most misunderstood – fast food in the world. Given that they serve it just about everywhere, it's also the least exotic, and certainly one of the most variable. Some say that pizza is like sex: even when it's bad it's still pretty good. Truth is, it can be terrible. But in Italy, the home of pizza, it can be sublime.

Making something this elemental is a precise art, and it's all in the base – toppings are kept plain in Italy, especially in Naples, where pizza was invented. Here even cheese is sometimes considered a luxury. The base must be thrown around within an inch of its life by the pizza-maker or *piazzaiolo*, until it is light and airy, rolled thin, spread with its topping, and then thrown into a wood-fired brick oven until it just begins to burn and blister – a pizza that doesn't have at least a few traces of carbon just isn't worth eating.

Neapolitan pizzas, thin-based but typically with a thick, chewy crust, are unusually venerated; even northern Italians, who hate everything from the South, acknowledge that these are the best. Roman pizzas are no slouch either, always served crispy-thin, and, as in Naples, with the simplest of toppings – although specifically Roman ingredients like cowgetter flowers may be added. Rome is also the home of *pizza bianca* – no topping really, just sprinkled with herbs and drizzled with oil – and fantastic by the slice (*al taglio*).

You can of course get versions of the above from your supermarket, or perhaps order up a pie from the nearest delivery spot and never leave the comfort of your own home. But without making the trip to Italy you won't know what it's like to eat the real thing – and there are so many great places to do it. Some of the country's best pizzerias are the most basic, with limited menus and rough-and-ready service. One thing to remember: although you can of course get pizza any time, proper pizzerias only open in the evening. Expecting to have one for lunch will mark you out as a hopeless tourist!

213 Music, dance and drama in ancient Aspendos

TURKEY It's a hot summer's evening; overhead is a soft, purple-black and star-strewn sky. The incessant chirrup of cicadas mingles with the murmur of thousands of voices – Turkish, German, English, Russian – and the popping of corks, as the 15,000-strong audience settles down, passes round wine and olives and eagerly awaits the entertainment ahead. All are perched on hard, solid marble, still warm from the heat of the day, but the discomfort is a small price to pay to experience what a Roman citizen would have 1800 years ago, when this theatre, the largest and best preserved in Asia Minor, was built.

The views from the semicircular auditorium, its forty tiers cut into the hillside, are magnificent. At sunset, the fading light on the remains of this once wealthy and powerful city and the Pamphylian plain beyond shows it at its best. There's a faint taste of the nearby Mediterranean on the breeze and the Taurus mountain range stands in splendid silhouette to the north.

The stage lights play across the facade of the multilevel stage building, ornamented with Ionic and Corinthian columns, niches that once sported marble statues and elaborate friezes and pediments. The lights dim and the massed ranks of spectators fall silent. Slowly the intensity of the lights increases and the show begins. Maybe it's Verdi's *Aida*, set in ancient Egypt, whose pomp and splendour match the setting perfectly.

Afterwards, close to midnight, throngs of people – having suspended disbelief for a few memorable hours – disgorge into the night, scrambling not for their chariots but for cars and buses as reality sets in and the ancient entertainments are left behind.

214 Heading into deepest mafia country

ITALY The deep south, toe-end region of Aspromonte is still considered by many Italians to be out of bounds. For it is here, among the thick forests, crenellated mountain peaks and tumble-down villages, that the *n'drangheta*, or Calabrian mafia, based their empire until the 1990s. The organisation had its origins in landless nineteenth-century peasant workers who stole livestock, and by the 1980s mafia means of extracting cash had extended to regular kidnappings of local businessmen, who would be held for ransom in the dense woodland of the mountain slopes. The glare of publicity eventually drove the various ringleaders out of villages such as San Luca, and still keeps many potential visitors away.

That means that the delights of this unexplored corner of Calabria can be seen without fear of stumbling across a mafia don or a coach party. The Pietra Cuppa, or "Valley of the Large Stone", is known to locals as the Uluru of southern Italy. A vast behemoth of granite jutting out of the slopes on the Ionian Sea side of the mountains, local folklore insists that it's possible to see six human faces in the surfaces of the rock. Elsewhere, endless mountain roads corkscrew their way around the area, occasionally opening up to reveal all-but-abandoned villages clinging to the sides of cliff faces. Many have succumbed to the effects of poverty and random rock falls to create incredible ghost towns. The population of the upper half of San Luca village vacated en masse in the early 1970s, leaving villas, churches, shop fronts and gardens to the forces of nature ever since. Now whole days can be passed exploring these remains.

Accommodation in the Aspromonte mountains is limited to a rustic cabin owned by local farmer Antonio Barca. Here, perched on top of a steep hill, miles from the nearest village, evenings are spent drinking homemade wine on the veranda and eating vast platefuls of polenta and lamb chops, cooked by Antonio's wife Teresa.

Italy's last undiscovered corner is several universes away from Venice and Versace. The national staples of natural beauty and political corruption still hold sway here, but the lack of visitors, the deserted winding roads and the thrill of being at the very bottom end of the country's toe all contribute to this being a very different – and now completely safe – Italian experience.

GREECE Work off that moussaka with a hike up the most monumental of the Greek mountains – Mount Olympus. Soaring to 2920m, the mountain is swathed in mysticism and majesty, mainly due to its reputation as the home of the Ancient Greek gods. Reaching the peak isn't something you can achieve in an afternoon – you'll need at least two days' trekking, staying overnight in refuges or tents. You don't need to be a climber but you do need to be prepared: it's a tough climb to the summit, and requires a lot of stamina and some degree of caution: the weather may be stiflingly hot at the bottom, but there could still be a blizzard blowing halfway up. Passing sumptuous wildflowers and dense forests on the lower slopes, the rocky, boulder-strewn terrain and hair-raisingly sheer drops of the summit are well worth the struggle. Just watch out for Zeus's thunderbolt on the way up.

215 Conquering Mount Olympus

216 Braving the midday sun in rock-hewn Lecce

ITALY In a mid-August heatwave, the heel of Italy is not a place many people would choose to be. Still less standing in the centre of Lecce's Piazza del Duomo, a heat-sink square paved with burning-hot stone flags, surrounded by scorching stone buildings and overlooked by a sun that seems as hard and unrelenting as the rock itself. In such conditions the day begins at thirty degrees, and rises smoothly through the forties before topping out at a temperature that should be measured in gas marks, not degrees centigrade.

Squinting up at the towering stone facade of the Duomo and the adjacent bishop's palace, however, it all starts to make sense. Here, and on the surfaces of churches and palaces all over the city, the stone breaks out in exuberant encrustations, as if the very heat had caused the underlying architecture to boil over into fantastical shapes and accretions.

In fact, it wasn't the heat that caused Lecce's stone to crawl with decoration. It was a rare combination of time and place. The city lies beside a unique outcrop of soft sandstone in the razor-hard limestone that forms the tip of the heel of the Italian boot – and stonemasons' chisels take to this *pietra* Leccese like hot knives to butter. And at the very time the masons were setting to work, in the early sixteenth century, the flamboyant ornamentation of the Baroque style was taking hold in Italy. Lecce, the city they call the Florence of the South, was the fervid, sun-struck result.

217 The peace of Paestum

ITALY The travel writer Norman Lewis called it a "scene of unearthly enchantment", and Paestum is still one of southern Italy's most haunting ancient sites. Its three Greek temples brood magnificently over their marshy location just south of Naples, where, despite the proximity of the city, there are relatively few visitors. Perhaps everyone goes to Pompeii? Whatever the reason, the site is an overgrown and romantic joy, only partially excavated and still the domain of snakes, lizards and other wildlife rather than large numbers of visitors. The splendid museum holds some fantastic finds from the site, including a marvellous mosaic of a diver in mid-plunge that is worth the price of entry alone. Afterwards you can fumble your way back through the undergrowth for a lounge and a swim on some nice nearby beaches lined by scruffy campsites.

218 Haggle with horror in Istanbul

TURKEY The phrase "shop till you drop" might have been invented by a Turk, with Istanbul's Kapalı Çarşı (Grand Bazaar) in mind, for this Ottoman-era labyrinth of shops, stalls and alleys is truly the prototype for all shopping centres worldwide – a humming magnet for consumers that boasts as many as 4000 outlets selling everything from carpets, tiles and pots to mundane household items, food, antiques – you name it. There are no prices; instead *pazarlık* (haggling) is the norm, deals being done over long sessions fuelled by tea and mock horror at insulting offers. Visit here not hoping to snag a bargain, nor necessarily even to buy anything at all – despite the many entreaties from the market traders. A lack of self-induced pressure will mean you're more like to find something you like. You will certainly have a much better time.

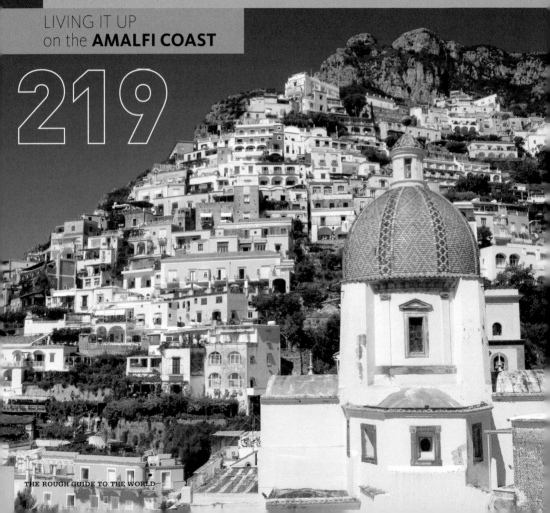

ITALY The Amalfi Coast, playground of the rich and famous, exudes Italian chic. The landscape is breathtakingly dramatic: sheer, craggy cliffs plunge down to meet the shimmering blue water and tiny secluded coves dot the coastline, accessible only by very expensive yacht. Setting off down the coastal road, you can't help but fancy yourself a bit of a jetsetter.

The drive itself deserves celebrity status; you may think you've seen coastal roads, but this one's in a class of its own, hewn into the sides of the mountain and barely wide enough for two large cars to pass comfortably, let alone the gargantuan buses that whiz between the main towns. On one side rises an impenetrable wall of mountain, on the other there's nothing but a sheer drop to the sea. Overcome the instinct to hide your head in your hands and embrace the exhilaration – this is not a ride

to miss. The road snakes its way along Europe's moneyed edge, plunging headlong into dark, roughly-hewn tunnels, curving sharply around headlands and traversing the odd crevice on the way. Every hair-raising bend presents you with yet another sweeping vista.

Don't get so caught up in the drive that you forget to stop and enjoy the calm beauty of the effortlessly exclusive coastal towns. Explore the posh cliffside town of Positano or stroll the peaceful promenades and piazzas of elegant hilltop Ravello. And in more down-to-earth Amalfi, just below, readjust to the languorous pace of resort-town life at a café before heading off to enjoy the town's sandy beach. Presided over by a towering cathedral adorned with glittering gold tiles and a lush and peaceful cloister, it's the perfect antidote to the adrenaline rush of the coast road.

LIVING IT UP
on the **AMALFI COAST**

219

220 Tackling Old Mr Three Heads

SLOVENIA It's said that every Slovene has to climb Mount Triglav, the country's highest (2864m) and most exalted peak, at least once in their lifetime. They're joined by hikers and climbers from many nations, who arrive in droves each summer. The mountain's nickname, Old Mr Three Heads (Triglav means "Three Heads"), originated with the early Slavs, who believed that it accommodated a three-headed deity who watched over the earth, sky and underworld.

The most difficult approach is via the north face, a stark 1200m-high rock wall that's certainly not for the faint-hearted. Most hikers opt for the route from Lake Bohinj further south; watched over by steeply pitched mountain faces, this brooding body of water is the perfect place to relax before embarking on the mountain trail ahead. Starting at the lake's western shore, you pass the spectacular Savica Waterfall, before a stiff climb over the formidable Komarča

cliff, and then a more welcome ramble through meadows and pastureland. Beyond here lies the highlight of this route: rich in alpine and karstic flora, the Valley of the Seven Lakes is a series of beautiful tarns surrounded by majestic limestone cliffs. The views are glorious, though by this stage most hikers are hankering after the simple comforts of a mountain hut.

Not only is Triglav a tough nut to crack in one day, but these convivial refuges are great places to catch up with fellow hikers as well as refuel with steaming goulash and a mug of sweet lemon-infused tea. Most people push on at the crack of dawn, eager to tackle the toughest part of the ascent, entailing tricky scrambles, before the triple-crested peak of Triglav looms into view. Once completed, according to tradition, there's just one final act for first-timers, namely to be "birched" – soundly thrashed across the buttocks with a branch.

221 Nuts, socks and mistletoe brandy: joining the truffle train in Buzet

CROATIA Even the most committed of culinary explorers often find the truffle an acquired taste. Part nut, part mushroom, part sweaty sock, the subtle but insistent flavour of this subterranean fungus inspires something approaching gastronomic hysteria among its army of admirers. Nowhere is truffle worship more fervent than in the Croatian province of Istria, a beautiful region where medieval hill towns sit above bottle-green forests. Summer is the season for the delicately flavoured white truffle, but it's the more pungent autumnal black truffle that will really bring out the gourmet in you. A few shavings of the stuff delicately sprinkled over pasta has an overpowering, lingering effect on your tastebuds.

The fungus-hunting season is marked by a plethora of animated rural festivals. Biggest of the lot is held in the normally sleepy town of Buzet, where virtually everyone who is anyone in Istria gathers on a mid-September weekend to celebrate the Buzetska Subotina, or "Buzet Saturday". As evening approaches, thousands of locals queue

for a slice of the world's biggest truffle omelette, fried up in a mind-bogglingly large pan on the town's main square. With the evening rounded out with folk dancing, fireworks, alfresco pop concerts and large quantities of *biska* – the local mistletoe-flavoured brandy – this is one small-town knees-up that no one forgets in a hurry.

Buzet's reputation as Istria's truffle capital has made this otherwise bland provincial town a magnet for in-the-know foodie travellers. The revered fungus plays a starring role in the dishes at *Toklarija*, a converted oil-pressing shed in the nearby hilltop settlement of Sovinjsko Polje, whose head chef changes the menu nightly in accordance with what's fresh in the village. One of the best meals you're likely to eat is in the neighbouring hamlet of Vrh, where the family-run *Vrh Inn* serves fat rolls of home-made pasta stuffed with truffles, mushrooms, asparagus and other locally gathered goodies. With the ubiquitous mistletoe brandy also on the menu, a warm glow of satisfaction is guaranteed.

222 Called by Rumi: dervishes in Istanbul

TURKEY A few years ago my wife and I had borrowed an old wooden house in Istanbul from a carpet-dealing friend. It was beloved by cats, and at dawn it echoed to the call of half a dozen minarets. There was a salon at the top of the narrow house with a tiny balcony where we could bathe our baby daughter in a washing-up basin filled with mineral water. This was necessary as the builders had walked out without plumbing the sink, which drained out over your lap and onto the floor if used, and Istanbul's tap water is lethal. Although there was a historic mosque on the edge of the neighbourhood, it was otherwise undisturbed by visitors, a quiet little residential enclave where the women would let down baskets from their apartment windows to be filled up by the grocer's boy. In the evening you could wander out through a hole in the walls and watch the long line of ships that were anchored off the Marmara shore, awaiting crews, cargoes and their chance to sail up the narrow straits of the Bosphorus. We were adopted by the local taverna, where white rice was served free of charge to our daughter and the

young waiters bossed us around shamelessly about proper child-care. One evening for a change in mood we were walking down the İstiklal Caddesi, Istanbul's main shopping street in the dusky gloom. Above the bustle of the shop-keepers and drinkers we caught the haunting sound of a single flute. Drawn by this music, we passed through a gate in the high stone walls, and, feeling increasingly nervous, walked through a garden of eighteenth-century turbaned tombs towards the source of the sound. As if in a dream, rather than being expelled by a security guard we were welcomed and shown into a beautiful octagonal hall. It was the founder of the dervish order Rumi's birthday, and on this day the Mevlevi Dervishes are allowed to celebrate with their music and whirling dances. I have been back many times since, but nothing can equal that first mysterious beckoning and the almost illicit celebration of the unworldly beauty of the mystical poet. It is said that the sound of the flute always transmits a hidden desire to be returned to the reed bed, which Rumi likened to the soul searching for its home.

223 Live like a doge: one night at the Danieli

ITALY Venice has more hotels per square kilometre than any other city in Europe, and for more than 150 years one particular establishment has maintained its status as the most charismatic of them all – the *Danieli*. Founded in 1822 by Giuseppe Dal Niel, it began as a simple guesthouse on one floor of the Palazzo Dandolo, but within twenty years it became so popular that Dal Niel was able to buy the whole building. Rechristened, the hotel established itself as the Venetian address of choice for visiting luminaries: Balzac, Wagner, Dickens, John Ruskin and Proust all stayed here, and nowadays it's a favourite with the Film Festival crowd and the bigwigs of the art world who assemble for the Biennale.

So what makes the *Danieli* special? Well, for a start there's the beauty of the Palazzo Dandolo. Built at the end of the fourteenth century for a family that produced four of the doges of Venice, the *palazzo* is a fine example of Venetian Gothic architecture, and its entrance hall, with its amazing arched staircase, is the most spectacular hotel interior in the city. The rooms in this part of the *Danieli* are furnished with fine antiques, with the best of them looking out over the lagoon towards the magnificent church of San Giorgio Maggiore. This is the other crucial factor in the *Danieli's* success – location. It stands in the very heart of Venice, right next to the Doge's Palace, on the waterfront promenade called the Riva degli Schiavoni, and in the evening you can eat at the rooftop *La Terrazza* restaurant, admiring a view that no other tables in town can equal.

All this comes at a price, of course; the *Danieli* is one of the most expensive places to stay in this most expensive of cities. There are three parts to the hotel: the old Palazzo Dandolo, known as the Casa Vecchia; an adjoining palazzo; and a block built in 1948. The best rooms, with lagoon views, are in the Casa Vecchia. If your lottery ticket has come up, however, you might want to consider the delirious gilt and marble extravagance of the Doge's Suite – yours for a mere €4000 a night.

224 Techno and turbo-folk: having a blast in Belgrade

SERBIA It is the quintessential Balkan city, a noisy, vigorous metropolis whose nightlife is as varied as it is exciting, and whose sophisticated citizens really know how to party hard. Belgrade has every right to proclaim itself the good-time capital of Eastern Europe. As good a place as any to start is Strahinjića bana, known as "Silicone Valley" thanks to the number of surgically enhanced women who parade up and down here. You can get the evening going with a glass of hoppy Nikšićko beer or a shot of Šlivjovica (a ferocious plum brandy) in one of the many über-hip bars packed cheek-by-jowl along this fantastically lively street. From here it's time to hit *Anderground*, a venerable techno joint located in the vast catacombs beneath the Kalemegdan citadel. Complete with a funky chill-out zone, this vibrant place is typical of the city's clubs, and though the scene is in a constant state of flux, good dance venues are the rule rather than the exception.

To experience a different side to Belgrade's nightlife, head down to the banks of the Danube and Sava rivers which, during the summer months, are lined with a multitude of river rafts (*splavovi*), housing restaurants, bars and discos. These places can get seriously boisterous, but are popular with devotees of Serbia's infamous turbo-folk music, a brilliantly kitsch hybrid of traditional folk and electronic pop.

If this type of music presses your buttons – and it is worth experiencing at least once – you can also check out one of the city's several *folkotekes*, discos specializing in turbo-folk. Another quirky, yet somewhat more restrained, Belgrade institution is the hobby bar; these small, privately owned cafés or bars are run by young entrepreneurs ostensibly for the entertainment of their pals, though anyone is welcome to visit. The next morning the chances are that you'll be good for nothing more than a cup of strong Turkish coffee in one of the many cafés sprawled across Trg Republike – before doing it all over again in the evening.

225 Monasteries in the air

GREECE When scouting around for a secluded refuge from the cares of the world, it's perhaps not surprising that a group of eleventh-century Greek monks should have hit upon Meteora (literally, "suspended in the air"). These otherworldly, towering sandstone pinnacles, jutting upwards from the plains of Thessaly, take the notion of remoteness to another level. In those days, access to the monasteries was by way of nets hoisted heavenwards by hand-cranked windlasses; nowadays, hard-core climbers get their kicks by making the same journey up nigh-on vertical pillars of rock with names like the Corner of Madness. For those who prefer to take the stairs, the six monasteries are also accessible by steps hewn into the rock in the 1920s. Well-worn trails zigzag between monasteries, their rust-coloured roof tiles in cheery contrast to the desolate greyness of the wind-blasted rock. Inside, you'll find superb frescoes and late Byzantine art; outside, top-of-the-world views.

226 Hot coals for Constantine

GREECE In a handful of sleepy farming villages in northern Greece, the fire-walking ritual is an annual celebration of a thirteenth-century miracle, when locals rescued icons from a burning church – without being burned themselves. By nightfall, the towering bonfire in the main square has dwindled to glowing embers. Every light is put out and all eyes are on the white-hot coals – and the cluster of people about to make the barefoot dash across them. Fire-walkers limber up for the main event with rhythmic dancing, which escalates into frenzied writhing as they channel the spirit of St Constantine, believed to shield them from harm. Clutching icons for further protection, the fire-walkers step out onto the coals, stomping on the smouldering embers with gusto, as though kicking up autumn leaves. An inspection of feet after the rite reveals miraculously unmarked soles, a sign of St Constantine's divine protection – and an excuse for a slap-up feast.

227
Sauntering through the ruins of Ani

TURKEY The ruins of Ani are a traveller's dream – picture-perfect scenery, whacking great dollops of history, and almost nobody around to see it. While Turkey as a whole has been enjoying ever more popularity as a tourist destination, the number heading to its eastern reaches remains thrillingly low, lending an air of mystery to its attractions. Of these, none are more enchanting than the rosy-pink ruins of Ani, spectacularly located amidst a grassy expanse of undulating hillocks.

In 961, Ani became capital of a Bagratid Armenian kingdom that ruled over much of what is now southeastern Turkey. Though now firmly under Turkish rule, the ruins lie a stone's throw from the modern-day border – macho types may find it impossible to resist sending a projectile over the stunning gorge that divides Turkey from Armenia. However, the two nations are still at loggerheads on certain issues, and Ani is patrolled by the Turkish *jandarma*; whole areas remain out of bounds despite the recent political thaw.

Considering the centuries of neglect, some of Ani's buildings are in amazing condition, a testament to the masterful Armenian stoneworkers of the time, and the inherent qualities of *duf*. Still used extensively in Armenia today, this pinkish rock can assume near-transcendent hues of rose, tangerine and cinnamon during sunrise and sunset. Most visitors find themselves pointing their cameras at Prkitch, an eleventh-century church that's mercifully a lot easier to photograph than it is to pronounce: known in English as the Church of the Redeemer, it was cleaved in two when struck by lightning in 1957, making it quite possibly the only church in the world that can be seen in cross-section with the naked eye.

Time has been kinder to Tigran Honents, a fresco-filled church just down the hill from Prkitch, and cathedral located just to the west – the latter is topped with a minaret that the brave may choose to ascend for an eagle-eye view of one of Turkey's most unspoilt areas.

CHEWING THE FAT:
a glutton's tour of Bologna

ITALY Bologna is "La Dotta" or "The Learned" for its ages-old university, one of the first in Europe; "La Rossa" or "The Red" for the colour of its politics. But its most deserving nickname is "La Grassa" or "The Fat" for the richness of its food. Even fiercely proud fellow Italians will acknowledge, when pressed, that Bologna's cooking is the best in the country.

This gourmet-leaning university city doesn't expect starving students to shell out a month's rent for a fine meal, either. It's the last major Italian centre where lunch with wine barely breaks €10 a head, and €25 will buy a de luxe, multicourse dinner. The only people who should be wary are vegetarians and calorie counters: dishes here are meaty and diet-busting – the Bolognese traditionally chow down on cured hams, game and creamy pasta sauces. Smells of smoked meat waft onto the sidewalk from the old-fashioned grocery-cum-canteen, *Tamburini*, off the main square; it's staffed with old, white-uniformed men, brandishing hocks of ready-to-slice prosciutto amid a clatter of dishes at lunchtime as dozens of locals jostle around the dining room. The Via delle Pescherie Vecchie nearby is still jammed with traditional market stalls, fallen produce squishing on the street and sharp-voiced women heckling the stall holders over prices.

But Bologna's love of food is clearest through its drinks: specifically, at cocktail hour, when in bars you can load up for free on *stuzzichini*, Italy's hefty answer to tapas, for as long as you nurse that G&T. With its cream sofas, sparkly chandelier and thirty-something crowd, the *Café de Paris* serves a buffet of watermelon slices and tortilla wraps, while browsing the bars and restaurants nearby will turn up both simple snacks and fancy nibbles such as dates wrapped in ham or Martini glasses full of fresh chopped steak tartare.

229 Island-hopping on the Aegean

GREECE There's an indefinable scent that, in an instant, brings the Greek islands vividly to mind. A mixture, perhaps, of thyme-covered slopes cooling overnight and the more prosaic smells of the port, of fish and octopus, overlaid with the diesel exhaust of the ferry that's carrying you there. A moment at night when you can sense approaching land but not yet see it, just moonlight reflecting off the black Aegean and sparkling in the churning wake.

Travelling between the islands by boat, it feels like little has changed in hundreds of years. Dolphins really do still leap around the prow, days are stiflingly hot, nights starlit and glassy. The ferries on the Aegean may be modern but the old adventure stubbornly refuses to die.

There are well over a thousand Greek islands, perhaps a tenth of them inhabited. Almost all of those have some kind of ferry connection, and no two are the same. From party islands like Íos or Mýkonos to the sober, monastic atmosphere of Pátmos, from tiny rocks to the vastness of Crete, there's an island for every mood. And there's a visceral thrill in travelling by sea that no plane or coach or car can ever match. Sleeping on deck under the stars; arriving in a rock-girt island port at dawn; chaos as cars and trucks and human cargo spill off the ship; black-clad old ladies competing to extol the virtues of their rooms. Clichéd images perhaps, but clichés for a reason – this is still one of the essentials of world travel, uniquely Greek, hopelessly romantic.

230 Locked up in Ljubljana

SLOVENIA Fancy being banged up for the night? Well, be Celica's guest. Born from the gutted remains of a former military prison, Ljubljana's *Hostel Celica* (meaning "cell") possesses a dozen or so conventional dorms, but it's the twenty two- and three-bed rooms, or, more precisely, cells, that makes it so unique.

Different designers were assigned to come up with themes for each one, resulting in a series of funky and brilliantly original sleeping spaces – one room features a circular bunk bed, for example, and in another a bunk is perched high above the door. That's to say nothing of the wonderfully artistic flourishes, such as the colourful murals and smart wooden furnishings, that illuminate many of the rooms. Surprisingly, the cells are not at all claustrophobic, though some authentic touches, such as the thick window bars and metal, cage-like doors, remain – there's little chance of being robbed here.

The hostel stands at the heart of a complex of buildings originally commissioned for the Austro-Hungarian army and which later served as the barracks of the former Yugoslav People's Army. Following Slovenia's declaration of independence in 1991, the complex was taken over by a number of student and cultural movements, evolving into a chaotic and cosmopolitan cluster of bars, clubs and NGOs collectively entitled Metelkova.

Despite repeated attempts by authorities to regulate, and even demolish, the site, the community has stood firm as the city's alternative cultural hub, with club nights, live music (everything from punk and metal to dub-techno) and performance art all part of its fantastically diverse programme. Indeed, if you don't fancy the short stroll into Ljubljana's lovely old town centre for a few drinks, this makes a lively place to hang out before stumbling back to your cell. Just don't throw away the key.

231 Monastic Mount Áthos

GREECE Leaving the boat I'd caught in Ouranoúpoli, the last Greek-Macedonian village before the border with the monastic republic of Áthos, I disembark at a small harbour. I toil uphill onto the peninsula's endangered cobbled-trail system, and find myself deep in broadleafed forest – without mobile reception. An anxious hour ensues before a signal reappears; it's essential to reserve a bed in advance at most of the mountain's twenty fortified monasteries.

Lunch, four hours later, is at Hilandharíou. The young monks at this thirteenth-century Serbian monastery are amazingly courteous considering NATO recently flattened their country. Despite losing my way on overgrown paths, I reach shipshape Stavronikíta on the north coast by nightfall, where I am offered a meal of soup, salad, bread and an apple – typical fast-day fare.

My room comes complete with snoring roommate; seeing my hesitation, the guest-master takes pity and lodges me in private quarters – until 3.30am, when a *símandro* (hammered-plank-bell) announces obligatory matins. After a 6am coffee and biscuit, I'm sent on my way – hospitality is for one night only – munching

on the nuts and sesame cake Áthos trekkers use to keep their strength up.

Father Iakovos, the kindly, multilingual librarian at tenth-century Iviron, greets me. I mention the disgraceful state of Áthonite paths, and he offers me Philip Sherrard's monograph on their spiritual meaning. After lunch, a monastic jeep gives me a lift to Áthos's spectacularly rugged, roadless tip, where I stay at a primitive *kellí* (agricultural colony).

Next morning, in the echoing corridors of Ayíou Pávlou monastery, a small boy, brought along by his father, cries inconsolably for his mum – unluckily for him, the only woman allowed on the Holy Mountain is the Holy Virgin.

Dawn after my last overnight at Grigoríou, on the fourth day of July trekking, finds me filthy; Áthonite guest quarters have no bathing facilities. (A particularly ripe medieval Orthodox monk, challenged about his hygiene, retorted, "I am washed once in the blood of Christ. Why wash again?"). Below the trail that takes me back to the boat, I find a secluded cove, strip naked, and plunge into the satiny Aegean.

232 Cappadocia: Land of the Fairy Chimneys

TURKEY An expanse of undulating, cave-pocked, tunnel-riddled rock at the centre of Turkey, Cappadocia is a landscape like no other. It's one of those rare places that can draw quality snaps from even the most slapdash photographer, with a rocky palette that shifts from terracotta through pink and honey to dazzling white, the orange fires of sunrise and sunset adding their own hues to the mix. From Uçhisar's castle to the cliff-hewn churches of Çavusin, there are heavenly views at every turn – surreal stone towers up to fifty metres in height pop up along innumerable valleys; some resemble witches' hats, others are mushroom-shaped, a couple defy gravitational logic and a few are markedly phallic, but to locals they're all the *peribacalar* – or "fairy chimneys".

Although the countryside is ideal for hiking, cycling or an aimless ramble, there's no need to stay on the surface. You can delve below ground into one of many underground cities, built up to 4000 years ago and once home to Christians feeling persecution,

among other groups, or float up in a balloon to watch the sun rise over the peaks. From on high you'll also see the entrances to thousands of caves which pepper the area like Swiss cheese – some towers are honeycombed with up to twenty cave-levels, hand-hewn from the rock hundreds of years ago. Before the tourist trade, the indentations found in many caves were used to harvest pigeon dung, which was then used as fertilizer in local fields. Other caverns, particularly those lining the green Ihlara Valley, served as churches to what was once a large Christian community. Although still host to the odd family, hermit or teashop, most of the caves lie empty, and some intrepid travellers save on accommodation costs by slinging their sleeping bags in out-of-the-way grottoes. However, in towns such as Çavusin and Ürgüp, or the relaxed backpacker capital of Göreme, there are a few caves that have been converted into hotels and guesthouses, letting you live the troglodyte dream without neglecting your creature comforts.

233 In the footsteps of Odysseus on Ithaca

GREECE In Homer's epic poem, the hero Odysseus needs ten years to return home to Ithaca after the Trojan War. I needed just over an hour on the early-morning ferry from Lefkas. But from the moment I set foot in the harbour of Frikes, I felt there was something special about this sleepy, rugged island. The craggy coast zigzagged south to Kiuni, an amphitheatric bay lined with swanky yachts and smart tavernas. It was pleasant enough, but I knew I'd have to embark on a little adventure of my own to really slip under Ithaca's skin.

Homer describes Ithaca as a "rocky severe island good for goats". The reason why became clear as I climbed the wildly overgrown donkey trail weaving uphill from Kiuni, where oak and pine canopies provided shade from the blistering sun. I cut a path through the thicket, keeping track of the faded blue-and-yellow signs to Anoyi and listening to the out-of-tune toll of hundreds of goat bells. Locked in a time warp, these forgotten woods are marvellously eerie and evocative of Odysseus's island. Before the

main coastal road sprang up in the nineteenth century, the island had been combed by mule trails like this, the definition of a road then being a path wide enough for two laden donkeys to pass.

Mount Niritos loomed large, but my eyes were drawn to bizarre rock formations studding the boulder-strewn plateau, in particular Heracles, a striking 8m megalith. Arriving in Anoyi, a near ghost town, I was forced to look up again – this time at a free-standing Venetian campanile that dwarfed the deserted square. Further north, Stavros's shady square was the perfect spot to sip a glass of local white and rest my weary feet. The bougainvillea-clad houses blushed pink as the sun set over the glassy Ionian Sea. It was poetic stuff and Homer's mythical verses had never seemed so appropriate:

I am Odysseus, Laertes' son, world-famed
For stratagems: my name has reached the heavens.
Bright Ithaca is my home: it has a mountain,
Leaf-quivering Neriton, far visible.

234 The murals of Tirana's tower blocks

ALBANIA Tirana's torrid twentieth century was dominated by one colour: a Communist red so deep that the country severed ties with the Soviet Union because brutal dictator Enver Hoxha believed the USSR had turned anti-Marxist since Stalin's death. The capital's skyline is still dominated by the concrete apartment buildings thrown up in the postwar period but, under wildly popular city mayor Edi Rama, these bleak structures have been daubed in all manner of murals, patterns and multicoloured stripes.

Formerly a painter himself, and armed with a lifelong passion for Picasso, legend has it that one of the first things Rama did when he took office in 2000 was order in paint. Now, after encouraging tenants and housing cooperatives to get involved in brightening up this most maligned of cities, Tirana has been transformed into a riot of purples, yellows, greens, and yes, even a little red.

Venturing into the side streets, the injection of colour seems to have bled into the atmosphere of neighbourhoods such as Bloku. Formerly a gated area for use only by Hoxha's favoured elite, the streets now thrive 24 hours a day with slinky and swaggering cocktail bars, coffee houses serving up potent espressos (a hangover from the country's Italian occupation) and alfresco opportunities galore to people watch with a bottle of the fine local beer, Korca.

"The city was without organs", Rama proclaimed. "My colours will have to replace those organs." After decades of all kinds of repression, the artistic impulses of this lovably chaotic city are now free to run riot, making this one of the best places in Europe to spend a weekend putting down the hammer and sickle and picking up the paintbrush and easel – or a coffee or beer – instead.

Classical drama at Epidavros

GREECE There's no better place to experience classical drama than the ancient theatre at Epidavros, just outside the pretty harbour town of Nafplio in the Greek Peloponnese. Dating back to the fourth century BC, it seats 14,000 people and is known above all for its extraordinary acoustics – as guides regularly demonstrate, you can hear a pin drop in its circular orchestra (the most complete in existence) even if you're sitting on the highest of the theatre's 54 tiers. It's a venue for regular performances of the plays of Sophocles and Euripedes between June and September every year. Occasionally these are in English, but whether you understand the modern Greek in which they are usually performed or not, the setting is utterly unforgettable, carved into the hill behind and with the brooding mountains beyond.

235

Striking oil in Edirne

TURKEY If you enjoy watching grown men dressed in leather and doused in oil grappling with each other, the Kirkpinar oil wrestling championships, held just outside Edirne every July since 1924, are definitely for you. Competitors are smeared all over with a special variety of olive oil before each bout, and the object is to pin your opponent's shoulders to the ground or prise out a verbal submission. Over a thousand wrestlers take part in the tournament, and you can either watch the 45-minute bouts as they happen, or just enjoy the fairground atmosphere that prevails, with Gypsy bands, dancing bears and lots and lots of kebabs.

237 Studenica's magic monasteries

SERBIA Serbia is ready for rediscovery. The steep wooded hills of the countryside south of Belgrade are beautiful and host a network of medieval monasteries located in deliberately out-of-the-way spots. Most boast well-preserved frescoes that the Serbs keenly tout as examples of their superior civilization before the Ottomans. But the real allure is in the locations – magical spots where the peace is disturbed only by the clinking of goat bells. Studenica is perhaps the greatest of them all, sitting in a gorgeous location 12km from the nearest town – Uscé – in the high alpine pastures of central Serbia; there's a hotel up there too so you can experience the location at its most exquisitely peaceful. Other monasteries include Ravanica, easily accessible on a day-trip from the capital; harder-to-get-to Kalenić; Sopoćani, whose frescoes are especially fine; and Mileşeva, southwest towards the Bosnian border, which was the last resting place of St Sava, founder of the Serbian Orthodox Church.

238 Roam Ostia Antica

ITALY Rome's best ancient Roman sight isn't in fact in the city, but a half-hour train ride away at Ostia, where the ruins of the ancient city's port (now-landlocked Ostia was once on the coast) are fantastically well preserved. Ostia was the beating heart of Rome's trading empire, but it is relatively free of the bustle of tourists you find in the city proper. There are marvellously preserved streets with shops and upstairs apartments, evocative arcaded passages and floor mosaics, and even an old café with outside seats, an original counter and wall paintings displaying parts of the menu. There's a small theatre and a main square that would have been full of traders from all over the ancient world, with mosaics of boats, ropes, fish and suchlike denoting their trade. Afterwards, climb up onto the roofs of the more sumptuous houses and enjoy the view that once would have taken in one of the ancient world's busiest harbours.

239 Face to face with the gods in Sicily

ITALY Gorgeous bays and smouldering volcanoes, boisterous markets and fabulous food, Sicily has the lot. But what's less well-known is the fact that, amid the energy and chaos of the contemporary island, it is also home to some of Italy's oldest and most perfectly preserved classical sites, sublimely located buildings that bring a distant era of heroism, hedonism and unforgiving gods to life.

Starting in the far west of Sicily, the fifth-century BC Greek temple of Segesta, secluded on a hilltop west of Palermo, enjoys perhaps the most magnificent location of all, the skeletal symmetry of its Doric temple and theatre giving views right across the bay – not to mention the *autostrada* snaking far below. Further east, just outside the south-coast town of Agrigento, there are more Doric temples, this time from a century earlier, dramatically arrayed along a ridge overlooking the sea. They would have been the imposing

setting for blood-curdling ceremonies, yet walk a bit further and you're back in the Catholic present, at the tiny Norman church of San Biagio. Inland from here, you can view the vivid mosaics of the Villa Romana just outside Piazza Armerina – sumptuous works from the fourth century AD that show manly Romans snaring tigers, ostriches and elephants, and a delightful children's hunt with the kids being chased by hares and peacocks.

Then, on the east coast, there are the marvellous theatres of Taormina and Siracusa. The former once staged gladiatorial combats and has views that encompass sparkling seas and Mount Etna – usually topped by a menacing plume of smoke. Siracusa's Greek Theatre is one of the biggest and best preserved of all classical auditoriums; it's used every summer for concerts and Greek drama, and a starlit evening at either theatre is the perfect way to round off your classical tour.

240 Enjoying Da Vinci's Last Supper

ITALY It has always been busy, and boisterous crowds still line up around the Santa Maria delle Grazie convent in Milan, sometimes for hours in the summer. But in recent years viewing Leonardo Da Vinci's *Last Supper* has been imbued with a renewed sense of wonder, mystery and, above all, conspiracy. Worn, heavily thumbed copies of Dan Brown's 2003 bestseller *The Da Vinci Code* give some indication of what's on their minds: does the image of John really look like a woman? Is there a triangle (the symbol for "holy grail") between Jesus and John? Put such burning questions aside for a moment, and use your precious fifteen minutes to focus on the real wonder inside – Da Vinci's exquisite artistry.

The Renaissance master was in his forties when he painted his depiction of Christ and the twelve disciples, a mural that also served as an experiment with oil paints, a decision that led to its decay in Da Vinci's own lifetime. It might be a shadow of its former self, but the epic 21-year restoration, completed in 1999, has

nevertheless revealed some of the original colours, and Da Vinci's skills as a painter; his technique is flawless, the painting loaded with meaning and symbolism. Light draws attention to Jesus, who sits at the centre, having just informed his disciples that one of them will betray him. The genius of the painting is the realism with which Da Vinci shows the reaction of each: Andrew on the left, his hands held up in utter disbelief; Judas, half in shadow, clutching his bag of silver; Peter next to him, full of rage; and James the Greater on the right, his hands thrown into the air.

Housed in the sealed and climate-controlled refectory of the convent, the focus on just one great work, combined with the laborious process of booking a slot and lining up to get in (25 at a time), heightens the sense of expectation. Once inside, there's usually a dramatic change in atmosphere – viewers become subdued, often overwhelmed by the majesty of the painting, and just for a second they stop looking for that elusive grail.

241 Rafting the Tara Canyon

MONTENEGRO Eighty kilometres long, and with an average depth of 1100m, the Tara river gorge is Europe's largest canyon, not to mention one of its most spectacular natural wonders. By far the most exhilarating way to get up close and personal with the Tara is to raft it, the most popular excursion being the three-hour trip between Splavište and Šćepan Polje, some 18km distant.

Once you've been kitted out in boots, life jacket and helmet, and then clambered aboard the sturdy rubber boat with around ten other equally mad souls (thankfully, a steersman is included), the thrills and spills get under way. Well, sort of. The early stages of the river are characterized by a series of soft rapids and languid, almost still waters, the silence broken only by the occasional rumble of a waterfall spilling from the steeply pitched canyon walls. But after passing beneath the magnificent Tara Bridge – a 165m-high, 365m-long, five-arched structure built in 1940 – things take a dramatic turn. The sudden increase in gradient means faster currents, which in turn means more powerful rapids. Approaching Miševo vrelo, the deepest section of the canyon, your skills as an oarsman are put to a severe test, as the foaming waters toss the raft every which way and you bounce, shake and struggle to keep balance. For those feeling vulnerable, straps on the side of the raft – somewhat unflatteringly termed "chicken lines" – are there to assist.

The river eventually relents, just in time for the home stretch. Exhausted and hungry, it's time for some Durmitor lamb, cooked in milk and prepared *ispod sača* – the traditional Montenegrin way meaning "under the coals". Served with potatoes and *kajmak* (sour-cream cheese), and washed down with a glass of local rich-red Vranac wine, it's the perfect way to round off a day on the river.

242 Take the Iron Way over the Alps

ITALY An exhilarating sense of triumph overtakes you as you climb the crest of a jagged, snow-laced limestone peak. From your roost above the valley floor, Cortina's campanile and the hotel where you had breakfast this morning are barely visible. The most spectacular climbing routes in the Dolomites are now within your grasp. You've suddenly joined the ranks of the world's elite alpine climbers – or so you would like to think. Actually, most of the credit goes to the cleverly placed system of cables, ladders, rungs and bridges known as Via Ferrata, or "Iron Way".

These fixed-protection climbing paths were created by alpine guides to give clients access to more challenging routes. During World War I, existing routes were extended and used to aid troop movements and secure high mountain positions. But today, hundreds of Via Ferrata routes enable enthusiasts to climb steep rock faces, traverse narrow ledges and cross gaping chasms that would otherwise be accessible only to experienced rock jocks.

With the protective hardware already cemented into the rock, you can climb most Via Ferrata routes without a rope, climbing shoes or the rack of expensive hardware used by traditional rock climbers. With just a helmet, harness and clipping system, you fix your karabiner into the fixed cable, find your feet on one of the iron rungs and start climbing. It's an amazingly fun way to conquer some stunning vertical terrain and quickly ascend to airy alpine paths.

Via Ferrata climbing doesn't require polished technique, exceptional strength, balance or even prior rock-climbing experience, although the sustained ascent of several hundred vertical metres means decent aerobic fitness is a distinct advantage. Once you put aside any fear of heights, you'll find secure and sure-footed excitement in this aerial playground.

243 Touring the Tuscan hill-towns

ITALY The ancient hill-town, with its crumbling houses and bell towers rising above a landscape of vineyards and olive groves, is one of the quintessential images of Italy, and nowhere in the country provides more photogenic examples than the area around Siena.

The Chianti region, immediately to the north of Siena, has numerous pretty little hill-towns, with Castellina in Chianti making the obvious target for a half-day trip. Colle di Val d'Elsa is as accessible, and while the industrial zone of the lower town mars the view a little, the upper town is a real gem. The most famous of all the Sienese satellites, however, is San Gimignano, whose tower-filled skyline is one of Europe's great medieval urban landscapes. On the downside, in high season the narrow lanes of San Gimignano get as busy as London's Oxford Street, so if you're touring in summer and don't relish the crowds, head instead to windswept Volterra, a dramatically situated place whose Etruscan origins are never far from the surface. Like Pitigliano, in the far south of Tuscany, Volterra is more a clifftop settlement than a hill-town – walk just a few minutes from the cathedral and you'll come upon the Balze, a sheer wall of rock down which a fair chunk of Volterra has tumbled over the centuries.

Some 40km south of Siena lies Montalcino, as handsome a hill-town as you could hope to find; famed for the mighty red wines produced in the surrounding vineyards, it's also very close to the ancient abbey of Sant'Antimo, one of Tuscany's most beautiful churches. From Montalcino you could loop to the even more handsome Montepulciano, which is ranged along a narrow ridge and strewn with Renaissance palaces – and is the home of another renowned wine, the Vino Nobile di Montepulciano. East of here, on the other side of the river plain known as the Valdichiana, lofty Cortona is reached by a 5km road that winds up from the valley floor through terraces of vines and olives. Clinging so closely to the slopes that there's barely a horizontal street in the centre, Cortona commands a gorgeous panorama; climb to the summit of the town at night and you'll see the villages of southern Tuscany twinkling like ships' lights on a dark sea.

BOSNIA Two decades on from the break-up of Yugoslavia, the Bosnian capital of Sarajevo contains few visible reminders that it was the scene of one of the most prolonged sieges in modern history. There is no central monument to the fallen, and certainly no signs leading to Snipers' Alley – the central thoroughfare that achieved international notoriety due to its vulnerability to enemy fire.

Which is probably why the tunnel museum, 13km southwest of the centre in a tranquil garden suburb, has become such a compelling destination for locals and visitors alike. Located in the house of the Kolar family, the museum marks the southern end of the cramped underground passage that for long stretches of the siege marked Sarajevo's only link with the outside world.

From spring 1992 until autumn 1995 Sarajevo was almost totally surrounded by Serbian forces, the only exception being the UN-controlled Sarajevo airport, which was out of bounds to both sides. The only way to break the blockade was to dig a tunnel beneath the airport runway. The resulting passage emerged right beside the Kolars' house – from where a well-defended supply route ran towards Bosnian-controlled positions in the south.

Three generations of Kolars were involved in the construction and maintenance of the tunnel, and visiting this self-financed museum you also take an intimate voyage into one family's wartime experience. Mementos and photographs are displayed in an exhibition space that feels like a cosy living room – come in winter and you'll find one of the Kolars' cats dozing in front of the heater.

A short stretch of the tunnel has been preserved beneath the house, the first few metres of which you are free to explore. For the city of Sarajevo, this claustrophobic 1.6m-high passage made the difference between survival and surrender, bringing food and military supplies into the city, and providing an escape route for civilians and the wounded – it was used by four thousand people a day. The tunnel's 800m length doesn't sound like a great deal in terms of distance, until you gaze out across Sarajevo airport from the Kolars' back garden and realize what a slow subterranean trudge it must have been.

244

Going underground
in Sarajevo

Kayaking
IN THE BAY OF KOTOR

245

MONTENEGRO Jet skis tearing through the inky bay and imposing cruise liners anchored outside medieval Kotor confirm that Europe's southernmost fjord (actually a submerged canyon) is best viewed from the water. But there's no need to sign your independence away to an Adriatic cruise – lazily kayaking around the Bay of Kotor is a wonderful way to take in the mountainous panorama that surrounds this jewel in Montenegro's increasingly popular seaboard.

Drifting towards the fortress walls and Venetian-Gothic church spires of Kotor's Old Town, in the shade of imposing Mount Lovćen, you'll feel as though you've been framed in a postcard. Idyllic villages dot the shore, while shingle beaches present tempting opportunities to rest your biceps and cool off in the sparkling water. Gliding across the calm bay aboard a kayak, finding a satisfying rhythm as your paddle slices through the sparkling water, pale stone buildings loom in and out of view and you pass restaurants selling deliciously fresh coastal specialities such as *punjene lignji* (stuffed squid) and *dagnje*

bouzzara (mussels in a tomato and onion sauce).

Depending on your itinerary (and your stamina), you might stop at Risan – the bay's oldest settlement, whose intriguing Roman history is preserved in a number of extraordinary mosaics in the Villa Urbana museum. Perched 3km further along the bay from Risan, Perast is another worthy destination where kayakers can exercise their feet. Though its diminutive size betrays little of its former significance, the town was a naval stronghold under the Venetian Empire. A fleet of around a hundred ships was based here, and the town was the site of the first nautical school in the Mediterranean, established in 1700 and the *alma mater* of many victorious Russian and Venetian naval leaders. Striking defensive towers, grand Baroque houses and palaces from Perast's maritime heyday line the waterfront, and fascinating Orthodox and Catholic churches stand along the historic streets. Returning to your faithful kayak, take inspiration from the ghosts of seafaring past as you paddle your way back through the dramatic bay.

246 Doing penance in the Sistine Chapel

ITALY You've seen them a thousand times before you even get there. Michelangelo's ceiling and wall frescoes of the Sistine Chapel are perhaps the most recognizable pieces of art in the world, reproduced so much that they've become part of the visual furniture of our lives. Getting to this enormous work isn't easy; indeed, it's almost an act of penance in itself, waiting in endless queues and battling flag-following tour groups. But none of that, nor the simple entrance to the chapel, can prepare you for the magnificence of what lies beyond.

Despite the crowds, the noise and the periodic chiding of the guards, seeing these luminous paintings in the flesh for the first time is a moving experience. The ceiling frescoes get the most attention, although staring at them for long in the high, barrel-vaulted chapel isn't great for the neck muscles. Commissioned by Pope Julius II in 1508, they depict scenes from the Old Testament, from the Creation of Light at the altar end to the Drunkenness of Noah at the other, interspersed with pagan sybils and biblical prophets, who peer out spookily from between the vivid main scenes. Look out for the hag-like Cumean sybil, and the prophet Jeremiah, a self-portrait of an exhausted-looking Michelangelo. Or just gaze in wonder at the whole decorative scheme – not bad for someone who considered himself a sculptor rather than a painter.

Once you've feasted on the ceiling, turn your attention to the altar wall, which was decorated by an elderly Michelangelo over twenty years later, depicting in graphic and vivid detail the Last Judgement. The painting took him five years, a single-handed effort that is probably the most inspired large-scale work you're ever likely to see. Its depiction of Christ, turning angrily as he condemns the damned to hell while the blessed levitate to heaven, might strike you as familiar. But standing in front of it, even surrounded by crocodiles of people, still feels like an enormous privilege.

247 Gorging on frogs and eels in the Neretva Delta

CROATIA Nowhere along the Adriatic coast are landscape and food so closely linked as in the Neretva Delta, an hour's drive north of Dubrovnik. Standing in lush green contrast to the arid mix of limestone and scrub that characterizes much of the Croatian coast, the delta is a dense patchwork of melon plantations, tangerine orchards and reedy marsh. With a shimmering grid of irrigation channels spreading across the plain, local farmers get to their fields by boat: it's not uncommon to see a row of stone-built waterside houses with a parked motor launch bobbing up and down outside each one.

The waterways of the delta teem with frogs and eels, and hunting for these slithery creatures is an age-old local preoccupation. Together they provide the backbone of a distinctive delta cuisine, and the area is fast gaining cult gastronomic status among Croatian foodies eager to reconnect with earthy regional traditions.

The hub of the Neretva Delta is the workaday river port of Metković, although the homely *konobe* (inns) in out-of-town villages like Vid, Prud and Opuzen are the best places to eat. It's in rustic establishments like these that frogs can fill a page or two of the menu, with the white meat of their hind legs either fried in breadcrumbs, grilled with garlic, or wrapped in slivers of *pršut*, the delicious local home-cured ham. However it is the tangy, succulent eel that is the real delicacy, especially when used as the key ingredient of *brudet* – a spicy red stew that's often accompanied by a glossy yellow mound of polenta.

Aiding the delta's emergence as a tourist trail for in-the-know travellers is the ultra-modern archeological museum in Vid, a reed-fringed village built on the ruins of the once prosperous second-century Roman market town of Narona. A quick examination of the imposing statues that once graced Narona's Temple of Augustus, followed by a leisurely lunch in a waterside inn, makes for the perfect delta day out.

248 Venice: Europe's first modern city?

ITALY In Venice you are constantly coming upon something that amazes: a magnificent and dilapidated palace, a lurching church tower, an impossibly narrow alleyway that ends in the water. The coffee-table books don't lie – this really is the most beautiful city in the world. The thing is, it's so beautiful that you might not see just how remarkable it is.

Weaving your way through the city, you have to remind yourself that every single building is a miracle of ingenuity; the urban fabric of Venice is extraordinarily dense, but the walls have been raised on nothing more than mudflats. The canalscapes are undeniably picturesque, but they're an extremely efficient circulatory system as well – freight in Venice goes by water, leaving pedestrians in complete control of the land. Venice was also a pioneer of industrial technologies; the glass factories of Murano were one of the Continent's earliest manufacturing zones, while the dockyards of the Arsenale were Europe's first production line, operating so smoothly that a functioning battleship could be assembled in the course of a day. Socially and politically, too, Venice was in the vanguard. At a time when most other European states were ruled by monarchs and hoodlums, Venice was a republic, and it lasted for a thousand years.

At its zenith, this was a metropolis of some 250,000 people (about four times the present population), with an empire that extended from the Dolomites to Cyprus and trading networks that spread across Asia. And trade was what made this one of Europe's great cities: the main post office was once the HQ of the German merchants, the natural history museum occupies the premises of the Turkish traders, and all over the city you'll find traces of its Greek, Albanian, Slavic, Armenian and Jewish communities.

Of course, the monuments of Venice attract tourists in their millions. Most, however, see nothing more than St Mark's Square. To escape the crowds, and see the place clearly, you just have to stroll for ten minutes in any direction and lose yourself in the world's most remarkable labyrinth.

249 Worship the cathedrals of the megalithic

MALTA Ggantija, Hagar Qim, Mnajdra, Ta' Hagrat, Ta' Skorba and Tarxien. Not the most recognizable names, but these Maltese locations host some of the world's most ancient buildings. Better known by their official title of the Megalithic Temples of Malta, the seven sites (two are at Ggantija) are listed as a UNESCO World Heritage Site, and most of them date back to around 3600 BC, before even the more famous Pyramids at Giza and England's Stonehenge.

On the main island of Malta, Tarxien is the most visited site of the seven, considered by some to be the cathedral of European megalithic culture. Discovered in 1914 by a farmer who had grown increasingly curious about the rocks that kept ruining his plough, the temple held a wealth of prehistoric artefacts, including the Magna Mater (or the "Fat Lady", as she's lovingly referred to by the locals). Estimated to have stood more than 2.5m tall when complete, only the lower half of the statue was found during excavations. The original is now housed in the archeology museum in Valletta, with a replica standing on the site of its discovery, but a visit to Tarxien will capture your imagination.

The mystery of why the temples were built – and how – continues to baffle experts worldwide, but the beauty of the spiral and dotted motifs that are carved into the stones, and the simple yet structurally sound building methods and intricately interwoven passageways, make you not really care.

250 Celebrating the Biennale

ITALY Several European cities hold major contemporary art fairs, but Venice Biennale has more glamour, prestige and news value than any other cultural jamboree. Nowadays it's associated with the cutting edge, but it hasn't always been that way. First held in 1895 as the city's contribution to the celebrations for the silver wedding anniversary of King Umberto I and Margherita of Savoy, in its early years it was essentially a showcase for salon painting.

Since World War II, however, the Biennale has become a self-consciously avant-garde event, a transformation symbolized by the award of the major Biennale prize in 1964 to Robert Rauschenberg, one of the *enfants terribles* of the American art scene. The French contingent campaigned vigorously against the nomination of this New World upstart, and virtually every Biennale since then has been characterized by controversy of some sort.

After decades of occurring in even-numbered years, the Biennale shifted back to being held every odd-numbered year from June to November so that the centenary show could be held in 1995. The main site is in the Giardini Pubblici, where there are permanent pavilions for about forty countries that participate at every festival, plus space for a thematic international exhibition. The pavilions are a show in themselves, forming a unique colony that features work by some of the great names of modern architecture and design: the Austrian pavilion was built by the Secession architect Josef Hoffmann in the 1930s, and the Finnish pavilion created by Alvar Aalto in the 1950s. Naturally enough, the biggest pavilion is the Italian one – it's five times larger than its nearest competitor.

The central part of the Biennale is supplemented by exhibitions in venues that are normally closed to the public. This is another big attraction of the event – only during the Biennale are you likely to see the colossal Corderie in the Arsenale (the former rope-factory) or the huge salt warehouses over on the Záttere. In addition, various sites throughout the city (including the streets) host fringe exhibitions, installations and performances, particularly in the opening weeks. And with artists, critics and collectors swarming around the bars and restaurants, the artworld buzz of the Biennale penetrates every corner of Venice.

251 Soldiers, monks and frescoed squid in Kosovo's monasteries

KOSOVO When it declared independence from Serbia in 2008, Kosovo hoped for a fresh start. But breaking with the past has not been easy: the scars of war are still there, from burnt-out houses to war memorials. Of course, there is much in Kosovo's history to preserve as well as to forget: a whole string of different cultures have made their mark, from the medieval Serbian kingdoms to the Ottoman Empire. But all too often Kosovo's cultural heritage has been understood only through the prism of today's ethnic divides.

Visiting the UNESCO-listed medieval Serbian Orthodox monasteries of Gračanica in central-eastern Kosovo, or Dečani and Peć in the western corner of this diamond-shaped country, gives an instant flavour of the richness of Kosovo's inheritance. But the NATO soldiers standing guard serve as a sharp reminder of the legacy of distrust from 1998–99, when both Christian and Muslim places of worship came under fire.

The Patriarchate of Peć, framed by the mountains of the Rugova Gorge, contains splendid, 2.5m frescoes of archangels – but also silver and icons rescued from nearby churches hit by ethnic rioting in 2004. In the candlelit chapels of Gračanica, just ten minutes' drive from the capital Pristina, a lively fresco of the Garden of Eden depicts the denizens of land and sea – including an oddly conspicuous squid – but books for sale show the damage done to Kosovo's churches in graphic detail, and fresh-faced Swedish soldiers stand guard in sentry boxes by the gate.

Still, there is hope that the remnants of distrust will, with time, disappear. Just 20km from Peć, at the foot of the hills that lead west to Montenegro, lies Visoki Dečani Monastery, a fourteenth-century Byzantine edifice with more than a thousand frescoes. Here, the emphasis is on what unites visitors, not what divides them. Guests attending the Thursday evensong or Sunday morning services queue to take the eucharist and kiss the icons, and after a leg-aching two hours with standing-room only, everyone is invited for a home-made meal in the refectory. As tourists, soldiers and monks gather together to eat and drink – there's even home-made plum brandy going – the differences between them seem a lot less important than the similarities.

ITALY Milan is synonymous with shopping: boutiques from all the world's top clothes and accessory designers are within a hop, skip and a high-heeled teeter from each other. The atmosphere is snooty, the labels elitist and the experience priceless.

The city has been associated with top-end fashion since the 1970s, when local designers broke with the staid atmosphere of Italy's traditional fashion home, the Palazzo Pitti in Florence. It was during the 1980s, however, that the worldwide thirst for designer labels consolidated the international reputation of home-grown talent such as Armani, Gucci, Prada, Versace and Dolce & Gabbana.

You don't need to be rich to feel part of it. These days the stores themselves make almost as important a statement as the clothes. In-house cafés are springing up, as are exhibition spaces, even barbers and spas. For a handful of euros you can sip a cocktail at *Bar Martini*, in the Dolce & Gabbana flagship store at Corso Venezia 15; enjoy an espresso and a monogrammed chocolate at the *Gucci Café* inside Milan's famous nineteenth-century Galleria Vittorio Emanuele II; or drink prosecco at the tables outside the *Armani Café*, at Via Manzoni 31, part of the four-storey temple to all things Giorgio. And, as you're here for the experience, why not head for the ultimate in bling at *Just Cavalli Food*, in Via della Spiga, where the leopardskin-clad clientele floats down in a cloud-lift to the boutique's café, which is lined with a saltwater aquarium swimming with brightly coloured tropical fish.

Shopping with style
IN MILAN

252

NEED to know

181 See ⊕www.carnevalediivrea.it for more.

182 Mystra can be reached by bus from Spárti or Néos Mystrás. It's open daily 8am–8pm (2pm in winter).

183 The restaurant is at Via dei Macci 111 (⊕www.teatrodelsale.com).

184 There are particularly well-known, and extremely popular, midnight mass celebrations on Crete, Ídhra, Corfu and Pátmos. Ferries and accommodation will be very busy; book well in advance if you want to spend Easter at Loutró.

185 Cottages in the Kornati National Park (⊕www.kornati.info) sleep two to six and can be booked through UK agencies Croatia for Travellers (⊕www.croatiafor travellers.co.uk) and Bond Tours (⊕www.bondtours.com) or travel agents in Murter – try Lori (⊕www.touristagency -lori.hr). Apartments on Palagruža can be booked through Croatia for Travellers or Adriatica (⊕www.adriatica.net). Transfers are from Korčula.

186 Pescasseroli lies on the single paved road that runs through the heart of the park, and is served by buses from Avezzano (on the Pescara–Rome rail line), Naples and – in summer only – Rome itself.

187 Šutka is 30min by bus from central Skopje – numbers #19 and #20 run here from the post office and train station respectively. Alternatively, it's only 100 MKD by cab.

188 See ⊕www.galleriaborghese.it/nuove/einfourbino .html.

189 The Duomo is on Via Duomo, 10 minutes' walk from the city's main train station.

190 The Guča festival takes place over four or five days in August. See ⊕www.guca.rs.

191 See ⊕www.firenzemusei.it.

192 Tri Volta, Ghetto and Puls are officially only open until midnight, but sometimes serve later.

193 Troy is best accessed from Çanakkale. Tours cost 30YTL upwards, and dolmuşes leave every twenty minutes.

194 Reserve online at ⊕www.cappelladegliscrovegni.it.

195 Buses run regularly from the regional capital, Aosta. ⊕www.parks.it/parco.nzionale.gran.paradiso; ⊕www .pngp.it; ⊕www.granparadiso.net.

196 Postojna can be accessed by bus or train from Ljubljana. ⊕www.turizem-kras.si.

197 The Colosseum is open daily from 9am.

198 From Sultanahmet take a tram to Karaköy then the Tünel funicular railway to the bottom of Independence Street; both close at around 9pm. Return to Sultanahmet by taxi after midnight.

199 The mud baths are accessible by boat only, with mixed bathing 11am–6pm. The pools can get busy in high season (roughly June–Aug), although there are quieter, outlying pools – ask your skipper.

200 St John's Co-Cathedral; Mon–Fri 9.30am–4.30pm, Sat 9.30am–12.30pm (last entry 30min before closing); ⊕www .stjohnscocathedral.com.

201 ⊕www.comune.marinadigioiosaionica.rc.it has details on the area.

202 Most buses between Split and Zagreb stop at the Plitvice Lakes. ⊕www.np-plitvicka-jezera.hr.

203 Climbing Stromboli is permitted only with a registered guide. ⊕www.magmatrek.it has details.

204 To get from Ohrid town to the Albanian border, first hop in a bus or shared taxi for the trip to Struga (30min), from where it's a 15km cab ride to the border crossing. There are only half a dozen buses back from Sveti Naum to Ohrid town, so check the schedule before you leave.

205 There are tours of the Palazzo Farnese in French and Italian every Monday and Thursday at 3pm, 4pm and 5pm. Book in advance, either by email to ⊕visitefarnese@farnese-italia.it, or by going to the consular office at Via Giulia 250, ⊕+39 (0) 6 6889 2818.

206 Pompeii can be reached easily by train from Naples. See ⊕www.pompeiisites.org for more information.

207 The truffle season runs from the end of September to the beginning of November, and Alba celebrates with its own fair for gourmets. More information can be found at ⊕www.tuber.it.

208 Buses run regularly to Durres from Tirana, taking around an hour.

209 To see anything, stake your claim by lunchtime in the standing-room area of the piazza; ⊕www.initaly.com/info/ palio/paliotix.htm has info on limited seated tickets.

210 Marsaxlokk is easily reached by public transport from the capital Valletta (bus 27; approx 35min).

211 Vaporetto tickets (€6.50) can be bought at most landing stages, or on board, but consider a 24hr pass (€18). The sleek water-taxis are incredibly expensive but the intrepid (and experienced) could rent a private boat; ask at the tourist office or try ⊕www.brussaisboat.it.

212 The perfect Roman pizza: Dar Poeta, Vicolo del Bologna 45 (⊕www.darpoeta.com). The perfect Neapolitan pizza: Di Matteo, Via dei Tribunali 94 (⊕www.pizzeria dimatteo.it).

213 The Aspendos Festival takes place for three to four weeks, starting in mid-June. Try ⊕secure.dobgm.gov.tr/ or ⊕www.aspendosfestival.gov.tr

214 Aspromonte can be accessed at any time of year except Dec–Feb, when snow can make roads impassable: Go to ⊕www.parks.it/parco.nazionale.aspromonte for more information on the park. The Barca farmhouse (⊕www .misafumera.it). San Luca can be reached only by car and is about 35 km away from the coastal town of Reggio Calabria, which is served by the Italian rail network.

215 The best map to use is Road Edition's no 31 Olympos, 1:50,000.

216 See ⊕www.turismo.provincia.le.it.

217 Paestum is open 9am to 1hr before sunset; €6.50. It can be reached by bus from Naples and Salerno.

218 Istanbul's Kapalı Çarşı is open Mon–Sat 9am–7pm and admission is free. Weekdays are quieter times to visit.

219 The Amalfi Coast is in Campania, southwestern Italy.

220 The tourist office in Ribčev Laz (see ⊕www.bohinj .si), 20km from Mount Triglav as the crow flies, can offer advice.

221 The Buzet tourist office (⊕www.buzet.hr) has details of the Buzetska Subotina festival. Toklarija, Sovinjsko Polje 11, ⊕+385 (0) 52 663 031.

222 See ⊕www.mevlana.net.

223 Hotel Danieli is at Riva degli Schiavoni 4196; reservations at ⊕www.danieli.hotelinvenice.com.

224 Anderground is at Pariski 1a (daily 10am–4am). Strahinjića bana, Obilićev venac and Njegoševa ulica offer the greatest concentration of bars and cafes.

225 You'll need a full day to explore Meteora (⊕www .meteora-greece.com); the town of Kalampaka, 20min by bus, is your best bet for an overnight stay.

226 Fire-walking festivals take place towards the end of May in the villages of Langadas, Ayia Eleni, Meliki and Ayios Petros in northern Greece.

227 Ani is 45km from Kars, a town accessible by bus from many Turkish cities, as well as twice-weekly trains from Istanbul. The ruins are best visited by taxi – aim for three hours at the site plus two getting there and back, and bargain hard. After paying the small entry fee the ruins are yours, though the sun can be fierce, so bring water.

228 Tamburini, Via Caprarie 1, ⊕www.tamburini.bo.it; Café de Paris, Piazza del Francia 1, ⊕+39 (o) 51 234 980.

229 The starting point for almost all Greek island travels is Athens' port at Piréas. Timetables change constantly and are subject to the weather. ⊕www.gtp.gr is a good starting

point, but the only truly accurate information is at the port, on the day: simply turn up and buy a ticket.

230 Hostel Celica is located on Metelkova ulica. See ⊕www.souhostel.com for more information.

231 Only ten males are admitted to Mount Áthos each day, for a maximum of four days. Contact the Mount Áthos office in Thessaloniki (⊕+30 2310 252 578).

232 Göreme and Ürgüp have regular bus connections to cities all over Turkey, although you often get dropped in the town of Nevsehir – 20km to the west – even if you have a ticket to Göreme.

233 From May to September, there are ferries twice daily between Vathy, Ithaca, and Sami, Kefalonia (1hr), and once daily between Frikes, Ithaca, and Nidri, Lefkas (1hr 30min).

234 It won't cost you anything to walk around Tirana, but guided tours are available from local agency Albania Holidays (⊕www.albania-holidays.com).

235 Epidavros is open daily 8am–7pm (winter until 5pm). Entrance costs €6. Plays are performed on Fri & Sat eve June–Aug.

236 ⊕www.kirkpinar.com has everything you need to know about the Kirkpinar championships, past and present.

237 Buses run from Belgrade to Ravanica. Otherwise, a hire car is a better bet, although Kraljevo (200km south of Belgrade) and the nearby village of Ušće have some useful bus links.

238 Trains (50min) run from Rome's Termini station to Ostia Antica.

239 Information and tickets for performances are available from the tourist offices at Taormina (⊕www.gateztaormina .com) and Siracusa (⊕www.comune.siracusa.it).

240 See ⊕www.cenacolovinciano.org for more.

241 Rafting is available April–Sept; Tara Tours (⊕www.tara -grab.com) offer half-day and longer excursions.

242 The Gruppo Guide Alpine ⊕www.guidecortina.com offers guided day trips, or you can stay at scenic mountain huts and go from one route to another.

243 Go to the official tourist board website (⊕www .turismo.toscana.it) for more info on Tuscany.

244 The tunnel museum is 12km southwest of the centre of Sarajevo at ul. Tuneli 1, Donji Kotorac. Tours are arranged by the tourist office, Zelenih Beretki 22, near the National Gallery.

245 Kayak Montenegro (⊕www.kayakmontenegro.com) offers guided day-trips around the Bay of Kotor from Herceg Novi as well as rentals and tailored tours.

247 There are several family-run inns 3–4km north of Metković; try Konoba Narona (⊕+385 (0) 20 687 555) and Djudja i Mate (⊕+385 020 687500), both in Vid, and Konoba Vrilo in Prud (⊕+385 020 687139). Djudja i Mate also offers cosy B&B accommodation. Regular buses (1hr 20min) run from Dubrovnik to Metković, from where you can continue by local bus or taxi to the outlying villages.

248 Venice is popular all year, so book your room well in advance. The tourist office's website (⊕www.turismo venezia.it) gives details of accommodation of all types.

249 For more on Malta's megalithic sites, visit ⊕www .heritagemalta.org. The Fat Lady and other artefacts are housed in the National Museum of Archaeology, Valletta.

250 Information on tickets and other Biennale practicalities is available at ⊕www.labiennale.org.

251 Buses from Skopje (2hr) depart several times daily, and Kosovo airport is regularly served by flights. To reach Pejě/Peć or Dečan/Dečani, take a bus from Pristina (2hr 30min); to Gračanica/Graçanice, take a taxi (10min) from Pristina. You'll need to show your passport to enter Dečani and Peć.

252 The top-name fashion stores are concentrated in the "Quadrilatero d'Oro" or "Golden Quadrilateral".

GOOD to know

TOP TUCK-INS

Gorgonzola One of the great Italian cheeses, hailing from Lombardy, blue-veined and either creamy (*dolce*) or sharp (*piccante*).

Lahmacun Street vendors in Turkey hawk these delicious small "pizzas" with meat-based toppings.

Mezes An extensive array of cold appetizers in all shapes and sizes.

Porchetta Basically roast pork, with lots of stuffing and crackling, and sold from open-air stalls in Umbria, Tuscany and Lazio.

Prosciutto di San Daniele The greatest of the great cured hams from Parma and around (actually from Friuli).

Truffles Italy produces twenty percent of all black truffles, a delicacy of Umbria, and virtually all white truffles (from Piedmont).

Tyrópites and spanakópites Cheese and spinach pies respectively, on sale everywhere in Greece.

Flower power The Turkish drink of *salep* is derived from the tubers of various orchids; its popularity has led to the decline of Turkey's wild orchid population, and its export is now illegal.

ATLANTIS

The Atlantis myth is one of the most famous of all "lost world" legends, an island state first mentioned by Plato. According to him Atlantis lay "beyond the pillars of Hercules", and eventually sank into the ocean around 9000 years before his birth. Speculation on its location has focused on numerous places, including Crete, Sardinia and Santorini in the Mediterranean.

ITALIAN FOOTBALL

English workers brought **football** to Italy in the 1890s, with James Richardson Spensley establishing Genoa in 1896, and Alfred Edwards AC Milan three years later; both clubs still incorporate the cross of St George in their team badges. Italy's national team (known as the "Azzurri" for their dark blue shirts) went on to win the World Cup four times (1934, 1938, 1982 and 2006). Italy's clubs have won 28 major European trophies, more than any other nation. Their Serie A is

one of the best leagues in the world, despite being rocked by a match-fixing scandal in 2006. The league is traditionally dominated by AC Milan and Internazionale (also from Milan), and Juventus from Turin (historically Italy's most successful team), although the two principal Rome teams, Roma and Lazio, have enjoyed some success in recent years.

INVENTIONS

Galileo Galilei (1564–1642) was born in Pisa and is regarded as the father of modern astronomy and science, making major breakthroughs in scientific method and theory, improving the telescope and discovering several of Jupiter's moons.

> *"The Balkans produce more history than they can consume"*
>
> **Winston Churchill**

BEST HOTELS

Ajia Hotel, Istanbul, Turkey A Bosphorus palace with an elegant modern interior. @www.ajiahotel.com.

Bauer il Palazzo, Venice, Italy This boutique hotel in Venice enjoys an unbeatable location in a grand palazzo on the Grand Canal. @www.ilpalazzovenezia.com.

Grand Hotel a Villa Feltrinelli, Gargnano, Italy A sumptuous palace dating from 1892 and beautifully restored, right on the shore of Lake Garda. (@www.villafeltrinelli.com)

Hotel de Russie, Rome, Italy This could just be the capital's best-located and most luxurious hotel, with a fantastic courtyard garden and a gorgeous terraced garden full of butterflies. (@www.hotelderussie.it)

Marmara Bodrum, Bodrum, Turkey A dazzling retreat with all the luxuries you could ask for, including, of course, a Turkish bath. (@www.themarmarahotels.com)

Melenos Lindos Hotel, Rhodes, Greece A boutique hotel featuring impressive

antiques and beautiful gardens. (@www.melenoslindos.com)

Punta Tragara, Capri, Italy Where better to stay on Capri, high above the Faraglioni rocks, and with a stunning poolside restaurant. (@www.hoteltragara.com)

Sea Captain's House, Santorini, Greece Set on pumice cliffs overlooking the Aegean, this soothing whitewashed paradise offers all modern luxuries. (@www.sea-captains-house.com)

Riva Hotel, Hvar, Croatia A lovely and luxurious harbourside hotel located on a stunning Adriatic island. (@www.suncanihvar.com)

Villa San Michele, Fiesole, Italy. Set in a fifteenth-century monastery, this small luxury hotel just outside Florence is pure class. (@www.villasanmichele.com)

DO ITALIANS DO IT BETTER?

Giacomo Casanova (1725–1798), a Venetian, claimed in his autobiography to have slept with 122 women, and Italians are often stereotyped as the world's greatest lovers. However, a Durex Sex Survey placed Italy twentieth in terms of frequency of sex (106 times per year compared to the winner, Greece, at 138 times).

AT THE MOVIES

Bicycle Thieves (1948) This neo-realist Italian classic is many people's favourite film of all time.

La Dolce Vita (1960) Federico Fellini's most celebrated film, satirizing the vacuity of the Sixties era in Rome.

Z (1969) Banned in Greece during the dictatorship, this tense political thriller about the assassination of a left-wing politician won an Oscar for Best Foreign Language Film.

Time of the Gypsies (1989) Ethereal, compassionate and witty film about this most marginalized of races by Bosnian director Emir Kusturica, featuring a sublime soundtrack.

The Talented Mr Ripley (1999) A disturbing tale of deception, obsession and murder, set in Venice, Rome, and along the coast near Naples.

HUNTING FOR BARGAINS IN BUDAPEST • A MINDBLOWING MUSEUM: ST PETERSBURG'S HERMITAGE • TRACKING CARNIVORES IN THE CARPATHIAN MOUNTAINS • HORRORS OF THE HOLOCAUST: VISITING AUSCHWITZ • ECCENTRIC ARCHITECTURE: WANDERING THE STREETS OF RIGA • ST PETERSBURG'S WILD WHITE NIGHTS • FISH STEW WITH A DIFFERENCE • CAVORTING WITH THE KUKERI • JOURNEYING TO THE END OF THE DANUBE • VULTURE-WATCHING IN THE MADZHAROVO NATURE RESERVE • ROAMING THE BOULEVARDS OF EUROPE'S TWILIGHT ZONE • PAYING TRIBUTE TO THE DEFENDERS OF THE MOTHERLAND • PONDERING ARMAGEDDON AT THE PLOKŠTINE MISSILE BASE • RIDING HORSEBACK THROUGH SNOW IN TRANSYLVANIA • SOVIET EXHIBITIONISM IN MOSCOW • ON THE DRACULA TRAIL IN TRANSYLVANIA • SIPPING A REAL BUD IN ČESKÉ BUDĚJOVICE • TRIAL BY TROLLEYBUS: SIMFEROPOL TO YALTA • MOUNT ELBRUS: CLIMBING EUROPE'S MIGHTIEST PEAK • HIKING IN THE TATRAS • NIGHTCLUBBING BACK IN THE (OLD) USSR • STANDING AT THE HEART OF MOTHER RUSSIA • THE GREAT ESCAPE • HIGH ON A HILL WITH A LONELY GOATHEARD • SEARCHING FOR LOST EMPIRES IN KAMIANETS-PODILSKYI • CROSSING CULTURAL BOUNDARIES IN KRAKÓW • TAKING A TRIP ON THE MOSCOW METRO • FOLLOWING MIKHAIL BULGAKOV'S FOOTSTEPS IN KIEV • SOOTHE YOUR TROUBLES AT THE HOTEL GELLERT • BEAVERING AWAY IN LAHEMAA NATIONAL PARK • WOODEN CHURCHES: "MASS" TOURISM WITH A TWIST • THE TALE AND TONGUE OF ST JOHN OF NEPOMUK • GOLDEN MOULDY: DRINKING TOKAJ IN ANCIENT CELLARS • SPENDING A NIGHT AT THE CELLS IN LIEPĀJA • HUNTING FOR BARGAINS IN BUDAPEST • A MINDBLOWING MUSEUM: ST PETERSBURG'S HERMITAGE • TRACKING CARNIVORES IN THE CARPATHIAN MOUNTAINS • HORRORS OF THE HOLOCAUST: VISITING AUSCHWITZ • ECCENTRIC ARCHITECTURE: WANDERING THE STREETS OF RIGA • ST PETERSBURG'S WILD WHITE NIGHTS • FISH STEW WITH A DIFFERENCE • CAVORTING WITH THE KUKERI • JOURNEYING TO THE END OF THE DANUBE • VULTURE-WATCHING IN THE MADZHAROVO NATURE RESERVE • ROAMING THE BOULEVARDS OF EUROPE'S TWILIGHT ZONE • PAYING TRIBUTE TO THE DEFENDERS OF THE MOTHERLAND • PONDERING ARMAGEDDON AT THE PLOKŠTINE MISSILE BASE • RIDING HORSEBACK THROUGH SNOW IN TRANSYLVANIA • SOVIET EXHIBITIONISM IN MOSCOW • ON THE DRACULA TRAIL IN TRANSYLVANIA • SIPPING A REAL BUD IN ČESKÉ BUDĚJOVICE • TRIAL BY TROLLEYBUS: SIMFEROPOL TO YALTA • MOUNT ELBRUS: CLIMBING EUROPE'S MIGHTIEST PEAK • HIKING IN THE TATRAS • NIGHTCLUBBING BACK IN THE (OLD) USSR • STANDING AT THE HEART OF MOTHER RUSSIA

Eastern Europe
253–286

Beavering away in
Lahemaa National Park

258 St Petersburg's wild
White Nights

ESTONIA

RUSSIA

LATVIA

Spending a night at the
cells in Liepāja · 286

LITHUANIA

RUSSIA

BELARUS

POLAND

280 Following Mikhail Bulgakov's
footsteps in Kiev

CZECH REP.

278 Crossing cultural
boundaries in Kraków

UKRAINE

269
Sipping a real Bud
in České Budějovice

SLOVAKIA

MOLDOVA

HUNGARY

273

259

ROMANIA

Nightclubbing back in
the (old) USSR

Fish stew with
a difference

255

Tracking carnivores in the
Carpathian Mountains

260
Cavorting with the kukeri

BULGARIA

253

Hunting for bargains
in Budapest

HUNGARY One result of Eastern Europe's economic transformation is that shopping is no longer a voyage into the unknown. Familiar international brands fill the malls, and local crafts lie hidden behind shelves of mass-produced souvenirs. Luckily, a parallel culture of flea markets and craft fairs is still going strong, and if you happen to be in Budapest over the weekend then there's no better city in which to indulge in a rummage.

Dedicated browsers should head first for the bustling flea market held outside the Petőfi Csarnok, a cultural centre in the middle of the Városliget park. With traditional porcelain sold next door to pirate DVDs and hand-operated meat-mincers, it's a bit of a mixed bag. You'll usually turn up the odd bit of folk art if you prowl the stalls for long enough; the embroidered pillowcases here are certainly better quality than those in Budapest's central souvenir shops. Fans of hammers, sickles and furry hats may be disappointed to discover that there's not as much communist-era memorabilia on display as

there used to be, although Red Army-issue gas-mask fetishists are unlikely to walk away empty-handed.

While it's the jewel-or-junk unpredictability of Petőfi Csarnok that makes it so enjoyable, serious seekers of collectables will want to head for the Ecseri antiques market on the city's southeastern fringes. A century or so of Budapest's domestic history stands piled up in the dense bazaar-like warren of stalls. If you haven't got room to stow a hat-stand in your luggage, there are plenty of smaller items that might appeal: china, cutlery, vintage postcards and piles of magazines from the 1920s and 1930s.

Those really serious about their shopping should time their visit to coincide with the monthly WAMP design-fair, an open-air market on the central Erzsébet tér featuring cutting-edge work by local designers. If you're looking for something that will bring out the individual in you, then the affordable accessories on display here should help do the trick.

254 A mindblowing museum: St Petersburg's Hermitage

RUSSIA The Hermitage's collections run the gamut of the ancient world and European art. Where else could you find Rubens, Matisse, prehistoric dope-smoking gear and the world's largest vase under one roof?

The museum occupies the Imperial Winter Palace and the Old and New Hermitages, added by successive tsars. To avoid the crowds, start by checking out the little-visited ancient Siberian artefacts in the palace's dingy ground-floor west wing. The permafrost preserved burial mounds that contained mummified humans and horses, even chariots, all discovered by Soviet archeologists 2500 years later. They even found a brazier encrusted with marijuana – Altai nomads used to inhale it inside miniature tents – which was still potent.

Next, luxuriate in the State Rooms, glittering with gold leaf and semi-precious stones. The Malachite Drawing Room has an underwater feel, awash with the eponymous green stone. On certain days, the English Peacock Clock spreads its bejewelled tail in the Pavilion Hall, whose decor fuses Islamic, Roman and Renaissance motifs. By this time the tour groups are thinking of lunch, making it a good time to investigate the art collection.

The adjacent Old and New Hermitages are stuffed with antiquities and artworks and it's difficult knowing where to turn. Old Masters are on the first floor – Botticelli, Van Dyck and twenty paintings by Rembrandt (including *Danaë*, restored after a deranged visitor slashed it) – plus works by Velázquez and Goya. If you prefer more modern art, be overwhelmed by Renoirs, Van Goghs and Gauguins – all "trophy art" taken from Nazi Germany in 1945. The Post-Impressionist collection on the top floor has a superb array of Matisses and Picassos, acquired by two Muscovite philanthropists in the 1900s. Matisse's *Music* and *Dance* were commissioned for his patron's mansion, whose owner feared that the nude flautist might offend guests, and painted out his genitals – which the Hermitage's restorers have carefully restored.

Merely glancing at each item in the collection, it would still take nine years to see the whole lot. With not quite so much time on your hands, you may prefer to browse what you missed in one of the many catalogues, from the comfort of a nearby café.

255 Tracking carnivores in the Carpathian Mountains

ROMANIA Bloodthirsty vampires, howling werewolves and medieval hamlets lashed by vicious storms – welcome to the popular, and mostly mythical, image of Transylvania. This beautiful and ancient region (from the Latin for "Beyond the forest"), nestled in the breathtakingly dramatic horseshoe curve of the Carpathian Mountains, is the location for the greatest reservoir of large-carnivore species outside Russia. It's home to Europe's biggest refuge for grey wolves, of which there are now an estimated two thousand, while more than five thousand brown bears roam the wooded slopes. It's all a far cry from the time when Nicolae Ceaușescu, a fanatical hunter, offered bounties equivalent to half a month's salary to those who killed a wolf. Once the mad, megalomaniac president realized that Romanian bears were actually quite valuable, he afforded them protected status – albeit so that he could shoot them himself.

Among the many fascinating wildlife programmes on offer in Romania, few are as popular or capture the imagination quite so much as wolf- and bear-tracking. The techniques to do this include following their prints in the soft mud or snow, sighting their droppings or looking out for telltale signs, which might include a flattened patch of grass where a bear has had an afternoon snooze, a log overturned in the frantic search for food or a tree stump that has been scratched for ants. Any animals that are caught, are tagged with a small radio transmitter that enables their behaviour and movement to be closely monitored. Due to the vastness of the terrain and the highly elusive nature of wolves and bears, there's certainly no guarantee of a sighting, but it's the tantalizing prospect of a brief encounter that makes the exhaustive search so worthwhile.

256 Horrors of the Holocaust: visiting Auschwitz

POLAND One thing that will stick in your mind is the hair. Mousy, dark clumps of it and even a child's pigtail still wound like a piece of rope, all piled together like the relics from an ancient crypt. But there are no bones here. The hair in this room was deliberately, carefully, shaved from the heads of men, women and children, ready for transportation to factories where it would be turned into haircloth and socks. This is Auschwitz, the most notorious complex of extermination camps operated by the Nazis.

No one knows how many people died here: estimates range from 1.1 million to 1.6 million, mostly Jews. They starved to death, died of dysentery, were shot or beaten. And then from 1941, the Final Solution, death by cyanide gas ("Zyklon-B"): twenty thousand people could be gassed and cremated each day.

Auschwitz still has a chilling, raw atmosphere, as if the Nazis had simply walked away the day before. You'd think the gas chambers would be the worst place – imagining the ashy smoke billowing from the chimneys, and then inside, the agonizing struggles of the naked prisoners as the gas poisoned their blood. But the horror of Auschwitz doesn't hit you at once, it spreads over you slowly, like an infection, so that the more you see, the sicker you feel, until you can't take any more. The camp video is loaded with images too horrible to take in: plastic-like bodies being bulldozed into pits, bags of bones with faces. It's a terrible place, full of terrible, haunting memories. But everyone should go – so that no one will forget.

257 Eccentric architecture: wandering the streets of Rīga

LATVIA Walking along Alberta iela in Rīga is a bit like visiting an abandoned film studio where a Biblical epic, a gothic gore-fest and a children's fairy tale were being filmed at the same time. Imperious stone sphinxes stand guard outside no. 2, while malevolent gape-mouthed satyrs gaze down from the facade across the street. Further down at no. 11, a grey apartment block with steep-pitched roofs and asymmetrical windows looks like an oversized farmhouse squatted by a community of Transylvanian counts.

Alberta iela is the most spectacular street in a city that is famous for its eccentric buildings – products of a pre-World War I construction boom that saw architects indulge in all manner of decorative obsessions. Most influential of the local architects was Mikhail Eisenstein, father of Soviet film director Sergei. Responsible for the sphinx-house at Alberta iela 2, Eisenstein filled his designs with Egyptian-, Greek- and Roman-inspired details, producing buildings that looked like extravagantly iced cakes adorning the party-table of a deranged emperor. The most famous of his creations is just around the corner from Alberta iela at Elizabetes 10, a purple and cream confection with a scarily huge pair of female heads staring impassively from the pediment.

An imprint of equal substance was left on the city by Latvian architect Eižens Laube, who brought the folk architecture of the Baltic country cottage to the city. The apartment block at Alberta iela 11 shows his trademark, with shingled roofs and soaring gables that produce a disconcerting half-breed borne of gingerbread house and Gotham City. Something of an architectural equivalent to the Brothers Grimm, Laube's creations add a compellingly moody character to the bustling boulevards of Rīga's main shopping and business districts.

Rīga's Art Nouveau-period apartment blocks seem all the more incongruous when you consider that they were built to house the stolid middle-class citizens of a down-to-earth mercantile city. Judging by the sheer number of stuccoed sprites, mythical animals and come-hither mermaids staring out from the city's facades, psychoanalysts would have had a field day analyzing the architectural tastes of Rīga's pre-World War I bourgeoisie.

258 St Petersburg's wild White Nights

RUSSIA Imagine spending all day sightseeing, taking a shower and a nap, and then looking out of the window to see the sky as bright as midday. Your body kicks into overdrive, and the whole day seems to lie ahead of you. The streets throng with people toting guitars and bottles of champagne or vodka; naval cadets and their girlfriends walking arm in arm, and pensioners performing impromptu tea-dances on the riverbank. The smell of black tobacco mingles with the perfume of lilac in parks full of sunbathers. It's eight o'clock in the evening, and St Petersburg is gearing up for another of its White Nights.

Freezing cold and dark for three months of the year, St Petersburg enjoys six weeks of sweltering heat when the sun barely dips below the horizon – its famous *Byele Nochy*, or White Nights. Children are banished to dachas in the countryside with grandparents, leaving parents free to enjoy themselves. Life becomes a sequence of *tsusovki* (gatherings), as people encounter long-lost friends strolling on Nevsky prospekt or feasting in the Summer Garden at midnight.

To avoid disrupting the daytime flow of traffic, the city's bridges are raised from 2am onwards to allow a stream of ships to sail upriver into Russia's vast interior. Although normally not a spectacle, during White Nights everyone converges on the River Neva embankments to watch, while bottles are passed from person to person, and strangers join impromptu singsongs around anyone with a guitar or harmonium – chorusing folk ballads or "thieves' songs" from the Gulag. Those with money often hire a boat to cruise the canals that wend through the heart of the city.

The bridges are briefly lowered during the middle of the night, allowing queues of traffic fifteen minutes to race across. Keeping in lane is entirely ignored, with drivers jockeying for position as if it was a chariot race. By this time, people are stripping off and jumping into the Neva – those too prodigiously drunk to realize go swimming fully clothed.

259 Fish stew with a difference

HUNGARY It's famed for its goulash, but there is far more to Hungarian cuisine than this dish alone. The speciality of southern Hungary is *halaszlé*, a blisteringly hot crimson-coloured soup with huge chunks of carp, catfish and zander floating around in it. With the Danube, Drava and Tisza rivers yielding the fish, and the paprika produced on the surrounding plains, *halaszlé* is something of a regional cultural trademark, cropping up in bus-station buffets and village pubs as well as the finest restaurants.

The unofficial capital of *halaszlé* is the Danube-hugging town of Baja, a popular staging post on the way to the fish-teeming wetlands of the Forest of Gemenc. Soup cauldrons are bubbling away throughout the year in the restaurants of Petőfi Island, a popular recreation spot reached by bridge from Baja's main square.

Each establishment keeps the details of its *halaszlé* recipe a closely guarded secret, but the results are broadly the same: huge bowls of rich red liquid served with belly-expanding portions of pasta – the latter frequently smeared with liberal portions of cream cheese. The roughly hewn lumps of fish will probably have bones, skin and fins still attached; picking out the succulent white meat only adds to the sense of epicurean ritual. All in all it's a messy business. You may well laugh at the kiddie-style bib offered to you by waiting staff, but refusing it could have fatal consequences for your favourite shirt.

Southern Hungary's consumable riches don't just stop with the fish: incendiary brandies from the local cherry, apricot and pear orchards make for an irresistible range of aperitifs. And Unicum, the coal-black herbal concoction distilled in regional capital Kecskemet, is guaranteed to settle your stomach no matter how much of the stew you've managed to get through.

260

Cavorting with the kukeri

BULGARIA When it comes to the rich folk heritage of Eastern Europe, few events carry the visceral punch of Bulgaria's annual kukeri processions. In archaic rites dating back to pre-Christian times, men gather to scare off the evil spirits of winter by donning shaggy animal disguises and dancing themselves into a state of exhaustion. Colourful and cacophonous, these celebrations are a million miles away from the sanitized folklore shows of the resorts, and are of enormous ritual significance for those who take part.

The rites are still enacted in the villages south of the Bulgarian capital Sofia, and are easy to catch if you know when and where to go. January 14 is the big date in the Pernik region, where each village has a troupe of kukeri or "mummers", charged with cleansing the community of evil and ensuring fertility in the coming year. Costumes differ from one place to the next, although they invariably feature grotesque masks resembling demons or wild beasts. Most

kukeri wear cowbells around their waists, throwing up a clanking wall of sound once they start jumping and gyrating around the streets. The processions can take all day to weave their way through their home villages, with participants stopping off for a round of home-brewed brandies and festive cakes in the households they bless en route.

Outsiders are welcome – although to ensure the good will of the kukeri you may have to offer sweets or small coins to the masked urchins who guard the entrance to each village. Some of the most compelling celebrations take place in the former uranium-mining village of Eleshnitsa on Easter Sunday. Dancers clad in huge sheepskin headdresses strut their way around the village square, with a thunder-like rumble of drum beats echoing off the surrounding buildings. Thousands of locals attend; you'll find it hard not to be drawn into the round of folk dancing that follows.

261 Journeying to the end of the Danube

ROMANIA Few rivers are as richly evocative as the Danube. Strauss made it the star of his signature waltz, and the lyrics added to his melody reflect most people's perception of the waterway's meandering course – the sweeping vales, craggy hillsides and lofty castles of a bygone age, augmented by the spires of beautiful Vienna. This is merely the first capital city to be mopped up by the Danube – Bratislava, Budapest and Belgrade also feature on its nine-nation journey from the Black Forest to the Black Sea, but few of their inhabitants are likely to be aware of the surprise that lies at the end of the river.

Just before arriving in the Romanian town of Tulcea, the Danube finally becomes too great for the land to handle. It then splits into a wide, ever-evolving delta of wetland marsh, eventually spanning over 60km between the northernmost and southernmost of its three main arms. With little here but reeds and sandbars, the area does little to encourage human habitation, but our feathered friends are in their element – throughout the year the delta plays host to gargantuan flocks of pelicans, whooper swans, great white egrets and many more.

Those who want to savour one of Europe's most idyllic corners can take a ferry from Tulcea to the Black Sea villages of Sulina or Sfantu Gheorghe. Neither are yet accessible by road, and their timeless air is further heightened by straw-roofed houses and street-wandering livestock. Few trappings of the modern day are in evidence, and it's hard to find anything but traditional Romanian food – try some Black Sea fish with a plate of mămăligă, the polenta-like national dish. Boatmen are on hand to punt adventurous visitors around the reeds, heading down narrow canals and chasing off a sea snake or two before, if you're lucky, depositing you on the coast at a prime bird-watching area. There are few more stirring sights than a pinkish wave of a million pelicans, all staring out over the mysterious Black Sea.

262 Vulture-watching in the Madzharovo Nature Reserve

BULGARIA You are crouched in juniper bushes exuding the smell of gin when suddenly the wind shifts and a foul odour sweeps through the gorge. From their perch halfway up the cliffs, three vultures launch themselves onto the thermals before plunging into the thickets of *Salix* trees, emerging with their talons and beaks laden with rotting flesh. Refocusing your binoculars, you track them back to their nests, where they start to feed a ravenous brood of chicks.

Vulture-watching at Bulgaria's Madzharovo Nature Reserve isn't your standard ornithological experience. Vultures are ugly, vicious creatures that feed on carrion; their intestinal systems have evolved to handle any microbe nature can throw at them. The Arda Gorge is one of the few breeding grounds in Europe for Egyptian, griffon and black vultures; here twitchers can also spot eight kinds of falcons and nine kinds of woodpecker as well as black storks, bee-eaters, olive-tree warblers, and several species of bats.

All this wildlife is right on the doorstep of an ex-mining town of crumbling concrete low-rises – a juxtaposition of magnificent nature and man-made stagnation that's all too common in the Rhodope Mountains.

With its forests of pine and spruce, alpine meadows, crags and gorges, this is one of the wildest and most beautiful regions of Bulgaria. Travelling to the reserve through its villages, you're struck by the degrees of separation between its Christian and Pomak (Slav Muslim) inhabitants, with some villages exclusively one, others a mixture of both – signified by churches and mosques, miniskirts and veils. With villages half-depopulated by the flight of able-bodied adults to richer nations of the European Union, and remaining subsistence farmers too poor to afford pesticides or herbicides, the land is as ecologically rich as it is economically blighted.

263 Roaming the boulevards of Europe's Twilight Zone

TRANS-DNIESTER Our bus now within sight of the "border", a youngish man sitting one seat ahead chooses this moment to break the silence. "Are you foreign?" he asks. A nod is the only possible response. "Welcome... to the Twilight Zone." His mysterious greeting delivered, the man returns to face the front, but then swings back for an equally deadpan punchline: "...and I'm not joking."

Trans-Dniester is a self-declared republic on the eastern flank of Moldova, and modern Europe's closest approximation to the former Soviet Union. Though once Soviet, Moldova's people and language have always been far more similar to those of neighbouring Romania, but this skinny sliver of land east of the Dniestr River is largely made up of Russians and Ukrainians. Following the Soviet collapse, Moldova's subsequent independence and a minor war, Trans-Dniester chose to go it alone, but even though it now has its own leader, currency, anthem and flag, it remains unrecognized by the outside world. For this reason, most governments advise against entry, for which the border police – possessing no real authority but some very real weapons – may choose to charge you anything from one to one hundred dollars, depending on their mood. A few words of Russian will go down very nicely, as will a bottle of vodka or whisky.

After squeezing through Bendery, a city just over the border, the bus dives into the capital, Tiraspol, at one point passing a gleaming football stadium – conspicuous by its presence in Europe's poorest corner, it's the most visible example of misused government funds. Tiraspol itself is remarkably laid-back, though it thankfully fulfils a few of those Soviet-era stereotypes: a wartime tank is the city's focal point; red stars and nationalist slogans are everywhere you look; and you'll probably see the odd civilian sporting a Kalashnikov, or a fleet of missiles on their way to the Ukraine. When you've wandered its wide boulevards enough for one day, head for the *Hotel Druzhba*, the town's most atmospheric place to stay (think of a Soviet version of *The Shining*). Follow the gaze of the Lenin statue and you won't miss it. It's unlikely that you'll forget it either.

264 Paying tribute to the defenders of the Motherland

BELARUS For the Belarusians, World War II was a catastrophe. In all, during the brutal three-year Nazi occupation of the then Soviet republic, almost a quarter of the population died – a tragedy that has left a profound imprint on succeeding generations. Nowhere does the nation's sense of grief retain a greater rawness than at the colossal war memorial, constructed with typical Soviet bombast, at Brest Fortress, close to the Polish border. In 1941, as today, Brest stood on a political and ideological fault line between East and West, a frontline German target during the terrifying opening assault of Operation Barbarossa. The bravery of the Soviet counter-attack became a heroic symbol of resistance for a beleaguered nation, despite the reality that the defence proved short-lived and futile, merely delaying the inevitable descent into barbarity.

It's a sombre half-hour trudge along a broad, empty boulevard out to the fortress complex on the edge of town, the eye drawn towards the monumental concrete slab carved with a giant Communist star that serves as the entrance. As you pass through, radio broadcasts, Soviet songs and the deafening thunder of artillery ring through the tunnel. Once inside, remains of the original fortress – much if it shelled to oblivion – are sparse. Instead it's a massive icon of Socialist Realist art that dominates the tableau: carved into another gigantic concrete block is the head of a huge, grim-faced soldier, jutting muscular jaw set in defiance. It's a staggeringly powerful piece of work, lent added poignancy by the eternal flame that burns beneath, and the neat tiers of memorials that lead up to it, many garlanded in beautiful wreaths. A haunting choral rendition of Schumann's *Träumerei* plays on a permanent loop.

Elsewhere, it might be tempting to dismiss this oversized monumentalism as a piece of Soviet kitsch. But here, where the scars of tragedy are never deep below the surface, it's impossible not to be bowed into mournful silence.

265 Pondering Armageddon at the Plokštine missile base

LITHUANIA It's not often you're invited to join a guided tour of a nuclear missile base, especially when you're in the middle of one of northeastern Europe's most idyllic areas of unspoiled wilderness. However, this is exactly what's on offer at the friendly tourist information centre at Plateliai, the rustic, timber-built village in the centre of western Lithuania's Zemaitija National Park.

Long popular with a happy-go-lucky bunch of Lithuanian hostellers, campers and canoeists, the park is famous for its emblematic Baltic landscape. Calm grey lakes are fringed by squelchy bogs, forests of silver birch and intricately carved wooden crosses which sprout from farmhouse gardens like totem poles. It's perversely appropriate that Soviet military planners chose this tranquil spot as the perfect place to hide a rocket base. Located at the end of a harmless-looking gravel track, the Plokštine base is virtually invisible at ground level, its low-lying grey-green domes blending sympathetically with the local landscape of stubby coniferous shrubs. There's no front door: an innocuous-looking metal panel opens to reveal a staircase, descending into an abandoned world of concrete-floored, metal-doored rooms, linked by passageways which bring to mind the galleries of an underground cave system.

Built in 1962, the installation at Plokštine was one of the first such sites in the then Soviet Union, housing four nuclear missiles capable of hitting targets throughout western and southern Europe. Closed down in 1978 and left to rot, it's now eerily empty of any signs, panels or technical equipment that would indicate its previous purpose.

Until, that is, you come to one of the silos themselves – a vast, metal-lined cylindrical pit deep enough to accommodate 22 metres of slender, warhead-tipped rocket. The missile itself was evacuated long ago, but peering into the abyss from the maintenance gallery can still be a heart-stopping experience. Especially when you consider that similar silos, from North America to North Korea, are still very much in working order.

266 Riding horseback through snow in Transylvania

ROMANIA The track to the Centrul de Echitaţie takes a sharp left off the road leaving Poiana Brasov, Romania's popular ski resort in the southern Carpathian mountains. The transformation is dramatic: the noise and bustle of skis, ski-lifts and open-air cafés dies away, and suddenly you're in the rural hinterland, where horses are still crucial to agrarian life. The world of salopettes and goggles is replaced by one of stables and deep forests; fresh snow coats the tiered fields, from which just a few hardy stalks peek up, casting tiny blue shadows against the white.

The Centrul de Echitaţie is a family-run horse centre whose farm buildings huddle in the shelter of pine trees and firs. It may seem deserted, but after a few knocks at reception you'll be greeted by a member of the brood with whom you can discuss what kind of ride you'd like – either on horseback or a horse-drawn sleigh. Go for the former and you'll be led by one of the boys to the stables and then out into the glistening fields.

Sure-footed and warm, the horse gives a reassuring rhythm to the journey, and your guide will make regular checks that everything's OK. The hush that snow brings makes everything feel closer and more still; the silence only broken by the horse's breath and the crunch of hooves in snow. This relaxed, unhurried pace takes you deeper into clumps of forest – where frost sparkles on branches already weighed down by snow – and beyond onto open hillsides. As long shadows stretch out, and as the wind whips up, you'll be ready to turn back, at peace with the world and looking forward to a warming mug of hot wine.

SOVIET EXHIBITIONISM
in Moscow

RUSSIA For a taste of all the Soviet Union once promised and an illustration of what it has come to, there's nowhere better than the all-Russian Exhibition Centre, known by its acronym VDNKh. This enormous park in northeast Moscow is a glorious illustration of Soviet hubris, an exuberant cultural mix 'n' match vision of a world where sixteen republics join hand in socialist hand to present a cornucopia of human achievement, ranging from agricultural tools and farm animals to atomic energy.

Opened in 1939 as the All-Union Agricultural Exhibition, the grounds were extended in the 1950s to include culture, science and technology, and continued to expand until 1989. Nevertheless, the overall atmosphere is of prewar optimism, when all progress was good and man was master of the world, living in a kind of mechanized agricultural paradise where even the streetlights were shaped like ears of corn.

Set around the gaudy gold fountain of the Friendship of Nations, pavilions for the former Soviet socialist republics and areas of economic achievement make a gesture towards national building

styles while remaining unmistakably Stalinist. Particularly striking are the Ukraine Pavilion, a sparkling mosaic and majolica jewelbox; the Uzbekistan Pavilion, patterned with interlocking geometric designs; and the stylish, Art-Deco-influenced Grain Pavilion. Beyond, a copy of the rocket which took Yuri Gagarin into space points skywards in front of the Aerospace Pavilion. Built in 1966, the pavilion's railway-station-like hangar and glass dome are still breathtaking in their vastness.

It's a little disappointing to find the working models of hydroelectric power stations and the herds of prize cattle long gone, and even the famous Soviet worker and collective farm girl monument vanished recently amid rumours that it's been melted down for scrap metal. But the casual traders and cheap beer stands that now fill VDNKh lend the place a certain raffish charm. Perhaps it's fitting that the monumental worker and farm girl have been replaced by a succinct image of today's Russia: rows of salesmen from the Caucasus selling everything from Belarusian bras to cheap Chinese trainers under the Aerospace Pavilion's unlit light bulbs.

268 On the dracula trail in Transylvania

ROMANIA Few figures capture the imagination as dramatically as Dracula, the bloodthirsty vampire count from deepest, darkest Transylvania – at least that's how Bram Stoker portrayed the mythical version in his 1897 novel. The real Dracula was in fact the fifteenth-century Wallachian prince Vlad Țepeș, better known as Vlad the Impaler. Although he was never accused of vampirism, his methods of execution – spread-eagled victims were bound and a stake hammered up their rectum, then raised aloft and left to die in agony – earned him a certain notoriety, especially among his long-time adversaries, the anti-crusading Turks, who were terrified of him.

Inevitably the legend of Dracula is touted for all its worth, but finding anything meaningful associated with Vlad is tricky. Aside from his birthplace in the delightful town of Sighişoara – now a high-class if kitschy restaurant – the most played-up Dracula connection is in the small southern Transylvanian town of Bran. Looking every inch like a vampire count's residence, the splendidly sited Bran Castle is hyped as Dracula's haunt and encompassed by an army of souvenir stalls flogging vampire tack. The more mundane reality, however, is that Vlad may have laid siege to it once.

Dracula's real castle lies in the foothills of the stunning Făgăraş mountains in northern Wallachia. Located just north of the village of Arefu, a steep hillside path – an exacting climb up 1400 steps – brings you to Poienari Castle, one of Vlad's key fortresses and where, allegedly, his wife flung herself out of a window, exclaiming that she "would rather have her body rot and be eaten by the fish of the Arges" than be captured by the Turks. Aside from some reasonably intact towers, this surprisingly small citadel is now little more than a jumble of ruins. However, its dramatic setting ensures an authentically spooky atmosphere, no doubt the sort that Bram Stoker had in mind when penning his masterpiece about the ultimate horror icon.

269 Sipping a real Bud in České Budějovice

CZECH REPUBLIC The best Czech pubs are straightforward places: tables, benches, beer mats and an endless supply of the best lager in the world. And there are few more atmospheric venues for drinking the stuff in than Masné kramy, the complex of medieval butchers' stalls in the southern Bohemian town of České Budějovice (Budweis in German).

Walk into the long central hall, sit down and place a beer mat in front of you. Soon enough a waiter will walk round with a large tray of frothing beer mugs and slap one down on your table. As you near the end of the glass, before you've even begun to worry about catching the waiter's eye, you'll have been served another. At which point it becomes clear why the Czechs don't go in for pub crawls. With table service the norm, you need serious strength of will (and a clear head) to get up and leave. Little surprise then that the Czechs top the world beer consumption league, downing approximately a pint a day for every man, woman and child in the country.

There's another reason why Masné kramy is a great place in which to quaff the amber nectar – they serve Budvar, produced by the only major Czech brewery not owned by a multinational. Instead, the brewery still belongs to the Czech state, primarily to stave off a takeover bid by Anheuser-Busch, the world's largest beer producer, responsible for the hugely inferior American Budweiser, or Bud as it's universally known. Litigation over the shared name has been going on for nearly a century, and looks set to continue well into the future. For the moment, however, Budvar is in safe hands and continues to be brewed according to traditional techniques. So enjoy the taste – smooth, hoppy, slightly bitter, with an undercurrent of vanilla – while the going's good.

270 Trial by trolleybus: Simferopol to Yalta

UKRAINE Bounce, bounce. Squeak, squeak. I've got an elbow in my ear, an unknown child on my lap and the cardboard box wedged under my seat, taking up all my legroom, is making strange cheeping noises. Of course there are easier ways of getting to the seaside. On the other hand, the Simferopol–Yalta trolleybus route in Crimea, at 86km and 742m – over the Angarskiy pass – is the world's longest and highest trolleybus line, so this journey is an event in itself. I wonder if the rest of the jam-packed passengers, clinging on for dear life round hair-raising bends, are also consoling themselves with that fact.

The line was completed in 1961 to ferry Soviet holidaymakers from the rail terminal at Simferopol to the Black Sea coast. I'm lucky enough to ride in a pleasingly rotund Skoda 9Tr, one of the original trolleybus fleet. There are odd moments when the trolleybus poles become detached from the overhead electric wires and the driver has to get out and haul them back into place using ropes, a process a bit like upside-down fishing.

We squeak and bounce through vine-covered villages and slow down for the long climb to the Angarskiy pass, where the silvery Crimean mountains open out on either side. Then there's the exhilarating cruise down, down, down – enough to make your ears pop – to the coast. After more than two hours of extreme discomfort in the close proximity of bossy fat grandmothers, wriggling children, and men who clearly breakfasted on vodka and garlic, the final appearance of the satiny blue Black Sea is nothing short of miraculous. Salty breezes blow in through the windows, and I find I'm almost sorry to reach Yalta. I give up the child – to whom I've become rather attached – and can't resist asking the owner of the squeaking box under my seat what's in there. It's full of cheeping yellow chicks. I still wonder why he was taking them to the seaside.

RUSSIA "Are you ready?" asks my guide as we clamber off the snowmobile at Pastuckhov Rocks. I'm not sure if I am. I'm on Mount Elbrus – at 5642m, Europe's highest mountain. It's snowing. I've been training for the climb for weeks, but now it's actually starting I freeze. "Come on," he laughs, chucking a snowball in my direction.

The peak of Mount Elbrus towers over the western Caucasus, close to the border with Georgia. The mountain's icecap feeds over twenty glaciers, serving the chilly Baksan, Kuban and Malka rivers. You can travel by cable car or snowmobile to a height of around 3000m, from where the summit is fairly accessible.

We pass clean white meadows, black rock and glacial valleys. Freezing fog gives way to a big blue sky. Later, as I throw my crampons down on the summit, I reach down to make a snowball to throw back at my guide and realize that the sun has melted the snow at the top; we are standing on a grassy plain.

Mount Elbrus:
climbing Europe's mightiest peak

271

272 Hiking in the Tatras

POLAND The country's traditional attractions – Warsaw's lively old town and Kraków's gorgeous squares – are worthwhile stops, but it's easy to forget that there is another Poland, a genuine wilderness of high (and often snowbound) peaks, populated by lynx and bears. The Tatras Mountains are as beautiful as any national park in Europe, and their numerous trails – from vertiginous ridge-walks to forested rambles – are enormously popular with the locals, who troop here in their thousands in summer. The hamlet of Kuźnice, just south of the resort of Zakopane, has a cable car that climbs to almost 2000m above sea level (it feels a lot higher); from here, the very heart of the Tatras, marked trails for walkers of all abilities pick their way among the pinnacles.

273 Nightclubbing back in the (old) USSR

MOLDOVA Hemmed in between Romania and Ukraine, tiny Moldova has not gained a great reputation as an oasis of hedonism over the years. And arriving in temperatures of -20°C in Chisinau, the capital city of this landlocked nation, it appeared from the miles of unspeakably bleak Soviet-era tenement buildings, driving snow and belching car exhausts, that the closest I was going to get to excess was necking a glass or two of vodka from under my hotel bed sheets.

This fear was only confirmed when my cab driver told me that the best place in town on a Monday was the *Military Pub*. The thought of a spartan, female-free basement full of inebriated and underpaid soldiers was hardly appealing, but when your hotel room is so cold that the bedding is dusted with a layer of frost – as I found mine was – then you haven't really got an option. At least, not in Chisinau.

The first inkling that my night in the "Pub" was going to be an interesting one was the huge Soviet-era army tank slap-bang in the middle of the dancefloor. The DJ, complete with his decks, was hidden inside it blasting out some deep house, which was being lapped up by the hordes of sultry, beautiful, smiling women and their slightly more bashful, chain-smoking boyfriends. A giant portrait of Lenin hung above the DJ-booth tank. Sandbags were lying everywhere. The atmosphere was raucous but friendly – and there wasn't an army uniform in sight.

Every few minutes, a huge bell hanging above the bar would be rung vigorously by one of the grinning staff, the signal for an urgently frugging dancer to be dragged off the floor and plonked on top of the bar where he or she would be forced to down a dark green-coloured shot of a local spirit that seemed to give everyone who drank it the sudden urge to take all their clothes off and run outside. By my reckoning, it was now down to -25°C. Strange behaviour maybe, but it somehow seemed so in keeping with this utterly unnoticed corner of Eastern Europe.

274 Standing at the heart of Mother Russia

RUSSIA Stand in the middle of Moscow's Red Square and in a 360-degree turn, the turbulent past and present of Russia is encapsulated in one fell swoop: flagships of Orthodox Christianity, Tsarist autocracy, communist dictatorship and rampant consumerism confront each other before your eyes.

Red Square, is, well, red-ish, but its name actually derives from an old Russian word for "beautiful". It might no longer be undeniably so – its sometime bloody history has put paid to that – but it continues to be Moscow's main draw. In summer, postcard sellers jostle with photographers, keen to capture your image in front of one of the many iconic buildings; but in winter, you step back in time a few decades as Muscovites, in their ubiquitous shapki fur hats, negotiate their way through piles of snow, while the factory chimneys behind St Basil's Cathedral churn out copious amounts of smoke.

It's hard to avoid being drawn immediately to St Basil's, its magnificent Mr Whippy domes the fitting final resting place of the eponymous holy fool. Should retail, rather than spiritual, therapy, be more your bag, try GUM, the elegant nineteenth-century shopping arcade, which now houses mainly western boutiques, way out of the pocket of the average Russian, but very decent for a spot of window-shopping or a coffee, or just to shelter from the elements outside. If you think that the presence of Versace and other beacons of capitalism would have Lenin spinning in his grave, you can check for yourself at the mausoleum opposite, where his wax-like torso still lies in state. Despite the overthrow of communism, surly guards are on hand to ensure proper respect is shown: no cameras or bags, no hands in pockets and certainly no laughing. Putin's police officers are never far away, casting a wary eye over it all – perhaps having learned a thing or two from Lenin's bedfellows and disciples (including Uncle Joe), who are lined up behind the mausoleum under the imposing walls of the Kremlin.

275 The great escape

POLAND At first sight the area of pine forest stretching south of Żagań betrays few signs of the iconic place it occupies in popular culture. Yet this tranquil corner of western Poland was once home to an archipelago of German prisoner-of-war camps, most famous of which was Stalag Luft III. Built to intern escape-obsessed allied airmen, the camp went on to inspire two of the best-loved tunnel-digging movies ever made.

The first of these films was *The Wooden Horse* (1950), a true story of how plucky prisoners used a vaulting horse as a cover for their tunnelling activities. This was eclipsed in 1963 by *The Great Escape*, the all-star, epic retelling of a mass break-out that occurred in March 1944.

A museum at the edge of the forest recalls the history of the camps in disarmingly understated style, focusing on the fates of all of Żagań's POWs rather than the heroics of the few. Devotees of *The Great Escape* may be disappointed by the absence of any pictures of Steve McQueen attempting to cross the Swiss border on a motorcycle – but McQueen's character was in fact invented by Hollywood scriptwriters to increase American interest in the story.

The real-life Great Escape was masterminded by RAF Squadron Leader Roger Bushell, who aimed to get hundreds of prisoners out of the camp via three tunnels codenamed Tom, Dick and Harry. The first two were discovered by the Germans, but on the night of March 24, 1944, a total of 76 prisoners made their way out of Harry and into the surrounding woods.

The site of Harry is marked by an engraved boulder a half-hour's walk from the museum. It's a popular spot for laying wreaths and to reflect: only three of the great escapees ever reached the UK; of those recaptured, fifty were executed by the Germans to serve as an example to other prisoners.

276 High on a hill with a lonely goatherd

BULGARIA Most people tend to use an alarm clock, but in rural Bulgaria you can rely on the goats to get you out of bed. In the east Bulgarian village of Zheravna, an age-old Balkan ritual is enacted daily between 6 and 7am, when the local goatherd takes the beasts to pasture, collecting them one by one from the individual households where they spend the night. Bells clanging raucously as they pass, it makes for a novel dawn chorus.

With tumbledown stone houses leaning over crooked cobbled alleyways, Zheravna is a perfect example of a village whose rustic character has remained largely unchanged since the nineteenth century. Goat farming is no longer the most lucrative of industries, however, and rural depopulation has all but emptied the place of its young. Nowadays, the renovation of old houses and the development of rustic B&Bs points at a tourist-friendly future.

Zheravna is far from being the only remote community whose combination of highland scenery, historic architecture and hospitable landladies has made it a crucial stop-off on any village-hopping itinerary. Lying at the end of a potholed mountain road in Bulgaria's rugged southwest, Kovachevitsa is a bewitching knot of half-timbered houses and full of no-frills accommodation: just don't expect to see "vacancy" signs hanging outside gateways or tourist offices taking reservations. Instead, Kovachevitsa's mayoress hangs around at the village tavern keeping an eye open for any approaching cars bearing registration plates she doesn't immediately recognize. She then guides the newcomers to the house of a granny she knows who has a double bed made up and ready. Breakfast will include locally made herbal teas, and yoghurt so healthy it could add years to your life.

There's not a great deal to do when you get here, although that is undoubtedly part of the attraction. Lolling around in wildflower-carpeted meadows and meditating in the middle of a pine forest are just two of the activities on offer. If stuck for ideas you could always follow the goats, whose taste for invigorating air and gourmet grasses will lead you up into some exhilarating wilderness areas.

SEARCHING FOR **LOST EMPIRES** IN KAMIANETS-PODILSKYI

UKRAINE There can't be many Catholic cathedrals that have a minaret standing right outside the front door – but then this is Kamianets-Podilskyi, a town that has over the centuries seen more than its fair share of regime change.

At a time when the seventeenth-century Polish-Lithuanian commonwealth was engaged in decade-spanning struggles with the Ottoman Empire, Kamianets was the border fortress that frequently proved pivotal to whole campaigns. With many of its grizzled battlements still in good shape, it remains a one-stop history lesson in the struggles that shaped Europe's southeastern margins.

The town's position is as dramatic as they come, sitting on a rocky plateau surrounded by the looping gorge of the River Smotrych. Kamianets's ridge-top fortress is certainly one of the most romantic-looking castles you're likely to visit, its pointy-tipped cylindrical towers spearing upwards like something out of a medieval manuscript.

North of the fortress, the Old Town is an engaging agglomeration of cobbled alleys, cast-iron street lamps and pastel-coloured houses. It was traditionally divided into four quarters: Polish, Ukrainian, Armenian and Jewish. Standing in mute testimony to this multicultural past are some magnificent churches and a gorge-hugging restaurant that turns out to be a former synagogue. The communities themselves have largely disappeared: the Armenian presence faded as east-west trade routes dried up, Poles were forced out by Soviet power in the 1920s, and Kamianets's Jews were murdered during a two-day Nazi killing spree in August 1941. Even the Ukrainians find themselves outnumbered by newer arrivals, and today Russian is the language you will hear most on the streets.

Although popular with Ukrainian and Polish tourists, the town sees little in the way of visitors from further afield – so if you're looking for one of Eastern Europe's true historical jewels, come to Kamianets.

POLAND Poland's oldest football team, Cracovia Kraków, serves as a metaphor for the multicultural history of the city. During the interwar years, Cracovia was nicknamed the "Yids" because significant members of Kraków's Jewish community were on both the terraces and the team sheet. It also happened to be the favourite team of local boy Karol Wojtyła, who would later become Pope John Paul II.

Before World War II, many of Cracovia's supporters came from Kazimierz, the inner-city suburb where Poles and Jews had lived cheek-by-jowl for centuries. Most of Kazimierz's Jews perished in the nearby camps of Płaszów and Auschwitz, but their synagogues and tenement houses remain, providing a walk-round history lesson in Jewish heritage and culture. Kazimierz's complex identity is underlined by the presence of some of Kraków's most revered medieval churches. In May the suburb's narrow streets swell with the solemn, banner-bearing Corpus Christi processions that are among the best-attended events in the Polish Catholic calendar.

Today Kazimierz's Jewish population is a tiny fraction of what it was in the 1930s, but the district retains a vibrant melting-pot atmosphere – thanks in large part to its varied population of working-class Poles, impoverished artists and inner-city yuppies. The most dramatic change of recent years has been its reinvention as a bohemian nightlife district, full of zanily decorated cellar bars, pubs that look like antique shops and cafés that double as art galleries. With the area's non-conformist, anything-goes atmosphere drawing increasing numbers of the open-minded, tolerant and curious, Kazimierz is emerging once more as a unique incubator of cultural exchange.

279 Taking a trip on the Moscow metro

RUSSIA After a few vodkas my Russian neighbour unfailingly produces the two English phrases he learned in his Soviet childhood. One concerns friendship between nations, the other, that the Moscow metro is the greatest in the world.

This second assertion isn't far from the truth. The Moscow metro was designed as an eighth wonder of the world, a great egalitarian art gallery for the proletariat, combining utility and beauty as it ferried workers around the city, beguiled them with sculpture and chandeliers, and indoctrinated them with Soviet propaganda. Even now it's hard not to believe, just a little bit, in the Soviet dream when you step out of a clean, quick underground train (one every two minutes) into the fabulously ornate stations. Perhaps that's why hard-bitten Muscovites never seem to raise their eyes from their hurrying feet, and it's easy to spot the tourists.

With twelve lines and over 170 stations, the problem is where to start exploring. The *Koltsevaya*, or ring, is the most distinctive and navigable metro line. Built in the 1950s, its twelve stops include some of the finest stations, and as it's a circular line, it's hard to get lost. Park Kultury was the first station to be built on the line, and is decorated with bas-reliefs of workers enjoying sports and dancing. Travelling anti-clockwise, pretty, white and sky-blue Taganskaya is a mere prelude to Komsomolskaya, one of the most awesome stations on the whole system. Komsomolskaya connects to railway terminals for St Petersburg and Siberia, and the vast chandeliers suspended from the Baroque ceiling are designed to impress.

Towards the end of the circuit, Novoslobodskaya is the loveliest station of all. In the light of its jewel-bright stained-glass panels, even infamously surly Muscovites seem to smile and, recalling my Russian neighbour's English phrases, you may even start believing in friendship between nations. Which takes us neatly to Kievskaya, adorned with mosaic depictions of historical events uniting Russia and Ukraine, and the last stop on your circular journey.

280 Following Mikhail Bulgakov's footsteps in Kiev

UKRAINE Of the many authors who tried to dredge some meaning from the anguish and absurdity of life in the Soviet Union, few inspire as much devotion as Mikhail Bulgakov. Best known for *The Master and Margarita*, a phantasmagorical journey through 1930s Moscow, his earlier novel *The White Guard* is a sweeping evocation of Kiev, the city of his birth – and if you're keen to get to grips with its complex history, stow this book in your backpack.

Set in the winter of 1918–1919, the book describes a city at the mercy of German, Ukrainian-Nationalist and Bolshevik armies. Army doctor Bulgakov was himself caught up in the events described, and his street-level portrayal of Kiev could almost be used as a guide to the Ukrainian capital of today.

No streets were more vividly evoked by Bulgakov than Andriivskyi uzviz ("St Andrew's Descent"), the cobbled alley that zigzags steeply downhill From St Andrew's Church to the city's riverside quarter of Podil. Lined with nineteenth-century buildings, this charming relic of old Kiev is nowadays the part of the city that tourists want most to look around.

Halfway down the street is the Mikhail Bulgakov museum, occupying the house in which the writer lived from 1906 to 1919. It's also the house described in *The White Guard* as the home of Bulgakov's fictional alter ego Aleksei Turbin. Blurring fact and fiction in a way that would have surely appealed to the author himself, the display sets Bulgakov's authentic possessions alongside the kind of personal effects that might have belonged to his characters. One of the rooms is entered via a wardrobe, as if to underline the fact that this is a museum of the imagination.

The museum is also deliciously disorientating in quite unintended ways. Exhibits are unlabelled, accompanying brochures are in Russian only, and even on the rare occasions when an English-speaking guide is on hand, you'll be abandoned in mid-explanation if a more important-looking group turns up for a tour. The man who wrote *The Master and Margarita* could not have wished for a more fitting tribute.

281 Soothe your troubles at the Hotel Gellert

HUNGARY You might be impressed by the stately location of the *Hotel Gellert*, just over the "Liberty Bridge" on the western bank of the Danube, anchoring the old section of Buda. You might enjoy this picturesque scene especially after dark (and you'll certainly feel compelled to take pictures) on your way back across the bridge from a night out in Pest: the entire, rambling building, frontlit, glows like some giant Art Nouveau birthday cake at the base of craggy Gellert-hegy cliff. You might be awed by the grand staircases leading from the lobby; charmed by the cosy, hideaway bar and its array of Hungarian liquors; spun around by the long corridors and various turns getting to and from your room (especially after a drink or two of Unicum at the aforementioned bar); satisfied by the size of the room - better still if it comes with a view of the river in front or hills behind. But none of this is by itself necessarily a reason to stay. There's a greater motivation for that.

Wake up early to find out, and pull on the robe that hangs in the closet. Go to the excruciatingly slow, caged elevator on your floor. Tip the lift operator as you reach the bottom, exit and pick your way through the milling crowd to see what they're all waiting for. Don't be embarrassed about your state of relative undress - soon you'll all be in the same boat. Then - behold the glory of the Gellert baths.

The grandeur of the vaulted entry hall, its tiling, statuary and skylit ceiling, is a worthy precursor to the pools themselves. First, the segregated areas: a dip in the 34°C waters, while admiring the magnificent mosaics and ornamental spouts; a sit-down in the aromatic sauna; a bracing splash in a tiny, freezing cold bath; a plunge into another pool, this one 38°C . . . repeat the ritual again, then finish with some invigorating laps in the colonnaded central pool, the one place where the sexes intermingle. Consider doing the backstroke to enjoy best the light streaming through the retractable stained-glass roof above. And think about extending your stay another day or two.

BEAVERING AWAY IN
Lahemaa National Park

ESTONIA Visitors to Lahemaa National Park, a 725-square-kilometre area of pastureland and wilderness that runs along Estonia's northern seaboard, are often frustrated by never setting eyes on the forest-roaming bears, moose and lynx that guidebooks promise. The best they can hope for is the fleeting glimpse of a deer or rabbit – hardly the thing of which travellers' tales are made. Beavers, however, are a different matter. Although they're just as elusive as many of their peers (you'd probably need infrared vision and the patience of Job to see one), evidence of them is everywhere.

My own induction into beaver-world occurred at the Oandu beaver trail, a well-marked nature walk that begins on the eastern fringes of the park. Embracing dense forest, desolate bogs, coastal wetlands and archaic fishing villages, Lahemaa is the best possible introduction to this Baltic country's unspoiled rural character.

Leading through thick woodland, the trail crosses several streams where log-built dams and freshly gnawed tree trunks indicate the presence of a highly industrious animal. Beavers are the architects of the animal world, endlessly redesigning their environment until it meets their bark- and twig-munching requirements. The main mission of a beaver's life is to carve out a feeding area by felling trees, building a dam, and flooding an area of forest that other herbivores are loath to enter. Free of competition, it can then stuff its face with all the vegetal matter trapped in its semi-sunken realm.

These beaver-created landscapes can be found throughout the Baltic States. The Pedvale open-air sculpture park in Latvia even includes a "Mr Beaver" in its list of featured artists – a real-life furry prankster who mischievously flooded part of the grounds.

Despite two years of trawling through the protected areas of the Baltics, the only beaver I set eyes on was the tombstone-toothed cartoon character who appeared nightly to advertise toothpaste on Lithuanian television. When I finally came face to face with one, it was basking in Mediterranean sunshine in the middle of a Croatian zoo. It would be nice to think that, somewhere in a dank Baltic forest, there's a birch tree with his name on it.

SLOVAKIA You have to see the task of finding the all-important *kľúč* (key) as part of the experience when visiting the wooden churches of Slovakia's Carpathian foothills. Sure enough, there's nearly always a little sign (in Slovak) pinned to the wooden door, telling you which house harbours it, but finding the right one in a village without street names and only fairly random house numbers is a feat in itself. It's a sure way to get to meet the local head-scarved *babičky* (grannies), but don't expect to get to see too many churches in one day.

The churches look like something straight out of an East European fairy tale, or a Chagall painting: perched on slight hillocks by the edge of the woods, looking down on their villages, their dark-brown shingled exterior sprouting a trio of onion domes. Most were built in the eighteenth century when the influence of Baroque was making itself felt even among the carpenter architects of the Carpathians. Once inside, you can't help but be struck by the musty murkiness of the dark wooden interiors. At one end a vast and vibrantly decorated iconostasis reaches from the floor to the ceiling, its niches filled with saints. Elsewhere, a local folk artist allows his imagination to go wild in a gory depiction of the *Last Judgement*, with the damned being burned, boiled and decapitated with macabre abandon.

Despite the fact that the churches are often locked, they're still very much in use, mostly by the Greek Catholic church. Should you happen upon one when there's a service, note that Mass is celebrated in Old Slavonic.

Wooden churches:
"mass" tourism with a twist

283

284 The tale and the tongue of St John of Nepomuk

CZECH REPUBLIC As you shuffle along with your fellow tourists round the chancel of Prague's main cathedral, there's not a lot to see beyond the remains of a few medieval Czech kings with unpronounceable names – Břetislav, Spytihněv, Bořivoj. That is, until you find your way virtually barred by a giant silver tomb, which looks for all the world as if it has been abandoned by a bunch of Baroque builders upon discovering it was too big to fit into one of the side chapels. Turning your attention to the tomb itself, you're faced with one of the most gobsmackingly kitsch mausoleums imaginable – sculpted in solid silver, with airborne angels holding up the heavy drapery of the baldachin; and you notice the saint's rather fetching five-star sunburst halo, and back to back with him, a cherub proudly pointing to a glass case. On closer inspection, you realize the case contains a severed tongue.

Jesuits were nothing if not theatrical, and here, in the tomb of their favourite martyr, St John of Nepomuk, the severed tongue adds that extra bit of macabre intrigue. Arrested, tortured and then thrown – bound and gagged – off the Charles Bridge, John was martyred in 1393 for refusing to divulge the secrets of the queen's confession to the king. A cluster of stars appeared above the spot where he was drowned – or so the story goes – and are depicted on all his statues, including the one on the Charles Bridge. The gruesome twist was added when the Jesuits had his corpse exhumed in 1715 and produced what they claimed was the martyr's tongue – alive and licking so to speak – and stuck it in the glass case. Unfortunately, science had the last say, and in 1973 tests proved that the tongue was in fact part of his decomposed brain. Sadly, the object you now see on his tomb is a tongue-shaped replica.

285 Golden mouldy: drinking Tokaj in ancient cellars

HUNGARY Eastern European wines receive few accolades. Apart from one, that is: the "wine of kings, the king of wines" was how Louis XVI described Tokaj, Hungary's most celebrated drink – indeed, so important is it to Hungarians that it's even cited in the national anthem.

Harvested among the rolling green hills of the Tokaj-Hegyalja region in northeast Hungary, the most famous variety of Tokaj is Aszú, a devilishly sweet dessert wine that owes its distinctive character to the region's volcanic loess soil and the prolonged sunlight that prevails here. More importantly, though, it's down to the winemaking techniques employed, whereby the grapes are left to become overripe, leading to botrytization – in layman's terms, decomposition (grandly termed the "noble rot"). This shrivels the grapes to raisin-sized proportions and gives them their concentrated sweetness.

Nothing beats a few hours in one of the cosy cellars lining Tokaj's narrow streets, the most venerable of which is the Rákóczi cellar, named after the seventeenth-century prince Ferenc Rákóczi. Reposed in 24 eerily cobwebbed, chandelier-lit passages are thousands upon thousands of bottles of the region's choicest wines. No less esteemed is the cellar of the same name located in the town of Sárospatak; it was here that Rákóczi would come to smoke his pipe, indulge in his favourite tipple and plot the downfall of the Habsburgs. Hewn out by prisoners from the castle dungeons, the kilometre-long cellar, chock-full of handsome oak barrels, is thickly coated with *penész*, the "noble mould" – everything's noble where Tokaj is concerned – whose presence is integral to the wine's flavour. Whether quaffing this most regal of wines in the open air, down a cellar, or on a boat, the taste of Tokaj is something you won't forget in a hurry.

286 Spending a night at the cells in Liepāja

LATVIA Being incarcerated in a foreign country is usually the stuff of holiday nightmares. Unless you want an insight into Latvian history, that is, in which case you're advised to buy tickets in advance.

The best place to book yourself in for a bit of rough treatment is the former naval prison in Karosta, the Russian-built port that stretches north from the seaside city of Liepāja. Built by the Tsarist Empire in the nineteenth century, Karosta subsequently served as a submarine base for the USSR, and is nowadays an enduring symbol of the half-century of Soviet occupation.

Formerly used as a punishment block for unruly sailors, the grim-looking red-brick prison is now the venue for "Behind Bars", a two-hour interactive performance that involves being herded at gunpoint by actors dressed as Soviet prison guards, then interrogated in Russian by KGB officers. Dimly lit and decorated in floor-to-ceiling shades of black, the prison interior is enough to dampen any hopes

of resistance. Sign up for one of the "Extreme Night" performances and you may well find yourself mopping the floors before bedding down in one of the bare cells, only to be brutally awoken by an early morning call.

And if the experience of being shouted at in Russian leaves you disoriented, then in a way that's the whole point: life for Latvians in the Soviet Union was a long slow process of humiliation administered by people who didn't bother to learn their language.

Once outside the prison walls, Karosta remains rich in historical resonances. A self-contained, Russian-speaking mini-city quite separate from the rest of Liepāja, it retains an onion-domed Orthodox cathedral and rows of grey housing blocks where former naval workers still live. Most poignant of all is the line of collapsing artillery bunkers behind the beach, mutely testifying to the decline of the empire that built them.

NEED to know

253 The flea market at Petőfi Csarnok (Sat & Sun; 8am–2pm) is in the middle of Városliget park; trolleybus #70 trundles past every 15–20min. Ecseri antiques market (Mon–Fri 8am–4pm, Sat 6am–3pm, Sun 8am–1pm) is in the southeastern suburbs; catch bus #54 from Boraros tér and get off at the Fiume út. stop. Dates for the WAMP design fair are posted on @www.wamp.hu.

254 The Hermitage (@www.hermitagemuseum.org) is on Palace Square, near Nevsky Prospekt metro.

255 Wolf- and bear-tracking excursions can be organized with Roving Romania (@www.roving-romania.co.uk).

256 Auschwitz is named after the Polish town of Oświęcim, around 50km west of Kraków – buses between the two are frequent. The Auschwitz-Birkenau Museum & Memorial is free; see @en.auschwitz.org.pl for the latest opening hours.

257 Alberta iela lies in the Centrs district of Rīga; see @www.rigatourism.lv.

258 The White Nights last from June 11 to July 2.

259 The best time to be in Baja is for the *halászlé* festival on the second weekend of July, when the town square is filled with locals cooking up a storm in big iron pots over open fires. For more information on Baja contact the local tourist information centre (☎+36 7942 0792).

260 The celebrations take place every January 14 in the villages of Yardzhilovtsi, Kosharevo and Banishte. The Sofia-based travel agent Lyuba Tours (@www.lyubatours.com) can organize day-trips to see them. Many of Bulgaria's kukeri take part in the Festival of Masquerade Games (@www.surva.org), held in Pernik every even-numbered year.

261 There are daily hydrofoils from Tulcea to both Sulina and Sfantu Gheorghe (both around 90min), though perhaps more in keeping with the surroundings are slower ferries (3–5hr), which run five times per week to each location.

262 From Plovdiv take a bus from the Yug terminal to the town of Haskovo (1hr 30min) to catch the 3pm bus to Madzharovo (2hr). The Nature Information Centre (@marin.kurtev@bspb.org) arranges guided tours of the reserve.

263 Tiraspol can be accessed on regular buses from Chisinau, the capital of Moldova, or Lviv in the Ukraine.

264 Brest is 4hr by train from either Minsk or Warsaw (change in Terespol from the latter); the fortress is open daily 8am–midnight (free). The film *Brestskaya Krepost* ("The Brest Fortress"), one of a new breed of patriotic, Kremlin-backed war epics, was released in 2010.

265 Check out @www.zemaitijosnp.lt for more about the tours.

266 The Centrul de Echitaţie (open daily; ☎+40 268 262 161) is about 2km down the road that leads from Poiana Brasov to Brasov. To get to Poiana Brasov from Brasov, take bus #20, which leaves every 30min from Livada Postei bus station and takes 30min.

267 For a virtual excursion of the park in English, see @www.vvcentre.ru/eng/about_us/excursion.

268 Hourly buses go from Braşov to Bran Castle. For Poienari, take a bus from Curtea de Argeş to Arefu, from where it's 4km to the footpath that leads up to the castle. *Casa Dracula*, the restaurant occupying Dracula's birthplace, is at Str Cositorarilor 5.

269 České Budějovice is 150km south of Prague. Masné kramy is just off the old town square on Krajinská. The brewery is 2.5km north of the old town.

270 See @www.ukraine-travel-advisor.com/simferopol-airport.html for more information.

271 The nearest town to Mount Elbrus is Mineralnya Vody, a short flight from Moscow or Munich; it's a 4hr bus ride from the airport to the Baksan Valley at the base of Elbrus. For more information on the climb, visit @www.elbrus.org.

272 Zakopane is around 3hr by train or bus from Kraków.

273 The *Military Pub* is at No.7, Kiev Street (nightly until 6am).

274 Red Square can be reached from Ploshchad Revolyutsii, Aleksandrovskiy Sad, Biblioteka Imeni Lenina and Borovitskaya metros.

275 Żagań is a lengthy but enjoyable day-trip from the city of Poznań, from which you can take a bus or train to the town of Zielona Góra, followed by a local bus to Żagań. The Concentration Camps Museum (Muzeum obozów jenieckich; Tues–Fri 10am–4pm, Sat & Sun 10am–5pm; @www.muzeum.zagan.pl) is located 3km south of town – a taxi from Żagań bus station will cost around 20zł (€5).

276 In Kovachevitsa, *Kapsuzovi Kushti* (@kapsazovs_houses@yahoo.com) offers fully equipped rooms and has a fantastic restaurant. Or contact Sofia-based Zig-Zag Holidays (@www.zigzagbg.com) for accommodation throughout Bulgaria.

277 Despite being some way off the main transport routes, Kamianets is served by one direct daily train from Kiev, as well as direct buses from Kiev and Lviv. The enthusiast-run website @www.castles.com.ua provides an excellent historical lowdown.

278 The tourist information office is at ul. Jozefa 7 (@www.krakow.pl). The Cracovia stadium lies west of the town centre on al. Focha.

279 See @www.urbanrail.net/eu/mos/moskva.htm for information on ticket prices and routes.

280 The Bulgakov museum (daily except Wed; 10am–5pm) is at Andriivskyi uzviz 13.

281 *Hotel Gellert*, Szent Gellért tér, District XI, Budapest (@www.danubiushotels.com/gellert).

282 The Lahemaa National Park lies an hour's drive east of Tallinn. The national park visitors' centre (@www.lahemaa.ee) is in Palmse.

283 The churches are scattered across a remote part of Slovakia – the best way to reach them is to hike or hire a bicycle.

284 St Vitus Cathedral in Prague Castle is open daily. Charles Bridge can be visited any time of the day or night. For more on St John, see @www.sjn.cz.

285 The Rákóczi cellar in Tokaj is at Kossuth tér 15 (mid-March to mid-Oct daily 10am–6pm); the cellar in Sárospatak is at Erzsébet utca tér 26 (same times); a tasting of six wines plus nibbles costs around €10.

286 Both "Behind Bars" and "Extreme Night" can be booked through Karosta Prison (@www.karostascietums.lv), with prices ranging from 7–10Ls per person depending on how many take part. If you don't fancy the interactive experience, a simple guided tour of the prison costs 2Ls. Karosta is 4km north of central Liepāja and can be reached by bus #7 or #8.

GOOD to know

COOL AS A CUCUMBER

If a Czech thinks he's been asked an obvious question he may reply "I'm not here for the blueberries", whereas if involved in a boring activity may claim, "It's like throwing peas at a wall". A Bulgarian might warn you not to carry two melons under the same armpit. If a Russian tells you that you look like a cucumber, say thank you, but be upset if you are called an old horseradish. A pointless activity may be compared to "knocking pears out of a tree with your dick".

BEST DRINKS TO TRY

Vodka Drunk throughout the region, it supposedly aids digestion.

Beer Poles and Balts make lovely malty dark versions, but the Czechs, who invented it, have the best lager.

Brandy Moldovans modestly claim theirs is the finest in Europe.

Champagne Crimean, though no rival to French, is perfectly palatable – and far cheaper.

Wine Bulgarian, Hungarian and Romanian vintages are very decent; best of all is Tokaj, the world-renowned Hungarian dessert wine.

Borovička A gorgeous Slovak sloe spirit, similar to gin, but more fiery.

"Don't walk around hot porridge!"

Czech saying

EUROVISION SONG CONTEST

No current Eastern European nation had managed to capture this most dubious of titles until Estonia emerged victorious in 2001. This kick-started an impressive run of success, with Latvia, in 2002, and the Ukraine, in 2004, both coming first. In 2003, Russian female duo T.a.T.u, caused a bit of a storm thanks to marketing themselves as a (faux) lesbian couple, finishing third. Russia eventually won in 2008, Dima Bilan triumphing with the help of US production legend Timbaland.

EAST EUROPEAN JEWS

Before World War II, Eastern Europe had the largest Jewish population in the world. Historically, Jews had suffered exclusion from many parts of Europe, but since 1791 had been allowed to live in the Pale of Settlement – an area established by Catherine the Great, which covered much of eastern Poland and Russia. In the twentieth century, this is where the majority of Europe's Jews still remained, many of them in *shtetls* – predominantly Jewish small towns – where they had been forced to live having been previously excluded from cities. With the Nazi takeover of Eastern Europe, aided by strong feelings of local anti-Semitism, all but a remnant of the Jewish population was murdered. Of the fraction who remained, many fought as partisans, or were able to hide undiscovered. Since the demise of communism there has been a rekindling of interest in Jewish life evident in the emergence of new cultural centres, renovated synagogues and theatres in many of the places where their loss was felt so strongly, in particular in the cities of Vilnius and Kraków.

FIVE OUTSTANDING NATURAL ATTRACTIONS

Carpathian Mountains, Romania/Ukraine Stunning hiking terrain, sheltering quaint villages and home to some fabulous wildlife, including wolves and brown bears.

High Tatras, Slovakia Jagged granite peaks rising spectacularly from the Poprad Plain.

Couronian Spit, Lithuania Dramatic landscape of pine forests, pristine sands and calm lagoons.

The Danube River Stretching from the Black Forest to the Black Sea, this majestic waterway is Europe's second longest (2857km) after the Volga in Russia.

Puszcza Białowieska, Poland A national park containing the last major tract of primeval forest left in Europe.

"A man goes into his local garage and asks, 'Do you have a windscreen wiper for my Škoda?' 'Sounds like a fair swap', replies the man in the garage"

One of many jokes about (now-improved) Czech car, whose name means "pity" or "shame" in Czech

ETIQUETTE

Bulgarians shake their heads when they mean "yes" and nod when they mean "no". In a Czech pub, never top up a new glass of beer with the remains of the previous one.

When a Russian lights a cigarette, wish him good health, however ironic it seems.

FIVE MUST-READS

• **Transylvania, Romania**
Bram Stoker's *Dracula*

• **St Petersburg, Russia** Fyodor Dostoevsky's *Crime and Punishment*

• **Sofia, Bulgaria**
Georgi Gospodinov's *Natural Novel*

• **Odessa, Ukraine**
Isaac Babel's *Odessa Tales*

• **Gdansk, Poland**
Günter Grass's *The Tin Drum*

DID YOU KNOW…?

The geographical centre of Europe is located 25km north of Vilnius in Lithuania.

MATCH THE REVOLUTIONS WITH THE COUNTRIES:

A Orange	**1** Poland
B Velvet	**2** Estonia
C Singing	**3** Czechoslovakia
D Solidarity	**4** Ukraine

(answers: A/4, B/3, C/2, D/1).

CAMEL TREKKING IN THE SAHARA • THE MEDERSA BOU INANIA: A STUDY IN STYLE • THE PYRAMIDS OF GIZA • HAVE A SWELL TIME IN TAGHAZOUT • DISCOVERING ROCK ART ON THE TASSILI N'AJJER PLATEAU • ENJOYING THE VIEW FROM THE FISHAWI CAFÉ • MOPPING UP A MOROCCAN TAJINE • HANGING OUT IN THE JEMAA EL FNA • DRIFTING DOWN THE NILE • SWEATING IT OUT IN A HAMMAM • DRIVING THROUGH THE DESERT • EXPLORE A BIBLICAL LANDSCAPE: CLIMBING MOUNT SINAI • GREETING THE PHARAOHS IN THE VALLEY OF THE KINGS • MOUNTAINS AND MIRAGES IN JEBEL ACACUS • HAGGLING IN THE SOUKS OF FES • TOURING TROGLODYTE VILLAGES • LOSING YOURSELF IN A GOOD BOOK AT THE BIBLIOTHECA ALEXANDRINA • EXPLORING THE ROMAN RUINS AT DOUGGA • LISTENING TO GNAWA MUSIC IN ESSAOUIRA • KEEPING COOL IN THE OLD TOWN OF GHADAMES • GILF KEBIR: THE LAND OF THE ENGLISH PATIENT • EXPLORING BENI-ABBÈS AND TIMIMOUN • EXPLORING THE DUNE LAKES OF UBARI • SEEING THE OLD CITY OF TLEMCEN • HIKING IN THE HOGGAR • STROLLING THROUGH THE RUINS OF LEPTIS MAGNA • STAYING WITH A FAMILY IN MERZOUGA • THE MOULID OF SAYYID AHMED AL-BADAWI • TRANS-SAHARA BY MOTORBIKE • DRIVING THE ROUTE OF A THOUSAND KASBAHS • GETTING TO KNOW THE SOUKS OF TRIPOLI • MOUNTAIN HIGH: A VISIT TO CHEFCHAOUEN • DIVING IN THE RED SEA CORAL GARDENS • CAMEL TREKKING IN THE SAHARA • THE MEDERSA BOU INANIA: A STUDY IN STYLE • THE PYRAMIDS OF GIZA • HAVE A SWELL TIME IN TAGHAZOUT • DISCOVERING ROCK ART ON THE TASSILI N'AJJER PLATEAU • ENJOYING THE VIEW FROM THE FISHAWI CAFÉ • MOPPING UP A MOROCCAN TAJINE • HANGING OUT IN THE JEMAA EL FNA • DRIFTING DOWN THE NILE • SWEATING IT OUT IN A HAMMAM • DRIVING THROUGH THE DESERT • EXPLORE A BIBLICAL LANDSCAPE: CLIMBING MOUNT SINAI • GREETING THE PHARAOHS IN THE VALLEY OF THE KINGS • MOUNTAINS AND MIRAGES IN JEBEL ACACUS • HAGGLING IN THE SOUKS OF FES • TOURING TROGLODYTE VILLAGES • LOSING YOURSELF IN A GOOD BOOK AT THE BIBLIOTHECA ALEXANDRINA • EXPLORING THE ROMAN RUINS AT DOUGGA • LISTENING TO GNAWA MUSIC IN ESSAOUIRA • KEEPING COOL IN THE OLD TOWN OF GHADAMES • GILF KEBIR: THE LAND OF THE ENGLISH PATIENT • EXPLORING BENI-ABBÈS AND TIMIMOUN • EXPLORING THE DUNE LAKES OF UBARI • SEEING THE OLD CITY OF TLEMCEN • HIKING IN THE HOGGAR • STROLLING THROUGH THE RUINS OF LEPTIS MAGNA • STAYING WITH A FAMILY IN MERZOUGA • THE MOULID OF SAYYID AHMED AL-BADAWI • TRANS-SAHARA BY MOTORBIKE • DRIVING THE

North Africa
287–319

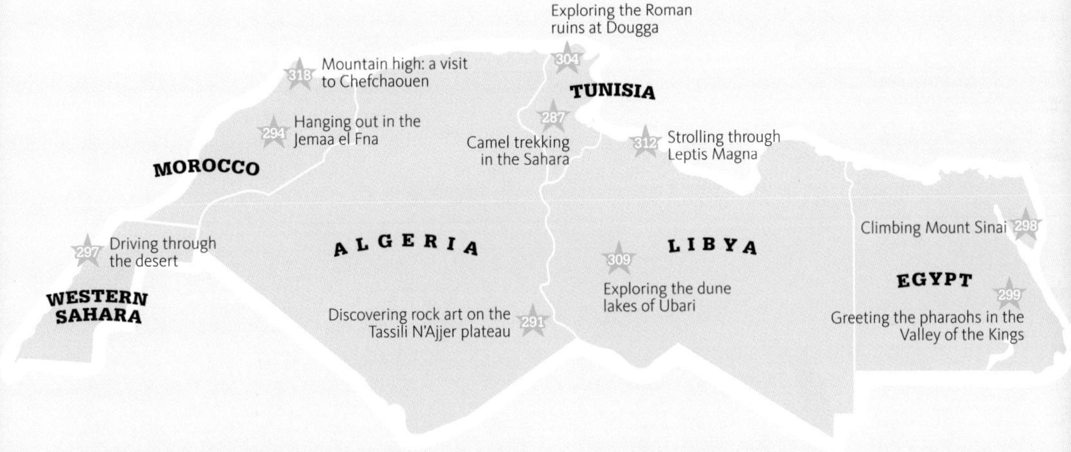

Exploring the Roman ruins at Dougga — 304

Mountain high: a visit to Chefchaouen — 318

TUNISIA

Hanging out in the Jemaa el Fna — 294

Camel trekking in the Sahara — 287

Strolling through Leptis Magna — 312

MOROCCO

Driving through the desert — 297

ALGERIA

LIBYA

Climbing Mount Sinai — 298

WESTERN SAHARA

Exploring the dune lakes of Ubari — 309

Discovering rock art on the Tassili N'Ajjer plateau — 291

EGYPT

Greeting the pharaohs in the Valley of the Kings — 299

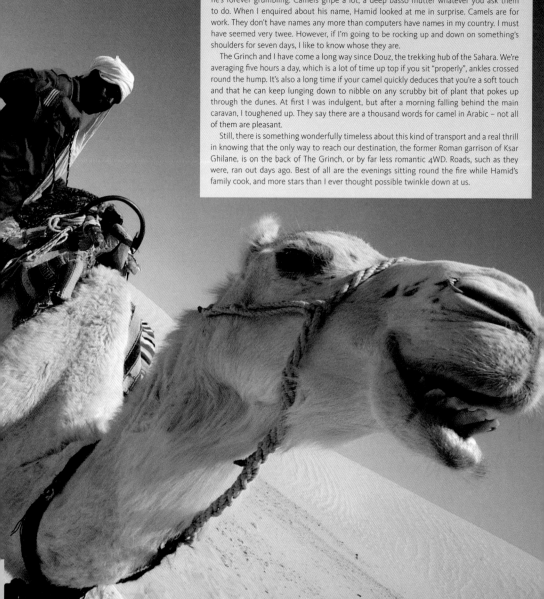

CAMEL TREKKING
in the Sahara

TUNISIA I had to insist on having control of my own camel. Too many of these treks resemble a ride at the zoo with a minder walking alongside holding the bridle. Hamid saw the advantage, though. If I went solo, he could send one of his sons home and I'd stop moaning that Lawrence of Arabia drove his own beastie.

The Grinch and I have been companions for four days now. I call him Grinch because he's forever grumbling. Camels gripe a lot, a deep basso mutter whatever you ask them to do. When I enquired about his name, Hamid looked at me in surprise. Camels are for work. They don't have names any more than computers have names in my country. I must have seemed very twee. However, if I'm going to be rocking up and down on something's shoulders for seven days, I like to know whose they are.

The Grinch and I have come a long way since Douz, the trekking hub of the Sahara. We're averaging five hours a day, which is a lot of time up top if you sit "properly", ankles crossed round the hump. It's also a long time if your camel quickly deduces that you're a soft touch and that he can keep lunging down to nibble on any scrubby bit of plant that pokes up through the dunes. At first I was indulgent, but after a morning falling behind the main caravan, I toughened up. They say there are a thousand words for camel in Arabic – not all of them are pleasant.

Still, there is something wonderfully timeless about this kind of transport and a real thrill in knowing that the only way to reach our destination, the former Roman garrison of Ksar Ghilane, is on the back of The Grinch, or by far less romantic 4WD. Roads, such as they were, ran out days ago. Best of all are the evenings sitting round the fire while Hamid's family cook, and more stars than I ever thought possible twinkle down at us.

288 The Medersa Bou Inania: a study in style

MOROCCO If you visit only one city in Morocco, you should visit Fes, a sensory-overloading tangle of shaded alleys, industrious souks and graceful architecture that shaped the country's history for a thousand years, and which remains the most complete medieval city in the Arab world. And if you visit only one building in Fes, you should visit the Medersa Bou Inania, a love song to intricacy and the finest Merenid monument in North Africa.

Like a lot of things in Fes, the *medersa* is all the more striking for its location. Squeeze through the throngs that fill the dusty lane of Talâa Kebira – the weary old men with their even wearier donkeys, the kebab sellers obscured by clouds of aromatic smoke – then duck down a step to your right, and you'll stumble across one of the most elaborate entrances in the medina, an ornate opening that hints at the extravagance within.

Bou Inania was a student college (*medersa* means "place of study"), and the large marble courtyard that greets you is a lesson in craftsmanship. Running around its perimeter, and splitting the walls aesthetically, a band of swirling Kufic script lends praise to Sultan Abou Inan, the fourteenth-century ruler who commissioned the *medersa* as the most important religious building in the city. Below this flows a striking mosaic of *zellij*, ceramic tilework based on complex geometric patterns; above, exquisite stucco climbs the walls, the work perhaps only bettered by the carvings that grace the courtyard's rich cedar doors and lintels.

But there is also substance to this style: Bou Inania is very much a functioning religious building, and from one corner you can see across to the prayer hall, the sound of chanting drifting through its doors and across the open courtyard.

289 The Pyramids of Giza

EGYPT The Pyramids at Giza were built at the very beginning of recorded human history, and for nearly five millennia they have stood on the edge of the desert plateau in magnificent communion with the sky.

Today they sit on the edge of the city, and it must be a strange experience indeed to look out of the windows of the nearby tower blocks to a view like this. The closest, the Great Pyramid, contains the tomb of Cheops, the Fourth Dynasty pharaoh who ruled Egypt during the Old Kingdom. This is the oldest of the group, built around 2570 BC, and the largest – in fact it's the most massive single monument on the face of the Earth today. The others, built by Cheops' son Chephren and his grandson Mycerinus, stand in descending order of age and size along a southwest axis; when built they were probably aligned precisely with the North Star, with their entrance corridors pointing straight at it.

You enter the Great Pyramid through a hole hacked into its north face in the ninth century AD by the caliph Mamun who was hunting for buried treasure. Crouching along narrow passages you arrive at the Great Gallery, which ascends through the heart of the pyramid to Chephren's burial chamber. Chances are you'll have the chamber to yourself, as claustrophobia and inadequate oxygen mean that few people venture this far. Occasionally visitors are accidentally locked in overnight.

The overwhelming impression made by the pyramids is due not only to the magnitude of their age and size but also to their elemental form, their simple but compelling triangular silhouettes against the sky. The best way to enjoy this is to hire a horse or camel and ride about the desert, observing them from different angles, close up and looming, or far off and standing lonely but defiantly on the open sands. Seen at prime times – dawn, sunset and night – they form as much a part of the natural order as the sun, the moon and the stars.

290 Have a swell time in Taghazout

MOROCCO Ice-cream headaches, chilly wetsuits in snow-covered car parks and blown-out waves beneath leaden skies; a north European winter can make the most dedicated surfer think twice. Why bother when in a few hours, many landlocked surfers could access perfect right-hand points, blue skies, 16°C water and the exoticism of Africa? Small wonder Taghazout is spoken of in revered tones.

The ramshackle fishing village, 20km from Agadir international airport, has come a long way. A hippy hangout in the 1960s, Taghazout – also spelled Tarhazoute or even Taghagant – is now known for great winter waves. Come late November, the first visitors arrive to join a clique of hardcore locals. By January, when low-pressure systems barrel west across the North Atlantic to lash northern countries with storm-force winds and rain, the breaks are busy with an accomplished international crew. And it's cheap, too,

when double rooms sourced from local families cost around 450dh a week and a tajine can be had for the price of a beer back home.

It takes serious waves to lure surfers from fabled breaks like Mundaka (in Spain) or Hossegor (in France). Taghazout's edge is its bounty. As well as several minor breaks, three right-hand points break off headlands in front of the village; waves like Anchor Point, whose flawless walled rights tumble for hundreds of metres, or Panoramas, which, by happy coincidence, concludes in front of a village bar. A few kilometres either side are breaks like Killers, a powerful reef-break named for the killer whales that cruise this coast, and Banana Point, a mellow, forgiving right-hander.

Indeed, there are only two negatives to this sunny surf Utopia. One is that popular waves plus small take-off zones can equal hassle in the water; as ever, observe the rules and show respect to the locals. The other is sea urchins – so bring your wetsuit booties.

291 Discovering rock art on the Tassili n'Ajjer plateau

ALGERIA The world's biggest open-air art gallery lurks in the heart of the Sahara, among the wind-carved ramparts of southeastern Algeria's Tassili n'Ajjer plateau.

Its caves and overhangs shelter countless prehistoric frescoes, laboriously engraved or painted onto the rock in shades of ochre, white and charcoal. When discovered in the 1930s, these images – including elephants, hippos and rhinos – helped illustrate the dramatic influence climate change has had on human development.

The most impressive concentration of rock-art sites is on the plateau above the remote oasis of Djanet. When, after an hour's steep hike, you finally encounter the frescoes for the first time, it's a humbling experience, heightened by the arid desolation. Was the Sahara once so green that where you stand, women would grind corn or milk cows beside flowing rivers, as some frescoes depict?

These scenes, some as fine as on any Greek vase, reflect the main theme of the rock paintings, that of the Neolithic Revolution, when humans progressed from eons of hunter-gathering to a settled lifestyle tending crops and domesticating animals. Not all such endeavours were ultimately successful, though – look out for engravings of giraffes on leads.

Elsewhere, figures with large round heads don't depict spacemen, as once theorized, but arcane gods, presaging the dawn of religious consciousness. Subsequently, the descendants of the ancient hunters are shown turning their bows and spears on each other as horse-drawn charioteers invade from the north. The story ends as the current arid phase takes hold, driving the people of the Tassili towards the Mediterranean and the Nile Valley. The rest, as they say, is history.

292 Enjoying the view from the Fishawi Café

EGYPT In a small alley in the heart of medieval Cairo is the famous *Fishawi Café*, where you sit on cane chairs at marble-topped tables in the narrow mirror-lined passage. Waiters carrying brass trays dart from table to table, weaving in and out among the street hawkers who offer you everything from a shoeshine to a woman's song accompanied by a tambourine, to necklaces of jasmine flowers.

Fishawi has been open every day and night for over two hundred years, and as you sip a thick black coffee or a sweet tea and perhaps enjoy the gentle smoke of a *narghile*, the Egyptian water pipe, you can immerse your senses in an atmosphere reminiscent of *The Thousand and One Nights*. All around you is Khan al-Khalili, a vast bazaar dating back to the fourteenth century, its shaded streets as intricate as inlay work, its shops and stalls sharp with spices, sweet with perfumes and dazzling with brass, gold and silver.

Fishawi is within hearing of the calls to prayer rising from the minarets of the Sayyidna al-Hussein, the principal congregational mosque of the city, and of the popular nightly celebrations that take place in the square outside throughout the month of Ramadan. Opposite the square, and far older, is the mosque of al-Azhar, the oldest university in the world and the foremost centre of Islamic theology.

Naguib Mahfouz, Egypt's Nobel Prize-winning novelist, was born and raised in the neighbourhood, and it provided him with the setting of many of his novels. For Mahfouz, the streets and alleyways around the *Fishawi Café* were a timeless world, which, as he wrote of Midaq Alley, a five-minute walk from the café, "connects with life as a whole and yet at the same time retains a number of the secrets of a world now past".

293 Mopping up a Moroccan tajine

MOROCCO Robert Carrier, one of the twentieth century's most influential food writers, rated Moroccan cuisine as second only to that of France. Which is perhaps a little hyperbolic, for, outside the grandest kitchens, Moroccan cooking is decidedly simple, with only a half dozen or so dishes popping up on most local menus. But no matter where you are in the country, from a top restaurant to a roadside stall, there is one dish you can depend upon: the tajine.

A tajine is basically a stew. It is steam-cooked in an earthenware dish (also called a tajine) with a fancifully conical lid, and most often prepared over a charcoal fire. That means slow-cooking, with flavours locked in and meat that falls from the bone.

What goes in depends on what's available, but a number of combinations have achieved classic and ubiquitous status: *mrouzia* (lamb or mutton with prunes and almonds – and lots of honey) and

mqualli (chicken with olives and pickled lemons), for example. On the coast, you might be offered a fish tajine, too, frequently red snapper or swordfish. And tajines can taste almost as good with just vegetables: artichokes, tomatoes, potatoes, peppers, olives, and again those pickled lemons, which you see in tall jars in every shop and market stall. The herbs and spices, too, are crucial: cinnamon, ginger, garlic and a pinch of the mysterious *ras al-hanut*, the "best in shop" spice selection any Moroccan stall can prepare for you.

There's no need for a knife or fork. Tajines are served in the dish in which they are cooked, and then scooped and mopped up – using your right hand, of course – with delicious Moroccan flat bread. Perfect for sharing.

And when you're through, don't forget to sit back and enjoy the customary three tiny glasses of super-sweet mint tea.

MOROCCO There's nowhere on Earth like the Jemaa el Fna, the square at the heart of old Marrakesh. The focus of the evening promenade for locals, the Jemaa is a heady blend of alfresco food bazaar and street theatre: for as long as you're in town, you'll want to come back here again and again.

Goings-on in the square by day merely hint at the evening's spectacle. Breeze through and you'll stumble upon a few snake charmers, tooth pullers and medicine men plying their trade, while henna tattooists offer to paint your hands with a traditional design. In case you're thirsty, water sellers dressed in gaudy costumes – complete with enormous bright red hats – vie for your custom alongside a line of stalls offering orange and grapefruit juice, pressed on the spot. Around dusk, however, you'll find yourself swept up in a pulsating circus of performers. There are acrobats from the Atlas Mountains, dancers in drag and musicians from a religious brotherhood called the Gnaoua, chanting and beating out rhythms late into the night with their clanging iron castanets. Other groups play Moroccan folk music, while storytellers, heirs to an ancient tradition, draw raucous crowds to hear their tales.

In their midst dozens of food stalls are set up, lit by gas lanterns and surrounded by delicious-smelling plumes of cooking smoke. Here you can partake of spicy *harira* soup, try charcoal-roasted kebabs or *merguez* sausage, or, if you're really adventurous (and hungry), a whole sheep's head, including the eyes – all beneath the looming presence of the floodlit, perfectly proportioned Koutoubia minaret to the west, making a backdrop without compare.

294

HANGING OUT IN THE

Jemaa el Fna

295

DRIFTING *down the Nile*

EGYPT Often called "the gift of the Nile", Egypt has always depended on the river as a life source. Without the Nile, the country could not survive, and would not have nurtured the great civilizations of its pharaonic past. Snaking the full length of the country, it flows from south to north and boats of all varieties ply it day and night. For an authentic – and uniquely Egyptian – taste of river life, opt for a voyage on a felucca.

These traditional, lateen-rigged wooden vessels – used on the river since antiquity – are small: a group of six will fit comfortably. Bargaining and gathering supplies before the cruise can be frenetic, but as soon as your captain guides the boat out onto open water, the bustle fades away. There's then nothing to do but lie back and soak up the atmosphere.

It's an experience that feels timeless. Drifting gently down the Nile in a traditional wooden boat, shaded from the African sun by a square of colourful cloth, watching the fields and palm groves slide past, kids waving from the banks. Nothing could be more seductive. It isn't timeless, of course: the cloth will likely be polyester, the kids have trinkets to sell and you'll see Japanese pickups parked in the shoreside villages – but one can dream...

296 Sweating it out in a hammam

TUNISIA Chances are that if you're in Tunisia you'll fancy visiting a *hammam*, the North African equivalent of a Turkish bath. And why not? It's where the locals come for gossip and a deep clean, and they always find it amusing when nervous foreigners turn up to try it out.

Be warned: the *hammam* experience covers the gamut of comfort, from a luxuriant pampering in the better hotels to a no-frills affair in the village bathhouse. The former is like a spa: you'll be ushered into a mosaic-tiled steam room to sit and gently perspire, after which a burly masseur awaits, ready to gloss you with scented oils and grind out those stress knots. It's invigorating and not in the least bit intimidating, but doesn't score too highly for atmosphere or insight into Tunisian life.

Those seeking authenticity should ask where the locals go – usually an innocuous domed building in the town's old quarter. The interior is often dim, the darkness pierced only by shafts of sunlight falling through slits of glass, and a hubbub of voices floats out to the entrance, where you pay and are shown the changing area. Armed with two buckets and a bowl you proceed into the steam room, where the murmur rises to a raucous chatter. Don't worry about the stares. Take a seat (watch out for broken tiles, clumps of hair or worse), look calm, get sweaty and watch what the others are doing. One bucket is for hot water, the other cold; you mix the two in the bowl to get the right temperature, before scrubbing yourself with a worn-out mitt and washing with soap.

If you're lucky, someone officious may shout something indiscernible in Arabic and point you towards a slab. This means you're due to be scoured by a maniac with a loofah until all your dead skin comes off. You may even get a brutal massage afterwards. Then it's out into the light, blinking, dazed and feeling slightly violated, but with a renewed sense of kudos.

297 Driving through the desert

WESTERN SAHARA The Sahara desert presents a challenge for anyone wanting to cross Africa by road. The only sensible way to get from North Africa to West Africa overland is to travel from Morocco to Mauritania, through the disputed province of Western Sahara. The single-lane highway hugs more than 1200km of Atlantic coast, allowing you to skirt around the inhospitable Saharan interior and enjoy the sea breeze.

A desert can sometimes feel like a beach gone wrong; it's all sand and no sea. Along this road, however, you are nearly always in sight of sandy cliffs tumbling down to the boisterous Atlantic Ocean. The road is flat, straight and empty for hours at a time. The only vehicles are occasional buses and an array of hard-working Series 1 Land Rovers, made in Britain in the 1940s.

A former Spanish colony, Western Sahara has been shared between Morocco and Mauritania since the 1970s. Its people, the Saharawi, have been seeking independence for more than fifty years. Morocco now controls most of the territory, within a 2000km sand wall known as the "berm". A UN-backed referendum on independence has been repeatedly delayed, while 100,000 Saharawi remain in refugee camps in Algeria.

On the coast road, the view doesn't change much as the hours and days tick by. There are only three towns of any size, each flanked by police checkpoints. Rolling into Boujdour, you can't miss a plethora of Moroccan flags, flapping in the relentless wind. No need to brace yourself for an imminent royal visit though; this is how the Moroccan authorities ensure that everyone is clear exactly which country they are in. In the cafés lining the main street, men in billowing robes and tightly wrapped headgear sip on glasses of sugary mint tea.

Heading south, the last leg is from a petrol-station-cum-hotel to the Mauritanian border. The area around the border is heavily mined and crossing it means a nerve-wracking drive across 8km of rocky no-man's-land. The trick, it's said, is to follow the tracks of a vehicle bigger and heavier than yours.

298 Explore a biblical landscape: climbing Mount Sinai

EGYPT The interior of the Sinai peninsula is a stark, unforgiving place. Beneath a strikingly blue sky lie parched mountains, rocky outcrops and great expanses of barren sand, interspersed with isolated oases and crisscrossed by medieval pilgrimage routes. It is, in the truest sense, a landscape of biblical proportions.

In the south of this region, just a few hours' drive from the booming tourist resort of Sharm el-Sheikh, rises the magnificent 2285m Mount Sinai, venerated by Christians, Muslims and Jews alike as the site of God's unveiling of the Ten Commandments. Although there is some doubt about whether this red-and-grey granite peak is actually the site mentioned in the Bible, it is undeniably awe-inspiring – particularly the views from the summit, reached via 3750 knee-crunching "Steps of Repentance", or the easier but longer "camel path". Despite the crowds of pilgrims, travellers and Bedouin guides (and their camels), a night camped out here under a star-filled sky allows you to wake up to one of the most beautiful sunrises imaginable.

Almost as atmospheric – and considerably more comfortable – is a stay at the guesthouse in the grounds of the imposing St Catherine's Monastery, which stands at the foot of Mount Sinai. Dating back to 337 BC, this active Greek Orthodox monastery looks more like a fortress than a place of religious devotion. Behind its forbidding walls is what is reputed to be the burning bush from which God spoke to Moses, as well as a library containing innumerable priceless texts and manuscripts, including fragments of the world's oldest Bible, the 1600-year-old Codex Sinaiticus.

299 Greeting the pharaohs in the Valley of the Kings

EGYPT They're badly lit, hot and claustrophobic. They're packed with sweating, camera-toting tour groups. But nowhere else can you get so vivid a glimpse of ancient Egypt than in the 3000-year-old tombs where the ancient dynasties of Thebes laid their rulers to rest – in the Valley of the Kings.

Thebes' temples were built on the east bank of the Nile, to greet the rising sun and celebrate life. But where the sun set was a place of death. Here, the pharaohs sank tombs into the rock to hide their embalmed bodies, decorating the subterranean passageways with images of the gods they would meet after death on their journey to immortality.

The Valley of the Kings is huge, located across the river from the busy town of Luxor and hemmed between crags in an arid desertscape under the scorching sun. Its light is glaring, the heat exhausting, the air dry as dust. There are dozens of tombs, so you need to choose judiciously: Tutankhamun is an obvious draw, but Tut was a minor pharaoh and his tomb is relatively small (and commands a hefty surcharge).

Instead, go for Ramses III – one of the grandest and longest tombs, running for almost 200m under the rubbly hills. As you descend narrow steps to the tomb entrance, the walls close in. Pass through the dim gateway and the floor drops further: you're in a narrow, gloomy shaft, with images of scarabs, crocodiles and dog-headed gods for company. Further down into the musty depths, you come face to face with the garishly colourful wall-paintings for which these tombs are famous: the sun god Ra journeys through the twelve gates of the underworld, harpists sing and pictorial spells weave magic to protect the dead pharaoh in the afterlife.

300 Mountains and mirages in Jebel Acacus

LIBYA The prehistoric rock art in Libya's Jebel Acacus depicts a world that no longer exists. It's found only in the under-hangs and caves, where the inhabitants lived and painted the world around them thousands of years ago: elephants, giraffes, ostriches, lions, deer, buffalo, as well as hunting scenes, human rituals and epic battles. What a contrast today: the vistas now are of a silent, empty land of extraordinary beauty – bare mountains, rocky pinnacles, vast gorges, sand dunes – all radiant with vibrant colours, shades of orange, black, brown, azure (and not a wisp of cloud).

The lush landscape of forests and big game vanished 5000 years ago when the Sahara Desert dramatically dried up. The only stirrings now are the hum of the wind, and the mirages – which are intense, like tongues of flames skidding across the surface, giving the land a rarefied, uncertain quality, as if everything is morphing into something else.

There is much at Jebel Acacus to fire the imagination: among them the ever-changing perspective of the landscape and the sparse flora and fauna, which exists in some valleys despite the 400m-deep water table. The plants, looking monstrous and weird, are well adapted to this unforgiving environment; no camel could munch on the thorny acacias, or the bitter desert melons, or the hallucinogenic plant known as *felesles*.

301 Haggling in the souks of Fes

MOROCCO Everywhere you look in Fes's medina – the ancient walled part of the city – there are alleys bedecked with exquisite handmade crafts. Here the city's distinctive ceramics jostle for space with rich fabrics, musical instruments and red tasselled fezzes (which take their name from the city). Most of these items are made in the medina itself, in areas such as the carpenters' souk, redolent of cedarwood, or in the rather less aromatic tanneries, where leather is cured in stinky vats of cow's urine and pigeon poo, among other substances. In the dyers' souk, the cobbles run with multicoloured pigments used to tint gaudy hanks of wool, while nearby Place Seffarine, by the tenth-century Kairaouine Mosque, reverberates to the sound of metalworkers hammering intricate designs into brass.

Should you wish to buy, however, it's not a matter of "how much?", "here you go", "bye". Love it or hate it, haggling is de rigueur. These crafts are made with love and patience, and should not be bought in a rush. Rather, the shopkeeper will expect you to dally awhile, perhaps enjoy a cup of tea – sweet, green and flavoured with Moroccan mint – and come to an agreement on a price. This is both a commercial transaction and a game, and skilled hagglers are adept at theatrics – "How much? Are you crazy?" "For this fine piece of art? Don't insult me!"

Know how much you are prepared to pay, offer something less, and let the seller argue you up. If you don't agree a price, nothing is lost, and you've spent a pleasant time conversing with the shopkeeper. And you can always go back the next day to reopen discussions.

Touring troglodyte villages

TUNISIA When Tunisia gained its independence in 1956, its then president, Habib Bourguiba, proclaimed a new nation in which "people will no longer live in caves, like animals". He was addressing the reality that across the arid far south of the country, people did live in caves, not uncommonly with their livestock. Gradually, these people were moved into new houses put up by the government, and most of the old dwellings were abandoned.

Visit the troglodyte villages today, however, and you'll see they're enjoying a new lease of life – some even offer tourist accommodation. Many are stunningly sited. At Chenini, Douiret and Guermessa, set in a jagged prehistoric landscape, you're confronted by mountainsides riddled with cave dwellings and guarded by rugged stone forts. At nearby Ghoumrassen, three folds of a rocky spur are studded with caves, under the gaze of a whitewashed mosque. Yet more scenic is Toujane, built on two sides of a gorge, with breathtaking views. Anywhere you spot oil stains down the hillside signifies caves housing ancient olive presses; visit after the olive harvest and you may well see some of these being powered by donkeys.

But the big centre for troglodyte homes is Matmata, whose people live, to this day, in pit dwellings. Signs outside some invite you to visit, and for a few dinars you can descend into a central courtyard dug deep into soft sandstone, which serves to keep the rooms – excavated into the sides – comfortably cool in summer and warm in winter. Better still, Matmata has three hotels in converted pit dwellings, including the *Sidi Driss*, which was used as one of the locations in *Star Wars* – here you can dine where Luke Skywalker once did.

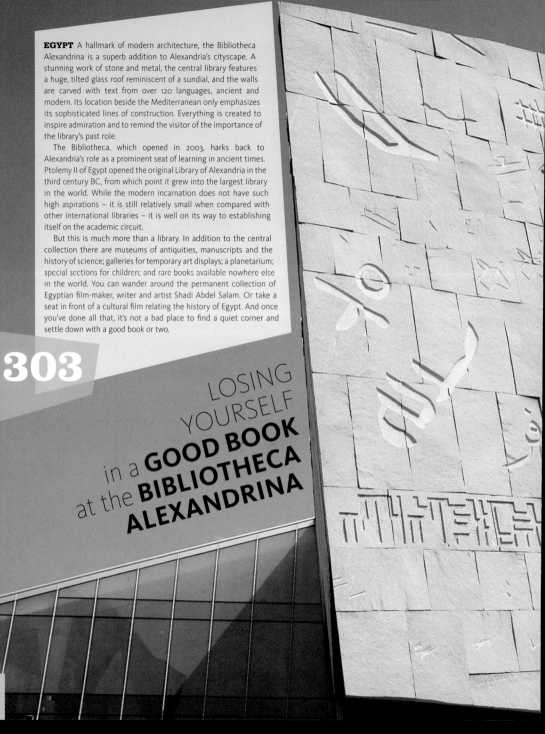

EGYPT A hallmark of modern architecture, the Bibliotheca Alexandrina is a superb addition to Alexandria's cityscape. A stunning work of stone and metal, the central library features a huge, tilted glass roof reminiscent of a sundial, and the walls are carved with text from over 120 languages, ancient and modern. Its location beside the Mediterranean only emphasizes its sophisticated lines of construction. Everything is created to inspire admiration and to remind the visitor of the importance of the library's past role.

The Bibliotheca, which opened in 2003, harks back to Alexandria's role as a prominent seat of learning in ancient times. Ptolemy II of Egypt opened the original Library of Alexandria in the third century BC, from which point it grew into the largest library in the world. While the modern incarnation does not have such high aspirations – it is still relatively small when compared with other international libraries – it is well on its way to establishing itself on the academic circuit.

But this is much more than a library. In addition to the central collection there are museums of antiquities, manuscripts and the history of science; galleries for temporary art displays; a planetarium; special sections for children; and rare books available nowhere else in the world. You can wander around the permanent collection of Egyptian film-maker, writer and artist Shadi Abdel Salam. Or take a seat in front of a cultural film relating the history of Egypt. And once you've done all that, it's not a bad place to find a quiet corner and settle down with a good book or two.

303

LOSING
YOURSELF
in a **GOOD BOOK**
at the **BIBLIOTHECA
ALEXANDRINA**

304 Exploring the Roman ruins at Dougga

TUNISIA The columns and arches of the crumbling Roman city loom above, its winding passages hinting at secret spaces. Below stretches the countryside, the slopes patterned with olive trees and dotted with the occasional dwelling. But this is North Africa, not northern Italy, and in a country more renowned for beach holidays and desert safaris.

Modern Tunisia is unmistakably Arab, but two millennia ago it was the heart of the Romans' North African empire. Just 140km from Sicily, the region grew rich selling grain and olive oil to its Mediterranean neighbours, and the cities were large and lavish. Dougga, a couple of hours south of the modern-day capital of Tunis, was one of the biggest. The Romans usually built on flat terrain but here they took a pre-existing Carthaginian township perched on a hilltop and made it their own. The citizens built their homes in the lower reaches, saving the higher regions for the municipal goods: the peak features a cluster of public buildings made of golden stone, including a theatre, a market, and several temples, the biggest of which is dedicated to Jupiter, the king of the gods. The only clue of an earlier age is a mausoleum tower dating from the ancient African Numidian civilization.

The ruins are in remarkably good repair, considering that the local people lived among them until the early twentieth century. They now live a few miles away in Nouvelle Dougga, but many remain connected to the site through work. Some Roman remains are one part scattered stones, nine parts imagination; Dougga is not one of them.

305 Listening to Gnawa music in Essaouira

MOROCCO It's midnight in Essaouira, and a castanet-like rhythm is drifting over the ramparts on the steely Atlantic breeze.

Tucked into a courtyard is a group of robed musicians playing bass drums, reed pipes and *qaraqebs*, metal chimes which are clacked together in the fingers. Their leader, the *maalem*, plucks a three-stringed gimbri lute. Singers in tassel-topped caps weave a polyrhythmic chant into the sound. The group is surrounded by a respectful audience: some standing, some preferring to sit cross-legged.

Suddenly, the beat quickens and one of the chanters launches into a dazzling sequence of lunges, jumps and cossack-like knee-bends. Finally, he spins on the spot, his long tassel whirling like a helicopter blade. An audience member joins in and ends up collapsed on the ground, seemingly in some kind of ecstatic trance.

This is a *lila*, one of the intimate musical gatherings that take place each night during the city's annual Gnawa music festival. The Gnawas (or, in French, Gnaouas) are a spiritual brotherhood of healers and mystics whose ancestors, animist West Africans, were transported to Morocco as slaves. Their hypnotic music, a blend of sub-Saharan, Berber and Arab influences, is key to their rituals.

As well as these late-night sessions, the festival offers large-scale concerts. From early evening each day, crowds of locals gather around the stages in Place Moulay Hassan and other main squares to hear bands from all over North and West Africa. But it is the starlit *lilas* that make the festival unique. And it's hard to imagine a more romantic setting for them than the rugged, windswept fortifications that protect the city from the sea.

By day, Essaouira has a different kind of romance. Seagulls soar over the sun-bleached rooftops and swoop down onto the shore, where fishermen sort their catch. The ramparts bake in the sun. This is the time for the festival's more energetic visitors to browse the souks for glass beads, leather slippers and drums. Others, meanwhile, just snooze in the cool courtyard of a riad, waiting for another evening's magic to unfold.

306 Keeping cool in the old town of Ghadames

LIBYA The houses in Ghadames, a pastel-coloured town in the Sahara Desert, are as dense as honeycomb – it's possible for the women to travel about town by walking on the rooftops (keeping separate from the men) – and its covered alleys are like an underground maze. One can imagine the inhabitants milling about in dark corners, but now Ghadames belongs to ghosts: government handouts have enticed its former 6000 Berber inhabitants to modern houses outside the old town. The desolation is part of the allure; only occasionally will you meet other tourists.

The best approach is to wander aimlessly and marvel at the old town's intelligent design; the way, for example, water was tapped from aquifers and channelled to the inhabitants in stringent allocations. There is much to see – public baths, old mosques, groves of date palms – and there are birds everywhere, hoopoes and doves and other colourful desert species. The decor inside some of the houses is so intense – geometric designs blooming across the walls, trunks and rugs covering the rest of the interior, and many, many mirrors, strategically placed to amplify light from the skylight – that sometimes it looks overdone for tourists' awe. But actually this is typical, as the inhabitants still maintain the houses as summer retreats. The air-con in their modern abodes can't cope with the fifty-degree heat, and only Ghadames's natural-cooling design offers a reprieve. And so the old town continues to endure, as it has done for hundreds of years.

307 Gilf Kebir: the land of The English Patient

EGYPT The Cave of the Swimmers depicted in the film *The English Patient* exists, in the far southwest of Egypt – the most arid corner of the Sahara, and an area even nomads avoid. Discovered by Count Laszlo de Almasy, the real "English Patient" in 1933, a couple of "swimming" figures survive on the flaking walls, and today rock-art sites depicting long-extinct animals and abstruse rituals are still being discovered. This is the Gilf Kebir, unoccupied since Neolithic times. Legends abound of lost oases and invading armies swallowed by the sands. On the desert floor, World War II fuel cans mingle with the earliest pottery and Paleolithic stone axes, from a time when humans first took to their feet.

308 Exploring Beni-Abbès and Timimoun

ALGERIA As you race along the strip of road south of the Atlas Mountains, the presence of the Sahara in all its vastness begins to dawn on you. It's almost comforting to reach the oasis of Beni-Abbès, where you can camp in the endless, swaying groves of date palms near the water, or stay in town beneath the colossal dunes. Further south, and almost impossibly exotic in its high red walls, the remote outpost of Timimoun, deep in the desert away from the main trans-Sahara route, exerts a more severe appeal, but it is a fabulous and little-visited destination, with a wonderful old centre of shady alleys full of crafts workers. To the north of town, irrigated palm groves and gardens stretch over a dry salt lake, with more villages to explore, many with inhabitants of West African ancestry.

309 Exploring the dune lakes of Ubari

LIBYA One of the Sahara's many natural wonders lies west of Sebha in southwestern Libya. The vast Idhan Ubari – or Ubari Sand Sea – spills out in all directions like a huge barrier, but exploring the interior in a 4WD leads to the unexpected sight of half a dozen palm-rimmed lakes twinkling at the feet of immense dunes. Where the water comes from is still unknown – some lakes are warm, others cold, and once a long-gone tribe survived here off lake shrimps mashed with dates. The best known is Lake Gabroun, but the prettiest is Um el Ma (Mother of the Waters), many people's idealized image of a Saharan oasis.

310 Seeing the old city of Tlemcen

ALGERIA The mountain stronghold of Tlemcen is one of northern Algeria's pre-eminent cities, and one of the Islamic world's great centres, stuffed with mosques (with visiting hours for non-Muslims). Its architecture is redolent of the Andalusian period, centuries before the European carve-up of North Africa. Inside the city walls, the visually arresting interior of the eleventhth-century Grand Mosquée, inspired by the Mezquita in Cordoba, Spain, includes multiple rows of columns and arches. Tlemcen's old centre is a warren of narrow alleys, strictly explorable on foot only, and seething with commercial energy, including cabinet-making, embroidery, jewellery-making and leather-working.

ALGERIA Rising from the very centre of the Sahara, on a vast, brooding plateau, the peaks of the Hoggar spire towards a shimmering blue dome of sky. The heat is relentless, and yet the arid air removes every trace of perspiration as soon as it forms on your brow. Keep your *cheche* (headscarf) wrapped across your mouth and you can breathe moist air: it's a good trick. This is a waterless, inhospitable environment – a surreal, otherworldly landscape of volcanic plugs rearing vertically for hundreds of metres, where silence reigns.

In the Hoggar, you can explore, or climb, in some of the most remote peaks and wadis (dry water courses) in the world, and find examples of the rock art left here thousands of years ago when the region was fertile, hunter-gatherer country.

Today the solitude leaves the Hoggar largely uninhabited, save for the nomadic Tuareg, reliant entirely on their herds and their ability to endure hardships that would destroy most people in a couple of days. It was a fascination with the Tuareg that drew Charles de Foucauld, a French priest, to a remote vantage point on the high col at Assekrem in the central Hoggar – the small stone chapel where he lived as a hermit for sixteen years at the beginning of the twentieth century is the best-known target for hikers.

"The view is more beautiful than can be conveyed or imagined", de Foucauld wrote of his isolated home. "The very sight of it makes you think of God, and I can scarcely take my eyes from a sight whose beauty and impression of infinitude are so reminiscent of the Creator of all; and at the same time its loneliness and wildness remind me that I am alone with Him."

A hundred years later, you stand and stare, from the lonely col, gazing at the infinite geological wonders across your field of view. The great outdoors doesn't get much greater.

312 STROLLING THROUGH THE RUINS OF LEPTIS MAGNA

LIBYA North Africa is dotted with Roman remains, but the one that beats them all is Leptis Magna, arguably the most impressive Roman site outside Pompeii.

Leptis Magna reached its zenith under local boy Septimius Severus, who rose to become emperor in 193 AD, and died in battle eighteen years later in a far-flung province called Britain. Fittingly, if there's one superlative edifice at Leptis Magna, it's the amazing four-way arch Septimius commissioned. One of the first monuments you encounter, it is nearly forty metres tall, and bears a plethora of superb, recently restored marble reliefs. Septimius also endowed the city with the more imposing of its two forums, squares where people met to socialize and conduct business.

So well preserved is the city's luxurious bathhouse, endowed by Septimius's predecessor, Hadrian, that it's easily recognizable as a direct ancestor of the *hammams* found across North Africa. Walking through, you follow the route that bathers took, from the frigidarium (cold room) through the tepidarium (warm room, but actually more like an open-air swimming pool) to the caldarium (hot room), where they would sweat out the grime and scrub it off – just as in today's *hammams*.

Elsewhere, there's an enormous amphitheatre (for gladiatorial and other sporting events, more likely than not involving Christians and lions), a hippodrome (for horse races) and a substantial, well-preserved theatre to take in. There's also a good museum with commentaries in English. But one of the very best things to do at Leptis Magna is simply to wander the maze of colonnaded streets, so intact that you can imagine toga-clad Romans approaching at every corner.

313 Staying with a family in Merzouga

MOROCCO Waking up in a nomad's black-wool tent, surrounded by mile upon mile of ochre-coloured sand dunes, the first thing that strikes you is the silence: a deep, muffled nothing. The second is the cold. You'll appreciate the three glasses of mint tea by the fireside before you help saddle up the camels for the day's trek.

Despite the chilly mornings, January is the best month to visit southern Morocco's Erg Chebbi dunes. The skies are big and blue, the horizons crisp and, best of all, the hordes who descend here later in the year blissfully absent.

The *Chez Tihri* guesthouse is a rarity in a corner of the country notorious for its highly commoditized versions of the desert and its people: an auberge run by a Tamasheq-speaking Amazigh (Tuareg) where you actually feel a genuine sense of place. Built in old-school kasbah style, its crenellated pisé walls, adorned with bold geometric patterns in patriotic reds and greens, shelter a warren of cosy rooms, each decorated with rugs, pottery and lanterns, and interconnected by dark, earthy corridors.

As well as being a congenial host, Omar Tihri, dressed in imposing white turban and flowing robe, is a passionate advocate for Amazigh traditions and culture, and living proof that tourism can be a force for good in this region. A slice of the profits from *Chez Tihri* go towards funding a women's weaving cooperative, in addition to a small school where Tamasheq-speaking children, who are poorly catered for by state education in the area, learn French and Arabic.

314 The Moulid of Sayyid Ahmed al-Badawi

EGYPT The Egyptian year is awash with *moulids* (festivals honouring local saints), but they don't come much bigger than the Moulid of Sayyid Ahmed al-Badawi, when the otherwise nondescript Nile Delta city of Tanta is besieged by some two million pilgrims, who converge on the triple-domed mosque where al-Badawi is buried.

Moulids are especially associated with Sufis – Islamic mystics who use singing, chanting and dancing to bring themselves closer to God. Some fifty Sufi brotherhoods put up their tents around Tanta and set to work chanting and beating out a rhythm on drums or tambourines, as devotees perform their *zikrs* (ritual dances). In the less frenetic tents, you can relax with a *sheesha* (water-pipe) or a cup of tea, while scoffing festive treats such as roasted chickpeas and sugared nuts. The atmosphere is intense, the crowds dense and pickpocketing rife (so leave your valuables at home).

Tanta doesn't have much in the way of accommodation, and most people just bunk down in the tents, but if that doesn't appeal and you can't get a room, it's near enough to Cairo to take in on a day-trip. Wherever you stay, make sure that you're here for the spectacular last-night parade, when the Ahmediya, the Sufi brotherhood founded by al-Badawi himself, takes to the streets in a colourful blur of banners.

315 Trans-Sahara by motorbike

ALGERIA–NIGER Riding across Africa, two stages stand out: the clammy, bug-ridden byways of the Congo Basin – where "infrastructure" is just a good score in Scrabble – and the Sahara. The latter's appeal is uncomplicated: the stark purity of landforms stirred by dawn winds; the simplicity of your daily mission – survival; and the brief serenity of hushed, starlit evenings. It's just you, your bike and the desert.

Disembarking at Algiers is chaos, but muddle through and by nightfall you'll emerge in the ravines of the Atlas, where the desert unrolls before you. By Ghardaia things are warming up and near El Meniaa breathtaking dunes begin spilling over the road. Settlements now appear maybe only once a day and so become vital staging posts. Other travellers, too, acquire a hallowed status: fellow pilgrims on the desert highway.

Some days the road is washed away, submerged in sand or lost in a dust storm, but you soldier on. You pass through the Arak Gorge, a portal to the white sands and granite domes of the haunting Immidir plateau. By now your apprehension has subsided and you dare to relax. Within days the volcanic peaks of the Hoggar rise and you roll into Tamanrasset; chugging down the main street you look at the locals and they look back, at a dusty wanderer on a horse with no name.

It's time to focus on the final leg – four days across the long-dreaded piste to Agadez. Those first few moments riding the loaded machine on the sands will be a shock but you must be assertive, gunning the throttle across soft patches, resting where you can.

The Niger border is a crossroads: monochrome sobriety meets the colourful exuberance of sub-Saharan Africa. Brightly clothed women mix with mysterious nomads and, for you, an ice-cold beer in the shabby *Hotel Sahara* washes away the desert dust.

316 Driving the route of a thousand kasbahs

MOROCCO East of Marrakesh, up over the dizzying Tizi n'Tichka pass, runs one of the oldest trading routes in history, snaking out across the Sahara and linking the Berber heartland with Timbuktu, Niger and old Sudan. The gold and slaves that once financed the southern oases are long gone, but the road is still peppered with the remains of their fabulous kasbahs – fortified dwellings of baked mud and straw – and as it sprints out into the Sahara, it passes great sweeping palmeries of dates, olives and almonds, their lush greens a vivid contrast to the barren desert. The cream of the architectural crop is at Aït Benhaddou, near the start of the route. Although most of the inhabitants have moved to the modern village across the river, it's a magical place, its stunning collection of crenellated kasbahs, their crumbling clay walls glowing orange in the soft light of late afternoon, among the most intricately decorated of the deep south.

317 Getting to know the souks of Tripoli

LIBYA Tripoli is one of the world's safest big cities, and has excellent souks: a fine combination that encourages you to wander freely. Most of the souks, or market quarters, are located in the arched alleys of the medina – the walled old city of Tripoli right by the port – and each has its own speciality and character, from the noisy clamour of the coppersmiths' souk to the colour and commerce of tailors' and shoe shops and the aroma of vegetable, fish, spice and meat stalls along Souk al-Turk. When it comes to buying, there's refreshingly little hard sell, and no need to haggle like crazy. Gold and silver, sold by weight, are good purchases, as are Berber wool rugs in geometric patterns, and more domestic items that often make the best souvenirs, like baskets and leather, local robes (*galabeyas*), pottery and metal utensils, and charms and folk medicine from across the Sahara.

318 Mountain high: a visit to Chefchaouen

MOROCCO "So why did you come, then?" Given that Chefchaouen is renowned across Morocco and beyond for its hashish, *kif* (marijuana) and *majoun* (marijuana cake), you can perhaps forgive the local touts for their exasperation; for why else would you come to this ancient corner of the Rif? The idea that you'd want to get high on Chefchaouen's otherworldly aura alone perhaps doesn't quite cut it in the cross-cultural stakes.

Had they rumbled his Rabbi disguise, the zealous natives might well have asked the same question of French monk Charles de Foucauld (see *311*), the first Christian to breach the walls of what was then (in 1883) a militantly anti-European outpost. When the Spanish finally took control in 1920, they found not only descendants of the Muslims and Sephardic Jews they'd kicked out of Spain centuries earlier but also the medieval dialect, Haketia, they'd brought with them. The place is still a world apart today, and even if some of the locals automatically assume you're here to sample their wares, they'll warmly welcome you into their once-forbidden city all the same. You might even cross one of the ornate thresholds of the medina, rooted in the diaspora from Spain, with architectural echoes of Al-Andalus despite the defiantly Maghrebi locale.

Washed in swathes of pastel blue, the stone passages, dead ends and doorways are more luminous and dream-like than perhaps any other old quarter in North Africa, aglow with mountain light. Aromas of baking bread, mint tea and cumin fill the air. Getting lost is a given, and a must; the medina's centuries-old momentum will deposit you into the main square in its own unhurried time, for here lies another dream-world, at least at night, when the tea shops and restaurants assume the guise of exotic grottos, twinkling and beckoning. Over it all presides the sheer rock of Jebel al-Kalaa, hanging in an electric-blue sky so crisp you can feel it crackling, across a landscape coloured with the same Indian hemp crop that's grown here for centuries.

Diving in the Red Sea coral gardens

EGYPT The Ras Mohammed National Park is one of the Red Sea's prime diving areas. Of the variety of starting points, Anemone City, a sloping underwater plateau covered with sea anemones hosting cute but ferocious pairs of clownfish, makes for one of the best introductions. Once you've descended to 20m, you swim through the blue towards the 700m vertical wall of Shark Reef, a kaleidoscopic natural aquarium. Home to countless species, from gaudily striped butterflyfish to long-horned unicornfish, the wall is also a nursery for baby fishes, flapping their fins madly just to remain stationary.

Nearby is the coral garden at Yolanda Reef and the wreck of the *Yolanda* itself, which sank carrying bathroom supplies. Now assimilated by the sea and encrusted with coral layers, its cargo of toilets lies adorned with stinging green fire corals. A blue-spotted ray rises from the sandy bottom and drifts gracefully away. Before you know it your air's nearly done; time to re-enter the world above.

NEED to know

287 Several operators specialize in camel-trekking; try Siroko Travel (www.sirokotravel.com).

288 The Medersa Bou Inania (Mon–Thurs, Sat & Sun 8.30am–noon & 1–6pm, Fri 8.30–11am & 1–5pm; 10dh) is at the western end of Talàa Kebira, the upper of two main lanes that traverse the medina.

289 The Pyramids are 11km west of Cairo and can be reached by bus or taxi. The site is open daily: summer 6.30am–midnight; winter 7am–8pm.

290 From Agadir airport, buses (to Essaouira) or taxis go to Taghazout. Most accommodation is through local host families; alternatively try *Auberge Amouage Taghazout* (ⓣ 00 212 (0) 2820 0272). Board and wetsuit hire from outlets in the village costs around 190dh per day. Surf-camps/surf schools offer weekly packages with board-hire, lessons, travel, accommodation and a meal for 3800–5000dh.

291 Most Tassili treks are part of an organized tour; see www.sahara-overland.com. Written confirmation of your place on a tour is required to obtain an Algerian visa.

292 The *Fishawi Café* is behind the *El Hussein* hotel in Khan-el-Khalili and is open 24hr.

293 A variety of tajines are available from places all over Morocco, from hole-in-the-wall eateries to upmarket restaurants.

294 The rooftop terraces of the *Café de France* and *Restaurant Argana* afford great views over the Jemaa el Fna. Be aware that pickpockets operate in the square; usual cautions apply.

295 Aswan lies 900km south of Cairo. The Aswan tourist office can recommend felucca captains and prices.

296 *Hammams* typically cost around 3TD for a steam bath; double that with a massage. Women usually bathe in the afternoon, men in the morning and evening. Some are single sex only. Good ones to try are Hammam Sahib et Tabaa in Tunis (close to Place Halfaouine) and Hammam Sidi Bouraoui in Sousse (off Rue Aghlaba).

297 Many nationalities can travel in Morocco and Western Sahara without a visa and can buy a Mauritanian visa on the border (€20). It's possible to cross the Western Sahara by public transport or taxi, but if you're driving yourself an excellent website to use is www.sahara-overland.com.

298 St Catherine's Monastery (daily except Fri & Sun 9am–noon, closed on Greek Orthodox holidays) charges £E17.50 to enter the St Catherine's Protectorate area, plus £E85 to hire a compulsory guide to climb Mount Sinai. For more information see www.egypt .travel.

299 Luxor is 700km south of Cairo. Boats cross the Nile, from where you can proceed by bus or taxi to the Valley of the Kings.

300 The only permitted travel to Jebel Acacus is with a tour; try Wahat Umm Algouzlan, 1st Circle Road, Alfidaiq, Denghazi (ⓣ 00 218 61 222 3420, ⓔinfo @libyato.com).

301 For upmarket accommodation, try the *Ville Nouvelle*, while there's a cluster of budget places around Bab Boujeloud.

302 Troglodyte accommodation ranges from Matmata's de luxe *Hôtel Diar el Barbar* (ⓣ 00 216 75 240 074) to simple guesthouses in Douiret and Toujane.

303 The Bibliotheca Alexandrina is at El Shatby 21526. See www.bibalex.org for more.

304 Dougga is just over 100km from Tunis; to get there by public transport, take the bus from Tunis to Taboursouk and transfer to a *louage*.

305 The four-day Festival d'Essaouira Gnaoua et Musiques du Monde (www.festival-gnaoua.net) is held annually in June. All concerts are held in public spaces and are free.

306 There are now flights to Ghadames from Tripoli, or you can take a bus via Nalut.

307 For information on tours to the area, see www .sahara-overland.com.

308 For information on travelling to Beni-Abbès and Timimoun, visit www.algeria.embassyhomepage .com.

309 The usual jumping-off point for the Ubari lakes is Tekerkiba, where there are a couple of places to camp and eat; otherwise there's a youth hostel in nearby Fjeij.

310 Tlemcen is a town close by the Moroccan border, and is well connected with the rest of Algeria by bus and train, as well as by air with Algiers.

311 The base for the Hoggar is the modern town of Tamanrasset. Point Afrique (www.point-afrique .com) organizes expeditions.

312 Leptis Magna is 3km east of Khoms, though it makes an easy day-trip from Tripoli.

313 *Auberge Chez Tihri* (www.tuaregexpeditions .com) lies 2km north of Merzouga.

314 Tanta is 95km north of Cairo. The Moulid of Sayyid Ahmed al-Badawi takes place over eight days in October.

315 The best time to cross the desert is between November and March.

316 You can stay at several refurbished kasbahs along the route; the most atmospheric is *Kasbah Ellouze* (ⓣ 00212 6796 5483, www.kasbahellouze.com).

317 As well as the medina, spare some time for Tripoli's wonderful Jamahiriya museum – one of the world's best archeological collections.

318 Chefchaouen is most easily accessed by the twice-daily bus from Tangier (3hr). Despite the apparent tolerance in town, be aware that cannabis possession is illegal and any foreigner caught indulging can expect the full force of Moroccan law.

319 For more information, go to Red Sea Diving College (www.redseacollege.com).

GOOD to know

AFRICAN EXPLORERS

The colourful exploits of European adventurers such as David Livingstone, Mungo Park and Richard Francis Burton are well known, but arguably the world's greatest explorer is actually from Africa. In the fourteenth century, Morocco's **Ibn Battuta** travelled over 100,000km over a thirty-year period. In addition to much of Africa, Battuta's claim to have been all over the Middle East, Central and Southeast Asia and China, far outstripped the travelling credentials of his near-contemporary, Marco Polo.

RETURN OF THE MUMMY

Egyptologist Zahi Hawass is a leading voice in the archeological **repatria-tion** movement – the campaign to get artefacts, many looted in colonial times, returned to their places of origin. The Rosetta Stone at the British Museum is perhaps the most significant, but it may only be a matter of time before the increasing sophistication of DNA testing and genealogical techniques lead to demands for the return of many of the embalmed nobles and dignitaries – mummies – whose haunting faces can be seen in museums around the world.

"A stone from the hand of a friend is an apple"

Moroccan proverb

HOT SPOT

The highest **temperature** ever recorded was in the Libyan town of Al 'Aziziyah on September 13, 1922, when the mercury reached 57.7°C (135.9°F) – in the shade.

POT SPOT

"Wanna buy hashish? Very nice. Cool, my friend. Have a little piece." You can't visit Morocco and escape at least one **drugs** offer, often hundreds. Most of the hash – resin rubbed from marijuana plants grown on Rif mountain cannabis farms – is filched surplus from the huge quantities destined to be smuggled to Europe and beyond.

SAHARA SCALE

The biggest desert in the world (or, to geographers who insist on including Antarctica, the second biggest), the **Sahara** defies imagination. At nearly ten million square kilometres, it would easily swallow the USA. Crossing the middle, from north to south, takes a good four days of steady driving, over largely trackless wastes: even today, there's no continuous tarmac. By the time you reach the outpost of Tamanrasset, halfway across, you're further from Algiers than Algiers is from London. Big dunes (known as barkans) are comparatively rare, but there are some monsters in southern Algeria, where they can reach more than 450m high – taller than New York City's Empire State Building.

SENSITIVE CARTOGRAPHY

In 1975, King Hassan II of Morocco organized a mass, popular march into the phosphate-rich region of **Western Sahara**, nominally a Spanish colony at the time, to claim it for Greater Morocco. More than a quarter of a million Moroccans joined the procession, and, despite international protests and UN resolutions, tens of thousands of Moroccans have since emigrated into the Sahrawis' homeland. The Polisario armed resistance movement, with its sprawling refugee capital at Tindouf, deep in the desert, has repeatedly struck back, usually with Algerian assistance, to little avail. A UN-sponsored autonomy referendum, long overdue, is still supposed to be held, one day, but as the years go by, the question of who is and who isn't a Sahrawi gets harder to ascertain. Meanwhile, Moroccan security police still examine the maps and guides of travellers to check they're not carrying any misleading information.

TANGIER: HOME OF THE BEATS

The year Jack Kerouac's *On The Road* was first published, 1957, coincided with a wave of interest from writers and artists in the bohemian lifestyle supposedly on offer in the international port city of **Tangier**. Kerouac and Allen Ginsberg stayed at the *Hôtel el Muniria*, where William Burroughs wrote *Naked Lunch* in room 9.

SACRED SERPENTS

The **asp**, also known as the Egyptian cobra, was worshipped in ancient Egypt. The snake was seen as a symbol of power, and its image adorned the crowns of the pharaohs.

NILE FEVER

The dancing known in the West as belly dance is an Egyptian form known as **raks sharki**. A long-established solo performance repertoire, it holds a major place in the hearts of millions of Egyptians and is often performed at weddings and other family occasions.

"The whole world is in revolt. Soon there will be only five kings left: the King of England, the King of Spades, the King of Clubs, the King of Hearts, and the King of Diamonds"

King Farouk
Egypt's last reigning monarch

ISABELLE EBERHARDT

Nineteenth-century European society threw up some extraordinary individuals, few more so than **Isabelle Eberhardt**. Born into a radical family in Geneva in 1877, she went to Algeria when she was 20 to start a new life with her widowed mother, who died soon after they arrived, leaving Isabelle to fend for herself. She soon spoke fluent Arabic and travelled widely in the desert, dressed as a man, and, eschewing her European anarchist background, following the pious code of Wahhabist Islam. At the same time, she continued to pursue a passionate and uninhibited lifestyle that recklessly toyed with the mores of her adopted home. The fascinating and inspiring *Diaries of Isabelle Eberhardt* are a highly recommended read if you're travelling in North Africa. Eberhardt was killed in a flash flood in the Sahara in 1904.

THE MANUSCRIPTS OF CHINGUETTI • THE MYSTERIOUS RUINS OF DJADO • DRIFTING UP THE NIGER • PARTYING WITH THE TUAREG AT THE FESTIVAL IN THE DESERT • BIG BEAKS AND HASTY UNDERTAKERS: WATCHING HORNBILLS • HOBNOBBING WITH AFRICA'S FILM-MAKING JET SET • BIRD-WATCHING IN THE VERDANT VOID • THE GOLD COAST: SUN, SEA AND SLAVE FORTS • ADMIRING THE CATCH ON SANYANG BEACH • GETTING DOWN TO BUSINESS IN CONAKRY • CYCLING A RING ROAD WITH A DIFFERENCE • DEMYSTIFYING VOODOO IN OUIDAH • SOAKING IN WIKKI WARM SPRINGS • CROSSING THE DESOLATE SANDS WITH THE PEOPLE OF THE VEIL • SACRED SPACE: THE GRAND MOSQUE IN DJENNÉ • SPOTTING RAINFOREST ORCHIDS IN A PROG-ROCK PARADISE • IN SEARCH OF THE BEST CHOCOLATE IN THE WORLD • CLUBBING IN DAKAR • SEEING THE JUNGLE THROUGH THE EYES OF THE BAKA • ISLAND-HOPPING OFF THE AFRICAN COAST • STREET FOOD, HIGHLIFE AND SHRINES IN ACCRA'S OLD TOWN • UPRIVER BY BOAT, AFRICAN QUEEN STYLE • RUNNING AGROUND IN THE BIJAGÓS ISLANDS • SPOTTING SMALL HIPPOS ON BIG ISLAND • TREKKING IN DOGON COUNTRY • RIDING THE WAGONS ON THE WORLD'S LONGEST TRAIN • PEAKING ON FOGO • THE MANUSCRIPTS OF CHINGUETTI • THE MYSTERIOUS RUINS OF DJADO • DRIFTING UP THE NIGER • PARTYING WITH THE TUAREG AT THE FESTIVAL IN THE DESERT • BIG BEAKS AND HASTY UNDERTAKERS: WATCHING HORNBILLS • HOBNOBBING WITH AFRICA'S FILM-MAKING JET SET • BIRD-WATCHING IN THE VERDANT VOID • THE GOLD COAST: SUN, SEA AND SLAVE FORTS • ADMIRING THE CATCH ON SANYANG BEACH • GETTING DOWN TO BUSINESS IN CONAKRY • CYCLING A RING ROAD WITH A DIFFERENCE • DEMYSTIFYING VOODOO IN OUIDAH • SOAKING IN WIKKI WARM SPRINGS • CROSSING THE DESOLATE SANDS WITH THE PEOPLE OF THE VEIL • SACRED SPACE: THE GRAND MOSQUE IN DJENNÉ • SPOTTING RAINFOREST ORCHIDS IN A PROG-ROCK PARADISE • IN SEARCH OF THE BEST CHOCOLATE IN THE WORLD • CLUBBING IN DAKAR • SEEING THE JUNGLE THROUGH THE EYES OF THE BAKA • ISLAND-HOPPING OFF THE AFRICAN COAST • STREET FOOD, HIGHLIFE AND SHRINES IN ACCRA'S OLD TOWN • UPRIVER BY BOAT, AFRICAN QUEEN STYLE • RUNNING AGROUND IN THE BIJAGÓS ISLANDS • SPOTTING SMALL HIPPOS ON BIG ISLAND • TREKKING IN DOGON COUNTRY • RIDING THE WAGONS ON THE WORLD'S LONGEST TRAIN • PEAKING ON FOGO • THE MANUSCRIPTS OF CHINGUETTI • THE MYSTERIOUS RUINS OF DJADO • DRIFTING UP THE NIGER • PARTYING WITH THE TUAREG AT THE FESTIVAL IN THE DESERT • BIG BEAKS AND HASTY UNDERTAKERS: WATCHING HORNBILLS •

West Africa
320–346

CAPE VERDE ISLANDS
Island-hopping off the African coast
339

Riding the wagons on the world's longest train
345

MAURITANIA

MALI

Trekking in Dogon country

NIGER

SENEGAL

Upriver by boat, African Queen style
341

THE GAMBIA

344

GUINEA-BISSAU

GUINEA

Hobnobbing with Africa's film-making jet set
325

Soaking in Wikki Warm Springs

Getting down to business in Conakry
329

BURKINA FASO

NIGERIA

332

SIERRA LEONE
343

Spotting small hippos on Big Island

CÔTE D'IVOIRE

GHANA

LIBERIA

TOGO

BENIN

CAMEROON

338

Seeing the jungle through the eyes of the Baka

SÃO TOMÉ & PRINCÍPE
336

EQUATORIAL GUINEA

In search of the best chocolate in the world

320 The manuscripts of Chinguetti

MAURITANIA Al-Habot's house is a house like any other in the warren of lanes that makes up the old mud-walled desert town of Chinguetti. A heavy wooden door creaks open onto a courtyard and your guide reaches for a foot-long key carved from tamarisk to unlock a smaller portal. Inside the dimly lit cavern are piles of boxes containing manuscripts dating back to the twelfth century, when Islam first reached this region. Finely penned Arabic scripts, still readable today, offer guidance on grammar or etiquette. Other parchments record civil disputes or manifests, for Chinguetti has been a key staging post on trans-Sahara trade routes for over a thousand years.

321 The mysterious ruins of Djado

NIGER Timbuktu? Forget it. A far more intriguing mystery lies hidden on the far side of Niger's Ténéré Desert; here, among vast plains, abandoned villages and intriguing cave art, the mud-brick citadel of Djado rises from palm-fringed pools crammed with bright-green reeds, like some unworldly goblin's castle. Explore the honeycomb of sand chocked passages inside; there's no one around. Eventually, you'll emerge atop the crumbling ramparts and comprehend the isolation: a barren plateau to the east; infinite sand sheets unrolling westwards. When was Djado built? Why was it abandoned? The hot wind stirs the palms but keeps its secrets.

322 Drifting up the Niger

MALI The shore is awash with colours and voices. People clamber aboard like pirates, vaulting over barriers and passing down goods and livestock in exchange for wardrobes and other essential items. Just time to get a few more sheep stowed and we are off.

The "big" boats have been ferrying people up and down the River Niger since 1964, playing a vital role in Malian society by providing the only form of access to some villages and transporting traders to sell their wares. In their heyday, the boats were packed with a thousand passengers; floating villages with people marooned in their cabins or sleeping amongst the cargo. These days you are likely to see more goats than people on board.

It takes six days to drift from Koulikoro, near the capital Bamako, to Gao, a Sahelian city 1300km to the north, stopping along the way to explore the bustling market towns of Mopti and Niafunké, home of the late, great Malian musician, Ali Farka Touré. When it's not possible to go ashore, boys pull up in dug-out canoes to sell provisions to passengers – the warm aroma of exotic food wafts across deck from their small charcoal stoves.

The richness of the experience of travelling on the "big" boat is spending time with the locals, sharing stories and exchanging views. And there's no better way to get close to Malian life, as you slip through the scenery, past villages clinging to the cliff side and sand dunes reaching down to the water's edge. Fishermen on *pirogues*, camels on the bank, hippopotamuses in the shallows: it all passes slowly by.

PARTYING WITH THE TUAREG at the **FESTIVAL IN THE DESERT**

MALI Way back in pre-Islamic times, Tuareg nomads would have gathered in the desert to settle disputes, race camels and entertain one another with displays of swordsmanship, music and dance. Today, Mali's Festival in the Desert combines these traditions with the chance to hear a dazzling range of sounds under the clear desert sky. The music and the setting among the rolling white dunes of the southern Sahara are hard to beat, but it's the people – men in richly coloured robes perched on camels bedecked with tassels, women in black, their faces stained with indigo – and the sea of white tents where families have set up camp with their livestock that make the event so unforgettable.

By day most of the action takes place in and around a shallow natural amphitheatre where women drum, clap and sing and tribesmen dance, swiping swords through the air as they skip and sway to the hypnotic rhythms. Stalls nearby sell metal and leatherwork, beads of glass and amber and moon-faced fertility dolls. Here you can have a cloth-seller tie you a turban against the burning sun, or learn about nomadic life as you bargain over glasses of bittersweet Tuareg tea.

After nightfall, as temperatures plummet, you'll be wrapping up warm and planting yourself close to one of the charcoal braziers among the dunes. The festival's main acts pump out an astonishing range of music – recent years have seen appearances by bands from Africa, Europe, North America and as far afield as the South Pacific. You'll hear everything from the pure, limpid tones of the harp-like *kora*, through western dance music, to timeless desert blues of the kind made famous by the late Ali Farka Touré.

323

THE GAMBIA Just like its people, the avian population of this small West African nation are a welcoming lot. There's a remarkable abundance and variety of birds to be found, and a great many are colourful, conspicuous individuals with a "look at me!" attitude – it's bird-nerd heaven. Spotting them is as easy as stepping out onto your veranda: every hotel garden is alive with jaunty little finches, doves, sunbirds and glossy starlings. But the adventurous will want to hire a guide and head off on the kind of walk where you get burrs in your socks and need frequent swigs from your water bottle. In some areas, you can clock up a hundred or more species in a few hours: common wetland birds such as kingfishers, pelicans, herons and egrets, and savannah-dwellers such as vultures and rollers are practically guaranteed – as are many bird-watchers' favourites: the hornbills.

As endearing as they are faintly ridiculous, hornbills' beaks seem too large for their bodies, and their flapping, gliding flight looks nothing short of haphazard. What's more, they take parental paranoia to grand extremes: if it's breeding season (July and August), you may see a male incarcerating his female and her brood in a nest sealed with mud, high up in a tree, where they'll stay until the young are strong enough to survive on their own.

The most lugubrious fellow of all is the Abyssinian ground hornbill. Nearly a metre tall, cloaked in black and with a beak of Gothic proportions, it strides through the open grassland with the undignified haste of an undertaker who's late for an urgent appointment. It's by far the largest – and the most impressive – of the hornbills, so if you manage to spot one, you've really scored. And before you know it, you'll be posting gloating field notes on the internet like a true convert.

BIG BEAKS AND HASTY UNDERTAKERS:
watching hornbills

324

325 Hobnobbing with Africa's film-making jet set

BURKINA FASO In an attempt to reinvent Ouagadougou, the government in Burkina Faso has taken the drastic decision to raze most of its centre to the ground. The residents of the apartment blocks that now lie in rubble have been relocated to outlying neighbourhoods, while architects ponder how to make the Burkinabè capital the envy of West Africa. The plan is for a gleaming new centre, although arguably Ouaga's true renaissance began when FESPACO first rolled into town forty-odd years ago.

It might not be the most likely cultural centre, but this stifling Sahelian city, known largely for its catchy name, hosts the continent's biggest film festival – one explicitly dedicated to African film-making. The biennial event is a great time to be in Ouaga. Several understated cinemas, wisely left intact by city-planners, show Africa's latest cinematographic offerings, from touching pastoral tales to riotous comedies, and festival-goers get the chance to rub shoulders with film stars and directors.

After the screenings, Ouaga's restaurants fill up with people from all corners of Africa and the world beyond. Over glasses of French wine, lively discussions revolve around the contenders for the Étalon de Yennenga, the festival's most prestigious award, given to the film that best symbolizes the cultural identity of Africa. And in the seething, sweaty *cabarets* (bars), local bands play as large divas dressed in vibrantly coloured *boubous* and kaftans try in vain to teach tourists to dance.

FESPACO is a democratic and unpretentious gathering, a real melting pot that's the antithesis of the glitz and glamour of events such as Cannes. Forums, debates and other events provide visitors with relatively easy access to film-makers, which means that in Ouaga, rather than a mere autograph, fans stand to get phone numbers, email addresses and maybe even the chance to establish lasting friendships with the big names of Africa's silver screen. And who knows, perhaps one day Ouagadougou will even have the kind of infrastructure that wouldn't look out of place along the Côte d'Azur.

326 Bird-watching in the verdant void

MAURITANIA Once known to French colonialists as Le Grande Vide ("The Great Void"), Mauritania covers more than one million square kilometres of Saharan dunes – nearly a third of the entire country is desert. Brush the sand aside, however, and you'll discover that Mauritania's national parks – set about verdant coastal wetlands – make for some of the most spectacular bird-watching in the world, with opportunities for sighting more than 500 individual species, many of them endangered or threatened.

Parc National du Banc d'Arguin, located on the western fringes of the Sahara, comprises thousands of acres of shallow seagrass beds and intertidal flats and creeks. Together, these grounds are home to millions of families of migrating birds who nest and raise their chicks in these areas from April to July and again between October and January. Around a third of all waders using the East Atlantic flyway winter here. Birds to watch out for include flamingoes, pelicans, herons and cormorants, as well as European spoonbills, godwits and terns. Small shorebirds are particularly numerous, gathering in large flocks around coastal settlements – keep an eye out for the sanderling and ruddy turnstone. Look down and around, meanwhile, and you'll see a unique ecosystem of marine and animal life that includes seals, tortoises, dolphins and crabs, as well as jackals and gazelles.

The prodigious flocks scatter across the vast 290km-long coastline during the day, so it's best to head out at dawn to catch them before they make for the offshore islets. For the most intimate viewing, visit one of several native Imragen villages, where an early-morning guided boat trip lets you get up close to great waves of birds flying low over the water on their way to feeding grounds.

327 The Gold Coast: sun, sea and slave forts

GHANA In 1471, Portuguese merchant seamen arrived on the palm-lined shore of the Gold Coast and bought a fort at Elmina. Over the next four hundred years they were followed by British, Dutch, Swedes, Danes and adventurers from the Baltic. Gold was their first desire, but the slave trade soon became the dominant activity, and more than three dozen forts were established here, largely to run the exchange of human cargo for cloth, liquor and guns. Today, thirty forts still stand, several in dramatic locations and offering atmospheric tours and accommodation. Here you can combine poignant historical discovery with time on the beach – a rare blend in this part of the world.

One of the biggest forts is the seventeenth-century Cape Coast Castle, which dominates the lively town of the same name. Just walking through its claustrophobic dungeons, where slaves were held before being shipped across the Atlantic, moves some visitors to tears – the scale of the cruelties that took place here is near-incomprehensible.

A particularly good time to visit the town is September, when the huge harvest festival, the Oguaa Fetu, takes over – a noisy, palm-wine-lubricated parade of chiefs, fetish priests and queen mothers. If you want to be made particularly welcome, bring along some schnapps, the customary gift for traditional rulers, with whom you may well be granted an audience.

Elmina, now a bustling fishing port, is home to the photogenically sited St George's Castle and Fort St Jago, eyeballing each other across the lagoon. St George's offers a worthwhile historical and cultural exhibition, and in the town itself you can ogle several intricate traditional shrines – pastel-coloured edifices of platforms, arches and militaristic figurines.

Some of the best beaches are at Busua, which has a low-key resort an easy walk from the cutely perched Fort Metal Cross. A day-trip to the far western coast, between Princestown and Axim, brings you to an even finer stretch of beaches and sandy coves punctuated with jungle-swathed headlands.

328 Admiring the catch on Sanyang beach

THE GAMBIA With pockets full of treasure – a sand dollar urchin, a cowrie, a piece of wave-bitten wood – we're padding along off Sanyang beach. It's late in the day, and we hardly recognize the place, even though we were here just a few hours ago, strolling in the opposite direction. In the monochrome midday heat, the shoreline had been near-deserted. It's since become a boat park, a fish market, a playground for bright-eyed kids and a scavenging site for squabbling seabirds. The whole scene is a riot of colour.

A few brightly painted *pirogues* are still heading home on the incoming tide, their 12m lengths dipping into the water, heavy with the day's haul. It takes strength to manhandle them onto logs and roll them up the beach. Once ashore, prize catches such as small sharks or whip-tailed rays are held up and admired, and quick deals are struck as the quarry is divided among the crew

members or offloaded to traders.

The fishermen's wives and daughters, their heads wrapped in vivid cotton *tikos*, squat beside buckets of greasy-skinned bonga fish, scraping scales onto the sand or slicing open sea snails to reveal oozing grey innards. The metallic tang of salt and blood mingles with the eye-wateringly pungent aroma of dried fish wafting across from the smokehouses.

We're only a few kilometres from the busiest Gambian resorts. Fifteen minutes' drive and we'd be hearing a different kaleidoscope of sounds – the snap and sigh of beer bottles opening, the hairdryer-whirr of tourists getting ready for the evening ahead. But, right now, there's nothing I'd rather be listening to than these fishermen shouting good-natured jokes while the gulls wheel and call overhead.

329 Getting down to business in Conakry

GUINEA Conakry has seen real turmoil in recent years, with extreme poverty, a large refugee population and a series of government coups afflicting Guinean society, but nightlife here still ranks among the best in Africa. For years, an ethos of creativity and hedonism has pervaded the capital, supported by a seemingly endless array of drinking and dance joints that offer everything from local folksy sounds to simmering international DJ parties.

Nights out on the town are all about moving your body to Guinean music – soft lilting tunes that explode into gorgeous, grooving dance workouts melding Caribbean zouk and African *mbalax*, infused with the region's trademark trebly electric guitar. There's not much point heading out before midnight, and you should dress to impress – suit and tie for men, black, form-fitting dance gear for women – at least if you want to fit in with your African peers. You'll find plenty of alcohol, but few posers.

To start, escape downtown Ville and explore some of the low-key spots north on the peninsula. *KSK* in Ratoma is a large, blingy disco

run by a group of Liberian refugees and a super spot to start a party. Avoid the upstairs VIP room and its overpriced bubbly and stay downstairs, where DJs spin up-and-coming Guinean pop and rap. Next, in Coléah, try *Petit Paris* – a crowded, sweaty and very local little *boîte* that gets packed with svelte Guinean twenty-somethings, the occasional foreigner and a coterie of prostitutes checking themselves out in the mirrors. Nearby here is *La Paillote*, Guinea's most vibrant venue during the Sekou Touré era and now exuding no small amount of nostalgia, with members of former star orchestras hanging out during the week in the early evening; you can be sure of meeting old band members telling stories over a beer. For live music, a good downtown bet is *Bembeya Jazz*, a long-established mirrored club with a central raised stage that still hosts regular performances of the *ngoni* (banjo), the *balafon* (vibraphone) and the *kora* (a cross between a harp and a lute), while Friday evenings often see local groups perform at around 9pm on the small square opposite the BICIGUI bank on Ave de la République in downtown Ville.

330 Cycling a ring road with a difference

CAMEROON The green, hilly Western Region, straddling the fault line between English- and French-speaking Cameroon, is one of Africa's most verdant corners, a spectacularly beautiful bubble-wrap landscape of grass-swathed volcanic hills, rivers, lakes and forests. The single "main road" that circles round the region in a 200km red-earth loop makes a perfect route for a superb week of cycling.

Start from the cacophonous, English-speaking town of Bamenda, then pedal north for an hour or two to Bafut, of naturalist Gerald Durrell's *Bafut Beagles* fame – his book recounts his visit collecting zoo animals here in the 1950s, when he stayed with the traditional ruler, the Fon of Bafut. His son, the present *fon* (chief), encourages visits to the thatched-roofed palace complex and, if you're here at the end of the dry season, you can participate in the riotous, palm-wine-lubricated grass-cutting ceremony.

Further north, one or more wooden bridges on the Ring Road

are often down – usually busted by heavy lorries – so your much laughed-at mode of transport (locals think it hilarious for tourists to cycle) will prove a wise, as well as fun, choice. In the village markets, look out for fantastic arrays of fruit and veg – the best, intensely flavoured, green-skinned, orange-fleshed mangoes to be had anywhere, and avocados the size of boats. You'll also, less cheerfully, pass Lake Nyos where, in 1986, a freak cloud of naturally occurring carbon dioxide belched from the lake one night and asphyxiated thousands of people and animals.

At Dumbo, past the lush pastures of the Grassfields, you have the option of completing the Ring Road round to Bamenda or setting off north to Nigeria, down a vertiginous escarpment of boulders, tree roots and twisting paths. If the latter takes your fancy, you can hire a porter in Dumbo for the two-day hike – he'll even carry your bike, padded and trussed up and balanced on his head.

331
Demystifying voodoo in Ouidah

BENIN Despite the fact that Ouidah boasts one of West Africa's most beautiful beaches, the Atlantic walkway is not its main attraction. Situated 40km west of Cotonou, Benin's de facto capital, this former centre of West Africa's slave trade is the home of voodoo's eleventh supreme chief, the Daagbo (His Majesty) Tomadjlehoukpon II Metogbokandji. For visitors and locals alike, Ouidah is one of the region's most important centres of this oft-misunderstood belief.

Voodoo, Benin's official religion, isn't about sticking pins in dolls fashioned in the form of your mother-in-law or ex-boyfriend. Nor is it about the evil spells or devil worship that Hollywood makes it out to be. It's actually a faith with over fifty million followers worldwide, all worshipping a Supreme Being and hundreds of lesser gods and spirits.

In Ouidah, the cityscape is detailed with evidence of its influence. Fetishes – any man-made object that has been occupied by a spirit – lurk among the faded Portuguese-style buildings and along the grassy road to the beach. You may notice them because they look out of place in their environment, or are covered in the bloody, waxy remains of a recent animal sacrifice.

About a kilometre down a dirt track from town lies the Sacred Forest of Kpassé, guarded by a dozen or so statues honouring the various divinities of the gods. Several are made from old motorcycle parts, but the most striking lies near the entrance, a roughly metre-high horned creature with an enormous phallus, symbolizing strength and fertility. When ceremonies to the snake god Dangbé (also known as Dan) are not under way in Ouidah's Temple of the Python, opposite the Ouidah Basilica, visitors can creep inside its cement walls to have their photos taken with sleepy and harmless pythons slung around their necks.

The town also hosts a voodoo festival each January, and various ceremonies are held throughout the year, when costumed dancers and those "fortunate" enough to be temporarily possessed by spirits sway to the beat of drums, summoning the gods. And, if you're really lucky, you might get invited in for an audience with the Supreme Chief himself, regally perched in an imitation La-Z-Boy and sipping a Fanta. Imagine the Pope being so hospitable.

NIGERIA Bathing in the near-perfect natural pool at Wikki Warm Springs, part of Nigeria's remote Yankari National Park, is one of West Africa's most gratifying experiences. Below the park lodge, down a steep path, the upper Gaji stream bubbles up from a deep cleft beneath a rose-coloured, sandstone cliff.

Twelve million litres a day, at a constant 31°C, flood out over sparkling sand between a dense bank of overhanging tropical foliage on one side and the concrete apron that serves as a beach on the other – the one dud note in an otherwise picture-perfect environment, though the concrete helps keep the crystal-clear water clean. Floodlighting makes the springs equally idyllic at night, giving them a satisfyingly theatrical appearance, like an elaborate New Age interior design piece. A good deal larger than most swimming pools, the springs are the ideal place to wash away the frustrations of travelling in Nigeria.

Should you tire of simply drifting on your back above the gentle current, you can explore the woods around the lodge for their abundant birdlife. It's also possible to go on a guided game drive with Yankari's rangers, bringing you into close contact with the park's savannah mammals, including several species of antelope, a variable population of elephants and, it's said, even lions. If, as occasionally happens, the viewing isn't up to much, returning to Wikki Warm Springs, and that delightful initial immersion, is ample compensation.

Soaking in Wikki Warm Springs

332

333 Crossing the desolate sands with the people of the veil

NIGER The Sahara is the world's largest desert, and arguably the most desolate, inhospitable place on Earth. It's roughly the size of the USA, yet has a population of less than a million people, and its vast expanse divides North Africa from sub-Saharan Africa in a great swath of dunes, sand seas, mountains and plateaus.

How do you get to experience this natural wonder? Well, not surprisingly the traditional caravan routes in northern Africa have long since been supplanted by more modern modes of transport. But a camel journey across the Sahara is not just a retro-chic way of "doing the desert", it adds up to an authentic and intimate experience that gets to the core of the desert's appeal. You become immersed in the landscape at a natural pace, savouring the simplicity, space and silence.

The journey begins a day's drive from Agadez in northern Niger. Camels grumble as loads are lashed to their backs, but saddles are mostly unoccupied. Forget the romantic image of the dromedary's lolling gait transporting you effortlessly over the sands. A camel is more mule than horse so you'll be on foot most of the time. Your Tuareg guide will show you how to put on the traditional turban or *tagelmoust* worn by all desert men, and soon you'll adapt to their pace, rising at dawn, strolling towards a shady noontime rest, and camping again around mid-afternoon when the camels are unloaded to forage for food. You cover 15km a day, stopping for mint tea at scruffy encampments where half-naked kids chase the goats and girls giggle shyly from behind their indigo shawls. The landscape is more diverse than you might expect, with the 2000m-high blue-grey peaks of Niger's Aïr Mountains merging with the amber-pink sand sheet of the Ténéré Desert far beyond the eastern horizon – the classic Saharan combination.

Tuareg nomad culture is alive and well in the Aïr despite a hostile government in the distant capital, Niamey. But "Tuareg" is in fact a derogatory Arabic term. From southwest Libya to Timbuktu in Mali these proud nomads describe themselves collectively as Kel Tagelmoust: "the People of the Veil".

334 Sacred Space: the Grand Mosque in Djenné

MALI is a treasure box of a country, where fishermen ply the River Niger in brightly painted *pirogues*, *kora*-playing *jalis* sing songs written for the rulers of an ancient, glittering empire and the faithful worship in spectacular mosques of timber and mud.

Djenné's Grande Mosquée is the most famous of all. Beautifully simple but with a potent presence, it exudes the kind of gravitas shared by all the world's great sacred buildings. But there's also something gloriously organic – sensuous, even – about its curves and crenellations; and it's a fitting focal point for a community which guards its traditions fiercely while embracing a brand of Islam that is neither repressive nor restrictive. Djenné itself is steeped in history and works hard to maintain its meticulously preserved state. Mud-built houses need regular attention, and at the end of each rainy season the whole town pitches in to make good the building's russet facades. Several hundred workers scale the walls of the Grande Mosquée with the help of the timber struts that sprout from the minarets like bristles.

Visit the Grande Mosquée on a Monday and it's abuzz with activity of a different sort. In the large, dusty marketplace in front of the mosque, traders preside over pyramids of knobbly bitter tomatoes and sacks of pungent dried fish, Fula women with heavy gold earrings pore over brightly patterned cotton fabrics and rickety donkey carts weave through the crowds. The market is thoroughly absorbing. But to appreciate Djenné more deeply, you'll need to stay on after the hubbub has dispersed, and savour that last, golden hour of the day when the call of the muezzin wafts over the city, just as it has every evening for seven hundred years.

335 Spotting rainforest orchids in a prog-rock paradise

SÃO TOMÉ AND PRÍNCIPE The island nation of São Tomé and Príncipe is Africa's second smallest country, after the Seychelles. Marooned in the sweltering Gulf of Guinea, just 250km from the equatorial rainforests of Gabon, its size hasn't stopped it being blessed with remarkable biodiversity.

Volcanic eruptions sculpted the archipelago's landscapes into dramatic crags and made them exceptionally fertile. Both of the main islands – São Tomé to the southwest and Príncipe to the northeast – are steep-sided, their heights cloaked in humid forest. On São Tomé, mist-shrouded towers of basalt add a surreal touch. Exploring the remoter corners feels like stepping into a prog-rock album cover, or the set of a *Lord of the Rings* spin-off.

Head into the virgin rainforest of Obô National Park and you can't fail to be wowed by the sheer variety of plant species. The Jardim Botânico de Bom Sucesso, the starting point for guided tours through the park, gives you an excellent overview, its fine array of native flora, carefully tended by local horticulturalists. Obô itself, which covers much of central and southeast São Tomé including the 2024m Pico de São Tomé, is home to giant begonias and over 150 types of tree fern – more than anywhere else in Africa. Birds and insects gravitate here: as you make your way along the mountain tracks, butterflies dance in the sunlight and African grey parrots squawk and chatter overhead.

Orchid aficionados will be in their element. Around 130 species have been identified on the islands to date, a quarter of them endemic, the descendants of plants whose seeds found their way here from the African mainland millions of years ago and have evolved in isolation ever since. Visit Obô in the rainiest months, March to April or September to December, and many of them will be in bloom. Some, such as *Cribbia pendula*, are inconspicuous, so spotting them is a pleasant challenge. Others are more colourful: *Bulbophyllum lizae* is a delicate yellow, *Polystachya biteaui* is as pretty as lily-of-the-valley, but a delightful dusty pink.

336 In search of the best chocolate in the world

SÃO TOMÉ & PRÍNCIPE You know you're in a country far from modernity when one of the main problems facing landowners is reforestation. São Tomé, the smallest nation in Africa, has largely been forgotten by the outside world since Portuguese colonizers packed up and left in the mid-1970s.

Away from São Tomé town – where the faded colonial-era buildings try their best to decay with elegiac ease, despite the occasional tree bursting out of a rooftop – and into the awesomely lush interior, the occasional remain of a long-abandoned train track is the only clue that you are about to stumble upon one of the many old plantation or roca buildings. Built by Angolan and Portuguese slaves, these grandiose structures helped make São Tomé one of the world's leading coca and coffee producers at the turn of the twentieth century. The owner's residence of the large Augustino Neto plantation looks something like a minor Inca fortress but, like most others on the island, it is derelict – independence and subsequent Marxist governments have brought coca production to its knees.

There are, however, smaller signs of life elsewhere. Individual entrepreneurs are slowly arriving at this tiny island, drawn to try and work with São Tomé's exceptionally fertile soil. Italian Claudio Corrallo has started a tiny coca plantation on the even smaller neighbouring island of Príncipe, where his chocolate is so luxurious that it is bought by Fortnum and Mason in London. He'll tell you how his cottage industry has cultivated coca species that many thought extinct, and ask him nicely, as I did one sweltering afternoon, and he might even give you some coca powder. A tiny teaspoon mixed with boiling water sipped on his rotting veranda in a chipped and battered mug is an explosion of rich and sumptuous flavour. This is sweetness taken straight from the raw coalface of chocolate production, and as Claudio reminds me, though he really doesn't need to, "the taste is out of this world".

337 Clubbing in Dakar

SENEGAL "Nanga def?" "Jama rek." The throaty greeting and response of the Wolof language is all around us as we hustle to get into a soiree at one of the busy clubs in Dakar, Senegal's dusty capital. Under the orange glow of street lamps, some outrageously upfront flirting is going on. It pervades the warm, perfume-laden air like static.

Inside, the lights swirl, the simple stage fills, the high, clear lead vocals surge through a battering of drums and the floor becomes a mass of shaking hips, bellies, arms and legs. It's no place to be shy – but there's no better place in Africa to get over shyness quickly.

Nightlife in Dakar is dominated by big-name musicians and their clubs. The city, staunchly Muslim (most Senegalese are devoted followers of Sufi saints) yet keenly fun-loving, is a magnet for musicians from across West Africa, drawn by a thriving CD market, famous venues and the best recording facilities in the region. The principal sounds are *mbalax* – the frenetic, drum-driven style popularized by Youssou N'Dour and his Super Etoile band – and hip-hop, whose ambassadors Daara J introduced the Senegalese streets to the world.

Going out in Dakar is not only about music and mating: clued-up Dakarois are obsessed with the mercurial fashion scene. However you wear it, your look is very important; go for bold and shiny and you won't fail to impress. Increasingly, you'll see girls in T-shirts and leggings, or even skinny harem pants and tunics, both daring innovations in a country where yards of beaten damask cloth is still a byword for glamour.

338 Seeing the jungle through the eyes of the Baka

CAMEROON Hot and sticky, with impenetrable green stretching as far as the eye could see. If first impressions really do count, then our relationship with the equatorial rainforest, in the extreme southeastern corner of Cameroon, looked like it wasn't going to last. But then our Baka guide led us into the jungle – and we immediately knew that this was the start of something beautiful.

The Baka are one of the many bands of so-called Pygmies that inhabit the forests of southern Cameroon. Believed to be the original inhabitants of the equatorial rainforest, they have for centuries lived as nomadic hunter-gatherers in harmony with their surroundings. Sadly, European ivory traders, loggers and the introduction of a Western market economy have gradually made it impossible for the Baka to maintain their traditional lifestyle, and they now find some financial solace in guiding clumsy tourists through the rainforest.

We were heading for a clearing – *bais* in Baka – where a stilted platform had been erected to watch, in safety, wildlife pass under-neath, following our guide in awe as he moved quickly and stealthily through the forest, stopping mid-stride whenever something caught his attention. Then, standing completely motionless, one foot still dangling in the air, he would crane his neck and track the sounds – the crack of a breaking branch or the shuffling of leaves – as they came ever closer. Even with the smallest noise, he would turn around, smile at us and mouth, "colobus", or "snake", and we'd go "huh?", not realizing it was anything more than a leaf turning in the wind or a seed falling from a tree.

Watching our guide in his element was highlight enough, but then, halfway to the *bais* he suddenly froze and whispered "gorilla", following up with an unmistakable hand gesture to make it clear he wanted us to stay absolutely still. Right in front of us, bushes were shaking, and as the noise became louder, so did the thumping of our hearts. In an instant, a beautiful silverback exploded from the undergrowth, rushing past. And then, just as quickly, he was gone. And we headed deeper into the jungle.

CAPE VERDE Follow the pointing finger of Senegal westwards and, 400km off the African coast, you reach the archipelago of Cape Verde, home of soulful world-music superstar Cesaria Evora. This nation of nine small islands remained uninhabited until 1462, when it was colonized by the Portuguese. The new arrivals brought in slaves from the mainland to work their sugar-cane fields. Not quite African and not quite European, Cape Verde today is almost Brazilian in feel.

Start in Praia, the capital, dramatically sited on a plateau on the largest and greenest island, Santiago, and offering relaxed street life, a small museum and a scattering of restaurants and clubs. From here, take the thirty-minute flight to Fogo ("Fire") island, dominated by a vast volcanic crater, where Cape Verde's only vineyards flourish. It's surmounted by the cone of a more recent volcano, steep but climbable, with sweeping views across the Atlantic from the summit that fully justify the effort.

The flat desert islands of the east – Sal, Maio, Boa Vista – have the best beaches, azure seas and windsurfing schools. On Boa Vista you can rent a jeep and drive to the uninhabited south coast, where turtle tracks are almost the only sign of life, and images of Robinson Crusoe spring irresistibly to mind.

Out on the northwest fringe of the archipelago lies the canyon-grooved mass of Santo Antão, where local buses cut precipitous routes along nineteenth-century cobbled roads overlooking the ocean. It's one of the more fertile islands, and you can enjoy superb hikes along rural farmers' paths. Nearby is São Vicente, noteworthy for playing host to an exuberant Carnaval every February, and the international Baia das Gatas music festival every August. Sate your hunger on pork or tuna, in a hybrid of Portuguese and African styles, washed down with shots of *grogue*, a powerful, aromatic sugar-cane rum.

339 Island-hopping
off the African coast

STREET FOOD, HIGHLIFE AND SHRINES IN ACCRA'S OLD TOWN

GHANA If you spend most of your time in Accra's central business district around Adabraka, or in the commercial suburbs of Osu and East Ridge, you may overlook the Ghanaian capital's historic heart, the adjoining neighbourhoods of Usshertown and Jamestown. This atmospheric warren of streets and alleys lies just back from the Atlantic seafront behind the main coast highway. Ruled by King Tackie Tawiah III, the paramount chief of the Ga people, Old Accra (or "Ga Mashie" to its local inhabitants) is a generally safe area to wander through alone, though you'll get more out of the visit, and greater freedom to take photos, if you're accompanied by a guide.

Beneath corrugated-iron roofs and between tinder-dry clapboard walls – hand-painted with adverts for fish and phones and often lettered with the curious characters of the Ga language – the district resonates with the noise of things being made, discussions about things being sold and the growl and crash of r'n'b and highlife playing from straining sound systems. There are reminders of the Ga's pre-colonial religious and political systems here, too: look out for the Sakumo shrine by an old well on Orgle Street, where you might meet priests on the shady terrace (though you won't be allowed inside). Just around the corner, pause at the Gbese Mantse Palace, with its portrait of current *mantse* (neighbourhood chief) Nii Ay-Bonte II.

When you're tired of wandering, take a break at the small museum of slavery in Ussher Fort, on the clifftop. Nearby, Brazil House records the story of nineteenth-century Brazilian freed-slave returnees – the Tabon community (named after the Portuguese greeting "Ta bom?"). The veranda of neighbouring Franklin House is a good spot for gazing down on the busy beach, thronged with people and fishing boats. You can get street food and a cold soda on any corner: try *kenkey* (fermented, pounded maize), or *fufu* (pounded cassava, sometimes mixed with plantain), with chunks of smoked fish and scorching pepper sauce.

The best time to be in Old Accra is the second week of August, for the Ga harvest festival of Homowo. You'll find music, drumming, men in toga-like robes, processions of twins, and what anthropologists call "suspension of behavioural sanctions" – partying.

340

341 Upriver by boat, African Queen style

THE GAMBIA Mid-afternoon brings a silvery gloss to the upper reaches of the River Gambia. The sky is white, the air hot and still. It's a quiet time for wildlife-watching on the river, but if you have a four-hour journey ahead of you, it's the perfect time to set out. Your vessel is a traditional West African *pirogue* that's been kitted out as a cruise boat, with simple, awning-draped decks. It looks rather like a canal barge crossed with a tent. Upstairs, there's room to stretch out. You settle yourself on a mattress, your binoculars by your side, as the captain eases the speed up to a gentle potter.

This mighty river – one of the few navigable stretches of fresh water in this, the most accessible part of West Africa for western Europeans – was once a corridor for raiders and rogues. Between the sixteenth and nineteenth centuries, adventurers combed its vicinity for slaves and game, picking off elephants for their ivory and big cats for their skins.

Today, the elephants and cats have long gone, but little else has changed. Settlements are sparse. The tropical vegetation thickens as soon as your boat steers away from the small rice-growing town of Kuntaur, and by the time you enter the stunning, island-scattered River Gambia National Park, your immersion is complete. The river and its banks fill the view, crowded with lush evergreens, reeds and palms. In the distance, a horizontal fuzz of green marks the next lazy bend.

Gradually, your eyes become accustomed to the glare, allowing you to pick out birds among the foliage: rollers and bee-eaters by their vivid colours; African fish eagles by their imposing silhouettes. The ears and nostrils of river-dwelling hippos surface near the mid-river islands, where chimps hoot and holler. As the light softens and the day cools, other primates – golden-green *Callithrix* monkeys and russet-coloured red colobus – can be seen bounding between the upper branches. Occasionally, solo fishermen make an appearance, paddling their dugouts through the shade at the water's edge with strong, measured strokes. But otherwise, you and your companions have this remarkable wilderness entirely to yourselves.

342 Running aground in the Bijagós islands

GUINEA-BISSAU With only two trips a week, it was important that every last bit of cargo was crammed into the *pirogue*'s damp, cavernous hull. The boat listed slightly as it lurched out of Bissau and away from the mainland, a few over-ripe tomatoes rolling off the tarpaulin roof and into the capital city's harbour, but gained an even keel in open water. The blue expanse of sea was utterly flat and so shallow that mounds of sand poked above the surface like dunes. Off the port side, the distant mangrove swamps of Bolama could have been an oasis.

A bottle of palm wine on board was doing a wonderful job deflecting attention away from the cramped legroom and oily stench of fish, until the captain appropriated it for himself and his rudder-man. Moments later, a few more tomatoes rolled off the roof as the *pirogue* ran aground. A chorus of Bijagó expletives caught the attention of flamingoes sunning themselves on a nearby sandbar... and then silence, the boat rocking gently in the rising tides that would eventually set it free.

Bathed in the golden light of the sinking sun, the wildlife-rich island of Bubaque felt like the undiscovered fantasy of a wizened explorer. Wispy plumes of smoke rose from the wooded interior and cries of "branco, branco" greeted the *pirogue* at the small jetty – the arrival of a white person is still an event worthy of exclamation in this little-visited corner of West Africa. The cargo was unloaded onto the island's two cars, which then bumped along tracks through the bush to deliver bottles of Coke to the few hotels and a new generator for the hospital. Their raspy engines reverberated across the island and reached back down to the jetty, where the captain was snoring peacefully in his simple vessel under thousands of stars.

343 Spotting small hippos on Big Island

SIERRA LEONE Deep in the maze of waterways, woodland and farm plots of southeast Sierra Leone lies Tiwai Island Wildlife Sanctuary, sheltering an extraordinarily rich fauna.

Tiwai means "Big Island" in the local language, and this truly is the Africa of the imagination, the air saturated with the incessant chirrups, squawks and yelps of birds, chimpanzees, tree hyraxes, assorted insects and hundreds of other creatures, all doing their thing in twelve square kilometres of rainforest. In the background, you can hear the dim rush of the Moa River where it splits to roar around Tiwai through channels and over rocks.

As you weave along paths between the giant buttress roots of the trees, park guides will track troops of colobus and diana monkeys and should know where to find the chimps. The rarest and most secretive of Tiwai's denizens is the hog-sized pygmy hippo, which you're not likely to see unless you go jungle walking at night, when they traipse their habitual solitary paths through the undergrowth.

Exploring after dark with a guide is, in fact, highly recommended – take a lamp with plenty of kerosene, and a good torch. By night, the forest is a powerful presence, with an immense, consuming vigour: every rotten branch teems with termites, and all around you sense the organs of detection of a million unseen creatures waving at your illuminated figure as you stumble over the roots. You can also take a boat tour of the Moa river in a canoe or motorboat, watching out for rare birds and butterflies and looking for turtles below the surface.

Trekking in Dogon country

MALI When the research of French anthropologist Marcel Griaule first shed some light on the mysterious lives of Mali's Dogon people back in the 1930s, no one could have predicted that barely a generation later backpackers would be trudging along the Bandiagara escarpment, drinking Coke with village elders and filling their stomachs with the slimy green gumbo that Griaule had no doubt laboured over during his field trips. But a trek through Dogon country, exploring the spectacular villages built precariously on the rise of the escarpment, has become a highlight of any trip to West Africa. It's not necessarily an extreme activity, nor does it involve overly difficult tramping, but there's plenty of intrigue and adventure nonetheless. Just as the villages themselves have an enchanted air about them, hanging for dear life to the cliff-face, so the ways of the Dogon seem imbued with a near-magical quality.

The services of a good guide are indispensable in a land where simple mounds of earth are in fact sacred altars and random markings in the sand are really questions to the gods. As you wander from one village to the next under a hot sun that beats down on the escarpment and warms the sandy plain that stretches towards Burkina Faso, a palpable energy follows you. It seeps through the mud pillbox granaries, their thatched roofs peaked like witches' hats; it hovers over the *togu na* ("House of Words") during a village council meeting, and it makes you feel that you are in a strange place indeed. As darkness falls over the escarpment, this energy is sucked up by the caves overhanging the cliff-face to sleep with the skeletons of the Dogon who are buried there, and when morning comes it swoops back down on the village just as you are contemplating your first spoonful of yet another steaming gumbo breakfast.

345 Riding the wagons on the world's longest train

MAURITANIA Waiting beside the track in the dead of night, we are offered tea and encouraged to huddle round a small fire. Somewhere, out across the emptiness, our train is rattling towards us, a chain of wagons that seems endless – it can stretch for over 2km – that cuts its way through the Sahara Desert, transporting iron-ore from the Adrar to the Atlantic port of Nouadhibou.

We've been straining our eyes and ears since 6pm, but delays are frequent and tonight the thunder of wagons is not heard until 1am. Occasional trains have passenger carriages, but not ours. The locals rush to hoist us on top of the cargo – iron is the real business here and paying passengers fare little better than the rooftop stowaways – and someone starts laying down a bed of blankets for everyone. We bless their kindness, as the crushed ore looks far from comfortable and the desert night is far from warm. But despite our being wrapped in headscarves and countless layers of clothing, the cold soon works its way into the soul. The black soot that clouds the train is no less persistent. We are soon rocked to sleep beneath the star-lit sky by the rhythm of the carriages until the sun rises and the desert stretches out on either side. The morning quickly warms and the remaining journey seems as infinite as the Sahara. Hours are whiled away, sharing tea and staring into a sandy horizon. Finally, we roll into Nouadhibou, and start the long walk to the front of the train – and town.

346 Peaking on Fogo

CAPE VERDE First impressions of Fogo, rising in a cone 2800m above the ocean, are of its forbidding mass, the steep, dark slopes looming above the clouds. The small plane is buffeted on Atlantic winds as you dip onto the runway, perched high on dun-coloured cliffs above a thin strip of black beach and ultramarine sea.

Fogo ("Fire" in Portuguese) is the most captivating of the Cape Verde Islands, with its dramatic caldera and peak, its fearsomely robust red wine, its traditional music and the hospitable Fogo islanders themselves.

Up in the weird moonscape of the caldera, after a slow, shared taxi ride from the picturesque capital, São Filipe, you'll be dropped on the rocky plain at a straggle of houses made of grey volcanic tufa. One of a handful of charmingly rakish-looking guides will greet you, host you in his own home and, early next morning, take you up the steep path to the summit, Pico de Fogo, with its extraordinary panorama. The descent is better than any theme-park ride as both guide and guided leap and tumble through the scree in an entertaining, inelegant freestyle.

Shaking out the dust and volcanic gravel at the bottom, you'll fetch up at the local social club where an impromptu band – guitar, violin, keyboard, scraper and *cavaquinho* (a four-stringed mini-guitar) – emboldened by the consumption of much *vinho* and local hooch or *grogue*, often strikes up around the bar. Wind down your evening listening to Fogo's beautiful *mornas* – mournful laments of loss and longing that hark back to the archipelago's whaling past and to families far away.

NEED to know

320 Chinguetti is two days' drive from the capital, Nouakchott. A dozen or so families maintain libraries in their homes, preserving some 6000 manuscripts in total.

321 Djado is a three-day jeep drive from Agadez, the largest city in northern Niger. Consult your foreign office's website for advice on northern Niger's security situation.

322 In season (Aug–Dec) boats leave Koulikoro every Tuesday at 10pm, though delays are frequent.

323 The festival takes place in early January at Essakane, although 2010's was moved to a site near Timbuktu after security concerns – your foreign office should be able to offer advice on security in the area. For tickets and more information, go to Ⓦwww .festival-au-desert.org.

324 Prime bird-watching areas include the Tanbi Wetlands, Abuko Nature Reserve, Brufut Woods, Marakissa and Janjanbureh. Birdfinders (Ⓦwww.birdfinders.co.uk) offers specialist tours to The Gambia.

325 FESPACO (Festival Panafricain du Cinéma et de la Télévision de Ouagadougou; Ⓦwww.fespaco.bf) takes place in every odd-numbered year at the end of February and lasts for ten days. Book accommodation well in advance.

326 Parc National du Banc d'Arguin is two hours from Nouadhibou, near the Moroccan border. Several organisations in Nouakchott run bird-watching tours; try Randonnées Tours (Ⓣ+222 525 9535, Ⓔrt@toptechnology.mr).

327 Bus services (around 4hr) run along the main coastal highway from Accra.

328 Sanyang beach is an easy taxi ride from Banjul and the resort towns of Kololi, Kotu, Fajara and Bakau.

329 For club hopping, hiring a private car (around FG50,000) for the evening is easiest. Cover fees can vary, ranging from nothing to FG15,000, though this is often negotiable – especially for foreigners heading to the purely African places, where they remain something of a novelty.

330 Bamenda is accessible by bus from most Cameroonian cities. Ⓦwww.ibike.org/bikeafrica offers tours and advice on cycling.

331 Ouidah is an hour's taxi ride from the capital, Cotonou. The Temple of the Python is open daily.

332 Yankari can get crowded at weekends, especially over Christmas and Easter. The park lodge has basic rooms (reserve ahead through Ⓦwww.yankarigamereserve.com).

333 Tour agencies in Agadez can organize camel treks. Consult your foreign office's website for information on travel in northern Niger – the security situation has been unstable in recent years.

334 Djenné is 30km from the main road between the Malian capital, Bamako, and the junction town of Mopti. The interior of the mosque is open to Muslims only.

335 Specialist tour operators organizing bespoke trips to São Tomé and Príncipe include Cape Verde Travel (Ⓦwww.capeverdetravel.com) and Africa's Eden (Ⓦwww.africas-eden.com). The Jardim Botânico de Bom Sucesso (Ⓦwww.jardimbotanico.st) is 19km from the capital of São Tomé.

336 TAP (Air Portugal) fly once a week from Lisbon to São Tomé; see Ⓦwww.flytap.com for details.

337 Check out clubs *Thiossane*, to see if Youssou N'Dour is in town; *Le Kily (Kilimanjaro)*, home to local star Thione Seck; or *Just 4 You* for Orchestra Baobab and other great bands. The quarterly *221* magazine has all the latest listings.

338 The WWF office at Yokadouma (Ⓣ+237 6629 5931 or +237 5529 2484), 612km from the capital of Yaoundé, can arrange treks with Baka guides into all three of southeastern Cameroon's national parks. See Ⓦwww.panda.org for general information from the WWF.

339 You can get around the islands by ferry, but voyages can be rough and slow; alternatively, buy a multi-coupon domestic air ticket from TACV (Ⓣ+238 260 8200), the national airline, based in Praia.

340 Ghana Home Tours (Ⓦgoghanahometours.com) runs tours of Old Accra with an excellent local historian, Sam Baddoo.

341 Specialist operator Hidden Gambia (Ⓦwww.hiddengambia.com) offers touring holidays which include a *pirogue* trip on the River Gambia (from £499 for seven nights, excluding flights).

342 Passenger-carrying *pirogues* (dug-out canoes) leave Bissau twice weekly for the two main Bijagós islands of Bubaque and Bolama.

343 Contact the sanctuary to make enquiries about a visit: Ⓦwww.tiwaiisland.org.

344 The most popular trek is from Banani to Kani Kombolé and takes roughly two days.

345 Trains run three times a day between Zouérat and Nouadhibou, via Choum, and are operated by SNIM: Ⓦwww.snim.com/fr/train/article-train.html.

346 The national airline TACV (Ⓣ+238 260 8200) offers flights to Fogo.

GOOD to know

TRADING PLACES

One of the main factors that shaped the history of West Africa between the eleventh and seventeenth centuries was **trans-Saharan trade**. Gold from Buré (in modern-day Guinea), Bambouk (in modern-day Senegal) and Akan (in modern-day Ghana) was transported across the desert to North Africa, as were slaves, while salt from mines in the Sahara went south. Powerful desert trading outposts were created, such as Oualata and Aoudaghost (both in modern-day Mauritania), and, most famously, Timbuktu in Mali – once so wealthy that its streets were said to be lined with gold. Huge camel caravans, known as *azalaïs*, still transport salt mined in Taoudenni, in northern Mali, across the Sahara, though trucks and 4x4s increasingly supplant these ships of the desert.

GO IN STYLE

Ever felt the Western way of **death** was a little too... solemn? The Ga people from the Accra area in Ghana came to that conclusion some time ago, and for those who can afford it, several famous coffin-makers construct elaborate, glossily painted caskets in any design you like. Fish? Lion? Mercedes? A little too traditional perhaps. How about a mobile phone, or a mouse?

WHAT'S IN A NAME?

Most West African countries retain the names by which they were known in colonial times, or earlier, such as the Ivory Coast, Guinea and Nigeria. But certain nations chose names at independence that would give their new nationhood an extra shine. **Ghana** is named after the huge medieval empire of the same name, whose capital was in the southeast of present-day Mauritania, and as recently as 1983, the revolutionary government in Upper Volta threw out the old descriptive moniker referring to the country's main river and came up with **Burkina Faso**, an epithet that means "Land of Honourable Men".

AFRICAN BIRDWINGS

Africa's biggest butterfly, the **giant swallowtail** (*Papilio antimachus*), lives in the great rainforests of Guinea, Sierra Leone, Liberia and the Ivory Coast. You can occasionally see the splendid orange males – with their twenty-centimetre wingspan and long, narrow wings – on forest paths, where they suck moisture and minerals from the mud. The slightly smaller females are rarely spotted, as they prefer to stay in the treetop canopy.

"If you are in hiding, don't light a fire"
Ghanaian proverb

TAKE THE BANJUL CHALLENGE

Forget the Paris–Dakar, which is a big commercial event for men who want to kick up dust, get lost and blow away a few villagers. No, if you're a petrolhead with a conscience, you should check out the **Banjul Challenge**, which takes place every February. The rules are simple: you have to acquire your car for £100 or less, you have to drive it from the UK to The Gambia, and then you have to auction it and give away the proceeds to a local development charity. See ⓦwww.dakarchallenge.co.uk for this and other madcap races.

LARGER THAN LIFE

The largest Christian church in the world, at 30,000 square metres, is the **Basilica of Our Lady of Peace** in the Ivory Coast. It was built by the diminutive longtime ruler of the country, Félix Houphouët-Boigny, in the small town of Yamoussoukro where he was born, and which is now the country's capital. Asked whether a colossal cathedral was precisely what a developing country needed, Houphouët would have none of it: "I did a deal with God," he sniffed. "You would not expect me to discuss God's business in public, would you?"

DOGON STARSTRUCK

When, in the late 1930s, the reclusive Dogon people of Mali gave French anthropologist Marcel Griaule an insight into their customs and beliefs, it was apparent that they had a considerable knowledge of the **heavens**. They knew about Saturn's rings and four of Jupiter's moons, and claimed that Sirius, the brightest star as seen from Earth, was orbited by two other stars, one of which was extremely dense. Modern astronomers only identified this dense companion, Sirius B, in 1970, so how was it that this remote African tribe had known of it? The puzzle prompted Robert Temple to speculate, in his book *The Sirius Mystery*, that the Dogon must have been visited by extraterrestrials from Sirius.

"When an old man dies, it is as if a library burns down"
Amadou Hampaté Bâ (Malian writer)

BELIEFS

A wide range of indigenous beliefs coexist with Africa's two main faiths, Christianity and Islam. Traditionally, for example, the **Igbo** of southeast Nigeria believe that every man has two souls. Upon death, the life force perishes with the body, but the eternal ego survives in the form of a ghost, a shadow or a reflection. The spirit of a good Igbo will come back as a vigorous animal, such as a cow, leopard or elephant; a bad person might return as some kind of plant.

BATTLE OF THE SEXES

In 2005, Liberia's Ellen Johnson-Sirleaf became Africa's first elected **female president**, defeating football legend George Weah in the vote.

FOLLOWING THE GREATEST SHOW ON EARTH • CAMPING WITH HIPPOS IN MURCHISON FALLS • HUNTING FOREST ANTELOPE WITH THE BAKA OF DZANGA-SANGHA • TAKE THE PLUNGE IN THE BAY OF GHOUBET • A DAY BY LAKE KIVU • MARKET DAY IN KURCHI • DINOSAUR HUNTING BY LAKE TÉLÉ • BUSH AND BEACH IN BUJUMBURA • VISITING THE KIGALI GENOCIDE MUSEUM • THE POISON MONKEYS OF THE JOZANI • CLIMBING KILIMANJARO • MAKING A MEAL OF INJERA • IN THE FOOTSTEPS OF FRANCO: CHECKING OUT THE KINSHASA MUSIC SCENE • THE ANCESTRAL HOME OF THE IK – KIDEPO NATIONAL PARK • DROPPING IN ON THE CHURCHES OF LALIBELA • THE GORILLAS OF KAHUZI-BIEGA • A NIGHT ON THE EQUATOR WITH KENYA RAILWAYS • TREKKING IN THE SIMIEN MOUNTAINS • SCI-FI PLANTS OF MOUNT KENYA • REEF ENCOUNTER: ECO-LIVING ON CHUMBE ISLAND • LOSING THE CROWDS AT KATAVI NATIONAL PARK • THE REAL BATCAVE • SURF'S UP: WATCHING HIPPOS HIT THE WAVES • SWIMMING WITH TURTLES IN THE INDIAN OCEAN • LANGOUÉ BAI: THE LAST PLACE ON EARTH • MOUNTAIN BIKING WITH THE HERDS • WILDLIFE-SPOTTING IN NGORONGORO CRATER • SUSTAINABLE SAFARIS WITH THE MAASAI • THAT'S MAGIC: PEMBA'S DJINN • WHITEWATER RAFTING AT THE SOURCE OF THE NILE • THE GREAT AFRICAN MEAT FEAST • BULL-JUMPING IN THE LOWER OMO VALLEY • FULFILLING FANTASIES ON FRÉGATE ISLAND • EXPLORING STONE TOWN ON FOOT • VISITING A WESTERN LOWLAND GORILLA REHABILITATION CENTRE • TOURING THE SPICE ISLAND • MEETING THE MONKEYS OF KIBALE • EXPLORING THE MEROË PYRAMIDS • CRUISING TO KISANGANI • STORYTELLING ON THE SSESE ISLANDS • RED RIVER HOGS AND FOREST ELEPHANTS AT LOANGO NATIONAL PARK • FOLLOWING THE GREATEST SHOW ON EARTH • CAMPING WITH HIPPOS IN MURCHISON FALLS • HUNTING FOREST ANTELOPE WITH THE BAKA OF DZANGA-SANGHA • TAKE THE PLUNGE IN THE BAY OF GHOUBET • A DAY BY LAKE KIVU • MARKET DAY IN KURCHI • DINOSAUR HUNTING BY LAKE TÉLÉ • BUSH AND BEACH IN BUJUMBURA • VISITING THE KIGALI GENOCIDE MUSEUM • THE POISON MONKEYS OF THE JOZANI • CLIMBING KILIMANJARO • MAKING A MEAL OF INJERA • IN THE FOOTSTEPS OF FRANCO: CHECKING OUT THE KINSHASA MUSIC SCENE • THE ANCESTRAL HOME OF THE IK – KIDEPO NATIONAL PARK • DROPPING IN ON THE CHURCHES OF LALIBELA • THE GORILLAS OF KAHUZI-BIEGA • A NIGHT ON THE EQUATOR WITH KENYA RAILWAYS • TREKKING IN THE SIMIEN MOUNTAINS • SCI-FI PLANTS OF MOUNT KENYA • REEF ENCOUNTER: ECO-LIVING ON CHUMBE ISLAND • LOSING THE CROWDS AT KATAVI NATIONAL PARK • THE REAL BATCAVE

Central & East Africa
347–387

CHAD

SUDAN

Market day in Kurchi 352

ERITREA

DJIBOUTI 350 Take the plunge in the Bay of Ghoubet

ETHIOPIA

SOMALIA

Bull-jumping in the lower Omo Valley 378

CENTRAL AFRICAN REPUBLIC

The great African meat feast 377

GABON

CONGO

D.R. CONGO

UGANDA

KENYA

Whitewater rafting at the source of the Nile 376

Surf's up: watching hippos hit the waves 369

Visiting the Kigali genocide museum 355

RWANDA

Climbing Kilimanjaro 357

In the footsteps of Franco 359

BURUNDI

Swimming with turtles in the Indian Ocean 370

TANZANIA

SEYCHELLES

ANGOLA

347 Following the GREATEST SHOW ON EARTH

TANZANIA & KENYA Imagine squinting into the shimmering Serengeti horizon and seeing a herd of wildebeest trundle into view. They're moving slowly, stopping every now and then to graze on what's left of the parched savannah. At first, they number a couple of dozen, but as you watch, tens become hundreds, and hundreds become thousands. And still they come – a snorting, braying mass, relentlessly marching north in search of food. This is the wildebeest migration, and watching it play out on the sweeping plains of Tanzania's Serengeti National Park is unforgettable.

The statistics are staggering: in May each year, over 2.5 million animals, mostly wildebeest but also several hundred thousand zebras and antelopes, set out on a three-month journey from the short-grass plains of the southern Serengeti to Kenya's Masai Mara Game Reserve. On the way, they'll cover some 800km of open plains and croc-infested rivers, running the gauntlet of predators such as lions, cheetahs, hyenas and hunting dogs.

By June, the herds have passed deep into the park's Western Corridor and are nervously starting to cross the Grumeti River. This is the migration at its most savage – and the defining moment of countless wildlife documentaries – as the reluctant wildebeest gather at the riverbank, too scared to go any further, until the mass behind them is so intense that they spill down into the water and are suddenly swimming, scraping and fighting in a desperate attempt to get across. Many are injured or drowned in the mayhem, while huge Nile crocodiles pick off the weak and unwary.

Those that do make it are still some 65km from the Mara River, the last and brutal barrier between them and the rain-ripened grasses of the Masai Mara. Once there, they'll have three months to eat their fill before going through it all over again on the return journey south.

348 Camping with hippos in Murchison Falls

UGANDA A faint rustling woke me up. Had I rolled onto the floor of my tent? Or was it a nearby camper? No, there it was again. A sound of an animal, a quiet animal. Silence. And then stepping – or tugging? – on the grass. I wouldn't have heard it an hour earlier, when the *Red Chilli Rest Camp*'s generators had been humming. Even now, it was hardly distinguishable from the frogs and insects.

Could it be a lion? During the morning driving safari, the park rangers had said that the lions lived on the other side of the Nile, that the lions can't swim and that they certainly can't take the ferry that connects the two halves of Murchison Falls National Park here in northwestern Uganda. But later, at the open-air dining section of the rest camp, the bartender had mentioned that a female lived on our side, near the famous waterfalls.

"But we're camping outside!" I'd cried. "We're a lion lunch in a canvas wrapper!"

"Lions don't take tents", he'd said. But now there was another rustle – right in front of my tent. Crocodiles were on both sides of the Nile, I realized. The boat safari had taken us past a half-dozen sneering crocs earlier in the day.

The rustling ballooned into a fully-fledged racket. Surely the crocodile was ready to pounce. The leopard was going to take my carcass up a tree. The lion could smell me. Why hadn't I showered?

"If I'm going to be eaten by a wild animal, I want to know what's eating me", I thought. I zipped open the tent fly and shined my torch right onto a giant pink-and-grey...

Hippo bum... I pulled the zip down fast, and quaked silently. The hippo ignored me, kept munching grass, and then slowly moved off into the bush, following his nightly feeding trail that would take him back down the hill to the safety of the Nile.

349 Hunting forest antelope with the Baka of Dzanga-Sangha

CENTRAL AFRICAN REPUBLIC The Baka of equatorial Africa – one of the peoples the colonial-era explorers used to call pygmies – have an intimate and highly spiritual relationship with their forest home. In Dzanga-Sangha, a group of Baka villagers invite visitors to share a glimpse of this secret domain by joining them on a traditional hunting trip.

Dzanga-Sangha is a little-known reserve, tucked into the far southwest corner of a little-known country, Central African Republic. Step into its forest and you're immersed in a wraparound world of buttress roots, lianas and low-hanging branches. Butterflies dance like confetti in shafts of filtered sunlight. This tangled wilderness fits the term "trackless jungle" rather neatly, but the Baka are unfazed, their bare feet moving swiftly across the spongy carpet of fallen leaves. Those out in front yelp. The plan is to flush out a duiker, the small forest antelope that goes down very well on a Baka barbecue.

The back-up party – a mixed assortment of Baka men and women of all ages – begin to unroll hand-knotted nets between the trees, joining them together to form a trap which looks much like a very long, semi-circular tennis net. Up ahead, the yelps rise to a crescendo. If they die away, that means there's no catch this time; the nets are rolled up and the party races on to somewhere more suitable.

A series of unsuccessful attempts to chase an animal into the trap results in a pause for reflection. The Baka believe that if one of their number is nursing a guilty conscience, that can bring bad fortune. The solution is for the individual to make a confession to the forest spirits. With this, their luck may turn. For any duiker unfortunate enough to be caught, the end is swift and efficient. Butchered on the spot, the meat is carefully divided up between all the families in the hunting party. Not a scrap is wasted. Once each portion is parcelled up in leaves, the Baka move on, the forest reverberating with their songs.

350 Take the plunge in the Bay of Ghoubet

DJIBOUTI The locals will beg you not to. They'll tell you that forces unknown lie beneath the waters of the Bay of Ghoubet. But, after a day spent exploring one of the most inhospitably hot regions in the whole of Africa, the urge to dive in may just prove too tempting to resist.

One of the smallest and most obscure nations on the continent, Djibouti has some feisty neighbours in Somalia, Ethiopia and Eritrea, making its peaceful existence over the last fifteen years even more remarkable. Outside the crumbling streets of the tiny capital Djibouti Town, there is little sign of any human life in this former French colony (the last to be given independence by France, in 1977).

Nature has free rein, and its blunt power is demonstrated throughout the arid hinterland in the form of extinct volcanoes, tectonic plate fissures and Assal, a vast salt lake where it hasn't rained for over three years. You may see the odd local member of one of the nomadic Afar tribes that still exist in this barren landscape selling salt sculptures and gypsum crystals on the side of the lake, but you won't find anyone in the waters of Ghoubet.

Tiers of sun-bleached cliffs surround the bay. In the middle of the water lies Devil's Island. With a rock face punctuated with tiny holes, it looks every inch the lair of a barbaric and fearsome creature. The Afar claim nobody fishes or swims in the waters as there have been too many incidents of people getting mysteriously sucked under. Even Jacques Cousteau claimed to have encountered an unidentified large mammal here while diving in the 1960s.

The isolation is absolute. If there really is a Loch Ness Monster in this empty quarter of the Horn of Africa then it's certainly keeping a low profile at the moment. Though be wary: to take a refreshing swim to escape the heat here is to take your chances against an Afar legend that has yet to be disproved.

RWANDA Where the slopes of the Virunga volcanoes duck into the deep waters of Lake Kivu you'll find the pretty lakeside town of Gisenyi. After the emotional impact of the Rwanda's genocide memorials, and the intensity of gorilla-tracking, arriving in Gisenyi – with its warm days and cool nights, tropical gardens, tan-coloured sandy beaches and shabby, European architecture – always feels like the start of a holiday. And that's what the Belgians thought, at the end of World War II, when they inherited this former military post from the Germans. Exulting in its combination of equatorial climate and 1500-metre altitude, Rwanda's new colonial rulers created a mini Riviera, with villas, spa-style hotels and avenues lined with palms and gum trees.

These days, Gisenyi entertains Kigali's elite crowd for weekends of water-skiing and windsurfing. But the jewel of the area lies at Rubona, a 6km walk (or taxi ride) along the spectacular lakeside corniche, where the *Paradis Malahide* is the country's most charming hotel. Tucked in your wood-and-lava-rock cottage, you awake to the conversation of fisherpeople above the soft crash of waves. Start your day with a swim (float back and look north to see the active volcano, Nyiragongo) and then take a canoe across the bay to the local hot springs. Back on the mainland, the Belgians' old Bralirwa brewery (controlled by Heineken, who tap methane from the lake as a fuel) is behind the fishing harbour. It's just a ten-minute walk from the hotel, which can arrange a tour to see where all those huge bottles of Primus beer come from. Get a cab to Gisenyi town for a buffet lunch in the colonial *Stipp* hotel – roast meat, local fish and veg and huge avocados – which will set you up for afternoon watersports, or a laze by the pool, where you can count 100 species of birds. Evenings in Gisenyi and Rubona are sedate, but look out for Intore dance shows, the sanitized but still thrilling displays of traditional royal warriorhood.

A day by
Lake Kivu

351

352 Market day in Kurchi

SUDAN As your bus rattles south across the scorched plains of Kordofan, cooler and greener mountains rise up on the horizon, refuge of the Nuba, a medley of charismatic tribes.

The Nuba region (as distinct from Nubia) represents the ethnic fault line between north and south Sudan, but distinctions between "Arab" and "African" social spheres are fuzzy and complicated, shown nowhere better than when you arrive at the weekly market in Kurchi, held under the shade of a massive baobab tree. Kurchi attracts thousands of Nuba villagers from the nearby hills, many still largely unclothed and scarified in traditional style, as well as Fellata pastoralists and cow-riding Baggara Arabs.

The tree is the place where people meet to exchange news and gossip, and it's large enough to shade half a dozen tailors' stalls around its trunk, each with an ancient, well-oiled, foot-operated Singer sewing machine. Ramshackle stalls sell local fruit and vegetables – sorghum, sesame, mangoes, bananas, beans, squash, peanuts – and bread and home-grown tobacco, as well as imported goods from Khartoum. Blacksmiths and cobblers, secondhand clothes' sellers and traditional healers – known as *kujur* – all ply their trades in a milling sea of negotiations and networking, often lubricated by local sorghum beer, *marissa*, drunk from huge gourds. The gourds, or calabashes, make fine souvenirs, as do ladles made from the same fruit.

During the harvest season, or *sibir*, younger men use market day to look for partners, displaying their physical prowess and dressing themselves up outlandishly, using anything from traditional beads, ostrich feathers and magic ash to face paint and industrial goggles. They confirm their eligibility through wrestling tournaments, generally held in the late afternoon, when the commerce dies down. The celebrations by victorious champions and their entourages carry on well into the evening. Listen hard above the clatter and burble of a multitude of languages and you may be lucky enough to pick out home-made harps, clay-pot bass drums and shakers. The music is usually unplugged. Time your visit for a full moon and, unforgettably, you'll find dozens of people singing and dancing all night.

353 Dinosaur hunting by Lake Télé

CONGO Waking at dawn in the deep forest, you emerge from your tent to face clouds of tiny sweat bees and a breakfast of black coffee, tinned sardines and sticks of glue-like *foufou*, wrapped in banana leaves. The Congo Republic's official website invites visitors to this region, and even remarks on its semi-mythical attraction. But you will be a rarity at strange Lake Télé, Congo's Loch Ness, slap in the middle of 3000 square kilometres of forest, bounded by meandering creeks on three sides and logging concessions on the fourth. With no road access, and oddly missing from all the maps, the almost circular lake is surrounded by thick forest – home to the biggest population of gorillas in Africa, as well as elephants, hippos, pythons and crocodiles.

But the lake's strangest denizen is an unknown quantity, an amphibious, horned monster called *mokele mbembe*, the "river dammer'" often described as a living dinosaur. Colourful, mostly secondhand anecdotes, and some Japanese aerial footage of something that looks like a small motorboat creating a wake and then sinking rapidly, are about all the evidence for its existence. And yet it terrifies local people and has excited explorers and zoologists for centuries. The lake is approached along a creek by boat, and then by a long day's hike on a difficult trail.

Following your guide and porter you're quickly deep in the forest. Shafts of sunlight illuminate the dark leaf-litter on the ground, where flickering butterflies settle on gorilla droppings. Chimps hoot somewhere in the distance. Above you, buttress-rooted forest giants soar 60m or more through the foliage towards the light. There are few locals along the way – only rarely a group of Pygmy hunters comes this far south – and they're as fascinated to see you as you them. With biting-insects, roots to trip on, and stretches of swamp where you have to wade up to your thighs, this excursion is no picnic (except for the tsetse flies). And then suddenly the great, dark expanse of the lake is in front of you. Like Loch Ness, it's hard to put your camera down, or take your eyes away.

354 Bush and beach in Bujumbura

BURUNDI Bujumbura may not have a reputation for rest and recreation, but its fragile peace is convincing enough to short-stay visitors, and it has two fine assets. Tucked between the steep, green walls of the western branch of the Great Rift Valley, on the shores of Lake Tanganyika, little "Buj" has a national park at the edge of town – just like Nairobi. Unlike Kenya's sprawling capital, Buj's suburbs peter out onto dazzling beaches lapped by the blue waters, or occasionally thrashed by the rough waves, of Africa's deepest lake.

Coming from the airport, you don't even need to go into town: the Plage des Cocotiers, or coconut beach, is effectively at the end of the runway. If you come to the beach soon after sunrise, you'll find it near enough empty – an ideal spot (now that Gustave the giant croc has died) for clean and safe swimming and kite-surfing.

Later on, and especially at weekends, the bars and grilled meat stands open, there's beach volleyball and boat rides and even the occasional local guitar band on offer.

Taking centre stage on the sands is the surprisingly sustainable resort of *Hôtel Club du Lac* (which uses local materials and is air-cooled and partly solar-powered) – the best spot for sundowners. Just a few kilometres west of the beach, near the Congolese border, the road crosses the Rusizi River and you can drive your rented jeep or organize a river trip by *pirogue* downstream into the lush reedbeds and palm groves of the Rusizi National Park (notice the "Attention Crocodiles" sign at the gate).

It's just 3km to the river mouth and the lake: be sure to ask your captain to take you down the small channels on the eastern side of the estuary, where you can see hippos and plenty of birdlife, and where Gustave's smaller relatives wait for fish.

355 Visiting the Kigali genocide museum

RWANDA In 1994, while the world looked the other way, around one million Tutsis and moderate Hutus were murdered by Hutu extremists. The attempted genocide left a scar on the Rwandan nation which will be felt for generations, but the immediate wounds of that terrible three-month period have healed faster than most outsiders could have imagined. While leading *genocidaires* have faced UN trials, those who murdered their own neighbours under orders have undergone a process of reconciliation with survivors in local *gacaca* courts. The country itself has been transformed by its pragmatic government and is rapidly modernizing.

Tourism is an important part of development and it engages remarkably with recent events in Rwanda's genocide museum, the Kigali Memorial Centre, where you're likely to spend at least two very worthwhile but emotionally draining hours. On this hillside site, north of the city centre, eleven huge crypts have been constructed, the resting place for nearly a quarter of a million of the country's victims. The semi-subterranean exhibition

itself implicitly lays the blame for what happened on decades of colonial oppression, divide-and-rule policies, under-development and ultimately deliberate planning, while placing the slaughter in the context of humanity's history of genocide. Particularly poignant is the still-growing display of victims' photos, donated by their families, and the inexpressibly sad and beautiful sculptures by Rwandan artist Laurent Hategekimana. The memorial to the children who died is unbearably moving, focusing not on the huge numbers, but on fourteen individual lives, on little things like their favourite meals, and on how they were killed.

Outside, it's not always easy to be contemplative in the pretty memorial gardens, with the hum of Kigali's traffic in the background, but the sombre Wall of Names is a reminder of the arbitrariness of the genocide: although the Belgians divided people into Tutsi (owning ten cows or more) and Hutu (owning fewer than ten), the country shares one language and one culture and the division is a socially constructed one.

356 The poison monkeys of the Jozani

ZANZIBAR, TANZANIA For centuries, settlers have torn away at Zanzibar's indigenous forests to make way for the crops which made the island's fortune: cinnamon, cardamom, vanilla and, of course, cloves, once the most valuable spice of all. Only one stand of semi-natural evergreen forest remains. Happily, it's protected. It forms part of the Jozani Chwaka Bay National Park, which comprises 50 square kilometres of trees, saline grasslands and mangroves and is home to a unique species of red colobus monkey.

Considerable thought has gone into making the park accessible to visitors. With a guide you can explore the mangrove swamps around Pete Inlet and Chwaka Bay by strolling around a network of boardwalks. You may see crabs scuttling among the fresh green shoots, or schools of young fish in the pools – this intricate habitat, protected from the ocean swells, serves as a giant hatchery. You can also tour the paths of Jozani Forest to admire old-growth mahogany

trees and listen out for the screeches of the red colobus community.

The Kirk's red colobus (*Piliocolobus kirkii*) is called *kimi punju* in Swahili, meaning poison monkey. Legend has it that if a dog eats one, it will lose all its fur, perhaps because of the monkeys' uncanny ability to digest leaves which are highly toxic to other animals. Other features which mark it out from its mainland relatives include its idiosyncratic vocabulary of calls and its distinctive coat pattern, featuring a grey chest, dark shoulders and a russet-coloured back.

Despite their sinister local name, Zanzibari monkeys are harmless to humans and highly charismatic, with inquisitive, Yoda-like features. What's more, for all their rarity, they're very easy to find at Jozani. One troop has learned that if they hang around in the trees nearest the road, they're likely to score a treat or two from unscrupulous visitors. You'll almost always see them here, grooming each other endearingly or just perching among the foliage.

357 Climbing Kilimanjaro

TANZANIA The statistics are impressive. Measuring some 40km across and rising 5895m above sea level, Kilimanjaro is easily Africa's highest mountain.

But such bald facts fail to capture the thrill of actually climbing it: the days spent tramping from muggy montane forest to snowy summit, pausing occasionally to admire the views over the lush lower slopes and beyond to the dusty plains, or scrutinize the unique mountain flora; the blissful evenings gazing at the panoply of stars with fellow trekkers; and the wonderful esprit de corps that builds between yourself and your crew, a camaraderie that grows with every step until, exhausted, you stand together at the highest point in Africa.

Beguiling though the mountain may be, those contemplating

an assault on Kili should consider its hazards and hardships. For one thing, though it's possible to walk to the summit, it's not easy. An iron will and calves of steel are both essential, for this is a mountain that really tests your mettle. Then there are the extreme discomforts on the slopes, from sweat-drenched shirts in the sweltering forest to frozen water bottles and wind-blasted faces at the summit. And there's the altitude itself, inducing headaches and nausea for those who ascend too fast.

Such privations, however, are totally eclipsed by the exhilaration of watching the sunrise from the Roof of Africa, with an entire continent seemingly spread out beneath you. The sense of fulfilment that courses through you on the mountaintop will stay with you, long after you've finally said goodbye to Kili.

358 Making a meal of injera

ETHIOPIA Crunch! A grain of sand slipped between my teeth as I bit into my spongy *injera* dipped in spicy puréed chickpeas. The Ethiopian grandmother sitting across from me smiled at my surprise, perhaps assuming I was taken aback by the strong spiciness of the *shiro wat*. She teased me in Amharic, then tore off a piece of *injera* – using her freshly washed right hand – and deftly scooped up a pile of mushy lentils from her side of the platter we were sharing.

This was the Horn of Africa, where the staple grain is teff, ground on the spot and turned into a soft, yeast-free sour pancake-like bread that becomes both fork and plate. Sand is not a usual feature of Ethiopian cuisine, but this was a hut, a rural home – the owner's lounge doubling as a restaurant – near the Sudanese border. The grain had been fermenting in a pot in the unscreened home, in a town where goats, donkeys and buses travelled the central dirt road. A little sand was to be expected.

"Can we have *doro wat*?" I had a craving for a spicy chicken dish. The grandmother shook her head. "It's Wednesday", explained her son in English. A fasting day. "Fasting" in Ethiopia means eating only vegetarian food, and this happens every Wednesday and Friday as well as during Lent.

Tearing a spoon-sized piece of *injera* off a separate folded pancake, I used it to scoop up a dark red stew from one of the five puddles of coloured *wat* on the flattened bread. I popped the stew into my mouth and my eyeballs nearly blew.

"*Berbere*", chuckled the grandmother. Red pepper spice.

Never mind, I thought. It was still an exquisite experience. How often do you get to eat your plate?

359 In the footsteps of Franco: checking out the Kinshasa music scene

DEMOCRATIC REPUBLIC OF CONGO It all started with a guitar made from an old can, with stripped-down electrical wire for strings. The young François Luambo Makiadi – better known as Franco – was barely 11 when he was first spotted jamming on a makeshift instrument in the market district of 1940s Léopoldville, as Kinshasa was then known. Nurtured by a far-sighted local recording artist, Paul Dewayon, his canny blend of hard-nosed street cred and natural star quality put him straight on a path to success.

By his early twenties, Franco was the biggest star in Congolese dance music. Every night, he and his band OK Jazz would belt out a joyous blend of rippling guitars, shimmering drums and upbeat choruses – a sound that's as quintessentially African as mangoes, kola nuts and cowrie shells. He called his Cuban-influenced musical style "rumba odemba", after a favourite Congolese aphrodisiac.

Franco went on to open four nightclubs in Kinshasa, the most famous of which, the *Un Deux Trois* club in the district of Kasa-Vubu, just south of the city centre, was his professional headquarters. Throughout the last two decades of Franco's life, the 1970s and 1980s, Kinshasa was a throbbing live-music hub. Since then, much has changed, but despite its woes, the city remains a vibrant crossroads town and a place where musicians meet.

Even now, the seedy but lively Matonge district around Rond-Pont Victoire, between Kasa-Vubu and the centre, buzzes after dark. For a dose of raw-edged nightlife, head up to the rooftop terrace at the down-at-heel *Hôtel de Crèche*, near Rond-Pont Victoire: live bands play here most nights. Meanwhile in Gombe Commune, the more salubrious central district, well-heeled locals and expats pack out the dancefloor at *Chez Ntemba*, an after-midnight club. If you want to catch a big-name band, see the local press – near the Congo River, the swish *Grand Hôtel Kinshasa* and Halle de la Gombe sometimes host stars such as Werra Son, Youssou N'Dour and Papa Wemba, all of whom cite Franco as a formative influence.

360 The ancestral home of the Ik – Kidepo National Park

UGANDA While most visitors to Uganda look to the country's western highlands and Rift Valley Lakes, and particularly to the gorillas of Bwindi Impenetrable Forest, there's an alternative adventure at the opposite end of the country in the shape of Kidepo National Park. In the 1960s the American anthropologist Colin Turnbull visited this region, wedged in the far northeast between Sudan and Kenya, to study a group of starving hunters and farmers called the Ik, who had been pushed out of the newly created park – an area "still unsullied by civilization" according to the park authorities – and whose social bonds were disintegrating. Turnbull's grotesque study of a community in meltdown, *The Mountain People*, became a controversial bestseller.

Today, far from having become "extinct" as Turnbull expected, the Ik are hanging on in their beautiful district, no longer hunting, but scraping a living from their gardens and fields, though often caught in the violent raids and cattle rustling that goes on between the Karamojong and Turkana raiders from Kenya. Despite, or perhaps because of its remote and unstable character, Kidepo is emphatically worth the trip, and visitors to the park are not at any risk. The Kidepo Valley itself is a great plain of grasslands, surrounded by gaunt mountains, ribboned by streams shaded with shaggy fan palms. The southern part of the park, the richest area for plains animals, is made up of the Narus Valley, and this is where the superb *Apoka* lodge and neighbouring budget *Apoka* resthouse are located. The few visitors to Apoka nearly all fly, to avoid crossing through Karamojong bandit country – where AK47-toting warriors have replaced their naked, spear-carrying grandfathers who greeted Turnbull – but you can sometimes drive up in a police convoy, or use the route from Gulu and the west. Whichever way you come, you'll be treated to elephants, buffalo, tree-climbing lions, Uganda's only cheetahs, and the park's remarkable range of birdlife – more than 460 species, including the black variety of the splendid crowned crane – and a highland savannah environment barely studied by naturalists.

Dropping in on the churches of Lalibela

ETHIOPIA Lalibela, in Ethiopia's highlands, is so rural that it doesn't even have a bank. Yet in the thirteenth century it was the capital of the great Zagwe dynasty, one of whose last rulers, King Lalibela, embarked on a quest to build a Holy Land on Ethiopian soil.

Historians say he was inspired to build the town's famous rock-hewn churches after a pilgrimage to Jerusalem, while the devout claim that he was instructed by angels during a poison-induced sleep. Whatever the real reason, the town of Lalibela, built as a "new Jerusalem", leaves pilgrims and visitors alike humbled by the elegance of its churches. Gracing a rocky plateau and intricately carved, they mostly lie in two interconnected groups scattered along the "Jordan River", another biblical landscape feature that King Lalibela designed.

This major UNESCO World Heritage Site is hidden from view until you are literally upon it – a strategic choice, offering protection from marauders. The churches are monolithic, dug deep down into the rock. As you pass through carved gullies leading from one church to the next, you can look in on caves containing the skeletons of monks, or gaze up to cubby holes in the red rock face to see yellow-robed pilgrims reciting the Bible in Ge'ez, an archaic form of Amharic. The churches remain vibrant, their monks, nuns and priests fervently engaged with the Ethiopian Orthodox Church's demanding calendar. Every church has a hereditary guardian priest dedicated to this medieval world of incense, beeswax candles and ritual – though, incongruously, they all seem to keep sunglasses handy should you try a photograph using a flash.

362 The gorillas of Kahuzi-Biega

DEMOCRATIC REPUBLIC OF CONGO We set out on foot from the park headquarters at Tsivanga and spent the next two hours following a wildly gushing watercourse upstream, climbing steeply all the time. The trackers were somewhere up ahead of us, and messages were passed regularly on the radio. After a particularly strenuous uphill stretch, clutching at roots and branches to drag ourselves up a near-vertical slope, we heard a sudden stentorian roar as a fully grown male gorilla (known to the guides as Chimanuka) burst out of the undergrowth. I knew what I was meant to do. The park's chief guide had briefed us: "If a gorilla charges, stand still", he said. "Lower your head. Look submissive." He stared pointedly at me. "Better wear a hat. If they see your fair hair, they may think you're another silverback."

Yes, I knew what to do all right. But when Chimanuka sprang from the bush in all his glory, his solid muscle rippling in the dappled sunlight, I didn't stand my ground and lower my head. I jumped behind our Pygmy tracker and held my breath. This was a huge and magnificent animal, weighing 200kg and, when standing upright, getting on for 2m tall – I had never seen anything like it before.

Chimanuka must have charged us at least half a dozen times that morning. He seemed to enjoy it. The pattern went as follows: a charge would be followed by a period of chewing the cud. He would sit on his haunches, rolling his eyes and swiping the available vegetation with his long prehensile arms so as to grab any accessible fruits or succulent stalks. After ten minutes or so, he would rise and turn away from us to show off his magnificent coat (it really is silver), before crashing off again through the undergrowth. Shock and awe. That's what you feel when you first see a gorilla in the wild.

363 A night on the equator with Kenya railways

KENYA Constructed in the 1890s, Kenya's "Lunatic Line" (so named by the British press for the folly of building a line into the unexplored interior of Africa) has come to be one of Africa's best-loved train journeys. Your London-style cab pulls into the forecourt of Nairobi's scruffy but civilized railway station and an elderly porter beats his colleagues to the door. Minutes later, installed in your compartment, you feel the train pull out. It's 7pm sharp, and outside it is pitch dark.

Just after departure, a steward in a shiny-buttoned, frayed white tunic strides through the carriages ringing a bell – time for dinner: a kind of do-it-yourself version of silver service accompanied by waiters leaning with wobbling plates of tomato soup, tilapia fish and curry. So begins your 526km overnight journey across the savannah to the island city of Mombasa.

Three times a week, a diesel train pulls out of the capital, heading down to the coast. The following night it makes the return journey. Arrival is scheduled for the next morning, about 13 hours later, but passengers take care not to arrange any tight connections as delays and breakdowns are frequent.

Outside, with Nairobi's shanties left behind, the big, dark spaces begin. You peer into the nocturnal emptiness of the plains, where Maasai and Kamba herders traipse by day, tending their cattle among zebra, wildebeest, giraffe and ostrich, and you make a mental note to keep your eyes peeled over breakfast on the return journey. Back at your compartment, beds have been made up and sleep, with the incessant rocking of the carriage, comes quickly.

In the mild, grey light of pre-dawn, you awake to an awareness that the climate has changed: you're now out of the 1500m highlands and are dropping to the Indian Ocean coast. As you twist on your bunk to stare out of the window, tropical odours and humidity percolate through the carriages, together with a fresh brew of coffee. The equatorial sun rises as fast as it set as the train jolts at walking speed through the suburbs of Mombasa. With prayer calls in the air and Indian sweet shops on the streets, you disembark, already seduced by the coast's beguiling combination of Asia, Africa and Arabia.

364 Trekking in the Simien Mountains

ETHIOPIA The great mass of the Simien range – formed from one of Africa's ancient super-volcanoes – rears up in Ethiopia's remote, northern hinterland, broken into towering plateaux and peaks by a slew of rushing rivers and trailing waterfalls. In the heart of the mountains, the UNESCO Natural Heritage Site of Simien National Park is a spellbinding wilderness of fertile valleys and grassy moors, the jewel in Ethiopia's crown of natural attractions, offering one of Africa's, if not the world's, most spectacular hikes – an eight-day return trek to the snow-capped peak of Ras Dashen (4620m).

Once the fortified home of Ethiopia's Jewish community, the Simiens remain largely roadless, but are still traced by footpaths and scattered with Amhara villages. On the misty heights within the pristine national park live three large mammals unique to the region: the impressively horned and vulnerable Walia ibex (a nimble, shaggy goat that you only ever see hundreds of metres away on a sheer, high cliff-face); the critically rare and beautiful red-coated Simien wolf; and the remarkable, grass-eating Gelada baboon, which you are very likely to see grazing on the steep, alpine meadows, sometimes in parties numbering hundreds.

Foot-slogging and mules are the usual transport in the Simiens, and you'll soon get used to the steady pace and moderate height gains required at these altitudes, with stunning birdlife, such as the huge lammergeyer vulture, and giant African-alpine vegetation to distract you from your heaving chest and throbbing legs.

SCI-FI PLANTS
of MOUNT KENYA

KENYA The Kikuyu people venerated Mount Kenya as the dwelling place of God. They believed if they climbed to the peaks, they would find spiritual inspiration. Straddling the equator and piercing the clouds, Africa's second-highest mountain – the eroded remains of a vast, prehistoric volcano, towering 5199m from the plains – is a steeper and quicker climb than Kilimanjaro, and in terms of scenic variety and fauna and flora is perhaps the more inspirational of Africa's two giant mountains. It's certainly the less busy.

For most trekkers, the climax of seeing the sunrise from Point Lenana, among the jagged, glacier-studded peaks, is the literal highpoint of the experience. But try to love the climbing moments, too: on day three of the Naro Moru trail, once you've overcome the slightly daunting "vertical bog" and emerged into the high moorland, the wonders of alpine Africa's otherworldly flora, seemingly designed by some 1950s science-fiction writer, are all around you. Altitude and the equatorial location combine to nurture forms of vegetation that exist only here and at one or two other lofty points in East Africa. When you first see them, it's hard to believe the "water-holding cabbage" or "ostrich plume plant". This is a land of giant shrubs and weeds: giant heather, giant groundsel and giant lobelia. It turns out the cabbages on stumps and the larger, candelabra-shaped, tree-like plants are the same species, known as giant groundsel or tree senecio. The intermediate stage has a sheaf of bright yellow flowers. These enigmatic plants, though frail-looking, are slow growers and individuals may survive on these chilly, misty slopes for more than two hundred years.

The tall, fluffy, less abundant plants are a species of giant lobelia, popularly called the "ostrich plume plant", discovered by the explorer Teleki and found only on Mount Kenya. The furriness wich gives this giant lobelia such an animal quality acts as insulation for the delicate flowers. It is perhaps the only plant in the world that could fairly be described as cuddly.

Reef Encounter:
eco-living on Chumbe Island

366

ZANZIBAR It's difficult to know which way to look, snorkelling in the turquoise waters off Chumbe Island: at the oriental sweetlips, bobbing in unison around a huge coral fan? At the blue-spotted stingrays, shuffling under the sand along the bottom? Or at any one of the other four hundred or so species of fish that help make the island's reef, Tanzania's first marine protected area, one of the finest coral gardens in the world?

Overlooking the reef at Chumbe's western edge are seven palm-thatched eco-lodges; the rest of the island is a designated nature reserve of creeping mangroves and coral rag forest, left to the local wildlife – including the rare Ader's duiker and the endangered coconut crab, the largest land crab in the world. Everything about the lodges shouts "green": their roofs are designed to collect rainwater, which is then filtered before running through to the shower; hot

water and electricity are provided by solar power; toilets are of the composting variety; and the air-conditioning system is probably the most efficient you'll ever see – a pulley lowers the bedroom's tree-top front wall, cooling the room with a fresh sea breeze.

With a maximum of twelve guests at any one time, Chumbe is a real honeymoon hideaway – indeed, it's often used to round off a once-in-a-lifetime safari, maybe as an ecological appeasement for all those internal flights spent whizzing from one park to another on the African mainland. The only other visitors are schoolchildren from nearby Zanzibar, who visit the island on educational snorkelling trips. Watching them come back in off the reef, chatting excitedly about following a hawksbill turtle along the outer shelf or trying to outdo each other with the size of the groupers they've just seen, is almost as much fun as drifting above the coral yourself.

367 Losing the crowds at Katavi National Park

TANZANIA Unlike the parks of northern Tanzania, where increasingly one of the most common species is *Homo sapiens touristicus*, the remoter west of the country, close to Lake Tanganyika, feels more like central Africa, and is little visited.

The rich concentrations of wildlife in Katavi, which only gets a hundred or so visitors a month, include big herds of magnificent roan and sable antelope, some 4000 elephants and as many as 60,000 buffalo, among dozens of other species, supported by seasonally flooded grasslands. With flocks of waterbirds at the right time of year, and reliable numbers of hippos snorting and crocs sunning around palm-fringed Lake Katavi, it's a wonderful environment – best explored on foot, with an armed ranger you can hire on the spot.

368 The real Batcave

UGANDA Five enormous pythons setting up house with a giant monitor lizard doesn't sound like a marriage made in heaven. But, odd bedfellows as they may be, they're quite content to share their cave, tucked away in a corner of Queen Elizabeth National Park. The reason they're so content is very simple indeed: food. And lots of it.

The cave mouth is as wide as a pair of Chingford semis, not quite as high but definitely with more residents. Home to around a million fruit bats, this is the real Batcave, where what seems like rock is actually a mass of writhing and chattering flesh. It's also a one-stop hypermarket for the corpulent reptiles.

Mountains of guano, an incredible stench and astonishing body heat are the backdrop to the most impressive case of overcrowding on the planet.

369 Surf's up: watching hippos hit the waves

GABON Barely touched by tourism, and with a small and localized population leaving much of it as virgin rainforest, Gabon's lagoon-broken coast is one of the few places in the world where you can watch hippos in the sea – and not simply swimming from island to island, as they do in Guinea-Bissau. These hippos are surfers.

In the stunning Loango National Park, in order to get from one river mouth to another, the hippos swim out far enough to ride in again on the breaking waves – a remarkable adaptation that's safer, quicker and much more fun – and far cooler – than plodding along the shore or breaking through the jungle. And if the hippos don't fancy the conditions on any particular day, then there's always the elephants on the beach, the whales offshore, or the gorillas and chimps inland – all of which help make Loango unique in Africa.

370 Swimming with turtles in the Indian Ocean

SEYCHELLES A cluster of granite islands enveloped in deep-green tropical vegetation and edged with beaches of blindingly white sand that's so fine it squeaks when you walk across it, the Seychelles are the nearest thing on Earth to the Garden of Eden. The turquoise waters of the surrounding Indian Ocean are also one of the best places in the world to see marine turtles, especially the hawksbill, once severely endangered by the trade in its beautifully patterned shells, which were used to make combs, spectacle frames and the like. With most of the Seychelles' waters now a marine reserve, hawksbill numbers have bounced back locally, though the species is still threatened worldwide.

The best place to see them is on their home turf, so don mask, snorkel and fins – or full scuba gear – and get into the sea. Watching them flapping effortlessly past you into the blue is an incredible spectacle; they're sometimes curious, sometimes indifferent, but usually wary of letting you get too close – best to catch them asleep under coral overhangs or in shallow caves, where they can spend up to an hour dozing. If you're not prepared to get wet, try to time your visit during the October–February nesting season when, just after dark, you'll find females heaving themselves up the beaches to just above the high-tide line before using their hind flippers to scoop out a deep pit.

They then lay about fifty round, parchment-shelled eggs before shovelling all the sand back on top of them and making their way back down to the water. The eggs incubate in the sand (the sex of the entire clutch is determined by the surrounding temperature) until the young hatch around ten weeks later. Perfect hawksbills in miniature, they dig themselves out of the nest after dark and, using the moon as a guide, scuttle frenetically down the beach toward the sea like an army of wind-up bath toys.

371 Langoué Bai: the last place on Earth

GABON The Pygmy tribes of the Central African rainforest gave Langoué Bai its name, but it was Mike Fay who put it on the map. When, in 1999, the American ecologist set himself the task of walking from Bomassa in Congo to Loango in Gabon, a project he called the Megatransect Expedition, he already knew that the natural riches of this challenging wilderness were diminishing fast. Together with *National Geographic* photographer Michael Nichols, his mission was to monitor the impact of human activity on this beautiful but fragile environment.

Their work revealed a hidden world where forest elephants are glimpsed, fleetingly, through thick foliage, western lowland gorillas bathe waist-deep in the cool water of marshy clearings, and chimpanzees stare in astonishment at a primate they rarely see – man. Their data inspired the government of Gabon to protect a significant proportion of this, the second largest rainforest in the world, through the creation of thirteen new national parks.

Langoué Bai, a large natural clearing surrounded by dense vegetation, is a jewel in the heart of one of these parks: Ivindo. Well-watered and remote, the *bai* attracts a host of wildlife – not just forest elephants and endangered gorillas but also forest buffalo, antelopes (small, shy duikers and marsh-loving sitatungas) and red river hogs, whose tufty ears give them a comical, gremlin-like look. Hidden in the trees, viewing platforms built by Fay's colleagues at the Wildlife Conservation Society provide the perfect vantage point. It's a sweaty hour or two's trek from camp, but it's worth every step just to witness the spectacle of so many highly elusive species gathered together in one arena. No wonder Nichols and Fay dubbed this forest "The Last Place on Earth".

372 Mountain biking with the herds

KENYA How about a cool, low-key private game sanctuary, with delightfully eccentric lodgings built from mud, thatch, reclaimed timber and recycled ranch fencing? How about staying in your own cottage shaded by superb acacia trees, fronted by sloping lawns, close to a rushing river and not far from the Happy Valley of colonial days? *Malewa Wildlife Lodge*, set in Kenya's Kigio Conservancy, is such a place.

A recent, private venture that has converted a cattle ranch on the banks of the Malewa River into a thriving sanctuary for the kind of wildlife you can mingle with in relative safety, the Kigio Conservancy harbours a breeding herd of rare Rothschild's giraffe, good numbers of zebra, impala and waterbuck, and several charmingly inquisitive ostriches. Staying at the lodge, you can rent mountain bikes, or take horses, and head off through the bush for a few hours, following an easy network of tracks and landmarks. There are no large predators in the conservancy, which is fenced on three sides and bounded to the north by the river. The brown and churning Malewa itself wows kids and young-at-heart adults.

The forest-swathed riverbank near the lodge harbours troops of monkeys and dozens of species of birds, while a mini-suspension bridge gives access to the foothills of the Aberdare range, from where you can look out for the local pod of hippos. Head downstream and you come to a weir, waterfall and cliffs ideal for river-jumping.

The adventure doesn't end as night falls. Grab a torch to make your way through the bush to the dining room. The *Malewa Wildlife Lodge* chef conjures excellent meals from fresh local food, and they serve the best coffee in the Rift Valley. After dinner, you'll gather with the other guests to share animal stories by a huge fire. They have electricity at the office, but mostly your nights will be lit by the flicker of candles and kerosene lamps.

TANZANIA The tectonic forces that created East Africa's Great Rift Valley also threw up a rash of volcanoes, one of which blew itself to smithereens 2.5 million years ago. Its legacy, the 19km-wide Ngorongoro Crater, is a place that holiday brochures like to call "the eighth wonder of the world". They're not far wrong. Ngorongoro's natural amphitheatre is home to virtually every emblematic animal species you might want to see in Africa, and the crater's deep, bluish-purple sides provide spectacular backdrops to any photograph.

The magic begins long before you reach the crater. As you ascend from the Rift Valley along a series of hairpins, the extent of the region's geological tumult becomes breathtakingly apparent. Continuing up through liana-draped forest, you're suddenly at the crater's edge, surveying an ever-changing patchwork of green and yellow hues streaked with shadows and mist.

Living in the crater's grasslands, swamps, glades and lakes is Africa's highest density of predators – lions and leopards, hyenas and jackals among them – for whom a sumptuous banquet of antelope and other delicacies awaits. Glimpsing lions is an unforgettable thrill; just as memorable but far more unsettling is the macabre excitement of witnessing a kill. You'll also see elephants and black rhinos, the latter poached to the brink of extinction. Twitchers have plenty to go for, too, including swashes of pink flamingoes adorning the alkaline Lake Magadi in the crater's heart. If ogling wildlife from a vehicle doesn't do it for you, stretch your legs – and escape the crowds – on a hike through the Crater Highlands, in the company of an armed ranger and a Maasai guide.

Sustainable safaris with the Maasai

374

KENYA North of Mount Kenya, the Laikipia region, a vast sweep of rangelands, ridges and seasonal rivers, stretches out towards the northern deserts. Here, former ranches are converting to eco-tourism and conservation, and pastoral communities are setting up innovative experiments in tourist development.

Many places in Laikipia make efforts to limit their environmental footprint and *Il Ngwesi* – owned and run by the 6000-strong Il Ngwesi Laikipiak Maasai community – has taken the lead.

The lodge, located on a remote, bush-covered ridge, is delightful. It's a birdwatcher's paradise: you awake to a jaw-dropping dawn chorus, and birds – from drongos to hornbills – fill the air all day long, crowding the footpaths and branches, and often appearing in the rooms themselves. Six huge *bandas* (artfully rustic, thatch and tree-trunk cottages) are spaced out along the west-facing slope, their open-sided fronts graced with magnificent decks and chunky furniture made of polished branches. Banda number one has amazing views of the elephants that congregate around Il Ngwesi's magical waterhole, and, like number five, features a giant mosquito-netted four-poster bed that you can pull out onto the deck.

There's no wood burning or fossil-fuel use at Il Ngwesi – all electricity is supplied by solar power – and the community has a water-use association to monitor consumption and pollution, ensuring the local herds have plenty to drink and leaving enough for the lodge's beautiful infinity pool. Although strictly a private conservancy, the area swarms with wildlife, and game walks with Maasai guides and armed rangers are the norm. It's especially satisfying that all the money goes back into the community, which – among other things – has enabled them to bring back rhinos, formerly hunted out of the area, and to track and monitor at least one pack of highly endangered African wild dogs.

THIS STONE WAS LAID BY HER EXCELLE
MRS PRUDENCE BUSHNELL THE U
AMBASSADOR IN RECOGNITION OF THE
ASSISTANCE GIVEN TO THE
IL NGWESI COMMUNITY BY THE FOLLOWIN
USAID
WORLD BANK
GOVERNMENT OF KENYA
KENYA WILDLIFE SERVICE

375 That's magic: Pemba's djinn

ZANZIBAR There's no better place to seek help from the potent East African spirits than verdant Pemba Island, with its lush low hills, primeval forest, mangrove-lined creeks and unspoilt beaches and islets. The place quietly reeks with the supernatural and is home to the area's *djinn*: form-changing spirits. Popo Bawa – half bat and half man, but without any Hollywood blockbusters to his name – is an infamous resident. He flies into homes late at night and does dastardly things to men as they slumber in their beds; look out for groups of men sleeping outside in their porches or on the streets – a telltale sign of a recent "attack".

A charm placed at the base of a fig tree or the sacrifice of a goat are usually enough to keep Popo Bawa away. Respect the culture and tradition and, if lucky, an invitation to a sacrificial ceremony might just come your way.

376 Whitewater rafting at the source of the Nile

UGANDA A nearby memorial celebrates Gandhi – some of his ashes were placed here – but even with him present, peace isn't assured. At Jinja, minutes after it calmly ebbs from Lake Victoria, the world's longest river roars into life as the White Nile.

After basic whitewater training, our instructor describes rapids ranging in strength from grade 1 (gentle) to grade 5 (life threatening). Hair of the Dog, Overtime, The Bad Place – they'll all be ridden.

The grade 2 rapids are a livid, turbulent stream. It's only a taster for the next set – a grandaddy grade 5. A rush of adrenaline revved by fear precedes the spectacular frothing outrage. The elements are unleashed, magnificent super-nature lets rip and a deafening roar magnifies the strange euphoria of being eaten alive by the Nile.

377 The great African meat feast

KENYA Ask any expat East African what food they miss most and they'll tell you *nyama choma*. In The Gambia, it's known as *afra*; and in South Africa it's what you have at a *braai*. All over the continent, roast or grilled meat is the heart of any big meal and, whenever possible, it is the meal.

A meat feast is also the only occasion in Africa when you'll find men doing the cooking – charring hunks of bloody flesh clearly answering a visceral male need that kings of the barbecue the world over would admit.

Most people don't eat meat often, subsisting on a simple starch dish for their regular meal of the day, so it's perhaps not surprising that when the occasion demands or provides a banquet, meat is the main fare. In Kenya or Tanzania, unless you happen to be invited to a wedding or funeral, you'll go to a purpose-built *nyama choma* bar, where flowing beer and loud music are the standard accompaniments, with greens and *ugali* (a stiff, corn porridge, like grits) optional. The choice is usually between goat and beef, with game meat such as impala, zebra or ostrich available at fancier places. If you select one of these, usually with an all-you-can-eat price tag equivalent to about a week's average wages, you should cannily resist the early offerings of soup, bread and sausages, leaving space for the main events.

After roasting, your meat is brought to your table on a wooden platter, chopped up to bite-size with a sharp knife, and served with a small pile of spiced salt and a hot sauce of tomato, onion, lime and chilies. You eat with your fingers, of course. You'll need a good appetite, strong jaws and plenty of time – to wait for your chosen roast, to chew and digest, to pick your teeth while downing a few more beers and to honour the dance requests that inevitably come your way, no matter how full you might feel.

378 Bull-jumping in the lower Omo Valley

ETHIOPIA It's seeing the casual violence of the girl-whippers, rather than the slightly comic jumping itself, that stays with you after witnessing a Hamar bull-jumping ceremony. After an hour's drive along rutted tracks deep in the bush, you leave your 4WD and trek with your guide for another hour along barely visible paths. You hear the gathering long before you see it: a din of chattering voices blended with claps and whistles and the toots of the Hamars' little trumpets. Arriving at the designated clearing at the hottest time of day, you find impromptu groups of stamping dancers forming and reforming – the women's ochre-rubbed hair braids flapping in unison, their legs wreathed with metal rattles. The dancers barely acknowledge visitors. The dusty air smells of cow dung, wood smoke, perspiration and the coffee prepared as part of the ritual.

There's organization in the chaos, but it's at first hard to discern, especially when, in a parody of male-female relations, the girls (sisters and cousins of the initiates) tauntingly approach their feather-headdressed male peers to be ritually swiped with canes, each stripe borne without flinching, and often drawing blood. Laughing and flirting, they compete for scars as signs of devotion to their brothers.

The day draws to a climax with the main event: a group of steers is rounded up and dragged into a row, side by side. Out of the crowd dashes a naked youth, who has to leap onto the end bull and complete four runs across their backs without tripping, in order to become a *maz*, a young adult. It's a compelling scene, all its complex meanings layered over centuries of social evolution and oral tradition. There are few parts of Africa where such events are still the norm, but throughout the lower Omo Valley, tribal communities from some twenty different language groups – still unconnected by mobile phone signals or roads and almost entirely self-reliant – maintain their old customs, including the dramatic stick fights and lip discs of the Mursi and the intricate, personalized body art of the Kara.

Tourism in South Omo is a rare opportunity to connect with a pre-modern Africa, and is at last being organized, at least in part, by local people.

379 Fulfilling fantasies on Frégate Island

SEYCHELLES They say there is pirate's treasure buried here. Pure white fairy terns nest in the branches of the tangled banyan trees. Fruit bats with metre-wide wings emerge from the forest at sunset, chattering like schoolchildren as they feast on papaya and custard apples. Giant tortoises creep among the pandanus palms, and bright green geckos perch on the trunks of the swaying bamboo. Seven beaches of purest white sand are lapped by the turquoise Indian Ocean, and just fourteen villas perch on the granite rocks that make Frégate one of the most beautiful islands in all of the Seychelles.

The island is private with a capital "P". Bill Gates stayed here, and Liz Hurley jetted in to Frégate for her honeymoon. Pierce Brosnan once hired the entire island after finishing a Bond film. Every villa has its own outdoor Jacuzzi, an outdoor shower, two marble bathrooms, and bedrooms where rich teak woodwork, tropical

daybeds and swathes of silk and muslin create a luxurious cocoon where anyone can hide from the real world. Sleek motor yachts are on hand ready to take the guests out on diving excursions or to try their hand at deep-sea fishing in search of wahoo and kingfish.

Frégate Island is not your typical hotel. Privately owned, and conserved, it is home to one of the world's rarest birds: the magpie robin, rescued from the brink of extinction when there were less than thirty individuals. Now, the little black and white birds are breeding successfully, and mating pairs have been transported to nearby islands to help increase their chances. There are turtles, too, nesting on the soft moonlit beaches at high tide.

Neither is it your typically flat coral island. At sunset, the pink granite boulders catch the light and from the top of the island's own miniature peak, Mount Signal, the Indian Ocean is an endless expanse of blue.

380 Exploring Stone Town on foot

ZANZIBAR There's a strong echo of the Middle East in the winding alleys and grand palaces at the heart of Zanzibar's historic capital. This is no coincidence – Stone Town was built by the Omani Arabs, who colonized the archipelago in the early seventeenth century and ruled it for almost two hundred years.

In 1841, Sultan Seyyid Saïd of Oman made Stone Town his capital in order to nurture Unguja Island's lucrative trade in cloves, ivory and, most notoriously, slaves. Sixty thousand captives were "processed" in Stone Town every year, and the Sultan received a tax on each sale, investing a significant part of the proceeds in showy architecture.

In the late twentieth century, post independence, Stone Town neglected its mansions and palaces, leaving their hand-plastered coral limestone facades to the mercy of the punishing tropical climate. But in recent years, a wave of conservation programmes has gained momentum, spurred on by Stone Town's

recognition by UNESCO as a World Heritage Site of historical and architectural significance.

If you have a few hours to spare and are feeling moderately adventurous, then leave your map (and your valuables) behind and set off on foot, just taking each alleyway as it comes. Each twist in the medina-like labyrinth will yield new discoveries – intricately carved teak or sesame wood doorframes, elaborate balconies, Swahili doors studded with ornate brass knobs and souk-like curio shops piled high with textiles, beads and paintings.

To appreciate the sheer ambition of the city founders, stroll along the seafront west of the harbour. Impressive by any standards are the four-storey Old Dispensary, now restored; the Old Customs House, home to Stone Town's highly creative Dhow Countries Music Academy; the Arab-style Palace Museum, former home of the Sultans; and the famous Beit al-Ajaib or House of Wonders, a vast late nineteenth-century palace.

381 Visiting a western lowland gorilla rehabilitation centre

GABON Evengué Island, home of the Fernan-Vaz Gorilla Project (FVGP), lies in a broad coastal lagoon deep in the wilderness, 250km south of Libreville. To reach it, you take a light aircraft to the hamlet of Omboué, then continue by boat, skimming across the smooth, silver-grey water. Herons and palm-nut vultures flap overhead. The ever-increasing sense of remoteness is significant: isolation is key to the project's success.

Gabon's western lowland gorillas are critically endangered. Unlike many of the world's great apes, their natural habitat is well preserved, but bushmeat poachers, exotic pet hunters and the deadly ebola virus all threaten their survival. FVGP rescues orphaned gorillas from zoos or the black market, gives them veterinary care and shelters them from danger. Depending on their circumstances, they either receive life-long sanctuary or are prepared for re-release, a process which takes at least two years.

For a world-leading primate project, Fernan-Vaz is remarkably

low-key. Its leader, young Canadian vet Nick Bachand, talks visitors through the project's objectives in a basic shack then leads them to the sanctuary on foot. There's a simple briefing: try to avoid sudden noises, movements or eye contact with the animals. After that, you're led into the observation area. The gorillas you're introduced to are the permanent inmates – those which, for behavioural or health reasons, would never survive in the wild. They don't seem to begrudge this: they live a peaceful, companiable life in a large, leafy enclosure. There's a generous gap between the viewing platform and the fence, but you still feel breathtakingly close. And when the silverback pummels his palms against his chest in true alpha male fashion, you're left in no doubt as to his power and strength.

You won't be allowed to see the re-release candidates, but you'll hear news of their progress. The project's greatest success is the transfer of six youngsters from the sanctuary to their own island in the summer of 2009 – a first step towards total rehabilitation.

ZANZIBAR Caressed by the warm waters of the Indian Ocean and cleansed by its monsoon, Zanzibar – East Africa's "Spice Island" – feels worlds apart from the Tanzanian mainland just 40km away. A millennia of trade with lateen-rigged dhows (sailing vessels) introduced numerous peoples from faraway climes, all of whom contributed to the Swahili culture and language and also brought most of the ingredients that infuse one of Africa's most distinctive, and delicious, cuisines.

There's nutmeg and cloves from the Moluccas; cardamom, rice and peppercorns from India; aromatic Sri Lankan cinnamon; and sweet basil (and hookah pipes) from Persia. Portuguese caravels carried chilli, vanilla and cassava from the Americas; Indonesians arrived with bananas, turmeric and coconuts; the Arabs introduced coriander and cumin; and Chinese fleets unloaded ginger, along with porcelain and silks for the wealthy.

A spice tour is de rigueur for visitors, but it's on the plate that Zanzibar's fragrant culinary marriage really shines. At nightfall in Stone Town's waterfront Forodhani Gardens, dozens of cooks set up trestle tables and charcoal stoves to prepare nightly banquets that would please any sultan, all in the flickering light of oil lanterns, and at bargain prices. Feast on octopus stewed in coconut sauce, along with fresh lobster, shrimp, prawns, king fish (diced and grilled), whole snappers and even shark. Cool your throat with tropical juices like coconut straight from the shell, tangy tamarind, mango, papaya, pineapple, banana and sugar cane – though you'll have to bear the banshee-like wails of an ancient iron press to sample that one.

Top off your meal with a tiny cup of Omani-style coffee laced with cardamom, and a glob of *halua*, a sticky, gooey confection made from wheat, pistachios, saffron and cardamom, and unbelievable amounts of sugar – the perfect sweet finale to a spicy feast.

382

TOURING the
SPICE ISLAND

383 Meeting the monkeys of Kibale

UGANDA It's unnerving to hear a bass drum being thumped when a) you're deep in a tropical forest and b) there is no one present to beat it. But exciting things happen in Kibale Forest National Park. And there's nothing more thrilling than when you find who it is that's responsible for the noise: wild chimpanzees. Kibale contains the highest concentration of primates in the world; there are twelve species in total but it is the chimps that enchant the most. After beating on flying-buttress roots with their feet, they decide on other scare tactics. Unsettling screams echo through the forest canopy – it's an exhilarating din. But the acoustics have got nothing on their terrific aerial acrobatics and displays of great ape machismo. And then they're off, moving through the branches at high speed, and it's impossible to keep up.

384 Exploring the Meroë Pyramids

SUDAN Egypt is famed for its great pyramids, but Sudan has many more. The most striking examples make up the ancient ruined city of Meroë. For nearly a thousand years from 600 BC, the little-known Kingdom of Kush prospered here alongside the Nile, once successfully repelling an attack by Alexander the Great and for centuries interring its rulers in the small but distinctively slender pyramids. Some thirty survive today, while all around small dunes in turn entomb the rubble. Meroë gets few visitors, so chances are you'll have this incredible site all to yourself.

385 Cruising to Kisangani

DEMOCRATIC REPUBLIC OF CONGO For decades, drifting down the Congo River was one of the classic African adventures. But the journey on its longest navigable part, between Kinshasa and Kisangani, was all but impossible to undertake during the country's horrific civil war. Some eastern parts of the country remain wracked by conflict, but relative peace now reigns in the west, and the barges are making the journey more regularly, with some tour operators offering two-week or more trips on their own vessels.

If you want to try it independently, get to one of the ports along the Congo and ask about boats leaving: you'll need to be fully self-sufficient, proofed against mosquitoes, happy to munch on manioc sticks and bushmeat and, just in case, a good swimmer. The rewards are remarkable river scenes that few foreigners have ever witnessed, and the joyous welcome of locals on the river who are just glad to know you want to be there.

386 Storytelling on the Ssese Islands

UGANDA The Ssese Islands of Lake Victoria are a sleepy, sibilant archipelago, yet slumber doesn't do them justice. "Ssese" is a corruption of "tsetse", the fly that carried the disease that at one point devastated the entire region. Kalangala, the main town on Buggala Island, still snoozes even though it is repopulated now. But there's action at the local beer stall; Kasiim, a small righteous man, will be telling fearful stories loaded with folklore and superstition. Join his enraptured audience gathered around the beer-crate table, charmed by tales of magic, gravely nodding and eyes popping to the fabulous night-time entertainment.

GABON For all his shortcomings, the late President of Gabon, Omar Bongo, had a shrewd grasp of the value of his nation's mighty forests. In 2002, he successfully ring-fenced over ten percent of Gabon's pristine wilderness from loggers, miners, hunters and farmers by creating thirteen new national parks, with one stroke of the pen.

One of the most accessible of these parks is Loango. But accessible, here, is a relative term. Getting to Loango takes time and money, whether you choose to fly (tricky since the 2009 change of regime) or hop on a boat from Port-Gentil, the nearest town. If you're new to safaris and keen to find the quickest, easiest route to a plain teeming with zebras, lions and giraffes, then Loango isn't for you. But if you're prepared to a suffer a long journey for a wildlife-watching experience that's unlike anything else Africa has to offer, it might be your kind of place.

Loango's unusual juxtaposition of habitats, including undeveloped beach, savannas and forest, makes it an outstanding place to visit. Its population of large mammals and reptiles ebbs and flows in a seasonal relay: for most of the year, there's a good chance of seeing something remarkable, be it breaching humpback whales (July to September), breeding Nile crocodiles (October to January) or nesting leatherback turtles (November to February). The park's hippos, famous for frolicking in the Atlantic surf, appear between November and January, while forest elephants patrol the shore from February to April.

Forest elephants, which are daintier than their better-known cousins, are somewhat unpredictable. They're partial to a hallucinogenic root, *ibago*, which grows wild in Loango's forests. If, as your guide drives you around the park, you come across an elephant that's under the influence, you could be in for an unnervingly close encounter. Less alarming, but just as intriguing, are the red river hogs – Loango's answer to warthogs. They're comical-looking, with very tufty ears. With care, you can creep up on them on foot as they trot through the grasslands. It's a thrilling experience in a continent where opportunities to watch unusual wildlife, out of range of dangerous predators, are rare indeed.

Red river hogs and forest elephants
at Loango National Park

387

NEED to know

347 The best time to see the migration in the Serengeti is between December and July; for the river crossings, visit in June (Grumeti) and July or August (Mara). Check out ⊛ www.wildwatch.com/sightings/migration.asp for up-to-date reports on the location of the herds.

348 Large two-bed safari tents at *Red Chilli Rest Camp* (⊛ www.redchillihideaway.com/paraa.htm) cost USh35,000.

349 Africa's Eden (⊛ www.africas-eden.com) build a visit to Dzanga-Sangha into their 13-day Africa's Best Kept Secret tour, which also includes Loango National Park in Gabon and the island of Príncipe.

350 It's best to go with a tour group into the wilderness of Djibouti. Companies such as Explore (⊛ www.explore.co.uk) offer trips including a 10-day Djibouti Seatrek. You may be told that you have to get a visa in advance to visit Djibouti but it's actually very straightforward to buy one on arrival by air.

351 The *Paradis Malahide* (⊛ paradismalahide.com) can organize most aspects of your stay in Gisenyi.

352 You need a travel permit to visit the Nuba mountains, available from the Ministry of the Interior in Khartoum. The best time to visit is October to January, after the rains and during the annual harvest festival.

353 Check security information before visiting this part of Congo. Permits to visit Lake Télé are issued in Brazzaville at the Ministère de l'économie forestière et de l'environnement; expect delays. To reach the lake, fly Air Congo to Impfondo, or go by river barge, and then make arrangements locally.

354 Coconut beach is a 15min taxi ride from central Bujumbura. Rusizi National Park ($3 entry fee) is open daily from dawn to dusk.

355 The Kigali Memorial Centre is open daily 10am–6pm (donations accepted) and is a partner of the UK-based Aegis Trust (⊛ aegistrust.org), which works to prevent crimes against humanity.

356 Jozani Chwaka Bay National Park (daily 7.30am–5pm; $8) lies 38km east of Stone Town; you can get there by public transport by taking a *daladala* from the Darajani terminal on Creek Road. A visit to the park is included in many guided tours of the island.

357 The best times to make the ascent of Kilimanjaro are January to mid-March and June to October. Climbers must sign up with a trekking agency. Treks last 6 to 8 days.

358 Injera has a slightly sour taste, and is best accompanied with a drink of *tej* (a honey wine) or Ambo (a brand of fizzy water).

359 Kinshasa's live music venues include *Hôtel de Crèche, Rond-Pont Victoire* (☎ 099 993 3003); *Chez Ntemba*, Place du 27 Octobre, Gombe; *Grand Hôtel Kinshasa*, Gombe (⊛ www.gh.cd); and *Halle de la Gombe* (Centre Culturel Français de Kinshasa), Gombe ⊛ www.ccf-kinshasa.org).

360 The fee for Kidepo National Park is $30 per 24hr period. Uganda Wildlife Authority game drives cost USh4000 (US$2) per kilometre.

361 A three-day pass covering all eleven churches costs around Br165. Hiring a guide is worthwhile, at around Br110 per day.

362 For further information on Kahuzi-Biega National Park, contact the Gorilla Organization (⊛ www.gorillas.org).

363 Most Kenyan travel agents will make train reservations for you, or your can book in person at the station.

364 A guide and scout can be hired at the entrance to the national park. Avoid the rainy season (June–Sept).

365 Climbing Mount Kenya is possible all year round. Many Nairobi operators and agents can offer tours, or you hike independently with a local guide. Kenya Wildlife Service (⊛ kws.go.ke) has information on fees and mountain accommodation.

366 *Chumbe Island Eco-Lodge* (⊛ www.chumbeisland.com) is reached by boat from Zanzibar. All profits from the lodge go back into the conservation of the island.

367 Access is easier by public transport than in your own vehicle: get to Mpanda by rail, then catch a vehicle to the village at the park headquarters. Armed rangers cost US$20 per day (plus park entrance of US$20/day).

368 Queen Elizabeth National Park is 5 hours from the capital, Kampala. Accessing the cave is best done with a local guide.

369 See ⊛ www.operation-loango.com for more info on Loango National Park.

370 Many resorts offer turtle-watching trips in season; one of the easiest places to see them is Cousine Island.

371 You can visit Langoué Bai with World Primate Safaris (⊛ www.worldprimatesafaris.com), whose trip includes a stay at *Langoué Bai Camp*, a rustic forest base run by Wildlife Conservation Society researchers.

372 See ⊛ www.kigio.com for more information.

373 Crater safaris are easily arranged in Arusha, several hours' drive to the east.

374 *Il Ngwesi* is approximately 90 minutes' rough drive from the nearest road. See ⊛ www.ilngwesi.com for more information.

375 Pemba Island is easily accessed from Zanzibar, either by ferry or by air.

376 Several white-water-rafting companies operate out of Jinja; try Adrift (⊛ www.adrift.ug) or Nile River Explorers (⊛ www.raftafrica.com).

377 Standard practice at meat bars is to go to the kitchen and order by weight direct from the butcher's hook or out of the fridge. *Carnivore*, on Langata Road, is Nairobi's best-known and biggest *nyama choma* bar.

378 Bull-jumping usually takes place at the end of the harvest season, between July and September. South Omo is best visited with a local guide and a 4WD vehicle. Check out ⊛ omovalleytravel.com, ⊛ mursicommunity.org, ⊛ abebatoursethiopia.com or ⊛ soratours.com. Mursi Online (⊛ mursi.org) is an excellent resource.

379 *Frégate Island* (⊛ www.fregate.com) is a 20-minute helicopter hop from the international airport on Mahé. Villas cost from €2600 per night for two people on a full-board basis (3 nights min stay).

380 Stone Town is 7km north of Zanzibar's international airport, which is served by direct flights from Dar es Salaam, Arusha, Mombasa and Nairobi.

381 You can visit the Fernan-Vaz Gorilla Project (⊛ www.gorillasgabon.com) with its ecotourism partner, specialist tour operator Africa's Eden (⊛ www.africas-eden.com).

382 Zanzibar is a 20-minute flight from Dar es Salaam, and under 3 hours by ferry.

383 Kibale Forest National Park is best reached from Fort Portal, either on local buses or with organized day tours.

384 Meroë is a two-day train ride north of capital, Khartoum.

385 The journey between Kinshasa and Kisangani takes two weeks. Alternatively, Go Congo (⊛ www.gocongo.com) runs an adventure tour in a 34m river cruiser.

386 Ferries to the islands leave from Bukakata; timings are erratic, so be prepared to hang around.

387 Specialist tour operator Africa's Eden (⊛ www.africas-eden.com) offers safaris in Loango National Park from €2510 for 9 days, including transport from Libreville.

GOOD to know

SWAHILI TIME

Time calculations in Swahili are made from dawn to dusk, which, with minor variations east and west, are pretty close to 6am and 6pm throughout the Swahili-speaking region of Kenya, Tanzania, Uganda and eastern Congo. So, *saa moja* ("one o'clock") is seven o'clock and *saa nane* ("four o'clock") is ten o'clock. You add *asubuhi* (morning), *jioni* (evening) and *usiku* (night) to be more precise. It sounds confusing, but once you've learnt your Swahili numbers, it soon becomes automatic to subtract six for Swahili time. Watch out, however, for Swahili-speakers practising their English and forgetting to add six when they arrange an appointment.

"Never argue with a fool: people may not notice the difference"

Popular Kenyan aphorism

LAKE VICTORIA

Africa's largest lake, **Victoria Nyanza,** spreads across approximately 69,000 square kilometres – approximately, because the surface area varies seasonally and the fringes are so choked with water hyacinth that it can be hard to determine the shoreline – making it the largest lake in Africa and the second largest freshwater lake in the world, equivalent in area to the size of Ireland.

CONFINEMENT, EURO-STYLE

The **Maasai** term for the first white people who visited their districts spoke directly of the Victorian obsession with modesty. Unlike the Maasai, who rarely wore much at all, and never more than a simple cloth or blanket, the Europeans went by the colourful appellation *iloridaa enjekat* – "those who confine their farts".

RUNNING HIGH

Although **athletes** from North Africa are rapidly gaining ground, it is still the **East Africans** who dominate middle- and long-distance running. Academics have long tried to explain the endurance of athletes from countries such as Ethiopia and Kenya. Some researchers believe that living and training at high altitudes produces great athletes. For others, it's all a matter of genetics: in the late 1980s, for example, the Nandi people comprised less than two percent of Kenya's population, but made up two-fifths of the nation's elite runners.

INDEBTED

Although some countries in East and Central Africa have been given debt relief, several, including Kenya and the Democratic Republic of Congo, are still among the continent's most heavily indebted. The region's countries have **national debts** of between $400 million and $30 billion, totalling nearly $90 billion between them – burdens that mire them in the deepest poverty.

SOUKOUS

The variety of **Congolese music** called **soukous**, with its high-tempo beat, thumping bass lines and ringing guitars, is among the most popular – and sexy – of Africa's many musical styles. **Soukous** has its roots in Cuban music, particularly rumba, which became popular in the booming cities of Leopoldville (now Kinshasa) and Brazzaville during the early 1940s. For a time, the indigenous music industry boomed, but these days, with the average Congolese income at less than US$1 a day and music often being sold on bootlegged CDs, the stars of **soukous** are making the most of their money in the West.

FIVE LEGENDARY CONGOLESE MUSICIANS

Papa Wendo The first star of African rumba.

Joseph Kabasele Leader of African Jazz, one of the big bands that transformed

the African take on Cuban rumba into soukous.

Franco Luambo Nicknamed the "Sorcerer of the Guitar", Franco was the front man of OK Jazz, African Jazz's big rival during the 1950s.

Tabu Ley Rochereau Tabu Ley's band African Fiesta dominated Congolese music in the 1960s.

Papa Wemba The best-known soukous musician around today, with a stunningly pure, high voice.

"He who waits until the whole animal is visible spears its tail"

Swahili proverb

THE BIG FIVE IN THE TWENTY-FIRST CENTURY

"Safari" is Swahili for "journey" (*kusafiri* meaning "to travel"); it entered the English language in the nineteenth century, when Europeans first visited Africa on game-hunting expeditions. Today, the lion, elephant, rhino, leopard and buffalo are still known as the **"big five"** – a phrase originally coined in recognition of their trophy value, but one which has somehow outlived the rifle into the digital camera age (don't forget your battery charger and spare memory cards).

LAND OF THREE COUNTRIES

Somalia has had no recognized central government since 1991. The capital Mogadishu is a hornet's nest of warring clan militias – you go there at your peril. In the north of the country, **Puntland** (capital Bosaso) is a self-declared autonomous federal region of Somalia, while in the northwest, **Somaliland** (capital Hargeisa) has declared outright independence.

SWIM WITH PENGUINS AT BOULDERS BEACH • HIKING THE FISH RIVER CANYON • A TASTE OF THE SWEET LIFE AT KANDE BEACH BAR • LEARNING THE WAYS OF A WILDLIFE RANGER • MALOLOTJA: A BIG PLACE IN A SMALL COUNTRY • DIGGING AND DANCING ON A PIONEER PROGRAMME • WALK WITH WHALES AT THE FOOT OF AFRICA • TOURING A TOWNSHIP • DREAMING IN COLOUR: BALLOONING OVER THE NAMIB • CROSSING THE MAKGADIKGADI PANS • PADDLING THE GREAT, GREY, GREASY ZAMBEZI • GETTING HOT AND BOTHERED ON THE DRAKENSBERG • MUNCH ON A MOPANE WORM • TRACING MANDELA'S ROOTS IN THE WILD COAST • ON THE TRAIL OF DEAD DODOS AND PLUMP PIGEONS • ACROSS THE GREAT KAROO • LAUGHING ON THE EDGE WITH TOWNSHIP COMEDIANS • LIVING WITH THE KUNDA • LOOKING FOR LIONS IN MADIKWE • ENJOYING THE SHOW IN ETOSHA NATIONAL PARK • TSINGY'S BREAD KNIFE FOREST • WATCHING THE DESERT BLOOM IN NAMAQUALAND • TRICKY TOPOGRAPHY: THE OKAVANGO DELTA • TAKING A WALK ON THE WILD SIDE • CAPE CROSS: THE SEAL DEAL • TROU AUX CERFS: INSIDE THE STAGS' CRATER • ON YOUR BIKE: CYCLING THROUGH THE NYIKA PLATEAU • WINGING IT OVER LUANGWA • WARRIORS AND MAIDENS: THE REED DANCE OF LUDZIDZINI • DIVING WITH MANTA RAYS IN THE QUIRIMBAS ARCHIPELAGO • FIND A TINY SLICE OF HEAVEN ON NOSY VE • DIVE THE GREAT SARDINE RUN • DISCOVERING THE LOST CITIES OF THE SWAHILI • LEARNING ABOUT ELEPHANTS IN THE BOTSWANAN BUSH • GOING ON A FROG SAFARI IN ZULULAND • PONY-TREKKING IN THE MOUNTAIN KINGDOM • COUNTING FISH IN LAKE MALAWI • THE SMOKE THAT THUNDERS • BIRDING BY LAKE ST LUCIA • MULANJE: MORE THAN JUST A MOUNTAIN • VISIT THE HOUSE OF THE SPIRITS • TRACKING RHINO IN DAMARALAND • BUSANGA: THE PLAINS TRUTH • CLIMBING TABLE MOUNTAIN • SWIGGING THE MOST REMOTE BEER ON EARTH • SAMPLING WINES IN THE WESTERN CAPE • UP THE TSIRIBIHINA IN A DUGOUT CANOE • EXPLORING THE SKELETON COAST • JUNGLE OPERATICS: THE LEMURS OF ANDASIBE-MANTADIA • RAFTING THE STAIRWAY TO HEAVEN • GIVING SOMETHING BACK AT GULUDO BEACH LODGE • ON A SWING AND A PRAYER: THROUGH THE TSITSIKAMMA FOREST CANOPY • SWIM WITH PENGUINS AT BOULDERS BEACH • HIKING THE FISH RIVER CANYON • A TASTE OF THE SWEET LIFE AT KANDE BEACH BAR • LEARNING THE WAYS OF A WILDLIFE RANGER • MALOLOTJA: A BIG PLACE IN A SMALL COUNTRY • DIGGING AND DANCING ON A PIONEER PROGRAMME • WALK WITH WHALES AT THE FOOT OF AFRICA • TOURING A TOWNSHIP • DREAMING IN COLOUR: BALLOONING OVER THE NAMIB • CROSSING THE MAKGADIKGADI PANS

Southern Africa
388–439

Diving with manta rays in the Quirimbas Archipelago 317

Living with the Kunda 305

A taste of the sweet life at Kande Beach Bar 390

ZAMBIA

MALAWI

Munch on a mopane worm

Crossing the Makgadikgadi Pans

ZIMBABWE 400

MOZAMBIQUE

MADAGASCAR

Cape Cross: the seal deal 412

BOTSWANA 397

On the trail of dead dodos and plump pigeons 402

NAMIBIA

RÉUNION

MAURITIUS

Finding a tiny slice of heaven on Nosy Ve 418

The Reed Dance of Ludzidzini 416

SWAZILAND

SOUTH AFRICA

LESOTHO

Touring a township 395

Swim with *penguins* at BOULDERS BEACH

388

SOUTH AFRICA Think of a penguin and it's hard not to see icy wastes. Yet penguins can be found as far north as the scorched Galapagos Islands, and on family-friendly Boulders Beach, close to Cape Town, you can actually swim amongst them.

The African penguin population has been decimated in recent centuries, their eggs eaten by humans, who also compete for fish stocks, and habitat threatened by pollution, yet this colony of 2,500 birds (one of only two groups on the African mainland) is growing.

Seeing the animals requires no tracking, no luck and no guide – just get out of your car at the Boulders Beach car park, half-an-hour's drive from central Cape Town, and you'll see them sunning themselves on the great granite rocks that give the beach its name, or walking around on the beach itself. The calm, clear water, protected from the Atlantic swells and strong winds by the smooth boulders, offers glimpses of the black and white birds flying through the water, using their flightless wings as efficient flippers, heading out into the mountain-encircled bay to fish. The birds are surprisingly nonchalant, and you can easily get to within a metre of them – providing a perfect photo opportunity – as they waddle their way down to the surf.

Don't expect companionship as you swim in shared waters, though. The penguins streak past at up to 25km/h and fish way off the coast, returning to regurgitate their meals for their chicks, which you can see in the plentiful nesting sites above the beach.

The azure water may lull you into Mediterranean fantasies, but Cape Town's waters are cool even in midsummer. During the winter, especially from August to October, you might not be tempted to swim, but can still roam the beach, or stand on the boulders themselves, looking past the penguins into False Bay, where southern right whales arrive from the Antarctic every year to calve.

389 Hiking the Fish River Canyon

NAMIBIA Africa's biggest ravine and one of southern Africa's great hiking trails, the Fish River Canyon is a mega-rent in the Earth's crust more than half a kilometre deep, twenty kilometres wide and one hundred and fifty kilometres long, snaking south to vent its river into the mighty Orange River. The Grand Canyon is bigger, but Fish River, ranked second in the world, is still unfathomably vast, the result of tens of millions of years of erosion, and on a scale that is more accessible. The area's astounding natural beauty and the ease with which you can walk – it takes five days to traverse the canyon – and camp here, together with the birdwatching opportunities, have made it one of Namibia's greatest outdoor attractions.

390 A taste of the sweet life at Kande Beach Bar

MALAWI Kande Beach is an apt name for this little piece of backpacker paradise in northern Malawi. For life is sweet here, whether you're getting stuck in to some of the many waterbound activities on Lake Malawi or just snoozing on a beachfront hammock. But perhaps the sweetest pleasure of all is to be had at the famed *Kande Beach Bar*. Grab a cold one and settle in under the shade of the open wood-framed bar – lake shimmering just beyond, music softly playing in the background. As the sun sets and the revelling steps up a notch, the only sour note is knowing you can't stay for ever.

391 Learning the ways of a wildlife ranger

SOUTH AFRICA Two weeks ago, it would have been just another pile of poo. But now, a fortnight into your ranger-training course, this tower of dung is so much more than that. Now, it means elephants have passed through here recently, maybe within the last few hours. It means that the herd is heading west, looking for fresh foliage. And it means that if you swing your Land Rover around and take the dusty track behind you, you'll have a good chance of beating them to the waterhole. And the guests in the back of your 4WD will have yet another great tale to tell the folks back home.

The wildlife ranger-training course in Kruger National Park is the epitome of "hands-on" learning. You'll spend eight hours a day in the bush, discovering how to take a game drive effectively, understanding animal behaviour, brushing up your tracking skills, and getting used to handling a high-calibre rifle. You'll drive along rutted roads, you'll sit up-front in the tracking seat to scan the undergrowth for antelope, and you'll have one of the most incredible months of your life.

392 Malolotja: a big place in a small country

SWAZILAND Another false summit. Defeated, you lever the pack from your back and slump into the shade of a sugar bush, porcupine quills strewn at your feet like some primitive offering. Bird calls drift up from the canopy below: the chirrup of bulbuls, the growling of a turaco.

Down in the forest, the trail had been all cool, green-filtered light. Up here on the shattered slopes, the sun has you pinioned to the hillside like a beetle on a sand dune. An unseen baboon barks its alarm from the ridgetop. But the rush of the falls is a siren call. One more push?

The grandeur of Malolotja belies the bijou dimensions of Swaziland. This, the biggest park in southern Africa's tiniest nation, protects a muscular wilderness of peaks, grasslands and gorges, with vistas that stretch far beyond the country's borders. Highlights include the world's oldest iron-ore mine, the 90m

bridal-veil cascade of Malolotja Falls and the "potholes" – a terraced series of circular plunge pools that lure footsore hikers deep into an echoing ravine. Hiking trails embroider the wild ridges and forested clefts. And every stream swells the exuberant Malolotja River, which carves its way downwards and northwards until it hits the Komati and turns east for the Indian Ocean.

For birders, Malolotja means the blue swallow – southern Africa's rarest bird and just one of a fine cast of avian A-listers. Other wildlife is rich, but elusive: alert hikers might meet mountain reedbuck skittering across the rocky slopes, an otter lolloping along the riverbank or maybe a shy serval stalking the marsh. Plants, too, are prolific: orchids in the grasslands, cycads in the forests, aloes and coral trees spotting the hillsides with scarlet. It's not "Big Five country", give or take the occasional leopard print. But whatever you find, you'll have it all to yourself.

393 Digging and dancing on a pioneer programme

MADAGASCAR As someone who'd never wielded a shovel in his life, I was pretty pleased with my first day's efforts on the Azafady Pioneer programme. Azafady makes a point of pitching its volunteers into the thick of things, which in my case meant digging a well in a remote Malagasy village, bounded on one side by forested hillsides and on the other by the most idyllic beaches I'd ever set eyes on. Not that we had much chance to gaze at the scenery. Half-buried in red dust and mud, most of the day was spent digging and slapping on trowels of cement under the watchful eye of our local project coordinator.

Sometimes, volunteering initiatives seem geared more towards benefiting the volunteers themselves than the communities they are ostensibly there to help. But this isn't the case with Azafady, where the work carried out – supporting NGOs on a range of health, sanitation and environmental schemes – really does make a positive impact on the environment and lives of local people. It's an award-winning project that provides a very special way to get

under the surface of life on La Grande Île. Moreover, all the profits are ploughed back into sustainable development.

After an intensive seven-day orientation course, where you're taught the basics of local Malagasy dialects, the volunteer work proper begins. Ours involved planting fruit trees, making puppets and writing songs to help teach children about the importance of washing their hands before eating. Out in the forest, we spent days collecting rare seeds, surveying the impact of logging and assisting with studies of birds, plants and lemurs.

The hands-on nature of the work means it can be physically demanding at times, but Azafady makes sure there's enough downtime for its volunteers to surf and, more importantly, hang out with the local people they work with. There were some amazing parties on the beach outside Ambinanibe, the village where we dug the well. Fuelled by bottles of warm Three Horses beer, we were shown how to drum, sing bawdy songs in the local lingo and, best of all, do the *mangaliba* – the sexiest dance in the Indian Ocean.

394 Walk with whales at the foot of Africa

SOUTH AFRICA If size really does count, then whales are the biggest attraction in South Africa. In most places on the planet you need to get on a boat to get a decent glimpse of these amazing creatures, but in South Africa they come so close to shore you can easily see them with your naked eye. One of the very best places anywhere for land-based whale watching is the De Hoop Nature Reserve, in the Western Cape, close to the continent's southernmost tip, where in the breeding season (roughly June to November) hundreds of female southern right whales come to calve and suckle their offspring.

You can stay in cottages in the nature reserve, but the most rewarding way to come into contact with the mammals is the five-day Whale Trail, which covers the 55km from Potberg to Koppie Alleen, traversing beaches and cliff edges with terrific views from dusk to dawn. During the season, you're treated to so many whale sightings that by the end of the trail you become almost blasé. But

not quite. It takes a lot to beat the vision of a southern right blowing fine spray out of the water as it breathes or exposing its tail above the water surface like some massive dark sail. Breaching, the whales create an enormous swell, leaping clear of the water and sometimes twirling in the air before returning to the deep with an enormous splash. You'll often also see seals scouting for fish and dolphins riding the surf, while on land there are some eighty mammal species, from small yellow mongooses to antelope and mountain zebras.

The hike is a "slackpacking" trail that requires only basic fitness. Your supplies and kit are taken by road to each night's accommodation – comfortable, fully equipped cottages, each one in splendid isolation. The porterage means when you're not gawking at whales, you can really enjoy the endemic fynbos vegetation, which incorporates an extraordinary diversity that includes fine-leafed heathers, minute insectivorous plants, giant proteas and orchids. And, best of all: only one group at a time is allowed on each day's section.

Touring a township

SOUTH AFRICA I'm listening to a group of children singing folk songs in a timber-shack assembly hall. It's tiny – far too small for a school of this size – and very basic. But compared to the old shipping containers that serve as classrooms, it's generous.

When the kids segue into *Nkosi Sikelel 'i Afrika*, I feel a lump rise in my throat. Who could fail to be moved by these earnest young voices singing South Africa's unmistakably poignant anthem? Blinking hard, I gulp back my emotions and know, without looking round, that my companions are doing the same.

Some of us had misgivings about joining a guided tour of Langa and Khayelitsha. We'd be travelling around the oldest and largest of the black townships in Cape Town's poverty-stricken Cape Flats. Would we feel like voyeurs, intruders or cultural imperialists? By just dipping in for a day, would we be reinforcing the outdated social divisions that first brought the townships into existence?

The reality turns out to be more complicated. Brian, our guide, himself a township resident, doesn't shield us from the difficulties that the communities face: overpopulation, unemployment, inadequate health care. As we drive past Guguletu cemetery, fresh graves bear testament to one of the bitterest problems – it's believed that eight out of ten residents may be HIV positive.

But there's another message. Our itinerary is all about meeting people – albeit in rather contrived circumstances. We visit places and projects where motivated individuals are chipping away at the heavy burden of deprivation that keeps the townships on their knees. There's Maureen Jacobs, the head teacher, who's giving kids from the informal settlements a start in life; Rosie Gwadiso, founder of a community kitchen, who sends children to school nourished instead of hungry; and Golden Nongawuza, who runs a workshop making ornamental flowers out of recycled tin cans. "This gives you an introduction," says Brian. "Come back in a year or so and you'll see how much more will have changed for the better."

NAMIBIA Yellow ochre, burnt sienna, raw umber, salmon pink. The early morning landscape that's unfolding beneath us summons a litany of colours remembered from old paintboxes. Spice colours, too – cinnamon, turmeric, nutmeg, powdered ginger – and palest blond, the colour of bone, straw or freshly-cut wood.

If you picture the desert as a stark, monochrome place, you couldn't be further from the truth. As our balloon floats over crumpled hills, powdery dunes and saltpans dotted with skeleton trees, the rich subtlety of the desert palette is so beautiful that I'm determined to imprint it on my memory. I feel like an Inuit searching for new words to describe the colour of snow.

Here, nature is sculptor. The Namib, widely considered the world's most ancient desert, was carved by water and wind. From the air, your eye can trace the rhythmic alignment of the eighty-million-year-old dunes, like ripples in a storm-blown sea.

Incredibly, a few species manage to survive in this near-barren environment. We drift over a towering dune the colour of clotted cream and peer down to watch a long-shadowed oryx climbing the ridge on slow, stiff legs. It's the kind of antelope that Picasso might have dreamed up – its facial markings bold, its horns strikingly graphic. On the plain at the foot of the dune, a male ostrich races across the sand, feathers fluffed up like a bustle. Beyond, a small herd of zebra mill about under heat-wizened camelthorn trees.

"I'm taking her higher", says our pilot. There's a roar from the burner, and the balloon begins to ascend. The scene below softens and recedes, and the luminous African sky grows larger and larger. And I turn my gaze to the endless horizon.

396

Dreaming in colour:
Ballooning over the Namib

397 Crossing the Makgadikgadi Pans

BOTSWANA We stand at the edge of a sea of grass looking out onto the saltpan. "A flat and featureless expanse of sun-baked clay," says our guidebook. It's not far wrong. We can see our route ahead: twin tyre tracks meandering sketchily towards the horizon, disappearing into the blinding heat-haze. But this is where we stop. Going onward requires expedition-style gear: winch, GPS, satellite phone. One wrong turn and you're through the crust, axle-deep in treacherous silt. The next vehicle might be days or weeks.

This was once a lake. On Kubu Island, a baobab-studded granite outcrop to the south, ancient beaches record the lapping waves of another era. Fossilized aquatic creatures are strewn among the shingle – as are Stone Age arrowheads, relics of a people who once called this desolation home. But during the subsequent millennia, geology intervened: seismic forces tilted the centre of Botswana,

diverting its rivers and cutting off the lake from its supply. Today, the pans receive an annual trickle – the overspill from the Okavango. Briefly, they become glassy sheets of shallow, salty water.

Wildlife here is nomadic. Hit the right season, and you'll find springbok and zebra massing on the grasslands, pans washed pink with flamingoes, and wandering lions adding their throaty voice to the nocturnal soundtrack. At other times, the plains seem empty – just the odd ostrich stalking the horizon, dodging the dust devils. But tracks and signs tell of meerkats, springhares and other permanent residents that quietly eke out a precarious living.

Other parts of Botswana may have bigger game, but if it's wilderness, isolation and sheer space you crave, then the Makgadikgadi Pans are hard to beat. Here, on the northern frontier of the Kalahari, it's a big place for feeling small.

398 Paddling the great, grey, greasy Zambezi

ZIMBABWE When Rudyard Kipling wrote of an archetypal African river all set about with fever trees, he was referring to the Limpopo, which defines the southern border of Zimbabwe. Yet the Zambezi, which heads through the north of the country, is larger, grander and far more crocodile- and hippo-infested than its rival. It took Victorian missionary and explorer David Livingstone three years to travel the 2500km from its source in Zambia to its mouth in Mozambique by dug out. Today, canoeing through wilderness areas, downriver from Victoria Falls, where the spray of the plunging Zambezi can be seen 20km off, offers the rawest experience of African wildlife you will ever encounter.

Apart from your own small, guided group on the waters of the Lower Zambezi, in the Mana Pools National Park, you won't see any buildings or people for several days. You'll skim past herds of grazing buffalo and antelope as well as elephants, which stand on their hind legs to tug at delicious seed pods high up on acacia trees. And a

quiet canoe can get preciously close to birdlife; vermilion carmine bee-eaters swoop in and out of nests burrowed into sandy banks and black egrets, green-backed and goliath herons stalk the shallows for fish and frogs.

Everything is carried on your canoe, including a tent, though you may spend some nights with only a mosquito net spread over your mattress as chilling predator growls and roars split the night. Territorial male hippos, not always keen to let canoes pass through their domain, are far more frightening than the 5m crocodiles that slide into the water as you paddle by, keeping close to the river guide. The paddling itself is not strenuous and, in colonial style, canoe safaris are actually quite luxurious – meals are prepared by the camp cook, and you dine under the stars, white tablecloth and all.

The people you do meet tend to be exceptionally friendly and easy-going – they may be governed by a despot, but the benefits of tourism are appreciated on the ground.

399 Getting hot and bothered on the Drakensberg

SOUTH AFRICA It's hot and it's dry and the mountains are huge. They just hang there – craggy, grey and wholly unsympathetic. We've been heading up towards the Amphitheatre for an hour or so and the damn thing hardly seems any closer. The Afrikaners called this range, fronted by a cliff face of almost unimaginable vastness, the Dragon Mountains, or Drakensberg. In Zulu, they are Ukhahlamba, "the Barrier of Spears", hundreds of kilometres of flat-topped peaks that are the remnants of a once vast southern African plateau.

You can get up and down in a day; that's what Witness, our chef at *Tendele Camp*, said. We've already given him our supplies, and by the time we get back tonight he'll have prepared supper and have it set out beside the bungalow. For the moment, though, I chew on a piece of biltong and realize that I'm getting through my water bottles too fast. This is an epic struggle between mountain and man, and the man is very hot indeed.

Fortunately, as we stumble through a wooded section of the Tugela Gorge, there's a stream cascading over huge basalt boulders. I don't just drink. I fill my hat and upend it over my head. Fifteen minutes later, we're ready to start again.

I know what lies ahead: the notorious chain ladder up the last section of the Amphitheatre. Rusty and dented from thousands of sweaty bodies, it's the only way to get on top of towering Mont aux Sources (3254m). Lesser men have balked at its hundred rungs up a near vertical rock face.

Still, the view from the top is breathtaking; that's what Witness claims and he's been doing this route since childhood. Wringing out my damp headgear, I follow the rest of our small band of brothers. We've still to reach Tugela Falls, the second highest waterfall in the world, plunging down 948m in five dramatic leaps. Only we'll be going up, not down. Tonight, we will have such stories to tell Witness.

Munch on a mopane worm

400

ZIMBABWE First things first: it's a caterpillar, not a worm. This revelation may or may not improve your appetite. But to many Zimbabweans – especially those living in the low-lying, mopane tree belt – this protein-packed invertebrate is a staple.

Trawl through the local markets and you'll see them by the thousand, heaped in bright plastic buckets or piled on the rickety stalls among mounds of beans and dried *kapenta* sardines. Take a closer look at one. It's grey and wrinkled; the size of your little toe. Now try a nibble. There's no real taste – it's more like dried wood than anything animal. Add a little salt, though, and you have the perfect bar snack; the insect equivalent of a pork scratching.

Those you find in the market have already been prepared, their tail ends pinched off and noxious gut contents squeezed out, then dried in the sun. For a good meal you'll need a decent portion. The vendor will scoop them up in an old tin can and wrap them in a twist of newspaper. Now you can take them home, rehydrate them in warm water, and fry them with some onion, tomato and a dash of chilli. Served the traditional way, with a portion of *sadza* (maize meal porridge), they make a cheap, tasty and nutritious dinner.

This dish – or a version of it – is eaten across a wide swathe of southern Africa, wherever the mopane tree grows. And it is on the butterfly-shaped leaves of this drought-resistant species that the emperor moth, *Imbrasia belina*, lays its eggs. When they hatch, the caterpillars work voraciously through the foliage until they are big enough to pupate, which they do underground over winter. It's at the fifth, and fattest, larval stage that local people harvest them, picking them from the leaves before drying or smoking them.

Once just a subsistence food, mopane worms now fuel a wider industry that has become vital to the local economy. OK, so they may not appeal to the first-timer. But perhaps appetite is all in the mind; after all, a bowl of prawns is hardly a thing of beauty. Forget the name and just tuck in.

401 Tracing Mandela's roots in the Wild Coast

SOUTH AFRICA True to its name, South Africa's Wild Coast is one of the country's most unspoilt areas – a vast stretch of undulating hills dotted with traditional African villages, lush forest and kilometres of undeveloped beaches. Arguably the best place to taste the Wild Coast is at *Bulungula Lodge*, a joint enterprise between the people of Nqileni Village and seasoned traveller and development worker Dave Martin.

Idyllically sited along the mouth of the Bulungula River, Nqileni and the lodge lie in a remote region of the former Transkei, the notionally "independent homeland" to which Xhosa-speaking black South Africans were relegated under apartheid. One consequence of South Africa's racial policies was the neglect suffered by the Wild Coast, but this also meant it escaped the intense coastal development that has ravaged many former whites-only coastal areas.

With a dearth of formal jobs, people in the Transkei still live rural lives in thatched adobe huts, growing maize, fishing and cooking on wood fires, while young lads still herd cattle, pretty much as Nelson Mandela did when he was a boy some seventy years ago. Wander around Nqileni and you may be invited into someone's house for a slug of traditional beer or asked to take part in everyday business, such as mud-brick making or maize stamping.

Bulungula also gives a livelihood to members of the community, who take visitors exploring on horseback or canoeing up the Xhora River to look for malachite kingfishers, or teach them how to fish with a throw net. You can meander along the beach to watch whales and dolphins or have one of the villagers take you out on an all-day expedition to beautiful Coffee Bay. At night, the skies are so clear and the shooting stars so plentiful that, according to the lodge's owner, "if you look at the sky for half an hour without seeing one, you can stay the night for free."

402 On the trail of dead dodos and plump pigeons

MAURITIUS Island life has its upsides and its downsides. Some of the animals which washed up on the world's remotest shores in distant millennia were lucky – finding themselves in a food-rich, predator-free habitat, they thrived. On Mauritius, reptiles, birds and bats evolved into complacent creatures of considerable proportions. But their peaceful nature was their downfall. As soon as humans showed up, it was all over.

The disappearance of the dodo, the poster bird of extinct species, was total: only sketches and scraps of bone survived. Archeologists have done their best to piece together images of this metre-tall flightless pigeon from skeleton fragments found in centuries-old rubbish tips; at the Dodo Gallery of the Natural History Museum in the capital, Port Louis, you can view some of their attempts.

Dead it may be, but there's no escaping the dodo on Mauritius. It's everywhere – on tablecloths, fridge magnets and even on the passport stamp you receive at the airport. The islanders seem almost proud of being more famous for their extinct wildlife species than their living ones. But these days, they're a lot more conservation-minded than the sixteenth- and seventeenth-century seafarers who (together with their pigs and monkeys) munched their way through the entire dodo population, or the twentieth-century settlers who nearly polished off another Mauritian endemic, the pink pigeon.

On Ile aux Aigrettes, a small woodland reserve in a lagoon off the southeast coast, the Mauritian Wildlife Foundation is taking great pains to protect the few pink pigeons which remain. The pigeon, *Columba mayeri*, is naturally plump and reluctant to fly: their population had plummeted to under a dozen in the early 1990s before naturalists, including the Durrell Wildlife Conservation Trust, stepped in to intervene.

You can visit Ile aux Aigrettes by motorboat, but for a truly magical approach hop into a kayak at the *Shandrani* hotel and paddle your way across the turquoise water. There's usually just enough of a current to give your shoulders a gentle workout. Once ashore, a guide leads you along paths lined with rare flora: little by little, rangers are replacing non-native species with endemics thanks to funds raised from visitors. You'll almost certainly spot some pink pigeons, sunning themselves in a clearing with the smugness of a bird which knows it's onto a good thing.

403 Across the Great Karoo

SOUTH AFRICA Take on the 1400km drive between Cape Town and Johannesburg and you'll discover there's an awful lot of nothing in South Africa's interior. This immense semi-desert is called the Great Karoo, meaning "place of thirst", and it stretches from the southwestern Cape Mountains northeast to the Orange River. The name is apt: summer heat is fierce here, the winter cold biting, rain is elusive and the soil all but barren. Slow, creaking windmills struggle to bring water to the surface, and the baked, red-brown earth is roamed only by skittish knots of springbok or small merino sheep. The human inhabitants and are thinly spread: those that do brave the desolation live on remote farms or are huddled in squat, whitewashed settlements which seem to drift like rafts in an arid ocean.

You can – as most do – speed along the straight, featureless N1 highway at a steady 120 km/h. Every few hours you'll come upon a sterile service station offering some shade, a refrigerated drink and the chance to scrape the accumulated layers of insects from your front windscreen.

Alternatively, you could stop off for a while: the total emptiness is quite awe-inspiring. Sitting in the shade of their verandas, locals will tell you that after a few days, or maybe weeks, you'll come to relish the crispness of the air, the orange and ochre colours of the rocks on the flat-topped hills at sunset and the tenacious succulents and desert flowers that defy the heat and drought. There are few places on Earth where you can see so much sky; at night, there are so many stars that even the familiar constellations get lost in the crowded galaxies. The water-starved Karoo is called Great for a reason.

404 Laughing on the edge with township comedians

SOUTH AFRICA "You can probably guess that I'm from the Cape Flats – born and fled that is!" So starts another night of impassioned, edgy and often bitingly satirical comedy from some of South Africa's rawest young comedy talent.

The townships of Cape Town aren't known as hubs of comedy, but the Starving Comics, an almost exclusively black and mixed-race group of young funny men and women, most of whom hail from troubled areas such as Mitchell's Plain and Gugulethu, aim to change that perception. After decades in the international wilderness during apartheid, when comedy from the US and Europe was all but impossible to watch, this clutch of new comics have a voracious appetite for international skits and stars, and are deadly serious about giving South Africa a distinctive comic voice.

So this means an eclectic cluster of moneyed bohos, grizzled old Afrikaners, township residents and tourists can be found in a variety of modestly sized venues above bars and in tiny theatres across Cape Town on any given night to hear comics blaze a trail through comic journeys both satirical and surreal that can take in everything from political corruption to ice-rink etiquette.

To watch a gig with the Starving Comics is to be reminded that it's possible to create comedy out of absolutely anything – even issues as tragic as the South African crime rate and the legacy of apartheid. It's not the slickest comedy experience. Performers forget their lines, audiences are sometimes barely in double figures and getting info in advance about gigs can be difficult. But this is comedy at its rawest, bravest and most exciting. Even if, after watching these guys, you may never feel the same way about Nelson Mandela's rugby shirt ever again.

405 Living with the Kunda

ZAMBIA Waking up in a comfortable and traditional African hut in the early light of dawn, children and animals rousing around you, the sounds of women preparing the first meal of the day carried on the still morning air – such is the experience of living with the Kunda.

The villagers of Kawaza, a small hamlet on the fringes of Zambia's South Luangwa National Park, earned their livings from subsistence agriculture and working in safari lodges until they started offering tourists the chance to experience village life by spending a night or two with them. From the income this generates, the villagers – the village guides, the traditional healer we visited, and the drummers and dancers who performed a spectacular evening display for us under the moonlight – are paid. The remaining balance goes into a central fund, which the community allocates to projects such as Kawaza's village school. Six years ago the school had 327 pupils and four teachers – now there are 551 pupils and sixteen teachers.

Kawaza village consists of immaculate thatched huts or bandas surrounded by patchwork fields of crops. It's a happy place full of playful children, women going about their daily work and men discussing the issues of the day. You can't help but feel incredibly grounded in the village – maybe because somewhere in our ancient past our relatives lived in a similar way. I spent two nights there, and it's the most positive – not to mention authentic – travel experience I've had.

We spent the days in the village playing football with the kids – using a ball made out of crushed paper tied up with string – and simply sitting and talking with the locals, including an old lady from the village called Elimina Banda, who says she is happy to see whites in the village and would like to spend all day with them. "There was a time when I was scared of them," she says, "but not now."

406 Looking for lions in Madikwe

SOUTH AFRICA An indistinct crackle on the ranger's radio broke the peace of our unhurried journey back to the lodge. Danie translated over his shoulder, ear straining for more reports as he cajoled the Land Rover into picking up a bit more speed. "Two of the unattached young lions are on the move. This is their territory and we've had an idea for a few days that there was another male trying to move in. There's a bit of light from the moon tonight. There could be a rumble."

The radio crackled again and we took a sharp turning. "Hold on," said Danie. "They're heading for the waterhole."

We drove hard for a few minutes. The sunset had all but drained from our surroundings, twilight dimming to evening monochrome. At the waterhole there was another vehicle. We drew alongside softly. A ranger in the same uniform as Danie shook his head quickly, then motioned with his hands that we take different routes.

Every movement in the bush made us twitch. The Land Rover bumped slowly over the rutted track. Then we came round a corner, and stopped suddenly. Danie flicked off his headlights, and with his foot on the clutch slid the gearstick into reverse. The lions were 30m away.

They sat on their haunches, peering into the bush away from us, their dark manes bristling. By comparison, the pride we'd seen earlier that day seemed lethargic and uninterested.

No one dared breathe. One of the lions lifted his head and, starting from somewhere around the end of his tail, let out a grumbling, tumbling growl which built into a massive, full-throated, primal roar. The sound left the air around us shaking.

A reply rose from further away. Our pair pushed up onto all fours, then moved off purposefully. In seconds they had slipped into the dark shadows of the bush.

"Good luck, guys," said Danie. He flicked on the lights. "I think we'd best leave them to it."

407 *Enjoying the show* in **Etosha National Park**

NAMIBIA Just this morning, through the dust and glare, eighty nodding zebra had filed out of the thorn scrub, the leaders forced belly-deep into the waterhole by the jostling ranks behind. Now, darkness assembles a new cast. The first player enters stage right: a black rhino, huffing from the shadows, calf at her heels. She pauses at the moan of a distant lion – radar ears rotating and nostrils scouring the breeze. Then, with a stamp and a snort, she steps up to drink.

It's a safari truism that the real thing is not like the TV version: the animals don't simply queue for your viewing pleasure. Except, perhaps, at Etosha. Namibia's premier national park has a string of spring-fed waterholes that, in the dry season, suck the wildlife from the surrounding bush. And with floodlights at each of the three main camps, you get to see the nocturnal action, too. You'll have to share it with others, mind: Etosha is safari central. But the wildlife is unbeatable.

On this September night at Halali Camp, black rhino is just for starters. Next, a herd of forty elephants arrives, taking over the waterhole with their lumbering frolics. Then, as the jumbos ghost away into the night, a single male lion pads in from stage left. He drinks long and deep before departing purposefully – on a mission. Four hyenas soon follow, giggling in some edgy dispute. Meanwhile, hares, eagle owls and other night creatures come and go, while a honey badger sniffs around the rocks where I perch.

Next morning, out on the road, Etosha is all horizons: dusty plains, blinding saltpan, bleached skies. The place has none of Okavango's lushness or Serengeti's grandeur. It's just huge and harsh, with herds – everywhere – trudging across its flat immensities. No point trying to follow them. Just pack your sandwiches, pick a waterhole and wait: they'll come to you.

Tsingy's *bread-knife* forest

MADAGASCAR Some of the butterflies are so large they hardly look able to get off the ground. But the lemurs and hairy crabs aren't interested in them, nor are the lime green *parrots*. They're too busy fussing through the *tsingy*.

These serrated limestone rock formations, sharp as bread-knives, cut up through the landscape of western Madagascar, creating baroque grottos and pinnacles. Dry and seemingly inhospitable, they are home to extraordinary wildlife. Even fat baobabs manage to grab hold in this alien environment. But extraordinary beauty is also found in the detail: miniature red ants and tiny jewelled orchids dazzle against jagged bone-coloured stone.

409 Watching the desert bloom in Namaqualand

NAMIBIA & SOUTH AFRICA Spring in Namaqualand brings the kind of miracle for which time-lapse photography was invented. After the brief winter rains, mile after mile of barren-looking semi-desert is transformed, within days, into a sea of flowers – a dazzling display that sends butterflies, bees and long-tongued flies into a frenzy.

Namaqualand, a thirsty, rocky region encompassing South Africa's northwestern corner and Namibia's extreme south, supports over 4000 wild floral species, a quarter of them endemic. It's this diversity that gives the annual display so much charm. The key lies below the surface: seeds and bulbs can lie dormant through many years of drought, and when conditions suddenly improve, the plants grow roots of differing length, so numerous species can exploit relatively small stretches of terrain.

The least showy of the plants are the succulents, some shaped like fingers, others (such as lithops) like pebbles. These cling to life on the ground, where the colour of the gravel can mean the difference between extinction and survival – a few chips of white quartz may be sufficient to lower the local air temperature by a degree or so, just enough for a plant to cope.

Intriguing though the succulents are, it's the colourful blooms that draw the crowds. Visit on a sunny day in a good year and you'll see meadow after meadow sprinkled with aloes and lilies, daisies and gladioli, purple ruschias, golden ursinias and gaudy vermilion gazanias, as bright as hundreds and thousands on a fairy cake.

It's a photographer's dream – and a heaven for painters, too. If Claude Monet had set up his easel near Springbok instead of Argenteuil, the Namaqualand daisy would by now be every bit as famous as the Val d'Oise poppy.

410 Tricky topography: the Okavango Delta

BOTSWANA The vast Okavango River flows for 1600km through three countries, yet never reaches the sea. Instead, it hits the vast, ultra-flat plain of arid nothingness that is northern Botswana. It's like a strange contest – desert versus river – and here the desert wins. With no gradient to guide it, the water spreads out over 15,000 square kilometres, then gives up and seeps away or evaporates in the heat. Nothing like it happens anywhere else on Earth. The river simply disappears.

The Okavango Delta is a birder's paradise and a cartographer's nightmare. No one seems able to decide if it should be green or blue on a map. The waters rise and fall in tune with distant rainfall patterns, creating a bewildering maze of islands, waterways and lagoons, much of which disappears underwater during floods, only to reappear in a quite different arrangement when the waters recede.

The best way to see the delta is in a *mokoro*, the local variety of canoe; a poler will guide you, often along waterways that are precisely the width of a hippo's body, for the simple reason that they have been formed by the daily migration of hippos from the lagoons, where they bask during the day, through the reeds to the shore, where they graze all night.

The water is utterly clear, with hundreds of tiny fish darting just below the surface. The hippo-made waterways snake and curve through the tall reeds, which seem to glow in the low, bright African sun, occasionally opening out into wide lagoons, each of which is only the most minuscule fraction of this endless, mysterious landscape of not-quite-land, not-exactly-water. The only sound is the swish of the pole in the water, and the croak of frogs, happily proclaiming that they have found frog heaven.

411 Taking a walk on the wild side

ZAMBIA Call me a safari snob, but to my mind the Big Five are seriously overrated. Leopards may be gorgeous, but they're maddeningly elusive – set your heart on finding one and you're heading for disappointment. Elephants are entertaining, but if you've seen them pull a forest to pieces you'll know how thuggish they can be. Lions are forever grumbling at each other, rhinos are miserably shy, and buffalo are just bulky, belligerent cows.

But show me a trap set by an antlion and talk me through the way this crafty little larva nabs its prey, and I'm all ears. Stop beneath a fig tree, break open one of its fruit and explain the intricate symbiotic relationship it enjoys with a fig-wasp, and I'll listen intently. Crouch beside a fallen branch to point out a chameleon, its eyes swivelling madly, its tail perfectly coiled, and I'm enthralled.

One of the very best ways to enjoy the African wilderness is to forget about the Big Five and go out walking with somebody who knows his quails from his queleas and his *munga* from his *mutemwa*. Africa has plenty of first-rate guides, but Zambia's walking-safari guides are the *crème de la crème*. Find one you click with and he'll turn everything, from the commonest shrub to the tiniest bug, into a discovery worth pages of your travel journal.

Exploring on foot is a much more subtle experience than charging around in a vehicle. While you probably won't get close to the kind of wildlife that considers humans a threat, your ears, nose and eyes will tune in to every rustle, whiff and movement, just in case. And if you do spot something larger than a squirrel, it's a heart-thumping experience.

It's almost as thrilling, though, to examine signs of animal activity – spoor, dung, flattened vegetation – and work out what happened next. Any guide worth the name can read tracks in the dust as clearly as a morning newspaper.

Let the canopy-topped Land Rovers and zebra-striped minibuses charge off in search of marauding lions and stampeding buffalo – I'd rather keep my feet firmly on the ground, and walk.

412 Cape Cross: the seal deal

NAMIBIA You'll smell them before you hear them: a pungent oily aroma wafting off the Atlantic Ocean. You'll hear them before you see them: a chorus of grunts and snorts carried on the breeze. And then you finally clap eyes on them – a writhing mass of spray-shrouded seals stretching far along the Skeleton Coast. The colony at Cape Cross is overcrowding in action, with up to 100,000 cape fur seals gathering here at any one time. Word has it that this is actually a beach, but you'd never know it underneath all that blubber. Large bulls fight for territory; pups fight just to stay alive. And just offshore, the breaking waves bubble with hundreds more seals, waiting for a scrap of sandy space on which to wedge themselves.

413 Trou aux Cerfs: inside the stags' crater

MAURITIUS Up in the hilly heartland plateau of Mauritius, the extinct volcanic crater of Trou aux Cerfs ("Stags' Crater") rises incongruously from the centre of the Indian Ocean island's highest town, Curepipe. A superb escape from urban life (and the heat at sea level), there's a road to the rim, and around it, from where you get stunning panoramas of the island, including the sheer peaks of the Trois Mamelles ("Three Breasts") rising to the west. The inner slopes are thickly wooded, and there's a good chance you'll see some of Mauritius's unique birdlife, including the endangered pink pigeon. Down on the crater floor, the lake varies seasonally from pristine to weed-choked, but it's deep, so watch your step.

414 On your bike: cycling through the Nyika Plateau

MALAWI Now the going gets tougher. The red dirt track has narrowed, and your wheels crunch as you enter the dense miombo woodland of the Rukuru Valley. Splintered branches strewn across the track tell of recent elephants. The Chisanga Falls are somewhere below: a chance to wash the dust off jolted limbs. But beyond them lies a climb of 40km, back onto the escarpment where camp awaits.

Just thirty minutes earlier you had been on top of the world – or at least on top of the Nyika Plateau, which must feel pretty similar. Grazing zebra had lifted their heads to stare as you'd passed them on your two-wheeled steed. Eland antelope, ever cautious, had filed away along the distant ridge. They're still filing now, 5km behind you, silhouetted against a towering cloudscape.

"It doesn't look like Africa," comes the refrain from first-timers. Certainly, the undulating treeless terrain up top can be more suggestive of the moors than the tropics. But what do you expect at 2500m? The logbook at *Chelinda Lodge* tells of a young couple who, only last week, cycled around a corner to find a leopard lying on the track. That was certainly enough "Africa" for them.

There's a final day's hard pedalling ahead, but tonight will be spent at a campfire beneath the stars with a continent laid out below you: Zambia to the west, Tanzania to the north and, lying far below like a darkened pool, Lake Malawi to the east.

ZAMBIA "Over there," bellows John into your headphones, "that's part of the original course." He indicates a sun-cracked crescent of clay down to your left. "Hang on, I'll show you."

You hold your breath and clutch your camera as the microlight makes a low pass over the river. Its angular shadow sweeps ahead, scrambling crocs from the bank and sending hippos snorting through the shallows. A saddle-billed stork hangs for a second in your flight path before lurching away with ponderous wing beats.

Then suddenly you're whisked up again and the valley rolls out in pin-sharp detail, buffalo filtering through the mopane woodland like ants through broccoli. Down below, the Luangwa snakes to the horizon in contours of sand, its dry-season flow reduced to a broken chain of pools and channels that wink at the dawn. Such is the clarity of light that you could swear the distant escarpment walls – yesterday just a smudge of heat-haze blue – have advanced across the valley floor overnight.

South Luangwa is Zambia's premier national park. You can explore its rugged terrain on foot and by vehicle, scouring the rutted plains and thorny thickets for game. But this aerial perspective is a revelation, the park arrayed in an exquisite model-railway mosaic of oxbows, palm stands and forest islands. Imagine if Livingstone had seen it like this.

You're losing height – and a glimpse of thatched roofs beside the riverbank reveals *Tafika*. This is your camp and the home of your pilot, John Coppinger, the only licensed microlight operator in the valley. Beyond is the red-earth airstrip where you took off fifteen minutes earlier, parked Land Rover at one end, elephants ambling across the other.

But you're not done yet. John is pointing again and you follow his gaze to a line of golden shapes emerging from the thickets, casting exaggerated feline shadows across the sand. Lions. A big male brings up the rear, massive head swinging from side to side. He stares up as you pass – now low enough to see the tufted tail and narrow haunches – then trudges onward towards the river.

Winging it over Luangwa

415

Warriors and maidens:
The Reed Dance of Ludzidzini

SWAZILAND Seen from the rugged heights of Hangman's Rock, the scale of the pageantry is breathtaking. Column upon column advances across the cattle-cropped sward onto the parade grounds of Ludzidzini, the Queen Mother's royal village, before dissolving into the pulsating mass of bodies already assembled there. Panning out towards the horizon you see still more arriving, snaking like huge, multi-coloured millipedes over the contours of the Ezulwini Valley. The noise laps against the escarpment, drifting towards your elevated perch like the roar of distant surf.

Soon you are down among the spectators on the valley floor, where at close quarters it all becomes rather more real. Ranks of dancers bear down from all sides. Bare-breasted girls stamp and sway in step, anklets rattling, as the confusion of colour and flesh blurs into a chanting kaleidoscope. Details flash past: the oranges impaled on ceremonial knives; the crimson headdresses of turaco feathers marking out those of royal descent. Ahead of each column strides its warrior escort, adorned with cow tails and clutching knob-stick

and shield. His glance is contemptuous of cameras, although the girls behind him seem to be taking things less seriously: there is giggling in the ranks, flashed smiles and shared jokes. It's Swaziland's biggest holiday, and after seven days of tramping the hillsides, cutting reeds and camping out, they're determined to enjoy the party.

Cultural historians will tell you about the origins of the Umhlanga (or Reed Dance): how the maidens have travelled from across the kingdom to cut reeds at various sacred locations, then marched to the Queen Mother's *kraal* – carrying their bundles – in a symbolic celebration of chastity and tribute; how the date varies from year to year according to ancestral astrology. They might also marvel at how the event's popularity defies the apparent decline of traditional culture elsewhere in the region.

On the ground, though, who can tell what's really happening? Understanding and description are overwhelmed by a sea of colours, faces and voices. It's dusty, noisy, chaotic and utterly thrilling: celebration at its most African.

417 Diving with manta rays in the Quirimbas Archipelago

MOZAMBIQUE You have to be fairly wealthy to holiday in the Quirimbas Archipelago in northern Mozambique, but it's not a place for spoilt, petulant types with exacting demands and trolleyloads of luggage. The islands are home to a handful of lodges specializing in back-to-basics barefoot luxury, with the emphasis firmly on the "barefoot". No need for designer heels here – but a good pair of fins will definitely come in handy.

From the mainland town of Pemba, a light aircraft carries you and your single bag (the most you're permitted to bring) over a wilderness of dazzling beaches and intricate reefs. From above, the archipelago has a pristine, faraway charm that's irresistible. By the time you touch down, you're itching to sink into the soft sand.

Even more alluring is the prospect of exploring offshore. The islands are surrounded by the vivid turquoise waters of the Quirimbas National Park, created in 2002 on the recommendation of the WWF. Thanks to the cooperation of local communities and lodge-owners, the park, which includes 1500 square kilometres of ocean and island habitats, is one of the best, and least exploited, scuba diving destinations in southern Africa.

While the coral gardens teem with colourful fish, manta rays are without a doubt the star attraction. These balletic megafish are the subject of extensive studies elsewhere in Mozambique; take the plunge, and you might be lucky enough to encounter one face to face. Though related to sharks, they're filter-feeders and harmless to humans: in fact, some appear positively friendly. Flowing through the blue with easy sweeps of their wings, which can measure up to 7m in span, they may approach close enough for you to check out the cleaner wrasses hitching a ride on their bellies. And if you meet one that's supremely relaxed, or just plain curious, it may circle you as you hover in the water – a truly captivating moment.

418 Find a tiny slice of heaven on Nosy Ve

MADAGASCAR Trekking through Madagascar's backcountry and paddling its interior is a wonderful way to spend your time, but sooner or later you'll want to rest your aching muscles and swap your well-worn hiking boots for a pair of makeshift flip-flops. And there are few better places to do it than the unspoiled tropical beaches and aquamarine waters of the Mozambique Channel.

Situated a few kilometres south of the Tropic of Capricorn, on the southwestern shores of Madagascar, lies the picturesque fishing village of Anakao. Accessible only by boat, it sits by a crescent-shaped white sand beach, nestled between spiny forests and rolling dunes and guarded by an armada of brightly coloured *pirogues* and herds of wandering goats. This tiny slice of heaven is dotted with a string of bungalows, cooled by gentle trade winds and lapped by the calming surf.

A trip to this remote locale is not complete until you've hired a fisherman to take you by *pirogue* to the nearby island of Nosy Ve. Rumoured to have been a former pirates' haunt in the seventeenth century – some say their bones are still scattered about – it's deserted now, and offers superb snorkelling amongst schools of colourful angelfish, parrotfish and tangs that dart through the small offshore coral. The beach, strewn with seashells of every conceivable shape, size and colour, is a stunning place for a stroll – you can return with your pockets full to a mouth-watering meal of freshly caught lobster and fish grilled on a makeshift barbecue by your captain.

As the late afternoon winds pick up speed the captain signals, and it's time to return. An hour or so later you'll be back at your bungalow in time to witness another spectacular sunset framed over the waters that separate you from Africa. Lazing in your hammock, you'll be serenaded to sleep by millions of flickering stars and that wafting offshore breeze.

419 Dive the great Sardine Run

SOUTH AFRICA It may be a humble creature, but the sardine can put a pride of lions or a herd of buffalo to shame. Almost every year around June, enormous shoals of the fish, millions strong and kilometres long, swim up the South African coast towards Mozambique. Although little is known about this epic piscine migration – apart from the fact that the sardines travel on a cold south-to-north current – it is one of nature's greatest spectacles.

Among the best places in the country to witness the Sardine Run is KwaZulu-Natal's south coast, along which lies the scuba-diving town of Umkomaas. For most of the year, the dive operators here offer trips to a reef called Aliwal Shoal, one of the country's outstanding dive sites, but when the sardines are running, the attention shifts to viewing this awesome event at the closest quarters possible. Advanced divers don their wet suits and, informed of the shoals' latest coordinates by the KwaZulu-Natal Sharks Board, launch boats to take them to the heart of the action.

Once under water, it becomes apparent that the sardines have company. They have been tracked by thousands of hungry sharks, dolphins and game fish such as bluefish and tuna intent on gorging themselves silly on an incredibly easy target. The rare, once-in-a-lifetime highlight for the diver is when dolphins herd part of the shoal into a compact mass, known as a "bait ball", pushing the fish towards the surface where they, along with their hungry co-predators, indulge in a feeding frenzy, darting towards the hapless sardines with gaping mouths. Meanwhile, above water, Cape gannets, albatrosses and other seabirds plunge like missiles into the dark patches in the sea, emerging with bunches of fish in their dripping beaks.

Discovering the lost cities of the Swahili

MOZAMBIQUE Strangler figs wrap their fingers around once-elegant doorways, lofty ceilings gape at the sky and ornamental balconies rust in the sun. The grand mansions of Vila do Ibo – the Stone Town of Ilha do Ibo, in northern Mozambique's Quirimbas Archipelago – are earmarked for World Heritage status, but their coral-stone facades are in such an advanced state of disrepair that you'd be forgiven for thinking it's already too late to save them.

The remains of the town are highly atmospheric, nonetheless. Exploring on foot, you can almost picture the scene two or three hundred years ago, when the air was full of the scent of spices and the yells of visiting seafarers. Its setting is as beautiful as ever: a gently curving beach where lateen-rigged dhows, timeless symbols of the Swahili coast, glide by just as they have for centuries.

In medieval times, the South Equatorial Current brought ships carrying gold, ivory and spices to Ibo to stock up on fresh water before continuing their voyage to or from India. Muslim traders from the Arab world were the first adventurers to spot the island's potential, settling here to peddle amber, ivory and turtle shell. Later, Portuguese slave traders made it their base: by the late eighteenth century, Vila do Ibo had become a prosperous and well-fortified provincial capital. Then, in the early twentieth century, everything changed; the traders and officials moved away to a new mainland settlement, Porto Amélia, now Pemba, abandoning Ibo to the rigours of cyclones and extreme humidity. Today, the forts which once defended the city serve only as workshops for local silversmiths, who melt down old coins to make jewellery to sell to visitors.

Another of Mozambique's lost cities, Ilha de Moçambique in Nampula Province, has already made it onto the World Heritage list. It, too, was once an important Swahili trading post, but in the decades since independence it has decayed into a picturesque ruin. Its large sixteenth-century fort, Fortaleza de São Sebastião, still watches the coastline, but was badly battered by Cyclone Jokwe in 2008 – retribution, some might say, for the many crimes it disguised during the island's days as a hub of the slave trade.

421 Learning about elephants in the Botswanan bush

BOTSWANA Elephant lesson number one: the world's mightiest land mammals are chatty creatures, but they keep their gossip amongst themselves. Many of the sounds they make, though audible by other elephants up to 10km away, are far too low-pitched for the human ear to detect.

I learnt this from the man sharing my saddle: the elephant handler who's my guide for the afternoon. Apparently, there's much, much more to an elephant's vocal range than the ear-splitting trumpeting we all remember from *The Jungle Book*. I particularly like the peculiar noise that sounds like a stomach-rumble, but is actually voiced – that's an elephant expressing blissful contentment.

You get a whole new perspective on elephants from the back of one – and a whole new perspective on the bush, too. You're higher than you would be in the back of a Jeep and, with no rattling engine or grinding gears to distract you, you can concentrate on the full gamut of elephant noises, along with bird calls, the screeching of insects and even the snorting of zebras and gazelles. Most grazing herbivores turn tail and flee at the sight of humans on foot, but the elephant-plus-human combo doesn't seem to faze them: they stay put, and chew on.

In many ways, an elephant makes the perfect alternative to a 4WD. Eco-friendly and even-tempered, they tackle the terrain with ease, only pausing in their stride when a particularly tasty looking tree catches their eye.

Which leads nicely on to elephant lesson number 99. Elephants love their snack breaks, and safari elephants are no exception. After all, what to you is a thrilling ride in pristine bush is, to them, a pleasant amble through an open-air salad bar.

422 Going on a frog safari in Zululand

SOUTH AFRICA The South African bush looks different by torchlight. Reed beds and acacia branches stand out in sharp relief, a mesh of clean lines and crisp angles. Beyond the beam, the middle-distance is unimaginably black. Your eyes strain to make out the details, then give up. Your ears take over.

Frogging is all about tuning in. Across wetland regions throughout the tropics, frogs greet the seasonal rains with a nightly symphony in which different species perform distinctive roles. Experienced listeners can isolate and identify each one. Of South Africa's 115 known species of frog, some, like the delightfully perky-looking tinker reed frog, emit a metallic, staccato sound, while others trill like a mobile phone. Bullfrogs belt out a full-throated belch. You can probably guess what kind of noises the chirping frog, the clicking stream frog and the snoring puddle frog make.

All this vocal exhibitionism is, as you'd expect, part of a mating game. The males are the protagonists, laying noisy claim to territory and females. In the Amazulu Private Game Reserve, KwaZulu Natal, voyeurs can witness their moves at close quarters by joining an after-dark walking safari, led by an expert guide.

African walking safaris are, by definition, thrilling; setting out by night adds an unforgettable extra dimension. Leave your trekking sandals behind – wellington boots are the footwear of choice. You will squelch through the mud around rain-soaked waterholes, watching as your guide's torch beam traces a variety of clinks, chirrups and quoips to the source. There can be much searching: amplified by its balloon-like vocal sac, the racket made by even the most minuscule of frogs can cover a considerable range.

Some individuals choose prominent perches and are conspicuous enough to be spotted, and blasé enough to be observed very closely. It's important to try not to touch their delicate, permeable skin, which doubles as a breathing membrane. Instead, aim the beam of your torch onto their jewel-bright colours, and prepare to be dazzled.

423 Pony-trekking in the mountain kingdom

LESOTHO Landlocked within South Africa, the mountain kingdom of Lesotho is a poor but magical place.

A lot of the magic is encapsulated in those two words – mountain kingdom. Lesotho is one of Africa's few surviving monarchies, proud of its distinctive history, and the whole country lies above an altitude of 1000m, its highest peaks soaring into a distinctly un-African realm of mists and dank cloud. Back in the nineteenth century, the dominant figure in the country's history, King Moshoeshoe (pronounced Mo-shweh-shweh) acquired a pony stolen from a farm in the Cape.

Its suitability for Lesotho's hilly terrain was soon clear, and the people, the Basotho, quickly became a nation of horse riders. They remain so today. Few of the scattered villages of the mountains are reached by any road, tarred or otherwise. Everywhere is connected by paths, and to get anywhere you need to walk or ride.

Pony trekking isn't really an "activity", something to do instead of canoeing or birdwatching; get atop a horse here and you're participating in Basotho life. There's nothing prim about it either; no one will comment on your posture or how you hold the reins, and given that the paths only go uphill or downhill, you'll do a lot more plodding than prancing.

You'll greet passing locals, breathe mountain air, village woodsmoke and the scent of clammy horse sweat, and hear the ringing shouts of barefoot children rounding up goats on the hillside – accompanied, all the while, by the steady clip-clop of your sure-footed pony picking its way along the path.

424 Counting fish in Lake Malawi

MALAWI On satellite images of the Rift Valley, Africa's third-largest lake looks like a long, dark gash in a crumpled curtain. But visit Lake Malawi on a bright day, and it's luminous. The turquoise waters stretch way beyond the horizon. It's as vast as a sea but benign, its sandy shore lapped by the gentlest of waves.

Explore beneath the surface and you'll soon be drifting through granite archways among clouds of brilliantly coloured cichlids. These small fish, prized by aquarium-keepers, are abundant in Lake Malawi. Scientists have counted over 1500 endemic species; as evolutionary hotspots go, the lake is almost as fascinating as Madagascar or the Galapagos.

If you're new to diving, it's a dream. It's far more fun to work through your drills on the sandy bottom of a warm lake than on the cold, hard tiles of a swimming pool. As you practise flooding your mask and clearing it again, the fresh, clear, chlorine-free water won't sting.

The lake has advantages over the ocean, too. There are no awkward currents or underwater menaces to spook you, no moray eels, jellyfish or sharks. You'll need less weight on your belt to help you sink. And once you're back on dry land, there's no salt to rinse off your gear – just head down to the campfire where, after dark, you can swap stories under the stars.

425 The Smoke That Thunders

ZIMBABWE You know that a place is special when it can inspire true love. Over 500 million litres of water crashes every minute from heights of up to 450m at Victoria Falls; it creates an intangible but potent magic. Many visitors are happy to stand and stare, surrounded by a fine spray of warm mist, or amble along the paths that cut through the surrounding rainforest. Those looking for thrills and spills can white-water raft the mighty Zambezi, from which the falls flow (see *437*), or take a 110m plunge from the bridge between Zambia and Zimbabwe – the roar of the falls, and likely your screams, ringing in your ears. For a different perspective, book a hot air balloon, microlight or helicopter ride and marvel at the bird's-eye view of what the locals call Mosi-oa-Tunya – "The Smoke That Thunders".

426 Birding by Lake St Lucia

SOUTH AFRICA Safari in South Africa is not all about lions, leopards and laughing hyenas. The Greater St Lucia Wetlands has its hippos and its crocs, but it's the staggering number of birds that makes this northeastern corner of KwaZulu Natal so special.

Over 500 species pass through each year, drawn by the park's unique cocktail of world-class wilderness: dune-backed beaches, tidal estuaries, coastal forest, swamps, saltwater marshes and dry thornveld, all bordering the 360-square-kilometre Lake St Lucia, one of South Africa's most important waterbird breeding areas.

On the lake's western shore, a number of self-guided trails lead off through the vegetation. African broadbills chase butterflies through the forest, southern banded snake eagles circle overhead, and Neergaard's sunbirds flit between succulent bunches of weeping boer-beans. In the Greater St Lucia Wetlands, small really is beautiful.

Mulanje:
more than just a mountain

427

MALAWI If variety's the spice of your life, a trip to Malawi is hard to beat. You might luxuriate at the lake or spot an elephant or three, but you should not neglect the country's iconic western highlands.

Rising out of the plain, emerald-green tea estates sprawling at its feet, Mount Mulanje is a stunning massif that offers something for everyone. Extreme sport fans can coincide their visit with the Porter's Race, which takes place every July – a 25km scramble up to the central plateau, along and down again, completed in just over two hours by the winners. The cerebral can sit at its base with Laurens van der Post's *Venture to the Interior*, in which he describes a harrowing encounter with the mountain and the death of one of his companions. Naturalists can hunt out the endemic Mulanje cedar trees, their branches festooned with strands of pale green lichen so long you could knit with it, and serious rock climbers can attempt the sheer west face of Chambe, one of the longest climbing routes on the continent.

The average visitor, though, is someone with a modicum of fitness and two or three days to spare. There are numerous starting points all around the massif, with guides and porters for hire at each. Three to four hours' slow plodding (all the ascents are steep) takes the hiker up narrow, winding paths, through patches of forest populated with rare blue monkeys, and on to the 2000m plateau where there are a number of simple wooden huts. Each hut has a watchman who will light a fire for you to cook your meal on, and heat water so that you can wash away the day's exertions. After a night tucked into your sleeping bag, you can go on to conquer one of the peaks – many go for Sapitwe, at 3002m the highest in South-Central Africa – or continue across the plateau through swathes of montane grassland to a different hut, admiring the endless panorama of peaks and vistas that unfolds along the way.

Visit the house of the spirits

SOUTH AFRICA It's art, myth and archeology, it's visually stunning and you can reach back through the millennia and immerse yourself in its marks and contours. South Africa's rock art represents one of the world's oldest and most continuous artistic and religious traditions. Found on rock faces all over the country, these ancient paintings are a window into a historic culture and its thoughts and beliefs. In the Cederberg range alone, 250km north of Cape Town, there are some 2500 rock art sites, estimated to be between one and eight thousand years old.

The paintings are the work of the first South Africans, hunter-gatherers known as San or Bushmen, the direct descendants of some of the earliest *Homo sapiens* who lived in the Western Cape 150,000 years ago. Now almost extinct, their culture clings on tenuously in tiny pockets of Namibia, northern South Africa and Botswana.

If you're looking to dig deeper, the easy-going Sevilla Trail gives you the opportunity to take in ten rock art sites along a stunning 4km route. The animals that once grazed and preyed in the fynbos (literally "fine bush") vegetation of the mountainous Cederberg are among the major subjects of the finely realized rock art paintings, which also include abstract images and monsters as well as depictions of people and therianthropes – half-human, half-animal figures. You'll see beautifully observed elephants, rhinos, buffaloes, oryx, snakes and birds, accurately portrayed in sinuous outline or solid bodies of colour – often earthy whites, reds and ochres. Frequently quite small, they're dotted all over rock surfaces, sometimes painted one over the other to create a rich patina.

Archeologists now regard many of the images as metaphors for religious experiences, one of the most important of which is the healing trance dance, still practised by the few surviving Bushman communities. The rock faces can be seen as portals between the human and spiritual world: when we gaze at Bushman rock art we are gazing into the house of the spirits.

429 Tracking rhino in Damaraland

NAMIBIA Did you know that the footprint of a black rhino can measure a full 30cm from toe to hefty heel? Nor did I until I found myself standing in the middle of one in northern Namibia's Damaraland, my size nines dwarfed by the dusty imprint. A big male had passed here in the night, maybe as little as two hours previously. Our guide finished inspecting the considerable pile of dung teetering on the trail a few metres up ahead, slung his high-calibre rifle onto his shoulder and gestured for us to move on. We were heading east, in the direction of the tracks, for a rendezvous with a BMW-sized beast.

Damaraland is the only place in the world where you can find free-roaming black rhino. But you've got to know where to look. And the trackers from *Palmwag* – a mobile tented camp set amidst the grassy plains and light scrub of a million-acre private reserve –

know exactly where to look. Noticing a stack of steaming spores is easy enough; spotting an acacia bush that's been crumpled by the hooked lips of a browsing black rhino isn't – and it's that sort of proficiency that pretty much guarantees you sneaking up on one just a few hours after leaving camp.

Rhinos have terrible eyesight, but their hearing and sense of smell are acute. As we approach a mother and her calf from downwind, the previously innocuous dry scrub suddenly becomes one giant, crackling boobytrap. We inch ourselves closer and closer, until we can make out oxpecker birds picking insects off the mother's back. She's immense, yet beautiful – 900 kilos of rippling muscle, ribs shifting as she digests the shrubbery. No one talks. I don't breathe. And then they have moved on, and we start talking – and breathing – again.

430 Busanga: the plains truth

ZAMBIA The slimline feline slinks away through the sea of grass, all seesaw shoulders and switching tail. Two elegant wattled cranes, picking at a patch of burnt ground, pay no heed – but a rummaging warthog breaks off to stare, poised rigid for flight.

You're itching to follow. A cheetah is a rare sight, especially in Zambia. But the terrain is treacherous. Only your guide can tell where the firm ground gives way to swamp and once already this morning he's had to dig you out of trouble. With no other vehicle on the horizon, no shade to speak of and – judging by the abundant tracks – only the local lion pride to keep you company, this is no place to get stuck.

You take a swig from your water bottle and check out the surroundings. The map, which shows Busanga Plains smuggled discreetly into the remote northwest corner of central Zambia's Kafue National Park, gives little sense of scale. But perched out here in the middle, the grasslands seem limitless, their

irregular punctuation of palm islands and termite mounds simply emphasizing the immensity. A binocular sweep reveals animals in all directions: not vast herds, but a wall-to-wall scattering of grazers – puku, lechwe, wildebeest – all munching their way across the great salad bowl. Many more will join them as the dry season begins to bite.

To the south a low line of miombo woodland shimmers in the heat haze, reminding you of the vast hinterland and yesterday's battles with the tsetse flies as you'd lurched and jolted your way here. To the north you can see where the grassland gives way to water, each flash of blue littered with the white forms of egrets, storks and pelicans.

"Zambia's Okavango," they call this place. Out on the water this afternoon, drifting among the grunting hippo pods, the comparison will seem even more apt. But for now you're happy to soak in the one big difference. No people.

431 Climbing Table Mountain

SOUTH AFRICA If the skies are clear on your first day in Cape Town, drop everything and head straight for Table Mountain. It's an ecological marvel, and a powerful icon for the entire African continent. What's more, the views from the top are unmissable – as long as the celebrated "tablecloth" of cloud stays away.

For Capetonians, Table Mountain is a backdrop and an anchor, both physically and spiritually. Close to the South African coast, it was one of the beacons that Nelson Mandela and his fellow inmates fixed upon during their incarceration on Robben Island, just offshore.

The mountain's famous plateau is part of a short upland chain that stretches from Signal Hill, just west of the city centre, to Cape Point, where a lighthouse marks the meeting of the Indian Ocean and the Atlantic. The obvious, and most popular, route to the top is to take the aerial cableway – a sizeable cable car that, thrillingly, gently rotates on the ascent. But if you'd rather work a little

harder, you can tackle one of the hiking trails that snake their way up the cliffs.

Visit in the South African spring or summer and the fynbos vegetation, unique to the Cape, will be in full bloom. You'll see plenty of pretty daisies and heathers in the tussocky wilderness, while proteas, sundews and watsonias add splashes of red, white and pink. Botanists have identified over 1470 plant species on the mountain – there's more floral diversity here than in the entire United Kingdom. The wildlife scores top marks for entertainment value, too. Stars of the show are the dassies, placid creatures that look a bit like monster guinea pigs and are more than happy to pose for photos.

And then there's that view. You may only be a thousand metres up, but gaze out over the city to the ocean beyond and you'll feel on top of the world.

432 Swigging the most remote beer on Earth

TRISTAN DA CUNHA The *Albatross Inn* does a rather decent lobster quiche as a bar snack. The lager isn't bad either. It's a good job really, because there's nowhere else to get a drink or a bite to eat for 2815 kilometres. This is the only pub on the most remote inhabited island on Earth.

Tristan da Cunha is one of the far-flung hotchpotch of islands that make up what's left of the British Empire. None, however, are as isolated. Situated in the middle of the notoriously rough patch of the South Atlantic Ocean known as the Roaring Forties, its closest landmass is southern Africa, some 540km nearer than South America. The island has no airport and can only be reached by fishing vessel from Cape Town; a trip that can take upwards of six days with no guarantee of being able to dock in the island's tiny harbour because of the often torrid weather.

The sole settlement is the evocatively named "Edinburgh of the Seven Seas" which is where, in a motley collection of tin-roofed bungalows, the 261 resident islanders live and work, mainly as fishermen of Tristan's number one export: crayfish. Everything is dwarfed by the volcano that rises over 1700m above sea level. It is rarely climbed by locals, and there are signs everywhere of the 1962 eruption, not least the huge pile of volcanic debris that still lies just outside the village. In the wake of the eruption, the islanders were evacuated to the UK, where they spent two unhappy years before being allowed to return.

With no mobile phones, one shop, one school, one policeman and one available TV channel many things about Tristan remain unchanged by the twenty-first century. The accent spoken is a curious, and almost incomprehensible, dialect of early eighteenth-century seafaring English; everyone's birthday is celebrated by a party in the Prince Phillip Hall next to the *Albatross*; and absolutely nobody seems to have any desire to leave their epically remote home. "People think we're stranded here," the barman tells me over yet another slice of quiche. "But it's not true. We're happy, and we're here because we want to be."

433 Sampling wines in the Western Cape

SOUTH AFRICA We're sitting around the elegant dining table of a 200-year-old Cape Dutch manor house, set in beautiful countryside near Paarl. Our host, effusive wine expert Katinka van Niekerk, has us under strict instructions to sample the heavenly wines before us in a pre-planned order. Before each mouthful, we must eat something of a particular flavour or texture – curry for spice, cheese for sweetness, bread to neutralize the palate once again – and note the effects. It's fascinating stuff.

When we're asked to wash down a piece of bread and Marmite with a mouthful of vintage Pinotage, master winemaker Razvan Macici, who has joined us for this session, grimaces. The Marmite represents the flavour known as umami, also found in soy sauce, Parmesan and certain mushrooms. It wrecks Pinotage, the signature Cape red. But the same wine with a chunk of roast lamb tastes like a dream. Earlier in the day we toured the massive Nederburg estate, admiring the ranks of vines which stretch away to the purple-tinged Drakenstein Mountains, sniffing the heady, oaky aromas of the barrel rooms and marvelling at the cellars' hi-tech temperature-controlled steel tanks. Then it was time for our first tasting. We all eyed the spitoons rather squeamishly and went for what seemed, at the time, the more decorous option – raising each glass to our noses to inhale the bouquet and then taking delicate sips.

It's amazing how quickly all those sips add up. So it is that when, replete from our wine-and-food-pairing lunch, we stagger out onto the lawn to enjoy the sunshine and spring flowers, we're all merrily speaking double Dutch.

434 Up the Tsiribihina in a dugout canoe

MADAGASCAR The early morning daylight filters through the tent and slowly warms your aching body. You awaken to the muffled sounds of roosters crowing and the echo of beating drums from a neighbouring village. A faint whiff of smoke entices you out of your slumber and onto the sandy riverbank to join the guides and a few curious onlookers around a crackling campfire. Together, you share fried eggs, fresh fruit, stale baguettes and a cup of strongly brewed coffee. Another day on the Tsiribihina River has begun.

After breakfast, the guides pack camp and load the wooden *pirogues*. Within minutes, you're drifting down the muddy waters and into the heartland of Madagascar. Exploring this fascinating country is not complete until you've experienced a few days on this remote waterway, meeting local villagers, paddling alongside impressive landscapes and discovering Malagasy folklore.

The sun burns overhead as you glide past thatched-hut villages, where excited children bound into the waters waving and screaming "bon voyage". Gradually, the landscape transforms from low-lying flood plains lined with green rice paddies to sparsely covered rolling hills and thick forests, the river slicing through deep gorges before widening once more as it drains into the Mozambique Channel. Along the way, you make chance encounters with wildlife: Verreaux's sifaka forage high in the canopies and enormous flying foxes flutter by while river crocodiles lurk in the murky waters below. Hundreds of exotic birds vie for your attention: metallic-coloured kingfishers dart along the shoreline, white egrets hitch a ride on floating mats of hyacinths and a majestic harrier hawk wheels on the horizon.

At the end of a long day's journey, you reach camp on the shores of yet another sandbank, arriving just in time to witness a spectacular sunset framed against a rugged mountainous backdrop. While dinner is prepared, you set up the tents and begin to wind down for the evening. Dancing fireflies and singing katydids give way to a night sky filled with flickering stars.

NAMIBIA There's a good reason why Namibia's extreme northwest is called the Skeleton Coast. Its treacherous conditions have scuppered ships – the beach is littered with rusting iron and weathered timbers from long-abandoned wrecks – and whales, too, have met their end here, their massive vertebrae bleaching on the shore, lapped by the tides.

As a visitor, you'll need an eye for detail to appreciate the allure of this bleak and barren place, where the chilly Atlantic meets mountainous dunes and endless, grey-white gravel plains, and distant wind-sculpted rocks cast unearthly shadows. Look carefully and you'll begin to realize that the desert is not as devoid of life as it might seem. Walking through the rugged landscapes with a guide, you'll learn how beetles, lizards and sidewinder adders survive on the moisture brought by the early morning mists. You may begin to distinguish the different lichens – delicate smudges of black, white and ginger which decorate slabs of quartz and basalt. Drought-resistant succulents like the bizarre, pebble-like lithops and the ragged, ancient-looking *Welwitschia mirabilis* cling to life in the gravel. Among the few mammals hardy enough to survive in this environment are black-backed jackals and noisy, malodorous colonies of Cape fur seals, the latter a potential target for hungry lions, which very occasionally can be seen prowling the shoreline. Perhaps the best way to enjoy the desert's strange beauty is from the air. Soar over the landscape in a light aircraft and you feel like an astronaut over an alien world, the scene below mottled and textured like a vast abstract painting.

EXPLORING THE

Skeleton Coast

435

436

JUNGLE OPERATICS:
the lemurs of Andasibe-Mantadia

MADAGASCAR Close your eyes and imagine the haunting song of a humpback whale. Add heat, humidity and air infused with damp vegetation and moss that tingles your nasal passages. Sounds improbable, doesn't it? Now open your eyes: you're in a Madagascan rainforest listening to a group of indri, the largest of the island's lemurs, proclaiming rights to their territories like arboreal opera singers.

This is the sound of Madagascar. In the early mornings, the forests of Andasibe-Mantadia National Park ring out with the indri's eerie, wailing chorus. It wafts through the canopy in wave after glorious wave, sending shivers down your spine and making every nerve-end jangle.

A number of indri family groups here have become thoroughly accustomed to people. With the help of a local guide, they're easily seen, and their cute teddy-bear looks, striking black-and-

white coats and comically inquisitive manner make them hugely endearing – most people fall for them immediately.

When you first come upon them, the indri are likely to be high in the canopy, shrouded by a veil of foliage, but it pays to be patient and wait (something many people don't do), as they regularly descend to lower levels and are quite happy to sit and munch their leafy breakfasts while you watch in wonder from close by.

Eleven other lemur species live in the national park, and there's a good chance of seeing several of these, too. One of the most remarkable is the diademed sifaka, its orange and silver fur contrasting vividly with the dark recesses of the forest. You can see both indri and diademed sifakas many, many times, and remain fascinated: these are arguably the most beautiful primates on the planet.

437 Rafting the Stairway to Heaven

ZAMBIA Ever thought it might be fun to be trapped inside a giant washing machine as it switches from rinse to spin? Perhaps not. But after a dozen drenchings and umpteen mouthfuls of river water, you might just find yourself tumbling headlong down the Stairway to Heaven, yelling like a maniac, high on the thrill of just staying alive.

Dropping 8m over a 10m distance, the Stairway is one of the steepest of the world-class rapids that churn up the mighty Zambezi just below Victoria Falls. But it's by no means the scariest. The names the rafters give the toughest runs – Gnashing Jaws of Death, Overland Truck Eater, Double Trouble, Oblivion – say it all.

The Lower Zambezi rafting route begins in one of the most dramatic midriver locations on Earth. You paddle across the foam-marbled water of the Batoka Gorge – the steep-sided ravine that receives the full fury of the 1.5km wide, 100m high falls. Behind you, water crashes against water and hurtles into the heavens as spray. It's a nerve-jangling display of natural energy.

The first three rapids come hard and fast, then there's a sharp left turn as the gorge zigzags downhill. Before you know it, you're tackling Morning Glory, the first big challenge, where a "hole" almost as wide as the river threatens to swallow you in one gulp.

Survive this and, thanking the river gods for their kindness, you can prepare for the Stairway. But you'll never be truly ready for Rapid 18: Oblivion. This one eats rafts for breakfast – the chances of making it through its three monster-sized waves without your raft being flipped are only one in four. They say that a baptism in the Zambezi purifies the soul: one tussle with Oblivion and you'll be praying for mercy.

438 Giving something back at Guludo Beach Lodge

MOZAMBIQUE Translucent turquoise water swarming with rainbow-coloured fish, sand the colour and consistency of finely ground pearls, a hinterland of irrepressible tropical greenery... it sounds like paradise. But for the inhabitants of this remote stretch of the Mozambique coast, still licking its wounds after four decades of civil war, life isn't a beach. Infant mortality runs at one in three, and – thanks to rampant malaria, a shortage of clean water and poor sanitation – average life expectancy struggles to exceed forty years.

It was exactly this glaring juxtaposition of beach idyll and grinding poverty that inspired a team of young British entrepreneurs to establish a tourist resort with a difference on the deserted seashore near Guludo village, just north of the Quirimbas National Park. But instead of carving out an exclusive enclave, the primary aim of the project was to provide a sustainable means of alleviating hardship in the neighbourhood: 55 local people have been trained to work in the tourist lodge, and one day they'll run the place entirely.

Guludo Beach Lodge was designed to have minimal impact on the environment. Its nine "rooms" are thatched, tented shelters, or, with raised inner platforms, private, but open to the sea breezes and views, and equipped with luxurious beds, mozzie nets and alfresco marble bathrooms. All the wonderful food is sourced locally, and all waste is recycled.

Far from being screened from local conditions, guests are actively encouraged to visit Guludo village, patronize handicraft businesses there, play in the weekly locals-versus-staff football match, and generally get involved in the development projects financed by the resort. Five percent of the lodge's profits are channelled directly into schemes such as well excavation, health and sanitation workshops, support and training for midwives and – most ambitiously – the construction of a new school for the village.

439 On a swing and a prayer: through the Tsitsikamma forest canopy

SOUTH AFRICA Skip back a few millennia and we were all arboreal primates. We'll never know for sure what those ancestors of ours looked like. But in Tsitsikamma National Park, you can discover the primate within by swinging through the canopy – 30m up.

In fact, whizzing is a better word, for instead of bombing through the forest on the end of a vine, Tarzan-style, you're strapped into a high-tech harness and sent careering along a steel cable that's strung between two trees. But you can yodel as much as you want.

Each cable slide – there's a circuit of eleven – leads to a timber platform high up in a mighty outeniqua forest. Here, as you catch your breath, a guide sorts out your karabiner clips, gives you a few nature notes and gets you ready for the next slide.

The platforms and slides may stir up childhood memories of monkeying around in tree houses, but in fact they're state of the art. Cleverly engineered using tensile forces, leverage and rubber blocks instead of bolts to keep the trees as pristine as possible, the whole circuit is based on a system designed by ecologists working in the Costa Rican rainforest. They used their cables to collect specimens and data. Trust the adventure-mad South Africans to use theirs just for fun.

The longest and steepest slides are the best: with a good shove, you can hurtle along at up to 50km/h, hyped with excitement. But on the gentler ones, there's more time to enjoy the scenery: the light and shade playing on the foliage above, the intricate forms of the giant ferns below, the passing birds and staring monkeys. Or you can just soak up the rich, unfamiliar smells – the musty whiff of decaying vegetation mixed with the damp freshness of new growth – and the heart-pounding sensation of exploring a new domain.

NEED to know

388 Boulders Beach is on the itinerary of every Cape Peninsula tour and is easy to reach in your own car. Sanccob (Ⓦwww.sanccob.co.za) is dedicated to the preservation of African penguins. For accommodation in the area, see Ⓦwww.simonstown.com.

389 Hiking along the canyon is only allowed May–Sept to avoid flash floods. Numbers are limited: book as far in advance as you can at Ⓦwww.nwr.com.na.

390 For more information about Kande Beach, go to Ⓦwww.kandebeach.com.

391 For more details, see Ⓦwww.ecotraining.co.za and Ⓣtinyurl.com/kruger-ranger.

392 Malolotja Nature Reserve is 30min drive from the capital, Mbabane, and 90min from Matsapha airport.

393 Volunteers on Azafady's ten-week Pioneer programme are required to raise a minimum donation of £2000. For more, see Ⓦwww.azafady.org.

394 In the whale season, booking is essential, preferably a year ahead. CapeNature's website (Ⓦwww.capenature.co.za/reserves.htm) has information about the Whale Trail, including booking details.

395 Calabash Tours (Ⓦwww.calabashtours.co.za) in Port Elizabeth and Cape Capers (Ⓦwww.tourcapers.co.za) in Cape Town run township tours.

396 For early morning hot-air-balloon safaris over the desert near Sossusvlei, followed by a champagne breakfast on the ground, try NamibSky Adventure Safaris (Ⓦwww.balloon-safaris.com).

397 In a 4WD, you can reach the Makgadikgadi Pans from the main tar road between Nata and Maun: the two largest pans, Sowa and Ntwetwe, lie to the south; Nxai Pan to the north.

398 Air Zimbabwe flies from Harare and Victoria Falls to Kariba, the start of most river expeditions. The wildest stretch goes from Mana Pools National Park, lasting 4–6 days. Visit in April–Nov, outside the rainy season, and use a reputable river safari company: try Ⓦwww.natureways.com and Ⓦwww.zambezi.com.

399 *Tendele Camp* (Ⓦwww.drakensberg-tourism.com/tendele-camp-royal-natal.html) offers bungalows with mountain views. For more information on hiking in the Drakensberg, visit Ⓦwww.drakensberg-tourism.com.

400 Dried mopane worms are sold at markets across Zimbabwe, as well as in parts of South Africa, Namibia, Zambia and Botswana. You can also buy them tinned – usually in brine or tomato sauce – in supermarkets.

401 *Bulungula Lodge* (Ⓦwww.bulungula.co.za) has dorms and twin rooms.

402 The Natural History Museum (Mon, Tues, Thurs & Fri 9am–4pm, Sat–Sun 9am–noon; free) is in Port Louis. Excursions which include a tour of Ile aux Aigrettes (Ⓦwww.ile-aux-aigrettes.com; Ⓦwww.mauritian-wildlife.org) can be booked at several hotels including *Shandrani* (Ⓦwww.beachcomber-hotels.com).

403 It takes about 12hr to drive between Cape Town and Jo'burg on the N1: the tiny towns of Richmond and Hanover are roughly halfway. See Ⓦwww.northerncape.org.za for more.

404 The Starving Comics perform almost daily at various venues in and around Cape Town including *Zula Sound Bar* (194 Long Street) on Mon nights. Contact the venue on +27 21 424 2442.

405 Visit Ⓦwww.kawazavillage.co.uk for more information. Bookings can be made through Ⓦwww.robinpopesafaris.net.

406 Madikwe (Ⓦwww.tourismnorthwest.co.za/on-safari) is one of a handful of game reserves in South Africa large enough to accommodate free-ranging lions. To visit, you'll need to base yourself at one of its private lodges.

407 Etosha National Park (Ⓦwww.etoshanationalpark.co.za) is about 400km north of Namibia's capital, Windhoek. The three national park rest camps have shops, fuel and plentiful accommodation.

408 Anjajavy, a useful base for exploring the *tsingy*, is a very remote spot, that's realistically only accessible by air – the *Anjajavy Hotel* (Ⓦwww.anjajavy.com) runs a regular transfer from the capital, Antananarivo.

409 Since rainfall and temperatures vary from year to year, it's impossible to be sure when and where the show of flowers will be at its peak, but the best displays are usually from mid-Aug to mid-Sept.

410 Most lodges in the Okavango Delta run *mokoro* safaris. Visit Ⓦwww.okavango-delta.net for more.

411 Zambia's South Luangwa National Park is one of Africa's best walking-safari destinations. Outhts operating there include The Bushcamp Company (Ⓦwww.bushcampcompany.com).

412 Bull seals are rarely seen outside of the breeding season (Oct). Nov–Dec is the best time to see pups.

413 See Ⓦwww.mauritius.net.

414 Nyika Plateau National Park lies 350km north of Malawi's capital, Lilongwe. It's a long slog by road to the top, or a short flight to Chelinda, the park headquarters, where there's a campsite, chalets, an upmarket lodge and mountain bikes for hire.

415 Microlight flights over South Luangwa National Park are available between May and October from *Tafika Camp* only (Ⓦwww.remoteafrica.com). The 15min flights can be arranged on site as part of a standard Remote Africa safari that explores Luangwa by vehicle and on foot. Other top Luangwa safari operators: Ⓦwww.robinpopesafaris.net and Ⓦwww.normancarrsafaris.com.

416 The Umhlanga is held in late August or early September, the precise date varying from year to year. There is plentiful accommodation in the nearby Ezulwini area and admission to the festivities is free – though you will need a permit for photography. Find out more at Ⓦwww.welcometoswaziland.com.

417 Excellent bases for diving in the Quirimbas include *Medjumbe Island Resort* (Ⓦwww.medjumbe.com, from US$515 per person per night, full board), *Vamizi Island* (Ⓦwww.vamizi.com, from US$390) and, on the mainland, *Guludo Beach Lodge* (Ⓦwww.guludo.com, from US$255 – see 438).

418 Anakao is accessible from the city of Toliara, in the south of the island, via a 55km rough dirt road or by boat. Most hotels provide a transfer by land and sea – be prepared for an extremely bumpy ride. Contact Safari Vezo at Ⓔsafarivezo@netclub.mg for travel to and accommodation in Anakao.

419 For updates on shoal coordinates, contact the Sardine Hotline (Ⓣ+27 (0)82 284 9495; Ⓦwww.shark.co.za). Note that in some years the sardines do not run at all. Umkomaas-based Meridian Dive Centre (Ⓦwww.scubadivesouthafrica.co.za) offers Sardine Run dive trips.

420 The most straightforward routes to Pemba (for Ibo) and Nampula (for Ilha de Moçambique) are via Maputo, Dar es Salaam, Nairobi or Johannesburg. Tour operators offering trips include Ⓦwww.imagineafrica.co.uk and Tribes Travel Ⓦwww.tribes.co.uk.

421 Botswana has two great elephant-safari operations: Elephant Back Safaris at *Abu Camp* (Ⓦwww.abucamp.com), and Living with Elephants (Ⓦwww.livingwithelephants.org).

422 KwaZulu Natal's *AmaKhosi Safari Lodge* (Ⓦwww.amakhosi.com) offers frog safaris from Nov–March as part of the activity programme included in its full board rate. Good bases for do-it-yourself frog watching elsewhere in eastern South Africa include Chrissiesmeer in Mpumalanga province.

423 A good place to arrange treks is *Malealea Lodge* (Ⓦwww.malealea.co.ls), an hour's drive south of the capital, Maseru.

424 You can dive in Lake Malawi all year round, but be wary of bilharzia (schistosomiasis): avoid reedbeds in calm water close to shore.

425 See Ⓦwww.zambiatourism.com/travel/places/victoria.htm for more on the falls.

426 The Zululand Birding Route (Ⓦwww.birdingroutes.co.za/zululand/zbr-home.html) have guides.

427 The nearest large town is Blantyre, where trips to Mulanje can be arranged. For information, try the Mountain Club of Malawi Ⓦwww.mcm.org.mw.

428 You don't need to book to walk the trail, but you do need a permit, which can be obtained from *Traveller's Rest Farm* (Ⓦwww.travellersrest.co.za), which also has accommodation and lays on horse trails.

429 *Palmwag Rhino Camp* is run by Wilderness Safaris (Ⓦwww.wilderness-safaris.com) in conjunction with Save the Rhino (Ⓦwww.savetherhino.org).

430 Access to Busanga Plains is by air from Lusaka or Livingstone, or by road through the park (4WD only). Wilderness Safaris (Ⓦwww.wilderness-safaris.com) operate three upmarket lodges – all closed during the wet season (Dec–April), when the region is inaccessible by road.

431 To make the most of the mountain, book a place on one of Hoerikwaggo Trails' guided hikes (Ⓦwww.hoerikwaggotrails.com).

432 Shipping vessels leave twelve times a year from Cape Town to Tristan da Cunha. To enquire about permission to visit the island, go to Ⓦwww.tristandc.com.

433 Many wineries around Stellenbosch, Franschhoek and Paarl open their cellars to the public from November to March: see Ⓦwww.stellenboschtourism.co.za for more information.

434 Numerous outfitters can be hired in Antananarivo or at Miandrivazo; Belaza Tours (Ⓦwww.gassitours.com) offers a variety of tours of the river.

435 A package trip includes guided nature walks and 4WD excursions. For accommodation, try the *Skeleton Coast Camp* (Ⓦwww.wilderness-safaris.com), a luxury tented camp reachable by air.

436 Try Ⓦwww.papyrustours.co.uk, Ⓦwww.wildlifeworldwide.com or Ⓦwww.theultimatetravelcompany.co.uk.

437 The river is at its lowest (and calmest) between mid-July and mid-Jan. Safari Par Excellence (Ⓦwww.safpar.com) runs trips out of Livingstone.

438 For more on *Guludo Beach Lodge* see Ⓦwww.bespokeexperience.com.

439 A Tsitsikamma Canopy Tour is available via Stormsriver Adventures (Ⓦwww.stormsriver.com).

GOOD to know

SNOW IN AFRICA

Lesotho is one of the few parts of Southern Africa that regularly gets serious **snowfalls**, especially in the highlands between May and July, when even main roads can be blocked for days. There's some informal skiing in the kingdom near the 3220m Mahlasela Pass, but for a proper ski resort, head to Tiffendell in South Africa's Drakensberg – here artificial snow makes up for unreliable cover, despite freezing-cold conditions.

ORIGINAL PEOPLES

The original inhabitants of Southern Africa were speakers of ancient **Khoi-San** languages incorporating various unusual click sounds now found in the languages of several South African peoples who arrived later, such as the Zulu and Xhosa. The San hunter-gatherers, formerly known as Bush-men, and the herding Khoi or Khoikhoi, once known as Hottentots (both names are now considered offensive) are believed to be among the world's most ancient cultures.

STATE OF MULTI-CULTURALISM

Zambia has 78 different **language groups**, or "tribes" as they're unselfconsciously referred to in the country. Most of the population speak Bantu languages, with the Bemba and Tonga together forming about a third of the population. There are small communities of Zambians of European and Asian descent and the country has welcomed dispossessed white farmers fleeing Zimbabwe.

POOR ZIMBABWE

Potentially one of Africa's richest countries, Zimbabwe's government under independence-leader-turned-mad-dictator **Robert Mugabe** has thrown it all away. A programme of "land reforms" saw rich white farmers flung off their properties, which, with no planning, then failed to produce the maize Zimbabweans relied upon; vindictive politics denied a voice to the opposition while the government failed the most basic tests of competency; tourism and investment dried up; and the annual inflation rate rocketed to over two million percent in 2008, making the vast majority of the population destitute – most transactions are now carried out in foreign currencies.

GREAT ZIMBABWE

Despite the gloom about its current predicament, the ruins of Zimbabwe's Great Zimbabwe, with its haunting, curved walls and pillars built of carefully interlocked dry stones, are a magnificent reminder of the depth of African history. There were in fact hundreds of *zimbabwes* (the word means "stone house towns" in Shona) built during the slow advance of Bantu-speaking peoples across Southern Africa between the eleventh and fifteenth centuries AD. Great Zimbabwe was just one of the biggest, symbolizing the dominance of the Monomotapa state that constructed it.

> *"A baby that does not cry out, dies on its mother's back"*
>
> **Xhosa saying**

LIFE IN THE WORLD'S BIGGEST AQUARIUM

Lake Malawi's famous tropical fish – the **cichlids** – are one of Malawi's most popular sights – and one of the country's biggest exports. Ranging from tiny slivers a few centimetres long to the predatory and torpedo-like **Champsochromis caeruleus** that's as big as your forearm, the rarer varieties can sell to fish fanciers for hundreds of dollars. In certain parts of the lake, over-fishing has resulted in an increase in the population of snails carrying the disease **bilharzia**, so there are now sound economic as well as environmental reasons to conserve fish stocks.

THREE KINGS OF AFRICA

The powers of the kings of Morocco and Lesotho are limited by their country's constitutions, but no such check seems to be placed on Africa's last absolute monarch, **King Mswati III of Swaziland**, who has ruled in an authoritarian – and eccentric – style since 1986. In 2001, he signed a decree banning newspapers, stating afterwards: "I must admit that when I signed this decree, I did not read it at all. I just signed it." Another decree banned women under 18 from having sex, in an attempt to combat the country's massive HIV problem (around forty percent of Swaziland's population is HIV-positive), but just two months after imposing the ban the king himself broke it in marrying his ninth wife, who was 16 – for which he fined himself a cow.

SOUTHERN SANDS

The **Namib Desert** in Namibia has existed for at least 80 million years, making it the world's oldest desert. The region's other desert, the **Kalahari** in southern Botswana, is better vegetated, thanks to occasional rainfall, and supports the traditional hunter-gatherer lifestyle of the San.

> *"If you want to make peace with your enemy, you have to work with your enemy. Then he becomes your partner"*
>
> **Nelson Mandela**

KUNG FU ISLAND

Decades of British involvement (an "arms in exchange for anti-slavery" agreement from their base on neighbouring Mauritius) led to the Protestant baptism of the queen of the dominant Merina people on the formally French island of **Madagascar** in 1869, and there's been a strong Anglican presence ever since. On an island of multiple surprises, it seems unpredictably fitting that a century after the queen's baptism, not only was the government Marxist, but the opposition coalition rallied under the banner of Kung Fu clubs with tens of thousands of Bruce Lee-mad members demonstrating on the streets.

HAUNTING THE DEAD CITIES • FIGHTING OFF THE CATS IN ACRE • TREKKING THE DESERT MOUNTAINS OF WADI HALFAYN • RELAXING IN A DAMASCUS HAMMAM • WALKING AROUND THE OLD CITY OF JERUSALEM • FLOATING ON THE DEAD SEA • DISCOVERING MADA'IN SALEH • KRAK DES CHEVALIERS: THE FINEST CASTLE IN THE WORLD • HEARING THE GROANS IN HAMA • PEARL DIVING IN THE PERSIAN GULF • DIVING IN THE GULF OF AQUABA • BOBBING ABOUT ON THE MUSANDAM FJORDS • SUNSET OVER PALMYRA • THE BURJ AL ARAB SHOWS OFF IN DUBAI • SAND-SKIING IN THE DUNES • TAWI ATTAIR: THE SINGING SINKHOLE • FEELING DWARFED BY BAALBEK • FROM SKI SUIT TO SWIM SUIT IN A SINGLE DAY • WANDERING OLD SANA'A • TAKING TEA IN ISFAHAN • FROLICKING WITH DOLPHINS OFF MUSCAT • FEASTING ON LEBANESE MEZE • SHOPPING IN THE CITY OF GOLD • CHECKING OUT THE BAUHAUS ARCHITECTURE IN TEL AVIV • TAKING A TRIP TO IRAQI KURDISTAN • WALK ROUND A GOLAN HEIGHTS GHOST TOWN • WALKING THE SIQ TO PETRA • SEARCHING FOR DRAGON'S BLOOD • THE ABODE OF SILENCE: THE MOST BEAUTIFUL DESERT ON EARTH • SAMPLE BEIRUT'S CUTTING EDGE CULTURE • CARVING A PATH THROUGH PERSEPOLIS • BEDOUIN CAMPING AT WADI RUM • FINDING THE REAL DUBAI ON A DHOW • FISH SUPPERS ON THE RED SEA • GETTING ACQUAINTED WITH ARABIC SWEETS • BARGAINING IN THE ALEPPO SOUK • HEAR THE LANGUAGE OF JESUS • SOAKING UP THE MASJID I-IMAM • ON THE INCENSE TRAIL IN ARABIA FELIX • BLAZING A TRAIL AT DANA NATURE RESERVE • OFF-ROADING FOR REAL: ACROSS THE DUNES TO KHOR AL-ADAID • WATCH GALLOPING CAMELS AND THEIR ROBOT RIDERS • SWIMMING THE WADI SHAB • MASADA: CONQUERING HEROD'S HILLTOP PALACE • VISITING THE HANGING VILLAGE OF HABALAH • HAUNTING THE DEAD CITIES • FIGHTING OFF THE CATS IN ACRE • TREKKING THE DESERT MOUNTAINS OF WADI HALFAYN • RELAXING IN A DAMASCUS HAMMAM • WALKING AROUND THE OLD CITY OF JERUSALEM • FLOATING ON THE DEAD SEA • DISCOVERING MADA'IN SALEH • KRAK DES CHEVALIERS: THE FINEST CASTLE IN THE WORLD • HEARING THE GROANS IN HAMA • PEARL DIVING IN THE PERSIAN GULF • DIVING IN THE GULF OF AQUABA • BOBBING ABOUT ON THE MUSANDAM FJORDS • SUNSET OVER PALMYRA • THE BURJ AL ARAB SHOWS OFF IN DUBAI • SAND-SKIING IN THE DUNES • TAWI ATTAIR: THE SINGING SINKHOLE • FEELING DWARFED BY BAALBEK • FROM SKI SUIT TO SWIM SUIT IN A SINGLE DAY • WANDERING OLD SANA'A • TAKING TEA IN ISFAHAN • FROLICKING WITH DOLPHINS OFF MUSCAT • FEASTING ON LEBANESE MEZE • SHOPPING IN THE CITY OF GOLD • CHECKING OUT THE BAUHAUS

The Middle East
440–484

LEBANON

Sample Beirut's
cutting-edge culture — 469

SYRIA

443 — Relaxing in a Damascus
hammam

464 — Taking a trip to
Iraqi Kurdistan

459 — Taking tea in
Isfahan

IRAQ

IRAN

**ISRAEL & THE
PALESTINIAN
TERRITORIES**

JORDAN

471 — Bedouin camping
at Wadi Rum

KUWAIT

449 — Pearl diving in the
Persian Gulf

BAHRAIN

Shopping in the — 462
City of Gold

451 — Bobbing about on the
Musandam Fjords

SAUDI ARABIA

QATAR

UAE

OMAN

The Abode of Silence : the most — 468
beautiful desert on Earth

Wandering Old Sana'a — 458

YEMEN

440 Haunting the Dead Cities

SYRIA I was half expecting some togaed Roman to pop his head out of a side window and ask me what the heck I thought I was doing on his land. This is Serjilla, one of the best preserved and most complete of the "Dead Cities", a network of Roman towns and villages that once thrived in the fertile plains of northern Syria, profiting, it seems, from a combination of Byzantine-Empire trade routes and their suitability for olive-oil production.

Serjilla, like its neighbours, has been abandoned for more than a millennium – but it doesn't feel that way: you can explore Roman houses that were virtually complete, pop into church and visit the baths and the temple, while those Roman ghosts look on with disdain.

441 Fighting off the cats in Acre

ISRAEL & THE PALESTINIAN TERRITORIES The Middle East isn't all desert, desert, desert. Take a break from sand and head for the water: stand on the walls of Acre and watch the sun sink into the Mediterranean.

Acre is one of the most evocative Palestinian towns inside Israel. There are ancient walls, mosques, gardens and museums here, but this old Crusader stronghold is a fabulous place to simply wander through. It has survived as a fabulous skein of tight alleyways and atmospheric markets, wreathed around – of course – by the fragrance of fresh-caught fish, for sale in the souk and offered at a dozen restaurants down by the old port. Fight off the cats to get your share.

442 Trekking the desert mountains of Wadi Halfayn

OMAN In the last few decades Oman has leapt from medieval times into the modern world. Tiny mountain villages are now linked by paved roads, so everyone drives. The villagers love it, and so do hikers keen to explore the old paths that once provided vital trade links over steep ridges into neighbouring valleys. They're now deserted but for the occasional goat herder and a few – very few – hikers.

Craggy peaks, long views and isolation make trekking here an appealing prospect, but coping with minimal water quickly synchs you with the rhythm of the desert. Between villages you have to rely on random pools, and dinner and breakfast may be just dates and crackers washed down by the contents of your water bottle. A small oasis the next day makes a great spot for a rehydrating lunch out of the scorching midday sun.

One particularly spectacular three-day loop starts up the Wadi Halfayn valley, where broken irrigation channels and abandoned terraces attest to Oman's rapid urbanisation. Sporadic flashes of paint on rocks mark a tortuous route up into the mountains, over a pass

then down to the small village of Al Manakhir. A thin smattering of gnarled pines partly shade the route onwards to the palm-girt village of Hadash, heralded by a lone tower which once fortified this route. The guidebook talks of a route from Hadash into Wadi Bani Rawahah, but an almost sheer 600m-high ridge of mountains blocks the way. It seems highly improbable, but up the route goes – with a few stretches of airy ledges and a couple of rickety tree trunks that have been fashioned into primitive ladders for scaling the steeper sections. From the col it is a 1400m descent down Wadi Bani Rawahah and back to the road. A restorative Coke will never be more welcome.

A far easier option is the three-hour Balcony Walk, which threads its way along an easy but spectacular path into a deep canyon on Jebel Shams, Oman's highest peak at just over 3000m. It ends at a tiny cluster of rough houses tucked under a massive overhang. Until around thirty years ago people eked out a living directing a single small spring across precipitous terraces. They may have upped sticks for the cities, but the now-untended trees still bear fruit.

443 Relaxing in a Damascus hammam

SYRIA Hammams, or "Turkish" steam baths, are often inconspicuous from the street, with nondescript, run-down facades. Inside, though, the best of them – like the Hammam Nur ad-Din in Damascus – are architecturally splendid, with fountains, grand, tiled halls and coloured glass set into domed roofs to admit shafts of sunlight. Gloomy warrens of passages snake off from the entrance into the steamy distance, flanked by sweatrooms and plunge pools. The Nur ad-Din has been in operation since the twelfth century and the sense of history here is every bit as powerful as it is in the ruins and museums outside.

After depositing your clothes in a locker and donning a towel-cum-loincloth – modesty is always preserved for men, although women can strip off completely – head first for a scaldingly hot sauna, your body stewing in its own juices as you lie on a marble slab

working up the mother of all sweats. Public hammams are always single-sex: some admit only men, while others may publicize set hours for women (and children), when male staff are replaced by female counterparts.

An ice-cold shower follows, after which you can expect to be approached by a heavily built, no-nonsense attendant bearing a rough-textured glove, used to scrub every inch of your body and loosen layers of dirt and dead skin you didn't even know you had.

You may then be offered a massage, which often involves much pummelling and joint-cracking. With your circulation restored to maximum and every sinew tingling, seemingly endless rounds of soaping, steaming, splashing and cold plunging follow, for as long as you like, at the end of which you'll be swaddled in towels and brought a refreshing glass of sweet tea to aid recovery. Sheer heaven.

ISRAEL & THE PALESTINIAN TERRITORIES For a place so dear to so many hearts, and so violently fought over, the walled Old City of Jerusalem is not as grandiose as you might imagine; it's compact and easy to find your way around, though you'll stumble at almost every turn over holy or historic sites. The streets hum with activity: handcarts, sellers of religious artefacts, Jews scurrying through the Muslim quarter to pray at the Wailing Wall, and Palestinian youths trying to avoid the attentions of the Israeli soldiers patrolling the streets.

The three biggest attractions are the major religious sites. The Church of the Holy Sepulchre is a dark, musty, cavernous old building, reeking of incense, and home to the site of the crucifixion. Pilgrims approach the church by the Via Dolorosa, the path that Jesus took to his execution, observing each Station of the Cross and not infrequently dragging large wooden crosses through the narrow streets, where local residents pay them scant attention.

Heading through the heart of the Old City, past a meat market, piled high with offal and sheep's heads, you emerge blinking into the sun-drenched esplanade that fronts Judaism's holiest site, the Western ("Wailing") Wall, last remnant of the ancient Jewish Temple that was originally built by King Solomon and later rebuilt by Herod. From here, you can nip into the Western Wall Tunnels that run under the city's Muslim Quarter; with subterranean synagogues, underground gateways and ancient aqueducts, they're fascinating to explore.

Around the side of the Wailing Wall, up on Temple Mount, is the Dome of the Rock, Islam's third-holiest site. This is the spot where Abraham offered to sacrifice his son to God, and where Mohammed later ascended to Heaven upon a winged steed. The perfect blue octagon topped with a golden dome is a fabulous gem of Ummayad architecture, immediately recognizable as the symbol of Jerusalem.

The wealth of sights in this ancient, entrancing city is overwhelming, so don't forget to make time on your wanderings for more mundane pleasures: a cardamom-scented Turkish coffee at the café just inside the Damascus Gate, or hummus at *Abu Shukri's*, arguably more divine than the relics that surround it.

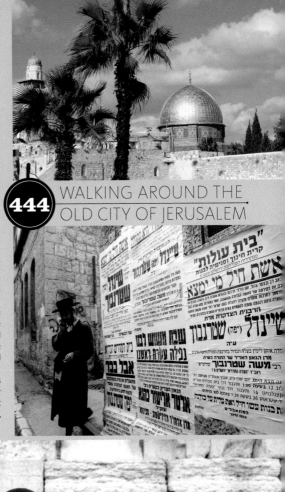

444 WALKING AROUND THE OLD CITY OF JERUSALEM

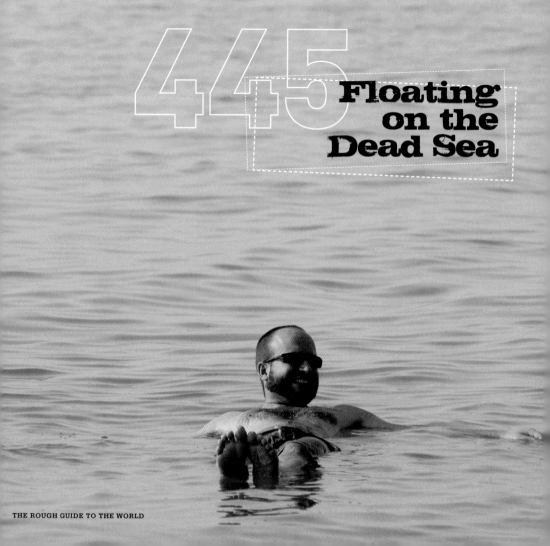

JORDAN I peered past my toes at the burning sun, framed between craggy mountains opposite. Bobbing gently, outstretched and motionless on the surface of the sea, I felt like a human cork. I tried to swim, but my body rode too high in the water and I ended up splashing ineffectually; droplets on my lips tasted horribly bitter, and the water in my eyes stung like mad.

At 400m below sea level, the Dead Sea – hot, hazy and the deepest blue – is the lowest point on Earth and is named for its uniquely salty water, which kills off virtually all marine life. Normal sea water is three or four percent salt, but Dead Sea water measures over thirty percent. The lake is fed mainly by the River Jordan, but due to geological upheavals it has no outflow; instead, the sun

evaporates water off the surface at the rate of millions of litres a day, leading to salt and minerals – washed down from the hills by the river – crystallizing onto the beach in a fringe of white.

The high salt content makes the water so buoyant that it's literally impossible to sink. As you walk in from the beach you'll find your feet are forced up from under you – you couldn't touch the bottom if you tried – and the water supports you like a cradle. Floating is effortless.

The heat was oppressive and the air, with an unmistakable whiff of sulphur, lay heavy in my nostrils. All sound was dampened by a thick atmospheric haze of evaporation, and the near silence was eerie. As I lay, taking in the entire surreal experience, I realized just how aptly named this place is: the Dead Sea really feels dead.

445 Floating on the Dead Sea

446 Discovering Mada'in Saleh

SAUDI ARABIA Rocky, remote and allegedly accursed, Mada'in Saleh, deep in the Arabian Desert, is the location of the magnificent Nabatean city known in ancient times as Hegra. With its great, rock-cut facades carved from warm golden sandstone, this city was once an important stop on the powerful Arabian tribe's incense trail.

Built in the first century AD on the fringes of Nabatean territory, Hegra lay at a junction of trade routes. Camel caravans travelling north from the incense towns of Arabia would stop here; animals would be rested, merchants would do business, taxes would be collected. With the constant traffic and trade, Hegra prospered, and the ruins here are suitably grand.

Roaming Mada'in Saleh you'll see all the styles typical of Nabatean architecture, set against breathtaking desert landscapes. Ornate, classically influenced tombs are carved into the cliffs, displaying impressively intricate workmanship; their detailing, preserved in the dry desert air, remains crisp and sharp. Standing beneath these towering funerary edifices, you'll feel the heavy, silent heat pressing down upon you. The Nabatean people, who were conquered by the Romans and slid into obscurity after the trade routes shifted, maintain a ghostly presence.

447 Krak des Chevaliers: the finest castle in the world

SYRIA When T. E. Lawrence was not yet "of Arabia", but merely of Oxford and still only 20, he went on a summer's walking tour of Crusader castles. Writing home after spending three days at Krak des Chevaliers, he described it as, "the finest castle in the world: certainly the most picturesque I have seen – quite marvellous". What immediately struck him was that it was "neither a ruin nor a show place", and that it had remained "as formidable as of old". The wonderful impression that Krak made on Lawrence early in the twentieth century, the genius and the grace of its construction, strikes the visitor as much as ever today.

As you approach along the Homs-Tartus highway, you notice the trees bent eastwards, forever blown by draughts of Mediterranean air sucked through the Homs Gap by the rising heat of the interior. This is the only point between Turkey and Israel at which the otherwise unbroken line of coastal mountains allows access between the deserts and plains of Syria and the sea. Where the gap narrows and the mountains press against you like a wall, you see Krak riding aloft on a spur of the Jebel al-Sariya, like a vast battleship on station, forever cresting a giant wave.

The standard of the Knights Hospitaller would have fluttered from the top of the Warden's Tower, where a spiral staircase rises to a voluminous chamber, the Grand Master's apartment, dating from the mid-thirteenth century and decorated with delicate pilasters, Gothic ribbed vaulting and a frieze of five-petalled flowers carved in stone. From here there is a splendid view of the concentric circles of Krak's defences spiralling around you, an encircling curtain wall with a line of round towers, then within this and rising higher, a tighter ring of protective walls and towers surrounding a central court.

In the end, Krak was not taken; it was given away. During the last years of the Frankish states the Hospitallers could not raise sufficient manpower, and the castle was reduced to a lonely outpost facing a still-gathering enemy. Finally, after Krak had been in Christian hands for 161 years, and after a month's siege by the Egyptian Mameluke sultan, Baybars, the remaining knights accepted his offer of safe conduct and, in 1271, rode to Tartus and the sea for the last time.

448 Hearing the groans in Hama

SYRIA As we came into the centre of Hama, a pleasant city in an idyllic location on the Orontes River south of Aleppo, the sound of groaning filled our ears. In 1982, an Islamist uprising here was brutally suppressed by the Syrian army; the medieval old quarter was bombed and tens of thousands died. It felt to us like the city hadn't really recovered. A generation on, people still tread gingerly.

And always the sound of groaning. All along the riverbank stand giant wooden waterwheels, or norias, seventeen of them, up to twenty metres high – relics of an Ottoman irrigation system. They are elegant examples of early technology, but as they turn, the grinding of wood on wood produces a hair-raisingly mournful sound. Hama is filled with groans.

449 Pearl Diving in the Persian Gulf

BAHRAIN The largest of their kind in the world, Bahrain's 650 square kilometres of oyster beds have attracted divers since ancient times. Before oil was discovered, the country's economy was dependent upon these little sea treasures, which provided riches where the desert landscape could not.

Pearl diving was done without equipment – divers descended on a weighted rope and spent only one minute under water at a time. Though no longer the industry it was, visitors can now experience this tradition for themselves – unlike the divers of long ago, those lucky enough to find a pearl today are allowed to keep it for themselves.

450 Diving in the Gulf of Aqaba

JORDAN Tucked between the arid lands of northern Africa and the Arabian Peninsula, the Red Sea is one of the world's premier diving destinations, and leading off from its northern tip the Gulf of Aqaba boasts some of its best and least-damaged stretches of coral. The long Egyptian coastline is filled with brash, bustling and rather commercial resorts, and Israel's slender coast around Eilat can get uncomfortably crowded, but the unsung Jordanian resort of Aqaba offers a tranquillity and lack of hustle that, for many, makes it top choice in these parts.

Diving from Aqaba is simple and rewarding: the reef begins directly from the shallows and shore dives are the norm; only 100m offshore you can explore coral walls and canyons, shipwrecks and ethereal undersea gardens.

The water here is nearly all ways warm and the reefs exquisite. Wide fields of soft corals stretch off into the startlingly clear blue gulf, schools of anthias shimmering over the various fans, sea fingers and sea whips. Huge heads of stony, hard corals grow literally as big as a house, their limestone skeletons supporting an abundance of marine life, including turtles, rays and moray eels. Endless species of multicoloured fish goggle back at you from all sides. Seabass, lionfish and groupers patrol the fringing reef of First Bay, while shoals of barracuda circle the sunken Lebanese freighter *Cedar Pride*. The views along the sheer wall of the Power Station are worth the dive alone – though, if the fates are really smiling on you, you might be lucky enough to spot a shark circling in the depths below.

451 Bobbing about on the Musandam Fjords

OMAN The scenery is majestic: towering mountains plunge like runaway rock into the turquoise water 2000m below, and crystal-clear waterways knife their way through craggy cliffs.

These are fjords alright, but not as most visitors know them. There are no snow-capped peaks around here, no gushing waterfalls or fertile slopes. Instead, a heat-haze hangs over the Hajar, and the waters are plied not by 3000-ton ferries but by the occasional fishing dhow, bobbing its way towards Khasab harbour with a bounty of grouper and spiny lobster. Welcome to the Musandam Peninsula, an isolated entity, cut off from the rest of Oman by the United Arab Emirates and jutting out into the Strait of Hormouz. It's a strikingly rugged region, dominated by the Hajar Mountains, which, having snaked across the UAE, topple off into the Gulf of Oman.

Such grandeur is best appreciated from below, from one of the sheltered fjords, or *khors*, that riddle the peninsula. What better way to start the day than by setting sail from Khasab in a traditional wooden dhow, maybe a *landj*, a *batil* or the larger *mashuwwah*? And what more relaxing way to spend it than by propping yourself up amongst the Persian carpets and thick, lolling cushions, and gazing out at the tiny villages that cling to the cliff face, and at the humpback dolphins that cavort alongside your boat.

SYRIA Sunsets make the desert come alive. The low, rich light brings out textures and colours that are lost in the bleached-out glare of noon. It had been a hot, dusty day, but now, perched on a summit high above the desert floor, with the sun at our backs, the views made it all worthwhile.

Spread out below us was the ruined city of Palmyra. For most of the second and third centuries AD, this was one of the wealthiest and most important trading centres in the eastern Roman Empire, perfectly positioned between Persia, India, China and Rome.

We'd spent the day exploring its fabulously romantic array of semi-ruined temples and tombs, their honey-coloured stonework bronzed by the desert sun. Inside the huge Temple of Bel, we'd stood where the Palmyrenes' chief deity was worshipped alongside the gods of the moon and the sun, then walked the length of Palmyra's Great Colonnade, an ancient street more than a kilometre long, flanked by tall columns and set amidst the sandy ruins of temples, marketplaces, a theatre and other buildings which once formed the core of the city.

Overlooking us from the west were the ramparts of a ruined, seventeenth-century Arab castle. As sunset approached, we'd ventured up here. It was then that Palmyra's most evocative tale hit home.

At the height of the city's wealth and influence, in 267 AD, Queen Zenobia led her army against the might of Rome, rapidly seizing the whole of Syria and Egypt. The legions hit back, eventually sacking Palmyra in 273 and parading Zenobia in chains through the streets of Rome, but those few short years of rebellion created a legend: Zenobia as the most powerful of Arab queens, Palmyra as her desert citadel.

The **Burj Al Arab** *shows off* in Dubai

UNITED ARAB EMIRATES Dubai is a desert turned Disney. What was once a sleepy fishing village is now a futuristic cybercity, with sparkling skyscrapers, shopping malls, water parks, golf courses and hotels so flashy that Elton John would be proud to call them home. The iconic *Burj Al Arab* is a striking 28-storey symbol of new-world bling. The gleaming building, one of the tallest hotels in the world, is shaped like a billowing sail – and to say it dominates the skyline is an understatement. At night, surrounded by choreographed fountains of water and fire, it is truly spectacular.

Start as you mean to go on with a Rolls-Royce pick-up from the airport and you will swiftly get the picture. Huge tropical aquariums and backlit waterfalls dominate the lobby, the carpets are a whirl of lurid reds, greens and blues, and on-site stores glitter with diamonds and emeralds. Modestly marketed as "the world's first seven-star hotel", it has a helipad on the roof (where Federer and Agassi played out a vertigo-inducing exhibition tennis match) and more than 1200 staff poised to satisfy your every whim.

The bedrooms are all gigantic suites, their decor the epitome of Arabian kitsch. We're talking mirrors above the beds, leopard-print chairs and gold-tapped Jacuzzis in every bathroom. The 42-inch TV screens are framed in gold, and the curtains and doors can be operated electronically. If all this doesn't quite cut it for you, the two show-stopping Royal Suites come with their own private elevators, cinemas and rotating beds: a bargain at $28,000 per night.

When it comes to food, naturally your personal butler can rustle up anything you desire, or you might prefer to take a three-minute trip in a simulated submarine to the underwater restaurant. Oh, and don't miss a drink in *Burj Al Arab*'s famous bar, situated on the 27th floor, 200m above sea level. From here you can gaze across at The Palm and The World – extraordinary man-made islands shaped like their namesakes and prime real estate to some of the wealthiest people on the planet. Dubai may not be for everyone, but if you've made it here, embrace the ostentation, wallow in the excess and smile.

454 Sand-skiing in the dunes

QATAR Skiing in the desert? You don't have to go to Dubai's super-cooled ski dome to experience it. Launching yourself down the slopes under a scorching desert sun is possible in Qatar (pronounced something like "cutter"), a small Gulf country midway between Kuwait and Dubai – but forget about snow machines and fake icicles. Here, the ski slopes are all natural.

Jaded ski bums looking for a new thrill should take a 4WD trip to Khor al-Adaid – known as Qatar's Inland Sea. This is a saltwater inlet from the blue waters of the Gulf which penetrates far into the desert interior and is surrounded on all sides by monumental formations of giant, silvery sand dunes.

These are almost all crescent-shaped barchan dunes. Both points of the crescent face downwind; between them is a steep slip face of loose sand, while the back of the dune, facing into the breeze, is a shallow, hard slope of wind-packed grains.

This formation lends itself particularly well to sand-skiing or, perhaps more commonly, sand-boarding, both of which are almost identical to their more familiar snow-based cousins – without the woolly hats but with a softer landing for novices. The 4WD delivers you to the top of the dune, whereupon you set off down the loose slip face, carving through the soft sand to the desert floor; friction is minimal, and this kind of dry, powdery sand lets you glide like a dream.

And Khor al-Adaid comes into its own as sunset approaches. With low sunshine illuminating the creamy-smooth slopes and glittering light reflected up off the calm surface of the khor's blue waters, a surreal, almost mystical quality settles on the dunes. Après-ski with a difference.

455 Tawi Attair: the singing sinkhole

OMAN At the edge of an emerald highland plain patrolled by Jabali tribesmen and their herds of camels and cattle lies the opening to Tawi Attair ("the Well of Birds"), one of the largest sinkholes in the world. A massive, gaping limestone cavity 150m in diameter and 211m deep, the well was formed eons ago when a cave roof collapsed into itself; today, it could house half the Empire State Building. Thousands of visitors come here each year to witness numerous bird species swooping in and out once the torrential *khaleef* (monsoon) has drenched the Omani plains.

Work your way through the marshy grasses towards the edge of the pit and gaze down: bedecked with specks of green foliage amidst crumbling mounds of dirt and the occasional falling rock, the craggy walls are swimming with hundreds of birds – raptors, swifts and rock doves – their warbles and chirps welling up in a harmonious flurry of sound. From the side of the opening, carefully follow the stony path down to the small platform for better views of the deep abyss 80m below – you'll need a powerful torch to see all the way down to the bottom, where an aquamarine pool funnels into a complex and intertwined system of sub-aquatic caves.

The platform is the best vantage point to hear the famed birdcalls of the well's diverse residents – exotic, isolated species such as the Yemen serin, Bonelli's eagle and African rock bunting, among many, many others. Once the birds embark on their flight towards the sky, their coos hushed, the silence down here is uncanny, trumping even that of the vast desert above.

456 Feeling dwarfed by Baalbek

LEBANON One of the wonders of the ancient world, the Roman archeological site of Baalbek – a place that, in the words of Robert Byron, "dwarfs New York into a home of ants" – holds awe-inspiring temples, porticoes, courtyards and palatial stone stairways. The Greeks and Romans called it Heliopolis, "The City of the Sun", a name it shares with another great Classical city in Egypt – but this phenomenal site has no equals.

Avoid the midday heat and crowds by arriving late in the afternoon, when you're likely to catch the sky as it turns a purplish orange, flanked by Mount Lebanon and the colossal Temple of Jupiter. Ascend the temple's restored steps – which long ago stretched to twenty times their current breadth – to the chiselled portico, once covered in cedar and supported by twelve massive Corinthian columns. The central door gives onto a hexagonal courtyard encircled with exedrae, small, carved recesses in the walls where Romans would come to ponder the world. Further on, past the inner sanctum, the main court is overshadowed by six elephantine stone columns – the largest in the world – below which two large open basins served to bathe cows and bulls for sacrificial rites and above which once towered a massive Roman basilica.

Even more striking is the towering Temple of Bacchus just next door – larger than the Parthenon and once a Mecca for decadent orgies and pagan sacrifice rituals. Dozens of engraved, fluted columns shoot up off the podium into the sky, while the portico above is adorned with colonnades, friezes of lions and bulls and ornately carved grapes and poppies; the temple is appropriately attributed to the god of wine and pleasure. Looking on, the sacred cella is impeccably decorated with an assortment of windows, columns and niches.

Exit through a tunnel below the acropolis for Baalbek's other sites: the Temple of Venus; the Ummayad Grand Mosque; and the Hajar al-Hubla, the largest cut block of stone known to man. Forged from local crystalline limestone, it supposedly took 40,000 men to move and its power has reportedly made barren women fertile.

457 From ski suit to swim suit in a single day

LEBANON The best things come in small packages, but few small packages contain quite as much as Lebanon. In a single day you can swish your way down the slopes in the morning before losing the salopettes and donning your shades at the seaside in the afternoon.

Though boasting neither the altitude nor the acreage to qualify as a major international resort, Lebanon's skiing is great fun. Best of all, the resorts all lie within a day's trip by car from Beirut, meaning you don't have to risk long and expensive journeys for nothing. The best plan is to check out the resort's snow conditions in advance then head out early the following morning – either taking a hire car along the boisterous roads or travelling with a tour company – to catch the snow before Lebanon's Levantine sun turns it all to humus.

The pick of the bunch, with the most-developed infrastructure and facilities, is Faraya Mzaar, northeast of Beirut, with the powder-friendly Cedars, southeast of Tripoli, close behind. Many resorts also offer cross-country skiing and snow-shoeing, and there's a good variety of pistes, though most are short. The most important thing to remember is that in Lebanon looking good is almost as important as skiing.

To work on your tan, head to Lebanon's best beaches, which can be found south of Tyre and near Byblos. In Beirut the best public beach, Ramlet al-Bayda, is grubby, and the well-maintained private beach clubs are generally your best bet – they have heated pools (in case you find the winter sea chilly) and are home to much shimmying and strutting. After a day on the slopes, there's no better way to unwind, and there's still time for a spot of shopping in Beirut's boutiques, a beer followed by fresh fish at one of the city's bars or restaurants and more shimmying and strutting at the booming nightclubs. Best of all, you'll return from your skiing trip with a perfect tan, much to the chagrin of your panda-eyed Alpine friends.

458 Wandering Old Sana'a

YEMEN Nestled by Yemen's al-Surated mountain range, the city of Sana'a is said to have been built by Noah's son. Modernity has since thankfully stayed well away from the city's old quarter, where traditional architecture has endured for over a thousand years.

Begin your day at the *medina*'s southeastern portico, the Bab al-Yaman, which still welcomes local traders on their way to Turkish coffee-houses for a strong shot of local brew. From here, head north to marvel at the Grand Mosque (al-Jama'a al-Kabir), just one of fifty city mosques, and the home of the largest collection of Islamic manuscripts in Yemen. Non-Muslims aren't allowed in, but admiring the beautifully constructed minarets and domes all over the city won't cost you a thing. Continue on to the Souk al-Milh (salt market), where you'll be confronted with a beguiling collection of stalls purveying coffee, incense, spices and cloth.

From here, notch your head back to take in a vista of the nearly 15,000 ancient tower-houses of Old Sana'a. You can amble about the old city for hours without seeing a single "new" structure. The buildings range in height from six to eight storeys and are made of locally quarried dark basalt stone with whitewashed facades of chalk and limestone, which protects against rain. The exteriors display a gorgeous melange of traditional Yemeni and Islamic styles, with windows done in artful friezes. At the very top of each building, framing the *manzar* (attic), are the rooms that look out across the city, windowed with moon-shaped stained glass. Some call them the world's first skyscrapers, and Yemeni families still live in them today as they have for centuries.

Once you've had your fill of traditional architecture, rest yourself in a resplendent evening bath at the Hammam Abhar, Sana'a's finest. But after the sun has set, return once more for a walk through Old Sana'a: at nighttime, the entire *medina* is bathed in gorgeous, golden hues emanating from the weathered stained-glass windows.

459 Taking tea in Isfahan

IRAN You could easily devote a day to exploring Isfahan's great Maydan Naqsh-i Jahan, a vast rectangular space dotted with gardens, pools and fountains and ringed by arcades, above which rise the domes of the adjacent mosques. Separate from the bustle of this cultured city, it has even managed to cling onto its original polo goals, though the game hasn't been played here for centuries.

The square is always busy with people. It spreads south from the sprawling Bazar-e Bozorg, packed with shops offering Isfahan's most famous export – hand-woven Persian carpets. As you stroll the square you may well find yourself engaged in conversation by an eminently courteous Iranian with impeccable English, who turns out to have a brother/uncle/cousin with a carpet shop – where, of course, there's no charge for looking...

Even if you're able to resist the charms of the carpet bazaar, you won't be able to ignore the square's exquisite seventeenth-century Islamic architecture. To the south is the Masjid i-Imam mosque, its portal and towering dome sheathed in glittering tiles of turquoise and blue, while to one side, the smaller Sheikh Lotfollah Mosque – marked by a dome of cream-coloured tiles which glow rosy pink in the afternoon sun – is, if anything, even more stunning, with fine mosaics and a dizzyingly decorated interior. Opposite, the Ali Qapu Palace – an ex-royal residence – boasts a sensational view over the square from its high terrace.

Either way, be back at one of the terrace teashops as sunset approaches. The square fills with Isfahani families strolling or picnicking on the grass, and you get a grandstand view over the scene, sipping *chay* (tea) as floodlights turn the arcades, domes and minarets to gold.

460 Frolicking with dolphins off Muscat

OMAN Lightly wedged along a coastal strip between the Hajar Mountains and the blue waters of the Gulf, Muscat has been called the Arabian Peninsula's most enigmatic capital for its bewildering mixture of conservative tradition and contemporary style. Muscat itself – the walled, seafront quarter that hosts the Sultan's Palace – is one of three towns comprising the city. Inland lies the busy modern area of Ruwi, while a short walk along the coast from Muscat is Mutrah, site of the souk and daily fish market. But the city's unmissable attraction is the astonishing display of marine acrobatics to be seen daily just offshore.

Dolphins are the star performers, dancing and pirouetting on the water in the sparkling sunlight. From various points along the coast near Muscat, tour operators run dolphin-watching trips, departing around 6.30 or 7am. The early start is worth it, as each morning numerous pods of dolphins congregate beside the little boats including common, bottlenose and the aptly named spinner dolphins, which delight in somersaulting out of the water with eye-popping virtuosity, directly under your gaze. Adults and youngsters alike take part, seemingly showing off to each other as well as the goggling humans; nobody knows why they spin, but they do it every morning, before sliding off into deeper waters. Whales have also been sighted close to shore in the winter months (Oct–May), amongst them humpbacks and even killer whales.

And if that's not enough, you can return at sunset for more dolphin-watching, or alternatively even take to the water yourself for a closer look: kayaking with the dolphins, morning or evening, is a real treat. Paddling a short distance into the midst of the frolicking beasts brings you close enough to interact with them, their squeaks and clicks filling the air as they come and investigate who or what you might be.

461 Feasting on Lebanese meze

LEBANON Lebanese food is one of the great pleasures of travel in the Middle East, and the mainstay of this cuisine is meze. This array of dishes, served simultaneously on small plates as a starter or main, has spread around the world. But to get a real sense of it, it's worth going to the source.

The concept extends far back into history: the ancient Greeks and Persians both served small dishes of nuts and dried fruits with wine as an appetizer, a tradition which continued (with a non-alcoholic beverage) throughout the medieval Arab period.

Today, good restaurants might have thirty or forty choices of meze on the menu, ranging from simple dishes of herbs, olives and pickled vegetables, *labneh* (tart yoghurt), and dips such as hummus and *baba ghanouj* (aubergine), up to grander creations like *kibbeh* (the national dish of Lebanon, a mixture of cracked wheat, grated onion and minced lamb pounded to a paste, shaped into oval torpedoes and deep-fried), *tabbouleh* (another Lebanese speciality: parsley and tomato salad with cracked wheat), *shanklish* (spiced goat's cheese) and *warag aynab* (stuffed vine leaves). *Kibbeh nayeh* (lamb's meat pounded smooth and served raw) is perhaps the most celebrated of all meze, while mini-mains such as lamb or chicken shish kebabs, charcoal-roasted larks and even seafood are also common. Everything is always accompanied by unlimited quantities of hot, fresh-baked flat bread, used for scooping and dipping.

Meze exist to slow down the process of eating, turning a solitary refuelling into a convivial celebration of good food and good company. Sitting at a table swamped in colours and aromas, and eating a meal of myriad different flavours and textures, is nothing short of sensuous delight – as, indeed, it's intended to be.

462 Shopping in the City of Gold

UNITED ARAB EMIRATES Dubai's nickname, the "City of Gold", is well earned: gold jewellery is sold here at some of the world's most competitive prices, and shopping among the constant flow of customers, many here for their marriage dowries, is an exceptional experience.

The Gold Souk is a fascinating warren of tiny shops and stalls clustered together in the old quarter of Deira. Visit in the cool of early evening when the souk is at its best, with lights blazing and window-shoppers out in force. Every corner is crammed with jewellery of every style and variety; spotlights pick out choice pieces and racks holding dozens of sparkling gold bangles and chains dazzle the eye.

Buying is a cagey but good-natured process: treat it as the chance to have a friendly chat with the shopkeeper, talking about family, work, life – anything but the item you've got your eye on. Then ask to see a few pieces, while surreptitiously assessing quality and sizing up your adversary, before lighting on the piece you knew you wanted from the start.

When the time comes to discuss money, bear in mind that the gold price fluctuates daily – and every shopkeeper in the souk knows the current price to several decimal places. Whereas in the West gold jewellery is sold at a fixed price, in Dubai the cost of each item has two separate components: the weight of the gold and the quality of craftsmanship involved in creating it. The former is fixed, according to the daily price-per-gram (listed in the newspaper) set against the item's purity; the latter is where bargaining comes into play, with you and the shopkeeper trading prices – always with a smile – until you reach agreement.

It takes a cool head, amidst all that glittering gold, not to be dazzled into paying over the odds, but the experience is more than worth it.

Checking out the
Bauhaus architecture
in Tel Aviv

ISRAEL & THE PALESTINIAN TERRITORIES Tel Aviv is a city with chutzpah, a loud, gesticulating expression of urban Jewish culture. Revelling in a Mediterranean-style café culture, it has dozens of bars and clubs, all aimed squarely at the under-30s. It doesn't seem likely to have much in the way of architectural interest – it was only founded in 1909 – or so you'd think. Take a closer look and Tel Aviv reveals a wealth of buildings constructed in the International Style, inspired by the German Bauhaus school. Not as grandiose as its predecessor, Art Deco – indeed, deliberately understated in contrast – the style has its own charm, and abounds in Tel Aviv as nowhere else in the world.

Wandering the streets, you don't at first see the architecture, but then you start to notice it, and suddenly you'll see it everywhere – it really is a signature of the city. The International Style's beauty lies not in ornamentation or grand gestures, but in its no-nonsense

crispness: lines are clean, with lots of right angles; decoration is minimal, consisting only of protruding balconies and occasionally flanged edges, designed to cast sharp shadows in the harsh Mediterranean sunlight. It wears whitewash especially well, giving the whole of Tel Aviv an almost Hockneyesque feel with its straight white lines and hard edges, as if someone had turned up the contrast button just a mite too high.

Check it out on Rehov Bialik, a small residential street in the very centre of town. Take a stroll on Sederot Rothschild, a fine 1930s avenue with some very classic Bauhaus buildings. A further wander around the streets in between Bialik and Rothschild yields still more examples of the genre, as does a visit to the more workaday district of Florentin. As cool and stylish as its cafés, Tel Aviv's architecture reflects the city itself – young, brash and straight to the point. It may not impress at first, but it definitely grows on you.

464 Taking a trip to Iraqi Kurdistan

IRAQ So much for George W. Bush's famed "Axis of Evil". Iran is easy to enter if you've the patience to wait for a visa, North Korea can be visited on package tours from Beijing, and now, with very little effort, you can get to Iraq from Turkey. There are few more exciting stamps to have in your passport, though would-be adventurers should note that the mighty four-letter word is barely legible in the visa.

The only part of Iraq currently open to tourists is the Kurdish enclave to the north, by far the safest part of the country and, indeed, largely supportive of the 2003 war. However, it's not without its dangers – you're highly advised to do your research beforehand, and to keep a low profile once inside Iraq. Getting there, however, is simple: just turn up at the Turkish border town of Silopi and you'll soon be met by a taxi driver willing to arrange the necessary documentation for your visa and to escort you across the border. You'll be dropped off in the frontier town of Zakho, a pleasant enough place in which you'll get a taste of Kurdish friendliness and hospitality, though for those who want to sightsee rather than merely claim their visa stamp, there are some enticing places further afield.

Dohuk is the next town of importance, a youthful place whose safe and tranquil vibe makes it a favourite with American soldiers on leave. There's even a small amusement park here, though travellers will probably prefer the teeming bazaar. The road then climbs east to an area that confounds most impressions of Iraq – who'd have thought raging waterfalls, snowcapped peaks and grassy ravines would be on the agenda? Amadiya is a mountain village offering gorgeous views and fresh air, though those who press on to the Iranian border will find that the scenery becomes ever more sumptuous. Heading south you'll come across wonderful Erbil, an ancient city whose now-decrepit citadel may be the oldest continuously inhabited place on Earth. Museums, mosques, bazaars pungent with spice, and even a bar or two – you may well wish to prolong your stint in Iraq.

465 Walk round a Golan Heights ghost town

SYRIA One of the most contentious spots on Earth, the mountains on Syria's southern border have been occupied by Israel for forty years. The hilltop town of Quneitra was evacuated in 1973, and the Syrians refused to rebuild it, leaving it as a permanent monument to the Israeli action. Almost every single building was flattened by the departing Israeli army, giving the streets an eerie feel, and a cool breeze blows through this ruined hilltop town. The grey concrete roofs of the small houses still lie flat on the ground, around the occasional larger building, left standing, but gutted internally.

Each building tells a story. The shutters on some of the shops weren't even pulled down, apparently because the owners fled in such a hurry when fighting broke out. You can walk into the bullet-ridden hospital for a view of the Israeli soldiers just metres away on the other side of the divide. On the lush green peaks in the distance there are Israeli early warning towers, protecting the settlers who have moved in to take advantage of some of Syria's most fertile land.

When the Israeli occupation began, Syrian families were literally cut in half. Some haven't seen their relatives for forty years, and because the two countries are still technically at war, there are no direct phone lines. That's where the Shouting Valley comes in. A few miles along the border from Quneitra, at Ain Tineh, Syrians regularly gather with loud-hailers to shout across the border, and catch up on the latest family gossip.

In Quneitra and the Shouting Valley you'll need to be accompanied by someone from the Syrian secret service – just to make sure you don't cause an international incident by jumping the fence. At the UN-controlled border in Quneitra, there's a peace park, where visiting heads of state have planted trees. If you're visiting the region and want to understand the anger on both sides of the divide, a visit to this sobering memorial to conflict is essential.

466 Walking the Siq to Petra

JORDAN Tucked away between parallel rocky ranges in southern Jordan, Petra is awe-inspiring. Popular but rarely crowded, this fabled site could keep you occupied for half a day or half a year: you can roam its dusty tracks and byways for miles in every direction.

Petra was the capital of the Nabateans, a tribe originally from Arabia who traded with, and were eventually taken over by, the Romans. Grand temples and even Christian-era church mosaics survive, but Petra is best known for the hundreds of ornate classical-style facades carved into its red sandstone cliffs, the grandest of which make the tombs of the Nabatean kings.

As you approach, modern urban civilization falls away and you are enveloped by the arid desert hills; the texture and colouring of the sandstone, along with the stillness, heat and clarity of light bombard your senses. But it's the lingering, under-the-skin quality of supernatural power that seems to seep out of the rock that leaves the greatest impression.

As in antiquity, the Siq, meaning "gorge", is still the main entrance into Petra – and its most dramatic natural feature. The Siq path twists and turns between bizarrely eroded cliffs for over a kilometre, sometimes widening to form sunlit piazzas in the echoing heart of the mountain; in other places, the looming walls (150m high) close in to little more than a couple of metres apart, blocking out sound, warmth and even daylight.

When you think the gorge can't go on any longer, you enter a dark, narrow defile, opening at its end onto a strip of extraordinary classical architecture. As you step out into the sunlight, the famous facade of Petra's Treasury looms before you. Carved directly into the cliff face and standing forty metres tall, it's no wonder this edifice starred in *Indiana Jones and the Last Crusade* as the repository of the Holy Grail – the magnificent portico is nothing short of divine.

467 Searching for dragon's blood

YEMEN The island of Socotra – Yemeni territory, though it lies closer to Somalia than Arabia – is the most far-flung and unique destination in the Middle East. Cut off from the mainland for half the year by monsoon winds and high seas, Socotra has developed a unique ecosystem. Much of its flora is endemic to the island – odd flowers, strange plants, weirdly shaped trees. Add in the misty mountains and sense of isolation, and Socotra looks and feels like a prehistoric world.

Coming into the capital, Hadibo, you'll be struck first by the mountains – sheer pinnacles of granite soaring into the clouds behind the town. Next you'll squint sceptically at the bizarre bottle-shaped trunks of the cucumber trees in the foothills, as the feeling of entering a bizarre parallel universe heightens. But the real curiosity here, perching on the crags of the mountains, are the outlandish *Dracaena cinnabari*, or dragon's blood trees – Socotra's most famous residents.

Also called inside-out-umbrella trees, they resemble giant mushrooms in silhouette, with a thick trunk sweeping up to a broad cap of dense foliage, supported by spoke-like branches. They look like something out of *Alice in Wonderland* – or one of Willy Wonka's absurd creations. Blink hard, but they're really there.

Socotrans still gather the reddish dragon's blood tree sap, known as cinnabar – once used as a cure-all by the Romans. It was employed in alchemy and witchcraft in medieval times; Europeans believed that this mysterious crimson resin was the authentic dried blood of dragons and it's considered a magical ingredient in Caribbean voodoo. Hold a piece up to the sun – when it begins to glow blood-red, you'll understand why.

468 The Abode of Silence: the most beautiful desert on Earth

SAUDI ARABIA The Empty Quarter is well named. Covering an area the size of Belgium, Holland and France combined, it is almost entirely devoid of life. With its constantly-changing colour, vast, ever-shifting dunes and eerie silence, it's quite simply the most mesmerizing desert in the world.

Since ancient times, frankincense and spice caravans – sometimes in the form of hundreds of plodding camels – risked sandstorms, quicksand, tribal wars and vast well-less stretches. European explorers dreamt of conquering this challenging terrain, and wrote of whole raiding parties swallowed by the sands.

Once home to the fascinating Bedu, who regarded the dunes with reverence, the desert today hosts the Arabian oryx, endemic to the region and one of the most beautiful creatures on Earth, around two dozen species of plants (many of which lie dormant beneath the surface, ready to spring to life on the slightest suggestion of rain) and hundreds of species of insects.

Visiting the Empty Quarter requires serious preparation. With few if any useful maps, very little chance of meeting another human being, and extremely low chances of survival in the case of stranding, you need to travel well prepped and well equipped. Most visitors choose to join a tour run by any of several reputable local tour companies. Knowledgeable and experienced, they can also organize the many permissions and passes required for a foray into the Empty Quarter. Guides, tents and even camels can also be arranged.

When you're in the midst of the sands, the desert's Arabic name, Rub al-Khali (the "Abode of Silence"), seems utterly apposite. Devoid of bird song, the sound of grazing or the slightest sign of human habitation, it is instead the 55-degree heat which seems to hum. Darkening as the day grows long, the sand dunes turn a deep crimson at dusk, resembling a giant damask cloth thrown from heaven across the Earth.

469 Sample Beirut's cutting-edge culture

LEBANON It's the most happening place in the Middle East. In Beirut, you can lean over the shoulders of some of the Arab world's most exciting artists, take in thrilling gigs and explore a decidedly hip bar and club scene.

Start your day with a tour of the city's politically-charged street art. The roads around the American University, as well as east Beirut, are home to ever-changing images. Expect to see Banksy-style stencil art advocating revolution, the end of religious politics or gay rights. It's passionate, often experimental and always controversial.

As well as visual art, there are varied live music shows every night, with even the more popular bands often playing in tiny, packed-out bars for free. You might hear Arabic rhythms over the top of a saxophone, or electronic soul in French and Arabic. Band-of-the-moment Mashrou' Leila ("The Overnight Project") mix Arab folk with rock to hypnotic effect, while Palestinian refugee group Katibe Khamseh ("The Fifth Battalion") play funky and impassioned hip-hop.

To plan your night you'll need to pick up some of the flyers dumped at the entrance to *Ta Marbuta* in Hamra or at the *Art Lounge* bar in Karantina. Then head across town to walk up the hilly Monot Street, home to the popular *Facebook Pub* and the city's see-and-be-seen crowd. But Monot is losing its edge to Gemmayze, at the bottom of the hill, a change kick-started by a red-neon-lit bar called *Torino Express*. With a DJ pressed up against the window, it maintains its exclusivity by its sheer size – only a lucky few can squeeze in to this little Lebanese legend.

The bars start emptying out after midnight, when queues start to form at *BO18* and *Sky Bar* – clubs which attract superstar DJs like Judge Jules and Fred Baker. *BO18* is in a converted bunker, and when the sun rises over the Mediterranean, the roof peels back and the party steps up a gear. The open-air *Sky Bar*, meanwhile, has a 360-degree view of the city lights, framed by the mountains and the never-ending shoreline and patronized by Armani-clad, Hummer-driving playboys. It may all feel a little too cool for school, but Beirut can rival London or New York on a good day.

Carving a path through Persepolis

IRAN You begin to feel the historical weight of Persepolis as you drive down the tree-lined approach, long before reaching the actual site. Here, on the dusty plain of Marvdasht at the foot of the Zagros Mountains, the heat is ferocious, but nothing can detract from the sight before you: a once-magnificent city, looming high above the plain on a series of terraces.

Enter through the massive, crumbling stone Gate of All Nations, adorned with cuneiform inscriptions that laud the mighty Persian emperor whose father built the city across a gap of 2500 years, "I am Xerxes, king of kings, son of Darius...". Walking between great carved guardian bulls standing to attention on either side of the gate, you come out on a vast terrace, stretching almost 500m along each side.

It's not the scale, though, but the details – specifically the carvings – that make Persepolis special. Wherever you look, they indicate what went on in each area: in private quarters, bas-reliefs show servants carrying platters of food; in the Hall of Audience, Darius is being borne aloft by representatives of 28 nations, their arms interlinked. Everywhere you can trace the intricately worked details of curly beards and the even more impressive expressions of body language that show the skill of the ancient artists.

The centrepiece is the ruined Apadana Palace, where you come nose to nose with elaborately carved depictions of the splendours of Darius the Great's empire – royal processions, horse-drawn chariots and massed ranks of armed soldiers. Look closer and you'll spot human-headed winged lions, carved alongside esoteric symbols of the deity Ahura Mazda. Begun around 518 BC by Darius to be the centrepiece of his vast empire, Persepolis was a demonstration of Persian wealth and sophistication – and it shows.

Bedouin camping
at **Wadi Rum**

471

JORDAN My Bedouin guide settled forward over his *ribaba*, a simple traditional stringed instrument. As he drew the bow to and fro, the mournful, reedy music seemed to fill the cool night air, echoing back off the cliff soaring above us. The fire threw dancing shadows across the sand. A billion stars looked down.

"Bedouin" means desert-dweller. It's a cultural term: Bedouin today, whether they live in the desert or not (many are settled urban professionals), retain a strong sense of identity with their ancestral tribe. You'll find this desert culture across the Middle East, but to get a feel for its origins you need to travel into its homeland – which is why I'd come to southern Jordan, specifically Wadi Rum.

Here, the dunes and desert vistas form one of the classic landscapes of the Middle East – the backdrop for the movie *Lawrence of Arabia*. Granite and sandstone mountains rise up to 800m sheer from the desert floor. The heat during the day is intense: with no shade, temperatures down on the shimmering sand soar. Views stretch for tens of kilometres; the silence and sense of limitless space are awe-inspiring.

I'd come to spend a night camping. Camels were available as transport, but I'd opted instead for a jeep ride. Bumping out into the deep desert, we headed for camp: a distinctive Bedouin "house of hair" – a long, low tent hand-woven from dark goats' hair and pitched in the sands – would serve as quarters for the night.

As blissful evening coolness descended, the sun set over the desert in a spectacular show of light and colour, and the clarity of the unpolluted air produced a starry sky of stunning beauty.

472 Finding the real Dubai on a dhow

UNITED ARAB EMIRATES Glamorous, fast and flash, Dubai excites admiration and contempt in equal measure. In a frenzy to find new, post-oil industries fast, the diminutive emirate has turned to tourism, buying, borrowing or stealing the world's most popular attractions. It now boasts a snow dome where you can take to the slopes in the sweltering heat of summer, pristine golf courses that unfurl across the desert like great green carpets, dozens of tropical islands fashioned Creation-like from the sand and the sea and a Venice complete with canals and gondoliers.

If you're looking for culture and traditions under the high-rises and Vegas-style attractions, charter a dhow for a cruise along the city's historic Creek. A piece of history in itself, the dhow has linked the Gulf with Asia and Africa for millennia. Built upon its bows are the fortunes not just of its daring merchant seamen, but also of their city. Unmistakable for its squat shape and distinct, lateen sail, the beautiful boat still plays a key role, transporting the spices, fish, fruit and vegetables of olden times alongside TVs, fridges, air-conditioners, power-showers and bootlegged liquor.

A cruise up the Creek takes you right through the city's history. Stone, Bronze and Iron Age settlements sprang up on both its sides, living off rich fishing waters. Later came the *barasti*, the famous mud and palm-frond huts of the early pearl divers, who risked their lives until 1929, when the Wall Street Crash and the introduction of the Japanese cultured pearl devastated the industry. On both sides of the Creek rise neat grids, the buildings of the oil-boom rising like giant chess pieces: offices, hotels and private residences, each more lavish than the last. Around them, in low-rise sprawls, are the quarters of the Asian immigrants who built them, with their temples, shrines, fabric shops, flower markets and teahouses. Drifting past the sights, smells and sounds of this city, you might just rediscover the one thing Dubai's accused of losing but can never buy: its soul.

473 Fish suppers on the Red Sea

YEMEN One of the joys of travel in the Middle East is the food. But outside the towns and cities, the variety of dishes is more limited and you may start to mezze-out. Served day after day, meal after meal for breakfast, lunch and dinner, these appetizers can become, well, rather unappetizing.

Here's a tip: when in Yemen, do as Yemenis do: head for the coast. Lying dog-legged across the Red and Arabian seas, Yemen's long shoreline means you're never too far from it – and all its piscine glory. If you're unsure where to start, simply follow the signs to the port or, in the larger towns or cities, the fishing harbour. Next, seek out the fishermen's boats walloping on the water. Then follow your nose. Emitting smoky, saliva-inducing smells and often lit up with a single, dangling neon light, barrel-like clay ovens sit on the edge of the water.

There, illuminated ghost-like above them, the face of your waiter-cum-chef, who will ask for your order. A swift "Hamour!" (a species of grouper with thick, flaky white flesh) should do the trick and, before you know it, a fish not dissimilar to one of Nemo's movie mates is being scooped straight out of the sea, where they're kept since the morning in little pens or nets.

After a quick clean with the flick of a knife and a final rinse in sea water, the fillet is sprinkled inside and out with salt and hot, carmine-coloured pepper. Then, with a satisfying slap, it's fixed to the inside wall of the oven.

After just minutes in the tandoor, the fish is extracted with the aid of a long, pointed stick and turned onto a newspaper. Served with folded *khobz* (unleavened, chapati-like bread), along with *mukbusa* (a rough paste made of honey, butter and either bananas or dates), it's a meal not to be missed. It's probably the freshest, healthiest and most succulent version of fish and chips you'll ever have had.

474 Getting acquainted with Arabic sweets

JORDAN Whenever I go back to Jordan (which is often), my first appointment is in downtown Amman. There, up an unpromising-looking alleyway alongside a bank building, is a hole-in-the-wall outlet of Habiba, a citywide chain devoted to *halawiyyat* (literally "sweets", or sweet pastries and desserts). I join a line – there's always a line – and, for the equivalent of a few cents, I get a square of *kunafeh*, hot and dripping with syrup, handed to me on a paper plate with a plastic fork. It is a joyous experience: for the Ammanis hanging out and wolfing down the stuff, it's everyday; for me, it's like coming home. Habiba's *kunafeh* is worth crossing continents for.

Kunafeh is the king of Arabic sweets. Originating from the Palestinian city of Nablus, it comprises buttery shredded filo pastry layered over melted goat's cheese, baked in large, round trays, doused liberally with syrup and cut up into squares for serving. It is cousin to the better-known *baklawa*, layered flaky pastry filled with pistachios, cashews or other nuts, also available widely.

However, you're rarely served such treats in Arabic restaurants: there's not a strong tradition of postprandial desserts. Instead, you'll need to head to one of the larger outlets of Habiba, or their competitors Jabri or Zalatimo, patisseries with a café section.

Glass-fronted fridges hold individual portions of *Umm Ali*, an Egyptian milk-and-coconut speciality, sprinkled with nuts and cinnamon, and *muhallabiyyeh*, a semi-set almond cream pudding, enhanced with rosewater: comfort food, Arab-style. Choose one to go with a coffee and perhaps a water-pipe of flavoured tobacco.

Or get a box of assorted sweets – *baklawa*, *maamoul* (buttery, crumbly, rose-scented cookie-style biscuits), *burma* (nut pastries baked golden brown), *basma* (delicate lacy pastries also filled with cashews) and other delectably sticky and aromatic varieties – the perfect gift if you're lucky enough to be invited to someone's home. Forget, too, about Western-bred inhibitions: in the Arab world, as far as *halawiyyat* are concerned, consumption is guilt-free!

475 Bargaining
in the Aleppo souk

SYRIA "Best price to you, my friend!" are familiar words to anyone who's tried to strike a deal in a Middle Eastern souk. To buy here you have to bargain.

Shopping in these bazaars is, for many visitors, the epitome of the Middle Eastern experience. With busy, narrow, shop-lined lanes crowded with people and the aroma of food and spices mingling with the stink of animals, souks are packed with sights, sounds and smells and full of atmosphere.

Aleppo's souk is one of the best. You can get lost here time and time again, roaming the dimly lit lanes past windows full of gold jewellery and stalls piled high with rope or soap or ice cream. Hit the wall as donkey-carts and minivans force a path through the shoppers; linger among the perfume shops, sample fresh almonds and finger exquisite silks.

If you're after a particular item, play it cool. Work out the most you would be prepared to pay – then take the time to chat. In the souk, shopkeepers are never in hurry; they want to talk, pass the time of day, offer you a glass of tea and a sit-down – whether you're a customer or not.

Eventually you can casually enquire how much the item costs. The first price quoted will be twice, perhaps three or four times, as much as the shopkeeper would be prepared to accept, so counter it with a low offer of your own. In response he'll tut, knit his brows, perhaps wag a finger at you – it's all part of the game.

There are only two rules to bargaining: never lose your temper, and never let a price pass your lips that you're not prepared to pay. And don't forget: the "best price" never is. In the souk, everyone's a sucker.

HEAR THE LANGUAGE OF **JESUS**

SYRIA Aramaic is spoken in just a handful of places on Earth. And the beautiful, hilly village of Maaloula, just north of Damascus, is one of them. A trip here involves an hour-long ride on one of the most kitsch buses you'll ever board, complete with flashing lights inside and out, valentine's hearts, a horn that plays a song every time it's pressed and teddy bears dangling from each window.

When you step out at Maaloula, the colourful theme continues. Stone-washed houses in blue, green, red, white and pink cling to the steep slopes. Between two of the peaks is a mountain pass reminiscent of Petra, which gives this stunning place its name – Maaloula means "the entrance" in Aramaic. And crowning the village is the Mar Sarkis Monastery. Dating back to the fourth century, this Greek Catholic monastery is one of Christianity's oldest, and is dedicated to Saint Sergius – a Roman soldier executed for his religious beliefs. Inside, the nuns will happily recite a few lines in Aramaic before selling you some of the country's tastiest wine.

Things don't stop there: nearby Saint Thekla Monastery is a Lourdes-like place of miracles. Syria's Christians – who make up ten percent of the country's population – believe the sick can be cured here, and around the shrine at the back of the monastery, the lucky ones have placed silver offerings to show their thanks.

The Muslims and Christians of this isolated village consider themselves the guardians of the language of Jesus – they've been speaking Aramaic here for at least three thousand years, and while threatened, a government-sponsored academy in the town is helping keep it alive. Currently, around fifty families use Aramaic as their first language. And three times a year they take over the town to hold religious festivals, which attract an estimated 30,000 people from across Syria. The song and dance in these colourful autumn celebrations is the best way to hear this ancient language. In the most stunning of the three events, the Festival of the Fires, a bonfire is lit at the top of the mountain, illuminating singing and dancing that continues late into the night. The street-parties include plenty of local food, and – of course – the legendary Maaloula wine.

477 Soaking up the Masjid i-Imam

IRAN Known to the Persians as Nisf-e-Jahan ("Half the World"), Isfahan – a two-time capital of the Persian Empire – is home to the crowning jewel of Islamic architecture, the stunning Masjid i-Imam mosque. It is said that if you visit all the mosques in Iran, you should visit this one last, as its beauty will supplant your memory of all others.

Built over 26 years, the Safavid-era mosque sits on the southern edge of the Maydan Naqsh i-Jahan, a massive fountained square in central Isfahan where horseriding and polo were once put on for the shah and his court. Stroll around the outside of the mosque to take in the wild collection of diverse motifs, colours and calligraphic designs that adorn the various portals, walls and vaults. In the centre of it all is a beguiling, 54m-high bulbous dome. On either side of the main prayer hall courtyard are the halls of a *medrese*, an important Islamic school in use until the nineteenth century.

Enter the mosque through its enveloping front portal, its foundation of white marble supporting a facade of rich floral calligraphy, moulded niches, gorgeous azure tilework and slender, rocket-like patterned minarets that shoot up 48m towards the heavens, their balconies still reverberating with the trebly calls to prayer of Isfahan's muezzins. Follow the corridor through to the inner courtyard, where a reflective washing pool is encircled by four porched, blue-and-yellow walls, each leading to its own *iwan* (vaulted space). The southern entrance gives way to a central sanctuary, whose domed ceiling – the same dome you just saw from the outside – is bedecked with golden rose floral designs surrounded by breathtaking mosaics. The usual silence of Islamic holy places is likely to be broken here by the clapping hands and giggles of children testing out the dome's renowned echo. To capture a memorable photograph of the whole thing, visit the Ali Qapu pavilion, just across the square, home to views that are simply magnificent.

478 On the incense trail in Arabia Felix

OMAN In antiquity, the Romans knew southern Arabia – the area of modern Yemen and the far southwestern tip of Oman – as Arabia Felix, meaning fortunate. This rugged land was so named for its fabulous wealth, derived from trade in exotic goods such as spices, perfumes, ivory and alabaster (most of them brought from India) and, above all, locally cultivated frankincense and myrrh.

The incense trail was followed, in ancient times, by camel caravan from Salalah, regional capital of Oman's Dhofar region and traditionally regarded as the source of the world's finest frankincense, to Petra in Jordan.

Plunging into the alleys of Salalah's souk is a heady experience. Here, hemmed in by coconut groves, stalls and shops are crammed tightly together, offering everything from snack foods to textiles and jewellery. The air is filled with the cries of hawkers, the sweet smell of perfumes and the rich, lemony scents of frankincense and myrrh.

Prohibitively expensive commodities in the ancient world, frankincense and myrrh were offered by two of the wise men as gifts to the newborn Christ. They were also essential to religious ritual in every temple in every town. Buying them today is a fascinating business: shopkeepers will show you crystals of varying purity, sold by grade and weight; sniff each before choosing. Coals and an ornate little pottery burner complete the purchase.

After Salalah, you can follow your own incense trail and, if spending several months on a camel to Petra doesn't appeal, try driving west towards the Yemeni border on a spectacular coast road that skirts undeveloped beaches before climbing into mountains lush with frankincense trees – or head for the lost city of Ubar, legendary centre of Arabia's frankincense trade, reputed to lie near Shisr, the location of Oman's most highly prized groves.

479 Blazing a trail at Dana Nature Reserve

JORDAN When you think of eco-friendly travel, the Middle East might not immediately spring to mind. In environmental terms, the region is a disaster, characterized by a general lack of awareness of the issues and poor – if any – legislative safeguards. But Jordan is quietly working wonders, and the impact in recent years of the country's Royal Society for the Conservation of Nature (RSCN) has been striking: areas of outstanding natural beauty are now under legal protection and sustainable development is squarely on the political agenda.

The RSCN's flagship project is the Dana Nature Reserve, the Middle East's first truly successful example of sustainable tourism. Until 1993, Dana was dying: the stone-built mountain village was crumbling, its land suffering from hunting and overgrazing and locals were abandoning their homes in search of better opportunities in the towns.

Then the RSCN stepped in and set up the Dana Nature Reserve, drawing up zoning plans to establish wilderness regions and semi-intensive use areas where tourism could be introduced, building a guesthouse and founding a scientific research station. Virtually all the jobs – tour guides, rangers, cooks, receptionists, scientists and more – were taken by villagers.

Today, over eight hundred local people benefit from the success of Dana, and the reserve's running costs are covered almost entirely from tourism revenues. The guesthouse, with spectacular views over the V-shaped Dana Valley, continues to thrive while a three-hour walk away in the hills lies the idyllic *Rummana* campsite, from where you can embark on dawn excursions to watch ibex and eagles.

But the reserve also stretches down the valley towards the Dead Sea Rift – and here, a memorable five-hour walk from the guesthouse, stands the *Feinan Wilderness Lodge*, set amidst an arid sandy landscape quite different from Dana village. The lodge is powered by solar energy and lit by candles; with no road access at all, it's a bewitchingly calm and contemplative desert retreat.

480

OFF-ROADING FOR REAL:
across the dunes to Khor al-Adaid

QATAR In southern Qatar, the roads simply stop, swallowed by fuming waves of sand. Every weekend, countless Qatari 4WD enthusiasts make the pilgrimage to the desert to push their vehicles to the limit and find solitude in a shifting world of shimmering heat and rolling dunes.

Moussad introduced himself with a beaming smile, which matched his white *thobe* (floor-length white robe) and headscarf. He ushered the four of us – all excited Westerners – into his latest-model Toyota Landcruiser and took off for the dunes.

Moussad is one of many tour drivers who whisk tourists out of Doha, Qatar's main city, down to the desert for a day of adventure. After an hour's drive south on a pot-holed freeway, huge sand dunes loomed on the horizon marking the end of the road. Numerous 4WDs were parked up in the shadows, their drivers scurrying from tyre to tyre letting out air for better traction on the slippery sand.

Loud hip-hop and techno blared from the assembled entourage of expensive cars, Qatar's modern day equivalent of the camel – gone are their plodding steeds of yesteryear, exchanged for faster, gruntier and air-conditioned contemporaries that are thirstier and also tend to roll more often.

Moussad cranked the volume up and charged into the desert, roaring up near-vertical walls of sand and carving down steep slopes sideways, skilfully riding the dunes in his 4WD like a surfer riding a wave or a snowboarder riding a mountain, but with added horsepower.

As the day came to an end, deep shadows accentuated the desert's sensuous curves. The sun hung low in the sky like a red orb and reflected across Khor al-Adaid, the inland sea bordering Saudi Arabia.

481 Watch galloping camels and their robot riders

KUWAIT A stampede of two-year-old camels tears down the racetrack, their sinewy tan bodies stirring up brown dust as they speed along, trying to outpace the other camels nearby. Crops flick across their backsides – but this is not the work of an overzealous jockey. Instead, strapped across the back of each camel ride remote-controlled robots, limbless mechanical boy-sized torsos bucking with every stride.

Keeping pace in the Kuwaiti desert just beyond the track railing, a fleet of modern "ships of the desert" – SUVs and minivans – pursues the dromedaries. In them sit the camels' owners, expertly manoeuvring the whips by remote control.

Radio-controlled jockeys are new, having spread across Kuwait and several other Arabian countries after laws banning child jockeys – some of whom were as young as four – were passed. In Kuwait, they take the form of wrapped cylinders with faceless sock monkey-heads. At some events, plastic human-shaped heads adorn the robots.

The robots and chase cars are all products of the modern world. But camel racing is part of Kuwait's cultural heritage, and the audience, sitting atop overstuffed, black leather armchairs and comfortably ensconced in an air-conditioned glass pavilion, is still full of men dressed in traditional Kuwaiti robes and white headdresses. Children of businessmen and sheikhs frolic on the maroon carpets. Strangers are offered tea – "One hump or two?" – or even camel's milk.

A distant pounding echoes and the crowd quiets down. The camels are coming. Teacups are set aside as attention shifts from the flat-screen television monitors showing distant action to the finish line right in front of the clubhouse. It's a close call, but the jockeys seem far from fazed.

482 Swimming the Wadi Shab

OMAN If Adam and Eve had carried Omani passports, they'd probably have bitten into their poison apple somewhere in the waters of Wadi Shab. Arguably the country's most enchanting destination, the edenic Wadi Shab ("Gorge of Cliffs" in Arabic) runs full of water for much of the year thanks to a series of flash floods and torrential rains. Here, the region's barren rocky desert plains give way to a heavenly oasis decorated with natural, shallow pools of aquamarine water, verdurous plantations and cascading waterfalls, with caverns, grottoes, crevices and sheer rock faces providing a haven from the beating sun.

From the fishing village of Quriyat, follow the bumpy coastal track alongside stretches of white beach to arrive at the wadi, bordering a lake. Hop in one of the small rope-pulled ferries to traverse the lagoon, plying your way through the oleander and brush, from where you'll enter a steep, rifted valley, overgrown and shaded with trees, grasses and date palms. Lazily wade through the azure waters – which should only come up to your knees – before making your way up for a hike along the craggy, winding hills, during which you might even come upon an Omani family, ready to offer traditional dates and coffee. After a good two hours of medium-intensity trekking, you'll arrive at a cave that drops down to a shimmering pool of water. Perch yourself on the ladder and climb down for a well-earned swim with schools of iridescent kingfishers. Now the tricky part: you'll need to swim through a small keyhole opening in the cavern rock to access a small subaquatic channel. But it's a worthy endeavour, as the channel leads to a second cavernous pool that empties into the mouth of the wadi itself, where the idyllic, sandy Fins Beach is adorned with fishing boats and makes a perfect spot for a picnic – assuming you've remembered to waterproof your packed lunch.

483 Masada: conquering Herod's hilltop palace

ISRAEL & THE PALESTINIAN TERRITORIES The steep cliffs rising out of the Judean Desert look like an unlikely place for a fortress, but there, 400m up, overlooking the Dead Sea, sits the legendary stronghold of Masada. Masada was first fortified by Herod the Great in the late first century BC, who was apparently so scared his people would revolt that he built this virtually impenetrable fortress. There's a cable car for those who don't fancy taking one of the various different paths that lead up the hill, but to get the feeling that you really conquered Masada, opt for the ancient snake path, which winds its unsheltered way up the eastern side – an exhausting forty-minute walk. Your reward is an archeological site that appears to dangle over the edge of the precipice, and tremendous views across the desert and the Dead Sea.

484 Visiting the hanging village of Habalah

SAUDI ARABIA Appearing to dangle from a 250m cliff face over a deep valley, the deserted village of Habalah is a truly unique settlement. It takes its name from "habl", meaning "rope" – a reference to the ladders that the long-gone inhabitants used to descend to their dwellings from the plateau above.

These days, a cable car runs visitors down to the village, offering outstanding views over the dramatic Arabian landscape along the way. Built out of the rock on which they stand, the houses offer a fascinating insight into traditional Saudi life, and give a whole new meaning to the phrase "living on the edge".

NEED to know

440 Serjilla lies 7km east of Bara. The nearest facilities are in Idleb.

441 Acre is 25km north of Haifa, served by buses and trains from there and Tel Aviv.

442 The trekking season runs Dec–Feb. Bus services are limited, so renting a car works better. *Adventure Trekking in Oman*, by Anne Dale and Jerry Hadwin, is the best text and has reasonable maps.

443 Hammam Nur ad-Din (daily 8am–midnight) is strictly men-only. Hammam al-Qaimariyya (daily 7am–midnight) is one of several in Damascus with women-only hours (noon–5pm).

444 *Abu Shukri*'s is at the fifth station of the cross on the Via Dolorosa, near the Damascus gate.

445 There are hotels and public beaches on the eastern shore near Swaymeh (Jordan) and on the western shore at Ain Feshkha (in the Palestinian Territories), Ein Gedi and Ein Bokek (both in Israel).

446 See ❂www.saudiembassy.net for information on visas; a small number of tourist visas are issued each year to organized groups.

447 Visit the Krak des Chevaliers as soon as it opens (8.30am) to avoid the crowds.

448 Hama is 47km north of Homs, served by trains and buses between Damascus and Aleppo.

449 Visit the Museum of Pearl Diving in Manama for an insight into the tradition.

450 Tour operators worldwide have diving packages to the Red Sea, and dive centres in Aqaba offer PADI and other international diving courses. Try ❂www.aqabadivingseastar.com, ❂www.rdc.jo, ❂www.aquamarina-group.com or ❂www.diveaqaba.com.

451 Khasab Travel and Tours (❂www.khasabtours.com) runs half- and full-day cruises on the Musandam Fjords; otherwise, try Shaw Travel (❂www.shawtravel.com), who include the Musandam Fjords in some of their Oman itineraries.

452 Regular buses shuttle between the main terminal in Damascus and Palmyra's bus stand; the journey takes 3hr. The site is unfenced, though some of the temples have set hours (generally 8am–sunset). For more information, visit ❂www.syriatourism.org.

453 See ❂www.jumeirah.com/en/hotels-and-resorts/destinations/dubai/burj-al-arab.

454 Khor al-Adaid lies 75km south of Doha, the Qatari capital. No roads run even close. The only way to get here is in a 4WD vehicle organized by any of several tour companies based in Doha: try ❂www.gulf-adventures.com or ❂www.nettoursdubai.com.

455 Tawi Attair is located in southwest Oman. You'll need a 4WD to access the area, which you can hire in nearby Salaha.

456 Buses from Beirut to Baalbek take 2–3hr – see ❂www.baalbeck.org.lb for details.

457 Lebanon's ski season runs late Dec–early April. For current information on runs, resorts, weather conditions and lift prices, check out the website ❂www.skileb.com. All resorts can provide ski and boot rentals as well as classes.

458 The Hammam Abhar is open Mon, Wed & Thurs for men and Tues, Fri & Sat for women. In recent times, Al-Qaeda-linked activity has made Yemen a dangerous place to travel – check the situation with your foreign office.

459 The I-Imam Mosque, Sheikh Lotfollah Mosque and Ali Qapu Palace are all open daily (approx. 8am–sunset).

460 Operators offering dolphin-watching trips include ❂www.arabianseasafaris.com and ❂www.zaharatours.com.

461 The country's finest meze restaurants are in the town of Zahlé, just over an hour's drive east of Beirut.

462 Most shops in the Deira Gold Souk follow similar hours (daily 9am–10pm).

463 Even when Israel and Palestine are consumed by conflict, Tel Aviv can seem a world away from trouble, but it's best to check the situation before you travel.

464 The typical taxi fare from Silopi is $20 for the trip and $10 for paperwork, though ensure that your driver agrees to take you to central Zakho, or you may be unceremoniously dropped at the border. Zakho and Dohuk have plenty of accommodation for around $30 per room, and some establishments are quite slick despite being far more used to traders than tourists.

465 You need to get a permit from the small Interior Ministry (Mon–Wed, Sat & Sun 8am–2pm) building on the north side of Maliki Square in Damascus. To get to Quneitra, take a microbus from Soumaria (the main international bus and taxi station) to Khan Arnabah, before getting a taxi on the final stretch through the checkpoints into Quneitra. See ❂www.golan.sy.

466 Petra (daily 6am–sunset) is 240km south of the Jordanian capital, Amman. The adjacent town of Wadi Musa has restaurants and hotels. Check out ❂petranationaltrust.org.

467 Socotra lies 500km south of the Yemeni coast, reached most easily by scheduled flights from Aden or Sanaa. For more go to ❂www.socotraisland.org and ❂www.friendsofsoqotra.org.

468 Saudi Arabia is still one of the world's most inaccessible kingdoms. Non-business visitors can visit as a group travelling with a recognized agency. See ❂tinyurl.com/visitsaudi and ❂www.saudiembassy.net.

469 *Ta Marbuta* is in a side street behind the Antoine Bookshop in the centre of Hamra, *Art Lounge* is opposite the Forum de Beyrouth in the Karantina area (a 10min taxi ride from Achrafiyeh), *Torino Express* is in the heart of Gemmayze, *BO18* is near the Forum de Beyrouth (you'll need a taxi to find it) and *Sky Bar* is on

the top floor of the *Palm Beach Hotel* which is walking distance from Hamra or Downtown.

470 Persian voyages (❂www.persianvoyages.com) can organize a trip to Iran. All visitors require a visa.

471 Wadi Rum lies 300km south of Amman. The best online resource is ❂www.jordanjubilee.com.

472 Various Dubai travel companies offer dhow cruises, including Al-Boom Tourist Village (❂www.alboom.ae), which offers various trips at different prices including lunch and dinner cruises. Al-Mansour (❂www.radissonblu.com/hotels/united-arab-emirates) organizes dinner cruises accompanied by traditional Arab food and music.

473 Fish suppers cost as little as a couple of dollars to take away; a few more served on a table at a simple restaurant. A fresh fruit juice such as pomegranate or red grape makes a great accompaniment. Towns with restaurants offering particularly good fish suppers include Jizan, Al-Hudayda and Al Khawkha on the Red Sea coast. In recent times, Al-Qaeda-linked activity has made Yemen a dangerous place to travel – check the situation with your foreign office.

474 Habiba, Jabri and Zalatimo (❂www.zalatimosweets.com) have numerous stores across Amman.

475 Aleppo is 350km north of Damascus and is accessible by plane, train and bus. Most shops in the souk are open 9am–6pm (closed Fri).

476 Buses to Maaloula go from Abasseen Square in Damascus, next to the football stadium, a 15min walk north of Bab Touma.

477 The mosque is open to visitors daily 8am–5pm (until 7pm during the summer), but it is closed on Friday mornings.

478 Salalah is 1000km southwest of Muscat, served by regular worldwide flights.

479 Check out ❂www.rscn.org.jo.

480 There are numerous tour companies in Qatar offering 4WD trips into the desert; Arabian Adventures (❂www.arabian-adventureqatar.com) is well established and drivers often speak English.

481 Kuwait Camel Racing Club is in Kabd, an hour's drive west of Kuwait City. Races are held most weeks Nov–May, generally on Saturdays – call ahead for the schedule (☎ +965 539 4014 or 4015).

482 Wadi Shab is on the coastal rough between Muscat and Sur and requires a 4WD vehicle to access.

483 Buses run to Masada (❂tinyurl.com/visitmasada) from Jerusalem, Tel Aviv, Beersheba and Eliat.

484 Habalah is located about 75km from Abha, near Saudi Arabia's southwestern tip. Non-business visitors can only come as a group travelling with a recognized agency. See ❂tinyurl.com/visitsaudi and ❂www.saudiembassy.net.

GOOD to know

CITIES

The title of the world's **oldest** continuously occupied city is disputed by several Middle Eastern contenders, including Damascus in Syria, the Palestinian city of Jericho and Jbeil (Byblos) in Lebanon. Cairo, with a population around 17 million, is the **largest** city in the Arab world.

RAILWAYS

The train service running today between Damascus and Amman is a remnant of the **Hejaz Railway**, built by the last Ottoman sultan in 1908 from Damascus to the holy city of Medina, in the Hejaz region of Arabia. The scenic stretch of line from Tel Aviv to Jerusalem, which was built by the British (as the Jaffa–Jerusalem Railway) in 1892, also still has a regular scheduled service. The line was recently upgraded.

Currently, the only railway on the Arabian Peninsula runs from Dammam to Riyadh, though plans are afoot to extend the line to Jeddah, thus connecting the **Red Sea** and the **Gulf**.

> *"Squeeze the past like a sponge, smell the present like a rose and send a kiss to the future"*
>
> **Arab proverb**

DRINK

The Middle East's best-known tipple is **arak**, an aniseed spirit most famously distilled in Lebanon, which – like Israel – also has a thriving wine industry. **Shiraz** once stood at the centre of a renowned wine region. Its name lives on as one of the world's most famous grapes (aka Syrah), though the city itself now lies in Iran, where the production of alcohol is effectively banned. The Middle East's only microbrewery, producing **Taybeh** beer, is located near the Palestinian city of Ramallah.

MOUNTAINS

At 5671m, **Mount Damavand**, in Iran, is higher than any European peak. The summit is reachable in three days of steep walking. **Mount Sinai** (2285m), in Egypt, is venerated by Jews, Christians and Muslims as the place where God revealed the Ten Commandments to Moses. It's a popular spot from which to watch the sun rise. Near Bcharre, on the slopes of **Qornet as-Sawda**, the highest mountain in Lebanon (3090m), stands the last surviving forest of Lebanese cedar trees.

LITERATURE

Naguib Mahfouz is the only writer in Arabic to win the Nobel Prize for Literature, in 1988. His most famous works, including *Midaq Alley* (1947) and *Children of Gebelawi* (1959), evoke Cairo's street life amidst a cast of colourful characters.

S.Y. Agnon is the only writer in Hebrew to win the Nobel Prize for Literature, in 1966. *The Bridal Canopy* (1931) and *Only Yesterday* (1945), two of Agnon's best-known books, use a surreal style to explore conflicts between Jewish tradition and modernity.

Simin Daneshvar's *Suvashun* (1969) explores themes of modernity in her home town of Shiraz, and is the best-selling novel ever written in Persian.

WILDLIFE PRESERVATION

The Arabian **oryx** is a beautiful, long-horned white antelope that is indigenous to the Middle East. Throughout the twentieth century hunting drastically reduced its numbers, until the last wild oryx was shot in Oman in 1972. **Captive breeding** programmes in the USA, Jordan, Qatar and Oman ensured the survival of the species and oryx have now been reintroduced to the wild in Israel, Jordan, Oman and Saudi Arabia, all of which – along with Qatar and the UAE – maintain herds in wildlife reserves.

INVENTIONS

The **Sumerians**, an ancient people from southeastern Iraq, developed a network of city-states well before 3000 BC – the world's first civilization. Sumerian inventions include the **wheel**, **writing** and **agriculture.** The Sumerian clock, based on a sexagesimal system (60 seconds, 60 minutes, 12 hours), is still in use today.

Around the fifth century BC, mathematicians at Babylon, in Iraq, invented **zero**.

Byblos (or Jbeil, in Lebanon) was the source of the world's first **alphabet**, developed around 1200 BC.

> *"Don't sleep in silk sheets until you've walked across the desert"*
>
> **Persian proverb**

A TRUE DIVA

The Egyptian diva **Umm Kalthoum** (also spelled in a number of other ways, including Oum Kalsoum and Om Kolsum; 1904–1975) remains the best-loved singer in the Arab world, outselling many contemporary stars. At her peak – the 1950s to 1970s – she was able to empty the streets of Cairo and other Arab cities, as people stopped everything to listen to her monthly radio concerts. These were nothing short of epic, often consisting of a four- or five-hour performance of a single song – generally on the themes of love, loss and yearning – to an orchestral accompaniment. An estimated **four million mourners** attended her funeral.

COFFEE

Coffee originated in Ethiopia but was first cultivated as a crop in Yemen a thousand years ago, from where it spread to Mecca, then Cairo, Constantinople and into Europe. The chocolatey-coffee flavour of mocha originated in a natural variety of arabica bean grown near the Yemeni port of Al-Mokha.

SIDESTEPPING ASH AND LAVA ON KILAUEA • MIGHTY REAL IN LAS VEGAS • RIDING HIGH ON THE BLUE RIDGE PARKWAY • RECONSIDERING THE WILD WEST IN MONUMENT VALLEY • STROLLING THROUGH DOWNTOWN SAVANNAH • IN HIGH SPIRITS ON THE BOURBON TRAIL • FINDING PARADISE ON KAUAI'S NORTH SHORE • SPENDING A WEEKEND IN WINE COUNTRY • SCOPING OUT THE SCENE ON MIAMI'S OCEAN DRIVE • SLEEPING NEAR THE CORNER IN WINSLOW • CHASING STORMS IN TORNADO ALLEY • CATCHING A BASEBALL GAME AT WRIGLEY FIELD • CELEBRATING FANTASY FEST IN KEY WEST • HITTING THE TRACK AT THE INDIANAPOLIS 500 • WOLF-WATCHING IN YELLOWSTONE NATIONAL PARK • A BILLION-DOLLAR CIRCUS FOR THE TWENTY-FIRST CENTURY • HIKING HALF DOME IN YOSEMITE • FEELING THE BLUES AT A DELTA JUKE JOINT • THE QUINTESSENTIAL SNACK IN AMERICA'S FOOD CAPITAL • A NIGHT AT THE LOBSTER POUND • JUMPING THROUGH HOOPS TO SEE THE HULA • CASTLES OF SAND: ACTING LIKE A KID AT CANNON BEACH • BED, BARRACUDA AND BREAKFAST: JULES' UNDERSEA LODGE • CHECKING THE PROGRESS OF THE CRAZY HORSE MEMORIAL • ANGLING FOR BROWN BEARS AT BROOKS FALLS • WITNESSING POWER IN ACTION ON CAPITOL HILL • SEA KAYAKING IN PRINCE WILLIAM SOUND • CEDAR POINT: THE ROLLER COASTER CAPITAL OF THE WORLD • MAKING A MESS WITH MARYLAND CRABS • LEAVING IT ALL BEHIND ON THE APPALACHIAN TRAIL • BURNING MAN FESTIVAL • LEAF-PEEPING ALONG ROUTE 100 • CRUISING THE INSIDE PASSAGE • GAZING AT A NANTUCKET SUNSET • GETTING IN LINE AT MARDI GRAS • TOURING GRACELAND • TRUSTING IN TUSTY ON THE ALASKA MARINE HIGHWAY • GOING NATIVE IN THE LAND OF THE BLUE-GREEN WATER • CALIFORNIA IN A CONVERTIBLE: DRIVING THE LENGTH OF HIGHWAY 1 • STALKING THE PILGRIM FATHERS OF PLYMOUTH • GOING BATTY IN AUSTIN • PAYING HOMAGE TO COUNTRY MUSIC • BIKING THE GOLDEN GATE BRIDGE • DEATH BY ICE CREAM AT BEN & JERRY'S • HANG-GLIDING THE OUTER BANKS • TRAVELLING THE TURQUOISE TRAIL • UP CLOSE WITH ALLIGATORS ON THE ANHINGA TRAIL • RIDING THE SLICKROCK IN MOAB • PLAYING BALL AT THE FIELD OF DREAMS • SKIING AT SNOWBIRD AND ALTA • GOING TO THE SUN IN GLACIER NATIONAL PARK • EATING BARBECUE IN TEXAS HILL COUNTRY • ATTENDING A CEREMONIAL DANCE AT TAOS PUEBLO • PADDLING IN THE PACIFIC • LUNCHING ON CREOLE CUISINE IN NEW ORLEANS • TRACING CIVIL RIGHTS HISTORY IN MONTGOMERY • TAKING THE A-TRAIN THROUGH MANHATTAN • GETTING GOSPEL IN HARLEM • LOST FOR WORDS AT THE GRAND CANYON • SNOWSHOEING ON SAWTOOTH • ON THE TRAIL

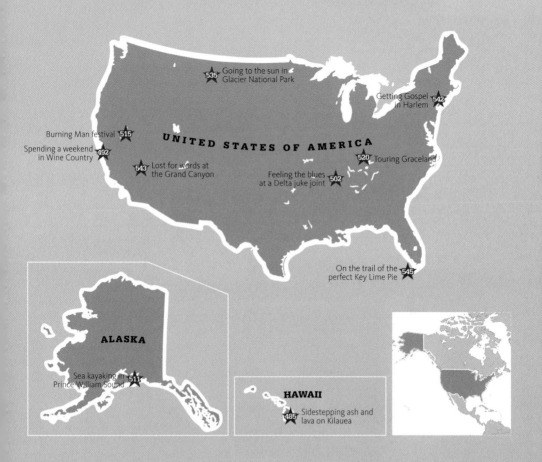

535 Going to the sun in Glacier National Park

Getting Gospel 542 in Harlem

Burning Man festival 515

Spending a weekend 492 in Wine Country

UNITED STATES OF AMERICA

543 Lost for words at the Grand Canyon

520 Touring Graceland

Feeling the blues 502 at a Delta juke joint

On the trail of the 545 perfect Key Lime Pie

ALASKA

Sea kayaking in 511 Prince William Sound

HAWAII

485 Sidestepping ash and lava on Kilauea

HAWAII The Hawaiian islands are the summits of volcanoes rooted 20,000ft below the Pacific. Kilauea, on the Big Island, is the youngest of these volcanoes, and it's been erupting continuously ever since 1983. Mark Twain described its crater as a dazzling lake of fire, but the action these days is lower down its flanks, where molten lava explodes directly into the ocean.

I parked my car where the Chain of Craters Road, which winds from the crater down to the sea, was abruptly blocked by fresh black lava. No path set off beyond; instead I picked my way through broken slabs, and stepped across mysterious cracks, dodging the vapours that hissed from gashes in the rock. I finally found myself ten feet above the crashing waves, on a precarious "bench" of lava. Down at sea level, a sluggish river of incandescent rock churned into the water, amid plumes of steam and evil-smelling gases. Other hikers prodded at the eggshell crust with sticks, to see if they could break through to the river beneath their feet and set the wood ablaze.

I stayed until the sun went down, and the molten glow of the lava was the only light. A small cone of fine ash had formed at the seafront. As I climbed it, my feet sank deep with every step, and sent a fine powder slithering around me. From the top I looked down into a fiery orange pool that gently bubbled and popped, sending up phlegmy strings of rock.

There were three or four people nearby, silhouetted against the orange clouds. A sudden thud from below, solid as a hammer stroke, made my knees buckle. As I turned, the volcano nonchalantly spewed a shower of rocks high into the air. Now I felt entitled to run, though wading through thick volcanic ash felt more like a slow-motion nightmare. I struggled to speed up, all too aware that it was a matter of pure luck whether any of the lumps overhead would hit me.

As it turned out, a glowing boulder larger than my head thumped down six feet away. I crept back to examine it, bright orange on the black moonscape, then stumbled away through the night.

485

Sidestepping ash and lava on Kilauea

NO PARKING

486 Mighty Real in Las Vegas

NEVADA New York City has its skyscrapers, Cairo its pyramids, Paris the Eiffel Tower, Venice its canals. Las Vegas? It's got all the above, and then some.

People travel round the globe in search of the authentic. But you won't find this in Vegas. In its place are simulacra, kitschy homage and pure, unadulterated spectacle. Here, in the middle of the Nevada Desert, hotel entrepreneurs play an ever-higher-stakes game of "Can you top this?", and everything has to be newer, bigger and brighter than before. In fact, the newness of everything is a fake, too. What's new really means what's been done before and re-imagined. The Forum Shops at *Caesars Palace*? A cunningly themed shopping mall that's an indoor re-creation of Rome's open-air bazaar, where the "sky" (well, the ceiling) changes as the day goes on. Nobu Matsuhisa's inviting namesake restaurant in the *Hard Rock Hotel*? A splashier replica of his original, internationally acclaimed raw-fish emporium in Manhattan. It's no wonder that so much of the big-ticket night-time entertainment is centred on magicians and gravity-defying acts like Cirque du Soleil. The whole of Las Vegas is an illusion, and one that to most people is utterly irresistible – and, just as importantly, unabashedly, trashily American. Who needs the whiff of authenticity when you've got all this in one place? The smoky glass pyramid of the *Luxor*, from which emanates the world's most powerful beam of light, is heralded by an enormous sphinx. The choreographed fountains at the giant lake in front of the *Bellagio* can't help but thrill. You can ride on a gondola at *The Venetian* – inside the hotel – or a roller-coaster at *New York-New York*. Most importantly, you can sustain the illusion for as long as you want – or can afford. No wonder no one ever wants to leave.

487 Riding high on the Blue Ridge Parkway

VIRGINIA & NORTH CAROLINA Slicing through some of the most stunning scenery in the country, the Blue Ridge Parkway winds its way along the crest of the Appalachian Mountains, from Shenandoah National Park in Virginia to Great Smoky Mountains National Park between North Carolina and Tennessee. Once dotted with isolated frontier communities where bluegrass was born, today you'll find traces of the region's history – like old gristmills, abandoned wooden barns and ramshackle diners – scattered along the road, but in truth much of what has been preserved is aimed squarely at the tourist trade. What the parkway is best for is simply a heavy dose of nature at its finest.

The first part of the drive cuts through northern Virginia, and here the ridge is very apparent, sometimes narrowing to a ledge not much wider than the road. The central section is much less dramatic – the land is heavily farmed and the road busier with local traffic, especially around Roanoke. But the lower highway, which snakes through North Carolina, is the most spectacular part. There's plenty of kitschy development here (the town of Blowing Rock is a full-scale resort, with shopping malls and themed motels), but the views are astonishing – at nearby Grandfather Mountain, on Hwy-221 one mile south of the parkway, a mile-high swinging bridge hangs over an 80ft chasm with 360-degree views.

Further south, near Mount Pisgah, the road reaches its highest point. As you ascend towards it you'll have numerous chances to stop at overlooks, or just pull onto the shoulder, for breathtaking vistas: hazy blue ridges, smothered in vast swathes of hickory, dogwood and birch, and groves of mountain ash bursting with orange berries.

488 Reconsidering the Wild West in Monument Valley

ARIZONA When you think of the American West, it's hard to conjure a more iconic image than Monument Valley, with its awesome mesas, spires of jagged sandstone and arid, desert-like plains. This is the Wild West of popular culture – a vast, empty landscape that dates back to antiquity and can make you feel at once tiny and insignificant and completely free and uninhibited. These qualities have made it the perfect location for Westerns, which is perhaps why it seems so familiar: *Stagecoach*, *The Searchers* and *How the West Was Won* are among the numerous movies that have been filmed here.

But while Hollywood favours heroic cowboys on stallions, you won't be restaging the gunfight at the OK Corral while here (head south to Tombstone, Arizona for that). Instead, this is sacred Indian country managed by the Navajo Nation, and to visit the area today is to experience the West through their eyes. From the Anasazi petroglyphs in Mystery Valley to the traditional hogans still inhabited by local Navajo, every rock here tells a story. The valley's most famous formations – like the twin buttes of the Mittens, with their skinny "thumbs" of sandstone, and the giant bulk of Hunt's Mesa – can be seen from the circular, seventeen-mile track (starting at the Visitors' Center) that's usually smothered in red dust. Navajo guides, who fill you in on local history and culture, lead 4WD rides around the track, as well as longer, usually overnight, expeditions on foot. These may start before dawn, allowing you to reach the top of a mesa before it gets too hot and watch the sunrise across a land where sand and rock stretch endlessly before you to the horizon.

489 Strolling through downtown Savannah

GEORGIA When an intrepid British Utopian named James Oglethorpe founded Savannah in 1733, he thought he could tame the local marshes and alligators without the aid of slaves or – more preposterous – hard liquor. The latter ban fell by the wayside less than twenty years later, and Savannahians have been devoted to immoderation ever since. Any walking tour of the three-square-mile downtown historic district should, for tradition's sake, be accompanied by a cold beer in a perfectly legal "to-go cup". (The traditional local tipple, Chatham Artillery Punch, is more safely appreciated sitting down, however.)

One element of Oglethorpe's vision that did stick was the city's layout – a repetition of grids and squares that have become 21 miniature parks, each offering a different proportion of dappled shade, fountains and monuments. The squares are most alluring in the spring, when the azalea, dogwood and honey-rich magnolia trees are in full bloom. But even in the thick of an August heat wave, when the air is like a sauna and the greenery is growing wildly up the cast-iron balconies, the squares offer a respite from the untamed mugginess. The sunlight shimmers through craggy oak boughs and Spanish moss, the cicadas drone and cars motor laconically around the cobblestone streets. The stately homes that face each square represent all of the most decadent styles of the eighteenth and nineteenth centuries: Neoclassical, Federal, Regency, Georgian, French Second Empire and Italianate.

"The Belle of Georgia", as the city is known, hasn't always been so; for much of the twentieth century, decadence had slipped into outright decay. But in 1955, seven elderly ladies banded together against developers to prevent the 1821 Davenport House from being turned into a parking lot, and the Historic Savannah Foundation was born. Fortunately, no such effort is required of today's casual visitor – you can just stroll, sip your drink and watch the centuries roll by.

490 In high spirits on the Bourbon Trail

KENTUCKY What is the spirit of the United States? Ask an average citizen or, worse, a politician, and you may get a rambling metaphysical reply longer than the Bill of Rights. Ask a seasoned bartender, however, and you'll get that rarest of responses, the one-word answer: bourbon.

The country's sole native spirit and, thanks to a congressional declaration, its official one as well, bourbon is a form of whiskey. Technically speaking, the grain used to make bourbon must be at least 51 percent corn, and it must be aged for a minimum of two years inside charred, white-oak barrels – though both the percentage and years are typically much greater. And while bourbon can be produced elsewhere, the spirit of the spirit resides in Kentucky, home to the finest distilleries as well as, according to local legend, its birthplace, where late eighteenth-century settlers in Bourbon County combined their extra corn harvests with local iron-free water to make the fabled whiskey.

The best place to find out more is along the Bourbon Trail, a meandering route through the rolling hills of central Kentucky that links several distilleries and historic towns. Must-sees include Loretto, where you can watch the deliciously smooth Maker's Mark being produced in a picture-perfect setting laced with green pastures and well-preserved nineteenth-century buildings like the Master Distiller's House, and the Jim Beam Distillery an hour's drive away in Clermont, whose pedestrian main brand is augmented by several "small batch" potions, like the fiery Knob Greek and silky Basil Hayden's, which can be sampled on-site.

Tucked in between the two of these is friendly Bardstown, the state's second-oldest city and best base along the Bourbon Trail, home to the Oscar Getz Museum of Whiskey History and September's lively Bourbon Festival. Book a bed at the *Old Talbott Tavern*, whose former guests have included Abraham Lincoln and Daniel Boone, and you'll only have a few steps to walk after an evening spent using your newfound knowledge comparing local bourbons at the bar.

491 Finding paradise on Kauai's north shore

HAWAII Kauai is the Hawaii you dream about. Spectacular South Seas scenery, white-sand beaches, pounding surf, laid-back island life – it's all here. While the other Hawaiian islands have the above to varying degrees, none has quite the breathtaking beauty nor sheer variety of beguiling landscapes of Kauai. And none has a shoreline as magnificent as the Na Pali Coast ("the cliffs" in Hawaiian), where lush valleys are separated by staggering knife-edge ridges of rock, some towering almost 3000ft tall and all clad in glowing green vegetation that makes them resemble vast pleated velvet curtains.

The one road that circles Kauai peters out on the North Shore. Shrinking ever narrower to cross a series of one-lane wooden bridges, it finally gives up where lovely Ke'e Beach nestles at the foot of a mighty mountain. Swim out a short distance here, and you'll glimpse the mysterious, shadowy cliffs in the distance, dropping into the ocean.

Now deserted, the remote valleys beyond the end of the road once supported large Hawaiian populations, who navigated the fearsome waves between them in canoes. The only way to reach the valleys these days is on foot. One of the world's great hikes, the eleven-mile Kalalau Trail is a long, muddy scramble: one moment you're perched high above the Pacific on an exposed ledge, and the next you're wading a fast-flowing mountain stream. Your reward at the far end – an irresistible campsite on a long golden beach, where you can breathe the purest air on Earth, explore the tumbling waterfalls of Kalalau Valley and then gaze at the star-filled sky into the night – is a little slice of heaven.

492 SPENDING A WEEKEND IN
Wine Country

CALIFORNIA With its rolling green hills, bucolic landscapes and small towns heavy on antique charm, California's Wine Country, centring on Napa and Sonoma valleys, is one of the most beautiful places in the West. Beyond touring the wineries – Beringer, Silver Oak, Stag's Leap, Robert Mondavi and many more, all of which allow you to sample the goods – there's no shortage of things to see and do. Come here for a weekend retreat (preferably not at the peak of summer, when the hordes descend), and your first instinct might be to pack in as much as possible. But in a place where the main point is to relax, indulge and melt away the stresses of modern life, that's the last thing you should do.

Instead, aim for just a few choice tastes of the good life. Start with a spot of nature, either driving the Silverado Trail (parallel to Hwy-29), taking in the mountains and vineyards along the way, or enjoying a peaceful walk through the woods in Jack London State Historic Park, once ranchland owned by the famed naturalist writer. Next, rest your aching bones and revitalize your senses by checking into one of the luxury spa resorts near Calistoga. At Dr Wilkinson's Hot Springs, dip yourself in a mix of heated mineral water and volcanic ash, or at Mount View Spa, enjoy the mud baths and herbal applications, as well as aromatherapy, hydrotherapy and other refined New Age treatments that pamper both the body and soul.

Round out your experience with a great, even legendary, meal at one of the region's many gourmet restaurants; these days the area is known as much for food as the vino. Foremost among these is Thomas Keller's *French Laundry*, an icon of California Cuisine known for its blend of fresh local ingredients and creative, spellbinding presentation. It won't come cheap and you'll have to reserve months in advance, but it's reason enough to visit.

Miami's Ocean Drive

FLORIDA At sundown, the main promenade of Miami's hedonistic South Beach was like a gigantic movie set, where several different films were being shot simultaneously.

A 1978 Mustang pulled up outside the *Kent Hotel* and three Latino men, designer shirts unbuttoned almost down to the navel and sporting heavy gold chains, stepped out in what could have been a scene from *Scarface*. A bronzed male rollerblader in a "Gold's Gym" tank top weaved between the pedestrian traffic that crept past the thoroughfare's swanky cocktail lounges, thrusting his hips from left to right, a gasping Pomeranian struggling to keep up. Cheesy gay porn sprang to mind. Crossing the road in the direction of the beach brought the area's famed Art Deco buildings perfectly into view – a strip of pastel yellows, blues and oranges bathed so dramatically in the fading sunlight that you could have been standing in the middle of a Disney cartoon.

As sunbathers gradually left the beach, a couple of real-life Barbie dolls with tiny waists and enormous chests lingered on the sand to be filmed for some dubious Internet site. The poolside at the *Clevelander* began to fill up with Spring Break schmoozers and girls with plenty of potential for going wild. Electronic music that earlier had drifted gently from hotel lobbies was now being pumped out in energetic beats, heralding the transformation of twilight's languorous Ocean Drive into night-time's frenetic strip of revelry – clubbers flashed synthetically manufactured smiles as they hurried to the latest place to be seen. Pretty hostesses talked to you when you stopped to have a look at the expensive restaurant menu they were touting, and the waitress at the *Kent* scribbled her number on a napkin when the three Latinos from the Mustang slapped down a generous tip.

Just another day in the neighbourhood.

494 Sleeping near the Corner in Winslow

ARIZONA The Eagles may have sung about "standin' on the corner in Winslow, Arizona" – Standin' on the Corner Park supposedly marks the spot – but things at this desert outpost have been pretty sleepy since interstate I-40 supplanted Route 66.

Strange place, then, to find the most magical hotel in America. La Posada is the masterpiece of pioneering Southwestern architect Mary Jane Colter. For the last and greatest of the Fred Harvey company's railroad hotels, she was given the opportunity to create a showpiece property from the ground up, with complete control over everything from the overall design to the interior decor.

Although in reality the whole place was built in 1929, Colter gave it an intricate backstory, a romantic previous life as a Spanish-style hacienda – laid out by a Hispanic cattle baron in the 1860s, it was expanded as he grew rich, and finally "converted" into a hotel. The sprawling complex combined Mexican antiques and local craftsmanship with the Art Deco trimmings and fancy innovations expected by 1930s travellers. With the decline of the railroads, La Posada closed in 1957; Colter herself died a year later, after sadly observing: "There's such a thing as living too long."

Forty years later, however, La Posada reopened, restored by enthusiasts who proclaim: "We are not hoteliers – for us this is about art." This is no lifeless museum, however; it's bursting with earthy Southwestern style and imaginative adornments, not least the dazzling modernist canvases by co-owner Tina Mion that bedeck the public spaces. Each guest room is individually furnished – fittings range from hand-carved four-poster beds and inlaid wooden floors to deeply luxurious Jacuzzis – and named after illustrious former guests from John Wayne to Shirley Temple.

A fabulous restaurant, designed to mimic the dining car of the Santa Fe Railroad's Super Chief, and using Colter's original Pueblo-influenced tableware, serves contemporary Southwestern cuisine, using ingredients like Navajo-raised lamb and wild turkey. And irresistibly, this is still a railroad station, even if the former ticketing area and waiting rooms now serve as cosy public lounges; doors from the lobby lead straight to the platform, and the distant sound of train whistles provide a haunting backdrop to your slumbers.

495 Chasing storms in Tornado Alley

KANSAS, NEBRASKA & OKLAHOMA The central plains may not seem the likeliest of places to find a weather wonder, but every long, hot summer these cornfield-flat states play witness to some of the most powerful storms on Earth. In fact, Mother Nature gets so aggressive around here, and with such consistency, that the area – along with Texas – has been dubbed "Tornado Alley" thanks to the record number of funnel and wedge tornadoes that batter its turf each year. This is ideal twister-tracking territory. Behind every great storm is an even greater equipped team of daredevil stormchasers who specialize in stalking tornados across the central plains from vans loaded with the latest in GPS systems, Doppler radars, satellites and lightning-detector sensors. You can join these professionals on the hunt, keeping an eye on the skies as they try to anticipate growing storms. With every cloud-gathering there is a tingle of expectation, and the hope that this is the one they're looking for: a supercell. The Holy Grail of high winds – spreading as far as a mile wide and reaching up to 300mph – this is the biggest and baddest of them all.

496 Catching a baseball game at Wrigley Field

ILLINOIS Home to an iconic, ivy-covered outfield wall, Chicago's Wrigley Field is where America's pastime reaches its apotheosis. Though it dates to 1914, it's neither the oldest nor the smallest ballpark in the major leagues to Boston's equally famed Fenway Park, opened two years earlier). And as for team play... well, the kindest thing to say is that the stadium and the fans that fill it have borne witness to some hard times: the home-team Chicago Cubs haven't won a World Series since 1908, the longest such streak by four decades. But for baseball purists, there's no better place to properly enjoy a game.

Nicknamed "The Friendly Confines" by Cubs' legend Ernie Banks, the idiosyncratic park anchors the buzzing neighbourhood of Wrigleyville. The stadium melds perfectly with its surroundings: along Waveland Avenue, fans wait just outside the low outfield wall hoping to catch a stray home-run (and throw it back on the field, if it's hit by the opposing team), and the views from adjacent apartment rooftops – some sporting grandstands – are better than from the faraway seats in mega-parks elsewhere. If you can't get a ticket, pull up a stool at Murphy's Bleachers or Sheffield's, two of Wrigleyville's finer watering holes – you'll be surrounded by fans decked out in Cubs' colours.

Inside the park, the game feels more like a mammoth picnic than a high-stakes competition, particularly during summer afternoon contests. (The park didn't add lights until 1988, and the majority of Cubs' home games are still played during the day.) It's no stretch to say that fans expect to have fun rather than win: after all, why should things change now? So get a cheap seat with the so-called "Bleacher Bums" and join in the raucous sing-along of "Take Me Out to the Ball Game" during the seventh-inning stretch. If the Cubs don't win, it's really not such a shame.

497 Celebrating Fantasy Fest in Key West

FLORIDA The saucy climax of Key West's calendar, capping the end of hurricane season in October, is a week-long party known as Fantasy Fest. The old town is transformed into an outdoor costume bash, somewhat tenuously pegged to Halloween; really, it's a gay-heavy take on Mardi Gras, with campy themes (past ones have included "Freaks, Geeks and Goddesses" and "TV Jeebies") and flesh-flashing costumes.

The week is punctuated with offbeat events, like the pet costume contest where dogs and their owners dress the same, and a sequin-spangled satire of a high school prom. On Saturday, the final parade slinks down the main drag, Duval Street, on a well-lubricated, booze-fuelled route.

It's not surprising that such an irresistibly kitschy shindig should have emerged and endured in Key West. Save San Francisco, there's nowhere in America more synonymous with out and proud gay life than this final, isolated, all-but-an-island in the Florida Keys – the town's been a byword for homocentric hedonism since the sexually liberated 1970s. But in many ways, Key West's queer reputation is misleading. Sure, it's still a gay hotspot, as the thong-sporting go-go boys, who wield their crotches like weapons in bars along Duval Street, attest. But what drew the gay community here in the first place was the town's liberal, all-inclusiveness; be who you want to be, the locals say, whatever that is. It's all summed up by the town's official motto: "One Human Family". Indeed, Key West welcomes everyone, from President Truman, who holed up in the so-called Little White House here in the 1940s to an oddball bar owner like "Buddy" today, who built his ramshackle café-cum-pub, *B.O.'s Fish Wagon*, out of piles of junk. After a few days, these kind of visual quirks seem quite standard – except maybe that pet costume contest.

498 Hitting the track at the Indianapolis 500

INDIANA "Gentlemen, start your engines!" With that, the crowd noise crescendos to a deafening roar and 33 cars line up to await the start of the most thrilling speedway race in the world. The numbers boggle the mind: five hundred tension-filled laps, speeds topping off around 230mph, more than half-a-million spectators, $10 million-plus in prize money. The Indy 500 is an electrifying experience, not to mention the event that best embodies the American obsession with getting somewhere *fast* – in this case, right back where you started.

Visitors come for the glitz and glamour as well as the star-power of legends like Mario Andretti, hailed as the greatest driver of all time, who conquered Indy in 1969 and now watches his sons, grandson and nephew compete. But the race is not without its homespun midwestern charm: rather than a champagne spray, the winner's celebratory libation is ... milk, a tradition since 1937, after three-time winner Louis Meyer chugged a glass of buttermilk in Victory Lane the year before. The garage area is still referred to as Gasoline Alley, even though the cars run on methanol, and the final practice race is known as "Carb day", despite the switch to fuel-injection systems.

If the earsplitting noise and heart-stopping speeds don't provide enough of a rush, pivoting your foot on the accelerator of a real 600 horsepower V-8 Nascar certainly will. The BePetty School of Racing allows you to experience first hand the thrill of Indy-car racing on the actual Indy track. After being kitted out in racing suits, each class of around twenty aspiring Andrettis is given a crash course in safety, driving instructions and an introduction to the philosophy of "trust the car" before competing for the fastest average lap speed. If your blood's not racing when you step out of the car, you must be made of stone.

499 Wolf-watching in Yellowstone National Park

WYOMING Waking at ink-black 4am to groggily don layers of long underwear is an inauspicious start to a day. And huddling with strangers on a roadside layby a half-hour later, shivering against the well-below-freezing temperature, hardly sounds better. But as a crack of light on the horizon grows and an eerie chorus of hair-raising howls rises from the gloom ahead, your discomfort is soon forgotten. The morning's wolf-watch is already a success. When it was founded in 1872, Yellowstone was celebrated as a wonderland of gushing geysers, where elk and bison roamed freely. But while visitors flocked to the world's first national park to glory in the steady steam of Old Faithful, indigenous animals believed to be a danger to man were trapped and killed at virtually every opportunity. Grey wolves were particularly feared, and the last pack was exterminated in 1926. For nearly seventy years, wolves, once the continent's most abundant predator, were absent from the country's most prized ecosystem.

It took until the winter of 1995 for the first group of Canadian grey wolves to be trucked in under the Roosevelt Arch. Although the reintroduction programme has been a runaway success, the population has been in decline in recent years and, at the time of writing, less than a hundred wolves now roam here. Despite this, a single pack in Yellowstone can live within less than fifty square miles, and the park is still the most reliable place in the wild for watching wolves. The Lamar Valley, where the wolves were all originally released, remains the best spot to catch a glimpse of these complex and social creatures, who rely on teamwork to take down prey in bloody battles but also to raise new pups each spring. Even if you're not fortunate enough to see a wolf, you'll get to interact with the omnipresent wolf-watching parties clustered along the park's highways, exchanging stories of favourite wolves and dramatic hunts between peeks through a line of spotting scopes.

A billion-dollar circus for the twenty-first century

NEVADA If you're heading to Las Vegas to see tassels, feathers and high-kicking showgirls, you're fifty years too late. Things may have been like that when the Rat Pack ruled the roost, but these days, the city's biggest stars are the postmodern Canadian performance troupe Cirque du Soleil, currently running an amazing seven shows.

That the Cirque and the Strip make such a heavenly pair is thanks to the sheer amount of money sloshing around Las Vegas. Selling nine thousand tickets per night, for $100 or more, gives Cirque a million dollars a day to splash out on dare-devil acrobats, flamboyantly inventive costumes and unbelievable special effects. Each show takes place in its own purpose-built theatre, and for anyone interested in the performing arts, the results demand to be seen. What they lack in terms of plot, or even dialogue – the absence of which certainly helps non-English-speaking visitors – they make up for in jaw-dropping spectacle.

Although their highest-profile show is *Love*, a glorious celebration of The Beatles at the *Mirage*, you'll get a better sense of Cirque mastery at *O*, in the *Bellagio*. Its name is a pun on the French for "water", and any part of the stage can suddenly be submerged; seconds after you watch someone walk across a particular spot, a high-diver may plunge fifty feet headfirst into it. A colossal pirate ship, crewed by fearless trapeze artists, swings high over the heads of the audience, and from the aisle beside your seat graceful footmen launch themselves into the air amid swirls of velvet drapery.

Kà, at the *MGM Grand*, is even more astonishing. A martial-arts extravaganza that also incorporates wonderful puppetry and sumptuous costumes, it's the most expensive theatrical production ever staged, anywhere. The set is quite extraordinary; the stage floor can rise, swivel and pivot in every direction. One minute it's a steep cliff-face, to which the performers cling for dear life; the next they simply fall, mid-battle, into the abyss below.

With their flair for making every spectator feel like a participant, and a constant interplay between actors and audience involving planted stooges as well as genuine volunteers, Cirque offers an engrossing experience that's both exhausting and exhilarating in equal measure.

CALIFORNIA Even if you start out at dawn from Yosemite Valley, after five hours you're still not at the top of Half Dome, whose looming, truncated form ("like it had been sliced with a knife") makes it one of the most iconic mountains in North America. The sun is beating down, you're dehydrated and the most challenging section is still ahead. In front of you, rearing up at an impossibly steep angle, lies a vast curving sheet of virtually smooth gray granite. There's no way you'd get a grip in even the best sticky-rubber hiking boots but, fortunately, some determined souls have forged the way, drilling holes in the ancient rock and attaching a series of cables and wooden steps. Help yourself to a pair of leather gloves stashed at the base of the "staircase", grab the cables and haul your way up the final 400ft to the 320-acre summit plateau. It's an exhilarating finish to a superb hike.

From the top, nearly 9000ft up, the dramatic views will render you speechless. Those who dare can edge toward Half Dome's lip and dangle their feet over the side, while the very brave (or very foolish) may inch out along a projecting finger of rock for a vertiginous look straight down the near-vertical face. But neither is necessary to appreciate how far you've come – just turn to gaze back at your route along a section of the famed 212-mile John Muir Trail; even the two magnificent waterfalls you passed – the Vernal and Nevada falls – look puny from this height. Then take in the snowy spine of the Sierra Nevada mountains, the rippling granite sheets that run up to the summit of Cloud's Rest and the wonderland of forests and alpine meadows that comprise Yosemite National Park. Sit back, take a deep breath and enjoy the view.

501 Hiking Half Dome in Yosemite

FEELING THE BLUES
at a **Delta juke joint**

502

MISSISSIPPI The ceilings are often made up of half rotted wood, half plastic sheeting and rain drops are collecting in buckets on the stained carpet floor. If you want a drink, your choices are simple: beer or whiskey served in a plastic cup. From the outside on a weekend night these places often look abandoned, with assorted junk piled up against the front wall. But open the door after 10pm, and you'll find one of the most influential musical genres of the past century in full swing, with a hard drinking, hard partying crowd grooving and shaking to some of the Delta's finest bluesmen – who are usually stuffed into a corner with their battered guitars and primitive PAs, but making enough noise to be heard three zip codes away.

The blues originated in the early 1900s in the cotton fields of the Mississippi Delta and juke joints flourished as the only places where black people could gather and hear this new music, invented by black workers in the sordid working conditions of the fields.

Rough shacks with few amenities, sporadic opening times and often far from the centre of town, many of the joints still operating today have changed little from the times when the likes of Robert Johnson, the king of the Delta blues singers, performed in the 1930s.

Live music is guaranteed on weekends and could come from gnarled white country boys with one battered slide guitar, dungarees and a ZZ Top-esque beard, or from nattily attired black bluesmen armed with electric guitars, drums and bass.

The Delta is still a racially divided area – the poorest region of the poorest state in the US. *Red's*, on the outskirts of Clarksdale in a residential area straight out of *The Wire*, and *Po'Monkey's*, located in a field a few miles from Merigold, are patronized by an eclectic mixture of predominantly local characters. Expect to embrace conversation with music lovers, beer swillers and tall-tale tellers, all of whom need little excuse to hit the dance floor. A visit to a juke joint remains one of the most grittily authentic nights out in the States – just be sure to avoid hitting those buckets as you dance.

503 The quintessential snack in America's food capital

NEW YORK The long list of things to try is staring you in the face. Overstuffed pastrami sandwich at *Katz's Deli*. Foot-long hot dog out at *Nathan's* on Coney Island. Eight-course tasting menu costing a couple of hundred dollars at *Jean Georges*, or *Per Se* or *Gramercy Tavern*. Soup dumplings for next to nothing at any number of Chinatown holes-in-the-wall. Brunch at an impossibly cute West Village café. The bistro burger, washed down with a $2 McSorley's, at *Corner Bistro*. Then again, this is why you came to New York.

But there's one grave omission, one that may well be the most "New York" dish of all. And it's got everything to do with the water. At least that's what they say: a crusty yet chewy New York bagel, first boiled in that water before being baked, is just better because of it. Whether that comes near to the truth, no snack is more symbolic of the city than a bagel with cream cheese, piled high with lox (smoked salmon), a few slices of tomato and red onion and perhaps some capers for effect. You can find bagels nearly everywhere, of course, and many claim to be the best, but no one does it quite like *Russ and Daughters*.

It's not a restaurant or diner but an "appetizing" store, family-owned to boot, that has spent four generations brining, baking, whipping and generally perfecting the art of righteous Jewish food. It's mostly known for its smoked fish, and you can't go wrong with any of their salmon offerings (or their whitefish or sable, for that matter). But the salty belly lox, cured rather than smoked, may be most toothsome of all. Lay it over their own home-made, soul-satisfying cream cheese, smeared on a garlic bagel, also made in-house, and you've got the best accompaniment to a cup of coffee and the *New York Times* known to man.

504 A night at the lobster pound

MAINE You're seated at a picnic table at the *Lobster Shack at Two Lights*, which has be one of the most picturesque spots in the country: an unassuming, clapboard restaurant with a storybook lighthouse to the left and craggy cliffs pummelled by an unruly sea to the right. Maine's slogan is "The Way Life Should Be", and here, along its gorgeous, corrugated coastline, you can't help but agree. That is, of course, if you're able to think of anything other than the red, hot challenge in front of you – one freshly steamed Maine lobster, waiting to be cracked open.

Eating Maine lobster is a culinary rite of passage for visitors to the state. It requires tools (nutcracker, teeny-tiny fork), patience and enough hubris to believe that you can look cool even while wearing a disposable bib. It's smart to bring along an experienced lobster slayer; your first lobster can be intimidating, and it's nice to have a bit of guidance (as well as someone to take that requisite embarrassing photograph).

When you're ready to begin, crack the claws in half, pull out the meat with your little fork and dip it in the melted butter. Lobster meat comes well-defended, so be wary of sharp points along the shell. The tail follows the claws: tear it from the body, pushing the meat from the end. Finally (if you're feeling emboldened), pull off the legs to suck out the last bit of flesh. There is no other meat like lobster – tender, sweet, elusive – and in Maine, where lobster is king, the crimson crustacean is celebrated with parades, festivals and an energetic devotion that's shared by everyone.

At its best, a lobster dinner should be an all-around sensory experience. Breathe in the salty ocean breezes. Listen for the booms coming from the lighthouse. Finally, lick the butter off your fingers, remove the bib and give your dining partner a high five – you've just taken part in a Maine institution.

505 Jumping through hoops to see the hula

HAWAII In a state filled with some of the country's most lavish resorts, where you generally go to sleep late and relax on the beach, it's well-nigh perverse to camp in a park, rise before sunset and head on a bus to the top of a mountain – meant to be off-limits to the general public – for the ceremonial beginning of a hula festival. Of course, coming to Molokai in the first place, the Hawaiian island best known for its leper colony, seems somewhat perverse, too. But everything here is so refreshingly unpretentious and uncommercialized that the appeal is soon obvious. As does that of the hula festival, Ka Hula Piko; this is, after all, where the art purportedly began. The sound of the conch shell signals the start. The dancers' movements steadily increase in intensity. The celebration continues under the trees at Papohaku Beach Park, not far from a beautiful strand of golden sand abutting crashing crystal-blue waters. The pre-dawn wake-up call becomes a distant memory.

506 Castles of sand: acting like a kid at Cannon Beach

OREGON Dreaming of a forum for your long-repressed artistic abilities? Hoping to construct a life-size sand-version of Elvis, Jesus or someone else close to your heart, then have it washed away with the afternoon tide?

The annual Sandcastle Day in Cannon Beach offers just the opportunity – along with the chance to have your creation gawked at by thousands of onlookers, in America's oldest sandcastle-building competition. Others may have surpassed it in size since its debut in 1964, but there's something to be said for taking part in the original.

The field is limited to 150 entrants, so you may have some qualms about taking the place of an expert, but don't worry too much; unless you've won in a comp before, you won't be eligible for the "masters" competition – where the architects get serious with their sand.

507 Bed, barracuda and breakfast: Jules' Undersea Lodge

FLORIDA *Jules' Undersea Lodge* – named after intrepid aqua-explorer Jules Verne – began life as a research lab off the coast of Puerto Rico in the 1970s; it was moved to the Florida Keys and converted to its current use in 1986 by a pair of diving buffs and budding hoteliers.

A pod that sits a few feet above the lagoon floor, the lodge has just two smallish guest bedrooms, fitted out with TVs, VCRs, phones and hot showers, plus a fully equipped kitchen and common room. All very ordinary – except, of course, that you are 21 feet below the sea. Expert scuba divers can spend up to 22 hours exploring the marine habitat each day – safety regulations permit no longer than that; first-timers, meanwhile, need only take a three-hour tutorial on the basics of underwater swimming and survival before they can duck down for check-in.

(Fitful types will sleep with the fishes far more restfully knowing that there's 24-hour safety monitoring from land nearby.)

Guests – or "aquanauts" as the lodge-owners call them – must swim down to reach the lodge, which, shaped like a figure of eight, has a small opening on the base in the centre. Your first point of arrival is into a wet room; the disconcerting sensation is much like surfacing from a swimming pool, except, of course, that you're still under water. Compressed air keeps the sea from flooding in.

Once ensconced in this enclave, most guests spend their time gazing out of the enormous, 42-inch windows in the lodge's hull: these vast portholes make a spectacular spot to spy on its surroundings. *Jules' Undersea Lodge* is anchored in the heart of a mangrove habitat, the ideal nursery for scores of marine animals, including angelfish, parrotfish and snapper; meanwhile, anemones and sponges stud the sea floor. Anyone too busy fish-spotting to whip up a spot of dinner needn't worry, as there's a chef on hand who can scuba down to prepare meals; or, for late night munchies, a local takeaway joint offers a unique delivery service – perfectly crisp, underwater pizza.

508 Checking the progress of the Crazy Horse Memorial

SOUTH DAKOTA Angered by the completion of Mount Rushmore in 1941, a group of Lakota Sioux chiefs led by Henry Standing Bear asked sculptor Korczak Ziolkowski to build a monument to the Native American legend known as Crazy Horse: victor of The Battle of the Little Big Horn; a leader who never signed a treaty; and a warrior who never surrendered. Mount Rushmore, just seventeen miles down the road, was big – this had to be bigger. As Henry Standing Bear put it, "we want to let the white man know we have heroes too."

The first thing that hits you when you gaze upon the memorial, deep in the Black Hills of South Dakota, is indeed its enormity. While the images of Mount Rushmore were carved onto the existing rockface, Ziolkowski reshaped an entire mountain, blasting, drilling and carving, slab by slab, an image of the revered warrior atop his horse, his arm stretched over the land that he fought to defend

in the 1870s. The modern Orientation Center is over a mile from the 563ft peak, so initially you won't even grasp the memorial's true dimensions, but take a bus to its base and you're guaranteed to be utterly mesmerized.

It's not just the proportions that are overwhelming. The audacious, seemingly hopeless, timescale of the project makes the great Gothic cathedrals of Europe seem like prefabs. When Ziolkowski died in 1982, his family continued the work he had begun 34 years earlier; Crazy Horse's face, with its finely shaped nose and eyes, measures 87ft tall and was completed as recently as 1998. Today, his horse is gradually taking shape through a series of blasted-out ridges, but it's impossible to estimate when everything will be finished. No matter though: time seems to have little significance here, as the construction work – careful, reverential – has become almost as sacred as the monument itself.

509 Angling for brown bears at Brooks Falls

ALASKA If you've ever seen a photo of a huge brown bear standing knee-deep in rushing water, poised to catch a leaping salmon in its mouth, there's a 95 percent chance it was taken at Brooks Falls, a stalling point for the millions of sockeye salmon that make their annual spawning run up the Brooks River. Each July, at the height of the migration, bears flock in to exploit the excellent feeding possibilities, and with viewing platforms set up a few feet from the action, watching them is both exhilarating and slightly nerve-racking. It's easy to feel as though you're right in the middle of a wildlife documentary.

At any one time, you might see a dozen or more jockeying for position. Such proximity causes considerable friction among these naturally solitary animals, but size, age and experience define a hierarchy that allows posturing and roaring to take the

place of genuine battles. Fluffy and defenceless babies are highly vulnerable to fatal attacks from adult males, so the mothers go to great lengths to ensure they're secure, sending their cubs to the topmost branches of nearby trees and then fishing warily close by. Daring juveniles like to grab the prime fishing spot atop the falls, but become very nervous if bears higher up the pecking order come close – successfully holding pole position might mean moving up the rankings, but the youngster risks a severe beating. Some older and wiser bears prefer wallowing in the pool below the falls: one regular visitor dives down every few minutes and always seems to come up with a flapping sockeye in his mouth. Come the end of the salmon run, the bears head for the hills, only to return in September for a final pre-hibernation gorge on the carcasses of the spent fish as they drift downstream.

Witnessing power in action on **Capitol Hill**

510

WASHINGTON DC Dominated by massive monuments, museums, war memorials and statues, Washington DC represents the purest expression of political might. But the seat of government of the world's only superpower is a surprisingly accessible place – it's by the people, for the people, after all – and though certain security measures may seem an obstacle, you shouldn't miss the chance to see the corridors of power, and maybe even catch a glimpse of the action.

Wherever you go in DC, it'll be hard to avoid the looming, cast-iron dome of the US Capitol building. From its marvellous Rotunda (styled after Rome's Pantheon) to the stately figures of National Statuary Hall, you won't be disappointed (and may be slightly awed) by the country's centre of legislative power – pick up a ticket for a free tour at the kiosk on the building's southwest side. For an up-close look at the angry speech-making and partisan posturing of Congress, however, you'll need to get a special pass in advance of your trip.

Although the president and his advisors stay well out of the public eye, you can still tour the White House; make reservations in advance to check out the richly draped, chandeliered East Room, the silk-trimmed and portrait-heavy Green Room, the oval, French-decorated Blue Room and a glittery display of presidential china.

Perhaps the most rewarding spot for actually seeing the American government at work is the US Supreme Court. The building itself is stately enough, with its grand Greek Revival columns and pediment, but the real sight is all nine justices arrayed behind their bench, meticulously probing the lawyers making their arguments. From these arguments the Court writes its opinions, affirming or striking down existing laws and at times making history before your very eyes.

ALASKA As you manoeuvre your way towards the towering face of one of Alaska's many tidewater glaciers, the gentle crunch of ice against the fibreglass hull of your kayak sounds faintly ominous. It's nothing, though, compared to the thunderclap that echoes across the water when a great wall of ice peels away from the glacier and sends waves surging toward you. Your first reaction is quite naturally a jolt of fear, but no need to panic: if you're at least 500 yards away from the glacier face (as any sensible paddler is), the danger will have dissipated by the time whatever's left of the waves reaches you.

Watching glaciers calve while paddling round a frozen margarita of opaque blue water and brash ice is an undoubted highlight of sea kayaking in Prince William Sound. Perhaps better still are the opportunities for viewing marine life here. Seals often loll around on icebergs close to glaciers, while sea otters swim in the frigid waters, protected by the wonderfully thick fur that made them prized by the eighteenth-century Russian traders who partly colonized Alaska. In deeper water, look for pods of orcas cruising the waterways in search of their favourite food, seals (no wonder they hang back on the icebergs) You might even spot a few humpback whales, which congregate in small groups and breach spectacularly on occasion. Keep a splash-proof camera handy at all times.

Even if you miss out on a great action photo, there is considerable pleasure in just gliding around the generally calm waters of the fjords, where cliffs clad in Sitka spruce and Douglas fir rise steeply from the depths. For full atmospheric effect, stay in a simple Forest Service cabin or camp out on a small beach or at a designated campsite in one of the state marine parks; it's a wonderfully relaxing way to while away a few days – falling sheets of ice aside, of course.

SEA
KAYAKING
in Prince 511
William
Sound

512 Cedar Point: the roller coaster capital of the world

OHIO The air of anticipation on the platform is palpable, but you're trying not to think about what comes next. You scan the crowd for a sympathetic face, but to no avail; everyone is feverish with excitement. Are they all mad? The train rounds the corner suddenly, its brakes exhaling along with its passengers. It comes to a rest alongside you, bringing into sharp relief your seat and its present occupant, a girl who is sobbing. Your knees buckle slightly and you step in. The safety bar locks over your lap: there is no going back. Above the rallying cries of your fellow riders, one question screams inside your head: "Why am I here?"

"Here" is Cedar Point, the roller coaster capital of the world, which sits on the shores of Lake Erie in Sandusky, Ohio, seventy miles west of Cleveland. Though the carnival atmosphere, corn dogs and freedom to act like a five-year-old are all compelling reasons to spend a day at this massive amusement park, the real draw is the profusion of rides. From antique cars and bucking horse carousels to a giant swing set and the sinister Demon Drop – an experience not

unlike a ten-storey freefall – nearly seventy rides stand ready to spin you, soak you, flip you upside down and heave you to and fro. None, however, manages to do so quite so frighteningly as the undisputed headliners, the roller coasters. Seventeen dot the park – more than anywhere else on the planet – including a fair share of the fastest, steepest and longest thrill rides ever designed, like the perennial favourite, the Magnum XL-200.

The train climbs the Magnum's first hill with a cold determination. You can see nothing but the blue sky above. Now is not the time to steal a glance over the side, but you can't help it and so you do and immediately wish you hadn't. For far longer than seems sensible, the train presses up the hopelessly narrow track. Abruptly the screams begin in earnest, portents of the 60-degree descent. On cloudless days like this one it's possible to see Canada from the ride's zenith 205ft off the ground, but it's hard to focus when your life is passing before your eyes. Ninety heart-pounding seconds later it's all over and you're still in one piece. There's only one place to go: back in line.

513 Making a mess with Maryland crabs

MARYLAND Hands stained red with Old Bay seasoning, fingers so slick with crab fat you can hardly clutch your beer, maybe a few stray bits of shell stuck in your hair or to your cheek – that's the sort of dishevelled look which you should be aiming for at a Maryland crab feast.

"Picking" hard-shell steamed blue crabs is a sport Marylanders attack with gusto from May to October – though anyone will tell you that the heaviest, juiciest number-one "jimmies" are available only near the end of the summer. That's when the most popular crab restaurants up and down the bay have lines out of the door, and every other backyard in Baltimore seems to ring with the sound of wood mallets smacking on crab legs.

It's simplicity itself: a bushel or two of crabs in the steamer with some beer and lashings of spicy Old Bay, and yesterday's newspaper

laid out on a big picnic table, along with a few rolls of paper towels. What else? Only more beer (cold this time), some corn on the cob, a hot dish or two ... nothing to distract from the main attraction.

Then it's down to business. The process starts with yanking what can only be described as an easy-open pull tab on the crab's under-shell. From there, dig out the yellowish fat called "mustard", as well as the gills, then snap the hard-back shell in half and proceed to scoop out the sweet, succulent flesh. Soon you'll be whacking the claws just so with a wooden mallet and gouging the meat out with a knife.

It's easier than it sounds, and the crabmeat is certainly a powerful motivator for thorough picking (and fast learning). In the process, you can't help but marvel at man's cleverness when it comes to eating critters with the prickliest of defences. But maybe that's just the beer talking.

514 Leaving it all behind on the Appalachian Trail

GEORGIA–MAINE Hiking the Appalachian Trail, the epic trek that stretches 2186 miles from the peak of Springer Mountain in Georgia to the top of Mount Katahdin in Maine, changes your perspective on life, whether you want it to or not. When your house weighs a pound, your job involves walking from sunrise to sunset and your nights are filled with strangers' stories round roaring campfires, the mundane routines of the modern world are replaced with the realities of survival: water, gear, aching joints and the insatiable rumbling in your stomach.

A popular saying on the AT is that the only thing that separates a hiker from a hobo is a thin layer of Gore-Tex. So why do so many choose to spend upwards of four months walking a distance that could be covered by a car in two days?

As you plan your route across the snowcapped peaks of the

Smokies at the end of winter, then the indigo waves of the Blue Ridge Mountains in early spring, the grassy green mounds of the Shenandoahs in the heat of mosquito season and finally the striking profiles of the Presidentials in early fall, you find there's a sublime satisfaction in mapping out your future, one mountain at a time. (Most thru-hikers walk from south to north, to catch the best weather.)

But the trail is really about those countless days when you walk twenty-five miles through three thunderstorms and over six mountains, and arrive at your campsite feeling exhausted yet triumphantly alive. That and the sleepy towns to which you hitchhike for supplies, where welcoming locals ply you with pitchers of beer at the local bar and blueberry pancakes for breakfast and offer lifts to buy new shoes for the next leg of your trip.

515 Burning Man festival

NEVADA Picture a nudist miniature golf course, an advanced pole-dancing workshop and a bunch of neon-painted bodies glowing in the night, and you may be getting close to imagining what Burning Man is all about. Every year during the last week of August, several thousand digerati geeks, pyrotechnic maniacs, death-guild Goths, crusty hippies and too-hip yuppies descend on a prehistoric dry lakebed in the Nevada Desert to build a temporary autonomous "city" – one that rivals some of Nevada's largest in size and leaves no trace when it disbands. Known as Black Rock City, it's not the ideal place to consume a heady cocktail of alcohol and drugs – temperatures are scorching – but the thousands of anarchists, deviants, techno-heads, trance-dancers and freakish performance artists that arrive here from all over the world give it their best shot.

Art and interactivity are at the very core of the Burning Man ethos. Basically, this is the most survivalist, futuristic and utterly surreal show on Earth, where the strangest part of your alter ego reigns supreme. Leashed slaves with foot fetishes wander around offering footbaths, faceless Pythia give advice in oracle booths, flying zebras circle, caged men in ape suits pounce and motorized lobster cars tool about. Some of Burning Man's participants see the event as a social experiment and others a total free-for-all. But the main goal is the same: you're there to participate, not observe. Burning Man allows all the black sheep of the world to graze together, so the more experiential art you share, gifts you give, bizarre costumes you wear or free services you provide, the better.

The highlight of the week is the burning of a 50ft-tall effigy of a man, built from wood and neon and stuffed with fireworks. After all the laser-filled skies, electroluminscent wired bodysuits and fire-breathing mechanical dragons that illuminate the skies every evening for the rest of the week, it's almost an anticlimax, but it's still certainly a sight to behold. If you fancy making a smaller-scale statement, you can choose whatever alter ego or fantasy you desire. Just pack your politically correct non-feathered boas, body paint and imagination, and you're all set.

516 Leaf-peeping along Route 100

VERMONT Route 100 is beautiful year-round – winding its way through quintessential New England scenery, it skirts tidy chocolate-box villages dotted with white-steepled churches, clapboard houses and home-made sweet shops, all nestled beneath the Green Mountains. But from late September to early October, when the leaves start to change colour, the road is transformed into a 200-mile, skin-prickling display of arboreal pyrotechnics; it's as if the entire state has been set ablaze. Even the most die-hard cosmopolitan will find it hard not to be seduced by the spectacular scenery, as dizzying peaks give way to a conflagration of vermilion sugar maples, buttery aspens, scarlet sourwoods and acid-yellow ashes.

This yearly riot of colour can be appreciated whether you choose to ever leave your car or not. Gliding along a winding stretch of open road, crawling through an impossibly picturesque nineteenth-century town, or off-roading along serpentine country lanes, the explosion of unreal-looking leaves is inescapable – and unadulterated (no billboards or malls are allowed along the route). For an up-close look, pull off Route 100 and head into Green Mountain National Forest to walk along part of the 265-mile Long Trail, which has countless leaf-peeping opportunities alongside rugged, mountainous terrain, flowing streams and placid ponds.

517 Cruising the Inside Passage

ALASKA There's little better than sitting on deck and nursing a warm nightcap sometime around 11pm, as the sun slowly dips towards the horizon and you cruise past mile after gorgeous mile of spruce- and hemlock-choked shoreline. If you're lucky, whales will make an appearance; perhaps just a fluke or a tail but maybe a full-body breach. This is Alaska's Inside Passage, flanked by impenetrable snow-capped coastal mountains and incised by hairline fjords that create an interlocking archipelago of over a thousand densely forested islands.

Gliding into port at successive small settlements, you can't help but think these towns insignificant after the large-scale drama of the surrounding landscape. They cling to the few tiny patches of flat land, their streets spilling out onto a network of boardwalks over the sea. Shops, streets and even large salmon canneries are perched picturesquely along the waterside on spruce poles.

Everything is green, courtesy of the low clouds which cloak the surrounding hills and offer frequent rain. The dripping leaves, sodden mosses and wispy mist seem to suit ravens and bald eagles. You'll see them everywhere: ravens line up along the railings overlooking the small boat harbours while bald eagles perch, solitary and regal, in the trees above.

The next stop is Glacier Bay National Park, a vast wonderland of ice and barren rock where massive tidewater glaciers push right into the ocean. The ship lingers a few hours as everyone trains their eyes on the three-mile-wide face where walls of ice periodically crumble away and crash into the iceberg-flecked sea. The schedule is pressing and it is time to move on, and the moment you turn away, the loudest rumble of the day tells you you've just missed the big one.

518 Gazing at a Nantucket sunset

MASSACHUSETTS You spent the morning beside a peppermint-striped lighthouse, and then meandered past shingled, rose-covered cottages. For lunch, you feasted on freshly steamed lobster and sweet corn on the cob. But in truth, you only really feel like you've arrived in Nantucket once you've sauntered along one of its long stretches of sugary white sand, with the moorlands and breezy dunes to your back, and to the west, a gorgeous, swirly pink sun slipping into a glowing sea.

Difficult to access – it's a two-hour, no-land-in-sight boat ride south from mainland Cape Cod – and primarily a summertime destination, the tiny island is imbued with a catch-it-while-you-can ambience. It's as if the sun and surf have filtered out the details of life on the mainland, shaping the island into a quiet, sandy idyll. There's not really much "to do" in Nantucket, but that's where its charm lies – content yourself with ice-cream cones and seashells, salty sea air and bike rides to the beach.

As the evening fog rolls in – the island is famous for it, even owing its nickname, "the Grey Lady", to the mist – beach-weary folk head for Nantucket Town, packing into the drugstore for creamy milkshakes from its time-worn soda fountain where the stools still spin.

Nantucket wasn't always a land of leisure. During the eighteenth and nineteenth centuries, it served as a hub for the whaling trade, a dangerous industry marked by meagre pay and gruelling years at sea. Evidence of this hard-working heritage is well preserved in the pretty sea captains' homes and cobblestones that line Main Street.

More than anything, windswept Nantucket is a wistful sort of place. As you board the ferry to go home, you'll long not only for simpler days, but also for the chance to come back again.

LOUISIANA America's most over-the-top and hedonistic spectacle, Mardi Gras (the night before Ash Wednesday) in New Orleans reflects as much a medieval, European carnival as it does a drunken Spring Break ritual. Behind the scenes, the official celebration revolves around exclusive, invitation-only balls; for such an astonishingly big event, it can seem put on more for locals than the raucous crowds who descend on the town, but you'll hardly be wanting for entertainment or feeling left out.

Following routes of up to seven miles long, more than sixty parades wind their way through the city's historic French Quarter. Multi-tiered floats snake along the cobblestone streets, flanked by masked horsemen, stilt-walking curiosities and, of course, second liners – dancers and passersby who informally join the procession. There's equal fun in participating as there is in looking on.

Whichever way you choose to see it, you'll probably vie at some point to catch one of the famous "throws" (strings of beads, knickers, fluffy toys – whatever is hurled by the towering float-riders into the crowd); the competition can be fierce. Float-riders, milking it for all it's worth, taunt and jeer the crowd endlessly, while along Bourbon Street, women bare their breasts and men drop their trousers in return for some baubles and beads.

As accompaniment, the whole celebration is set to one of the greatest soundtracks in the world: strains of funk, R&B, New Orleans Dixie and more stream out of every bar and blare off rooftops – no surprise, of course, considering the city's status as the birthplace of jazz.

You might have thought that all of this madness would have been curtailed in the wake of Hurricane Katrina, but like New Orleans, the party carries on in the face of long odds; indeed, the year following, many of the weird and wonderful costumes were made from the bright blue tarps that have swathed so much of the city since the storm.

Getting in line at
Mardi Gras 519

520 Touring Graceland

TENNESSEE As pilgrimages go, touring Graceland isn't the most obvious religious experience. The Memphis home of legendary rock 'n' roll star Elvis Presley doesn't promise miraculous healing or other spiritual rewards. But for those who perceive truth in timeless popular music – as well as in touchingly bad taste – a visit to the home of "the King" is more illuminating than Lourdes.

From Elvis's first flush of success (he bought the house in 1957 with the profits from his first hit, "Heartbreak Hotel") to his ignominious death twenty years later, Graceland witnessed the bloom and eventual bloat of one of America's biggest legends. Just as he mixed country, gospel and rhythm and blues to concoct the new sound of rock 'n' roll, Presley had an "anything goes" attitude towards decorating. The tiki splendour of the jungle room, which has green shag carpeting on the floor and the ceiling, is only steps from the billiards room, where the couch and the walls are covered in matching quilt-print upholstery. In the living room, a 15-ft-long white sofa sets off a glistening black grand piano. (The audio tour commentary, from Lisa Marie Presley, is understandably preoccupied with her father's impetuous shopping habits.)

Amid all the glitz, though, you can still glimpse an underlying humility. A modest, windowless kitchen was one of the King's favourite rooms, and the blocky, colonial-style house itself is nothing compared to today's mega-mansions, especially considering he shared the place with his extended family for decades. The quiet, green grounds are a respite from the less-than-attractive patch of Memphis outside. And even after passing through a monumental trophy room and a display of Elvis's finest jewel-encrusted jumpsuits, you can't help but think that this was a man who hadn't strayed too far from his rural Mississippi roots.

Serious pilgrims pay their respects at Elvis's grave, which is set in the garden at the side of the house. Around the mid-August anniversary of the singer's death, tens of thousands flock here to deposit flowers, notes and gifts – a homage to a uniquely American sort of saint.

521 Trusting in Tusty on the Alaska Marine Highway

ALASKA It's America, but not as you know it. There are no malls, ball games, Tex-Mex or frappuccino lights. Indeed, there are scarcely any shops at all, which is why, when the *Tustumena* – the Alaska Marine Highway's state ferry from Bellingham, Washington, to Dutch Harbor in the Aleutian Islands – calls four times a year, the locals surge towards the docks with delight.

She's no luxury liner: a few of the 174 passengers manage to book berths and the rest just pitch tents on the deck or lay sleeping bags on the floor among the snoring bodies of strangers. But because the "Trusty Tusty" – as locals call her – is small, she can squeeze through narrow passageways that cruise ships can't, and visit communities that no dressed-for-dinner passenger could ever hope to see.

In Chignik (population: 80), midway down the south coast of the Alaska Peninsula, passengers flock to *Janice's Donut Hole* for pastries – she's been baking since 6am on this lucrative day – while the locals of this restaurant-less community rush to the ferry to buy cheeseburgers that the ship's chef has cooked up especially for them. At King's Cove, 270 miles to the west, passengers feast on fresh salmon chowder and between stops, the onboard naturalist points out a colony of sea otters here, a humpback whale there and relates the history of this remote territory: in 1942, the Japanese invaded the Aleutian Islands of Attu and Kiska.

As the days pass – it takes three days and four nights to travel between Homer and Dutch Harbor – the scenery becomes more dramatic: flower-filled meadows turn to rugged outcrops before emerald-green hills until, on the final evening, the *Tustumena* passes the three volcanoes of Unimak island: Roundtop, Isanotski and Shishaldin. Southwest Alaska's weather is famously moody, but if you're lucky, you'll see them capped with snow, basking against a brash, tangerine-coloured sky.

522 Going native in the land of the blue-green water

ARIZONA A stunning Shangri-la of turquoise waterfalls and lush vegetation, little-known Havasu Canyon lies deep in the heart of the Grand Canyon. It doesn't belong to the national park, however, for the simple reason that it's the ancestral home of a small group of Native Americans. One anthropologist called this "the only spot in the United States where native culture has remained in anything like its pristine condition."

Havasu Canyon receives virtually no rain, but every drop of water that falls for miles around funnels down into this narrow gorge, to feed the year-round torrent of Havasu Stream. Known as the "people of the blue-green water", the Havasupai have farmed here for centuries but today depend as much on tourism as agriculture, ferrying visitors on horseback down the demanding eight-mile trail from the nearest road, and running a simple lodge and campground. Their village, Supai, is a bedraggled affair that has been repeatedly battered by flash floods; the compelling reason to visit is a few miles deeper into the canyon, in the glorious succession of waterfalls. These too are frequently reshaped by flooding; thus Navajo Falls disappeared in 2008, to be replaced by two brand new cascades.

Towering Havasu Falls survives, however. Here the stream foams white as it hurtles over a 170ft cliff to crash into shallow terraces filled with clear turquoise water. Bizarre rock formations all around are formed from travertine – the same stuff that clogs the inside of domestic kettles – which also coats the riverbed and gives the water its astonishing blue-green glow.

Weary hikers can swim here and at the base of the even taller Mooney Falls, which you descend via footholds chiselled into the rock, while clutching a precarious iron chain. Splashing beneath these mighty cascades, knowing you're in a remote oasis at the bottom of the Grand Canyon, is a quite extraordinary thrill.

523 California in a convertible: driving the length of Highway 1

CALIFORNIA Highway 1 starts in little Leggett, but most people pick it up in San Francisco, just after it has raced US-101 across the Golden Gate Bridge and wiggled its way through the city. Roll down the rooftop on your convertible – this is California, after all – and chase the horizon south, through Santa Cruz and misty Monterey and then on to Big Sur, one of the most dramatic stretches of coastline in the world, where the forest-clad foothills of the Santa Lucia Mountains ripple down to a ninety-mile zigzag of deeply rugged shore.

You could easily spend a week in one of the mountain lodges here, hiking in the region's two superb state parks or watching grey whales gliding through the surf, but SoCal's sands are calling. Gun the gas down through San Luis Obispo and swanky Santa Barbara until you hit Malibu, from where – as the Pacific Coast Highway – the road tiptoes around Los Angeles, dipping in and out of the beachside suburbs of Santa Monica, Venice and Long Beach.

Highway 1 eventually peters out at San Juan Capistrano, but most people pull off a few miles shy, finishing their journey in Los Angeles. Leaving Malibu's multi-million-dollar condos behind and easing gently into the downtown LA traffic, it'll suddenly dawn on you that the hardest part of the journey is still to come – at some point soon, you're going to have to say goodbye to the convertible.

524 Stalking the Pilgrim Fathers of Plymouth

MASSACHUSETTS The rock sits, rather humbly, under a tiny Greek portico on the Plymouth shore, a relatively small chunk of granite smothered in sand and littered with coins and the odd cigarette butt. It's more pebble than rock, and easy to miss. Yet this is the vaunted spot where the first settlers of the United States disembarked in 1620. Or is it?

Visitors can be forgiven for being seriously underwhelmed. Plymouth Rock is confusing; it remains at the heart of America's most enduring foundation myth, one that claims this small, unexceptional New England town as the first settlement of the United States, yet the rock was only "identified" by a church elder in 1741, who said he'd heard the story from his father (the Pilgrims never mentioned it). Plymouth's claim as "America's Hometown" also ignores dozens of settlements from Florida to Virginia that were established years before the Pilgrims stumbled ashore.

Wander along the otherwise unremarkable waterfront and you'll get a better sense of history at the authentic replica of the Pilgrim's ship, the *Mayflower*. Built in Britain, the *Mayflower II* was given to America as a gesture of goodwill in 1957. On board, modern-day crew members and role-playing "interpreters" in period garb, field questions about the arduous journey across the Atlantic.

The rest of modern Plymouth little resembles its early incarnation – to get a sense of that you need to drive a few miles out of town to the Plimoth Plantation, an earnest recreation of the settlement circa 1627. Here, more role-playing actors try to bring you back in time – replete with English accents and a seventeenth-century Puritanical world view. But the site also includes a reproduction of a modest Wampanoag village, where exchanges are less structured and the Native American staff (wearing traditional clothes but not role-playing) are keen to chat about Indian customs. Indeed, after being ignored for decades, the Wampanoags' role in the Pilgrim story is commemorated in the site museum (the tribe effectively kept the settlers alive that first year and took part in the first "Thanksgiving"). Yet the virtuous, hard-working Pilgrims retain an icy grip on the American imagination – many still believe that it was here, in the 1620s, that America really got started.

525 Going batty in Austin

TEXAS Every evening from mid-March to early November Austin plays host to one of urban America's most entertaining natural spectacles, as Mexican free-tailed bats perform at the city's Congress Avenue Bridge. They emerge from the bridge's deep crevices just after sunset, flapping and squeaking in a long ribbon across the sky. An eclectic mix of townies and tourists watches from the south bank of Town Lake, from boats, from blankets at the Austin American-Statesman's observation centre and from the bridge itself. Picturesque from any spot, the bats' game of follow-the-leader is most impressive when you stand beneath the ribbon and look up – that's when the sheer number of these creatures hits home. During the summer, the best viewing season, more than 1.5 million bats reside here, making it the largest urban bat colony in North America. Caves elsewhere in Texas host larger colonies, but in Austin there is a certain wonder in watching natural and man-made worlds collide harmoniously.

526 Paying homage to country music

VIRGINIA Along a highway disguised as a country road in the town of Hiltons, the Carter Family Fold showcases acoustic mountain music in a place where time stands still. Here it might as well be 1927, the year of the "Big Bang" in country music, when the original Carter Family sang about hard times and wildwood flowers. The children of Sara and A.P. Carter constructed and nurtured this unique structure, built right into the hillside. An on-site museum in A.P.'s old grocery store contains snapshots of "Mother Maybelle", a lock of Sara's hair and the clothes June Carter Cash and Johnny Cash wore when they entertained at the Nixon White House. And during the weekly concerts, the site still evokes a direct connection to them, to their famous forebears who are honoured here, and to all of the music that came from these mountains.

527 Biking the Golden Gate Bridge

CALIFORNIA Like a bright-orange necklace draped across the neck of San Francisco Bay, the Golden Gate Bridge is said to be the most photographed man-made structure in the world, and no wonder: you can snap a postcard-worthy picture of it from almost any hilltop in the city. But to really experience the span, you need to get close. You need to feel it. And the best way to do that is by biking it. The eight-mile trip from Fisherman's Wharf over the bridge to Sausalito is truly spectacular and, just as important, truly flat.

Rent some wheels at the base of Hyde Street Pier, then cruise through manicured Aquatic Park. It's a short climb to Fort Mason Park, where you can catch eerie glimpses of Alcatraz through the thick cypress trees. Swoop down to Marina Green, past the legions of kite flyers and the small harbour, and you'll soon be gliding past Crissy Field, replete with newly planted sea grasses, sand dunes and the occasional great blue heron. Grab a grass-fed beef hot dog from the popular *Let's Be Frank* cart, then press on to the end of the path, where at historic Fort Point you can peer up into the bridge's awesome latticework underbelly.

You'll have to double back a few hundred yards to the road leading up to the bridge approach. But the steep ascent is worth it as you serenely pedal past the mobs of tourists and onto the bike and pedestrian path. As the crowds thin out, you can contemplate the bridge's stunning Art Deco lines and mind-boggling scale. The towers rise 65 storeys and contain 600,000 rivets apiece. The 3ft-wide suspension cables comprise 80,000 miles of pencil-thin steel wire. More darkly, over a thousand people have jumped to their deaths from this very trail.

There's one last viewing platform on the Marin County anchorage, after which it's time to drift downhill along the twisting road to the quaint town of Sausalito, where you can catch the ferry back to San Francisco. Though it hardly seems possible, the view from the ferry landing may be the most magnificent of the whole journey, especially at sunset, when the white lights of the city glow against the darkening bay.

528 Death by ice cream at Ben & Jerry's

VERMONT In the late 1970s, a couple of hippy drop-outs decided they'd like to make ice cream for a living. They took a $5 correspondence course, bought a cranky ice-cream machine and opened a scoop shop on the concourse of a shabby gas station in Burlington, Vermont. Ben Cohen and Jerry Greenfield had a talent for mixing tasty stuff into their ice cream – chunks of real chocolate, cashew nuts and cookies all went into the blender.

Today, Vermont is known for its green hills, ski slopes and picture-perfect clapboard villages. Yet the state's most popular attraction is Ben & Jerry's manufacturing plant just outside the sleepy town of Waterbury. To be sure, it's an intriguing enterprise; a quirky video describes the unlikely origins of the venture and, though Unilever-owned, the company is proud of its small size, eco-friendly philosophy and community involvement. But there's really only one reason everyone comes here; that super-chunk, fudge-soaked, biscuit and marshmallow choco-rich ice cream that is the most addictive product ever sold (legally) in the US.

Guided tours run above the factory floor where machines turn cream, sugar and other natural ingredients into over fifty flavours, but does anyone really care about output levels and local dairy farms? The real highlight is the free taster at the end – rare or brand-new flavours are dished out here. Think coconut double-chocolate chip and peanut butter cookie dough. Nirvana for ice-cream addicts.

The shop outside presents a real opportunity to indulge. Don't feel self-conscious and order that single scoop; you'll soon observe seniors and six-year-olds alike walking out with plates stacked high with multi-flavoured dollops of ice cream and toppings. Before you leave, waddle over to the Flavor Graveyard to mourn the likes of Tennessee Mud, Rainforest Crunch and the short-lived Cool Britannia (strawberries and shortbread).

One fact is sure to boggle your mind as you drive away; each employee can take home a tub of ice cream every day, for free. Most do not – apparently, there really is a limit on how much ice cream you can eat.

529 Hang-gliding the Outer Banks

NORTH CAROLINA There are few coastal spots in America as magnificent as Carolina's Outer Banks. Your main goal here should be contemplating the fragility of the shifting sands and unique ecosystems, hitting deserted beaches along the southern portions of the barrier islands, in Cape Hatteras, Ocracoke Island and largely undeveloped Cape Lookout. Getting off – and above – beach level is an experience not to be missed: there's a hang-gliding school in Jockey Ridge State Park where you can soar over the largest sand dunes in the eastern US, in Nags Head. Once airborne you may well consider what fired the imagination of Orville and Wilbur Wright, who launched their historic flight just a few miles north.

530 Travelling the Turquoise Trail

NEW MEXICO A stunning 52-mile stretch of Highway 14 – known as the Turquoise Trail – links Santa Fe and Albuquerque. It's a day-tripper's delight: start with a bit of ghost town charm in Cerrillos, where you'll be greeted by little more than tumbleweed, dirt roads and empty western storefronts complete with hitching posts. Continue south, taking in golden hills, desert meadows and swaths of startling blue sky, and head to the mining town-cum-artist enclave Madrid. Here you can shop for turquoise jewellery, check out local art and visit the Old Coal Mine Museum. Top off your trip with a beer at the *Mine Shaft Tavern*, an old roadhouse-style saloon that boasts the longest bar in New Mexico.

531 Up close with alligators on the Anhinga Trail

FLORIDA Stepping onto the concrete Anhinga Trail, you can't help but doubt its reputation as serious gator territory. Leading straight from a car park and with a friendly little visitor centre at its head, the half-mile circular pathway smacks of the type of "nature trail" on which you'd be lucky to catch sight of a sparrow. But don't judge it hastily – the Everglades is full of surprises.

Located way down in Florida's tropical south, the Everglades National Park covers 1.5 million acres of sawgrass-covered marshland and swamp, the largest subtropical wilderness in the United States and the perfect home for the American alligator. So as you stroll along admiring the exotic birdlife, don't let your guard down: all around you, massive carnivorous reptiles are lurking in the shallows, blending effortlessly into their surroundings. Almost comically prehistoric-looking, they sunbathe inches from the path or sometimes even stretched across it, motionless and slit-eyed, with seemingly hundreds of long, pointed teeth glinting in the hot Florida sun.

The sheer number of lazing alligators is remarkable, but your effortless proximity to them is even more incredible. In fact, you nearly forget you're in the wild – it all seems far too zoo-like (or even museum-esque, since the animals don't stir); and then, almost before you realize it, and with truly incredible speed, an alligator moves – and the enjoyable awe and excitement you were feeling morphs into sheer terror. When they take to the water and adopt that classic alligator pose – only eyes, teeth and powerful, ridged tail visible as they glide quietly and quickly towards their prey – it's nigh-on impossible to stop yourself from leaping away down the path, burning to tell someone of your near-death experience.

532 Riding the Slickrock in Moab

UTAH The allure of the small town of Moab, 238 miles southeast of Salt Lake City and 325 miles from Denver, lies not in the inspiring desert landscape that surrounds it, nor the stunning moonscape of ochre rocks, deep folded canyons, mesas or spires. Nor is it the spectacular landforms in nearby Arches National Park, the gurgling Colorado River, which swoops past town, or the landscape of mesas and buttes that stretch out before a backdrop of the snow-capped La Sal Mountains. No, what makes the place really remarkable is the incredible grip offered by the sandpapery surfaces of a group of contorted sandstone rocks near town – the location of the exceptional Slickrock mountain-bike trail.

From a distance these rocks look smooth, their neat shapes resembling a giant basket of eggs, but up close they offer bikers traction that's positively unreal, and with it a powerful sense of possessing superhuman skills. You'll be able to glide across areas where you'd usually expect the bike to slip out from under you and astonish yourself with the grades you can climb and descend – all adding up to a mind-blowing roller-coaster ride in wonderful desert surroundings. It's all so extraordinary that the trail – little more than a series of dots daubed on the rock to form a 10-mile loop – has become the most famous ride in the mountain-biking world. But perhaps best of all, it doesn't really matter how experienced a mountain biker you are: the Slickrock experience is accessible to anyone who can ride a bike, thanks to a 2.5-mile practice loop that never strays more than a half-hour's walk from the parking lot.

533 Playing ball at the Field of Dreams

IOWA "If you build it, they will come." So runs the memorable line from the movie *Field of Dreams*, an idealized ode to America's national pastime in which an Iowa farmer is inspired to construct a baseball diamond slap bang in the middle of his cornfield. And ever since the movie's set was carved across a pretty little family farm at Dyersville in Iowa, that's exactly what they've done. Within a few weeks of the movie's release in 1989, and with the diamond still in place from filming, the first visitor arrived, travelling over 1000 miles from his home in New York just to sit in the bleachers behind right field.

Since then, over a million people have come to this tiny corner of the rural Midwest, drawn by some strange compulsion to bat a few balls, play a little catch and fulfil a dream or two. In the late summer of 1997, I was one of them, stashing my weathered but trusty mitt into the glove compartment and driving north with a college friend in search of our own piece of baseball mythology. It was early September, the corn surrounding the field was high and green – just as it is in the movie – and as we pulled into the bijou car park, a pick-up game was just getting going. A family from California was manning the bases, and a kid from nearby Indiana was practising his curveballs from the mound, so we took our places in the outfield. After fielding a couple of grounders (my friend) and dropping a fly ball (me – I still blame the glare of the sun), we retired to the bleachers as the young pitcher moved onto his frighteningly quick fastballs.

Is this heaven? No, it's Iowa, a place where, for a few hours on a soft summer's day, you can enjoy the simple pleasures of a little make-believe.

Skiing at Snowbird and Alta

534

UTAH Squeezed side-by-side at the upper end of Little Cottonwood Canyon, the Alta and Snowbird resorts first linked their lifts in 2002 and ever since, their nearly 5000 combined acres have added up to the finest downhill skiing experience in North America. Like two brothers forced to share a bedroom, the resorts have learned to co-exist while maintaining their distinctive characters.

Alta, an old silver mining town, opened its slopes in 1939. Not much has changed since then, and therein lies Alta's charm: while other resorts loudly embrace all things modern, anachronistic Alta tenaciously holds onto its old-world lodges, creaky double-chair lifts and ban on snowboarding, prizing tradition over convenience at nearly every turn. Opened forty years later, brash Snowbird next door welcomes boarders and any other daredevils willing to ride the thrilling aerial tram zipping nearly 3000 vertical feet up to

the crest of hidden peak. Steep-and-deep is the quickest way to describe the riding here, where a ski-it-if-you-can ethos prevails.

Granted, you won't find a hip village like nearby Park City or the glitzy crowds that flock to Aspen and Vail in Colorado at either resort. Instead you'll encounter laid-back downhillers happy to spend their time exploring a spine-tingling collection of chutes, cirques, cliffs and knee-knocking steeps that can leave even the most hardcore enthusiast humbled. Softening the inevitable spills, an epic 500 inches of yearly snowfall forms light, fluffy pillows. So much snow can dump at once, in fact, that breakfast is often accompanied by the deep, pleasing boom of World War II-era howitzers blasting away at fresh drifts, readying the slopes for a morning filled with first tracks through heavenly bottomless powder.

535

MONTANA Sitting at the northern edge of America's Rocky Mountains, magnificent Glacier National Park's craggy cliffs, awe-inspiring peaks and beautiful deep-blue lakes are, true to the park's name, a result of massive tongues of ice invading the land from the north some 20,000 years ago.

While the trails that wind through this magical terrain are stunning – leading you past colourful mountain meadows, towering columns of rock up to 1.6 billion years old and all manner of elk, bighorn sheep and mountain goats, as well as grizzly and black bears – you can also gaze at some of the park's best, and most harrowing, views along the Going-to-the-Sun Road.

Cutting across the middle of the park, connecting the wooded groves of Montana's Rockies with the sprawling dry expanse of the Great Plains, the road offers an eye-popping jaunt over the Continental Divide, where at Logan Pass (6680ft) there's a Visitors' Center and a chance to stretch your legs in the shadow of the park's mighty peaks. By the time you get there, you'll have ascended through gently rolling foothills from charming, low-lying Lake MacDonald to a sudden series of switchbacks that rise ever higher with each mile.

The stunning views from the road as it contours along the jagged face of the Rockies feature sheer precipices that drop far down into shadowy forests, frozen rivers of ice framed by stark canyon walls and splashing waterfalls fed by snowmelt. While the road can be perilous at times, its narrow width straining to accommodate passing cars and its sheer-edged drop-offs not allowing much room for driving error, a white-knuckle ride is simply not possible, due to the slow speed of traffic during the peak summer season and most drivers being so overcome by the visual splendour that they forget about things like speed, direction or destination.

536 Eating barbecue in Texas Hill Country

TEXAS If you think barbecue is a sloppy pulled-pork sandwich or a platter of ribs drowned in a sticky, sweet sauce, a Texan will happily correct you. In the rolling hills around Austin – where pecan trees provide shade, pick-up trucks rule the road and the radio is devoted to Waylon, Willie and Merle – you'll find barbecue as it should be: nothing but pure, succulent, unadulterated meat, smoked for hours over a low wood fire. In fact, at one veteran vendor in Lockhart, *Kreuz Market*, the management maintains a strict no-sauce policy, so as not to distract from the perfectly tender slabs of brisket. Your meat, ordered by weight, comes on butcher paper with just crackers to dress it up.

Thankfully, this austerity applies only to the substance – not the quantity – of the meat. Gut-busting excess is what makes barbecue truly American, after all, especially at places like the legendary *Salt Lick*, southwest of Austin near the town of Driftwood. The all-you-can-eat spread here includes heaps of beef brisket, pork ribs and sausage, all bearing the signature smoke-stained pink outer layer that signifies authentic barbecue. On the side, you get the traditional fixin's: German-style coleslaw and potato salad, soupy pinto beans, sour pickles, plain old white bread and thick slices of onion.

So whether you visit *The Salt Lick*, *Kreuz Market* (those anti-sauce hardliners in Lockhart), *Black's* (another Lockhart gem, which has conceded to a light sauce), *Louie Mueller BBQ* (in an old wood-floor gymnasium in Taylor), *City Market* (in Luling) or any of the other esteemed purveyors a local barbecue fetishist points you to, don't ever forget: it's all about the meat.

537 Attending a ceremonial dance at Taos Pueblo

NEW MEXICO The sun shines down from the cloudless turquoise sky, but your feet are cold. You stamp them impatiently, squint your eyes against the glare and tuck your mitten-swaddled hands under your armpits. The rest of the crowd seems unconcerned, even though the scheduled starting time was surely hours ago, so you continue breathing in the freezing air, fragrant with wood smoke, and watching your breath cloud in front of you. Inside the adobe church Christmas Mass has come and gone, and people mill around the open plaza greeting friends and chatting quietly, the elders and women settling into folding chairs with blankets over their laps or wrapped around their shoulders. Some begin to pay holiday visits inside the mud buildings that rise up, in haphazard stacks, three or four storeys high.

And then, from the direction of Taos Mountain, which stands beyond the soft edges of the ancient pueblo, you hear a distant drone. The murmuring crowd goes quiet. The muffled drumbeats grow clearer, now accompanied by the rhythmic shimmer of bells, and you forget about your feet. The waiting throng forms a border around the pueblo's sacred dance space, instinctively giving prime spots to residents of this thousand-year-old settlement. The crowd parts easily as a procession of men arrives – they are no longer men but deer, their antlers swinging, their dainty hooves picking at the earth. The drums boom, the chanting swells and the transformation is complete – the circle is a forest glade, and hunters trace the edges, taking aim with their symbolic arrows.

Hours pass, or perhaps only minutes, and then the drums stop. The illusion lifts: these are mere men, some boys, labouring under slippery elk hides, many of which look as though they were butchered only this morning. Shirtless, the men are breathing hard from the rigour of the hunt, giddy and sombre at the same time. The women now take their place in the circle, making delicate hand motions with switches of piñon tree, and you stamp your feet again, tuck your hands tighter and surrender once more to the heart-pounding drums.

538 Paddling in the Pacific

CALIFORNIA Although just an hour north of LA by boat, the Channel Islands National Park feels a world away. Whether you're enjoying a hiking trail along the islands' rugged contours or dipping into the waters for a look at some of the two thousand marine creatures on view, the natural splendour of this 250,000-acre preserve is an unexpected delight. Spoiled for choice, you can fish or scuba dive in the crystal-clear Pacific waters, take a close-up look at intriguing caves, coves and shipwrecks or, in the late winter and early spring, watch the world's largest pod of migrating blue whales cavorting offshore.

Part of the fun is sailing between each of the islands: volcanic outcrops whose cliffs and crags were carved by glaciers during the last Ice Age. On most tours, one-mile-square Anacapa will be your first stop and you'll make your entrance past dramatic Arch Rock – a 40ft-high, wave-cut natural bridge. With rocky headlands and steep promontories over the sea, Anacapa also has an attractive beach near Frenchy's Cove (a good base for scuba divers and snorkellers). To the west, the much larger Santa Cruz is the largest and highest of the islands, rich in its fauna – from bald eagles and scrub jays to native foxes – and diverse landscapes, with forbidding canyons and lush green valleys. It's a fine place to hike or camp, as is Santa Rosa further west, with its alluring grasslands and steep ravines. Off Santa Rosa's northwest tip, San Miguel is most notable for being crowded with barking elephant seals and sealions. Only for the most gung-ho nature explorers, the place is frequently foggy and windy, and its surrounding rocks make for a white-knuckle sailing trip (park-approved boat tours only). South of the main group lies the smallest island, Santa Barbara, with its own sealions, kestrels, larks and meadowlarks – a beautiful, lonely outpost that almost makes you forget the teeming metropolis a short hop away.

539 Lunching on Creole cuisine in New Orleans

LOUISIANA New Orleans is a gourmet's town, and its restaurants are far more than places to eat. These are social hubs and ports in a storm – sometimes literally, in the case of the French Quarter kitchens that stayed open post-Katrina, dishing out red beans and rice to the stubborn souls who refused to abandon their beloved city. Above all, they are where New Orleans comes to celebrate itself, in all its quirky, battered beauty. And no restaurant is more quintessentially New Orleans than *Galatoire's*, the grande dame of local Creole cuisine.

Lunch, particularly on Friday and Sunday, is the meal of choice; set aside an entire afternoon. Reservations aren't taken for the downstairs room (the place to be), so you'll need to come early and wait in line. In true New Orleans fashion, this bastion of haute Creole style sits on the city's bawdiest stretch, Bourbon Street. Picking your way through the morning-after remnants of a Bourbon Saturday night – plastic cups floating in pools of fetid liquid, a distinctive miasma of drains and stale booze and rotting magnolias

– brings you to a display worthy of a Tennessee Williams play. Seersucker-clad powerbrokers puff on fat cigars, dangling dainty Southern belles on their arms; immaculately coiffured women greet each other with loud cries of "dawlin'!" Inside – or downstairs at least – it's like time has stood still: brass ceiling fans whir overhead, giant old mirrors reflect the lights cast by Art Nouveau lamps and black-jacketed waiters, who have worked here for ever, crack wise with their favourite diners.

It's the same century-old menu, too: basically French, pepped up with the herbs and spices of Spain, Africa and the West Indies. Lump crabmeat and plump oysters come with creamy French sauces or a piquant *rémoulade*, a blend of tomato, onion, Creole mustard, horseradish and herbs; side dishes might be featherlight soufflé potatoes or fried eggplant. To end with a kick, order a steaming tureen of potent *café brûlot* – jet-black Java heated with brandy, orange peel and spices – prepared tableside with all the ceremony of a religious ritual.

540 Tracing civil rights history in Montgomery

ALABAMA The struggle for African-American civil rights – one of the great social causes of American history – played out all across the South in the 1950s and 1960s. To try to gain a grasp on its legacy, and a sense of how the fabric of the country has changed as a result, make your way to Montgomery, Alabama, the culmination of the so-called Selma-to-Montgomery National History Trail.

Start at the state capitol building (which looks like a cross between the US Capitol and a plantation manor), where you can almost hear Dr Martin Luther King Jr in 1963 declaring at the end of the four-day Selma-to-Montgomery civil rights march, "however difficult the moment, however frustrating the hour, it will not be long, because truth pressed to earth will rise again." To experience more of King's spirit, take in a passionate Sunday service at the Dexter Avenue King Memorial Baptist Church, where today's

ministers use King's example to inspire both parishioners and casual visitors. The church's basement holds a mural depicting scenes from King's life, as well as his preserved desk, office and pulpit. His birthplace, for those interested, is in the Sweet Auburn district of Atlanta, Georgia.

The Rosa Parks Museum honours the Montgomery event that started it all. Parks's refusal in 1955 to accept a seat at the back of a Montgomery bus in essence sparked the civil rights movement; her inspiring story is told through photographs and dioramas, and you can step onto a replica of that city bus. Most poignant, though, is the civil rights memorial, centred on a black-granite table designed by Maya Lin and inscribed with the names of forty activists killed by racist violence from 1954 to 1968. The events described on the table are as good an overview of the era as you're likely to find.

541 Taking the A-train through Manhattan

NEW YORK It may be just a dirty, run-of-the-mill inner-city commuter train, but ever since 1941 when Duke Ellington's band immortalized the A-train – the subway from Brooklyn through the heart of Manhattan and into Harlem – the route's been associated with jazz, the Harlem Renaissance and the gritty glamour of travelling through New York. The iconic tin-can carriages – long a favourite location for TV cop dramas – rattle along on this express route, taking you to some of Manhattan's most varied neighbourhoods.

Wherever you choose to board the train, getting out at Jay Street in Brooklyn Heights, and stopping at one of the cafés on leafy Montague Street for a long, lazy brunch starts the day in true New York style. From here, the Brooklyn Bridge beckons; cross on foot and enter downtown Manhattan, taking in the spectacular views of the skyline as you traverse the sparkling East River, the Statue of Liberty just visible to your left.

Rejoin the A-train at Park Place and head up the line. Jump off at West 4th Street and browse the boutiques alongside funky West Villagers; stop at Columbus Circle, emerging at the southwest corner of Central Park for a leafy stroll. From here it's a nonstop express trip whizzing under the Upper West Side – sit in the front carriage for a driver's-eye view of the glinting tracks as they disappear beneath the train.

Your final stop is Duke Ellington's own journey's end: 145th Street for Harlem's Sugar Hill. High above the city, with hazy views back along Manhattan's straight avenues, this was the more upmarket part of the neighbourhood during the Jazz Age. Today, well into its second renaissance, the area's art and music scenes thrive, nowhere so much as in its classic jazz clubs. Stick your head into *St Nick's Pub*, known to the greats as *Lucky's Rendezvous*, and catch some improv – Duke would definitely approve.

NEW YORK The church is overflowing, humming with whispers. Smartly dressed ladies with wide-brimmed hats, neat dresses and flowers, men in immaculate suits, and little boys and girls sparkling in their best clothes. The choir, dressed in deep red and gold robes, fills the raised platform above the altar, facing the congregation and backed by vivid stained glass – the pastor enters, and the service begins. There are prayers, and a sermon of course, but it's the choir that drives worship here; entrancing, invigorating music that soon has the whole congregation clapping, whooping and praising the Lord. Soloists belt out hymns and spirituals, moving some to tears, before the tempo picks up and a chorus of voices joins in. Sometimes they hum, softly, building up to a crescendo of sound and rhythm that seems to envelop the whole church; the singers clap and dance, and the congregation joins in, everyone on their feet. Make no mistake, this is a religious service and not a show, but the quality on display is astounding – every member of the choir is a powerful, accomplished artist, and the soloists seem to hold everyone spellbound. As the waves of music blast the congregation, hats slide, suits are loosened and everyone seems uplifted – even the tourists jump and clap.

Getting Gospel in Harlem

Harlem is chock-full of churches and almost every one features Gospel music on Sundays. The choir at Abyssinian Baptist Church, the second oldest black congregation in the US, is the best in the city, and has long attracted steady streams of curious visitors. The Abyssinian started becoming the religious and political powerhouse that it is today when it moved to Harlem in 1920 – under charismatic pastors such as Reverend Adam Clayton Powell, Jr (1937–1970), also the first black Congressman from New York, it became the largest Protestant congregation in the US and remains a hugely influential centre of African-American spirituality and activism. Gospel tours are big business, but entry is free and you can easily visit alone – get there early. Just remember that this is a place of worship and that you should dress accordingly: shoulders should be covered before entering and no flip-flops, shorts or tank tops allowed.

543 Lost for words at the Grand Canyon

ARIZONA If a guidebook tells you that something is "impossible to describe", it usually means the writer can't be bothered to describe it – with one exception. After pondering the views of the Grand Canyon for the first time, the most spectacular natural wonder on Earth, most visitors are stunned into silence. Committed travellers hike down to the canyon floor on foot or by mule, spending a night at *Phantom Ranch*, or hover above in a helicopter to get a better feeling for its dimensions. But it is still hard to grasp. The problem isn't lack of words. It's just that the canyon is so vast and so deep, that the vista stretches so far across your line of vision, up, down and across, giving the impression of hundreds of miles of space, that it's a bit like looking at one of those puzzles in reverse – the more you stare, the more it becomes harder to work out what it is or where you are. Distance becomes meaningless, depth blurs, and your sense of time and space withers away.

The facts are similarly mind-boggling: the Grand Canyon is around 277 miles long and one mile deep. The South Rim, where most of the tourists go, averages 7000 feet, while the North Rim is over 8000 feet high – its alpine landscape only adding to the sense of the surreal. On the canyon floor flows the Colorado River, its waters carving out the gorge over five to six million years and exposing rocks that are up to two billion years old through vividly coloured strata. It's this incredible chromatic element that stays with you almost as much as the canyon's size, with the various layers of reds, ochres and yellows seemingly painted over the strangely shaped tower formations and broken cliffs. Think of it this way: the Grand Canyon is like a mountain range upside down. The country around the top is basically flat and all the rugged, craggy elements are below you. The abruptness of the drop is bizarre and, for some, unnerving. But the Grand Canyon is like that: it picks you up and takes you out of your comfort zone, dropping you back just that little bit changed.

544 Snowshoeing on Sawtooth

IDAHO Tucked beneath the serrated peaks of the Sawtooth Range – part of the Rocky Mountains, and as far removed from the haunt of the Hollywood stars down the road as it's possible to imagine – you'll discover perfect snowshoeing trails, for all levels of ability, snaking their way through Idaho's silent winter forests.

For millennia, Native Americans used snowshoes as a means of getting around in winter – the tennis racquet-like extensions to your feet spread your weight, allowing you to move through deep snow that would otherwise swallow you to the knee or beyond. Modern snowshoes are lightweight, and it takes seconds to fasten the bindings to your boots before you're all set to head off and explore. There's not really any special technique – just lift your feet slightly higher than normal. Marked routes on the scenic North Valley Trails can be accessed from Galena Lodge, north of Ketchum: the Cowboy Cabin Trail is perfect for first-timers; dazzling views of the surrounding icy mountains and meadows unfold on Pioneer Cemetery Loop; or for something a bit more heart-pumping, challenge yourself on Tilt a Whirl or Psycho Adventures. You can take a guide, but pretty much anyone can enjoy snowshoeing here under their own steam and renting shoes for the day is far cheaper than skiing.

The palpable silence of the forests will occasionally be broken by a soft "whump" as a pillow of snow slips from a tree branch, or by the gentle tick of snowflakes landing on your shoulders, but despite this almost eerie lack of noise there is still plenty of life here. Look out for the tracks of squirrels, rabbits, hare and deer and listen for the occasional tweet of winter wrens and mountain bluebirds, which are tough enough to survive winter in the mountains.

At the end of the day, there's nothing quite like heading back to civilization, icy dusk descending and a well earned hot bath awaiting. Pity those poor squirrels who are out there all night though...

545 On the trail of the perfect Key Lime Pie

FLORIDA The only portrait of "Lee" Ida Mae Neil hangs on the wall of the old Customs House in Key West. She faces sideways, dressed in white, her veiny arms the only sign of decades of lime squeezing; making key lime pie is very hard work. Neil moved to Key West in 1944, eventually becoming the undisputed "Queen of Key Lime Pies" and today, the beloved pie is the Florida Keys' best-known culinary export, made from the tiny, green citrus fruits that every local seems to grow in their backyard.

Highway 1 connects the Florida mainland with Key West, a spectacular ribbon of causeways and bridges that soars above sandy bars, mangroves and channels thick with giant mantra rays and sharks – it's also your route to the best key lime pies in the country. Aficionados are divided: graham-cracker or pastry crust? Meringue on top or whipped cream? The one thing that everyone can agree on is that adding green food colouring is taboo. Authentic key lime pie is always light yellow.

The gluttony begins in Key Largo, where the *Key Lime Tree* offers thick, piquant creations made with condensed milk. Heading south, Marathon is home to *Porky's Bayside Restaurant*; skip the barbecue and go straight for the coronary-inducing, deep-fried key lime pie. This time it's the batter that's top secret. Key West, at the end of the road, is pie central. The *Key West Key Lime Pie Co* serves all sorts of fancy, custard-like, frozen versions, including mango, pineapple and coconut. For classic fluffy meringue toppings, head to the *Blond Giraffe Key Lime Pie Factory*; they also do whipped cream. *Kermit's Key West Key Lime Shoppe* serves pie with a consistency somewhere between gelatin and cake, a perfect blend of sugary and tart, but the insider's choice is the *Rooftop Café*: the top layer of meringue and the gooey graham-cracker base sandwich a tangy core made with fresh lime juice and traces of melted butter. It's easy to get hooked, but at least you're never far from the Keys, where kayaking, swimming and snorkelling offer a chance to burn off those calories.

NEED to know

485 Kilauea is part of Hawaii Volcanoes National Park (🌐www.nps.gov/havo).

486 The Strip, a four-mile stretch of hotel-casinos along Las Vegas Boulevard (19 of the 25 largest hotels in the world call Vegas home), is the city's beating heart.

487 The parkway starts at Rockfish Gap near Waynesboro, Virginia, just off I-64, and ends 469 miles later near Cherokee, North Carolina, on Hwy-441.

488 Monument Valley Visitors' Center (🌐www.navajonationparks.org) is off Hwy-163, near the Utah border.

489 Walking tours cover everything from local architecture to legends; visit 🌐www.savannahvisit.com.

490 For Bourbon Trail info, visit 🌐www.kybourbon.com.

491 Direct flights connect Lihue with Honolulu, San Francisco and Los Angeles. See 🌐www.hawaiistateparks.org for info on hiking in the Na Pali Coast State Park.

492 Dr Wilkinson's Hot Springs, 1507 Lincoln Ave, Calistoga (☎+1 707/942-4102, 🌐www.drwilkinson.com); Mount View Spa, 1457 Lincoln Ave, Calistoga (☎+1 707/942-6877, 🌐www.mountviewhotel.com); Jack London State Historic Park, Glen Ellen (🌐www.jacklondonpark.com); The French Laundry, 6640 Washington St, Yountville (☎+1 707/944-2380, 🌐www.frenchlaundry.com).

493 South Beach occupies the southernmost part of Miami Beach; Ocean Drive runs south-north for 10 blocks.

494 La Posada, 303 E 2nd St, Winslow (☎+1 928/289-4366, 🌐www.laposada.org).

495 Two of the most experienced stormchasing operators are Violent Skies (🌐www.violentskiestours.com) and TRADD (🌐www.traddstormchasingtours.com).

496 Visit 🌐www.cubs.com for Wrigley Field ticket information. Murphy's Bleachers, 3655 North Sheffield Ave (🌐www.murphysbleachers.com); Sheffield's, 3258 North Sheffield Ave (🌐www.sheffieldchicago.com).

497 For more info on Fantasy Fest, check out 🌐www.fantasyfest.net.

498 The Indianapolis 500 (🌐www.indy500.com) is held over Memorial Day weekend at the Indianapolis Motor Speedway; you'll need to pre-order tickets.

499 For more information on wolf-watching in Yellowstone, visit 🌐www.yellowstoneassociation.org.

500 See 🌐www.cirquedusoleil.com. Cirque's other shows are Mystère at TI, Zumanity at New York-New York, Viva Elvis at the Aria, and Criss Angel's Believe at Luxor. All typically play five nights per week; ticket prices $70–165.

501 The round-trip hike to the top of Half Dome is 17 miles (9–12hr, 4800ft ascent).

502 Juke joints don't tend to have websites, phones or set opening hours. For the most up-to-date information on what's on in the various venues in the Delta, call the "Cat Head" music and crafts store in Clarksdale on ☎+1 662-624-5992.

503 Russ and Daughters, 179 E Houston St (☎+1 212/475-4880, 🌐www.russanddaughters.com).

504 Lobster Shack at Two Lights, 225 Two Lights Rd, Cape Elizabeth (5 miles south of Portland; ☎+1 207/799-1677).

505 The festival takes place in May in Molokai on the western tip of the island. Admission is free.

506 See 🌐www.cannon-beach.net for more info.

507 Jules' Undersea Lodge, Key Largo Undersea Park, 51 Shoreland Drive, mile marker 103.2, Key Largo (☎+1 305/451-2353, 🌐www.jul.com).

508 The Crazy Horse Memorial (🌐www.crazyhorsememorial.org) is in South Dakota's Black Hills, on Hwy-16/385.

509 Brooks Falls (🌐www.nps.gov/katm) is a twenty-minute walk from Brooks Camp. Getting to Brooks Camp from Anchorage involves a flight to the town of King Salmon, then a short float-plane flight.

510 US Capitol (Mon–Sat 8.30am–4.30pm; 🌐www.visitthecapitol.gov); White House (🌐www.whitehouse.gov/about/tours-and-events); Supreme Court (Oct–April arguments 10am & 1pm; 🌐www.supremecourt.gov).

511 Alaska Sea Kayakers (☎+1 907/472-2534, 🌐www.alaskaseakayakers.com), in Whittier, rents sea kayaks and runs guided day-trips and multi-day tours.

512 Cedar Point (☎+1 419/627-2350, 🌐www.cedarpoint.com) is open daily 10am–10pm, late-May to early Sept.

513 Annapolis's Cantler's Riverside Inn, 458 Forest Beach Rd (☎+1 410/757-1311, 🌐www.cantlers.com), or Kelly's, 2108 Eastern Ave (☎+1 410/327-2312) and Costas Inn, 4100 Northpoint Blvd (☎+1 410/477-1975, 🌐www.costasinn.com), both in Baltimore, will do the trick.

514 Visit 🌐www.appalachiantrail.org for more info.

515 The official website, 🌐www.burningman.com, has ticket info, photos and a helpful "First-Timers' Guide".

516 Early October is prime leaf-viewing time. See 🌐www.foliage-vermont.com for updates.

517 Several companies, including Celebrity (🌐www.celebritycruises.com), Holland America (🌐www.hollandamerica.com) and CruiseWest (🌐www.cruisewest.com), run cruises through Alaska's Inside Passage.

518 The Steamship Authority (☎+1 508/693-9130, 🌐www.steamshipauthority.com) and Hy-Line Cruises (☎+1 800/492-8082, 🌐www.hy-linecruises.com), run ferries to Nantucket from Hyannis, Cape Cod.

519 See 🌐www.mardigrasneworleans.com for more info.

520 Graceland, 3734 Elvis Presley Blvd, Memphis (☎+1 800/238-2000, 🌐www.elvis.com/graceland).

521 For more information on the Alaska Marine Highway, go to 🌐www.dot.state.ak.us/amhs.

522 For all details, see 🌐www.havasupaitribe.com. Visitors pay $35 entrance fee, plus $17 to camp, or $145 for a lodge room. Getting from the road to the village costs $70 by horse or $85 by helicopter; hiking is free.

523 To experience life on the road in true Golden State style, rent a convertible; you can slip behind the wheel of a Chevrolet Corvette with San Francisco-based Specialty Rentals (🌐www.specialtyrentals.com).

524 Mayflower II is docked at the State Pier on Water Street in Plymouth (April–Nov daily 9am–5pm; $10, combo ticket with Plimoth Plantation $28; ☎+1 508/746-1622, 🌐www.plimoth.org). The Plimoth Plantation is three miles south of town off Rte-3 (April–Nov daily 9am–5pm; $24, combo ticket with Mayflower II $28; ☎+1 508/746-1622, 🌐www.plimoth.org).

525 The Austin American-Statesman Bat Observation Center is on the southeast side of the bridge.

526 Concerts are every Saturday night at the Carter Family Memorial Music Center (🌐www.carterfamilyfold.org).

527 Blazing Saddles Bike Rentals & Tours is at 2715 Hyde St at Beach (☎+1 415/202-8888, 🌐www.blazingsaddles.com).

528 Half-hour tours are offered at the factory, one mile north of I-89 on Rte-100 in the village of Waterbury Center (every 30min daily; July to mid-Aug 9am–9pm; mid-Aug to late Oct 9am–7pm; late Oct–June 10am–

6pm; $3, under 12s free; ☎+1 866/BJ-TOURS, 🌐www.benjerry.com/scoop-shops/factory-tours).

529 Jockey's Ridge State Park, US 158 Bypass, mile marker 12. Kitty Hawk Kites (☎+1 877/359-8447, 🌐www.kittyhawkkites.com) provides instruction and equipment.

530 Old Coal Mine Museum, 2814 Hwy-14, Madrid (🌐www.turquoisetrail.org/stops/detail/old-coal-mine-museum); Mine Shaft Tavern, 2846 Hwy-14, Madrid (☎+1 505/473-0743, 🌐www.themineshafttavern.com).

531 The Everglades (🌐www.nps.gov/ever) are best visited during the dry season (Nov–April).

532 Several stores in town offer bike rentals and shuttles to trailheads; the best times to visit are spring and fall.

533 For more on playing ball at the Field of Dreams, visit 🌐www.fieldofdreamsmoviesite.com.

534 Visit 🌐www.alta.com and 🌐www.snowbird.com for full details on lift tickets, accommodation and transport.

535 The most popular entrance to Glacier National Park (🌐www.nps.gov/glac) is near West Glacier town, off Hwy-2.

536 In Lockhart: Kreuz Market, 619 N Colorado St (☎+1 512/398-2361); Black's Barbecue, 215 N Main St (☎+1 888/632-8225). In Luling: City Market, 633 E Davis St (☎+1 877/526-2271). Near Driftwood: The Salt Lick, 18300 FM 1826 (☎+1 512/858-4959). In Taylor: Louie Mueller BBQ, 206 W 2nd St (☎+1 512/352-6206).

537 Ceremonial dances are performed at Taos Pueblo (🌐www.taospueblo.com) about ten times a year.

538 Information on transportation and outfitters is provided by the National Park Service (☎+1 805/658-5730, 🌐www.nps.gov/chis), which also operates a visitor centre at 1901 Spinnaker Drive (daily 8.30am–5pm; free) in Ventura on the nearby California coast. Camping permits are $15 per night (info at ☎+1 877/444-6777).

539 Galatoire's, 209 Bourbon St (☎+1 504/525-2021, 🌐www.galatoires.com). Jackets required for men after 5pm and all day Sunday.

540 Alabama state capitol, 600 Dexter Ave (☎+1 334/242-3935); Dexter Avenue Church, 454 Dexter Avenue; Civil Rights Memorial, 400 Washington Ave (🌐www.splcenter.org/civil-rights-memorial); Rosa Parks Museum, 252 Montgomery St (☎+1 334/241-8615, 🌐montgomery.troy.edu/rosaparks/museum).

541 The A-train runs from Queens through Brooklyn and Manhattan to Inwood-207th Street.

542 Abyssinian Baptist Church, 132 Odell Clark Place. Tourists are welcome at the Sun 11am service only (1hr 30min; free). Mount Nebo Baptist Church, 1883 Adam Clayton Powell, Jr Blvd at W 114th St is less touristy.

543 The South Rim is open 24 hours a day, 365 days a year, the North Rim from mid-May to mid-October. See 🌐www.nps.gov/grca for more information.

544 Snowshoes can be rented at Galena Lodge, one of the Rocky Mountains' prime venues for snowshoeing and cross-country skiing. Fly into Boise from where it's a four-hour drive to Sun Valley/Galena Lodge. Useful websites: 🌐www.galenalodge.com, 🌐www.visitidaho.org.

545 Key Largo: Key Lime Tree (☎+1 305/853-0378). On Marathon: Porky's Bayside Restaurant, 1400 Overseas Highway (☎+1 305/289-2065). On Big Deer Key: Key West Key Lime Pie Co, 225 Key Deer Blvd (☎+1 877/882-7437). In Key West: Blond Giraffe Key Lime Pie Factory, 107 Simonton St (☎+1 305/296-9174); Kermit's Key West Key Lime Shoppe, 200 Elizabeth St (☎+1 305/296-0806); Rooftop Café, 310 Front St (☎+1 305/294-2042).

GOOD to know

CITIES

The **most populous US cities** are New York City (8.3 million people), Los Angeles (3.8 million), Chicago (2.8 million) and Houston (2.2 million), followed by a close race between Philadelphia and Phoenix (both around 1.5 million); the latter is also the country's fastest-growing major city. Among the **fastest-shrinking** major cities are Detroit, Boston, Cincinnati and St Louis; New Orleans, which lost a great deal of its population after Hurricane Katrina, has started to see growth again, and recent estimates put the population at around 330,000, or just under three quarters of its pre-Katrina levels.

EXTREME CLIMATE

The lowest, hottest and driest points in the US are all in **Death Valley**. Badwater Basin is 282 feet below sea level, while the ironically named Greenland Ranch reached 135°F in 2001 (the highest temperature ever recorded in the US and the second-highest in the world). Death Valley's overall average precipitation is less than two inches per year.

"Whoever wants to know America had better learn baseball"

Jacques Barzun

ELVIS IS EVERYWHERE

Elvis Presley had 31 #1 songs between Billboard's US charts and the UK top 40, the first of which was the bluesy **"Heartbreak Hotel"**, in 1956; the most recent was a remix of **"A Little Less Conversation"**, in 2002 (which only hit #50 in the US). Coincidentally, Elvis made 31 movies during his lifetime, sharing the screen with everyone from Walter Matthau and Bill Bixby to Barbara Stanwyck and Mary Tyler Moore. More than 600,000 visitors make the pilgrimage each year to visit the King's home, Graceland, in Memphis, Tennessee.

FIVE UNUSUAL FESTIVALS

World Grits Festival, St George, SC (mid-April). Consuming corn porridge in the grits-eating capital of the world.

Solstice Parade, Seattle, WA (mid-June). Nude bike-riding.

Redneck Games, East Dublin, GA (early July). Hillbilly Olympics, featuring seed spitting and bobbing for pigs' feet.

Lumberjack World Championships, Hayward, WI (late July). Climbing, sawing and rolling logs.

Punkin' Chuckin', Millsboro, DE (early Nov). Hurling pumpkins by catapult.

THANKSGIVING

Thanksgiving has been officially observed in the US since the Civil War, though its legend dates back to 1621 as part of a goodwill ceremony between English Pilgrims and Wampanoag Indians in Plymouth Plantation. These days a traditional menu includes:

One large turkey

Bread or mushroom stuffing

Mashed potatoes with gravy

Sweet potatoes/yams

Cranberry sauce

Creamed onions

Green beans or Brussels sprouts

Waldorf or other salad (Waldorf salad is typically apples, celery, walnuts and mayonnaise)

Rolls or biscuits

Pumpkin/pecan/apple pie(s)

PRESIDENTS

There have been 43 US presidents but since one, Grover Cleveland, was elected twice (non-consecutively), Barack Obama is considered the 44th president. Presidents serve four years in a term and have a two-term limit.

Gerald Ford is the only person in US history to have served as vice president and president **without having been elected** to either position; he was appointed to both positions after the resignations of Spiro Agnew and Richard Nixon, respectively.

Because US presidents are elected by electoral votes and not popular votes, four men have become president **without receiving the most votes** from the people: John Quincy Adams (1824), Rutherford B. Hayes (1876), Benjamin Harrison (1888) and George W. Bush (2000).

"In America, anyone can become president. That's one of the risks you take"

Adlai Stevenson

GREAT AMERICAN NOVELS

Invisible Man *Ralph Ellison*. The greatest, and most depressing, portrait of race relations in mid-twentieth-century America.

The Sound and the Fury *William Faulkner*. The quintessential Southern writer's masterwork, told from four different perspectives in four wildly different styles.

Moby Dick *Herman Melville*. A gripping tale of survival, salvation and society on the high seas, scientific detail sitting alongside frantic action sequences.

The Adventures of Huckleberry Finn *Mark Twain*. Still complex and challenging after 120 years, the signature tale of life on the Mississippi River in antebellum America.

Slaughterhouse Five *Kurt Vonnegut*. The most experimental of the country's greatest novels, blending a brutal wartime saga with time travel and a fractured narrative.

DRIVE OR BIKE?

Four of the five busiest urban freeways are in **Los Angeles** – the 405, 5, 10 and 101 – along with Atlanta's I-75. The 405 carries nearly 400,000 cars a day. The average American drives more than 8300 miles and emits two to five tonnes of **carbon dioxide** per year. According to *Bicycling* magazine, Portland, Oregon, is America's top city for cycling. The worst are Atlanta, Houston and Boston.

GETTING WET ON THE WEST COAST TRAIL • CATCHING A WAVE ON VANCOUVER ISLAND • CRUISING GEORGIAN BAY • DRIVING THE ICEFIELDS PARKWAY • GETTING LOST WITHIN THE WALLS OF VIEUX-QUÉBEC • FOLLOWING THE YUKON QUEST • PADDLING YOUR WAY THROUGH ALGONQUIN PROVINCIAL PARK • EXPLORING ANCIENT CULTURE ON HAIDA GWAII • ICE SKATING ON THE WORLD'S LARGEST RINK • DRIVING THE CABOT TRAIL • REDEFINING REMOTE ON THE HUDSON BAY TRAIN • SEA KAYAKING IN THE MINGAN ARCHIPELAGO • SKI FROM THE SKY IN THE ROCKIES • CYCLING ON THE P'TIT TRAIN DU NORD TRAIL • TRACKING DOWN POLAR BEARS IN CHURCHILL • RAFTING THE TATSHENSHINI • SPEND THE NIGHT IN ISOLATION AT BATTLE HARBOUR • FLOAT ON LITTLE MANITOU LAKE • LIGHTING UP THE SKY IN MONTRÉAL • EATING LIKE A NEWFOUNDLANDER IN ST JOHN'S • STRIKING IT LUCKY IN DAWSON CITY • TAKING AFTERNOON TEA IN VICTORIA • SEEING OLD RIVALS IN AN ICE-HOCKEY GAME • RELIVING THE WILD WEST AT THE CALGARY STAMPEDE • FORM A LASTING IMPRESSION AT NIAGRA FALLS • WATCHING THE TIDE ROLL AWAY IN THE BAY OF FUNDY • SPYING WHALES AND SPOTTING PUFFINS IN THE ATLANTIC • GETTING WET ON THE WEST COAST TRAIL • CATCHING A WAVE ON VANCOUVER ISLAND • CRUISING GEORGIAN BAY • DRIVING THE ICEFIELDS PARKWAY • GETTING LOST WITHIN THE WALLS OF VIEUX-QUÉBEC • FOLLOWING THE YUKON QUEST • PADDLING YOUR WAY THROUGH ALGONQUIN PROVINCIAL PARK • EXPLORING ANCIENT CULTURE ON HAIDA GWAII • ICE SKATING ON THE WORLD'S LARGEST RINK • DRIVING THE CABOT TRAIL • REDEFINING REMOTE ON THE HUDSON BAY TRAIN • SEA KAYAKING IN THE MINGAN ARCHIPELAGO • SKI FROM THE SKY IN THE ROCKIES • CYCLING ON THE P'TIT TRAIN DU NORD TRAIL • TRACKING DOWN POLAR BEARS IN CHURCHILL • RAFTING THE TATSHENSHINI • SPEND THE NIGHT IN ISOLATION AT BATTLE HARBOUR • FLOAT ON LITTLE MANITOU LAKE • LIGHTING UP THE SKY IN MONTRÉAL • EATING LIKE A NEWFOUNDLANDER IN ST JOHN'S • STRIKING IT LUCKY IN DAWSON CITY • TAKING AFTERNOON TEA IN VICTORIA • SEEING OLD RIVALS IN AN ICE-HOCKEY GAME • RELIVING THE WILD WEST AT THE CALGARY STAMPEDE • FORM A LASTING IMPRESSION AT NIAGRA FALLS • WATCHING THE TIDE ROLL AWAY IN THE BAY OF FUNDY • SPYING WHALES AND SPOTTING PUFFINS IN THE ATLANTIC • GETTING WET ON THE WEST COAST TRAIL • CATCHING A WAVE ON VANCOUVER ISLAND • CRUISING GEORGIAN BAY • DRIVING THE ICEFIELDS PARKWAY • GETTING LOST WITHIN THE WALLS OF VIEUX-QUÉBEC • FOLLOWING THE YUKON QUEST • PADDLING YOUR WAY THROUGH ALGONQUIN PROVINCIAL PARK • EXPLORING ANCIENT CULTURE ON HAIDA GWAII •

Canada
546–572

561 Rafting the Tatshenshini

Redefining remote on the Hudson Bay Train **556**

Eating like a Newfoundlander in St John's

Sea kayaking in the Mingan Archipelago **557**

565

C A N A D A

Reliving the Wild West at the Calgary Stampede

569

563 Float on Little Manitou Lake

546 Getting wet on the West Coast Trail

Paddling your way through Algonquin Provincial Park **552** **554** Ice skating on the world's largest rink

568 Seeing old rivals in an ice-hockey game

546 Getting wet on the West Coast Trail

BRITISH COLUMBIA Between raging Pacific gales and steady rainforest downpours, chances are you're going to get wet. Very wet. But it's the rain that has made the primordial landscape of the West Coast Trail, a 77km hike along a remote and rugged stretch of western Vancouver Island, almost magical for its lushness of life. Deep shades of green colour much of what grows here, from thick stands of evergreen trees and giant ageless cedars to the smooth rocks dappled with emerald moss and billowing kelp strands floating just beneath the water's surface.

Though only 52 people each day are permitted to embark on the trail, you won't be alone as you wade across rivers, negotiate log bridges and climb up and down ladders. Expect to catch glimpses of seals, sealions, great blue herons, bald eagles and migrating grey whales. Just don't expect to stay dry.

547 Catching a wave on Vancouver Island

BRITISH COLUMBIA For some of the wildest surfing in the world, head to the shipwreck-strewn west coast of Vancouver Island, also known as "the graveyard of the Pacific". Flanked by the lush temperate rainforest of the 130km-long Pacific Rim National Park, the waters here are ferocious. Swells reach up to six metres, and epic storms uproot trees, sending drifting logs down the face of waves. Whales have been known to sneak up on unsuspecting surfers, diving under their boards and lifting them clean out of the water. As if that weren't enough abuse, barking, territorial sealions often chase these thrill-seekers from the ocean back to shore. On land, it's just as wild – bald eagles soar between giant trees, and wolves and black bears forage for food amid piles of sun-bleached driftwood.

Even in summer, when swells ease to a gentle one to two metres, the water remains bone-chillingly cold, hovering around 13ºC. Still, plenty of wannabe wave riders flock to the chilled-out surf centre of Tofino to practise their "pop-ups", but a thick skin – or a thick wetsuit – is required.

Come winter, the waves start pummelling in from the Pacific with all the force of a boxer's knock-out punch. The wind whips off the snow-capped mountains, the ocean cools down to a shocking 8°C and hardy surfers hit the waves wearing 5mm-thick wetsuits as well as boots, gloves and protective hoods. For the novice, this is the time to peel off the wetsuit and watch the waves roll in from the blissful confines of a seaside hot tub.

548 Cruising Georgian Bay

ONTARIO The rocky little islets and crystal-blue waters of Georgian Bay, a long and wide appendage of Lake Huron, are the best parts of the wild and wonderful landscape that begins not far north of Toronto. Set sail, catch a water taxi or join a day-trip cruise from Honey Harbour to see what inspired the "Group of Seven" artists, who declared this true "painter's country", the lone pine set against the sky their favourite motif. Beausoleil Island, at the centre of Georgian Bay Islands National Park, makes for scenic hiking back on dry land, with thick maple stands in the south and glacier-scraped rock in the north.

ALBERTA "This wondertrail will be world renowned", predicted a 1920s surveyor when Highway 93 North – now better known as the Icefields Parkway – was only a fanciful idea. And sure enough, when it opened twenty years later, built as a Depression-era public works programme, the 230km road between Lake Louise and Jasper immediately became one of the world's ultimate drives.

It still is. The highway snakes through the cornucopia of snow-capped peaks that crown the Continental Divide, running right down the heart of the Rockies. Between the peaks lies an almost over-whelming combination of natural splendour: immense glaciers, blue-green iridescent lakes, foaming waterfalls, wildflower meadows, forests and wildlife from elk and moose to black and grizzly bears.

You could drive the whole highway in about four hours, but to do so would be to miss out on the many trails and viewpoints along the way, as well as the chance to appreciate properly all the subtle shifts in scenery and mood: rivers broaden or narrow, moving from churningx to sluggish; light changes according to the fickle mountain weather, sometimes bathing a distant set of peaks in a rosy pink almost otherworldly glow.

Several points along the route outstrip any superlatives. Bow Pass, at 2070m the road's highest point, is spectacular not only for the views but the delicate subalpine ecosystem that ekes out its existence at these windy, snowy heights. Here moss-lined paths lead between dark stands of towering fir and spruce while mountain heather and alpine forget-me-nots provide splashes of pink, yellow and white.

Far bleaker is the 325-square-kilometre Columbia Icefield itself – one of the largest accumulations of ice south of the Arctic Circle. Its rock-strewn moonscape has remained virtually unchanged since the last ice age, and at its edge you can watch 200-year-old snow slowly melting.

550 Getting lost within the walls of Vieux-Québec

QUÉBEC You'd be forgiven for mistaking Canada's most graceful downtown for somewhere in the middle of Europe. As you amble the cobbled streets of a centuries-old walled city, where the views encompass castle turrets and battlefields – and the main language spoken is French – it's easy to feel you've left North America far behind. Founded by the French in 1608, Québec City was taken in 1759 by the English in a historic battle on the Plains of Abraham, just outside the city walls; the victory also won them control of Canada. The fortifications survive today (making it North America's only walled city) and mark the boundaries of the old town, or Vieux-Québec. Its lovingly maintained, chaotic tangle of streets holds a treasury of historic architecture, fine restaurants and tiny museums. Pottering around its pedestrianized precincts – which are virtually untouched by minimarts, chain stores and fast-food restaurants – is the chief pleasure of a visit here.

The lower town, particularly the Quartier Petit-Champlain – a beautiful warren of narrow lanes and hidden staircases lined by carefully restored limestone buildings – is a good place to begin an aimless wander. It's easy to idle away hours soaking up the historic charm, listening to buskers and browsing refined boutiques, antique shops and studio-galleries where artists are often at work, before being tempted by the aromas that drift from the doorways of the many old-fashioned restaurants.

Luckily, the climbs up and down the steeply sloping streets and staircases around the town help justify indulging in rich, multi-course meals. After some Québecois foie gras, local duck, rabbit or wild game and creamy local cheeses, you'll need to hit the streets again to walk it all off.

551 Following the Yukon Quest

YUKON At the start of the Yukon Quest dogsledding race, a din has broken out. Dogs are barking, whining and howling as they're hooked up to their lines. They leap high in the air, hauling forward with all their might, trying to shift the weight that anchors them. Their ears are pricked, their tails wave, their tongues loll, their wide mouths grin. Anyone who suggests that sled dogs run against their will has never witnessed this – these dogs can't wait to get going.

The course of the Yukon Quest crosses 1600km of inhospitable winter wilderness between Fairbanks, Alaska and Whitehorse in Canada's Yukon Territory. In temperatures that can drop into the –40°C range, mushers and their dogs negotiate blizzards and white-outs, sheer mountains, and frozen rivers and overflow ice that snaps and cracks under paws and sled. Checkpoints are far apart (the more famous Iditarod race has twenty-five, but the Yukon Quest has just ten), with more than 300km between some of them, and teams have to camp beside the trail. Mushers must be able to care for themselves and their dogs no matter what the elements throw at them and, except at the race's halfway point in Dawson City, they're allowed to accept no outside help.

As the days progress, spectators observe the mushers' eyes go bloodshot and rheumy. Their hair becomes matted; their posture stoops. These men and women are enjoying little sleep. They may stop to rest their dogs for six hours in every twelve but by the time they've massaged ointment into their team's feet, melted snow for water and fed the dogs – who burn ten thousand calories a day when racing – and themselves, only a couple of hours remain. The curious spectator might wonder what could motivate these people to endure such hardship. But then darkness falls, the moon rises and the northern lights weave a tapestry of green and red against the night sky and the answer is clear: it's the world's most beautiful racetrack.

552 Paddling your way through Algonquin Provincial Park

ONTARIO The day may start like this: the rain eases and the mist on the lake begins to dissipate as the early sun breaks through the trees and onto your secluded campsite. You awaken to the melodious songs of warblers overhead, to the unspoiled wilderness of Algonquin Provincial Park.

After breakfast you ponder the day's route, put your canoe in the water and push off to explore this dense, forested park's extensive network of interconnected lakes, rivers and portages; with some 1500km of paddling circuits, exploring by canoe is an essential part of understanding what makes Algonquin tick. As you slide along glassy ponds and seemingly bottomless lakes, you begin to get a truer sense of the dramatic landscape: thick stands of maples, towering red pines, black spruce bogs, granite ridges and sandy beaches.

But it's not all magnificent landscapes – you'll have chance encounters with wildlife as well: the canoe drifts by a lone moose foraging chest-deep in a marshy wetland; a black bear appears along the far shore, but the distance between the two of you feels close enough; an industrious beaver constructs his lodge; and a family of merganser ducks paddles alongside you before diving into the water to grab a fishy meal with their long, thin bills.

At the end of a long day's paddle the blue skies give way to a star-filled night and you settle around the crackling campfire to a plate of freshly caught lake trout. A new cast of characters croon their forest tunes: haunting calls of loons ricochet around the lakeshore, wolves howl in distant highlands. A barred owl hoots its distinctive "Who cooks for you? Who cooks for you all?" call, but you're not hearing things – after all, in a place where you could easily go for days without human contact, the only voice you're likely to hear is nature's.

EXPLORING ANCIENT CULTURE ON
Haida Gwaii

BRITISH COLUMBIA Soaking in natural hot springs on a rainforest island while a pod of humpback whales swims past... suddenly the "Canadian Galápagos" moniker, occasionally used to describe the remote archipelago of Haida Gwaii, doesn't seem so far-fetched.

Cast some 150km off the west coast of British Columbia, Haida Gwaii is a place where the world's largest black bears forage on deserted beaches, black-footed albatross show off their enormous wingspan, and sea stars the size of coffee tables and the shades of disco lights sprawl languidly on rocks.

Only two thousand people a year make the journey to the pristine national park in the southern portion of the islands. Here, it takes eight people to hug a thousand-year-old cedar tree, months to kayak around the 1750km of coastline and a lifetime for an archeologist to uncover artefacts left untouched by a 10,000-year-old civilization. There is an underlying eeriness to this place that was, until recently, home to thousands of Haida – the most sophisticated and artistically prolific of British Columbia's aboriginal peoples.

These days, moss-covered beams of longhouses and decaying totem poles are the lingering remains of the ancient Haida villages, whose populations left after being drastically reduced in an 1880s smallpox epidemic. The most haunting and remote of the deserted villages is SGang Gwaay, a mist-shrouded UNESCO World Heritage Site on the southernmost tip of the park, where the world's largest collection of Haida mortuary poles stare defiantly out to sea.

Looking up at this forest of tree trunks – expertly carved with the wide-eyed features of bears, frogs, beavers, eagles, ravens and whales – is to gaze into the weather-beaten face of history. However, as is the wish of the Haida, there is little attempt at preserving the totems. Some day soon the poles will lean, fall, rot and – like everything else here – return to nature.

SKATING on
the world's largest rink

ONTARIO Yes, Paris has the elegance of the Seine. Fine, London has the bustling Thames. And OK, Rome has the historic Tiber. Great waterways all, no doubt about it – but none of them is a match for what you can do on the ribbon of snow and ice that is Ottawa's Rideau Canal in winter.

Because when the chill hits, an 8km stretch of water running through the heart of the city freezes and becomes the world's largest natural ice-skating surface, the size of ninety Olympic-sized ice rinks. This is the signal for hearty Ottawans to bundle up, strap on their skates and head out onto the ice to play, glide past the sights of the nation's capital and even commute to work. It's all part of an annual ritual that has become a favourite winter pastime.

Completed in 1832, the whole of the Rideau Canal is actually much longer than the segment you can skate on in Ottawa. Its 202km-length connects the capital with Kingston, to the southwest, via a series of canals, rivers, lakes. In winter, though, the canal is best experienced in Ottawa during the annual Winterlude Festival, held during the first three weekends of February.

In the crisp bright of a Canadian winter the canal is a hive of activity. Thousands glide – and sometimes totter – about, a quick game of pond hockey breaks out on a more isolated stretch, figure skaters spin, speedskaters skim by, all metronome-like consistency, and everybody vies for a glimpse of world-renowned sculptors carving masterpieces from blocks of snow and ice.

As daylight gives way to an even chillier darkness, floodlights light up the canal and the icy spectacle becomes cosier and even more magical. Children – overbalanced either by lack of practice or thick winter clothing – zip precariously along, steaming cups of hot chocolate are sipped, kisses are exchanged and BeaverTails (don't worry – they're the fried, sweet pastry variety) are eaten. Everyone, it seems, is totally oblivious to the subzero temperatures. Who needs a beach when you can have this much fun on ice?

555 Driving the Cabot Trail

NOVA SCOTIA Weaving its way through some of the most mesmerizing scenery in Canada, the Cabot Trail makes a 300km loop around the northern tip of Cape Breton Island, a scintillating coastal drive that takes in jagged cliffs, pristine lakes and mist-draped forests; it's also one of the best places in Canada to go whale-watching, with numerous lookout points and tour providers located along the trail. En route you'll discover remnants of Cape Breton's rich colonial past. On the west coast, La Région Acadienne is a French-speaking enclave established by Acadian settlers in 1785, while on the east coast a strong Gaelic culture thrives in the form of ceilidhs, fiddle-players and festivals, brought over by Scottish Highlanders in the nineteenth century.

Begin your journey on the trail at the Hwy 105 access point (Exit 7), which snakes northwest over the hills before slipping along the Margaree River Valley, whose soft, green landscapes are framed by bulging peaks. Further north lies the awe-inspiring Cape Breton Highlands National Park, a mix of deep wooded valleys, untouched headlands and boggy uplands. The trail continues to hug the coast before cutting right through the park, offering captivating views at every turn, but to make the most of the landscape you need to get hiking; 25 trails are signposted from the road. Some are easy woodland strolls, while others offer more demanding climbs to bubbling cascades and towering coastal viewpoints. One of the most popular is the 9.2km-long Skyline Loop Trail (2–3hr), which clambers up the coastal mountains a few kilometres up the coast from the Acadian settlement of Chéticamp.

At the top end of Cape Breton the road threads its way across the base of Cape North, where you can make a detour to Meat Cove, a wonderfully picturesque bay at the end of a pockmarked gravel road; on the way, visit the windswept spot where John Cabot, for whom the trail is named, may have "discovered" North America in 1497. Fine strips of sand await on the eastern side of Cape Breton; in the summer you can swim at places like Ingonish Beach, soaking up the raw scenery and fresh, Atlantic breezes.

556 Redefining remote on the Hudson Bay Train

MANITOBA There's something deeply alluring about travelling somewhere you can't reach by car – a truly remote place, far from anywhere. The tiny settlement of Churchill, shivering by the shores of the great Hudson Bay in Canada's north, is just such a place; its only land connection to the rest of the world is a 1600km railway that begins in the prairie town of Winnipeg. You start your journey in the agricultural heartland of Canada and end it in a frozen wasteland where only arctic mosses and lichen can grow. It's a startling transformation – a real journey to the edge of the world.

The train itself oozes character with its 1950s stainless steel carriages, polished chrome fixtures and an old-fashioned dining car. This is the place to get chatting to your fellow travellers, among them gnarled fishermen and trappers, Cree and Chipewyan aboriginal people and even a few Inuit. Most of them know this land like the back of their hands, and will readily tell you the names of the flora and fauna you pass by. They'll also fill you in on the minor scandals associated with the various communities along the line: the embezzling mayor who ended his days trapping furs to earn his crust; the village where a Mountie was shot dead by a Cree outlaw a hundred years ago.

The journey includes two nights on the train; waking up from your second night, pull open the blind and you'll feel as if you're on another planet: gone are the verdant forests, replaced by stunted, shrivelled stumps which peter out altogether as you enter the Barrenlands – a region of fierce winds, bitter cold and permanently frozen soil. And then you pull into Churchill and the phrase "end of the line" takes on a whole new meaning. Way up here, in Canada's subarctic, you'll feel farther from civilization than you ever thought possible.

557 Sea kayaking in the Mingan Archipelago

QUÉBEC On the map, the Mingan Archipelago, stretching 150km from Longue-Pointe-de-Mingan to Aguanish, looks like a trail of biscuit crumbs scattered in the Gulf of St Lawrence. But from the vantage point of your sea kayak, cruising through the channels that separate this collection of forty uninhabited islands and nearly a thousand islets and reefs, it's a much different story. First, it's impossible to miss the tall rock monoliths that guard the bays. The sea has worn the rock into smooth curves and, from a distance, these towering hunks of stone look very much like people; from closer to shore, they resemble abandoned flying saucers placed one on top of the other. Second, much of what you're paddling around to see actually lurks beneath the surface. The waters here are a feeding ground for the largest mammal on Earth, the blue whale, as well as for minke, fin, beluga and humpback whales – keep your eyes trained on the horizon, looking for the telltale puff of water vapour blown by a whale as it surfaces. But don't ignore what's right around you: seals pop their heads through the waves, like periscopes, no more than a few strokes away. Their big brown eyes set in moustachioed faces stare at you curiously before the animals disappear back into the deep with a flash of silver underbelly.

Beneath your paddles the water is so clear that it magnifies the seabed. Bright orange sea stars, deep red urchins and lime green kelp crust the sea floor, the rock worn into underwater monoliths or crazily paved ledges. As sunset stains the sea pink and purple, you'll need to pick an island and a beachside campsite. Civilization feels a galaxy away as you laze around the campfire or scramble up a clifftop for a last gaze out at sea, hopeful of spotting a whale silhouetted against the sinking sun.

558 Ski from the sky in the Rockies

BRITISH COLUMBIA The small town of Golden, between Glacier and Revelstoke national parks near the British Columbia-Alberta border, doesn't seem like much as you pass through. But descend on to a snowy peak in the area from a helicopter, skis in tow, and you're likely to form a totally different opinion.

Heliskiing got its start in the Rocky Mountains of BC, and this is still one of the best places on Earth to take part in this terrifically expensive, fairly dangerous and undeniably thrilling activity. It's a pristine mountain wonderland filled with open bowls and endless tree runs, all coated in a layer of light and powdery snow. Accessing these stashes by helicopter, with its odd mix of mobility and avian fragility, only intensifies the feeling of exploration and isolation. From the air, you'll eagerly envision making your signature squiggles and carve lines in the untouched powder fields. And once the helicopter recedes into the distance, leaving you alone atop the mountain, you'll feel every inch the pioneer.

After you've adjusted to the rhythm and bounce of skiing or riding this light powder, you might find yourself on a good day descending twice the typical distance as at a top ski resort.

You're also likely to discover that the deeper the snow and steeper the grade, the more exhilarating the run. Cornices and drop-offs that seemed foreboding from the helicopter will be a daring enticement; trees that from a distance looked impossibly dense reveal tempting paths; you'll drop into pitches that would have been unthinkable on harder snow, plunging in and out of chest-deep powder again and again. But be warned: all this may be enough to transform you into one of the many diehards who sign up for their next heliskiing adventure the moment they reach base.

559 Cycling on the P'tit Train du Nord trail

QUÉBEC After a day of pedalling, a long downhill coast is a moment to be savoured. On either side the forest is a blur of green tinged with gold and the breeze ruffling your hair smells faintly of pine and earth. The treetops almost form a tunnel around the trail but in the glimpses of sky loom crinkled mountains, and off to the right, screened by foliage, roars the frothing fury of the Rivière Rouge, the Red River.

In the silence of the forest it's hard to imagine that fume-belching locomotives once thundered along the same route as your bicycle tyres. The P'tit Train du Nord was a busy railroad for eighty years, carrying Montréalers to the resorts of southwest Québec's Laurentian region before closing in 1989. But instead of abandoning the route to the forest, the rail bed was transformed into a magnificent cycling trail that winds for 200km through wooded splendour, especially beautiful in the autumn. Many of the original railroad station houses have been converted into cafés, information booths and facilities for cyclists, their decorative wooden gables and shady terraces restored with vibrant paint and blooming baskets.

The northern half of the trail is wild and remote, crossing numerous rivers dyed chestnut-brown by minerals and passing blue-black lakes close enough to wet your wheels. Small villages full of silver-steepled churches and impossibly cosy cottages cluster around the southern half of the trail. But whichever part you choose to ride (if not the whole course), nearly every bend holds an inviting picnic spot to laze in or a shady pool to revive sore feet and aching muscles.

560 Tracking down polar bears in Churchill

MANITOBA Signs warning "Polar Bear Alert – Stop, don't walk in this area" dot the city limits of Churchill, Manitoba. Beyond them lie wide expanses of the bleak and often frozen Hudson Bay or the treeless, endlessly flat tundra. It's this location on the threshold of two forbidding environments that makes the town the unchallenged "polar bear capital of the world".

Local polar bears spend most of their lives roaming the platform of ice covering Hudson Bay to hunt seals. But by July the ice melt forces the bears ashore to subsist on berries, lichen, seaweed, mosses and grasses. This brings the animals close to your doorstep; indeed, during the summer Churchill's "Polar Bear Police" typically remove over a hundred bears from the town. It's challenging and very dangerous work: although cuddly-looking, these creatures are also the largest land carnivores in existence. They can run at 50km/h and a single whack of their foot-wide clawed paws can kill. Being unaccustomed to humans, they'll also quickly size you up as potential prey.

It's better to wait until later in the year, and from the relative comfort of a tundra buggy (a converted bus that rides high above the ground on giant balloon tyres), to do your bear-watching. At the beginning of October, around two hundred polar bears gather near town to wait for the bay to freeze. With temperatures beginning to drop below zero and winds gusting up to 60km/h, the prime viewing season begins.

Lean and mean from the meagre summer diet male polar bears spend the autumn sparring with one another for hours, standing on their hind legs to launch fierce swipes and rather more gentlemanly (for a polar bear, anyway) chest-punches. Females steer clear of these shenanigans, particularly when with cubs, and spotting a mother lying back on a snowbank nursing her offspring – making tenderness and brute force temporary bedfellows – is a surprisingly touching scene.

YUKON The morning sunlight streams over the mountaintops, casting its warm rays on your wilderness campsite. Moments later you awaken to the calling of white-crowned sparrows as the thunderous crash of icebergs calving from nearby glaciers ricochets across the valley. A whiff of smoke entices you out onto the pebbled shore for breakfast around a crackling campfire. You take a deep breath and stretch – another day of rafting on the famed Tatshenshini River is about to begin.

These silt-laden waters are a paddlers' paradise, with the most magnificent portion coursing 213km through the heart of the St Elias Mountains, which extend from the southern Yukon across to northern British Columbia and on into the Gulf of Alaska. But long before anyone shrugged on a waterproof jacket, stowed their pack and grabbed a paddle, the river and surrounding region were home only to the Champagne and Aishinhik aboriginal peoples and wildlife – lots of wildlife.

There's still no shortage of things beaked, toothed and clawed here, and the inevitable sightings and full-on encounters are thrilling: grizzly bears lumber along gravel river beds, hoary marmots scramble up scree slopes and schools of glinting salmon swim in the murky waters below. Meanwhile, rufous hummingbirds hover overhead, swallows dart along the shoreline and a pair of bald eagles tend to their chicks atop a towering spruce tree.

Putting in at tiny Dalton Post, Yukon, for the start of a ten-day expedition that ends at Dry Bay, Alaska, you'll soon be floating through the same territory prospectors did during the late 1800s Klondike gold rush, when the river was a busy thoroughfare. Yet you'd barely know anyone had ever been this way – the whole region remains gloriously untouched, surrounded as it is by Canada's Kluane National Park, BC's Tatshenshini Provincial Park, the Yukon's Kluane Wildlife Sanctuary and the US Glacier Bay National Park. Journeying through these, you'll pass through steep-sided mountain canyons, negotiate rapids, drift past razor-sharp cliffs and thick stands of pristine wilderness and come within touching distance of 10,000-year-old icebergs – the river system, after all, passes through the largest non-polar ice field in the world.

After another long and rewarding day's paddle, you glide up to the riverbank in time to witness the spectacular sunset framed against a backbone of majestic peaks. After a hearty meal and a round of trading tales with your companions you crawl into your tent, bone-tired but already dreaming about what the river holds in store for you tomorrow.

561 Rafting
the TATSHENSHINI

NEWFOUNDLAND & LABRADOR Stuck out in the Labrador Straits, the jagged knot of granite that is Battle Harbour feels like it's perched at the end of the world. Established in the 1770s, the island soon became one of North America's busiest saltfish, salmon and sealing ports. Today the fishing boats are long gone; only a red-roofed church and a clutch of clapboard cottages dot the hillside above the rickety wharf. Just offshore, shimmering blue-white icebergs float gently southwards, slowly melting into bizarre shapes and twisted pillars. Humpback whales chase herring and capelin right up to the rocky shoreline, their gaping jaws bursting out of the water, full of fish; minke whales bask a little further out, while killer whales sometimes glide just off the docks.

Spending the night here is a magical experience; the island's natural beauty is complemented by its equally evocative human elements – creaking bunkhouses equipped with oil lamps and wood fires, a museum built from old, salt-stained warehouses and friendly locals who seem to have stepped straight out of *Moby Dick*. Accents have changed little since the first settlers arrived from England's West Country in the 1800s; children ask their mothers "Where's me father to?", and old fishermen look at the sky and say "ee look like rain, don't ee?".

In its prime Battle Harbour was the scene of Robert E. Peary's first news conference after he reached the North Pole in 1909. Long-term decline began in the 1930s and most residents were relocated to Mary's Harbour on the mainland in the 1960s. Many of those still work here as guides, boatmen and volunteers, all of them part of an epic heritage project that has resulted in the smattering of historic buildings currently open to the public; stay the night in one of the artfully restored cottages and you'll have little more than the cracking of ice and the splashing of whales for company.

562

SPEND THE NIGHT IN ISOLATION at
BATTLE HARBOUR

563 Float on Little Manitou Lake

SASKATCHEWAN In the minds of most Canadians, Saskatchewan is the heart of the rather plain prairies: a land of vast skies and dull Trans-Canada Highway drives. But within easy reach of the highway lies a lake with world-class therapeutic waters that must rank as the province's, if not the country's, best-kept secret. Little Manitou Lake and the adjacent Manitou Springs resort offer a no-frills spa experience where you come out heavily coated with minerals and feeling much the better for it.

The lake's magnesium and iodine-rich waters are good for the skin, glands and joints, and overall a dip in the water is said to promote healing and be an effective treatment for some dermatological problems. But reasons to soak here go well beyond skin therapy, the relief of aches and pains or even the many claimed cures attributed to the waters: in short, it's just a whole lot of fun. The water has three times as much salt as seawater does and is denser than that of the Dead Sea, which means you'll find yourself bobbing on the surface, feet up. This unique sensation of effortless floating is as close as you'll likely get to the weightlessness of space; it brings with it all sorts of acrobatic possibilities, or just the chance to drift about on your back and comfortably read a newspaper.

The waters have long been celebrated, first by the aboriginal peoples who camped on its shores and named it for its healing properties, later by homesteaders who spread the news of the mineral-rich lake, and of course by the Manitou Mineral Water Company, which shipped it as a product across North America. But things have quietened down from its spa town heyday, so for once there are few to rebuke you for time spent aimlessly adrift.

564 Lighting up the sky in Montréal

QUÉBEC Summer is a celebratory time in Montréal. After the winter hibernation, Montréalers spill onto the street terraces and fill the parks at the first sign of fine weather. Keen to milk it for all it's worth, the city lays on all sorts of colourful outdoor parties – the calypso-tinged Carifiesta and the world's pre-eminent jazz festival – that keep you tapping your feet. But the constant crowd-pleaser just requires you to look skywards: the twice-weekly spectacular fireworks display, from mid-June to late July, which pays tribute to balmy nights in a normally frigid city.

The Montréal International Fireworks Competition has become synonymous with the city's summer months and sees music and pyrotechnics synchronized to tell a story, creating an ephemeral fantasy world. Fireworks companies representing different countries let off their arsenals at La Ronde – an amusement park on an island in the middle of the St Lawrence River – and the shows are stunningly artistic.

The thousands upon thousands of wheels, candles, fountains and rockets that light up the sky are intended to be viewed with the accompanying musical score (broadcast live on local radio). From there it's not too far a leap to imagine a profusion of red stars and comets set to the soundtrack of *Born Free* to be the rising African sun. Then again, you could just turn off the radio, tilt your head skyward and be thankful that summer has arrived.

565 Eating like a Newfoundlander in St John's

NEWFOUNDLAND Belbin's Grocery isn't your average supermarket. It might look like one, but this is St John's, Newfoundland's feisty capital, so you can expect a few surprises.

Here you'll find fish and brewis (pronounced "bruise"), a sort of fisherman's comfort food of soft-boiled salt cod blended with crumbled chunks of bread and drizzled with scrunchions, fried fatty pork that adds a bacon-like addictiveness to the mix. Or toutons, pieces of bread dough fried in pork fat and slathered with hot molasses – the aroma of these frying is what lures Newfoundlanders out of bed in the morning. And then there's the venerable jiggs dinner, a traditional and deceptively simple Sunday feast that's one of the most satisfying home-cooked meals you'll ever have. Each family has its own variation – even Newfoundland truckstops serve it according to the dictates of the local ladies in the kitchen – but expect a heap of corned or salted beef drenched in rich gravy and served with buttered cabbage, potatoes and a bevy of lightly boiled vegetables. Cod tongues, another local delicacy, are actually the chunks of gelatinous meat found behind and under the tongue of said fish. Animal lovers, meanwhile, should note seal-flipper pie really is made with seal flipper. The tender meat of this appendage is blended with carrots and turnip, mixed with a thick gravy and topped with a biscuit crust.

Newfoundland cuisine was traditionally based on fish and game (including moose), hearty protein-rich foods that kept Atlantic fishermen alive through icy winters, and you can still find many of the dishes listed above in the city's older cafés and restaurants. But today trendier restaurants like *Bacalao* in St John's are creating a newer, healthier cuisine based on these old ingredients, while artisan producers craft partridgeberry (loganberry) jams, as well as iceberg vodka – made with water chipped off Greenland bergs. Moose is rarely served (hunters can only sell it to restaurants cooked, making it difficult to serve fresh) but caribou meat from nearby Labrador is common, often turning up in burgers. Still, you can always pick up some "bottled moose": cooked chunks of the meat packed into jars and seasoned with salt and pepper – perfect for stew and a taste of Newfoundland once back home.

566 Striking it lucky in Dawson City

YUKON In the late 1890s, rumour spread that the streets of Dawson City were paved with gold. In the most hysterical gold rush stampede the world has ever known, tens of thousands of fortune-seekers packed their bags and headed north for this former patch of moose pasture just below the Arctic Circle. By the time they arrived, most of the claims had been staked, and the brothels, dance halls and theatres of this burgeoning city were busy mining every last cent from the dejected prospectors.

More than a hundred years on, the streets of Dawson City are still not paved with gold. In fact, they're not paved at all, and you need not bother panning for the few flakes of the yellow stuff left in the creeks just outside town. Instead, make the trek to appreciate the rough-and-tumble feel and gold-rush-era charm of which Dawson City still has plenty.

With its historic wooden false-fronted buildings, dirt streets, creaking boardwalks and midnight sun, it's easy to see how Dawson City inspired literary titans such as Jack London and Robert Service – not just to write about the place but to live here too.

As for striking it lucky, your best chance is at Diamond Tooth Gertie's Gambling Hall, Canada's oldest legal casino, where women in breathtaking corsets and ruffle skirts hustle up drinks while you bet your way to boom or bust. Having doubled your chips at the roulette table, it's customary to celebrate at the *Sourdough Saloon*, in the *Downtown Hotel*, where the house tipple is the sour-toe cocktail – a drink that includes a real pickled human toe in a shot of alcohol (local charitable frostbite victims keep the bar well-stocked). As the rule goes: you can drink it fast or drink it slow, but your lips must touch the toe.

567 Taking afternoon tea in Victoria

BRITISH COLUMBIA Silver cutlery tinkles against Royal Doulton china as piano music wafts over idle chatter. "Would you like one lump or two?" enquires the waitress politely as she pours the piping hot tea. You'll take two, you say, and sink back into the floral sofa, taking in this most splendid view of Victoria's Inner Harbour from the *Tea Lobby* in the *Empress Hotel*. Rudyard Kipling once took afternoon tea in this very room and described Victoria as "Brighton Pavilion with the Himalayas for a backdrop". You can't help but agree with him.

Indeed, this provincial capital on the southern tip of wild and windy Vancouver Island is doing its bit to keep the "British" in British Columbia. Vancouver itself may have embraced lofty glass condominiums and coffee, but across the Georgia Strait, Victoria has clung steadfastly to its English heritage, preserving its late-1800s and early 1900s-era architecture and keeping alive the age-old tradition of afternoon tea.

There are many quaint places in Victoria to indulge this whim – small, suburban teahouses surrounded by royal family memorabilia, or amid the floral finery of the Butchart Gardens – but none can match the palatial *Empress Hotel* for grandiosity or price. Shirley Temple, John Travolta and Queen Elizabeth II have all been spotted piling on the pounds here.

The multi-course ritual starts off innocently enough: seasonal fruit topped with Chantilly cream with a choice of eight tea blends. Then a three-tiered plate arrives, heaving with cucumber and smoked salmon sandwiches, raisin scones slathered with jam and clotted cream and, on top, a glorious selection of pastries oozing chocolate. If you're too self-conscious to indulge in the very un-English practice of stuffing yourself silly, you could always fall back on the distinctly North American custom of asking for a doggy bag. It's all too good to just leave behind.

ONTARIO & QUÉBEC Saturday is known, on TV at least, as "Hockey Night in Canada" – pretty much all you need to know in terms of the country's fanaticism for one of its national games (lacrosse is the other one, but it has a long way to go before arousing the same level of passion that hockey does).

Perhaps it's the nature of the game itself. You'll have to focus hard to track the movement of the puck and the hurried but fluid way the teams shift players – frequently – in the middle of it all. And with those skaters hurtling around at 50km/hr and pucks clocking speeds above 160km/hr, this would be a high-adrenaline sport even without its relaxed attitude to combat on the rink. As an old Canadian adage has it, "I went to see a fight and an ice-hockey game broke out".

To maximize your exposure to the madness – and the bone-crunching body checks that send players smashing into the rinkside Plexiglas – try to get a seat near the ice for a game matching old rivals. Any of the six Canada-based teams will do, but when the Montréal Canadiens, the most successful team in hockey history, and the Toronto Maple Leafs meet – mirroring the country's Francophone and Anglophone divisions – you'll get a real feel for the electricity a match can generate. You may even see a hockey game break out.

Seeing old rivals in an ice-hockey game

568

ALBERTA For ten days each year, during the middle of July, the usually conservative city of Calgary loses its collective head (or finds a new cover for it, at least). Virtually everyone turns out in white Stetsons, bolo ties, blue jeans and hand-tooled boots. Indeed, everything seems, well, more western – which for a city like Calgary means shifting gears into serious cowboy overdrive. It's all a signal that the self-proclaimed "Greatest Outdoor Show on Earth" – the Calgary Stampede – has begun.

For Canada's rural folk – who often live on isolated farms or in tiny communities – this is the opportunity to bring their culture into the big city and really let rip. For the half-million visitors from elsewhere, it's a chance to witness the ultimate Wild West carnival, said to be North America's roughest rodeo.

Many activities, both kitschy and quite serious, vie for your attention. The main event is the daily rodeo competition, featuring the likes of bronco and bull riding, wild-pony racing, calf-roping, steer-wrestling and barrel-racing. But what sets the Stampede apart from other rodeos is the presence of the ludicrously dangerous, hugely exciting, chuck-wagon races: several teams of horsemen pack a stove and tent into these covered wagons, then hurtle around the dirt track at breakneck speeds.

The non-rodeo action takes place at the festival's focal point, Stampede Park. Top attractions include a First Nations tepee village where you can try traditional foods; the satisfyingly obscure World Blacksmith Competition; and an Agricultural Building that's home to many a handsome cow and bull.

Finish each day with a dash of Stampede nightlife, yet another world unto itself. The drinking, gambling and partying at various bars and mega-cabarets goes on into the small hours, sustained by a seemingly endless supply of barbecued meat and baked beans.

569
Reliving the Wild West at the Calgary Stampede

570 Form a lasting impression at Niagara Falls

ONTARIO In 1860, thousands watched as Charles Blondin walked a tightrope across Niagara Falls for the third time. Midway, the Frenchman paused to cook an omelette on a portable grill and then had a marksman shoot a hole through his hat from the *Maid of the Mist* tugboat, 50m below. Suffice to say, the falls simply can't be beaten as a theatrical setting.

Like much good theatre, Niagara makes a stupendous first impression, as it crashes over a 52m cliff shrouded in oceans of mist. It's actually two cataracts: tiny Goat Island, which must be one of the wettest places on Earth, divides the accelerating water into two channels on either side of the US-Canadian border. The spectacle is, if anything, even more extraordinary in winter, when snow-bent trees edge a jagged armoury of freezing mist and heaped ice blocks.

You won't just be choosing sides – note that the American Falls are but half the width of Canada's Horseshoe Falls – but also how best to see the falls beyond that first impression. A bevy of boats, viewing towers, helicopters, cable cars and even tunnels in the rock-face behind the cascade ensure that every angle is covered.

Two methods are especially thrilling and get you quite near the action: the *Maid of the Mist* boats, which struggle against the cauldron to get as close to the falls as they dare; and the tunnels of the "Journey Behind the Falls", which lead to points directly behind the waterfall. Either way guarantees that your first impression won't be the last one to register.

571 Watching the tide roll away in the Bay of Fundy

NOVA SCOTIA & NEW BRUNSWICK There's an eeriness to the Bay of Fundy, never more so than when the banking fogs that sweep in off the Atlantic shroud its churning waters, rendering its sea cliffs and coves barely visible in an all-pervasive gloom. Tourist brochures would lovingly call this "atmospheric", which it is. But what they tend to play up more are the bay's impressive stats: this is where the highest tides in the world come crashing in – there is up to 16m difference between high and low tide; in some places, the tide retreats four to five kilometres as it ebbs.

You don't need numbers, just your own eyes. Stand on the steps at Evangeline Beach in Grand-Pré and see young boys pedalling bicycles across far-reaching mud flats, then return a few hours later to find the beach deserted, the water three metres high and rising. You could build a giant IMAX movie screen on the mud flats at low tide and it would be completely submerged at high tide, just six hours later.

The effect comes in part from the bay's shape. At its mouth it is 100km wide, but it gradually narrows and shallows, producing a funnelling effect when the water comes in. Many of the rivers that lead off the upper bay are sites of tidal bores – basically the name for what occurs when the water rushes against the current. This is what people come to see.

When you first spot it from a distance, it may be subtle: just a faint line across a wide section of water. But as the river narrows and the water closes in, seeming to pick up speed, it's more like a moving wall – one that submerges islets, rides up high on floating docks and provides plenty of challenge for those foolish enough to break out surfboards or inflatable Zodiac boats.

572 Spying whales and spotting puffins in the Atlantic

NEWFOUNDLAND & LABRADOR Every spring and summer the waters off the coasts of Newfoundland and Labrador play host to the largest concentration of nesting seabirds and migrating humpback whales anywhere in the world. This spectacle unfolds just a few kilometres offshore, at the confluence of the warm Gulf Stream and the frigid Labrador Current. Here, where cod has been overfished to the point of near-elimination, nature enthusiasts come to experience the thrill of seeing hundreds of thousands of nesting seabirds, the feeding frenzy of 40-tonne whales and the occasional sighting of a 10,000-year-old iceberg drifting southwards from its Arctic home.

The way to observe all or part of this is on board one of the many passenger ferries that operate from Bay Bulls Harbour, bound for the Witless Bay Ecological Reserve. As your boat chugs towards the mist-shrouded islands, the patter of your guides and the jovial folk singing recede in deference to a loud hum, accompanied by an overpowering stench – its origin apparent only when the fog lifts. All of a sudden you're surrounded by what seems like millions of clown-faced puffins, penguin-like murres and black-legged kittiwakes diving in and out of the waters, delivering beakloads of capelin to their young.

The flurry of activity overhead nearly distracts you from seeing the telltale spray of a giant humpback in the distance. A short while later a guide announces that a small pod of minke whales has been spotted near the stern. Soon more dorsal fins slice through the gentle swells and the characteristic forked tails slap the seas as the whales submerge to feed. It's only now that you appreciate the immense size of these cetaceans as they follow alongside your boat.

The three-hour cruise is over far too quickly. Before you know it your guide asks, "Are you ready to become an honorary Newfoundlander?" Your intentions seem obvious as you quickly down a shot of Screech (the local rum) and kiss a stuffed puffin in front of a rowdy group of fellow passengers.

NEED to know

546 See ⊛ www.pc.gc.ca/pacificrim and ⊛ www.west-coasttrailbc.com for more details on planning a trip and general information on the trail.

547 See ⊛ www.westsidesurfschool.com and ⊛ www.surfsister.com for lessons.

548 Go to ⊛ www.gbcountry.com for lots of information and links on Georgian Bay.

549 Tours with Brewster Vacations (⊛ www.brewster.ca) include a ride on an Ice Explorer on the Columbia Icefield and a night's stay in a Jasper hotel.

550 See ⊛ www.quebecregion.com for information.

551 The race's official website (⊛ www.yukonquest.com) has past and future race details.

552 See ⊛ www.algonquin.on.ca for canoe rental details and ⊛ www.ontarioparks.com for more detailed information on the park.

553 For information on travelling to Gwaii Haanas National Park Reserve and Haida Heritage Site, see ⊛ www.pc.gc.ca/gwaiihaanas.

554 The National Capital Commission (☎ 613 239 5234 or 613 239 5000, ⊛ www.canadascapital.gc.ca) maintains the Rideau Canal and has information on ice conditions and events; the canal is usually open for skating from mid-January. You can rent skates at kiosks along the canal (C$16/2hr).

555 See ⊛ www.novascotia.com and ⊛ www.pc.gc.ca/capebreton for more information on the Cabot Trail.

556 The Hudson Bay train runs from Winnipeg to Churchill 3 days a week – see ⊛ www.viarail.ca for details.

557 Expédition Agaguk in Havre-Saint-Pierre (☎ 418/538 1588, ⊛ www.expedition-agaguk.com) rents equipment and also provides guides for trips around the islands.

558 Contact CMH Heli-Skiing (☎ 403/762 7100 or 1-800/661-0252, ⊛ www.cmhski.com).

559 The P'Tit Train du Nord takes 3–4 days, starting in Saint-Jérôme and ending in Mont-Laurier (⊛ www.transportduparclineaire.com).

560 Tundra buggy trips cost around C$80 per day, or you can book an all-inclusive five-day bear-spotting package with Wildlife Adventures – ⊛ www.wildlifeadventures.com.

561 Tatshenshini Expediting in Whitehorse (☎ 867/633 -2742, ⊛ www.tatshenshiniyukon.com) has details on package tours ranging from day-long rafting trips to 10-day expeditions.

562 Battle Harbour is open from mid-June to mid-September. For more detailed information call ☎ 709/921-6325 or 709/921-6216, or see ⊛ www.battleharbour.com.

563 Little Manitou Lake lies beside the small town of Watrous. The Manitou Springs Resort (☎ 306/946-2233 or 1-800-667-7672, ⊛ www.manitousprings.ca) is adjacent to the lake.

564 See ⊛ www.internationaldesfeuxloto-quebec.com

for schedule and ticket information.

565 Bacalao is at 65 Lemarchant Rd (☎ 709 579 6565, ⊛ www.bacalaocuisine.ca) and Belbin's Grocery is at 85 Quidi Vidi Rd (☎ 709 576 7640, ⊛ www.belbins.com). Blue on Water (☎ 709/574 2583, ⊛ www.blueonwater.com), another good restaurant for nouveau Newfoundland cuisine, is at 319 Water St.

566 Dawson City is a 1hr 15min flight from Whitehorse. *Diamond Tooth Gertie's Gambling Hall* is at 4th Ave and Queen St; the Sourdough Saloon is at 2nd Ave and Queen St.

567 Afternoon tea starts at noon at the Empress Hotel, 721 Government St (☎ 250/389-2727, ⊛ www.fairmont.com/empress).

568 Tickets need to be bought in advance for nearly all matches; check the club websites via links at ⊛ www.nhl.com.

569 Plan at least a year in advance for the annual Stampede: see ⊛ www.calgarystampede.com.

570 The *Maid of the Mist* leaves every 15–30min and the Journey Behind the Falls tour lasts 30–45min – see ⊛ www.niagaraparks.com.

571 Truro, Moncton and Saint John are all good bases for trying to watch a tidal bore – see ⊛ www.pc.gc.ca/fundy.

572 Gatherall's Puffin & Whale Watch Tours offers daily trips to the Witless Bay Ecological Reserve (⊛ www.gatheralls.com).

GOOD to know

PROVINCES AND TERRITORIES

Canada has ten provinces – Newfoundland & Labrador, Prince Edward Island, Nova Scotia, New Brunswick, Québec, Ontario, Manitoba, Saskatchewan, Alberta and British Columbia – and three territories – the Yukon, the Northwest Territories and Nunavut. The combined population is 34 million.

LISTEN TO THESE

Yer Favourites (2005) The Tragically Hip. Justly considered Canuck rock 'n' roll legends, the Hip's lyrics are marvellously image-rich, haunting and rousing all at the same time.
After the Gold Rush (1970) Neil Young. A lovely song cycle that defined his early blend of folk and hippie rock.
Funeral (2004) Arcade Fire. Second album *Neon Bible* (2007) is a cracker, but this laid down the template: ambitious, soaring indie rock with a cache of infectious melodies.

ROCKS AND LAKES

The **Canadian Shield**, a huge swath of terrain covering half of the country and roughly stretching around Hudson Bay, is made up of rock, some of it as old as the Earth itself.
Not counting the Great Lakes (Superior and Huron are the nation's biggest), the two largest **lakes** fully within Canada are both in the Northwest Territories: Great Bear (31,328 sq km) and Great Slave (28,568 sq km).

> *"If some countries have too much history, we have too much geography."*
>
> **Former PM Mackenzie King**

MEMORABLE HOTELS

Ice Hotel, Québec City, Québec. Constructed entirely of ice, this deep-frozen luxury item is open only three months of the year, so book an igloo-style room before the place melts.
King Pacific Lodge, Princess Royal Island, British Columbia. You can only get to this luxurious wilderness lodge set in the heart of the Great Bear Rainforest by floatplane (Ⓦwww.kingpacificlodge.com).
West Point Lighthouse, O'Leary, Prince Edward Island. Rugged 1875 lighthouse tower that holds a romantic, windswept B&B.

ROADSIDE ATTRACTIONS

Canadians generally aren't prone to using superlatives about themselves (unless in reference to ice hockey), which may be why so many smaller Canadian communities have trained the spotlight squarely on inanimate objects that they claim to be the world's biggest or greatest – these usually commemorate some aspect of the town's heritage or industry.
The world's largest **lobster**, for instance, is in Shediac, New Brunswick. Imagine the mighty battle that would ensue should that crustacean ever encounter the world's largest (and most sullen looking) **beaver**, which you can find in, of course, Beaverlodge, Alberta. Fancy a peek at the world's largest **easter egg**? Off you go to Vegreville, Alberta, then. On your way there, you may as well stop at nearby Glendon to admire the world's largest **pierogi**, pierced by the tines of an equally large fork. Those with tastes more musical should take a glance at the world's largest illuminated **fiddle**, in Sydney, Nova Scotia, while numismatists may want to make the pilgrimage to see all 13 tonnes of Sudbury Ontario's Big Nickel, the world's largest "**coin**".

MUST-SEE MOVIES

The Barbarian Invasions (2003). Québec's leading director Denys Arcand applies his dialogue-heavy realism to Montréal intellectuals and their politics, sexuality and mortality.
Exotica (1994). Perhaps the most existential film ever set in a strip club (in Toronto), imagined by Atom Egoyan in dramatic and eye-opening detail.
Away from Her (2007). Once best known as an actress, director Sarah Polley marked her arrival as a film-maker of considerable talent with this moving story of a man coping with his wife's Alzheimer's disease.

IT'S GOT WHAT IN IT?

Canada's most popular cocktail is the **Bloody Caesar**, a blend of sweet (tomato juice), sour (lime), spicy (Worcestershire sauce), bitter (celery salt) and salty. The source of that last element? Clam juice. Combined with tomato juice, it's sold as Clamato which, with a couple of dashes of vodka, completes the package.

GREAT BOOKS

Robertson Davies *The Deptford Trilogy*. Davies memorably spins picaresque tales of mystery and magic in the early twentieth century.
Alice Munro *The Love of a Good Woman*. A selection by Canada's most renowned short-story author, mainly set in the West.
Mordecai Richler *Barney's Version*. Richler's last – and perhaps funniest – novel follows the irascible, combustible Montréaler Barney Panofsky as he dissects in memoir form his past loves, losses and motivations.

> *"A Canadian is someone who knows how to make love in a canoe."*
>
> **Pierre Berton**

FRENCH CANADA

By the mid-1700s France controlled from what's now Canada down to the Mississippi River and Gulf Coast to the Caribbean. That rule ended in 1763, when Britain finally emerged as victors from the Seven Years' War.
Although Britain expelled Nova Scotia's **Acadians** (to places such as Louisiana, where they became "Cajuns"), most French speakers remained, and today form a **Francophone belt** that includes all of Québec and parts of Ontario and New Brunswick.

KICK BACK IN A CASA PARTICULAR • HAVE YOUR SPIRITS LIFTED ON A TAP-TAP • CLIMBING INTO THE CLOUDS ON THE ROUTE DE LA TRACE • EL YUNQUE'S FROG CHORUS • TASTE HAVANA'S BATTERED GLAMOUR • FIND YOUR NOOK ON AN ELEGANT ISLAND • GET ON BAD IN TRINIDAD • THE CAVE OF INDESCRIBABLE HORRORS • SNIFFING SULPHUR AT BOILING LAKE • KITEBOARDING IN CABARETE • SEA KAYAKING IN THE EXUMAS • GROOVING AT REGGAE SUMFEST • MEET THE PEOPLE: FAIR TRADE AND FRUIT PASSION • SUGARCANE, SALTFISH AND TRANQUIL SOUFRIÈRE • SPICE SHOPPING IN ST GEORGE'S • HIGH ADVENTURE ON GROS PITON • ARIKOK NATIONAL PARK: THE CARIBBEAN OUTBACK • LAND OF THE MIDNIGHT SON • GOURMET COFFEE IN THE BLUE MOUNTAINS • EXPLORE NELSON'S JUNGLE DOCKYARD • SWIM THE LIGHT FANTASTIC AT PUERTO MOSQUITO • SAVOURING THE FAMILIAR AT CRESCENT MOON • SUCKING UP THE KILLER BEES • SUGAR AND SPICE: TOURING RUM-MAKERS • FINDING INSPIRATION AT GOLDENEYE • SNORKELLING WITH TURTLES • DIVING BLOODY BAY WALL • GOING UNDERGROUND IN SANTO DOMINGO • DOING JUNKANOO • IN SEARCH OF THE CITADELLE • GET REAL ON TREASURE BEACH • WHALE-WATCHING IN SAMANÁ • BATHTIME IN VIRGIN GORDA • KICK BACK IN A CASA PARTICULAR • HAVE YOUR SPIRITS LIFTED ON A TAP-TAP • CLIMBING INTO THE CLOUDS ON THE ROUTE DE LA TRACE • EL YUNQUE'S FROG CHORUS • TASTE HAVANA'S BATTERED GLAMOUR • FIND YOUR NOOK ON AN ELEGANT ISLAND • GET ON BAD IN TRINIDAD • THE CAVE OF INDESCRIBABLE HORRORS • SNIFFING SULPHUR AT BOILING LAKE • KITEBOARDING IN CABARETE • SEA KAYAKING IN THE EXUMAS • GROOVING AT REGGAE SUMFEST • MEET THE PEOPLE: FAIR TRADE AND FRUIT PASSION • SUGARCANE, SALTFISH AND TRANQUIL SOUFRIÈRE • SPICE SHOPPING IN ST GEORGE'S • HIGH ADVENTURE ON GROS PITON • ARIKOK NATIONAL PARK: THE CARIBBEAN OUTBACK • LAND OF THE MIDNIGHT SON • GOURMET COFFEE IN THE BLUE MOUNTAINS • EXPLORE NELSON'S JUNGLE DOCKYARD • SWIM THE LIGHT FANTASTIC AT PUERTO MOSQUITO • SAVOURING THE FAMILIAR AT CRESCENT MOON • SUCKING UP THE KILLER BEES • SUGAR AND SPICE: TOURING RUM-MAKERS • FINDING INSPIRATION AT GOLDENEYE • SNORKELLING WITH TURTLES • DIVING BLOODY BAY WALL • GOING UNDERGROUND IN SANTO DOMINGO • DOING JUNKANOO • IN SEARCH OF THE CITADELLE • GET REAL ON TREASURE BEACH • WHALE-WATCHING IN SAMANÁ • BATHTIME IN VIRGIN GORDA • KICK BACK IN A CASA PARTICULAR • HAVE YOUR SPIRITS LIFTED ON A TAP-TAP • CLIMBING INTO THE CLOUDS ON THE ROUTE DE LA TRACE • EL YUNQUE'S FROG

The Caribbean
573–605

BAHAMAS

Kick back in a
casa particular [573]

CUBA

Diving Bloody
[599] Bay Wall

CAYMAN IS.

Grooving at [584]
Reggae Sumfest

JAMAICA

Have your spirits
lifted on a tap-tap

HAITI

Swim the light fantastic
at Puerto Mosquito

DOMINICAN
REPUBLIC

PUERTO
RICO [593]

BRITISH
VIRGIN IS.

ST BARTS

ANTIGUA

Explore Nelson's
[592] jungle dockyard

ST MARTIN/SINT MAARTEN

ST KITTS & NEVIS

[581] DOMINICA

Sniffing sulphur
at Boiling Lake

ST LUCIA

BARBADOS

ARUBA

BONAIRE

CURAÇAO

ST VINCENT

GRENADA [587]

Spice shopping
in St George's

Get on bad in Trinidad [579]

TRINIDAD
& TOBAGO

573 Kick back in a casa particular

CUBA By far the best option for accommodation in Cuba is to stay in a *casa particular* (private house), always abbreviated to "*casa*". It's also the best way to meet the country's famously gregarious and charming people: you can sip a *mojito* while getting a good dose of gossip from the owner, as well as the lowdown on the best nearby music venues, bars and festivals.

There are thousands of *casas* across the country. You'll find them in Viñales in the west, where simple village homes are backed by lush tobacco fields and tall limestone stacks; in angular tower blocks and historic homes in Havana; and in the paradisal seaside town of Baracoa in the far east. But one of the best is *Hostal Florida Center*, an airy nineteenth-century mansion located in urbane Santa Clara, burial place of Che Guevara.

Beyond the private rooms at the entrance to the house, owner Angel will take you to the open courtyard with its Art Deco tiled floor and luxuriant orchids, fruit trees and ferns, around which are high-ceilinged rooms for visitors. One of these is in Thirties style, featuring a fabulous antique black-laquered bed and dressing table, the other is colonial, with ornate mirrors, wrought-iron beds and delicate miniatures on the walls.

Dinner is served in the candle-lit courtyard: abundant home-cooked Cuban food at its simple but tasty best – organic chicken, corn on the cob, shredded beef or river prawns. After dinner you could take a stroll to the main square to see its colonial theatre and palaces, and the mint-green *Santa Clara Libre* hotel, pockmarked with bullets from the Battle of Santa Clara, a decisive victory for Castro's forces in 1958. Or just stay in Angel's verdant courtyard, pick a book from his shelves and order yourself another *mojito*.

574 Have your spirits lifted on a tap-tap

HAITI Your heart sinks as you hear it labouring up the hill, its engine chronically ill and crying "tap, tap, tap, tap". It reaches the brow and you see the most wretched pick-up truck imaginable, struggling for dear life under the weight of the small village stuffed in the back. You want to let it pass on by, but there will not be another one along for hours. So you reluctantly wave it down and clamber aboard. The mass of bodies shifts, creating a space where previously there was none, and you are absorbed into the community-on-wheels which passes for public transportation in Haiti.

The tap-tap continues its painful progress along the potholed road, creaking around tight corners and dislodging rocks that roll down the denuded hills. The slopes are brown, arid and dotted with the occasional palm tree: a lunar landscape with a tropical twist. Each bump and swerve threatens to dislodge the most precariously positioned passenger – which always seems to be you. You long for a cushion to ease the soreness in your buttocks or for some shade from the sun, but all you get is some music. A girl with a cage of chickens on her lap starts humming a gospel tune. The young voice gradually grows in confidence, rising above the clucking poultry and inspiring other passengers to add some words. Spontaneously, the whole village breaks into a rousing song praising the virtues of the Lord Jesus Christ their Saviour amidst the clouds of dust and exhaust fumes.

Surely no one deserves praise for your current discomfort, yet the resounding "hallelujahs" drown out the tap-tapping of the engine and instead of the scorching sun on your face you start to feel an uplifting warmth in your heart. It's a moment that embodies the tremendous spirit of the Haitian people, their camaraderie and optimism in the most difficult of circumstances. It's a moment that will remain, poignant and vivid in your memory, long after the hardships of your ride in a tap-tap have been forgotten.

575 Climbing into the clouds on the Route de la Trace

MARTINIQUE It may be blessed with fabulous beaches, enticing ruins and fine cuisine, but Martinique can seem more like a suburb of Nice than a Caribbean island to new arrivals. Traffic is painfully congested in and around the capital, Fort-de-France, resorts line the southern beaches and hordes of tourists hop from one (admittedly superb) rum distillery to another as if on a Rhône Valley wine tour. To escape the crowds, rent a car and head north into the hills; the Route de la Trace (aka N3) runs through increasingly lush slopes like a winding ribbon, ending at the far more tranquil north shore.

The road was created by Jesuits in the eighteenth century, so it's fitting that the first major sight on route is the Sacré Cœur de Balata, a smaller, weather-beaten version of its famous namesake in Paris. From here the road snakes through steep valleys and dripping forests of bamboo, tree ferns and mahogany, passing the Jardin de Balata, a sweet-smelling botanical garden.

Hiking trails lead off from car parks all along the road, yet the most rewarding comes at the end of the Route, beyond the town of Morne-Rouge. The vast dome of Mont-Pelée, the infamous volcano that destroyed the town of St-Pierre in 1902, looms over the whole island, asking to be climbed; it's an exhilarating hike to the top, the cool winds and tranquillity a million miles from the coastal resorts.

The volcano is still active, but carefully monitored and safe to climb. The walk begins from a small car park and café at the end of the Morne-Rouge road. You'll need at least four hours, as though the trail is not long it cuts a very steep path up to the rim. Once at the 1397m summit you'll literally be on top of the island, with a precipitous drop on one side and the rocky slope on the other. You can wander along the rim, soaking up the mesmerizing views of the Caribbean, but remember that the peak is often shrouded in clouds; even if it's sweltering on the beach, it's a different world up here.

El Yunque's **frog chorus**

576

PUERTO RICO "Ko-kee, ko-kee!" As the moon climbs over mist-cloaked El Yunque Rainforest, the shrill symphony of tiny voices swells – "ko-kee, ko-kee, ko-keeeeee!" – echoing through the tropical tangle of dewy palms, orchids and feathery ferns. Stand still on the damp trail, and the whistling chorus rises all around you. The din is the mating call of the petite coqui frog, which is endemic to Puerto Rico. Even though you could fit several in the palm of your hand, the noise they make is incredible, and El Yunque, with its tumbling waterfalls and mossy pools, is their concert hall. As the sun dips, the frogs climb to the tops of trees, where they begin their nocturnal ensemble. The males belt out "ko" to scare off rivals from their territory, followed by the proud, piercing "kee" to attract the ladies. As day breaks, they leap off the branches, spreading their arms and legs so that they float, parachute-like, to the ground, where they land with a quiet plop.

Taste *Havana's* battered glamour

CUBA First-time visitors to Havana can feel they are in a dream, coasting through a fantastic cityscape of colonial fortifications, Art Deco towers and Fifties hotels, uncluttered by advertising but punctuated by the bold colours and lines of painted propaganda. Part of their character comes from their decay, from the peeling layers of lemon-yellow and sea-green paint, chipped tiles and tumbling plaster.

Yet not everything is run down. Designated a UNESCO World Heritage Site for its architecture, the historic district of La Havana Vieja has in parts been well restored and forms a wonderful walkable grid of narrow streets, graceful squares and wide avenues lined with pastel mansions. Check out the Catedral de San Cristóbal, its wide facade decorated with the restrained swirls and classical columns of the Cuban Baroque style, and the Art Deco Bacardí building, which looms over the district's west side like a wild Gotham City creation, its trademark bat adorning everything from the brass door handles and cracked light fittings to the Gothic sculpture that crowns the roof.

West from the La Havana Vieja lies Vedado, bounded to the north by the long line of the sea wall (*malecón*), the city's promenade and the focus of its nightlife. Here you'll find the bulky *Hotel Nacional* with its twin arched towers and the shell-like form of concrete *Coppelia*, the city's enduringly (and endearingly) popular ice-cream parlour – in this impoverished city an ice cream is the closest most people get to a treat. In contrast, Havana's lavish pre-Revolutionary decadent era is recalled in the Fifties *Riviera* building, built by the mob as a casino hotel and still with its original sculptures, furniture and fittings miraculously intact.

Like the Italian cities which survived unblemished only because of centuries of poverty and neglect, Havana is a time capsule, one that makes life hard for locals who can't afford repairs each time hurricanes batter their homes. The limited conservation work shows how Havana could be restored to its proper place as the most glamorous city in the Caribbean – for now, it remains a fascinating hotpotch.

578 Find your nook on an elegant island

ST BARTHÉLEMY There are plenty of ways to do the Caribbean on a budget, but why suffer the concrete package hotels with their nasty food and Hawaiian shirt-wearing hordes when you could blow the nest egg on a once-in-a-lifetime experience in St Barts? This little gem of a desert island isn't exactly splashy, though – celebrities like Nicole Kidman and Uma Thurman make it out here for its understated elegance and the privacy that such a high price-tag can afford them.

The atmosphere here is decidedly low-key, and local zoning laws make sure it stays that way, forbidding big resort development along the main beaches and ensuring that buildings in the small capital town of Gustavia are a height shorter than the highest palm trees. While there is a handful of nice hotels sprinkled about, the way to do St Barts is to rent your own red-roofed villa in one of the many isolated nooks and crannies along the shore of this boomerang-shaped oasis.

The local population consists mostly of descendants of the original French settlers to St Barts, who led a hard-scrabble existence during the first centuries of its colonization, as the sandy soil didn't do much for large-scale agriculture. The high-end tourism industry has therefore been something of a diamond-encrusted life preserver to the locals, who operate a mix of excellent *boulangeries*, *crêperies* and restaurants that help make the St Barts experience exquisite. Dinner options range from super-hip, ambient Indian couch lounges to unpretentious beachfront diners with tasty Creole seafood.

You'll find a slew of archetypally pristine, white-sand beaches throughout the island, some of them accessible only by sea, which lends a sense of Robinson Crusoe seclusion that's hard to come by elsewhere in the Caribbean these days. And there's a Zarathustrian view from above on the west end of the island at Anse des Flamands that's about as majestic as you can get. Those seeking a bit of civilization can hop on over to doll's house-quaint Gustavia, its U-shaped harbour lined with designer boutiques from Gucci and Hermes to Louis Vuitton and Lacoste – a veritable Champs Elysées on the sand.

579 Get on bad in Trinidad

TRINIDAD & TOBAGO Trinidadians are famed for their party stamina, and nowhere is this dedication to good times more evident than in their annual Carnival, a huge, joyful, all-encompassing event that's the biggest festival in the Caribbean, and one which quite possibly delivers the most fun you'll ever have – period. And as carnival here is all about participation, rather than watching from the sidelines à la Rio, anyone with a willingness to "get on bad" is welcome to sign up with a masquerade band, which gets you a costume and the chance to dance through the streets alongside tens of thousands of your fellow revellers.

Preceded by weeks of all-night outdoor fetes, as parties here are known, as well as competitions for the best steel bands and calypso and soca singers, the main event starts at 1am on Carnival Sunday with Jouvert. This anarchic and raunchy street party is pure, unadulterated bacchanalia, with generous coatings of mud, chocolate, oil or body paint – and libations of kick-ass local rum, of course – helping you lose all inhibitions and slip and slide through the streets until dawn in an anonymous mass of dirty, drunken, happy humanity, accompanied by music from steel bands, sound-system trucks and the traditional "rhythm section" band of percussionists. Once the sun is fully up, and a quick dip in the Caribbean has dispensed with the worst of the mud, the masquerade bands hit the streets, their followers dancing along in the wake of the pounding soca. This is a mere warm-up for the main parade the following day, however, when full costumes are worn and the streets are awash with colour. The music trucks are back in earnest and the city reverberates with music, becoming one giant street party until "las lap" and total exhaustion closes proceedings for another year.

580 The cave of indescribable horrors

BAHAMAS The remote island of San Salvador in the eastern Bahamas has a little something for everyone – sun, sand, scuba and a dank hole in the ground some call the "Cave of Indescribable Horrors". Formally known as the Lighthouse Cave, locals will smile nervously and maybe wag a finger at the notion of leading you through its watery belly. You'll have better luck bribing the American students from the nearby marine science lab to take you.

From the antique, hand-cranked, kerosene-fuelled lighthouse perched atop Dixon Hill, an overgrown trail snakes down to an ominous gap in the ground with an unsteady rusty ladder poking out of the darkness. The entry chamber may seem a little spooky with its swooping bats, pungent guano and piercing stalactites, but it pales in comparison to what lurks ahead.

Wielding your waterproof torch like a gun, you muster up enough courage to enter a cool pool of chest-deep water and meander down a passageway that narrows to a dead end. To proceed you must hold your breath and duck under water, passing beneath a narrow but psychologically terrifying lip of limestone to pop out the other side into a pitch-black room. This is a perfect place to gather the troops, shut off all flashlights and either fabricate a tale about human sacrifices, or just contemplate that you are wet, cold and muddy and somewhere inside a fossilized sand dune when you could be at the beach with a good book and a fruity drink.

Exit through a crack in the rock, wade through more water, clamber up some caved-in ceiling and crawl on your belly through a three-metre tube and plop a few metres down into another pool of water. Just when you thought you were hopelessly lost you'll wind up back near the entrance, with a few rays of sunlight beckoning escape.

581 Sniffing sulphur at Boiling Lake

DOMINICA Reggae pumps from the speakers and foliage blurs through the windows of a Chinese-made minibus, recklessly winding into the mountains at six in the morning. "Make sure you have enough water," warns Rastafarian guide Seacat. "Dem shoes look like dey could melt. And watch out your silver don't turn black."

He grins, leading our groggy group of hikers along an elevated wooden water pipe that snakes through groves of sweet grapefruit and clusters of office plants, their familiarity tempered by the fact that they are growing berserk in their native habitat. A trail shoots uphill into the rainforest, a dense canopy of plants growing over plants that creates a dark yet serene environment for the next two hours of climbing. Nearing the peak, the dense flora thins into elfin trees and shrubs stunted by the powerful winds.

"Getting close," says Seacat, as we get our first whiffs of sulphur, a reminder that an active volcano lurked nearby. We clamber down into the caldera, appropriately named the Valley of Desolation for its scorched rock landscape. Mineral-encrusted fumaroles spew boiling multi-hued gasses, sounding remarkably like a fleet of small jet engines. The group instinctively gathers together, some hold hands, and everyone follows the guide's footsteps. In this freakish landscape, pterodactyls and dinosaurs would not appear out of place.

Inching toward a precipice overlooking a cauldron of bubbling muddy water nearly 70 metres across, we are enshrouded in steam and fog. Sulphurous gasses, reeking more powerfully than ever, turns silver jewellery to black. Seacat climbs down to the edge of the water to boil a few eggs, proving another point.

On the return, we take a refreshing swim through a steep, dark gorge to a small waterfall to rinse off the day's mud, soak weary muscles and postpone the white-knuckle ride out of the mountains and back to civilization.

582 Kiteboarding in Cabarete

DOMINICAN REPUBLIC Kiters from around the world come in droves to the broad, archetypally Caribbean cove of Cabarete off the north coast of the Dominican Republic. Some never leave, hanging out on the beach in a state of perpetual kite-slacker bliss, like lotus-eaters from Homer's *Odyssey*. Others shuttle in at weekends between stints at investment banking firms and crash at the high-end condos on the edge of town. All seem perpetually chilled, except for those moments when they're riding the Caribbean trade winds like a hundred little neon-coloured insects trained to do circus tricks for the nearby beach loungers. Life is good here.

And why not? Cabarete's bay seems engineered by a benevolent god of kiteboarding. Steady trade winds blow east to west, allowing easy passage out to the bay's offshore reefs and then back to the sand. Downwind, the waters lap onto the sardonically named Bozo Beach, which catches anybody unfortunate enough to have a mishap. The offshore reef provides plenty of surf for the experts who ride the waves here, performing tricks and some incredibly spectacular jumps. The reef also shelters the inshore waters so that on all but the roughest of winter days the waters remain calm. During the morning the winds are little more than a gentle breeze, and this, coupled with the flat water, makes the bay ideal for beginners, especially in summer when the surface can resemble a mirror. Then, as the temperature rises, the trades kick in big-time and the real show starts.

Increasingly, the kiteboarding community has left the built-up main village to the windsurfers and retreated west to so-called Kite Beach. Here you can experience Cabarete as it was fifteen years ago, a kiteboarder's paradise filled with fellow wind worshippers and a lively outdoor nightlife scene, including bonfires along the beach into the wee hours.

583 Sea kayaking in the Exumas

BAHAMAS "Wilderness" is not the first word that springs to mind when someone mentions the Bahamas; rum cocktails, high-rise hotels and limbo contests are the ready images. Yet a short hop from the wall-to-wall cruise ship carnival in Nassau lies the Exuma Cays, a chain of a couple of hundred mainly uninhabited islands stretching for more than 65km along the edge of the Great Bahama Bank. Separated by a tranquil sea, the low-lying chunks of honeycombed limestone rimmed by powdery white sand and covered in dense vegetation have seemingly been designed with one mode of exploration in mind: the sea kayak.

The Exuma Land and Sea Park, in the middle section of the cays, makes for an excellent starting point. Your ride begins at dawn, when the mirror-smooth sea takes on a delicate shade of pink. The languid morning hours are spent blissfully dipping your paddle into turquoise waters lit from beneath by sunlight reflected off a brilliant white sandy bottom and brimming with lush undersea gardens, coral reefs and a profusion of tropical fish. At midday, beach your kayak on an inviting swathe of sand and picnic under a palm tree. Snorkel over bright-hued clumps of coral, marvelling at the dazzling colours and patterns of the fish as they dart among the waving purple sea fans. Visit the colonies of metre-long iguanas sunning themselves on beaches scattered throughout the islands. Hike the footpath to the summit of Boo Boo Hill on Warderick Wells Cay and enjoy a commanding view down the length of the island chain as it trails off over the horizon, the sunset shifting through operatic tints of red, pink and purple.

At night, a bright moon looms overhead and an opulent canopy of stars appears close enough to pluck. Lying on the sand, you'll fall asleep to nothing but the periodic muffled thump of a coconut falling from a tree and the gentle lapping of the waves.

Grooving at
Reggae Sumfest

JAMAICA As you might expect from Jamaica's flagship music festival, Sumfest is one of the best reggae shows in the world. If you're expecting a bacchanalian free-for-all of campfires on the sand, you'll be sorely disappointed – it's a four-day series of concerts and sound-system jams. But if you're interested in seeing the hottest names in Jamaican music past and present, with a few international R&B or hip-hop acts thrown in for good measure, then you're in for a serious treat.

It's best to arrive in Montego Bay a week or so before the event – held in late July or early August – and head for the beach to rid yourself of that fresh-off-the-plane pallor, and to attend pre-festival events: the Blast-Off beach party on the Sunday before the festival starts, and the Monday street Party with DJs and outdoor jams.

Once the festival is under way, the island's stage shows start late, carry on until dawn and involve some serious audience participation – or lack of it, if a performer fails to please the famously fickle local crowd. And it's doubtful you'll find a better high than standing under the stars in a grassy bowl by the Caribbean with the music echoing out over the bay.

585 Meet the People: Fair Trade and Fruit Passion

CUBA With his sticking-out ears and Groucho Marx moustache, Lucio Parada Camenate makes an unlikely revolutionary hero, but as the face of Fruit Passion, his mugshot appears on juice cartons across the world, wherever Fair Trade products are marketed – much to the evident amusement of his colleagues, who tease him mercilessly for being *famoso*.

Lucio is one of several guest-star guides featured on Fair Trade's "Meet the People" tour of Cuba – part holiday, part crash course on the culture and society of Fidel Castro's economically disadvantaged island. Visiting coffee plantations, citrus orchards and juice factories – not to mention primary schools and maternity wards – may not sound as alluring as slurping *mojitos* by the poolside in Fuertaventura, but the reality turns out to be just as much fun as it is instructive.

Being pitched into the middle of ordinary people's lives lets you experience first hand the pervasive impact of the US trade embargo, and the ways in which Fair Trade initiatives have been able to circumvent it. Holiday pleasures of a more conventional kind are also included in the packed itinerary – from visiting salsa bars in Havana to trekking across mountains draped in rainforest – but it's the encounters with Cubans themselves that stand out.

One evening, we were trundled on an ox cart down five kilometres of bumpy track to a small wooden farmhouse for a typically Cuban family hog roast. Everyone from the 96-year-old patriarch, Clemente, to his great-grandchildren scampering around after the chickens, was delighted to share a meal with visitors from Canada and Europe. Afterwards, while the women were given an impromptu salsa lesson indoors, the rum and guitars appeared on the veranda, and glasses were raised in a toast to "Libertad, Independencia y Comercio Justo!" – "Freedom, Independence and Fair Trade!".

586 Sugarcane, saltfish and tranquil Soufrière

ST LUCIA Lazing on one of St Lucia's manicured beaches, it's easy to forget that the island has a rich and turbulent history. Fought over by the French, Spanish and English, there's plenty of heritage squashed in between the dense jungle slopes and five-star resorts.

To really get away from the tourist trail you need to drive south, bypassing the capital Castries, into the sun-baked Roseau Valley, a swathe of billowing sugarcane plantations. Beyond here, the road drops down to Anse La Raye, a totally unspoiled St Lucian village, nestled between green headlands on the edge of a pristine bay. The streets are crammed with weathered clapboard cottages, some brightly adorned in gingerbread style, all with corrugated iron roofs and neatly tended gardens. Fishing shacks and small boats line the beachfront, while schoolkids play football on the sand.

Just inland, the island's colonial legacy is on view at La Sikwi Sugar Mill, built in 1876 and now in a state of refined decay. The casual tours take in lush, blossom-strewn gardens humming with butterflies, trees laden with cacao pods, coconuts and bananas, and the old weather-beaten, vine-smothered ruins themselves. Inside you'll find the original sugar kettles, huge cauldrons of iron where cane juice was boiled for hours before turning into crumbly brown sugar.

Back on the coast road, *La Plac Kassav* is an essential St Lucian food experience; little more than a small shack, perched high above the sea, it produces traditional cassava breads in a variety of flavours (such as saltfish and yam). You can also watch the baking process, where cassava root is pounded and the dough cooked in a huge cauldron over an open-wood fire.

Keep driving south and you'll end up at Soufrière, dating from 1746 and the oldest town in St Lucia. It's a tranquil place today, filled with an appealing blend of modern houses and clapboard huts. The town faces a sharply defined bay at the end of a jungle-smothered valley, and the views from the coastal road as you enter are spectacular – a world away from those cocktails and beach umbrellas.

587 Spice shopping in St George's

GRENADA Nutmeg, mace, cinnamon and ginger. It doesn't quite ring like parsley, sage, rosemary and thyme, but the island of Grenada – one of a few worldwide to lay claim to the moniker "Spice Island" – might still be glad to adopt it as its theme song. And Grenada produces thyme as well, come to think of it. Though Hurricane Ivan knocked out much of the island's agriculture industry in 2004, the recovery effort has been great and the central market in the capital, St George's, once again bristles with activity. It's a riot of sounds and smells: this is the place to get sacks of exotic spices, bottles of local rum, cacao, tropical fruits and vegetables, perhaps even a nutmeg-infused medicinal ointment.

588 High adventure on Gros Piton

ST LUCIA High adventure in the Caribbean usually comes in the form of charter flights between islands, but not so on St Lucia. Standing sentinel on the southwestern coast are the twin peaks of the Pitons, two of the tallest and most striking mountains in the West Indies. Gros Piton, at 798m, is the taller of the two and makes for a challenging and dramatic day-hike, its steep trail winding past a former cave hideout of slave freedom fighters and through a dense tropical landscape home to several colourful bird and butterfly species. Set out early to avoid climbing in the stifling midday heat, and at the summit you'll be rewarded with breathtaking views of Petit Piton and the azure Caribbean below.

589 Arikok National Park: the Caribbean outback

ARUBA Massive boulders, towering cacti, ancient petroglyphs, abandoned gold mines and secluded limestone grottoes dot the hilly interior. There are glitzy beaches a few short kilometres away, but Arikok National Park, a bizarre desert-like landscape in the northeastern corner of resort-heavy Aruba, has little in common with the rest of the island save the blazing tropical sun. Indeed, walking its dirt paths can feel more like wandering the Australian outback.

As you traverse some of the 34km of self-guided trails you gain a sense of the untamed beauty: patches of reddish-orange rocky outcrops interspersed with gnarled divi-divi trees and herds of wandering goats give way to rolling sand dunes and a rugged shoreline sprinkled with white sandy coves ideal for a picnic retreat from the midday desert heat. Nearby, limestone caves are adorned with Arawak Indian rock drawings and beautiful flowstone formations, while burrowing owls, rattlesnakes and lizards guard the ruins at the Miralamar gold mine.

In the stifling afternoon heat you find yourself at the base of Cerro Arikok (176m), the second-highest peak on the island. A 1.5km pathway guides you through an example of what the typical Aruban countryside would have looked like in the nineteenth century. Along the way, you'll pass aloe plants growing alongside other endemic thorny shrubs, large diorite boulders and a petroglyph of an ancient bird left behind by the Amerindians. Halfway through your trek you come across a partially restored *casa di torta* farmhouse, a small traditional country home constructed with dried cactus husks and glued together with layers of mud and grass. A short stroll uphill brings you to the peak and a stunning panoramic view of the surrounding park and its unique natural treasures.

590 Land of the midnight son

CUBA It's a sweltering Saturday night in Santiago de Cuba, and the entire *barrio* seems to be packed into *La Casa de las Tradiciones*. A mist of rum, beer and sweat fills the air of the much-loved club, while dozens of pairs of feet pound the flexing plywood floors. The wail of a trumpet rides above the locomotive percussion – maracas, congas and *guiros* all chugging along in rhythmic, rumba unison.

The *cajón* player raises his hand, silencing the band and the room. From somewhere among the revellers, a reed-thin voice salvages the melody, this time with less urgency but more emotion. The aged *cantor* takes the stage, his voice bolstered by an upright bass, violin and *tres*. Momentary transfixion melts into sinuous shuffle-steps as the audience swoons to his rousing *son*. The rest of the band joins in again, and soon the crowd is echoing the singer's refrains as his voice soars with the vigour and vibrato of someone half his age.

As dawn steadily approaches and the performance winds down, word arrives of a nearby wedding reception. Eager celebrants spill outside and navigate the barely lit streets between tiny houses, cement bunkers with corrugated tin roofs and the flickering eyes of stray dogs. Along the way, party-goers rush into their homes and emerge with bottles of bootlegged *ron* and a cornucopia of musical instruments.

Arriving at the scene, they're welcomed with cheers and the neighbourhood fiesta surges with renewed energy. One man hammers away at a *bata* drum while a teenage girl plonks a pair of wooden *claves*. An older fellow raises an ancient trumpet to his lips; it's dented, with only the memory of a sheen left, but sits in his hands as if he's held it since birth. Then he wades into the roiling *descarga*, horn crowing wildly as morning begins to glow at the edges of the sky.

591 Gourmet coffee in the Blue Mountains

JAMAICA For most people, Jamaica is synonymous with reggae, Rastas and beach-bound relaxation. Yet the island is also a paradise for coffee lovers, its Blue Mountain beans some of the most sought after – and delicately flavoured – in the world.

Only coffee grown above a certain altitude can claim the coveted trademark, and there's now a clutch of guesthouses and quality hotels where you can experience this high, rugged landscape – and a fresh daily brew – first hand. *Strawberry Hill Hotel* is traditionally chosen by the international glitterati, while *Forres Park* is a lower-key B&B below a coffee plantation, but there's no better option than the magnificent *Lime Tree Farm*. This small and luxurious family-run hotel, built high upon a remote ridge, is only accessible by a perilous track local villagers politely refer to as a road. The slopes descend on three sides, a beautiful panorama stretching past vast terraces of red coffee berries, interspersed with eucalyptus, fuchsias, begonias and orchids. Hummingbirds flutter about, while the murmur of coffee pickers is just audible as they call to one another across the hillsides. In the distance, the glint of white surf is the only indication you're near to Caribbean waters.

The cool, moist climate here – the mountains rise up to 2256m – is a far cry from the dogged heat of the coast. This is a reliably friendly and unhurried land, and excitement comes in the form of hiking trails through plantations and forest, and staggering views every few minutes. Guided walks teach you about the planting and picking of some of the world's finest coffee bushes, while a tour of the Jablum coffee factory, perched on the mountainside at Mavis Bank, demonstrates the process from berry to cup, its several million beans drying out in the sunshine.

The vast majority of Blue Mountain coffee is sold to Japan, leaving its price in Europe and North America sky high – all the more reason to pick up a few bags at source. Known for its rich aroma, smooth feel in the mouth and a total absence of the bitter aftertaste so common in standard blends, it's no wonder people save these beans for a special occasion.

Explore
Nelson's jungle dockyard

592

ANTIGUA Long before his famous victory at Trafalgar, a fully limbed Horatio Nelson cut his teeth in the Caribbean. He wasn't there on holiday; the 27-year old captain arrived in Antigua in 1784 and stayed for three years, ruffling feathers and generally having a miserable time, claiming he was "most woefully pinched" by mosquitoes. Determined not to get soft, he drank a quart of goat's milk a day, and had six pails of salt water poured over him at dawn.

Like most islands in the Caribbean, Antigua is best known these days for its picture-perfect beaches, but the island offers more than windsurfing and sunbathing. Thanks to the Royal Navy, it is home to the only working Georgian-era dockyard in existence, a rare window into the world of Nelson dating back to the 1720s. This southeastern corner of Antigua is unusually rugged, which made it an excellent refuge from Caribbean storms, French privateers and freeloading pirates, and Nelson's Dockyard is now a national park in sheltered English Harbour, hemmed in by lush jungle slopes.

The dockyard is a sleepy, languid place, hosting the odd beach escapee and plenty of yachties from the nearby marina. Wander down to the water after a drink at *Admiral's Inn*, a pitch and tar store erected in 1788 that's now a gorgeous hotel and restaurant. The restored colonial buildings along the way mix classic Georgian architecture with the Caribbean: thick stone blocks, wooden shutters and plenty of palm trees. The 1769 sawpit shed is the oldest part of the Dockyard, while the joiner's loft, boathouse, blacksmith's workshop and the copper and lumber store all date from the late eighteenth century. The cordage and canvas store is marked with graffiti, said to have been left by the future King George V when he was here in 1884; disappointingly, the young royal simply wrote: "A Merry Xmas and a Happy New Year 2 You All".

Finally, in the Dockyard Museum, once an officer's house, exhibits tell the story of English Harbour from its original Arawak inhabitants to the 1950s. Inside you'll find "Nelson's Room", with a life-sized portrait of the great commander and what is supposed to be his bed – minus mosquito net.

593 Swim the light fantastic at Puerto Mosquito

PUERTO RICO Tucked away on the south coast of Vieques, an unspoiled tropical island best known for its beaches, the placid waters of Puerto Mosquito look fairly ordinary by day, fringed by scrubby hills and thick mangroves. But when night falls everything changes. You have to see it to believe it: fish, boats and kayaks leave ghostly trails in the darkness, water falling like sparks of light from paddles and trailing arms. If you get a chance to swim, things become even stranger; as you splash around in the warm lagoon, bodies are engulfed by blue-green luminous clouds, while droplets spill off hands and hair like glittering fireflies.

Thanks to harmless microscopic creatures known as dinoflagellates, Puerto Rico is home to the truly spellbinding phenomenon of bioluminescent bays. It's hard to believe, but CGI is not involved; the natural effect is produced when the little creatures release a chemical called luciferin, which reacts with oxygen to create light (experts are divided on why this happens;

it's either a defence mechanism or an attempt to attract food). Dinoflagellates are found all over the tropics, but the lagoon at Puerto Mosquito has a particularly intense concentration: it's shallow, has a narrow mouth that acts like as valve, the salinity is perfect (with no freshwater source or human contamination) and the mangroves provide a crucial nutrient boost. Though you can visit the bay on your own it's much more enriching to use one of the local tour operators.

Tours usually begin with an introductory talk, followed by a bone-shaking bus ride through the scrub to the waterside. From here enthusiastic guides take small electric pontoon boats for one-hour loops around the lagoon, providing a non-stop commentary on local history and botany. If it's a dark night, you'll already see signs of luminescence, but it's when the boat stops for a twenty-minute swim in the middle of the bay that things really get weird. Don't be shy; jump in and prepare to be amazed.

594 Savouring the familiar at Crescent Moon

DOMINICA If, when you arrive at *Crescent Moon Cabins*, nestled high in lush Morne Trois Pitons National Park, you find it has a familiar feel, it should: this is the Caribbean retreat you've always dreamed of. Blissfully secluded and smartly incorporated into the surrounding rainforest, this ecological gem features spring water pumped daily, an ever-expanding organic garden and cabins beautifully designed from local wood – all powered by wind generators. After a day spent hiking to the nearby volcanic crater and serene mountain lakes, and cooling off in the soothing pools of a 60m-high waterfall, you can follow the winding footpath back to your cabin and admire the sweeping vistas of the ocean and jungle valley from the veranda. You could linger here until the day's end, were it not for the sweet aromas that signal dinner is about to be served. In fact, it's quite possible your dreams didn't do this place justice.

595 Sucking up the killer bees

NEVIS *Sunshine's Bar and BBQ* is a ramshackle hut with just a couple of picnic tables on Pinney's Beach, but once you've tasted the signature rum drinks and burned your lips on the spicy charred shrimp you won't care what it looks like. The owner himself serves up the syrupy "killer bee", a special rum punch made from a secret and lethal recipe (though its name hints at the inclusion of honey among the closely guarded ingredient list) – sip it slowly while you wait for the food. Then, sitting under the shade of a palm-frond umbrella or in the steeply shelving sand, take your first, delicious bite. In the heavy, humid air of the West Indies the sharp heat of the shrimp, straight from the fire pit, hits you first and then intensifies as the insanely hot spices sear your taste buds. Cool your toes in the gently lapping water and soothe your burning mouth with a long gulp of ice-cold rum punch – now you're living like an islander.

596 Sugar and spice: touring rum-makers

PUERTO RICO Rum is history on this island. Track down its greatest rum-making dynasties and you might meet Fernando Fernandez, heir to the family that has been making Ron de Barrilito since 1880. His office lies inside the shell of a graceful windmill built in 1827, surrounded by aged photographs of his grandfather and dusty bottles of what many believe to be the finest rum in the world. The rambling *hacienda* outside contains cellars crammed with white-oak barrels of rum, once used to mature Spanish sherry, the air thick with the burnt, sweet aroma of sugar molasses. Workers bottle the rum by hand, slap on the labels and then pile them, delicately, onto trucks for distribution.

Real connoisseurs drink Barrilito on ice – a spicy, rich spirit that goes down like fine Cognac – but the top rum-maker in Puerto Rico is Don Q. The brand was created by the Serrallés family, who started selling rum in 1865 in the southern coastal city of Ponce. Casa Don Q is their San Juan outpost, housing a small exhibition about the

company, and a bar where you can sample fine Don Q rum for free.

Then there's Casa Bacardí. Visit this slick tourist centre inside the "cathedral of rum", the vast Bacardí distillery across San Juan Bay, and you'll enter another world – Cuba, to be precise. The Bacardí family started making rum in Santiago de Cuba in 1862, and now utterly dominate the world market. Hand-held audio devices and enthusiastic guides help you navigate the seven sections of the centre. Special barrels allow you to "nose" the effects of wood barrelling, ageing and finishing, as well as the various Bacardí brands on offer: sweetly scented apple and melon flavours and the rich, addictive aroma of coconut-laced rum – *piña colada* in a bottle. Mercifully, there are two free drinks waiting for you at the end of the tour. Bacardí abandoned Cuba in 1960 and now has headquarters in Bermuda, but while you can argue about where it came from or who made it first, there's no doubt that today the home of rum is Puerto Rico.

597 Finding inspiration at Goldeneye

JAMAICA It has been the scene of many an iconic James Bond moment, from the London double-decker bus chase through the palms to Ursula Andress emerging goddess-like from the sea. And though the island doesn't make a huge deal of its connection with Bond creator Ian Fleming, who wrote most of his famous novels on Jamaican soil, there are a few places where you can pick up 007's trail. Named by the Spanish for the golden light that bathes the area, the village of Oracabessa, on the island's north coast, was chosen by Fleming as the site for his Jamaican home, Goldeneye.

These days, his classy bungalow forms the centrepiece of one of Jamaica's most beautiful and exclusive hotels, a homage to all things chic and a far cry from the bowing obsequiousness of the all-inclusive "tourist prisons". Swathed in lush greenery, the property sits atop a bluff overlooking the Caribbean, with its own private beach and a teeming reef within paddling distance. And whether you bed down in Fleming's old pad, with its luxurious outdoor bathroom and his old Remington typewriter still on his desk, or go for seclusion at Naomi Campbell's fabulous cottage right on the water, it's pretty much guaranteed that as you sip a sundowner, you'll find the same inspiration as Fleming himself: "Would these books have been born if I hadn't been living in the gorgeous vacuum of a Jamaican holiday? I doubt it."

598 Snorkelling with turtles

BONAIRE After months of planning and years of dreaming you've finally arrived at a small, uninhabited cay off the coast of Bonaire. Beneath the crystal-blue waters awaits a spectacle unparalleled in the marine world. Immense schools of tropical fish in every conceivable shape, size and colour swim alongside sea turtles and dolphins in and around the most impressive coral and sponge gardens in the Caribbean.

The waters surrounding this tiny boomerang-shaped island, 80km north of Venezuela, were made a marine park in 1979. Here, deep ocean currents carry nutrient-rich waters to the surface, nourishing the magnificent reef communities. These same currents bring minimal rainfall to Bonaire, which in turn reduces surface run-off to create the clearest waters imaginable.

Once under water you immediately hear the continuous grinding of parrotfish grazing on the algae that grows on top of coral heads. Within seconds, a dazzling spectrum of reef fish comes out of hiding from the delicate stands of soft and hard corals. Schools of brightly coloured butterflyfish, angelfish and damselfish swim in and out of the crevices and between colonies of elkhorn and staghorn corals. Several metres below, purple sea fans and the tentacles of anemones sway back and forth as the swift current pushes you along. You take a deep breath through your snorkel and submerge to the seafloor where you peek into nooks and crannies to spy on wrasse, tangs and other fish. You spot the slender body of a trunkfish, carefully hidden amidst the branches of sea rods, patiently waiting for its prey to drift by. A lunging moray eel emerges out of hiding, warning you not to get too close, while a triangular-shaped boxfish hovers nearby.

Before you realize it the captain signals it's time to return on board. As you prepare to board the craft you take one final glance at your underworld surroundings just in time to spot two hawksbill turtles cruising by through the magical sea.

599 Diving Bloody Bay Wall

LITTLE CAYMAN The reeftop is fairly flat and relatively shallow – around 8m deep – but when you swim to the edge you are looking into the abyss, 2000m straight down a vertical wall of coral.

Bloody Bay Wall is over 3km long and dotted with coral arches, chimneys and sand chutes. Giant barrel sponges as tall as a man cling to the wall, while barracuda, Nassau groupers and turtles patrol the wall. The waters around Little Cayman are among the clearest in the Caribbean, let alone the world, and floating over the drop-off is a unique experience – as close to skydiving under water as you can get.

600 Going underground in Santo Domingo

DOMINICAN REPUBLIC Originally used by the indigenous Taino people for religious ceremonies, this massive, multi-level underground cave now attracts those who worship a different type of deity – the DJ. In a city full of hot clubs, *La Guacara Taina*, or simply "The Cave", is Santo Domingo's best, attracting world-class musicians and hordes of ravers. Decadence awaits as you descend into the club, passing bars, stalactites and scantily clad, well-to-do locals. If the intricate lightshow and three throbbing dance floors don't pull you out into the crowd, you can pass the evening sipping your Presidente in one of the smooth rock alcoves in the back.

BAHAMAS The country's most important and spectacular party, Junkanoo is a blast to the senses. It's organized pandemonium, held in the pre-dawn hours on two days each year – December 26 and New Year's Day. It has its roots in Africa, and is reminiscent of New Orleans' Mardi Gras and Rio's Carnival, but really, Junkanoo is distinctively Bahamian. There is no other festival like it – not in the Caribbean, not anywhere.

Parades flood the streets of Nassau in a whirling, reeling mass of singing and dancing chaos, as competing groups or "crews" rush out to meet the dawn, moving toward one another from all directions rather than following each other in the semi-organized fashion of the modern parade. Various groups and societies compete to have the biggest and loudest floats, which means you'll see stilt-dancers, clowns, acrobats, go-go girls, goatskin drummers and conch and cowbell players, all blaring out their tunes in an awesome celebration of life that can only have originated in the Caribbean.

The distant beats of Goombay drums indicate that the paraders are shifting into formation, and this is your cue to join the spectators jockeying for the best views, climbing trees and spilling onto balconies and the verandas of stores, hotels and houses. Under the Christmas lights, the crowds reach a frenzy of anticipation. The first cowbells are heard soon after, everyone swigs from bottles of rum and fireworks crackle in the background. Behind, in Nassau Harbour, the looming cruise ships form almost a surreal counterpoint to the phantasmagoric crowds, who are now stamping and clamouring in time to the music. Then, as if from everywhere and nowhere, Junkanoo crews – some numbering a thousand – flood the streets in a swirling, kaleidoscopic mass of singing and dancing.

602 In search of the Citadelle

HAITI High in the hills above the northern plains sits an imposing fortress, an architectural marvel that would be among the Caribbean's top destinations were it not for the grave lack of tourists in Haiti. Constructed in the early 1800s following the successful revolt of Haiti's massive and angry slave population, the Citadelle La Ferriere was designed to house and protect the new black royal family of Henri Christophe and 5000 soldiers for up to a year in the event of a French retaliatory attack, which never came.

Travelling to the Citadelle is an adventure in itself, taking nearly an hour to traverse 20km of motorway riddled with craterous potholes, pedestrians and roadside repairs. In the peaceful town of Milot visitors can expect to be descended upon by a horde of would-be guides. Although the Citadelle is easy enough to get to, guiding is important to the local economy and each visitor will end up with one, like it or not. Some offer sad horses that look as though they should be carried up the hill, not vice versa.

During the two-hour ascent you'll be immersed in a day in the life of Haitian rural poverty – families living in one-room shacks without running water yet boasting proud smiles. A lively entrepreneurial spirit thrives along this cobblestone trail, with vendors and kids selling fresh fruit, handmade dolls and artefacts. There is even a small vodou peristyle, or temple, along the way and anybody hanging about will be happy to show you the sacred space for a small donation.

Entering the Citadelle via massive doors through nearly 10m-thick walls, the massive interior reveals moss-covered staircases, chambers and cisterns, topped by panoramic views of Haiti's sadly deforested yet strikingly beautiful landscape. Hundreds of cannons of all shapes, sizes and nationalities, salvaged from shipwrecks off the treacherous coast, are aimed toward unseen enemies, while thousands of rusting, unused cannonballs remain stacked into pyramids, a testament to the revolution's ultimate success.

603 Get real on Treasure Beach

JAMAICA In countries whose main income is from tourism, holidaying can be a somewhat surreal experience – and Jamaica is no exception. The big resorts are dominated by fenced-off all-inclusive hotels, the best bits of beach are pay-to-enter and most visitors' only interaction with Jamaicans is ordering a beer or a burger. It's easy to see why savvier tourists are heading away from the white sand and gin-clear waters of the resort-packed north to the black sand and breakers of the south.

In Treasure Beach, sustainable, community-based tourism is the order of the day. Locals have taken control of development, opening low-key hotels and guesthouses instead of selling up to the multinational chains, ensuring that the tourist dollar goes into the community rather than some corporate bank account. Instead of themed restaurants and bars selling flavoured margaritas and bongs of beer, you'll find laid-back, locally run

outfits where you can feast on Jamaican home-cooking, learn the art of dominoes Caribbean-style or sip a white rum while the regulars teach you the latest dancehall moves. And thanks mostly to community group BREDS – named after "bredrin", the patois term for friend – tourism has had a tangibly positive effect: funds raised by visitor donations and an annual triathlon and fishing tournament have, among many other achievements, bought an ambulance (essential in a place where few have a car and the nearest hospital is 24km away), upgraded the local school and given financial aid to low-income families whose lives were ripped apart by 2004's Hurricane Ivan. A cheering thought as you hop in a fishing *pirogue*-cum-tour boat to head up the coast to the *Pelican Bar*, a rickety shack built on a sandbar a mile out to sea – easily the coolest drinking spot in Jamaica, with not a flavoured margarita in sight.

604 Whale-watching in Samaná

DOMINICAN REPUBLIC No Caribbean experience can top sitting on a seaside veranda in the sleepy town of Samaná, sipping a *cuba libre servicio* – two Cokes, a bottle of aged rum and a bucket of ice – as you watch a series of massive humpback whales dive just offshore. Thousands of whales – the entire Atlantic population – flock to the Samaná waters each winter to breed and give birth. And no matter how long you relax there, looking out at the swaying palms backed by a long strand of bone-white sand, you never cease to be surprised as one whale after another sidles up the coastline and emerges from the tepid depths of the Samaná Bay before coming back down with a crowd-pleasing crash.

Samaná, on the Dominican Republic's northeast coast, is refreshingly free from package tourists. The modest expat community is almost all French, and they've set up a series of laid-back outdoor restaurants and bars along the main road. A lot of

the native Dominicans are from the United States originally – free black men and women who moved here in the early nineteenth century when the country was a part of Haiti, the world's first black republic.

Samaná also once held an allure for the Emperor Napoleon, who envisioned making its natural harbour the capital of his New World empire. While he never carried out his grand plans, look out over Samaná today and you can still imagine the great Napoleonic city destined to remain an emperor's dream: a flotilla of sailboats stands to attention behind the palm-ridged island chain, and in place of the impenetrable French fortress that was to jut atop the western promontory is a small, whitewashed hotel.

For now, though, Samaná remains passed over, which means you can have its natural beauty, tree-lined streets and, above all, its spectacular whale population, pretty much all to yourself.

605

Bathtime in Virgin Gorda

BRITISH VIRGIN ISLANDS In the extreme southwest of Virgin Gorda, a bizarre land- and seascape of volcanic boulders known as The Baths offer a prehistoric twist on the archetypal Caribbean beach. These granite rocks, some the size of houses, stretch from the wooded slopes behind the sands right on into the clear aquamarine sea, forming a series of striking grottoes, pools and underwater caves through which you can swim, snorkel or just bob around in. The usually calm waters and sun-streaked private nooks can help make a day at the beach seem like a visit to the largest, most outlandish bathtub imaginable.

NEED to know

573 For accommodation ideas, see ⊛www.cuba casas.net. Well-known *casas* like *Hostal Florida Center* (+53 4220 8161) are dogged by touts, who will pretend the *casa* is full and try to take you elsewhere. Don't be put off – if you have a booking make sure you get through the front door. If you haven't booked ahead, look out for the blue symbol outside the establishment which shows it is legal.

574 A tap-tap can be anything from a pick-up truck to a brightly painted, North American-style school bus. They leave when (very) full and, together with *camions* (open-backed trucks), cover the length and breadth of Haiti.

575 For more info on Martinique, go to ⊛www .martinique.org; for the Jardin de Balata check ⊛www .jardindebalata.fr. Avis, Budget, Europcar and Hertz all have offices at the airport and in Fort-de-France.

576 There are several places to stay in the rainforest, from budget cabins for US$35 a night to luxury villas for US$150 upwards. See ⊛www.elyunque.com for more.

577 You won't need any transport to get you around Old Havana, and it's possible to walk to Vedado along the *malecón*. Otherwise, look for a metered taxi near one of the large hotels. You can visit the bar in the Bacardi building for a drink, and ask at reception to be taken up the tower for the views.

578 There are no direct flights to St Barts from the North American or European mainland; you're best flying to St Martin and then catching an island-hopper to St Jean Airport, which lies snug in the centre of the island's inner curve. Try ⊛www.saint-barths.com for information on villa rentals.

579 The main parades in the capital, Port of Spain, take place on the Monday and Tuesday before Ash Wednesday.

580 It's best to explore the cave with a knowledgeable guide; check with the Gerace Research Center (⊛www.geraceresearchcentre.com) for more information.

581 Plenty of guides organize treks up to Boiling Lake; Seacat and his partner Roots also arrange excursions throughout the island. Contact them at ©sea cat55@hotmail.com.

582 The international airport at Puerto Plata is 20km west of Cabarete. All the major windsurfing and kiteboarding equipment manufacturers have schools and equipment rental along the town's main strip.

583 The main transport hub in the Exuma Cays is Staniel Cay, easily reached from Nassau; for trips departing from Great Exuma, you can fly into George Town from Florida.

584 The official festival website (⊛www.reggae sumfest.com) has full details.

585 For more, see ⊛meetthepeople.skedaddle.co.uk.

586 To tour St Lucia you need to rent a car; there are plenty of outlets at the airport, Castries and Rodney Bay, and most of the larger resorts can also arrange rental.

587 ⊛www.grenadagrenadines.com has more details on St George's.

588 The Pitons Tour Guide Association (☎+1 758 459 9748) leads hikes of Gros Piton from the Interpretive Centre in Fond Gens Libre, near Soufrière.

589 Arikok National Park lies 20km east of the capital city of Oranjestad.

590 *La Casa de las Tradiciones*, between Rabí no.154 and Princesa y San Fernando, Santiago de Cuba, features live *son* and other varieties of Cuban music.

591 *Lime Tree Farm* (⊛www.limetreefarm.com), *Forres Park* (⊛www.forrespark.com) and *Strawberry Hill Hotel* (⊛www.islandoutpost.com) all offer tours as well as accommodation.

592 Nelson's Dockyard is open daily 9am–5pm. The national park also includes the fortifications at Shirley Heights and the new multimedia centre at Dow's Hill.

593 Island Adventures (⊛www.biobay.com) offers boat tours of Puerto Mosquito. Tours usually begin at their office, west of Esperanza on PR-996, daily 8–10pm. Avoid heading down on a full moon, when it's impossible to appreciate the effect. Vieques is connected to Puerto Rico by plane and ferry; see ⊛www .gotopuertorico.com.

594 *Crescent Moon Cabins* (⊛www.crescentmoon cabins.com) is located halfway between the capital Roseau and Melville Hall Airport.

595 *Sunshine's* is on Pinney's Beach, on the northwest corner of the island, and is open seven days a week for lunch and dinner during high season (mid-Dec to mid-April); ⊛www.nevisisland.com. has more info.

596 To visit the makers of Ron de Barrilito, contact the tourist office at La Casita in Old San Juan (☎+1 787 722 1709). Casa Don Q faces the marina near La Casita, across from Pier 1, while the Casa Bacardí Visitor Center (⊛www.casabacardi.org) lies across San Juan Bay.

597 To book at *Goldeneye*, visit ⊛www.islandoutpost .com.

598 ⊛www.infobonaire.com has lots of information on snorkelling.

599 For more info, check ⊛www.divecayman.ky.

600 *La Guacara Taína*, Av Mirador del Sur, Santo Domingo (☎+1 809 533 1051).

601 See ⊛www.caribtickets.com for information.

602 From the northern city of Cap Haitien you can take a private taxi or the public bus to the town of Milot, where you'll start your ascent to the Citadelle.

603 For info on Treasure Beach, visit ⊛www.treasure beach.net. For more on BREDS, visit ⊛www.breds.org.

604 Fly into Puerto Plata's international airport, from where it's a 4hr bus ride to Samaná village. Check with Victoria Marine (⊛www.whalesamana.com) for a whale-watching boat tour.

605 Check ⊛www.bvitourism.com for more.

GOOD to know

PIRATES & PLUNDERERS

Welsh-born, Jamaica-based privateer **Sir Henry Morgan** was the terror of the Spanish fleet in the latter half of the seventeenth century, routinely undermining their attempts to control the region by destroying their ships and plundering their treasure. Today his malevolent grin graces every bottle of Captain Morgan rum.

Legendary pirate **Anne Bonny** was born in Ireland in the early 1700s and later moved with her husband to the Bahamas. Soon after, she eloped with "Calico Jack" Rackham, who introduced her to the seafaring life. Female pirates were not unheard of – there may even have been another on Rackham's ship – and some historians contest the popular belief that Bonny concealed her gender, showing just how formidable she was.

"At sunset Martin Alonzo called out with great joy from his vessel that he saw land, and demanded of the Admiral a reward for his intelligence"

Christopher Columbus
on the discovery of San Salvador, Bahamas

JAMAICAN FAITH

Jamaica is purported to have the highest number of churches per capita in the world. Many are Anglican, thanks to the island's history of British rule, but others are Moravian, Baptist, Methodist, Adventist and Pentecostal.

TROPICAL EATS

Acra Fish fritter made with saltfish, eggs and a combination of vegetables, popular in Martinique.
Lambi Ubiquitous Caribbean stew made with the flesh of the conch, a large marine gastropod.
Saltfish Salted and dried fish, usually mackerel or cod, used in a variety of Caribbean (particularly Jamaican) dishes.
Soursop Related to the cherimoya, this large fruit is said to combine the flavours and textures of strawberry, coconut, banana and pineapple.
Stinking toe Sweet-tasting but foul-smelling (hence the name), toe-shaped fruit used in Caribbean (especially Jamaican and Antiguan) cooking. Also an ingredient in folk medicines.

MIGHTY WINDS

Caribbean islands are frequently visited – and ravaged – by hurricanes, particulary in the "season" from June to November. The Great Hurricane of 1780 killed over 22,000 people in Barbados, Martinique and Sint Eustatius. Abaco, in the Bahamas, is considered the Caribbean's historic **hurricane capital**, having withstood eighteen big ones since 1851. Since 1944, however, it's received fewer than **Grand Bahama**, which sees one roughly every four years. Indeed, since 1944, **Nevis** has taken the brunt of the Caribbean's heaviest storms, with Hurricane Lenny severely depressing the island's economy in 1999. In general, the eastern Caribbean sees fewer hurricanes than the rest of the region – and **Bonaire** and **Curaçao** get the fewest, with only eleven named storms passing through in the last 150 years.

PARLEZ VOUS CREOLE?

In addition to the European languages imported by the Caribbean's major colonizers – French, Spanish and English – many islanders also speak variations of these, called **patois** or **Creole**. Often mistaken for mere "simplifications" of European languages, they are distinct dialects with their own grammatical and syntactical rules. While French is the official language of Haiti, *kreyol* is what Haitians really speak. Papiamento, from the Dutch Leeward Islands, comes primarily from Portuguese, but is influenced by Spanish, Dutch, West African dialects and Arawak, an indigenous language of the region.

NATURE UNDER FIRE

The Puerto Rican island of **Culebra**, a National Wildlife Refuge, has been protected since US President Theodore Roosevelt established a bird refuge there in 1909. Today, it's still home to a huge variety of birds and other life, but between World War II and 1975, the US Navy used it for bombing and gunning practice. Another Puerto Rican island, **Vieques**, is now used for similar purposes. On **Bequia**, in the Grenadines, the long-standing tradition of harpooning **whales** is still legal. Natives are permitted by the International Whaling Commission to take four whales per year using traditional methods and weapons. **Guana Island**, in the British Virgin Islands, is said to be the Caribbean locale least disturbed by humans.

ISLAND PEAKS

Pico Duarte, in the Dominican Republic, is the Caribbean's tallest mountain at 3087m. The island of St Lucia is well known for its twin mountains (once active volcanoes), **Petit Piton** and **Gros Piton**, rising 734m and 798m above sea level.

"Reason, I sacrifice you to the evening breeze"

Aimé Césaire

RUM

Since Europeans first colonized the Caribbean with West African slaves, rum has been one of the region's most important exports. Sugar cane grows abundantly in the hot climes, and molasses, a by-product of sugar refinement, was collected by British ships for distillation into rum. Ships would cross the Atlantic to deliver rum to Europe, and then, on their way back to the Americas, swing by West Africa to pick up more slaves to work in the cane fields.

On British Admiral Horatio Nelson's journey back to England from Antigua, where he'd been an administrator, a barrel of rum was on hand to preserve his body in case he died of fever.

TURTLE-WATCHING IN TORTUGUERO • SURFING AT LA LIBERTAD • HOPPING ABOARD THE COPPER CANYON RAILWAY • SOLENTINAME: THE ORANGE (AND YELLOW, AND RED, AND BLUE…) REVOLUTION • CIRCLING LAGO ATITLÁN • WHALE-WATCHING IN BAJA CALIFORNIA • IN SEARCH OF GRILLED RODENT • TAKING A DIP IN THE YUCATÁN'S CENOTES • FLOATING THROUGH THE MAYA UNDERWORLD • HONOURING THE DEAD IN JANITZIO • RUSTIC LUXURY IN THE BELIZEAN FOREST • SOUNDWAVES ON THE CARIBBEAN'S SECRET SHORE • FLOATING THROUGH XOCHIMILCO • A GLIMPSE OF THE MURALS OF BONAMPAK • GALLOPING THROUGH GUANACASTE • MARKET DAY IN OAXACA • EXPERIENCING THE DARIÉN WITH THE EMBERA • DANCING DRAMA WITH THE MAYA • ALL ABOARD THE CHICKEN BUSES • VACATION LIKE A DRUG LORD IN TULUM • THINGS THAT GO BUMP IN THE NIGHT • FROM SEA TO SHINING SEA: CRUISING THE PANAMA CANAL • ISLA DE OMETEPE BY MOTORCYCLE • MAKING PEACE WITH TEQUILA IN TEQUILA • EXPLORING THE SURREAL RAINFOREST ARCHITECTURE OF LAS POZAS • TREKKING IN CORCOVADO NATIONAL PARK • FLOATING DOWN THE NEW RIVER TO LAMANAI • BEING SERENADED BY MARIACHIS IN GUADALAJARA • PADDLING GLOVER'S REEF • DAWN AT TIKAL • BIRDWATCHING ON THE PIPELINE ROAD • KAYAKING IN THE SEA OF CORTÉS • ON THE TRAIL OF PANCHO VILLA • HEADING TO MARKET IN THE GUATEMALAN HIGHLANDS • MEETING THE MONARCHS IN MICHOACÁN • INDULGING IN THE JUNGLE • REVEL IN ECO-LUXURY AT MORGAN'S ROCK • ENCOUNTERING KUNA CULTURE • RIDING DOWN THE RÍO SAN JUAN • A TASTE OF MOLE POBLANO IN PUEBLA • SEARCHING FOR JAGUARS IN COCKSCOMB BASIN WILDLIFE SANCTUARY • DIVING AT PALANCAR REEF • A RIVER RUNS TO IT: PACUARE JUNGLE LODGE • CORN OF PLENTY • ISLA BARRO COLORADO: THE APPLIANCE OF SCIENCE • SAMPLING FISH TACOS IN ENSENADA • CHASING WHALE SHARKS NEAR UTILA • STELAE STORIES OF COPAN • NEW YEAR ON CAYE CAULKER • MEXICO CITY'S MURALS • UNRAVELLING THE MYSTERIES OF MONTE ALBÁN • TURTLE-WATCHING IN TORTUGUERO • SURFING AT LA LIBERTAD • HOPPING ABOARD THE COPPER CANYON RAILWAY • SOLENTINAME: THE ORANGE (AND YELLOW, AND RED, AND BLUE…) REVOLUTION • CIRCLING LAGO ATITLÁN • WHALE-WATCHING IN BAJA CALIFORNIA • IN SEARCH OF GRILLED RODENT • TAKING A DIP IN THE YUCATÁN'S CENOTES • FLOATING THROUGH THE MAYA UNDERWORLD • HONOURING THE DEAD IN JANITZIO • RUSTIC LUXURY IN THE BELIZEAN FOREST • SOUNDWAVES ON THE CARIBBEAN'S SECRET SHORE • FLOATING THROUGH XOCHIMILCO • A GLIMPSE OF THE MURALS OF BONAMPAK • GALLOPING THROUGH GUANACASTE • MARKET DAY IN OAXACA •

Mexico & Central America
606–656

MEXICO

638 On the trail of Pancho Villa

629 Making peace with tequila in Tequila

618 Floating through Xochimilco

647 Diving at Palancar Reef

641 Indulging in the jungle

BELIZE

HONDURAS

624 All aboard the chicken buses

GUATEMALA

607 Surfing at La Libertad

NICARAGUA

649 Corn of plenty

EL SALVADOR

COSTA RICA

PANAMA

631 Trekking in Corcovado National Park

622 Experiencing the Darién with the Emberá

606 Turtle-watching in Tortuguero

COSTA RICA It's a clear, moonless night when we assemble for our pilgrimage to the beach. I can't understand how we are going to see anything in the blackness, but the guide's eyes seem to penetrate even the darkest shadows. We begin walking, our vision adjusting slowly.

We've come to Tortuguero National Park, in northeast Costa Rica, to witness sea turtles nesting. Once the domain of only biologists and locals, turtle-watching is now one of the more popular activities in ecotourism-friendly Costa Rica. As the most important nesting site in the western Caribbean, Tortuguero sees more than its fair share of visitors – the annual number of observers has gone from 240 in 1980 to over 50,000 today.

The guide stops, points out two deep furrows in the sand – the sign of a turtle's presence – and places a finger to his lips, making the "shhh" gesture. The nesting females can be spooked by the slightest noise or light. He gathers us around a crater in the beach; inside it is an enormous creature. We hear her rasp and sigh as she brushes aside sand for her nest.

In whispers, we comment on her plight: the solitude of her task, the low survival rate of her hatchlings – only one of every 5000 will make it past the birds, crabs, sharks, seaweed and human pollution to adulthood.

We are all mesmerized by the turtle's bulk. Though we are not allowed to get too close, we can catch the glint of her eyes. She doesn't seem to register our presence at all. The whirring sound of discharged sand continues. After a bit the guide moves us away. My eyes have adapted to the darkness now, and I can make out other gigantic oblong forms labouring slowly up the beach – a silent, purposeful armada.

607 Surfing at La Libertad

EL SALVADOR It's not surprising that the beach in La Libertad is packed on Sundays. The port town is less than an hour's drive from the choked capital of San Salvador, its oceanfront restaurants serve the finest *mariscada* (creamy seafood soup) in the country and, of course, there's *el surf*.

The western end of the beach here has one of the longest right point breaks, prosaically called *punta roca* (rocky point), in the world. On a good day – and with year-round warm water and consistent and uncrowded waves there are plenty of those – skilled surfistas can ride a thousand yards from the head of the point into the beach. Amateur surfers, meanwhile, opt for the section of gentler waves, known as *La Paz*, that roll into the mid-shore.

It's rare to walk through the town without seeing one of the local boys running barefoot, board under arm, down to the sea or hanging outside the Hospital de las Tablas while a dent or tear is repaired. Some, like Jimmy Rottingham, whose American father kick-started the expat surf scene when he arrived in the 1970s (witness the psychedelic surfboards on the walls of *Punta Roca* restaurant), have become semi-professional.

If you're looking for quieter, cleaner breaks, join the foreign surfers who head west to beaches such as El Zonte. Now a backpacker heaven, the point break here used to be a secret among locals and students from Santa Tecla. The village's best surfer, El Teco, was inspired to jump on a board after watching *Hawaii Five-O*, later polishing his technique by observing pelicans surfing the waves. Even if you miss out on *olas de mantequilla* (waves like butter) or suffer too many *wipeadas*, there's always the Zonte scene: at weekends the capital's hip kids come to party amid bonfires, fire dancers and all-night drumming.

608 Hopping aboard the Copper Canyon Railway

MEXICO As the countryside – by turns savage, pristine, lush – flashes past the windows of the *Chihuahua-Pacific Express*, Mexico reveals a side of itself that is both spectacular and unexpected.

"El Chepe", as the train is known, traverses the country's most remote landscape, a region of rugged splendour called the Copper Canyon. Spanning six prodigious canyons and a labyrinth of some two hundred gorges, this natural wonder is four times the size of the Grand Canyon. Harsh, inaccessible and thoroughly untamed, the canyons are sparsely populated only by the Rarámuri, an indigenous agrarian people.

El Chepe's journey commences on Mexico's Pacific coast, in Los Mochis, then trundles through 75km of arid, cactus-strewn wasteland to placid El Fuerte, the gateway to the canyons. From here, the track climbs, the air cools and the scenery shifts: for the next six hours you roll past one incredible vista after another. In a continual skyward ascent, El Chepe plunges in and out of tunnels, rattles over bridges and makes hairpin turns.

Colossal stone cliffs, folds of rock and serpentine rivers flicker by. Above you, mountains rise like fortified cities, while gaping chasms open on either side. Then, all at once, the stone corridor yields to a sweeping plateau of pine-scattered towers and stratified monoliths.

At Divisadero, 300km from Los Mochis and 2000m above sea level, three canyons converge to form an astonishing panorama. The train makes a brief stop here, giving you time to snap some pictures and breathe in the ozone and pine. Creel, another 60km along, is the place to stop for extended excursions – forests, gorges, waterfalls and hot springs all lie within easy reach.

The 655km expedition concludes on the desert plains of Chihuahua, though it feels as if you've travelled further. Stepping off the train, you're as likely to feel humbled as you are exhilarated.

Solentiname:

the orange (and yellow, and red, and blue...) revolution

NICARAGUA Breached by extinct and not-so-extinct volcanoes, haunted by vampire bats and frequented by some of the most dangerous sharks in the world, the opaque waters of Lake Nicaragua, southeast of the capital Managua, offer some of the more adventurous destinations in the country's fast-emerging tourist industry. The bow-tied island of Ometepe may get much of the press but it's the Solentiname Archipelago, clustered in the lake's southeastern corner, which really offers a trip off the edge of Central American civilization.

You won't find a regular and convenient ferry crossing from the mainland, in fact you wouldn't really want to hang around much on the mainland at all, given that the point of departure is the terminally mildewed, desperately down-at-heel port of San Carlos. If you're lucky, your arrival might coincide with the twice-weekly boat, a mere 15km whizz across the lake to a series of untouched islands which, lo and behold, are more famous for their art than their beaches or budget PADI courses. For, back in the day, Solentiname was home to a community of peasant painters and nascent revolutionaries headed by poet-priest Ernesto Cardenal, himself once a pivotal figure in the country's iconic socialist movement, the Sandinistas.

The simple church on Mancarrón where Cardenal preached is a touching monument to the primitivist art he pioneered, and though he left in the late 1970s the creative community remains, earning a crust from the life-affirming colour and guileless lines of their canvases. The reality of the landscape they portray isn't quite so dreamlike – how could it be? – but it is untamed and teeming with life, both aquatic and avian, much of which still other artisans stylize in wood carvings: willowy egrets and barking parrots, wily caimans and vibrant fish. It's likewise a landscape more pristine even than the most undeveloped corners of the Caribbean; the few islands which are inhabited have no electricity, no running water and no paved roads, much less any conventional tourist facilities to speak of. What little accommodation there is relies on solar power, just as the night stars shine free of light pollution, in an enclave where art and nature work luminous wonders.

GUATEMALA Ever since Aldous Huxley passed this way in the 1930s, writers have lauded the natural beauty of Lago Atitlán. Ringed by three volcanoes, the lake is also surrounded by a series of Maya villages, each with its own appeal and some still quite traditional, despite the influx of visitors. A week spent circumnavigating Atitlán is the ideal way to experience its unique blend of Maya tradition and bohemian counterculture.

Start at the main entry point, Panajachel, which was "discovered" by beatniks in the 1950s and remains the most popular lakeside settlement. The hotels and shopping (especially for textiles) are excellent, even if the place has become something approaching a resort.

By contrast, Santiago Atitlán remains close to one hundred percent Tz'utujil Maya and has a frenetic and non-touristy market that fires up early each Friday morning. It's a riot of colour and commerce as a tide of highlanders overloaded with vegetables and weavings struggles between dock and plaza. Elsewhere, drop by the textile museum, the parish church and the shrine of the Maya pagan saint Maximón, where you can pay your respects with offerings of liquor and tobacco.

Neighbouring San Pedro is another Tz'utujil village, but in the last decade or so has become Guatemala's countercultural centre, with a plethora of language schools and cheapo digs for backpacking bong-puffers and bongo drummers. Even if this puts you off, you can content yourself with the village's wonderful restaurants and a hike up nearby San Pedro volcano.

It's a short hop to San Marcos, for some New Age vibes at the renowned *Las Pirámides* meditation-cum-yoga retreat. Last stop is Santa Cruz, where a few great guesthouses make the ideal base for days spent idling in a hammock and admiring the perfect lake views.

Circling
Lago Atitlán

610

611 Whale-watching in Baja California

MEXICO Whale shapes are picked out in fairy lights; whalebones are hung on restaurant walls and garden fences; posters, flyers and sandwich boards depict whales outside every shop and bar – even the name of the supermarket here, La Ballena, means whale.

If you didn't already know, you might guess that Guerrero Negro, a flyblown pitstop halfway down the long, spindly peninsula of Baja California, is the main base for whale-watching in Mexico. Every November, California grey whales leave Alaska en masse and migrate south to calve, arriving in the warm waters of Mexico in January and February. The lagoon close to Guerrero Negro is where most end up – and the tour to see them, with a guaranteed sighting at close quarters, is one of Mexico's most unforgettable experiences. And it goes like this. By the time the small boat reaches the middle of the glassy-smooth lagoon and the captain switches off the engine, all its

excitable passengers have been silenced. Someone spots a distant, cloudy spray – then a great grey body, studded white with barnacles, rises out of the water and curves back in with a deep, resounding splash, leaving a trail of smooth rings across the surface of the water. The little boat rocks and shakes, and curious whales come closer.

Round and round they swim, nine metres of pure elegance twisting, flipping, rolling and spouting, their brand new offspring gliding alongside – the boat's passengers can almost touch them. And the whales are often joined by dolphins, aquatic bodyguards swimming in perfectly synchronized pairs to protect the whale calves, and by sealions, their cheeky whiskered faces nearly stealing the show. Then just as suddenly as the mammals arrived, they disappear back into the deep. The lagoon settles and, moved to silence or even tears, a boatload of awestruck tourists motors back to shore.

612 In search of grilled rodent

BELIZE The petite coastal country of Belize brings to mind sandy islands, oiled tans and tropical drinks with little paper umbrellas. What doesn't come to mind is grilled rodent. But, gibnut is one of Belize's traditional dishes – and it reveals an intriguing side to a nation known more for its cayes than its cuisine. Gibnut (also called "paca" elsewhere in Central and South America) is a nocturnal rodent that's hunted in the northern and western jungles of Belize. It's then grilled, carved up and plated as a local delicacy. Belizeans, particularly those who grew up in rural areas, have been dining on it for years – but gibnut first came into the international spotlight when it was served to Queen Elizabeth II at a state dinner in Belize. When news reached the UK that the Queen had been served rat, the press corps were apparently scandalized (plus, the headline sold plenty of newspapers), and gibnut got its nickname, "Royal Rat". So, what does it taste like? On the plate, gibnut looks like pork – slightly fatty, and often tender

enough to cut with the side of a fork; in the mouth, its wild nature comes through, with a pungent, earthy gameyness. In fact, as many chefs report, when hunters haul in gibnut to the kitchen, the odour is so powerful and rank that it has to be dunked in a vat of lime juice for the day. Tracking down gibnut is also part of its appeal. Most tourist-geared restaurants don't offer it, but just asking around will bring huge grins to the faces of Belizeans – and directions to the nearest family restaurant that serves it. Dig in to gibnut and ease into the Caribbean night at the one-room *Nerie's II*, in Belize City. The setting is wonderfully Belizean traditional: chalkboard menu; plastic table covers; an out-of-date calendar hanging askew on the wall; Belizean reggae spilling out of crackly speakers; a sticky bottle of Marie's hot sauce next to your plate; and a chilled Belikin beer cracked open for you as soon as you drain your last one. Spend awhile here, and you may even be in the mood for a second helping of gibnut.

613 Taking a dip in the Yucatán's cenotes

MEXICO The Yucatán Peninsula can be unpleasantly muggy in the summer. At the same time, the low-lying region's unique geography holds the perfect antidote to hot afternoons: the limestone shelf that forms the peninsula is riddled with underground rivers, accessible at sinkholes called cenotes – a geological phenomenon found only here.

Nature's perfect swimming spots, cenotes are filled with cool fresh water year-round, and they're so plentiful that you're bound to find one nearby when you need a refreshing dip. Some are unremarkable holes in the middle of a farmer's field, while others, like Cenote Azul near Laguna Bacalar, are enormous, deep wells complete with diving platforms and on-site restaurants.

The most visited and photographed cenotes are set in dramatic caverns in and around the old colonial city of Valladolid. Cenote Zací, in the centre of town, occupies a full city block. Half-covered by a

shell of rock, the pool exudes a chill that becomes downright cold as you descend the access stairs. Just outside town, Dzitnup and neighbouring Samula are almost completely underground. Shinny down some rickety stairs, and you'll find yourself in cathedral-like spaces, where sound and light bounce off the walls. Both cenotes are beautifully illuminated by the sun, which shines through a hole in the ceiling, forming a glowing spotlight on the turquoise water.

Even more remarkable, however, is that these caverns extend under water. Strap on a snorkel or scuba gear, and drop below the surface to spy a still world of delicate stalagmites. Exploring these ghostly spaces, it's easy to see why the Maya considered cenotes gateways to the underworld. The liminal sensation is heightened by the clarity of the water, which makes you feel as if you're suspended in air.

BELIZE Caves were considered sacred by the ancient Maya, offering a gateway to their ancestors and the spirit world. Called "Xibalba" – literally "frightening" – they would enter with respect, to offer sacrifices, paintings and pottery to appease the Gods. Central America's largest cave systems lie in today's Belize, and now a new type of adrenalin-fuelled visitor is to be found exploring this subterranean underworld.

Belize's first and still its longest cave tubing expedition – run by master adventure outfit Caves Branch – follows a spectacular seven-mile route through gigantic limestone caverns, narrow passageways, and mysterious chambers carved out of the foothills of the Maya Mountains, and strewn with artefacts and wall markings left from ceremonies up to three thousand years ago. The Maya entered these underground rivers by canoe, but today giant inflatable rubber tubes are the floating transport of choice. The adventure begins at Caves Branch HQ, a rustic, communal scattering of purpose-built cabañas, luxury treehouses, pools, Jacuzzis and massage huts on the river bank, tucked beneath a towering rainforest canopy. Seated comfortably in tube, you set off in groups of up to twelve and glide slowly down-

river, thick foliage either side, fully-clothed and damp from the intense humidity. The cave mouth looms up ahead and an eerie silence replaces excited chatter. Expert guides are quick to reassure, however, and headlamps illuminate the initially startling darkness. Cool and moist, small sections of the caverns have to be negotiated on foot by clambering up pathways. Sparkling crystal rock formations glisten and shadow dance in the odd shaft of jungle sunlight and you can't help but remember you're following in the footsteps of a long-gone civilization.

Deep underground and with headlamps off, you descend through the pitch blackness, pulled earthwards down low-grade rapids with water gushing all around as you swirl past soaring stalagmites and dripping stalactites. With adrenalin pumping, the day is swallowed up in a baffling sense of timelessness. At once you're at the liberty of the sacred cave underworld, an exhilarating, scary, yet strangely calming experience. You're expelled suddenly back into bright sunlight, the jungle cacophony of the daytime almost deafening in your ears. You may be soaked to the skin, but laughter engulfs the whole group as you float back to the overworld.

Floating through the
Maya underworld

614

HONOURING THE DEAD IN JANITZIO

615

MEXICO Mexicans believe that the thin veil between the land of the living and the world of the spirits is at its most permeable on the night of November 1, as All Saints' Day slips silently into All Souls' Day. This is the one time each year, it is said, when the dead can visit the relatives they have left behind. Mexicans all over the country aim to make them feel welcome when they do, though nowhere are the preparations as elaborate as on the island of Janitzio in Lago Pátzcuaro.

Market stalls laden with papier-mâché skeletons and sugar skulls appear weeks in advance; the decorations and sweets go on shrines set up in people's homes. Dedicated to the departed, the shrines come complete with a photo of the deceased and an array of their favourite treats – perhaps some cigarettes, a few *tamales* and, of course, preferred brands of tequila and beer.

When the big day comes, you don't want to arrive too early at the cemetery – it isn't until around 11pm, as the witching hour approaches, that the island's indigenous Purhépecha people start filtering into the graveyard. They come equipped with candles, incense and wooden frames draped in a riot of puffy orange marigolds. Pretty soon the entire site is aglow with candles, the abundantly adorned graves slightly eerie in the flickering light. So begins the all-night vigil: some observers doze silently, others reminisce with friends seated at nearby graves. It is a solemn, though by no means sombre, occasion. Indeed, unlike most cultures, Mexicans live with death and celebrate it.

By early morning the cemetery is peaceful, and in the pre-dawn chill, as sleep threatens to overtake you, it is easier to see how the dead could be tempted back for a brief visit, and why people return year after year to commune with the departed.

616 Rustic luxury in the Belizean forest

BELIZE The story goes that Francis Ford Coppola built *Blancaneaux* as a place to write, and it's hard to imagine a more inspiring base than this luxuriously rustic resort in Belize's Mountain Pine Ridge Forest Reserve. Just two or three hours' drive from the airport – or a short hop in your private plane – and you're poised for an idyllic few days where nature comes with all mod cons. Everything here seems designed to showcase the natural environment. Thatched cabañas scattered through the lush gardens, furnished with Central American textiles and artworks, feature decks and bathrooms half-open to the elements; thankfully, bedrooms are secured against mosquitoes and other nasties.

Twice a day, honeymooners and hikers alike troop up to the restaurant for tasty American breakfasts and Italian dinners, cooked using ingredients from the on-site organic garden. Staff will happily make you a packed lunch to enjoy while out exploring. Several of Belize's sights are within easy reach by 4WD, chief among them the ancient Maya city of Caracol – still under excavation – where you might find yourself wandering the overgrown ruins alone but for your driver-guide. Armed with every fact there is to know about Belizean history and wildlife, he'll regularly stop the car en route to point out a king vulture, perhaps, or to let you sniff the fragrant bark of a tree used in traditional medicines.

With so many activities to choose from, you'll need to set aside time to enjoy *Blancaneaux* for its own sake: lazing in a hammock overlooking the jungle, taking a dip in the natural pools formed by the Privassion Creek as it runs through the grounds, or hanging out in the bar, chatting with the guides about whether to go horseriding, hiking or mountain-biking tomorrow.

However you spend your days, be sure to get up one morning while it's still dark. As the sky lightens and a misty scene comes into focus, parrots fly past, screeching an alarm over the sound of the rushing river. Sitting snuggled in a fleece on your deck, watching the jungle awaken before you in all its cawing, chirruping and whirring glory, is worth getting out of bed for.

617 Soundwaves on the Caribbean's secret shore

COSTA RICA At the southeastern end of Costa Rica's Caribbean coast, a tiny spur of rainforest and golden sand butts into the warmth and verdant wetness of Panama. This is the little-visited and low-key Gandoca-Manzanillo Wildlife Refuge. Unlike Costa Rica's more visited national parks, there are no shrieking scarlet macaws, no ringing three-wattled bellbirds, no volcanoes, no pounding Pacific surf – and not many tourists either. You can bask on the expansive arc of Manzanillo beach, sheltered by its massive green wall of coastal rainforest, and hardly see or hear another person.

What you will see – and hear – are animals: everywhere. On the beach, every footfall disturbs sapphire-blue land crabs, scurrying to hide in their sandy holes. In the shallows, you might spot a jumping devil ray, its wings spread like a menacing angel before it splashes back into the water. On the forest trails you'll hear the eerie shrieks of howler monkeys – which inspired Christopher Columbus to name the adjacent headland Punta Mona, or "Monkey Point"; you may glimpse the improbably bright chestnut-mandibled and keel-billed toucans too. At night, guides take you to see leatherback turtles; torches can hardly illuminate the expanse of the carapace, but sit quietly beside a laying female and you'll hear the gentlest popping as she lays her eggs.

The inshore coral reefs offer fine snorkelling and diving (there are some sleepy local dive centres), and fishermen can take you in search of the local dolphins – bottlenose, Atlantic spotted or the rare, tiny tucuxi. Once the boat's engine is cut, there's nothing to hear but the surge of the dolphins' leaping or the sudden insuck of blowhole air as they surface. Ask the boatman why dolphins breach like this and you might get a truly Caribbean reply: "him jus' jump up and taalk to I". It's the best kind of conversation.

618 Floating through Xochimilco

MEXICO Spend a few days in the intoxicating, maddening *centro histórico* of Mexico City, and you'll understand why thousands of Mexicans make the journey each Sunday to the "floating gardens" of Xochimilco, the country's very own Venice.

Built by the Aztecs to grow food, this network of meandering waterways and man-made islands, or *chinampas*, is an important gardening centre for the city, and where families living in and around the capital come to spend their day of rest. Many start with a visit to the beautiful sixteenth-century church of San Bernardino in the main plaza, lighting candles and giving thanks for the day's outing. Duty done, they head down to one of several docks, or *embarcaderos*, on the water to hire out a *trajinera* for a few hours. These flat, brightly painted gondolas – with names such as *Viva Lupita*, *Adios Miriam*, *El Truinfo* and *Titanic* – come fitted with table and chairs, perfect for a picnic.

The colourful boats shunt their way out along the canals, provoking lots of good-natured shouting from the men wielding the poles. As the silky green waters, overhung with trees, wind past flower-filled meadows, the cacophony and congestion of the city are forgotten. Mothers and grannies unwrap copious parcels and pots of food, men open bottles of beer and aged tequila; someone starts to sing. By midday, Xochimilco is full of carefree holidaymakers.

Don't worry if you haven't come with provisions – the *trajineras* are routinely hunted down by vendors selling snacks, drinks and even lavish meals from small wooden canoes. Others flog trinkets, sweets and souvenirs. And if you've left your guitar at home, no problem: boatloads of musicians – mariachis in full costume, marimba bands and wailing ranchera singers – will cruise alongside or climb aboard and knock out as many tunes as you've money to pay for.

619 A glimpse of the murals at Bonampak

MEXICO For almost a century, scholars studying ancient Maya culture believed the Maya to be pacifists, devoted to their arcane calendar and other harmless pursuits. It wasn't until 1946, when a few Lacandón Maya led an American photographer to a ruined temple at Bonampak, deep in the Chiapas jungle, that they had any reason to think differently.

As the party entered the narrow building perched at the top of the temple and torchlight played across its interior, the ancient Maya flickered into living colour. A series of murals covered the walls and ceilings of three rooms, depicting the Maya in fascinating detail. Lords paraded in yellow-spotted jaguar pelts and elaborate headdresses, while attendants sported blue-green jade jewellery.

More remarkable was the quantity of bright-red gore splashed on scenes throughout the rooms: severed heads rolled, prisoners oozed blood from mangled fingers, sacrifice victims littered the ground. On one wall, the eighth-century king Chan Muan glowered mercilessly at writhing captives, while on another his soldiers engaged in a frenzied battle.

The artistry of the murals was undeniable: even the most gruesome images – such as the king's wife threading a thorn-studded rope through her tongue – were balanced by lush colours and captivating precision. But the discovery, while offering unparalleled insight for anthropologists and Maya experts, must have been somewhat unsettling, too: to see Chan Muan poised to lop the head off a prisoner was astounding.

Visiting the Bonampak murals is slightly easier now than it was when they were found sixty years ago, but only just. They remain buried far enough in the humid Lacandón forest that you can still feel – when you step into the dimly-lit rooms – a sense of drama and revelation. If you can't make it out to Chiapas, there are reproductions in the National Museum of Anthropology in Mexico City, where the colours are brighter but the ambience lacking.

620 Galloping through Guanacaste

COSTA RICA This is not the Costa Rica you may have imagined: one glance at the wide-open spaces, the legions of heat-stunned cattle or the mounted *sabaneros* (cowboys) trotting alongside the Pan-American Highway reveals that Guanacaste has little in common with the rest of the country. Often called "the Texas of Costa Rica", this is ranching territory: the lush, humid rainforest that blankets most of the country is notably absent here, replaced by a swathe of tropical dry forest. It's one of the last significant patches of such land in Central America.

Given the region's livelihood, it's only fitting that the best way to tour Guanacaste is astride a horse. Don't be shy about scrambling into the saddle – many of the working ranches in the province double as hotels, and almost all of them offer horseback tours, giving you a chance to participate in the region's *sabanero* culture. From your perch high above the ground, the strange, silvery beauty of the dry forest appears to much greater advantage – in the dry season, the trees shed their leaves in an effort to conserve water, leaving the landscape eerily bare and melancholy. You'll be able to spot all kinds of wildlife, from monkeys and pot-bellied iguanas to birds and even the odd boa constrictor (though the horses may not be impressed by this one).

For a different sort of scenery, head to the area around still-active Rincón de la Vieja, where you can ride around bubbling mud pots (*pilas de barro*) and puffing steam vents, all under the shadow of the towering, mist-shrouded volcano.

Some of the region's ranches-cum-hotels even let guests put in a day's work riding out with their hands, provided their fence-mending and cattle-herding skills are up to scratch. Regardless of your level of equestrian expertise, once you've had a gallop through Guanacaste, you'll never look at sightseeing on foot the same way again.

621 Market day in Oaxaca

MEXICO Oaxaca is pure magical realism – an elegant fusion of colonial grandeur and indigenous mysticism. From the Zócalo, the city's main square, streets unfold in a patchwork of belle époque theatres, romantic courtyards and sublime churches.

While the city's colonial history reaches its zenith in the breathtaking Iglesia de Santo Domingo, pre-Hispanic traditions ignite in its kaleidoscopic markets. The largest of these is the bustling Mercado de Abastos, which bombards the senses with riotous colours, intoxicating aromas and exotic tastes.

Indigenous women dressed in embroidered *huipiles*, or tunics, squat amidst baskets overflowing with red chillis and *chapulines* (baked grasshoppers), weaving *pozahuancos*, wrap-around skirts dyed with secretions from snails. Stalls are piled with *artesanía* from across the region. Leather sandals, or *huaraches*, are the speciality of Tlacolula; made from recycled tyres, they guarantee even the most intrepid backpacker a lifetime of mileage.

Hand-woven rugs from Teotitlán del Valle, coloured using century-old recipes including pomegranate and cochineal beetles, are the most prized. The shiny black finish on the pottery from San Bartolo Coyotepec gives it an ornamental function – a promotion from the days when it was used to carry mescal to market.

Street-smart vendors meander the labyrinthine alleyways, offering up the panaceas of ancient deities – *tejate*, the "Drink of the Gods", is a cacao-based beverage with a curd consistency and muddy hue. (A more guaranteed elixir is a mug of hot chocolate, laced with cinnamon and chilli, from Mayordormo, the Willy Wonka of Oaxaca.) The stalls around the outer edges of the market sell shots of mescal; distilled from the sugary heart of the cactus-like maguey plant and mixed with local herbs, it promises a cure to all ailments. With a dead worm at the bottom as proof of authenticity, it's an appropriately mind-bending libation for watching civilization and supernaturalism merge on a grand scale.

PANAMA Enveloped in the thick blackness of night, the sounds of the rainforest assail your senses: against a chorus of cicadas and crickets, a panoply of other nocturnal creatures chirp, trill, squeak and rustle in the undergrowth. Tucked under a mosquito net four metres off the ground, on the floor of a traditional wood-and-thatch house on stilts, you slide into your first night's sleep in the Darién jungle.

Comprising vast swathes of near impenetrable tropical wilderness straddling the border between Panama and Colombia, the Darién has achieved near mythical status with its potent allure of outstanding natural beauty, inaccessibility and danger: from deadly pit vipers to guerillas and para-militaries, and vampire bats to drug-traffickers, the rainforest commands respect. A magnet for nature-lovers, boasting a staggering array of wildlife, it is also home to several thousand indigenous Emberá. Once semi-nomadic hunter-gatherers, adept at pursuing their prey with poison-tipped arrows and blowpipes, the scattered communities of the Emberá now lead a more settled existence, welcoming tourists, sharing their traditional culture and knowledge, and even their homes. Learn about the intricacies of basketry and wood-carving, for which they are world-renowned; try fishing from a *piragua* – a wooden dugout canoe, keeping an eye out for crocs and caimans; or have your body painted with the indigo dye of the jagua fruit, providing a temporary two-week tattoo and convenient natural insect repellent. Engage a guide to venture into the rainforest itself – preferably at dawn when the dazzling birdlife is at its most active and the heat tolerable. Several villages have trails leading to harpy eagle nests, where a patient stake-out may be rewarded by a sighting of arguably the world's most powerful raptor; instantly recognizable by its imperious slaty-grey cloak and regal crest, it boasts a 2m wingspan and talons the size of a grizzly bear's claws. Like the endangered harpy eagle, the Emberá way of life is under threat; sensitively managed ecotourism may help preserve their culture and guarantee future visitors a similarly rich and unforgettable experience.

Experiencing the Darién
with the Emberá
622

623 DANCING DRAMA WITH THE MAYA

GUATEMALA A riot of colour, music, dance, alcohol, religion and tradition, every Maya village in Guatemala celebrates its patron saint's day with a life-affirming fiesta. You'll find the village square packed with trinket-selling traders, a fairground with dodgy-looking rides, festival queens wearing exquisite *huipiles* (blouses made from hand-woven textiles) paraded on floats and an endless array of machine-gun-style firecrackers and *bombas* (ear-drum-splitting fireworks which provoke all the stray dogs in town to bark at the moon – night or day).

Alongside standard-issue bands (complete with a strutting lead singer) belting out the latest Latino hits, traditional dances are performed. These enact a custom of history-telling through dance drama. Masked performers wearing fantastical plumed headdresses and elaborate and gaudy costumes skip to the beat of the *marimba* (a kind of xylophone), flute and drum. The *Baile de la Conquista* (Conquest Dance) recounts the struggle between the Spanish and Maya. Tecún Umán, the K'iche king, confronts the conquistadors but is killed in battle and the Maya are converted to Christianity. Though the drama narrates a tragedy for the Maya, the dancers manage to inject humour into the tale as the arrogance of the invaders is ridiculed. By performing this dance the spirits of their defeated ancestors are released.

In some areas of the western highlands, even more arresting spectacles take place. The most astonishing of all, the *Palo Volador*, is only performed in Cubulco, Chichicastenango and Joyabaj. Men climb to the top of a 20m pole, then swallow-dive to the ground, with only a cord tied around both feet to break their fall, spiralling slowly to the ground in ever-increasing circles. This ritual is said to signify the descent of the hero twins into hell to fight the Lords of the Underworld in the Maya creation epic.

As a spectacle, Maya fiestas are a total assalt on the senses as dance and custom, noise and costume combine in an orgy of celebration, which is as much about honouring highland ritual as it is about having one hell of a party.

624 All aboard the chicken buses

GUATEMALA *Camionetas* ("chicken buses") start their lives as North American school buses, Bluebirds built to ferry under-eights from casa to classroom. Once they move down to these parts, they're decked out with gaudy "go faster" stripes and windshield stickers bearing religious mantras ("Jesús es el Señor"). Comfort, however, is not customizable: bench seat legroom is so limited that gringo knees are guaranteed a bruise or two, and the roads have enough crater-sized potholes to ensure that your gluteus maximus will take a serious pounding. But you choose to hop aboard in Antigua anyway, just to say you've ridden one if for no other reason.

Pre-departure rituals must be observed. Street vendors stream down the aisles, offering everything from *chuchitos* (stuffed maize dumplings) to bibles. Expect a travelling salesman-cum-quack to appear and utter a heartfelt monologue testifying how his elixir will boost libido, cure piles and insomnia (which won't be a problem on the journey ahead). Don't be surprised to find an indigenous family of delightful but snotty-nosed, taco-munching kids on your lap and a basket of dried shrimp under your feet; on the chicken bus, there's no such thing as "maximum capacity". A moustachioed driver jumps aboard, plugs in a tape of the cheesiest merengue the marketplace has to offer, and you're off. The exhaust smoke is so dense even the street dogs run for cover.

Antigua to Nebaj doesn't look much on a map – around 165km or so – but the route passes through four distinct Maya regions, so you look out for the tightly woven zig-zag shawls typical of Chichicastengo and the scarlet turban-like headdresses worn by the women of the Ixil. Considering the way the bus negotiates the blind bends of the Pan-American Highway, you'll take anything to divert your attention.

With some luck, after five hours you arrive in Nebaj, a little shaken, slightly bruised, but with a story to tell.

625 Vacation like a drug lord in Tulum

MEXICO Even drug kingpins – perhaps especially drug kingpins – need a little time away from it all. The late Pablo Escobar, the Colombian drug lord once ranked by Forbes as the seventh richest man in the world, favoured beach getaways. In the 1980s, he built an airy, eight-bedroom mansion just footsteps away from the ocean in the one-street town of Tulum, about 100km south of Cancún on Mexico's Caribbean coast.

In 1993, after Colombian police killed Escobar in a shootout in Medellín, his Tulum mansion, nicknamed *Casa Magna*, became the property of the Mexican government. Over the next decade, as the town evolved into an ecofriendly, yoga-centric beach paradise, *Casa Magna* fell into disrepair. Finally, in 2005, Mexico leased the house to the owners of *Amansala*, a Tulum resort best known for its yoga-and-fruit-shake bikini bootcamps. *Amansala*'s owners – Americans Melissa Perlman and Erica Gragg – painstakingly renovated the villa, replacing its rustic drug-dealer style with minimalist Asian beach-chic.

Ironically, the former kingpin's party house has become perhaps the quietest, most understated resort in what's now known as the "Mayan Riviera". This is the place to sit back and enjoy the white sand, gentle waves and warm water of the Caribbean – and a wide array of the most comfortable beach furniture on Earth.

Take care when choosing a bedroom, however, as *Casa Magna*'s rooms are numbered, essentially in order of desirability, from one to eight. The secluded room one must have been Pablo's – its two private decks offer views of both the ocean and the sunset. The dark, viewless room eight, on the other hand, was surely the domain of tag-alongs and lowly members of his extended posse. If the room available is numbered higher than six, you may want to seek alternative accommodation – luckily, the equally stunning *Casa Magna Two*, Pablo's second vacation home, is just down the road.

626 Things that go bump in the night

COSTA RICA The thick cloud hangs heavily amongst the branches, leaving a trail of moisture as it swirls slowly through the dense foliage of Monteverde Cloudforest Reserve. The blurry silhouette of a creature gradually emerges through the fine mist, advancing down the track towards you. As more figures appear, you recognize their outlines: a swarming group of greatly spotted tourists.

Ever since *National Geographic* declared that Monteverde might just be the best place in all of Central America to see the resplendent quetzal – a striking emerald bird, revered by the Aztecs and Mayans alike – the neat trails of this vast reserve have been swamped with ecotourists and twitchers intent on catching a glimpse of a shimmering tail feather. Visitor numbers are limited, but at times you could be forgiven for thinking that most of the wildlife is of the camera-toting kind. There is one excellent way, however, of escaping the crowds.

Each night, when a hush has fallen on the forest, a small group sets out from the reserve office to walk the deserted trails with just an expert guide – and a flashlight or two – for company. In the dark, your sense of hearing peaked by the inky blackness, you can almost hear the jungle breathing. Many of Monteverde's animals are nocturnal, and as the guide scans his torch across a pair of toucans, their beaks nestled firmly in their feathers for the night, his beam lands on the furry face of a cuddly looking kinkajou, a comic-book member of the racoon family, steadily navigating the lower branches. As it heads off on the forage for food, you stand stock-still to soak up the silence. The only sound is the crunching of leaf-litter as a rather hefty tarantula makes its way across the forest floor. By morning, he'll be safely hidden out of sight, as the tour groups arrive to take over the trails once more.

627 From sea to shining sea: cruising the Panama Canal

PANAMA The Panama Canal, a narrow channel surrounded by virgin jungles teeming with toucans and white-faced capuchin monkeys, takes only a day to traverse. But during that day you'll experience an amazing feat of engineering and cross the Continental Divide. Politically fraught from its inception and burdened by the death of nearly 30,000 workers during its construction, the 80km canal, opened in 1914, is a controversial yet fascinating waterway which offers safe passage to over 14,000 vessels per year.

Your trip begins in the Caribbean near the rough-and-tumble town of Colón, which prospered during the canal's construction but has since declined, its ramshackle colonial buildings and hand-painted signs frozen in time. Once on board, ships enter the narrow Gatún locks; the canal rises over 25m above sea level as it crosses the Panamanian isthmus, so you start and end your journey in a series of locks, which elevate and then lower you from the ocean on either end.

On the far side, the enormous, sparkling Gatún Lake was formed by a flooded jungle valley and serves as an intersection for shipping freighters, cruise ships, local pleasure boaters and environmentalists, drawn by the lake's isolated islands – basically the tops of mountains that remained above water level. They and the surrounding rainforest are home to thousands of species of wildlife, including monkeys, sloths, lizards and a variety of tropical birds, all of which you'll see from the boat. With the lake behind you, you enter the narrowest part of the canal – the Gaillard Cut. Blasted out of solid rock and shale mountainside, this channel is so perilously close that it's impossible for two large ships to pass; as you enter, your clothes stick to your skin in the hot, heavy equatorial air, and the rainforest feels very close by. Listen for the calls of the myriad birds, loud and distinct above the engine's low-speed hum, and scan the banks, where you'll pick out crocodiles floating menacingly in the shallows.

After nearly 14km of slow, careful progress, you emerge at the Miraflores Locks, beyond which lies the Pacific. As you exit the final chamber and pass under the Bridge of the Americas at Balboa, the bright lights and skyscrapers of Panama City appear on your left. From the timeworn streets of Colón to the bustling metropolis ahead, you have truly travelled from one side of the world to the other.

628 Isla de Ometepe by motorcycle

NICARAGUA When it comes to getting around Central America with speed and ease, there are two extremes: a luxury coach and a motorcycle. The former option allows tourists to turn off their minds as they and fifty others ride across the land in supreme comfort. The latter option involves a little effort, a lot of wind in one's face and journeys quite unlike any other.

On Nicaragua's Isla de Ometepe, the largest of four hundred islands sprinkled across Lago de Nicaragua, there are no luxury coaches disembarking from the island's ferry port. Which begs the question, how will you navigate around this 250-square-kilometre, hourglass-shaped island? With only one half-unpaved and bumpy road that circles the island, the choice is an easy one – rent a 125cc dirt bike from an enterprising Ometepean.

As you loop around the island, you'll pass plantain plantations and several small villages, giving you a chance to see rural Nicaraguan life up-close. Two towering volcanoes – Concepción at 1640m and Madera at 1340m – dominate the landscape, and a hike up to Madera's crater makes for an excellent and challenging break from the road. Riding a dirt bike also gives easy access to pre-Columbian petroglyphs and stone statues, made by the indigenous Chorotega people, the San Ramón waterfalls on the southern slope of Madera, and prime swimming spots at Ojo de Agua spring and Charco Verde Beach, the latter tucked majestically between the two volcanoes. So hit the road, easy rider, but mind the stray dogs, wandering pigs and sharp turns.

629 Making peace with tequila in Tequila

MEXICO My first taste of tequila in Tequila was terrible – rough as guts and horribly strong. We were on a tour of one of the area's many distilleries, and the sample had been extracted straight from the production line. My stomach swooped uncomfortably as I looked at the steaming piles of blue agave cactus pulp. Definitely not going back for seconds.

Things began to look up when we entered the distillery's ancient storage sheds: this was where they kept the good stuff as it aged. As yet another round of samples went around, the guide explained the subtleties of the various styles and how best to appreciate them (no, the gringo accompaniments of salt, lime and bare skin are not obligatory). A few sips and my stomach, still nervous about receiving more of the fresh stuff, began to settle – my conversion was under way.

Light-headed but not entirely sated, we headed back to Guadalajara, where we repaired to *La Maestranza*, a dimly-lit bar festooned with old bullfight memorabilia: half a dozen stuffed bulls' heads were arranged above the row of tequila bottles on the top shelf of the bar, as if to drive the point home. Someone ordered us a round of *banderas*, a trio of hefty tumblers that together form the green, white and red of the Mexican flag – the first is half-filled with fresh lime juice, the second with tequila, and the third with *sangrita*, a slightly sweet combination of spicy tomato juice and orange juice. Some chose to savour theirs, conforming to the recommended sequence (the sweetness of the *sangrita* settles the astringency of the tequila), others knocked them back without a second thought, then rapidly ordered another round. And another. All in all, I think that first taste was deceiving.

Exploring the surreal rainforest architecture of Las Pozas

MEXICO The lush forests of the Sierra Gorda mountains don't just hem in Las Pozas, they are taking over this whimsical fantasy hamlet arranged along a series of nine river pools (*pozas*) that give the place its name. Epiphytes cluster on unfinished platforms, banana plants sprout behind half-built walls and the bare frame of an iron staircase-to-nowhere rusts elegantly in the torpid humidity. The small team of gardeners slump hats-over-faces in the midday shade, but as the day wanes they'll be back at work keeping the stone-set pathways for the trickle of visitors that make it out this way.

Las Pozas is hardly on Mexico's gringo trail, but the idle few get lured here by tales of the eccentric Edward James. Born to an aristocratic English mother and her railroad-rich American husband, James liked to claim he was actually the illegitimate son of Edward VII. It was the sort of assertion that suited his image as a *bon vivant* and patron of the arts. He bought the entire 1938 output of his friend Salvador Dalí, and Picasso apparently described James as being "crazier than all the Surrealists put together. They pretend, but he is the real thing." James moved to Mexico in the early 1950s, created a small zoo, ran an orchid-growing business and, through the 1960s and 1970s, set about building his surreal fantasy world, often with a parrot on his shoulder.

There doesn't seem to have been much of a plan, though ambition runs through the names he gave the buildings – "The House With Three Stories That Might be Five" and "The House Destined To Be a Cinema". Nonetheless, there's a sense of enchantment as you wander past mildewed columns supporting nothing at all, peek inside useless buildings and stumble into 2m-high concrete hands, but watch out for unexpected drop-offs. Nothing was properly finished, though James did partly live in a hideaway apartment four floors up. He died in 1984 leaving Las Pozas to his long-time Mexican helper, though failing to assign funds for its upkeep.

Spend a few hours exploring James's magical legacy before taking an exhilarating dip in the *pozas*.

Trekking in Corcovado National Park

COSTA RICA The road to Corcovado National Park was once paved with gold – lots of gold – and although most of it was carried off by the Diqui Indians, miners still pan here illegally. These days, though, it's just an unpaved track that fords half a dozen rivers during the bone-rattling two-hour ride from the nearest town, Puerto Jiménez, and which runs out at Carate, the southern gateway to the park.

The journey in doesn't make an auspicious start to a hike in Corcovado – and it gets worse. Trekking here is not for the faint-hearted: the humidity is one hundred percent, there are fast-flowing rivers to cross and the beach-walking that makes up many of the hikes can only be done at low tide. Cantankerous peccaries roam the woods, and deadly fer-de-lance and bushmaster snakes slip through the shrub.

But you're here because Corcovado is among the most biologically abundant places on Earth, encompassing thirteen ecosystems, including lowland rainforests, highland cloudforests, mangrove swamps, lagoons and coastal and marine habitats. And it's all spectacularly beautiful, even by the high standards of Costa Rica.

Streams trickle down over beaches pounded by Pacific waves, where turtles (hawksbill, leatherback and Olive Ridley) lay their eggs in the sand and where the shore is dotted with footprints – not human, but tapir, or possibly jaguar. Palm trees hang in bent clumps, and behind them the forest rises up in a 6om wall of dense vegetation.

Corcovado has the largest scarlet macaw population in Central America, and the trees flash with bursts of their showy red, blue and yellow plumage. One hotel in the area offers free accommodation if visitors don't see one during their stay – it's never happened. And after the first sighting of the birds flying out from the trees in perfectly coordinated pairs, the long journey to reach Corcovado seems a short way to come.

631

632 Floating down the New River to Lamanai

BELIZE "It looks fake," says the Canadian, peering through his sunglasses at a reptilian hump in the distance. Our paint-flecked boat – *Mrs Cristina* – glides closer, nosing marshy reeds. Captain Ignacio cuts the engine, and water ripples gently over the ridged torso, which remains motionless.

"Yeah, it's just a piece of driftwood," says the New Yorker, handing the binoculars over.

And with that, the baby crocodile pushes off with a muscular thrust of its tail, leaving a solitary, expanding water ring in its wake. A prescient sign – we're floating down the New River to the Maya site of Lamanai, whose name comes from "submerged crocodile".

Like many of Belize's splendid Maya ruins, Lamanai lies deep in the jungle – but it also overlooks the New River Lagoon, so most visitors journey here on a riverboat from Orange Walk, just as we were doing.

And getting here really is half the fun. Though the river waters are eerily placid, the steamy jungle along its banks are not: howler monkeys scamper overhead, emitting guttural howls, while a great blue heron extends its long neck, and flaps regally into the sky. As we float near a strange black cluster quivering on a tree branch, the swarm disbands, and hundreds of bats fly off every which way.

An old barge, heavy in the water with its load of molasses, slowly drifts past us. On the deck sit three sun-browned beefy locals in sunglasses who raise their hands in unison. Around a bend, in the distance, lies the Mennonite settlement of Shipyard – the men in wide-brimmed hats and women in ankle-length dresses an arresting image, particularly against the tropical backdrop of Belize.

Our boat pulls up to the wooden dock at the Lamanai entrance, and it begins to rain – fat, heavy drops as we clomp single-file, stumbling over muddy roots. We're sweating in our windbreakers, mosquitoes are biting and it all seems like a lot of effort – and then the first majestic temple looms into view.

Once the sun comes out, we start on the thigh-aching slog up the 35m "High Temple", which was the largest structure in the Maya world when it was first constructed in 100 BC. We pull on a slippery rope, heaving up one massive step, then another. At the top, panting, we gaze out at the jungle canopy, a magnificent 360-degree panorama of dewy, tangled green stretching into the horizon. From up here, anything seems possible. Until you look at the climb down.

633 Being serenaded by mariachis in Guadalajara

MEXICO Saturday night in downtown Guadalajara, Mexico's second city: the Plazuela de los Mariachis, squeezed into a corner of the colonial heart of the city, reverberates with the sounds of instruments being tuned. You'll no doubt recognize the violins, trumpets and guitars; more exotic to the ear – and unique to the music you're about to hear – are the *vihuela*, a small plinky guitar with a bowed back, and the *guitarron*, a large bass guitar. For time-honoured tunes, you're in the right spot: Guadalajara, also the most traditional of Mexico's cities, is also the birthplace of mariachi, the country's famous musical export.

A smartly dressed couple – he with hair slicked back and she in her best dress – start the festivities with a request for an old love song. The mariachis line up around their table, forming a wall of *charro* (nineteenth-century cowboy) outfits: large bow ties, gleaming belt buckles, jackets and trousers decorated with embroidery and silver fastenings. A trumpeter raises his instrument to his lips, and the first familiar notes of "Cielito Lindo" ("Ay, ay, ay, ay, canta y no llores") float over the square. Another song follows, then another. The couple get to their feet and begin to waltz slowly between the packed café tables. Several troupes join the fray, serenading elderly couples, students, young lovers, fascinated travellers. Each group competes to be louder and more flamboyant than the next, and the noise – a melodious cacophony – is ear-splitting.

Fittingly, the evening winds down with several howled rounds of one of the most popular mariachi tunes: "Guadalajara, Guadalajara, tienes el alma de provinciana, hueles a limpia rosa temprana" ("you have the soul of the provinces, you smell of fresh early roses").

634 Paddling Glover's Reef

BELIZE The Caribbean coastline of Belize is something of a paradise cliché. The second largest coral reef in the world, all 320km of it, runs the length of the country, sheltering around 1200 small islands, or "cayes", in its calm inshore waters – some are developed tourist resorts, others low-key backpacker haunts and uninhabited, palm-shaded sandbanks. As if this wasn't enough, three of the Caribbean's four coral atolls (extinct volcanoes) are close offshore, providing stupendous diving. Cliché, indeed.

The Blue Hole may be the most famous of these atolls, but the best developed is Glover's Reef. About 50km off Dangriga, it spans 35km from north to south, and is encircled by deep, stunning walls of coral. A handful of cayes pepper the central lagoon; under water, they're surrounded by several hundred colourful patch reefs.

To explore Glover's by sea kayak couldn't be more perfect. The cayes in the central lagoon are a good place to start out – each has a white-coral beach, and all are easy to reach. Many visitors elect to go as part of a guided tour, but it's also possible to spend a few days on your own, meandering from caye to caye, camping and living on barbecued grouper and lobster. More adventurous kayakers can head miles out to sea through calm swells, where, although you leave your human companions behind, you're never alone – pelicans, nesting ospreys and other seabirds are always close by. Snorkelling straight off the kayak reveals staggering underwater biodiversity – sea turtles, parrotfish, rays and dolphins all make frequent appearances, and whale sharks haunt the waters around Glover's in the spring. If laid-back Belize has really got under your skin, opt for a kayak with a kite sail, which allows you to sit back and follow the trade winds through the cayes. Bliss.

635 Dawn at Tikal

GUATEMALA The dense jungles of northern Guatemala, once the heartland of the Maya civilization, were home to dozens of thriving cities during Classic Maya times (250–909 AD). Tikal was arguably the greatest of them all, controlling an empire of vassal states and trade routes between the southern highlands and the Caribbean. The symbols of its dominance – six great temples – still stand.

Impressive at any time of day, Tikal shows itself to full advantage in the hours around sunrise. Because of the nature of the terrain – the extreme humidity of the forest usually shrouds the sun's early rays – it's rare actually to see the sun come up over the jungle. But even without a perfect sunrise, as the ruins of this Maya city come to life around you, dawn is still a magical time.

As day breaks, head for the top of Temple IV or Temple V. An ocean of green unfurls before you, the jungle canopy broken only by the chalk-white roofcombs of the other pyramids, soaring over the giant ceiba and zapote trees. The forest's denizens gradually begin to appear, emerging from their night-time resting places. Flocks of green parakeets career over the temple tops and keel-billed toucans hop along bromeliad-rich branches. Howler monkeys are at their most vociferous at dawn, their roars echoing around the graceful plazas and towering temples. Many of the animals that live in Tikal have become accustomed to seeing humans, so you're virtually guaranteed to come across packs of playful racoon-like coati snuffling through the undergrowth or the startling blue-chested ocellated turkey strutting around in search of its first feed of the day. As the sun climbs higher in the sky and the heat of the day increases, things begin to calm down. By 9am, when the large tour groups roll in, nature's activity has all but faded away, until the jungle awakes the next morning.

636 Birdwatching on the Pipeline Road

PANAMA The logbook at Parque Nacional Soberanía's headquarters reads like a "who's who" of exotic bird species. There are mealy Amazons, purple-throated fruitcrows, shining honeycreepers and red-capped manakins; ocellated antbirds make a regular appearance, alongside grey-headed chachalacas, thick-billed motmots and the diminutive tropical pewee. Each entry is more gushing than the last – someone had almost torn through the page describing their chance encounter with a rufous-vented ground cuckoo – but if there's one place on Earth that's guaranteed to send twitchers into a feathery frenzy, it's the 17km-long trail at the heart of Soberanía: a dirt track they call the Pipeline Road.

During World War II, the US government built a pipeline along the Panama Canal to transport fuel from the Pacific to the Atlantic in the event the waterway was attacked. The backup was never needed and the "road" constructed to maintain the pipeline barely used. Over time, it was swallowed by the rainforest. But nature's gain was also man's, and the thin stretch of track now provides some of the finest bird-spotting on the planet, with over four hundred recorded species.

The Pipeline Road, or Camino del Oleoducto, runs through a range of habitats, from second-growth woodland to mature rainforest. A network of side tracks, creeks and rivers can be followed into the surrounding forest, but the road itself is a rich hunting ground, especially in the soft light of dawn or the cool hours around dusk, when activity is at its greatest. Army ant swarms attract birds by the hundred, while the trail is a popular location for leks – an incredible avian dance-off where males gather at the same spot each season for the purposes of elaborate (and very competitive) courtship displays. Just don't be surprised if you find yourself rushing back to HQ, pen at the ready.

637 Kayaking in the Sea of Cortés

MEXICO Standing on the east coast of Baja California, surveying the peninsula's near-lifeless ochre landscape, it's hard to imagine that a frenzy of nature lies just steps away. But launch a sea kayak into the glistening surf of the Sea of Cortés and you'll find yourself surrounded by rich and varied wildlife – a veritable natural aquarium.

The remote and ruggedly beautiful Baja coastline has become a favourite destination for sea kayakers – and for good reason. The calm waters of the Sea of Cortés make for easy surf launches and smooth paddling. Hundreds of unexplored coves, uninhabited islands and miles of mangrove-lined estuaries play host to sealions, turtles and nesting birds. Just the shell of your kayak separates you from dolphins, grey whales, coral reefs and over six hundred species of fish as you glide through placid lagoons, volcanic caves and natural arches.

It's a good idea to keep your snorkelling gear handy – should you ever tire of the topside scenery, you can make a quick escape to an even more spectacular underwater world. Rookeries of sealions dot island coasts, and if you approach them slowly, the pups can be especially playful, even mimicking your underwater movements before performing a ballet of their own.

Back on land, as you camp on white sand beaches and feast on freshly made *ceviche* (citrus-marinated raw fish) under the glow of a glorious sunset, you'll have time to enjoy some peace and quiet before pondering your next launch.

MEXICO Few Mexican folk heroes command so much reverence as Francisco "Pancho" Villa, the ruthless bandito turned revolutionary, though facts about his life remain surprisingly obscure. You won't find much in San Juan del Río, Durango, where he was born around 1878 and became an outlaw whilst still a teenager; his early criminal career tends to be glossed over. Instead, it's the Mexican Revolution that provides Villa's greatest monuments, beginning with the old silver town of Zacatecas – scene of his decisive victory over the Huerta regime in 1914.

Today the pinnacle of the Cerro de la Bufa, the jagged ridge that overlooks Zacatecas, is crowned with a grandiose bronze statue of the General; his battle horse rears up, nostrils flaring and hooves flaying, as Villa holds his rifle aloft in a sign of absolute defiance. Nearby, tourists pose for photos in sombreros and peasant garb while a cable car floats across the pink and white rooftops. The adjacent museum honours his win with a collection of period photos – some showing harrowing scenes of piled up dead bodies. For a more romantic view, wander back down the hill to Los Dorados de Villa in the Plazuela de García, a cosy cantina of tiled walls and exotic birds, named after "Los Dorados", Villa's young followers – dashing photos of the desperados line the walls.

To get a better sense of Villa's flamboyant personality, make for the desert city of Chihuahua. He bought an opulent mansion here, now the Museo Casa de Villa, and it remains crammed with the General's possessions; his incredibly elaborate saddles – worthy of a president – and a 1915 poster, urging "gringos" to head south and ride with Villa for "gold and glory". Finally, there's the bullet-riddled car (a black 1919 Dodge Roadster), in which Villa was assassinated in 1923. He was gunned down in the town of Parral, further south, and here the Museo Francisco Villa commemorates the hero with yet more displays of revolutionary effects and antique weapons. Fitting perhaps, that in Mexico at least, Villa's death generates more interest than his birth.

On the trail of **PANCHO VILLA**

638

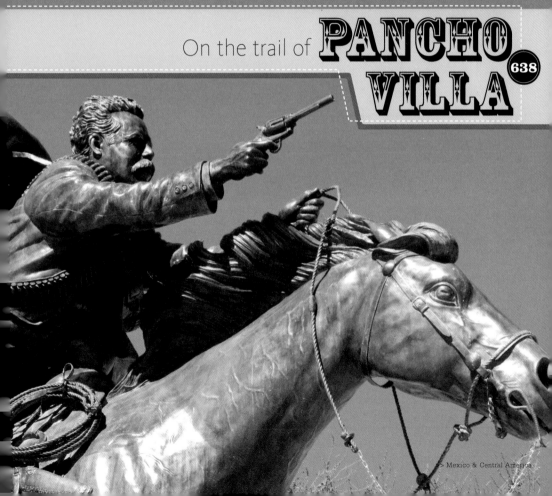

HEADING TO MARKET in the
Guatemalan highlands

639

GUATEMALA The market town of San Francisco el Alto adopts its suffix for good reason. Perched at 2610m atop a rocky escarpment, it looks down over the plain of Quetzaltenango to the perfect volcanic cone of Santa María that pierces the horizon to the southwest.

But on Friday mornings, few of the thousands that gather here linger to take in the view; instead, the largest market in Guatemala's western highlands commands their attention. Things start early, as traders arrive in the dead of night to assemble their stalls by candlelight and lanterns, stopping periodically to slurp from a bowl of steaming *caldo* broth or for a slug of *chicha* maize liquor to ward off the chilly night air.

By dawn a convoy of pick-ups, chicken buses and microbuses struggle up the vertiginous access road, and by sunrise the streets are thick with action as blanket vendors and tomato seekers elbow their way through lanes lined with shacks. There's virtually nothing geared at the tourist dollar, unless you're in desperate need of a Chinese-made alarm clock or a sack of beans, but it's a terrific opportunity to experience Guatemala's indigenous way of life – all business is conducted in hushed, considered tones using ritualistic politeness that's uniquely Maya.

Above the plaza is the fascinating animal market, where goats, sheep, turkeys, chickens and pigs are inspected as if contestants at an agricultural show. Vendors probe screeching porkers' mouths to check out teeth, tongues and gums, and the whole event can descend into chaos as man and beast wrestle around in the dirt before a deal can be struck.

640 Meeting the monarchs in Michoacán

MEXICO Early morning in the mountains of Michoacán. There's a stillness in the wooded glades and a delicate scent of piny resin in the air. Mostly oyamel firs, the trees are oddly coated in a scrunched orange blanket – some kind of fungus? Diseased bark? Then the sun breaks through the mist and thousands of butterflies swoop from the branches to bathe in the sunlight, their patterned orange and black wings looking like stained-glass windows or Turkish rugs – the original Mexican wave. The forest floor is carpeted with them. Branches buckle and snap under their weight. And there's a faint noise, a pitter-patter like gentle rain – the rarely heard sound of massed butterflies flapping their wings.

The annual migration of hundreds of millions of monarch butterflies from North America to this small area of central Mexico – no more than 96 square kilometres – is one of the last mysteries of the scientific world. For years, their winter home was known only to the locals, but in 1975, two determined American biologists finally pinpointed the location, and now visitors (mainly Mexican) flock here during the season to witness one of nature's most impressive spectacles. In the silence of the forest sanctuary, people stand stock-still for hours at a time, almost afraid to breathe as millions of butterflies fill the air, brushing delicately against faces and alighting briefly on hands.

No one is entirely clear why the butterflies have chosen this area. Some say it's the oyamel's needle-like leaves, ideal for the monarch's hooked legs to cling onto; or that the cool highland climate slows down their metabolism and allows them to rest and lay down fat before their arduous mating season. The Aztecs, however, had other ideas, believing that the butterflies – which arrive in Mexico shortly after the Day of the Dead on November 1 – were the returning souls of their fallen warriors, clad in the bright colours of battle.

641 Indulging in the jungle

BELIZE It's all in the mud. Plumbed from the earth and brimming with minerals, this is the kind of rich goop that you'll happily smear on your body parts, then submit to its rejuvenating tingle while reclining in a breezy cabana, eyes closed against the warm sun, and hold on – is that a howler monkey? The *Maruba Resort and Jungle Spa* sits amid the dewy tropical foliage of Belize, where it offers pampering with a primal edge: retreat into a palm-shaded hideaway for the signature "mood mud" body scrub rooted in ancient Maya customs, then zone out to the low thrum of piped-in drumbeats mingled with the rustling of wild critters foraging in the undergrowth. At the *Maruba* – as in much of Belize – it's the lush outdoors that makes all the difference. And let's face it – there's something especially hedonistic about a pedicure in the jungle.

The splendid Maya site of Altun Ha lies near the *Maruba*, so you can trek up giant stone temples in the early light of day, then wind down with a scalp massage and an African honey bee scrub. As night falls, sip rum punch from a hairy coconut with the top lopped off. As you might expect, the primitive-meets-posh *Maruba* is all very decadent – think gleaming mahogany ceilings, billowing silks, feather beds, wafting incense and hibiscus-strewn, mosaic bathrooms – but it's done with a wink. Quirky, jungle-chic details abound: a carved penis as a toilet paper holder in the lobby bathroom; palm fronds as placemats; rough-hewn walls studded with recycled glass bottles of Belikin beer and Fanta. In the ecological spirit of Belize, little goes to waste at this largely self-sustaining resort, where the natural surroundings are respectfully incorporated at every turn. So, not only will you emerge with your pores clean and glowing, but your conscience too.

642 Revel in eco-luxury at Morgan's Rock

NICARAGUA The largest area of virgin rainforest north of the Amazon, endless miles of pristine coastline, 76 national parks brimming with wildlife, six active volcanoes – Nicaragua is an ecotourist's fantasy. After decades of political turbulence, the largest country in Central America is set to become the buzz word for adventurous travellers with a conscience – like Costa Rica before the swarm.

Leading the way in terms of environmentally-friendly accommodation is the country's first five-star resort, *Morgan's Rock Hacienda and Ecolodge*. The hacienda's fifteen chalets are built like stupendous treehouses, with open sides offering gorgeous views onto a private beach where giant leatherback turtles lay their eggs; wake in the night to witness hundreds of flapping babies (seasons vary, but usually from August to February). Simple furniture is handmade by regional artisans, the friendly staff are locals and the open-air showers are heated by solar panels.

This is a hotel that takes the "eco" part of its billing incredibly seriously. Behind the scenes, *Morgan's* is a clean dream of organic living. The owners of the hacienda have planted almost 1.5 million trees and have set aside eight square kilometres of primary forest for conservation – home to spider monkeys, armadillos and sloths, as well as dozens of exotic birds, and brought alive on awesome wildlife tours by trained biologists. Endangered animal species are being reintroduced, whilst existing animals are protected from hunters. Then there is the restaurant, which offers some of the freshest, purest food you will ever taste – including organic algae-fed shrimp, cheese made from the hacienda's cows and sweet home-made rum.

Luxurious ethical travel doesn't come better than this. Enjoy moonlit walks on the beach or wallow in the saltwater pool, happy in the knowledge that what's good for you is also good for the planet. It's back-to-nature bliss.

643 Encountering Kuna culture

PANAMA It's often said that there's an island for every day of the year in the San Blas archipelago. In fact, there are slightly more than that in this chain of coral atolls that stretches for 375km along the Caribbean coast of Panama. This is Kuna Yala, the autonomous homeland of the Kuna Indians, one of the most independent indigenous cultures in Central America. Even if you haven't heard of the Kuna before, you've probably seen them: the women, wearing piratical headscarves, gold nose rings and colourful traditional costumes, are the pin-ups of the indigenous world. With palm-fringed beaches and coral reefs, Kuna Yala is the stuff of Caribbean dreams, but it is the Kuna themselves, with their rich cultural traditions, that most people come here to see.

In some ways, visiting Kuna Yala gives a feel of what the Caribbean must have been like before European colonists arrived. No outside development is allowed – non-Kuna cannot own land or property. You'll need to ask permission of a community's headman, or *sahila*, if you wish to visit a particular town or island, and you must be accompanied by a Kuna guide. Around forty of the islands are inhabited; some are home to several thousand people, while others are narrow sandbanks sheltering only a few families.

Despite the regulations, you can still explore Kuna culture and your natural surroundings pretty widely. Travelling by motorized dugout canoe, your guide will take you to pristine beaches and reefs where you can swim and snorkel, as well as to other island communities. You may even be lucky enough to witness a traditional religious ceremony or join a fiesta in a communal hall (*casa de congreso*), where poet-historians sing myths and legends from hammocks, leaving you with a lasting impression of the Kuna heritage.

644 Riding down the Río San Juan

NICARAGUA It was the end of a hot day in earthquake-flattened Managua. "There," I hissed in frustration, pointing at a poster on the wall, "that is where I want to go."

I had seen the photograph before, slapped up on café, bar and shop walls all over Nicaragua. The prize-winning photo, chosen by the tourist board to promote the country's pristine beauty, does not show the colonial streets of Granada. Nor does it illustrate the volcanoes of Ometepe or the cayes off the Caribbean coast.

Instead, it depicts a bend in a wide blue river, fringed by green meadows and dotted with small boats. The waterway is the 170km-long Río San Juan, which starts at Lago Nicaragua, runs along the country's border with Costa Rica and finally spills into the Caribbean Sea.

The river has a rich – if tumultuous – history: it once carried supplies from Spain to its new colony and was besieged by pirates who came to capture Granada. Now better known for its ecotourism opportunities, the Río San Juan is surrounded by some of the most peaceful wilderness in Central America. Hundreds of species of wildlife live along its banks, from caimans, herons, manatees and jaguars to howler monkeys, sloths and flocks of rainbow-coloured parrots – don't forget your camera.

Remote as the river is, carved into dense rainforest, there is one notable pocket of civilization. In contrast to the small collection of ramshackle fishing villages along its banks, and sleazy San Carlos at its head, the old Spanish fort of El Castillo, two and a half hours downstream, shimmers like a mirage. Its waterfront is lined with wooden homes on stilts, their porches covered in carefully tended plants and connected by a meandering lane. The lovely setting is framed with a ruined castle atop a grassy knoll. And at the end of the village, as it seeps gently back into the forest, is the bend in the river in the photograph.

645 A taste of mole poblano in Puebla

MEXICO Visitors to Mexico may find some of the country's culinary offerings a bit odd – not only do fried grasshoppers, baked maggots and raw ant eggs occasionally appear, but the national dish, *mole poblano*, combines two flavours, chilli and chocolate, that would seem to have little use for each other. *Mole* (or *mólli*), a Nahuatl word, means "mixture", of which there are actually dozens in Mexico; *mole poblano*, the most revered, comes from Puebla.

A rich sauce normally served with turkey or chicken, *mole poblano* can boast upwards of thirty ingredients; the most cherished recipes are guarded like state secrets. Fruits, nuts and spices are toasted over a fire, ground by hand and mixed into a paste. The chocolate, added at the last minute, is in its traditional unsweetened form, powdered cacao seeds. The dish was created in the seventeenth century in the kitchens of the Convento de Santa Rosa for a banquet. It's still made for special occasions: no wedding in Puebla is complete without the women spending days preparing their *mole poblano* in huge black cauldrons. Among Cholulteca families, a live turkey is considered the guest of honour at wedding receptions; the bird is slaughtered the next day to serve as the base for the newlyweds' first *mole*.

A prime time to sample the sauce is during the Festival of Mole Poblano, held on three consecutive Sundays each July, when local restaurants compete to have their mole judged the city's best. The dish also stars on menus across the city on the fifth of May, or Cinco de Mayo, a national holiday that celebrates the defeat of Napoleon's invading army in Puebla in 1872. After the festivities, join the crowds and top off the night by feasting on the city's savoury speciality.

646 Searching for jaguars in Cockscomb Basin Wildlife Sanctuary

BELIZE Looking for tigers? Head to India. Lions or cheetahs? You'll want to be in southern Africa. If it's jaguars you're after, though, few places are more spectacular than the rainforests of Belize.

Here, in the Cockscomb Basin Wildlife Sanctuary, the world's only jaguar reserve, the enormous, elusive wildcats roam freely through four hundred square kilometres of pristine jungle.

According to local guides, sunrise is the best time to glimpse jaguars. Almost every day, eager cat-spotters set out in the small hours from Maya Centre, an indigenous Mopan Maya community and the hub for trips into the reserve. In the half-light, the rainforest teems with wildlife. The trees form a cavernous canopy above your head; in combination with the thick undergrowth, the vegetation can overwhelm – and the atmosphere is intensified by sightings of red-eyed tree frogs, tarantulas, bats and iguanas. Gibnuts – small, rat-like

creatures – rustle through the scrub. Keep an eye out for the four other species of wildcats that also call the reserve home, including margay, who favour the canopy, and pumas, who slink through the surrounding mountains. As the forest warms up, four thousand species of flowering plants spring into bloom, and toucans, king vultures and scarlet macaws flit through the trees.

You've come for the jaguars, though, and as the sun climbs in the sky, you still haven't seen one. Let's be honest – you're far more likely to see the eyes of a gibnut shining from the undergrowth than you are the glamorous yet camera-shy felines. It's the hunt that makes Cockscomb so special. You know they're there, and they know you know it – if your paths happen to collide you'll be rewarded with a sight very few people are lucky enough to witness. In the meantime, don't forget to enjoy the natural wonderland around you.

647 Diving at Palancar Reef

MEXICO The view from the boat is beautiful, with the variegated blues and greens of the Caribbean stretching toward the Yucatán coast on one side, and palm trees bowing over Cozumel's pearly-white beach on the other.

From the surface, though, you'd never know that the most stunning sight of all is directly beneath you: Palancar Reef, a 5km stretch of some of the globe's richest coral beds, and the kind of vivid world people tend to imagine only with the aid of hallucinogens. Teeming with marine life, Palancar is just one small part of the Mesoamerican Barrier Reef, which stretches from Mexico to Honduras, but it is in a prime position to flourish. Just off the southwest corner of the island of Cozumel, and part of a larger ring of coral around much of the island, it is washed by slow, steady currents that keep the water clear and bear nutrients from nearby mangrove swamps.

Bumped by clumsy snorkellers, battered by hurricanes and boiled by freakish spikes in water temperature, Palancar not only survives but prospers as a fascinating and complex ecosystem. Any diver, novice or expert could explore this reef for hours – or, if you're Jacques Cousteau, who put this place on divers' maps in the 1960s, years. Lobsters pick their way delicately along outcrops, feelers blown by the current, while blue-green parrotfish gnaw at the coral with their beaky mouths. (Their digestive system produces the powdery sand that slopes away into the deep-blue distance.) Striped clownfish hide in the protective tentacles of an anemone, immune to its toxic sting; mellow turtles graze on algae; a graceful ray glides by. All this happens as if in a dream, in near-complete silence – the only audible sound is the rush of your own breath. Lovely as the surface world is, when you come up for air, it will all seem impossibly drab.

648 A river runs to it: Pacuare Jungle Lodge

COSTA RICA Standing outside your palm-thatched river-view suite, its wooden doors opened on to the terrace to reveal a vast canopy, king-size, Egyptian-cotton sheets ruffling in the breeze, *Pacuare Jungle Lodge* seems like the archetypal luxury hideaway. But there's one big difference: you're dripping wet and are kitted out in a life jacket and helmet.

At some hotels, you arrive by limo; at *Pacuare*, you (and your guide) paddle there in a raft, negotiating several kilometres of the raging Río Pacuare in order to bed down for the night in your own private piece of paradise. Surrounded by rainforest, the lodge perches on a bend in the river and has to be one of the few five-stars in the world where you can truly say that getting there is half the fun.

The Río Pacuare's adrenalin-inducing mix of open canyons and narrow passages has made it one of the best whitewater-rafting rivers on Earth – when rapids are called "Double Drop" and "Upper Pinball"

you know they've earned their names – but the journey is as much about the scenery as the scintillation. Thundering waterfalls cascade down overhanging rocks, and the lowland tropical forest that borders the river spills right down to the water's edge, its thick undergrowth providing refuge for monkeys, sloths and an incredible array of birdlife.

There's more nature when you step out of the raft. A lot of so-called ecolodges only pay lip-service to the environment, but *Pacuare* wears its credentials on its sleeve: it part-funds a nearby jaguar research project and has started its own conservation effort by reintroducing howler monkeys into the surrounding area, two initiatives that have helped it become one of only 65 hotels recognized by the World Tourism Organization for good practice in sustainability and ecotourism.

Hopefully, the howler monkeys won't disturb you too much in the night – you'll need as much sleep as you can get for the return journey.

Corn of *plenty*

CORN ISLANDS Some 70km off the coast of Nicaragua, a far-flung Caribbean world away from film stars and offshore bank accounts, lie one of the Atlantic's most endearingly ramshackle outposts: the Corn Islands. You need neither an expense account flight nor a million-pound yacht to get there, nor an inheritance to pay for your stay. You do need the nerve to board a single-prop Cessna plane – either that or the stomach for a potentially rough, five to ten-hour ferry crossing. Once you've arrived, though, the mere prospect of a return journey may well seem unthinkable, as it must have done to the pirates, slaves and Miskito Indians who once took refuge here.

While construction is bringing a patina of modernity to Big Corn – the largest of the two islands – there's a definite end-of-the-English-speaking-world feel to the place, English-speaking because Britain once exercised a modicum of control over this often lawless swathe of the Atlantic. They likewise left their mark on the architecture, a painted muddle of wooden porches and washed-out charm, straggling past the main drag and out into miles of palm-stitched coastline. If you want an impression of how Big Corn must have once appeared minus its airport, electricity and island-round road, though, you need only hop on a boat for the high-seas scoot to Little Corn, just over one square mile of traffic-free rainforest that surely can't retain its "best-kept Caribbean secret" cliché for much longer. Though travel writers have only recently begun raving over it, this hideaway-within-a-hideaway has drawn divers and dreamers for years, some of whom have stayed and set up businesses like *Casa Iguana*, a bohemian ecohotel with heavenly sited cabins, and *Farm Peace and Love*, a biodynamic farm and unlikely oceanside trattoria serving storied renowned Italian cuisine to those who've made the effort of a cross-island trek to get there. Then there's the ocean itself, magnifying the pearl-white sand, bottle-green mangroves and bleached-blue firmament in a tie-dye riot of eagle rays, nurse sharks and parrotfish, all massing on one of Central America's most pristine reefs. Islands in the (main)stream these are not.

650 Isla Barro Colorado: the appliance of science

PANAMA Semi-hidden in the thick forest floor, a nervy agouti is on the forage for food. It stops to nibble on some spiny palm fruit, sandwiching each bite with anxious glances into the surrounding undergrowth. Less than five metres away from the unsuspecting rodent, and closing the gap with every stealthy stride, an ocelot moves in for the kill. The agouti enjoys its last few drips of sweet palm juice, and then...BANG. The cat gets the cream.

In the surrounding rainforest, several scientists from the Smithsonian Tropical Research Institute (STRI) monitor the moment, another important step in piecing together the relationship between ocelot and agouti, predator and prey. Further south, more scientists observe the family behaviour of white-faced capuchins; to the west, the evolution of Baird's tapirs is the focus. Welcome to Isla Barro Colorado, the most intensely studied tropical island on Earth.

Sitting plum in the middle of man-made Lago Gatún, roughly halfway along the Panama Canal, Barro Colorado is a living laboratory, fifteen square kilometres of abundant biodiversity – more than a thousand plant species, nearly four hundred types of bird and over a hundred species of mammals – that the island owes to the canal itself. Flooding the area to facilitate its construction chased much of the wildlife in the surrounding forests on to higher ground. The one-time plateau became an island, and the island became a modern-day Noah's Ark, the animals coming in two by two dozen to seek refuge in its dense rainforest covering.

The Smithsonian has run a research station on Barro Colorado for over eighty years, but only fairly recently have they opened their doors to tourists. It's been worth the wait, though – hiking through the rainforest in the company of expert guides, the jungle canopy abuzz with screeching howler monkeys and ablaze with red-billed toucans, is an incredible experience, even if the Hoffman's two-toed sloths, hanging lazily from the trees, seem distinctly underwhelmed by it all.

651 Sampling fish tacos in Ensenada

MEXICO The *taco de pescado* – Baja California's gift to locals, dust-caked off-road explorers and cruise-boat day-trippers alike – exemplifies the simple pleasures that make the peninsula so appealing.

Constructed by piling freshly fried pieces of white fish on two warm corn tortillas and topping with shredded cabbage, a little light mayo, a splash of hot sauce and a squirt of lime, the *taco de pescado* is Mexican food at its most basic and delicious. Like all great street food, fish tacos taste better when served somewhere devoid of any atmosphere – most choice locations lack a proper floor, ceiling, walls or any combination thereof. The quality of the tacos corresponds directly to the length of time it takes for the cook to get them to you, then for you to get them into your mouth.

Ensenada, a large fishing centre on the peninsula's northwest coast, is one of the best places to sample the *taco de pescado* – it's said that the dish was first concocted here by Japanese fishermen. Fifteen minutes inland from the port and the Mercado Negro fish market lies a well-established street vendor, *Tacos Fenix*. The three-person outfit operates from the pavement: one person preps the ingredients, a second mans the frying pan and the third handles the money and drinks. You don't have to know much Spanish (beyond *por favor* and *gracias*) to order; just listen and watch the people in front of you. And don't worry about the juices running down your hand after the first bite – getting dirty is part of the fun.

652 Chasing whale sharks near Utila

HONDURAS The island of Utila, off the coast of Honduras, isn't your ordinary scuba-diving base. Sure, there's plenty of stunningly beautiful marine life to be seen. It isn't the beautiful, though, that draws many diving enthusiasts here. Rather, it's the exotically monstrous – Utila is one of the few places on Earth that the whale shark, the world's largest fish, can be spotted year-round.

Whale sharks, which are harmless to humans, remain elusive creatures – relatively little is known about them, and their scientific name (*Rhincodon typus*) wasn't even established until 1984. Measuring up to fifteen metres (and twenty tonnes), they are filter feeders, sieving tropical seas for nutrients and migrating across oceans and up and down the coast of Central America. Oceanic upswells close to Utila consistently sweep together a rich soup of plankton and krill, making them a prime feeding ground for the immense creatures.

Most mornings, dive boats scour the seas north of Utila between reef dives looking for "boils": feeding frenzies created by bonito tuna rounding up huge schools of baitfish, or krill. Hungry sharks home in on the boils, gliding just below the surface, mouths agape as they scythe through the sea. Their blue-grey upper bodies are sprinkled with intricate patterns of white spots (which appear electric blue from a distance in the sunlight), interspersed with chessboard-style markings.

Often, they feed upright, an astonishing sight – watch as the great fish manoeuvre themselves into a vertical position, bobbing up and down and gulping sea water into 2m-wide mouths. If you like, you can slip into the water with them. But do it while you can – the chance to swim among them is usually fleeting, as the boils disintegrate rapidly and the sharks disappear as quickly as they came.

653 Stelae stories of Copan

HONDURAS It's hot, the air is thick with fragrant tropical aromas and the undergrowth is wrapping its verdant claws around everything in sight. It's a wonder, then, that Copan's 700-year-old stelae are still standing and that the tangled jungle hasn't completely taken over these intricately carved stone slabs that line the processional walkways between Copan's decaying pyramids.

The carvings on the stelae may at first simply look like big-beaked birds and stylized plants amid swirls and scrolls, but a closer investigation reveals these to be Maya hieroglyphs that tell the detailed stories of this long-gone civilization. Each depicts the illustrious King Waxak Lahun Ubah K'awil (also known as Eighteen Rabbit), the most powerful of Copan's leaders, in a variety of guises including his apotheosis as several Maya gods. He is remembered for his patronage of the arts and for sourcing some of the best craftsmen the Maya world had ever seen.

654 New year on Caye Caulker

BELIZE Forget the beer-soaked hordes in party hats and the sloppy midnight renditions of "Auld Lang Syne". And forget the far-fetched resolutions that you're going to break anyway. This year you've picked a wave-licked little island in the Caribbean to ring in the New Year.

"Go slow" is the motto on Caye Caulker, which is pretty much the only speed your golf cart will travel, barring the occasional burst to avoid an iguana crossing the sandy lane. Here, chilling out is a way of life, reggae the music and ten languorous paces the distance from your beach shack to the Caribbean Sea. Decisions are similarly weighty: snorkel or sunbathe? Hairbraiding or henna tattoo? It's this sun-warmed simplicity that shapes your last day of the year: you spend the morning floating on your back, then munching on shrimp kebabs from a beach grill, licking the tart juices from your fingers. After this, you get into a hammock for a foot massage, followed by a siesta under the rustling leaves of a fan palm. As night falls, you saunter to the split at the north end of the caye. Somewhere, the midnight countdown is being chanted by thousands, but here your only companions are the bright moon, the rhythmic whoosh of the waves and a chilled Belikin beer – and the New Year's resolution to do this every year.

655 Mexico City's murals

MEXICO Nothing prepares you for Mexico City. This sprawling, chaotic, ancient, beautiful, congested powerhouse buzzes like New York or Paris. In the central square, the Zócalo, they fly an enormous national flag which it takes ten soldiers to carry from the Palacio National each day.

Understanding the history of this 700-year-old capital isn't easy. But one Mexican artist holds the clue. Stepping inside the cool central arcade of the Palacio Nacional, you are confronted by Mexican history laid out in the giant murals of Diego Rivera. Above the main staircase the leaders of Mexican independence are all there: Father Hidalgo, Salvador Allende and later revolutionaries including Emiliano Zapata and Pancho Villa. It is an overwhelmingly bold piece of art, full of encyclopaedic detail, representing everyone from the ancient Maya to the rapacious conquistadors. Eagles, plumed serpents and raging volcanoes compete with peasants grinding maize, picking tropical fruit and holding hairless dogs.

Monte Albán

656

MEXICO Rising like a giant fist above the valleys of Oaxaca, magical, mystical Monte Albán is above all a statement of power. The Zapotecs built their city far from the valleys and without any natural water supply (water was carried up by hand and stored in vast urns). This wasn't a mistake – they wanted to emphasize their dominance of their people, and nature itself. Founded around 500 BC, most of the city was abandoned by 950 AD and though the Mixtecs later used it as a burial site, the main structures were only cleared and restored in the 1930s.

Approaching from the city of Oaxaca, the narrow road snakes its way through a series of terraced hillsides, now all overgrown scrub but once home to a thriving population of almost 20,000. What remains today is just the very centre of the site – the religious and political heart – and until you reach the top it's impossible to appreciate the sheer audacity of this place; a whole mountaintop was effectively levelled by hand to create this massive, man-made plateau on which the Zapotecs

constructed soaring pyramids, astronomical observatories and palaces.

You enter by the Plataforma Norte, but won't appreciate the true dimensions until you reach the Gran Plaza, the ceremonial focus of the city. Lined by sombre stone platforms, the best place to get your bearings is on top of the Plataforma Sur, a mighty square pyramid offering a fine overview of the site and mesmerizing panoramas of the surrounding countryside; the Oaxaca Valley is clearly visible, often shrouded by mist (or smog, sadly), as well as the rugged hinterland to the northwest. The building of Los Danzantes may offer a better insight into how all this was possible; the carved "dancers" here are actually nude male figures that may represent prisoners or, more likely, sacrificial victims. If you have time, explore the tombs to the northeast of the main site, linked by rough paths across the scrub – here, amongst the stone memorials to Zapotec rulers long forgotten, Monte Albán's sense of lingering mystery is most palpable.

NEED to know

606 Tortuguero National Park is 3–4hr north of Limón by boat. Independent travellers must buy tickets for the park and arrange for a certified tour guide.

607 Puerto La Libertad is 34km south of San Salvador; there are frequent buses. In La Libertad, you can rent boards from *Mango's Lounge* and Hospital de Tablas.

608 Rail services depart from Los Mochis and Chihuahua daily. Tickets are available from individual train stations or direct from Ferrocarril Mexicano (Ⓦwww .chepe.com.mx).

609 La Costeña airline (Ⓦwww.lacosteña.com.ni) flies daily to San Carlos from Managua. If your arrival doesn't coincide with the boat to Solentiname and you can't find a private ride, it's worth taking a side trip down the San Juan river to El Castillo.

610 Frequent *lancha* boats buzz across Lago Atitlán between each village.

611 Guerrero Negro is easily reached by bus from Tijuana or La Paz. There are numerous operators offering whale-watching tours in Guerrero Negro and the town of San Ignacio, 150km to the south.

612 Gibnut is served at traditional Belizean restaurants around the country. In Belize City, try *Nerie's II*, on Queen St at Daly St (daily until 10pm; ☎+501 223-4028). Call ahead to confirm, as gibnut is only offered a couple of nights each week.

613 Cenote Zací in Valladolid is in the block formed by *calles* 34, 36, 37 and 39. Dzitnup and Samula are 7km west of Valladolid on Hwy-180. There are also cenotes along the Carribean coast.

614 *Caves Branch Jungle Lodge* is located on Hummingbird Hwy, 90min drive from Belize City. Cave tubing costs US$15 for a simple bunkhouse to US$285 for a luxury treehouse with two bedrooms. See Ⓦwww. cavesbranch.com for more details.

615 The town of Pátzcuaro, on the shores of Lago Pátzcuaro, is the main staging point for boat trips to Janitzio; boats run throughout the night. Accommodation for the Day of the Dead should be booked at least six months in advance.

616 You can take a bus from Belize City to San Ignacio, the nearest town to *Blancaneaux* (Ⓦwww.coppola resorts.com).

617 The Refuge lies 12km south of Puerto Viejo. Kayaks, surf boards and nature guides can be hired through eco-resorts in the forest or budget places in Manzanillo village.

618 Xochimilco is 28km southeast of Mexico City, reachable from Tasqueña station.

619 Bonampak is a short hike from the village of Lacanjá Chansayab. You can also ride directly to the site in a Lacandón-run van from the Frontier Highway.

620 There are frequent buses to Liberia, the capital of Guanacaste province, from San José.

621 Saturday is market day in Oaxaca. The Mercado de Abastos is near the second-class bus station on Periférico.

622 Twice-weekly flights and several daily buses run from Panama City to the Darién. Contact a community in advance, just roll up, or take a 4–6-day trip with a tour operator from Panama City ($800–1500).

623 See Ⓦwww.mayaparadise.com/fiestas/fiestas.htm for comprehensive information about fiestas in Guatemala. The most traditional fiestas are in the western highlands. They are held all year round.

624 Antigua's main bus terminal is next to its market; set off for Chimaltenango, from where a *directo* leaves to Nebaj.

625 See Ⓦwww.casamagnatulum.com for more info.

626 Monteverde Cloudforest Reserve is 190km from San José and is run by the Center for Tropical Science (Ⓦwww.cct.or.cr/english). The centre's night walks leave daily at 6.15pm.

627 Panama Canal Tours (Ⓦwww.pmatours.net) and Canal and Bay Tours (Ⓦwww.canalandbaytours.com) offer full and partial transits of the Panama Canal (10hr, $165; 5hr, $115).

628 There are six ferries daily from San Jorge, which is a short taxi from the town of Rivas, to Ometepe.

629 Several distilleries around Tequila run tours; the most popular is José Cuervo (Ⓦwww.cuervo.com). *La Maestranza* is at Maestranza 179, Guadalajara.

630 Las Pozas is at Xilitla, 300km north of Mexico City. Stay at *Posada El Castillo* (Ⓦwww.junglegossip.com /castillo.html), James's house in Xilitla.

631 It's best to visit Corcovado during its dry season (Dec–March). Meals and camping space or lodging need to be booked six weeks in advance (☎+506 257-2239, Ⓔazucena@ns.minae).

632 Several companies offer trips to Lamanai down the New River, including Jungle River Tours, 20 Lover's Lane, Orange Walk (☎+501 302-2293, Ⓔlamanai mayatour@btl.net).

633 Every September, Guadalajara hosts performers from all over the world for the Festival de los Mariachis (Ⓦwww.mariachi-jalisco.com.mx).

634 Boats from Sittee River and Dangriga travel to the reef at least once a week; each caye within Glover's central lagoon has a dive operator that organizes tours or rents equipment.

635 Tourist minibuses run from every hotel in El Remate and Flores to Tikal National Park from 4.30am. There are three hotels in the park, and both towns also have plentiful accommodation

636 Parque Nacional Soberanía is a 45min drive from Panama City or 2km hike from the town of Gamboa, which is served by regular daily buses from the capital.

637 Tour operators in both Loreto and La Paz offer outfitting, guided expeditions and accommodation, with La Paz providing more rental options for the independent kayaker.

638 The statue of Villa and Museo de la Toma de Zacatecas (daily 10am–5pm; M$10) is on the summit of Cerro de la Bufa. Museo Casa de Villa is 2km east of Chihuahua at Calle 10 no. 3010 (Tues–Sat 9am–7pm,

Sun 10am–4pm; M$10). Museo Francisco Villa in Parral is at Juárez 11 and Barrera (Tues–Sun 10am–5pm; M$10).

639 San Francisco el Alto is 1hr by bus from Quetzaltenango.

640 The best place to see the butterflies is in the butterfly sanctuary near the village of El Rosario (mid-Nov to late March daily 9am–4pm; Ⓦwww.santuario -monarca.com.mx).

641 Find out more about Maruba at Ⓦwww.maruba -spa.com.

642 *Morgan's Rock* (Ⓦwww.morgansrock.com) is north of San Juan del Sur, a 2hr drive from Granada.

643 Daily flights leave Panama City for several islands in Kuna Yala as well as a cheaper daily 4x4 road transfer to Cartí.

644 Boats leave San Carlos for El Castillo daily. Two boats a week (Tues & Fri 5am; 10hr) travel the whole length of the river to the Caribbean Sea.

645 Puebla's best restaurant is *Mesón Sacristía de la Compañía*, 6 Sur 304. You can buy *mole* paste at the Mercado 5 de Mayo.

646 All buses between Dangriga and Punta Gorda pass Maya Centre. Julio Saqui (☎+501 520-3042, Ⓦwww .cockscombmayatours.com) runs Cockscombe Maya Tours and can arrange trips into the reserve.

647 Cozumel has scores of dive operators who will take you to Palancar Reef; Deep Blue (☎+987 872-5653, Ⓦwww.deepbluecozumel.com) is recommended.

648 *Pacuare Jungle Lodge* (Ⓦwww.junglelodge costarica.com) is near the town of Siquirres, southeast of San José. Two-night packages, including rafting in and out, start from US$375.

649 La Costeña (Ⓦwww.lacosteña.com.ni) flies twice daily to Big Corn from Managua. Weather permitting, the water taxi from Big Corn to Little Corn also runs twice daily. Ⓦwww.casaiguana.net is a reliable resource for all things Little Corn.

650 To visit Isla Barro Colorado, contact the Smithsonian Institute in Panama City (☎+507 212-8026, Ⓦwww.stri.org).

651 There are regular bus services to Ensenada from Tijuana. *Tacos Fenix* is on Calle Espinosa, at Calle Juárez.

652 Utila has several daily flights and a daily ferry connection with La Ceiba on the mainland. Utila Dive Center (Ⓦwww.utiladivecenter.com) is a highly recommended dive operator.

653 The nearby town of Copán Ruinas has plenty of accommodation, although Santa Rosa de Copán, around 50km east, is a much nicer place to stay.

654 Caye Caulker lies 35km northeast of Belize City; regular boats travel here from Belize City and San Pedro.

655 The Palacio Nacional is open daily 9am–4.30pm and entry is free.

656 Monte Albán (daily 9am–5pm; M$51) is 9km southwest of Oaxaca – most visitors make day-trips from the city. Buses run from Calle Mina every 30min (M$51 return) from 8.30am to 3.30pm, while official returns start at noon and finish at 5pm.

GOOD to know

RING OF FIRE
Mexico and Central America are home to almost one hundred **volcanoes** (most are found in Mexico, Costa Rica, El Salvador, Guatemala and Nicaragua) – the region is part of the "ring of fire", a zone of frequent volcanic eruptions and earthquakes that encircles the Pacific Basin. A handful of these volcanoes are still considered active, and it's possible to see spectacular light shows of molten lava at Arenal in Costa Rica and Picaya in Guatemala. Most, however, have long been dormant, leaving their slopes open to hikers.

"Love is blind. But not the neighbours"
Mexican proverb

THE MAYA
One of the western hemisphere's most sophisticated pre-Columbian civilizations, **the Maya** flourished in Mexico and northern Central America between 300 and 900 AD. An intricate calendar based on the solar year, an advanced form of hieroglyphics and enormous temples are just a few elements of their legacy.

COCKS AND BULLS
Cockfighting is a popular backwoods sport in Mexico (where it is legal and official arenas – *plazas de gallos* – exist). Birds are specially trained for months, substantial bets are laid and fights go on until one of two cocks is killed by the other (metal spurs are attached to their legs). **Bullfighting** is also still popular in Mexico; the world's largest bullfighting ring, Plaza México, is in Mexico City.

LANGUAGE
Spanish is the official language of Mexico and the countries of Central America, with the exception of Belize, where people speak a type of patois – English with a lilting accent, adjustments to grammar and phonetic spelling. The Amerindians of Mexico and Guatemala also have their own dialects. Mexican Spanish is very distinct, with drawn-out nasal cadences and lots of expression. Guatemalans tend to speak very slowly and clearly. Hondurans and El Salvadorans have strong regional accents, while Nicaraguans are known for the variety and richness of their slang. Panamanians speak a kind of Caribbean Spanish, similar to Cubans or Puerto Ricans.

ZÓCALO
The centre of every Mexican town, big or small, is its *zócalo* (main square). Evenings see food vendors wheeling their carts into the streets, balloon-sellers touting their wares, café tables filled with patrons and roving musicians breaking into their repertoires. Three of the most distinctive *zócalos* in Mexico are in Mexico City, Oaxaca and Veracruz.

MEXICO AT THE MOVIES
Mexico has a thriving film industry, one of the world's oldest. The home-grown film business saw its golden age during the 1940s, with stars such as Cantinflas (the Mexican Charlie Chaplin) and Dolores del Rio. In the 1950s and 1960s the country became known for its cult horror flicks, but more recent dramas like *Amores Perros* and *Y Tu Mamá También* have brought Mexico to the forefront of the international film scene.

POLITICAL MURALS
Wall paintings were made popular shortly after the Mexican Revolution by three artists: Diego Rivera, David Siqueiros and José Clemente Orozco. Their enormous, vibrant murals can still be seen today in government buildings – Rivera's *History of Mexico* in Mexico City's National Palace and Orozco's frescoes in the Hospicio Cabañas in Guadalajara are particularly memorable. In Central America, the civil wars of the 1970s and 1980s spawned a number of naïve paintings depicting revolutionaries and their tormenters. To this day, official political campaigns are hand-painted on the sides of buildings, walls and even telegraph poles throughout the region.

"It's better to be a living chicken than a dead cockerel"
Mexican proverb

FIVE FAVOURITE DISHES
Chiles en nogada, Mexico. Stuffed green peppers covered in a white sauce (walnuts and either cream cheese or sour cream) and pomegranate.
Pupusas, El Salvador. Small tortillas filled with cheese, beans and pork crackling, and served piping hot with tomato juice, hot sauce and *curtido* (pickled cabbage, beetroot and carrots).
Sancocho, Panama. A hearty chicken soup with yucca, plantains and other root vegetables and flavoured with coriander.
Anafre, Honduras. A fondue-like dish involving some or all of cheese, beans and meat.
Ron don, Nicaragua. "To cook", in local parlance – a stew of yucca, chayote and other vegetables, and meat; it's simmered for at least a day and traditionally eaten at weekends.

CORAL REEFS
The world's second-largest coral reef, the Mesoamerican Barrier Reef, lies off the Caribbean coast of Mexico, Belize, Guatemala and Honduras, making the region a magnificent aquatic playground. Hot spots for scuba diving and snorkelling include the Mexican island of Cozumel, Belize's cayes (tiny islands; home to three atolls and the Blue Hole, a collapsed cave made famous by Jacques Cousteau), and the Bay Islands of Honduras.

FIVE UNIQUE DRINKS
Seaweed, Belize. A strange, delicious blend of seaweed, milk, cinnamon, sugar and cream.
Guifiti, Honduras. A distilled moonshine flavoured with cloves that tastes a bit like toothache medication, available in the north-coast Garífuna villages.
Pitahaya juice, Nicaragua. Made from the fruit of a cactus, it's a virulent purple in colour – it'll probably stain your tongue.
Guaro, Costa Rica. An indigenous sugarcane-based spirit; Cacique is the biggest brand.
Hot chocolate, Mexico. Not the drink of your childhood – here it's spicy and semi-bitter, often flavoured with chilli powder.

WATCHING WILDLIFE IN THE DUSTY CHACO • WINE-TASTING IN MENDOZA • ARMADILLOS AND AMULETS: SAMPLING A WITCH'S BREW • NATURAL REJECTION IN THE GALÁPAGOS ISLANDS • RETAIL THERAPY AT OTAVALO CRAFTS MARKET • WILDLIFE SPOTTING IN THE BENI WETLANDS • GLITZ AND GOLDEN SANDS ON PUNTA DEL ESTE • ITAIPÚ: PLUGGING THE WORLD'S BIGGEST DAM • SWINGING STICKS AT THE ARGENTINE OPEN • DOWNING CAIPIRINHAS IN RIO DE JANIERO • SANDBOARDING AT HUACACHINA • FILL UP IN THE WORLD'S PIE CAPITAL • RUBBER BUSTS AND TOP HATS: OPERA IN THE AMAZON • THE ROAD TO RUINS: MACHU PICCHU • MOUNTAIN BIKING THE WORLD'S MOST DANGEROUS ROAD • WALKING ON ICE: THE PERITO MORENO GLACIER • SEEING THE SUN RISE IN THE VALLEY OF THE MOON • MAKING A PILGRIMAGE TO ISLA DEL SOL • GO BACK IN TIME IN PARATY • TREK TO THE LOST CITY • DINOSAUR HUNTING IN SUCRE • BEEF EATER'S PARADISE: THE ARGENTINE PARRILLA • SIZE MATTERS: IN SEARCH OF THE WORLD'S BIGGEST SNAKE • RAFTING ON SACRED WATERS IN THE URUBAMBA VALLEY • FINDING EDEN ON THE ALTIPLANO'S EDGE • LOOKING DOWN ON KAIETEUR FALLS • THE SECRET SENSATION OF POUSADA MARAVILHA • SEARCHING FOR THE PERFECT OYSTER ON ISLA MARGARITA • COMMUNING WITH AN AMAZON SHAMAN • SPEND LAZY DAYS AT PARQUE TAYRONA • EXPLORING QUICHUA CULTURE IN ECUADOR'S VOLCANIC HIGHLANDS • PARROT-WATCHING AT THE WORLD'S BIGGEST MACAW LICK • STAR-GAZING AT MAMALLUCA • SAVORING CEVICHE IN LIMA • TREASURE, TRINKETS AND TRASH IN NERUDA'S CASA • BRAVE THE DEVIL'S THROAT AT IGUAZÚ • WINE AND HORSES AT ESTANCIA COLOMÉ • CHASING CONDORS IN THE COLCA CANYON • ON THE TRAIL OF BUTCH CASSIDY AND THE SUNDANCE KID • SEEKING HEAT IN THE CHAPADA DIAMANTINA • SUMMITING AT SUNRISE ON VOLCÁN COTOPAXI • TAKING A RING-SIDE SEAT AT THE PENÍNSULA VALDÉS • THE FRENZY OF BOI BUMBA • SOARING OVER THE NAZCA LINES • CELEBRATE QOYLLUR RITI • PEACE AND PACHAMAMA IN TILCARA • MEET THE LOCALS ON THE AMAZON'S BACKWATERS • VISITING THE LAST PANAMA HAT WEAVERS • EXPLORING COLONIA DEL SACRAMENTO BY SCOOTER • HEAR GAUCHO TALES IN THE BEASTLY PANTANAL • TAPATI: FUN AND GAMES ON EASTER ISLAND • LIFE ON THE QUIET SIDE: HOMESTAYS ON LAKE TITICACA • TRAVERSING THE SALAR DE UYUNI • THERMAL SPRINGS AND THE DEVIL'S PONCHO: A PATAGONIAN ODYSSEY • CATCHING A LAUNCH AT THE CENTRE SPATIAL GUYANAIS • SWEPT OFF YOUR FEET IN BUENOS AIRES • NAVIGATING THE NARROW STREETS OF CARTAGENA • GOING DOWNHILL IN THE

South America
657–734

VENEZUELA

GUYANA

SURINAME

FRENCH GUIANA

Size matters: in search of the world's biggest snake — 679

COLOMBIA

Birdwatch and be watched — 719

The silent statues of San Agustin — 727

ECUADOR

Rubber busts and top hats: opera in the Amazon — 669

PERU

B R A Z I L

Parrot-watching at the world's biggest macaw lick — 688

BOLIVIA

Slave dances, a medusa Lucifer and bow-tied gringos — 734

Walk with giants at Serra da Canastra — 729

Watching wildlife in the dusty Chaco — 657

PARAGUAY

CHILE

URUGUAY

A R G E N T I N A

Swinging sticks at the Argentine Open — 665

Braving the wind at Torres del Paine — 730

657 Watching wildlife in the dusty Chaco

PARAGUAY All the faces in our safari party wear the same expression of awe as we stare at the jaguar strolling down the dusty track. This one looks a lot bigger than its TV counterparts, and we feel a healthy sense of respect now that there's nothing but a clear path separating it from us. With paws the size of dinner-plates and a head as big as a sack of potatoes, there is no doubt that he rules here, and we are tolerated by him just as we tolerate the gnats that buzz around our ears.

The scene plays out not in the virgin Amazonia, or the verdant Pantanal, but in the Paraguayan Chaco – one of the hottest, driest and most inhospitable environments on Earth. In spite of its image as a thorny, dusty wilderness, the unspoilt splendour of the High Chaco is one of the best places in South America for wildlife-watching. Here big mammals still roam about in large numbers and encounter humans so infrequently that they show no fear toward us. In fact, so few people visit that in 1976 the discovery of the pig-like Chaco peccary, or tagua, shook the zoological world – until then it was known only from fossils.

From November to March the Chaco defies its arid reputation as heavy rains stimulate plant growth, converting dry grasslands to lush wetlands – a haven for waterbirds such as the enormous jabiru and flocks of snow-white egrets. Caimans sun themselves on sandbanks and herds of capybara take advantage of the season of plenty to raise their young. As we watch, the jaguar moves off into the distance. Our driver restarts the engine to approach him. The jaguar turns abruptly, flashes us a look of contempt and disappears into the bush.

658 Wine-tasting in Mendoza

ARGENTINA Recently named the eighth "Great Wine Capital", putting it alongside more famous regions like Napa and Bordeaux, Mendoza is the main reason Argentina has become one of the best wine-producing countries. The area attracts top-flight vintners from around the world, but arguably the finest wines in the region are those of Argentine Nicolás Catena. Even if you've already had the bacchanalian pleasure of uncorking one of his US$100 bottles, nothing can match the excitement of visiting his otherworldly winery, Bodega Catena Zapata, where the grapes are harvested from February to April.

Rising like a Maya pyramid from the dusty flatlands that surround Mendoza, the adobe and glass structure stands against the breathtaking backdrop of the 6962m Aconcagua, the highest peak in the Americas. Descend through a pathway of stone arches into the building's cool, dimly lit sarcophagus, where the wine barrels are stored, and a long oak table is set with a sampler to quicken your pulse. It's the perfect setting for a taste of Mendoza's signature red grape, Malbec, which has prospered like no other in this dry, high desert *terroir*. For decades after being brought over from Europe by Italian immigrants like Catena's grandfather, the ruby-coloured grape was deemed too robust for all but the beefy Argentine palate. Now widening curiosity among wine consumers and more consistent growing techniques have made this fruity and full-bodied nectar a stalwart of the wine world.

With hundreds of tasting rooms within reach – many in the traditional bodegas are still free – there's no shortage of places to visit. So get an early start, and unless you want to topple over in a sun-kissed, drunken haze, abide by the sommelier's golden rule: swirl 'n' spit.

659 Armadillos and amulets: sampling a witch's brew

BOLIVIA At first glance, the bustling market seems much like any other in Bolivia: there are neat piles of fruit and vegetables, baskets of *empanadas* and alpaca-wool hats, jumpers, ponchos and socks for sale. But take a closer look at the stalls and a strange picture emerges. Among the everyday items are shrivelled llama foetuses, dried frogs, birds, armadillos, porcupines and turtles, boxes of herbs, remedies and potions, smouldering multicoloured candles, soapstone figures, and collections of amulets, charms and talismans.

The Witches' Market (the Mercado de Hechiceria or Mercado de las Brujas) sits on a cobbled street a few blocks back from Plaza San Francisco in La Paz, the world's highest capital city at more than 3800m above sea level. Although the Spanish conquistadors and missionaries brought Catholicism to Bolivia, they failed to completely supplant the indigenous population's traditional religious practices, such as the worship of Pachamama (Mother Earth). Instead, the two sets of beliefs blended together and today continue to find their expression in rituals that require an evocative array of ingredients.

At the market, the smell of incense hangs in the air, while the low hum of whispered requests from locals mingles with the excited chatter of foreign tourists. The stallholders or "witches", generally Aymara women clad in traditional Andean dress – long woven skirts, bright shawls and small black or brown bowler hats (known locally as *bombin*) – claim to cure almost any malady, and the methods they use have barely changed in hundreds of years.

The llama foetuses are buried under the foundations of most Bolivian homes as an offering to Pachamama, an apology for digging into her. Armadillos, meanwhile, are believed to dissuade burglars, while frogs bring about wealth. There are amulets and potions for those hoping for a happy marriage, to conceive or reinvigorate their sex life. Others promise good luck in business or protection against illness. For those with more complicated problems, or just a healthy sense of curiosity, there are even *yatiris* (spiritual healers) to be consulted – a memorable experience regardless of personal beliefs.

Natural rejection
in the Galápagos Islands

ECUADOR The utter indifference (some call it fearlessness) that most of the animals of the Galápagos Islands show humans is as if they knew all along they'd be the ones to change humanity's perception of itself for ever. It was, after all, this famous menagerie of accidental inmates, washed or blown from the mainland across a thousand kilometres of ocean and cut off from the rest of their kind, that started the cogs turning in Charles Darwin's mind. His theory of natural selection changed humankind's understanding of its place in the world, and by extension, some might say, its place in the universe.

Peering out to shore from your cabin, you little suspect that the neon sea and coral beaches mark not the fringes of paradise, but of hell solidified – a ferocious wasteland of petrified lava lakes, ash-striped cliffs, serrated clinker tracts and smouldering volcanoes. Even so, as you walk through this scarred landscape,

you find that life abounds, albeit peculiar life, the product of many generations of adaptation to a comfortless home. A marine iguana flashes an impish grin at you and, unlike its more familiar ancestors on the continent, scuttles into the sea to feed. On a rocky spur nearby, another one-of-a-kind, a flightless cormorant, which long ago abandoned its aerial talents for ones nautical, hangs its useless wing-stumps out to dry. With each island, new animal oddities reveal themselves – giant tortoises, canoodling waved albatrosses, lumbering land iguanas and Darwin's finches to name but a few – each a key player in the world's most celebrated workshop of evolution. And except for the friendly mockingbirds that pick at your shoelaces, most life on Galápagos is blank to your existence, making you feel like a privileged gatecrasher, one who's allowed an up-close look at a long-kept secret: the mechanics of life on Earth.

661 Retail therapy

at Otavalo crafts market

ECUADOR Just about every traveller is struck at some point by the panic-inducing realization that there are people back home expecting to be lavished with exotic gifts from faraway lands. If you happen to find yourself in Ecuador at this anxiety-ridden moment you're in luck: Otavalo's spectacular indigenous *artesanías* market is one of the largest crafts fairs on the continent and one of the most enjoyable alfresco shopping experiences to be had anywhere.

Up for grabs are handicrafts of every description – ceramics, jewellery, paintings, musical instruments, carvings and above all a dazzling array of weavings and textiles, for which the Otavalo Valley has long been famous. Looms in back rooms across the countryside clatter away to produce chunky sweaters, hats, gloves, trousers and tablecloths, while weavings of the highest quality, indigenous ponchos, blouses, belts and tapestries are still made by master-craftsmen using traditional means in tiny village workshops. Come Saturday, when the crafts market combines with a general produce, hardware and animal market to create a megabazaar that engulfs much of the town, people stream in from miles around for a day of frenzied trading.

The Plaza de Ponchos is the epicentre of the crafts melee, a blazing labyrinth of makeshift passageways and endless ranks of tapestries, jumpers, hammocks, cloths and shawls, amid which Otavaleños dressed in all their finery lurk at strategic points to tempt potential customers. But hard sell isn't their style; gentle, good-natured coaxing is far more effective at weakening the customer's resolve. Even the most hardened skinflints will soon be stuffing their bags with everything they never knew they needed and plenty else besides. The only tricky part is deciding who back home should get the two-metre rain-stick and who should get the sheepskin chaps.

662 Wildlife spotting in the Beni wetlands

BOLIVIA It's just a forty-minute flight from La Paz to the tropical lowlands of Beni, but the contrast couldn't be greater. From a window seat you'll see the snow-covered Andes give way to a dark green shadow of rainforest, before disembarking to the sweltering humidity of Rurrenabaque and rapidly shedding your high-altitude layers of clothes. This laid-back town sits in a shimmering heat haze on the banks of the Beni River, framed by shrub-covered hills. It's a fine base for trips into the lush wetlands of Bolivia's Amazon Basin, popular with travellers who idle in hammocks under palm-thatched canopies before visiting the jungle.

Local operators take small groups into the wetlands on three-day excursions, the knowledgeable guides pointing out wildlife as well as plants used by locals as remedies for fever, colds and flu. Tours glide down the Yacuma River's overgrown waterways in low-bottomed boats, eyes peeled for inquisitive yellow skull monkeys and magnificently plumed birds and wade through sticky, swamp-

like mud in search of anacondas. Accommodation is basic: you'll spend your nights on mattresses shrouded in mosquito nets within a wooden hut on stilts. But the boat quickly becomes your breezy second home as you cruise along vegetation-lined channels, past graceful, long-necked herons and sunbathing turtles. In the shady shallows between tangles of tree roots, you can hook piranhas on home-made fishing rods using cubes of raw meat as bait. Further upstream you can swim with playful river dolphins, coloured an improbable shade of dusky pink.

Douse yourself in repellent to watch the sky burn brightly as the sun sets over the flat pampas. Once night falls, glowing fireflies provide intermittent light; shine a torch into the murky, shrub-covered riverbanks and you'll catch the sinister white glint of unblinking caiman eyes. At dawn, the wetlands echo with the eerie rumble of howler monkeys waking up, and the clouds form perfect reflections on the calm, mirrored surface of the water.

663 Glitz and golden sands on Punta del Este

URUGUAY The continent's most exclusive beach resort by some distance, Punta del Este is Uruguay's answer to St-Tropez. There's a certain level of celebrity that's achieved simply by being here: if you don that outrageously expensive Sauvage swimsuit, act like you belong and hit the beach, chances are you may end up in the pages of a South American glossy mag. Punta is largely about glitzy casinos, all-night parties, designer sushi and fashionistas sipping frozen *mojitos*. It's the kind of place where you might spot Naomi Campbell and Prince Albert of Monaco on the same evening – though probably not in the same Ferrari convertible. Every January half a million visitors – mostly Argentines and Brazilians – cram themselves in between surfers' paradise Playa Brava and family-friendly Playa Mansa, so you can easily lose yourself in the crowds.

But there's another side to Punta. Leave the Quiksilver-clad

funboarders and world beach-volley tournaments behind and head for one of the infinite golden *playas* way beyond Punta Ballena, on the River Plate side of things. In Chihuahua, where you can sunbathe among the enormous straw-hued dunes, take cover in the secluded pine groves and venture into the tepid waters. At night, drive across the landmark roller-coaster bridge to La Barra – ignore the bronzed beauties queuing for flambéed lobster along the main drag – and race past the windswept ocean strands to José Ignacio. Here you can dine in discreet style right on the seafront, enjoying simply-barbecued squid and chilled Sauvignon Blanc, as the breakers crash onto the sand and the Atlantic breeze ruffles your hair. The shutterbugs will be busy snapping the heir to the Spanish throne at some heaving cocktail bar in Punta: they're welcome to their prize.

664 Itaipú: plugging the world's biggest dam

PARAGUAY & BRAZIL Colossal, gargantuan, mammoth, gigantic – it's difficult to find the right adjective to capture the sheer magnitude of the Itaipú Dam. The joint property of Paraguay and Brazil, it has been voted one of the seven wonders of the modern world by the American Society of Civil Engineers (who should know what they're talking about), and is arguably man's greatest ever feat of practical engineering, meeting the energy needs of most of Paraguay as well as a large chunk of southern Brazil. You don't need to be mechanically minded to appreciate it, however: the introductory video about the finer details of electricity generation might not hold your attention, but the sheer awe-inspiring scale of the structure certainly will.

It took sixteen years to build the dam, a project that was begun in the dark days of Paraguayan dictator Alfredo Stroessner's

dictatorship and finally completed in the early years of democracy; its inception created a reservoir so deep and wide that it completely flooded the Sete Quedas, a set of waterfalls comparable in size to those at nearby Iguazú. At 8km long and 195m high, standing next to it and looking up is as dizzying as you might expect. But to really feel insignificant, make a visit to the inside of the dam and the extraordinary one-kilometre-long machine room. It's like the inside of an anthill, with workers scurrying around, dwarfed by the sheer scale of their surroundings. The dam is at its most impressive when water levels are at their peak during the rainy season, when torrents of water rush down the chutes and the roar can be deafening. Whenever you're here, though, it's an amazing sight – and one that for once does justice to even the highest expectations.

665

Swinging sticks at the
Argentine Open

ARGENTINA It's the most prestigious polo club tournament in the world. But unlike pukka sporting events elsewhere, there's no snobbery involved in the invitations. Turn up at the ground in Buenos Aires's leafy Palermo district, hand over less cash than you'd spend on a beer in an upmarket London pub, and you'll find a seat in the stands.

Finding a seat in the saddle is more challenging. Many of the players of the Argentine clubs that participate in the Open share the same surname (the Heguy and Merlos families are particularly well represented), and there's no doubt that this is a rich man's sport. Individual ponies can sell for hundreds of thousands of dollars, and players use fresh mounts for each of the game's eight or more chukkas.

When the game begins and the tempo picks up, you get a sense of why they're needed. The noise is terrific as the horses' hooves pound the turf, turning up little puffs of dust as each foot slams into the ground, and the bulging muscles of their legs and rumps heave beneath their glistening coats. Astride them, the players seem almost to float as they whip their sticks around in dexterous circles and, leaning impossibly far from the saddle, clip the ball with backhand swipes that should surely dislocate their joints. Galloping flank to flank, they scorch along, pressing one horse against the other, piling its entire weight on that of the opponent, trying to push it out of the way – yet still, incredibly, the riders don't fall off.

The crowd, meanwhile, cheers and chats, and natters on its mobile phones. It's a mellow bunch of spectators of all ages, gently enjoying a sporting afternoon in the sun. And foreigners – fear not. You don't need to be a polo aficionado to enjoy this game. You don't even need to understand the rules. Any layman can see: in these men and horses, breeding and skill have come together to create a match of breathtaking bravado and beauty.

DOWNING CAIPIRINHAS IN
RIO DE JANIERO

BRAZIL What could be simpler than a *caipirinha*? Made with just *cachaça* (a rum-like spirit distilled from fermented sugar-cane juice), fresh lime, sugar and ice, the *caipirinha* (literally "little peasant girl") is served at nearly every bar and restaurant in Brazil. Neither insipidly sweet nor jarringly alcoholic, it's one of the easiest and most pleasant cocktails to drink.

Therein lies the problem: because it's so smooth, it's all too common to lose count of just how many you've quaffed. And as lots of bars mix the cocktail with the cheapest *cachaça*, chances are that the next day you'll have to deal with a thumping headache, scarcely a just reward for a hard day at the beach. So a true aficionado will only accept the cocktail made with *cachaça* that's good enough to sip neat.

There's no better place to find this than at Rio de Janeiro's *Academia da Cachaça*. Opened in 1985, when Brazil's aspirant whisky-drinking middle class tended to dismiss *cachaça* as the drink of the poor, the *Academia* has about a hundred varieties on offer, and the bar's friendly owners and staff enjoy nothing more than offering tasting hints to their customers.

As you enter you may well wonder what all the fuss is about. The green and yellow Brazilian-flag-themed decor is utterly unremarkable and the music inaudible. But the shelves on the walls of the tiny bar, lined with a bewildering selection of bottles, remind you why you've come.

The *caipirinhas* are everything one might hope for, with just the right balance of alcohol, tang and sweetness. After one or two, you may even feel ready to forego the sugar, lime and ice and start downing shots. Choosing a label is easy: if you don't listen to the house recommendations, the regulars around you will intervene to suggest their personal favourites. The spirit inspires debates, not unlike those over the finest single malt whiskies. The perfection of the *caipirinha*, on the other hand, is undebatable.

666

667 Sandboarding at Huacachina

PERU Huacachina appears like a mirage. In the northern stretches of the Atacama – the driest desert on Earth – the oasis is a precious sapphire in an unrelenting world of sand. As you drive from the dusty town of Ica, there is no hint of what is to come until your taxi reaches the crest of a hill, when suddenly the glory of the place is revealed. Your eyes are drawn to the water, palm trees and crumbling grandeur of the promenade, a reminder of the days when Huacachina was a secluded retreat for only the very wealthiest Peruvians. But once you've descended into the town huddled around the lake, your perspective changes entirely. The dunes, not the water, take centre stage: viewed from the oasis, they ascend dramatically in steep mountains of sand, some of them 300m high. From up there, all you wanted to do was be by the cool of the water. From down here, all you can think about is scaling an enormous dune and sliding down again.

Sandboarding sounds glamorous, but it's really pretty low-tech. You need to embark as early as possible to avoid being cooked by the sun. At a house where guinea pigs, chickens and children run free in the back room, a grinning, toothless woman will rent you a board and a candle. If someone in a dune buggy offers to take you up the hill, accept. Otherwise you have to climb: there is no ski-lift. Every step up is a heroic effort, immediately deflated by a half-a-step slide down again. Progress is slow. The sandboarding, however, is not: a well-waxed board will fly down the slope. Whether you're experienced enough to stand up and catch the dune or just sit down and cling to the board for dear life, it's an exhilarating ride. It's also exhausting. After an hour or two your perspective changes again, and you'll want to recuperate at a bar by the oasis – where you can start removing the sand that coats your body.

668 Fill up in the world's pie capital

URUGUAY Prince Charles ate it as a child. It's considered as British as drizzly rain and disappointing cricket results. Allied soldiers chomped it by the truckload during both World Wars. Yet the mighty Fray Bentos range of foods has its home in a charmingly elegiac corner of Uruguay.

Once known as "the kitchen of the world", and employing more than a quarter of the town's population, Fray Bentos's location in the cattle fields of Uruguay made a perfect location for the German- and British-owned Liebig Extract of Meat Company to build a vast factory in 1863. Every day thousands of cows and lambs were slaughtered in the abattoir to make corned beef and pies that went into tins and were exported to the UK and the rest of Europe. Such was its popularity that British soldiers during World War I referred to anything good as being "Fray Bentos".

Outdated equipment and a declining export market led to the factory being closed down for three decades until a Brazilian company started operating out of the town again in 2008 and began exporting the pies to the USA for the first time. The new plant is much smaller, leaving the original abattoir vacant – it's now been converted into the Museum of the Industrial Revolution, where tours explore the vast, spookily empty slaughterhouses and retro admin offices – untouched since the 1970s.

The rest of the town seems trapped in time, its central bandstand gathering dust. Sightseers might venture into a museum dedicated to the locally born artist Luis Solari, who made bizarre sketchings of humans with animal heads.

It's not a trip to recommend to vegetarians – the tour guide seems to relish telling macabre tales of cows' ear hair being exported to Europe to make brushes, and the pies on sale in the town are cheap enough to encourage some serious binge eating. But providing you're not planning a diet anytime soon, this is a fascinating, and highly eccentric, way to explore the centuries-old trading links between this quiet corner of one of South America's least known nations and the rest of the pie-loving world.

669 Rubber busts and top hats: opera in the Amazon

BRAZIL A noisy concrete forest of tower blocks and brightly lit malls, the remote Amazonian capital and duty-free zone of Manaus throngs with shoppers braving the hot, humid streets to buy cheap electronic goods. Glittering in the twilight and visible above the chaos and heat of downtown is a large dome whose 36,000 ceramic tiles are painted gold, green and blue, the colours of the Brazilian flag. The palatial building it presides over is a grand pink and white confection of *belle époque* architecture, the Teatro Amazonas.

Nothing could seem more out of place. Built in the late nineteenth century during the height of Brazil's rubber boom, the lavish opera house was designed by Italians to look Parisian (indeed, almost all the materials were brought over from Europe). Abandoned for many years when the rubber industry died and Manaus could scarcely afford its electricity bill, the theatre is now funded by a large state budget and hosts regular performances of jazz and ballet, though nothing is quite so singular as its staging of top-quality opera in the middle of the jungle.

The surreal experience begins the moment you enter the foyer and step onto a floor covered in gleaming hardwood; walls are lined with columns made from the finest Carrara marble and ornate Italian frescoes decorate the ceiling. Hundreds of chandeliers hang in falling crystal formations. It's as if you've been transported to a European capital. You're ushered through red velvet curtains by men dressed in tailcoats and top hats. The orchestra, the Amazonas Philharmonic, pick up instruments that have been specially treated to cope with the humidity of the jungle, and the chatter dissipates abruptly. The conductor raises his baton, and the first familiar notes of Wagner's *Ring Cycle* fill the auditorium, then seep out languidly into the steamy night.

670 The road to ruins: Machu Picchu

PERU There's a point on the Inca Trail when you suddenly forget the accumulated aches and pains of four days' hard slog across the Andes. You're standing at Inti Punku, the Sun Gate, the first golden rays of dawn slowly bringing the jungle to life. Down below, revealing itself in tantalizing glimpses as the early-morning mist burns gradually away, are the distinctive ruins of Machu Picchu, looking every bit the lost Inca citadel it was until a century ago.

The hordes of visitors that will arrive by mid-morning are still tucked up in bed; for the next couple of hours or so, it's just you, your group and a small herd of llamas, grazing indifferently on the terraced slopes. That first unforgettable sunrise view from Inti Punku is just the start: thanks to its remote location – hugging the peaks at 2500m and hidden in the mountains some 120km

from Cusco – Machu Picchu escaped the ravages of the Spanish conquistadores and remained semi-buried in the Peruvian jungle until Hiram Bingham, an American explorer, "rediscovered" them in 1911. Which means that, descending onto the terraces and working your way through the stonework labyrinth, you'll discover some of the best-preserved Inca remains in the world.

Sites such as the Temple of the Sun and the Intihuatana appear exactly as they did some six hundred years ago. The insight they give us into the cultures and customs of the Inca is still as rewarding – the former's window frames the constellation of Pleiades, an important symbol of crop fertility – and their structural design, pieced together like an ancient architectural jigsaw, is just as incredible.

671 Mountain biking the world's most dangerous road

BOLIVIA The reputation of the road linking La Paz with the tropical lowlands of Bolivia is enough to put most travellers off. But for downhill mountain bikers and all-round thrill-lovers, it's an irresistible challenge. The World's Most Dangerous Road, as this byway is colloquially known, is a stunning ride through some of the most dramatic scenery South America has to offer, and with a vertical descent of around 3500m over just 64km, it's one of the longest continuous downhill rides on Earth. A 2006 bypass, which most cars and trucks now use to avoid the most precipitous stretch, means the old road is now quieter for cyclists, although the route has got no less precipitous.

Starting amid the icebound peaks of the Andes at over 4000m above sea level, the road plunges through the clouds into the humid valleys of the Upper Amazon basin, winding along deep,

narrow gorges where dense cloudforest clings to even the steepest of slopes. The descent is an intense, white-knuckle experience, not made easier by the sight of so many stone crosses marking where buses and trucks have left the road. The surface is so bad that in most countries it wouldn't even be classified as a road. On one side, dizzying precipices drop down hundreds of metres to the thin, silver ribbon of a river below; on the other, a sheer rock wall rises into the clouds. In the rainy season, waterfalls cascade across the road, making its broken surface even more treacherous. At every hairpin bend, there's a risk a heavy lorry may lurch round the corner, leaving very little room for manoeuvre on a track only 3m wide.

By the time you're sipping beer and resting aching limbs by the pool in the tropical heat of Coroico, the resort town at the end of the ride, your only fear will be the bus ride back up to La Paz.

672 Walking on ice: the Perito Moreno Glacier

ARGENTINA Fed by one of the planet's largest freshwater reserves – the Southern Patagonian Icecap – the Perito Moreno Glacier is the world's biggest ice-cube dispenser. It looks like a gigantic frozen Blue Lady, thanks to centuries of compression which has turned the deepest ice a deep shade of *curaçao*, whose sapphire veins can be tantalizingly glimpsed through plunging fissures. This icy leviathan of a cocktail is one to linger over, surveying its infinite cracks and curves from the viewing platform across the Lago Argentino. One of the few advancing glaciers in the world, it does move, but at, well, glacial speed. It's noisy, too, squeaking and whining and sporadically exploding, as every few minutes a wardrobe-sized chunk splashes into the lake's chilly waters and bobs away as an iceberg.

But the spectacular event you'll be hoping to see, the *ruptura*,

when Perito Moreno lunges forward, forms a dam of ice and then violently breaks, happens only every four to five years. And throughout the 1990s it didn't happen at all...

A great way of getting to know this icy beast is to go for a walk on it. Standing on the glacier, you can see every crack and crevice, every tiny pinnacle. Even on a warm summer's day, the glacier remains chilly, so wrap up well. Protect your eyes and exposed skin from the immense white glare with sunglasses and a high-factor sunscreen. The ice can be slippery, but it's not dangerous as long as you stick to sensible footwear and snap on the crampons issued by all the tour companies offering glacier-treks. And when you've walked far enough, you'll be glad to know that most treks end up with a tumbler of whisky on the rocks, made with ice-cubes chipped out of the glacier, of course.

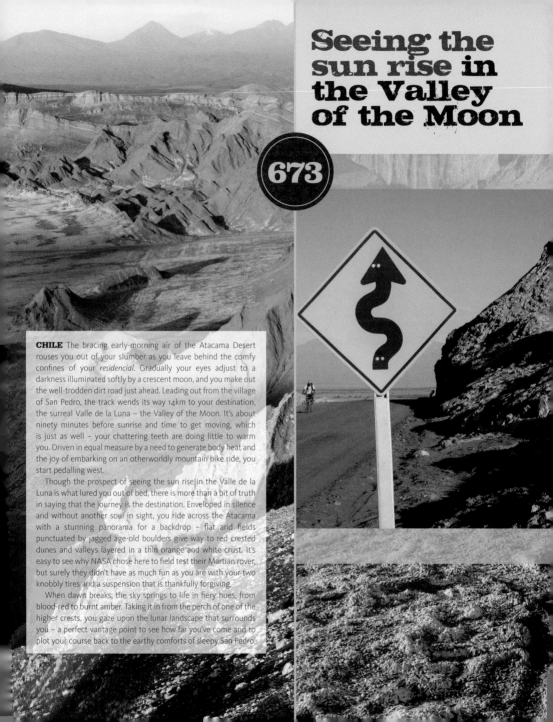

Seeing the sun rise in the Valley of the Moon

673

CHILE The bracing early-morning air of the Atacama Desert rouses you out of your slumber as you leave behind the comfy confines of your *residencial*. Gradually your eyes adjust to a darkness illuminated softly by a crescent moon, and you make out the well-trodden dirt road just ahead. Leading out from the village of San Pedro, the track wends its way 14km to your destination, the surreal Valle de la Luna – the Valley of the Moon. It's about ninety minutes before sunrise and time to get moving, which is just as well – your chattering teeth are doing little to warm you. Driven in equal measure by a need to generate body heat and the joy of embarking on an otherworldly mountain bike ride, you start pedalling west.

Though the prospect of seeing the sun rise in the Valle de la Luna is what lured you out of bed, there is more than a bit of truth in saying that the journey is the destination. Enveloped in silence and without another soul in sight, you ride across the Atacama with a stunning panorama for a backdrop – flat arid fields punctuated by jagged age-old boulders give way to red crested dunes and valleys layered in a thin orange and white crust. It's easy to see why NASA chose here to field test their Martian rover, but surely they didn't have as much fun as you are with your two knobbly tires and a suspension that is thankfully forgiving.

When dawn breaks, the sky springs to life in fiery hues, from blood-red to burnt amber. Taking it in from the perch of one of the higher crests, you gaze upon the lunar landscape that surrounds you – a perfect vantage point to see how far you've come and to plot your course back to the earthy comforts of sleepy San Pedro.

674 Making a pilgrimage to Isla del Sol

BOLIVIA Set against the parched grasslands of the Altiplano, where agriculture is dependent on irrigation and capricious rain, the deep, sapphire-blue waters of Lake Titicaca offer the promise of life and fertility. The Incas believed the creator god Viracocha rose from the waters of this lake, calling forth the sun and the moon to light up the world, from an island in its centre now called the Isla del Sol – the Island of the Sun.

Claiming their own dynasty also originated there, they built a complex of shrines and temples on the island, transforming it into a religious centre of enormous importance, a pan-Andean pilgrimage destination once visited by thousands of worshippers annually from across their vast empire.

Modern visitors can follow the same route as the pilgrims of Inca times, travelling by boat from the port town of Copacabana – itself a pilgrimage centre for the now nominally Christian population of the Bolivian highlands – through the waters of the world's highest navigable lake.

With no roads or cars on the island, the only way to visit the Inca ruins is on foot, trekking through the tranquil villages of the indigenous Aymara, who raise crops on the intricate agricultural terraces left by the Incas and still regard Lake Titicaca as a powerful female deity capable of regulating climate and rainfall.

The ruined temples themselves are small in comparison with Inca sites elsewhere in the Andes, but the setting more than makes up for this. The great rock where the sun and moon were created looks out on all sides across the tranquil expanse of the lake, which is in turn surrounded by mighty, snowcapped mountains, each of which is still worshipped as a god in its own right. Serene and beautiful, Titicaca's sacred Andean geography makes it easy to believe it could indeed be the centre of the universe.

675 Go back in time in Paraty

BRAZIL Despite its close links to Brazil's second city, Paraty, a few hours drive down the coast, feels a world away from Rio. There are no swarms of buses trailing exhaust to greet you, no *favelas*, few chattering street vendors and practically no party animals. It's deathly quiet, especially at night, when the sound of the tide hypnotizes you into sleep. Paraty (or Parati) was first discovered by the country's Portuguese colonists in 1502, and the laid-back burg has a wonderful rustic charm that belies its busy history. It's an awesome place to simply unwind, and with only a bit more effort you can set off on the pristine water for a schooner trip taking in three or four nearby islands or a scuba dive among the fish.

After its formal establishment as a city in 1667, Paraty was instrumental in the transport of gold from the hills of Minas Gerais state to Rio, and of slaves and equipment in the other direction. By the early 1800s, coffee had replaced gold, and by the middle of the century the sugar-cane-based spirit *cachaça* was the area's lifeblood, with 150 distillers. Production trailed off, but the residents still put on a major festival to celebrate the liquor every August. Almost everything was transported by water – the first proper road was only built in the 1970s, when Paraty was "discovered" once more.

Things are quieter now, and the city's relative isolation, along with the proximity of verdant nature reserves, more than sixty islands and hundreds of unspoiled beaches has turned the area into something of a tourist destination, though on a manageable scale. To fully appreciate your surroundings, hire a boat and driver at the pier to tour the bay or embark on a fishing expedition in search of dorado or king mackerel, two of the hundreds of species that live in these waters. Others can stroll among whitewashed buildings on cobblestoned streets, contemplate the colonial architecture of the handful of ancient churches here – the oldest, 1722's Igreja da Santa Rita, is especially beautiful – and transport themselves back to a time before *telenovelas* and stadium *futbol*.

676 Trek to the Lost City

COLOMBIA It's a challenging three-day trek through dense jungle to the Ciudad Perdida, the fabled ruins of a lost city hidden deep in the mountains of northern Colombia – and then another three days back. But the strenuous hike along steep trails sticky with mud is worth it just for the time you spend in the tranquil, unblemished cloudforest of the Sierra Nevada de Santa Marta, washing beside waterfalls in bracingly fresh pools and mastering the art of sleeping soundly in a hammock. Indiana Jones-style moments abound, from wading across the fast-flowing River Buritaca to inching along narrow ledges at the path's whim.

The only other people you'll encounter along the way are a few bemused Kogui tribesmen standing outside their circular thatched huts and youthful soldiers guarding occasional military outposts. Gaps in the trees afford glimpses of rolling peaks carpeted in vegetation, filling the landscape in every direction. It's easy to fixate on where you're placing your feet, but remember to pause to admire the view. After a day or two you'll start to distinguish the jungle's infinite textures and shades of green and appreciate the subtly contrasting hues of twisted vines and delicate leaves.

Walking six hours each day can be exhausting, but the group camaraderie carries you up the most gruelling slogs. Even the fittest trekker will be effortlessly outstripped by the nimble guide in wellies. Darkness descends around 6pm, so evenings are spent chatting as fireflies flicker. The dramatic climax to your journey involves hauling yourself out of the river to climb 1200 worn, moss-covered and perilously slippery steps hacked out of the rock.

Little remains of the Ciudad Perdida bar grass-covered plateaus edged with rocks. But you can picture how it looked before Spanish-brought illnesses devastated the Tayrona people, and marvel at their resourcefulness at establishing a thriving community in such a remote location. By day, sunlight dapples the paths, lending the place an aura of faerie, which becomes more eerie when damp white mist rolls in at night. Colombia's pre-colonial history is largely unknown, and in this ancient site your imagination is free to conjure up the mysterious past.

677 Dinosaur hunting
IN SUCRE

BOLIVIA It may be famed for its salt flats and Lake Titicaca, but the unsung hero of Bolivia is an experience like no other. Just over 5km from the city of Sucre, on the Altiplano's eastern edge, you can walk among dinosaurs without the aid of CGI or a celebrity voiceover. Here, on a near-vertical wall in an old limestone quarry, sits the largest collection of dinosaur tracks in the world: five thousand footprints from scores of different species dating back almost seventy million years.

It is thought dinosaurs, chased by predators or in search of food, paused at nearby watering holes. During the rainy season the area would have flooded, creating a layer of mud and sediment that acted to preserve the footprints. Across the years the tectonic plates moved and pushed the ground upwards, creating the 100m-high limestone wall that exists today, peppered with footprints and stretching for over a kilometre.

Discovered by local cement quarry workers in 1994, the site has evolved from an informal attraction to a fully-fledged dinosaur park, replete with towering, life-size models of different dinosaurs (including the iconic tyrannosaurus), an audio-visual display and a restaurant.

But the footprints are the key to the site's appeal. They're viewed from a platform a safe distance away, and while you miss out on touching the markings you do get to take in the size of the prints and imagine how frightening it would have been to stand surrounded by these awesome creatures. Once your eyes have worked out what is rock face texture and what are footprints you can pick out the different shapes and sizes of footprints, follow the baby dinosaur walking alongside its parent or try and spot the trackway of the young *Tyrannosaurus rex* (nicknamed Johnnie Walker by the archeologists studying the site) – at more than half-a-kilometre it is the longest ever track recorded. Happy hunting.

678 Beef-eater's paradise: the Argentine parrilla

ARGENTINA Argentines rich and poor base their high-protein diets around beef; they eat more of it per capita than any other people on Earth. And who can blame them? Succulent, juicy Argentine beef has a distinct, refined taste, redolent of the perfect pastures that the cattle graze upon – the incredibly fertile pampas, an emerald green carpet radiating out for hundreds of kilometres around Buenos Aires.

The beef's flavour is expertly brought out in its preparation. The traditional – in fact, practically the only – method is on a *parrilla*, a barbecue using wood (or occasionally charcoal, but certainly never gas). Almost sacred to Argentines, the *parrilla* is a custom that has its roots in *gaucho* (cowboy) culture: the fire is lit on Sundays, holidays, after football matches – pretty much at any excuse. In the countryside, ranch hands spread the embers along the ground; in the town, chefs use a metal pit. A grill is hung above and the food lined up – fat chorizo sausages and rounds of melting provolone cheese to start, followed by tasty *asado* ribs and, finally, huge slabs of steak.

The meat is of such quality that there's no need to drown it in sauces – the *parrillero* (cook) will lightly season it and offer up some *chimichurri* to add zip. Made of herbs, garlic and peppers in oil, *chimichurri* was purportedly invented by a Scottish (or Irish) *gaucho* named Jimmy McCurry (or Curry), who mixed the only ingredients he had to hand to spice up his diet. Vegetables are an afterthought, mostly restricted to fries and salad – the only essential accompaniments to a *parrilla* are bread and a bottle of rich, red Argentine Malbec (see 658).

The best *parrillas* are found outside Buenos Aires, closer to the source. Stay on an *estancia* (ranch), such as *El Ombú*, to enjoy beef reared on site, or seek out family-run *parrillas* found in pretty much every countryside town. Alternatively, upmarket city restaurants like *Cabaña Las Lilas*, in the capital's converted docks area, offer premium cuts of meat in more sophisticated surroundings.

679 Size matters: in search of the world's biggest snake

VENEZUELA At an average of 7m long and weighing up to 250kg, you'd think it'd be impossible for the green anaconda to find somewhere to hide. But gazing out over Venezuela's Los Llanos floodplain, probably the best place in the world to find these gargantuan serpents, all we can see are a couple of scarlet ibis and a herd of capybara. Felipe, our guide, assures us that they are out there, and we set off into the wetlands.

Anacondas entwine their prey in a horrific hug, unhinging their jaws and swallowing it whole; digesting their meal headfirst is easier for them, Felipe explains, as their prey's limbs tend to fold this way. With this nugget of gratuitously detailed information fresh in my mind, I follow him closely, keeping a comforting rodent shield of capybaras – the anaconda's snack of choice – between myself and the water. Fed by the Orinoco river, Los Llanos spills across 300,000 square kilometres of flooded savannah – almost a third of the country – but Felipe seems to know exactly which patch of reeds to head for. His expertise is complemented by the very latest in anaconda detection tools – a stick – and he sets to work, prodding the swampy foliage in front of him at regular (and cautious) intervals.

It seems to work – after half an hour, Felipe strikes ophidian oil. Quick as a flash, he grabs the tail, his assistant Carlos grabs the head, and the battle begins. The beast is a good 3.5m long, I estimate (from a good 4m away). I pluck up enough courage to inch closer until I can reach out and touch it. It's like patting a wet tyre: cold, damp and dense. After a few more minutes of sizing it up, the two men let it go, and it ripples off into the water. And then it's just Felipe, Carlos and me, and the seemingly endless watery horizon of Los Llanos.

680 Rafting on sacred waters in the Urubamba Valley

PERU Snaking along from the Andes out to the Apurimac in the Amazon basin, the mighty Urubamba is the main artery pulsing through the Inca heartland, winding between many of their most revered sites, making the river itself sacred. Not all the Urubamba is negotiable by craft, but one section, not far from the start of the Inca Trail, is perfect for a bit of gentle white-water rafting.

On the first stretch, a serene meander through the Urubamba Valley, novice rafters will have the chance to get used to the feeling of having nothing but inflated plastic between them and some fairly sharp rocks. This is a chance to enjoy the superb views of the snowy peaks of the Andes in the distance on one side, and the wooded slopes of the valley stretching up hundreds of metres on the other, where Quechua-speaking llama herders ply the steep trails of their ancestors and the distinctive black and white forms of condors can be seen wheeling far above. Blink and you'll miss the rows of ancient Inca grain stores, carved from rock and piled impossibly high on the emerald-green banks.

Don't be lulled into thinking this is naught but a pleasure boat, though. The roar of the rapids quickly gets louder as the raft moves faster. Following the instructor's command, you'll row harder and duck lower as the raft shoots down increasingly larger and faster falls. However secular you are, you may find yourself praying to the ancient spirits of the Incas as you go rushing down the final and biggest drop along this beginner's stretch. There are scarier, more dangerous river rapids in Peru for experienced rafters – the excellent class V rapids of the Colca Canyon, for instance – but none can rival the beauty and majesty of the sacred river of the Incas.

681

Finding Eden on the
Altiplano's edge

BOLIVIA You can't buy a return ticket to the Garden of Eden, but if you could, your final destination would almost certainly be the Middle East. Colonial Spain begged to differ; according to Eduardo Galeano's *Open Veins of Latin America*, one contemporary account located the biblical garden in the heart of the Amazon basin. It's the conquistadors who were nearer the mark, though, finding their own Eden further west in Sorata, Bolivia. Here, after an endless and desolate plain, the Altiplano jigsaws down into the kind of valley routinely trumped up in fairy tale and myth. That it's seemingly hidden from the world goes without saying, but it's the topography that dazzles, a cosmic wedge of terraces falling into mist, so ravishingly green after the whey-brown Altiplano they seem like, well, the hallowed allotments of Eden, if not quite the garden itself.

At the heart of it all, below the lottery of bijou maize plots and heaven-scented eucalyptus, sits Sorata, a beginning-of-the-world outpost populated by diggers, dreamers, eccentrics and entrepreneurs, its colonial piles crumbling contentedly under the gaze of almighty Illampu. At over 6300m tall, this ice-crowned mountain deity shadows every cobbled corner of town, its glacial heights all the more fantastical amid the bucolic setting, and one reason why the place remains popular among climbers and trekkers.

Yet Eden or no, once upon a time Sorata was itself a gateway to the heart of Amazonian darkness; Victorian explorer Colonel Fawcett, who inspired Conan Doyle's *The Lost World*, passed this way more than once on his journey to oblivion, while the town's predominantly German merchants made a killing on quinine and rubber hauled up from the jungle. These days the adventurous can still head east down the old trails, assuming they can tear themselves away from Sorata's sequestered cafés and glorious climate, an eternal spring with blissfully warm days and cool, quiet nights, themselves spent in a peerlessly eccentric choice of psychedelic cabin, time-warped colonial chamber or haunted art-deco hotel. You might not find Eden but you will find a cure for modernity, one that might just make your return ticket redundant.

>> South America

682

Looking down on
Kaieteur Falls

GUYANA From the vantage point of a Cessna, the great expanse of Guyana's rainforest interior looks like billows of green cloud. The little plane drones over the soft canopy, almost low enough that the passengers could blow and the trees would disperse like smoke, revealing whatever mysteries lie hidden beneath. About an hour out of Georgetown, just as the unbroken jungle scenery starts to get monotonous, the plane banks sharply to the right, losing roughly half of its altitude in a couple of seconds, and heads down towards a gorge bordered by thick forest. As the plane descends farther, a waterfall soon comes into view, cascading down the middle of the gorge, not in tumultuous rumbles of white foam, but in a single, rapier-like gush of water that seems to come from nowhere.

Enjoying the kind of splendid isolation that Niagara Falls can only dream of, Kaieteur Falls is five times as high as its North American rival, and infinitely more enigmatic. The narrow band of water that runs off the side of the Kaieteur Gorge plunges 226m past nesting swifts to the bottom, making the falls here the highest single-drop waterfall in the world. Flying close enough to hear the water's roar blend menacingly with the sound of whirring propellers, it all seems dark and forbidding down below. The plane's passengers may start to worry about those hardy souls who opted to walk through the rainforest for several days in order to reach the falls, getting their first glimpse of Kaieteur dropping on top of them – a somewhat intimidating experience when compared with the exhilaration of flying in, but no less awesome.

683 The secret sensation of Pousada Maravilha

BRAZIL Fernando de Noronha is an impossibly beautiful secret island just an hour's flight from Recife in northern Brazil. A pristine National Marine Park, it was once visited by Charles Darwin and is so eco-orientated that on some beaches no sun cream or flip-flops are allowed. It has long been a hideaway for the Brazilian jet set, and is all the more alluring because the number of visitors is limited to just 400 a day. Mention the island to any Brazilian and they will sigh with longing. UNESCO has measured the air as the second purest in the world after the Arctic.

Until recently, the island's only weakness was the lack of a decent hotel. So if you like your luxuries the *Pousada Maravilha*, owned by the scions of some of Brazil's wealthiest families, is reason to rejoice. There are just eight white, bright rooms, very contemporary, and all with billowy curtains and bouncy beds. Views stretch out onto a brilliant peacock-green ocean, and you can enjoy outdoor jungle showers, a private Japanese hot tub

and lazy-time hammocks. If you can bear to leave your room, the sleek infinity-edged pool is rock-star cool, with funky low-level day beds and more of those awesome views.

During the day your best bet is to hire a beach buggy, bomb around the quiet roads and discover the most breathtaking deserted beaches – many of them lurking at the end of bumpy, dusty tracks, and some with cavorting dolphins. Divers will delight in the gin-clear water – visibility up to 50m – and ridiculously rich marine life; those who prefer to stay on shore can watch baby green turtles hatch on the beach in the dead of night. Showtime runs from December to May.

Returning to the hotel is the ultimate treat. Candlelit massages are knock-out; suppers waist-expanding. The staff are so accommodating that they even check you in for your flight out, so you have to face the airport only minutes before departure. Heaven.

684 Searching for the perfect oyster on Isla Margarita

VENEZUELA Oysters provide a great source of inspiration for a food-driven odyssey. You can travel far and wide looking for the freshest, finest specimen; once discovered, you might consume it on the half-shell, or fried up in a *po-boy* sandwich, or perhaps as part of a shrimp and oyster omelette – a South Korean favourite.

Consider first what they are: sensitive little creatures that thrive in unpolluted areas, where fresh water and sea water mix and where temperatures aren't too hot in summer or too cold in winter. In short, relatively unspoilt and often unusually attractive stretches of coastline. So you'll not only enjoy the goods when you arrive, you may find a picture-perfect setting too.

These spots lie in a band across the globe, taking in wild oysters from the fjords of Norway and South Africa lagoon oysters, as well as European oyster plantations in Loch Fynne (Scotland), Whitstable

(England) and the 350-plus oyster farms on the Bassin d'Arcachon in France. But for our money, there's no cooler crustacean than mangrove oysters, and no more inspiring location in which to consume them than the coconut-grove-lined beaches of Isla Margarita, Venezuela.

These bivalves, which call the roots of the red mangrove home, are much smaller than other oysters – typically measuring no more than 4cm across – so knocking back a couple of dozen briny, salty-sweet ones for lunch (raw, of course, with a dash of citrus – the purist's choice), mandatory frosty Polar beer in hand, is no problem at all. While you're lazing on the beach, you only need to corral a vendor: armed with just a small blunt knife, a bag full of limes, a jar of fiery cocktail sauce and a plastic bucket full of lagoon water and mangrove oysters, these traders dispense a little bit of paradise.

685 Communing with an Amazon shaman

PERU Psychedelic tourism isn't everyone's cup of tea, but there is nowhere on Earth where so many shaman serve such magical brews as they do in Peru. Since the start of this millennium, an increasing number of travellers have sought the magical ayahuasca experience, whether from simple curiosity or in search of ancient wisdom. These night-long shamanic healing rituals, with roots over 3500 years old, often involve the ingestion of psychotropic hallucinogens, and can produce a life-changing experience.

The San Pedro cactus, a mescaline-based plant common on the coast and in the mountains of Peru, brewed for hours, can produce very profound and extremely vivid out-of-body experiences. Seen as "sacred medicine" and a "teacher", San Pedro has been used for millennia by priests and shaman to provide solutions to everything from physical sickness to broken-down relationships.

The ayahuasca vine, found in the rainforest, tends to provide an even stronger trip, notably when mixed with leaves in "jungle juice". The typical setting for a session with an *ayahuasquero*, or jungle

shaman, is to meet him at a rainforest lodge, usually a *tambo* (hut) on the edge of an Amazon tributary. The session starts at dusk in a small room or roofed platform. Shortly after sunset, the shaman offers his brew after blowing and smudging large billows of thick, tangy Amazon tobacco smoke over himself, his participants and, most importantly, the ayahuasca container. After giving each guest a bitter, small gourd-full, the scene settles down and soon the shaman begins to rattle, chant or drum.

The effects can be challenging – the drug's purging qualities mean many people vomit, while the colourful visions may be spiritual, sexual or just plain terrifying – but most people, helped by the shaman's guiding songs and vision, make it beyond this to a healing and ecstatic session. Many experience strange conversations or see loved ones from the past or present. The good vibes and endorphin-related elation continues into the next day. Watching dawn over the forest canopy with a river alive with fish and brimming with exotic birdlife is a cool way to start the rest of your life.

686 Spend lazy days at Parque Tayrona

COLOMBIA You'll have to hike through thick jungle to reach Colombia's best beaches, tucked away in a paradisal national park on the Caribbean coast. Parque Tayrona, an hour by bus from the mellow port city of Santa Marta, is famed for its vast swathes of verdant forest, swaying palms and pristine beaches, and enjoys a legendary status among locals and travellers.

With secluded bays so impossibly pretty you feel as if you're on a film set, you won't begrudge the arduous trudge to reach them. After forty minutes' march and muddy scrambles over rocks under a woodland canopy, the moment you first stumble upon a stunning vista of glistening turquoise sea and white sand is unforgettable.

Arriving at Arrecifes, you'll find a wide and gorgeous stretch of sand and plenty of accommodation, from spartan *cabañas* to pricey "EcoHabs" with plasma-screen TVs. Most people camp or string up a hammock, the cheapest and most picturesque option.

It's worth walking on to the park's quietest spots – not least because rip tides at Arrecifes make swimming dangerous. Nearby La Piscina is a natural swimming pool of limpid water in a sheltered cove, and at El Cabo San Juan del Guía two coconut-laden palms lean over two perfect sandy bays, hinged on a wooden tower perched on a rocky outcrop. Beyond lies a long, semi-deserted nudist beach, where you can work on your all-over tan and cool off in the vigorous waves.

Your most arduous choices in Tayrona will be deciding which beach to lounge on and what time to crack open a beer. There's a ruined indigenous village at El Pueblito, a ninety-minute uphill hike from El Cabo, but most people are content to just swim, sunbathe and snooze in a hammock. Stay as long as you can and congratulate yourself on finding this relaxed, tropical idyll.

687 Exploring Quichua culture in Ecuador's volcanic highlands

ECUADOR You're at an altitude of 3900m, shivering in the cold as the sun rises behind you. Below, a saw-edge precipice encircles a still, emerald-green lake 3km in diameter. Lower still, fertile plateaus creased with deep, shadowed valleys are picked out by the golden dawn light and, beyond, snow-capped peaks fringe the horizon.

This is the dormant volcano of Quilotoa, high in the Andes' central highlands. In the late 1940s, its altitude, beauty and proximity to the equator led a young American here who believed himself to be a reincarnation of John the Baptist. He called himself Johnny Lovewisdom and stayed on the lake shore for a year, pursuing his belief that it's possible to live on rarefied air and sunlight alone.

There is an undeniable spirituality about this beautiful place, something partly fostered by the culture of the Quichua people, who lead a traditional farming life, and have dotted the landscape with tiny shrines. Their religion is Catholicism blended with indigenous beliefs: the Virgin Mary is identified with Pachamama, the female Earth deity

with whom a drop of any drink is shared by pouring it on the ground. A public bus is the best way of exploring the local area and culture on the Quilotoa Loop, a string of Quichua villages a half-day trip from Quito. If you can stomach the twists and turns as it hurtles along the bumpy hillside tracks, the views are much better from the roof. Anyway, when you're getting squashed between sacks of potatoes and crates of clucking chickens, it's probably more comfortable.

If you take a bus to the top of the pass, Quilotoa can be tackled as a challenging day-walk down to the villages in the valley below. The trail starts along the crater rim, winding between wild lupins and grasses, descends past farms and fields, plunges down a precipitous canyon and finally ends up by a handful of hostels in the village of Chugchilán. The walk's not particularly long, but it tells on the lungs, and the steep slopes are hard going. It's at this point that staying at the *Black Sheep Inn*, a beautiful ecolodge, pays dividends: it boasts a home-made, wood-fired sauna and a hot tub to ease your aching limbs.

688 Parrot-watching at the world's biggest macaw lick

PERU Crawling out of a mosquito-netted bed and into a canoe an hour before dawn isn't everyone's idea of a good time. But, in this verdant corner of the Amazon, it gives you the chance to reach one of nature's great sights – the spectacle of hundreds of exotic birds arriving at a remote island in the Tambopata river for breakfast.

This island, not far from the Bolivian border, is just yards away from the world's biggest macaw lick – a place where flocks of bright parrots come most days to eat clay and minerals which aid their digestion of otherwise inedible jungle fruits. Usually, at least one group of eco-tourists or birdwatchers can be found sitting quietly in a row of deck chairs, their binoculars, telescopes and cameras pointing towards the 30m-high river cliff well before the sun rises.

The jungle is quiet except for the constant drone of insects, the occasional bull frog call and water lapping along the river's edge. Then, the first flock will be heard, perhaps the high-pitched squawks

of a squadron of some sixty blue-headed parrots, flying and working together, patrolling the area around the cliff to make sure there is no danger from predators like spider monkeys. If the coast appears clear, other parrots start to gather. By the time day arrives, several pairs of scarlet or chestnut-fronted macaws will follow. Within an hour the entire cliff is studded with brilliant colour. The birds use their strong beaks to peck away at the soft cliff face, holding on fast with their strong feet. If the highly sensitive parrots become aware of their audience or any threat they fly off en masse, a swathe of rainbow in the deep blue sky.

By 8 or 9am, groups usually head back to the lodge, eager to get their own breakfast. And while the parrots may be the highlight of your trip, there's plenty more on offer. By day, you can see monkeys, sloths, wild boar and deer; after dark, guides take visitors on the river to look for caimans, flying fish and tarantulas.

Star-gazing
at Mamalluca

CHILE In the northern half of Chile, the driest place on Earth, clouds are virtually unknown and the skies are of the brightest blue. At night, far away from the lights of major settlements, you can look up at a dark vault simply shimmering with stars. The near-perfect visibility almost every night of the year makes the region ideal for observing the universe – indeed, there are more astronomical observatories here than anywhere else on Earth – but you don't need to be an astronomer to get a great view.

Some of the world's most powerful computerized telescopes sit here, among the plains and hills, but you can also catch sight of constellations such as the Southern Cross and familiar heavenly bodies like Jupiter or Mars at more modest observatories, such as Mamalluca. Set aside one evening, resist that extra *pisco sour* and book one of the regular stargazing tours that depart in the wee hours. These take you high up on Cerro Mamalluca, where the darkness is absolute and the air is crisp. There's the classic visit – a short talk giving you a grounding in basic astronomy, followed by a few minutes looking through a telescope – or the Andean Cosmovision tour, in which guides explain how the pre-Columbian peoples interpreted the night sky, and perform native songs, with flutes and drums accompanying mystic verses, speaking of a local cosmology dating back thousands of years.

690 Savouring ceviche in Lima

PERU Located on the edge of the barren Atacama Desert, Lima is among the driest cities on the planet, with miles of hot red rocks stretching inland beyond its limits. You'd be forgiven for assuming its residents eke out a scorched, *Road Warrior*-style existence, but, as descendants of the Inca, innovators of irrigation systems and aqueducts, Peruvians have made their capital surprisingly verdant.

Lima's foliage finds sanctuary in manicured parks, as should you: they're perfect venues for picnicking with old travelling friends or new *limeño* acquaintances. Savoury *anticuchos* and spicy *papas a la Huancaína* make a marvellous menu, but if you can pull together a few kitchen utensils and an ice-filled cooler, nothing completes the feast better than a freshly made *ceviche*.

Something like fish salad, *ceviche* is "cooked" in an acidic bath of lemon and lime juice and diced onion, tomato, coriander and *ají* pepper, leaving the fish soft, moist and cool. Peruvians are proud of their national dish, and its preparation is a familiar ritual. Though other countries have tried to claim it, *peruanos* know it's as unique to their heritage as Machu Picchu and the Nazca lines. They've even mythologized it: *leche de tigre*, the bracingly sour "tiger's milk" that remains after the fish has been devoured, is a potent aphrodisiac.

So find a shady spot – one with a picnic table is best – and don't forget the *choclo* (boiled, large-kernel corn cobs) and sweet yams, *ceviche*'s traditional accompaniments. Once the work's been divvied up and completed, sit back for a couple of hours while the fish marinates. Savour the afternoon light, the warm chatter of nearby families, perhaps a slight breeze off a man-made pond. Take an icy sip of a *pisco sour*, and try to remember those desert dunes you heard about, now so very far from this lush oasis.

691 Treasure, trinkets and trash in Neruda's casa

CHILE One morning Pablo Neruda looked out of the window and spotted a chunk of driftwood being tossed about in the Pacific Ocean. He walked down to the beach behind his home, Casa de Isla Negra, and waited patiently for the surf to carry it to the shore. This "present from the sea" was turned into the desk on which many of the poems that earned him the 1971 Nobel Prize were written.

The desk remains in the study of his wonderfully eccentric house, a few hours drive west of Santiago, which was turned into a museum after his death. While his other homes were ransacked by supporters of General Pinochet shortly after the military coup, Casa de Isla Negra survived largely unscathed. When soldiers arrived late at night to search the house, Neruda reputedly remarked: "Look around. There's only one thing of danger for you here – poetry."

Today, the house has the feel of a treasure trove. An inveterate hoarder, Neruda crammed the place with bric-a-brac, kitsch collectables and bits of junk that he had picked up on his travels – including coloured glasses, seashells, Hindu carvings, a full-size model horse, African masks and ships in bottles. The house perfectly sums up Neruda's tangle of contradictions, and offers as good an insight into the man as any of his poems. He was fascinated by the sea – Casa de Isla Negra was built to resemble a ship, with narrow hallways, porthole-like windows and low ceilings – but could not swim, and rarely ventured onto a real ship. Similarly, he loved to collect musical instruments, but was unable to play any of them.

On September 23, 1973, Neruda died of cancer, two weeks after the coup that claimed the life of his great friend, and the elected President of Chile, Salvador Allende. Alongside his poetry, Casa de Isla Negra survives as lasting tribute to a man considered Chile's, and arguably South America's, greatest poet. His most famous work, the melancholic and erotically-charged *Twenty Love Poems and a Song of Despair*, is the perfect accompaniment to a visit here, with a line from "Poem 20" particularly appropriate: "Love is so short, forgetting is so long."

692 Brave the devil's throat at Iguazú

ARGENTINA & BRAZIL Upon first seeing Iguazú Falls, all Eleanor Roosevelt could manage was "Poor Niagara". Every year, tens of thousands of visitors from around the world try to evaluate the sheer dimension of this natural miracle – a collection of more than two hundred cascades thundering over an 80m cliff – and usually fail. However you spell it – Iguazú, Iguaçu or Iguassu – the Guaraní name, translating as "Big Water", is something of an understatement. Situated on the border of Brazil, Argentina and Paraguay, the falls are surrounded by lush tropical forest that's home to more than 2000 species of flora, over 500 bird species and approximately 80 different mammals.

Many marvel at these massive falls from the relative dryness of the Brazilian side, but you are advised against looking down at them from a Brazilian helicopter for ecological reasons. Armchair travellers might watch these gushing waterfalls rival Robert De Niro and Jeremy Irons for the leading role in the 1986 epic film *The Mission*. But the true way to experience the rapids, or *cataratas* as the locals call them, is to land right in the action and get soaked to the skin. Leave your digital camera and your iPod in your hotel room; think twice before wearing that new crimson top that might run or the T-shirt that gets transparent when wet; don't even bother with the waterproof gear the guidebooks tell you to bring. Just give the boat crew the kick they never tire of: take a soothingly tepid bath in the world's biggest open-air shower, the ominously named Devil's Throat, the most majestic of Iguazú's many cascades.

693 Wine and horses at Estancia Colomé

ARGENTINA *Estancias* are Argentina's proud answer to *haciendas*: working ranches with prize land stretching to the horizon, a stable full of thoroughbred horses and a distinctly noble flavour. Recently, a number of *estancias* have allowed guests to share their comforts while enjoying a back-to-nature experience. One such, the luxurious *Colomé*, is unusual in that it's also a winery. Not just any winery, but one of the world's highest, more than 2300m above sea level. The first grapevines, planted by the conquistadors in the sixteenth century, flourished thanks to the region's cool nights, warm, sunny days, and just the right amount of rain. Argentina's last remaining Spanish aristocrats ran the place in the nineteenth century. And then, as the world entered the new millennium, an ecologically minded Swiss entrepreneur turned *Colomé* into a luxury resort.

Nine modern suites form a neo-colonial quadrangle around a galleried patio and a gently gurgling fountain. Most afford sweeping views across to the snowcapped Andes, best enjoyed from a private veranda that looks directly onto a garden of native plants. *Colomé* manages to be spacious yet cosy – when the outdoor temperature drops, under-floor heating allows you to pad around barefoot. In any case, if you so wish, the butler will come with his bellows and light a fire in your very own hearth.

To discover the wild surroundings at a leisurely pace, tie on some chaps, mount a *criollo* steed and let Ernesto, a taciturn horse-whisperer from Chile, lead the way. Rides take you along dried-up riverbeds past thorny scrub with magnificent sierras as a backdrop. Flocks of parrots screech overhead. Gaudy butterflies sip at cactus blooms. Back at the ranch, you can meditate in the Zen room, take a dip in the turquoise pool or admire the soothing works of avant-garde artist James Turrell. And, most important of all, lose yourself in a ruby glass of 2004 Colomé Malbec, while lounging in the *gaucho* bar. Then dinner is served...

694 Chasing condors in the Colca Canyon

PERU The rays of the morning sun begin to evaporate the mist that shrouds the depths of Peru's Colca Canyon. You've come out in the early hours to see the condor, or Andean vulture, in action, and as the mist dissipates, you can see hundreds of others have done the same. Many cluster at the mirador or Cruz del Condor. Others perch above pre-Inca terraces embedded into walls twice as deep as the Grand Canyon. Audacious visitors clamber to the rocks below to see the condor, but a short hike along the rim of the canyon allows for a viewpoint that is less precarious and just as private.

Wrapped up against the cold, you whisper excitedly and wait for the show to begin. Suddenly, a condor rises on the morning thermals, soaring like an acrobat – so close you think you could reach out and touch its giant charcoal wings. It scours the surroundings, swooping lower and then higher, then lower again, in a roller-coaster pursuit of food. Soon it is joined by another bird, and another, in a graceful airborne ballet.

Eventually, the birds abandon the audience in their hunt for sustenance, and the mirador becomes home to a less elusive species. Peruvian women, brightly dressed in multilayered skirts, squat on their haunches, hawking food, drinks and souvenirs – everything from woolly Andean hats to purses embroidered with the condor.

The panpipe sounds of "El Condor Pasa" are played so often in Peru that they become the theme tune for many trips. Simon and Garfunkel might have made the song famous with their cover version, but it's the eponymous bird that deserves a place in your Peruvian holiday.

695 On the trail of Butch Cassidy and the Sundance Kid

BOLIVIA No one really knows how Butch Cassidy and the Sundance Kid spent their final days. Rumours still abound, enhanced by the 1969 Hollywood classic starring Paul Newman and Robert Redford. But this much is true: the outlaws pulled their last heist, stealing the $90,000 payroll of a mine company, in Bolivia. To pick up their trail, start in the easy-going southern Altiplano town of Tupiza, set in a lush valley that slices through striking desert. It was in the leafy main square that the gunslingers devised their plan to overtake the payroll transport, and locals can show you where they lived – in a house just behind the mansion of the mining family they were to rob. From there, take a scenic jeep tour 100km northwest to the dusty village of San Vicente, where Butch and Sundance, the military hot on their heels, sought shelter. It is here, according to the prevailing belief, that the pair met their end inside a simple adobe home after a gunfight with a small military patrol. But will a close inspection of the hut and a visit to their unmarked grave in the cemetery be enough to convince you?

696 Seeking heat in the Chapada Diamantina

BRAZIL If it weren't for the *forró* band playing in its tiny plaza, Lençois, at the heart of Brazil's vast Parque Nacional da Chapada Diamantina, could be an outpost in the American Southwest. Then again, a cold *caipirinha* and a crispy chicken *picadinho* aren't so easily found in Arizona. The dry, rugged *sertão* of northeastern Brazil offers something unique: a Martian landscape of rifts and ridges, ideal for hiking or bouldering and dotted with modest but vibrant villages still scraping by since the days this area was mined for diamonds. Climb the 300m-high, vaguely camel-shaped mesa called Morro do Pai Inácio – named for a legendary lover who threw himself from its edge – or watch a stream make a similar plunge from the top of Cachoeira Glass, the country's tallest waterfall. When the sun reaches its apex, take cover in any of several grottoes that puncture the plain. Whatever you do, bring plenty of liquids, for the heat – like the otherworldly terrain – is mind-altering.

697 Summiting at sunrise on Volcán Cotopaxi

ECUADOR A shard of sunlight cracks open the horizon, spilling crimson into the sky and across the last icy crest, glittering like a crown of diamonds above you. Your exhausted legs can barely lift your snow-encrusted boots and the crampons that stubbornly grip the ice, but you're almost at the top. Gasping in the thin air, you haul yourself from the chilly shadow of night into the daylight. As the sun bursts across your face, a spectacular dawn spreads out before you.

The perfect cone of Volcán Cotopaxi, regarded by early explorer Alexander von Humboldt as "the most beautiful and regular of all the colossal peaks in the high Andes", at 5897m is one of the highest and most magnificent active volcanoes in the world. From the refuge at 4800m, tucked just below a girdle of ice and snow encircling the peak, it's around seven gruelling hours to the summit on a route that picks its way between gaping crevasses and fragile seracs, over ladders and up vertical ice. For some it's just as well that much of this steep climb is done unseen at night; hopefuls must rouse themselves from a fitful and breathless slumber at midnight to climb before the heat of the day makes the glacier unstable. The payback is arriving at the summit just as the sun rises, when you're treated to mind-blowing views of Cotopaxi's yawning crater, the giant peaks of the Andes in the distance, and through the clouds, glimpses of Quito sleeping far below.

698 Taking a ring-side seat at the Península Valdés

ARGENTINA "SHWOCK!" Or should that be "SHWAP!"? It's difficult to pin down precisely the slapping sound that emanates when six tonnes of blubbery wet flesh collides, but while I was still working out if it actually wasn't more of a "SHWACK!" than either, the two huge bull elephant seals thundered together again, sending gallons of sea water flying in their titanic battle.

The object of their affection, a fertile female with a twinkle in her coal-black eyes, had spent the last twenty minutes preening her coat to the height of seductive softness but was now far more concerned with keeping her month-old pup well clear of the thriving mass.

This is October on the Península Valdés, a scrubby blob of land clinging to the side of Argentina's Atlantic coast that, other than being the only continental breeding ground for southern elephant seals, also happens to be one of the world's most significant marine reserves. The strip of sand on which the seals try proving their prowess is also crammed with some of the area's 20,000-strong sealion population.

Along the coast, a colony of Magellanic penguins have pocked the rugged hillside with their burrows, coming ashore each afternoon to make their comical but arduous waddle up the hill and home, while up to half of the world's southern right whales frolic in the peninsula's sheltered waters.

At the shingle spits of Caleta Valdés, and around wild Punta Norte, further up the coast, the sight of ominous black dorsal fins cruising just offshore is the precursor for one of nature's most incredible sights: killer whales storming the shingle banks, beaching themselves at up to 50km/h in an attempt to snap up a baby sealion or young elephant seal.

Back at the beach, though, mother and pup are still dodging the fighting fatties. Behind them both – and both as impressed with her perfect pelt – two more gigantic males square up, clashing with such force that the sand shakes. And this time, there's no doubt that it's a "SHWACK!"...

699 The frenzy of Boi Bumba

BRAZIL One of South America's greatest parties, Boi Bumba is a riot of colour, dancing, pageantry and parades on Parintins Island, deep in the Amazonian jungle, and as remote as any major festival, even in Brazil, gets – it's a two-day boat journey from "nearby" Manaus. Surrounded by more than 1000km of rainforest on all sides, the isolated location is key to making the festival special. Whereas party-goers in Rio or Salvador gather for the parades and disperse anonymously into the city afterwards, in Parintins the sixty-thousand-plus crowd is contained by the Amazon itself – over the three-day frenzy, the festival becomes a private party of familiar faces and dancing bodies.

The origins of the event, which takes place every June, lie in the northeastern Bumba Meu Boi festival (it was introduced to Parintins by emigrants from the state of Maranhão), telling the story of Pai Francisco, his wife Mae Catarina and their theft of a prize bull from a wealthy landowner. But it tells it on a huge scale, in a purpose-built forty-thousand-seat stadium called the Bumbódromo. Here, two competing teams, Caprichoso and Garantido, parade a series of vast floats made up of giant statues and animal heads, some 30m tall. Serpents, jaguars, macaws and other rainforest creatures switch places like actors in a play, wheeled on by troupes dressed in Indian costumes and surrounded by one-hundred-strong drum orchestras and scores of scantily clad dancers. Against this spectacular backdrop, a whole host of characters tell the story, led by the beautiful feminine spirit of the rainforest, the Cunhã-Poranga, and an Indian shaman, both of whom emerge in a burst of fireworks from the mouth of a serpent or jaguar on the most extravagant and dramatic of the floats. Fans of each group are fiercely partisan and roar their encouragement from the stadium stands throughout.

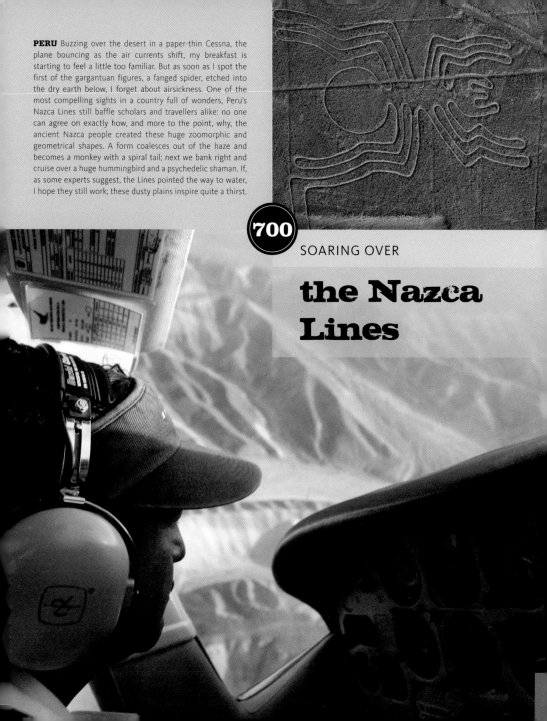

PERU Buzzing over the desert in a paper-thin Cessna, the plane bouncing as the air currents shift, my breakfast is starting to feel a little too familiar. But as soon as I spot the first of the gargantuan figures, a fanged spider, etched into the dry earth below, I forget about airsickness. One of the most compelling sights in a country full of wonders, Peru's Nazca Lines still baffle scholars and travellers alike: no one can agree on exactly how, and more to the point, why, the ancient Nazca people created these huge zoomorphic and geometrical shapes. A form coalesces out of the haze and becomes a monkey with a spiral tail; next we bank right and cruise over a huge hummingbird and a psychedelic shaman. If, as some experts suggest, the Lines pointed the way to water, I hope they still work; these dusty plains inspire quite a thirst.

700

SOARING OVER

the Nazca Lines

701 Celebrate Qoyllur Riti

PERU Most visitors to the ancient Inca capital of Cusco in southern Peru are drawn by the extraordinary ruined temples and palaces and the dramatic scenery of the high Andes. But the only true way to get to the heart of the indigenous Andean culture is to join a traditional *fiesta*. Nearly every town and village in the region engages in these raucous and chaotic celebrations, a window on a secret world that has survived centuries of oppression.

Of all the *fiestas*, the most extraordinary and spectacular is Qoyllur Riti, held at an extremely high altitude in a remote Andean valley to the south of Cusco. Here you can join tens of thousands of indigenous pilgrims, both Quechua and Aymara, as they trek up to a campsite at the foot of a glacier to celebrate the reappearance of the Pleiades constellation in the southern sky – a phenomenon that has long been used to predict when crops should be planted.

At the heart of the *fiesta* are young men dressed in ritual costumes of the Ukuku, a half-man, half-bear trickster hero from Andean mythology, and if you're hardy enough, you can join them as they climb even higher to spend the night singing, dancing and engaging in ritual combat on the glacier itself. Be warned, though, that this is an extreme celebration. Some years, pilgrims have died during the night, having frozen or fallen into crevasses, and when the pilgrim-celebrants descend from the mountain at first light, waving flags and toting blocks of ice on their backs, they bear the bodies, the blood sacrifice at once mourned and celebrated as vital to the success of the agricultural year ahead.

702 Peace and Pachamama in Tilcara

ARGENTINA High in the mountains close to the Bolivian border lies the enchanting Andean town of Tilcara, nestled in a narrow canyon of craggy rock striped in astonishing shades of crimson, violet, orange, green and pink. You don't need to be a geologist to appreciate this kaleidoscopic explosion of stone and sediment, and a sense of connectedness to the natural surroundings permeates this tranquil place, which combines comfort and tradition in fine style. Come here for a few days and you might find yourself staying for a blissful week.

At 2460m above sea level, the air in Tilcara feels pure and invigorating, and the fierce sunlight bouncing off whitewashed houses can dazzle. In the central market square, stalls are heaped with fluffy alpaca-wool sweaters to help you stay snug when the temperature plummets at night. Silver jewellery made by local artisans is inspired by pre-Columbian symbols, from cunning two-headed serpents to powerful condors in flight. Indeed, the city is located on an ancient Inca route and the community is proud of its indigenous traditions, celebrating Pachamama – the spirit of Earth – with a lively festival each August.

Intimate guesthouses fuse Andean design with modern comforts. You can sleep under heavy, antique blankets in welcoming *Rincon del Fuego* or stay in traditional stone and adobe *cabañas* at *Alas del Alma*, while at family-run *Uwa-Wasi* guests breakfast on home-made quince jam and fragrant *api* – a viscous purple corn drink flavoured with lemon and spices – beneath grape-laden vines in the garden.

Should relaxing in town not provide entertainment enough, it's a forty-minute bus ride to the small resort town of Purmamarca, where the views are staggering and the Hill of Seven Colours lives up to its rainbow name. Just outside Tilcara, the impressive ruined fortress of Pucará is populated by thorny, bulbous cacti – some an imposing five metres tall.

703 Meet the locals on the Amazon's backwaters

BRAZIL Of all the wonders of South America, none captures the imagination as much as the Amazon rainforest. Covering an area almost as large as the continental United States, and extending from Brazil into seven other countries, the Amazon basin is the most biologically diverse region on Earth, home to an astonishing variety of plant and animal life – rare birds and mammals, extraordinary insects and reptiles and millions of plant species – all woven together into a rich and complex natural tapestry.

Despite its immense size, the forest is disappearing at an alarming rate, and if you want to see the fabulous wildlife close up you need to head upstream by boat, taking either one of the many excursion boats or – better – a motorized dugout canoe. As you chug into the remote backwaters of the Amazon, every twist and turn offers the prospect of something to see: turtles or caiman crocodiles basking in the sun; pink river dolphins playing in the brown waters; flocks of brightly coloured macaws or toucans flying overhead; monkeys cavorting in the treetops on either side; perhaps even a giant anteater drinking along the riverbank.

For accommodation, you can camp out on the riverbank, with the nocturnal noise of the forest all around, or stay at one of a growing number of eco-lodges. Some of these are run by indigenous tribes, built in traditional style from natural materials harvested from the forest but with modern additions such as solar-powered lighting. Staying with indigenous hosts gives an insight into cultures that have developed over many centuries of living with the rainforest. You'll get a chance to sample traditional Amazonian food – minus the endangered animal species that are now hunted for photographs rather than food – and learn how people survive in a natural environment that to outsiders can seem extremely hostile. Best of all, you'll get to walk forest trails with an indigenous guide and tap in to their encyclopedic knowledge of the rainforest ecosystem. The guides may not know the scientific name of every species you encounter, but they can usually explain its behaviour, uses and place in local legend. In fact, many visitors find the lifestyle and culture of their Amazonian hosts as fascinating as any of the plants or animals they see in the rainforest.

704

Visiting the last **panama hat** weavers

ECUADOR Panama hats, as any Ecuadorian worth their salt will tell you, don't come from Panama. Authentic Panamas – or *sombreros de paja toquilla*, as they call them locally – are only woven in the Andean country, from the straw of the toquilla plant, which grows in the swamps near Ecuador's central coast. The origin of the misnomer comes from the hat's widespread use by the workers who built the Panama Canal from 1904 to 1914. Toquilla hats have been woven in Ecuador for at least five hundred years, but in the face of cheap Chinese competition, lower demand and the massive emigration of young Ecuadoreans, the traditionally woven Panama is now an endangered species.

It's well worth seeking out the last few artisans who create the very best *superfinos*. Most tourists on the trail go to Cuenca, a weaving centre in the southern highlands. A better option is to head west to Montecristi, which is to Panama-hat lovers what Havana is to cigar aficionados. It's no showroom: the dust-and-

concrete town is an inauspicious centre for the production of some of the most expensive headgear in the world. But ask around for a local *comisionista* (middlemen who travel around villages and buy hats from weavers) and arrange a trip to meet the weavers in nearby villages such as Pile.

The time to arrive is just after dawn, when the light is atmospheric and the heat and humidity are perfect for weaving. The contrast between the beautiful hats – the finest of which are woven so tightly they look like off-white cotton – and the conditions in which they are produced is stark. The weavers, who spend up to four months weaving each hat, live in ragged redbrick dwellings with rusting corrugated-iron roofs, linked by degraded dirt streets patrolled by strutting chickens and shuffling pigs. Be sure to visit the straw-cutters, too, and accompany them on a hike to see the plants growing. The more you see of the hats and the weavers, the better equipped you'll be to buy your own.

705

Exploring **Colonia del Sacramento** by *scooter*

URUGUAY Perched on a peninsula at the confluence of the Río Uruguay and Río del Plata, Colonia del Sacramento is perhaps the most picturesque town in all of Uruguay. One of the best ways to explore it is by scooter, zipping past the brightly coloured homes, tiny bars and craft stores that line the perfectly preserved maze of cobblestone streets in the Barrio Histórico. Cut through the lovely Plaza Mayor, where parakeets screech in the trees, and head for the town's lighthouse, El Faro, which sits next to the ruins of a former convent. Take a break from your scooter here, and ascend the top of this still-operating beacon to see a stunning panorama of the surrounding city and shoreline. Be sure to make it down before dusk, though, as you'll want to head to the sloping Calle de los Suspeiros (Street of Sighs) to watch the sun sink slowly into the silver water of the rivers – the street has some of the best views of sunset in the city.

706 Hear gaucho tales in the beastly Pantanal

BRAZIL Weary travellers twist in their hammocks as the sun rises; no one has slept much. All night long, the small campsite glade has resounded with the noise of snuffling, snorting and bashing through the undergrowth, broken only by a hideous high-pitched yelling and the sound of thrashing water. And then, the deafening squawking of the dawn chorus.

"The snuffling?" says one of the *gaucho*-cum-guides over *cafezinho* and toast. "That's the peccaries. It's normal." And the thrashing water? "Ah, you were lucky. That was an anaconda killing a cow in the stream over there." The stream we waded through last night on a so-called torchlit adventure? "Yes." And the birds? "Parrots – possibly. Parakeets. Or toucans. Storks. Roseate spoon-bills. Kingfishers. Snowy egrets. Red-crested cardinals . . ."

Some 650 species of bird inhabit the Pantanal, the world's largest freshwater wetland, alongside 3500 plant species, 250 types of fish, 110 kinds of mammal and 50 different reptiles. And when the waters of the Paraguay River recede in April, its grassy plains resemble nothing other than a vast, cageless zoo. Caimans, capybaras and giant otters wallow in the murky lagoons and rivers, jaguars and ocelots prowl the long grass, armadillos and anteaters forage for insects. And eight million cows graze.

The *gauchos* who roam the Pantanal on horseback comprise most of its human population, and make the most knowledgeable guides. They'll track down flocks of magnificent hyacinth macaws, roosting in trees and preening their violet feathers. They'll wrestle a crocodile out of the water for close-up viewing or point out the jabiru stork, as tall as a man, picking its way around the edge of a lily-choked pond. And in the evening they'll invite their visitors to sit round a blazing fire while they play accordions, pass round *yerba mate* tea and tell tales of life on the plains of the Pantanal.

707 Tapati: fun and games on Easter Island

CHILE Rapa Nui – Easter Island – is shrouded in mystery. How did its people get there? Where did they come from? How did they move those gigantic statues? Some of that enigma comes to life during January's fortnight-long Tapati, a festival that combines ancient customs, such as carving and canoeing, with modern sports, such as the triathlon and horse racing.

First, the islanders form two competing teams, representing the age-old clans, so if you want to participate, it's best to get to know one of the captains. The opening ceremony kicks off with Umu Tahu, a massive barbecue, followed by a parade of would-be carnival queens wearing traditional grass skirts.

Most of the sports events are for men only: one breathtaking highlight is the bareback horse race along Vaihu Beach. If you fancy your chances against the proud locals, be prepared to wear little more than a bandana, a skimpy sarong and copious body paint. Another event, staged in the majestic crater at Rano Raraku, has contestants – including the odd tourist – paddling across the lake in reed canoes, running round the muddy banks carrying two handfuls of bananas and finally swimming across, with huge crowds cheering them on.

Meanwhile, the womenfolk compete to weave the best basket, craft the most elegant shell necklace or produce the finest grass skirt; visitors are welcome to participate. Little girls and venerable matriarchs alike play leading roles in the after-dark singing and dancing contests. They croon and sway through the night until the judges declare the winning team, usually around daybreak.

But the true climax is Haka Pei, in which three-dozen foolhardy athletes slide down the steep slopes of Maunga Pu'i Hill – lying on banana trunks. Top speeds reach 80km/h, total chaos reigns and usually a limb or two is broken, but the crowds love it. Should they ask you to take part, learn two vital Rapa Nui words: "mauru uru", "no thanks".

708 Life on the quiet side: homestays on Lake Titicaca

PERU Set against a backdrop of desert mountains, the shimmering waters of Lake Titicaca have formed the heart of Peru's highland Altiplano civilizations since ancient times, nourishing the Pukara, Tiawanaku and Colla peoples, whose enigmatic ruins still dot the shoreline. More than seventy of Titicaca's scattered islands remain inhabited, among them the famous *islas flotantes*, floating islands created centuries ago from compacted reedbeds by the Uros Indians.

In recent decades, such attractions have made the lake one of Peru's top visitor destinations; as a consequence, only in the most remote corners can you still encounter traditional settlements that aren't overrun with camera-toting outsiders.

Yet merely by visiting such isolated places, aren't travellers running the risk of eroding the very ways of life they've come to see? Not in distant Anapia, a cluster of five tiny islets near the border with Bolivia, whose ethnic Aymara residents – descendants of the Altiplano's original inhabitants – make a living from subsistence agriculture and fishing, maintaining their own music, dance, costume and weaving traditions.

Fifteen Anapian families have got together to create their own homestay scheme. Each takes it in turn to host visitors, in the same way they've traditionally rotated grazing rights. Accommodation is simple, but clean and warm: you get your own room and bathroom but share meals with the host family on tables spread with brightly coloured homespun cloth. Potatoes are the main staple, and if you're lucky they'll be prepared *huatia*-style, baked in an earth oven with fresh fish and herbs from the lake shore.

Walking, fishing, sailing and rowing trips fill your time. Your hosts can also take you to the uninhabited island of Vipisque, where the Aymara rear vicuñas – small, cinnamon-coloured cousins of the alpaca, prized for their fine wool. From the hilltop at the island's centre, the view extends across Lake Titicaca to the icy peaks of Bolivia's Cordillera Real – one of South America's most magnificent panoramas.

709 Traversing the Salar de Uyuni

BOLIVIA Driving across the immaculate white expanse of the Salar de Uyuni, you'd think you were on another planet, so alien and inhospitable is the terrain. Some 3650m above sea level in the remote Andes of southwest Bolivia, the Salar is the largest salt flat in the world, a brilliantly white and perfectly flat desert that stretches over 10,000 square kilometres.

In some places the salt is over 120m deep, saturated with water, its thick surface crust patterned with strange polygons of raised salt crystals that add to the unearthly feel. When dry, the salt shines with such intensity you'll find yourself reaching down to check that it's not ice or snow. After a heavy rainfall, meanwhile, the Salar transforms into an immense mirror, reflecting the sky and the surrounding snowcapped peaks so pristinely that at times the horizon disappears and the mountains seem like islands floating in the sky. The best views are from Isla del Pescado, a rocky island at the centre of the Salar that's home to an extraordinary array of giant cactuses that somehow manage to thrive in this harsh saline environment.

To appreciate the sheer scale and surreal beauty of the landscape, it's worth taking the full four-day tour, travelling right across the Salar in a 4WD and sleeping in rudimentary huts and shelters on the shores of the lake; you can even stay in a hotel made entirely from salt. These trips also take in the Eduardo Abaroa Andean Fauna National Reserve, south of the Salar, a windswept region of high-altitude deserts, icebound volcanoes and mineral-stained lakes where you can see an unlikely variety of wildlife, including flocks of flamingoes and herds of vicuña, the delicate and rare wild relative of the llama.

710 Thermal springs and the devil's poncho: a Patagonian odyssey

CHILE The Carretera Austral – Chile's Southern Highway – begins nowhere and leads nowhere. Over 1000km in length, it was hewn and blasted through the wettest, greenest and narrowest part of the country. This sliver of Patagonia is a majestic land of snowcapped volcanoes, Ice Age glaciers, emerald fjords, turquoise lakes and jade-coloured rivers, set among lush temperate forest where giant trees seem to drip with rain the whole year long. The Carretera was built with the very purpose of settling this damp, secluded sliver of territory, but the only way to reach it from the rest of Chile is by boat or plane or overland from Argentina. Few roads can feel more remote.

Although some picturesquely rickety buses ply the route, they are irregular, unreliable and can't take you everywhere you'll want to go. It's far more rewarding to rent a 4WD pick-up truck, pack a can of fuel and plentiful supplies and drive yourself. The slippery, loose-gravel surface demands the utmost respect, so don't expect to average more than 50km/h. As the locals will tell you: hereabouts, if you hurry, you never arrive! Lashing rain, gales and passing vehicles – albeit few and far between – are the only likely hazards.

The pleasures, however, are many and varied: make pit stops to wallow in the thermal springs at Cahuelmó after the bone-rattling ride, enjoy the warm hospitality and delicious cakes at *Casa Ludwig* in Puyuhuapi, or feast on roast Patagonian lamb by the fireside at *El Reloj* in Coyhaique. Most of the route affords incredible views of the Andean cordillera, and along the way you'll see dense groves of southern beech and immense lakes like miniature seas, as well as the amazing "hanging glacier" in the Parque Nacional Queulat and the Capilla de Mármol, a magical grotto carved into the blue and white limestone cliffs looming from Lago Carrera. But the best bit is the feeling of driving through utterly virgin lands – especially the southernmost stretch that leads to pioneering Villa O'Higgins, completed only in 2002. The road seems to fly over the barren crags to the place where, according to local legend, the devil left his poncho.

711 Catching a launch at the Centre Spatial Guyanais

FRENCH GUIANA Completed in 1968, the Centre Spatial Guyanais (CSG) could form the backdrop to countless Bond films. Rocket launch towers, futuristic silos and other state-of-the-art technology poke out above the trees in the rainforest surrounding Kourou. Once a quiet, nondescript village in the French overseas *département* – and former penal colony – of Guyane (French Guiana), it was discovered that Kourou was the only place in the world where both polar and equatorial synchronous orbits could be achieved. Over the course of a few years, French Guiana was transformed from a Hell-on-Earth for France's hapless convicts (the penal colony was finally abolished in 1947) to the centre of the European Space Agency's satellite-launching operations.

Nowadays Kourou is bustling with technicians in jumpsuits scurrying about with clipboards in hand, and occasionally the French Foreign Legion patrols the perimeters, protecting the CSG from spies and other such threats. This isolated, surreal and, it must be said, slightly sinister space centre in the jungle outdoes anything that NASA's Florida-based Kennedy Space Center has to offer, at least as far as sci-fi-fantasy-meets-reality is concerned. *Ariane 5* rockets have been blasting off from the CSG since 1996, carrying payloads consisting mainly of satellites.

Launches take place in the early evening, just after the sun has set and the enigmatic, nocturnal sounds of the rainforest draw attention to the eerie coexistence of extreme technology and extreme nature. Hundreds, sometimes thousands, of people gather to watch the take-off. With an almighty roar, the rocket lifts into the sky, leaving a great plume of white smoke and a blinding sheet of fire in its wake that lights up the trees and warms the faces of the starry-eyed onlookers.

ARGENTINA When it first emerged in the city's brothels and slums sometime in the 1890s, the world's sexiest ballroom dance, the tango, horrified the genteel residents of Buenos Aires. Some of the city's more liberal-minded upper-class youths fell in love with tango, though, and brought it to Paris, where the dance's characteristic haunting melodies, seductive gazes and prostitute-inspired split skirts took the capital of passion by storm. By the 1910s tango's popularity had gone global, but Buenos Aires was and remains the spiritual and professional home of both the music form and dance.

If you want to keep a low profile, head to a tango show. Aimed squarely at tourists, these are glitzy, polished, expensive affairs where the dance is performed on stage by professionals. More earthy and authentic – and worth seeking out – are the *milongas*, or tango gatherings, where everyone takes part. These range from stately mid-afternoon affairs in the city's exquisite Art Deco tea salons to smoky, late-night events behind unmarked doors deep in the suburbs and youthful tango-meets-techno *milongas* in the city's trendy districts. Long-running *milongas* include the traditional Tango Ideal at the *Confitería Ideal* and the hip Parakultural events in Palermo.

For those who want to take part, some *milongas* are preceded by a tango lesson – you'll need several of these, and, if you're a woman, a killer pair of heels – before you can master the basics of the fairly complex dance. It's also perfectly acceptable to turn up, albeit smartly dressed, and simply enjoy the music while watching the dancers glide with apparent ease across the floor. Beware, though: the music and the locals may have you under their spell – and in their arms – faster than you may have anticipated.

Swept off your feet in Buenos Aires

712

>> South America

NAVIGATING
the narrow streets of
Cartagena

713

COLOMBIA The great riches that flowed through Cartagena during colonial times must have made the pirates and privateers that roamed the Caribbean salivate. Founded nearly five centuries ago as Cartagena de Indias – the Carthage of the Indies – this was one of the most strategically vital points in the Spanish empire. It was here that the galleon fleets would gather before making the perilous return journey to Spain, their holds laden with the gold and silver looted from the great civilizations of the Americas. Here, too, was the empire's main slave market, a clearing-house for the ill-fated Africans whose blood and sweat underwrote the entire colonial venture.

Though the Spanish have long since departed, Cartagena's colonial heritage is inescapable. The narrow, winding streets of the old walled city are still lined with grand mansions painted in the vibrant pastel hues of the Caribbean, with overhanging balconies draped in flowers and arched doorways that lead into cool courtyard gardens. Its nightclubs and rum shops pulsate with salsa, *cumbia* and reggaeton – African rhythms little changed from those brought over in the first slave ships. As you wander down these almost fantastical, decaying streets, it's easy to understand how this city inspired Colombia's greatest author, Gabriel García Márquez, to create his masterpieces of magical realism.

Stop for a coffee in the run-down artisans' neighbourhood of Getsemaní, or cool off with a freshly blended tropical fruit juice by the docks, and you could be rubbing shoulders with Marxist guerrillas plotting against the government, cocaine traffickers planning their next shipment, emerald smugglers cutting a deal or just a local hustler cooking up his latest scam. In the country of dreams, as the locals call it, anything is possible.

714 Going downhill in the Andes

ARGENTINA Skip the beach this year. Instead, embrace winter in July and get a tan on the sunny slopes of the Andes in the middle of Argentina's Lake District at Bariloche, a laconic town turned major South American skiing destination. Surrounded by spectacular forests, pristine rivers and lakes, rift valleys and towering alpine peaks, and with average seasonal temperatures around 4°C, it's no wonder that this is prime ski country for South Americans. Luckily, since the rest of the world hasn't quite caught on, you won't spend a fortune on rentals and lift tickets, or wait a lifetime in line.

Start by hitting the slopes at Cerro Catedral, the oldest, largest and most developed ski resort in South America, which features a vertical drop of 1070m and over 75km of marked trails, gullies and chutes – the longest run is 4km long – to say nothing of the off-piste possibilities, with back-country riding that can rival anything

in the French Alps or Colorado. Skiing is a lot less common in South America than elsewhere in the world, and mid-level skiers will find themselves in plenty of good company here. On the other hand, if you're a superstar on the snow, the more challenging pistes are much less crowded and yours for the shredding.

Unlike the massive resorts of US and European ski centres, Argentina's mountain destinations are decidedly more low-key in terms of their sprawl, though don't think for a moment that this means there is less going on. Argentines are well known for their indulgence in the refined institution of après-ski, and Bariloche's off-slope adventures include dozens of discos, casinos and wine bars, with ample restaurants for savouring Argentina's scrumptious cuisine. After all, what would a week (a month? an entire season?) on the slopes be without exploring the excellent winter nightlife?

715 Show no restraint in Rio

BRAZIL might not have a monopoly on exhibitionism, but it comes pretty damn close. There's no other country on the planet where the unbridled pursuit of pleasure is such a national obsession, transcending race, class and religion. Brazilian bacchanal reaches its apogee during Carnaval, when the entire country enters a collective state of alcohol-fuelled frenzy. Rio is home to the most glitzy and outrageous celebration of them all, an X-rated theatre of the absurd and the greatest spectacle of flesh, fetish and fantasy you are ever likely to see. For this four-day blowout before Lent the streets of the Cidade Maravilhosa are overrun with Amazonian-sized plumed headdresses, enormous floppy carrots, cavorting frogs, drag queens and head-to-toe gilded supermodels clad in impossibly tiny tassels, sequins and strategically applied body paint, challenging the ban on complete nudity.

The centrepiece of Carnaval is the parade of the sixteen samba schools (a neighbourhood association, there's nothing academic about it) down the kilometre-long parade strip of the colossal

Sambódromo (a specially constructed parade stadium). Samba schools often hail from the poorest communities and spend nearly the entire year preparing a flamboyant allegory of their chosen theme, which is dramatized through a highly choreographed display of impassioned songs, wild dances, gigantic papier-mâché figures, lavish costumes and pulsating percussion.

It doesn't take long for such organized celebrations to erupt with infectious delirium as the whole city voraciously indulges in sensual pleasure at every turn – Rio's denizens, also known as *cariocas*, have never been known for their temperance. The neighbourhood *blocos*, or parades, are the most accessible, authentic and impromptu way to immerse yourself in the city's sexually charged atmosphere. This is a freewheeling fantasy land in which trucks are converted to moving stage sets with bands and loudspeakers and anything goes. Even the most rigid of hips will gyrate freely, and as the night unravels, the more you'll have to try to forget in the *manhã*.

716 Enjoying isolation at the Termas de Puyuhuapi

CHILE It can take you days to reach the *Termas de Puyuhuapi* – but then getting there is all part of the fun. One of the most remote hideaways in the world, the luxurious lodge-cum-spa sits halfway down Chile's Carretera Austral, or "Southern Highway", a 1000km, mostly unpaved road that threads its way through a pristine wilderness of soaring mountains, Ice Age glaciers, turquoise fjords and lush temperate rainforest. The most exciting way to travel down it is to rent a 4WD – you'll rarely get above 30km/h, but with scenery like this, who cares?

Separated from the *carretera* by a shimmering fjord, the lodge is unreachable by land. Instead, a little motor launch will whisk you across in ten minutes. It's hard to imagine a more romantic way to arrive, especially during one of the frequent downpours that plague the region, when guests are met off the boat by dapper young porters carrying enormous white umbrellas.

The hotel is made up of a series of beautifully designed low-

lying buildings, constructed from local timber with lots of glass, that blend in handsomely with their surroundings. Having come quite so far to get here it would be a shame not to splash out on one of the eight shoreside rooms, with their mesmerizing views across the fjord. Inside, it's all understated luxury: flickering log fires, bare wooden floors, sofas to sink into, light streaming in from all directions.

You can take to the wilderness in a number of ways: go sea-kayaking (with dolphins, if you're lucky); learn to fly-fish in rivers packed with trout and salmon; take a hike through the rainforest to a nearby glacier. And afterwards soak your bones in the hotel's *raison d'être*, its steaming hot springs, channelled into three fabulous outdoor pools – two of them right on the edge of the fjord, the other (the hottest of all) enclosed by overhanging ferns. Lying here at night, gazing at the millions of stars above, you'd think that you were in heaven. And really, you'd be right.

ARGENTINA & BRAZIL Few sporting events rival the raucous spectacle of a football match in South America. From a small, local but enthusiastically supported game in the Andes to a clash of the titans in one of the great cathedrals of the sport in Brazil or Argentina, even those who can't tell a goal kick from a penalty kick won't fail to be impressed by the colour and passion – both on the pitch and in the stands.

Fans of the sport can look forward to fast, attacking football, individual star turns, lots of goals (especially in the Brazilian league; things tend to be tighter in Argentina), red cards aplenty and quite possibly a pitch invasion.

The bigger the team, the bigger the stadium, and the louder the roar of the crowd. Choose Rio's Maracanã, one the world's largest, São Paulo's Art Deco Pacaembú, or Buenos Aires's Bombonera ("chocolate box", for its shape) for a full-on assault of the senses – particularly if you time your visit for a local derby such as São Paulo v Corinthians or Boca Juniors v River Plate.

As well as their teams' jersey, fans will go armed with ticker tape, flags, flares, horns and drums. Don't be surprised if you can hardly see the players through the resulting clouds of red, blue or yellow. You certainly won't be able to miss the supporters' loud and decidedly colourful singing before, during and after the match, whether their team wins or loses, accompanied by entire brass bands and battalions of drummers. The frenetic, all-standing terraces (*popular* in Argentina, *geral* in Brazil) are the noisiest part of the stands, but first-time attendees are advised to head to the relative calm of the seating area (*platea* or *arquibancada* respectively). After a big game, follow the (winning) crowds to the boisterous after-match street parties.

watching a
football
match

717

718 Going to church in Chiloé

CHILE Never mind that just a thirty-minute ferry ride separates Isla Grande from mainland Chile. You sense it with your first step onto the principal island of the Chiloé archipelago: this is a land wholly unto its own. Though centuries-old legends of trolls and witches haunting its forests and secluded coves still linger, there's more to Chiloé's identity than mythical underpinnings. With its rural way of life and sleepy fishing villages of *palafitos* – wooden houses built on stilts above the sea – it's often regarded as a curiosity even among Chileans, but there's no better way to get to know Chiloé than by going to church.

Over 150 reverently maintained eighteenth- and nineteenth-century timber churches dot the islands, with the greatest concentration on Isla Grande. Start your journey in the north at Ancud, where the red- and orange-tiled Iglesia Pío X makes for an excellent introduction to the distinctive style – bold colours, arched porticoes and striking hexagonal bell towers – first created by Jesuit missionaries and the local indigenous population and later enhanced by Franciscan monks. As you make your way south, you'll pass delicate roadside shrines and quiet side roads that lead to solitary churches standing in an open field or presiding over breezy plazas. Though few of these aspire to the grandiose design of the yellow and eggshell blue of Iglesia San Francisco in Castro, the island's capital, they each shed light on the essence of Chiloé in their own way. The trick is to take your time exploring, and when you're done gazing upon the churches, be sure to turn around and take in what lies before them. Chances are it's the sea.

719 Birdwatch and be watched

SURINAME The strap of your binoculars chafes the back of your neck and the mosquitoes, constant companions in this nature reserve, form a pesky aura around your head. Yet you can't tear yourself away from what's locked in your sight: a flock of bright orange cocks-of-the-rock stripping a tree of Suriname cherries. A flurry of feathers to your left signals the arrival of a pair of sparrow-sized antbirds. They peer intently at your hiking boots, which are parked right in the marching path of their black, crawling prey. Leaving the little feasters to their work, you press deeper into the jungle until you're stopped dead by the piercing "whee-oo!" of an ornate hawk-eagle. With the discreetness of an Apache helicopter it lands on a branch and seizes you in its fierce glower – you must have ventured too near its nest. It's a funny thing they call birdwatching, when you're so often the one being watched.

720 Flying down to Rio

BRAZIL A tentative peek from the ramp reveals treetops far below and the beachfront high-rises of São Conrado in the distance. A safety briefing follows, and then, strapped side-by-side with your instructor, you charge down the ramp. After the initial surprise of realizing that you haven't plummeted to your death, you can start to enjoy the flight. Soaring past a sheer cliff face, feeling the wings flex as the sea breeze lifts you up, is an experience you will never forget. Then finally, cruising in over backyard swimming pools, you come in to land on the warm beach, which twenty minutes ago was about five kilometres away and half-a-kilometre below.

BRAZIL There's not meant to be any physical contact in this age-old, ritualistic melding of martial arts and breakdancing. Your instructor probably explained that, though unless you happen to speak Portuguese you probably didn't understand (and if you did, would you trust it to be true?). But you're ready to give it a whirl; who knows, you may even get to sing or play an instrument to help keep the beat – tambourine, drum, some kind of gourd with strung beads. Probably not the *berimbau*, a stringed bow struck while positioned against your stomach; that looks more difficult. In fact, it all looks difficult: how can the dancer-combatants fly and spin with such grace, spending as much time on their hands and airborne as on their feet? Maybe you should just passively observe, or head back to any number of street corners in Salvador, where *capoeiristas* cartwheel and kick encircled by onlookers. And save your own handstand prowess for another day.

Capoeira
up close

72.1

722 Tackling the Fitz Roy massif

ARGENTINA From the sandstone canyons of La Rioja to the granite peaks of Patagonia, Argentina's superb network of national parks form the backdrop to some of the continent's most diverse trekking. Most visitors, however, head south to the Andes, and the legendary Parque Nacional Los Glaciares, the northernmost section of which – the Fitz Roy massif – contains some of the most breathtakingly beautiful mountains on the planet.

At the centre of the massif, puncturing the wide Patagonian sky, is the 3405m incisor of Monte Fitz Roy, known to the native Tehuelche as El Chaltén, "The Mountain that Smokes", in reference to the whisps of cloud that almost continually drape from its summit. Alongside Fitz Roy rise Cerro Poincenot and Aguja Saint-Exupéry, whilst set back from them is the forbidding needle of Cerro Torre, a crooked finger standing in bold defiance of all the elements that the Hielo Continental Sur, the immense icecap that lurks behind the massif, can hurl at it. A series of excellent trails crisscross the massif, several of which can be combined into the Monte Fitz Roy/Cerro Torre Loop, a three-day jaunt done under the perpetual shadow of these imposing peaks.

723 Wake up and smell the coffee: the zona cafetera

COLOMBIA You've probably got an image of Colombia, even if you've been nowhere near it. More likely than not it's one of two things: that of shadowy, menacing drug cartels or of the proud, smiling face of coffee grower Juan Valdez. They're both a bit outdated, and the latter was in any case a fiction – a marketing tool used to promote Colombian coffee, which is the nation's biggest export, and second only to Brazilian coffee in worldwide production. However, you can get close to that homespun image of Colombia by going to stay at a coffee farm (*finca*) in the country's Tierra Paisa (also known as the *zona cafetera*, or Tierra Templada region). Plenty of these are still run by single families, looking for ways to supplement their modest incomes, and you'll spend much of your time learning about the history of the area and wandering around, perhaps on horseback, drinking in the atmosphere and mountain scenery.

724 Ice climbing in the Cordillera Real

BOLIVIA You're halfway up a sheer ice wall in the high Andes, with crampons on your feet, an ice axe in each hand and your stomach quavering somewhere around knee level, when you sense that there are some things humans were not meant to do. Yet if you don't mind the odd moment of panic, the Cordillera Real, strung across Bolivia between the barren Altiplano and the Amazon basin, is a wonderful place to begin mountaineering. For one thing, it's substantially cheaper than Europe or North America. More importantly, this harsh landscape, with its thin air, intimidating peaks and snow-covered ridges, is an unforgettable one, a world away from hectic La Paz and another planet from the one most of us live on.

725 Taking time over maté

URUGUAY The process is long, the preparation meticulous. The *matecito*, a wooden, hollowed-out gourd, is stuffed with yerba herb. A *bombilla*, a straw-shaped tube of silver, thrust into the leaves, then water – very hot but not boiling – trickled down its side, slowly, carefully, wetting the yerba from below.

"¿Como lo tomás?" the *cebador*, the *maté*-maker, asks you. "Amargo", you reply. Without sugar. The connoisseur's choice. You take a suck. Long and smooth. And bitter – a shock to first-timers, who are far better off taking it *dulce* (sweet). You pass it on, with your right hand, and clockwise, as tradition dictates.

A little more yerba, a little more water. The *matecito* is emptied, the process started afresh.

726 Fly fishing in Tierra del Fuego

ARGENTINA It may seem a long way to come to cast your line, but down in the toe of Argentina's boot the rivers run with gold. Well, with brown and rainbow.

The waters of the Río Grande boil with trout. Back, flick, cast, catch. Back, flick, cast, catch. It's like taking candy from a baby. And some fairly hefty candy at that, as the river is home to some of the most super-sized sea-running brown trout in the world, whose forays into the nutrient-rich ocean help them swell to weights in excess of 14kg.

Back, flick, cast, catch. The fly barely has time to settle on the surface before another monster gobbles it up and is triumphantly reeled up onto the bank.

727 The silent statues of San Agustin

COLOMBIA There's something at once romantic and rugged about riding, *gaucho*-style, past great rivers and waterfalls to ancient statues, your feet in iron stirrups. The locals in this mountainous region above the Río Magdalena in Colombia's Andean south claim the statues represent chiefs and shamans, as well as jaguars, eagles that communed with the sun and frogs that represented fertility. Some show grinning mothers presenting their newborn children to the gods for sacrifice.

The statue builders themselves remain shrouded in mystery. They disappeared in the fifteenth century, and are referred to as San Agustinas purely because all five hundred statues were found near the town of San Agustin. They were not patriarchal, selecting men and women as their chiefs and shamans, and carved wild-eyed figures holding containers of coca leaves and lime, suggesting intoxicants were used in search of esoteric knowledge. Yet no writings or buildings have yet been uncovered in this vast necropolis. The likelihood is that the Agustinas lived here for thousands of years before being carried off during an Inca invasion in search of slaves – and that they buried their sacred statues before they were captured. They lay there, silent and overgrown, for three hundred years, until Spanish missionaries arrived in the area and began uncovering the remnants of a long-dead civilization.

Over a hundred of the statues are found within an archeological park 2km above San Agustin. Most are less than 1.5m tall, caricatured figures with huge heads created by bold deep cuts into grey tufa. Often their teeth are filed into points and sometimes they support masks on heavy poles that reach down to the ground. We know that originally they would have been painted in red and yellow with white teeth and black eyes. The two statues accessible by horseback at La Pelota, a wooded hillside to the north of the archeological park, have traces of their original colour and stare angrily out at us. We can only guess at the lost world they represent.

728 Equatorial differences in Quito

ECUADOR If you find yourself in Quito, a visit to the equator is more or less obligatory – the middle of the Earth is only about a thirty-minute drive north from the Ecuadorean capital. As you get closer, the highland vegetation gives way to sandy plains punctuated by uninspiring brown hills. The "Mitad del Mundo" monument itself is even less exciting: a low-level metal-and-stone affair, it sits at the point determined by a French scientific expedition in 1736 to be latitude 0° 0' 0". The real treat here is to stand on the red-painted equator line, with one foot in each hemisphere. Doing so is more than just an unmissable photo opportunity: you can't help but be struck by a sense of reverence.

It all seems a bit unreal – and it may be: about 150m north, a short walk up the highway, is a rival museum, Inti Ñan, which claims that it sits on the location of the real equator line, a point well known to mystics from Ecuador's indigenous Quichua peoples since pre-Columbian times. There's no monument and everything has a very home-made feel, but you do get to interact with the magnetic forces at work here. A sink is produced, filled and then emptied of water to show you that instead of swirling, water at the equator runs straight down the plug. You can also balance an egg on a nail, since the forces of gravity are weaker. The passion of the guides involves more than the position of the equator line: Inti Ñan is about honouring traditional knowledge as much as scientific accuracy.

Ultimately, a visit to the equator would be incomplete if you didn't go to each of the museums, tipping your hat to the achievements of both early modern science and ancient heritage. Rather than transcendental cosmic awe, you're more likely to be somewhat comforted by the kitschy understatedness of it all, as if the Earth is having the last laugh.

Serra da Canastra

729

BRAZIL The mist has cleared and the wind is in your favour. You hold your ground – and your breath – as the outlandish animal ambles steadily closer. Her long nose breaks into view, parting the shivering grass heads. Now you can see her pickaxe front claws and the metre-long glory of her shaggy tail. And, best of all, her passenger: a myopic mini-me clinging tighter to mum's back with every bump in the trail.

At five metres – just as you're looking nervously to your guide – she stops. The wind has changed. Her outrageous hooter swings up, combing the breeze for your scent like some animated vacuum-cleaner nozzle. And then she's off, turning tail and harrumphing away down the hillside. You breathe again.

Among South America's menagerie of the weird and wonderful, few creatures come stranger than the giant anteater. And nowhere do you have a better chance of making its acquaintance than among the high, rolling grasslands of Serra da Canastra National Park.

Here, perched on a plateau in Minas Gerais Province, the beleaguered animals are safe from the hunters, traffic and loggers that have reduced their numbers across the continent and so more inclined to wander about in broad daylight. Just find an elevated spot and scan the slopes; sooner or later you'll spot that distinctive profile working a distant hillside. Every termite mound is scarred with their excavations.

It's not only anteaters that make Canastra special. This park marks the birthplace of the mighty Sào Francisco river, which gurgles up from a fern-choked hollow on the plateau to cross the grasslands and cascade off the escarpment into the forests below. Hike the river's upper reaches and you may meet a rare maned wolf – a fox on stilts, decked out with a horse's mane and tail – stalking elegantly through the long grass. Pick your way along the lower river and you might spy a party of Brazilian mergansers, one of the world's rarest ducks, bottle-green heads glinting as they bob and plunge among the rapids.

For now, though, you unwrap a sandwich and pull on another layer as the mist comes rolling back. Brazil is not all tropical rainforest and sun-kissed beaches. But that anteater might just be worth a little samba.

730

Braving the wind at Torres del Paine

CHILE You have to keep your head down. Despite the spray-laden wind, it's tempting to lift it above the rim of the boat and look ahead, so you can see the foam-capped waves racing past as the Zodiac inflatable roars upstream. Soon, in the distance, a towering peak of rock rises up. As you get closer you see shattering precipices and giant towers dusted with snow.

This is Torres del Paine, the citadel of Chile's epic south and one of the wildest national parks in the world. When the inboard of the Zodiac inflatable is finally switched off, all you can hear is the fury of the wind. The waves die down and the water reflects the massif in a pool as perfect as you could imagine, fringed by gnarled trees and blasted by bitter winds. Close by is a huge glacier, an offshoot of one of the largest ice fields in the world.

Then you set off walking, shifting the weight of your pack to get comfortable. There are other hikers around you, too – this isn't deserted wilderness by any means – but the largeness of the landscape can more than accommodate everyone. High up to the east, and overlooking the scrub and blasted forest, are the unnaturally sculpted Paine Towers themselves, and in front of you, dark-capped, are weird sculptures of the peaks of the Cuernos del Paine. If you're lucky you'll stumble across some guanacos, wild relations of the llama, or even a shy ñandú, the South American ostrich. But perhaps the best experience to be had here is simply to inhale the air, which is so crisp and thin that breathing is like drinking iced water.

731 The giants of Rapa Nui

CHILE An insignificant speck in the South Pacific, Easter Island, or Rapa Nui in Polynesian, is one of the most isolated islands in the world. South America lies 3600km to the east, and with the vast expanse of the Pacific never far from view, the sense of utter isolation can be unnerving. Yet despite its location, Easter Island is famous, thanks to its enigmatic *moai*, whose squat torsos and long, brooding heads loom sombrely over the island's coastline, their mysterious existence making them symbols of a lost civilization, fuel for crackpot Atlantis theories, evidence of alien intelligence or, more plausibly, proof of ecological disaster.

The *moai* might look familiar, but it's only when you visit the island that the overwhelming scale of their construction sinks in – it's littered with hundreds of them, most toppled over, face down in the tussock grass. The carvings, many 30m tall, have a majestic, serene quality that is certainly captivating, and it helps that many have been raised and restored, top knots and coral eyes included. They are thought to represent the ancestors of a Polynesian tribe that settled on the island some time before the eleventh century, and it's easy to see why their obsessive production intensified the drift towards catastrophe. No one knows why the carvers dropped their tools and abandoned their work so suddenly, or what caused this highly organized society to self-destruct, descending into anarchy, but by the time the first European ships arrived here in the eighteenth century, only a few impoverished villages remained. Today, the sleepy settlement of Hanga Roa exists only for tourists and virtually every morsel of food is imported on weekly flights from Chile.

So how did the Polynesians even find this place, never mind survive? The longer you stay, the more impossible it seems that people travelling thousands of kilometres in canoes could ever get here. By the time you leave, Easter Island's secrets will seem more unfathomable than ever, and those theories of alien intervention and lost Atlantis less cranky after all.

732 Honouring the Orixás in Salvador

BRAZIL Along the "Red Beach" of Salvador da Bahia, worshippers dressed in ethereal white robes gather around sand altars festooned with gardenias. Some may fall into trances, writhing on the beach, screaming so intensely you'd think they were being torn limb from limb. Perhaps in more familiar settings you'd be calling an ambulance, but this is Salvador, the epicentre of the syncretic, African-based religion known as *candomblé*, in which worshippers take part in *toques*, a ritual that involves becoming possessed by the spirit of their Orixá.

A composite of Portuguese Catholicism and African paganism, *candomblé* is most fervently practised in Salvador, but it defines the piquancy and raw sensuality of the Brazilian soul throughout the entire country. In this pagan religion, each person has an Orixá, or protector god, from birth. This Orixá personifies a natural force, such as fire or water, and is allied to an animal, colour, day of the week, food, music and dance. The ceremonies are performed on sacred ground called *terreiros* and typically feature animal sacrifices, hypnotic drumming, chanting and convulsing. Props and paraphernalia are themed accordingly; the house is decorated with the colour of the honorary Orixá, and usually the god's favourite African dish is served.

Ceremonies are specialized for each god, but no matter which Orixá you are celebrating, you can be sure that the experience will rank among the most bizarre of your life. If you attend a ritual for Ossaim, the Orixá of leaves, for example, chances are that you will be swept from head to foot in foliage. If pyrotechnics are your thing, better pay homage to Xango, god of fire, whose ceremony reaches a rather hazardous climax as bowls of fire are passed, head to head, among the participants. While animal sacrifice, one central aspect of the ceremony, may not be for the faint-hearted, music and feasting provide a more universally palatable denouement to the public "mass". After you enter the realm of *candomblé*, you may view Salàvador, and indeed Brazil, through an ethereal prism that challenges your accepted reason.

733 Getting high in Caracas

VENEZUELA After a day or two spent amidst the chaos of Caracas, you'll most likely be looking to escape from the city. But before you leave, don't miss the *teleférico* cable-car ride up El Avila mountain, one of the few places you can enjoy the Venezuelan capital's best offerings: beautiful Caribbean weather in a spectacular setting. The ride up is not for those with vertigo: it's an eighteen-minute journey, one of the longest such trips in the Americas, and it takes you hundreds of metres above breathtaking cloudforest scenery, where trees and plants vie for limited space. As soon as you get over the first ridge, the noise around you abruptly quietens. With every passing minute you journey further from the city's relentless mass of concrete and glass. Caracas shrinks below you, and nature gradually vanquishes the urban sprawl.

At the top, you emerge in a different world. Seen in its geo-graphical context, with a backdrop of tropical mountains, Caracas is deceptively attractive. On the other side, sharp slopes lead down to red-roofed cottages perched on the side of mountains and fields of flowers. Beyond them you can see the Caribbean Sea. The altitude makes the top sunny yet cool, and nature seems more vivid in comparison with the noisy capital. Birds are all around you, flying daringly close. Even the plants are different: highland varieties grow well here, 2100m above sea level. The attraction is not free from tat – there are several overpriced souvenir shops and, bizarrely, an ice rink – but it doesn't spoil the beauty of the place. Most locals head up here for sunset, choosing to spurn the view of twinkling hills opposite and snog furiously instead. A better option is late morning on a weekday, when El Avila is just beginning to heat up at the top and the path is blissfully deserted.

Slave dances,
a medusa Lucifer
and bow-tied gringos:

734

the Oruro Carnival

BOLIVIA It might not have the glamour of Rio, but the Andean outpost of Oruro can lay claim to the most outlandish carnival in all Latin America, a fiesta where the devil really is in the detail. This is a place where roots run deep, far below the city streets, where the pre-Columbian god of the underworld, Huari, holds jealous dominion over a mine-shaft labyrinth. When the week before Lent rolls around, Orureños bring that kingdom to life with an unparalleled eye for the satirical and the grotesque, lolloping through the crowds amid a cacophonous siren of Ben Hur-scale brass bands.

If the bulging, bloodshot eyes and slavering tongues of the *morenada* dancers – representing African slaves forced into lung-searing labour in the city's silver mines – affect a comic-book suffering, you can be sure the guy propping up the costume's incredible weight is suffering in turn, and will even have paid for the privilege. You can't take your eyes off the slow, hypnotic stomp of the choreography, but even this pales next to the *diablada*, the

showpiece showdown between Lucifer – a riot of demonic kitsch with antenna-like horns and medusa hairdo – and the Archangel Michael, accompanied by packed ranks of no-less-outrageous demons and libidinous she-devils.

Small wonder UNESCO has designated the spectacle a "Masterpiece of the Oral and Intangible Heritage of Humanity", but even that doesn't hint at the sheer scale of the thing: tens of thousands of dancers, crowds getting on for half a million and enough water-bombs to fill several reservoirs. Tourists are particularly juicy targets, yet while long-gone colonial overseers are wonderfully sent up in the bow ties and long noses of the *doctorcitos* parade, for a price and months of practice gringos can actually join in: you too can don a whip and a pair of jingle-jangle boots and high-step your way through the Afro-Bolivian *caporales* dance, or strut your stuff in a bouffant mini and jaunty bonnet. With a route of no less than four raucous kilometres, though, almost 4000m above sea level, be prepared to pant.

NEED to know

657 The High Chaco should not be attempted alone. @www.faunaparaguay.com offers expert-led eco-tours.

658 *Bodega Catena Zapata* is in Luján de Cuyo (@www.catenawines.com).

659 The Witches' Market is on Calle Linares. Ask for permission before taking photos and think twice before buying animal products – some are endangered species.

660 See @www.galapagospark.org.

661 The Plaza de Ponchos market in Otavalo is open every day, but is most impressive on Saturdays.

662 Fly with Amaszonas (@www.amaszonas.com) or take the 20hr bus from La Paz. Tour companies (try @www.indigenatour.com) operate from La Paz and Rurrenabaque. Avoid the flood-prone, insect-packed rainy reason (Nov–March).

663 Punta del Este's Laguna del Sauce airport is only 30min from Buenos Aires' Aeroparque Jorge Newbery. November and March are best for avoiding crowds.

664 The visitors' centre for the Paraguayan side of the dam is about 20km north of Ciudad del Este. Visits are by tour only (Mon–Fri 9.30am, 1.30pm & 3pm, Sat 9.30am).

665 The Argentine Open takes place in Palermo, Buenos Aires, in Nov/Dec. See @www.aapolo.com (Spanish only).

666 *Academia da Cachaça*, Rua Conde Bernadotte 26, Leblon, Rio de Janeiro (@www.academiadacachaca.com.br).

667 Ica is a 6hr bus ride from Lima; take a bus or taxi from Ica to Huacachina. Most of the local cafés rent sandboards.

668 Tours of the old Fray Bentos factory take place daily at 10am and 3pm – just turn up.

669 The Teatro Amazonas, which hosts an annual opera festival at the end of April, can be visited on a guided tour.

670 You can only hike the Inca Trail on a tour or with a licensed guide. In Cusco, try SAS (@www.sastravel.com) and United Mice (@www.unitedmice.com).

671 One-day bike trips are easy to arrange with operators in La Paz; the original and best is Gravity Assisted Mountain Biking (@www.gravitybolivia.com).

672 The nearest town to the glacier is El Calafate; the official website @www.elcalafate.gov.ar is a useful resource.

673 You can see the Valley of the Moon on a tour from San Pedro – there are lots of operators.

674 Boats to Isla del Sol depart every morning from the town of Copacabana.

675 Paraty is a bumpy 4hr bus ride from Rio. In town, stop by Paraty Tours (Av. Roberto Silveira 11, ⊕+55 24 3371 2651) or the official tourist bureau right next door. The comfortable local *pousadas* can usually help with recommendations.

676 Tours depart for the Ciudad Perdida from Taganga and Santa Marta – check out @www.sierratours-trekking.com.

677 Trucks to the Parque leave from outside the cathedral on Plaza 25 de Mayo, Sucre, several times a day.

678 *El Ombú* (@www.estanciaelombu.com); *Cabaña Las Lilas*, Av Alicia M de Justo 516.

679 Los Llanos is a 1hr flight from Caracas. The easiest time to find anacondas is the dry season (Nov–May).

680 Rafting trips can easily be arranged in Cusco. The rapids are Class III and suitable for beginners.

681 Sorata is served by buses from La Paz (4hr). In June–Aug, climbers arrive en masse and it's worth booking ahead.

682 Wilderness Explorers (@www.wilderness-explorers.com), in Georgetown, offers day-trips by plane. The falls are at their most dramatic in the wet season (April–Aug).

683 There are daily flights to Fernando de Noronha from Recife and Natal. See @www.pousadamaravilha.com.br.

684 The popular Playa El Agua and Playa Puerto Cruz, at the northern tip of Isla Margarita, are patrolled by vendors.

685 One-off sessions with a shaman are easy to arrange through lodges in Iquitos. Ayahuasca and San Pedro are legal in Peru, but both are strong hallucinogens and should be taken with a genuine shaman and treated with respect.

686 Officially a yellow fever vaccination is required to enter Parque Tayrona (@www.concesionesparquesnaturales.com).

687 The Quilotoa Loop is accessible by train (4hr) or bus (5hr) from Quito. See @www.blacksheepinn.com.

688 The Río Tambopata ($30 entry fee) is accessible from many of the lodges in the Puerto Maldonado region. Rainforest Expeditions (@www.perunature.com) have good facilities and guides in three eco-lodges.

689 The installations at Mamalluca (@www.mamalluca.org) are easily accessible from the city of Vicuña.

690 There are many ceviche-appropriate parks around Lima – Country Club el Bosque (Carretera Panamericana Sur Km 44.45) has picnic tables, tennis courts and a pool.

691 Casa de Isla Negra (Tues–Sun 10am–6pm) is 110km west of Santiago. For more, visit @www.neruda.cl.

692 The best close-up experience to be had is in the Parque Nacional, outside Puerto Iguazú (Argentina). The rainy summer season (Nov–March) is the best time to go. For more, consult @www.iguazuargentina.com.

693 *Colomé* (@www.estanciacolome.com) is in the far northwest corner of Argentina, 200km from the nearest airport at Salta. Arrange transport through Salta's Marina Turismo (@www.marina-semisa.com.ar).

694 Most Colca Canyon trips leave from Arequipa, approximately 5hr away.

695 Tupiza Tours, inside the *Hotel Mitru* (@www.tupiztours.com), can organize trips to San Vicente.

696 Lençóis is 6hr by bus from Salvador da Bahia. Once there, try Lentur (@www.lentur.com.br) for park day-trips.

697 Volcán Cotopaxi is in the Parque Nacional Cotopaxi, accessed from the Panamericana 41km south of Quito. Fully qualified guides are available through operators in Quito or Riobamba.

698 Elephant seals are at their most active Sept–Nov.

699 Boi Bumba takes place for three days every June. Visit @www.boibumba.com for more information.

700 Flights over the Lines are about US$60 for 45min.

701 Qoyllur Riti happens every year in early May. You can arrange transport to the start of the trek near the town of Ocongate with tour companies in Cusco.

702 Regular buses make the two-hour trip from San Salvador de Jujuy to Tilcara.

703 Trips are easy to arrange in towns like Manaus in Brazil, Iquitos in Peru or Rurrenabaque in Bolivia.

704 Montecristi is about 3hr by road from Guayaquil, Ecuador's biggest city.

705 "Moto Rent" shops are abundant in the Barrio Histórico; golf carts and bicycles are also available.

706 The Pantanal's dry season (April–Oct) is the best time to spot wildlife; a dozen lodges offer tours with *gaucho* guides, or try @www.ecoverdetours.com.br.

707 Tapati begins every year at the end of January. Lan Chile (@www.lan.com) makes the 5hr flight to Easter Island several times a week from Santiago.

708 Homestays on Anapia can be arranged at the jetty in Puno, a 2hr boat ride from the island, or as a package; try Insider Tours (@www.insider-tours.com).

709 Expeditions to the Salar by 4WD are easily arranged with local tour operators in Uyuni, 12hr from La Paz.

710 Jan and Feb are the best months to drive the route. *Casa Ludwig*, Av Otto Uebel, Puyuhuapi; *El Reloj*, Baquedano 828, Coyhaique.

711 Visit @www.cnes-csg.fr for launch dates. If you want to watch from the closest sites, request an invitation by writing to: CNES-Centre Spatial Guyanais, Service Communication, BP 726, 97387 Kourou Cedex.

712 Venues and times of *milongas* are constantly changing, so seek local advice; a good place to start is @www.tangobuenosaires.gov.ar.

713 It's much easier to fly to Cartagena than take the bus, as military roadblocks can cause lengthy delays.

714 Ski season lasts from late May until early October, with the peak season from mid-July to early August.

715 Carnival starts on the Friday before Ash Wednesday. Tickets for the Sambódromo can cost anywhere from US$200 for the bleachers to over US$1000 for a covered box.

716 *Termas de Puyuhuapi* (@www.patagonia-connection.com) offers transfers from Balmaceda airport.

717 The football year runs late July–early June, with a break in Dec and Jan, in both Brazil and Argentina. Tickets are available on match days, but buy ahead for the big games.

718 Ferries depart daily every 30min from Puerto Montt in the Lake District to Chacao at Isla Grande's northern tip.

719 Tours to the Central Suriname Nature Reserve can be organized through STINASU (@www.stinasu.sr).

720 For information on hang-gliding in Rio, email @justfly@alternex.com.br.

721 The Associacao de Capoeira Mestre Bimba, Rua das Laranjeiras 1, is Salvador's foremost dance school and sometimes has classes open to tourists.

722 The national park information centre is open daily 8am–8pm; ⊕+54 2962 493 004.

723 For stays on a coffee *finca*, see @www.ecoguias.com.

724 The Cordillera Real is a few hours' drive from La Paz – guides and equipment can be organized here or in Sorata.

725 Go to @noborders.net/mate for more about *maté*.

726 Fishing licences are available in Río Grande, from the Asociación de Pesca con Mosca at Montilla 1040 (⊕+54 2964 421 268).

727 The park is open Tues–Sun 8am–6pm. Arrive early to avoid school parties. Travel The Unknown (@www.traveltheunknown.com/tours) offer Colombian excursions.

728 A bus runs from Avenida América in Quito to Mitad del Mundo. For Inti Ñan, turn left from the Mitad del Mundo, walk uphill a few hundred metres and then follow signs left again.

729 Serra da Canastra National Park (@www.canastra.com.br) lies 8km from the town of Sao Roque de Minas and about five hours' drive from Belo Horizonte – the nearest airport. Access is best during the dry season (April–Oct).

730 Guided treks run to Torres del Paine from Puerto Natales, or you can travel to the park by bus or Zodiac.

731 Lan Chile (@www.lan.com) makes the 5hr flight to Easter Island several times a week from Santiago.

732 Visitors are admitted to *terreiros*, with "mass" usually beginning in the early evening. Trousers and long skirts should be worn, preferably white. For information on ceremonies in Salvador, contact the Federação Baiana de Culto Afro-Brasileiro, Rua Portas do Carmo 13 (⊕+55 3326 6969).

733 The *teleférico* in Caracas leaves from the intersection between avenidas Principal de Maripérez and Boyacá, a 15min taxi ride north from the centre.

734 March 4–8, 2011; Feb 17–21, 2012; Feb 8–12, 2013. If you want to join one of the troupes, the tourist office on Plaza 10 de Febrero (⊕+591 (0)2 525 0114) can put you in touch.

GOOD to know

EL DORADO

Despite centuries of exploration, legends persist of fabulous **cities of gold**, known as Paititi or El Dorado, hidden deep in the Amazon rainforest or the remote Andes. And substantial new ruins are still being discovered every few years. **Machu Picchu** is the most famous of these, but others include **Ciudad Perdida**, in Colombia, and **Vilcabamba**, **Kuelap**, **Choquequirau** and **Gran Pajaten**, all in Peru.

SOUTH AMERICA ON FILM

Blood of the Condor *(Yawar mallku)*, 1968. Scathing attack on the impact of US imperialism on the indigenous people of the Bolivian Andes.
Central Station, 1998. Heart-rending story of a Brazilian woman who abandons her cynicism to help a homeless boy search for the father he's never known.
City of God, 2002. Gripping portrayal of life and death among the teenage drug gangs in the slums of Rio de Janeiro.
The Motorcycle Diaries, 2004. Delightful adaptation of Che Guevara's diary, in which the future revolutionary and a friend travel across South America by motorbike in search of adventure.

"Those who serve a revolution plough the sea"

Simón Bolívar

CUISINE

With its mixture of European, African, Asian and indigenous influences, South America boasts some fantastic **food** alongside a fair dose of stodge. Don't miss Argentine beef, *ceviche* in Peru or *feijoada*, a classic Brazilian stew of black beans and meat. For the more adventurous, there's *cuy* (roast guinea pig) in Peru and Ecuador, and *hormiga culona* (big-butt queen ants with a nutty flavour) in northern Colombia.

FOOTBALL

It's often said that the unofficial religion of South America is **football** (*fútbol* in Spanish, *futebol* in Portuguese). Almost everywhere you go you'll find people watching, talking about and playing the sport. Practically every village has a football pitch, and it's not unusual to come across South Americans who are the proud owners of a pair of football boots but have no other shoes. Uruguay, Argentina and Brazil have produced a series of World Cup-winning teams, and the continent has also produced the two greatest footballers ever: Argentine Diego Maradona and Brazilian Edson Nascimento da Silva, better known as Pelé. Should Argentina's Lionel Messi continue his current trajectory, South America could have a mighty triumverate on its hands.

LIBERATORS

In most South American countries the wars of independence from Spain in the early nineteenth century are seen as national epics of sacrifice and heroism, and the leaders of that struggle are lionized as near-godlike figures. None is more revered than **Simón Bolívar**, known as "the Liberator", whose armies drove the Spanish out of Venezuela, Colombia, Ecuador, Peru and finally Bolivia, which was named in his honour. You'll find statues of Bolívar throughout South America, above all in his native Venezuela, where any disrespect to his image can still get you in serious trouble. Ernesto "Che" Guevara, who died in 1967 trying to start a continent-wide revolution, is accorded similar reverence.

COCA

Demonized in Europe and the United States as the raw material for the production of cocaine, the small green **coca leaf** has been used for thousands of years by the indigenous people of the Andes as both a mild stimulant and a key ingredient in traditional rituals and medicine. In Peru and Bolivia, where it's still legal, it's considered an important symbol of indigenous identity. When made into a herbal tea, it's also a useful treatment for altitude sickness.

LANGUAGE

South America is dominated by two main languages brought over by European conquerors in the sixteenth century: **Portuguese** in Brazil, and **Spanish** almost everywhere else. The exceptions are the small countries of Guyana, French Guyana (technically part of France) and Suriname, which are **English**, **French** and **Dutch**-speaking respectively. Throughout the continent, hundreds of indigenous languages are still spoken, some by only a few hundred people, others by nations of millions. These are particularly concentrated in the Andean regions of Peru, Bolivia and Ecuador, and in Paraguay, which has the highest level of bilingualism in the world.

"God is big, but the forest is bigger"

Brazilian proverb

HAMMOCK SIESTAS

The hammock, invented by the indigenous peoples of the Americas, is one of the greatest contributions to world civilization. Strung up anywhere there are trees, roof beams or upright poles, the hammock is both a perfect place to adjust to the local pace and a comfortable alternative to a bed.

FIVE GREAT READS

Of Love and Shadows *Isabel Allende* Powerful love story set in a country of arrests, disappearances and executions.
Dona Flor and Her Two Husbands *Jorge Armado* A potent supernatural romance plays out in the Brazilian state of Bahia.
Labyrinths *Jorge Luis Borges* Essays and short stories that encapsulate the unique approach of Argentina's greatest writer.
One Hundred Years of Solitude *Gabriel García Márquez* Epic tale of a Colombian family in love and at war – the definitive work of magic realism.
Conversation in the Cathedral *Mario Vargas Llos* Power, corruption and the search for identity in Peru.

CIRCUITING THE JOKHANG • BLOWN AWAY BY THE GREAT WALL • PAYING HOMAGE TO THE QUEEN OF HEAVEN • THE RITUAL OF A KAISEKI MEAL • UNSCROLLING THE LI RIVER • NAADAM: THE MANLY GAMES • CYCLING AROUND RURAL YANGSHUO • ROARING ON DRAGON-BOAT RACES • HILL TRIBES AND FINE TEAS: TREKKING THE BURMESE BORDER • BETTER THAN DISNEYLAND: THE GHIBLI MUSEUM • FACES FROM THE PAST: XI'AN'S TERRACOTTA ARMY • WALKING AMONG SILLA ROYALTY • CRACKING THE ICE FESTIVAL • A FLORAL WAVE OF CHERRY BLOSSOMS • GIVING THANKS WITH THE TSOU • MAKE MERRY AT SEOUL'S SWINGING NIGHT MARKETS • STEP AEROBICS: CLIMBING HUANG SHAN • EYEBALLING SOLDIERS IN THE "SCARIEST PLACE ON EARTH" • GETTING NAKED IN INAZAWA • UP CLOSE WITH PANDAS IN CHENGDU • CRUISING THE SINGING DUNES OF THE GOBI • VISITING HENAN'S MONA LISA • GETTING STEAMY IN A JJIMJILBANG • BATHING WITH SNOW MONKEYS • FILLING UP ON LITTLE EATS • VISIT THE BERLIN OF THE STEPPES • RELAXING IN TROPICAL TAKETOMI-JIMA • CRUISING THE THREE GORGES • WHITE NIGHTS ON THE WORLD'S EDGE • BUDDHIST BOOT CAMP AT HAEINSA TEMPLE • PAST MEETS PRESENT AT GION MATSURI • SKIING BESIDE VOLCANIC VENTS • CONQUERING THE PAMIRS • HANGING OUT IN SUPER-COOL SHINJUKU • TREKKING THROUGH TIGER LEAPING GORGE • HORSING ABOUT WITH THE MONGOLS • STEPPING BACK IN TIME IN RURAL YUNNAN • ACROBATICS AT THE ARIRANG MASS GYMNASTICS FESTIVAL • SWEET DREAMS JAPANESE-STYLE • SLURPING A TURKISH COFFEE IN YEREVAN • RIDING BY BUS TO DÊGÊ • SHARING ANCIENT ROADS WITH YAK HERDERS • STROLLING THE SHANGHAI BUND • SPACE-AGE TRAVEL: RIDING THE SHINKANSEN • HAVE A SAKE PARTY AT FUJI ROCK • SHOPPING AT THE MOTHER OF ALL MARKETS • GO FISHING WITH CORMORANTS IN THE FIRELIGHT • SVANETI - THE HIDDEN HEART OF THE CAUCASUS • VISIT THE REINDEER HERDERS OF SIBERIA • BEATEN AND BRUISED AT WUDANG SHAN • STARING INTO THE INFERNO • GETTING SOUSED AT SISTERS' MEAL FESTIVAL • TOURING TAMERLANE'S BLOODY CITY OF SAND • LOOK DOWN ON THE CITY OF THE FUTURE • EXPERIENCING THE NOMADIC LIFE • FEELING THE MAGIC OF CARPETS IN BAKU • ROLL UP YOUR SLEEVES AT A HAIRY CRAB BANQUET • SHOPPING FOR A NATIONAL TREASURE AT TOLKUCHKA MARKET • ADMIRING SUZHOU'S GARDENS • ON THE TEMPLE TRAIL IN SHIKOKU • JOUSTING FOR A TASTE OF BEIJING DUCK • LOSING TRACK OF TIME: BEIJING TO MOSCOW ON THE TRANS-SIBERIAN • SIPPING TEA IN THE LAND OF FIRE • PEAKING EARLY IN HONG KONG • TREKKING THROUGH THE VALLEY OF THE

Central & Northern Asia
735–803

Visiting the reindeer herders of Siberia **783**

RUSSIA

Visit the Berlin of the Steppes **760**

Horsing about with the Mongols **770**

KAZAKHSTAN

Sipping tea in the Land of Fire

UZBEKISTAN

AZERBAIJAN 797

Shopping for a national treasure at Tolkuchka Market

KYRGYZSTAN

792

Conquering the Pamirs **767**

MONGOLIA

NORTH KOREA

Getting steamy in a jjimjilbang

795

Jousting for a taste of Beijing duck

TURKMENISTAN

AFGHANISTAN

TAJIKISTAN

CHINA

757

Getting naked in Inazawa **753**

SOUTH KOREA

JAPAN

BHUTAN

737

Paying homage to the Queen of Heaven

TAIWAN

Circuiting the Jokhang

735

TIBET The Jokhang is the holiest temple in Tibetan Buddhism, and what it lacks in appearance – a very shabby facade compared with the nearby Potala Palace – it makes up in atmosphere. Located in the cobbled lanes of the Barkhor district, Lhasa's sole surviving traditional quarter, there's an excited air of reverence as you approach, with a continuous throng of Tibetan pilgrims circuiting the complex anticlockwise, spinning hand-held prayer wheels and sticking out their tongues at each other in greeting. A good many prostrate themselves at every step, their knees and hands protected from the accumulated battering by wooden pads, which set up irregular clacking noises. Most of the pilgrims are wild-haired Tibetan peasants reeking of yak butter and dressed in thick, shabby layers to protect against the cold; especially tough-looking are the Khampas from eastern Tibet, who almost always have one arm exposed to the shoulder, whatever the weather.

Devout they may be, but there's absolutely nothing precious about their actions, no air of hushed, respectful reverence – stand still for a second and you'll be knocked aside in the rush to get around. Inside, the various halls are lit by butter lamps, leaving much of the wooden halls rather gloomy and adding a spooky edge to the close-packed saintly statues clothed in multicoloured flags, brocade banners hanging from the ceiling, and especially gory murals of demons draped in skulls and peeling skin off sinners – a far less forgiving picture of Buddhism than the version practised elsewhere in China. The bustle is even more overwhelming here, the crowds increased by red-robed monks, busy topping up the lamps or tidying altars. Make sure you catch the Chapel of Jowo Sakyamuni at the rear of the complex, which sports a beautiful statue of the 12-year-old Buddha, and the Jokhang's flat roof, where you can look out over the rest of the city.

BLOWN AWAY by the Great Wall

CHINA The Great Wall is one of those sights that you've seen and heard so much about that you know reality is going to have a tough time living up to the hype. But having made it all the way to Beijing, it seems perverse to ignore this overblown landmark, so arm yourself with a thermos of tea and catch a bus north from the capital to Simatai, one of several sections of this 4800-kilometre-long structure which has been restored.

It's easy to find bad things to say about the Great Wall. The work of China's megalomaniac first emperor Qin Shi Huang, over a million forced labourers are said to have died building the original around 250 BC, and this seven-metre-high, seven-metre-thick barrier didn't even work. History is littered with "barbarian" invaders who proved sophisticated enough to fight or bribe their way around the wall's 25,000 watchtowers, most notably the Mongols in the thirteenth century, and the Manchus – who went on to become China's final dynasty – in 1644. Indeed, the Manchus were so unimpressed with the wall that they let the entire thing fall into ruin.

And yet, you'll be blown away. Not even swarms of hawkers and crowds of tourists can ruin the sight of this blue-grey ribbon snaking across the dusty, shattered hills into the hazy distance, beyond which one end finally runs into the sea, while the other simply stops in northwestern China's deserts. You can spend hours walking between battlements along the top – in places, following the contours of the hills up amazingly steep inclines – until restorations give way to rubble, and even then you can't quite believe that such a solid, organic part of the scenery is only an artefact, built by simple human endeavour. If ever proof were needed of Chinese determination, this is it.

737 Paying homage to the Queen of Heaven

TAIWAN First come the police cars and media vans, followed by flag-waving and drum-beating teams, along with musicians and performers dressed as legendary Chinese folk heroes, their faces painted red, black and blue, with fierce eyes and pointed teeth. Finally, carried by a special team of bearers, comes the ornate palanquin housing the sacred image of the Queen of Heaven. The whole thing looks as heavy as a small car: the men carrying the Queen are wet with perspiration, stripped down to T-shirts with towels wrapped around their necks. Ordinary pilgrims – people like us – follow up behind.

Every year, tens of thousands of people participate in a 300km, eight-day pilgrimage between revered temples in the centre of Taiwan, in a tradition that goes back hundreds of years. The procession honours one of the most popular Taoist deities, a sort of patron saint of the island: the Queen of Heaven, Tianhou, also known as Mazu or Goddess of the Sea. In true Taiwanese style, the pilgrimage is as much media circus as fervent religious experience, with the parade attracting ambitious politicians and even street gangs who in the past have ended up fighting over who "protects" the Goddess during the procession.

Becoming a pilgrim for the day provides an illuminating insight into Taiwanese culture – you'll make lots of friends, walk around 20km and eat like a horse. The streets are lined with locals paying respects and handing out free drinks and snacks, from peanuts to steaming meat buns. At lunch, you'll get a huge bowl of sumptuous noodles from a gargantuan, bubbling vat managed by a team of sprightly old ladies. As well as a constant cacophony of music and drums, great heaps of firecrackers are set off every few metres. Whole boxes seem to disintegrate into clouds of smoke and everyone goes deaf and is dusted with ashy debris. No one cares – the noise drives off ghosts and evil spirits, ensuring that the Queen can pass in spiritual safety, and in any case, it's all part of the fun.

738 The ritual of a kaiseki meal

JAPAN *Kaiseki-ryori*, Japanese haute-cuisine, was developed as an accompaniment to the tea ceremony; it has the same sense of ritual, meticulous attention to detail and exquisite artistry, all of which combine for a sublime sensory – if rather pricey – experience.

At a *kaiseki* restaurant the atmosphere is just as important as the food. Ideally, it will be in a traditional, wood-framed building. Kimono-clad waiting staff show you to a table set out on rice-straw tatami mats. A hanging scroll and a perfectly balanced flower arrangement, both chosen to reflect the season, enhance the air of cultural refinement. You look out on an immaculate Japanese garden with not a leaf or pebble out of place.

The food fits the occasion and setting. A full *kaiseki* meal usually consists of ten to twenty small dishes, perhaps featuring succulent slivers of raw fish with fiery wasabi relish, a few simmered vegetables, silky smooth tofu, delicious pickled items or tempura as light as air. Only the freshest ingredients are used to create a flawless array of seasonal delicacies designed to complement each other in every way – taste, aroma, texture and visual appeal.

No less care goes into selecting the serving dishes. Lacquerware, hand-painted ceramics, natural bamboo and rustic earthenware both offset their contents and present a harmonious whole. It's all exceedingly subtle and full of cultural references, but don't worry – anyone can appreciate the sheer craftsmanship and the hours of preparation that have created the feast before you.

It seems almost a crime to disturb the dramatic effect, but a *kaiseki* meal demands tasting. There isn't any particular order to diving in, just try to savour each delectable mouthful. The only firm rule is that rice and soup come last, as a filler – should you have any room to spare. And even in these august surroundings, it's perfectly acceptable to slurp your noodles.

739 Unscrolling the Li River

CHINA You know that Chinese scroll painting on the wall of your local takeaway, the one where a river with tiny boats winds between jutting, strangely shaped peaks, their tips blurred by clouds? Well, that could be a scene from along the Li River between Guilin city and the market town of Yangshuo in northern Guangxi province, an 80km-long stretch that has inspired painters and poets for at least the last thousand years.

Today it also inspires the tourist industry, but despite the river becoming increasingly clogged with armadas of cruise boats, the journey still allows a look at the timeless Chinese countryside.

As is often the case in China, however, those expecting a peaceful commune with nature will be disappointed. But get into the cheerful, noisy Chinese way of enjoying a day out, and it's great fun: loaded with food and drink, head up to the cruise boat's observation deck and watch while the scenery gradually reveals itself for your pleasure. At first it's all green paddy-fields and buffaloes wallowing in the shallows, then the peaks begin to spring up – isolated at first, and none of them much over 200 metres tall, but weathered into fantastic shapes. They all have names too, and legends: Waiting-for-Husband Hill, where a wife turned to stone waiting for her travelling husband to come home; you'll also drift past Fish-Tail Peak and the Penholder; then admire the rockface of Nine-Horses Fresco Hill. Tall bamboo screens the bank, source of the rafts which are poled fearlessly over the Li's shoals where cruise boats – flat-bottomed though they are – would founder. Cormorants sit on each raft, trained to retrieve fish for their owners; they get to eat every sixth one or stubbornly refuse to work. And then, around a bend, is Yangshuo and the trip ends; cameras are bagged and jaws are tightened at the sight of the many souvenir touts lined up along the pier.

740 Naadam: the Manly Games

MONGOLIA *Enin Gurvan Naadam* – Naadam, for short (literally, "Manly Games") – is one of the world's oldest and most spectacular annual events. After seeing it, you'll understand how the Mongols once conquered half the planet. Basically a sporting contest, the festival pits the nation's best athletes against each other in tests of skill in the "manly sports" of archery, horse racing and wrestling – the very talents with which Genghis Khan forged an empire. It's an experience you won't forget easily: you know you've done *Naadam* when you're squeezed into a nomad's tent, swilling Genghis Khan vodka with a pair of 300-pound wrestlers in their bikini briefs while a woman in traditional silk robes presents you with a platter full of sheep parts.

Held every July on Mongolia's vast grassy steppes, *Naadam* brings the country to a standstill. It's a time of rest as well as a celebration of sport and manly virtues. Life is hard on the steppes – herding livestock and moving encampments – and the festival offers Mongolians a chance to visit friends, discuss current events and enjoy life before the winter sets in.

741 Cycling around rural Yangshuo

CHINA For once, not being able to read the road signs or ask for directions in Chinese doesn't really matter, because in the lush rural landscape around Yangshuo you simply hop on your rented bicycle and follow the course of your chosen river. Stony tracks wind through the karst-spiked landscape along the Li and Yulong rivers, leading you into mud-brick villages and past sweet-scented orange and pomelo orchards and great stands of golden bamboo. You'll barely see a car the entire day, just cycles, carts and the occasional lumbering water-buffalo. Stop for a pot of invigorating ginger tea at a teashop jutting out over the water and then decide whether you've got the energy to cycle all the way home again; if not, simply haul your bike onto a bamboo raft and get ferried back downriver in relative style.

742 Roaring on dragon-boat races

CHINA Hong Kong's dragon-boat races commemorate the aquatic suicide of an upright regional governor, Qu Yuan, who jumped into a river in central China in 278 BC rather than live to see his home state invaded by a neighbouring province's army. Distraught locals raced to save him in their boats, but were too late; later on, they threw packets of sticky rice into the river as an offering to his ghost.

There are festivities all over China each year on the national holiday held to remember the uncompromising Qu Yuan, but the race in Hong Kong's Stanley Harbour is one of the best, with huge quantities of sticky rice consumed and some fierce competition between the dragon-boat teams, who speed their narrow vessels across the harbour to the steady boom of pacing drums. To soak up the best of the buzz, go down to the waterside with a cold beer and take in the festive atmosphere, though you'll need to get up early to catch the dedication ceremonies of the dragon-head prows. The celebrations carry on through the evening, with firecrackers and traditional dragon dances.

HILL TRIBES AND FINE TEAS:

trekking the Burmese border 743

CHINA It's not what you expect from China. Right at the country's southernmost edge, by the Burmese border, you'll find an amazing subtropical Southeast Asian landscape – rolling hills covered in virgin forest – and an astonishing set of cultures. This lush region is home to minority peoples, each with a culture, language and even building style so distinct that walking from one village to the next (the only way to get around) is like crossing into another country.

Bulang women wear black turbans decorated with shells, and the men sometimes have fierce facial tattoos; the shy, hill-dwelling Hani are polytheistic and the women sport spectacular coloured headdresses; the plains-dwelling Dai, close relatives to the Thai people, have a reputation for being cultured and easy going, though they are said to look down on other minorities as they have a written form to their language; and the animist Wa might have given up headhunting but maintain their reputation as crafty trackers.

Each group has a separate set of festivals, and if you're very lucky you'll get to see one – expect a colourful pageant and plenty to drink. It's rather easier to time your trip to coincide with one of the weekly markets held in the larger communities, when people come down from the hills, dressed in all their finery, to trade.

Walking in the forest between villages, prepare to be overwhelmed by a glut of visual detail, with brilliant colour provided by iridescent butterflies which fly tantalizingly just ahead, then close their wings as soon as you get your camera out. In areas under cultivation, you'll see a lush cubist terrain of rice terraces sliced into the hillsides, and plenty of tea plantations – this is the source of some of the country's finest teas, such as the half-fermented *pu'er cha*.

You meet Burmese jade-dealers, men hunting with homemade crossbows, teenage monks, and plenty of curious children. It's an absolutely fascinating region, singularly rich in culture and environment. Get there fast, before the forest is cut down for rubber, and the people fall prey to the pressures and enticements of modernity.

JAPAN Move over Mickey Mouse: in Japan it's a giant cuddly fur-ball called Totoro who commands national icon status. This adorable animated creature, star of *My Neighbour Totoro*, is among the pantheon of characters from the movies of celebrated director Miyazaki Hayao and his colleagues at Studio Ghibli – Japan's equivalent of Disney.

Just like Walt, Miyazaki had an ambitious vision that his movies could come alive in real life. The result – Ghibli Museum, Mitaka – is an opportunity to step into a world that, true to Miyazaki's words, "is full of interesting and beautiful things". On a far more intimate scale than Mickey's sprawling theme park across Tokyo Bay, this candy-coloured, stained-glass-decorated fantasy on the edge of western Tokyo's leafy Inokashira Park provides an unparalleled experience – a chance not only to learn about the art of animation but also to glimpse the genius of an Oscar-winning director.

You don't need to be familiar with Ghibli's movies, such as *Spirited Away*, *Howl's Moving Castle* and *Ponyo*, to enjoy the museum. Every little detail has been thought of – from the rivets on the giant robot soldier from *Castle in the Sky* on the roof to the straws, made of real straw, served with drinks in the *Straw Hat Café*. Amazingly detailed dioramas and Technicolor displays evoke the many steps needed to make an animated movie, and a child-sized movie theatre screens original short animated features, exclusive to the museum.

To make this charming experience even more special for visitors, only 2400 tickets are available daily, meaning everyone can move around the compact galleries comfortably – and kids won't feel crowded when romping around the giant cuddly cat bus, reading a book in the library or rummaging through the quirky gift shop.

BETTER THAN DISNEYLAND:

the Ghibli Museum

744

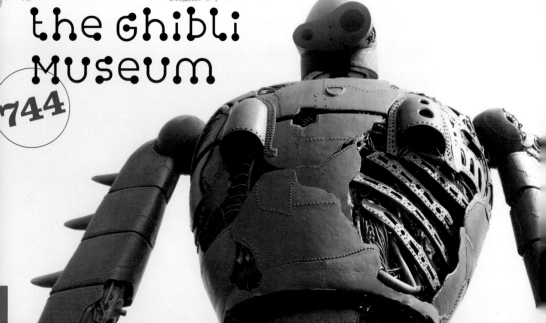

745 Faces from the past: Xi'an's Terracotta Army

CHINA Qin Shi Huang, China's first emperor, never did anything by halves. Not content with building the Great Wall, he spent his last years roaming the fringes of his empire, seeking a key to immortality. When (with inevitable irony) he died on his quest, his entourage returned to the capital near modern-day Xi'an and buried his corpse in a subterranean, city-sized mausoleum whose ceiling was studded with precious stones and where lakes and rivers were represented by mercury.

Or so wrote the historian Sima Qian a century after a popular uprising had overthrown Qin Shi Huang's grandson and established the Han dynasty in 206 BC. Nobody knows for sure how true the account is – the tomb remains unexcavated – but in 1974 peasants digging a well nearby found Qin Shi Huang's guardians in the afterlife: an army of over ten thousand life-sized terracotta troops arranged in battle formation, filling three huge rectangular vaults.

Make no mistake, the Terracotta Army is not like some giant schoolboy's collection of clay soldiers lined up in ranks under a protective modern hangar. The figures, twenty of which were displayed at London's British Museum in 2007 and 2008, are shockingly human; every one is different, from their facial features to their hands, hairstyles, postures and clothing. They are so individual that you can't help feel that these are real people, tragically fossilized by some natural disaster – more so in places where excavations are incomplete, leaving their half-buried busts gripped by the earth. Even their horses, tethered to the remains of wooden chariots, are so faithfully sculpted that the very breed has been established.

At the end, there's just one burning question: will they find a statue of Qin Shi Huang leading them all? A realistic statue over two thousand years old of China's first emperor – now that surely would be immortality.

746 Walking among Silla royalty

SOUTH KOREA In the centre of Gyeongju lies a gently undulating series of mysterious, grass-covered bumps. Though smaller and much softer to the eye, these mounds serve a similar purpose to the great Egyptian pyramids: tombs for great leaders from an ancient civilization, the impressive Silla dynasty, which ruled southeastern Korea for nearly a millennium, more than a millennium ago.

For some, the feeling of ancient power becomes quite palpable when walking through Tumuli Park, Gyeongju's district of burial mounds. Though close to the city centre, there's surprisingly little intrusion from the modern world – Gyeongju's more recent rulers chose to impose a cap on the height of buildings and encouraged the use of traditional roofing, all of which fosters a natural, relaxed feeling hard to come by in other Korean cities. As you walk around the park, you'll pass gentle green humps on your left and right – the

larger the bump, the more important the occupant. The largest is a double-humped mound belonging to a king and queen, and it's even possible to enter a slightly smaller one to see a cross-sectioned display of the surroundings of deceased Sillan nobility. These tombs have yielded wonderful treasures from the period, most notably an elaborate golden crown.

Gyeongju's pleasures do not start and finish with its tombs. Bulguksa, a temple dating from 528 AD and viewed by many as the most beautiful in the country, lies near to the east. It exudes vitality, and is surrounded by some staggering mountain scenery. Delving into the mountains on a meandering uphill path you'll eventually come across a grotto known as Seokguram. Here you'll see a stone Buddha that has long fixed his gaze over the East Sea – a perfect place to enjoy the sunset at day's end.

747 Cracking the Ice Festival

CHINA Getting out and about when the temperature dips to forty below may seem a little crazy, but that doesn't stop the thousands of visitors who every January don thick coats, hats and gloves and head to Harbin, capital of the wintery, northeastern province of Heilongjiang. That's when an army of builders from China, Russia, Europe, Asia and even Australia descend on the city, fire up their chainsaws, axes and chisels and kick off Harbin's month-long Winter Ice Festival by carving out all sorts of extraordinary sculptures in the city's parks from ice blocks cut from the Songhua River.

A surreal cityscape of cathedrals, pyramids, Thai palaces and Chinese temples rises in Zhaolin Park: most of the replicas are built to a reduced scale but are still so large you can wander through them, though some – including a section of the Great

Wall, which inevitably puts in an appearance – are life-sized. And as if a parkful of transparent, fairytale castles wasn't enough, at night everything is lit up splendidly in lurid colours by light bulbs embedded in the ice, drawing huge crowds despite the intense cold. Across the Songhua River, Sun Island is another park populated, this time, by snow sculptures. A few of these follow traditional Chinese themes (you'll usually find a giant Guanyin, the Buddhist incarnation of mercy), but most are more contemporary cartoon characters, overblown mythical creatures or fantastical inhabitants of the sculptor's mind. And then displayed among these are straightforward busts of famous celebrities, or just a life-sized sculpture of a horse, which – surrounded by such bizarre companions – are striking in their ordinariness.

748 A floral wave of cherry blossoms

JAPAN The arrival of the *sakura*, or cherry blossom, has long been a profound yet simple Japanese lesson about the nature of human existence. For centuries, poets have fired off reams of haiku comparing the brief but blazing lives of the flowers to those of our own – a tragically fragile beauty to be treasured and contemplated.

In Japan, spring sees the country gradually coated in a light pink shade, soft petals slowly clustering on their branches as if puffed through by some benevolent underground spirit. The *sakura-zensen*, or cherry blossom front, flushes like a floral wave that laps the country from south to north; this is followed ardently by the Japanese, who know that when the advancing flowers hit their locality, they'll only have a week or so to enjoy the annual gift to its fullest. This desire is most commonly expressed in the centuries-old form of countless *hanami* parties – the word literally means "flower viewing" in Japanese – which take place in the rosy shade of the *sakura-zensen* throughout the entire duration of its course. The

existential contemplation is often over in seconds, before the party's real *raison d'être*: consumption. Female members of the group are expected to provide the food, and then, of course, there's alcohol – *hanami* are often convenient ways for grievances to be aired in highly conservative Japan.

Hanami are typically friends-and-family affairs taking place in the most convenient location to the partygoers – often a park or river bank. Some of the most popular places are illuminated at night, and many are atmospherically decorated with red-and-white paper lanterns. Of course, the coming of the blossom can be enjoyed in any way you see fit; among the best places to go are Kiyomizu-tera, a gorgeous temple in Kyoto, Tokyo's Ueno Park or the castles in Osaka or Himeji, all of which are lent a dreamlike air by the arrival of the blossom each spring. A *hanami* party may even be possible in your own country – hunt down some sake, roll up some rice balls and become one with the nearest flowering cherry tree.

749 Giving thanks with the Tsou

TAIWAN Rarely visited by outsiders, the remote settlement of Dabang is hemmed in by jungle-smothered mountains that overflow with white plum blossoms in the spring. The village comes alive for the Mayasvi Festival, when red-robed members of the Tsou tribe gather outside the thatched village *kuba*, which looks a bit like a Polynesian longhouse, to slaughter a "mountain pig" – boar abound in these parts – and give thanks to the tribal gods. But this is not Fiji, Samoa or Tahiti. This is Taiwan, colonized by the Chinese in the seventeenth century but inhabited by Austronesian peoples for thousands of years.

More commonly known as aborigines or *yuanzhumin* ("original inhabitants") in Chinese, Taiwan's indigenous peoples represent just two percent of the island's 23 million people. The apparently small size of many tribes is deceiving – although the number of "pure" aboriginal people is small, many Taiwanese have aboriginal blood, often on the mother's side, but such ancestry is often covered up for fear of stigma.

The Alishan National Scenic Area in the heart of Taiwan was once

dominated by the Tsou tribe, and is today the best place to learn about them – it's still a wild, rugged area of crumbling ridges and dense forests, barely accessible by road. Yet with a bit of planning you can visit, staying at Tsou-run homestays, typically family homes, and eat sumptuous Tsou food. You can explore ancient mountain trails during the day, while at night villagers share stories over roasting pits.

Outsiders are welcome at the Mayasvi Festival, hosted annually in rotation by Tefuye and Dabang villages in February. Traditionally a celebration of warriors returning from battle, it still brings together the male members of the tribe for two days of singing, rites of passage and the blessing of newborn boys. They form a circle, and singing the old songs they give thanks to the God of War and the God of Heaven; finally a mountain boar is sacrificed in front of a spirit tree, each man dipping his spear into the pig's newly spilled blood. Later, the red cypress frame of the *kuba* and its hefty thatched roof are diligently repaired, and the feasting and drinking goes on long into the night.

750 Make merry at Seoul's swinging night markets

SOUTH KOREA You've heard the "city that never sleeps" cliché a million times, but as a description of Seoul, for once it holds true. Few cities are more genuinely open-all-hours than the South Korean capital – even on the coldest, quietest day of the year, you'll be able to throw back a beer, scoff raw fish, shop 'til you drop or give your favourite power ballad the karaoke treatment at any time, day or night. User-friendly? You betcha.

Nowhere is this nonstop consumerism more in evidence than Seoul's myriad night markets, of which Dongdaemun is the most popular by far. This is actually the name of a gorgeous oriental gate that once marked the city's eastern extremity; the gate remains, but has now been relegated to the status of ornamental traffic circle, and totally encircled by teeming markets of all forms. Within the space of a few hectic city blocks you'll find skyscraper shopping malls, underground clothing arcades, covered dining

streets, open-air fish markets and much, much more.

The focal point for most tourists is Gwangjang Market, which lies a few blocks to the west of Dongdaemun gate. Despite a near-total lack of English-language signage, most somehow find themselves in exactly the right spot, a covered crossroad-alley which ranks as one of the country's best places to eat, drink and be merry. You won't need any language skills to place an order – just look at the wild array of goods lined up in front of you, and point away. Among the items that may end up inside your stomach are *pajeon*, a kind of savoury pancake; *yuk-hoe*, strands of raw beef topped with sliced Korean pear; *sannakji bokkeum*, a dish made with still-moving baby octopi; and *makkeolli*, a creamy, refreshing rice wine, which makes a particularly useful bonding agent when you inevitably end up shooting the breeze with new-found friends.

CHINA The Chinese would say that "Where there is yin, there is yang"; Westerners would more prosaically opine "No gain without pain". At Huang Shan, Anhui province's Yellow Mountains, this means ravishing scenery tempered by steps, steps and more steps. All 15 kilometres of the path to the top of Huang Shan are cut into steps and paved in stone, which has been quarried, carried up here and laid by hand in an amazing human endeavour. It has also made the mountain accessible to generations of the country's greatest painters and poets, whose impressions have turned Huang Shan into a national icon of natural beauty, today attracting cartloads of tourists. The mountain's scenery of clouds, soaring granite monoliths and wind-contorted pine trees at first give the impression of a Chinese garden writ large. You soon realize, however, that the experience of visiting Huang Shan is what those gardens' designers

were trying to capture and fit into some rich patron's backyard, where it could be appreciated without the physical strain of eight hours of step aerobics.

In winter, when there are very few people, the mountain is overlaid with another layer of grandeur, but it's far easier to enjoy in spring or autumn – colourful times when nature is in compelling transition. The crowds are worse (though not as bad as they are during summer), but at least you can collectively share your pain while gasping ever upwards. The toughest moment of all is on finally reaching the "top", only to find there's no real summit, rather a plateau ringed in by little peaks which bring Huang Shan's height to within a whisker of 1900m. The finest sight here is watching the sun rise or set into a sea of clouds, alongside hundreds of other onlookers, all momentarily hushed by the incredible spectacle.

751.

STEP AEROBICS:
climbing Huang Shan

EYEBALLING SOLDIERS IN THE

752 "SCARIEST PLACE ON EARTH"

NORTH & SOUTH KOREA Your bus leaves central Seoul. The buildings soon start to decrease in size, before disappearing completely. Then, just ninety minutes from the capital, you see it – a barbed-wire fence that runs, in parallel to its spiky northern twin, from sea to sea across the Korean peninsula, separating South Korea from the hermit-like North, capitalism from communism, green from red. Between these jagged frontiers stretches a 4km-wide demilitarized zone (DMZ), across which the two countries aim undefined weapons at each other; bang in the middle of this is the village of Panmunjeom, where it's possible, under the escort of American infantry, to see now-nuclear North Korea at first-hand, and even take a few precious steps inside it.

This is the most heavily fortified border in the world, a fact that prompted a visiting Bill Clinton to describe it as "the scariest place on Earth". While he had the advantage of knowing the full scope and power of the surrounding weaponry, as well as what might happen should the fuses be lit, many visitors are surprised by the tranquillity of the place – there's birdsong among the barbed wire, and the DMZ is home to two small farming communities, one on each side of the Military Demarcation Line.

Your soldier-guide will take you by bus from Camp Bonifas – home to five thousand troops, and a single par-3 golf hole – to the DMZ itself, and before long you'll be in the Joint Security Area, where the two nation's soldiers stand almost eyeball-to-eyeball. Three small, sky-blue buildings here are shared by both sides, and by entering one and circumnavigating its central table you'll technically be able to straddle, walk across and take pictures of the border. The microphones on the table are left on, so whatever you say can be heard by the North Korean military; but there's no need to guard your words, as your guide himself will be a young pup, full of stories and propaganda – don't hesitate to ask questions. The scariest place on earth? Visit and see for yourself.

753 Getting naked in Inazawa

JAPAN Old men start to scream as the crush of naked flesh becomes so intense that steam is rising from the enormous crowd. It's only lunchtime and everyone's liver is saturated with sake. The chants of "*Washyoi! Washyoi*"! ("enhance yourself") rises to an ear-rupturing crescendo from the nine thousand men, all dressed in giant nappies, or *fundoshis*. Finally, just when it seems that the entire town of Inazawa is about to be ransacked by the baying mob, the Naked Man appears.

Dating back 1200 years, the Naked Man festival was originally a call to prayer, decreed by Emperor Shotoku in order to dispel a plague that was sweeping the region. The plan worked, so at a date determined by the lunar calendar each year (usually around February or March) men of all ages, though particularly those who are 25 and 42, which are considered *yakudoshi* or unlucky ages, gather in the narrow lane that leads up to the town's Shinto temple in order to touch the Naked Man and get rid of their own personal curses.

On the day of the festival, the volunteer Naked Man, minus even a *fundoshi*, must run through the crowd, all of whom are hoping to touch him in order to transfer all their bad fortune and calamity. The ordeal is terrifying. The crowds punch, kick, drag and crush anyone in sight in order to get near. The Naked Man himself disappears under the tidal wave of nakedness. It is only twenty minutes later that he emerges at the end of the temple lane: his hair ripped out, nose broken and with scars all over his body.

The spectacle is intense, frightening and utterly unique. Only a handful of Westerners have ever been brave enough to compete. It's strongly suggested that you watch from the sidelines – an exhilarating enough experience, and one that is more likely to leave you in full possession of your hair, teeth and sanity.

754 Up close with pandas in Chengdu

CHINA There's only one thing cuter than a giant panda: its cuddly, bumbling baby, the closest animal equivalent to a real live teddy. But these loveable black-and-white bears are one of the most reproductively challenged species on the planet, with exceptionally low birth rates. It's thought that there are fewer than two thousand of them left worldwide. The Giant Panda Breeding Research Base, just outside Chengdu in Sichuan, was established to preserve this cherished emblem of China, and has become a magnet for panda fans worldwide. It's extremely rare to see a cub in zoos, and it's virtually impossible to see any pandas at all in the wild – but come to the research base and you'll see plenty. And as over eighty cubs have been successfully bred here since 1987, you're almost guaranteed to see youngsters as well as adult bears. Most of the centre is covered in forest to replicate the mountain habitat of the bears, with naturalistic, spacious enclosures replete with trees and pools, and sleeping quarters designed to resemble caves.

There are no bars or railings here; instead, each enclosure is separated from the public pathways by a deep trench – come at feeding time and you can gaze unobstructed as mummy panda languidly chews her way through several heaps of bamboo shoots and leaves, slumped nonchalantly on the floor and occasionally throwing a bemused glance at her adoring admirers.

But there's no doubt who steals the show. Panda cubs come charging out of the compounds with surprising energy, romping over the grass and scrambling up the trees, invariably tumbling to the ground again and again as they make hilariously slapstick attempts to reach the top. While the adults like to lounge, babies love to play – and it simply doesn't get any cuter than this.

755 Cruising the singing dunes of the Gobi

MONGOLIA Climbing one of the world's largest sand dunes is hard work – every step towards the top involves a tiny slide back down – but reaching the crest is an extraordinary experience. The wind suddenly roars in your face and, 800m below, rows of tiny dunes stretch off to the horizon. It takes your breath away, so you duck back down, and lie in the calm of the crest of the dune. Sand trickles around you as it's blown from the top, and the mountain hums – a low, sonorous bass that reverberates inside your chest.

The massive Khongor sand dunes, also known as the "singing dunes", are about the deepest you're likely to reach in the Gobi Desert on a typical week-long round trip from Ulan Bator. This can be a punishing journey: the vast majority of the country is empty wilderness, and hurtling off-road at 65km/h in a Soviet-era van in the dusty heat can be trying on your patience and your backside.

The rewards, though, are breathtaking. The landscape that unfolds outside the dusty windows is extraordinarily varied. There are dusty plains of red gravel, dotted with camels and the rusting remains of unknown machinery; green, rolling grassland carpeted with herbs and coloured heathers; and outcrops of red rock in bizarre, wind-sculpted shapes. You'll pass the huge crimson canyons of the "flaming cliffs" of Bayanzag, and a long natural canyon, Yolin Am, that is so narrow and so deep that ice remains there even in the height of summer.

The daily routine of relentless driving between these major sites is broken into small moments that are equally memorable. Although the Gobi is a wilderness, you're never more than thirty minutes' drive away from a nomadic family's yurt, and you're likely to meet quite a few locals. The people here are friendly, and though English is rarely spoken, it's not a barrier to interaction: sitting around a fire under the vast starry sky, handing round enormous measures of vodka, brings a sense of togetherness that transcends the cultural gap.

756 Visiting Henan's Mona Lisa

CHINA The term "Buddhist cave art" sounds worthy and dull, conjuring an image of a bald, bearded recluse brightening up his lonely mountain retreat with some crude daubings. But though the medium here is sculpture, Chinese cave art is closer to the illuminated manuscripts of medieval Christian Europe: holy images depicted in a cartoon format which manage to be comic, exciting and – occasionally – even realistic, without losing the importance of an "inner message".

In China, the idea of carving rockfaces with religious scenes seems to have arrived with the Tobas, one of several regional dynasties who shared power between the break-up of the Han empire in 220 AD and the country's reunification four centuries later under the Tang. They imported Central Asian, Indian and Greek influences into Chinese art, while their Buddhist fervour and that of their Tang successors inspired an extraordinary trail of rock art sites stretching from northwestern Silk Road oases to the central Chinese heartlands, where the art form reached a peak at Longmen Caves.

There are over 100,000 figures chiselled into a honeycomb of grottoes at Longmen, a task that took even the industrious Chinese four hundred years to complete. Most of the spectacularly carved figures are life-sized or smaller, but the biggest and best is a seventeen-metre-high Buddhist trinity whose main figure's ears alone (at over two metres long) humble you into insignificance, while almost making you laugh at the proportions. But the Buddha's expression – of calm, powerful insight – is, like the Mona Lisa's smile, full of unselfconscious spirit.

757 Getting steamy in a jjimjilbang

SOUTH KOREA Although the word "sauna" may have certain connotations, the family-oriented Korean subspecies represents one of the most distinctive ways – and certainly the cheapest – to spend a night in the country, as almost all are open 24 hours a day.

Your *jjimjilbang* journey starts at the reception desk. After handing over some cash, you'll receive nightclothes and a locker key, then be directed to the single-sex changing areas; these are commonly accessed by lift and on separate floors, populated by Koreans in varying states of relaxation and undress. Your own clothing sacrificed and locked away, you're free to head to the pool area; here you'll find several pools and steam rooms, but it's incredibly bad form to jump into either without a preliminary shower – free soap is provided. After this, it's up to you: there are usually several pools, ranging from icy to skin-boiling, and some are even infused with giant tea-bags.

On exiting the pool area you'll find a towel and a free-to-use array of hairdryers, cotton buds and scents on the way back to your locker. Don the kindergarten-style T-shirt and shorts given to you earlier (often pink for women and baby blue for the gents) and head to the large, unisex common area; these usually contain televisions, internet terminals, water dispensers, massage rooms and snack bars. A cushioned mat will serve as your bed, and though you're free to sleep pretty much wherever you want – like cats, the Koreans can nod off anywhere, in any position – you'll usually be able to track down a sensible little corner, and can doze off with the knowledge that you've just enjoyed a quintessentially Korean experience.

758 Bathing with snow monkeys

JAPAN Should you choose to imagine a monkey, for whatever reason, it's likely to be surrounded in your mind's eye by tropical vines or thick jungle, trading screams with the parrots or chowing down a banana. Snowy peaks would not usually be on the agenda, but Japan is home to a particular breed of macaque that positively revels in the stuff. These clever monkeys share a number of common bonds with human beings – they're one of the only two animals known to wash their food before eating it, and no other primates live further north. Also, like their occasionally more intelligent two-legged cousins, many macaques counter the winter cold by hunting down a source of warmth; in Japan, you're never far from a hot spring, and one of the country's most magical winter sights is the view of a horde of apes silhouetted in the mist of an outdoor pool.

With a number of hot springs and other hydrothermal features – though most have been straddled by resorts and cut off from the outside world by a ticket booth – Japan offers its snow-loving macaques a place to escape the freezing temperatures. The winter coincides with the mating season, and it's hard to say what's more amusing – monkeys engaging in poolside trysts, or the Japanese pretending not to notice.

Tourists head to places such as Jigokudani in Yamanouchi to catch glimpses of the bathing apes, especially the loveable baby macaques. Given their schedules, the monkeys are usually the first to arrive, their faces standing out against the snow – pink Easter Island statues in balaclavas of fur. Bear in mind that though their eyes may appear dispassionate, it's unwise to look directly into them for too long, lest it be taken as a sign of aggression. In contrast, their postures can sometimes be eerily human as they plonk themselves into the water, slouched over the poolside in contented silence, and then perch on an outer stone to cool off.

TAIWAN Crowded alleyways, blaring scooter horns and a mix of Mandopop and Nokia tunes may not sound like an appealing night out, but there's a reason why Taiwan's night markets pack people in – some of the best food in Asia.

The Taiwanese love food so much, they've perfected what's known in Chinese as "little eats" (*xiaochi*), tasty snacks served in small portions – think Chinese takeaway meets tapas. The places most associated with *xiaochi* are night markets held all over the island; most get going in the evening and don't typically close till after midnight. Each stall has a speciality, a "little eat" it likes to promote as food fit for an emperor. But royal lineage is unimportant, as is language: just point, pay and devour.

At Shilin, Taipei's best and biggest night market, a typical evening starts with a few warm-up laps, perhaps grabbing a couple of appetizers along the way: a sugar-glazed strawberry, fried pancake with egg, or succulent Shilin sausage served with raw garlic and eaten with a cocktail stick. Suitably inspired, it's time for a little more chopstick work: many stalls own a cluster of plastic tables and chairs where you can slurp and munch while seated. Classic dishes include slippery oyster omelettes covered in luscious red sauce, and addictive *lu rou fan*, juicy stewed pork on rice. Still hungry? Try some celebrated regional specialities: *danzi mian* from Tainan (noodles with pork, egg and shrimp), or deep-fried meatballs from Changhua.

Serious connoisseurs – or more likely those with adventurous palates – can opt for the really scary stuff. Most infamous are *chou doufu*, cooked in pig fat and better known as stinky tofu, the smell of which sickens newcomers but the taste of which is sublime (the fried, crispy outer layer perfectly balances the fluffy tofu underneath), and *lu wei*, a savoury blend of animal guts, simmered in broth, and often eaten cold. Try this, washed down with a cold Taiwan beer, and you're certain to win the respect of the incredulous Taiwanese sitting next to you.

759 FILLING UP ON LITTLE EATS

KAZAKHSTAN Astana beggars belief. This new city, thrown up with a mix of determination and flair last seen when Peter the Great forged St Petersburg out of a Baltic swamp, is the second coldest capital in the world, after Ulan Bator in Mongolia. Why did newly independent Kazakhstan want to build its new capital on steppe-land where temperatures plummet to -40°C in winter? True, the old capital, Almaty, 1000km to the south, was prone to earthquakes and lacked space for expansion, but some suspect the real reason was to bring ethnic Kazakhs up to the north of the country so that its Russian-speaking population didn't form an enclave.

The city is the project of President Nursultan Nazarbayev, who has ruled Kazakhstan since the fall of the Soviet empire. A gilded imprint of his hand rests on the top of the Bayterek, a spiky space-age tower representing the poplar tree in which, according to legend, the magic Samuruk bird laid its egg. Visitors are encouraged to place their hand in his and make a wish, whereupon the Kazakh national anthem plays.

Yet this is only one of a number of statement buildings across this extraordinary city. Astana's planners have claimed they want to create a new Eurasian capital of culture rather than a purely administrative capital like Ottowa or Canberra.

Other recent buildings include a glowing glass Pyramid of Peace designed by Norman Foster, which is supposed to double as an underground opera house. Conspiracy theorists believe it is actually a piece of Masonic symbolism designed to herald a new world order. Others reckon it was constructed on its artificial hill so that President Nazarbayev has something to look at from his huge blue-domed marble palace. Foster is also building Khan Shatyry, a 50m-high "royal tent" that will enclose an entertainment complex, while the distinguished Japanese architect Kisho Noriaki Kurokawa was brought in to design the airport and much of the town planning. Money seems to be no object in Astana. As long as the petrodollars keep flowing in, this is a city that can genuinely say "Make it so."

761 Relaxing in tropical Taketomi-jima

JAPAN On tiny Taketomi-jima the traditional bungalow homes are ringed by rocky walls draped with hibiscus and bougainvillea. From the low-slung terracotta-tiled roofs glare *shiisa*, ferocious, bug-eyed lion figures. The only traffic is cyclists on rickety bikes negotiating the sandy lanes, and buffalo-drawn carts, hauling visitors to the beaches in search of minuscule star-shaped shells.

This is Japan – but not as you might know it. Taketomi-jima is one of the hundred-plus subtropical islands of Okinawa that trail, like scattered grains of rice, some 700km across the South China Sea. Cultural influences from China, Southeast Asia and the US, who occupied Okinawa until 1972 following WWII, have all seeped into the local way of life, providing a fascinating counterpoint to the conformity and fast-paced modernity of mainland Japan.

Fringed by soft, golden beaches, the islands are popular with Japanese looking for some R & R. Taketomi-jima especially is often besieged with daytrippers, as it's just a short ferry ride from the mountainous Ishigaki-jima, the main island of the Okinawan sub-collection known as the Yaeyamas. The trick is to stay on after the masses have left. Take up residence in one of the many family-run *minshuku* – small guesthouses with tatami mat floors, futons and rice-paper shoji screens. After a refreshing bath, slip into the *yukata* (cotton robe) provided and dig into a tasty dinner of local delicacies, and then wander down to the beach to watch the glorious sunset.

On returning to the *minshuku*, it's not unusual for a bottle or two of Okinawa's pungent rice liquor *awamori* to appear. Locals strum on a *sanshin* (three-stringed lute) and lead guests in a gentle sing-along of Okinawan folk favourites. As the *awamori* takes effect, don't be surprised if you also learn a few local dance moves.

762 Cruising the Three Gorges

CHINA There's something about China that's constantly cutting you down to size: the density of the crowds, the five thousand years of history, the complexity of the language, the awkwardness of chopsticks... But often it's the scenery alone, no more so than at Qutang Gorge, the first and most ferocious of the famous Three Gorges that together flank a 300-kilometre-long stretch of the Yangzi. "A thousand seas poured into one teacup" was how the poet Su Dongpo described this narrow, steep-sided canyon – though that was before the river had been domesticated by the dynamite and dams that have cleared hidden shoals, raised water levels and slowed the flow. Yet it's not to be scoffed at even today, and you won't find much excuse to hide in your cabin for the duration of the three-day cruise between Chongqing and Hubei provinces (not that a spartan four square metres of lumpy mattress and a blocked toilet costing the price of a three-star hotel room is any competition). The landscape demands to be admired. The best of it isn't on the Yangzi but the offshoot Daning River, through the Little Three Gorges – a cool stretch of lime-blue water with monkeys and prehistoric coffins hanging from perpendicular cliffs. But where to attach superlatives? The Wu Gorge, framed by mountains which drop sheer from their peaks to the water? Or Xiling Gorge, seventy-six kilometres of cliffs with names such as Ox Liver or Horse Lung? Or the final, man-made obstruction, the 1983-metre-long, 185-metre-high Three Gorges Dam – which, this being China, is naturally the largest in the world.

763 White nights on the world's edge

RUSSIA The inhabitants of Russia's far north have a hard time of it in the winter months, seeing just two hours' daylight in December, but the summer more than makes up for it, with sunlit days stretching into magical "white nights". St Petersburg's White Nights festival is an established tourist draw, but more adventurous travellers can head north towards the Arctic Circle and the remote Solovetsky Archipelago in the Karelia region. Situated on the White Sea, in the uppermost part of the world's biggest country, these islands seem close to the tipping-point of the world.

Whether you are walking along the sand beaches of the White Sea, dawdling by the shores of the hundreds of lakes dotting the islands, or taking a boat trip to spot white whales, the sense of space and timelessness is incredible. From the Middle Ages till the Bolsheviks seized power, monks sought out this place for solitary contemplation; when communism fell, they returned, and today the exquisite monastery on the main island, pure white with silver onion domes, is again a site of active worship.

But there were darker times in the interim. The Soviet authorities saw the potential of the islands' remote location, and in 1923 created a Camp of Special Significance, where political opponents could be subjected to the near-constant winter darkness, isolation and bitter cold. Solovetsky became, as the great dissident Alexander Solzhenitsyn put it, "the mother of the gulag".

Today, the camp is remembered in a museum inside the Kremlin on the main island. On top of Sekirnaya Gora ("Hatchet Mountain") you can also see the Church of the Ascension, which was used for solitary confinement – an incongruously picturesque spot a pleasant 12km walk from the monastery. But perhaps most striking is the prison dating from the late 1930s, today abandoned and neglected, where visitors can wander at will. The two-tone walls, door numbers and scrawled graffiti heave history out of the untouchable past and into vivid Technicolor.

However you spend your days on the Archipelago, one impression is liable to linger long after you've left: the otherworldly, eerie feel of days that last 22 hours and nights than never fully fall.

764 Buddhist boot camp at Haeinsa temple

SOUTH KOREA It's 2.30am on Sunday. Your head is spinning, and you feel like you might fall over, or even throw up. No, this is not another night out in one of Seoul's rowdy bars – it's an ordinary evening at Haeinsa, one of South Korea's most beautiful and famous Buddhist temples. Unlike other temples, where foreigners are introduced to "Buddhism lite", Haeinsa – meaning "Temple of Reflection on a Smooth Sea" – is not for the faint-hearted. It is a kind of Buddhist university, or rather Buddhist boot camp, for trainee monks and game foreigners.

On a typical weekend trip, you arrive on Saturday afternoon and immediately cast off your worldly attire – and all your worldly cares – in favour of baggy, unflattering grey monk pyjamas. Then it's straight into temple etiquette and meditation practice. No unnecessary talking, no unnecessary touching, no unnecessary thinking – just clear your mind and adhere to the rules. Bedtime is at 9pm. That's for a good reason, as you have to get up at 2.30 in the morning. After waking up and donning your grey outfit in a daze, it's out into the cold night for a monk's ritual.

First you head to the main dharma hall, where you're expected to perform 108 bowing moves, an effort that takes almost an hour. That's a lot of kneeling and standing in the middle of the night – not easy for unpractised backs and heads. Then, at 4am it's time to walk down a quiet mountain path to a marble meditation area. Here, you sit on the edge of what looks like it should be a pond, legs crossed. Clearing your mind is much easier in this environment. Staying awake is not. But luckily monks are on hand to prod slumping backs.

After what seems like hours spent in meditation, you head back to the dharma hall for a simple breakfast before watching the rising sun illuminate this beautiful temple. Your body may be battered and exhausted, but your soul definitely feels lighter.

765 Past meets present at Gion Matsuri

JAPAN It can be a weird place, at least to the uninitiated. Sometimes, Japan is the epitome of modern, urban life; at others, it's as if the country is stuck in the Middle Ages. Nowhere is this more evident, or perhaps more jarring, than in Kyoto, and there's no better time to be here than during the annual ten-day Gion Matsuri every July – a series of events dating back over a thousand years that culminates in a massive, full-on procession through the modern main streets of the old capital. Thousands of people of all ages line the route: youngsters in colourful summer kimonos, wobbling precariously on wooden sandals while they pose for pictures or chat on mobile phones, and tour buses full of middle-aged country folk, videocams out waiting to capture the moment when the floats – some of them two storeys high, and dragged by locals in loincloths – come by in a compelling drone of drums, bells, voices and flute.

766 Skiing beside volcanic vents

RUSSIA An average ski run in Kamchatka is not like that of your regular ski resort; it's not unusual to get in more than 10,000m of "vertical" in a single day. You're pumped full of adrenalin before you even start, thanks to the half hour ride to your first run in a huge, ramshackle Russian-built MI-8 helicopter.

Your guide will head down an enormous, open powder-field running 180m or more down the flanks of a volcano and you're then free to follow, with almost infinite space in which to lay down your own tracks. You may pass beside hissing volcanic vents (the most recent eruptions in Kamchatka occurred in 2010) or alongside glinting blue glaciers or just bliss out on endless turns in shin-deep fluff. You may even end up on a Pacific beach where you can take a frigid skinny dip.

And then you'll clamber back into the helicopter to do it all over again – and again, and again.

767 Conquering the Pamirs

TAJIKISTAN Standing at a skyscraping crossroads – the Himalaya, Karakorum, Hindu Kush and Tien Shan ranges meet here – the magnificent Pamirs remain one of the most unexplored places on the planet. Known as Bam-i-Dunya ("Roof of the World"), this vast, rugged stretch of Central Asia boasts astounding crested peaks and stretches of undulating fields. Visitors can camp with nomads and ride bareback across the steppe – and hike and climb a unique land.

While most of Tajikistan's hundred-odd mountains have never been scaled, you can climb Peak Lenin (recently renamed Ibn Sina Peak), at 7134m the third-highest mountain in the former Soviet Union. The peak is one of the world's easiest mountains over 7000m to climb due to its easy access and 16 relatively uncomplicated routes. As the classic ascent has few steep sections, ropes, harnesses and extensive high-altitude experience are not necessary – though several exposed ridges and a clutch of glaciated areas make winter mountaineering experience and use of an ice axe and crampons essential.

Although helicopters remain one option for reaching base camp, it's better to acclimatize yourself culturally by trekking from village to village in the lower altitudes. Here you'll encounter bands of Sunni Muslim shepherds tending families of sheep, goat and yak, and traditional families living unfathomably isolated existences (if any of them offer you the local delicacy of sheep lungs soaked in yak milk, say yes without any hesitation and swallow very quickly). Situated on a raised meadow of alpine flowers between two steep river valleys on the Tajik–Kyrgyz border, the lush green Edelweiss meadows of base camp lead to a heavily glaciated ascent towards several steep, exposed stretches of ridge that open south towards the Hindu Kush.

The climb to the summit traverses a range of terrain, including wide and steep snow-covered spurs and icy, crevassed slopes, while above, barren shards of rock shoot off sheer into the sky. The summit is crowned by a number of plaques, including one of Lenin himself, and offers unsurpassed views across the Pamirs, beyond which stretch China's Muztag Ata peak and the Karakoram range linking Pakistan to Ladakh in northern India and the Tibetan border.

Hanging out in
super-cool **Shinjuku**

768

JAPAN Shinjuku isn't for the faint-hearted. But if you're new to Tokyo and want a crash course in crazy, it's the first place you should come to. Sure, Asakusa has more history and Roppongi has better nightlife, but neither can compete when it comes to dealing out high-voltage culture shocks.

On the west side of Shinjuku station, which heaves with commuters and the smell of strong espressos, things are typically well-ordered. This shimmering business district is home to some of Japan's tallest skyscrapers (as well as more than 13,000 bureaucrats) and there are enough high-rise megastores to have you craning your neck in disbelief. It's a hardworking part of the city, where success is measured by the number of hours you spend at the office, and exploring it for the first time feels like stumbling through an ultra-efficient city of the future. But cross to the other side of the train tracks, and things couldn't be more different.

Here, chaos rules. Under the hot neon lights of Kabukichō, in the eastern part of Shinjuku, you'll find stand-up noodle bars snuggled next to strip joints and love hotels. Huge video screens pump noisy adverts into roadside bars, *Blade Runner*-style, and street hawkers skulk in the shadows by jazz clubs and theatres. To escape these guys, who'll try anything to get at your yen, head to an all-night karaoke bar where you can croon until your sake-soaked vocal chords feel like they're on fire. Or squeeze down the oddball alleyways of the Golden Gai district, which attracts artists, musicians and filmmakers with a ramshackle heap of more than 250 bars – each with its own unique theme. Chances are, you'll still end up singing the night away.

When the morning sunlight starts to extinguish Shinjuku's nocturnal glow, you can take a stroll through the cherry blossom trees of Shinjuku Gyoen – Tokyo's finest park – and give yourself a well-earned pat on the back. Consider yourself initiated.

769

Trekking through
Tiger Leaping Gorge

CHINA "A stony path winds up to cool hills", or so goes a Chinese poem. Well, it was never truer than where a youthful Yangzi channels violently through Tiger Leaping Gorge in Yunnan province, the stony path in question winding up to the foothills of an ash-grey, spiky range – though the peaks, at over 5000m high, spoil the comparison by actually being mountains. Of course, poetry also doesn't mention anything as mundane as what it's like to lug a backpack around for three days at this altitude: rather tiring. Nor does it explain the 100-metre-wide gorge's dramatic name: "A tiger was being chased, and it leaped across the river to escape" is the villagers' well-rehearsed answer.

Altitude and names aside though, trekking through the gorge is fantastic. The Chinese don't usually have a romantic view of nature; rather they see the Great Outdoors as being frighteningly empty, unless livened up by tour groups, cable cars, stone staircases, strategically placed pavilions, souvenir hawkers and noodle stands. But here there is nothing – just the mountains, the path, the gorge and a huge, blue sky. Occasionally you'll see a farmer or some goats; every few hours' walking throws up a couple of houses. You sleep along the way at small villages, and can sit outside under a gloriously luminous Milky Way while an unlikely number of satellites race in straight lines across the night.

Horsing about
WITH THE MONGOLS

MONGOLIA For Mongols, life has always been portable – homes, families and livelihoods are all carried on horseback. There's no better conveyance for this rolling grassy terrain than their well-trained steeds, and certainly no other way to immerse yourself in this last great nomadic culture. To enlist in this itinerant life you'll saddle up for the grassy steppe of the Darhat Valley, where horsemen and herders find prime summer pastures.

From an encampment on the shores of Lake Khovsgol, a day's horse trek across the Jigleg Pass leads through forests of Siberian larch trees laced with magenta fireweed before descending into the Darhat Valley – but this is just the beginning. Throughout your days on horseback you will come upon isolated encampments dotting the grassy expanse, each with several gers, the traditional lattice-framed, felt-covered home of nomadic herders. Mongols are quick to invite you inside where you'll witness their shamanistic rituals

as they call for rain or predict the future from the shoulder bone of a sheep. As you sit on the felt-lined ger floor, they'll reach for a leather bag and pour you a bowl of *airag*, a fermented horse-milk beverage – think fizzy sour milk with a kick. It's an acquired taste, but it quenches thirst and a swig will help wash down that morsel of roasted marmot you've been gnawing. Evenings will be spent in comfortable ger camps and in tents with all the accoutrements of catered camping.

As you approach the southern skirt of the valley you can expect to encounter the Tsaatan, a tribe that both rides and herds reindeer. The Darhat Valley is their favoured home for summer grazing before they retreat to the more protective forest highlands in the winter.

With fresh horses, you'll leave the Darhat through mountainous birch woods, bringing you back to Lake Khovsgol – the conclusion of your passage into a vanishing, but still vigorous, way of life.

771 Stepping back in time in rural Yunnan

CHINA In Xishuangbanna, in the far south of Yunnan province, the earth is a rich, rust red and the foliage an intense, glowing green. This area of China, just a few kilometres from the Burmese border, is about as rural as you can get, and a far cry from the hurly-burly of the urban boom. Here, there is no machinery and no roads, and the people tend their crops with rudimentary tools, just as they have for centuries.

I was trekking through this overgrowth with my guide. We were heading for a village inhabited by the Hani tribe, whose ancestors migrated south from the Tibetan plateau thousands of years ago. Every couple of hours we came upon a different village tucked away in a clearing between the trees: first an Akha settlement, then one belonging to the Bulang tribe. Near the Hani village, we found a white waterfall tumbling into a clear, icy pool that we jumped into to wash off the coating of red dust acquired on our long humid hike.

Later in the evening, we met our hosts at the Hani village. The houses here are topped with decorative horns. The story goes that more than two thousand years ago, during the Warring States period, a general helped the Hani people and they've honoured him ever since by decorating their houses with the horns from his helmet. The eldest son of the family in whose hut we were staying was out helping a neighbour build his home. There are customs to observe: no modern tools are used and the house's construction is measured out precisely into nine days. On the evening of the ninth day, the new homeowner threw a party to thank his neighbours for their help. Later we cooked meat, vegetables and rice and ate on low stools seated around the family's fire. Looking out from our perch in the lush, leafy jungle, modern China was nowhere to be seen.

772 Acrobatics at the Arirang mass gymnastics festival

NORTH KOREA When it comes to collective displays, North Korea is in a league of its own. And there is nothing more collective than the Arirang festival – a jaw-dropping mass gymnastics display performed in Pyongyang, the capital of the world's most isolated, tightly controlled state.

Walking into the huge May Day Stadium in Pyongyang, you are first confronted with a giant human billboard. Opposite the main entrance sit about 20,000 school children holding books with 170 colourful flip-pages, which they open in perfect unison throughout the ninety-minute performance: a backdrop to the display.

Through this performance, Kim Jong-il's regime is able to create the socialist paradise it has not been able to produce in reality. Into the arena march literally tens of thousands of performers – elaborately dressed female dancers, soldiers doing tae kwon do, labourers and cows and six-year-old children bouncing around in swimming costumes. There are even motorbikes riding across high wires above the stadium.

The performers swirl, leap, sashay, march, jump and shout around the stadium, enacting the traditional Korean "Arirang" love story interwoven with motifs of hardship under Japanese colonialism, the tragedy of the separation of the Korean peninsula, but mainly the prowess of the North Korean state, which George W. Bush once labeled part of the "axis of evil".

Sitting among crowds of North Korean families, you'll be caught up in the incredible spectacle. It's hard to believe that so many performers could move in such precise unison, so many spectators could cheer at exactly the right time and that a country would spend so much money on gymnastics rather than rice.

773 Sweet dreams Japanese-style

JAPAN From the discreet entrance way to the tatami-mat guestroom, everything about a *ryokan*, a traditional Japanese inn, oozes understated elegance. You'll need a little knowledge of etiquette – and a few yen – to stay in one for the night, but both are amply rewarded.

Sliding open the wooden front door, identified by a modest sign if at all, you enter a world of tinkling *shamisen* music and kimono-clad staff. Exquisite hanging scrolls and painted screens contrast with rustic woodwork and a seemingly casual arrangement of seasonal flowers soft-lit through *shoji* paper screens. It's an artful, quintessentially Japanese blend of refinement and simplicity.

Your shoes replaced with simple slippers, you'll be led along hushed corridors to your individually styled guestroom. It's stockinged feet only now on the rice-straw tatami mats. There's no sign of bedding, just a low table in an almost bare room. Attention is focused on the alcove, with its wall hanging and minimalist flower arrangement, and on the garden. For the full-blown *ryokan* experience, it's essential for the guestroom to look out on a traditional garden, no matter how small. Again it contains nothing flamboyant – no garish flowers, but a harmonious arrangement of moss, stone and neatly trimmed trees and bushes. If you are lucky, the forms and colours will be intensified by a recent rain shower: nature idealized.

The same attention to detail and sense of aesthetics is apparent in the food served. You'll be brought trays overflowing with meticulously balanced and presented seasonal delicacies. With its array of serving dishes and its delicate aromas a *ryokan* meal is as much a feast for the eyes and nose as for the taste buds. Don't just tuck in; savour the moment.

And the senses are in for one last treat before bedtime. The traditional Japanese bath is a ritual in itself. The basic rule is to scrub down thoroughly at the taps, then ease yourself into the cypress-wood tub full of piping hot water. Then simply soak. It's absolute bliss. Returning to your room you'll find your futon has been laid out for you. Sleep comes in an instant, soothed by the gentle beat of the bamboo water-dripper nodding back and forth in the garden.

774 Slurping a Turkish coffee in Yerevan

ARMENIA The break-up of the Soviet Union gave the world an impressive array of new capitals. Some have since become familiar fodder on travel itineraries – think Tallinn's Baltic charm, Kiev's bulbous cathedrals and Riga's drunken Brits. Others, for better or worse, remain something of a mystery.

Step forward Yerevan, capital of Armenia, a city swaggering into a new era, and making a mockery of the usual Soviet stereotypes of drab, grey skies and drab, grey architecture. Lofty and landlocked, Yerevan is one of the sunniest of the ex-Soviet capitals, and for most of the year the azure-blue firmament is punctuated only by the awe-inspiring shape of Mount Ararat. This fabled 5137m peak is where Noah's floating zoo is said to have come to rest after the floods, and although it now lies just across the border in Turkish territory, the fact that it can be seen from so many parts of Yerevan makes it one of the main symbols of the city.

One other unmissable feature here is the liberal, almost ubiquitous use of duf, a sumptuously coloured stone used in the construction of the vast majority of Yerevan's buildings. Its precise hue shifts from peach to pink to rose depending upon the weather and time of day, though the fiery tones that emerge under the rising and setting sun are particularly magnificent.

Nowhere is this more apparent than on Northern Avenue, a sleek pedestrianized thoroughfare in the very centre of the city – half a kilometre of soft, pinkish stone regularly inset with the cafés and boutiques of a burgeoning middle-class, it would look stylish in any European city, and makes a grand place to people-watch over a coffee, served Turkish-style from a conical metal pot. The same could be said of most of Yerevan – indeed, on a summer afternoon it can seem as if the whole city is out, dressed for a fashion shoot, getting a caffeine fix.

775 Riding by bus to Dêgê

CHINA Bored with western Sichuan's pandas, pristine blue lakes, raw mountain scenery and Tibetan monasteries? Well then, for what is likely to prove one of the most adrenaline-packed eight hours of your life, ride the public bus from Ganzi to Dêgê. You start 3500 metres up in a river valley at the foot of the Que'er Shan range, Ganzi's dusty sprawl of tiled concrete buildings disappearing abruptly around a corner behind you, the bus packed to capacity with raucous crowds of Tibetans. The road – like all roads here if you're riding west towards the Himalayan Plateau – heads ever upwards, crossing a wide pass festooned with bright prayer flags at the head of the valley, at which point the Tibetans all cheer and hurl handfuls of paper prayers out the windows like clouds of confetti. Beyond is the halfway town of Manigange, where the passengers get out and (despite their Buddhist leanings) consume vast quantities of meat dumplings and butter tea – the latter revolting as tea but satisfying

if thought of as soup. Back into the bus, the journey continues past brown glaciers hemming in the holy lake of Yilhun Lhatso and boulders carved in Tibetan script with "*Om Mani Padme Hum*", and the valley reaches a rounded conclusion beneath some particularly wicked-looking, spiky, snow-bound peaks. Unfortunately, the road goes on, winding back on itself as it climbs up... and up... and up. The Tibetans are no longer so boisterous; several are blatantly chanting prayers, thumbing rosaries with their eyes screwed up tight. Up among the peaks now, the bus is suddenly exposed to the wind as the road wobbles through the narrow, 5050-metre-high pass and around a corner so tight that at night you'd be over the edge before you even knew that there was a corner to turn. On the far side, the road slaloms down a virtually vertical rockface to the valley far below, and then, after all that excitement, your heart rate can settle on the unadventurous final stretch to Dêgê, just an hour away.

776 Sharing ancient roads with yak herders

BHUTAN To trek in Bhutan is to visit not only another land but also to encounter another time – a rare privilege. Buffering China to the north and India to the south, the terrain ranges from the 7000m peaks of the Himalayas through high-altitude meadows and forests and on to the jungle-covered foothills of the south. Bhutan has no illusions about its preciousness, having guarded its borders for centuries it now restricts access to only a few thousand visitors annually and charges US$200 a day per visitor. This exclusivity means many Bhutanese villagers living high in the mountains have never seen Westerners before.

While the urban centres of this mountainous Himalayan country

are modernized, many Bhutanese living in remote areas lead an ancient way of life where walking is the primary mode of transport and shipments of school supplies and general goods from the major towns are delivered by horse and cart, taking several days to arrive. Visitors trekking in Bhutan use ancient pathways to access such remote areas and will witness a way of life that has remained unchanged for generations. You can embark on hikes of any length and all levels of difficulty; from easy day-walks stopping at temples along the glorious but flat Bumthang Valley, to the gruelling 24-day Snowman trek across the far North. Along the way, you'll see nomadic yak-herders and processions of maroon-clad monks.

CHINA If Europeans ever made a real impact on China it was in the part they played in turning interwar Shanghai into one of the busiest, raciest cities in the world. Haunt of aristocrats, businessmen, gangsters and untold millions of beggars, prostitutes and day-labourers who barely managed to scrape together their daily bowl of rice, Shanghai through the 1920s and 30s was almost a caricature of itself – consequently the city was deliberately run down by the Chinese Communist government that took over in 1949. Today, however, Shanghai is booming again, with a growth in hyper-modern architecture and commercial dealings which is beginning to rival its fellow former colonial construction, Hong Kong.

And yet it's still one of old Shanghai's landmarks that is used as a benchmark of how the city is changing. Running south along the west bank of the Huangpu River for a couple of kilometres, the road known as the Bund was once Shanghai's docks and commercial heart in one, lined with European Neoclassical warehouses, banks and expensive hotels, some of which survive among the modern cityscape. Walking south, you pass the former British and Russian consulates and waterside Huangpu Park, infamous for signs once allegedly barring "dogs or Chinese" and now one of the best places to promenade and watch the latest high-tech developments springing up over the river at Pudong district. Further on are the one-time headquarters of Jardine Matheson (which made its original fortune in the opium trade) and the Art Deco *Peace Hotel*, known as the Cathay Hotel through the 1930s when its jazz band was the talk of the town. Incredibly, some of the musicians' descendants still provide a nightly show. Beyond here are the Bank of China, Customs House (still functioning), the Hong Kong and Shanghai Bank (HSBC), and *Dongfeng Hotel*, once the men-only Shanghai Club whose 33-metre-long mahogany bar is sadly no more. Wind up your walk nearby with a meal at *M On The Bund*, where the views (if not the Mediterranean-style food) are outstanding.

Strolling
the 777
Shanghai Bund

SPACE-AGE TRAVEL:
riding the Shinkansen

JAPAN A sleek, space-age train glides into the station precisely on time. When it pulls to a stop the doors align exactly in front of each orderly queue of passengers. The guard, wearing immaculate white gloves and a very natty peaked cap, bows as you climb aboard. Where but Japan could a train journey start in such style?

Japan's high-speed Shinkansen, popularly known as the "bullet train", is the envy of the world, and while it's not cheap, it's something you just have to experience once. The Tokaido–Sanyo line runs from Tokyo west to Kyoto and Hiroshima – 900km – and the fastest *Nozomi* trains cover this in just four hours. In places, they reach 300km per hour, yet the ride is as smooth as silk.

It's only by looking out of the window that you get a sense of speed; neat rows of houses flicker by, gradually giving way to rice fields, woods and the occasional temple, as you leave Tokyo's sprawling metropolis behind. If the weather's clear, you'll catch Mount Fuji's iconic, snow-capped cone.

Meanwhile, inside the train all is hushed calm. People sleep, punch messages into mobile phones (calls are forbidden), or tuck into *eki-ben*, takeaway station meals that are an art form in themselves.

Before you know it, you're pulling in to Kyoto's monumental new station – eyesore or emblem, depending on whom you ask. No time for the city's myriad temples now, though. The doors swoosh shut and you're off again. Osaka brings yet more urban sprawl, but after Kobe the tracks run along the coast, offering tantalizing glimpses of the island-speckled Inland Sea as you near Hiroshima, journey's end.

In a country where cutting-edge design coexists alongside ancient traditions and courtesies, the bullet train is a shining example of the extraordinary attention to detail and awesome teamwork that lies at the heart of Japanese society. Far more than a mere journey, riding the Shinkansen provides a glimpse into what makes Japan tick.

JAPAN In many ways, the Fuji Rock festival will be familiar to any seasoned Western festival-goer. Major international acts like Franz Ferdinand and Massive Attack headline stadium-scale stages, and smaller local bands play anything from Japanese drumming to experimental electronica at fringe locations. There's unexpected downpours and mud baths, and impossibly early mornings as the sun turns your tent into an oven. But all of this comes wrapped with the charms of Japanese culture, both softening and enriching the experience.

The night before the official first day, the festival kicks off with a *bon-odori* folk dance. The happy crowd honours the ancestors by stomping in a circle around a drummer, raising and lowering their hands. When the festival proper gets underway, food and drink stalls line all the main routes between the stages, but there's more sushi than burgers on the menus. There's alchohol, of course, but as well as beer stands, there are sake stalls where you can sample a variety of rice wines you'd never see outside Japan. Despite all the drinking, there's no aggression, and a warm welcome for the occasional foreigners. Above all, people are here because of their passion for music: many choose to quietly stand and watch, and moshing is carried out enthusiastically but with due regard for others. Most impressively, the entire site is rubbish-free: there are bins for sorting and recycling waste everywhere, including dedicated chopstick bags.

Pristine portaloos fully stocked with toilet paper on the fourth day is an extraordinary sight, and if the main areas feel a touch hectic you can get a cable car up the mountain, leaving the rockers and ravers far below, to enjoy noodles or ice cream at the top. But the on-site *onsen* is perhaps the most delicious local detail. It's a common form of relaxation that's popular throughout Japan: a large, natural hot-tub fed by volcanic springs. Sitting with your head just above the water and gazing at a small zen garden of artfully arranged rocks and gravel, you can watch your hangover drift away with the steam into the cool mountain air.

Have a sake party at
Fuji Rock

780 Shopping at the mother of all markets

CHINA They call it the "Mother of all Markets", and so they should: every week, 100,000 nomads, villagers and traders from all over Central Asia converge on Kashgar, the last sizeable place you'll come to in China if you're heading northwest along the ancient Silk Road. They're here to take part in the Yekshenba Bazaar, the Sunday Market, which fills the teahouses and dusty lanes of this Muslim city with a blur of noise and smells that went out of fashion elsewhere in the world after the Middle Ages. The heart of the market is a trampled area to the east of the city, where customers and traders haggle with melodramatic flair over the merits of horses, sheep, camels and donkeys. Just when it seems as if someone is about to get a knife in the ribs, the shouting and fist-shaking gives way to satisfied nods, money changes hands, and the new owner leads his purchases away. Beyond all this horse trading is the covered market, a maze of shaded stalls better-stocked than a Western shopping mall, whose owners sip tea, chat with their friends, and do their best to catch your eye so that they can beckon you over. They are masters of soft sell; each in their friendly, persuasive way makes it hard to escape without buying something. "Need some kitchenware – a new cleaver, some pots and pans? No problem, I have these. How about a carpet? This one, from Khotan, perhaps – or how about a fine kilim, handmade by nomads? Some Iranian saffron then; yes, more expensive than gold. A pity to come so far and leave empty-handed." But with the goods on display ranging from musical instruments to wooden chests inlaid with tin (used for carrying gifts to prospective brides), and enough food to last a lifetime – where to start?

781 Go fishing with cormorants in the firelight

JAPAN The scene is straight from a centuries-old woodblock print or scroll painting. Aboard a flat bottomed boat, the *usho* (lead fisherman) dressed in a water-repellent straw skirt, dark cotton kimono and linen headscarf, expertly handles up to twelve cormorants on long leashes. The slender-necked birds dive into the river, hunting *ayu*, sweet freshwater fish, which are attracted to the light of the fire blazing in the braziers hanging from the boat's prow and the rhythmic thump of oars or drums.

Having caught the fish, the cormorant is prevented from swallowing anything larger than tiddlers by a constricting ring around its throat. The *usho* tugs the bird aboard to relieve it of its catch, as the other two members of the fishing team guide the boat down the river.

This is *ukai* – the 1300-year-old Japanese tradition of fishing with cormorants at night. It may not look like a particularly enjoyable experience for the birds, but by all accounts they are very well cared for by their masters – even treated like members of the family

– and can live up to twenty years.

Protected by the Imperial Household Agency, *ukai* is practiced every year only in a few select places, including the castle town of Inuyama, 25km north of Nagoya, as a spectacle for tourists and those interested in traditional culture. The actual fishing by a flotilla of boats typically lasts around thirty minutes, but an *ukai* jaunt is not just about catching fish. Around two hours before fishing commences, the audience boards long, canopied boats, decorated with paper lanterns, which sail upriver and then moor to allow the enjoyment of a pre-show bento box meal. If you don't want to pay extra for this it's also possible to bring your own food and drink. Sometimes a boat will drift by selling beer, snacks and fireworks – another essential *ukai* component.

You can watch the show for free from the riverbank, but this way you won't experience the thrill of racing alongside the fishing boats, with the birds splashing furiously in the reflected light of burning pine logs, leaving a trail of sparks in the night air.

782 Svaneti – the hidden heart of the Caucasus

GEORGIA The isolated Svaneti region of northern Georgia is as beautiful as it is remote. True to the traditions of the Caucasus, its inhabitants have always been independent-minded, and for centuries frustrated outside attempts at control with the help of the sturdy defensive towers that still punctuate its hillsides. Yet today Svaneti is a place with a sense of peace that is a far cry from the breakaway Russian republics of Chechnya and Dagestan to the northeast. Locked under snow for much of the year, in summer defiant green hillsides emerge as if new-made by the thaw and the bright white meadow flowers echo and amplify the snows on the peaks of the Greater Caucasus mountains all around.

The village of Ushguli, sitting at the head of the Inguri gorge, with Georgia's highest peak, Mount Shkhara, as the backdrop, claims to be Europe's highest inhabited spot, at 2300m above sea level. Actually a collection of four tiny villages, Ushguli is home to just seventy families. It is reachable only by 4x4 – it's two hours from Mestia, the town where most visitors stay, which is eight hours from Zugdidi, where the overnight train from Tbilisi stops. Svan drivers take bends at high speed, and the roads are lined with shrines. But the journey is one worth braving.

Walking, biking, or horseriding out from Ushguli or Mestia gives stunning views of alpine valleys, deep gorges and distant peaks. The walk from Mestia to the Ushba glacier is particularly memorable: starting in gentle alpine forest, you pass guards inspecting passports on the route north to Russia, and end by scrambling over a post-apocalyptic landscape of raw black rock before finally arriving at a unique picnic spot – a crack in the rock and ice that is deep enough to sit in, sited just below the final scramble to the mouth of the glacier.

Svaneti's welcoming homestays offer unstinting hospitality, including enormous meals of home-made delicacies like *khinkali* (light meat dumplings in pleated dough), home-made yogurt and honey, and aubergine with walnuts. Crammed round the family table with visitors from around the world, it is easy to feel like travellers from an earlier century thrown together in some untouched spot. For now, that is just what this small corner of the Caucasus remains.

Visit the **reindeer** **herders** of Siberia

783

RUSSIA Still and white at the far northeastern tip of Siberia, Chukotka is nine time zones and nine hours by plane from Moscow. It's so remote that locals call the rest of Russia "the mainland". The territory is almost the size of Britain and France combined, but has only around 50,000 inhabitants. No highways connect their few communities. To travel out from Anadyr, Chukotka's capital, you must charter a boat, helicopter or plane – or in winter, you can wrap up in boots and parka, and travel across the tundra by snowmobile.

The only sounds you'll hear as you cross this bitter yet beautiful land are the thrum of the snowmobile's engine and the occasional flapping of pure-white ptarmigan, alighting in small flocks from tundra shrubs. While humans are few here, wildlife is plentiful. Chukotka is home to snow sheep and wolves; Wrangel Island, off its northern coast, is the world's largest polar-bear breeding ground. And then there are the reindeer. In this remote region, they outnumber humans by three to one.

The thermometer reads -20°C: the snowmobile's heated handlebars keep your hands warm but breathe on your helmet's visor and the moisture freezes, a veil of tiny ice crystals obscuring your view. For hour after hour, you fly over frozen hummocks and hurtle across solid turquoise lakes. Drive for a few days, past a coastal Eskimo village where you're offered whale to eat and a rusting Cold War radar station that still points towards Alaska, past tumbledown gulag buildings where political prisoners perished under Stalin's Terror, and you'll find the reindeer and their herders.

The reindeer provide the Chukchi with clothing, tents and food as they move from pasture to breeding ground. These people aren't used to tourists; they don't speak English and they've no souvenirs to sell you. Instead, they offer steaming tea, hunks of boiled reindeer meat and fresh, salty cakes of bread they've just baked over the fire.

Back on your snowmobile, heading towards civilization, you feel that some tiny part of you has changed. The journey has been long and hard, and you're happy to be heading to home comforts – yet you feel a wrench as you leave the tranquillity of the tundra, one of the few true wildernesses left on earth.

784 Beaten and bruised at Wudang Shan

CHINA If in your travels around China you hope to find a place where bearded mystics totter around mountain temples, unwinding after performing amazing feats of martial prowess, then head for Wudang Shan ("Martial Mountain") in Hubei province. Mythologized versions of this place can be seen in big-screen martial-arts epics such as *Crouching Tiger, Hidden Dragon*, which made such a significant impression in the West; if domestic critical response was more muted, it's only because people here were already used to this sort of thing. But there's no doubt that kung fu is a growth industry in modern China, not least because of the need for security: crime rates have mirrored the explosion in personal wealth with today's more capitalist-driven, free-market society, and the demand for bodyguards has increased too. Students can study kung fu privately, at martial art academies (where many hope to become film stars), and even at Wudang Shan, which is one of the homes of traditional Chinese kung fu.

There is a catch, however. Firstly, to study full-time at one of Wudang's temples you have to become a Taoist monk, which – what with the accompanying sexual abstinence, spartan living conditions and religious doctrine – might not appeal. Secondly, these people are serious. Not necessarily vicious, but you'll have to get used to being hit with fists, fingers, palms, feet, sticks and and an escalating number of weapons. Turn up casually, however, and you'll probably find people willing to spend an hour or two teaching you some basics of their systems without involving too much hand-to-hand combat. And even if you're not in the slightest bit interested in getting into a scrap, the mountain and its temples are a rare treat, with stone paths rising through thin woodland to the magnificent sight of the mountain's summit completely ringed by a fortress-like stone wall, a group of gold- and green-tiled temples rising within.

785 Staring into the inferno

TURKMENISTAN It's like standing on the edge of Hell. Huge flames leap out from a massive crater and fire balls explode, sending rocks cascading down the sides to the unseen pit, the jagged edges threatening to give way and send onlookers there too.

Here, in the middle of the desert in northern Turkmenistan, lie nine craters formed when the Soviet gas explorers came searching for energy. Some bright spark had the idea of setting one alight, and for the last two decades it has burned continuously, creating an orange glow that can be seen for miles at night and smelled from just slightly closer. There can be few attractions stranger than these Darvaza gas craters, and that's saying something considering the idiosyncracies of Turkmenistan, home to one of the world's most bizarre personality cults.

Setting up camp in the desert, our party looked out for giant zemzen desert lizards and waited for night to fall. Once the sky had descended into inky darkness, our guide revved his 4WD, ready to crash through the dunes. Banging into sand walls and dropping into sand holes, we careered through the emptiness towards the craters. As we got closer, the glow became brighter and the heat and smell hit us as soon as we got out of the car. Beholding this burning, furious pit in the middle of all the nothingness, I had a more vivid understanding of the saying "a snowball's chance in hell".

786 Getting soused at Sisters' Meal Festival

CHINA "Make him do it again!" insisted a young policeman who had just missed his chance to photograph me spilling a pint of home-made rice wine down my front. For the second time. Well, it's not every day that you get carjacked by a score of beautiful girls dressed in exquisitely embroidered silk jackets and enough silverware to sink a battleship, and forced to quaff from a buffalo-horn's worth of raw spirit if you want to carry on your way. "Don't touch the horn" warned a friend, "or you'll have to drain it!" So I stood with my hands behind my back while one of the girls held up the wine and tried to get me to sip. But buffalo-horn goblets are not designed for Westerners – a mouthful went in, but my big nose bumped the edge, and my shirt got the rest. The crowd loved it.

Such are the hazards of attending the Miao people's Sisters' Meal Festival at Shidong, Guizhou province, the time of the year when all marriageable girls from the local villages pick a husband. This was the third and final day, by which time I'd already got involved in vigorous group dances, had fireworks thrown at me (nothing personal – just part of the action) during a riotous late-night dragon-lantern competition, and narrowly missed being trampled by the loser at a buffalo-wrestling contest. Now all 20,000 participants were heading to a nearby river to wind the festival up with some dragon-boat races. The roadblock was eventually passed, but not before the policeman had got his photos, I'd sunk a skinful, and the world had become decidedly fuzzy around the edges. My final hazy memory after the boat races ended is of the whole crowd forming rings and dancing and singing until dawn.

Touring Tamerlane's bloody city of sand

UZBEKISTAN For centuries, the Silk Route served as the conduit to the most extensive trade network in the world, linking Europe to the far stretches of East Asia across the Persian Empire. Smack in the middle of it all lay the Uzbek city of Samarkand, an exquisitely decorated settlement that has attracted the interest of many conquerors, including Alexander the Great, Genghis Khan and Tamerlane. Tamerlane crowned it his capital in the late 1300s and hired the world's best craftsmen to construct the imposing and impossibly beautiful Registan, a Persian term meaning "City of Sand". If that sounds poetic, it's worth bearing in mind that the sand was reportedly sprinked on the ground to soak up the blood in the central square after Tamerlane's victims' heads had been set on spikes.

Amid the dusty, somewhat grungy downtown of modern Samarkand, the jaw-dropping, elephantine Registan lies at the terminus of six main roadways, its grand central plaza bounded by a triumvurate of *madrasas* (Islamic theological colleges) covered in bright, geometrically patterned tiles. The greatest of the three is Central Asia's oldest surviving Islamic structure, the *madrasa* of Ulug Bek, built in 1420, with shining star motifs on its towering *pishtak* (portal). On either side, paired minarets perfectly frame the building and its central courtyard, bordered by four dozen *hujira* (students' quarters). Just opposite is Shir Dor, a *madrasa* built two hundred years later whose portal features an unusual cross between a tiger and a lion with a human face. A third *madrasa*, Tillya Kari, completes the ensemble, with rich gilding on its dome, facade and mihrab; the interior is completely covered in gold leaf, which was applied by attaching the leafing to animal skins and beating it into the walls with a mallet.

The courtyards of each *madrasa* are now occupied by vendors selling carpets, crafts and souvenirs – and if you're lucky, cold drinks. Puttering about the grounds are trinket vendors, carpet sellers and devout Muslims, praying to Allah and searching for inspiration in one of the most evocative, gorgeous structures ever built by human hands.

788 Look down on the city of the future

CHINA Gaze at Shanghai's avant-garde architecture, tangled flyovers and massive new shopping and housing districts, all of which seem to have sprung up with magical haste, like mushrooms after rain, and you can see the city of the twenty-first century emerging. The best place to see all this is from above – from very high above, on the observation deck at the top of the World Financial Building, to be precise. This blunt, tapering tower with a hole near the roof – locals nickname it "the bottle opener" – is, at 492m, the tallest building in China, its 100th-floor observation deck the second highest in the world.

Though Shanghai is often compared to *Blade Runner*'s dystopian city, the journey up the tower is more reminiscent of the space station in *2001*, as greeters usher you along hushed corridors to the pod-like lift. Emerging a minute later, with your ears well and truly popped, you are confronted with a 360-degree view of the urban sublime. Space is at a premium in Shanghai, so the city has built

up rather than out – by population it's four times denser than New York. Those claustrophobic streets and jostling showcase buildings make for an astonishing cityscape.

To the south is Pudong: twenty years ago this was mostly paddy fields, but today it's new-build as far as the eye can see, with the unreal sheen of an architectural model. Right next to you you're looking down on one of the most beautiful modern buildings in Asia, the pagoda-like Jinmao Tower. Below, barges ply the Huangpu River, an example of the trade that is the source of the city's wealth. Across the water are the fusty colonial-era buildings of the Bund, where Art Deco classics such as the *Peace Hotel* show why the city was once nicknamed the Paris of the East.

One caveat, though – this is not a place for the nervous. Hardened glass tiles in the floor allow you to look right down beneath your feet and, rather disconcertingly, a sign asks you not to jump on them.

789 Experiencing the nomadic life

KYRGYZSTAN Sleeping in a yurt is akin to sleeping in a sheep's stomach. It's warm but damp, smells of wool and is filled with strange gurgling noises. Staying at the lush lakeside summer residence of Krygyz nomads – a row of round woollen tents with an open cauldron for cooking and a pen for the goats – there's little to do but enjoy this itinerant style of life.

Spending time in a *jailoo* (pasture) in Son Kul, a bone-jarring eight-hour drive in an old Soviet truck from the capital Bishkek into the centre of Kyrgyzstan, is like stepping back into the past to the days when life was simple, as long as Genghis Khan wasn't around.

Kyrgyz families have been moving around these sweeping pastures with their yurts for centuries, folding up the rugs and the walls and carting the huge circular roof frame from meadow to meadow, taking their animals to greener fields or simply opting for a change in summer scenery.

Inside the yurt, traditional Krygyz *shyrdak* rugs hang from the walls as colourful insulation. The spokes in the wooden wheel-like roof ascend to the apex of the cone, while a little hat sits on top of the cone on the outside, flung on or off for ventilation or warmth.

Arriving at night we settled on the hand-made felt rugs of the central yurt and enjoyed a magnificent feast of flat Kyrgyz bread, chunky soup, *plov* (rice and meat), *laghman* (noodles) and endless glasses of vodka, each one preceded by an elaborate toast.

The next morning, saddled up on awaiting ponies, we explored the hills beyond the camp, riding up through the hushed valleys to imposing peaks overlooking the glacial lakes, as we galloped across the wide pastures back to the yurts. Along the way we bought *kymys*, fermented mare's milk, from a farmer sporting a high, peaked traditional woollen hat. The fizzy beverage nipped the back of my throat – the perfect way to quench a Kyrgyz pasture thirst.

790 Feeling the magic of carpets in Baku

AZERBAIJAN In a business where antiquity is a mark of quality, it is fitting that Baku's carpet-sellers ply their trade in the Old City. These narrow lanes and winding streets, enclosed within medieval fortress walls, used to be the sum total of Baku. But during the first oil boom in the mid-nineteenth century, the city started to ooze out of its confining inner walls and the Outer City was born. In its heyday, the Old (or "Inner") City had 707 shops for its 7000 inhabitants, but nowadays it is much quieter. The carpet-sellers remain, their colourful rectangles with intricate and beautiful patterns draped over the ancient walls as they sit drinking tea on the lookout for business.

"Welcome! No charge to look. Welcome!" And you are being led down a narrow flight of stairs into a grotto piled high with rugs from Iran, Afghanistan, Pakistan and several other exotically named 'stans of the Caucasus and Central Asia – not forgetting Azerbaijan itself, which has a long and proud tradition of carpet making. More tea is poured and the merchant's son rolls out carpets woven a generation

or two ago. Each piece tells its own story. The missing tassels on one might have been caused by the burning coals of a water pipe, knocked over during the wild festivities at an Azeri wedding. And maybe the faded patch in the middle of another was the result of a million prayers to Allah.

The merchant's keen eye notices you giving one piece a lingering look. With the passion and authority of a curator at a museum he launches into a vivid description of a carpet nearly a century old, coloured with dyes from octopus, saffron and pistachio, and made with only the finest sheep's wool and camel's hair. The merchant's son holds the carpet high above his head while the customer, gazing at the soft, deep hues, is overcome by a gentle feeling of happiness. A carpet does not have to fly to be magic, and eventually you emerge from the grotto back onto the cobbled streets of the Old City carrying an old rug which is about to begin another chapter in its chequered life.

Roll up your sleeves at a HAIRY CRAB BANQUET

CHINA The supreme delicacy in Shanghai cuisine is, to be honest, an ugly little critter. Hairy crabs (called mitten crabs in the west) are about the size of a fist, greyish-green, and their legs are covered in bristles. They're usually caught and served from after the Mid-Autumn Festival in September till around the end of November – as the old verse tells it: "When autumn winds blow, crabs get itchy feet, chrysanthemums turn yellow and crab roe grows sweet". The very best are grown in Yangcheng and Tai Lakes in nearby Suzhou; the ones from Tai Lake are said to be meatier, but those from Yangcheng have the tastiest roe.

At a crab banquet, first you are shown your crab, trussed up in reeds and clicking indignantly, then it is taken away and cooked, to be returned to you still whole, but now a delightful blushing pink in colour. You'll need to roll up your sleeves – eating crabs Chinese-style is a pretty visceral experience. The Chinese joke that if you're on a date with someone you're not sure about, you should go to a crab restaurant, as the job of dissecting the things will fill in any uncomfortable pauses. First you have to take the shell off, exposing the soft fleshy parts. If you're lucky, you'll have a female stuffed with delicious red roe. You eat everything but the lungs (the gill-like greyish bits), dipping the meat in a pungent sauce of soy, ginger and vinegar.

Finally, you pull its legs off, snap them, and, using the instruments provided, scoop out what you can from inside. This is the most fiddly part, but it's worth it. Hairy crabs are regarded as being cooling to the body, so are taken with a good "warming" wine as an accompaniment: *hua diao* rice wine from Shaoxing is traditional, but a good Chardonnay does the job nicely.

791

>> Central & Northern Asia

792

Shopping for a national treasure at Tolkuchka Market

TURKMENISTAN "Water is a Turkmen's life, a horse is his wings, and a carpet is his soul". A proverb from days of yore it may be, but it's difficult to over-egg the role that carpets play in modern-day Turkmenistan. The national flag features the carpet *guls* (rug designs) of the country's five major tribes, Ashgabat's most popular cultural centre is the Carpet Museum and on the last Sunday in May, the whole country grinds to a halt to celebrate Carpet Day. In short, nothing gets a Turkmen going like the perfect weave.

The museum shop is a good place to start your browsing, but for the finest designs, join the locals at Ashgabat's Tolkuchka Market, a sprawling bazaar on the outskirts of town at the edge of the Karakum Desert. Soft *kilims* lie alongside *beshirs* and *kerkis*, huge *yomuds* are

splayed across the floor (the more knots in their finely trimmed ends, the pricier the pile), and *Teke* rugs tower in neat, folded rolls. But the finest of all, the carpet of connoisseurs, are the stunning *Akhal-Teke*, intricately designed wefts that dazzle in their symmetry. Mostly woven with a red background, the rarer blue designs can sell for several thousand dollars.

You won't be the first to leave Turkmenistan wishing that you'd left more rug room in your suitcase. Marco Polo came here in the thirteenth century and was sufficiently moved to declare that Turkmen carpets were the most beautiful in the world – seven hundred years later, and the quality of the craftsmanship is still beyond compare.

793 Admiring Suzhou's gardens

CHINA Since Marco Polo wrote of Suzhou's skilful artisans and sages in his book of travels in the thirteenth century, even Westerners have known about this cultured city. Incredibly, it still occupies an elevated position in the modern Chinese psyche: a popular saying lists Suzhou's virtues as its beautiful women, silk, and – especially – gardens, the design of which dates back over a thousand years to the Song dynasty.

It's unlikely that Polo ever visited a Suzhou garden; they were attached to family mansions, designed by wealthy merchants and scholars as private, contemplative retreats. Most pack a lot of detail into a very small space, and their construction was a genuine art, using carefully positioned rocks, pools, walls, windows and trees to create a sense of balance, harmony and proportion, where literature could be studied or a friend entertained over a cup of wine.

Well, that was the original idea, but holding on to any such lofty notions today is asking to be crushingly disappointed by the daily hordes of tourists that pack out these delicate, interlinked courtyards. Get around a few, however – about ten are open to the public – and you'll still sense echoes of what they were originally planned for, though the famous and complementary Wangshi Yuan (best viewed in moonlight), Shizi Lin with its naturally shaped rocks, and watery Zhuozheng Yuan are constantly seething with people. If you're lucky and arrive first thing in the morning before the crowds arrive, however, you might even find a few minutes to yourself at the relatively unknown Canglang Ting and Ou Yuan gardens, and maybe catch just a brief glimpse of a more refined time.

794 On the temple trail in Shikoku

JAPAN Japanese temples have an air of magic about them. Though somewhat austere in comparison to those of other Asian nations, less has long been more in Japan. A good sunset can draw simmering shades of gold from the bareness, while dusk can make white flashes of paint hover against dark, brooding backgrounds – like an anime come to life. Paper doors and windows play similar optical tricks within the buildings, filtering the light of the outside world into a soft, mind-cleansing cream.

While the former capital of Kyoto is arguably home to the most ornate temples in the country, some of the most atmospheric are located in the nooks and crannies of small towns or farming communities. Those truly in the know head to Shikoku – this smallest and most bucolic of Japan's four main islands is home to a mammoth eighty-eight-temple pilgrimage, which takes around three months to complete on foot. The overwhelming majority follow the route in a car or on a bus tour, but in warmer months you're sure to see staff-wielding pilgrims, or *henro-san*, pacing the route, as well as hikers who don traditional white costumes along with their backpacks.

Few will have the time or inclination necessary to complete the whole pilgrimage, but the number of temples on it – only a fraction of the total number on the island – means that opportunities for shorter treks are plentiful. Though each temple has its merits, one of the most commonly visited is Zentsu-ji, the birthplace of Kobo Daishi, in whose memory the pilgrimage is made. Despite its official status as number seventy-five on the clockwise course, the temple is one of the first you'll come upon after crossing the Seto Ohashi, a series of bridges slung across the spectacular island-peppered sea between Shikoku and the main Japanese island of Honshu. From there, green Shikoku and its temples are yours to discover.

795 Jousting for a taste of Beijing duck

CHINA Beijing 1985: Mao has been dead for nine years but China is still reeling from the effects of his restrictive policies, which have held the country's economy back at almost pre-industrial levels. People shuffle around dispiritedly in blue Mao suits, bicycles outnumber cars about a thousand to one, the air is heavy with the smell of charcoal burning in braziers and the most modern buildings are functional, grey, communist-inspired concrete blocks. The only shops selling anything other than daily necessities are the "Friendship Stores", full of imported luxuries such as televisions and the locals that dream about earning enough money to own one. Restaurants serving anything other than bland, uninspiring food are extremely thin on the ground, with one very notable exception: the *Quanjude Roast Duck* restaurant, founded in 1864 and recently resurrected after being closed down during the Maoist era. Enter most restaurants in China and you're herded into a special "foreigners' only" section out of sight of indigenous diners (for whose benefit it isn't clear), but not here: for Chinese and foreigners alike it's a free-for-all, where only the quick and strong get fed. The dining hall is so crammed with tables that there's barely room to fit the chairs in, and that's a big problem because all available room – absolutely every inch – is occupied by salivating customers hovering like vultures beside each chair, waiting for the person sitting down to finish their meal and begin to get up. The ensuing moments of hand-to-hand combat, as three people try to occupy the half-empty seat, end with the victor knowing that they are about to enjoy a cholesterol-laden feast. First comes the duck's skin, crispy brown and aromatic; next the juicy meat, carefully sliced and eaten with spring onion slivers, all wrapped inside a thin pancake; and lastly, a soup made from duck bones and innards. And all for ¥12 – less than two dollars for a night's entertainment.

796 Losing track of time: Beijing to Moscow on the Trans-Siberian

CHINA TO RUSSIA On the fourth day I stopped caring about time. I thought it was the fourth day, in fact it was the third. Beijing was a receding memory, Moscow impossibly distant. I had slipped into the habit of sleeping for four hours and then getting up for four hours, it didn't matter whether it was light or dark. Life inside the train bore no relation to the outside world – Siberia – which barreled past, cold, unwelcoming and as predictable as wallpaper: birch trees, hills, birch trees, plains, birch trees.

"I hate those trees," said the elderly German in my compartment. "I want to cut them all down."

Occasionally we passed an untidy village of wooden cabins but mostly the only human touch to the epic landscape was the telegraph poles at the side of the track.

My first Russian was a young guy in a shell suit with a moustache and an anarchy tattoo. "The Beatles", he said, on hearing I was British.

"The Rolling Stones", I countered.

He nodded "The Doors".

"Pearl Jam?" I inquired.

"Nirvana", he parried. "Napalm Death".

Once or twice a day the train stopped and I'd emerge for fresh air, dizzy and blinking, onto a platform swarming with frenzied shoppers. Traders stood in the carriage door and the townsfolk, who had waited all week for two minutes of consumerism, rioted to get to them. To save time the traders threw money over their shoulders into the corridor to be collected by colleagues. They sold World Cup T-shirts, plastic jewellery and Mickey Mouse umbrellas. Even the man from the dining car had a cupboard of trainers, which was perhaps why he could only offer gherkins and soup in his official capacity.

I played cards then slept, battleships, slept, charades, slept. It was an invalid's life – a long slow delirium in comfortable confinement. But on the seventh day when grey housing blocks started appearing and Moscow was imminent, I suddenly felt nostalgic for that easy sloth. When I finally got off, something felt terribly wrong; it took me a while to figure it out – oh yes, the ground wasn't moving.

797 Sipping tea in the Land of Fire

AZERBAIJAN The teashop was unexceptional in almost every respect. It was a long, single-storey building with a rudimentary toilet at one end and a couple of outdoor tables at the other. The setup was like hundreds of cafés all across the Muslim world, except that this teashop was situated next to a hillside that was on fire.

At a table covered in brightly coloured plastic veneer sat an elderly man with his two grandchildren. The man was sipping from a glass of black tea, the kids had cherry juice. The teashop tables overlooked a relatively unimpressive hill that more closely resembled a ridge, less than 10m in height. The striking thing about this hill was the fire burning at its base: not a bonfire or a barbecue, the lower part of the

incline was alight, but it wasn't a bushfire either. There was nothing obviously combustible in view. Large, bright orange flames simply leapt out of the rocks. The slope itself was ablaze, caused by natural gas seeping through fissures in the rock. The fire had been alight for nearly fifty years, the old man told us.

Here you could sip your tea outside all through the winter, he said, gesturing with his glass towards the flames. As the temperature dropped, all you had to do was move your table closer to the blazing incline. It was a bizarre spectacle, like drinking tea beside a trapdoor to Hades. It shouldn't have been surprising – "Azerbaijan" means Land of Fire. I just hadn't expected it literally.

798 Peaking early in Hong Kong

CHINA If you like to get on top of everything in your travels, then Hong Kong's summit to conquer is the 552m-high Victoria Peak: the only thing on the island that outstrips the eighty-eight-storey IFC2 Tower. And unlike everything else to do in the downtown area, not only is the Peak (as locals call it) not man-made, but it's also free, at least if you walk up.

It is, however, a great walk through a cross-section of the city, taking you from the harbour, underneath the HSBC Tower and along elevated walkways, around the knife-like Bank of China Tower, into Hong Kong Park. Continue uphill and exit the park near the jaguar cage, then follow ever-steeper inclines between high-rise apartments until the pavement turns into a concrete path and winds up into shady rainforest. Here you'll be overtaken by joggers

gasping themselves into an early grave, while the path climbs for another forty minutes past some exclusive, isolated houses (Hong Kong's costliest real estate), and then you're there.

If this all sounds a bit much, then the Peak Tram is a more stylish, faster and less exhausting way to ascend the Peak. In use since the 1880s, the Tram sidesteps the legwork but still gives the feel of the Peak's severe gradients in the way you sink back into your wooden seat as the carriage is hauled upwards. Whichever method you use to conquer the Peak, however, you'll find that reaching the summit brings some sense of let-down in a horrible concrete viewing platform, despite which you'd have to be very hardened not to find the views of Hong Kong's towering architecture and splendid harbour inspiring.

RUSSIA Penetrating Kamchatka's remote and rugged terrain to discover one of the world's most restless regions of seismic hyperactivity has never been easy. With no roads or nearby settlements, the spectacular Valley of the Geysers wasn't discovered until 1941. Not even Russians were permitted to travel to this far-eastern peninsula until after the fall of communism. Today, a trek through the Kronotsky Reserve on the peninsula's eastern edge leads you into this land of fire and ice, and brings you face to face with the full range of Kamchatka's volcanic phenomena.

You'll be dropped into the heart of the million-hectare bioreserve by helicopter, cruising over several of Kamchatka's 29 active volcanoes along the way. Your trek involves ten days and 130km of moderately strenuous hiking through coastal mountains, forests, bush thickets and some forest-less highlands. As you navigate this landscape down to the Pacific shore you'll circuit active glacier-flanked volcanoes and encounter piping fumaroles, belching mudpots and bubbling cauldrons.

Through forests of Siberian pine you'll descend into the Uzon Caldera, a marshy depression scattered with scalding lakes, warm streams and over a thousand hot springs. Steaming waterfalls cascade into rivers running with red salmon, migratory birds find green vegetation in April and bears coming out of hibernation warm themselves by simmering mud cauldrons.

From a forested ridge you descend into the Valley of the Geysers along the steamy banks of the River Geyzernaya, one of dozens of rivers that bisect the reserve en route to the Pacific shore. You don't immediately sense what's going on underfoot, as dozens of tributaries feed a concentration of hot springs below the surface.

Over twenty major geysers fill the narrow valley, each performing on its own timetable: some erupt every ten minutes, while others take 4–5 hours between show times. Some pulse in an erect column while others surprise you with a side shot – stick to the boardwalk or you might be nailed by an unexpected burst of scalding water.

Your onward descent to the Pacific shore leads through bushy and mossy tundras to an abandoned fur-trading outpost where, if all goes according to plan, your helicopter awaits for the return ride. Kamchatka's never-ending volcanic display is a reminder that earth's creation is a work in progress.

799 Trekking through the Valley of the Geysers

800

JAPAN Forget the comical Western stereotype of gargantuan men in nappies slapping each other around – sumo is serious business. Few sports have as long a pedigree, and sumo has been around for a millennium. The basic object of the fighters is to force their opponent out of the ring, or get them to touch the ground with any part of their body other than their feet. The enormous body mass involved ensures that fights are brief but blazing, though these guys are no mere spheres of flesh – to see a *rikishi* hoist up to 200kg of squirming human by the belt and carry it out of the ring is nothing short of astonishing.

Six tournaments, or *basho*, take place across the year – one every odd month – and last for fifteen days. Good *rikishi* progress though the ranks to *makuuichi*, the highest level; here, the top 42 wrestlers fight once per day, their main aim the posting of a positive tournament record of at least eight wins. The very best rise to *yokozuna* level and national superstardom, before a ceremonial cutting of their top-knotted hair on retirement.

Your ticket entitles you to nine hours of fight-time and hundreds of bouts; since many spectators only come for the *makuuchi* fights at the end, it's often possible to pinch a first-class seat for much of the day. Keep in mind that ringside seats come with an element of risk. Arriving early also increases the chances of sharing your train journey in with a wrestler or two; many are more than willing to chat, though the super-formal dialect drilled into them at their training "stable" can be impenetrable even for Japanese-speakers. One certainty is that you won't be able to miss them.

801 Climbing Fuji

JAPAN The Japanese call it *Fuji-san*, as if they're politely addressing a neighbour. Most famously glimpsed on winter days when the clouds clear and the symmetrical snow-capped cone is etched against a brilliant blue sky, Mount Fuji is the site of an annual pilgrimage. During the climbing season from July to September tens of thousands take on the dormant volcano's crumbling black ash slopes and trudge through the night to the summit of Japan's highest mountain (3776m).

Fuji is divided into ten stations, with the first being at sea level and the tenth the summit. A paved road runs to Kawaguchi-ko, the fifth station, a Swiss chalet-style gift shop about halfway up the volcano. This is where many people begin the ascent on foot, and at a steady pace it's a six-hour climb from here to the top. However, there's no rush: the true Fuji experience is more about the shared camaraderie of the climb rather than setting speed records.

The common approach is to start climbing in the afternoon aiming for one of the mountain huts at the seventh or eighth station levels. Here you can get dinner, meet fellow climbers and rest, waking in the dead of night to complete the final stages of the climb before dawn, which can be as early as 4.30am. The tiny lights of climbers' torches, like a line of fireflies trailing up the volcanic scree, will guide you to the summit. Having witnessed the *goraiko* (Buddha's Halo) sunrise, you'll then have an opportunity to take part in the time-honoured tradition of making a phone call or mailing a letter from the post office. A circuit of the crater is also in order, keeping your fingers crossed that this is not the day that Fuji decides to reawake.

802 Keeping typhoons at bay in Taipei

TAIWAN Towering a vertiginous 508m over Taiwan's largest city, Taipei 101 is an unlikely construction. Taiwan experiences a vicious typhoon season and is one of the most seismically active parts of the planet. For anyone who has experienced even a low-rise apartment block shaking like a pile of jelly, mixing earthquakes with tall buildings might seem more than a touch foolhardy.

Yet the designers of Taipei 101 managed to come up with a solution: their main innovation was to hang a 660-tonne steel pendulum, known as a tuned mass damper, from the 89th floor to offset strong winds and tremors. The damper is the world's largest and can be viewed from the observation deck. Don't worry though: if all else fails remember that the building is divided into eight canted sections, considered a lucky number in Chinese tradition, and that the whole project was approved by a Feng Shui master.

Shooting up to the 89th-floor observation deck of Taipei 101 in the world's fastest elevators, it's easy to lose all sense of perspective. To start with, the lift you're in is moving at over 60km per hour. Pressurized like an aircraft cabin, it takes just 37 seconds to travel the 382.2m from the 5th-floor entrance to the observatory. Once you've arrived, the disorientation is compounded by a mind-blowing mismatch of scale: looming over the modern heart of Taipei, the tower dwarfs everything around it. You'll feel far closer to the jagged mountains to the south, and to the thick clouds that frequently collect over the Taipei Basin – half the tower is often shrouded within one. You can only marvel at the dramatic view that Taipei 101's innovative designers have made possible.

803 Playing beachball at Beidaihe

CHINA With its faintly Mediterranean atmosphere, what better place to while away a warm summer day than Beidaihe, on the coast just a few hours from Beijing?

There was once a time when foreigners in China were the only people with a handle on beach life, and the Chinese would sit in uncomfortable family groups, ill at ease in their bathing gear, worried about wading out of their depth in the water and looking as if they knew that it should all be fun, but wondering how to go about it. China's non-steroid-enhanced swim team's performance at the 2004 Olympic Games in Athens swept all that away. Now, fired by national pride, the water beckons the athletic, while the less-competitive parade in surprisingly skimpy swimsuits, sunbathe, or play beachball between huge granite statues of heroic workers.

Most people here are ordinary, aspiring youngsters and *nouveaux riches* from Beijing, though the occasional cruising black Audi with dark windows harks back to a time when the sand and surf were reserved for the sole enjoyment of the party elite. Back along the promenade, shops sell exactly the sort of seaside kitsch you'd expect from the setting (fluorescent swimsuits, animal sculptures made of seashells), while private villas sport ludicrously overblown architectural flourishes. The best places to hang out, once you've had enough of the beach, are the many excellent restaurants, where you can down a cold beer and make your choice from seafood so fresh that it's still flapping around in a bucket.

NEED to know

735 The Jokhang opens daily 8am–6pm. As with all Tibetan temples, circuit both the complex and individual halls anti clockwise.

736 Many sections of the Great Wall are accessible as day-trips from Beijing; regular tourist buses run to Badaling (daily 9am–4.30pm), Mutianyu (daily 8am–4pm) and Simatai (daily 8am–4pm).

737 Check ⓦmazu.taichung.gov.tw for details.

738 Kyoto is the place to sample *kaiseki* cuisine – try *Nakamura-ro* or *Hyotei*.

739 Li River cruises depart Guilin year-round and can be organized through CITS (ⓦwww.cits.net).

740 Check out the website ⓦwww.naadam-festival.mn for further details on the festival.

741 For tips on where to cycle in the Yangshuo area, see ⓦ www.yangers.com.

742 See ⓦwww.dragonboat.org.hk for more details, particularly of the date, which varies each year.

743 You'll need a guide, which you can find by asking in the backpacker cafés in Jinghong, the nearest city. You'll pay around $30 a day, all inclusive. Be prepared to walk 10–20km a day, eat whatever the locals do (the home-cooked food is delicious), sleep on the floor in village houses, wash in cold water and use the local latrines.

744 The Ghibli Museum (ⓦwww.ghibli-museum.jp/en) is in Mitaka, Tokyo. Book well in advance via the website.

745 The Terracotta Army (daily 8am–6pm) is 28km east of Xi'an and can be reached in 1hr on bus #306 from Xi'an's train station.

746 Gyeongju is served by buses and trains from all over Korea.

747 You can reach Harbin from Beijing by train (9 daily; 17hr) or plane (13 daily; 1hr 30min). The Winter Ice Festival lasts from January 5 until February 5.

748 Though the exact dates vary each year, the *sakura* usually blossoms in late March or early April.

749 To find out more about the Tsou check the Alishan website at ⓦ www.ali-nsa.net. Most Tsou today speak Chinese as their first language, but learning a few words will go down well. The most commonly used is *aveoveoyu* (sounds like "aview-view-you"), literally "my heart is happy" and used both as a greeting and for "thank you".

750 Gwangjang Market is best accessed via Jongno 5-ga subway station, which sits on line 1 – come out of exit 8 and the market will be on your right.

751 To reach Huang Shan, you need to take a train, bus or plane to Tunxi, 50km southwest, and then a minibus to the mountain's base at Tangkou. Further minibus taxis run from Tangkou to the start of trails at Ciguang Ge or Yungu Si. See ⓦwww.huangshantour.com.

752 Several tour companies run tours of the DMZ; the best is USO (ⓦwww.uso.org/korea).

753 The Naked Man festival generally falls between Jan and March; confirm dates at ⓦwww.seejapan.co.uk.

754 The Chengdu Giant Panda Breeding Research Base (ⓦwww.panda.org.cn) is located 10km outside Chengdu in Sichuan province.

755 There are lots of tour operators in Ulan Bator. The more expensive options include a tour guide, driver, and yurt (and occasional hostel) accommodation; the cheapest option is to hire your own van and driver and take a tent. Shop around, and make sure you meet the driver or tour guide before setting off. Expect to wash infrequently.

756 The Longmen Caves (daily 7am–6.30pm) are 13km south of Louyang city, reached from Louyang's train station on bus #81.

757 There are several *jinjiibang* in every Korean city of note; any tourist office or taxi driver can direct you.

758 You can see snow monkeys throughout Japan, but your best chances are in Jigokudani, or "Hell's Valley".

759 Shilin Night Market in Taipei is opposite Jiantan

MRT station, and is open daily.

760 ⓦ www.airastana.com flies direct to Astana from many Asian and European airports, including London.

761 Taketomi-jima is reached by ferry from Ishikaki on Ishikagi-jima, which has direct flights to Tokyo and Osaka.

762 Passenger boats run year-round through the Three Gorges, though spring and autumn provide the most colourful scenery. Book tour-boat berths through online agents such as ⓦ www.chinahighlights.com.

763 Take the overnight train from St Petersburg to Kem, then the boat to the main island, Solovki (2hr 30min). Regional information is at ⓦwww.pomorland.info. Take cash and warm, waterproof clothes.

764 For more, check ⓦeng.templestay.com.

765 Contact the Kyoto Tourist Information Centre (ⓣ+81 (0)750 343 6655) for event information.

766 For packages, check out ⓦwww.eaheliskiing.com.

767 Central Asian climbing is best July–Sept. You'll need to apply for a Gorno Badakshan O.A. Permit in Dushanbe, the Tajik capital. ⓦwww.keadventure.com, ⓦwww .centralasia-adventures.com) and ⓦwww.asiamountains. net all organize expeditions to Peak Lenin. Get a Kyrgyz visa in advance if you want to cross the border.

768 Shinjuku's railway station is served by the Tokyo Metro, Toei Subway, and several inter-city lines.

769 The full trek takes at least two days, though three is recommended. Spring and autumn are the best months for walking as summer can be wet, with potentially dangerous landslides.

770 The best time for horse trekking is late June to mid-Sept. ⓦ www.boojum.com offers trips from Ulan Bator.

771 Jinghong is the main town of the region, reachable in an hour from Kunming by air, or around 16hr by bus.

772 No independent travel is allowed to North Korea, but ⓦwww.koryogroup.com operates regular tours.

773 Kyoto is the best place to sample the *ryokan* experience. Book well in advance for *Hiiragiya* (ⓦwww .hiiragiya.co.jp) or *Yoshikawa Ryokan* (ⓣ+81 (0) 75 221 5544).

774 Yerevan is easily accessible by plane, day-long bus or overnight train from the Georgian capital, Tbilisi. The Turkish border, just 20km from the city, has been closed since 1993 but may reopen by the time you read this.

775 Buses (8hr) run daily from Ganzi to Dêgê.

776 Visitors to Bhutan must be part of an arranged tour. Many companies offer treks in the country, among them Himalayan Kingdoms (ⓦwww.mountainkingdoms.com) and Karakoram Experience (ⓦwww.keadventure.com).

777 The Bund is south of Suzhou Creek on the western bank of the Huangpu River.

778 The Japan Rail Pass (ⓦwww.japanrailpass.net) must be purchased before arriving in Japan as it's only available to foreign visitors.

779 Fuji Rock (ⓦwww.smash-uk.com) is in mid-July each year. There are (expensive) ski-resort hotels for the less camping-inclined. If you're camping, try to get there as early as possible to find a (rare) flat pitch.

780 Kashgar's Yekshenba Bazaar takes place every Sunday about 2km from the city centre off Ayziret Lu.

781 The *ukai* season in Inuyama runs from June to mid-Oct. During the peak months (July & Aug), make a reservation ⓦwww.kisogawa-kankou.com). Ukai is also practiced in the nearby city of Gifu, in Kyoto and in Ozu.

782 Take the overnight train from Tbilisi, arriving in Zugdidi around 5.30am, then a minibus to Mestia, centre of Upper Svaneti (6–8 hours). Take walking boots, torches, warm clothes and cash (Georgian lari). Most homestays offer full board – try Nino Ratiani (ⓦtinyurl.com /y6ypchy) or Dato Ratiani (ⓦlileo-ushguli.blogspot.com).

783 Chukotka is remote, there is virtually no infrastructure for independent tourists and, if you get it wrong, the temperatures are deathly. For organized tours, try Go

Russia (ⓦwww.justgorussia.co.uk). Note that you need a special permit to visit Chukotka on top of a Russian visa.

784 Wudang Shan is in northwestern Hubei; from the nearest train station at Shiyan (25km west), catch a bus to Wudang town at the bottom of the mountain and then a minibus to Nanyan temple, about halfway up. A tiring 2hr track leads from Nanyan to the summit.

785 Getting to the craters is a difficult, bumpy ride across sand dunes. Experienced drivers can be found in Darvaza, on the highway between the capital of Ashgabat and the Uzbek border town of Konye-Urgench.

786 Contact CITS (ⓦwww.cits.net) in Kaili, who can advise on dates, accommodation and guides.

787 Visit at dusk, when the buildings are bathed in amber and locals crowd the plaza. Haggle for ticket prices – aim to knock a good 40 percent from the asking price.

788 The World Financial Building is in Pudong, not far from the Lujiazui subway stop. The entrance to the observation deck (daily 8am–10pm; $25) is in the southwest side of the building.

789 For more on yurting, see ⓦ www.cbtkyrgyzstan.kg.

790 Haggling is recommended. No matter what a carpet-seller might say, an export certificate (or "carpet passport") is required to take antique carpets out of Azerbaijan. These certificates are available from the State Museum of Azerbaijan Carpet and Applied Art (ⓦwww .azercarpetmuseum.azeurotel.com), though the seller can usually obtain the certificate on your behalf.

791 Everyone in Shanghai has a favourite crab restaurant, but the crab harvest has been hit hard by water pollution, and unscrupulous counterfeiters abound, so don't order it just anywhere. A reliable staple is *Wang Baohe*, at 603 Fuzhou Lu (ⓣ+86 (0)21 6322 3673), where set crab meals start at about $30 a head.

792 The carpet museum is open daily except Sun 10am–6pm; the market takes place on Sundays.

793 The gardens are scattered through the centre of Suzhou, though you'll need to take a taxi if you plan to visit several in one day (daily 7.30am–4.30pm).

794 It takes two months to walk the 1400km between the 88 temples on the Shikoku pilgrimage route. Zentsuji is just outside the small port of Marugame, in the north of the island.

795 *Quanjude Roast Duck* restaurant, 32 Qianmen Dajie, Beijing ⓣ+86 (0) 10 6701 1379.

796 You can buy tickets at the CITS office in the *Beijing International Hotel*, but you'll have to get a transit visa for Russia as well. See ⓦ www.transib.net for information.

797 ⓦwww.azerbaijan.az/portal/Culture/Cuisine/cuisine _e.html has more on the importance of tea to Azerbaijanis.

798 The Peak is on Hong Kong Island. The tram runs daily 7am–midnight; get to the lower Tram terminal on Garden Rd by bus #15C from outside the Star Ferry terminal.

799 Kronotsky Reserve is accessed by helicopter from Petropavlovsk; entrance is restricted and by permit only. The Valley of the Geysers is closed from mid-May to early July to protect breeding and nesting activity. July and August offer the best weather.

800 Six *basho* a year take place in alternate months. Tokyo's Ryogoku Kokugikan arena has tournaments in Jan, May and Sept. The March, July and Nov *basho* take place in Osaka, Nagoya and Fukuoka, respectively.

801 Apart from adjusting to the altitude, there's little that's technically difficult about climbing Fuji. During the climbing season, regular buses connect Kawaguchi-ko station with the fifth station.

802 For details, check ⓦwww.taipei-101.com.tw.

803 Beidaihe is on the east coast, about 2hr 30min from Beijing by train (7 daily). The beaches stretch for around 5km along the south side of a broad peninsula, easily walkable from town or reached by buses #6 or #34.

GOOD to know

HORSEPLAY

Kumis, or fermented mare's milk, is an important beverage to Mongols and the people of the Central Asian steppes. *Kumis* production requires great skill – it's tricky to milk a horse – and the beverage is traditionally fermented in a horsehide pouch.

AGE-OLD ACCOMMODATION

Hoshi Ryokan, a traditional Japanese establishment in the heart of Ishikawa Prefecture, Japan, is the **world's oldest hotel**; it has been receiving guests since AD 717.

TEA

Tea has been drunk in China for at least three thousand years and was introduced to Japan in the ninth century. There are three main types, depending on how the leaves are processed: green tea, where the leaves are picked and dried directly; black tea, where the leaves are fermented before being dried; and oolong tea, which is semi-fermented.

"Great souls have wills; feeble ones have only wishes"

Chinese proverb

TABLE MANNERS

In **Afghanistan,** if bread is dropped on the floor while eating at a table, it should be picked up, kissed and put to one's forehead before it is returned to the table-top. In **Russia** it is considered rude to look into someone else's plate or cup. In **China** you should never stick chopsticks into a bowl of rice, leaving them standing upwards, as this resembles the incense sticks that some Asians use as offerings to deceased family members.

DANGEROUS FOOD

Takifugu (or, colloquially, **fugu**) is a highly toxic pufferfish served as a delicacy in Japan. Because of its poisonous nature, only specially licensed chefs can prepare and sell it to the public, and would-be fugu chefs have to apprentice for two to three years before taking an official fugu-preparation test. Even then, only about one-third of applicants pass the rigorous examination. Ironically, many actually find the fish to be flavourless, eating it solely for the allure of cheating death. Eighteenth-century poet Yosa Buson summed it up with a haiku:

I cannot see her tonight
I have to give her up
So I will eat fugu

GOING, GOING....

Despite some improvements in the last two years, the **Aral Sea** in Central Asia is surely the world's largest man-made disaster: a once vast natural lake, it has not only been heavily polluted from weapons testing and industry, but it has also been reduced in size by sixty percent over the last forty years (mainly as a result of river diversion), and whole villages and fleets of ships lie stranded in the sand, hundreds of miles from water.

CHINA ON FILM

A Chinese Ghost Story (1987) One of the seminal Hong Kong films of the 1980s – part horror film, part love story, part martial-arts blockbuster.
Beijing Bastards (1993) One of the best of China's "underground movies".
Hero (2002). Martial arts epic, its action arguably superior to the lauded *Crouching Tiger, Hidden Dragon.*
Blind Shaft (2003) Deemed too controversial for domestic release, this great *film noir* is a telling indictment of runaway capitalism.
Kung Fu Hustle (2004) A melange of surreal comedy, pastiche, slapstick and kung fu.

WHERE IS EVERYBODY?

Mongolia has the lowest population density of any country in the world – just two people per square kilometre.

BUDDHISM IN BHUTAN

Buddhism in **Bhutan** originated in neighbouring Tibet, and today most Bhutanese follow either the Drukpa Kagyu or the Nyingmapa school of Tibetan Buddhism. The **Bhutanese** government closely regulates outside influences and tourism in part to preserve its traditional Buddhist culture, making the Himalayan nation one of the least-visited and most isolated countries in the world.

GETTING TO KNOW THE DALAI LAMA

- "Dalai" means "ocean" in Mongolian, while "Lama" is Tibetan for "spiritual teacher".
- The Dalai Lama is believed to be the incarnation of the Bodhisattva Avalokiteshvara.
- Familiarity with the possessions of the previous Dalai Lama is regarded as the main sign of the reincarnation.
- The first Dalai Lama was born in 1391.
- The current Dalai Lama – the 14th – won the Nobel Peace prize in 1989.

"In a mad world, only the mad are sane"

Akira Kurosawa

SERVICE WITH A SMILE

Nyotaimori, the art of eating sushi off of a naked woman, is a Japanese practice dating back to the late nineteenth century. Before their shift, servers bathe in fragrance-free soap and splash themselves with cold water to keep body temperature down for the food.

ON THE EDGE IN THE ANDAMANS • RIDING THE ROCKET ACROSS THE GANGES DELTA • EXPLORING THE THAR DESERT BY CAMEL • WASH AN ELEPHANT IN THE RAPTI RIVER • LAKESIDE ROMANCE IN RAJASTHAN • TRACING THE TURTLE ARRIBADA AT ORISSA • ELBOWING THROUGH THE CROWDS FOR ESALA PERAHERA • DODGING THE CROWDS ON THE SIKLES TREK • WATCHING A KATHAKALI PERFORMANCE IN KOCHI • MORNING PRAYERS AT DISKIT MONASTRY • SLIDING ALONG THE HIMALAYAN ICE HIGHWAY • GLITZ, LEATHER AND WILLOW: THE IPL • SUFI GROOVES: QAWWALI AT NIZZAMUDDIN • BAREFOOT BLISS AT SONEVA GILI • VISITING GHANDI'S PEACEFUL ASHRAM • TAKING TEA IN DHARAMSALA • PICTURING A LOST CIVILIZATION AT AJANTA • DIVE WITH REEF SHARKS AND WRASSE IN THE INDIAN OCEAN • WALKING TO PARADISE AT GOKARNA • HAULING IN DINNER IN GOA • THE DANCING GODDESS OF KERALA • BROWSING ENGLISH VEG IN THE ASIAN HILLS • CROWD-WATCHING AT KARTIK PURNIMA • TOY TRAINS AND TIGHT CURVES: THE DARJEELING UNLIMITED • INDIA'S ACROPOLIS: A SHRINE TO THE FISH-EYED GODDESS • LOWERING THE FLAG AT THE INDIA-PAKISTAN BORDER • TREKKING TO THE SOURCE OF THE GANGES • WATCHING ELEPHANTS GO WILD IN UDA WALAWE • CRUISING THE KERALAN BACKWATERS • INTO THE BLUE: TRACKING WHALES IN THE INDIAN OCEAN • FINDING PERFECT POWDER IN KASHMIR • BOLLYWOOD GLAMOUR AT THE MUMBAI METRO • SURF BOATS ON THE SOUTHERN SEAS • EATING A BANANA-LEAF LUNCH IN CHIDAMBARAM • FISHING FOR BARRACUDA OFF MEDHUFUSHI • WATCHING THE SUN RISE OVER ACHYUTARAYA TEMPLE • TAKE A DAWN LAUGHTER YOGA SESSION IN MUMBAI • SADHU-SPOTTING AT THE KUMBH MELA • GET HIGH ON MOUNTAIN POLO • THE JUGGERNAUTS OF PURI • EVEREST: THE HARD WAY • EXPLORING GALLE FORT'S DUTCH HERITAGE • MAKING SACRIFICES AT A TANTRIC TEMPLE • CITY OF LIGHT: ON THE GANGES IN VARANASI • VISITING THE TAJ BY MOONLIGHT • RHYTHM MADNESS AT THE THRISSUR PURAM • BUNGEE JUMPING THE BHOTE KOSHI • STAYING WITH A FAMILY IN THE HIMALAYAS • FINDING ENLIGHTENMENT IN BUDDHISM'S BIRTHPLACE • MAKE LIKE KIPLING ON THE ELEPHANT SHOW • JOURNEYING OVER THE ROOF OF THE WORLD • MEDITATING IN THE HIMALAYAS • GETTING SWEPT AWAY AT DURGA PUJA • CHRISTMAS SHOPPING IN KUTCH • CROSS THE HIMALAYAS TO YOUR OWN SHRANGRI-LA • MEETING SHIVA AND ST THOMAS ON ADAM'S PEAK • SIKHS, SABRES AND A GIANT CANTEEN: THE GOLDEN TEMPLE • ON THE EDGE IN THE ANDAMANS • RIDING THE ROCKET ACROSS THE GANGES DELTA • EXPLORING THE THAR DESERT BY CAMEL • WASH AN

The Indian Subcontinent
804–860

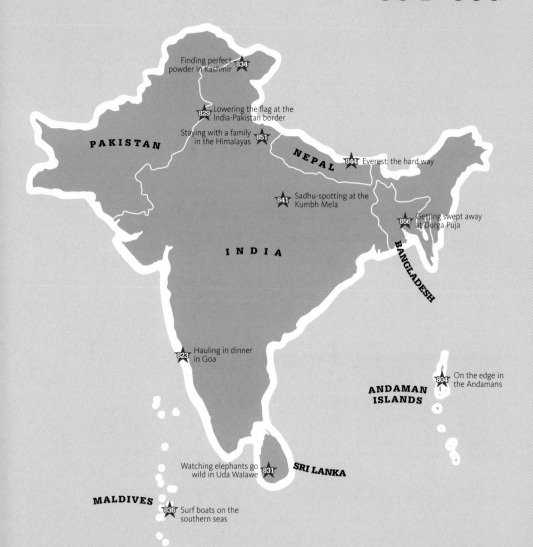

Finding perfect powder in Kashmir **834**

Lowering the flag at the India-Pakistan border **829**

Staying with a family in the Himalayas **851**

PAKISTAN

NEPAL

Everest: the hard way **844**

Sadhu-spotting at the Kumbh Mela **841**

Getting swept away at Durga Puja **856**

INDIA

BANGLADESH

Hauling in dinner in Goa **823**

On the edge in the Andamans **804**

ANDAMAN ISLANDS

Watching elephants go wild in Uda Walawe **831**

SRI LANKA

MALDIVES

Surf boats on the southern seas **836**

804 On the edge in the Andamans

INDIA There had been an unseasonal downpour and the jungle was literally steaming. Slicks of red mud had spilled over the road in places, repeatedly forcing the bus into first gear. Every time it slowed I noticed the policemen riding shotgun at opposite ends of the vehicle un-shoulder their Enfield rifles and study the forest like hawks. Through the 1990s, the Andaman Trunk Road, which links the largest islands in this remote archipelago 1000km off the east coast of India, was repeatedly attacked by Jarawa aboriginal people, angry at encroachments on their territory by settlers and loggers. Arrows and spears had rained through bus windows; travellers had been killed.

Since then, relations between the Jarawa and the mostly Tamil incomers from the mainland had calmed down, but the two still kept their distance. Waiting at a ferry jetty, a stony silence fell as three Jarawa men paddled out of the mangroves in a dugout. More African-than South Asian-looking, they all wore bands of frayed cotton around their heads. Not a glance, let alone greeting, was exchanged.

The far north of the Andamans has about it the air of a frontier zone. Infrastructure is minimal, accommodation basic and the beaches are out of this world. Permits restrict which islands you're supposed to visit, but local fisherman may be willing to take you out in boats to little islets where you can camp wild on shell-white sand beside turquoise bays fringed with coral reefs.

Smith Island is one of the most exquisite. A twenty-minute crossing from the tiny port of Arial Bay, it was uninhabited last time I was there, save for a small colony of deeply tanned Westerners living out an Alex Garland fantasy on a remote sandbar. The talk was all of wild elephants, secret springs and the wonders visible off the reef: marine turtles, dugongs and giant manta rays that swooped out of the blue depths like spectres. After a couple of nights grilling fish over driftwood fires, I began to understand why most had decided to stay until the rains came. In fact, it wouldn't surprise me if some were still there, paddling around Jarawa-style.

805 Riding the Rocket across the Ganges Delta

BANGLADESH The arterial Ganges and Jamuna, merging 60km west-southwest of Dhaka, feed hundreds of subsidiary rivers that radiate across the vast Ganges Delta, dissecting the land into a series of contiguous islands. This is the final stage in the odyssey of divine water, infused with an essence of the Subcontinental millions who have used and venerated it along its courses.

A Conrad-esque journey aboard one of the Rocket service's paddle-wheeled boats lets you join the flow of life on this awesome network of waterways. Your odyssey begins in the evening at Sadarghat, Dhaka's teeming main hub for river traffic, approached through the labyrinthine Old Quarter. From the *ghat* – perhaps the most compelling location in the capital – you can take in the panorama of bustling activity playing itself out on land and water against the backdrop of the striking cityscape on the far bank. It's an intoxicating blend of the old and the new: people bathe among beds of water

hyacinth, swarms of gondolier-like craft weave among wallowing cargo vessels, and the call of the muezzin mingles with the ferment of voices rising from the riverside market.

Night descends fast, and your first proper sight of rural Bangladesh is likely to come on the following morning. The verdant fields unfurl along the river bank, brightly-dressed women, children cavorting in the shallows, fishermen, dolphins and a thousand other ingredients forming a truly mesmerizing canvas.

Rocket boats are not pleasure cruisers that cocoon their passengers, but working parts of the transport infrastructure bringing you up close to the surrounding world. The nine stops between Dhaka and Khulna, when the boat comes alive with the transfer of people, animals and goods, offer the rare privilege of seeing in detail riverside habitations, ranging from clusters of huts nestled in pockets of jungle to the port of Mongla with its towering cranes and ocean-going freighters.

806 Exploring the Thar Desert by camel

INDIA In defiance of its old Rajasthani name, Marusthali (Land of Death), the Thar is the most densely populated of the world's great deserts. From the cities on its fringes all the way to the India–Pakistan border, the vast sand flats spreading across the northwest of the Subcontinent are dotted with myriad tiny mud and thatch villages, most of them many kilometres from the nearest stretch of tarmac. A train line and national highway wind in tandem to Jaisalmer, the Thar's most remote and beautiful citadel town, but from there on, the only way to reach the desert's more isolated settlements is by camel.

Riding out into the scrub, two metres off the ground, with the honey-coloured ramparts and temple towers of Jaisalmer fort receding into the distance, you enter another kind of India – one of wide, shimmering vistas, endless blue skies and, when the rolling gait of your camel ceases, profound stillness. The landscape is no great shakes: apart from a few picture-book dunes blistering up here and there, the Thar is monotonously flat.

Rather, it's for the flamboyance of the desert settlements that most visit this stark borderland. Perhaps as compensation for the sandy drabness of their world, the villagers adorn their children, their animals, houses, carts, shrines – and themselves – in elaborate style. Adobe walls are enlivened with elegant ochre and red geometric patterns, kitchen utensils with squiggly green and blue lacquerwork, moulded mud interiors, clothes and furniture with fragments of sparkling mica, cowry shells or embroidery.

Packs of jubilant children scamper out of every village as soon as a line of camels hoves into view. And the same pack follows you out again afterwards, which is perhaps why trekking camps tend to be in the middle of nowhere, well beyond foraging range. At sunset, saddle sore and a little sunburnt, you can sit back and reflect on the day's encounters as the desert glows red in the dying light. Sprawled on a rug beside a flickering campfire, with a pan of smoky dal and rice bubbling away under the starriest of skies, the Thar can feel a lot less like a "Land of Death" than a wholesome, blissful retreat.

Wash an elephant in the Rapti River

NEPAL Each day, at around 11am, a strange combination of sounds – excited laughter, lots of splashing and the occasional burst of trumpeting – can be heard drifting through the village of Sauraha in southern Nepal. Elephant bath time has begun.

This ritual takes place in the Rapti River, which separates Sauraha from Chitwan National Park, home to the endangered one-horned rhino. After a busy morning carrying tourists around the park and the nearby Community Forest reserves, a procession of dusty pachyderms are led by their mahouts to the river for a good scrub down – and, for a small fee, travellers are welcome to join in the fun.

After they have waded in, the elephants shoot jets of water into the air from their trunks, wallow on their sides while layers of mud are scraped off and, from time to time, dump unsuspecting riders into the river. In theory it is only the elephants that are there to be washed, but in practice anyone in the vicinity is given a good soaking too. This magical experience produces a childlike glee in even the most sober and straitlaced adult – and the elephants appear to enjoy it almost as much.

Before taking part in bath time, it's worth visiting the Elephant Breeding Project, 4km west of Sauraha, where elephants are trained to work in the park. It is home to several adult male elephants, a harem of females for them to breed with and usually a number of impossibly cute babies. While it can be difficult to tear yourself away from the calves, the small information room contains a list of verbal commands that should prove useful during bath time – if you manage to master the pronunciation. *Mail* means "stand up", *baith* means "sit down" and, perhaps most appropriately, *chhop* means "spray water".

807

Lakeside romance
in Rajasthan

INDIA India is teeming with wonderful places to stay, many of them tiny, old family-run homes transformed into romantic bolt holes. It is rare, however, to find a large modern-day hotel with equal measures of soul, style and glamour.

The *Oberoi Udaivilas* in Rajasthan has changed all that. Situated in the achingly romantic city of Udaipur, it is reached by canopied boat across shimmering Lake Pichola – arrive at dusk for the full effect. The grand Mewar-style building is a blaze of tinkling fountains, butter-coloured domes, reflective marble pools, pavilions and balconies. At night, flickering candles reflected in the water, the whole place evokes a bygone era of palaces and princes.

Despite all the must-do sightseeing in the area, it is hard to leave the hotel. Peacocks roam in the gardens, telepathic staff couldn't be cheerier, the shop is pashmina central and rooms offer divine decadence. The beds are vast, the marble baths deep, and local furniture and fabrics are beautifully crafted. You can even enjoy your very own mini infinity-edged pool, perfect for lazy lengths, with views of the City Palace, and a telescope to boot. If all this isn't enough, the hotel's Banyan Tree spa is a haven of *ayurveda* and aromatherapy. Every treatment begins with a foot scrub in rose-scented water, after which you can be wrapped in tomato or scrubbed with rice, enjoy marvellous massages or go yogic with the experts. As for the food – rejoice in fresh vegetables picked from the garden and fabulous meals ranging from fragrant curries to sophisticated Thai extravaganzas. Old hand or neophyte, you'll feast like there is no tomorrow – here is a hotel that satisfies everybody.

809 Tracing the turtle arribada at Orissa

INDIA We'd known they were on their way since breakfast time, when news that the arribada had formed a couple of kilometres out to sea had crackled through our shortwave radio from the spotter ship. First reports suggested that numbers were good. The Indian coastguard had forecast a steady onshore breeze blowing from the Bay of Bengal until dawn, and the military firing range nearby, forewarned of the invasion, had agreed to suspend artillery tests and cut its lights. After a week of scanning the eastern horizon, the stage was set for one of the world's great annual wildlife spectacles.

The first olive ridleys reached us around sunset. After their epic swim across half of the planet's oceans, the pregnant females arrive exhausted and silent, allowing the surf to wash them as far up the incline as possible before starting their struggle with the undertow and soft sand. Within half an hour, the beach is entirely covered: a huge undulating sweep of hump-backed shells, glistening under a full moon.

An estimated 240,000 marine turtles crawled on to Gahirmatha beach that night, watched by barely thirty or so people from the Greenpeace Turtle Witness Camp, which campaigns to protect the nesting site.

By the time they'd laid their batch of eggs, many were too drained to move, submitting with watery-eyed indifference to the attentions of us onlookers. Then, as if in response to some pre-arranged signal, the whole arribada suddenly started lumbering seaward again, leaving behind them an empty beach crisscrossed with myriad prints.

The cool of early morning allowed us a few hours' sleep back at camp before we too had to begin our journeys homewards, in the opposite direction: via the crowded cities of coastal Orissa. Bumping along in the back of a local bus, I tried to work out where I'd be in forty days' time when the tiny turtle hatchlings would emerge from their nests and scuttle into the waves to start their long and perilous swim to the Pacific.

810 Elbowing through the crowds for Esala Perahera

SRI LANKA In terms of noise and colour, there's nothing else quite like Kandy's Esala Perahera, an extravaganza dating back to the fourth century AD and the early days of Buddhism in Sri Lanka. It takes place over the last ten days of the Buddhist lunar month of Esala to honour the Buddha's tooth – according to legend, a devotee snatched one of his teeth from his funeral pyre around 300 AD and smuggled it to Sri Lanka, where it was laid in a golden urn and carried around in celebratory procession. The festival involves a series of spectacular night-time *peraheras* (parades) with drummers, dancers, torch-bearers, whip-crackers, fire-eaters and over a hundred costumed elephants.

The parades start between 8pm and 9pm, though you'll need to be in place at least an hour before. As dusk approaches, the flood of humanity lining the route turns into a solid, almost impenetrable mass. The smell of jasmine, incense, frangipani – not to mention the spicy picnic suppers everyone is tucking into – is intense, and the trees, shop fronts and streetlamps drip with tinsel and coloured lights.

You'll hear the *perahera* before you see it. Depending on the night, there might be up to a thousand drummers, and the boom of their instruments carries far across the city, heightening the sense of anticipation that precedes the elephants – scores of them, decorated in golden balaclavas, beautiful silks and silver thread. Surrounding them are brightly attired dancers, drummers or torch-bearers, each either carrying a bundle of sticks that have been dipped in oil or swinging burning coconut husks from chains. Troupes of dancers, acrobats and musicians accompany the procession, along with men wielding huge whips, which they crack every minute or so to scare away demons.

Near the head of the parade is the mighty Maligawa tusker elephant, the beast entrusted with the job of carrying the Tooth Relic (or a replica thereof). Kitted out more ostentatiously than all the other elephants put together, he marches through the streets with stately dignity, his appearance triggering wild cheering in the crowds, many of whom have waited for hours just to catch a glimpse of him.

811 Dodging the crowds on the Sikles Trek

NEPAL If you've ever longed to hike the land of the yak and yeti, but lack the endurance of hardened adventurers such as Sirs Edmund Hillary and Ranulph Fiennes, there's a trek out there just for you. Mid-West Nepal's five-day Sikles trip is an ideal eco-trekking route and an excellent alternative to the famed – and far too overtourished – Annapurna Circuit. It explores an untrampled corner of the Annapurna Conservation Area, and offers beguiling views of the peaks of Annapurna II, III and IV, Manaslu and the dozen summits of the monolithic Lamjung Himal.

The erstwhile hippy base of Pokhara is the departure point for the rickety tin bus that jounces trekkers north for several hours, across blacktop highway and potholed byroad, alongside the Mardi Khola River towards the thickly forested ridges of highland Nepal. Foot hits ground in a succession of terraced fields that quickly steepen towards the tiny hillside settlement of Ghalekharka. From this base, a steep, dense jungle of orchids, rhododendrons and the occasional

bloodsucking leech leads towards Sikles's most demanding ascent – the slog up to the wooded col of Tara Top, a plateau with dusk and dawn views of most of the Annapurna massif and the Himalayan foothills that drop to the Ganges and the plains of India. At an elevation of just over 3000m, the views of the snowy Eastern Annapurnas from this small knoll are rarely bettered, even on more formidable treks.

From here, follow the river's west bank down to a ridge above the trek's namesake village of Sikles (1980m), one of Nepal's largest Gurung settlements and home to many families of Gurkha soldiers. Up here are magical scenes: uniformed schoolgirls with red ribbons in their hair skipping down the hillside; giant oxen trailing them; and guides and porters, heads bowed, praying silently in front of the jagged peak of Machhapuchhre, a mountain considered sacred by locals. As day draws to a close, kick back as impossibly tall mountains unveil themselves against a clear blue sky, dotted with cushions of puffy white cloud, bands of setting sunlight slicing across their peaks.

INDIA "Clang", goes the rusty bell, "clang", and the blanket posing as a curtain begins to shake.

It's dark in the theatre – the limited illumination from the candles at the front of the stage is just enough to catch the mirror-work on what I assume must be part of a costume shuffling in the wings – and the air is heavy with sandalwood incense.

"Clang", goes the bell again. The blanket is thrust to the ground and a brighter candle appears stage right, but it's the centre of the stage that draws my attention now, for there stands a nightmareish version of the Sugar Plum Fairy. His face is a gaudy green with cherry-red lips and eyes accented with kohl, his bodice a huge gold bib from which his many skirts puff out like a vast tutu made from tablecloths. His headgear is not unlike a Middle Eastern water pipe with a halo of gold and jewels. As we watch, his eyes flicker and flutter and his mouth contorts into a variety of grins and grimaces. Who is he? Why, the prince out hunting cobra, of course.

We had come to Ernakulam, in Kerala, to see a *kathakali*, or "story play" performance, an ancient Hindu method of recounting tales from the *Ramayana* and *Mahabharata*. In this wordless theatre every concept or emotion has a corresponding facial expression or hand position – the performer contorts his face from one painful-looking, blinking attitude to another and gesticulates around the stage, the embodiment of a god or demon.

Watching a **kathakali** **performance** in Kochi

812

813 Morning prayers at Diskit Monastery

INDIA To join in morning *puja* (prayers) in a Ladakhi Buddhist monastery, high in the Himalayas, is to enter frozen time.

It's cold outside, even though the sun has hit the Nubra Valley floor. Long, cool shadows fall over yawning monks and novices flagged in plum-coloured robes. Incense is lit and syncopated chanting, more football terrace than enlightened warbling, begins.

Breakfast – butter tea dispensed from a dented kettle and porridge from a galvanized bucket – momentarily interrupts the rhythmic mantra. The simple, moving chorus starts once more, but with *puja* over there's a stampede past jewelled doors for a morning game of soccer.

814 Sliding along the Himalayan Ice Highway

INDIA On the frozen river, silence has substance. It's tangible because it means the way ahead is solid, and therefore safe. More than the crack of splintering ice, travellers on this hazardous artery – the only winter route through the Great Himalayan range from the remote region of Zanskar to Ladakh, in the Indus Valley – learn to dread the lap of open water. "This one Tsarak Do . . . 'Running Place'". My guide, Namgyal Tenzing, wrapped in a wine-coloured wool *goncha*, ice dusting his hat and eyelashes, peers upriver through a mist of falling crystals. "Very cold place. Zanskar people is running here. Never stop. No good." This, however, is precisely what I and my three Zanskari companions are about to do.

After eight hours skidding over shattered plate ice, our only chance of shelter turns out to be a rock hollow on the opposite bank. But between us and it, the ice is tinged tell-tale green, and we can all hear the gurgles of a living river beneath our feet.

The crossing, however, turns out to be straightforward, and in no time at all we're huddled around a driftwood fire that spits wild sparks into the night. Later, as we lie wedged together in the cave, I can hear freshly formed ice fizzing downstream, and the mountains, ghost-like against the star-strewn sky, begin to glow with the first moonlight.

Depending on weather conditions, it can take anywhere between four and ten days – or even longer – to cover the length of the frozen river, which the locals call Chaddar. Given the dangers involved, it's amazing that so many use it to escape their snowbound homeland in midwinter. But for foreigners, the route repays its rigours ten times over. Quite apart from being one of Asia's last true adventures, it offers the chance to experience the inner Himalaya as few outsiders see it: medieval Buddhist monasteries and thatched-roof villages, half-buried under fresh powder snow; frozen waterfalls; herds of ice-encrusted yaks; and monks performing masked *cham* dances – all set against a vast amphitheatre of white peaks.

There are two talismanic words you'll be glad to hear, loud and often, along the way. Stepping gingerly out onto the river the morning after our freezing night in the cave, Namgyal strikes the surface with his stick, scrutinizes the spangle of blue bubbles beneath and calls out "gala dukh!" – "good ice!".

INDIA In 2008, cricket in the Subcontinent went glam – and the parade shows no sign of slowing. With nail-biting cricketing action in twenty-over innings and teams owned by Bollywood royalty and business tycoons, the Indian Premier League has added a dramatic and showy new twist to a decidedly traditional sport.

From the day the event is announced to its spectacular opening ceremony and much-hyped finale, the IPL dominates the Indian psyche completely. The drama unfolds with a high-powered auction, some international stars reaching over a million dollars as the IPL lives up to its cash-rich reputation in style. While some may grumble that money is the name of the game, the appeal of seeing promising young guns in the midst of big money and big names sweeps the vast majority of fans along. Each franchise – teams include the Kolkata Knight Riders, Deccan Chargers and Rajasthan Royals – can include up to four non-Indians in their eleven, and passionate fans scream advice to brothers-in-arms who would otherwise face off as members of opposing international sides.

Once the games begin, the pent-up excitement becomes palpable. The first thing that strikes you is the rush of sound – loud cheering from the crowds and the latest Bollywood melodies. This is cricket shorn of some of its subtleties, but with the spectacle ramped up to the max. Matches seem like one big party, high-risk cricket, cheerleading, celebrities and slow-motion replays ensuring things never let up. Celebrations reach their peak as the teams take positions on field, and every wicket, six or boundary is followed by revelry in the stands. Even the riotously-hued players aren't immune to the merry-making and some can be seen shaking a leg between innings.

A trip to the IPL is like a trip through India. The excitement, colour, chaos and non-stop drama offer a vivid insight to the new Subcontinent and the flights of fancy that run through its veins. The eager crowd – men, women and children – can't get enough.

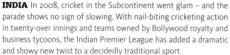

GLITZ, LEATHER AND WILLOW:
the IPL

815

816 Sufi grooves: qawwali at Nizzamuddin

INDIA The shrine, or Dargah, of the Sufi mystic Nizzamuddin Auliya, India's most revered Muslim saint, is one among many ancient vestiges rising from the modern sprawl of south Delhi. Sandwiched incongruously between a six-lane flyover and a faceless concrete suburb, it stands at the centre of a warren of narrow alleyways, mosques, onion-domed tombs and shanty huts. To step into this medieval enclave is to enter a kind of parallel reality where little has changed since Nizzamuddin's burial here in 1325.

From all over the city, large crowds descend on the Dargah on Thursday evenings to worship at the saint's candlelit mausoleum. Rubbing shoulders with the devotees are a collection of Sufi ascetics, or *pir zadas*, dervishes, henna-bearded Islamic scholars and priests, who rock back and forth over worn copies of the Koran, murmuring prayers, chatting or fanning braziers of incense.

A sudden drum roll announces the start of the evening's *qawwali* performance. As many as a dozen *qawwals* may be lined up, sitting cross-legged before the entrance to the tomb in long Peshwari frockcoats and lamb's-wool hats. A couple play harmonium, one will play tabla; the rest provide clapping percussion and chorus, taking it in turns to sing lead.

The *qawwals*' job is to inspire *hal* – spiritual ecstasy – among the worshippers by singing songs of devotion, songs whose rhythms and melodies will stir even those who may not understand a single word of their poetry. As the music gradually picks up pace and volume, the crowd becomes more and more moved by its hypnotic beats. Hands rise into the air, heads turn towards the darkening sky and, if the *hal* is upon them, dervishes slip into trances and start to spin or convulse, possessed by adoration of the saint. Such gatherings can last all night, breaking up only at dawn after one final, tumultuous cadence.

It's a testament to the spirit of tolerance at the heart of Sufism that the worshippers at Nizzamuddin's tomb invariably include members of all Delhi's faiths: Sikhs, Hindus and Buddhists, as well as Muslims. In this age of religious fundamentalism, the unifying power of *qawwali* remains undimmed.

817 Barefoot bliss at Soneva Gili

THE MALDIVES For being in, on and with the sea, the wonderful water-world of the Maldives is hard to beat. A necklace of palm-topped, sandy white islands in the Indian Ocean, from your sea-plane they look for all the world like Tiffany-blue floating poached eggs. Wonderfully secluded, these amazing atolls are home to some of the most luxurious, beautiful and expensive hotels in the world, each occupying its own small island.

Soneva Gili epitomizes the very best in barefoot luxury. If your idea of a hot hotel is marble bathrooms, golf courses and tables groaning under the weight of silver, you've got the wrong place. We're talking *Robinson Crusoe* meets *World of Interiors*, a simple idyll finessed with lavish touches.

At *Gili* your shoes are gently removed upon arrival, the clocks are set an hour forward for maximum sunshine and your food, spa, CD and pillow preferences are all established ahead via email. The wooden villas are castaway fantasies, spacious and deeply private, with walk-in wardrobes for all those clothes you'll never wear, breezy day rooms and two bathrooms – one inside, one beneath the stars. Stay in a villa on stilts over the shimmering sea and you can row your own little canoe back to your room, sleep outdoors lulled by a balmy breeze and order room service by speedboat – very James Bond.

Most pleasures here seem to be horizontal – sunbathing, swimming, snorkelling, scuba diving. You can also be dropped off at a deserted island for the day (hammocks and picnics provided), head off for a day of pampering at the spa, or simply chill in the pristine peace of your private pool.

The food is also sensational, much of it grown in the resort's own vegetable garden, with bread straight from the oven, sushi and oysters, zingy fresh fish and French wines. Feast in the candlelit privacy of your veranda or on a remote starlit sand-spit that's here today, gone tomorrow.

818 Visiting Gandhi's peaceful ashram

INDIA Occupying a peaceful plot on the western bank of the Sabarmati River in Gujarat is an evocative tribute to a man who changed the course of history. Mohandas Karamchand Gandhi, born in Porbandar in western Gujarat, led the campaign for Indian independence and will forever symbolize nonviolent protest.

The Mahatma ("Great Soul") established the Sabarmati Ashram in 1917, bringing together people who would work to secure India's freedom. Symbolically located between a jail and a crematorium – Gandhi believed a *satyagrahi* (someone engaged in passive resistance) inevitably ended up in one of these two places – the ashram soon became the centre of the Indian independence movement.

Although no longer in operation, it has become a pilgrimage site drawing hundreds of thousands of visitors a year. In keeping with Gandhian philosophy, it's a modest place, but one with unmistakable authority. The simple, single-storey whitewashed buildings and neatly tended gardens have an incredibly serene air that invites contemplation, in stark contrast to the crowded, pollution-choked city outside. Many come here simply to sit and think in the peaceful grounds, but there is also an auditorium for talks and film screenings, a photo gallery, library and archive, and an appropriately pared-back museum. Among the exhibits is a letter from Gandhi to Hitler urging him to avoid war, and a moving collection of personal possessions, including some wooden shoes, pristine white clothes and a pair of round spectacles.

The ashram was the starting point for the famous Dandi March on March 12, 1930, which catalysed the resistance movement in India. Gandhi led 78 people on a 388km walk to the Gulf of Cambay in protest against the British Salt Law, vowing not to return to the ashram until India was free. Although the country gained independence on August 15, 1947, Gandhi was assassinated before he could set foot in the ashram again.

Today, the Sabarmati Ashram commemorates the great achievements of the past, but in a state that has suffered bitter violence in recent years, it also stands as a potent symbol of hope.

819 Taking tea in Dharamsala

INDIA The bowl is placed gently in my hands. I look down at the thick, yellow liquid and sniff. It smells oily and rancid: yak butter tea. Three Tibetan women with browned, etched faces sit, like me, cross-legged on the floor. It's quiet except for their deep slurps – this is the equivalent of their morning coffee. The Himalayas loom all around us here in Dharamsala, the mountain home of the Dalai Lama and the Tibetan government in exile. The sun climbs in the sky, and I look out of the window as the snowy peaks slowly come in to focus. My Tibetan friends smile at me encouragingly. I close my eyes and gulp the tea: congealed fat catches in my throat and salt puckers my lips. I force a few more sips, then cradle the bowl in my lap. An acquired taste, to be sure.

Yak butter tea, they say, was made for life in the mountains – fat to insulate you against the chill, salt for rehydration and black tea to keep you going. Our days in Dharamsala start at dawn. We gather on the rooftop, facing in the four sacred directions, the colourful prayer flags whipping over our heads. It's winter, and from here we can see the white mist swirling through the shivering pines, and down the village's steep stone streets. The wind whips past maroon-clad monks circling the Buddhist temple, and around the spinning gold-and-red prayer wheels. It chills us as we later trek the mountain trails, the altitude leaving us breathless. Not until the sun sets do we return home, where we stretch our weary limbs, and warm up near the stove. A cup of yak butter tea, I think, would hit the spot.

820 Picturing a lost civilization at Ajanta

INDIA Even now, with the approach road marred by postcard stalls and car parks, the Ajanta Caves in northern Maharashtra have about them the aura of a lost world. Hollowed out of the sides of a horseshoe-shaped ravine, deep in an arid wilderness zone that has always been forbiddingly remote, the complex remains hidden from view until you're almost directly beneath it. When Lt Alexander Cunningham of the 16th Bengal Lancers stumbled on the site by chance during a tiger hunt in 1813, the excavations had lain forgotten for more than a thousand years – their floors a midden of animal bones and ash from aboriginal hunting fires, their exquisite frescoes blackened by soot.

These days, the worn, rock-cut steps to the caves are fitted with metal handrails, and electricity has replaced the candles used by Cunningham's party, but from the instant the guide first swings his arc light over the murals adorning the walls you're plunged into another time. It's a moment few visitors forget. Once your eyes have adjusted to the swirls of earthy red, yellow, blue and black pigments, scenes of unimaginable sophistication emerge from the gloom:

sumptuous royal processions; elaborate court and street scenes; snowcapped mountains; sages; musicians; stormy seascapes and shipwrecks; marching armies; and a veritable menagerie of animals, both real and imagined.

But it's the intimacy of the art that really captivates. The beautifully fluid tableaux seem to glow with life. Kohl-rimmed eyes light up; well-toned torsos, draped with jewellery, still look sexy; dance poses ooze sensuous grace, humour and vitality; and you can almost smell the aroma of a lotus blossom being raised by the smiling Bodhisattva Avalokitesvara in Cave 1 – India's own Mona Lisa.

For the pilgrims who would have filed past these sacred Buddhist treasures thousands of years ago, the art would have fired the imagination with a power equivalent to that of modern cinema. These must have been the Bollywood movies of their era, complete with resplendently bejewelled heroines and strong, compassionate heroes, backed up by a supporting cast of thousands – and if the images are anything to go by, the soundtrack would have been amazing too.

821 Dive with reef sharks and wrasse in the Indian Ocean

THE MALDIVES Its white-sand beaches and luxurious resorts are undoubtedly special places to unwind, but many people make the long journey to the Maldives with a snorkelling mask in their suitcase and PADI certification card in their wallet. The brilliantly turquoise waters hold over two thousand species of fish, including serpent-like moray eels, bulbous napoleon wrasse and huge, elegant manta rays.

With visibility of up to 40m, diving in this remote archipelago, 700km southwest of Sri Lanka, is understandably big business, and established dive centres at most resorts offer reef and drift diving, as well as the opportunity to dive at night – which promises intrepid divers intimate encounters with sharks and rays.

Reef sharks are one of the main attractions in the Maldives and are reassuringly unlikely to be aggressive towards divers. Often sighted gracefully skimming the edges of the reef, the grey reef shark, distinguished by a lighter strip on its dorsal fin and a black flash across the edge of its tail, can reach up to two metres

in length. Once immediate thoughts of *Jaws* have been banished, gliding through the sparkling Indian Ocean only metres from a great predator as it slinks its way around the coral is thrilling.

If you'd rather stay closer to the shore, snorkelling over the threshold of the shallow water is also a spectacular experience. Swimming out from an immaculately sandy beach, with the sun warming your back and your breath whispering through your snorkel, the reefs suddenly and dramatically drop away to reveal shoals of tropical fish and vividly coloured coral, while the chattering sound of feeding parrotfish resonates under water.

At an average of only 1.5m above sea level, the 1190 islands of the archipelago just peer above the surface of the Indian Ocean. Sadly, as water levels rise, the islands' future is increasingly threatened – and the extraordinary underwater world lying beneath the sand banks is likely to be easily accessed for only a few more decades. Plan your reef-shark rendezvous soon.

INDIA Goa tends to be where most people head when they fancy a beach break in India. There is, however, one special little town a couple of hours further south down the coast, where you can hit the sands without feeling like you've left the country entirely behind.

As the site of one of India's most revered Shiva shrines, Gokarna has been an important Hindu pilgrimage destination for thousands of years. Like a lot of India's religious centres, it's locked in a charismatic time warp: worn and dilapidated, but full of old-world atmosphere. Brahmin priests still saunter around bare-chested, swathed in white or coral-coloured *lunghis*, and the main market street is always thronged with stray cows and bus-loads of pilgrims squelching their way from the town's sacred beach to the temples after a purifying dip in the sea.

A lone Rama temple, overlooking Gokarna's seafront from the edge of a headland wrapped in waxy green cashew bushes, marks the start of a path to an altogether different kind of beach scene. Backed by coconut groves and forested hills, the series of beautiful bays to the south is where the hardcore hippy contingent forced out of Goa by the 1990s charter boom regrouped and put down roots.

Of all of them, Om Beach, where a pair of twin coves and their rocky outcrops replicate the sacred Hindu symbol for "Oneness and Peace", is the most famous. Further south, the path continues beyond steep, grassy clifftops dotted with miniature palms and red laterite boulders to a string of even more gorgeous side coves with names like "Full Moon" and "Paradise". This far away from civilization, the jungle descends right to the sand line, while the sea crashes in wild and clean. Fish eagles patrol the foreshore and dolphins regularly flip out of the waves.

Admittedly, the kind of ersatz Indian behaviour beloved in these hideaways isn't for everybody. But if the ostentatious chillum-smoking, yoga posing and mantra-chanting does start to grate, rest assured you can always slip one of the local fishermen a fifty-rupee note and have him whisk you back to town to watch the real thing.

Walking to
Paradise at
Gokarna 822

HAULING IN DINNER
in GOA

823

INDIA Though a cable winch (or a modern boat) would be more efficient, the Goan fishermen of Benaulim bring in their catch the old-fashioned way and, if you're strolling by, they'll probably wave you over to help. Two long ropes stretch all the way up the beach, with heavy branches attached at intervals; on the other end is their net, sometimes floating 500m from the shore and visible only as a massive swirl of water and seabirds. You and a dozen fishermen brace your backs against the branches and take straining steps in reverse toward the line of palms.

The old wooden fishing boat that rests on the sand, with the Portuguese name *Bom Jesus* painted on its prow, is both a reminder of the tiny state's colonial past and evidence of its peculiar culture. Like most of India, Goa had a sophisticated indigenous society for more than a millennium before Europeans arrived, but its modern character is the result of spice-hunter Vasco da Gama's arrival here

at the turn of the fifteenth century. Though the Indian army finally drove the Portuguese out in the 1960s, Goans today are proud of their unique identity: partly Lusophone, largely Catholic and with an intriguing and delicious fusion of Portuguese and Indian cuisine. These traits have attracted travellers to Goa for decades, as much to admire its cathedrals and colonial architecture as to throw massive raves on its famously lovely beaches.

It's not party time in Benaulim, though; the sand slips out beneath your feet and you must be conceding 3m for every one you gain. Either the waves don't want to give up their bounty so easily, or the fish aren't keen on being dinner. Groaning, yelling, laughing and grimacing, your team could keep at this for hours until the net is hauled in, though by this point you may have turned over your position to someone else. Stick around, though, and you'll see what's likely to end up on your plate that evening in a fish curry.

824 The dancing goddess of Kerala

INDIA A sudden intensification of the drumming and cymbal rhythms heralds the appearance of the Teyyam. The crowd of villagers falls silent. Bare-chested and wrapped in white cotton *lunghis*, the men and boys stand on one side, the women, in coloured silk saris with garlands of jasmine strung in their hair, stand on the other. Excitement, tempered with apprehension, flickers across their faces, turning in an instant to wide-eyed awe as the deity finally emerges from behind the village shrine.

It's hard to convey the electric mix of terror and adoration the Teyyam's costume inspires. A huge confection of gold-painted papier-mâché, metal jewellery, appliqué hangings, cowry-shell anklets and ornate necklaces, surmounted by a vast corona of silver foil and crimson fur, its focal point is an elaborately made-up face with curly chrome fangs protruding from its mouth.

This is as close to the goddess as some of these people will ever get. Age-old caste restrictions still bar them from access to Kerala's most revered Tantric shrines, but at this moment Muchilôttu Bhagavati, a local form of the Hindu goddess of death and destruction, Kali, is herself manifest among them, her spirit glaring through the Teyyam's bloodshot eyes, animating its every move and gesture.

Twisting and spinning through a succession of poses in the firelight, the apparition really does feel like a visitor from another realm. Temple drumming and chants accompany her graceful dance around the beaten-earth arena, which grows in intensity through the night, culminating in a frenzied possession. Only when the first daylight glows through the palm canopy does the deity retire, blessing her devotees as she does so.

825 Browsing English veg in the Asian hills

SRI LANKA Sri Lanka has many unexpected sights, but few are as surreal as early morning in Haputale. As dawn breaks, the mists that blanket the town for much of the year slowly dissipate, revealing the huddled shapes of dark-skinned Tamils, insulated against the cold in woolly hats and padded jackets, hawking great bundles of English vegetables – radishes, swedes, cabbages and marrows – while the workaday Sri Lankan town slowly comes to life in the background, with its hooting buses and cluttered bazaars. As the mists clear and the sun rises, the tangled ridges of the island's hill country come slowly into view to the north, while to the south the land falls dramatically away to the lowlands below, with the far-off view of the coast and its sweltering Indian Ocean beaches faintly visible in the distance. As an image of Sri Lanka's unexpected juxtapositions, Haputale has few peers, and to stand shivering on a hilltop within a few degrees of the equator, watching a scene reminiscent of an English market town crazily displaced in time

and space, is to understand something of the cultural and physical contradictions of this fascinatingly diverse island.

The contradictions continue in the countryside beyond Haputale, as the road twists and turns up into the sprawling British-era plantations of the Dambatenne Tea Estate, whose antiquated factory is filled with the ingenious Victorian mechanical contraptions which are still used to process the leaves brought in from the surrounding estates. For the British visitor particularly, there is always the faint, strange nostalgia of seeing the legacy of one's great-great-grandparents preserved in a distant and exotic tropical island. But there is also the subversive awareness that the hillsides of Haputale, once colonized by the British, have now reached out and quietly conquered distant parts of the world in their turn, filling the teabags and chai shops of countries as varied as England, Iran and India, with a taste that is purely and uniquely Sri Lankan.

826 Crowd-watching at Kartik Purnima

INDIA In this era of "Readymade Suitings and Shirtings", traditional Indian dress is definitely on the decline. There is, however, one place you're guaranteed to see proper old-fashioned finery at its most flamboyant. Each year, during the full-moon phase of Kartika month, tens of thousands of Rajasthani villagers hitch up their camel carts and converge on the oasis of Pushkar, on the edge of the Thar Desert, for a bathe in the town's sacred lake, whose waters are said to be especially purifying at this time. As well as a redemptive dip, the festival also provides an opportunity to indulge those other great Rajasthani passions: trading livestock, arranging marriages – and generally strutting one's stuff.

Kartik Purnima has in recent times been rebranded as the Pushkar Camel Fair by the region's entrepreneurial tourist office, and the vast sea of neatly clipped beige fur undulating in the dunes around the town during the festival does present one of India's most arresting spectacles. But it's the animals' owners who really steal the show. Dressed in kilos of silver jewellery, flowing pleated skirts and veils dripping with intricate mirrorwork and embroidery,

the women look breathtaking against the desert backdrop, especially in the warmer colours of evening, when the sand glows molten red and the sky turns a fantastic shade of mauve. The men go for a more sober look, but compensate for their white-cotton *dhoti* loincloths and shirts with outsized, vibrantly coloured turbans and handlebar moustaches waxed to pin-sharp points.

Traditional Rajasthani garb looks even more wonderful against the backdrop of Pushkar's sacred steps, or *ghats*, spread around the lake. For the full effect, get up before dawn, when the drumming, conch-blowing and bell-ringing starts at the temples, and position yourself on one of the flat rooftops or peeling whitewashed cupolas overlooking the waterside. When the sun's first rays finally burst across Nag Pahar ("Snake Mountain") to the east, a blaze of colour erupts as thousands of pilgrims gather to invoke Brahma, the Supreme Creator Being of Hindu mythology, by raising little brass pots of sacred water above their heads and pouring them back into the lake. It's a scene that has changed little in hundreds – even thousands – of years.

the Darjeeling unlimited

INDIA Thank the Raj. It was the Brits who laid the foundational tracks of the Indian railway system, whose lines today comprise the largest locomotive network in the world: nearly 65,000km of track, 7085 stations and 1.6 million staff. The most romantic – and affordable – way to explore India is by train, venturing into a bygone world of steam locomotives and dilapidated rail cars, and chugging past rural villages that have hardly changed for hundreds of years.

One of the least known – and most adventurous – routes is the Darjeeling Himalayan Railway, a tiny, steam-fuelled locomotive that more than deserves its nickname "The Toy Train". The string of narrow-gauge railway cars ply the hilly Himalayas of West Bengal, from New Jalpaiguri north of Calcutta up to Darjeeling, an early nineteenth-century station near the Nepali border, established for workers and servants of the East India Company.

Built in 1881 and ascending some 1800m of gauge track, the 82km route takes around seven hours, rarely exceeding 16km/h. Past Siliguri Junction, the train climbs slowly (and noisily) at a steady gradient. The rail cars switchback, zigzag, and, on several occasions, cross the very track they have just veered off after making 180-degree hairpin turns. The most nail-biting section of the journey is the aptly named Agony Point outside Tindharia, where the train wraps around one of the tightest track curves in the world. Through the carriage windows stretch tea plantations, rainforests and endless plateaus of green and umber fields: Sukna, where the landscape morphs from flat plains to wooded lower slopes; Rangtong, where a deciduous forest sprawls off into the distance; Kurseong, with its colourful, bustling bazaar stalls; and Ghum (2258m), the summit of the line and the highest railway station in the Indian Subcontinent.

Finally, as the train reaches Darjeeling station, you enter a relaxed new world: clean, alpine air, a colonial setting of convent schools and palaces and – in the distance – the soaring Himalayan peaks of Kanchenjunga Mountain, at 8586m the third highest in the world.

India's Acropolis:
a shrine to the **fish-eyed goddess**

INDIA Rising from the surrounding plains of tropical vegetation like man-made mountains, the great temples of the Chola dynasty utterly dominate most major towns in Tamil Nadu. For sheer scale and intensity, though, none outstrips the one dedicated to the fish-eyed goddess, Shri Meenakshi, and her consort, Sundareshwara, in Madurai. Peaking at 46m, its skyscraping *gopuras* stand as the state's pride and joy – Dravidian India's Empire State, Eiffel Tower and Cristo Redentor rolled into one. The towers taper skywards like elongated, stepped pyramids, their surfaces writhing with an anarchic jumble of deities, demons, warriors, curvaceous maidens, pot-bellied dwarves and sprites – all rendered in Disney-bright colours, and topped with crowns of gigantic cobra heads and gilded finials.

Joining the flood of pilgrims that pours through the gateways beneath them, you leave the trappings of modern India far behind. A labyrinth of interconnecting walkways, ceremonial halls and courtyards forms the heart of the complex. Against its backdrop of 30,000 carved pillars unfolds a never-ending round of rituals and processions. Day and night, cavalcades of bare-chested priests carry torches of burning camphor and offerings for the goddess, accompanied by drummers and musicians blasting out devotional hymns on Tamil oboes. Shaven-headed pilgrims prostrate themselves on the greasy stone floors as queues of women clutching parcels of lotus flowers, coconuts and incense squeeze through the crush to the innermost sanctum.

Perhaps the most amazing thing of all about the Meenakshi Temple is that these rituals have taken place in the same shrines, continually and largely unchanged, since the time of ancient Greece. Nowhere else in the world has a classical civilization survived into the modern era, and nowhere else in India are the ancient roots of Hinduism so tangible. It's as if Delphi or the Acropolis were still centres of active worship in the dot-com era.

829 Lowering the flag at the India–Pakistan border

INDIA & PAKISTAN Relations between India and Pakistan have long been tense and bloody, but a trip out to Wagh in the Punjab on the Indian side of the border will make you wonder whether it's nothing but a sibling rivalry.

It's a short walk from the car park to the border, and you'll pass the customs and passport offices before reaching the tiered seating for the daily lowering of the flag ceremony, pitched somewhere between an Olympic event and a school concert.

There was already a large crowd assembled when I arrived, and I sought out an inconspicuous seat on the far end of the bleachers. The border area was punctuated with tall, moustachioed, plumed sentinels looking splendid in their red-and-gold trimmed khaki uniforms. Several turbaned young men were gathered near the front of the guards, looking smart in their tailored trousers and crisp white shirts and dancing with their arms around each other with as much enthusiasm as if their team had won the cricket. A group of middle-

aged Israeli women joined in for a bit of pan-continental unification-style dancing, much to the bemusement of the Indian men.

Excitement among the crowd began to build. Chants of "Hin-doo-stan" on our side were matched in volume by the equally growing numbers of Pakistanis – somewhat less colourfully attired than their Indian counterparts, in their white *kurtas* and skull caps – shouting "Pak-is-tan" like a call and response game from the other side of the divide. This went on for some time, heightening the air of anticipation before the Indian guards began to march – not too dissimilarly to Basil Fawlty, with the flamboyance of flamenco dancers – along the famed border gate to the flag and eventually lowered it. Not to be outdone, the Pakistanis countered with their own colourful march, though on this occasion it was clear the Indian guards won the day. Totally surreal to a Westerner's eyes, the grandiose choreography was a reassuringly good-natured symbol of national pride right at the heart of a distressing conflict.

830 Trekking to the source of the Ganges

INDIA Of all India's holy rivers, the Ganges – or "Ganga" as it's known in Sanskrit – is considered by Hindus to be the holiest. And of all the sacred sites along its course, the most sacred is the spot, high in the Garhwal Himalaya, where its waters first see the light of day.

Aside from bringing you much spiritual merit (a mere wind-borne droplet of Ganga water is believed to purge the body of a hundred lifetimes of sin), the pilgrimage to the river's source provides the fastest possible route into the heart of the world's highest mountain range. Winding through rhododendron and deodar cedar forests, a paved road runs nearly all the way from the Indian plains to Gangotri, at an altitude of 3200m.

From here on, you have to join the ragged procession of pilgrims and ash-smeared sadhus as they cover the final 20km leg: a long day's walk over a moonscape of grey dust and scree. Laden with sacks of offerings and supplies, many chant the 108 honorific titles of the river as they walk: "Imperishable", "A Sun Among the Darkness

and Ignorance" or "Cow Which Gives Much Milk". And for once, the earthly splendour of the surroundings still lives up to its mythology.

Having crossed a rise on the valley floor, the full glory of the Gangotri Glacier is suddenly revealed, snaking away to a skyline of snow peaks. A 400m vertical wall, grey-blue and encrusted with stones, forms the awesome snout of the ice floe – Gau Mukh, the "Cow's Mouth". For the community of sadhus who live semi-naked in this freezing spot year-round, nearly 4000m above sea level, there's nowhere on Earth more uplifting. Come here at dawn, and you'll see them plunging into the icy water surging from the foot of the glacier, wringing it out of their long dreadlocks and settling down on the eroded rocks of the river bank to meditate or practise yoga. Even without the magnificent mountain backdrop the source would be one of the most enthralling places on Earth. But with the crystal-clear mountain light, the rituals and the vast amphitheatre of rock and ice rising on all sides, the atmosphere is nothing short of transcendental.

831 Watching elephants go wild in Uda Walawe

SRI LANKA It's a hazy dawn in Uda Walawe National Park and the thirty orphans at the Elephant Transit House are waking up to a day that will see seven of them spend their last few hours here. Each year, dozens of baby elephants from Sri Lanka's 4000-strong population get separated from their herds, or fall into wells or ditches. The transit house nurses them back to health and provides the care they need to overcome the trauma. Release days – which happen roughly annually – are special events, with government ministers in attendance, orange-robed Buddhist monks honouring the occasion and a crowd of tourists and locals looking on.

On this occasion, the first of the radio-collared youngsters to go into the truck, 5-year-old Baby Blue – found living in a buffalo herd – complains noisily at being pushed on board. His carer pats his trunk and murmurs in his ear, while funnelling milk into his mouth. Once he's aboard, four other young males and two females follow more willingly. They're all given leafy sugar-cane

tops to keep them busy. A dusty half-hour ride takes the orphans to the release site, where a lurching water truck pulls up alongside and hoses them down with a shower of water mixed with elephant dung, to rid them of their human odour.

The release, when it comes, is quick but strangely moving. Baby Blue barges forward through his peers and stomps off into the bush, shaking his ears at onlookers and shrieking with delight. The less experienced orphans follow, uncertain what to do in a place with no apparent barriers. After a minute they find a gap in the thick bush and follow each other further into the park. The radio-tracking Land Rover sets off down the nearest bush road in pursuit. The next morning, the trackers report the elephants have walked 4km and are still in one group. Within weeks, most of them have integrated into the park's herds. It's all over for another year, when the next batch of youngsters will be ready to brave a new life in the bush.

832 Cruising the Keralan backwaters

INDIA Kerala's Kuttinad backwaters region is, in every sense, a world apart from the mainstream of Indian life. Sandwiched between the Arabian Sea and the foothills of the Western Ghat Mountains, its heart is a tangled labyrinth of rivers, rivulets and shimmering lagoons, enfolded by a curtain of dense tropical foliage. This natural barrier screens Kuttinad from the roads, railways and market towns that dominate the rest of the coastal strip, making it blissfully tranquil for such a densely populated area.

Innumerable small vessels glide around Kuttinad, but easily the most romantic way to explore it is in a *kettu vallam*, or traditional Keralan rice barge. Hand-built from teak and jackwood and sporting canopies made from plaited palm leaves, they're beautiful craft – whether propelled along gondolier-style using long poles or by less environmentally-friendly diesel engines.

Views constantly change as you cruise along. One minute you're squeezing through a narrow canal clogged with purple water hyacinth; the next, you're gliding over luminous, placid lakes fringed by groves of coconut palms. Every now and then, a whitewashed church tower, minaret or temple finial will reveal the presence of a hidden village. Some settlements occupy only the tiniest parcel of land, barely large enough for a small house. Others have their own boatyards, vegetable gardens and ranks of cantilevered Chinese fishing nets dangling from the river bank.

Dozens of *kettu vallam* cruise firms compete for custom in towns such as Alappuzha and Karunnagapalli, some offering top-of-the-range rice barges complete with designer cane furniture, gourmet kitchens and viewing platforms scattered with cushions and lanterns. Alternatively, you could eschew such luxury in favour of a more authentic mode of transport: one of the stalwart municipal ferries that chug between Kuttinad's major towns and villages. Aside from saving you the equivalent of the average annual wage of most of your fellow passengers, arriving in one of these oily beasts won't provoke the frenzied response from local kids that can shatter the very tranquillity that makes Kuttinad so special.

833 Into the blue: tracking whales in the Indian Ocean

SRI LANKA It's only 7.30am, and the sun is already beating hard on the wooden deck of the *Spirit of Dondra*. The boys at the wheel have moved fast, and now, several kilometres out to sea, Mirissa's pretty, palm-backed fishing harbour has almost receded from view.

The driver cuts the engine, and our naturalist and guide recaps – as if we needed it – why we're here. "Sri Lanka is perhaps the best place in the world to see the largest creature that's ever lived: the blue whale," he explains. "Our waters lie on the whales' route between the Horn of Africa and the Bay of Bengal. And here at the island's southernmost point", he continues, jabbing at the mesh of lines on the map, "where the continental shelf is only just offshore, is the best place of all to see them. It's an ideal lunch stop for the whales – and perfect whale country for us."

We skim off again, across the eddying ocean. A pod of dolphins joins us for the ride, leaping in formation. But there's barely time to enjoy them before a commotion from the viewing deck above, and a cry of "Whale, whale!" from a crew member. The boat picks up speed and within minutes we're closing in on our target. It's the whale-spout we spot first: a towering spray, some three storeys high, of thin white foam, which holds its shape, then melts away in seconds.

We continue our course, and then suddenly come to a halt. No more than 20m away, the ocean surface ruptures and a giant beast breaches, its enormous body rolling through the water. The awestruck audience gasps in unison, then a rapt chorus accompanies the clamour of camera shutters: "Oh, my God – it's huge!". After a few seconds, the whale dips down and for a few moments there's calm. Then the ocean swells and the whale breaches again, this time, incredibly, joined by an even larger companion – so close we can see the markings on its underside. The pair dive in tandem, and then perform their *pièce de résistance*: each whale simultaneously hauls its massive tail – the width of a small aircraft – out of the water, flukes in classic pose, then plunges it back into the churning ocean with a resounding crash.

834 Finding perfect powder in Kashmir

INDIA The subject of a long-standing bitter territorial dispute between India and Pakistan, Kashmir was dubbed "the most dangerous place on Earth" after a particularly heated period in the 1990s involving not-so-veiled nuclear threats between the two countries. A few other places have since clinched that dubious title, but talk of the region still largely remains focused on its politics, obscuring the fact that Kashmir, with its verdant valleys and towering mountains, makes the Alps look like a cheap film set.

It's on those mountains that perhaps its biggest secrets – at least to snowboarding junkies – can be found. The Himalayas jut into Kashmir from Nepal, boasting light, dry powder in absurd quantities, but very few visitors around to take advantage of it. Its remoteness means that, if you're lacking a plane ticket, you might have to travel for days on a combination of trains, buses and Jeeps filled with chickens to see for yourself.

Thankfully it doesn't disappoint. Kashmir, or rather the small ski town of Gulmarg, seems set to explode onto the ski resort radar. Opened in 2005, its gondola is, at just shy of 4000m, the third highest in the world, and the powdery terrain that spreads out before it is limitless and untracked.

From the top, head to Apharwat's high northwest and southeast shoulders, before descending the mountain's multiple ridges, faces and bowls. Or descend over the backside of the mountain on a 1700m run that takes you through forests dotted with snow-leopard and hill-fox tracks.

Topping it off are some very unresort-like qualities: you'll ride a pony back to a hot shower and a warm bed; if it's chicken for dinner you can pick one from the yard. The secret won't keep for long.

Bollywood glamour
at the MUMBAI METRO

835

INDIA If you've never seen a Bollywood movie before, think John Travolta and Olivia Newton-John in *Grease*, then pump up the colour saturation, quadruple the number of dancing extras, switch the soundtrack to an A.R. Rahman masala mix and imagine Indo-Western hybrid outfits that grow more extravagant with every change of camera angle.

Like their classic forerunners of the 1970s and 1980s, modern Bollywood blockbusters demand the biggest screens and heftiest sound systems on the market, and they don't come bigger or heftier than those in the Metro BIG in Mumbai, the *grande dame* of the city's surviving Art Deco picture houses. A palpable aura of old-school glamour still hangs over the place, at its most glittering on red-carpet nights, when huge crowds gather in the street outside for a glimpse of stars such as Shah Rukh Kahn or Ashwariya Rai posing for the paparazzi in front of the iconic 1930s facade.

A sense of occasion strikes you the moment you step into the Metro BIG's foyer, with its plush crimson drapery and polished Italian marble floors. A 2006 revamp transformed the auditorium into a state-of-the-art multiplex, complete with six screens, lashings of chrome and reclining seats, but the developers had the good sense to leave the heritage features in the rest of the building intact. Belgian crystal chandeliers still hang from the ceilings, reflected in herringbone-patterned mirrors on the mid-landing, with original stucco murals lining the staircases.

While the Metro may have had a makeover, the same quirky conventions that have styled Indian cinema for decades still very much hold sway – in spite of Bollywood's glossier modern image and bigger budgets. So while the waistlines have dropped and cleavages become more pronounced, the star-crossed hero and heroine still have to make do with a coy rub of noses rather than a proper kiss.

Down in the stalls of the Metro BIG, meanwhile, the new decor hasn't subdued behaviour in the cheaper seats. Shouting at the screen, cheering every time the hero wallops someone, and singing along with the love songs are still very much part of the experience – even if overpriced popcorn has supplanted five-rupee wraps of peanuts.

836

Surf boats on the southern seas

THE MALDIVES Imagine a series of perfect tropical reef breaks populated by parrotfish, turtles and manta rays, over which crystalline waves roll with regularity. Surf conditions like these are hard to find, but charter a surf boat in the Maldives and you can anchor off the break of your choice early in the morning, when waves like these will be there for the taking. When the late risers paddle out, simply clamber back onto your floating hotel and enjoy a leisurely breakfast while you sail away to more distant, isolated areas.

A two-week trip here in peak surf season (July/August) may net you fourteen consecutive days of head-high surf. You'll never need to wear more than board shorts, a rash vest and plenty of sun cream, and it's easy enough to get in five sessions a day, since you're literally living next to the breaks. Downtime can be spent snorkelling the reefs, chilling out on deck with a book or snoozing in the sea breeze.

837 Eating a banana-leaf lunch in Chidambaram

INDIA "Step in!", reads the sign. "For: idly-wada-dosai-utthapam-appam-pongal . . . and rice plate!" You might not know what any of these promised gastronomic delights are, but the aromas of freshly cooked spices, smoky mustard oil, simmering coconut milk and sandalwood-scented incense billowing into the street are enticement enough to do just as the sign says.

In the temple towns of Tamil Nadu, where regional cooking styles have been refined over centuries in the kitchens of the great Chola shrines, "meals" or "rice-plate" restaurants are where most working men – and travellers – eat. Some are swankier than others, with air-conditioning instead of paddle fans, but none serve tastier or more traditional south Indian food than *Sri Ganesa Bhawan*, in the shadow of the famous Nataraja Temple in Chidambaram.

For lunch, space in the old-fashioned dining room is always at a premium – you'll probably find yourself squeezing onto a table

of pilgrims, hair neatly oiled and caste marks smeared over their foreheads, who'll greet you with a polite wobble of the head. Once seated, a boy in a grubby cotton tunic will unroll a plantain leaf, which you sprinkle water on. This acts as a signal for a legion of other, older boys in less grubby tunics to swing into action, depositing ladles of rice, fiery rasam broth and lip-smacking curries onto your plate.

The dishes are always consumed in the same set order, but chances are you won't have a clue what this is – much to the amusement of your fellow diners, who will by now be watching you intently. Mixing the various portions together with the rice, yoghurt, buttermilk and sharp lime pickle, and then shovelling them into your mouth with your fingers, requires a knack you won't get the hang of straight away. Not that it matters. Underscored by the tang of tamarind, fried chilli, fenugreek seeds and fresh coconut, the flavours will be surprising, delicious and explosive regardless of how you combine them.

838 Fishing for barracuda off Medhufushi

MALDIVES Early in the morning the *dhoni* leaves Medhufushi, chugging past Muli Corner, where the Australian surfer dudes are already paddling out. Slipping through a natural gap in the atoll on which these islands sit, the boat soon reaches deep water, its flimsy canvas awning flapping in the warm breeze.

Very soon flying fish are passing, propelling themselves effortlessly 20m through the air. Dolphins come alongside to do somersaults, two swimming in tandem in front of the *dhoni* like horses in imaginary shafts. Meanwhile the barefoot crew, young Ismail and old Ali Nasser, bait two lines with tuna scraps, then let them out about 20m behind each boat, their lead weights decorated with pom-poms of pink binder twine. Captain Ibrahim keeps the boat on a steady course as the guests pull on their white protective gloves and take hold of twine that is attached to the line.

Fishing is the second most important industry in the Maldives after tourism, and the seas around this archipelago abound in tuna, grouper, barracuda and squirrelfish. Soon there is a tug on the line

being held by a German woman. She starts to pull it in, the twine coiling down behind her onto the deck. Suddenly, 10m away, there's a flash of silver and pink in the water. A long body breaks the surface – a metre-long barracuda, the body completely streamlined except for its large posterior fins. These fish can grow up to 2m long, but even the scale models have fearsome-looking jaws. The crew help pull the bucking silver fish in and unhook its jaw. It thrashes as it is dropped in the battered green cool box on the deck.

The shock of landing the first fish soon passes. An air of competition develops between the guests. Ibrahim goes round in slow circles until the cool box is over half full, then Ismail brings everyone coffee and the boat begins to chug back towards the atoll. This far out the sight of the surf breaking on Muli Corner is impressive: it's clear how much the atoll protects its islands from the powerful waves. Ismail takes supper orders from the guests – for an extra $10 they can have their barracuda cooked for them on the beach tonight.

839 Watching the sun rise over Achyutaraya Temple

INDIA When Vijayanagar, capital of India's last Hindu empire, was ransacked by a Muslim army after the Battle of Talikota in 1565, the devastation was total. Few temples, palaces, houses or human lives were spared. It was the sixteenth-century equivalent of a nuclear holocaust.

Today, the site still lies largely deserted and in ruins – save for the mighty Virupaksha Temple at its heart, in the village of Hampi. Ranged around a bend in the Tungabhadra River, the small bazaar village and archeological remains occupy a landscape of surreal beauty. Hills of smooth granite boulders, eroded through time, are separated from each other by swathes of brilliant green banana groves, which conceal colonnaded walkways leading to hidden temples and bathing tanks. Because they were so comprehensively destroyed, the monuments possess an aura of greater antiquity than they perhaps deserve, but this only adds to the charisma of the place.

You can spend days wandering between sites, clambering up flights of rock-cut steps to reach forgotten shrines, deciphering mythological friezes on the walls of collapsed palaces, or catching coracles across the river to visit caves inhabited by dreadlocked sadhus. The definitive Hampi experience, however, has to be watching the sun rise from Matanga Hill, just east of the village's long, straight bazaar. Having scaled the flight of steps leading to the tiny temple crowning its summit, a wondrous view opens up. Immediately below you, the *gopuras* and walled enclosures of the Achyutaraya Temple rise through the morning mist like a vision from a lost world, framed by a vista of boulder hills stretching to the horizon.

And if that weren't a perfect enough way to start your day, an entrepreneurial chai-wallah has set up shop on the temple rooftop, so you can enjoy the awesome spectacle over a cup of delicious hot tea.

840 Take a dawn laughter yoga session in Mumbai

INDIA As dawn breaks in India's largest and noisiest city, there's a hubbub on Chowpatty beach that sounds altogether stranger than the car horns, bus engines and tinny radios that provide the usual rush-hour soundtrack. Standing on the pale yellow sands of the beach, a group of men and women are twirling their arms in the air like portly birds trying to take off. Dressed in a mix of saris, t-shirts and punjabis, they take their cue from Kishore Kuvavala, a man with a smile as wide as the Ganges, and the leader of the Chowpatty Beach Laughter Yoga Club.

Invented by Indian doctor Madan Kataria in the mid-Nineties, laughter yoga now has thousands of devotees. Many sessions, such as Kuvavala's, are free for anybody to join, providing newcomers don't mind an early start. Propelled by the philosophy that laughter gives humans huge spiritual and medical benefits, the session is book-ended by prayer and breathing sessions, and its main objective couldn't be simpler – to set your giggling, howling, chortling and smirking instincts free.

Kataria soon found out after starting his original group that simple joke-telling wasn't enough – not least because his devotees ran out of gags. So these days, laughter yoga clubs rely on physical comedy: stirring an imaginary bowl of lassi, laughing at yourself in an imaginary mirror, pretending to be an aeroplane and doing a giant hokey-cokey are all part of the forty-five minute Chowpatty beach session, which ends with a huge call and response shout-a-thon. It's hard to let yourself go, but look around at the hordes of men and women roaring without restraint and soon you'll be producing laughter of a volume and tone that would get you thrown out of most bars.

It certainly seems to be working. Laughter yoga clubs have now sprung up across the USA and Europe. The smiles on the faces of our motley crew of policemen, pensioners, students and office workers as they leave for work tell their own story. As Kishore explains at the end of the giggle-fest. "No need for lie-ins – but every need for laughter!"

841 Sadhu-spotting at the Kumbh Mela

INDIA At first I thought it was a severed head, smeared with cow dung, ash and sandalwood paste. But then its eyelids fluttered open. A murmur of amazement rippled through the crowd of onlookers. Buried up to his neck, dreadlocks coiled into a luxurious topknot, the sadhu then began to chant. Around him, smoke curled from a ring of smouldering camphor lamps, fed periodically by a couple of saffron-clad acolytes whose task it was to hassle the crowd for baksheesh.

"How many days is Baba-ji sitting in this way?" I asked one of them.

"Eight years, more than," came the reply.

You see many extraordinary things at the Maha Kumbh Mela, India's largest religious festival, held once every twelve years around the confluence of the Ganges, Jamuna and (mythical) Saraswati ivers, near Allahabad. But the penances performed by these wandering Hindu holy men are the ones that make you wince the most.

Standing on one leg or holding an arm in the air until it withers are two popular self-inflicted tortures. Sticking skewers through the genitals or dangling heavy bricks from the penis are others. Most sadhus who gather at the Kumbh, however, gain celestial merit in less ostentatious ways. For them, the simple act of bathing at the confluence during the festival is the fastest possible track to liberation from the cycle of rebirth.

The monastic orders, or Akharas, to which they belong, erect elaborate tented camps ahead of the big days. Watching each process to the river banks in turn, led by their respective pontiffs enshrined on gilded palanquins and caparisoned elephants, is the great spectacle of the Allahabad Kumbh. Stark naked, their bodies rubbed with ash and vermillion, the lines of dreadlocked sadhus march military-style through the early-morning mist, brandishing maces, spears, swords, tridents and other traditional weaponry associated with their Akhara.

When they finally reach the waterside, the shivering ranks break into an all-out sprint for the shallows, ecstatically shouting invocations to the Hindu gods, Shiva and Rama. Arguments over pecking order often erupt between rival Akharas, and those traditional weapons are sometimes put to traditional uses, turning the foreshore into a bloodbath. Onlookers should avoid getting too close.

842 Get high on mountain polo

PAKISTAN The highest and most isolated polo tournament in the world, the Shandur Polo Tournament is staged every July in the Shandur Pass, in the far north of Pakistan, between six teams from each end of the pass. It's a fantastically remote place for a sporting event, 3700m up and nine hours' rocky and precipitous drive from Chitral to the west or thirteen hours from Gilgit in the east – you have to either be a keen polo fan, or determined traveller, to make the journey.

But around ten thousand people do so every year, including the Pakistani president. Whether you like polo or not, the trip is unforgettable, and the tournament, surrounded by some spectacular mountain scenery, completely unique.

843 The juggernauts of Puri

INDIA There are chariot festivals in other parts of India, but as the home of Lord Jagannath and one of the most significant stops on the Hindu pilgrimage trail, the one held in Puri, in the state of Orissa, is by far the biggest. They build three vast chariots from scratch here every June, garishly painted and draped with coloured cloth, and a crowd of thousands pulls them from the Jagannath Temple to the outskirts of town and back again – a magnificent, devotional procession that is joined by thousands more. Orissa may be one of India's poorest states, but this is one of the country's greatest events by any standards – and just for good measure, the passion of its followers and the size of the chariots has bestowed on the English language the word "juggernaut".

Everest:
THE HARD WAY

NEPAL By the time you're halfway up the notorious Lamjura Pass – which rises in one lung-busting, 2km-high staircase of green, terraced hillside from steamy river to airy ridge – you'll be asking yourself why. Why did I ever think of walking to Everest Base Camp? Why did I carry so much stuff? And why did I not fly in to Lukla, halfway up, like all the other trekkers?

At the top of the pass, feelings can change dramatically. It's not just the glass of spicy-sweet *chiya* tea from a trailside lodge that does it, nor even the nip of home-distilled *raksi*. It's the astonishing prospect. Behind lies two days' tough walking, stretching back to where the tarmac ended. On either side, stony slopes festooned with prayer flags rise into a thin sky. Ahead, the eye – and the path – climbs and falls over ridge and succeeding ridge towards Everest.

Another two or three days of switchbacking past Buddhist monasteries and ramshackle villages brings you to Lukla. Here, an improbable airstrip, perched on the side of the gorge, receives the vast majority of Everest trekkers. From Lukla, all trekkers toil on up together through stony Khumbu, the fabulous high heartland of the Sherpa people. And all trekkers, as long as they can stand the thin air, arrive at either the great glacier beside Everest Base Camp or the heady peaks and lakes of Gokyo.

The Everest trek is a transformative, uplifting experience, however you do it. Walking in on the old route from Jiri, however, offers something extra. You'll find a greener and maybe more authentic side of Nepal, where the lodges are smaller and where fellow walkers on the trail are often as not Nepalis. You'll be fitter – you'll have come the hard way. And you'll really feel you've earned your Everest.

845 Exploring Galle Fort's DUTCH HERITAGE

SRI LANKA Battled over for centuries by South Indian kingdoms and European powers, Sri Lanka's palm-fringed coastline is studded with a network of sturdy colonial fortresses. Constructed by the Portuguese, expanded by the Dutch and later occupied by the British, many are off-limits, occupied by the military; others lie in picturesque decay. But one citadel remains splendidly preserved, having survived invasion and tsunami, its mighty bastions and pepperpot towers enclosing a maze of tranquil streets virtually unchanged since its days as the town's Dutch quarter.

Perched between bustling Galle and the glittering Indian Ocean, Galle Fort's soot-blackened, moss-covered walls loom immediately into view as you leave the city's chaotic bus and train stations. Enter via the tunnel-like Old Gate, inscribed with the date (1669) and crest (VOC, reckoned to be the world's oldest logo) of the Dutch settlers. Once inside, a historic vista unfurls like a movie set. An aimless wander through the backstreets will take you past dozens of gorgeous ornate-gabled houses, many still fronted by pillared verandas, with windows protected by heavy louvred shutters. The crumbling facades

of traditional family dwellings, their ochre paint stripped by sea breezes, stand cheek-by-jowl with beautifully restored mansions, many belonging to wealthy expats from the West, Galle's new invaders.

A five-minute walk from the Old Gate lies the Muslim quarter, many of whose residents, clad in long white robes and hand-woven skullcaps, are descendants of Arab traders, though a few Hindu families live alongside them. Climb to one of the delightfully homespun rooftop cafés hereabouts for some spectacular views across the fort's huddle of red rooftops, above which the stumpy spire of St Andrew's Church and gleaming white dagoba of the Buddhist temple stand prominent. It's a beautiful panorama; Sri Lanka's ethnic mix in microcosm.

From here it's a short amble to the fort's slender British-built lighthouse, the starting point for a circuit of the ramparts, best savoured in early evening when the townsfolk turn out en masse to enjoy the spectacular reddish-purple ocean sunsets. A carnival scene of gossiping locals and street peddlers, young lads playing cricket and courting couples sheltering coyly beneath umbrellas, it's one of the happiest sights in Sri Lanka.

846 Making sacrifices at a Tantric temple

NEPAL The Kathmandu Valley nestles at 1300m above sea level in the Himalayan foothills, like a giant bowl. It cradles not just the city of Kathmandu, Nepal's capital, but an astonishing array of temples. Among the most compelling is Sankhu Bajra Yogini, its golden pagoda roofs gleaming above the surrounding trees, halfway up the forested hillside of the valley's rim. This is the home of one of Nepal's most fearsome goddesses: the *yogini*, or female spirit, of the thunderbolt *vajra*.

Hindus know her as Durga, the most ferocious of eight terrifying mother goddesses. Buddhists call her Ugratara, a female aspect of Buddhahood characterized by her habit of dancing on corpses. Both agree that her Tantric powers are capable of bringing a devotee great benefit, or causing great destruction – and traditionally, she demanded blood sacrifice. In an upper chamber of the temple, you can still see the giant frying pan with which an ancient king offered parts of his own body to her.

Nowadays, the goddess is said to prefer gifts of rice, fruit and flowers, and her temple complex is perfectly serene, set at the top of an endless-seeming series of stone steps. You can look down on terraced rice- and mustard-fields, and taste the tree-scented sweetness of the Himalayan air. You'll probably see a few fellow pilgrims and the temple's red-robed guardian; you may even see a holy man in one of the neighbouring meditation caves. You'll surely hear the ringing of bells, and the chatter and scampering of the resident monkeys.

All is peaceful now, yet the dark side of the goddess is not entirely forgotten. As you climb the stone steps, look out for a curious, triangular stone, about the size of a man, halfway up. It represents Bhairab, the terrifying demon consort of the goddess. On the average day it's not just daubed with holy red powder and flowers; it shines darkly with the fresh blood of animal sacrifice. In Nepal, the Tantric traditions are very much alive.

847 City of Light: on the Ganges in Varanasi

INDIA The sun had barely risen above the river banks, but already the cremation *ghats* were hard at work. Four corpses, tightly bound in cotton and still soaked from their final cleansing dip in the Ganges, were laid out on wood pyres, ghee and garlands of orange marigolds piled on top of them. While gangs of small, dark, muscular men fed the flames, grieving relatives looked on, murmuring prayers with palms pressed together and heads bowed. The surrounding buildings were black with soot.

Varanasi – or Kashi ("City of Light") as it was known in ancient times – is Hinduism's holiest city. Infamous across India for its squalor, its old core is a teeming warren of narrow alleyways, intricately carved doorways opening on to hidden, high-walled courtyards and shrines. Wander around for long enough and you'll eventually emerge at the *ghats*, or sacred stone steps, which spread around the mighty bend in the river here. From dawn until dusk, they present a constantly animated canvas of bathers, sadhus, tourists, hawkers, stray cows and priests plying their age-old trade under ragged parasols – all set against a magnificent backdrop of crumbling temples and palaces.

The best way to enjoy the spectacle is to jump in a rowing boat at Asi Ghat, in the south of the old city, just before sunrise. Paddling north as the first rays of sunlight infuse the riverfront with a reddish glow, you glide past the dark stupas of Buddha Ghat, Rewa Ghat's distinctive leaning towers, and the candy-striped steps of Vijayanagar Ghat. Manikarnika, the cremation *ghat*, is where the boatmen generally turn around.

Out on the river, visitors are insulated from the hassle of guides and trinket sellers, but not necessarily from Varanasi's still less savoury aspects. Poor Hindus who can't afford enough wood for their pyres will often have their charred remains shoved unceremoniously into the water – it's not unusual to find your boat bumping into a bloated body part, or even something eating one.

The *ghats* themselves are most atmospheric just before dark. Watching the priests' cane lanterns flickering to life and mingling with the reflections of the afterglow, Kashi feels every inch the mystical "Threshold of Eternity" it has always been for Hindus.

848 Visiting the Taj by moonlight

INDIA When it comes to viewing the Taj Mahal, there isn't really an unflattering angle or wrong kind of weather. Even the Dickensian smog that can roll off the Jamuna River in midwinter only serves to heighten the mystique of the mausoleum's familiar contours. The monsoon rains and grey skies of August also cast their spell; glistening after a storm, the white marble, subtly carved and inlaid with semi-precious stones and Koranic calligraphy, seems to radiate light.

The world's most beautiful building was originally commissioned by Mughal Emperor Shah Jahan in the 1630s as a memorial to his beloved wife, the legendary beauty Arjumand Bann Begum, or Mumtaz Mahal ("Elect of the Palace"), who died giving birth to their fourteenth child. It is said that Shah Jahan was inconsolable after her death and spent the last years of his life staring wistfully through his cusp-arched window in Agra Fort at her mausoleum downriver.

The love and longing embodied by the Taj are never more palpable than during the full-moon phase of each month, when the Archeological Survey of India opens the complex at night. For once, the streams of visitors flowing through the Persian-style Char Bagh Gardens leading to the tomb are hushed into silence by the building's ethereal form, rising melancholically from the river bank.

Shah Jahan's quadrangular water courses, flanking the approaches, are specially filled for full-moon visits, as they would have been in Mughal times. The reflections of the luminous walls in their mirror-like surfaces seem to positively shimmer with life, like the aura of an Urdu devotional poem or piece of sublime sitar music. At such moments, it's easy to see why the Bengali mystic-poet Rabindranath Tagore likened the Taj Mahal to ". . . a teardrop on the face of Eternity".

849 Rhythm madness at the Thrissur Puram

INDIA Kerala is famous for its extravagant festivals, and none is more grand – or more frenetic – than the annual Puram in the central Keralan town of Thrissur. Caparisoned elephants, ear-shattering drum orchestras, lavish firework displays and masked dance dramas are common to all of them, but at Thrissur the scale of proceedings – not to mention the suffocating pre-monsoon heat – creates an atmosphere that can, to the uninitiated at least, seem to teeter on the brink of total insanity.

Two rival processions, representing the Tiruvambadi and Paramekkavu temples, form the focal point. Each lays on a phalanx of fifteen sumptuously decorated tuskers, ridden by Brahmin priests carrying silver-handled whisks of yak hair, peacock-feather fans and bright pink silk parasols. At the centre of both lines, the elephants' attendants bear golden images of their temple deity, like soccer players brandishing a trophy from an open-top bus victory parade. Alongside them, ranks of a hundred or more drummers mesmerize the crowd with rapid-fire beats, accompanied by cymbal crashes and wailing melodies from players of the double-reeded *khuzal*.

The *melam* music passes through four distinct phases of tempo, each double the pace of the last, with the fastest rhythm of all acting as a cue for those astride the elephants to stand up and brandish their feather fans and hair whisks in coordinated sequences. Meanwhile, the cymbals crash louder, the *khuzals* reach fever pitch and *kompu* trumpets blast away at their loudest and most dissonant.

Just at the point you think things couldn't get any more tumultuous, fireworks explode in the background – to great roars from the crowd. Many people punch the air, some randomly, while others are clearly *talam branthans*, or rhythm "madmen", whose thrusts follow every nuance of the drum patterns. When the fastest speed is played out, the slow march returns and the procession edges forward another few steps before stopping to begin the whole cycle again.

850 Bungee jumping the Bhote Koshi

NEPAL The worst part is the wait. Standing on a footbridge spanning a spectacular Himalayan gorge, it's impossible not to glance down at the churning Bhote Koshi River, which races down from the nearby Tibetan border. Every so often a cheer – or a scream – sounds, as someone plummets towards the water on the end of a disconcertingly thin rubber rope. The locals gathered at the far end of the bridge exchange wry looks, before returning to their conversations.

Operated by The Last Resort, a tented camp and adventure sports centre, this 160m bungee jump is one of the highest in the world – to put it into context, the Statue of Liberty only measures 93m from its base to the tip of the flame. When your turn comes, a reassuringly thorough member of staff checks, and double-checks, the safety harness, then ushers you towards the jumping-off point. With a final nervous wave at the cameraman (who has been recording your comments for posterity), and perhaps a quick prayer, you shuffle to the edge, vainly attempt to compose yourself, and jump as high as you can.

The mountains ahead appear briefly in your line of vision, before vanishing as you plunge down at what feels like an impossible speed. The river and the valley walls become little more than a blur, giving the strange sensation of both dramatic speed and slow-motion travel. For a few terrifying, exhilarating moments you feel as though you're flying. Finally, the rope goes taut and the bounces slow to a stop, leaving you twirling gently above the water. A long pole is hoisted up from the river bank for you to clasp, and you're pulled down onto a bed to wait for the adrenalin rush to subside. As your heart rate slowly returns to normal, a sense of elation prevails – particularly when you realize the camp bar is just a short stumble away.

851 Staying with a family in the Himalayas

INDIA As one of the holiest Hindu pilgrimage sites in the Indian Himalayas, Baijnath is busy year-round, but over the festival of Makar Sankranti, in mid-January, all hell breaks loose as villagers from the surrounding valleys pour in to town for the famous annual livestock fair. Most desirable among the animals traded on the muddy market ground here are the ponies brought in by the nomadic Bhotiyas, who pasture them on the grasslands of the Tibetan Plateau before leading them down to market in the winter.

The names, uses and cost of other exotic merchandise – borax, musk pods, dried apricots and salt horns – are explained to me by my companions from the village of Sonargaon, a few hours' bus ride further north into the mountains. I've been staying with a family for a month as part of a grassroots volunteer programme called ROSE (Rural Organization for Social Elevation), and this trip to the bright lights of the Makar Sankranti fair has been one of its highlights.

ROSE was set up as a development initiative to alleviate some of the hardships of rural life in the Kumaon region, where around 75 percent of people are landless farmers. Paying guests of the scheme get to work on a range of community-inspired projects that funds raised by them beforehand – along with bed-and-board money – help to pay for. During my stay I lent a hand to digging new latrines, planting trees and delivering smokeless, wood-free stoves to deforested villages. I also helped out with daily chores in the fields and at home: feeding the cattle, planting barley and potatoes and fixing roofs ahead of the summer rains.

Working alongside your hosts in this way leaves a vivid sense of how such small improvements might make a real difference. But the stay wasn't all toil. At the end, the eldest son from my host family arranged for a team of porters to trek with us further north into the mountains, to the snout of the Pinadri Glacier, overlooked by some of the highest peaks in the entire Indian Himalayas.

INDIA In 528 BC, Prince Siddhartha Gautama settled under a bodhi tree and – after withstanding threats of flood, fire, thunder and lightning from the evil Mara, as well as the temptations of Mara's beautiful daughters – found enlightenment. He later became known as the Buddha, and the Mahabodhi Temple, which marks the spot of his deliverance, has since become the world's most significant Buddhist pilgrimage site.

Bodhgaya, the town that has sprung up around the temple, maintains a wonderfully serene air, despite being located in Bihar – India's poorest state – an anarchic place, riven with caste conflict. Between November and February, large communities of exiled Tibetans – including, from time to time, the Dalai Lama – join red-robed monks, pilgrims and curious travellers here, giving the place a truly cosmopolitan feel. Devotees have built a number of elaborate, sometimes incongruous, modern temples and monasteries in various national styles, among them Thai, Japanese, Bhutanese and Tibetan. The site includes innumerable meditation centres, a 25m-high Buddha statue set in an ornamental garden, and an increasing number of hotels, from austere monastic guesthouses to luxury five-star establishments.

The focal point of it all is the imposing Mahabodhi Temple, a sixth-century construction with an elegant single spire surrounded by a collection of smaller stupas and shrines. At the heart of the temple complex is the bodhi tree itself, a distant offshoot of the original, which was destroyed by Emperor Ashoka before his conversion to Buddhism. Beside the tree, which is festooned with multicoloured threads and encircled with Tibetan butter lamps, is the *vajrasana* (thunder seat), a sandstone block on which the Buddha reputedly sat. Many people come here to meditate, but the spot invites quiet contemplation whatever your religious beliefs, particularly as the afternoon draws to a close, when the crowds disperse, the sun descends and ritual chants drift over on the breeze.

INDIA In the heart of India, the vast landlocked state of Madhya Pradesh boasts some of the world's best tiger reserves. You have a better chance of spotting a big cat here than anywhere else in India; moreover, you get to do so in a landscape that is simply stunning. Several of these parks claim – erroneously – to have provided the inspiration for Rudyard Kipling's *The Jungle Book*, and although the author never actually visited the areas in question, the scenery – meandering streams, creeper-clad deciduous forests and grassy *maidans* (meadows) – is undeniably Kiplingesque.

Madhya Pradesh's finest reserve is the 940-square-kilometre Kanha National Park, home to hordes of monkeys, gaur (the world's largest wild cattle), numerous species of deer, including the "12-horned" barasingha, sloth bears, wild boar, pythons, porcupines and leopards, but the tigers are by far the park's biggest draw. Safaris kick off in Jeeps – locally referred to as "gypsies" – and drivers and naturalists scan the ground for pugmarks and listen

for warning cries from other animals. When a sitting or sleeping tiger is spotted, an "elephant show" is declared: visitors exit their vehicles and clamber onto elephants, who, urged on by their mahouts, crash chaotically through the jungle in hot pursuit.

Some travellers initially feel the experience is a little contrived, but at the first thrilling flash of yellow and black markings it's impossible to remain a cynic. Untroubled by the elephants or their human passengers, the tigers stalk about proudly, turning occasionally to the spectators to conduct what feels like a cool appraisal. You get the unsettling feeling you're being sized up for lunch. When they decide they've had enough, the tigers simply slope off into the undergrowth.

While tigers face no predators in the natural world, land encroachment, development and poaching continue to reduce their numbers in India and elsewhere, making any sighting – however fleeting – a huge privilege.

854 Journeying over the roof of the world

INDIA–TIBET "Unbelievable is it Not!" reads a road sign at Tanglang La – at 5360m the highest point on the Manali–Leh highway. Looking north from the thicket of prayer flags fluttering above the pass, you'll probably find yourself agreeing. Between you and the white line of the Karakorams in the distance, stretches a vast, bone-dry wilderness of mountains and snow-dusted valleys – not a view you'd normally expect from a bus window.

The 485km route from Manali in Himachal Pradesh to Leh in Ladakh is the great epic among Indian road journeys. With an overnight stop at altitude under a makeshift parachute tent en route, it takes two days to cover, carrying you from the foothills of the Himalayas to the margins of the Tibetan Plateau. Weather conditions can be fickle – blizzards descend even in mid-summer – and facilities along the way are rough and ready, to say the least. But the privations pale into insignificance against the astonishing scenery.

The first, and most formidable, of the obstacles to be crossed is Rohtang La, "Pile of Bones Pass". Straddling one of the most sudden and extreme climatic transitions on the planet, Rohtang overlooks lush green cedar woods and alpine meadows on one side, and on the other a forbidding wall of chocolate- and sand-coloured scree, capped by ice peaks trailing plumes of spindrift.

Once across, settlements are few and far between. Nomadic shepherds and their flocks are sometimes the only signs of life on gigantic mountainsides streaked purple, red and blue with mineral deposits. Packed under snow for most of the year, the road surface deteriorates as you gain altitude, crumbling to loose shale and dizzying voids.

You cross lofty Tanglang La late on the second afternoon, reaching the first Ladakhi villages soon after. Swathed in kidney-shaped terraces of ripening barley, each is surveyed by its own fairy-tale Buddhist monastery, with spinning prayer wheels and golden finials gleaming from the rooftops in sunlight of an almost unearthly clarity.

855 Meditating in the Himalayas

NEPAL People have looked to the mountains for spiritual consolation for millennia. "I will lift up mine eyes unto the hills," say the Psalms, "from whence cometh my help." For Nepalis, the link is especially powerful. The Himalayas are where the Hindu gods go to meditate and replenish their *tapas*, or spiritual "heat", and the Buddhist peoples of Nepal's Himalayan regions regard many of the highest peaks and lakes as sacred.

Many trekkers come to Nepal to make personal pilgrimages. When you stand on a ridge festooned with colourful prayer flags torn ragged by the wind, or look down on the luminous, glacial blue of a Himalayan lake, or when with aching lungs, cracked lips and a spinning head you come to the top of the highest pass yet, it's hard not to feel your own spiritual store hasn't been warmed just a little. Of course, you can always just emulate the gods: find a high place, fix your eyes on the Himalayas, breathe and begin the search for mindfulness.

For spiritual discipline, perhaps the richest possibilities are found in the Kathmandu valley, Nepal's heartland in the Himalayan foothills. The valley has been described as a living *mandala*, or spiritual diagram – its very geography mapped out by temples, devotional stupas and holy caves and gorges. Pashupatinath, where Kathmandu's dead are burned by the river, attracts pilgrims from across India. Many Western travellers make for neighbouring Boudha, the vibrant Tibetan quarter, where the painted Buddha eyes on the great white dome look out across throngs of Buddhist monasteries and where, at dawn and dusk, the violet air echoes with the sounds of horns and bells, and the murmured mantras of the faithful.

856 Getting swept away at Durga Puja

BANGLADESH Hindus constitute just nine percent of Bangladesh's population, but the Durga Puja in Dhaka is at least as gripping as its Indian counterparts. Indeed, a consciousness of minority status seems to amplify the devotees' passion, and the close-knit Hindu enclaves concentrate the celebrations, creating a rarefied, otherworldly atmosphere. But the enclaves are not ghettos, and the Puja is not exclusively for Hindus: instead it is at once a religious event and a vibrant carnival.

The centrepieces of the individual *pujas* – religious rituals that show respect to Hindu gods and goddesses – are the beautiful, exquisitely painted clay effigies of Durga, best seen in Shankharia Bazaar, the largest Hindu quarter in Old Dhaka, where the drama of street life at Puja time is intense. A canopy of saffron drapes filters and softens the light, bathing the entire bazaar in an amber glow, and the numerous sites of worship, the market stalls, the artisans, the creaking wooden Ferris Wheels, the troupes of singers, musicians and dancers – sometimes performing on a bamboo dais under which you walk – all of this gives the impression of a fantastic elongated temple having opened its doors to a throbbing street fair.

On the evening of the tenth day, the Puja erupts into an outpouring of frenzied activity. Galvanized by the eerie fanfare of conch-shell horns and the rolling thunder of ceremonial drums, columns of chanting devotees swarm towards Sadarghat, carrying aloft their effigies. Tens of thousands of people line the river bank and crowd around the *ghat* as a relentless succession of Durgas arrives at the water's edge, where priests superintend their consecration and anoint their bearers with a smear of sandalwood ash. The goddesses are then loaded aboard diminutive boats that pitch and roll violently as the accompanying men dance and punch the air. In mid-stream the precious cargo is given to the water, and the sodden appearance of the returning men – delirious as they clamber up the steps of the *ghat* – hints at the mayhem beyond the reach of the light.

INDIA It had taken me an hour of skidding around sandy lanes in the humid late-November heat to find the place. Road signs are nonexistent in Kutch, and addresses vague, yet everyone seems to know exactly where you're headed, waving you in the right direction even before you've had time to stop your bike and ask.

I needn't have had any misgivings about turning up uninvited at the house of a renowned lacquerworker – they seemed to be expecting me. "Sit, sit," said a smiling granddaughter, spreading a mat on the beaten-earth floor next to the maestro. Glasses of hot chai appeared, along with a carved wooden spoon which the old man, his head wrapped in a huge white turban, started to spin on a lathe he manipulated with his toes. As its handle whirred, bands of brightly dyed wax were applied from zinc crayons, then deftly mixed into swirling patterns. "Fifty rupees!" announced the granddaughter when the wax had cooled. I didn't seem to have much choice in the matter, but considered the spoon a bargain anyway.

Kutch, a pan-shaped island off the northwest coast of Gujarat, is scattered with countless tiny craft villages – a legacy of the local ruling family's welcoming refugee policy. Over the centuries, castes and tribal minorities fleeing persecution were permitted to settle here, bringing with them a wealth of arts and crafts traditions.

I rode north next to visit a Harijan ("Untouchable") village famed for its embroidery. A gaggle of young girls, sumptuously attired in rainbow-woven bodices and silver neck rings, greeted me at the edge of their compound. Prompted by their shyer older sisters and mothers, they unfurled rolls of multicoloured stitchwork, sparkling with tiny mirrors. Later, they took me to a neighbouring Muslim village, where I watched a master block-printer make some of the most gorgeous textiles I'd ever seen, and finished up buying copper bells from a blind music teacher.

Buying work direct from the producers is a great way to really get under the surface exoticism of life in this remote corner of India. What's more, Kutchi craft villages offer a stimulating alternative to Christmas shopping at the mall – the lacquered spoon was a big hit with the in-laws.

CHRISTMAS SHOPPING

IN KUTCH

857

858 Cross the Himalayas to your own Shangri-la

INDIA In the far northeast of India, lodged between Tibet and Bhutan in the tiny state of Arunachal Pradesh – "the land of dawn-lit mountains" – lies a lonely valley. Here, high up on a spur, is Tawang Gompa, India's largest Buddhist monastery. Although you can get here by helicopter, the most rewarding way to reach Tawang is by joining the locals and wedging yourself into a *sumo*. These shared Jeeps – packed to bursting point with people and possessions – shuttle along the 345km road to the city of Tezpur in Assam, an exhausting journey that takes anything from 12 to 24 hours, depending on the weather.

Along this winding route of orchid groves, primeval forests, glacial streams and ice-blue lakes, darkly humorous road signs with phrases like "Be gentle on my curves" and "Overtaker, meet undertaker" warn drivers to take care at the wheel. The numerous military bases strewn along the route are potent reminders that the region remains a bone of contention between India and China – the latter occupied the

area during the 1962 Chinese-Indian war and still lays claim to it. At the breathtakingly high (4300m) Sela Pass, the *sumos* stop at a tiny wooden hut, the *Tenzing Restaurant*, where passengers crowd round a wood-fired stove and drink cups of salted yak-butter tea.

From here, the road curls down into an isolated valley, and eventually Tawang itself, a sleepy end-of-the-road town filled with Buddhist prayer wheels and flags. A few kilometres beyond is the monastery itself. A colourful fortified complex, it was the birthplace of the sixth Dalai Lama and remains home to around five hundred monks, as well as a priceless collection of Buddhist texts and historic manuscripts.

The monastery is most atmospheric in the late afternoon, when the setting sun bathes the place in a rich orange light. As you gaze down at the valley below, with its isolated *ani gompas* (nunneries), tiny hamlets, glistening lakes and sheer mountain slopes, it is hard to escape the feeling that you've found your own Shangri-la.

859 Meeting Shiva and St Thomas on Adam's Peak

SRI LANKA Sacred sites are easily accessible in Sri Lanka; you can barely move a step without tripping over giant Buddha statues, temples and rock paintings. But the most rewarding of all requires a night-time expedition to a pilgrim's mountain.

At 2243m, Adam's Peak is far from the highest place on the island, but as the holiest it draws thousands of pilgrims each year, all of whom pant their way up 4800 stone steps to worship at the indentation in the rock at the top. Most of the pilgrims are Buddhists, who believe it is the footprint of the Buddha. However, this is an all-purpose religious peak: Muslims attribute the footprint to Adam, Hindus to Shiva and Christians to St Thomas. In fact, pilgrimages here pre-date all the religions and have been taking place for thousands of years.

It's a 7km path from Dalhousie up through the cloudforest where leopards are said to prowl. Rock steps and handrails guide pilgrims

up the steepest sections although none of it is especially scary. From May to November you may well have the mountain to yourself, and the averagely fit take around four hours for the climb. In the pilgrimage season from December to April, when the weather is also at its best, the path is illuminated by a necklace of lights and endless tea stalls offer refreshment along the way.

At the top offer a prayer in the tiny temple around the footprint, ogle the sunrise and then head across to the opposite side of the summit to take in a remarkable phenomenon – if you are lucky. The ethereal sight of The Shadow of the Peak occurs when the rising sun casts the perfectly triangular shadow of the mountain onto the clouds below for a few short minutes. It's a magical view to carry in your mind through the pain of the next few hours, when knees and thighs howl in protest throughout the descent, and during the next couple of days – when your gait becomes an inelegant waddle.

860 Sikhs, sabres and a giant canteen: the Golden Temple

INDIA The gates of the Sikhs' holiest shrine, the Golden Temple in Amritsar, are open to all. Given the desecrations inflicted on the complex by the Indian army in 1984 and 1987, this is an extraordinary fact, and vivid testament to the spirit of inclusiveness and equality at the heart of Sikhism.

Originating in the sixteenth century, the youngest of India's three great faiths drew its converts mainly from the oppressed and disenchanted underclasses of Islam and Hinduism. Philosophically and stylistically, it's very much an amalgam of the two, and nowhere is this hybridity more apparent than in the architecture of the shrine that forms the nerve centre of the temple.

Seemingly afloat on a serene, rectangular lake, the temple's centrepiece, the Harmandir, is adorned with a fusion of Mughal-style domes and Hindu lotus motifs. Smothered in gold leaf, it looks at its most resplendent shortly after dawn, when sunlight begins to illuminate its gilded surfaces and the reflections in the lake shimmer. Before approaching it, pilgrims are supposed to bathe and then perform a ritual *parikrama*, or circumambulation of the

gleaming marble walkway surrounding the lake. En route, returning Sikh expats in sneakers and jeans rub shoulders with more orthodox pilgrims wearing full-length *shalwar-camises*, beehive turbans and an armoury of traditional sabres, daggers and spears. Despite the weaponry on display, the atmosphere is relaxed and welcoming, even dreamy at times, especially when the temple musician-priests are singing verses from the Adi Granth, Sikhism's holy text, accompanied by tabla and harmonium.

Perhaps the most memorable expression of the temple's open-hearted spirit, though, is the tradition of offering free meals at the Guru-ka-Langar, a giant communal canteen next to the temple entrance. Foreign tourists are welcome to join the ranks of Sikh pilgrims and the needy from neighbouring districts who file in and sit together cross-legged on long coir floormats. After grace has been sung, the massive job of dishing up thousands of chapatis and buckets of spicy, black-lentil dal begins. By the time all the tin trays have been collected up and the floors swept, another crowd will have gathered at the gates for the cycle to begin again.

NEED to know

804 You can fly to the Andaman Islands from Chennai (Madras) . You can also get there by ferry via Chennai or Kolkata (3–5 days).

805 Operated by the Bangladesh Inland Water Transport Corporation, the Rocket service, covering the 354km route between Dhaka and Khulna, runs all year.

806 Camel treks can be arranged through any Jaisalmer hotel or tourist office, but try to avoid those which use touts; Adventure Travel (@www.adventurecamels.com) and Sahara Travels (@www.mrdesertemeritus.com) are both dependable. Early Dec–end Jan is the best time to go.

807 Regular buses travel to Sauraha from Kathmandu, Pokhara and Sonauli, on the Indian border. For more on the park, see @www.chitwannationalpark.org.

808 For reservations at *Udaivilas* visit @www.oberoiudaivilas.com.

809 The arribada usually takes place around February or March. You will need your own transport to reach Gahirmatha beach – Chandbali is a good base for day-trips and you can obtain a permit here. Check with the OTDC tourist office in Bhubaneswar or Puri, to see if the turtles are expected before you set off. See @www.greenpeace.org/india/campaigns/save-our-seas/turtle-camp-orissa for more info.

810 Esala Perahera takes place in Kandy over 10 days, usually between late July and mid-August. See @www.daladamaligawa.org for info.

811 Himalayan Encounters (@www.himalayanencounters.com) runs the fully supported Sikles Trek (also known as Lamjung & Tara Top Trek) from mid-Sept through May. Intrepid Travel's (@www.intrepidtravel.com/nxa) Nepal Adventure trip includes a five-day trek to Sikles.

812 *Kathakalis* are usually performed as part of Ernakulam's annual festival in Jan/Feb, but tourist-oriented shows also take place year-round; see @www.cochinculturalcentre.com.

813 Diskit is a 6hr bus journey from Leh, but there are only three buses a week (Tues, Thurs & Sat 6am).

814 The frozen river is practicable for around 6 weeks during January and February; a few trekking agencies in Leh, such as Dreamland Trek & Tour (@www.dreamladakh.com), offer it as a package.

815 The IPL usually takes place in the first quarter of the year, with bidding in Jan and matches running March–April. Tickets to the matches can be booked online – see @www.iplt20.com.

816 Nizzamuddin is 6km south of Connaught Circus along the Mathura Road. Visitors should dress modestly and cover their heads.

817 The island is 15 minutes by speedboat from Male airport. See @www.sixsenses/Soneva-Gili/.

818 The Sabarmati Ashram is open daily 8.30am–6.30pm. For more information visit @www.mkgandhi.org/gandhiyatra/sabarmati.htm

819 Dharamsala is 12hr from Delhi by bus; there are usually several every day.

820 The Ajanta Caves are open Tues–Sun 9am–5.30pm. Most visitors base themselves in the city of Aurangabad, 108km southwest, travelling by bus or Jeep taxi.

821 The water is clearest Dec–March, but May–Sept is the best time to see manta rays, as a rise in plankton attracts them to the reefs. @www.divesitedirectory.co.uk lists dive spots in the Maldives.

822 Gokarna is most easily accessible via the Konkan Railway, which connects Mumbai with Kerala.

823 Benaulim is 15min by public bus from Margao, Goa's "second city".

824 Buses leave the Punjabi city of Amritsar for Wagha every 45min, although it's worth booking a taxi for the round trip.

825 Haputale can be reached by train from Colombo (9hr) and Kandy (5hr 30min). Accommodation is limited to a handful of guesthouses: try the excellent *Amarasinghe Guest House* (@+91 (0) 57 2268175).

826 Kartik Purnima is usually held in early Nov. Check @www.rajasthantourism.gov.in for the exact dates.

827 A ticket for The Toy Train (@www.dhrs.org) costs Rs247 (about £3) each way in first class. The trip also forms part of larger luxury excursions, such as Abercrombie & Kent's two-week Temple & Dragons tour to Bhutan (@www.abercrombiekent.com).

828 Madurai, in the south of Tamil Nadu, can be reached by plane from Mumbai (3hr 20min) or the state capital, Chennai (1hr).

829 Theyyattam rituals are held across the north of Kerala from October through May. The simplest way to find one is to visit the tourist office in Kannur (Cannanore).

830 Gangotri is accessible from May to October. Most visitors stay in the dorm of the state-run Tourist Bungalow (no phone), in Bhojbasa, 5km from the glacier.

831 Uda Walawe National Park lies south of the island's central hill country. For information about visiting the Elephant Transit Home, and orphan releases, see @www.dwc.gov.lk/library/Np_udawalawa.html.

832 *Kettu vallam* cruises can be arranged through most upscale hotels. Prices vary, but in early December or mid-January you can expect to pay Rs4500–6500 for a 22-hour cruise on a non-a/c, two-bedroom boat.

833 Mirissa Water Sports (@www.mirissawatersports.com) offers 3hr whale-watching tours for around $70 per person, leaving from Mirissa fishing harbour, about 4hr drive south of Colombo. The whale-watching season runs Dec–April.

834 From Srinagar it's a 2hr, 200km taxi ride to Gulmarg. Dec–April is the best time to visit, although check the security situation with your foreign office.

835 Mumbai's Metro BIG Cinema is at Dhobi Talao Junction, at the top of Azad Maidan, a short cab ride from CST (VT) Station. For details, see @www.bigcinemas.com.

836 You should be a good intermediate or advanced surfer with experience of surfing reefs, as there are no beach breaks in the Maldives. Xoxxisurf (@www.xoxxisurf.com) offers one-week surf-boat charters.

837 *Sri Ganesa Bhawan*, on West Car St (no phone), serves lunch between 11.30am and 2.30pm.

838 Most resorts in the Maldives offer deep-water fishing excursions; for advance information see @www.tourisminmaldives.com and @www.oceanmaldives.com.

839 Hampi is a 30min bus ride from the town of Hospet, which is served by mainline trains from Hyderabad, Goa and Bangalore.

840 The Chowpatty beach laughter club meets every morning at 7am at the eastern end of Chowpatty beach in South Mumbai. For more information on Kishore Kuvavala, see @www.essenceoflaughter.com.

841 The next Kumbh Mela to take place at the sacred confluence near Allahabad will be in 2013.

842 The Shandur Polo Tournament takes place every year during the second week of July. A tent village is set up at the pass during the tournament.

843 *Z* (@+91 (0) 6752 222554), on CT Rd near the beach, is a decent backpacker's hostel in Puri.

844 Jiri is 12hr by bus from Kathmandu, and Jeeps continue by rough track towards Bhandar, which can save a day or two's walking. The Jiri route takes three to four weeks to Everest Base Camp and back (though you can always fly back out of Lukla, 35 dizzy minutes by plane from Kathmandu).

845 It's a picturesque 3hr journey along the coast by road or rail to Galle from Colombo. Fun to explore at any time of year, the fort is at its most animated during the annual Literary Festival (@www.galleliteraryfestival.com) in late January, when a string of global literati descends on the town and accommodation is booked out well in advance.

846 To get to the temple, a crowded bus (or a taxi) can take you for a hectic half-hour from the centre of Kathmandu to the thriving Tibetan Buddhist settlement at Boudha; from there it's another 5km along increasingly rural roads to the ancient, brick-built town of Sankhu. The temple lies 2km outside town – the last kilometre on foot, up those endless stone steps.

847 Boat rides cost anything between Rs150 and Rs600, depending on demand and your ability to haggle.

848 The Taj Mahal is open from 6am to 7pm daily, except Friday. Over the 4 days of a full moon (except on Fridays and during Ramadan), you can also visit between 8pm and midnight; tickets must be booked a day in advance at the Archeological Survey of India office, 22 Mall Rd (@www.asi.nic.in).

849 Puram usually takes place on one day in April/May; check with the state tourist office, @www.keralatourism.org, for exact dates.

850 The Last Resort is a 3hr drive from Kathmandu. For more information, visit @www.thelastresort.com.np.

851 Other than for the festival, the best time to visit Kumaon is in early spring (March–April) or late summer (Sept–Oct). See @www.rosekanda.info for more info.

852 The Mahabodhi Temple is open daily 5am–9pm. The town of Gaya, 13km away, is the nearest transport hub, with an international airport, railway station and bus connections to elsewhere in Bihar. For more information, see @www.tourismbihar.org.

853 Kanha National Park is open from November until the start of the monsoon season. The nearest city is Jabalpur, a 5hr drive away, which has an airport and train station. See @www.mptourism.com.

854 The Manali–Leh highway is only open between late June and mid-September, although buses tend to run as long as the passes remain free of snow.

855 *Gompas* (monasteries) such as Boudha's Shedrub, the "White Monastery" (@www.shedrub.org), and nearby Kopan (@www.kopan-monastery.com) run teachings on Tibetan Buddhism in English, as well as meditation courses. For serious Hindu meditation, try the Osho Tapoban Forest Retreat Centre (@www.tapoban.com) and Nepal Vipassana Centre (@www.dhamma.org).

856 The Durga Puja falls in Sept or Oct, depending on the lunar cycle –search for the dates on @www.bdonline.com/tourism.

857 Bhuj, the capital of Kutch, is accessible by train from Ahmedabad. Guides and transport for trips out to the craft villages north of town can be arranged with the tourist officer in Bhuj's Aina Mahal.

858 The Tawang Gompa is open daily from dawn to dusk. The best times to visit are during Losar – the Buddhist New Year, in February or early March – and the Torgya Festival in January, when dancing and celebrations are used to ward off evil spirits and natural disasters. Foreign tourists require a Restricted Area Permit, in addition to an Indian visa, to visit Arunachal Pradesh. For further information, visit @www.arunachaltourism.com.

859 Dalhousie is 30km southwest of Hatton, which is on the main rail line from Colombo and Kandy.

860 Both the Golden Temple and Guru-ka-Langar are open 24hr. Although meals are served free of charge, small donations are welcomed.

GOOD to know

RELIGION

Around 80 percent of India's population follows **Hinduism** – less an orthodox faith than an amalgam of disparate religious rituals and practices dating back four or five millennia. **Islam** came to India, via Afghanistan and Central Asia, in the tenth and eleventh centuries and is now the religion of one in ten Indians. The rest of the population are Christians, Sikhs, Bahá'ís, Jains and Buddhists. In Nepal Hindus also dominate, comprising around 75 percent of the population, while the Buddhist community makes up 20 percent; **Tibetan Buddhism** is most widely practised. In Pakistan, 96 percent of the population are Muslims (of which nearly 77 percent are Sunni Muslims) and the remainder Shi'a; Bangladesh is 80 percent Muslim; and in Sri Lanka, nearly 77 percent of the people are followers of Buddhism.

BORDER CONFLICT

Since Partition in 1947, India has become embroiled in four major military confrontations with neighbour Pakistan, in addition to dozens of minor skirmishes. The conflict is fuelled by ongoing border disputes over Kashmir. In 2001, the two nuclear powers seemed on the verge of all-out war after Muslim extremists, allegedly armed by Pakistan, stormed the Indian parliament building. An estimated one million men-at-arms were involved in the ensuing standoff.

"The butterfly counts not months but moments, and has time enough"

Rabindranath Tagore

AYURVEDA

Ayurveda, literally "Science of Life", is a four-thousand-year-old holistic healing system still widely practised in India. It recognizes three constitutional types: **Vatta** (wind); **Pitta** (heat); and **Kapha** (earth and water). Disease is regarded as an imbalance between these three elements, so it's the imbalance rather than some infection that's treated, using a mixture of herbal remedies, massage, dietetics and lifestyle counselling.

SUCH GREAT HEIGHTS

Mount Everest, in the Himalayas on the border between Nepal and China, is the world's highest peak at 8848m. Attaining the summit has long been the ultimate mountaineering challenge. New Zealand's Sir Edmund Hillary and Tenzing Norgay, a Sherpa mountaineer from Nepal, were the first people to complete the ascent in 1953. Other Everest records include the first ascent by a woman (in 1975) and by a blind person (2001). Climbing Everest has now become something of an aspiration for wealthy professionals – the current going rate for the trip is around $65,000.

However, scaling Everest is a dangerous endeavour, and at the close of 2009, 216 people had lost their lives in the attempt, a fatality rate of almost ten percent. About one-third of the total deaths are suffered by the local Sherpa population, many of whom serve as guides. For them, Everest has spiritual significance and there are many taboos relating to it, one of which is a ban on sex for anyone attempting the summit – it is thought to bring bad luck.

FIVE INDIAN DISHES TO DIE FOR…

Biryani Tender lamb slow-baked in spicy saffron rice – a speciality of Hyderabad.
Paturi maach Steamed Bengali *bekti* fish in mustard and green chilli sauce.
Malai kofta Cheese and potato dumplings served in a creamy lentil gravy – a typical north Indian Mughlai favourite.
Pepper-garlic crab Mouthwatering Konkan seafood speciality.
Masala dosa Rice- and lentil-flour pancake with a tangy potato filling, originally from the temple town of Udipi, Karnataka.

BETELMANIA

Wherever you go in India you'll see people spitting long squirts of **betel juice** onto pavements, street corners and walls. The ubiquitous crimson spittle is a by-product of the country's number one bad habit: chewing *paan*, a preparation based on areca nut and intensified with tobacco and lime paste. At any given time, hundreds of millions of Indians may be under its mildly narcotic influence.

NUMBER CRUNCHING

714 million: the number of voters in India, the world's largest democracy.
1 million: number of machines required to count their votes in 2009.
10: the number of members of the royal family assassinated by the Crown Prince of Nepal in 2001, before he took his own life.
15,000: the number of guests at former Tamil Nadu Chief Minister Jayalalitha's son's wedding.
7th: the population of Bangladesh is the world's seventh largest; its 144,000 square kilometres make it one of the most densely populated countries.
300 million: the estimated number of cows in India.
-7258m: the lowest point of the Indian Ocean, the Java Trench, near Sumatra.

"It is the habit of every aggressor nation to claim that it is acting on the defensive"

Jawaharlal Nehru

FIVE BOLLYWOOD CLASSICS

Mother India (1957) Golden-Age classic whose lead actors, Nargis and Sunil Dutt, caused a scandal by later marrying – Sunil had played Nargis's son in the film.
Mughal-e-Azam ("The Greatest of the Mughals"; 1960) Epic tale of love and betrayal in the seventeenth century, as a spoilt prince falls for a court dancer, with tragic consequences.
Sholay (1975) This spaghetti western-inspired flick was the most successful Bollywood movie of all time, starring the legendary "Big B" himself, Amitabh Bachchan.
Monsoon Wedding (2001) Mira Nair's witty, award-winning depiction of a swanky Punjabi wedding in Delhi.
Rang De Basanti ("Paint it Saffron", 2006) The heroes of Indian independence provide the inspiration for five actors-turned-activists in a vigorous and controversial drama of corruption and cover-ups.

TAKE A SLOW BOAT DOWN THE MEKONG • A NIGHT IN THE RAINFOREST • THE REVOLTING KINGS OF KOMODO • PADDLING INTO SECRET LAGOONS • FEELING FRUITY IN THE MEKONG DELTA • DAWN OVER KELIMUTU IN FLORES • SAND AND SPICE ON KO SAMUI • PARTYING AT THE ATI-ATIHAN FESTIVAL • CONQUERING SOUTHEAST ASIA'S HIGHEST PEAK • MEETING THE RELATIVES: ORANG-UTANS IN SUMATRA • DIVING THE TUBBATAHA REEF • SAFFRON AND GOLD: FALLING UNDER THE SPELL OF LOUANG PHABANG • FIGHT NIGHT IN BANGKOK • JOINING THE PARTY AT AN IBAN LONGHOUSE • KARST AND CREW: OVERNIGHTING ON HA LONG BAY • HIKING IJEN VOLCANO WITH THE SULPHUR MINERS • IRONING OUT THE KINKS • THE HILLS ARE ALIVE: TRIBAL TREKKING • PUZZLES AT THE PLAIN OF JARS • SNAKES EVERY WHICH WAY IN HANOI • TAKE A FREIGHT TRAIN • ANCIENT AYUTTHAYA BY BOAT, ELEPHANT AND BICYCLE • PEEKING AT PARADISE IN ARU • MOPEDS AND MAGIC • VISITING THE TUOL SLENG GENOCIDE MUSEUM • BEDAZZLED AT BANGKOK'S GRAND PALACE • THE BUZZ AROUND CHIANG MAI • BUNAKEN'S MARINE MEGALOPOLIS • CANDLES IN THE WIND: THE LOY KRATHONG FESTIVAL OF LIGHT • EXPLORING THE TEMPLES OF ANGKOR • BUDGET BEACH-CHIC • GREAT DATES AND TEMPLE CEREMONIES • BALINESE THEATRICS • SHOPPING AT CHATUCHAK WEEKEND MARKET • GET AWAY FROM IT ALL IN THE GILIS • TUBING THE NAM XONG • SNIFFING OUT THE CORPSE FLOWER • JUNGLE BOOGIE IN SARAWAK • BOROBUDUR: THE WORLD'S BIGGEST BUDDHIST STUPA • CLIMBING THE STAIRWAY TO HEAVEN IN BANAUE • FOUR THOUSAND ISLANDS AND FISH FOR DINNER • MOONLIT MANOEUVRES THROUGH HOI AN • STALKING THE CREATURES OF THE NIGHT • MOTORBIKING THE NORTHWEST LOOP • TRIBAL FUNERALS IN SUMBA: BLOOD, BONES AND BURIALS • ISLAND-HOPPING IN THE BACUIT ARCHIPELAGO • ALL ABOARD THE EASTERN & ORIENTAL EXPRESS • VOLCANIC ACTIVITY: SUNRISE ON MOUNT BROMO • TACKLING POL POT'S LEGACY WITH THE VSO • SEA-GYPSIES, TURTLES AND FROGFISH • HIKE THROUGH HISTORY ALONG THE KOKODA TRAIL • LONG LIVE THE EMPEROR: THE IMPERIAL MAUSOLEUMS OF HUÉ • DANCING UNDER A FULL MOON • TAKE A SLOW BOAT DOWN THE MEKONG • A NIGHT IN THE RAINFOREST • THE REVOLTING KINGS OF KOMODO • PADDLING INTO SECRET LAGOONS • FEELING FRUITY IN THE MEKONG DELTA • DAWN OVER KELIMUTU IN FLORES • SAND AND SPICE ON KO SAMUI • PARTYING AT THE ATI-ATIHAN FESTIVAL • CONQUERING SOUTHEAST ASIA'S HIGHEST PEAK • MEETING THE RELATIVES: ORANG-UTANS IN SUMATRA • DIVING THE TUBBATAHA REEF • SAFFRON AND GOLD: FALLING UNDER THE SPELL OF LOUANG PHABANG • FLIGHT

Southeast Asia
861–913

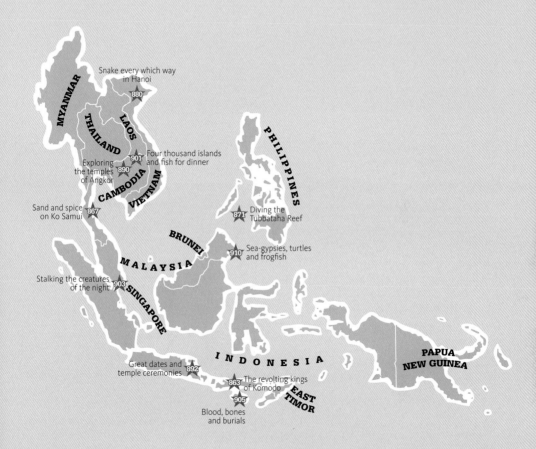

Snake every which way
in Hanoi
880

Four thousand islands
and fish for dinner
901

Exploring
the temples
of Angkor
890

Sand and spice
on Ko Samui **867**

Diving the
Tubbataha Reef **871**

Sea-gypsies, turtles
and frogfish **910**

Stalking the creatures
of the night **903**

Great dates and
temple ceremonies **892**

The revolting kings
of Komodo **863**

Blood, bones
and burials **905**

MYANMAR

THAILAND

LAOS

CAMBODIA

VIETNAM

PHILIPPINES

BRUNEI

MALAYSIA

SINGAPORE

INDONESIA

EAST
TIMOR

PAPUA
NEW GUINEA

861 Take a slow boat down the Mekong

LAOS Cargo-hold hell used to be the order of the day for travellers taking the slow boat through Laos, squashed between chickens and sacks of rice. But the ride's become so popular that there are now specially designed backpackers' boats running the 300km route from the Thai border east to Louang Phabang. They even have proper seats and a toilet – both pretty handy when you're spending two long days on the river. It's still a cramped, bottom-numbing experience, though, with over a hundred passengers on board, and an average speed that's very slow indeed.

In truth you wouldn't expect a trip on Southeast Asia's longest and most important river to be plain sailing. Here in northern Laos, approximately halfway down the river's 4000km journey from its source on the Tibetan plateau to its delta in southern Vietnam, the Mekong is dogged by sandbanks and seasonal shallows. It can be tough to navigate, as passengers in the hurtling, accident-prone speedboats often discover. Better to take it slowly: bring a cushion and enjoy the ride.

Little about the river has changed over the decades. The Mekong has always been a lifeline for Laos, Southeast Asia's only landlocked nation, and villagers continue to depend on it for fish, irrigation and transport, even panning its silt in search of gold. Limestone cliffs and thickly forested hills frame its banks, with riverside clearings used for banana groves, slash-and-burn agriculture and bamboo-shack villages. The largest of these, Pakbeng, marks the journey's midpoint, where everyone disembarks for a night on dry land. A ramshackle place for such an important river port, Pakbeng offers an unvarnished introduction to Laos, with rudimentary guesthouses and just four hours of electricity a day. Roll on the civilized comforts of Louang Phabang, a mere eight hours downriver.

862 A night in the rainforest

MALAYSIA You probably won't get much sleep on your first night in Taman Negara National Park – not because there's an elephant on your chalet doorstep or the rain's dripping through your tent, but because the rainforest is unexpectedly noisy after dark. High-volume insects whirr and beep at an ear-splitting pitch, branches creak and swish menacingly, and every so often something nearby shrieks or thumps. Taman Negara is a deceptively busy place, home to scores of creatures including macaques, gibbons, leaf monkeys and tapirs, as well as more elusive tigers, elephants and sun bears. Not to mention some three hundred species of birds and a huge insect population.

Many rainforest residents are best observed after dark, either on a ranger-led night walk or from one of the twelve-bed tree-house hides strategically positioned above popular salt licks. But a longer guided trek also offers a good chance of spotting something interesting and will get you immersed in the phenomenally diverse flora of Taman Negara, which supports a staggering 14,000 plant species, including 75m-high tualang trees, carnivorous pitcher plants and fungi that glow like lightbulbs. The rewarding six-hour Keniam–Trenggan trail takes you through dense jungle and into several impressive caves, while the arduous week-long expedition to the cloudforests atop 2187m-high Gunung Tahan involves frequent river crossings and steep climbs. With minimal effort, on the other hand, you can ascend to the treetops near park headquarters, via a canopy walkway. Slung some 30m above the forest floor between a line of towering tualang trees, this swaying bridge offers a gibbon's perspective on the cacophonous jungle below.

863 The revolting kings of Komodo

INDONESIA There are few expeditions more disquieting than visiting Indonesia's Komodo Island. Approaching by boat, it appears staggeringly beautiful – the archetypal tropical hideaway. But doubts about the wisdom of what you're about to do surface as soon as you step ashore and discover that you're sharing the beach with the local deer population: if they're too frightened to spend much time in the interior, is it entirely wise for you to do so?

Your unease only grows at the nearby national park office, as you're briefed about the island's most notorious inhabitant. From the tip of a tail so mighty that one swish could knock a buffalo off its feet, to a mouth that drips with saliva so foul that most bite victims die from infected wounds rather than the injuries themselves, Komodo dragons are 150kg of pure reptilian malevolence.

They are also – on Komodo at least – quite numerous, and it doesn't take long before you come across your first dragon, usually basking motionless on a rock or up a tree (among an adult dragon's more unpleasant habits is a tendency to feed on the young, so adolescents often seek sanctuary in the branches).

So immobile are they during the heat of the day that the only proof that they're still alive is an occasional flick of the tongue, usually accompanied by a globule of viscous drool that drips and hangs from the side of their mouths. Indeed, it's this docility that encourages you – possibly against your better judgement – to edge closer, until eventually those of sufficient nerve are almost within touching distance.

And it's only then, as you crouch nervously on your haunches and examine the loose folds of battle-scarred skin, the dark, eviscerating talons and the cold, dead eyes of this natural-born killer, that you can fully appreciate how fascinating these creatures really are, and that there is nothing, but nothing, so utterly, compellingly revolting on this planet.

THAILAND The first time you enter a *hong* you're almost certain to laugh with delight. The fun begins when your guide paddles you across to the towering karst island and then pilots your canoe through an imperceptible fissure in its rock wall. You enter a sea cave that reeks of bats and gets darker and darker until suddenly your guide shouts, "Lie back in the boat please!" Your nose barely clears the stalactites and you emerge, with your toes first, into a sunlit lagoon, or *hong*, right at the very heart of the outcrop.

Hong ("rooms" in Thai) are the *pièce de résistance* of southern Thailand's Phang Nga Bay. Invisible to any passing vessel, these secret tidal lagoons are flooded, roofless caves hidden within the core of seemingly solid limestone islands, accessible only

at certain tides and only in sea canoes small enough to slip beneath and between low-lying rocky overhangs. Like the islands themselves, the *hong* have taken millions of years to form, with the softer limestone hollowed out from the side by the pounding waves, and from above by the wind and the rain.

The world inside these collapsed cave systems is extraordinary, protected from the open bay by a turreted ring of cliffs hung with primeval-looking gardens of inverted cycads, twisted bonsai palms, lianas, miniature screw pines and tangled ferns.

And as the tide withdraws, the *hong*'s resident creatures – among them fiddler crabs, mudskippers, dusky langurs and crab-eating macaques – emerge to forage on the muddy floor, while white-bellied sea eagles hover expectantly overhead.

Paddling into
secret lagoons

864

865
FEELING FRUITY in the **Mekong Delta**

VIETNAM If you're looking for a classic Southeast Asian scene, Vietnam's Mekong Delta, south of Ho Chi Minh City, will do the trick. This is an area of vivid green rice paddies, conical-hatted farmers and lumbering water buffaloes, of floating markets and villages built on stilts. Lush orchards overflow with mangoes, papayas and dragonfruit; plantations brim with bananas, coconuts and pineapples. And through it all wind the nine tributaries of the Mekong River, which nourish this fruitbasket of Vietnam, the waters busy with sampans, canoes and houseboats. It is the end of the run for Asia's mighty Mekong, whose waters rise over 4000km away in the snows of the Tibetan plateau and empty out here, into the alluvial-rich plains fringing the South China Sea.

For the fifteen million people who live in these wetlands, everything revolves around the waterways, so to glimpse something of their life you need to join them on the river. Boat tours from the market town of My Tho will take you to nearby orchard-islands, crisscrossed by narrow palm-shaded canals and famous for their juicy yellow-fleshed sapodilla fruits. At Vinh Long, home-stay programmes give you the opportunity to sample the garden produce for dinner and spend the night on stilts over the water.

Chances are your host-family catch fish as well – right under their floorboards in specially designed bamboo cages, so the daily feed is simply a matter of lifting up a plank or two. Next stop should be Can Tho, the delta's principal city, to make the ride out to the enormous floating market at Phung Hiep.

Here at the confluence of seven major waterways, hundreds of sampans bump and jostle early each morning to trade everything from sugar cane to pigs – and of course mountains of fruit.

866 Dawn over Kelimutu in Flores

INDONESIA There's something magnificently untamed about Flores. As with almost every island in this part of the Indonesian archipelago, Flores is fringed by picture-postcard beaches of golden sand. But to appreciate its unique charms you have to turn away from the sea and instead face the island's interior. Despite its relatively small size (a mere 370km long and, in places, as narrow as 12km), only the much larger Indonesian landmasses of Java and Sumatra can boast more volcanoes than this slender sliver of land.

Unsurprisingly, Flores' jagged volcanic spine has played a major part in the island's development. The precipitous topography contributes to torrential wet seasons, which in turn provide a tropical countenance – not for nothing did the Portuguese name this island "Cabo das Flores", the Cape of Flowers. The rugged peaks have also long separated the tribes on the island – an enforced segregation that has ensured an inordinate number of different languages and dialects, as well as many distinct cultures.

The highest volcanic peak on the island is the towering 2382m Gunung Ranaka, while its most volatile is the grumbling, hot-headed Ebulobo on Flores' south coast. But the prince among them is Kelimutu. Though just 1620m high, the volcano has become something of a pilgrimage site. Waking at around 4am, trekkers pile onto the back of an open-sided truck for the thirty-minute ride up the volcano's slopes, from where a short scramble to Kelimutu's barren summit reveals the mountain's unique attraction: three small craters, each filled with lakes of startlingly different colours, ranging from vibrant turquoise to a deep, reddish brown.

With the wisps of morning mist lingering above the water's surface and the rising sun bouncing off the waters creating an ever-changing play of light and colour, dawn over Kelimutu is Indonesia at its most beguiling.

867 Sand and spice on Ko Samui

THAILAND Ko Samui is perhaps an unlikely spot to learn the art of Thai cooking. Given the choice between lapping up rays on a patch of sand, palms and waterfalls in the Gulf of Thailand or arming yourself with a sharp cleaver to take on a mound of raw pork and fiery chilies, most people will surely opt for the former – especially when the best plate of food you're likely to have in your life costs about a buck at the local market.

Yet the packed schedule at the Samui Institute of Thai Culinary Arts suggests otherwise. The school focuses on central Thai food, considered the classic style among the country's four regional cuisines, with its coconut-milk curries and flavoursome balance of hot, sour, salty and sweet.

The classes begin with a discussion of the ingredients (and how to substitute for those hard to find outside Southeast Asia), work up to wok skills and end with a feast of your own making, an array of tempting and delicious stir fries, curries and soups.

Walk into the school's unassuming shophouse just off Samui's Chaweng Beach and you may wonder whether you've been shanghaied into a tropical *Iron Chef* gone awry. A sea of tiny bowls bursting with cumin seeds, tamarind, coriander root, galangal and shrimp paste lie scattered across the prep tables, and you've got a little more than two hours to whip up three dishes. But before panic sets in, the lead chef calmly explains how to chiffonade a kaffir lime leaf, and soon enough, you're grinding out a proper chili paste in a mortar and pestle with the steady hand of a market lady who's been at it for fifty years.

It can't be this easy, can it? You chop a few more chilies, toss in an extra dash of fish sauce, swirl the wok and – *aroy mak* – you've just duplicated that *tom yum kai* (spicy shrimp soup) you saw at the market. So what if it cost a few dollars more?

868 Partying at the Ati-Atihan festival

THE PHILIPPINES You need serious stamina for the three days and nights of non-stop dancing that mark the culmination of Ati-Atihan, the most flamboyant fiesta in the fiesta-mad Philippines. No wonder the mantra chanted by participants in this marathon rave is *hala bira, puera pasma*, which means "keep on going, no tiring". If you plan on lasting the course, start training now.

Ati-Atihan, which takes place during the first two weeks of January in Kalibo – an otherwise unimpressive port town on the central Philippine island of Panay – actually lasts for two weeks. But it's the final three days that are the most important, with costumed locals taking to the streets in a riot of partying, music and street dancing. And it's this the tourists come for – 72 sleepless hours of alcohol-fuelled, intoxicating mayhem acted out to the deafening ranks of massed tribal drums.

Don't expect to just stand by and watch – the locals have an unwritten rule that there are no wallflowers at Ati-Atihan – and if you don't take part, they'll make you. Even if all you can muster is a drunken conga line, you can take the edge off your nerves with a few glasses of *lambanog*, a vigorous native aperitif made from leftover jackfruit or mango fermented in cheap containers buried in the earth – the "zombie flavour" is especially liberating.

Ati-Atihan is still partly a religious festival, held to celebrate the child Jesus (Santo Nino). In recent years it has morphed into a delightful hodgepodge of Catholic ritual, indigenous drama and tourist attraction. It's the one time of the year when Catholic Filipinos aren't afraid to push the boat out, especially for the final-day fancy dress parade that sees thousands of people in costumes so big and brash they almost block the street.

If you're feeling a little rough after all this, do what many others do and head up the coast to the beautiful little island of Boracay, where you can sleep off your hangover on one of the finest beaches in the world.

869 Conquering Southeast Asia's highest peak

MALAYSIA It's a hell of a slog up Malaysian Borneo's Mount Kinabalu, but every year thousands of visitors brave the freezing conditions and altitude sickness to reach the 4095m-high summit. The reward is a spectacular dawn panorama across granite pinnacles rising out of the clouds below you, and the knowledge that you've conquered the highest peak between the Himalayas and New Guinea.

Your two-day expedition up the southern ridge begins at Kinabalu Park headquarters, where you meet your obligatory guide and gulp at the multiple jagged peaks ahead. You need to be equipped as for any mountain hike, prepared for downpours and extreme chill at the summit, but Kinabalu's appeal is that any averagely fit tourist can reach the top. The steady climb up to the Laban Rata mountain huts is a five-hour trek along a well-tramped trail through changing forest habitats. Beyond 1800m you're in dense cloudforest, among a thousand species of orchids, 26 types of rhododendron and a host of insect-hungry pitcher plants. By 2600m most of the vegetation has given up, but you stagger on to 3300m and the long-awaited flop into bed. Day two starts at 2.30am for the final push across the glistening granite rock face to Low's Peak, Kinabalu's highest point. It's dark and very cold; for three hours you can see no further than the beam of your headtorch and, despite the handrails and ropes, the climb is tough; some have to turn back because of pounding altitude headaches. But when you finally reach the summit, your spirits will rise with the sun as the awesome view comes into focus, every horizon filled with the stark grey twists of Kinabalu's iconic peaks, and the mile-deep chasm of infamous Low's Gully at your feet.

870 Meeting the relatives: orang-utans in Sumatra

INDONESIA Sandwiched between the raging Bohorok River and the deep, silent, steaming jungle, the Bukit Lawang Orang-utan Sanctuary, on the vast Indonesian island of Sumatra, offers the unique opportunity of witnessing one of our closest and most charming relatives in their own backyard.

Having crossed the Bohorok on a precarious, makeshift canoe, your first sight of these kings of the jungle is at the enclosures housing recent arrivals, many of whom have been rescued from the thriving trade in exotic pets, particularly in nearby Singapore. It's here that the long process of rehabilitation begins, a process that may include learning from their human guardians such basic simian skills as tree-climbing and fruit-peeling.

Most of these activities are done away from the prying cameras of tourists, but twice a day park officers lead visitors up to a feeding platform to wait, and to watch. The sound of rustling foliage and creaking branches betrays the presence of a rangy, shaggy silhouette making its languid yet majestic way through the treetops.

Orang-utans literally force the trees to bend to their will as they swing back and forth on one sapling until the next can be reached. Swooping just above the awestruck audience, they arrive at the platform to feast on bananas and milk, the diet kept deliberately monotonous to encourage the orang-utans – all of whom have been recently released from the sanctuary – to look for more diverse flavours in the forest.

Once the ape has proved that it's capable of surviving unaided, it will be left to fend for itself in the vast, dark forests of North Sumatra. Its rehabilitation will be considered complete. Sadly, at Bukit Lawang there never seems to be a shortage of rescued apes to take its place.

871 Diving the Tubbataha Reef

THE PHILIPPINES If you're looking for some of the most adventurous and thrilling scuba diving in the world, Tubbataha Reef Marine Park in the Sulu Sea is the place to start. Well out of sight of land and almost 200km southeast of Puerto Princesa in Palawan, this World Heritage Site is only accessible on live-aboard boats when seas are favourable between March and June. Its very isolation means it's not overrun by package-tour divers, and even during these peak months you'll probably be on one of only a handful of small boats in the area. The reef – actually a grouping of dozens of small reefs, atolls and coral islands covering more than 300 square kilometres – is one of the finest in the world, with daily sightings of the big pelagics that all divers dream of.

Rise at dawn for a quick dive among the turtles and small sharks before breakfast. Afterwards there's time for a visit to Shark Airport, where sharks "take off" from sandy ledges like planes, before it's back to the boat for lunch and a snooze. You can do deep dives, night dives, drift dives, all kinds of dives. Or you can simply fossick gently along some of the shallower reefs, home to so many varieties of coral and fish that it's hard to know where to look next.

For a real buzz, dive deep over one of the many coral walls that seem to plunge into infinity, and hang out for a few minutes with giant manta rays, black-tip reef sharks and, just possibly, cruising hammerheads. You also stand a good chance of getting up close and personal with a whale shark, the harmless gentle giants of the sea known in the Philippines as *butanding*.

Of course, there's life beyond diving at Tubbataha. For a change of scene, you can snorkel around some of the atolls, picnic on the beach at the ranger station, or just kick back on deck and watch dolphins and tuna perform occasional aerial stunts.

872 Saffron and gold:
FALLING UNDER THE SPELL OF LOUANG PHABANG

LAOS The pace of life is deliciously slow in Louang Phabang, but if you opt for a lie-in you'll miss the perfect start to the day. As dawn breaks over this most languorous of Buddhist towns, saffron-robed monks emerge from their temple-monasteries to collect alms from their neighbours, the riverbanks begin to come alive and the smell of freshly baked baguettes draws you to one of the many cafés. It's a captivating scene whichever way you turn: ringed by mountains and encircled by the Mekong and Khan rivers, the old quarter's temple roofs peep out from the palm groves, its streets still lined with wood-shuttered shophouses and French-colonial mansions.

Though it has the air of a rather grand village, Louang Phabang is the ancient Lao capital, seat of the royal family that ruled the country for six hundred years until the Communists exiled them in the 1970s. It remains the most cultured town in Laos (not a hard-won accolade it's true, in this poor, undeveloped nation), and one of the best preserved in Southeast Asia – something now formalized by World Heritage status. Chief among its many beautiful temples is the entrancing sixteenth-century Wat Xiang Thong, whose tiered roofs frame an exquisite glass mosaic of the tree of life and attendant creatures, flanked by pillars and doors picked out in brilliant gold-leaf stencils. It's a gentle stroll from here to the graceful teak and rosewood buildings of the Royal Palace Museum and the dazzling gilded murals of neighbouring Wat Mai.

When you tire of the monuments, there are riverside caves, waterfalls and even a whisky-making village to explore, and plenty of shops selling intricate textiles and Hmong hill-tribe jewellery. Serenity returns at sunset, when the monks' chants drift over the temple walls and everyone else heads for high ground to soak up the view.

>> Southeast Asia

873 Fight night in Bangkok

THAILAND The Thai people are predominately Buddhist, and through much of their country Siddhartha's spirit is palpable. Even in the noisy and overcrowded capital city, hard-faced nationals will soften their features and treat visitors with a respect given all living creatures. The exception that proves the rule is the brutal national sport of *muay thai* or Thai boxing – where knees batter ribs while gamblers wager their salaries on who will fall, and when.

Vendors surround Bangkok's Lumphini Stadium three nights out of seven, peddling wares and heated snacks to patrons streaming into a theatre of controlled violence. Past the ticket booth is a mere hint of a lobby, its walls pierced with numbered archways too small for the seating areas behind them. A rhythmic thudding from deeper inside triggers a bottleneck at the edges of the arena, the narrow entryways imparting a final suggestion of order before releasing spectators into the clamour beyond. In the ring the pre-fight display has already begun. Like many of the martial arts, *muay thai* has its roots in national defence, and the fighters perform awkward dances before the bell in honour of a kingdom which was never at any point conquered by foreign invaders.

Drums pulse behind tense woodwind sounds as the early rounds get under way, each fighter cautiously feeling for weakness in his opponent's defence. The crowd is equally patient, watching carefully for an advantage they can use against the bookmakers. At the end of the second round all hell breaks loose. In the stands men are waving and shouting, signalling with contorted hands the amounts they're willing to lose. Within two minutes the fighters must retake the ring, and when they meet there are no more feints or dodges. Each attack is without pause. The music quickens. Blows are harder now, exchanged at a furious rate. The crowd raises its voice at every strike. Against the shin, into the ribs. Ferociously. Relentlessly. And then a step backward and to the left reveals enough space to slip an instep up to the loser's jaw. Patrons make good on their markers while a stretcher carries away the unconscious also-ran. With ten fights a night, there's simply no time for compassion.

874 Joining the party at an Iban longhouse

MALAYSIA It's always polite to bring gifts to your hosts' house, but when visiting a Sarawak longhouse make sure it's something that's easily shared, as longhouses are communal, and nearly everything gets divvied up into equal parts. This isn't always an easy task: typically, longhouses are home to around 150 people and contain at least thirty family apartments, each one's front door opening on to the common gallery, hence the tag "a thirty-door longhouse" to describe the size. These days not everyone lives there full time, but the majority of Sarawak's indigenous Iban population still consider the longhouse home, even if they only return for weekends.

Many longhouses enjoy stunning locations, usually in a clearing beside a river, so you'll probably travel to yours in a longboat that meanders between the jungle-draped banks, dodging logs being floated downstream to the timber yards. Look carefully and you'll see that patches of hinterland have been cultivated with black pepper vines, rubber and fruit trees, plus the occasional square of paddy, all of which are crucial to longhouse economies.

Having first met the chief of your longhouse, you climb the notched tree trunk that serves as a staircase into the stilted wooden structure and enter the common area, or *ruai*, a wide gallery that runs the length of the building and is the focus of community social life. Pretty much everything happens here – the meeting and greeting, the giving and sharing of gifts, the gossip, and the partying. Animist Iban communities in particular are notorious party animals (unlike some of their Christian counterparts), and you'll be invited to join in the excessive rice-wine drinking, raucous dancing and forfeit games that last late into the night.

Finally, exhausted, you hit the sack – either on a straw mat right there on the *ruai*, or in a guest lodge next door.

875 Karst and crew: overnighting on Ha Long Bay

VIETNAM Spend a night afloat among the limestone pinnacles of Ha Long Bay, and you'll witness their many moods as their silhouettes morph with the moonlight, mist and midday sun. Scores of local boat companies offer this experience, for the spectacularly scenic bay is a World Heritage Site and Vietnam's top tourist destination.

Regularly referred to as the eighth natural wonder of the world, the 1500 square kilometres of Ha Long Bay contain nearly two thousand islands, most uninhabited outcrops that protrude from the Gulf of Tonkin. Their intriguingly craggy profiles have long inspired poets, wags and travel writers to wax lyrical about Italianate cathedrals, every type of creature from fighting cocks to bug-eyed frogs, even famous faces, but the bay's creation myth is just as poetic. "Ha Long" translates as "the dragon descending into the sea": legend tells how the islets were scattered here by the celestial dragon as a barrier against invaders.

Even the most imaginative visitor might tire of interpreting the shapes for a full two days, so overnight trips offer different angles on rock appreciation. As well as lounging on island beaches by day and swimming the phosphorescent waters by night, there are plenty of caves and floating villages to explore, and endless fresh seafood to enjoy. Some tours allow you to paddle yourself around in a kayak, while others feature forest treks and cycle rides on Cat Ba Island, the largest in the bay.

Hiking **Ijen volcano** *with the sulphur miners*

INDONESIA The ragged-edged smoking cone of the Ijen volcano defines the extreme east of Java. It always pays to get up before dawn if you're climbing volcanoes, so you can reach the summit before the clouds roll in. But even if you start hiking Ijen at 2am you'll have plenty of company, for this peak defies its Indonesian name Gunung Ijen ("lonely mountain").

The volcano spews out sulphur, which is hacked out of the steaming caldera by hundreds of freelance miners, who get up at an ungodly hour to collect the foul-smelling yellow element. Only those who rise early enough are able to amass enough of the limited sulphur to make a day's pay (US$5).

Starting from the isolated national park post at Pos Paltuding, a steep trail ascends the shoulder of the mountain, passing through tropical forest that's home to gibbons and patrolled by eagles. You'll pass a steady stream of miners, who joke and chatter as they balance loads of up to 80kg across their backs in bamboo baskets, their steady progress fuelled by a diet of *kretek* (clove) cigarettes and black tea. The path switchbacks higher and higher until you emerge above the tree line and a spellbinding view of the neighbouring volcanic peaks of Merapi (2802m) and Raung (3332m) opens up. Little grows up here except some hardy bushes, their growth stunted by the howling wind and cold. Finally you reach an exposed viewpoint on the lip of the crater, the electric blue lake below only revealed periodically as gases and steam billow around the cone.

For most visitors this is enough, but it is possible to descend into the crater itself where the miners harvest sulphur (the "brimstone" of biblical times), which is mainly used by the cosmetics industry, and is added to fertilizer. Be warned: the vapours can be overpowering. Ijen miners wear no more than cotton scarves to protect themselves from the noxious fumes, but many do live to a ripe old age – one man in his mid-70s still does the hike most weeks.

877 Ironing out the kinks

THAILAND One of the many great things about having a Thai massage is that there's no oil or lotions involved, so you don't need to strip off and there's none of that embarrassing tussle with paper knickers; you can also get your massage pretty much anywhere. This could be at a temple – in particular at the famous Wat Pho in Bangkok, historic centre of Thai massage therapy – at a hotel spa, or, most enticingly (and cheaply), on the beach. A two-hour session under a palm tree will cost you no more than $10, the soothing soundtrack of gently lapping waves will be genuine, and you should emerge feeling like you've had a good yoga workout, both relaxed and energized, but without having made any of the effort yourself.

It can be a shock the first time a Thai masseur uses elbows on your back, then brings heels, feet and knees into play, pulling and pushing your limbs into contorted yogic stretches. But it's all carefully designed to exert a gentle pressure on your vital energy channels, and it's what distinguishes the Thai approach from other massage styles, more concerned with tissue manipulation.

Thais will visit a masseur for conditions that might send others scuttling to the pharmacist – to alleviate fevers, colds and headaches, for example. But healthy bodies also benefit; it's said that regular massage produces long-term well-being by stimulating circulation and aiding natural detoxification. And it's certainly an idyllic way to while away a few hours on the beach.

The hills are alive:
tribal trekking

THAILAND Exhilarating though the ridgetop views often are, it's not the scenery that draws travellers into the hills of northern Thailand, but the people who live in them. There are some four thousand hill-tribe villages in the uplands of Chiang Mai and Chiang Rai provinces, peopled by half a dozen main tribes whose ancestors wandered across from Burma and China. They have subsistence-farmed up here for two hundred years and continue to observe age-old customs and beliefs, making visiting them a fascinating, and popular, trip.

The trekking between villages is moderately taxing – you're in the hills after all – but the trails are well worn and a good guide will bring the landscape alive, pointing out medicinal plants and elusive creatures along the way. The highlights, though, are the villages themselves, clusters of stilted bamboo huts close by a river, invariably wreathed in wood-smoke and busy with free-ranging pigs and chickens. Village architecture varies a little between tribes, particularly where animist shrines and totems are concerned, for each group lives by distinct traditions and taboos. But the diverse costumes are more striking: the jangling headdresses of the Akha women decorated with baubles hammered out of old silver coins; the intricately embroidered wide-legged trousers worn by the Mien; and the pom-poms and Day-Glo pinks and greens favoured by the Lisu. Many hill-tribeswomen make their living from weaving and embroidering these traditional textiles, and buying direct is a good way of contributing to village funds.

878

879 Puzzles at the Plain of Jars

LAOS After three hours trudging along steep forest paths, you come to a surreal sight. Hundreds of megalithic stone jars, large enough for someone to a crouch inside, are strewn all around. This group of 416 jars is the largest at the aptly named Plain of Jars, whose current tally stands at 1900 jars in 52 clusters, plus fifteen jar-making sites. They were made by a vanished civilization and their presence indicates that the mountains were prosperously settled at the time. Today the Xieng Khoung province is on the rise again, this time as a tourist hub.

Little is known about the jar-makers, except that the plateau was a strategic and prosperous centre for trade routes extending from India to China. Nearly 2000 years ago, possibly earlier according to new evidence, these jars functioned as mortuary vessels: a corpse would be placed inside the jar until it decomposed down to its essence, then cremated and buried in a second urn with personal possessions. Now all that remains here are the empty jars, set in clusters on the crests of hills, an imposing and eerie legacy.

At Phukeng, you can see where the jars were made. Dozens of incomplete jars lie on the mountainside where they were abandoned after cracking during construction. It's a sight that evokes the magnitude of the effort: after many weeks spent gouging a jar from a boulder with hammer and chisel, the creators then had to haul the load of several tons (the largest jar weighs six tons) across the undulating, grassy, pine-studded landscape to the "cemetery" 8km away. How the jars were transported is another puzzle that serves to deepen the enigma that pervades the Plain of Jars.

880 Snake every which way in Hanoi

VIETNAM When the man bringing your meal to the table is missing most of his fingers and the main ingredient is not only still alive but also long and writhing and – hang on, is that a cobra? Well, that's when you know this is no ordinary dining experience. Eating at one of Hanoi's snake restaurants is as much a theatrical performance as a meal out.

The decor is way over the top. From a grungy side-street you enter a world of exuberant woodwork with mother-of-pearl inlay glowing in the lantern light. Bonsai plants are scattered artfully while off to the side glass jars containing snake wine hint at what's to come.

When everyone's settled, the snake handler – he with very few fingers – presents the menu. He kicks off with cobra, the most expensive item on the menu (and a choice photo-op), then runs through the other options, all very much alive and hissing. Traditionally, your chosen snake is killed in front of you, though it will be dispatched off-stage if you ask. The guest of honour (lucky you?) then gets to eat the still-beating heart.

The Vietnamese say it contains a stimulant and that the meat is an aphrodisiac. The jury's out on both counts, however, because of the copious amounts of alcohol everyone consumes. By way of an aperitif you get two small glasses of rice wine, one blood red, the other an almost fluorescent, bile-ish green . . . which is in fact exactly what they are.

Things get decidedly more palatable as the meal starts to arrive. In a matter of minutes your snake has been transformed into all manner of tasty dishes: snake soup, spring rolls, dumplings, fillets, even crispy-fried snake skin. Absolutely nothing is wasted. It's washed down with more rice wine, or beer if you'd rather, and to round things off, some fresh fruit and green tea – with no snake sorbet forthcoming.

881 Take a freight train

CAMBODIA The train was travelling at top speed when the accident occurred. After decades of service the rail line finally snapped, buckling in front of the locomotive and forcing it off the track. Mercifully the top speed in question was a shade under twenty miles per hour, and the passengers were able to disembark safely and push the vehicle back. After a spot of ad hoc welding under an unforgiving sun, the line was back in service, and the train rolled into Phnom Penh the following afternoon – sixteen hours late, but just about in one piece. If you want your trains to take you smoothly, safely and efficiently from A to B, head to Japan. If you want the diametric opposite, come to Cambodia.

Cambodia's trains largely exist to transport freight, rather than people – most sport just one passenger carriage, which may itself be filled with livestock or other goods. Some passengers, indeed, find it preferable to sit on top of the train, clambering up in the manner of an action-movie stuntman, then clinging on for dear life as the carriage wobbles its way forward. Any discomfort is mitigated by cheery locals, waving from the fields, and stupendous views of the Cambodian countryside – on the way from Sihanoukville to Phnom Penh, the line aims straight at photogenic Mount Bokor for what seems like an eternity, then spends almost as long inching its way around the picturesque peak.

The train schedules are far from fixed, while the journey itself is sometimes free – on the day of the aforementioned accident, none of the passengers had been required to buy tickets because the stationmaster was asleep in his bedroom, which doubled as the station's ticketing booth. Such loose schedules call for the occasional burst of creativity – from some stations, late-arriving passengers can be whisked up to the train aboard a rail-adapted Honda cub. Taking the bullet train? Way too predictable.

882 Ancient Ayutthaya by boat, elephant and bicycle

THAILAND Founded in 1351 on an island at the confluence of three rivers, the former Thai capital of Ayutthaya once dazzled at the heart of a refined and hugely prosperous kingdom, the glint from its golden temple spires visible several kilometres away.

These days the tones are more muted. In the two and a half centuries since the city was ravaged by its Burmese neighbours, the corncob towers have crumbled and tilted, lichen has invaded the weatherworn bricks and many seated Buddhas have lost their heads. The heart of the Old City is now a graveyard for temples, a patchwork of parkland crossed by extravagantly wide boulevards and bordered by the concrete shophouses of the modern town.

Bicycles are the obvious way to explore and the Buddhist reliquary of Wat Phra Mahathat the place to start. Climb its collapsed central pagoda for a lesson in elegant city planning, then return to the saddle to seek out Wat Ratburana's gracefully tapered stupas and the beautifully restored lacquered and gilded interiors of Wat Na Phra Mane.

Fittingly, many visitors choose to tour the three stupas of the royal monastery, Wat Phra Si Sanphet, on elephant back. Dressed in the reds and golds of the Ayutthayan court, the elephants and their mahouts evoke an era of princely duels and royal pageantry – and allow modern-day tourists a regally elevated perspective.

The Old City's encircling rivers provided Ayutthaya with natural defences, and there is much pleasure in rounding off a day's sightseeing with a boat tour, stopping at perimeter temples such as Wat Chai Watthanaram to admire the artful symmetries of towers, stupas and colonnaded halls designed to look their best from the water. The rivers are still very much working waterways, busy with barges lugging rice and sand down to the modern Thai capital, Bangkok, and lined with the teakwood stilt houses of present-day Ayutthayans. In among the homes and shrines are plenty of riverside restaurants, ideal last stops for a glass of Chang "Elephant" beer and the welcome chance to sample some royal Thai cuisine.

883 Peeking at paradise in Aru

INDONESIA So here I was in the middle of the jungle in Aru, at the end of the end of everywhere in the southeastern Indonesian province of Maluku, trying to find *cenderawasih*, the greater bird of paradise. These are gorgeous creatures, about the size of a thrush and with a similarly brown body, but one topped by a metallic green cap and, in males, a fantastic fountain of long, fluffy-looking golden feathers, which are proudly swished and shaken in territorial dancing displays.

But they were proving elusive: this was my fourth attempt within a year, after the others had ended in ferry strandings, political violence and a plane crash. I had now spent three days being taken ever-deeper into the forest's vine-tangled depths by hunters who I could barely communicate with, leaving me with tick bites aplenty but no sign of birds of paradise. We hadn't even heard their noisy "wok-wok-wok-wok" call, which sounds as melodic as a tin alarm

clock going off, and has caused locals to brand them *burung bodoh*, the stupid bird, because the racket they create makes them easy to track down and shoot.

But I was having fun, and now it was 6am on day five, my last, and I was being led into the forest once again by 60-year-old Bapak Gusti. He'd collared me in the village the evening before and casually mentioned that he owned a tree, just a short walk away, where the birds displayed every morning. I had nothing to lose by this point; my only worry was that this – like all the other "short walks" I had undertaken here – would actually last six hours, and the boat out would leave without me. But I was wrong: within twenty minutes, he had led me to a tree where, on a bare branch 30m up in the canopy, three male birds of paradise were displaying their hearts out, their plumage glowing as bright as the sunlight which brushed the treetops.

884 Mopeds and magic

THE PHILIPPINES The islands of the Philippines are so friendly and laid-back that independent travel is a breeze. A moped is ideally suited to exploring a place where so much life is lived outdoors. Pick a smaller island like Siquijor and you don't even need a map, and although there aren't many filling stations, you're never far from a village store, where you can buy soft drinks, snacks and huge Pepsi bottles full of petrol.

Cruising around at a leisurely pace, it's hard not to smile back at the succession of children yelling greetings, as the sun gently warms your back and the wind cools your face. Between villages on the coastal road you'll pass green fields and drive over carpets of rice that have been laid out to dry on the hot road surface. Everywhere, you'll see jeepneys: artistically decorated buses, covered in chrome and neon, and packed with schoolchildren, farmers, businessmen, and sacks crammed with food.

Head into the jungled interior, and it gets much quieter. Here, the dark tunnels of vegetation and trees that you drive through suggest a hint of Siquijor's reputation throughout the Philippines as a centre for witchcraft and healers (it's possible while you're here to arrange a session with a shaman to consult on anything from bad luck to kidney problems).

You'll also find unexpected panoramic views of the sparkling sea. Near the unfortunately named village of Poo, there's a sequence of waterfalls where you'll have to negotiate your way between local children somersaulting into the plunge pools.

Because it's off the usual tourist circuit, Siquijor is pleasantly quiet, and has wonderfully clear beaches. But it also has just the right amount in common with other places: at the end of the day, there's always an opportunity to watch the sun set from a bar, sipping a cold San Miguel beer, with your toes in white sand.

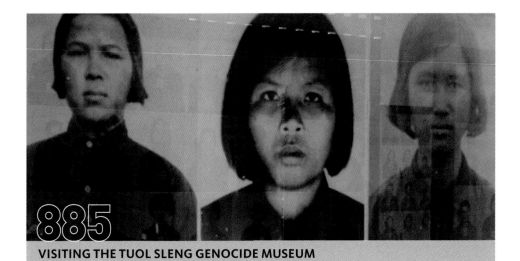

885

VISITING THE TUOL SLENG GENOCIDE MUSEUM

CAMBODIA Everyone over 30 in Cambodia has lived through the genocidal Khmer Rouge era. The woman who runs your guesthouse in downtown Phnom Penh; the moto driver who tried to rip you off on the ride down from the Thai border; your Angkor temples tour guide; the waiter at the seaside café in Sihanoukville. At the Tuol Sleng Genocide Museum you'll learn something of what that means.

A former school on the outskirts of Phnom Penh, Tuol Sleng, code-named S-21, was used by the Khmer Rouge to interrogate perceived enemies of their demented Marxist-Leninist regime. During the Khmer Rouge rule, from 1975 to 1979, some fourteen thousand Cambodians were tortured and killed here, often for the crime of being educated: for being a teacher, a monk, or a member of the elite; for wearing glasses; for being a discredited cadre.

We know this because the Khmer Rouge were meticulous in their documentation. When the Vietnamese army arrived at S-21 in January 1979 they found thousands of mugshots of former prisoners,

each of them numbered, along with reams of typed "confessions".

Those black and white photographs fill the downstairs walls of the museum today. There are rows and rows of them: men, women, children, even babies. Only seven prisoners survived S-21; one of them, Ung Pech, became the museum's first director. When the museum opened to the public in 1980, thousands of Cambodians came here to look for evidence of missing relatives.

The interior of the prison has in part been left almost as it was found. Tiled floors, classrooms crudely partitioned into tiny cells, shackles, iron bedsteads and meshed balconies. Elsewhere, graphic paintings by another survivor, Vann Nath, depict the torture methods used to extract confessions; some of these confessions are also reproduced here.

Once they'd been coerced into admitting guilt, prisoners were taken to the Choeung Ek Killing Fields and murdered. Choeung Ek, 12km southwest, is now the site of another memorial. Both provide graphic evidence of these recent horrors.

THAILAND As befits a former royal residence, there's bling aplenty at the Grand Palace, whose main temple, Wat Phra Kaeo, dazzles with its shimmering walls and gables covered all over in gilt and coloured glass mosaics. Join the hundreds of Thai pilgrims and step inside to pay homage to the teeny Emerald Buddha, the holiest icon in the country. The figurine is just 60cm high, elevated atop a towering golden pedestal, and is dressed according to the season: a golden shawl in winter, a monk's robe for the monsoon and a crown for summer. Things get even more surreal in the colonnades that encircle the temple, where an exuberant kilometre-long mural depicts the complicated ups and downs of the Ramayana story, an ancient epic tale of good versus evil, whose cast includes a monkey king, a demon with ten heads and otherwordly air-borne creatures.

887 The buzz around Chiang Mai

THAILAND The motorbikes of Chiang Mai are beautiful things. Renting them is easy and cheap, and they let you get around like a local, even if you have a poor sense of direction. Pick a morning, strap on your fisherman pants from the night market and, if you're brave, make room for a friend. Fly east to hilltop Wat Doi Saket to have your mind blown by trippy murals teaching Buddhist morality – illustrated with traffic signs. Buzz back along the "Handicraft Highway" to visit paper, celadon, wood and silk workshops. South of the city, get lost among the ancient chedis of Wiang Kum Kam, then rocket north to canoodle with baby elephants and watch their mothers make modern art at Mae Sa Elephant Camp. Once you've got the hang of all this, zip west up Doi Suthep mountain for lovely views of the countryside you've just explored. If the bike's motor hasn't turned your legs to jelly, climb the 300 stairs to Wat Phra That Doi Suthep, ding the bells in the courtyard for good luck – and beware speeding *songthaew* buses on the way back down.

888 Bunaken's marine megalopolis

INDONESIA The reefs at Bunaken Marine Park on Sulawesi teem with over 400 species of hard corals, rare pygmy seahorses, glorious gobies, decorator crabs and hairy frogfish. Coral walls, currents upwelling from deep nearby waters and huge schools of plankton feeders draw in shoals of different fish species, not to mention hordes of divers. Strict environmental regulations and cooperation with the local community have made Sulawesi, and the surrounding islands, one of the world's best diving destinations, and underwater photographers and marine biologists consistently rate Bunaken and the nearby Lembeh Strait as the globe's busiest macro-critter capital.

889 Candles in the wind: the Loy Krathong Festival of Light

THAILAND In the days leading up to Thailand's annual Loy Krathong Festival of Light, pretty little baskets fashioned from banana leaves and filled with orchids and marigolds begin to appear at market stalls across the country. On festival night everyone gathers at the nearest body of water – beside the riverbank or neighbourhood canal, on the seashore, even at the village fishpond. Crouching down beside the water, you light the candle and incense sticks poking out of your floral basket, say a prayer of thanks to the water goddess, in whose honour this festival is held, and set your offering afloat. As the bobbing lights of hundreds of miniature basket-boats drift away on the breeze, taking with them any bad luck accrued over the past year, the Loy Krathong song rings out over the sound system, contestants for the Miss Loy Krathong beauty pageant take to the stage and Chang beer begins to flow.

890 Exploring the temples of Angkor

CAMBODIA The sun was setting on the town of Siem Reap as I clung to the back of my moto driver. Threading our way through traffic, we rode out until town finally gave way to forest and we entered the Angkor site. In front of us were the iconic lotus-bud towers of Angkor Wat, looking like giant pine cones, resplendent in the light. Sunset is the best time to view west-facing Angkor Wat, from the top of nearby temple-mountain, Phnom Bakheng, when the greying stone of the towers glow red under the glare of the dying sun.

The secret of Angkor is to explore the galleries and enclosures at your own pace. Wander the corridors and you'll stumble across aged monks performing blessings on curious tourists; wafting bundles of burning incense over their bodies and loudly clapping a cupped palm across their backs. The outer walls of the temple are covered with bas-reliefs retelling stories of Hindu battles and mythology, whose intricately etched bodies are worn smooth by thousands of hands. And all around is the echo of children playing in the cool passageways and juvenile hawkers who sell cold drinks and trinkets out of plastic carrier bags.

The next morning I went back to see Angkor Thom, with its lichen-covered towers revealing exquisite faces carved into rock: fat, curvaceous lips smiling benevolently beneath half-closed eyes. Thick jungle once shrouded this lost twelfth-century Khmer kingdom. Its painstaking restoration involved numbering and cataloguing each and every stone block before setting it back into its original position.

The destructive force of nature and time on stone is no more evident than at Ta Prohm, the temple left to the jungle. Here huge tree trunks, hard as cement, spill out over the scattered blocks like the creamy bellies of snakes. It's a wonderfully peaceful place, and once you're done exploring the doorways and the curious shapes of the forest entwined with boulders, sit back, kick off your shoes and listen to the insects whirring in the sun and birds squawking in a soothing blend of background noise.

891 Budget beach-chic

THAILAND Old-school travellers complain that Thailand has gone upmarket, swapped its cheap sleeps for identikit villas and sacrificed the beach-shack-and-hammock vibe for apartments with swimming pools. They've got a point. Thailand is prospering: new boutique hotels entice you with minimalist curves and luxurious fabrics, and at $150 a night, a five-star suite can seem like an affordable indulgence.

But the rudimentary bamboo beach huts still exist and arguably there's no better way to experience the pleasures of Thailand's gorgeous strands. With over 3000km of coastline and scores of accessible islands you've got plenty of beaches to choose from, the default option being squeaky white sand and luminous turquoise water. Staying in a wooden hut you're often all but camping: you'll see the sand beneath your feet through the slats of the wonky planked floor; you'll hear the waves lapping the shoreline just a few metres from your ill-fitting front door; and there's no need for a fan when you prop open the woven rattan shutters and let the breeze waft through.

Make your own shell mobiles, hang your sarong as a door curtain and string up your hammock to rock to and fro. It's your very own eco home and worth every bit of the modest daily sum that buys you residency.

892 Great dates and temple ceremonies

INDONESIA It's mid-afternoon and you're sitting in an outdoor café when suddenly the street is closed to traffic and a procession of villagers comes streaming by. Women with delicate frangipani blossoms woven into their hair balance lavish offerings of food, fruit and flowers on their heads and walk with grace and poise, while men march by playing musical instruments or sporting ceremonial swords. All are making their way to one of the village temples to honour its gods and celebrate the anniversary of its dedication.

Bali is home to over 10,000 temples of varying sizes, each one of which has a dedication ceremony at least once during the course of the Balinese year of 210 days. Each anniversary celebration, known as an *odalan*, is carried out on an auspicious date set by a local priest and usually lasts three days. In preparation the temple is cleaned, blessed and decorated with flowers, silk sarongs and colourful umbrellas. Women spend hours weaving elaborate headpieces and decorations from palm leaves while men carve ornate objects from wood. Streets leading to the temple are lined with vivid flags, banners and long, decorated bamboo poles (*penjors*) that arch overhead with woven garlands of dried flowers and ornaments fashioned from young palm leaves. Worshippers from around the island arrive en masse to celebrate with prayer, ceremonial dance, drama, musical performances and food to entice the gods and spirits.

Celebrations take place inside the temple walls: fragrant hair oils and smoke from sandalwood incense fill the air as the chimes of bells and the shimmering sounds of the gamelan orchestra electrify the atmosphere. In one corner worshippers kneel before an altar filled with offerings to recite prayers and be blessed with holy water and rice, while in another spectators are treated to an elegant dance of girls in golden costumes. Shadow-puppet performances recount ancient tales while barong dances ward off evil sprits. All this activity competes with the sizzling smells of saté being grilled over coconut husks and the laughter of lads gambling with cards.

893 Balinese theatrics

INDONESIA On the island of Bali, a Hindu enclave in the Muslim majority nation of Indonesia, the gods and spirits need regular appeasing and entertaining. Offerings of rice and flowers are laid out twice a day in tiny banana-leaf baskets and on special occasions there is ritual music and dancing. Temple festivals are so frequent here that you've a good chance of coming across one, but there are also dance performances staged for tourists at the palace in Ubud, the island's cultural hub. Even though the programme has been specially tailored, there is nothing inauthentic about the finesse of the palace performers. And the setting – a starlit courtyard framed by stone-carved statues and an elaborate gateway – is magnificent.

Every performance begins with a priest sanctifying the space with a sprinkle of holy water. Then the gamelan orchestra strikes up: seated cross-legged either side of the stage, the 25 musicians are dressed in formal outfits of Nehru jacket, traditional headcloth and sarong. The light catches the bronze of their gongs, cymbals and metallophones, the lead drummer raises his hand, and they're off, racing boisterously through the first piece, producing an extraordinary syncopated clashing of metal on metal, punctuated by dramatic stops and starts.

Enter the dancers. Five sinuous barefooted young women open with a ritualistic welcome dance, scattering flower petals as an offering to the gods. Next, the poised refinement of the Legong, performed by three young girls wrapped in luminous pink, green and gold brocade, the drama played out with gracefully angled hands, fluttering arms and wide flashing eyes. Finally it's the masked Barong–Rangda drama, the all-important pitting of good against evil, with the loveable, lion-like Barong stalked and harassed by the powerful widow-witch Rangda, all fangs and fingernails. With typical Balinese pragmatism, neither good nor evil is victorious, but, crucially, spiritual harmony will have been restored on the Island of the Gods.

894

SHOPPING at
Chatuchak
Weekend Market

THAILAND Want to feel like a local on a weekend in Bangkok? Then you need to go shopping. Specifically, you need to go to Chatuchak Weekend Market and spend a day rifling through the eight thousand-plus stalls of what some claim to be the world's biggest market. It's certainly a contender for the world's sweatiest and most disorientating, with a quarter of a million bargain-hunters crammed into an enormous warren of alleyways, zones, sections and plazas. The maps and occasional signs do help, but much of the pleasure lies in getting lost and happening upon that unexpected must-have item: antique opium pipe, anyone?

Alongside the mounds of secondhand Levis and no-brand cosmetics you'd expect to find in Southeast Asia's most frantic flea market, there's also a mass of traditional handicrafts from Thailand's regions. Fine silk sarongs from the northeast, triangular cushions and mulberry-paper lamps from Chiang Mai, and hill-tribe jewellery and shoulder bags are all excellent buys here. But what makes Chatuchak such a shopaholic's dream is its burgeoning community of young designers. Many of Asia's new fashion and interior design ideas surface here first, drawing professional trend-spotters from across the continent.

The clothing zone is the obvious beacon, with its hundreds of mini-boutiques displaying radical-chic outfits and super-cute handbags, while the lifestyle zone brims over with tasteful ceramics and sumptuous furnishings.

Need a break from the achingly fashionable? Then wander through the pet section, perhaps lingering to watch Bangkokians' poodles getting their weekly grooming treatments, before enjoying a blast of natural beauty among the orchids and ornamental shrubs. You can treat your tastebuds for a handful of change at any number of foodstalls specializing in everything from barbecued chicken to coconut fritters, and there's even a tiny jazz café for that all-important chillout between purchases. And don't let aching feet call a premature end to the day: simply get yourself along to the foot-massage stall in Aisle 6, Zone B.

895 Get away from it all in the Gilis

INDONESIA To get to the Gilis you have to cross the churning waters of the deep Lombok Strait, infamous for its whirlpools, nauseating swells and fierce underwater currents. But your valiant efforts to get there pay off the moment you arrive: the islands' remote charm descends and entices you to explore a little further.

Collectively referred to as the Gilis, the trio comprises Gili Trawangan, Gili Meno and Gili Air, each of which has its own characteristic charm. The smallest and most tranquil of the three, Gili Meno, is perhaps the most picturesque, with pure white sand beaches framed against the warm turquoise waters, while Trawangan, the largest, is well known for its party atmosphere. A bit of both can be found on Gili Air, which has the largest population (one thousand people). All three offer mile upon mile of powdery beaches, plenty of snorkelling and diving opportunities and unlimited time under the tropical sun.

The biggest range of accommodation is found on Trawangan, from rustic backpacker shacks to exclusive resorts. Stylish bungalows are the norm on Air, while it's basic accommodation only on Meno. All three are known for their food: you can dine on everything from traditional Indonesian dishes such as chicken satay to freshly caught seafood grilled over the burning embers of coconut husks. On all the islands motorized vehicles are banned. Instead, horse-drawn carts known as cidomos add to the laid-back atmosphere, shuttling guests to and fro on the narrow dirt roads.

There's no shortage of activities – Trawangan offers everything from sea kayaking to scuba diving while cycling and beachcombing are best on Gili Air, which also offers superb sunset views of the volcanoes of Gunung Rinjani and Gunung Agung.

Daylong excursions in glass-bottom boats to the deepwater coral reefs can be arranged on all three. As the evening darkness descends the power generators are switched on. While others dance the night away on open-air patios and pubs, you may elect to withdraw to the tranquillity of the beach and simply gaze up at the stars.

896 Tubing the Nam Xong

LAOS Fast-flowing water, vertiginous zip wires and floods of cheap alcohol. It sounds like a recipe for disaster. And sometimes it is – people have died tubing the Nam Xong. But for most, floating effortlessly down this majestic river in an old tractor inner tube is one of Asia's ultimate backpacker experiences.

From Vang Viang, the nearest big town to the drop point, it's simple enough to get started. Cling to the back of a spluttering tuk-tuk, hold your breath as you fly through a few miles of chest-tightening road dust and, eventually, you'll arrive white-knuckled at the riverbank. Then hand over your cash (a few dollars should cover it) and clamber into your makeshift rubber ring. When you push gently off the embankment with warm, squidgy sand between your toes, take a second to look up. The Nam Xong is penned in by towering limestone karsts, and bobbing along its cloudy brown surface feels like floating into a forgotten land.

But instead of hearing the birdsong that filled this valley for millennia, you'll be greeted by the throb of dance music echoing off the rock face. And before long, locals will appear on the water's edge, throwing ropes, bamboo poles and life rings your way to lure you to their bars. It's unlikely you'll be invited alone – these days the whole 4km route is packed with partying, sunburnt travellers – and you can guarantee the Beer Lao will be flowing as fast as the rapids.

Some barmen even hand out free shots of Lao Lao, a fiery local rice whisky, in a bid to make your head spin. You won't need it though – there are frayed rope swings and rusting zip wires waiting to test your nerves round every bend. But for the best thrill, check out the Nam Xong's *pièce de résistance*: a 30m-high waterslide that curls up like an Olympic ski jump, firing you skywards for a final stomach-dropping free fall into the drink. The whole experience is a scream – just don't lose your head.

897 Sniffing out the corpse flower

INDONESIA When the English naturalist Joseph Arnold smelt rotting flesh during an 1821 expedition to the steamy jungles of Sumatra, he must have feared the worst. Back then, this was cannibal country. Blood-thirsty local tribes were known to capture their most hated enemies, tie them to a stake, and start feasting on their roasted body parts. So imagine his surprise when he learnt that the stench was coming not from a dead explorer, but a plant that produces the world's biggest flower. *Rafflesia arnoldii* (named after Arnold and Sir Stamford Raffles, who led the expedition) can produce blooms up to one metre across – and they carry the stink of death.

No surprise then, that Arnold's find has been nicknamed the "corpse flower" by those who've caught a whiff of it. There aren't many who can say they have, though – this is one of Southeast Asia's most endangered species. And despite each flower weighing in at around 11kg, they're notoriously difficult to come across. They're parasitic, for one thing, and can only take root beneath the dark green tendrils of undisturbed grape vines. And even when a plant does begin to thrive, its meaty-red flower lasts just days. If you want to see one in bloom, you'll have to learn to follow your nose.

But why would a plant evolve to smell like rotting meat? Well here in Sumatra, where the race for survival is tough, it pays to be ingenious. Flies are lured into the corpse flower's spongy interior by the promise of somewhere to lay their eggs, only to find they've been deceived.

When they eventually get bored, they'll take off in search of somewhere better. And maybe, just maybe, they'll drop pollen from one plant onto another. When you consider how unlikely this is to happen, you'll realize that your chances of seeing the corpse flower are pretty slim. But what better excuse to go sniffing around one of the last great rainforests?

898 Jungle boogie in Sarawak

MALAYSIA Afternoon, the first day of Sarawak's Rainforest Music festival. People are mingling ahead of show time when the famous Malagasy band Tarika will perform.

For now though, a local Melinau musician with a hat made of bark and bird feathers strums the lute-like sape as we wander around the site, comprising a dozen small longhouses which open daily for demonstrations of local culture. The music mingles with the screech of tropical birdlife, the scampering of chickens and the sing-along refrains of local children.

As evening progresses, crowds arrive from the nearby city Kuching, primed for the evening's fun. We first gorge ourselves on a Dyak feast of local delicacies: baked fish in banana leaves, spicy fried pork, rice and a salad dressed in lime and chili. Dusk swiftly becomes night as the festival hits its stride with sets from international folk, jazz and world fusion artists. I'm reminded of WOMAD in the early days, and expect to spot a beady-eyed Peter Gabriel on the lookout for new talent, hunting perhaps an upriver Iban rapper with a fleet of gongs and pipes for accompaniment.

By the time the opening night of the three-day jamboree draws to a close, and with the tropical heat cooled by a refreshing southwesterly, we are on our feet jiving crazily to Tarika lead singer Hanitra's robust sounds. We have made – or at least bumped into – many new friends from all over the world.

Some have been coming to the festival for years, know the bands and appreciate the attention this little outpost of Malaysian camaraderie gets over this hot, hot weekend. Others, though, confess to not knowing what has hit them – how is it that all this world-class music is being performed in a tiny little jungle enclave at the bottom of a narrow road in a place called the Damai Peninsula?

We head for bed, luckily a comfortable hotel room with a balcony that's only a five-minute stagger away, to awake not just to a hangover but to the delicious promise of another two days of groovesome beats deep in the jungle.

899 Borobudur: the world's biggest Buddhist stupa

INDONESIA On one level, the Buddhist monument at Borobudur is just one huge stone comic strip: the life of the Buddha told in a series of intricate reliefs carved around a gigantic stupa-shaped structure rising from central Java's fertile plains. But it's also a colossal representation of the Buddhist cosmic mountain, Meru. Built sometime around the ninth century AD by the short-lived Saliendra dynasty, occupying some 200 square metres of land and incorporating 1.6 million blocks of local volcanic rock, it is the largest monument in the southern hemisphere.

Much of Borobudur's appeal, however, comes not from its enormity but from the little details: the delicately sculpted reliefs, eroded down the generations but still identifiable and alive with warriors, maidens, the devout and the debauched, as well as elephants, turtles and other creatures. Beginning at ground level, pilgrims would walk clockwise around the monument, studying the frieze as they went, before moving up to the next level. Borobudur can be viewed as one enormous 34.5m-high educational tool: a complete circuit would take the pilgrims and monks, most of whom would have been illiterate, through the life of the Buddha.

Starting from his earthly existence, represented by the friezes on the first four tiers, it ends with his attainment of Nirvana (or "nothingness") at the tenth and top level, here represented by a large, empty stupa. The friezes on the first four "earthly" tiers are, on an artistic level, the most remarkable, but it is the upper five galleries that tend to linger in the memory, as the outside walls disappear, allowing you to savour the views over the lush Javanese plateau to the silent, brooding volcanoes beyond.

900 Climbing the stairway to heaven in Banaue

THE PHILIPPINES Lay them out end-to-end and they'd stretch from Scandinavia to the South Pole. No wonder the tribes of Ifugao province, in the beautiful northern Philippines, call the Banaue rice terraces their stairways to heaven.

The terraces are one of this country's great icons, hewn from the land two thousand years ago by tribespeople using primitive tools, an achievement that ranks alongside the building of the pyramids. Cut into near-vertical slopes, the water-filled ledges curve around the hills' winding contours, their waters reflecting the pale green of freshly planted rice stalks. And unlike other old wonders of engineering, the terraces are still in the making after two millennia. Employing spades and digging sticks, generations of Ifugao farmers have cultivated rice on thousands of these mountainside paddies. Constantly guarding them against natural erosion, the farmers have fortified the terraces with packed-earth and loose-stone retaining walls, supporting an elaborate system of dykes.

A few kilometres up the road from Banaue town is a popular lookout point that offers a sweeping vista down a wide valley with terraces on both sides. It's a great view, but it's not the only one. The only way to really get to know the landscape is on foot. Dozens of narrow paths snake their way past thundering waterfalls into a dazzling green hinterland of monolithic steps.

If you're looking for rural isolation and unforgettable rice-terrace scenery, the 15km trek from Banaue to the remote tribal village of Batad shouldn't be missed. Batad nestles in a natural amphitheatre, close to the glorious Tappia Waterfall. Accommodation here is basic, but it doesn't matter. In the semi-dark, after a long trek and a swim in the falls, you can sit on your veranda, listening to the hiss of cicadas and the squawk of giant bats, transfixed by the looming silhouettes of the surrounding mountains.

901

FOUR THOUSAND ISLANDS

and fish for dinner

LAOS At sunset, everyone plops into the nearest hammock to enjoy the show. Just after 6pm the sky fires orange behind the distant hills and the muddy River Mekong assumes a warm apricot glow. Palm trees and mangroves frame the view and frogs and cicadas provide the soundtrack. Another languid day on the tiny island of Don Det draws to a close.

Life is slow and traditional in this tranquil corner of southern Laos. The four thousand islands of the Si Phan Don archipelago splinter across a broad, landlocked sweep of the River Mekong just shy of the Cambodian border. Most are just minuscule outcrops but Don Det, Don Khon and Don Khong are inhabited. Islanders grow rice but mostly earn their living from fish, and from the increasing number of tourists drawn to this laid-back idyll.

As so often in Southeast Asian backwaters, the pleasures of a stay in Si Phan Don are low key: a round-island cycle ride through villages of stilted wooden homes and centuries-old Buddhist temples; a drift down the Mekong in an inner tube; a dinner of

aromatic fish steamed in banana leaves.

But the Mekong is far from equanimous at this stage of its mammoth 4000km journey to the South China Sea. Unnavigable rapids pepper Si Phan Don, long thwarting any attempt to use the river as a trade route from Tibet to the ocean. Cross the old railway bridge that connects Don Det to sister island Don Khon (part of a defunct nineteenth-century project to try and bypass the rapids) and you'll see the Mekong in a different mood. Somphamit Falls is where the river gets angry, roaring and spluttering through broiling rapids before plummeting via a series of massive cascades into Cambodia.

Astonishingly, the islanders sometimes fish these scariest of waters, balancing on bamboo scaffolds above the whirlpools and dancing between boulders to hurl their nets off the slippery rocks. It's something to think about as you sway gently in your hammock, contemplating the sunset and relishing the thought of a plate of tasty fish for dinner.

VIETNAM Once a month, on the eve of the full moon, downtown Hoi An turns off all its street lights and basks in the mellow glow of silk lanterns. Shopkeepers don traditional outfits; parades, folk opera and martial arts demonstrations flood the cobbled streets; and the riverside fills with stalls selling crabmeat parcels, beanpaste cakes and noodle soup. It's all done for tourists of course – and some find it cloyingly self-conscious – but nevertheless this historic little central Vietnam town oozes charm, with the monthly Full Moon Festival just part of its appeal.

Much of the town's charisma derives from its downtown architecture. Until the Thu Bon river silted up in the late eighteenth century, Hoi An was an important port, attracting traders from China and beyond, many of whom settled and built wooden-fronted homes, ornate shrines and exuberantly tiled Assembly Halls that are still used by their descendants today. Several of these atmospheric buildings are now open to the public, offering intriguing glimpses into cool, dark interiors filled with imposing furniture, lavishly decorated altars and family memorabilia that have barely been touched since the 1800s. Together with the peeling pastel facades, colonnaded balconies and waterside market, it's all such a well-preserved blast from the past that UNESCO has designated central Hoi An a World Heritage Site.

The merchant spirit needs no such protection, however: there are now so many shops in this small town that the authorities have imposed a ban on any new openings. Art galleries and antique shops are plentiful, but silk and tailoring are the biggest draws. Hoi An tailors are the best in the country, and for $200 you can walk away with an entire custom-made wardrobe, complete with Armani-inspired suit, silk shirt, hand-crafted leather boots and personalized handbag. And if you've really fallen under Hoi An's spell, you might find yourself also ordering an *ao dai*, the tunic and trouser combo worn so elegantly by Vietnamese women.

903 Stalking the creatures of the night

SINGAPORE Darkness engulfs the sky, blanketing trees, the path and those out walking. From the mysterious shadows, sounds of people – breathing, treading on twigs, murmuring in the distance – filter through. Then suddenly an intimidating roar penetrates the din. Welcome to Singapore Zoo's night safari, the world's first nocturnal zoo.

Walk one of three trails – Fishing Cats, Forest Giants and Leopards – or jump on a tram and travel two road loops to catch oblivious nocturnal creatures going about their usual business. You might find the shadowy corners of the trails a little disorientating, especially when you look up to find yourself face-to-face with a giant flying squirrel. Unlike other zoos, there aren't any big cats lazing around waiting for a keeper to bring them their meal. Here you'll witness them actually prowling around hunting for their supper – this is about as close to a real safari as you can get within the confines of a zoo.

The safari park is broken into eight geographical zones, home to over 1000 animals. In addition to the zones, there's an animal show, a fragrant walk (over 4000 plants line your entrance to the zoo) and cultural performances (including highlights from Borneo tribal dancers).

Many of the walk-through exhibits are likely to get your heart pumping faster: the Forest Giants trail, home to plants of all shapes and sizes, also has flying lemurs, owls and tree shrews, so if you're at all uneasy about having a creature come within centimetres of you, this is not the exhibit – or the zoo – for you.

904 Motorbiking the northwest loop

VIETNAM Vietnam's most spectacular mountain scenery is in the extreme north, shadowing the border with China. It's an astonishing landscape of evergreen mountains, plunging river valleys, high passes and hill-tribe villages. The bad news is that public transport is woefully inadequate and car hire costly, so two wheels are your best option. Main roads are virtually all paved, though there are rough sections.

The classic route begins in the featureless lowland town of Lao Cai, which is connected to Hanoi by highway and train. From here it's a three-hour run to Bac Ha, a lonely mountain village that hosts one of the best hill-tribe markets in Vietnam each Sunday. The stars of the show are the Flower Hmong women, who wear incredibly intricate hand-woven clothes made of Technicolor textiles.

The next leg of the trip entails a return journey to Lao Cai followed by a steep climb up to Sapa via some towering rice-paddy terraces. Sapa is a graceful old French hill station, replete with colonial architecture and good restaurants. It sits on a high ridge overlooking a valley, and on clear days the views are sublime. Moving west from Sapa involves a precipitous climb up to the Tram Ton Pass (1900m), the highpoint on this journey, where you're virtually guaranteed a soaking from the rainclouds that permanently cling to the peaks.

On the western side of the pass the weather usually improves, and as the road descends in altitude you'll probably find yourself peeling off layers as the sun comes out. Eventually you'll reach a flat-bottomed valley where the villages are famous for their rice wine.

The next stretch to Dien Bien Phu is magnificent, as the road clings to the banks of a river valley, which narrows to squeeze through a limestone gorge in sections. Dien Bien Phu, where the Viet Minh inflicted an epochal defeat on the French in 1954, has some fascinating museums and battle monuments and is a great place to recharge and get your bike checked over, before heading back to Hanoi.

905 Tribal funerals in Sumba: blood, bones and burials

INDONESIA The island of Sumba is curiously overlooked by most travellers. But with cinnamon and sandalwood trees, colossal tombstones and an indigenous religion (Marapu) that involves bloody funeral sacrifices it's an isolated but fascinating place. A century or so ago, slaves would have accompanied their masters to the grave, but today the Jakarta government limits sacrifices to a few large animals per ceremony.

Local tourism officials will keep you informed about upcoming events and advise you about the protocol. Foreigners are usually made very welcome but it's essential to take a few gifts: sugar and tobacco are preferred. Attire is important. You'll be supplied with a sarong (made from *ikat* fabric) and a turban-style headdress. It's customary to chew *sirih* (betel nut), a mild stimulant, which is mixed with lime. This provides a mild buzz, tastes like spicy chalk dust and gives you a somewhat rabid appearance thanks to its scarlet colour and foaming consistency. You gob out the foul residue.

On the day of the event, hundreds, often thousands, of neighbouring villagers arrive to pay their respects. Guests are fed, watered and given *sirih*. The main ceremony begins with the pounding of drums and sounding of gongs. Buffaloes (and sometimes pigs and horses) are led into the village square and one-by-one put to the sword to satisfy the Marapu gods. It's a grisly sight, as a turban-wearing executioner delivers a *coup de grâce* with a machete blow to the neck and blood waters the earth. All parts of the animals are shared and eaten (even buffalo skulls are retained as trophies). The grave is lined with precious *ikat* and a stone tombstone erected.

Bizarrely, it's quite regular for funerals to be completed many years after a death, when the family can afford it. Some canny folk even pay in advance (and attend) their own funeral. So if you meet a chief who seems in rude health but is getting buried in the morning, accept his invitation with a smile.

906

THE PHILIPPINES If you thought Alex Garland's tropical-island classic *The Beach* was inspired by Thailand, think again; it was the Philippines, particularly the spectacular islands and lagoons of the Bacuit archipelago in Palawan, where tourists are still relatively thin on the ground but surely won't be for long. It's not hard to see why Garland was so bewitched by this place: 45 stunning limestone islands rise dramatically from an iridescent sea. Most have exquisite palm-fringed beaches, so you shouldn't have too much trouble finding your own piece of paradise for the day. All you need to do is pack yourself a picnic, hire yourself an outrigger boat – known locally as a banca – and ask the boatman to do the rest.

Start by chugging gently out to Miniloc Island, where a narrow opening in the fearsomely jagged karst cliffs leads to a hidden lagoon known as Big Lagoon, home to hawksbill turtles. A couple of minutes away, also at Miniloc, is the entrance to Small Lagoon, which you have to swim through, emerging into a natural amphitheatre of gin-clear waters and the screech of long-tailed macaques.

Other islands you shouldn't miss? Well, take your pick. Pangalusian has a long stretch of quiet beach; Tres Marias has terrific snorkelling along a shallow coral reef; and Helicopter Island (named after its shape) has a number of secluded sandy coves where your only companions are monitor lizards and the occasional manta ray floating by.

The culmination of a perfect day's island-hopping should be a sunset trip to Snake Island, where you can sink a few cold San Miguels (take them with you in an ice box) and picnic on a slender, serpentine tongue of perfect white sand which disappears gently into shallow waters that are ideal for swimming.

Island-hopping
in the
Bacuit archipelago

907 All aboard the Eastern & Oriental Express

SINGAPORE–BANGKOK First, tea is served. In a fancy teapot, with biscuits, by a butler dressed in pristine white uniform. You gaze lazily out of the window as porters labour in the crushing afternoon humidity, blissfully cool in your air-conditioned cabin. Then the train eases out of the station: the skyscrapers of Singapore soon fall away, and you're across the Straits of Johor and into the lush, torpid palm plantations of Malaysia.

This is the *Eastern & Oriental Express*, the luxurious train service that runs between Singapore and Bangkok, the last remnant of opulent colonial travel in Southeast Asia – evoking the days of posh British administrators, gin-sloshed planters and rich, glamorous dowagers rather like the set of a Merchant Ivory movie.

To be fair, you're more likely to meet professionals from San Francisco or Hong Kong on the train today. There are a couple of stops to break the three-day journey – a rapid but absorbing trishaw ride through old Penang, and an evocative visit to the bridge over the River Kwai – but it's the train itself that is the real highlight of the trip.

If you feel the need to stretch your legs, the observation car offers a 360-degree panorama of the jungle-covered terrain, and there's a shop selling gifts to prove you've been. Then there's the elegant dining car. Eating on the train is a real treat, superb haute cuisine and Asian meals prepared by world-class chefs. Many choose to wear evening dress to round off the fantasy and after dinner retire to the bar car, where cocktails and entertainment await, from mellow piano music to formal Thai dance. A word of warning: after all this, reality hurts. Standing on the chaotic platform of Bangkok's Hualampong station, you might long to get back on board.

908 Volcanic activity: sunrise on Mount Bromo

INDONESIA It's not the most famous, the most active or the biggest volcano in the world, but Indonesia's 2392m-high Mount Bromo is one of the most picturesque – in a dusty, post-apocalyptic sort of way. The still-smoking and apparently perfectly symmetrical cone rises precipitously out of a vast, windswept, sandy plain. This is the Sea of Sand, actually the floor of an ancient crater (or caldera), stretching up to 10km in diameter and with walls towering some 300m high.

Though the locals will try to persuade you to take their horse, it's an easy enough walk to the summit, with no climbing ability required. Setting off an hour before sunrise, you follow a path across the Sea of Sand to the foot of Bromo's vertiginous cone. A small matter of 249 concrete steps up past crowds of others with the same idea – it's one of Java's most popular attractions – leads to the crater rim and a view down onto the fumaroles belching noxious sulphuric fumes. But the rewards of climbing Bromo are not olfactory, but visual: if the gods of climate and cloud-cover are on your side, a flamboyant golden sunrise awaits, casting its orange glow over the vast emptiness of the sandy basin, with Java's lush green landscape stretching to the horizon beyond.

909 Tackling Pol Pot's legacy with the VSO

CAMBODIA Thirty years after Pol Pot's notorious Khmer Rouge, the VSO (Voluntary Service Overseas) now runs one of its largest country programmes in Cambodia, with ninety volunteers working to improve health and education systems and help build secure livelihoods. I joined their programme in Kampong Cham, working with an NGO to help improve the local school curriculum through creative techniques such as art therapy and dance. The aim is to encourage children to express themselves and in time challenge the legacy of the Khmer Rouge, who left behind a culture of fear and conformity.

Part of my role in schools was encouraging communication between boys and girls. Marital breakdown and domestic violence are common and high school drop-out rates for girls especially are high; tackling this together with local leadership seemed to me a really tangible benefit of volunteering. We would mix boys and girls in the classroom so they could talk to each other more freely, and then introduce art or dance activities where they would role-play everyday events and talk about what they had learned.

Over the year, I was inundated with invitations to people's homes and was even befriended by Buddhist monks keen to get me on board as a catalyst for reopening a street children's centre. I was eager to learn and feel at home myself and this sharing process affected me as much as my local counterparts, challenging the taboos of my own culture in return.

Towards the end of the placement, my Khmer became pretty fluent, giving me an insight into local life that I would have missed otherwise. I loved listening to conversations about me on the bus – "Where is she from?", "Why is she on her own?", "I think I've seen her around on her bicycle", and my personal favourite, "Doesn't she have a nice nose?" – and I'd pipe up halfway through the journey speaking my Khmer and, to my enjoyment, the whole bus would fall about laughing.

MALAYSIA Every diver who comes to Sipadan will see something that they haven't seen before. Famous for its large resident population of green and hawksbill turtles as well as healthy numbers of reef sharks and magnificent coral, Sipadan is Malaysia's only oceanic island. Sitting in the Sulu Sea off the northeastern coast of Borneo, it's also a great base for exploring the nearby shoals of Kapalai and the island of Mabul, well-suited for voyeurs who are tantalized by the mating habits of mandarin fish and frogfish and other cryptic reef dwellers like sea-wasps. Above water, on Mabul you'll also meet the indigenous "sea-gypsies" – the Badjao – who live either in stilt-houses perched over the lagoon or on their tiny fishing boats which ply the Sulu Sea as far as the Philippines.

Sea-gypsies, turtles and frogfish

910

911 Hike through history along the Kokoda Trail

PAPUA NEW GUINEA As you trek along Papua New Guinea's Kokoda Trail, winding north 96km from Owers' Corner to Kokoda, it can feel like every step has its own story. During World War II, Australian troops used the route to prevent the Japanese, who had landed on the northern beaches, from taking Port Moresby on the southern coast. Though the trail's military pedigree attracts both war buffs and nostalgics, it's also justly famous for some of the most rugged and remote terrain in the South Pacific. Climbing up to 2200m as it tops the Owen Stanley Range, the path traverses orchid-decked jungles, lush river valleys and the settlements of the Koiari and Orokaiva tribes. Like the help these people gave Allied troops during the war, the smiles you share with the villagers won't easily be forgotten.

912 Long live the emperor: the imperial mausoleums of Hué

VIETNAM The broad, peaceful outer courtyard sweeps you past an honorary guard of immaculate stone mandarins towards the first of a series of elegantly roofed gateways, through whose triple doorways you get a perfectly framed view of Emperor Minh Mang's mausoleum complex. Archways look wistful in peeling ochre paint; slatted lacquer-red shutters offer tantalizing angles on lotus ponds, pavilions and artfully placed bonsai trees; and ceramic rooftop dragons add a touch of kitsch in pastel pinks, greens and yellows. Look carefully and you'll see the Chinese character for "longevity" picked out in blue, red and gold – Minh Mang, who designed his own mausoleum, left nothing to chance.

913 Dancing under a full moon

THAILAND The tourist party season in Southeast Asia traditionally gets under way at the end of the year with huge, head-thumping parties at Hat Rin Beach on Thailand's Ko Pha Ngan island. Hat Rin has firmly established itself as Southeast Asia's premier rave venue, especially in the high season around December and January, but every month of the year at full moon travellers flock in for the Full Moon Party – something like *Apocalypse Now* without the war. Tens of thousands of party fiends from all corners of the world kick up the largely good-natured, booze- and drug-fuelled mayhem, dancing the night away on the squeaky white sand.

To make the most of a Full Moon Party, get yourself to Hat Rin at least a couple of days in advance. That way you'll be able to make the most of the stunning beach location, soak up the growing buzz as the crowds pour in and, more importantly, snag yourself somewhere to stay. Most party-goers make it through to the dawn, and some can still be seen splashing in the shallow surf towards noon, when the last of the beach DJs pull the plug.

NEED to know

861 Slow boats leave when full and run from Houayxai on the Thai–Lao border to Louang Phabang, and vice versa.

862 Taman Negara (Ⓦwww.wildlife.gov.my) is 250km from Kuala Lumpur and can be reached by bus or, more enjoyably, by train and boat.

863 Most trips to Komodo (Ⓦwww.komodonational park.org) are organized from Labuanbajo, on the coast of neighbouring Flores.

864 Phang Nga Bay covers some 400 square kilometres of coast between Phuket and Krabi. A reputable sea-canoeing trips operator around the bay is John Gray's Sea Canoe (Ⓦwww.johngray-seacanoe.com).

865 My Tho is a 90min bus ride from Ho Chi Minh City. Homestays can be arranged at local tourist offices or through Sinhbalo Adventure Travel in Ho Chi Minh City (Ⓦwww.cyclingvietnam.net).

866 Regular flights from Bali serve Flores' three main airports: Labuanbajo, Maumere and Ende.

867 Classes are held twice daily at SITCA, on Sui Colibri.

868 Kalibo is a 1hr flight south of the Philippine capital, Manila. Hotels are usually full for Ati-Atihan, so book well in advance.

869 Kinabalu Park headquarters (Ⓦwww.sutera sanctuarylodges.com) issues permits and organizes guides and porters. Book accommodation in advance. Kinabalu Park is a 2hr bus ride from Kota.

870 Bukit Lawang is a 3hr bus ride from Medan. The sanctuary is only open to visitors during the twice-daily feeding sessions at 8am and 3pm.

871 Philippines-based dive operators such as Scuba World (Ⓦwww.scubaworld.com.ph), Dive Buddies (Ⓦwww.divephil.com) and Asia Divers (Ⓦwww.asiadivers.com) organize trips out of Puerto Princesa.

872 Louang Phabang is served by flights from Bangkok, Chiang Mai and Vientiane. You can also reach it by bus and boat from Vientiane and by boat from the Thai–Lao border at Chiang Khong/Houayxai.

873 Lumphini Stadium, on Thanon Rama IV, stages fights on Tues, Fri and Sat eves. Take the subway to Lumphini station or the Skytrain to Sala Daeng and then a taxi.

874 The easiest way to arrange a night in a longhouse is via a tour company based in the Sarawak capital, Kuching; Borneo Transverse (Ⓦwww.borneo transverse.com.my) or Borneo Adventure (Ⓦwww.borneoadventure.com).

875 Most people arrange all-inclusive tours of the bay from Hanoi, about 150km away. April–Oct is the best time to visit.

876 Banyuwangi is the nearest large town to Ijen. The tourist board here (Ⓣ+62 (0) 333 424 172) can organize trips in a 4WD. The path is easy to follow; it takes around two hours to reach the summit.

877 Bangkok's Wat Pho has been the leading school of Thai massage for hundreds of years, and masseurs who train there are considered the best in the country. Wat Pho runs massage courses in English (Ⓦwww.watpomassage.com).

878 Insensitive tourism has caused many problems in hill-tribe villages, and exploitation by travel companies is widespread, so choose your trekking company wisely. In Chiang Mai, both Eagle House (Ⓦwww.eaglehouse.com) and the Trekking Collective (Ⓦwww.trekkingcollective.com) are recommended operators.

879 Daily public buses connect Luang Prabang and Vientiane with Phonsovan. *Auberge de la Plaine des Jarres* (Ⓔauberge_plainjars@yahoo.fr) is the province's best hotel, with private wooden bungalows.

880 Hanoi's most famous snake restaurants are in the suburb of Le Mat, including the reliable *Quoc Trieu* (Ⓣ+84 (0)4 827 2988).

881 Cambodia's patchy train services have run into further trouble, with no trains at all in 2009. There are plans to resuscitate crossings with Vietnam and Thailand in order to make a train journey from London to Singapore possible; see Ⓦseat61.com for news.

882 Ayutthaya is 80km north of Bangkok and served by frequent trains. Many guesthouses and restaurants rent bicycles and organize tours.

883 Aru's major settlement, Dobo, is two days from the Maluku district capital, Ambon, with Pelni, the Indonesian state shipping line.

884 The nearest international airport is on Cebu island; the trip to Siquijor can just about be done in a day, by getting a bus to the south of Cebu, and island-hopping by ferry from Cebu to Negros island to Siquijor. The best months to visit are Dec–May, outside the typhoon season.

885 The Tuol Sleng Genocide Museum (daily 7.30–11.30am & 2–5pm) is off Street 13 on the southern fringes of Phnom Penh.

886 Wat Phra Kaeo, or the Grand Palace, is open daily 8.30am–3.30pm.

887 Queen Bee, at 5 Thanon Moonmuang near Tha Pae Gate (Ⓦwww.queen-bee.com), has reliable motorbikes and insurance coverage.

888 For more information, check Ⓦwww.divenorth sulawesi.com.

889 One of the best places to experience Loy Krathong is in Sukhothai, the first Thai capital, 400km north of Bangkok, where the ruins of the ancient capital are lit up by fireworks.

890 The Angkor site is 5km from Siem Riep; to visit you need a pass valid for one, three or seven days.

891 Thailand's best old-style beach huts are *KP Huts*, scattered through a shoreside coconut grove on Ko Chang (Ⓣ+66 84 099 5100); *Island Hut* on Ko Mak (Ⓣ+66 87 139 5537); and *Bee Bee Bungalows* on Ko Lanta (Ⓣ+66 81 537 9932, Ⓦwww.diigii.de).

892 Foreigners are invited to attend temple ceremonies, however you must respect local customs and ensure you are appropriately dressed with a sarong, headpiece and footwear.

893 Dance performances are staged nightly at Ubud Palace, about 30km from Bali's international airport.

894 Chatuchak Weekend Market (Sat & Sun 7am–6pm) is in north Bangkok, near Mo Chit Skytrain and Kamphaeng Phet subway stations.

895 The fastest and easiest way to travel to the Gilis from Bali is on the high-speed charter boat from Benoa Harbour (8am & 10am). See BlueWater Safaris (Ⓦwww.bwsbali.com) for latest details.

896 Vang Vieng is easily accessible by bus and *songthaew*, whether you're travelling from Vientiane or Louang Phabang. Laos Travel Plan (Ⓦwww.laostravelplan.co.uk) offers organized tours to the Nam Xong river and surrounding areas.

897 Tourists can hire a guide to point out the corpse flower from the office at the Batang Palapuh reserve, 12km north of Bukittinggi.

898 The yearly festival takes place in the first half of July; check Ⓦwww.rainforestmusic-borneo.com for more details.

899 Borobudur (daily 6am–5.30pm; Ⓦwww.borobudurpark.com) is served by frequent buses from Yogyakarta, 40km southeast, and can be visited as a day-trip. An overnight stay, however, allows you both to watch the sunset and to visit early the next day before the crowds arrive.

900 It's a bumpy 7hr bus ride from Manila to Banaue, where guides for treks can be hired.

901 Access to Don Det is by a 15min ferry-ride from the mainland pier at Nakasang. Minivans and public buses take around three hours to reach Nakasang from the southern Lao city of Pakse.

902 Hoi An is around 700km south of Hanoi. The nearest airport and train station are in Da Nang, a 30km taxi ride away.

903 For further information on Singapore Zoo's night safari, check out Ⓦwww.nightsafari.com.sg.

904 Rent a bike in Hanoi: Off Road Vietnam (Ⓦwww.offroadvietnam.com) are highly recommended and have good Hondas. Use a freight-train carriage (around US$15) to get your bike to Lai Cai. Carry a tool kit and spares.

905 Contact the tourist office (Ⓣ0387 21240) in Waikabubak for information about upcoming funerals. Staff will act as guides and help with introductions and etiquette (a small tip is appreciated).

906 There are daily flights from Manila to El Nido, departure point for the archipelago, with SEAIR (Ⓦwww.flyseair.com) and Islands Transvoyager Incorporated.

907 Singapore to Bangkok costs around US$2000 one way – see Ⓦwww.orient-express.com.

908 Mount Bromo is the main attraction of East Java's Bromo-Tengger-Semeru National Park. Most people stay in the nearby village of Cemoro Lawang, a 2hr bus drive from Probolinggo on Java's north coast.

909 For more information, visit Ⓦwww.vso.org.uk.

910 For more information on diving Sipadan, check Ⓦwww.visitborneo.com.

911 The website Ⓦwww.kokodatrail.com.au has lots of information on the Kokoda Trail.

912 The Minh Mang mausoleums are part of Hué's imperial city, which is open daily 7am–5pm.

913 Ⓦfullmoonparty-thailand.com gives the dates of forthcoming parties and news of big-name DJs.

GOOD to know

RELIGION

Buddhism is the predominant faith in Cambodia, Laos, Singapore, Thailand and Vietnam. Buddhist **monks** are forbidden to have close contact with women, which means, if you are female, that you mustn't sit or stand next to a monk (even on a bus), brush against his robes, or hand objects directly to him. When giving something to a monk, the object should be placed on a nearby table or passed to a layman who will hand it to the monk.

Indonesia is the largest **Islamic** nation in the world. The most orthodox region of the country is in North Sumatra; elsewhere, local Islamic practices often display **animist**, Buddhist and Hindu influences. Most of Indonesia's many tribal communities are animists, especially in West Papua, Sumatra and Kalimantan. Though their beliefs and customs vary widely, animists share the view that nearly everything in the world has a spirit, in particular trees, plants, rocks and rivers.

TASTE SENSATIONS

Amok dt'ray *Cambodia*. Fish curry made with a rich coconut sauce and baked in banana leaves.

Làp *Laos*. A salad of raw minced meat spiced with garlic, chilli and fish sauce.

Lechon *The Philippines*. Roast pig stuffed with pandanus leaves.

Nem *Vietnam*. Fresh spring rolls stuffed with herbs, crabmeat, rice vermicelli and beansprouts.

Tom yam kung *Thailand*. Fragrantly spiced hot and sour prawn soup.

Durian *Thailand or Malaysia*. This fruit is something of an acquired taste and is notorious for its foul smell – somewhere between detergent and dogshit.

THE MIGHTY MEKONG

The **Mekong** is one of the great rivers of the world, the twelfth longest on the planet. From its source 4920m up on the east Tibetan Plateau, it roars down through China's Yunnan province, then snakes its way a little more peaceably through Laos, by way of the so-called Golden Triangle, where Burma, Thailand and Laos touch. From Laos it crosses Cambodia and continues south to Vietnam, where it splinters into the many arms of the Mekong Delta before flowing into the South China Sea, 4184km from where its journey began.

Don't try to get a haircut in Thailand on a Wednesday: most barbers are closed to avoid bad luck.

POPULATIONS

Brunei 400,000
East Timor 1 millon
Singapore 4.8 million
Laos 6.2 million
Cambodia 15 million
Malaysia 27 million
Burma 50 million
Thailand 68 million
Vietnam 86 million
The Philippines 96 million
Indonesia 230 million

COLONIALISM AND INDEPENDENCE

Thailand is the only Southeast Asian country never to have been colonized by a European nation.

Historically, the major Western players in the region have been: France, in Laos, Cambodia and Vietnam; Britain, in Burma, Malaysia and Singapore; and the Netherlands, in Indonesia.

Timor Leste (East Timor) became a new nation on May 20, 2002, having finally won autonomy from Indonesia. It had previously been under Portuguese rule for four centuries until Indonesia invaded the territory in 1975.

In 1898, America fought Spain for control of the **Philippines** and won. The Philippines finally gained independence on July 4, 1946.

ETIQUETTE

In Buddhist, Islamic and Hindu cultures, the **head** is considered the most sacred part of the body and the feet the most unclean. This means that it's very rude to touch another person's head or to point your feet either at a human being or at a sacred image. You should be careful not to step over any part of a person who is sitting or lying on the floor without first offering an apology. Shoes are nearly always taken off before going inside a home or place of worship.

After Brazil, Vietnam is the biggest coffee exporter in the world.

BUILDING SPECS

When designing a **traditional house** on the Indonesian island of Bali, the architect begins by noting down the vital statistics of the head of the household. The house-compound's walls, for example, must be the sum of a multiple of the distance between the tips of the householder's middle fingers when the arms are outstretched, plus the distance from his or her elbow to the tip of their middle finger, plus the width of their fist with the thumb stretched out.

The different structures of the compound are believed to reflect the human body: the family shrine is the head, the main pavilions are the arms, the courtyard is the navel, the kitchen and rice barn are the legs and feet, and the garbage tip is the anus.

WHERE ART MEETS NATURE – WAIHEKE ISLAND • DRIFTING WITH JELLYFISH IN MICRONESIA • HIKING SYDNEY'S SPIT TO MANLY WALKWAY • PLAYGROUND BULLIES IN THE SOUTH PACIFIC: THE ULTIMATE SHARK DIVE • SETTING SAIL AMONG THE BLISSFUL BAY OF ISLANDS • ON THE LOOKOUT FOR THE DUCK-BILLED PLATYPUS • WITNESSING THE POWER OF THE HAKA • WALKING ON THE WILD SIDE AT THE SYDNEY MARDI GRAS • SUPPING WINE IN SUN-DRENCHED MARLBOROUGH • BUZZING OVER THE BUNGLES • INDULGE YOUR TASTEBUDS AT QUEEN VICTORIA MARKET • TUCKING INTO A HANGI • RAINFOREST VIBES IN THE DAINTREE • TRAMPING THE MILFORD TRACK • GETTING TO GRIPS WITH ABORIGINAL ART • FOLLOWING IN GAUGUIN'S FOOTSTEPS • DIVING THE COOLIDGE • WORKING UP A THIRST AT WINEGLASS BAY • FROM PRISON TO PARADISE ON I'LLE DES PINS • GETTING HANDS-ON AT WELLINGTON'S TE PAPA • PARAGLIDING OVER THE PADDOCKS • KNOCKING BACK KAVA • A VOLCANIC TRIP UP MOUNT YASUR • DISCOVERING THE SECRETS OF KINGS CANYON • TAKING A TRIP TO HELL ON EARTH • ZEN AND THE ART OF RELAXATION, BYRON BAY • RIVER DEEP, MOUNTAIN HIGH: BUSHWALKING THE OVERLAND TRACK • WATCHING FOOTY AT THE MCG • ISLAND DREAMING: SAILING THE WHITSUNDAYS • GETTING HIGH ON THE GILLESPIE PASS • DOING THE CROCODILE ROCK IN KAKADU NATIONAL PARK • CRUISING DOUBTFUL SOUND • LEARNING TO SURF ON THE GOLD COAST • COAST TO COAST WITH THE TRANZALPINE • SYDNEY HARBOUR-MASTERING • WATCHING WHALES IN KAIKOURA • RIDING THE GHAN TO DARWIN • SWIMMING WITH WHALE SHARKS AT NINGALOO REEF • PADDLING THROUGH ABEL TASMAN NATIONAL PARK • A WALK ROUND ULURU • A WORLD AWAY ON THE LANDSBOROUGH RIVER • GOING ORGANIC IN THE NORTHERN TERRITORY • TAKING IN THE VIEWS ON THE TONGARIRO CROSSING • SPYING ON PENGUINS AND ALBATROSSES ALONG THE OTAGO PENINSULA • A TORCHLIGHT TOUR OF QUEENSLAND'S CRITTERS • SCUBA DIVING THE WRECKS AT POOR KNIGHTS ISLANDS • A FAR-FLUNG FLUTTER AT THE BIRDSVILLE RACES • SEA KAYAKING AROUND SHARK BAY • HEADING SOUTH FOR THE WINTER IN QUEENSTOWN • OCEAN TO OCEAN, CAPE TO CAPE, ACROSS AUSTRALIA BY 4WD • FINDING EDEN ON LORD HOWE ISLAND • DOUBLE-CROSSED IN THE SOUTH SEAS • KIWI SPOTTING IN TROUNSON KAURI PARK • FOUR-WHEELING THROUGH CROC COUNTRY: CAIRNS TO CAPE YORK • HELI-BIKING BEN CRUACHAN • THE LAST FRONTIER: WORKING ON A CATTLE STATION • FRESH BREAKS AND FRESH BEANS: SURFING UTOPIA AT RAGLAN • DINNER WITH THE DEVIL • LIFE BEYOND THE BEACH IN MELANESIA • CANYONEERING IN

Australia, New Zealand & the South Pacific
914–985

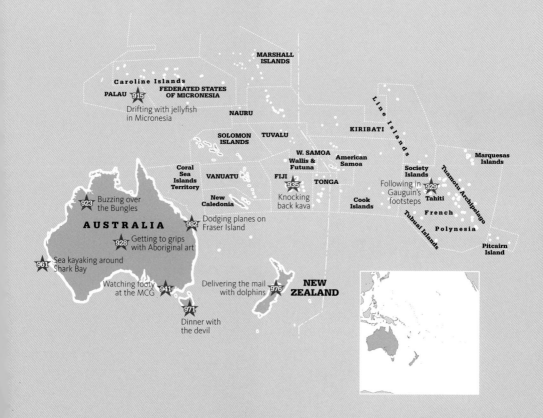

MARSHALL ISLANDS

Caroline Islands
FEDERATED STATES OF MICRONESIA

PALAU 915
Drifting with jellyfish
in Micronesia

NAURU

SOLOMON ISLANDS

TUVALU

KIRIBATI

Line Islands

Marquesas Islands

Coral Sea Islands Territory

VANUATU

W. SAMOA
Wallis & Futuna

American Samoa

Society Islands

Tuamotu Archipelago

FIJI 935
Knocking back kava

TONGA

Following in Gauguin's footsteps

929 Tahiti

New Caledonia

Cook Islands

French

923 Buzzing over the Bungles

Tubuai Islands

Polynesia

AUSTRALIA

982 Dodging planes on Fraser Island

Pitcairn Island

928 Getting to grips with Aboriginal art

961 Sea kayaking around Shark Bay

Watching footy at the MCG 941

Delivering the mail 976 with dolphins

NEW ZEALAND

971 Dinner with the devil

914 Where art meets nature – Waiheke Island

NEW ZEALAND Artists, writers and craftspeople have long flocked to Waiheke Island, which lies 35 minutes from Auckland by ferry. It may be the relative isolation that appeals, or perhaps the captivating combination of sandy beaches, verdant native bush, neatly rowed vineyards and alluring eateries. Whatever the reason, creative types thrive in this laidback environment, and there's ample opportunity to view the fruits of their labour around the island. The best place to start is Connells Bay Sculpture Park. Here, a 2km guided walk through bush and farmland takes you past a medley of stark sculptural works which amalgamate effortlessly with the surrounding lush vegetation. Pieces range from outlandish carbon-fibre structures to wood-carved monoliths reminiscent of Easter Island statues. With all of this framed by awe-inspiring vistas of the Hauraki Gulf beyond it's a true union of art and nature.

915 Drifting with jellyfish in Micronesia

PALAU They're all around you – literally millions of pulsating golden mastigia, like a swarm of squishy tennis balls in zero gravity. As you move your limbs to keep yourself afloat in this warm lake on one of Palau's Rock Islands, the jellyfish brush softly against your skin, then waft away as endless others take their place. They can barely sting – aeons spent in this saltwater lake without a single predator have weakened their defences – so there's no need to avoid them, and you couldn't even if you tried. And though beautiful, these creatures aren't as fragile as they look; the depths where they spend the night contain high levels of hydrogen sulphide, which is toxic to humans. Scuba diving is banned for this reason, but a mask and snorkel are all you need to explore the lake's upper reaches. Along with the mastigia, you'll also spot tiny gobies and cardinal fish hiding among the mangrove roots while up above, kingfishers perch imperiously on their branches.

916 Hiking Sydney's spit to Manly Walkway

AUSTRALIA Sydney's 10km harbour-side hike, running through bush above ragged cliffs and via sandy beaches, is surely the world's most scenic city walk. You begin at Spit Bridge, which spans the Middle Harbour, and end, an exhilarated three hours later, at the ferry wharf in Manly. Officially known as the Manly Scenic Walkway, the route is well signed and dead easy to navigate – just keep the sea on your right and let your eyes feast on the scalloped sandstone coastline and the enviable colonial homes that get this view day in and day out. If you're not quite ready for a dip at Clontarf Beach, just 1500m into the walk, you'll surely be tempted when you reach secluded little Washaway Beach, once an official nudist spot and still attracting the odd bare-buttocked bather. Tramping up to Grotto Point and later on to Dobroyd Head, through the the thick woodlands of Sydney Harbour National Park, provides a different view – the fabulous panorama of the harbour and its ocean jaws, the North and South heads.

917

PLAYGROUND BULLIES IN THE SOUTH PACIFIC:
the ultimate shark dive

FIJI Most divers catch a glimpse of a shark in Fiji, usually a small blacktip or nurse shark prowling the edge of the reef. But to see the big boys – 4m tiger sharks or mean-looking bulls – you need to take a deep breath and head to Pacific Harbour on the south coast of Viti Levu. Just offshore is a stretch of water that offers the world's ultimate shark diving experience – the chance to encounter up to eight species of the ocean's top predators with no cage or chainmail to protect you. While this could be considered a novel method of suicide, the dive has a flawless safety record and is a great way to learn about these much-maligned creatures.

Having signed a form acknowledging that shark diving "is an inherently risky activity", participants are given a detailed briefing (no swimming off on your own) before heading out to the Shark Reef Marine Reserve – a protected area funded by money raised from the dive. Here, experienced Fijian divers hand-feed the sharks,

while you view the action from a reef-ledge "arena" a few metres below. It's a bizarre sight: tuna heads and other scraps are served from a giant wheelie bin which soon attracts a swirling vortex of jacks, groupers and giant trevally. When the sharks arrive, the ocean hierarchy clicks into place like the queue at a deli counter. The schools of smaller fish defer to blacktips, which defer to grey reef sharks, which in turn defer to bull sharks. Like playground bullies, the bulls swoop in centimetres from the feeders, quickly snapping up the prize chunks and making low turns over the wide-eyed audience below. Occasionally one of the regular tiger sharks, "Valerie" or "Hot Lips" may make an appearance. You'll soon know about this, as even the bull sharks will make a swift exit. Heading back to shore you are left feeling more humbled than frightened by these graceful predators and keenly aware of the need to protect them for the next generation.

918 Setting sail among the blissful Bay of Islands

NEW ZEALAND We've lowered the sails, dropped anchor beside a gorgeous crescent of golden beach, and it's time for a swim before lunch. The waters are warm and clear in Northland's Bay of Islands, perfect territory for some gentle cruising and a touch of snorkelling. Our anchorage is just off Roberton Island where an isthmus is almost severed by a pair of perfectly circular blue lagoons. Mask on, I'm off to follow the undersea nature trail where points of interest have been marked on plaques.

After a lunch of fresh barbecued fish on deck we move slowly on past Black Rocks, bare islets formed from columnar jointed basalt – these rise only 10m out of the water but plummet a sheer 30m beneath, allowing us to inspect them at close quarters. We're aboard the *R Tucker Thompson*, a modern replica of a gaff rigged, square

topsail schooner built in Northland in the style of a North American halibut schooner. A majestic sight from afar, with the sails pushing out towards the open ocean, its even better aboard. You can help set the sails, ride the bowsprit, climb the rigging or just laze on deck playing the ship's guitar.

Occasionally dolphins will come and ride the boat's bow wave, but to really get close and personal with these fascinating mammals you need to get out on *Carino*, a smaller, modern yacht licensed for dolphin swimming. If a pod is spotted nearby, a handful of swimmers are immediately in the water splashing about and humming, trying to attract the dolphins' interest. Ever curious, dolphins seem to love the attention and are soon darting around, close but somehow always just out of reach.

919 On the lookout for the duck-billed platypus

AUSTRALIA When the first dried, stuffed specimens of Australia's platypus arrived in Britain in the early nineteenth century, they were dismissed by scientists as a badly executed hoax, clearly made from bits of other animals sewn together. In fact, the truth was even weirder: not only do platypus genuinely look like a cross between a duck and an otter, but they lay eggs, requiring a whole new order of mammals – monotremes – to be created.

All the more reason, then, to head up to Queensland's Eungella National Park and make a point of tracking one down. Platypus live in rivers and are reasonably common, but as they're extremely timid, vanishing at the slightest movement, you'll need a lot of patience to see one – dusk and dawn are the best times to try. A tried and tested

tracking method is to follow the trail of mud rising off the bottom of a stream, caused as their rubbery bills rummage along the bottom in search of shrimps and beetles. Once they've found a beakful they bob to the surface to eat, lying flat on their fronts with their webbed feet splayed as they chew and glance nervously around – then it's a swift roll headfirst down to the bottom again. At under 30cm in length, your first reaction on seeing one will be "they're not as big as I thought." In winter you might see a courting pair chasing each other around the water in tight circles; after mating, the female walls herself into a burrow, dug into the bank above the water line, to wait for the young to hatch. And if you're lucky, you might see them following her in a line, each holding on to the tail of the one in front.

920 Witnessing the power of the haka

NEW ZEALAND Few spectacles can match the terrifying sight of the All Blacks performing a haka before a test match. You feel a chill down your spine fifty metres away in the stands so imagine how it must feel facing it as an opponent. The intimidating thigh-slapping, eye-bulging, tongue-poking chant traditionally used is the Te Rauparaha haka, and like all such Maori posture dances it is designed to display fitness, agility and ferocity. This version was reputedly composed early in the nineteenth century by the warrior Te Rauparaha, who was hiding from his enemies in the sweet potato pit of a friendly chief. Hearing noise above and then being blinded by the sun when the pit covering was removed he thought his days were numbered, but as his eyes became accustomed to the light he saw the hairy legs of his host and was so relieved he performed the haka on the spot. It goes:

Ka Mate! Ka Mate! (It is death! It is death!)
Ka Ora! Ka Ora! (It is life! It is life!)

Tenei te ta ngata puhuru huru (This is the hairy man)
Nana nei i tiki mai whakawhiti te ra (Who caused the sun to shine)
A upane, ka upane! (Step upwards! Another step upward!)
A upane, ka upane! (Step upwards! Another step upward!)
Whiti te ra! (Into the sun that shines!)

Over the last decade or so, descendants of tribes once defeated by Te Rauparaha took umbrage at the widespread use of this haka at rugby matches and consequently a replacement, the Kapa o Pango (Team in Black) haka, was devised. Numerous Maori experts were consulted over what form the haka should take but controversy still surrounds the final throat-slitting gesture, which is supposed to symbolize the harnessing of vital energy. The Kapa o Pango and traditional Te Rauparaha haka are now used roughly equally, the uncertainty over what they'll be exposed to further unsettling the All Blacks' opponents. But whichever you manage to catch, both versions still illicit that same spine-tingling response.

921 Walking on the wild side at the Sydney Mardi Gras

AUSTRALIA Sydney is probably the world's most gay-friendly city and its annual Gay & Lesbian Mardi Gras Parade is a huge red- (or should that be pink?) letter day, drawing a bigger crowd than any other annual event in Australia. In essence, it's a full-on celebration of gay culture, and a joyous demonstration of pride; but it's enjoyable for people of any sexuality, provided partial nudity, G-strings, wild unleashings of inhibitions and senseless acts of kindness don't offend.

The parade route runs from Hyde Park, through the city's gay quarter, to Moore Park. Pumped-up marshals, searchlights, flares, fireworks, strobes and dance music from all the nearby clubs bring the throng to a fever pitch of anticipation – a perfect build-up to the gleaming Harley Davidsons of the Dykes on Bikes, who have heralded the start of the parade for many years. Vast floats, effigies and marching troupes follow in their wake – everything from two hundred drag Madonnas in cowgirl hats, to three hundred Barbara Cartlands in pink-sequined evening gowns, or mist-enshrouded boats carrying Thai princes and princesses. Up to half a million spectators of every age and gender line the route as the six thousand participants float, shimmy or line dance their way past.

Afterwards, Australia's biggest parade is followed by Australia's biggest party at Moore Park Entertainment Precinct. Tickets sell out fast, and touts will ask exorbitant prices. Whatever your sexuality, it's a pretty decadent affair, and – how can we put this? – voyeurs are not encouraged. But even if you can't get in, or just can't afford it, there are lots of places with plenty going on after the Parade. Just wander along the gay strip and the chances are you'll find every bar is jumping, and just as much fun as the last.

922 Supping wine in sun-drenched Marlborough

NEW ZEALAND When Marlborough's Cloudy Bay Sauvignon Blanc hit the international wine shelves in the late 1980s its zingy fruitiness got jaded tongues wagging. All of a sudden New Zealand was on the world wine map, with the pin stuck firmly in the north of the South Island. Half a dozen regions now boast significant wine trails, but all roads lead back to Marlborough, still the country's largest grape growing area, protected by the sheltering hills of the Richmond Range, and blessed with more than 2400 hours of sunshine a year.

Cellar doors around the region are gradually becoming more sophisticated, with their own restaurants and specialist food stores, but the emphasis is still mainly on the wine itself. And tasting it. To squeeze the very best from the area start by visiting Montana Brancott, the biggest and most established operation hereabouts. Take their winery tour to get a feel for how wine is made nowadays, then stick around for a brief lesson on wine appreciation. Even those familiar with the techniques will learn something of the qualities Marlborough winemakers are trying to achieve.

Next visit Cloudy Bay. Of course you'll want to try the famous Sav, still drinking well today and available for tasting. Somehow it always seems that little bit fresher and fruitier when sampled at source out of a decent tasting glass.

Come lunchtime, head for Highfield Estate with its distinctive Tuscan-style tower and dine in the sun overlooking the vines. A plate of pan-seared monkfish is just the thing to wash down with their zesty Sauvignon Blanc.

923 Buzzing over the Bungles

AUSTRALIA If you've never been in a helicopter then a flight over Purnululu National Park – or the Bungle Bungles as most people call it – makes a great initiation. This mass of orange and black striped beehive-like domes is amazing enough at ground level, but leaning out of the doorless cockpit, your foot on the landing rail, you'll have a grin as wide as the Fitzroy River as you swoop and soar over the maze of 200m-deep chasms between the "bungles". At one point you launch low off the plateau and in an instant the ground disappears, sending your stomach spiralling after it.

Each dome ranges from 10 to 40m high, but in total cover just a small part of the park's 25,000 square kilometres of lightly wooded hills and grassland. To local Aboriginal people Purnululu has been a sacred site for millennia, but the wonders of this remote region of northwestern Australia were only fully acknowledged in the 1980s when a TV crew came across it while filming a documentary. Recognizing these curious rock formations to be geologically unique, Purnululu National Park was created in 1987, with access purposely limited to small aircraft or high-clearance vehicles able to negotiate the twisting 53km access track.

The origin of the domes is still unclear. The theory of a meteor impact shattering the rock into the now weathered segments takes a knock when one sees mini-bungle formations elsewhere in the Kimberley. More mundane, but more likely, it's a result of deposition, uplifting and subsequent erosion. The banding, on the other hand, is a clear illustration of aeons of alternating sediments: the orange deposits (iron oxide) are not porous while the rock above and below holds water and supports the fragile-looking crusts of black lichen.

And "fragile" may well describe your knees as you climb out of the helicopter and wobble across the launch pad. Now you've seen them from the air it's time for a closer inspection on foot.

AUSTRALIA A visit to Queen Victoria Market, or "Vic Market", located on the northern fringe of the city centre, is a superb introduction to Melbourne's vibrant food culture and will have you rubbing shoulders with everyone from government ministers to the city's best chefs. Running for 128 years, it's one of the oldest markets in Australia and is liveliest at weekends when buskers compete with spruiking stallholders for your attention.

Follow your nose to the deli section, characterized by its strong smells and shops selling regional specialities such as Jindi Triple Cream Brie and Milawa's tasty goat's cheese, as well as lesser-known fusions like kangaroo biltong (South African-style dried meat). Arriving hungry you'll find the free tastings will put a stop to the pangs as quickly as they tempt you to lighten your wallet. Greek, Italian, French and Polish stalls stock everything from marinated octopus to juniper sausage, while speciality butchers sell emu and crocodile. If you're looking for more traditional meat offerings, head to the Meat and Fish Hall. Here, competition is fierce, with dozens of butchers supplying prime cuts from legs of lamb to Japanese-style Wagu beef, and fishmongers' stalls groan under an impressive array of seafood ranging from northern Australian wild barramundi, Victorian crayfish and fresh Tasmanian oysters.

The fruit and vegetable market reflects the seasons, dominated by root vegetables in winter and stone fruits in summer – the proximity of Southeast Asia means exotic fruits like mangosteens, rambutan and the pungent-smelling durian are also available. If you're after something less epicurean, however, try the German Bratwurst shop for a sauerkraut and mustard covered sausage, or the American Doughnut Van, serving up bags of jam-filled indulgence for a few dollars.

924 INDULGE YOUR TASTEBUDS AT **QUEEN VICTORIA MARKET**

925 Tucking into a hangi

NEW ZEALAND A suitably reverential silence descends, broken only by munching and appreciative murmurs from the assembled masses – the hangi has finally been served. Pronounced "hungi", this traditional Maori meal, similar to the luau prepared by the Maori people's Polynesian kin in Hawaii, is essentially a feast cooked in an earth oven for several hours. It can't be found on restaurant menus – but then again a hangi is not just a meal, it's an event.

To begin, the men light a fire, and once it has burned down, specially selected river stones that don't splinter are placed in the embers. While these are heating, a large pit is dug, perhaps two metres square and a metre and a half deep. Meanwhile the women are busy preparing lamb, pork, chicken, fish, shellfish and vegetables (particularly kumara, the New Zealand sweet potato). Traditionally these would be wrapped in leaves then arranged in baskets made of flax; these days baking foil and steel mesh are more common.

When everything is ready (the prep can take up to three hours), the hot stones are placed in the pit and covered with wet sacking. Then come the baskets of food followed by a covering of earth which serves to seal in the steam and the flavours. There's a palpable sense of communal anticipation as hosts and guests mill around chatting and drinking, waiting for the unearthing. A couple of hours later, the baskets are disinterred, revealing fall-off-the-bone steam-smoked meat and fabulously tender vegetables with a faintly earthy flavour. A taste, and an occasion, not easily forgotten.

926 Rainforest vibes in the Daintree

AUSTRALIA If you're only going to visit one national park in Australia you might as well make it the Daintree. The stunning rainforests here are thought to be the oldest on the planet and cascade dramatically down to the white-sand coast around Cape Tribulation. Here you'll find barely touched beaches offering world-class snorkelling, plus a few welcome signs of civilization: chic eco-resorts, gourmet restaurants and beachside bungalows.

Another part of the appeal is that Daintree's wild beauty has not been totally sanitized. Estuarine crocodiles still cruise among the mangrove swamps, the forests harbour plants with vicious stinging leaves, and the Coral Sea is home to box jellyfish, though fortunately only during the torpid wet season. Bright blue butterflies share the breeze with a variety of birds, from the giant, emu-like cassowary to kingfishers whose luminescent liveries will stop you in your tracks.

Decisions get no more fraught than choosing papaya or mango for breakfast or opting for either sustained relaxation or a bit of wilderness exploration. A wildlife-spotting boat trip up the Daintree River is a rewarding compromise, or a walk through the Mossman Gorge may give you an appetite for a crocburger (yes, it does taste like chicken). Alternatively, just head to the beach with a sarong and the latest copy of Australian *Hello* magazine. For the widest range of restaurants and cafés, base yourself in Port Douglas, also a good departure point for exploring the reef. Better still, push the boat right out and indulge yourself with a stay at the *Daintree Eco Lodge and Spa*. Set beside the river and surrounded by lush jungle, it offers exclusive treehouse accommodation and is renowned for its luxurious spa treatments. And there's no need to put ambient relaxation tunes on your iPod: the mellow sounds of a 100-million year-old rainforest are music enough.

927 Tramping the Milford Track

NEW ZEALAND You're going to get wet on this tramp. In fact it would be disappointing if you didn't. When the heavens open it seems like the hills are leaking; every cliff-face springs a waterfall and the rivers quickly become raging torrents.

The Milford Track lies in Fiordland National Park which gets at least five metres (yes, metres) of rain a year, making it one of the wettest places on Earth. But unless you are really unlucky it won't rain the whole time. Blue skies reveal a wonderment of magical scenery which explains why this four-day hike (or "tramp" as the locals call it) has become the most popular in the country.

The highest point, in terms of both altitude and views, is at the 1073m Mackinnon Pass. Deep glaciated valleys drop steeply away on both sides while weather-worn mountains rear up all around. It is a great place to eat your lunch, always keeping a wary eye out for kea, New Zealand's cheeky alpine parrot, who will be off with your sandwiches given even a quarter of a chance.

From the pass, it's possible to see most of the Milford Track route. Behind you is the valley of the Clinton River, along which you've just spent a day and a half tramping, after being dropped off by a small launch on the shores of Lake Te Anau. Ahead is the Arthur River, where the rain puts on its best display with two spectacular waterfalls. The story goes that when blazing the route in 1880, explorers Donald Sutherland and John Mackay came upon one magnificent fall and tossed a coin to decide who would name it on the understanding that the loser would name the next one. Mackay won the toss but rued his good fortune when, days later, they stumbled across the much more famous and lofty Sutherland Falls, at 580m the tallest in New Zealand.

928 Getting to grips with Aboriginal art

AUSTRALIA You don't need in-flight entertainment when you're flying across Australia because the view from the plane is always diverting. The endless, barely inhabited Outback spreads before you like a vast natural canvas: ivory-coloured saltpans merge into clumps of grey-green scrub; sienna, ochre and russet sands expand to the horizon, broken only by the occasional dead-straight line of an oil exploration track or the wiggle of a long-dried watercourse. It's like one enormous abstract picture and, in part at least, that's what informs many Aboriginal artworks, particularly the so-called dot paintings.

At the heart of many Aboriginal traditions are practices for surviving in the extreme conditions of the Outback and the need to pass on this knowledge to descendants. Historically, one way of doing that has been to draw a map in the dust, detailing crucial local features such as sacred landmarks, waterholes and food sources.

These sand paintings are elaborate and take days to create; they are also sacred and to be viewed only by initiated clan members before being destroyed. But in the early 1970s, a teacher at Papunya, northwest of Alice Springs, began encouraging young Aborigine kids to translate their sand-painting techniques onto canvas. In fact it was the elders who took to the idea – without divulging culturally secret information, of course – and a new art form was born.

Those early Papunya artists have been superseded by painters from throughout the central desert, the most successful using innovative abstract and minimalist styles in their bid to woo international collectors. Alice Springs now has two dozen art galleries devoted to Aboriginal art, with paintings priced between Aus$40 and Aus$40,000. Browsing these galleries is one of the highlights of a visit to Alice, and even if you don't bring a picture home, you'll come away with a different perspective on the Outback.

929 Following in Gauguin's footsteps

TAHITI Palms drooping languidly towards the ocean, vivid clumps of pink hibiscus and great patches of melon yellow and luminescent green. The "primitivism" Paul Gauguin found so appealing in Tahiti may be long gone, but the mesmerizing landscapes he painted are still here. In 1891, the artist sailed to the Pacific to escape "everything that is artificial and conventional". His hut in Mataiea on the south coast of Tahiti no longer stands, but the absorbing Musée Gauguin nearby has exhibits about his life and work. The best time to visit is in the morning when the botanical gardens outside the museum are often deserted and you can lounge under the canopy of a plump banana plant and imagine the artist creating his raw, expressive paintings, just across the river.

To continue the Gaugin trail, you fly to the fertile, ridge-backed island of Hiva Oa. Here you'll find a re-creation of his florid *Maison du Jour*, another small museum and finally, the flower-laden stone tomb where he was buried in 1903.

930 Diving the Coolidge

VANUATU There is no other wreck on Earth like the *SS President Coolidge*. This 210m-long ship is so huge you could dive here for a year and not see the half of it. Built in the 1930s as a luxury liner, the *Coolidge* was converted to carry troops in World War II. She met her end at Espiritu Santo in Vanuatu when the captain ran her aground and abandoned ship after hitting mines intended for the Japanese. All but two of the crew of 5000 disembarked safely, but the ship listed and slipped off the reef, flipping onto her side to lie 20m below at the shallowest point.

You start the dive by finning down the guide line into the deep blue, ending at the stern; from there, it's over the hull to where a hatch has been cut in the side. You're in darkness, following torchlight beams and rising bubbles along claustrophobic corridors. Slowly, your vision adjusts and the lights come back on. Down past dials, panels and machinery – the engine room – then there's a flash of grey and blue and you're on the sand outside the wreck, 60m down with half your air left. Time for a mellow ascent to the surface.

931 Working up a thirst at Wineglass Bay

AUSTRALIA Magical places are as much about the journey as they are the destination. That's true of reaching Tasmania from the mainland (skip flying in favour of the far-more-romantic overnight ferry crossing). And it's true of accessing this island state's most exquisite cove, Wineglass Bay.

Secluded within the Freycinet National Park, this perfect arc of white sand, midway along Tasmania's east coast, is reached along an invigorating ninety-minute trail. From the nearest vehicle access, at Coles Bay, you scale a steep track (scrambling up 600-odd rough bush steps) to the saddle between Mt Amos and Mt Mayson. From here a path leads to the Wineglass Bay lookout and the classic vista seen on every tourist poster in Tassie. As the smell of sea air and wildflowers fills your nostrils, it's hard to imagine the violence which gave the bay its name. In the 1820s, European whalers arrived, their harpoons staining the water dark-red with blood, like wine in a glass.

Fortunately, whales can still be seen in season, along with dolphins, seals and albatrosses, on half-day cruises around the bay.

Continuing downhill from the lookout brings you onto the beach where the brave can try a skin-tingling swim (Tassie's water temperatures are chilly by Aussie standards). But there's more to explore nearby. Spaced out in the dunes behind you are piles of shells, evidence of Aboriginal settlement dating back tens of thousands of years, while further south another trail leads to dazzling views of the craggy Hazards mountains.

If you want to experience the bay without the crowds it's worth spending the night at one of the campsites nearby. It's hard to beat being lulled to sleep by the sound of breakers rolling in, and if you wake up early enough there's the chance of spotting a bleary-eyed wombat or spiky echidna scuttling through the scrub before the day-trippers arrive.

From **prison** to *paradise* on
l'Île des Pins

932

NEW CALEDONIA If you have to go into exile somewhere, it might as well be the South Pacific, and this blob of an island at the southern end of French New Caledonia is a particularly bearable spot. Measuring just 14km by 18km the Île des Pins ("Island of Pines") was a penal colony in the nineteenth century, the last stop for many dissidents from the Paris Commune in the 1870s. It's interesting to share the impressions of one of the convicts transported here. Having acknowledged that he had ended up in a paradise, he immediately adds, with obvious bitterness, "but I saw nothing of its beauty" – and yearned only for the monochromes of northern France.

The modern-day visitor comes to the island by choice, of course, and can hardly fail to notice its beauty: stunning coastlines, with hot, white sand; warm, limpid water, pale blue as far as the reef, and a deeper blue beyond. The classic South Sea paradise. The most obvious place to test the water has to be the island's "la piscine naturelle", or natural swimming pool, where the sea enters a shallow bay through a narrow defile between jagged rocks and creates a calm, pristine pool, lined by sun-baked sand. You can wallow in safety while listening to the waves breaking in the distance.

But there's one thing stopping it all from becoming a cliché: the araucaria pines that so struck Captain Cook when moored offshore that he named the island after them. Although there are also plenty of swaying palms as well, it's these dark, spindly posts, soaring bolt upright into the sky, and adorned by minimal vegetation, that define and distinguish this place. And their forbidding, stark rigidity, in marked contrast to the friendly sway of the palms, creates a certain ambivalence. Do they really belong in paradise?

Before you leave, take in the island's ruined prison and monument and be thankful that you get to come and go as you please.

Getting hands-on at Wellington's **Te Papa**

NEW ZEALAND Spend any time in the Kiwi capital and you can't help but notice the bold, angular building amongst the yachts and seagulls of the waterfront. This is Te Papa, which translates as "Our Place", the Museum of New Zealand. Universally known by its Maori name, it was created in partnership with the nation's *iwi* (tribes) and presents a uniquely bicultural view of the country.

A far cry from the stuffy glass cases of the old museum it replaced, Te Papa exudes a radical modern approach not just in the design of the building but in the way the exhibits invite interaction and involvement. Like any good museum it works on several levels and yet, despite its size, it never feels overwhelming. You can easily waltz through in a couple of hours and get a comprehensive overview of what makes New Zealand tick. To make the most of your visit, linger over the superb Maori section with its robustly carved war canoe, traditional houses, collections of fearsome war clubs and intricately worked jade jewellery. Displays showcase how people have migrated to New Zealand, first using the stars to navigate the Pacific in double-hulled canoes, later in sailing ships, and more recently as immigrants from east Asia. And you shouldn't miss the *marae*, a Maori meeting place that is dramatically different from the red, black and white wood carvings you'll see elsewhere. Here semi-mythological figures are fashioned from warped plywood and shaded in an eye-catching array of pastel tones.

With more time on your hands, there's plenty to keep you occupied – drawers reveal smaller artefacts, a gallery showcases the best in Kiwi painting and sculpture, and "sound posts" encourage you to tune into wide-ranging views about the ongoing debate on New Zealand's founding document, the Treaty of Waitangi.

Te Papa is a great place for kids too, with all kinds of interactive, hands-on displays, the chance to feel the shudder of New Zealand's most powerful earthquake and even some high-tech rides.

More than a decade after its opening, over a million people pass through Te Papa's doors every year. Not bad, considering the country only has a population of four million.

933

934 Paragliding over the paddocks

AUSTRALIA Early starts are required to get the best out of paragliding over the vast farmland behind Mount Tambourine in Southern Queensland. The cool morning air, calm and still, gradually heats and begins to show signs of releasing every free-flyer's addiction – thermals. Bubbles of rising warm air lift the lucky ones clear off the ground's pull and rewards them with breathtaking views out over the plains towards the Great Dividing Range. Once at cloud base, the hopeful pilots take in the view of rich green pasture intersected by old red dusty scars and wait for 2pm, checking their watches anxiously until the strong coastal breeze hits like a wall and accelerates them and their gliders towards the horizon.

935 Knocking back kava

FIJI If you want to get to the heart of Fiji, drinking *kava* is a good place to start. First, you'll be invited to join a group, languidly assembled around a large wooden bowl. Then, a grinning elder will pass you a coconut shell, saying "tovolea mada" – "try please". You take a look – the muddy pool in the shell looks like dirty dishwater, but what the hell, you sip anyway. And then the taste hits you, a sort of medicinal tonic tinged with pepper. Resist the urge to spit it out and you'll gain the respect of your hosts. Passing the cup back you exclaim "maca!", which loosely translates as "thanks". Keep drinking, and you'll start to get numb lips, feel mildly intoxicated and if you're lucky, end up as tranquil as your new friends.

936 A volcanic trip up Mount Yasur

VANUATU The walk up to the continuously erupting Mount Yasur on Tanna Island takes about ninety minutes. A notice at the bottom warns against approaching the crater when there's a particular level of activity; usually it's safe to move on. The climb goes through tropical forest: rainwater trickles down every tree, then gushes down the path. Suddenly the forest gives way to a grim desert of rock and mud extending to the summit. The temperature drops markedly; a cool, dank mist blows in from the sea.

Yasur announces itself the closer you get. Every few minutes, there's a loud boom, then a few lesser booms. Just below the summit, a battered letterbox proclaims itself the world's only Volcano Post – it's quite literally a chance to send postcards from the edge.

At the rim, a pleasant waft of heat rises up and drives the mist away. But booms accompany tremendous eruptions of red-hot rocks – pyroclasts – that crash into the edge of the crater, and either fizzle or explode. The louder eruptions cause the ground to shake. Often the balls of fire soar high into the air; you'll have to guess where they're going to land. Most people, it seems, get lucky.

937 Discovering the secrets of Kings Canyon

AUSTRALIA If you're looking for adventure amidst the haunting scenery of Australia's Red Centre, you'd be hard-pushed to beat Kings Canyon in Watarrka National Park. The soaring, vertical walls of this sandstone canyon were carved out during a more humid climatic epoch, thousands of years ago. Today it lies in a scrubby semi-desert of scurrying lizards and gnarled trees. The main attraction here is the 6km walk taking you up and around the canyon's rim. Along the way you'll uncover a variety of wildlife and their habitats, from rocky crevices to palm-filled gorges, and can wander off the track as close as you dare to the very edge of the 100m cliffs.

Early morning is the best time to head out. You begin with a fifteen-minute stepped ascent that will get your heart pumping. But don't be put off; at the top the worst is over and from here the trail leads through the "Lost City", a maze of sandstone domes where information boards fill you in on the formation of the canyon.

Back on the signed track you clamber down into a palm-filled chasm which you'll need to summon the courage to cross via an impressive timber bridge. Spinifex pigeons and other birds dart overhead, while on the far side there's an easily missed ten-minute detour downstream to a shady pool. Most tour groups are content to sit here, eating their snacks, but the highlight of the walk and a secret known to few, is looking out from the very throat of the canyon above a dry waterfall. You can get there either by wading knee-deep round the right bank of the pool, scrambling over the rock above, or simply gritting your teeth and swimming across. Peering from the brink you get a perfectly framed view of the sunlit south wall and the canyon far below. Returning to the bridge, the walk takes you back to the very rim of the overhanging south wall above the jumbled, deep-ochre-coloured rocks, before descending gently back to the start point.

938 Taking a trip to hell on Earth

NEW ZEALAND You'll smell Rotorua before you even reach the city limits. It isn't known as the "Sulphur City" for nothing, and the unmistakable bad-egg aroma gets everywhere. Thankfully you get used to it after an hour or so. The whole city sits on a thin crust of earth underlain by a seething cauldron of waters and superheated steam that seem desperate to escape. Walking around you'll see puffs of vapour rising out of people's backyards, and stormwater drains venting sulphurous jets. Crypts predominate in the cemeteries as graves can't be dug into the ground, and on the shores of Lake Rotorua gulls are relieved of the chore of sitting on their nests – the earth is warm enough to incubate without assistance.

Close to town are a dozen or so dramatic geothermal wonders. Tourists have been coming for over a century to see the Pohutu

Geyser, which regularly spouts to 20m; around the turn of the millennium it performed continuously for an unprecedented 329 days. It still spouts several times a day, a spectacular show that's heralded by the smaller Prince of Wales Feathers geyser (10m). Mineral deposits turn lakes wild shades of orange and green, and steam forces its way to the surface to form boiling mud pools patterned with myriad concentric circles.

Weary bones are also well-catered for in Rotorua – just about every motel and campground has a hot pool in which to soak. Make a point of seeking out genuine mineral ones filled by therapeutic geothermal waters, whether it be hydrothermal pampering in sophisticated resorts or back-to-basics natural pools out in the woods under the stars.

939 Zen and the art of relaxation, Byron Bay

AUSTRALIA Back in the early 1970s, longboard surfers and yoga-loving hippies in "save the whale" T-shirts discovered Byron Bay, elevating it from a sleepy backwater to the coolest hangout on Australia's East Coast. It hasn't looked back since.

Today, the counter culture which made Byron's name continues to blossom. But things have changed: the town is still stuffed with quirky vegetarian cafés and shops selling windchimes, crystals and sarongs, but chic resorts with elegant spas have begun to outnumber the scruffy hippy hangouts. It's become a playground for both backpackers and cashed-up city escapees. Aussie soap and sport stars have become a common sight and you may even spot the odd A-lister; squeaky-clean Olivia Newton-John runs a wellness centre nearby. So if you like the idea of tapping into your nature-loving, spiritual side but balk at the thought of going right back to basics, Byron Bay may be just your sort of place.

Sign up for a yoga and surf retreat and you'll experience Byron at its best. With the services of professional yoga, meditation, pilates and wave-riding gurus on tap, you can divide up your time as you choose. Byron's teachers cater for all comers: if you've never tried to keep your balance on a longboard or bend your body into a cobra before, you will be in safe hands. It's a superb way to both relax and tone up – and the in-house cooks will rustle up enough healthy macrobiotic treats to fuel you through your exertions, however hard you choose to push yourself.

To get each day off to an invigorating start, you can be the first to greet the Australian dawn by heading down to Byron's lovely, long, sandy beach for a series of sun salutations on the shore, coordinating your breathing with the rhythmic roar of the surf. It certainly beats a sweaty studio with an ocean-wave soundtrack on the stereo.

AUSTRALIA Tasmania's Overland Track is one of the world's greatest long-distant walks. Stretching from the island's highest peak to Australia's deepest lake, you cross a magnificent alpine wilderness, unbroken by roads and adorned by brooding lakes, glacier-carved cirques and thundering waterfalls.

Stormy skies are frequent on Tassie, but even on the ground there's no shortage of drama with features named after their classical Greek counterparts – Mount Eros, the Acropolis and Lake Elysia – providing a fitting backdrop to the Olympian landscape. And though much of the 65km trail is boardwalk with bridged creeks, there's no escaping several muddy interludes – be prepared to get wet.

This is Tasmania, so fresh drinking water is plentiful and need not be carried; the daunting task is lugging enough food and stove fuel for the duration. Once you accept that, the exhilaration of wandering completely self-sufficient through the mountain wilderness fills you with a sense of deep satisfaction. Up above, raven-like currawongs and eagles cut through the skies, while below you quolls, cat-like relatives of the famous Tasmanian devil, and wallabies abound.

It takes about a week to tramp across the Overland's stirring range of landscapes, though you'll want to add a day or two for side trips to waterfalls, lakes and scrambling up peaks such as Mount Ossa, Tasmania's highest at 1617m, overlooking forests of King Billy pines and carpeted in fragrant wildflowers in early summer. Even then you're sure to have rain and even snow at some point, and eventually you'll stagger aboard the Lake St Clair ferry, aching, mud-caked but happy, for an uncelebrated return to civilization.

RIVER DEEP, MOUNTAIN HIGH:

Bushwalking the Overland Track

940

Watching footy

941

at the MCG

AUSTRALIA A Saturday "arvo" at the Melbourne Cricket Ground (MCG) reveals Melbourne at its best. All ages, races and classes are united by one passion: Australian Rules football, or simply "footy" as it's known in this sports-mad city. Resembling an eighteen-a-side brawl between vest-wearing beefcakes, footy is Melbourne's religion, and the locals have been passionate followers since the 1850s, when it was first invented here to keep cricketers fit in winter.

Every weekend the nearby railway stations and roads are clogged with fans heading in to "barrack" for their team. If you plan to see a game, choose one between traditional rivals such as Essendon and Carlton, two of Melbourne's oldest teams; the atmosphere will be electric with a guaranteed full house, split 50/50. The scene is tense but never violent, rowdy but not without humour, and you'll see just as many women as men cheering on their team.

The fun begins with rousing traditional team songs as players run onto the field, breaking through huge crepe-paper banners, while in the stalls big men wave pompoms in team colours. Played with what looks like a scaled down rugby ball, the aim is to score goals between the posts of the opposing goal. The catch is you cannot hold the ball or throw it so a lot of bouncing, tapping and kicking ensues, requiring great strength, athleticism and endurance: players have been known to run up to 20km in a match lasting 120 minutes and divided into quarters.

Feeling confused by all the action? Any fan sitting next to you will be happy to fill you in on the finer points of footy lingo from "screamers" to "floaters". Should you choose to support their team, you're likely to gain a lifelong mate. After all, nothing makes a devotee of a religion happier than a successful conversion.

942 Island dreaming: sailing the Whitsundays

AUSTRALIA There's a distinct feeling of déjà vu cruising in a sailboat among the Whitsunday Islands. Presently it comes to you: you've been here many times, in your lottery fantasies. This tropical idyll of turquoise seas lapping ivory sands against a backdrop of dense green foliage is ingrained in our imagination, be it some Jungian folk memory or saturation advertising. *The Beach* before it all turned sour. Paradise.

Just over 1200km north of Brisbane, this compact archipelago of seventy-odd islands lies just off Airlie Beach, a small resort described by locals as "a drinking town with a sailing problem". From here you have a delectable menu of islands to choose from: Hayman, which offers resorts so posh staff scurry unseen along tunnels; others like Long Island are more affordable; or you might prefer the Molle Islands, home to little more than a couple of basic campsites.

Sheltered by the Great Barrier Reef, the Pacific swell is dampened, but reliable light breezes remain, making the Whitsundays a sailing haven, and at an affordable price. Choose between a sedate three-day cruise, where you can laze aboard a spacious and comfortable crewed boat, or get stuck in and crew on a huge racing "maxi yacht" catering for partying backpackers.

Either way life becomes sybaritically simple. By day you commune with turtles, dolphins and even whales – up from the Antarctic to give birth before heading south again. Or go snorkelling on the lookout for morays and parrotfish (the northeastern tip of Hook Island is best). Come sunset you moor in one of the many unnamed bays while the chef prepares a fresh seafood meal. A shower is as simple as diving into the surrounding water, and your bed is the deck of the boat or the sand on the beach.

943 Getting high on the Gillespie Pass

NEW ZEALAND Clinging to the sheer cliff with a 15kg pack pulling on my back, I knew I couldn't afford to put a foot wrong: one slip on the scree and I'd plummet 500m. Forget bungee jumping and speed boats – if you want white-knuckle New Zealand, climb the Gillespie Pass. Below me, the steely grey crags of the Young Basin were shrinking, while above the almighty 2200m bulk of Mount Awful loomed large. When it comes to names, the Kiwis certainly know how to pick 'em.

After a series of tight switchbacks, I finally reached the Gillespie Pass: a rocky saddle speckled with brilliant wildflowers and random patches of snow. The tremendous panorama of the Southern Alps spread out in front of me, their peaks piercing the sky. Up here, only a lonesome kea shattered the silence with its shrill squawk. The feeling of being alone above the world was beyond words and a

million miles away from New Zealand's more populated hikes. This was hardcore. As if to prove my point, a bitter wind blew across from Mount Awful where threatening storm clouds were gathering. A hostile reminder that Siberia lay ahead.

The Siberia Valley is aptly named. Even when you're cocooned in a high-tech sleeping bag, the chill creeps in and grips you with its icy claws. Outside the moon illuminated the near-frozen river and the summit of Mount Dreadful (presumably Mount Awful's little brother). Shivering and sleepy, the final test of my mettle was the uphill climb to Crucible Lake the next morning. The boulder-strewn trek was tough, but the lake was awesome: a glacier-gouged crater filled with turquoise water and chinking icebergs. It looked like an alpine pasture struck by a meteorite. New Zealand boasts many great walks, but if you're seeking the real deal, this has got to be it.

944 Doing the crocodile rock in Kakadu National Park

AUSTRALIA "He was right by the base of that paperbark tree when the croc got him," says Nerida, our guide, as we unpack our picnic lunch on the edge of the West Alligator River. We're only a few hours drive out of Darwin and already this is her third crocodile tale, each new anecdote regaled with greater enthusiasm than the one before. Her eyes twinkle mischievously as she watches us quickly retreat back up the bank. "The poor guy didn't even have time to blink," she continues, with a deadpan delivery honed over countless tours. It's hard to tell if she has spiced up the story for us or not, but there's no doubting the reverential tone in her voice. Out here, I begin to understand, the crocodile is still king.

Nearly everyone you meet in Kakadu National Park has got a croc story to tell. And it's easy to see why: Kakadu is archetypal Outback – *Crocodile Dundee* was filmed amongst the gum trees here – and it exudes a feeling of raw nature. Acres of bleached eucalypti stand silhouetted against a rich sapphire sky; fertile floodplains and

billabongs, laced with water lilies and swollen from the recent rain, teem with some of the park's exotic wildlife: large goanna lizards, the blue-winged kookaburra, rare wallaroos and, of course, the saltwater crocodile, the park's most notorious resident.

After a few days spent exploring its woodlands, wetlands and sandstone escarpments, I was beginning to wonder if I would leave Kakadu without seeing a quick glimpse of a jagged tail. But stopping off on our drive back to Darwin for a cruise on the Adelaide River, I got it. The water was brown and still, and as our boat chugged upstream, a rugged outline broke the surface a few metres up ahead, scything through the water towards us. "A croc like that won't have got that old and that big without being more than a little clever," declares Nerida, checking that everyone onboard has their arms tucked firmly inside the boat. I just stare, transfixed, as nearly two hundred million years of immutable natural history glides slowly off into the distance.

945 Cruising Doubtful Sound

NEW ZEALAND The smell of frying bacon wafting from the galley brings the boat awake. And what a place to wake up. Deathly still, there's mist clinging to the sides of the cliffs which hem in Doubtful Sound; the only movement comes from the lone soul who has borrowed one of the boat's kayaks and is out exploring the shoreline. Cruises on Milford Sound may be more famous, but Doubtful Sound, in the far southwest corner of the South Island, is equally spectacular and, being off the main tourist route, is a more intriguing place to visit.

Just getting out here is half the fun. First you cruise across Lake Manapouri, a deep, glacier-hewn body now harnessed for hydroelectric power; the huge turbines are hidden like a Bond villain's lair beneath the mountains. Finally, a bus ride carries you over the 670m Wilmot Pass from where you get your first glimpse of Doubtful Sound, a hairline thread of water forcing its way inland through 20km of glorious scenery. So narrow is the fjord that explorer Captain Cook, who named the place, didn't actually enter – he felt it was so confined that he was doubtful he would be able to get out again.

After a hearty breakfast we're under way again, gently exploring narrow channels where the thick forest creeps right down to the shoreline. Before long we're joined by a small group of bottlenose dolphins. It is hard to work out if these are our friends from yesterday come back to play, or others from the resident pod. Either way, they seem to be having a great time riding the bow wave on their side gazing up at us as we lean over the rail.

946 Learning to surf on the Gold Coast

AUSTRALIA Mastering the art of riding a wave is not as tricky as it looks, and the southernmost coast of Queensland is one of the best surfing nurseries on the planet. Here the swell along the 40km beach from Coolangatta to South Stradbroke Island is untamed by the Barrier Reef's wave-dampening atolls further north. Between those two points you can't miss the high-rise blight of Surfers Paradise, Australia's domestic holidaymaking "Costa", but as far as you're concerned it's the reliable and easy surf that matters.

With tropical cyclones animating the Pacific swell, summer is the time to watch the surfing pros, while the temperate winter is the time to learn. From April to October the regular waves break safely over sand here and the warm, waist-deep water makes it all the more pleasurable. If you've got a good sense of balance, you'll be at an advantage; though most surf schools promise to have you at least standing on the board by the end of a typical two-hour session, and surfing properly in a day or two.

It mostly boils down to being in the right place at the right time. Learning to predict the break of a wave and positioning yourself in front of it can be most easily learnt on a short boogie board. The next big step on a full-sized board is getting from prone to on your feet in the blink of an eye – easy enough to practise on dry land but a lot trickier in the water. Soon enough, though, you'll be heading beachwards while adopting the classic surfer stance, even if the wave's only halfway up your shin. Get it right and you'll experience a taste of the bigger rush, the raw surge of adrenaline which is what surfing's all about. But everyone's got to start somewhere and for the novice surf junkie the beaches around Surfers Paradise couldn't be more aptly named.

947 Coast to coast with the TranzAlpine

NEW ZEALAND New Zealand's South Island is vertically split by the Southern Alps, a snow-capped spine of 3000m mountains. Only three road passes breach this barrier, and just one rail line – the TranzAlpine. Slicing 225km across the South Island from Christchurch, the island's biggest city, to the small west coast town of Greymouth, this unassuming train offers one of the most scenic rail journeys in the world.

Don't come looking for a luxury experience. This certainly isn't the *Orient Express*, but any shortcomings of the train itself will fade into the background when you take a look out of the window – the scenery is mind-bogglingly spectacular, especially in winter, when it's at its most dramatic with the landscape cloaked in snow.

As the train eases out of Christchurch, urban back gardens give way to the open vistas of the Canterbury Plains, acre upon acre of bucolic sheep country. After an hour the rail line cuts away from the main highway and charts its own course past the dry grasslands of the Torlesse Range, gradually climbing all the while.

The west of the South Island gets huge amounts of rain, the east very little. Here you're in a transition zone, and with every kilometre you'll notice the character of the vegetation change. Subalpine tussock gives way to damp beech forests before heading into the dripping west coast rainforest, thick with rampant tree ferns. Step onto the open-air viewing carriage for an even more intimate experience; photo opportunities abound.

At the little alpine community of Arthur's Pass you enter the 8km Otira Tunnel, burrowing under the high peaks and emerging at the former rail town of Otira. After losing height quickly along the cascading Taramakau River the train cuts to the tranquil shores of Lake Brunner before the final run down to Greymouth – just four and a half hours but a world away from Christchurch.

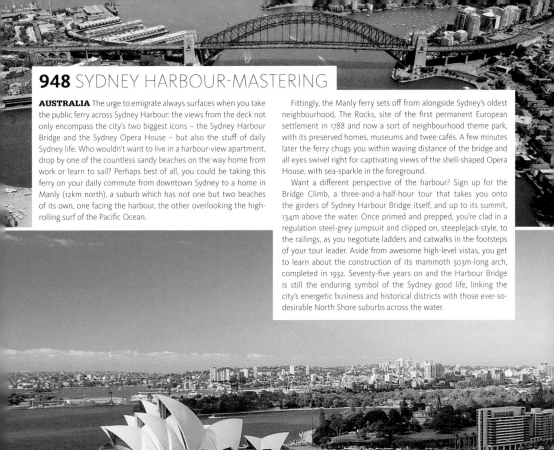

948 SYDNEY HARBOUR-MASTERING

AUSTRALIA The urge to emigrate always surfaces when you take the public ferry across Sydney Harbour: the views from the deck not only encompass the city's two biggest icons – the Sydney Harbour Bridge and the Sydney Opera House – but also the stuff of daily Sydney life. Who wouldn't want to live in a harbour-view apartment, drop by one of the countless sandy beaches on the way home from work or learn to sail? Perhaps best of all, you could be taking this ferry on your daily commute from downtown Sydney to a home in Manly (12km north), a suburb which has not one but two beaches of its own, one facing the harbour, the other overlooking the high-rolling surf of the Pacific Ocean.

Fittingly, the Manly ferry sets off from alongside Sydney's oldest neighbourhood, The Rocks, site of the first permanent European settlement in 1788 and now a sort of neighbourhood theme park, with its preserved homes, museums and twee cafés. A few minutes later the ferry chugs you within waving distance of the bridge and all eyes swivel right for captivating views of the shell-shaped Opera House, with sea-sparkle in the foreground.

Want a different perspective of the harbour? Sign up for the Bridge Climb, a three-and-a-half-hour tour that takes you onto the girders of Sydney Harbour Bridge itself, and up to its summit, 134m above the water. Once primed and prepped, you're clad in a regulation steel-grey jumpsuit and clipped on, steeplejack-style, to the railings, as you negotiate ladders and catwalks in the footsteps of your tour leader. Aside from awesome high-level vistas, you get to learn about the construction of its mammoth 503m-long arch, completed in 1932. Seventy-five years on and the Harbour Bridge is still the enduring symbol of the Sydney good life, linking the city's energetic business and historical districts with those ever-so-desirable North Shore suburbs across the water.

WATCHING WHALES
in Kaikoura

NEW ZEALAND It's 7.30am and we're just a kilometre off the coast of Kaikoura. I can still see the wharf where we embarked, backed by the snowcapped Seaward Kaikoura range, and yet below us is 1000m of ocean. This is exactly the sort of territory that many whale species like to call home. Most places in the world, a whale-watching trip involves hours powering out to sea to the whales' migration route, but here the whales are virtually on the doorstep.

Sperm whales and dusky dolphins are year-round residents, while blue whales, pilot whales and especially humpback whales all pass through. Regular visitors include southern right whales, so named because whalers found them to be the "right" whales to kill – they floated after being harpooned.

Weather permitting, trips run several times a day, and you're typically out among the leviathans within minutes. (Tour operators are so confident you'll see a whale that they'll refund eighty percent of your fee if you don't.) On the short journey out, big video screens have taken us into the virtual "World of the Whales" and their life in the depths of the Kaikoura Canyon and beyond, but we're here to see the real thing. Right on cue, someone spots a plume of spray, then a short dorsal fin. It is a humpback. The previously half-awake boat comes alive as everyone crowds the rails, camera in hand. Out of the corner of my eye I just catch a thirty-tonne barnacled beast surge out of the water, almost clearing the waves, with sheets of brine pouring off its sides. It crashes back with a surface-rending splash. We're all thrilled at our good fortune and are anticipating even greater displays when the whale decides it has had enough, and with a wave of its tail bids us adieu.

Riding the Ghan
to Darwin

AUSTRALIA In 2004 the Adelaide–Darwin *Ghan* train finally reached its destination about a hundred years behind schedule. Constructing a reliable rail link between these two towns took up most of the last century but around the start of the new millennium the government decided to plug the final 1500km gap from Alice to Darwin, completing a legendary transcontinental rail journey.

For most of the three-day, two-night northbound ride the train passes through uninhabited Outback that most people will only see out of a plane window. Just a couple of hours out of Adelaide and you're already lost on the vast Nullarbor Plain. Night falls and bleached saltpans glow eerily in the moonlight as you tuck yourself in to your comfy four-berth cabin. Next morning the view from the dining car reveals classic Outback colours: clear blue skies, grey-green scrub and rich orange sand. While you stare, doze or read the train passes close to the geographical centre of the continent, and by lunchtime squeezes through the West MacDonnell Ranges. Soon the driver's whistle heralds your arrival at the likeable desert town of Alice Springs where you're allowed a couple of hours' break.

Past Alice, the *Ghan* works its way through the ranges before spilling out onto the featureless 1000km Tanami Desert. The sun sets as you near Wycliffe Well roadhouse, famous for its UFO sightings. You peer keenly into the blackness but see only your reflection in the glass and so turn in. Dawn delivers you to the tropical Top End. Trees have reappeared for the first time since Adelaide, here interspersed with countless 2m-high termite mounds. The town of Katherine marks another first on this epic journey – the only flowing river for over 2000km – and then it's just an hour or two to journey's end in Darwin.

Sure, you could've flown here in a few hours, or driven and arrived feeling like week-old roadkill. But by rolling into town on the *Ghan* your carbon footprint is the size of a possum's front paw. And that is something to feel good about.

951 Swimming with whale sharks at Ningaloo Reef

AUSTRALIA Once a year the world's largest fish makes an appearance at the Ningaloo Reef fringing Western Australia's North West Cape. Its arrival is strategically timed with a moonlit night in late summer when coral polyps spawn en masse, ejecting millions of eggs into the tropical waters. Guided by some arcane instinct the hungry whale sharks are ready and waiting, mouths agape.

More whale than shark, this 15m-long gentle giant is twice the size of the great white of *Jaws* fame but entirely harmless to humans. It survives by cruising the world's oceans ingesting all the krill and plankton that its metre-wide mouth can scoop in. For the whale shark the weeks that follow the coral spawning are equivalent to being locked up in a sweetshop for a night.

Not surprisingly the North West Cape has become the world's prime destination for diving and snorkelling with these gentle giants. Spotter planes search for the telltale shadows and radio the boats below, which race into position ahead of the shark. After what may have been many hours of waiting, suddenly it's all action as you hurriedly don your kit. On the boat's rear platform they give the signal and you leap in, fins kicking hard, following the lead diver. As the bubbles clear a solitary grey silhouette looms out of the murk, its back speckled with white spots. With lazy sweeps of its tailfin, this oceanic behemoth glides gently by and for a couple of minutes, using your own fins, you do your best to keep up. This silent encounter with a shark longer than the boat you just jumped off should trigger alarm bells but strangely, as you swim alongside, you're mesmerized by its benign bulk until it dives effortlessly down into the abyss. You rise to the surface elated at having crossed paths with the biggest shark on the planet – and lived to tell the tale.

952 Paddling through Abel Tasman National Park

NEW ZEALAND Some people hike along the coast of Abel Tasman National Park, others cruise through its glassy waters, but by far the best way to explore New Zealand's smallest and most intimate national park is by sea kayak. The sheltering arm of Farewell Spit ensures the waters are seldom rough, so even inexperienced paddlers can head out for several days in relative safety.

Above all, this type of trip is about enjoying yourself at a relaxed tempo. Not only can you take to the shore at your own pace, but the kayak will carry all the wine, beer and tasty delicacies you'd want to bring along. A wide choice of golden beaches with designated camping spots are at your disposal for pit stops – spend the afternoon lazing on the sand, explore rock pools or take a dip. Pack a mask and snorkel and you'll be able to watch the shoals of fish weaving among the rocks and kelp beds.

One essential stop is the Tonga Island Marine Reserve, where the rocks come slathered with seals. These playful creatures have been known to come up to swimmers and cavort for a while before speeding off as fast as they arrived.

When you crave something a little more sophisticated than dinner cooked over a camp stove, wend your way up the delightful estuary of the Awaroa River, where a few lodges inhabit patches of private land. Stop in for a sandwich and an espresso or a beer on the deck; if you're feeling flush and hankering for white linen you can stay the night. A perfect finale to a glorious few days of relaxation.

953 A walk round Uluru

AUSTRALIA As you cruise westwards along the Lasseter Highway, you get your first glimpse of Uluru over cinnamon-red dunes while still 50km distant. Slowly the ochre-coloured monolith invades the empty horizon; it's hard to look at anything else. Then, just past the Uluru-Kata Tjuta National Park gates, you turn a bend, and suddenly it fills your field of vision. You simply have to stop and take a picture.

The Rock means different things to different people. To the Pitjanjarra people who've lived in its shadow for 20,000 years, "Uluru" is the name of a seasonal waterhole near the summit, formerly revealed only to initiates of the Mala wallaby clan during secret ceremonies. To them this iconic image of the Outback is no Mecca-like shrine, but a vital, resource-rich landmark at the intersection of various trails in the region. These "songlines" criss-cross the desert and any conspicuous natural features found along them were put into songs celebrating the "Dreaming" or Creation, to help memorize the way and so "learn the country".

To most tourists Uluru – or Ayers Rock (as it was named by explorer William Gosse in 1873 to honour his benefactor) – is still a climb to be conquered or a radiant landmark to be photographed en masse from the Sunset Viewing Area. But a far better way of getting into the spirit of the place is to take the 9km walk through waist-high grass around its base. Geologically the massif is a series of near-vertical strata inexplicably thrust up all around it. Looking rather like a weathered loaf of sliced bread, its grooves and cliffs vary with your perspective. Approaching the "slices" end-on reveals smooth gullies carved into the rock and feeding waterholes like Mutijulu Springs shaded by groves of casuarina oaks. A few kilometres further the steep flanks harbour caves and bizarre scalloped formations, some of them sacred sites fenced off from visitors: every bend in the track offers another startling profile. When you're back at the start of the circuit, hot and sticky from the sun, you can be satisfied that you've experienced the Rock and not merely stood on top of it.

954 A world away on the Landsborough River

NEW ZEALAND There's something about rafting South Island's Landsborough River that bends the mind. The water's crystal clarity reflects the light so the river becomes a luminous ribbon slicing through the mountains. It's pure, too: whenever you get thirsty you can simply dunk your cup in the ice cold water and drink it down.

Our trip began with a helicopter ride deep into New Zealand's Southern Alps. Glacier-laden mountains stood in stark relief against the blue sky. Unpacking the raft and supplies, the realization dawned that we were alone in the wilderness and civilization was three days away. The sun held sway for two days, igniting the river's intense turquoise colour, but the water was subject to changing moods. We tackled fuming rapids hungry to consume our meagre raft, followed by idyllic calm stretches where the forest loomed close and lofty mountains crowded the sky.

Each evening we set up camp beneath ancient beech trees swaying with moss and inhabited by curious native birds. A green silence settled over the forest as night fell, and we wandered beyond camp to where glow-worms pierced the darkness like earthbound stars, clustered in constellations amongst the dense undergrowth.

On our final day on the river, low storm clouds swallowed the mountaintops and a cold headwind bit through our wetsuits. The river rose to a muddy grey torrent and each paddle stroke took effort. We put our heads down and paddled into the wind, pitched in a silent battle against the elements.

It was with a mixture of relief and disappointment that we saw the waiting minibus come into view on shore. New Zealand's wilderness has a way of making you think the rest of the world no longer exists.

955 Going organic in the Northern Territory

AUSTRALIA It's 5am; dawn's mellifluous chorus of the early-waking birds propel me into consciousness even before the sun can wrap its (not so temperate) fingers around the eucalypts. The air, fresh with lemon and lime, wafts through the mosquito-net mesh that passes for the windows of my tin shack. Perfect timing – I can just about fit in a spot of breakfast before work.

Thus begins a typical day down on Wilderness Organic Farm, 50km north of Katherine in Australia's Outback, Northern Territory. Part of WWOOF (World-Wide Opportunities on Organic Farms), which was set up in 1971 and now has national organizations in 24 countries, this particular farm takes in willing workers for anything from a week to several months, providing them with a bed for the night and three meals a day (organic, of course) in exchange for five hours of daily work – anything from planting capsicum and

tomato seedlings, mulching lemon plants and harvesting mangoes to painting farm buildings, cooking and baking. Anything, basically, that might need doing in the daily life of a subtropical, Outback farm. And by "smoko", an archaic Aussie term for mid-morning tea break, you'll be glad you got the hard graft out of the way during the cooler part of the day, as temperatures soar to 40°C by 11am.

There's certainly never a dull moment when you're working and living with locals, migrant workers and backpackers from all over the world, swapping stories (and a few toasted marshmallows) around the campfire. Besides, work will be nothing but a distant memory by the time you've cooled off in the Edith River after lunch, eaten barbecued kangaroo with homebrewed mango wine for dinner, and been lulled to sleep by a symphony of cicadas under a star-puckered black canvas night.

956 Taking in the views on the Tongariro Crossing

NEW ZEALAND Alpine tundra, barren volcanic craters, steaming springs and iridescent lakes – the sheer diversity on the Tongariro Crossing makes it probably the best one-day tramp in the country. The wonderfully long views are unimpeded by the dense bush that crowds most New Zealand tracks, and from the highest point you can look out over almost half the North Island with the lonely peak of Mount Taranaki dominating the western horizon.

The 16km hike crosses one corner of the Tongariro National Park – wild and bleak country, encompassing the icy tops of nearby Mount Ruapehu, which is, at 2797m, the North Island's highest mountain. Catch the Crossing on a fine day and it is a hike of pure exhilaration. The steep slog up to the South Crater sorts out the genuinely fit from the aspirational, then just as the trail levels out, Mount Ngauruhoe (2291m) invites the keen for a two-hour side-trip up its scoria slopes. Ngauruhoe famously starred as Mount Doom in the *Lord of the Rings* films, and you can live out all your hobbit

fantasies as you look down its gently steaming crater. Getting back on track is a heart-pounding, hell-for-leather scree run back down the mountain – in just fifteen minutes you cover what took an hour and a half to ascend.

The gaping gashes and sizzling fissures around Red Crater make it a lively spot to tuck into your sandwiches and ponder the explosive genesis of this whole region. From here it is mostly downhill past Emerald Lake, its opaque waters a dramatic contrast to the shimmering surface of Blue Lake just ahead. With the knowledge that you've broken the back of the hike you can relax on the veranda of Ketetahi Hut gazing out over the tussock to glistening Lake Taupo in the distance. Rejuvenated, you pass the sulphurous Ketetahi Hot Springs on the final descent, down to the green forest and the welcome sight of your bus. Tired but elated you settle back in the seat dreaming of a good feed and the chance to relive the events of the day over a couple of beers.

NEW ZEALAND There's a knee-high, yellow-eyed penguin preening itself less than five metres away from me, and fifteen metres beyond him a sheep is grazing in lush meadows. It's an odd juxtaposition, probably one only to be found in New Zealand where, despite a lack of icebergs and glaciers, penguins abound. With two penguin species, a colony of seals and the world's only mainland royal albatross colony, the Otago Peninsula is a fantastic place for a day's wildlife watching.

At the Penguin Place viewing area, half a dozen of us huddle together in a strategically positioned hide covered with camouflage netting. As we walked over the hills we saw a couple of penguins slowly waddling up the beach returning home from their day's fishing, but it's only in the hides that we get to see them up close. Most of the four or five birds out this afternoon are just grooming and watching the world go by, but the setting feels so intimate that I could watch them for hours.

Dragging ourselves away, we head 10km up the road to Pilot's Beach where we wander among southern fur seals sprawled languidly along the shore. We'll be back here after dark to watch more penguins (little blues this time) toddle up the beach to their nesting holes in the bank.

On the hill above the beach, Taiaroa Head, we're guided into another hide, this one the converted remains of a WWII viewing tower. High on this grassy headland we can look out over a couple of dozen royal albatrosses – a truly majestic bird with up to a 3.5m wingspan. It's midsummer and their chicks are growing nicely, but still spend most of their time tucked under a parent's wing. With binoculars you can see their fluffy heads poking out, desperate to learn more about the big world out there. They'll get their chance soon enough and spend their lives circling the globe before returning here every two years to breed.

Spying on *penguins* and *albatrosses* along the

Otago Peninsula

958 A torchlight tour of Queensland's critters

AUSTRALIA If you're spending the night in rural Queensland, spotting nocturnal wildlife is as easy as picking up a powerful torch and pointing it at a tree. You have to know which kind of tree to choose, to some extent – but in favourite wildlife-watching areas such as the Daintree rainforest, Eungella National Park or Fraser Island, almost any tree will do.

Trees in flower or fruiting are a particularly good bet. Shine your spotlight into one of these and at least one pair of eyes may shine back at you. Possums and flying foxes are common in forested areas, and you may see sugar gliders – some of Queensland's smallest, cutest and most aerodynamic marsupials – feasting on eucalyptus sap or planing from tree to tree with limbs outstretched.

In grassy areas, a distant dark shape on the ground may turn out to be a pademelon or kangaroo. Some of these endearing herbivores are so accustomed to humans, and even to torch beams, that you can watch them at close quarters – only when truly alarmed will they break off their nibbling to bounce away to safety.

For one of Queensland's most sublime after-dark wildlife experiences, join a guided canoe trip on Lake Tinaroo, near Yungaburra, in the Atherton Tablelands. On a clear night, you'll be paddling under a dome of stars, the sound of cicadas filling your ears. Having crossed the smooth, dark water, you can trace your way along the rainforested banks where, if you're quiet, you'll spot bandicoots and brushtail possums. With a little luck, your torch beam may even pick out a Lumholtz's tree kangaroo. These rare creatures are climbers, not bouncers: perching in the rainforest canopy, they can easily be mistaken for monkeys, making them perhaps the most intriguing marsupials of all.

959 Scuba diving the wrecks at Poor Knights Islands

NEW ZEALAND Jacques Cousteau championed the Poor Knights Islands as one of the top ten dive sites in the world. And with their warm currents, crystal-clear visibility and a host of undersea attractions his judgement is understandable.

Dive boats spread themselves over fifty recognized dive sites that jointly cover New Zealand's most diverse range of sea life, including subtropical species such as Lord Howe coralfish and toadstool grouper, found nowhere else around the coast. Near-vertical rock faces drop 100m through a labyrinth of caves, fissures and rock arches teeming with rainbow-coloured fish, crabs, soft corals, kelp forests and shellfish. Blue, humpback, sei and minke whales also drop in from time to time, and dolphins are not uncommon.

A typical day might include an hour-long cruise out to the islands followed by a drift dive through a sandy-bottomed cave populated by stingrays and lit by shafts of sunlight. After lunch on board and perhaps some time paddling one of the boat's kayaks you'll head around the coast to a second dive spot, maybe working your way along a technicolor wall of soft corals and a few nudibranchs.

As if that weren't enough, the waters north and south of the reserve are home to two navy wrecks, both deliberately scuttled. The survey ship HMNZS *Tui* was sunk in 1999 to form an artificial reef, and proved so popular with divers and marine life that the obsolete frigate *Waikato* followed two years later. These form part of a Northland wreck trail which includes the remains of the Greenpeace flagship *Rainbow Warrior*, bombed by French government agents in 1985, just before it set out to campaign against French nuclear testing in the Pacific. Now colonized by new life it seems a fitting end to its quest to protect the ocean.

960 A far-flung flutter at the Birdsville Races

AUSTRALIA Come September, locals flee the dusty desert township of Birdsville, as a six-thousand-strong crowd descends for a weekend of hard drinking and, if they sober up for long enough to work out the odds, the chance to win a packet on the ponies running in the Birdsville Races. This is the archetypal, good-natured Aussie piss-up, in a bizarre Outback setting. The racegoers are a mix of young cowpokes making the most of their one opportunity of the year to whoop it up and meet folks they're not related to, and townies who have just driven 1400km from the coast on atrocious roads to get there. Even by Australian standards, that's a long way to go for a drink. Although you might see the odd fist-fight between drunken mates on account of the effort involved in reaching Birdsville, nobody has anything to prove by the time they arrive, and there's nothing left for it but to down a slab and party.

The Birdsville Races (officially known as the Birdsville Cup Carnival) kick off on Friday, though most people skip the trackside opening ceremonies in favour of spending the day easing themselves onto a liquid diet. After dark, the town fires up in fairground mode, with a host of sideshow attractions – whip-cracking competitions, guess my weight, arm wrestling, you name it – setting up along the main street. A huge, mainly male crowd materializes at the fundraising auction, impatiently watching all sorts of farm junk going under the hammer as they wait for the real attraction: the draw at the end to win a T-shirt off the back of a stripper.

Saturday is the day to hit the racetrack – a baking hot, shadeless stretch of dust and gravel 3km west of town. The races end mid-afternoon, when everyone retires for a wash-and-brush-up before heading back to town to celebrate – or drown their sorrows.

961 Sea kayaking around Shark Bay

AUSTRALIA The Peron Peninsula in Shark Bay, on the northwest coast of Western Australia, is well known for its regular dolphin visitations, and a beachside resort at Monkey Mia has grown around the spectacle. But there's much more to this UNESCO-listed reserve than meeting Flipper and the family, and the sheltered conditions make the Shark Bay area ideal for a sea kayaking adventure.

Paddling in a bay named after the ocean's deadliest predator may sound as sensible as skinny-dipping in Piranha Creek. Sure, there are tiger sharks out in the depths, but the abundant sea life means they're fed well enough not to bother you in the shallows. Besides the pleasures of gliding serenely across bottle-green waters and camping beneath paprika-red cliffs on whichever deserted beach

takes your fancy, marine-life spotting adds a "sea safari" element to your trip. Don't be surprised if before long a green turtle passes under your kayak, followed by rays the size of a tablecloth. And where there are rays there are usually sharks, but only frisky babies less than a metre long, maturing in the shallow nurseries before heading out to sea.

Battling the winds around Cape Peron there's a good chance you'll encounter dugongs grazing in the seagrass meadows, and as you cruise down the sheltered side of the peninsula flocks of cormorants, terns and pelicans will take to the air. Finally, if you've not seen any already, bottlenose dolphins are a guaranteed sight at Monkey Mia, which is also a great place for a day paddle.

962 Heading south for the winter in Queenstown

NEW ZEALAND Queenstown is definitely the place to savour the Southern Hemisphere winter. Always popular with Kiwis, the Southern Alps also draw Australians and addicts from north of the equator who can't get enough action in their own ski season.

As for the slopes, they're bald. None of your slaloming through trees here: this is all open vistas (and high winds when it blows). With more than 400 vertical metres of skiing and the longest pedigree of any Kiwi skifield, Coronet Peak is probably the more popular of the two fields. The Remarkables maxes out at 500 vertical metres and has its adherents, as much for the fine off-piste terrain as for the forgiving groomed slopes. For the freshest powder, you'll need to jump on a helicopter. Heli-skiing has a long

heritage in Queenstown and was first developed here in the 1970s. Today it offers a shortcut to over twenty 3000m-plus peaks ranging from remote razorback ridges to the majestic focal point of the Southern Alps, Mount Cook.

Back in town the après-ski is second to none. The restaurants are easily the match of those in Auckland and Wellington and the nightlife ranges from lively dance clubs to chic joints where you need to know the doorman to get in.

The season typically runs from early June into October, but the time to come is the last week of June for the Queenstown Winter Festival – a real riot with heaps of activities, crazy stunts and, of course, plenty of carousing.

963 Ocean to ocean, cape to cape: across Australia by 4WD

AUSTRALIA You're only going to do this once, so do it right. Driving from Cape Leveque, Western Australia, to Cape York on Queensland's northern tip is a two-month, 8000km odyssey so make sure you've packed your sense of adventure.

Broome, on the dazzling turquoise Indian Ocean, is a great place to start, right beside the pearly sands of Cable Beach. The journey kicks off with the suspension-mashing 700km Gibb River Road; starting near Derby, it cuts through the Kimberley region's untamed ranges, known as Australia's "Alaska". Along the way, turn-offs tempt you to idyllic waterfalls, like the Bell Creek Gorge where water rolls off a series of ledges into shallow inviting pools.

The Gibb finally spits you out at Kununurra township, where you can stock up on provisions and, hopefully, team up with another vehicle for the stretch ahead. Now comes the lonely 1500km all-desert stage into the Territory and down to Alice Springs, notable for the only traffic lights en route until Cairns.

Exploring Alice's hinterland and weaving among the majestic ghost gum trees along the shady Finke River track to Uluru (Ayers Rock) is an adventure in itself. Moving on from the Rock, scoot eastwards to the solitary Mount Dare homestead; fill up here and then head out across the dune fields of the Simpson Desert to join the pilgrimage to the legendarily remote *Birdsville Hotel*, Australia's best-known bush pub.

Have a drink, then head any which way northeast across Queensland's flat dusty interior. Finally, it's time to get ready for the 1000km creek-crossing climax of your journey: the "Trip to the Tip". Between you and the Pacific lies one of the most ecologically diverse habitats on the planet: creeper-draped rainforest teeming with tombstone anthills and day-glo snakes.

Watching the sunset over Cape York, your journey is complete; the red dust is now in your blood and what you've missed of the Australian Outback is a very short list indeed.

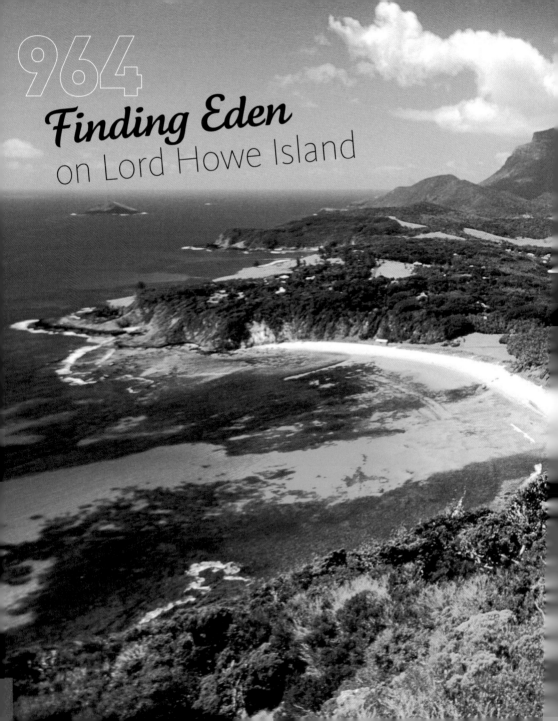

964

Finding Eden
on Lord Howe Island

AUSTRALIA From the summit of Mount Gower, Lord Howe Island lies before you – a Pacific paradise of swaying palms and turquoise lagoons that feels more Polynesian than Australian, despite being part of New South Wales. Wonderful as they are, the views don't come easy. The early botanists who first scaled the peak took several days to machete their way up to the 875m summit, and the route is now a strenuous guided walk. You'll understand why you need a guide when you see the track – an unlikely slice across a cliff face with nothing but air between you and rocks far below. Once you've clambered your way to the top you'll be pulsing with adrenalin though the thought of the return journey can make lunch up here a quiet, contemplative affair.

Many visitors are perfectly content to skip the tough ascent of Mount Gower in favour of snorkelling among the fish and sponges of the world's southernmost coral reef, or strolling along the island's Malabar Cliffs where red-tailed tropicbirds ride the thermals. Another nature show is on offer at Ned's Beach Marine Reserve. At low tide you can stand knee-deep amid a seething mass of metre-long king fish who come in to be fed each afternoon. For a closer look, grab a mask and fins from the beachside shack where you drop a few dollars in the honesty box – on this island everyone knows everyone's business and no one locks their car or even takes the key out of the ignition.

After a sundown beer overlooking the lagoon, everyone returns to Ned's Beach at dusk to watch ungainly muttonbirds crash out of the sky, land at your feet, then waddle off unconcerned to their burrow in the woods. It is a kind of innocence that chimes nicely on this slice of Aussie Eden.

965
DOUBLE-CROSSED in the **South Seas**

RAROTONGA The Cook Islands are not synonymous with hiking. Nor would you expect them to be; that's not why people make the journey to these South Sea idylls. But the cross-island walk in Rarotonga is well worth packing your boots for.

Most head out on a guided walk, not least because the trek is hard going. It certainly was for us; we just spotted the track on a map and set off ... from the finish line rather than the beginning. We noted the sign that read, "It is advised you start the cross-island walk from the other side", but encircling the island would take ages. This seemed the quickest way.

Before long the trail took us through tall, subtropical forest where tree roots had fashioned themselves into easy-to-climb stairs. It was like walking through a carved tunnel in an old cathedral. But soon we found ourselves scaling sheer slopes using any available tree root or liana for leverage. The vegetation got pricklier and sparser; still, we powered on and found our way to the top of the ridge, where the Needle, Te Rua Manga, stands. From here we could see the island's tallest peak as well as the golden beaches below and, in all directions, the infinite crystal sea.

Rather than continue cross-island, we doubled back – and soon found out why you're advised to head in this direction. For one, we finally saw the signposts on the trail. And two, the hike up to the ridge is much steeper the way we did it. Getting back to base proved a whole lot easier than coming up.

966 Kiwi-spotting in Trounson Kauri Park

NEW ZEALAND They're elusive creatures, these kiwi. In fact, New Zealand's national bird is so rare that it's almost never seen other than at the half-dozen places where guided night safaris raise the odds considerably. Heading out on foot, we hear the piercing cry of the male cutting through the inky darkness, closely followed by the husky female reply, but neither has yet seen fit to show its pointy face. The eeriness of the situation is enhanced by the vast walls of kauri trees that close in around us and the thick understorey of tree ferns which further block out the stars.

I can sense the kiwi are nearby, but these things can't be rushed. Not so long ago you'd have been lucky to hear them at all, as introduced stoats, rats, possums and feral cats and dogs had decimated numbers. But Trounson is one of several "mainland islands" where this diminutive relative of the ostrich is being brought back from the brink of extinction, with intensive trapping and poisoning keeping predator numbers low enough to allow indigenous species to flourish. And it's not just kiwi that benefit. Our guide introduces us to the ruru – a native owl known as the "morepork" for the sound of its haunting call – as well as the palm-sized, carnivorous kauri snail and the scary-looking, grasshopper-like weta, which can grow up to 10cm long. They're not dangerous, but no one wants to get too close.

Finally, a gentle scuffling in the leaf-litter comes closer and we get our first glimpse of a North Island brown kiwi, its slender beak probing the ground for food. Seemingly unconcerned by our presence, it wanders closer, its shaggy pelt looking more like fur than feathers. Then someone makes an unexpected move and the kiwi takes fright, skittering off into the darkness. Initial disappointment soon fades as another makes itself visible. That's it for the night, but even two sightings seem a rare privilege.

967 Four-wheeling through croc country: Cairns to Cape York

AUSTRALIA Most of us have little use for 4WDs, but in a particular corner of Australia these all-terrain machines can provide the sort of adventure they were truly built for. Cape York, Australia's northernmost point, is over 1000km from Cairns, with challenging driving that will demand all your concentration as you gingerly inch across tidal creeks inhabited by crocodiles.

From Cairns head out along the scenic Captain Cook Highway to Cooktown: the last settlement of any size on your "Trip to the Tip". Choose either the coastal route via Cape Tribulation, where Cook's *Endeavour* nearly sank in 1770, or, for a real adventure, the infamous "CREB Track" out of Daintree. Here's your chance to play with the transfer levers as you run along the CREB's tyre-clawing gradients to the *Lion's Den Hotel*, a classic "bush pub" dating back to 1875.

Past Cooktown the Lakefield National Park is Queensland's answer to Kakadu, with "magnetic" anthills aligned north–south to avoid overheating in the noonday sun, 180 species of birds and a rich colony of flying foxes.

But there's more. A tough, creek-ridden diversion leads east to the Iron Range National Park, where the creeper-festooned rainforests don't recede until Chilli Beach campsite on the Coral Sea. Ecologically this extraordinary park has more in common with New Guinea and is famed for the nocturnal green python and brilliant blue-and-red eclectus parrot.

Back on the main road die-hards avoid the newer bypasses to follow the Old Telegraph Track's numerous creek crossings. Eventually you arrive at Twin Falls, with its safe swimming holes, before reaching the 100m-wide Jardine River, a once demanding crossing now made easier by the nearby ferry. Then suddenly the road runs out near a rocky headland overlooking the Torres Straits. A sign marks the tip of mainland Australia and the end of your journey.

968 Heli-biking Ben Cruachan

NEW ZEALAND The helicopter drops you high on a mountaintop and swoops back down into the valley. Patches of snow lie on the ground, clouds hang low overhead and the air has a crisp, alpine bite. In every direction thrusting peaks stand in ranks around you, punctuated by fertile green valleys. Watching the helicopter diminish into a speck you take a deep gulp of alpine air before donning helmet, gloves and body armour. Pointing your front tyre downhill it's time to let gravity take care of the rest.

Ben Cruachan, a 2000m peak tucked behind the Remarkables, the mountain range that flanks the picturesque resort of Queenstown, is a favourite of many backcountry mountain bikers. It's no surprise why: it offers 1600 metres of pure downhill adrenalin. And that's after the rush of flying up to the top.

The trail follows a rough 4WD road down the ridgeline from the summit. Littered with loose shale, it demands both balance and patience to navigate. After a few kilometres the route veers left onto a vertiginious single track snaking 6km down a steep valley. The upper reaches of the track are fast and fun; further down, shallow streams cut across the trail and you need to concentrate hard to avoid flying over the handlebars when your tyres come to an abupt halt in a muddy bog .

Two hours after alighting on the mountain's summit, the crunch of gravel signals the final stretch into the Gibson wine valley. The race to the finish is on: a fast loose blast with the odd pothole and small jumps to negotiate. Once you've got your breath back you'll want to do it all over again, that or recover over a tasty Pinot Noir.

969 The last frontier: working on a cattle station

AUSTRALIA Director Baz Lurhmann did his best to make cattle droving look dramatic, even sexy, in the epic film *Australia*. But if you yearn to pull on your riding boots and start rounding them up like Hugh Jackman or Nicole Kidman you may be in for a reality check. Working on a real Kimberley cattle station is as tough as it gets: hot, sweaty, hard graft for long hours and low pay. You'll be sharing a bunkhouse and meals with rangy stockmen, and things like TV, telephones, the internet and even the radio are luxuries you'll have to learn to live without.

But when it's over and the aches have subsided, you'll look back with satisfaction. Instead of following the hordes along the usual backpacker trail you'll have participated in an iconic Australian activity. Apart from honing your riding skills, you'll learn how to brand a bull, build up plenty of muscle and experience life in the fabled "Nor'west".

The Kimberley is Australia's last frontier, a place where cattle stations run to a million acres and are on the margins of manageability. The rugged landscape and climate (which in turn floods then burns) make this some of the toughest cattle country on the planet. But eager hands are always sought so you'll be welcomed, particularly if you've an aptitude for working with horses or motorbikes. With a bit of luck you'll be part of the annual muster, when cattle are tracked down and driven in from the four corners of the property for transport to market. As well as horses, dirt- and quad bikes are used, all coordinated from above by helicopters equipped with radios, but you'll be just as useful on foot, coaxing the nervy beasts into mobile yards or triple-trailer roadtrains.

After working in a tight-knit team you may find it tough to leave at the end of your stay, and while the *Australia* fantasies may have faded you'll have plenty of real memories to savour.

970 Fresh breaks and fresh beans: surfing utopia at Raglan

NEW ZEALAND The laidback town of Raglan, about 150km southwest of Auckland, is beloved by in-the-know surfers for both its legendary left-handers and its bohemian vibe. Lines of perfect breakers appear like blue corduroy along the shore here, watched over by the majestic Mount Karioi or "Sleeping Lady".

For beginners, the best place to paddle out is sandy-bottomed Ngarunui Beach, 5km out of town. For seasoned surfers, the wildest rides are found at Manu Bay, around 8km from Raglan, which starred in the cult 1960s surf flick, *Endless Summer*. Manu's exposed point break provides one of the longest and most consistent waves on the planet and it regularly hosts pro surfing competitions. Ideally, it's best sampled at low tide when there are offshore, southeasterly winds, but you'll find it packed with grinning, wet-suited locals whatever the weather.

Once you've stashed your board and washed the salt from your hair, check out Raglan's artist-run galleries or its vibrant craft market, held twice a month. For a caffeine hit, follow the smell of freshly roasted beans to tiny *Raglan Roast*, squeezed next to a surf shop down tiny Volcome Lane. If your stomach begins to rumble grab some fish and chips down at the wharf or head to one of the cafés and pubs lining palm-shaded Bow Street. There's usually a band playing at one of them – don't miss local reggae legends Cornerstone Roots if they're in town.

If you find you can't drag yourself away from Raglan, check in at the *Solscape Eco Retreat* on Manu Bay. This sustainably run hostel offers accommodation in teepees and converted train carriages, provides its own solar water heating and lighting and, of course, rents boards and runs a surf school.

971 Dinner with the devil

AUSTRALIA Tasmania's Aborigines called them the "Nasty One" and colonial settlers thought them diabolical having heard their banshee shriek rip through the night. Even Warner Bros had it in for them, depicting the world's largest carnivorous marsupial as a whirlwind of fury and mischief. Considering such notoriety, it's ironic then that for most visitors the problem with the Tasmanian devil is spotting one. That's where Geoff King comes in.

A former cattle breeder turned evangelical conservationist, Geoff is the most committed devil-watcher you'll ever meet. A few times a fortnight, he feeds the Tasmanian devils that roam his 830-acre reserve near Arthur River on the island's gloriously untamed northwest coast. Devils need all the help they can get right now. Devil Facial Tumour Disease, a contagious cancer, nudged the species onto the Endangered list for the first time in 2008; not quite on the brink of extinction, perhaps, but close to the

edge. That it now affects over seventy percent of Tasmania makes disease-free refuges like Geoff's one of the last places to observe devils in the wild.

By nightfall, having watched wombats and wallabies, pademelons, blue-winged parrots and a quoll or two skitter away into the darkness, you hunker down in a shack on the foreshore. Night presses against the windows. Alone with the sound of the wind and waves, it feels at the edge of the world. Then a baby monitor radio on the mantelpiece gives a metallic cough and a pair of pink eyes set into a snout appear in the lamplight where the bait (roadkill found around the property) is staked outside. Dark shadows coalesce into the stocky shape of a devil, and jaws four times stronger than a pit bull tuck into a bonanza dinner. There's an audible crunch of bone from the speaker and to no one in particular Geoff murmurs affectionately: "Good boy."

Life beyond the beach
in Melanesia

FIJI For many people Fiji begins at the poolside bar and ends somewhere near the third sunlounger on the right. Yet the archipelago's largest island Viti Levu, or "Big Fiji", provides much more than tropical sun and coconut cocktails. Turn your focus inland and you'll find dramatic mountain scenery, exhilarating hikes and a fascinating tribal culture, all accessible by simply hiring a 4WD and hitting the dirt roads.

A few hours from Nadi, Fiji's tourism hub, the baking-hot sugarcane fields give way to the misty rainforest of the Nausori Highlands. Back in the 1860s, these mountains were inhabited by cannibal tribes; today, crater-sized potholes and the odd speeding truck are the main hazards to watch out for. Following the bone-shaking earth roads, and asking directions on the way, you will find the route to Navala, the most stunning village in Fiji. Looking like something out of a *King Kong* film set, all the homes here are *bures*, thickly thatched huts built with woven bamboo walls. Brightly coloured washing hangs between the huts and palm trees, the only traces of modernity supplied by the concrete church and school building. Given the setting, it's tempting to stay the night here and there's accommodation close by at *Bulou's Eco-Lodge*, a family-run homestay which offers en-suite *bures* as well as a small dorm.

Bulou's son Tui will introduce you to the village elders at Navala, and with luck you'll be invited to sup *kava*, Fiji's curious national drink, with the chief. Now accepted as a guest, it's up to you how you spend your time. With river trips on traditional *bilibili* rafts, jungle treks along ancient hunting trails or the ascent of Mount Tomanivi (Fiji's highest mountain at 1323m) on offer there's little chance of getting bored. Returning to *Bulou's*, the smell of home-cooked Fijian food will welcome you back and the lure of the beach resort will be far from your mind.

AUSTRALIA Canyoneering through Karijini National Park is an Indiana Jones-style adventure through a rarely seen world of towering red rock canyons, trickling waterfalls and hidden pools. Be prepared for half a day of walking then crawling, wading then swimming, climbing along ledges and up waterfalls and jumping into freezing pools. The trails are graded by how extreme the terrain gets. Classes 1–3 can be handled by most but 4–6 are where the excitement lies and should be tackled with a qualified guide.

One of the best is the "Class 4" Knox Gorge. Descending the steep track into the ravine you've little idea of what waits ahead. Paths and ledges peter out and you're forced to swim across a couple of pools until the walls narrow suddenly into a shoulder-wide slot that never sees sunlight. You enter the chasm, bridging over jammed boulders, deafened and disoriented by water running through your legs until it seems there is no way ahead. There is, but to continue you must hurtle blindly down the "do-or-die" Knox Slide into an unseen plunge pool below. Later, pumped with adrenalin and teeth chattering from the icy water, you look up to see tourists pointing and staring at you from a viewpoint, wondering how on Earth you got down there.

Canyoneering in Karijini

973

974 Exploring Waitomo's eerie underground world

NEW ZEALAND Waitomo, a tiny town in rolling sheep country, sits on a veritable Swiss cheese of limestone, with deep sinkholes, beautifully sculpted tunnels and wild organ pipes of stalactites all lit up by ghostly constellations of glow-worms. Their Harry Potter-esque scientific name is *Arachnocampa luminosa*, a reference to the almost magical bioluminescence they use to hunt and attract mates. More prosaically, you learn that they are not worms at all but the larvae of a humble insect, the fungus gnat. But the silk-like threads they produce to catch insects are nothing less than beautiful – hanging like fine gossamer from the stony roof.

Traditionally the way to see all this is on a gentle stroll through some of the shallower caverns where the Victorian explorers named the rock formations after animals, mythical creatures and household items. Coloured lights pick out the salient features before you take an otherworldly ride in a dinghy across an underground lake; the green pinpricks of light above your head resembling the heavens of some parallel universe.

Ever the adventure pioneers, New Zealand has also created another method of exploring the caves – blackwater rafting. Decked out in wetsuit, helmet and miner's lamp you head underground with a truck inner tube, then sit in it and float through the gloom (just remember not to watch *The Descent* beforehand). The few rapids are gentle and safe but the blackness gives that extra *frisson* of uncertainty. For an extra thrill you can try a hundred-metre-long abseil, waterfall jumps and even a little subterranean rock climbing. With small groups there's a genuine feeling of exploration as you negotiate tight squeezes and find your way into pristine chambers with that reassuring glow far up above.

975 River of no return: rafting the Franklin

AUSTRALIA Determine when you come and the river decides how long you'll stay. You're going to be soaked to the skin, cold and challenged by rapids with names like The Cauldron, Thunderush and Jawbreaker. And that's exactly why you're here.

The plan: you and nine others, including two all-knowing river guides, are to spend a week paddling, pinballing and peacefully drifting more than 100km through southwest Tasmania, one of the wildest and remotest parts of Australia. All the gear's provided: two inflatable rafts, camping equipment, wetsuits, helmets (to be worn at all times), waterproof-paddling jackets (unflatteringly called "cags") and, most importantly, lifejackets. The rest is up to the river.

Rafting the Franklin is one of the world's last true wilderness experiences, not least because the river has such a fearsome reputation. Its banks are so steep and its catchment so vast that any rain upstream (and it's plentiful in Tasmania) can cause river levels to rise 10m overnight, turning benign rapids into life-or-death obstacles for all but the most experienced river-travellers (that's where the guides come in); sometimes the team will even be forced to carry the fully laden rafts and gear along precarious, cliff-hugging tracks that skirt the most dangerous sections of river.

The good news is that no matter what the conditions – high water, low water or somewhere in between – you're in for the ride of your life. Most of the whitewater is Grade 3 and 4, but there are plenty of still and silent pools where you might spot a platypus or drift past stately 2000-year-old Huon pine trees.

It's humbling to spend days in such a place, travelling along the river by day and camping on its edges at night. And in losing track of time and the days of the week, you gain something else: that rare relief of being nobody of consequence in true wilderness.

976 Delivering the mail with dolphins

NEW ZEALAND The deep blue waters of Pelorus Sound are calm, the scenery along the sinuous waterways is wonderful and there's a fair chance of spying dolphins riding the boat's bow wave. But that's only part of the story. The real pleasure in riding the Pelorus Mail Boat is simply watching the day drift by as you chug between bush-clad hills around the waterways at the northern tip of the South Island.

There has been a mail service around the sounds since 1869, and while thirty-odd tourists a day help keep the business afloat, the *Pelorus Express* still has a vital role. Apart from the mail, it supplies a reassuring link to the outside world for this isolated group of small homesteads. It's a mixed bunch living here far from roads and shops – artists, retirees, entrepreneurs playing the stock market and even families whose kids receive their correspondence school papers by mail boat. The mail run is a much anticipated event and at most wharves skippers Nick and Val are greeted by at least one local. They always have a few minutes to stop and shoot the breeze and pass on local gossip. Dogs wait eagerly at wharf end awaiting a treat from Val's boxes of biscuits. There's often a little bartering: a few tomato seedlings from the garden centre back in town might be traded for a bag of oranges from a laden tree up by the homestead.

The waters of Pelorus Sound are also known for a gastronomic treat – the green-lipped mussel which grows here to epic proportions. Almost every bay has its mussel farm, and you'll usually spot a tender hauled up alongside while the deckhands winch up the ropes and slough off the juicy bivalves. When it is time for home, the passengers scan the water for those elusive dolphins while looking forward to a seafood feast back at the marina.

977 Learning the ancient art of bush medicine

AUSTRALIA In a country where a small spider can kill you it's reassuring to know Mother Nature has a softer side. Hidden in the prehistoric valleys of the Blue Mountains National Park in New South Wales are hundreds of plants used by Aboriginal peoples to cure everything from earache and fevers to snake bites and colds. The best chance you have of spotting them and learning about the art of bush medicine is to delve deep into the forest with an expert guide. Walking ancient hunting tracks used by indigenous peoples, far from the car parks and crowded viewpoints, you will discover a different side of this wonderful national park.

One of the first things you are struck by as you descend into the chiselled gorges of the park is the smell – an astringent mix of eucalyptus and tea tree, a result of the oils evaporating from these plants which also gives the air its blue haze. While you might think of tea-tree oil being used to zap the odd spot, Aboriginals used it widely, inhaling the infused oil to cure coughs and stuffing the raw leaves into cuts to prevent infection. Colonial settlers soon learnt about this miracle plant and tea-tree oil was even issued to Australian soldiers in WWII.

Descending further, the hum of cicadas gets louder and the air becomes humid as you enter the moss- and lichen-encrusted cloudforest. While you concentrate on the barely distinguishable path, your eagle-eyed guide will point out everything from bush pears, an ancient Aboriginal snack, to the aptly named headache vine, once crushed and rubbed directly into the skin to treat migraines. As the gradient steepens, you're glad of the guide ropes attached to the slippery stone walls. Nonetheless most people end up with an impromptu mud pack on their lower half before they reach the bottom of the creek. As the air grows warmer and your spirits start to flag, your ears will welcome the hiss of the nearby Wentworth Falls, signalling both the hike's end point and the prospect of an invigorating swim.

978 Waitangi: reliving the birth of a modern nation

NEW ZEALAND The birth of New Zealand as a modern country can be traced back to a small patch of landscaped grass just across the the Waitangi River from Paihia in the Bay of Islands. Here on February 6 1840, representatives of the British Crown and several dozen northern Maori chiefs met in a marquee to sign the Treaty of Waitangi. To this day it remains debatable whether the Maoris knew they were signing away their sovereignty, but sign they did, and the Treaty became not just New Zealand's founding document, but the cornerstone of the country's race relations to this day.

Arriving at the Treaty Grounds, you walk straight out onto that hallowed lawn with its views out over the Bay of Islands and its historic flagpole where Maori and British flags still fly. Inquisitive foreign visitors, and Kiwis in search of their heritage, gravitate towards the 1834 Treaty House, all neat white weatherboards and rooms containing material on the early colonial period.

When the Maoris arrived for the signing, most would have come by canoe – but few would have been as big as *Ngatoki Matawhaorua*, now in residence down by the shore. The world's largest wooden war canoe, it stretches more than 35m from prow to gloriously carved sternpost and took over two years to carve from a pair of massive kauri tree trunks. Eighty warriors are needed to paddle it during its annual outing on the anniversary of the signing of the treaty.

Lolling-tongue carved figures with iridescent seashell eyes greet you at *whare rununga*, or Maori meeting house, up beside the lawn – the only pan-tribal meeting house in the country.

For a deeper understanding of the *whare rununga*'s significance, return in the evening for the stirring Night Show. Through heartfelt dance, song and storytelling you'll get a primer in the richness of Maori legend and history, and learn a good deal about modern Maori life and how the treaty remains so essential to it.

979 What lies beneath: snorkelling at the Great Barrier Reef

AUSTRALIA "It's like being in another world!" may be the most predictable observation following a close encounter with the Great Barrier Reef, but it's only when you've come face to face with the extraordinary animals, shapes and colours here that you realize you've truly entered a watery parallel universe. And as a curious thick-lipped potato cod nudges your mask, you might also wonder, "who exactly is watching who?"

The Great Barrier Reef follows Australia's continental shelf from Lady Elliot Island, in southern Queensland, 2300km north to New Guinea. Its northern reaches are closer to land, so while it's 300km to the main body from Gladstone, Cairns is barely 50km distant, making this the best place for reef day-trips. Scuba diving may get you more quality time down below, but a well-chosen snorkelling location can reveal marvels no less superb without all the bother of training, equipment and lengthy safety procedures. Though commonly called the world's biggest life form, the Great Barrier Reef is more an intricate network of patch reefs than a single entity. All of it, however, was built by one animal: the tiny coral polyp which grows together to create modular colonies – corals. These in turn provide food, shelter and hunting grounds for a bewildering assortment of more mobile creatures.

Rays, moray eels and turtles glide effortlessly by, while fish so dazzling they clearly missed out on camouflage training dart between caves to nibble on coral branches, and slug-like nudibranchs sashay in the current. It all unfolds before you one breath at a time, a never-ending grand promenade of the life aquatic.

NEW ZEALAND After the thwump-thwump sound of the helicopter has receded down the glacier, I'm left standing in a beautiful white silence. With half a dozen others and a guide I've got the next couple of hours to explore the upper reaches of Franz Josef Glacier, one of a pair of blinding rivers of ice that cascade almost to sea level on the western side of the South Island's Southern Alps. In Maori legend these are Ka Riomata o Hinehukatere – "The Tears of the Avalanche Girl". The story goes that the beautiful Hinehukatere so loved the mountains that she encouraged her lover, Tawe, to climb alongside her. He fell to his death and Hinehukatere cried so copiously that her tears formed the glaciers.

The guide checks everyone has put on their crampons correctly, and, stout stick in hand, we set off slowly working our way through a labyrinth of seracs (ice towers) and crevasses. It is a bit of a shock to the system and initially nerve-wracking as I gaze down into the blue depths of the glacier with teetering blocks of ice looming above. But the guide seems to know what he's doing, continually assessing the changes on this fast-moving glacier. Most of the hikers have never been anywhere like this before so he charts a course that is safe but keeps us on our toes. Just as I am beginning to feel comfortable he ratchets up the exposure along a knife-edge ridge, just to make sure we're keeping our wits about us.

The ridge leads to a series of ice caves, features you couldn't hope to experience on hikes lower down the glacier. Deep blue and gently sculpted, they're wonderfully enticing, and the guide leads us through. A little scrambling, crouching and sliding against the slippery walls and we've made it. Feeling confident, a couple of us are keen for something more challenging, and we're shown a narrow hole that looks way too small to get through. Stripping off as much clothing as the temperature will allow we manage to worm our way into a glorious glowing grotto where we sit for a few minutes before struggling elated (and cold) back to the surface.

All too soon we hear the beat of the helicopter coming to whisk us back to town. Still, that means a steaming cup of hot chocolate is only fifteen minutes away – much needed after these dazzling few hours on the ice.

980 HELI-HIKING ON

Franz Josef Glacier

981 A walk through the woods in Waipoua Kauri Forest

NEW ZEALAND It may seem odd to drive for miles just to look at a bunch of old trees, but the kauri forests of New Zealand's North Island are special. To start with, the kauri trees are staggeringly, sensationally large. The tallest, Tane Mahuta (God of the Forest), towers some fifty metres above the earth; it's the same height as Nelson's Column in London's Trafalagar Square. Its long, straight trunk soars neck-achingly upwards, a smooth, brown cylinder unhindered by branches. Then, from near the top, spiky boughs spray outwards, covered in thousands of tiny, dark-green, oval leaves. The thin, gnarly branches look feeble compared to the massive trunk, and they betray the tree's age like the wrinkles etched onto an old man's face. But this tree is older than any man by far. It's reckoned to have started life some two thousand years ago; humans wouldn't even land here for another thousand years.

A walk through this protected sanctuary – European loggers and the gum trade greatly thinned the kauri ranks – takes you from Tane Mahuta to Te Matua Ngahere (Father of the Forest). This tree isn't as tall as Tane Mahuta, but it is phenomenally fat, more than sixteen metres wide. Personality oozes from every crack in its ancient bark. How many before you walked beneath its branches? Which now-extinct birds rested on its boughs? The tree replies with a far-distant rustle of leaves and continues its millennia-long watch.

982

Dodging PLANES on Fraser Island

AUSTRALIA Wipe the dust from your rear-view mirror and keep one juddering eyeball fixed on the sky behind you. At any moment a plane could drop down, flinging hot sand into your paintwork, and you'll be expected to give it enough space to land. On Fraser Island's 75 Mile Beach, you see, the highway doubles up as a runway – and pilots have priority. But nearly everywhere else on the world's largest sand island, you're better off in a 4WD.

Fraser Island is Australia at its most rugged and a tarmac-free zone. From the moment you roll off the ferry and begin trundling down the interior's steamy forest trails, you can expect to have your driving skills tested to the limit. As your tyres begin to slip into the powder-fine sand and the cabin begins to fill with the tangy smell of burnt clutch, you'll also need to look out for fallen trees, deep creeks and the resident population of hungry, pure-blood dingoes. It's not all slow and steady, though; when you hit the beach highway you can floor the accelerator, sending high-pitched tyre squeals through the rickety roll cage. The key to beach driving is to look out for treacherous patches of wet sand and remember not panic when you hear the "pop-pop-pop" of washed-up jellyfish being squashed under the wheels.

On a good day, it's possible to dash between multicoloured sand dunes, Aboriginal reserves and sparkling freshwater lakes in a single afternoon. But you won't see all of Fraser Island in a day, no matter how good your driving is, and that's why most visitors camp here overnight. So when you see a plane taking off, do give it plenty of room, but don't start to wish you were on board. After all, it's down here on the ground, with the dingoes and the dust, that you'll feel every jolt of the island.

983 Melbourne's street art revolution

AUSTRALIA Melbourne has always been a haven for serious culture buffs. But it would be wrong to mistake its seriousness for stuffiness. The Melbourne art scene, in particular, has a quirky, unfettered streak unrivalled by bigger, brasher Sydney. Book yourself onto a walking tour of the city's street art sites, and you can tap right into the wild side.

Melbourne's laneways – the alleyways off Flinders Lane and Little Bourke Street in the heart of the city – used to be places to dodge, not discover. Graffiti was a perennial problem. But in 2007, the city authorities hit on the idea of setting up a programme dubbed "Do Art Not Tags" to encourage licensed street art over mindless scrawling. Several laneway property owners went along with the scheme, and the result is an impressive array of vibrant murals, street sculptures and installations.

Hotspots such as Hosier Lane, Central Place, Caledonian Lane and Union Lane continue to evolve according to the whims of the city's now legitimate alternative artists. Facades, pavements, pipes and bins are daubed with everything from politically charged stencils to psychedelic graphics. It's easy enough to wander around the well-known sites under your own steam, but if you set out on a tour with an insider – such as an artist from the Blender Studios Collective – you'll be taken straight to the best of the recent additions while also hearing some of the back story.

The "Do Art" project has proved controversial, with hardcore creatives dismissing it as a sell-out, paving the way for property owners to start cashing in. Some of the artwork has even been vandalized, including a famous piece by British graffiti artist Banksy. But despite these undercurrents the alternative art movement continues to flourish. By ending your tour at Blender Studios, near the Queen Victoria Market, you'll have a chance to rub shoulders with some of the rising stars who are right at the heart of it.

984 Taking the plunge with AJ Hackett

NEW ZEALAND Ever since speed skiers and general daredevils AJ Hackett and Henry van Asch invented commercial bungee jumping, New Zealand has been its home, and Queenstown its capital. So if you're going to bungee what better place than here? And if it's the classic experience you're after, then the original Kawarau Suspension Bridge is your spot. At 43m it's only a modest jump by modern standards, but you're guaranteed an audience to will you on and then celebrate your achievement.

Diving off tall towers with vines tied around your ankles has been a male rite of passage in Vanuatu for centuries, but modern bungee started with the nutty antics of the Oxford University Dangerous Sports Club in the 1970s. The next leap forward was AJ Hackett's bungee off the Eiffel Tower in 1987. He was promptly arrested but soon started commercial operations in Queenstown.

So are you going solo or double? Dunking or dry? Shirt on or shirt off? Decisions made, you stroll out onto the bridge (looking oh so casual) while pumping rock or hip-hop starts building the adrenaline. Wrapping a towel around your ankles for protection, they'll attach the cord while feeding you some jocular spiel about the bungee breaking (it won't) or not being attached properly (it will be). You'll then be chivvied into producing a cheesy (or more likely rictus) grin for the camera before shuffling out onto the precipice for the countdown.

Three. Two. One. Bungee!

985 Slip into Broometime

AUSTRALIA The laid-back, romantic appeal of Broome stems partly from its uniqueness along the west Australian coastline. In many thousands of kilometres no other town matches its alluring combination of beautiful beaches, relative sophistication and a still resonant "frontier town" charm.

From its earliest days, Broome's had an ethnically diverse population: Timorese, Malays and Chinese came in their thousands to get rich quick when the pearl industry boomed here in the late 1800s. The world's largest oysters prospered in the tidal waters and shells were originally shovelled off the beach. With the invention of the diving helmet, Asian divers kept the supply going, but along with frequent cyclones the new-fangled technology caused many deaths, as a stroll around the town's different ethnic cemeteries reveals. Pearl farming continues today offshore, from securely guarded pontoons, and Broome remains the best place to buy these gems, particularly along Dampier Terrace.

The old Chinatown has been tastefully renovated, its once grubby tin-shack bordellos are now trendy boutiques, while a mile away the former master pearlers' bougainvillea-shrouded villas house galleries and coffee shops. Nearby, the 1916 Broome Picture House, the world's oldest open-air cinema, is still going strong. Bats flutter across the latest release on screen as you watch under starlight from communal canvas benches; the new air-con cinema round the corner just misses the point.

Nature has further blessed Broome with heavenly Cable Beach, 22km of palm-swaying indolence named after the telegraph cable that ran from here to Singapore. The classic vista from Gantheume Point lays red cliffs over ivory sands and a sea so hypnotically turquoise it should carry a health warning. Occasionally a watery illusion is created by the moon rising over the low-tide mudflats. Dubbed the "staircase to the moon", it sounds better than it looks, but you don't mind, you're on Broometime after all.

NEED to know

914 Connells Bay Sculpture Park offers tours by appointment only – contact ☎ www.connellsbay.co.nz.

915 See ☻ www.visit-palau.com for more details and links to diving operators.

916 You can pick up a map of the walkway from the Manly Visitor Centre (☻ www.manlyaustralia.com.au).

917 For full details on safety and dive experience needed see ☻ www.fijisharkdive.com.

918 For more information including yachting operators see ☻ www.northlandnz.com.

919 Platypus safaris in Eungella National Park are offered by ☻ www.reeforest.com.

920 For match schedules visit ☻ www.allblacks.com.

921 Sydney Gay and Lesbian Mardi Gras takes place mid-Feb to early March, see ☻ www.mardigras.org.au for full details.

922 Visit ☻ www.marlboroughtours.co.nz or ☻ www .winetoursbybike.co.nz for more information.

923 Purnululu National Park is open April–Dec, weather permitting. Helicopter flights are offered by ☻ www .slingair.com.au.

924 Queen Victoria Market is open Tues & Thurs–Sun, see ☻ www.qvm.com.au for further details.

925 If you can, try to get invited to a private hangi. Alternatively, Rotorua (www.rotoruanz.com) provides the widest range of commercial hangi nights.

926 If you want to stay in the park try ☻ www.daintree ecolodge.com.au or ☻ www.capetribbeach.com.au.

927 For more information, visit ☻ www.doc.govt .nz/parks-and-recreation; for guided hikes try ☻ www .ultimatehikes.co.nz.

928 One of the best Aboriginal art galleries in Alice Springs is run by the Central and Western Desert Art Movement; ☻ www.papunyatula.com.au.

929 The Musée Gauguin (☎ +689/57 10 58) is open daily 9am–5pm. Hiva Oa is one of the Marquesas Islands most easily reached by domestic flight on Air Tahiti (☻ www.airtahiti.aero).

930 The tourist board site (☻ www.vanuatu.travel) includes dive operators offering trips to the Coolidge.

931 See ☻ www.parks.tas.gov.au for details, including camping; and ☻ www.freycinetseacruises.com for whale-watching trips.

932 To stay on the island, try the *Nataiwatch* bungalows (☻ www.nataiwatch.com).

933 Te Papa (☻ www.tepapa.govt.nz) is open daily 10am–6pm and until 9pm on Thursday.

934 To get an early start on Mount Tambourine, book in at the cosy *Polish Place* (☻ www.polishplace.com.au).

935 Most resorts offer *kava* tasting sessions, but for a more authentic experience try a village tour with Adventure Fiji (☎ +672/2935).

936 For links to tour operators offering trips up Mount Yasur visit ☻ www.vanuatu.travel.

937 Allow 2.5 hours to enjoy the walk and take plenty of water. You can camp, lodge and eat at the *Kings Canyon Resort*, 10km past the canyon (☻ www.kings canyonresort.com.au).

938 Visit ☻ www.rotoruanz.com for more information.

939 *Samudra* –☻ www.samudra.com.au) offers full-board yoga and surf retreats. *The Byron* at Byron (☻ www.thebyronatbyron.com.au), a luxury lodge, offers complimentary daily yoga sessions and can arrange surfing lessons with local experts.

940 The best time to walk the Track is during February and March. See ☻ www.overlandtrack.com.au for

more information.

941 For more information, visit ☻ www.mcg.org.au.

942 Aussie Adventure Sailing (☻ whitsundays sailingadventures.com.au) offers outings on classic tall ships; Southern Cross (☻ www.soxsail.com.au) has tours on fast yachts.

943 You should be fit and have a head for heights to hike the Gillespie Pass in the Mount Aspiring National Park. For further information, contact the Makarora Visitor Centre (☻ www.doc.govt.nz).

944 ☻ www.environment.gov.au/parks/kakadu is a mine of information about the park.

945 Trips start from Te Anau or Manapouri in Fiordland National Park. Real Journeys (☻ www.realjourneys .co.nz) run excellent cruises.

946 For lessons, try Cheyne Horan School of Surf (☻ www.cheynehoran.com.au) or Australian Surfer (☻ www.australiansurfer.com).

947 The TranzAlpine (☻ www.tranzscenic.co.nz) operates daily from Christchurch to Greymouth and back, taking around 4hr 30min in each direction.

948 For ferry times, visit ☻ www.sydneyferries.info; for harbour bridge ascents, see ☻ www.bridgeclimb.com).

949 Trips are run by the Maori-owned Whale Watch Kaikoura (☻ www.whalewatch.co.nz); book in advance.

950 *The Ghan* (☻ www.gsr.com.au) leaves Adelaide for Darwin every Friday and Sunday at 5.15pm and takes 48 hours.

951 The best time to see whale sharks is between April and July. Licensed operators include Three Islands (☻ www.whalesharkdive.com) and Exmouth Diving Centre (☻ www.exmouthdiving.com.au).

952 Most people rent kayaks in Marahau, try ☻ www .oceanriver.co.nz or ☻ www.kahukayaks.co.nz.

953 For more information, visit ☻ www.environment .gov.au/parks/uluru.

954 Queenstown Rafting (☻ www.queenstownrafting .co.nz) offers multi-day guided trips down the Landsborough River; trips run from mid-Nov to end of March.

955 For more information, check out WWOOF's wesbite at ☻ www.wwoof.org.

956 The Tongariro Crossing typically takes 6–8hrs and requires a good level of fitness. See ☻ www.doc.govt.nz for updates on track conditions.

957 Although you can reach Otago easily under your own steam it's worth going on a tour – try ☻ www .elmwildlifetours.co.nz or ☻ www.wildearth.co.nz.

958 *Kingfisher Bay Resort* (☻ www.kingfisherbay.com) on Fraser Island offers night-time wildlife walks in the forest around the lodge. *On the Wallaby* (☻ www .onthewallaby.com), a budget lodge in Yungaburra, runs nocturnal canoe trips on Lake Tinaroo.

959 The Poor Knights Islands Marine Reserve is 25km off the east coast of Northland. For more information, visit ☻ www.diving.co.nz.

960 Check out ☻ www.birdsvilleraces.com for more information.

961 Visit ☻ www.sharkbay.org for more information.

962 Harris Mountains Heli-Ski (☻ www.heliski.co.nz) offer heli-skiing and heli-boarding around Queenstown, Wanaka and near Mount Cook. The season runs June–Oct.

963 For a long trip, you're best buying a 4WD bushcamper. Visit ☻ www.exploreoz.com for more advice on Outback four-wheeling.

964 Lord Howe Island (☻ www.lordhoweisland.info) is

a 1hr 50min flight from Syndey. The Mount Gower walk takes 8–10hrs.

965 Organized hikes can be arranged with Pa's Treks (☻ jillian@pasbungalows.co.ck). For more on the Cook Islands, see ☻ www.cookislands.travel.

966 Guided kiwi-spotting tours take place nightly, weather permitting, departing from the *Kauri Coast Top 10 Holiday Park* (☻ www.kauricoasttop10.co.nz).

967 You can rent a fully equipped 4WD bushcamper in Cairns: try ☻ www.apollocamper.com.au or www .britz.com.au; allow at least a fortnight for the return trip. Travel is only possible out of wet season from May to November.

968 Heli-biking trips up Ben Cruachan are run by Vertigo Bikes (☻ www.vertigobikes.co.nz) in Queenstown.

969 For more information on work opportunities, visit ☻ www.outback-australia-travel-secrets.com.

970 More information on Raglan (including surf cams) is available at ☻ www.raglan.net.nz. For details of *YHA Solscape Eco Retreat*, check out ☻ www.solscape.co.nz.

971 Eight-hour devil-watching tours (including dinner) at Geoff King's property can be booked through Kings Run Wildlife Tours (☻ www.kingsrun.com.au).

972 Four-wheel drives are available for hire at Nadi Airport. *Bulou's Eco-Lodge* is bookable through ☻ www .fijibure.com or direct on ☎ 679 628 1224.

973 West Oz Active (☻ www.westozactive.com.au) offers a range of tours into remote parts of Karijini.

974 Waitomo caving trips with glow-worm watching are run by ☻ www.absoluteadventure.co.nz and ☻ www.waitomo.com/black-water-rafting.aspx.

975 Rafting trips on the Franklin begin and end in Hobart, and guides are recommended: try ☻ www .franklinrivertasmania.com, ☻ www.raftingtasmania .com or ☻ www.tas-ex.com.

976 The Pelorus Mail Boat (☻ www.mail-boat.co.nz) runs from Havelock Tues, Thurs & Fri. There's a different route each day taking 7–9hrs. Bring your own lunch.

977 Blue Mountains bushwalks are offered year-round by River Deep Mountain High (☻ www.rdmh .com.au) based in Katoomba, Blue Mountains National Park.

978 The Waitangi Visitor Centre and Treaty House are open year-round (☻ www.waitangi.net.nz). You can book the Night Show through Culture North (☎ 09/402 5990).

979 For more information, visit ☻ www.greatbarrierreef .aus.net. For snorkel tours, try ☻ www.seastarcruises .com.au.

980 Franz Josef Glacier Guides (☻ www.franzjosef glacier.com) offers a range of guided hikes including heli-hiking.

981 Waipoua Kauri Forest is 50km north of Dargaville; Footprints Waipoua (☻ www.footprintswaipoua.co.nz) runs excellent walks to the kauri trees from Omapere.

982 Fraser Island is a 25–40min ferry ride from Hervey Bay, in the southern part of Queensland. Fraser Magic 4WD Hire (☻ www.fraser4wdhire.com.au), based in Hervey Bay, offers a range of self-drive options.

983 Melbourne Street Art Tours (☻ www.melbourne streettours.com) are run by artists from the Blender Studios Collective three afternoons a week.

984 AJ Hackett Bungy (☻ www.ajhackett.com) operate three bungee sites around Queenstown.

985 See ☻ www.broomevisitorcentre.com.au for more information.

GOOD to know

FIVE GREAT FILMS

Picnic at Hanging Rock (1975) Based on the mysterious disappearance of three schoolgirls at the titular Hanging Rock, this dream-like sensual film established the reputation of director Peter Weir.

Muriel's Wedding (1994) Set in fictional Porpoise Spit on the less fictional Gold Coast, Toni Collette made her big screen debut in this satire on the ghastlier side of suburban Australia.

Whale Rider (2002) This magical yet schmaltz-free story of a young girl defying her Maori elders became a global hit for New Zealand cinema.

The Proposition (2005) With a script by Aussie legend Nick Cave, this is as close as you'll get to a perfect Western, albeit one set in the red dust of the Outback.

Australia (2007) The stunning scenery of the Kimberley region of Western Australia was the real star of this hugely ambitious mix of wartime heroism and odd-couple romance.

WILD THINGS

crocs Australia's "Top End" is home to tens of thousands of saltwater crocodiles which despite their name can also live in freshwater – always pay attention to "no swimming" signs at creeks and rivers.

snakes Three quarters of the world's most venomous snakes can be found in Australia including the taipan, tiger snake and brown snake. Yet because so few people live in snake habitats the country has far fewer snake-bite incidents than India or Sri Lanka.

spiders if you're making a visit to an outdoor dunny (toilet), it's best to check under the seat: red back spiders (a relative of the notorious black widow) love these dark, musty places.

stingers Australia's tropical coastal waters attract stinging jellyfish between November and May. Always swim at patrolled beaches and wear a lycra stinger suit if they are available.

sharks There are shark attacks in Australia (around twenty in 2009) but these are still incredibly rare events when you consider the nation's love affair with the ocean and the presence of over 150 species of shark.

"A platypus is a duck designed by committee."

anon

LIVING THE DREAM

Aboriginal Dreamtime refers to a mythical age in the past when supernatural forces shaped the landscape of Australia. More than a creation story, Dreamtime also provides verbal maps of tribal territory and links natural features to the actions of Dreamtime ancestors, who often had both human and animal forms. These stories were often passed down in the form of drawings on the ground or on cave walls, or as dot paintings in the Central and Western deserts.

THE LONG WHITE CLOUD

In the Maori language New Zealand is known as Aotearoa, "the land of the long white cloud". This stems from the story of the hero Kupe who stumbled across the islands on his great voyage from Hawaiki, mythical homeland of the Polynesians. Having explored the coastline and battled a giant octopus he returned to Hawaiki and spread the news of his discovery. This led to the great migration of the Maori peoples in giant canoes or *waka* and the settlement of Aotearoa.

AUSSIE INVENTIONS

the boomerang – the most fun you can have with a wonky shaped bit of wood.

big things giant bananas, lobsters, sheep, you name it – an otherwise nondescript Australian town will have built one to put itself on the map.

the flat white – not a latte, not a cappuccino but somewhere in between.

plastic bank notes – almost impossible to forge and they'll even survive a spin cycle in your jeans.

sledging (cricket) – the dark art of insulting an opposing batsman.

Vegemite – sharp-tasting yeast-based spread, the great rival of British Marmite.

THE SPORTING YEAR

Both Australia and New Zealand grind to a halt during sporting events; if you can, try to see a Australia v New Zealand grudge match in either cricket or rugby. Better still, time your visit for the biennial Ashes cricket series between Australia and England.

Jan Australian Open Tennis, Melbourne (ⓦwww.australianopen.com)

Feb Rugby Union Super 14 season starts (ⓦwww.super14.com)

March Golden Sheers sheep shearing competition, New Zealand (ⓦwww.goldenshears.co.nz)

April World Surf Tour reaches New Zealand (ⓦwww.aspworldtour.com)

May Rugby League State of Origin matches begin (ⓦwww.nrl.com)

July Imparja Camel Racing Cup, Alice Springs (ⓦwww.camelcup.com.au)

August Isa Rodeo, Mount Isa, Queensland (ⓦwww.isarodeo.com.au)

Sept AFL (Aussie Rules) Grand Final, Melbourne (ⓦwww.afl.com.au)

Nov Melbourne Cup horse racing (ⓦwww.melbournecup.com)

Dec Sydney–Hobart Yacht Race (ⓦwww.rolexsydneyhobart.com)

"New Zealand is not a small country but a large village."

Peter Jackson

OCEANIA ODDITIES

•Fiji is the coup capital of the Pacific having had four abrupt changes of government since 1987.

•Three of the world's smallest countries are found in the South Pacific: Nauru (21 sq km) The Marshall Islands (180 sq km) and Palau (460 sq km).

•The traditional greeting in Tuvalu in the South Pacific is a face pressed to the cheek, and a deep sniff.

•The British Overseas Territory of Pitcairn Island, the last remnant of the British Empire in the Pacific, has just 67 residents.

•Rarotonga is the only country with a three-dollar bill.

BEHOLD THE NOTHERN LIGHTS • BEDDING DOWN IN AN IGLOO • WALKING ON THE ICE CAP • SNORKELLING WITH ORCAS • TREKKING ACROSS THE ARCTIC CIRCLE • SCRAMBLING UP OBSERVATION HILL • LIVING THE QUIET LIFE IN LOFOTEN • CHILLING OUT IN THE ICEHOTEL • HERDING REINDEER ACROSS THE TUNDRA OF LAPLAND • DIVING UNDER THE ICE IN RUSSIA'S WHITE SEA • THE ICE ROAD FROM INUVIK TO TUKTOYAKTUK • HUSKY DRIVING ALONG THE RUSSIAN BORDER • SPOTTING SEALS AND SKUAS • STUMBLING UPON A POLAR OASIS • VOYAGING INTO THE UNKNOWN • BEHOLD THE NOTHERN LIGHTS • BEDDING DOWN IN AN IGLOO • WALKING ON THE ICE CAP • SNORKELLING WITH ORCAS • TREKKING ACROSS THE ARCTIC CIRCLE • SCRAMBLING UP OBSERVATION HILL • LIVING THE QUIET LIFE IN LOFOTEN • CHILLING OUT IN THE ICEHOTEL • HERDING REINDEER ACROSS THE TUNDRA OF LAPLAND • DIVING UNDER THE ICE IN RUSSIA'S WHITE SEA • THE ICE ROAD FROM INUVIK TO TUKTOYAKTUK • HUSKY DRIVING ALONG THE RUSSIAN BORDER • SPOTTING SEALS AND SKUAS • STUMBLING UPON A POLAR OASIS • VOYAGING INTO THE UNKNOWN • BEHOLD THE NOTHERN LIGHTS • BEDDING DOWN IN AN IGLOO • WALKING ON THE ICE CAP • SNORKELLING WITH ORCAS • TREKKING ACROSS THE ARCTIC CIRCLE • SCRAMBLING UP OBSERVATION HILL • LIVING THE QUIET LIFE IN LOFOTEN • CHILLING OUT IN THE ICEHOTEL • HERDING REINDEER ACROSS THE TUNDRA OF LAPLAND • DIVING UNDER THE ICE IN RUSSIA'S WHITE SEA • THE ICE ROAD FROM INUVIK TO TUKTOYAKTUK • HUSKY DRIVING ALONG THE RUSSIAN BORDER • SPOTTING SEALS AND SKUAS • STUMBLING UPON A POLAR OASIS • VOYAGING INTO THE UNKNOWN • BEHOLD THE NOTHERN LIGHTS • BEDDING DOWN IN AN IGLOO • WALKING ON THE ICE CAP • SNORKELLING WITH ORCAS • TREKKING ACROSS THE ARCTIC CIRCLE • SCRAMBLING UP OBSERVATION HILL • LIVING THE QUIET LIFE IN LOFOTEN • CHILLING OUT IN THE ICEHOTEL • HERDING REINDEER ACROSS THE TUNDRA OF LAPLAND • DIVING UNDER THE ICE IN RUSSIA'S WHITE SEA • THE ICE ROAD FROM INUVIK TO TUKTOYAKTUK • HUSKY DRIVING ALONG THE RUSSIAN BORDER • SPOTTING SEALS AND SKUAS • STUMBLING UPON A POLAR OASIS • VOYAGING INTO THE UNKNOWN • BEHOLD THE NOTHERN LIGHTS • BEDDING DOWN IN AN IGLOO • WALKING ON THE ICE CAP • SNORKELLING WITH ORCAS • TREKKING ACROSS THE ARCTIC CIRCLE • SCRAMBLING UP OBSERVATION HILL • LIVING THE QUIET LIFE IN LOFOTEN • CHILLING OUT IN THE ICEHOTEL • HERDING REINDEER ACROSS THE TUNDRA OF LAPLAND • DIVING UNDER THE ICE IN RUSSIA'S WHITE SEA • THE ICE ROAD FROM INUVIK TO TUKTOYAKTUK • HUSKY DRIVING ALONG

The Polar Regions
986–1000

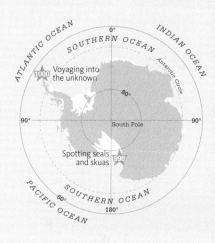

986 Behold the northern lights

SWEDEN They appear as shimmering arcs and waves of light, often blue or green in colour, which seem to sweep their way across the dark skies. During the darkest months of the year, the northern lights, or aurora borealis, are visible in the night sky all across northern Sweden. Until you see the light displays yourself, it's hard to describe the spectacle in mere words – try to imagine, though, someone waving a fantastically coloured curtain through the air and you've pretty much got the idea.

What makes the northern lights so elusive is that it's impossible to predict when they're going to make an appearance. The displays are caused by solar wind, or streams of particles charged by the sun, hitting the Earth's atmosphere. Different elements produce different colours, blue for nitrogen, for example, and yellow-green for oxygen.

The best place to view these mystical performances is north of the Arctic Circle, where temperatures are well below freezing and the sky is often at its clearest – two conditions that are believed to produce some of the most spectacular sightings.

For the quintessential northern lights experience, pack a couple of open sandwiches topped with smoked reindeer meat and a thermos of hot coffee to keep out the chill, then take a snow-scooter tour deep into the forests of Lapland – Kiruna, Sweden's northernmost city, is the best base. Park up beside a frozen lake and train your eyes on the sky. Try this between mid-December and mid-January, when there's 24-hour darkness north of the Arctic Circle, and the chances are you won't have to wait too long for your celestial fix.

987 Bedding down in an igloo

CANADA Tucked away between rolling hills and vast stretches of tundra in northern Quebec lies a series of igloos. These domed shelters were built by sealskin-clad Inuit elders, who carved snowblocks from windswept snowdrifts, using home-made snow knives and skills passed on from their ancestors. Igloos have long played a vital role in the lives of Inuit across northern Canada, where generations have gathered to share food, sing, dance and socialize while seeking refuge from the unforgiving elements of the Arctic winter. Today, igloos continue to safeguard hunters and have become the latest trend for adventure seekers.

To enter an igloo, you crawl through a narrow tunnel leading to the large domed enclosure. Sunlight, streaming in from a window fashioned from a block of clear river ice, fills the room to reveal a raised sleeping platform of snow, covered with willow mats and

caribou skins, which occupies the back half of the structure. Here, you sit back, remove your heavy parka and take it all in. Children giggle and play with a husky pup, while an elderly woman tends to the flame of her *qulliq*, a crescent-shaped lantern carved from soapstone and fuelled by seal blubber. A short while later you join the others around a plastic bag placed on the igloo floor where dinner is served. On the menu tonight: caribou stew and frozen Arctic char, eaten raw and considered a delicacy in this icy corner of the world.

After dinner and a round of cards you lie back in your sleeping bag and stare up at the spiralling blocks of snow while listening to muffled laughter and chatter from the elders. Within minutes the sounds of the kids throat-singing and the gentle flicker of the burning *qulliq* lull you to sleep.

988 Walking on the ice cap

GREENLAND Now get your head round this: the Greenland ice cap (also called the inland ice) is 2400km long – that's to say, it's the length of the journey from Greenland's east coast to London. It contains 2.85 million cubic km of ice (more than a billion Olympic swimming pools to you and me); if the whole lot were to melt most of the world's coastal cities would vanish under water, and several island nations would be wiped out. It covers a land area more than three times the size of France; and the oldest bits of ice are a staggering 250,000 years old.

The super-hardy like to ski from one side to the other, but for the rest of us, a simple summer stroll out onto the ice will do, for the ice cap is astonishingly accessible. Its edge lies just a 25km drive from Greenland's international airport at Kangerlussuaq. And there's a road that leads right there.

You leave the huddle of squat buildings that makes up Kangerlussuaq and drive out through spectacular rolling tundra. Small groups of musk oxen, with their stooped posture and strangely cute upturned horns, stand a short distance away and stare; occasionally a reindeer grazes, or an Arctic fox trots out in search of smaller fare. Then, rounding a bend in the road, you see it: a cliff of bluish-white ice in the distance soaring ever upwards. Drawing closer, you discern its spiralling peaks and diving crevasses, and the streaks of grey that smear the surface. And then you're there, walking out over this rugged, frozen mass of ice. There's no easy trail – the ice cap rolls and dips like an Alpine landscape in miniature and you must pick your own path. And if a comfy bed doesn't matter to you, pitch your tent on the edge of the inland ice, and wake in the morning to the thunderous calving of glaciers.

989 Snorkelling with orcas

NORWAY As you slide quietly over the side of the boat and put your face in the freezing water, it's hard to breathe – not just because your teeth are chattering, but also because there, below you in the blue, are six or seven killer whales that seem as curious about you as you are about them.

Tell your friends you're going snorkelling with "killer whales" north of the Arctic Circle in winter and they're likely to think you're a few minnows short of a school. But though orcas, as they're more properly known, have been known to eat prey larger than humans – including seals, dolphins, sharks, and even other whales – the ones in northern Norway mainly eat fish.

Prime orca-viewing time is October to January, when migrating shoals of herring lure 600–700 orcas to Tysfjord in northern Norway. You might even have a chance to see them feed. Norway's orcas have perfected a fishing technique called "carousel feeding": they herd the unsuspecting herring into a tight ball using air bubbles as a net, slap the ball with their tails to stun ten to fifteen fish at a time, then scoff them one by one.

Sure it's cold (winter water temperatures hover around 4°C) but there's plenty of gear to keep you warm: dry suit, warm inner suit, mask, snorkel, gloves and booties. And yes, you might feel a tad vulnerable drifting on the surface of the North Atlantic surrounded by a bunch of five-tonne marine mammals, a small rubber dinghy your only back-up. But all that's forgotten as soon as you spot a dorsal fin breaking the surface – and you realize you didn't just become dinner.

990 Trekking across the Arctic Circle

CANADA Bouncing along in a wooden *kamotik*, a traditional Inuit sled pulled by a snowmobile, you might have serious doubts as you think of what lies ahead: polar bears, hypothermia, avalanches and blizzards. You may question your sanity about trekking all the way to the Arctic Circle Marker in Auyuittuq National Park on Baffin Island. But in the end, you won't regret it for a moment.

Home to ten-thousand-year-old glaciers, towering granite mountains and awesome icy landscapes, Auyuittuq (pronounced "I-you-we-took") is an extraordinary place to explore on foot. Most visitors come during the summer to trek 97km through the scenic Akshayuk Pass, a corridor used by Inuit for thousands of years.

The guide drops you on the frozen shores at the Overlord Warden Station, the southern gateway to the park. Dwarfed by rugged snow-covered mountains, you are left alone to battle the elements. Within minutes the loud drone of the snowmobile disappears. Adrenaline pumping, you begin the 15km trek to the Arctic Circle, along the glacier-scoured terrain of the Weasel River Valley.

Guided by *inuksuit*, stone markers built by Inuit to navigate the land, you cross the turquoise-blue ice of braided streams, along the base of sheer cliffs a kilometre high and over boulders of every shape and size conceivable. Nearly five hours after starting out, you'll catch the first glimpse of the holy grail in the distance atop a gravel bed: a lonely *inukshuk* bearing a simple sign with the words "Arctic Circle" written in English, French and Inuktitut. Without fanfare or a welcome party you have reached your destination. A few moments surrounded by the great Arctic stillness is all the reward you'll need.

991 Scrambling up Observation Hill

ANTARCTICA Ice-locked into the France-sized Ross Ice Shelf lies Ross Island, a primary base for the British expeditions to Antarctica of a century ago. Many reminders of their efforts remain, including a stirring monument at the summit of the 230m Observation Hill, or "Ob Hill", so named because it was used as a lookout for ships returning to the ice; today station residents climb it for a view of their utterly alien, white surroundings.

The first third of the extinct volcano consists of loose scree, which must be scrambled up until you reach a road that winds partially around the hill to a decommissioned nuclear power plant. Here, most climbers turn to look for the first time at their temporary home – much like a new Manhattanite walks to the middle of the Brooklyn Bridge before gazing back at the city's towers. McMurdo Station, America's chief Antarctic research facility, looks like a small mining town from this vantage point, with curls of steam puffing from each building.

Ob Hill's next two thirds must be bounded up, billy-goat-style, over large, haphazardly strewn rocks. About 75m from the top a small, boulder-topped peninsula flattens out in front of the climber, offering the chance to take a breather and peer out at the frozen McMurdo Sound and, further off to the left, the imposing Royal Society mountain range. To the right looms the smoking cone of Mount Erebus, the world's southernmost active volcano.

Not until you nearly reach the top do you see the solid wooden cross which stands as a memorial to Captain Scott and his men. The stout cross is inscribed with a line from Tennyson's *Ulysses*, which serves as a sobering reminder of the sacrifices made so climbers can stand here today: "To strive, to seek, to find, and not to yield".

992 Living the quiet life in Lofoten

NORWAY Draped across the turbulent waters of the Norwegian Sea, far above the Arctic Circle, Norway's Lofoten Islands are, by any standard, staggeringly beautiful.

In a largely tamed and heavily populated continent, the Lofoten are a rare wilderness outpost, an untrammelled landscape of rearing mountains, deep fjords, squawking seabird colonies and long, surf-swept beaches. This was never a land for the faint-hearted, but, since Viking times, a few hundred islanders have always managed to hang on here, eking out a tough existence from the thin soils and cod-rich waters. Many emigrated – and those who stayed came to think they were unlucky: unlucky with the price of the fish on which they were dependent, unlucky to be so isolated and unlucky when the storms rolled in to lash their tiny villages.

Then Norway found tourism. The first boatloads turned out to be English missionaries bent on saving souls, but subsequent contacts proved more financially rewarding. Even better, the Norwegians found oil in the 1960s, lots and lots of oil, quite enough to extend the road network to the smallest village – the end of rural isolation at a stroke. The islands' villages have benefited from this road-building bonanza and yet kept their erstwhile charm, from the remote Å i Lofoten in the south through to the beguiling headland hamlet of Henningsvaer, extravagantly picturesque Nusfjord and solitary Stamsund.

Today, the Lofoten have their own relaxed pace and, for somewhere so far north, the weather can be exceptionally mild: you can spend summer days sunbathing on the rocks or hiking around the superb coastline. When it rains, as it does frequently, life focuses on the *rorbuer* (fishermen's huts), where freshly caught fish are cooked over wood-burning stoves, tales are told and time gently wasted. If that sounds contrived, in a sense it is – the way of life here is to some extent preserved for the tourists. But it's rare to find anyone who isn't less than enthralled by it all.

993 Chilling out in the Icehotel

SWEDEN The *Icehotel* is the only upmarket establishment in the world where you're guaranteed a frosty reception. Every October, huge chunks of crystal-clear ice are cut from Sweden's River Torne and pieced together, jigsaw style, in the village of Jukkasjärvi, on the river's northern bank. From December through to late spring, when the ice melts back into the river, the designer igloo opens its frozen doors to intrepid visitors, who travel deep inside the Swedish Arctic Circle for a night in this exceptionally cool hotel.

Pretty much everything in the entire complex, from the sculpted beds to the hotel's own chapel, is made out of ice; even the lights – intricately carved chandeliers – were once flowing water. While the overall effect is undoubtedly stunning, such sub-zero surroundings are hardly conducive to kicking back and relaxing, and there are plenty of (expensive) activities to keep your circulation going.

By day, you can scoot off across the powder behind a pack of exuberant huskies, with only the sound of your sledge's runners gliding through the soft snow for company. By night, you can hop on your own snowmobile and head out into the inky blackness in search of the northern lights, their technicolour brushstrokes delivered with an artist's flick across the pristine sky.

Back at the hotel, there's just enough time to hit the *Absolut Bar* for a zingy Wolf's Paw cocktail, served in glasses carved – you guessed it – out of ice, before turning in for the night. With room temperatures hovering at a balmy -5°C, the interior designers have wisely gone for reindeer pelts and expedition-strength sleeping bags instead of crisp linen and home-brand hand lotions. You won't get a wink of sleep, of course, but then if it's a cosy night's kip you're after you've definitely come to the wrong place.

994 Herding reindeer across the tundra of Lapland

FINLAND Ask most people to free associate with "reindeer", and you're likely to get "Christmas", "Santa" or "Rudolph" in response. But for Finland's nomadic Sámi people, the reindeer has been a fundamental figure in their existence for centuries. The Sámi eat and sell reindeer meat, use the skin and fur for clothing and blankets, and fashion their antlers into handicrafts and housewares. Semi-wild, reindeer are free to roam in large herding districts, easily outnumbering Lapland's human population. Each spring, Finland's 700 remaining Sámi herdsmen help thousands of these handsome beasts make their 200km migration from Finnish Lapland's central woodlands towards the mountainous regions of the northwest. Sign up to assist them, and you'll be in for an unforgettable adventure.

Each morning, you'll venture out by ski, sledge or *kelka* (snowmobile), racing through sun-dappled forests of birch and fir towards the fells, their trees marooned with snowdrifts the size of large igloos, fox tracks trailing off in the whiteness. Dressed to the hilt in warm clothes – it's cold 400km north of the Arctic Circle – you'll be working hard throughout the day, herding, counting, labelling, feeding, petting and listening to the distinctive low bellowing of reindeer hungry for dinner. Come evening, as the sun sets, kick back for a brief moment and relax as your Sámi driver speeds you onwards towards a local wilderness cabin for warm coffee – even by Scandinavian standards the Sámi drink a vast amount – and an evening meal of thick slabs of skillet-grilled reindeer sausage.

Though it's often the reindeer themselves who decide exactly where you'll end up each evening, herders and their apprentices can pitch the traditional Sámi *katas* (tents) anywhere. Once your bed is made, there's little to do besides huddle around a fire, share stories and gaze up at the sky as it morphs from deep amber to midnight blue to black, then settle in for a crisp, cold night of Arctic silence.

995 Diving under the ice in Russia's White Sea

RUSSIA How to go ice diving? 1. Fly to Moscow. 2. Board a 28-hour train north to Chupa, a polar station in the northernmost stretches of the European continent. 3. Head out by Chinese jeep to Polar Circle Lodge in the remote wilderness of northern Russia. 4. Zoom from the lodge out over the frozen White Sea by snowmobile. 5. Saw through the 1.5m-thick ice. 6. Jump in.

Russia's far north is a landscape of wonder and wandering once the colder months settle in and the unforgiving landscape freezes over, and ice diving in the White Sea – an open body of water that freezes over completely in the wintertime – is probably the most memorable time you'll ever spend under water. Although the winter air temperature in the Arctic can drop to an extremity-shrivelling −25°C, the water in the sea is thankfully a bit balmier: just below 0°C at ice level and only a few degrees colder towards the bottom.

With base layers, undersuit and dry suit on, the only part of your body to get cold will be your face, but make no mistake: it will be numb within seconds. Connected to the world above via a single safety rope, use your underwater torch to follow your guide down past ice hummocks, rifts, cavities and caves, minnowing under tall arches and vertical rocks overgrown with sea anemones and sponges. Underwater rocks abruptly disappear into the pitch-black depths of some of the sea's deepest parts, while kelp sways gently atop kelp gardens and sea urchins flutter about. In some parts you'll even come upon parts of shipwrecked fishing and patrol boats, while up above – visibility can reach a crystal-clear 50m – the masses of surface ice will appear as glowing green castles bobbing atop the air bubbles. After you surface, let yourself be guided along the frozen land by the glimmering northern lights above as you retire to a Soviet-era cottage for some real Russian hospitality, comradeship and – if you're lucky – a sauna in the buff.

996 The ice road from Inuvik to Tuktoyaktuk

CANADA Tuktoyaktuk is an Inuit community on the shores of the Beaufort Sea. In the summer, its thousand inhabitants can access the outside world only by air or water. During the dark Arctic winter, though, one aspect of life is easier for the people of Tuk. They can drive to their nearest town, Inuvik in Canada's Northwest Territories, on the 194km ice road that's carved into the surface of the Mackenzie River, and across the frozen ocean itself – and visitors can rent a jeep to visit them.

"You've gotta go slow", the manager of the car-rental firm advises first-timers. "Remember, it's all white out there". The cautious visitor chugs tentatively onto the ice. The road is wide, smooth and gleams like a figure-skating rink. Its route weaves with the meanderings of this waterway that has featured in the writings of explorers such as Mackenzie, Franklin and Stefansson.

Early in the journey, spindly trees poke out from the land to either side of the river's banks. Then the tree line is passed and they vanish. It's utterly silent – just the occasional thrum of a passing car resonates through the still air – but it's not entirely white. As your eye adjusts to the surroundings you'll pick out the buttery yellow of low sunlight on ice; the inky-blue shadows thrown by mounds of snow; the pink tinge in the sky as the weak sun dips. It's not all flat, either. Pingos – mounds of earth pushed up by frozen water trapped beneath the permafrost – loom like giant molehills and, as the road leaves the river and strikes out across the ice of the Beaufort Sea, the landscape is detailed in tiny, icy peaks and troughs, coloured palest violet and washed-out denim blue.

At last, the lone driver sees dark specks on the horizon: this is the settlement of Tuk, but even though it's visible to the eye, the traveller still has some way to go. This is a vast canvas and perspective has been sucked away into the white, icy air at the very top of the world.

FINLAND Outside in the frosty whiteness of the Arctic your team of three dozen harnessed huskies – gleaming in the late afternoon sunlight with their piercing blue eyes and sleek coats of fur – is busy howling, yelping, snarling and barking. The campfire lunch over, you're off again, thrashing through a magical northern scenery of Boreal taiga forest and swamp, then speeding across frozen lakes and fells. The only sound to break the eerie silence of the North is the *swish swish* of the sled's runners breaking the clumps of snow, and the howls and pants of excitement emanating from the front of the pack.

Driving a sled of huskies – four-paw-drive – is probably the best way to experience the sights, sounds and smells of the Arctic winter. Venturing out some 40km each day, you'll traverse the deep woods that run to the Russian and Norwegian borders, where tall pines drip blankets of snow onto trails that glisten a brilliant, blinding white. You'll be at the helm of your own dog sled, and though a guide will give tips on how to drive and tend to the dogs, it's up to you to learn how to work as a team. Come evening, you'll be taming, harnessing, rigging, feeding, watering and prepping the pack for the following day's mush; these friends and companions need to be shown who is boss and should be treated, in the words of one husky trainer, "as you would a hyperactive 5-year-old".

After a day's sledding, there's time for sauna and dinner at a wilderness lodge in a traditional lakeside Finnish log cabin, but it's then early to bed and early to rise; by day, concentration, alertness and peripheral vision is key. Still, it'll pay off: one thing that's nearly guaranteed is a unique wind-in-your-face exhilaration just about every moment you're out in the snow.

Husky driving along the Russian border

997

998 Spotting seals and skuas

ANTARCTICA On arrival, you're struck by the pristine desolation: everywhere, as far as you can see, is pure white. There are no trees, no plants, no smells and very little movement of any kind, save for the blowing snow. But the continent is not just one "big dead place", as it has been described – rather it's populated by all sorts of unique beasties, from seals to skuas. You just have to know where – and when – to look.

At the American McMurdo Station, on Ross Island, you'll occasionally spot short, fat Adélie penguins waddling in a self-important huff through town, looking like nattily attired, curious tourists. But the best place to spot them is out on the white, flat, endless expanse of sea ice where you'll see one rushing headlong, like the White Rabbit in Alice's *Adventures in Wonderland*, toward some very important date for which they are, invariably, late. The resident seals – fat, grey, impassive yet graceful – laze about in threes or fours out on the vast stretches of ice. Sometimes pups – aptly named, considering their happy, dog-like faces – are snuggled with the adults, who raise up from their flop and stare at you purposefully if you get too close.

And then there are the skua, scavengers that look like dirty gulls, with no natural predators. They are unafraid of humans, and will walk right up to you, entirely unruffled – or, if you're carrying food, the daring devils might even attempt to dive-bomb you. But it's best to revel in the chance to see these cantankerous creatures in their natural habitat – after all, you're the visitor; they, unlike humans, have no problem thriving in the harsh wilds of Antarctica.

999 Stumbling upon a polar oasis

CANADA Travelling by skidoo, you and your Inuit guide venture onto the sea ice off the coast of Baffin Island in Canada's eastern Arctic for a day's outing. Three hours later you spot a small body of water completely surrounded by ice and shrouded in mist. Nestled between two rocky islands, this mysterious marine "lake" is teeming with life – hundreds of eider and long-tailed ducks, and guillemots dive for food while in the distance a ringed seal keeps a close watch. Fresh tracks of an Arctic fox circle the perimeter of the ice edge where only days earlier a local hunter had spotted a wandering polar bear. You have stumbled upon a polynya.

Polynyas are areas of open water bordered by thick sea ice that recur year after year in the same location. There are a few dozen scattered throughout the Arctic Archipelago, ranging in size from less than a hundred metres across to a massive 40,000 square kilometres. A combination of wind and strong ocean currents keep these areas free of ice year-round. Although they account for less than five percent of the entire surface area of the Arctic Ocean, their presence is crucial to the survival of countless marine organisms.

As the spring sun glares down onto the reflective icy surface and penetrates deep into the water, billions of microscopic plankton suddenly burst to life, thanks to incoming solar radiation. This influx of energy triggers a chain of events many naturalists describe as one of the greatest spectacles in the Arctic. Millions of migratory seabirds and ducks join bowhead whales and large pods of narwhals and belugas to feed in the nutrient-rich waters.

Standing at the edge of the ice, and surrounded by a symphony of sound and colour, you begin to scan the horizon for more signs of life. A flock of at least three hundred king eiders flutter by while the tell-tale spray from a pod of belugas signal their return to the surface. This flurry of activity almost distracts you from spotting the two-metre spiralled ivory tusk of a narwhal as it pierces through the calm waters of this remarkable polar oasis.

1000 Voyaging into the unknown

ANTARCTICA Over a hundred years after the initial exploration of the continent, journeying to Antarctica still feels like stepping off the known world. Take a cruise to the crooked finger of land that points northward to South America and you'll encounter the other-planetary landscape and mysterious draw of this land beyond time – and for the most part still beyond civilization's reach.

Once through the Drake Passage – reputed to be the roughest body of water in the world – you feel the frozen land long before you actually see it. As you cross the invisible line of the Antarctic Convergence, a ribbon of coldwater current which circumnavigates the continent, the temperature plummets. Huge tabular icebergs appear – interpreting their fantastic shapes is at least half the fun. In the Gerlache Strait, sudden charcoal tors soar vertically from the water up to 450m and glaciers tumble vertically into the sea. From the ship you can brush against their hummocked layers of ice and try your hand at cataloguing their colours: cobalt, indigo and mint.

The tar-black Antarctic water teems with marine life: humpback and killer whales are fairly common, and if there is sea ice around you are guaranteed to see the silver-gold crabeater and nonchalant Weddell seals who can hardly be bothered to vacate a floe even as the ship splits it in two. Myriad penguins emit a serenade of squawks as the ship passes, and albatrosses and petrels are stalwart chaperones, flying level with the ship for days at a stretch.

Go ashore at the abandoned British Base B at Deception Island, flattened by a volcanic eruption, and the British Antarctic Museum at Port Lockroy, where a preserved-in-aspic 1950s base is on display, with tinned fruitcake and rice pudding from the explorer era.

On the whole, however, the Antarctic is a monumentally empty place, and a cruise down the peninsula gives you only a glimpse of this uninhabited continent, larger than Australia – but it's enough to draw you in. Even as it emits a *froideur*, there is an odd magnetism to the Antarctic; you'll feel its pull long after you've left.

NEED to know

986 In Kiruna, stay at the comfortable *Vinterpalatset* (Ⓦ www.vinterpalatset.se).

987 Spending a night in an igloo can be arranged in any Nunavik or Nunavut community – see Ⓦ www .nunavik-tourism.com or Ⓦ www.nunavuttourism.com.

988 Air Greenland flies six days a week from Copenhagen to Kangerlussuaq in summer. From Kangerlussuaq, you can take a guided tour to the ice cap with Albatros Travel Greenland (Ⓦ www.albatros-travel.dk). Visit Ⓦ www.greenland.com for more information.

989 The local Tysfjord tourist office runs snorkelling safaris between October and mid-January for 1700kr per person. See Ⓦ www.tysfjord-turistsenter.no for more.

990 You can get more infomation on the Auyuittuq National Park at Ⓦ www.pc.gc.ca. All visitors must register with Parks Canada.

991 Ocean Adventures (Ⓦ www.oceanadventures .co.uk) operates a thirty-day cruise that visits Mc-Murdo Station and several of the area's historic huts.

992 The Lofoten Islands can be reached by car ferry, passenger boat and plane from Bodø, in northern Norway.

993 Jukkasjärvi is 17km from Kiruna, the nearest domestic airport. Double rooms start at 1250kr. You can book online at Ⓦ www.icehotel.com.

994 Bundle up; the weather outside can range anywhere from –1º to –34ºC, and the blustery wind – and occasional heavy snowfall – won't make things any warmer. For information on joining the herd, visit Ⓦ www.visitinari.fi.

995 Ice diving is best between February and April. Some caution should be taken, such as acclimatizing your equipment to water temperature before beginning a descent. And remember: there is no such thing as bad weather – only inadequate gear. Ⓦ www.ice -diving.co.uk

996 The ice road is usually only open from February to April – see Ⓦ www.inuvik.ca for more up-to-date info.

997 Tinja Myllykangas operates Siperia Lapponica (Ⓣ +358 407 055 954 or contact Inari Event Lapland at Ⓦ www.visitinari.fi), a small, local company near Inari that raises and trains huskies, and leads regular husky safaris across Lapland during the colder months. There are regular flights from Helsinki to Ivalo airport, 40km south of Inari.

998 The website Ⓦ www.antarcticconnection.com has lots of info on Antarctic birds and wildlife and much else besides, including trips and cruises.

999 There are numerous polynyas in Canada's Arctic, and each village has outfitters who can arrange trips. Komeaortok Tours (Ⓔ ktoursoutfitting@yahoo. ca) organizes visits by snowmobile from Pangnintung, an hour's flight from Iqaluit, the capital of Nunavut.

1000 There are many Antarctic cruise operators but one of the best is Exodus (Ⓦ www.exodus.co.uk).

GOOD to know

SOUTHERN LIGHTS

From March to September, outside the period when Antarctica experiences 24-hour daylight, the *aurora australis*, or **southern lights**, can be seen in the skies above the continent. These curtains of coloured light are one of the greatest spectacles on earth.

THE "SNOW" MYTH

The idea that the Inuit of the Arctic have over 100 words for **snow** is a complete fabrication. The confusion lies in how you define a word. The Inuit language group uses multiple suffixes, called postbases, for word formation, which are added to roots to compose compounding words. Whereas English has one root word for "snow" – which is used for "snowball", "snowflake" and "snowstorm" – the Inuit have four: *aput* (snow on the ground); *gana* (falling snow); *piqsirpoq* (drifting snow); and *qimuqsuq* (a snow drift). The 100-plus words the Inuit use are actually just compounds; the reality is that the Inuit have about the same number of words for "snow" as we do in English.

POLAR EXPLORERS

With cruise ships now regularly visiting Antarctica in the Southern Hemisphere's summer, it is easy to think that the highest, coldest, windiest and driest continent has gone soft. But the South Pole was first reached less than a century ago. Some notable explorers include:

Roald Amundsen, Norway Leader of the first team to reach the South Pole, on December 14, 1911; he then made a successful return.

Robert Scott, UK Reached the South Pole 35 days after Amundsen. His party died of starvation just eleven miles short of a large food cache on the return journey.

Ernest Shackleton, Anglo-Irish Aboard the ship *Endurance*, Sir Ernest Henry Shackleton and crew attempted to sail across Antarctica, between the Weddell Sea and the Ross Sea, in 1914. This goal had to be abandoned when the ship was crushed by a floe of pack ice short of the continent. Shackleton then led his crew on an epic 639-day journey by sledge and boat to Elephant Island, just off the Antarctic Peninsula. From here he sailed with some of the men to South Georgia Island in the Falklands, where help was sought. Miraculously, not a man on the expedition was lost.

Edward E. Byrd, USA Byrd and three others were the first to fly over the South Pole in 1929.

Sir Edmund Hillary, New Zealand In 1958 the Everest conqueror led the third party to reach the South Pole overland, and the first with land vehicles, in this case converted Ferguson tractors.

Boerge Ousland, Norway Ousland became the first person to cross Antarctica unsupported (in 64 days), using a sled, skis and a sail in 1997.

"Better a live donkey than a dead lion"

Ernest Shackleton, after failing to reach the South Pole by 100km in 1909

THE ARCTIC CIRCLE

The **Arctic Circle** is an imaginary line that marks the latitude above which the sun does not set on the day of the summer solstice (usually June 21) and does not rise on the day of the winter solstice (usually December 21). North of this latitude, periods of continuous daylight or night last up to six months. The position of the Arctic Circle depends on the tilt of the earth's axis relative to the plane of its orbit around the sun, which is known as the "obliquity of the ecliptic". The average value of the tilt is currently decreasing by about 1.2cm per year, causing the Arctic Circle to drift towards the North Pole by some 15m each year.

TAKE YOUR THERMALS

The coldest place on earth is Vostok, Antarctica: it's registered at a fairly chilly -89°C.

HOW TO BUILD AN IGLOO

• Pack down a large, circular base area with snowshoes or skis, using a hand saw to cut blocks about 1m wide, 0.5m high and 20cm deep.

• Make the base layer of the igloo nearby, digging down into the snow to form the lower half of the igloo and an arched entrance tunnel.

• The second row of blocks should be cut bevelled at the bottom so the layers slant inward toward the middle until the igloo is about shoulder height.

• Cover the hole at the top with one single block, enlarge the inner chamber and build the entrance in the same manner as the main hut.

• Cut a couple of vents for circulation and bed down for the night!

"Water that does not move is always shallow"

Sami proverb

ON THE WING

The longest migration on earth is undertaken by **Arctic terns**: they fly 40,000km from the Arctic to the Antarctic – and back again.

THE ANTARCTIC TREATY

The Antarctic Treaty came into operation in 1961, having been ratified by the twelve countries involved with Antarctic science. It now has 44 signatories including the US, and aims to protect and preserve this unique wilderness, banning mineral extraction and military activity and promoting scientific discovery.

KEEPING WARM ON THE ICE

Emperor penguins huddle together in herds to keep warm in their freezing Antarctic habitat; there can be up to ten adults per square metre at the centre of the huddle, producing enough heat to release a cloud of steam.

Small print
Index

Author credits

001 Paul Gray	082 Keith Drew	162 Keith Drew	243 Jonathan Buckley
002 James Smart	083 Lucy White	163 Roger Norum	244 Jon Bousfield
003 Keith Drew	084 Matthew Teller	164 Sarah Eno	245 Lucy Cowie
004 Sarah Eno	085 Jan Dodd	165 Nikki Birrell	246 Martin Dunford
005 Melanie Kramers	086 Sarah Eno	166 Todd Obolsky	247 Jon Bousfield
006 Lucy White	087 Martin Dunford	167 Sarah Eno	248 Jonathan Buckley
007 Paul Gray	088 Martin Dunford	168 Roger Norum	249 Megan McIntyre
008 Paul Whitfield	089 Ross Velton	169 Alf Alderson	250 Jonathan Buckley
009 Robert Andrews	090 Martin Dunford	170 Oliver Schwaner-Albright	251 Sophie Middlemiss
010 Chris Scott	091 Nick Woodford & Tim Beynon	171 Keith Drew	252 Lucy Ratcliffe
011 Brendon Griffin	092 Matthew Teller	172 AnneLise Sorensen	253 Jon Bousfield
012 Robert Andrews	093 Jan Dodd	173 Felicity Aston	254 Dan Richardson
013 Lucy White	094 Ruth Blackmore	174 AnneLise Sorensen	255 Norm Longley
014 Donald Reid	095 Kerry Walker	175 David Leffman	256 Stephen Keeling
015 Robert Andrews	096 David Abram	176 AnneLise Sorensen	257 Jon Bousfield
016 Dave Dakota	097 Stephen Keeling	177 Helen Ochyra	258 Dan Richardson
017 Nick Jones	098 Martin Dunford	178 Tim Ecott	259 Jon Bousfield
018 Al Spicer	099 Kerry Walker	179 Roger Norum	260 Jon Bousfield
019 Mark Robertson	100 Stephen Keeling	180 Keith Drew	261 Martin Zatko
020 Paul Gray	101 James McConnachie	181 Martin Dunford	262 Dan Richardson
021 Hayley Spurway	102 Ross Velton	182 Martin Dunford	263 Martin Dunford
022 Donald Reid	103 Martin Dunford	183 Martin Dunford	264 Edward Aves
023 Sarah Eno	104 Greg Ward	184 Martin Dunford	265 Jon Bousfield
024 William Sutcliffe	105 Ross Velton	185 James Stewart	266 Ruth Hedges
025 Caitlin Fitzsimmons	106 Kerry Walker	186 James McConnachie	267 Lily Hyde
026 Tim Elcott	107 Jan Dodd	187 Martin Zatko	268 Norm Longley
027 Katy Bell	108 Stephen Keeling	188 Jonathan Buckley	269 Rob Humphreys
028 Tim Elcott	109 Martin Dunford	189 Martin Dunford	270 Lily Hyde
029 Martin Dunford	110 Brendon Griffin	190 Norm Longley	271 Kate Thomas
030 Polly Thomas	111 Keith Drew	191 Jonathan Buckley	272 James Smart
031 Alf Alderson	112 Martin Dunford	192 Jon Bousfield	273 Rob Crossan
032 Helena Smith	113 James Smart	193 Greg Langley	274 Alison Murchie
033 Mark Ellingham	114 Brendon Griffin	194 Jonathan Buckley	275 Jon Bousfield
034 James Smart	115 Brendon Griffin	195 Jeffrey Kennedy	276 Jon Bousfield
035 Polly Evans	116 Brendon Griffin	196 Norm Longley	277 Jon Bousfield
036 Paul Gray	117 Steven Vickers	197 Martin Dunford	278 Jon Bousfield
037 Alf Alderson	118 Brendon Griffin	198 Terry Richardson	279 Lily Hyde
038 Keith Drew	119 Harriet Mills	199 Martin Dunford	280 Jon Bousfield
039 Paul Gray	120 Matthew Hancock	200 Megan McIntyre	281 Andrew Rosenberg
040 Paul Whitfield	121 Brendon Griffin	201 Jeffrey Kennedy	282 Jon Bousfield
041 Donald Reid	122 Brendon Griffin	202 Martin Dunford	283 Rob Humphreys
042 Rob Coates	123 Matthew Hancock	203 Ros Belford	284 Rob Humphreys
043 James Smart	124 Brendon Griffin	204 Martin Zatko	285 Norm Longley
044 Diana Jarvis	125 Brendon Griffin	205 Martin Dunford	286 Jon Bousfield
045 Dave Dakota & Paul Gray	126 Matthew Hancock	206 John Fisher	287 Adrian Mourby
046 Donald Reid	127 Brendon Griffin	207 Siobhan Donaghue	288 Keith Drew
047 Mark Ellingham	128 Brendon Griffin	208 Ross Velton	289 Michael Haag
048 Kerry Walker	129 Brendon Griffin	209 Martin Dunford	290 James Stewart
049 Paul Whitfield	130 Brendon Griffin	210 Megan McIntyre	291 Chris Scott
050 Alf Alderson	131 Brendon Griffin	211 James McConnachie	292 Michael Haag
051 Neville Walker	132 Brendon Griffin	212 Martin Dunford	293 Mark Robertson
052 James McConnachie	133 Brendon Griffin	213 Terry Richardson	294 Dan Jacobs
053 Stephen Keeling	134 Matthew Hancock	214 Rob Crossan	295 Matthew Teller
054 Emma Gibbs	135 Geoff Garvey	215 Lucy White	296 James Rice
055 Emma Gibbs	136 Martin Dunford	216 James McConnachie	297 Emily Spry
056 Matthew Teller	137 AnneLise Sorensen	217 Martin Zatko	298 Juliana Barnaby
057 Neville Walker	138 Brendon Griffin	218 Martin Dunford	299 Matthew Teller
058 Brendon Griffin	139 Iain Stewart	219 Sarah Eno	300 Victor Borg
059 James Stewart	140 Brendon Griffin	220 Norm Longley	301 Dan Jacobs
060 Martin Dunford	141 Christian Williams	221 Jon Bousfield	302 Dan Jacobs
061 Shafik Meghji	142 Dave Dakota & Damien Simonis	222 Barnaby Rogers	303 Juliana Barnaby
062 Greg Langley	143 Kerry Walker	223 Jonathan Buckley	304 Caitlin Fitzsimmons
063 Ross Velton	144 Emma Gregg	224 Norm Longley	305 Emma Gregg
064 Ruth Blackmore	145 AnneLise Sorensen	225 Natasha Foges	306 Victor Borg
065 Helena Smith	146 Brendon Griffin	226 Natasha Foges	307 Chris Scott
066 James Stewart	147 Matthew Hancock	227 Martin Zatko	308 Richard Trillo
067 Keith Drew	148 Matthew Hancock	228 Mark Ellwood	309 Chris Scott
068 Martin Dunford	149 Martin Dunford	229 John Fisher	310 Richard Trillo
069 Martin Dunford	150 Christian Williams	230 Norm Longley	311 Richard Trillo
070 Lucy White	151 Brendon Griffin	231 Marc Dubin	312 Dan Jacobs
071 Lucy White	152 Brendon Griffin	232 Martin Zatko	313 David Abram
072 James McConnachie	153 Caroline Osborne	233 Kerry Walker	314 Dan Jacobs
073 James Stewart	154 James Proctor	234 Rob Crossan	315 Chris Scott
074 Matthew Teller	155 Keith Drew	235 Martin Dunford	316 Keith Drew
075 Adrian Mourby	156 Tim Ecott	236 Martin Dunford	317 Richard Trillo
076 Chris Straw	157 Andy Turner	237 Martin Dunford	318 Brendon Griffin
077 Martin Dunford	158 Roger Norum	238 Martin Dunford	319 Kate Berens
078 Kevin Fitzgerald	159 Richard Hammond	239 Robert Andrews	320 Chris Scott
079 Matthew Teller	160 Kate Thomas	240 Stephen Keeling	321 Chris Scott
080 David Abram	161 Keith Drew	241 Norm Longley	322 Suzanne Porter
081 Martin Dunford		242 Greg Witt	323 Miranda Davies
			324 Emma Gregg

325 Ross Velton	407 Mike Unwin
326 Roger Norum	408 Nick Maes
327 Richard Trillo	409 Emma Gregg
328 Emma Gregg	410 William Sutcliffe
329 Roger Norum	411 Emma Gregg
330 Richard Trillo	412 Keith Drew
331 Eliza Reid	413 Richard Trillo
332 Richard Trillo	414 Mike Unwin
333 Chris Scott	415 Mike Unwin
334 Emma Gregg	416 Mike Unwin
335 Emma Gregg	417 Emma Gregg
336 Rob Crossan	418 Claus Vogel
337 Richard Trillo	419 Ross Velton
338 Lone Mouritsen	420 Emma Gregg
339 Richard Trillo	421 Emma Gregg
340 Richard Trillo	422 Emma Gregg
341 Emma Gregg	423 Donald Reid
342 Ross Velton	424 Emma Gregg
343 Richard Trillo	425 Nikki Birrell
344 Emma Gregg	426 Keith Drew
345 Anna Paynton	427 Gill Harvey
346 Richard Trillo	428 Tony Pinchuck
347 Keith Drew	429 Keith Drew
348 Marie Jarvis	430 Mike Unwin
349 Emma Gregg	431 Emma Gregg
350 Rob Crossan	432 Rob Crossan
351 Richard Trillo	433 Emma Gregg
352 Richard Trillo	434 Claus Vogel
353 Richard Trillo	435 Emma Gregg
354 Richard Trillo	436 Nick Garbutt
355 Richard Trillo	437 Emma Gregg
356 Emma Gregg	438 David Abram
357 Henry Stedman	439 Emma Gregg
358 Marie Jarvis	440 Matthew Teller
359 Emma Gregg	441 Matthew Teller
360 Richard Trillo	442 Paul Whitfield
361 Beth Wooldridge	443 Matthew Teller
362 Stanley Johnson	444 Matthew Teller
363 Richard Trillo	445 Matthew Teller
364 Richard Trillo	446 Matthew Teller
365 Richard Trillo	447 Matthew Haag
366 Keith Drew	448 Matthew Teller
367 Richard Trillo	449 Emma Gregg
368 Nick Maes	450 Matthew Teller
369 Richard Trillo	451 Matthew Teller
370 David Leffman	452 Matthew Teller
371 Emma Gregg	453 Daisy Finer
372 Richard Trillo	454 Matthew Teller
373 Jens Finke	455 Roger Norum
374 Richard Trillo	456 Roger Norum
375 Nick Maes	457 Frances Linzee Gordon
376 Nick Maes	458 Roger Norum
377 Richard Trillo	459 Matthew Teller
378 Richard Trillo	460 Matthew Teller
379 Tim Ecott	461 Matthew Teller
380 Emma Gregg	462 Matthew Teller
381 Emma Gregg	463 Dan Jacobs
382 Jens Finke	464 Martin Zatko
383 Nick Maes	465 Sakhr Al-Makhadhi
384 Chris Scott	466 Matthew Teller
385 Richard Trillo	467 Matthew Teller
386 Nick Maes	468 Frances Linzee Gordon
387 Emma Gregg	469 Sakhr Al-Makhadhi
388 Barbara McCrae	470 Matthew Teller
389 Richard Trillo	471 Matthew Teller
390 Nikki Birrell	472 Frances Linzee Gordon
391 Keith Drew	473 Frances Linzee Gordon
392 Mike Unwin	474 Matthew Teller
393 David Abram	475 Matthew Teller
394 Tony Pinchuck	476 Sakhr Al-Makhadhi
395 Emma Gregg	477 Roger Norum
396 Emma Gregg	478 Matthew Teller
397 Mike Unwin	479 Matthew Teller
398 Barbara McCrae	480 Holly Wademan
399 Adrian Mourby	481 Marie Javins
400 Mike Unwin	482 Roger Norum
401 Tony Pinchuck	483 Marie Houghton
402 Emma Gregg	484 Matthew Teller
403 Donald Reid	485 Greg Ward
404 Rob Crossan	486 Andrew Rosenberg
405 Justin Francis	487 Stephen Keeling
406 Donald Reid	488 Stephen Keeling

489 Zora O'Neill
490 Stephen Timblin
491 Greg Ward
492 JD Dickey
493 Ross Velton
494 Greg Ward
495 Keith Drew
496 Stephen Timblin
497 Mark Ellwood
498 Caroline Lascom
499 Paul Whitfield
500 Greg Ward
501 Paul Whitfield
502 Rob Crossan
503 Andrew Rosenberg
504 Sarah Hull
505 Andrew Rosenberg
506 Andrew Rosenberg
507 Mark Ellwood
508 Stephen Keeling
509 Paul Whitfield
510 JD Dickey
511 Sara Lieber
512 Steven Horak
513 Zora O'Neill
514 Sara Lieber
515 Cali Alpert & Brad Olsen
516 Caroline Lascom
517 Paul Whitfield
518 Sarah Hull
519 Sean Harvey
520 Zora O'Neill
521 Polly Evans
522 Greg Ward
523 Keith Drew
524 Stephen Keeling
525 Madelyn Rosenberg
526 Madelyn Rosenberg
527 Shea Dean
528 Stephen Keeling
529 Andrew Rosenberg
530 Megan Kennedy
531 Sarah Eno
532 Christina Williams
533 Keith Drew
534 Stephen Timblin
535 JD Dickey
536 Zora O'Neill
537 Zora O'Neill
538 JD Dickey
539 Samantha Cook
540 JD Dickey
541 Alice Park
542 Stephen Keeling
543 Stephen Keeling
544 Alf Alderson
545 Stephen Keeling
546 Steven Horak
547 Phil Lee & Anna Roberts Welles
548 Phil Lee
549 Christian Williams
550 Christian Williams
551 Polly Evans
552 Claus Vogel
553 Janine Israel
554 Claus Vogel
555 Stephen Keeling
556 Janine Israel
557 Felicity Aston
558 Christian Williams
559 Felicity Aston
560 Christian Williams
561 Claus Vogel
562 Stephen Keeling
563 Christian Williams
564 Ross Velton
565 Stephen Keeling
566 Janine Israel
567 Janine Israel
568 Christian Williams
569 Christian Williams
570 Phil Lee
571 Melissa Graham
572 Claus Vogel

573 Helena Smith
574 Ross Velton
575 Stephen Keeling
576 AnneLise Sorensen
577 Helena Smith
578 Sean Harvey
579 Polly Thomas
580 Polly Thomas
581 Chris Hamilton
582 Sean Harvey
583 Natalie Foster
584 Polly Thomas
585 David Abram
586 Stephen Keeling
587 Andrew Rosenberg
588 Steven Horak
589 Claus Vogel
590 Seph Petta
591 Rob Coates
592 Stephen Keeling
593 Stephen Keeling
594 Steven Horak
595 Sarah Eno
596 Stephen Keeling
597 Polly Thomas
598 Claus Vogel
599 Tim Ecott
600 Megan Kennedy
601 Gaylord Dold & Natalie Folster
602 Chris Hamilton
603 Polly Thomas
604 Sean Harvey
605 Andrew Rosenberg
606 Jean Mcneil
607 Polly Rodger Brown
608 Richard Arghiris
609 Brendon Griffin
610 Iain Stewart
611 Polly Rodger Brown
612 AnneLise Sorensen
613 Zora O'Neill
614 Rob Coates
615 Paul Whitfield
616 Kate Berens
617 James McConnachie
618 Polly Rodger Brown
619 Zora O'Neill
620 Jean Mcneil
621 Caroline Lascom
622 Sara Humphreys
623 Iain Stewart
624 Iain Stewart
625 Mark Fass
626 Keith Drew
627 Lily Fink
628 Jonathan Yevin
629 Paul Whitfield
630 Paul Whitfield
631 Polly Rodger Brown
632 AnneLise Sorensen
633 Polly Rodger Brown
634 Rob Coates
635 Iain Stewart
636 Keith Drew
637 Gregory Witt
638 Stephen Keeling
639 Iain Stewart
640 Polly Rodger Brown
641 AnneLise Sorensen
642 Daisy Finer
643 James Read
644 Polly Rodger Brown
645 Polly Rodger Brown
646 Rob Coates
647 Zora O'Neill
648 Keith Drew
649 Brendon Griffin
650 Keith Drew
651 Jason Clampet
652 Iain Stewart
653 Diana James
654 AnneLise Sorensen
655 Tim Ecott
656 Stephen Keeling
657 Paul D Smith

658 Joshua Goodman
659 Adrian Mourby
660 Harry Adès
661 Harry Adès
662 Melanie Kramers
663 Andrew Benson
664 Paul D Smith
665 Polly Evans
666 Oliver Marshall
667 Hal Weitzman
668 Rob Crossan
669 Polly Rodger Brown
670 Keith Drew
671 James Read
672 Andrew Benson
673 Steven Horak
674 James Read
675 Todd Obo
676 Melanie Kramers
677 Sarah Cummins
678 Rosalba O'Brien
679 Keith Drew
680 Rosalba O'Brien
681 Brendon Griffin
682 Ross Velton
683 Daisy Finin
684 Dave Dakota
685 Dilwyn Jenkins
686 Melanie Kramers
687 Seb Bacon
688 Dilwyn Jenkins
689 Andrew Benson
690 Seph Petta
691 Shafik Meghji
692 Andrew Benson
693 Andrew Benson
694 Hannah Hennessy
695 Steven Horak
696 Seph Petta
697 Harry Adès
698 Keith Drew
699 Alex Robinson
700 Seph Petta
701 James Read
702 Melanie Kramers
703 James Read
704 Hal Weitzman
705 Megan Kennedy
706 Polly Rodger Brown
707 Andrew Benson
708 David Abram
709 Keith Drew
710 Andrew Benson
711 Rosalba O'Brien
712 Rosalba O'Brien
713 James Read
714 Roger Norum
715 Caroline Lascom
716 Melissa Graham
717 Rosalba O'Brien
718 Steven Horak
719 Seph Petta
720 Joe Tyrrell
721 Andrew Rosenberg
722 Keith Drew
723 Andrew Rosenberg
724 James Smart
725 Keith Drew
726 Keith Drew
727 Adrian Mourby
728 Hal Weitzman
729 Mike Unwin
730 Richard Danbury
731 Melissa Graham
732 Caroline Lascom
733 Hal Weitzman
734 Brendon Griffin
735 David Leffman
736 David Leffman
737 Stephen Keeling
738 Jan Dodd
739 David Leffman
740 Martin Dunford
741 Lucy Ridout
742 Martin Dunford
743 Simon Lewis

744 Simon Richmond
745 David Leffman
746 Martin Zatko
747 David Leffman
748 Martin Zatko
749 Stephen Keeling
750 Martin Zatko
751 David Leffman
752 Martin Zatko
753 Rob Crossan
754 David Leffman
755 Seb Bacon
756 David Leffman
757 Martin Zatko
758 Martin Zatko
759 Stephen Keeling
760 Adrian Mourby
761 Simon Richmond
762 David Leffman
763 Sophie Middlemiss
764 Anna Fifield
765 Martin Dunford
766 Alf Alderson
767 Roger Norum
768 Steven Vickers
769 David Leffman
770 David Leffman
771 Polly Evans
772 Anna Fifield
773 Jan Dodd
774 Martin Zatko
775 David Leffman
776 Lesley Reader
777 David Leffman
778 Jan Dodd
779 Seb Bacon
780 David Leffman
781 Simon Richmond
782 Sophie Middlemiss
783 Polly Evans
784 David Leffman
785 Anna Fifield
786 David Leffman
787 Roger Norum
788 Simon Lewis
789 Anna Fifield
790 Ross Velton
791 Simon Lewis
792 Keith Drew
793 David Leffman
794 Martin Zatko
795 David Leffman
796 Simon Lews
797 Nick Middleton
798 David Leffman
799 Greg Witt
800 Martin Zatko
801 Simon Richmond
802 Stephen Keeling
803 David Leffman
804 David Abram
805 Richard Wignell
806 David Abram
807 Shafik Meghji
808 Daisy Finer
809 David Abram
810 Dave Dakota & Gavin Thomas
811 Roger Norum
812 Diana Jarvis
813 Nick Maes
814 David Abram
815 Megha Gupta
816 David Abram
817 Daisy Finer
818 Shafik Meghji
819 AnneLise Sorensen
820 David Abram
821 Lucy Cowie
822 David Abram
823 Seph Petta
824 David Abram
825 Gavin Thomas
826 David Abram
827 Roger Norum
828 David Abram

829 Diana Jarvis
830 David Abram
831 Richard Trillo
832 David Abram
833 Edward Aves
834 Flip Byrnes
835 David Abram
836 Alf Alderson
837 David Abram
838 Adrian Mourby
839 David Abram
840 Rob Crossan
841 David Abram
842 Martin Dunford
843 Martin Dunford
844 James McConnachie
845 Edward Aves
846 James McConnachie
847 David Abram
848 David Abram
849 David Abram
850 Shafik Meghji
851 David Abram
852 Shafik Meghji
853 Shafik Meghji
854 David Abram
855 James McConnachie
856 Richard Wignell
857 David Abram
858 Shafik Meghji
859 Lesley Reader
860 David Abram
861 Lucy Ridout
862 Lucy Ridout
863 Henry Stedman
864 Lucy Ridout
865 Lucy Ridout
866 Henry Stedman
867 Lucy Ridout
868 David Dalton
869 Lucy Ridout
870 Henry Stedman
871 David Dalton
872 Lucy Ridout
873 Sean Mahoney
874 Lucy Ridout
875 Lucy Ridout
876 Iain Stewart
877 Lucy Ridout
878 Lucy Ridout
879 Victor Borg
880 Jan Dodd
881 Martin Zatko
882 Lucy Ridout
883 Flip Byrnes
884 Seb Bacon
885 Lucy Ridout
886 Lucy Ridout
887 Christina Markel
888 Tim Ecott
889 Martin Dunford
890 Karoline Densely
891 Lucy Ridout
892 Claus Vogel
893 Lucy Ridout
894 Lucy Ridout
895 Claus Vogel
896 Steven Vickers
897 Steven Vickers
898 Charles De Ledesma
899 Henry Stedman
900 David Dalton
901 Lucy Ridout
902 Lucy Ridout
903 Megan Mcintyre
904 Iain Stewart
905 Iain Stewart
906 David Dalton
907 Stephen Keeling
908 Henry Stedman
909 Rob Coates
910 Tim Ecott
911 Seph Petta
912 Lucy Ridout
913 Paul Gray
914 Nikki Birrell

915 Seph Petta
916 Lucy Ridout
917 Andy Turner
918 Paul Whitfield
919 David Leffman
920 Paul Whitfield
921 Chris Scott
922 Paul Whitfield
923 Alec Simpson
924 Chris Scott
925 Paul Whitfield
926 Chris Scott
927 Paul Whitfield
928 Chris Scott
929 Stephen Keeling
930 David Leffman
931 Catherine Le Nevez
932 Peter Chapple
933 Paul Whitfield
934 Scott Stickland
935 Stephen Keeling
936 Peter Chapple
937 Lucy Ridout
938 Paul Whitfield
939 Emma Gregg
940 Chris Scott
941 Chris Scott
942 Chris Scott
943 Kerry Walker
944 Keith Drew
945 Paul Whitfield
946 Martin Dunford
947 Paul Whitfield
948 Chris Scott
949 Paul Whitfield
950 Chris Scott
951 Lucy Ridout
952 Paul Whitfield
953 Chris Scott
954 Holly Wallace
955 Diana Jarvis
956 Paul Whitfield
957 Paul Whitfield
958 Emma Gregg
959 Paul Whitfield
960 David Leffman
961 Paul Whitfield
962 Paul Whitfield
963 Chris Scott
964 Paul Whitfield
965 Diana Jarvis
966 Paul Whitfield
967 Alec Simpson
968 Holly Wallace
969 Chris Scott
970 Catherine Le Nevez
971 James Stewart
972 Andy Turner
973 Alec Simpson
974 Paul Whitfield
975 Chris Scott
976 Paul Whitfield
977 Andy Turner
978 Paul Whitfield
979 Chris Scott
980 Paul Whitfield
981 Polly Evans
982 Steven Vickers
983 Emma Gregg
984 Paul Whitfield
985 Chris Scott
986 James Proctor
987 Claus Vogel
988 Polly Evans
989 Louise Southerden
990 Claus Vogel
991 Hunter Slaton
992 Phil Lee
993 Keith Drew
994 Roger Norum
995 Roger Norum
996 Polly Evans
997 Roger Norum
998 Hunter Slaton
999 Claus Vogel
1000 Jean Mcneil

Picture credits

Index by country

Index by theme